Encyclopedia of

INFORMATION SYSTEMS

S–Z   Volume 4

Encyclopedia of

INFORMATION SYSTEMS

S–Z   Volume 4

Editor-in-Chief

Hossein Bidgoli
California State University
Bakersfield, California

ACADEMIC PRESS
An imprint of Elsevier Science

Amsterdam   Boston   London   New York   Oxford   Paris   San Diego   San Francisco   Singapore   Sydney   Tokyo

Copyright 2003, ELSEVIER SCIENCE (USA)

Academic Press
An Elsevier Science Imprint
525 B Street, Suite 1900, San Diego, California 92101-4495, USA
http://www.academicpress.com

Academic Press
84 Theobalds Road, London WC1X 8RR, UK
http://www.academicpress.com

Library of Congress Catalog Card Number: 2001098280

International Standard Book Number: 0-12-227240-4 (set)
International Standard Book Number: 0-12-227241-2 (Volume 1)
International Standard Book Number: 0-12-227242-0 (Volume 2)
International Standard Book Number: 0-12-227243-9 (Volume 3)
International Standard Book Number: 0-12-227244-7 (Volume 4)

PRINTED IN THE UNITED STATES OF AMERICA
02   03   04   05   06   07   MM   9   8   7   6   5   4   3   2   1

To so many fine memories of my brother, Mohsen,
for his uncompromising belief in the power of education.

Contents

Volume IV

Contents

Contents   xiii

Contents by Subject Area

Contributors

Monica Adya
DePaul University
Expert Systems Construction

Sergio de Agostino
Armstrong Atlantic State University
Automata Theory

Manish Agrawal
University of South Florida
Electronic Commerce, Infrastructure for

Maryam Alavi
Emory University
Virtual Learning Systems

Johanna Olson Alexander
California State University, Bakersfield
Library Applications

Murugan Anandarajan
Drexel University
Global Information Systems

Timothy Anderson
Portland State University
Data Envelopment Analysis

Jay E. Aronson
University of Georgia
Expert Systems

Minoru Asada
Osaka University
Robotics

Reza Azarmsa
Loyola Marymount University
Desktop Publishing

Jerry Banks
AutoSimulations, Inc.
Discrete Event Simulation

Thomas T. Barker
Texas Tech University
Documentation for Software and IS Development

Richard J. Barnes
Marquette University
Value Chain Analysis

Tonya Barrier
Southwest Missouri State University
Systems Analysis

Michael Bedell
California State University, Bakersfield
Human Resource Information Systems

Izak Benbasat
University of British Columbia
Electronic Data Interchange

Seth D. Bergmann
Rowan University
Compilers

Hossein Bidgoli
California State University, Bakersfield
Electronic Commerce
Operating Systems

Robert Blanning
Vanderbilt University
Model Building Process

Michael H. Böhlen
Aalborg University
Temporal Data Model and Query Language Concepts

Marco Bruni
International Fund for Agricultural Development,
    United Nations
End-User Computing Tools

Ulla K. Bunz
Rutgers University
Research, Electronic

Bill M. Catambay
ExcaliburWorld Software
Pascal

Russell K. Chan
Pioneer Hi-Bred International, Inc.
Database Development Process

Senthilanand Chandrasekaran
University of Georgia
Java

Kaushal Chari
University of South Florida
Firewalls

Charlie Chien-Hung Chen
Claremont Graduate University
Global Information Systems

Peter C. Y. Chen
National University of Singapore
Engineering, Artificial Intelligence in

Zhengxin Chen
University of Nebraska, Omaha
Data Warehousing and Data Marts
Industry, Artificial Intelligence in

Elia Chepaitis
Fairfield University
Developing Nations

Chen H. Chung
University of Kentucky
Operations Management

Paul Chwelos
University of British Columbia
Electronic Data Interchange

Alan B. Craig
National Center for Supercomputing Applications
Virtual Reality

C. Brad Crisp
Indiana University
Organizations, Information Systems Impact on

Amit Das
Nanyang Technological University, Singapore
Knowledge Representation

Gordon B. Davis
University of Minnesota
Systems Approach

Jennifer DeCamp
MITRE Corporation and American University
Globalization

Albert S. Dexter
University of British Columbia
Electronic Data Interchange

Mary S. Doucet
California State University, Bakersfield
Control and Auditing
Public Accounting Firms

Thomas A. Doucet
California State University, Bakersfield
Control and Auditing
Public Accounting Firms

Edward J. Dudewicz
Syracuse University
Simulation Languages

Kevin Duffy
University of Texas, Arlington
Reengineering for Business Processes

Alexandra Durcikova
University of Pittsburgh
Statistical Models (Non-Optimization Models)

Amitava Dutta
George Mason University
Telecommunications Industry

Sean B. Eom
Southeast Missouri State University
Psychology

Daniel Felsenstein
Hebrew University of Jerusalem
National and Regional Economic Impacts of Silicon Valley

Robert G. Fletcher
California State University, Bakersfield
Advertising and Marketing in Electronic Commerce
Geographic Information Systems in Real Estate

Blaine T. Garfolo
San Francisco State University
Javascript

Edward J. Garrity
Canisius College
Success Measures of Information Systems

Eduardo Gelbstein
International Computing Centre, United Nations
Data, Information, and Knowledge
End-User Computing, Managing
Outsourcing

Leopoldo A. Gemoets
University of Texas, El Paso
Supply Chain Management

Joey F. George
Florida State University
Groupware

Jeff Gilchrist
Elytra Enterprises Inc., Yanier, Ontario, Canada
Encryption

William Go
Go & Associates
Law Firms

Steven H. Goldberg
Imagitas, Inc.
Year 2000 (Y2K) Bug Problems

Raymond Greenlaw
Armstrong Atlantic State University
Automata Theory
Internet, Overview
Object-Oriented Programming

William I. Grosky
University of Michigan, Dearborn
Hyper-Media Databases

Jiang Guo
California State University, Bakersfield
C and C++

Jatinder N. D. Gupta
University of Alabama, Huntsville
Globalization and Information Management Strategy

Dennis Guseman
California State University, Bakersfield
Service Industry

Ruth Guthrie
California Polytechnic University, Pomona
Program Design, Coding, and Testing

Robert R. Harmon
Portland State University
Marketing Information Systems

Laura Hecht
California State University, Bakersfield
Sociology

John H. Heinrichs
Wayne State University
Knowledge Management

Ellen M. Hepp
University of New Hampshire
Internet, Overview

Clyde W. Holsapple
University of Kentucky
Decision Support Systems

John-Paul Hosom
Oregon Health & Science University
Speech Recognition

Jamshid C. Hosseini
Marquette University
Value Chain Analysis

George P. Huber
University of Texas
Organizations, Information Systems Impact on

Lonnie J. Hudspeth
Florida A&M University
Knowledge Management

Ken Hultman
Synthesis, Inc.
Resistance to Change, Managing

Ray Hunt
University of Canterbury, Christchurch,
    New Zealand
Frame Relay
Network Environments, Managing
Transmission Control Protocol/Internet Protocol (TCP/IP)
Voice Communications

Magid Igbaria
Claremont Graduate University
Global Information Systems
Staffing the Information Systems Department
Virtual Organizations

James P. Ignizio
Resource Management Associates
Goal Programming

Jin H. Im
Sacred Heart University
Privacy

Lakhmi C. Jain
University of South Australia
Industry, Artificial Intelligence in

Christian S. Jensen
Aalborg University
Temporal Data Model and Query Language Concepts

Stephen Jodis
Armstrong Atlantic State University
Programming Languages Classification

Trevor H. Jones
Duquesne University
Disaster Recovery Planning

Jaak Jurison
Fordham University
Productivity

M. E. Kabay
Norwich University
Crime, Use of Computers in

Deborah Bayles Kalman
University of California, Irvine and Singapore
    Institute of Management
Extranets
Intranets

Abraham Kandel
University of South Florida
Medicine, Artificial Intelligence in

Shashidhar Kaparthi
University of Northern Iowa
Spreadsheets

Zaven A. Karian
Denison University
Simulation Languages

Bengt Karlöf
Karlöf Consulting
Benchmarking

Waldemar Karwowski
University of Louisville
Ergonomics

Dean Kashiwagi
Arizona State University
Information Measurement Theory (IMT)

Peter Keenan
University College, Dublin
Geographic Information Systems

Asterios G. Kefalas
University of Georgia
Cybernetics

Mohammed B. Khan
California State University, Long Beach
COBOL

Melody Y. Kiang
California State University,
    Long Beach
Neural Networks

Yong Jin Kim
State University of New York,
    Binghamton
Success Measures of Information Systems

William R. King
University of Pittsburgh
Management Information Systems
Strategic Planning for/of Information Systems

Bengt Klefsjö
Luleå University, Sweden
Total Quality Management

George J. Klir
State University of New York, Binghamton
Systems Science
Uncertainty

Richard E. Korf
University of California, Los Angeles
Search Techniques

Henry F. Korth
Bell Laboratories
Database Systems

Chun-Jen Kuo
State University of New York, Buffalo
Electronic Commerce, Infrastructure for

Jae Kyu Lee
Korea Advanced Institute of Science and
    Technology
Business-to-Business Electronic Commerce

Kenny K. F. Lee
Nanyang Technological University, Singapore
Manual Data Processing

Anita Lee-Post
University of Kentucky
Computer-Aided Manufacturing

Choon Seong Leem
Yonsei University
Service Industries, Electronic Commerce for

Dorothy Elliott Leidner
Baylor University
Virtual Learning Systems

Y. Daniel Liang
Armstrong Atlantic State University
Object-Oriented Programming

Bennet P. Lientz
University of California, Los Angeles
Project Management Techniques

Jeen S. Lim
The University of Toledo
Knowledge Management

K. B. Lloyd
Indiana University of Pennsylvania
Flowcharting Techniques

Claudia Loebbecke
University of Cologne
Digital Goods: An Economic Perspective

Kevin L. Lothridge
National Forensic Science Technology Center,
    University of Florida
Forensics

Pruthikrai Mahatanankoon
Claremont Graduate University
Virtual Organizations

Sathiadev Mahesh
University of New Orleans
Telecommuting

Mo Adam Mahmood
University of Texas, El Paso
Supply Chain Management

Alisha D. Malloy
Georgia State University
Copyright Laws

Theo Mandel
Interface Design and Development
User/System Interface Design

Salvatore T. March
Vanderbilt University
Data Modeling: Entity-Relationship Data Model

George A. Marcoulides
California State University, Fullerton
SAS (Statistical Analysis System)

Laura D. Marcoulides
California State University, Fullerton
SAS (Statistical Analysis System)

Merle P. Martin
California State University, Sacramento
Prototyping
Systems Implementation

Richard O. Mason
Southern Methodist University
Ethical Issues in Artificial Intelligence

Donna Weaver McCloskey
Widener University
Computer Assisted Systems Engineering (CASE)

Raymond McLeod, Jr.
University of Texas
Executive Information Systems

Brian McNamara
California State University, Bakersfield
Law Firms

Gene Mesher
California State University, Sacramento
Integrated Services Digital Network (Broadband and Narrowband ISDN)

Michael Metcalf
Berlin, Germany
FORTRAN

Zbigniew Michalewicz
University of North Carolina, Charlotte
Evolutionary Algorithms

John A. Miller
University of Georgia
Java

Kannan Mohan
Georgia State University
Copyright Laws

Ali R. Montazemi
Indiana University, South Bend
Computer-Integrated Manufacturing

Konrad Morgan
University of Bergen, Norway
Structured Design Methodologies

Yehia Mortagy
University of La Verne
Strategic Information Systems

Brenda J. Moscove
California State University, Bakersfield
Advertising and Marketing in Electronic Commerce
Sales

Krishnamurty Muralidhar
University of Kentucky
Monte Carlo Simulation

Uday S. Murthy
Texas A&M University
Accounting

Ata Nahouraii
Indiana University of Pennsylvania
Computer Hardware
Disaster Recovery Planning

Kichan Nam
Sogang University, Korea
Electronic Commerce, Infrastructure for

Günter Neumann
German Research Center for
   Artificial Intelligence
Artificial Intelligence Programming

Kenneth Nyberg
California State University, Bakersfield
Sociology

Joseph B. O'Donnell
Canisius College
End-User Computing Concepts

David L. Olson
University of Nebraska, Lincoln
Cost/Benefit Analysis
Optimization Models
Software Process Simulation

Gary M. Olson
University of Michigan
Computer-Supported Cooperative Work

Judith S. Olson
University of Michigan
Computer-Supported Cooperative Work

Joseph C. Otto
California State University, Los Angeles
XML (Extensible Markup Language)

Effy Oz
Pennsylvania State University
Ethical Issues

M. Tamer Özsu
University of Waterloo
Distributed Databases

Carmen de Pablos
Rey Juan Carlos University, Spain
Human Side of Information, Managing the Systems

Behrooz Parhami
University of California, Santa Barbara
Number Representation and Computer Arithmetic

June S. Park
University of Iowa
Wide Area Networks

Thomas M. Parks
Colgate University
Search Engines

A. Graham Peace
West Virginia University
Software Piracy

Douglas C. Pence
CPU Medical Management Systems
RPG (Report Program Generator Language)

Pedro David Pérez
Cornell University
People, Information Systems Impact on

Bryan Pfaffenberger
University of Virginia
Linux

Randal D. Pinkett
Building Community Technology (BCT) Partners,
    Inc.
Digital Divide, The

M. L. Plume
Framingham State College
SPSS (Statistical Package for the Social Sciences)

Aun-Neow Poo
National University of Singapore
Engineering, Artificial Intelligence in

Marshall Scott Poole
Texas A&M University
Group Support Systems

Daniel J. Power
University of Northern Iowa
Spreadsheets

Marlei Pozzebon
École des Hautes Études Commercial de Montréal
    and McGill University
Future of Information Systems

Andrew Prestage
Kern County Superintendent of Schools,
    Bakersfield, California
Operating Systems
Word Processing

Denis J. Protti
University of Victoria, Canada
Public Health

Stanislaw Raczynski
Universidad Panamericana, Mexico
Continuous Simulation

Sasan Rahmatian
California State University, Fresno
Transaction Processing Systems

H. R. Rao
State University of New York, Buffalo
Electronic Commerce, Infrastructure for

Jeremy Rasmussen
University of South Florida
Systems Design

H. Michael Rauscher
USDA Forest Service
Natural Resource Management

Kathryn Rea
The Consulting Edge, Inc.
Project Management Techniques

Keith M. Reynolds
USDA Forest Service
Natural Resource Management

Elizabeth Rhodenizer
Canadian Office of Critical Infrastructure Protection
    and Emergency Preparedness
Security Issues and Measures

Catherine M. Ricardo
Iona College
Database Machines
Relational Database Systems
Structured Query Language

Francesca Rizzo
University of Siena
Ergonomics

Donald Robbins
Indiana University of Pennsylvania
Disaster Recovery Planning

Lesley Anne Robertson
University of Western Sydney
Pseudocode

Michael L. Rodgers
Southeast Missouri State University
Internet Homepages

David Rodrick
University of Louisville
Ergonomics

Carlos Romero
Technical University of Madrid
Goal Programming

Michael Rosemann
Queensland University of Technology
Procurement

James Ross
California State University, Bakersfield
Sociology

Imre J. Rudas
Budapest Polytechnic
Hybrid Systems

Asghar Sabbaghi
Indiana University, South Bend
Computer-Integrated Manufacturing

Sowmyanarayanan Sadagopan
Indian Institute of Information Technology, Bangalore
Enterprise Resource Planning

A. Sakurai
Japan Advanced Institute of Science and Technology
Machine Learning

Michael Sampson
Institute for Effectivity, Christchurch, New Zealand
Electronic Mail

G. Lawrence Sanders
State University of New York, Buffalo
End-User Computing Concepts
Success Measures of Information Systems

George Gustav Savii
"Politehnica" University of Timisoara
Computer-Aided Design

Khalid Sayood
University of Nebraska, Lincoln
Data Compression

Marc Schoenauer
Ecole Polytechnique
Evolutionary Algorithms

Andrew F. Seila
University of Georgia
Java

Mark P. Sena
Xavier University
Enterprise Computing

Vikram Sethi
University of Texas, Arlington
Reengineering for Business Processes

Dale Shaffer
Lander University
Cohesion, Coupling, and Abstraction

Sushil K. Sharma
Ball State University
Globalization and Information Management Strategy

William Shay
University of Wisconsin, Green Bay
Standards and Protocols in Data Communications

Conrad Shayo
California State University, San Bernardino
Staffing the Information Systems Department

William R. Sherman
National Center for Supercomputing Applications
Virtual Reality

J. P. Shim
Mississippi State University
Multimedia

Charles Shipley
Armstrong Atlantic State University
Programming Languages Classification

Abraham Silberschatz
Bell Laboratories
Database Systems

Herbert A. Simon
Carnegie Mellon University
Decision Theory

Rahul Singh
University of North Carolina, Greensboro
Intelligent Agents

Robert M. Slade
Vancouver Institute for Research into User Security
Computer Viruses

William E. Snell, Jr.
Southeast Missouri State University
Internet Homepages

J. Solak
Indiana University of Pennsylvania
Flowcharting Techniques

Adriano Solis
University of Texas, El Paso
Supply Chain Management

Frederick N. Springsteel
University of Missouri, Columbia
Network Database Systems

David A. Starrett
Southeast Missouri State University
Internet Homepages

Constantinos J. Stefanou
Technological Educational Institution of
    Thessaloniki
System Development Life Cycle

Bernhard von Stengel
London School of Economics
Game Theory

Rod Stephens
Boulder, Colorado
Visual Basic

Theodor J. Stewart
University of Cape Town
Decision-Making Approaches

Jose Stigliano
International Fund for Agricultural Development,
    United Nations
End-User Computing Tools

Kevin J. Stiroh
Federal Reserve Bank of New York
Economic Impacts of Information Technology

Detmar Straub
Georgia State University
Copyright Laws

S. Sudarshan
Indian Institute of Technology, Bombay
Database Systems

Howard E. Sypher
Virginia Polytechnic Institute and State University
Research, Electronic

Pandu Tadikamalla
University of Pittsburgh
Statistical Models (Non-Optimization Models)

Joseph K. Tan
The University of British Columbia
Health Care, Information Systems in

Dong-Wan Tcha
Korea Advanced Institute of Science and Technology
Mobile and Wireless Networks

Horia-Nicolai Teodorescu
Romanian Academy and University of
    South Florida
Medicine, Artificial Intelligence in

Sergios Theodoridis
University of Athens
Pattern Recognition

Robert J. Thierauf
Xavier University
Corporate Planning
On-Line Analytical Processing

Marc P. Thomas
California State University, Bakersfield
Unix Operating System

Amrit Tiwana
Emory University
Copyright Laws

Marietta J. Tretter
Texas A&M University
Data Mining

Theodore L. Turocy
Texas A&M University
Game Theory

John Vargo
University of Canterbury, Christchurch,
    New Zealand
Network Environments, Managing
Voice Communications

Michalis Vazirgiannis
Athens University of Economics and Business
Data Modeling: Object-Oriented Data Model

Patrick Verlinde
Royal Military Academy, Belgium
Error Detecting and Correcting Codes
Information Theory

William P. Wagner
Villanova University
Knowledge Acquisition

Ming Wang
California State University, Los Angeles
Database Administration
Database Development Process
Server Classifications

Curt M. White
DePaul University
Multiplexing

Donna Wielbo
National Forensic Science Technology Center,
    University of Florida
Forensics

Jane K. Winn
Southern Methodist University
Electronic Payment Systems

Clive D. Wrigley
University of British Columbia
Electronic Data Interchange

Judy Wynekoop
Florida Gulf Coast University
Local Area Networks

Sangjin Yoo
Keimyung University
Data Flow Diagrams

Victoria Y. Yoon
University of Maryland,
    Baltimore
Expert Systems Construction

K. Yoshida
Hitachi Ltd.
Machine Learning

Vladimir I. Zadorozhny
University of Pittsburgh
Object-Oriented Databases

Fatemeh Zahedi
University of Wisconsin,
    Milwaukee
Quality Information Systems

Shu Zhang
Computer Science Corporation,
    Los Angeles
Server Classifications

Preface

The *Encyclopedia of Information Systems* is the first comprehensive examination of the core topics in the information systems field. We chose to concentrate on fields and supporting technologies that have widespread applications in academic and business worlds. To develop this encyclopedia, we carefully reviewed current academic research in the management information systems (MIS) field in leading universities and research institutions. MIS, decision support systems (DSS), and computer information systems (CIS) curriculums recommended by the Association of Information Technology Professionals (AITP) and the Association for Computing Management (ACM) were carefully investigated. We also researched the current practices in the MIS field carried out by leading IT corporations. Our work assisted us in defining the boundaries and contents of this project. Its articles address technical as well as managerial, social, legal, and international issues in information systems design, implementation, and utilization.

Based on our research we identified 10 major topic areas for the encyclopedia:

- Theories, methodologies, and foundations
- Hardware and software
- Database design and utilization
- Data communications, the Internet, and electronic commerce
- Social, legal, organizational, and international issues
- Systems analysis and design
- Office automation and end-user computing
- Management support systems
- Artificial intelligence
- Applications

Although these 10 categories of topics are interrelated, each addresses one major dimension of information systems design, implementation, and utilization. The articles in each category are also interrelated and com-

plementary, enabling readers to compare, contrast, and draw conclusions that might not otherwise be possible.

Though the entries have been arranged alphabetically, the light they shed knows no bounds. The encyclopedia provides unmatched coverage of fundamental topics and issues for successful design, implementation, and utilization of information systems. Its articles can serve as material for a wide spectrum of courses, such as systems theories, artificial intelligence, data communications and networking, the Internet, database design and implementation, management support systems, office automation, end-user computing, group support systems, systems analysis and design, electronic commerce, hardware and software concepts, programming languages, software design, and social, legal, organizational, and international issues of information systems.

Successful design, implementation, and utilization of information systems require a thorough knowledge of several technologies, theories, and supporting disciplines. Information systems researchers and practitioners have had to consult many sources to find answers. Some of these sources concentrate on technologies and infrastructures, some on social and legal issues, and some on applications of information systems. This encyclopedia provides all of this relevant information in a comprehensive four-volume set with a lively format.

Each volume incorporates core information systems topics, practical applications, and coverage of the emerging issues in the information systems field. Written by scholars and practitioners from around the world the articles fall into 10 major subject areas:

Theories, Methodologies, and Foundations

Articles in this group examine a broad range of topics, theories, and concepts that have a direct or indirect effect on the understanding, role, and the impact of information systems in public and private organizations. They also highlight some of the current research issues in the information systems field. These articles explore historical issues and basic concepts as well as economic and value chain topics. They address fundamentals of systems theory, decision theory, and different approaches in decision making. As a group they provide a solid foundation for the study of information systems.

Hardware and Software

These articles address important hardware and software concepts. The hardware articles describe basic hardware components used in the information systems environment. Software articles explain a host of concepts and methodologies used in the information systems field, including operating systems, high level programming languages, fourth generation languages, web programming languages, and methodologies for developing programs and commercial software.

Database Design and Utilization

The authors in this cluster cover database technologies within information systems. They examine popular database models, including relational, hierarchical, network, and object-oriented data models. They also investigate distributed database concepts, data warehousing, and data mining tools.

Data Communications, the Internet, and Electronic Commerce

Articles in this group explore several fundamental technologies, infrastructures, and applications of the Internet and data communications and networking. LANs, WANs, and client-server computing are discussed and security issues and measures are investigated. Fundamentals of e-commerce technologies and their applications are summarized as are business models on the Web. This collection of articles also presents several applications of data communications and networking, including group support systems, electronic data interchange, intranets, and extranets.

Social, Legal, Organizational, and International Issues

These articles look at important issues (positive and negative) in information systems design and imple-

mentation. These issues include social, organizational, legal, and ethical factors. They also describe applications of information systems in globalization and developing nations and introduce the obstacles involved for the introduction of information systems in a global environment. A thorough examination of these important topics should help decision makers guard against negative aspects of information systems.

Systems Analysis and Design

Articles in this group address tools, techniques, and methodologies for successful analysis and design of information systems. Among their subjects are traditional as well as modern systems analysis and design, software and program design, testing and maintenance, prototyping, and user/system interface design. Project management, control tools, techniques, and methodologies for measuring the performance and quality of information systems are introduced.

Office Automation and End-User Computing

The articles in this category examine ubiquitous information systems applications and technologies such as word processing, spreadsheets, long distance conferencing, desktop publishing, and electronic mail. They also discuss issues and technologies that affect methods for managing these productivity tools, including ergonomic factors and end-user computing.

Management Support Systems

These articles examine information systems technologies containing significant decision-making capabilities, such as decision support systems, group support systems, and geographic information systems. They also look at modeling analysis and the model building process which is essential for effective design and utilization of management support systems.

Artificial Intelligence

Articles in this range address the fundamentals of artificial intelligence and knowledge-based systems. This collection of articles highlight tools and techniques for design and implementation of knowledge-based systems and discusses several successful applications of these systems, including expert systems, machine learning, robotics, speech and pattern recognition and heuristic search techniques.

Applications

Information systems are everywhere. In most cases they have improved the efficiency and effectiveness of managers and decision makers. Articles included here highlight applications of information systems in several fields, such as accounting, manufacturing, education, and human resource management and their unique applications in a broad section of service industries, including law, marketing, medicine, natural resource management, and accounting firms. Although these disciplines are different in scope, they all utilize information systems to improve productivity and in many cases to increase customer service in a dynamic business environment.

Specialists have written this collection for experienced and not so experienced readers. It is to these contributors that I am especially grateful. This remarkable collection of scholars and practitioners have distilled their knowledge into a one-stop knowledge base in information systems that "talks" to readers. This has been a massive effort, but one of the most rewarding experiences I have ever taken. So many people have played a role that it is difficult to know where to begin.

I thank the members of the editorial board and my associate editors for participating in the project and for their expert advice and help with the selection of topics, recommendations for authors, and reviews of the materials. Many thanks to the countless number of reviewers who devoted their time advising me and the authors on how to improve the coverage of these topics.

I thank Dr. J. Scott Bentley, my executive editor, who initiated the idea of the encyclopedia back in 1998. After several drafts and a dozen reviews, the project got off the ground and then was managed flawlessly by Scott and Christopher Morris. They both made many recommendations for keeping the project focused and maintaining its lively coverage. I thank Ron Lee and Nicholas Panissidi, my superb support team at Academic Press, who took paper, diskettes, and e-mail attachments and made them into this final project. Ron and I exchanged several hundred e-mail messages to keep the project on schedule. I am grateful for all their support.

Last, but not least, I thank my wonderful wife Nooshin and my two lovely children Mohsen and Morvareed for being so patient during this venture. They provided a pleasant environment that expedited the completion of this project. Also, my two sisters Azam and Akram provided moral support throughout my life. To this family, any expression of thanks is insufficient.

Hossein Bidgoli

Guide to the Encyclopedia

The *Encyclopedia of Information Systems* is a comprehensive summary of the relatively new and very important field of information systems. This reference work consists of four separate volumes and 200 different articles on various aspects of this field. Each article in the Encyclopedia provides a comprehensive overview of the selected topic, intended to inform a broad spectrum of readers, ranging from computer professionals and academicians to students to the general business community.

In order that you, the reader, will derive the greatest possible benefit from the *Encyclopedia of Information Systems,* we have provided this Guide. It explains how the encyclopedia is organized and how the information within it can be located.

Organization

The *Encyclopedia of Information Systems* is organized to provide the maximum ease of use for its readers. All of the articles are arranged in a single alphabetical sequence by title. Articles whose titles begin with the letters A to D are in Volume 1, articles with titles from E to J are in Volume 2, articles from K to R are in Volume 3, and S to Z in Volume 4.

So that they can be easily located, article titles generally begin with the key word or phrase indicating the topic, with any descriptive terms following (e.g., "Crime, Use of Computers in" is the article title rather than "Use of Computers in Crime").

Table of Contents

A complete table of contents for the entire Encyclopedia appears in the front of each volume. This list of article titles represents topics that have been carefully selected by the editor-in-chief, Dr. Hossein Bidgoli, and his colleagues on the Editorial Board.

Following this list of articles by title is a second complete table of contents, in which the articles are listed according to subject area. The Encyclopedia provides coverage of ten specific subject areas, such as Management Support Systems and Database Design and Utilization. Please see the Preface for a more detailed description of these subject areas.

Index

A Subject Index is located at the end of Volume 4. This index is the most convenient way to locate a desired topic within the Encyclopedia. The subjects in the index are listed alphabetically and indicate the volume and page number where information on this topic can be found.

Article Format

Each new article in the *Encyclopedia of Information Systems* begins at the top of a right-hand page, so that it may be quickly located by the reader. The author's name and affiliation are displayed at the beginning of the article.

All articles in the Encyclopedia are organized according to a standard format, as follows:

- Title and Author
- Outline
- Glossary
- Defining Paragraph
- Body of the Article
- Cross References
- Bibliography

Outline

Each article begins with an Outline indicating the content of the article to come. This outline provides a brief overview of the article, so that the reader can get a sense of what is contained there without having to leaf through the pages. It also serves to highlight important subtopics that will be discussed within the article. For example, the article "Computer Hardware" includes sections for Input Devices, Output Devices, and Auxiliary Devices. The Outline is intended as an overview and thus it lists only the major headings of the article. In addition, second-level and third-level headings will be found within the article.

Glossary

The Glossary contains terms that are important to an understanding of the article and that may be unfamiliar to the reader. Each term is defined in the context of the particular article in which it is used. Thus the same term may be defined in two or more articles, with the details of the definition varying slightly from one article to another. The Encyclopedia includes approximately 2,000 glossary terms. For example, the article "Crime, Use of Computers in" includes the following glossary entries:

malware Contraction of "malicious software;" executable code intended by its writer to violate the information security of its victims. Examples include viruses, worms, logic bombs, Trojan Horses, and denial-of-service programs.

Trojan Horse Software having undocumented and unauthorized functions in addition to or instead of expected useful functions.

Defining Paragraph

The text of each article begins with a single introductory paragraph that defines the topic under discussion and summarizes the content of the article. For example, the article "Digital Divide" begins with the following defining paragraph:

THE DIGITAL DIVIDE is a phrase commonly used to describe the gap between those who benefit from new technologies and those who do not. The phrase was first popularized by the National Telecommunications and Information Administration (NTIA) in the U.S. Department of Commerce in their 1995 report, "Falling Through the Net: A Survey of the Have Nots in Rural and Urban America."

Cross-References

All the articles in the Encyclopedia have cross-references to other articles. These appear at the end of the article, following the article text and preceding the Bibliography. The cross-references indicate related articles that can be consulted for further information on the same topic, or for other information on a related topic. The Encyclopedia contains more than 1,500 cross references in all. For example, the article "Firewalls" has the following cross references:

Computer Viruses • Crime, Use of Computers in • Electronic Data Interchange • Electronic Mail • Encryption • End-User Computing, Managing • Ethical Issues • Internet, Overview • Network Environments, Managing • Privacy • Security Issues and Measures • Software Piracy • Wide Area Networks

Bibliography

The Bibliography appears as the last element in an article. It lists recent secondary sources to aid the reader in locating more detailed or technical information. Review articles and research papers that are important to an understanding of the topic are also listed.

The bibliographies in this Encyclopedia are for the benefit of the reader, to provide references for further research on the given topic. Thus they typically consist of a half-dozen to a dozen entries. They are not intended to represent a complete listing of all materials consulted by the author in preparing the article.

Sales

Brenda J. Moscove
California State University, Bakersfield

GLOSSARY

personal selling The face-to-face communication between buyer and seller necessary to persuade the prospective buyer to purchase goods and/or services that satisfy the buyer's needs. The modern concept of personal selling is broader including group sales, presentations, telemarketing, and e-commerce.
relationship selling The continuation of selling activities after the sale in order to build good customer relationships.
sales management The planning, implementing, controlling, and evaluation of the sales activities. Included in these activities are sales force recruiting, training, incentives, retention, and evaluation.
selling The communication, often persuasive, between the seller and buyer necessary to effect a transaction where the buyer purchases goods and services to satisfy his/her individual needs/wants or an organization's needs and wants.

I. BACKGROUND AND PURPOSE

The article on information systems for selling focuses on two areas: personal sales and sales management. The traditional definition of personal selling is the face-to-face communication between buyer and seller necessary to persuade the prospective buyer to purchase goods and/or services that satisfy the buyer's needs. However, changes in communication techniques and technology indicate the need to broaden the concept of personal sales to include group sales presentations, telemarketing sales, and e-commerce sales. Progressive companies are

building relationships with their customers. This means that the selling activities continue after the sale is made and information systems may include tracking the follow-up activities of salespersons. The main emphasis of the first half of the article is on face-to-face communications for personal selling, although many of the concepts can be adapted to group selling, telemarketing, e-commerce, and other sales situations.

Sales management is the planning, implementing, controlling, and evaluation of the sales activities. Included in sales management are activities such as sales force recruiting, training, incentives, retention, and evaluation. Also, territory and time management are essential topics. Sales forecasting and actual sales performance are also parts of the sales management process. The second half of the article discusses information systems focusing on selected sales management functions.

This article is intended to help readers think through the information process for sales rather than to be an all-inclusive listing of topics. It approaches the topic of information systems in sales from the perspective of what processes and decisions points should be considered when establishing such systems. It is intended to stimulate further discussion and thinking on the reader's part about how her system should be designed to be most helpful to the salespersons and sales managers for her organization.

II. INFORMATION SYSTEMS FOR THE SALESPERSONS

Salespersons use a sales information system to make their jobs easier and to make them more effective salespersons. Systems developed for individual organizations may differ in content. Before considering helpful information about customers, the sales call, and follow-up, the salesperson should consider what type of background information he needs in order to become a more effective salesperson. For example, the salesperson needs to study the industry and market conditions prevailing in the industry. He must be knowledgeable about the company. Information about the product/service offerings must be studied such as the product/service mix including features, advantages, and buyer benefits for each product and service. The salesperson also should note any product/service support offered by the company: point of purchase displays, calendar for special promotions/events, co-op advertising offers, inventory tracking, and automated customer reorder processes, for instance. Production and distribution information is essential: production capacity and limitations for the various product offerings, distribution systems and conditions affecting delivery, and special problems or opportunities presented by other departments in the company. The competition and their products/services and strengths and weaknesses must be analyzed in a similar manner. Some of the information may be available in the company's overall information system. Any other information needed specifically for selling should be built into the sales information system. The salesperson and sales manager should work together to outline and set the parameters for establishing an information system helpful to the sales force.

III. INFORMATION TO HELP THE SALES FORCE

There are several steps in personal selling and presentation where a formal information system can greatly enhance the salesperson's effectiveness. A major part of the sales information system is designed to facilitate the actual sales activities for the salesperson such as locating leads, giving the sales presentation, and building good customer relations.

A. Prospecting, Leads, and Customer Profiles

For outside salespersons, prospecting is an important activity. Also, prospecting can help salespersons in retail and other situations dealing with the final consumer. Prospecting involves looking for new customers and qualifying them. The result would be to eliminate the prospect from the potential pool of future customers or to qualify them as a lead. The salesperson gathers information about potential individuals and organizations that might be potential buyers. Prospecting information includes the name of the individual, organization, title, address, phone, and any other data needed for making a contact. For business and organizational potential customers, in contrast to consumers, the industry, size of the organization, revenue per year, number of employees, etc., aids in prioritizing the contacts. Other information, like the reputation of the organization, special needs of the organization related to the seller's products/services, and other interesting data should be placed in the system to form a quick profile of the prospect. For individuals, demographic information related to the sale of the company's products and services and other personal facts that can be quickly gathered are entered into the system.

Information about prospects, whether they are organizational buyers or individual consumers, can be gathered from published information sources, such as directories, databases, and trade publications, from people likely to know the individuals or companies under consideration, and/or from participation in trade shows. Often, present customers are good sources of information about prospects. The prospect should be contacted to establish interest and to gain an appointment. The date, time, and persons involved in the contact, including referrals where the salesperson has permission to disclose the source of the referral, should be recorded in the system. The result of the contact should also be recorded. Even if the person or company contacted is not interested, the information can be stored for future follow-up if the salesperson thinks the contact may be developed further some time in the future. Also, a brief record of contacts made and prospects eliminated from the pool should be kept to prevent wasting future time and duplicating efforts. Other information gathered during the prospecting stage for individuals and organizations that are eliminated from the prospect list may be deleted from the system.

A positive contact is called a *lead*. Thus, the purpose of prospecting is to produce a list of qualified leads (potential customers) for the salesperson. A potential customer is defined as a person or organization with the ability to make the buying decision, willingness to buy, and money to buy the product/service. For qualified leads, the salesperson now has the preliminary information in the system that was used for prospecting. She adds to the information provided as the time approaches for the initial appointment or contact. Personal information about the lead may be expanded: likes/dislikes, honors/awards, personality type (if known), and anything that may be helpful in establishing a relationship with the potential customer. A profile describing the lead is developed. If the lead turns into a customer, the profile can be expanded each time the customer is contacted. The profile becomes a tickler file to jog the salesperson's memory about the personal and organizational characteristics surrounding the sale. For example, the profile could indicate that the purchasing agent of company X likes to talk about football before talking business or that buyer Y does not like to chat and wants only to talk about the items being sold.

B. Planning and Delivering the Sales Presentation

Next, the saleperson must plan the sales call or, in the case of retail selling, the presentation. Usually, this activity is called the *preapproach*. The preapproach involves opening the sales presentation, the objectives for the presentation, and planning the sales presentation so that the potential customer's time is not wasted. The preapproach and subsequent activities discussed also apply to existing customers. If the person or company has not been contacted, make an appointment with the lead and record the details. Decide on the purpose(s) of the meeting. For example, it could be to introduce the salesperson and the company, products/services, learn more about the prospective customer and his needs and wants, and obtain a follow-up appointment. These may be legitimate purposes for the first sales contact with an organizational customer where it may take several calls to close the sale. The salesperson may wish to learn more about the buying process. What type of vendor analysis does an organization use in determining suppliers? Does the organization use a buying committee or a purchasing agent for specialized products/services? Or, the purpose could be to show a retail customer merchandise that has just arrived in an attempt to increase sales.

A list of topics to be covered in the meeting should be developed. The sales information system can include a generic listing of topics for companies in various industries and/or specific situations that would save the salesperson's preparation time. It can provide special forms with topical areas or questions to be completed as the salesperson plans individual presentations. If the meeting requires a formal sales presentation, the salesperson should plan the type of presentation to be included.

Formal sales presentations, generally, are categorized as prepared, formula, need satisfaction, and problem solving. The prepared presentation is memorized. Generally, a script is provided for the salespeople. Basically, the salesperson proceeds through the script with little deviation. Different scripts are used for individual products and services. The various scripts can be entered into the information system and accessed by each salesperson.

Formula and need satisfaction presentations call for questioning and listening on the salesperson's part to determine the needs and wants of the potential or actual customer. When the salesperson has discovered the needs and wants the prospective buyer has, he converts these to customer benefits and tailors the presentation around the information most likely to result in the sale. A generic list of topics and questions to be covered in order to discover the customer's wants/needs can become part of the information system. As the salesperson gathers additional facts and data from the potential buyer, he enters the information into the system to be used in subsequent sales contacts. For example, the salesperson may want to note which organizational buyers are driven by price, which are interested in buying into products and services using new technology, and which expect two-day delivery, etc. The information is converted into buyer benefits for specific individuals or organizations. A sophisticated system would include the ability to manipulate textual material to provide instant benefits for various comments that are likely to occur for specific products/services.

The problem-solving presentation involves multiple visits as a rule. The first meetings discuss problems that may occur in the buyer's organization. The salesperson spends time learning about the problems. Then, she prepares a plan to solve the problems. Subsequent visits are scheduled to present a proposal for solving the problems. This proposal includes a price for performing the job. Again, a generic listing of topics and questions to be included in the discovery process can be entered into the system. As the information evolves, it is added to the system. Finally, the proposal is developed. An experienced company or salesperson can develop a generic outline of possible points to include in a proposal to be used in similar situations, such as selling a specific product to companies in the same industry. Line items for preparing the bid can be included with the specific dollar amounts to be completed for each company's set of problems.

A section should be provided for recording buyer's questions and objections should be provided regardless of the presentation type. These are used for follow-up in subsequent meetings. The buyer's questions and objections must be answered in order to obtain the sale. This is where a textual system that can be manipulated easily by the salesperson comes in handy. Similar objections and comments may have been previously encountered; the same information may be used to counter them in the present situation, thus, saving the salesperson's time. These scenarios may be preserved in the information system.

Also, in the planning and follow-up stages, the information system is useful for preparing sales aids that can be shared with the buyer during the presentation. For example, the seller can develop a booklet of anticipated benefits that will appeal to the buyer and then use the booklet with the buyer during the presentation.

C. The Sales Record

The salesperson also must record the details of any sales made to various customers and follow through with placing the order. Information such as date of the order, quantity, item, price, delivery date, and special terms or conditions is included in the sales record. The sales record becomes a history of transactions with each customer. This record is used for tracking sales and providing information to each customer and the salesperson about the order status. It is helpful if the sales record contains various checkpoints that need follow-up actions by the salesperson. For instance, the date on which the goods should leave the warehouse should be noted; the salesperson should use that date for checking on the shipment of goods.

After-sales records include a schedule for making any follow-up calls to service the account and an action summary. The after-sales records are essential for relationship selling, which leads to customer retention. The system should be designed for manipulation of the data. The salesperson should be able to sort the data by date to obtain a daily, weekly, or monthly schedule of activities, by account, by product/services, prospect or customer location, and/or any other means that will increase the salesperson's effectiveness.

D. Time and Territory Management

The sales information system often is used to help the salesperson use his time more efficiently. These records can prioritize the sales activities by sorting prospects and accounts into priority levels. The leads and accounts with the greatest sales potential warrant more frequent contacts by the sales force. Thus, they may be classified as A accounts requiring weekly or monthly contact or as C accounts requiring contact every 6 months. Keeping track of the different categories of accounts and calling accordingly instead of trying to equalize the number of calls to each account produces better sales results.

The system helps in planning the most efficient travel routes for making daily or weekly sales calls, especially if it includes geographic information systems (GIS) software. In addition to travel distance and time, the salesperson must factor in the actual length of time needed to give a presentation or follow up with the customer or prospective buyer. Thus, time should be allocated to selling, nonselling, and travel activities. These information needs should be built into the sales information system.

E. Producing Sales Reports Requested by Management

Other facets of the salesperson's job involve completing reports required by sales managers. Several of these reports are discussed in detail under the Selected Sales Management Information section. However, they are highlighted to emphasize to the reader that the system design needs to provide an easy way for the salesperson to provide information to sales management.

1. Travel and Expense Records

Travel and expenses must be reported in the format required by management. These reports include a schedule of travel for a given period so that management can track the salesperson's activities. The amount of details required in these reports varies by company and management. Company A may require a weekly schedule showing where the salesperson will be staying while Company B requires a detailed schedule including daily appointments. Expenses reimbursed by organizations vary. The most common ones are travel and lodging, phone (including car phones), clerical, samples and promotional materials, entertainment, home PC and laptop, other equipment and supplies (fax, copy, postage, etc.), and auto expenses such as mileage allowances and maintenance.

2. Sales Forecasts

Management may require sales forecasting information from the sales force. The system should accommodate this information and subsequent manipulation. Sales forecasting concepts are discussed under sales management topics.

3. Sales Activity and Performance Reports

Sales reports and other measures of performance are another management requirement. Total sales, sales by customers, sales by product/service, average size of sales, number of sales made, actual sales versus quota, and number of calls made are examples of these reports. Also, the salesperson may be asked to report the number of new customers, total revenue generated by new customers, and/or total revenue generated by new customers, for example. The time interval for these reports varies by company. A good information system makes it possible for the sales force to produce many of these reports without reentering the data. This feature saves the salesperson's time.

4. Software Packages and Applications for the Sales Force

GoldMine Software Corporation focuses information entered into the sales information system around a contact. The company's contact records are the basis for generating many of the above reports. The software covers topics like creating records and establishing contacts, scheduling and viewing contact-based activities, reviewing the sales calendar, and completing the contact activity. GoldMine can be used to replace the Rolodex, manage the salesperson's calendar, and report results and transactions by contact. Thus, information is consolidated into one source.

Salespersons and managers also mention ACT and CALLPLAN software. Inputs include, but are not limited to, basic facts like sales visits usually performed in a given sales period, sales levels, sales margins, and estimated sales response to different levels of sales efforts. The salesperson generates response functions for each account. Different scenarios can be created based on variations in the sales efforts.

IV. SELECTED SALES MANAGEMENT INFORMATION

The information system for sales provides tools to manage the sales activity. The system should include data needed by sales managers to plan, implement, control, evaluate, and revise the sales plan and activities. Also, recruitment, training, and staffing are im-

portant sales management tasks. The information system should provide information to help managers make better decisions. Selected topics for sales managers are discussed. The topics are not intended to be an exclusive listing of all uses for a sales information system. Each system should be designed and adapted for the needs of individual organizations. Hence, a caution is issued that, if ratios, formulas, and models are incorporated into the system, they should be monitored to ensure that they work in the individual company situation. In many cases, these applications must be modified to fit the company's specific needs for sales information.

A. Recruiting and Training

Recruiting and training of the sales force aids can be built into the information system. Sales managers may find compiled lists of where to look for sales staff helpful. These lists can be from subscriptions, directories from trade and/or universities, recruiting services on the Web, or other sources. They are consulted whenever the organization needs additional salespersons or replacements. The most frequently used sources can be incorporated into the sales information system. *Pro forma* application job descriptions, job announcements, and interview forms may be included in larger systems. Computer models for combining test scores, interview results, ratings by references, and other data helpful for hiring decisions can be built into the information system particularly for larger organizations requiring large sales forces.

For organizations wishing to outsource training, data on existing training resources are available. Such data include the name of the organization providing the training and contact point, the type of training, the length of the training session, place of training, and the cost of the training session. Other details might be the method of delivery, on-line versus "live instruction," for example, or on-the-job versus centralized, in-house training. Comments about the outcome of any training offered may be included in the record. Often this information is reduced to cost–benefit analysis. Other types of training information may be incorporated into the system, like scenarios presenting various sales opportunities or problems. This material can be accessed and manipulated to provide in-house training materials to cover specific training needs. Costs for offering training in various locations are integral parts of some systems. A listing of locations, accommodations, and contacts for preferred training sites could reduce search time.

B. Size of Sales Force

Sales managers are responsible for determining the size of the sales force. If the company employs a large sales force and the sales needs are dynamic, a method for determining the number of salespersons can be considered for inclusion in the sales information system.

1. Breakdown Approach

One population-based method is the breakdown approach. This method incorporates data for the sales, population, and/or number of customers in a given area. The first step is to obtain an overall company sales forecast for a stated time period. The next step plugs in information about total average sales projected by salesperson (or territory—one salesperson per territory). The computation is:

Number of sales people

$$= \frac{\text{Forecasted sales}}{\text{Average sales per sales person}}$$

Other variations calculate the estimated population needed to support one retail store, the estimated number of retail stores in an area, and the number of retail stores that can be served by one salesperson in computing the breakdown. Additional considerations affecting sales include the type of organization specified for the sales force (geographic, product/service, industry), desired market coverage ranging from intensive to exclusive, and type of products/services sold.

2. Workload Method

Another method for determining sales force size is the workload method, sometimes called the buildup method. The workload method involves placing customers into categories, like key accounts, moderate accounts, and small accounts. Then the frequency of calling on each of the three categories is listed along with the length of each call. The workload to cover the entire territory is calculated; for instance, 8000 hours per year. The amount of time each salesperson has is listed (2000 hours per year). Then, the salesperson's time is allocated by task; for example: selling is 800 hours per year, nonselling is 600 hours per year, and travel is 600 hours per year. Using the selling time only, the number of sales persons needed per year is calculated:

$$\text{Number of salespeople} = \frac{8000}{800} = 10$$

C. Territory Management

The establishment of sales territories or reallocation of districts is more complex. These calculations can involve estimates of sales potential by total, individual customers, projected customers, industry, and/or product/service line; number of customers by product/service line, by industry, and/or size of organization; type of customer such as number of key accounts versus minor accounts, wholesale versus retail or final consumer compared to salesperson total sales; etc. Other factors to be considered include the objectives guiding the allocation of territories. For example, is the goal to equalize total sales potential, number of key accounts, physical size of the territory, or to minimize the travel time and expense? The territory boundaries and time period must be specified.

Established units for territory management may include state, trading area, county, or municipality designations. Metropolitan statistical areas, census track information, or zip codes can be incorporated into the territory management information, particularly for territories that are population based. *Potential Ratings for Zip Code Markets,* often referred to as PRIZM, details the 25,000 neighborhood areas in the United States and results in 40 clusters based on consumer behavior and lifestyles.

Organizational markets are often defined by industries where the Standard Industrial Codes (SIC) may be built into the information system. The use of GIS may be helpful in defining both consumer and organizational markets and sales territories. Needless to say, the data should be appropriate for decision making by the sales manager using information most closely related to the company's needs for territory management.

D. Managing the Incentive Plan

The sales manager may or may not be directly responsible for administering the sales compensation plan. In any case, he should be able to compute the salesperson's cost including salary, commission, draw accounts, bonus, expenses, and other monetary incentives like fringe benefits offered by the company. These computations are necessary for costing out the sales force and computing performance measures. In companies using combination plans (mixing salaries, quotas and different commission rates, bonuses, stock options, etc.), the information becomes more complicated.

E. Sales Forecasting

Accurate sales forecasting methods are difficult to develop, especially at the company and product/service levels. For industry sales, a fairly reliable figure can be obtained from the government, trade/professional publications, or other readily available source.

At the company level, managers must determine the level of forecasting. Examples of the levels of forecasting that may be included in the sales information system are (1) the estimate of market potential sales or the expected sales of goods/services at the industry level for a certain country or region, (2) the estimate of sales potential or the share of the market the company can expect, and (3) the sales potential or share of the market the company can expect for a product/service or line of products/services. Forecasting is usually a top management or market planning activity with some input from sales; therefore, a detailed discussion is beyond the scope of this article. The main methods of forecasting are presented conceptually because forecasts are important for the sales manager in decision making and in setting performance standards to evaluate the sales force performance. Thus, some of the forecasting techniques should be included in the sales information system.

The first step in forecasting is for management to determine the method of forecasting and source of information for the various levels of forecasts. For instance, a specific government publication may be used as the source for an industry forecast. The source remains constant from year to year. Consistency in applying forecasting techniques is important. A forecast may be prepared for overall company sales. Finally, a forecast for individual product/service lines or individual products/services may be required. At the product/service level, the company will need to compute its own forecasts.

1. Buying Power Index

At the company level, the Buying Power Index (BPI) may be useful especially for certain categories of retail product/services. This method of forecasting involves the use of the BPI published in *Sales & Marketing Management,* "Survey of Buying Power." The BPI is computed for various categories of consumer purchases. It links income, population, and retail sales in specified categories. The BPI is used to indicate the share of total market demand in a geographical area. Weights are applied during the calculation: 5 for income (I) expressed as the percent of disposable personal income in the geographical area, 2 for population (P) expressed as a percent of total U.S. population, and 3 for retail sales (R) expressed as the percent of total retail sales. For further information about the BPI, see the "Survey of Buying Power." The formula is:

$$\text{BPI} = \frac{5I + 2P + 3R}{10}$$

To use the BPI, management must determine whether or not the BPI actually correlates with industry sales in the area. This figure is not very applicable to infrequently purchased, high-cost consumer goods or industrial products. If the index does not apply, the company may wish to develop its own index for estimating demand.

2. Users' Expectations Method

An alternative method of forecasting is the users' expectations method, also frequently referred to as the buyers' intentions method. This method surveys customers or potential customers about their intention to purchase specific products/services over a given time period. Responses are then used to determine the sales forecast or market share for the time period for a specific product category.

3. Sales Force Composites

Another forecasting technique is the sales force composite method. Each member of the sales force estimates the sales from his customers or territory for a given time period. The figures are then adjusted by management to reflect management's judgment about the accuracy of the figures. The figures are then added to form estimates for various levels: company, branch, region, salesperson, etc.

4. Jury of Executive Opinion

A fourth method is the jury of executive opinion. Top executives of the company are consulted for their estimates of sales for the stated time period. Their estimates are refined and combined into projections for the company, product/service lines, individual products/services, and level of operation desired like territory or branch.

5. Time Series

A time series relies on historical information about sales and demand in order to project future sales. The pattern of sales from the past is used to predict future sales. Time series analysis works best when conditions are stable; it is not too reliable for businesses operating in dynamic environments. It is, however, easy to use and explain.

6. Statistical Demand Analysis

Statistical demand analysis involves looking at the relationships between sales and other factors affecting sales. If a relationship can be discovered, the results can be used to predict future sales. The variables and relationships are stored in the system.

7. Test Markets

The most accurate forecasting method is test marketing where actual sales results can be measured. Certain locations are selected, a controlled market test is conducted, and results are projected into other locations in which the company does business. The test market parameters and constraints should be incorporated into the system for future reference.

8. Comments about Forecasting Methods

All forecasting methods have flaws. The subjective methods, especially the jury of executive opinion and sales force composite methods, are used more than the statistical methods like time series and statistical demand analysis. Often the results of forecasts derived from different methods are combined to achieve a more accurate forecast. The forecasting process, unless otherwise noted, should be consistent for year to year and territory to territory.

F. Sales Analysis

Sales analysis ranges from simple to complex. Sales analysis can be as simple as listing total company sales for a stated time period. The data are merely enumerated and not compared against any standard. It can be complex like a comparative system requiring looking at hundreds of sales-related figures and making various comparisons—among data groupings, between data groupings, with external data, or over various time periods.

Several questions must be answered in order to build a sales analysis component into the sales information system. First, the type of evaluations system must be determined—simple or comparative. If the system will be comparative, what are the comparisons to be examined? Frequent comparisons are based on

quotas, last year's or forecasted sales, and by territories. Another question is what types of reports and controls are needed? Reporting methods include all data available on the topic or reporting deviations from the norm. A further question concerns the sources of information to be used. Information can be obtained from sales invoices, salesperson reports such as call reports, warranty cards, store audits or scanner data, diary panel data, etc. A final concern is what sales breakdowns are needed? Sales information can be reported by geographic regions or sales territories, product/services, package size, customers or customer size, channel of distribution, sales method, size of order, and terms of sale. Again, this listing is not intended to be comprehensive but only to give examples of ways to report sales information. The marketing and sales managers must determine the type of sales reports needed. For example, do they need reports by type of sale such as cash or charge, product/service category, and/or type of customer (retail, wholesale, industry, use, etc.)? Does the sales manager or organization need simple or comparative reports?

G. Sales Performance Measures

Measuring sales performance is a vital part of the sales manager's job. Often, minimum standards or norms are established for the various criteria allowing the manager to manage by exception. In other words, in looking at performance, the reports generated will flag problem areas where performance falls below the norms and point out performance well above the required standard. Such information is used by management to treat problems before they become a crisis and to look at exceptional performance in order to determine whether any of the practices could be incorporated into training that would enhance sales for less successful salespeople. Data deviating from the norms established are used to indicate more detailed reports that are needed in order to further examine problem areas. The time period and other constraints on the data must be defined.

A way to determine information needed for analyzing sales force performance is by thinking in terms of inputs and outputs. For instance, inputs could include data related to calls, time and time utilization, expenses, and nonselling activities. Outputs could include data related to orders and accounts.

Another perspective is to consider the two types of criteria used for evaluating sales performance. The first type is quantitative and the second is qualitative. Examples of quantitative criteria, which are easier to build into the information system, include sales volume, which is normally reported in terms of total revenue, market share, percentage increases, and actual performance compared to quotas set. The average number of calls per day, week, or month is another example. The number of new customers obtained and size of new orders may be tracked. Gross profit in terms of product/service line or individual products/services, customer or customer type, and order size can be specified. Other factors such as discounts, allowances, and cost of returns are included.

Qualitative criteria, which are descriptive instead of quantitative, are included especially if the descriptive terms can be converted to weights, rankings, scales, and other more quantitative measures. Qualitative criteria could include selling skills, such as listening, questioning, product knowledge, product benefits, obtaining customer participation, handling objections, using trial closes, and closing the sale. Time and territory management skills may be defined and included in the system. Personal traits such as motivation, initiative, teamwork, appearance, self-improvement, and care of company equipment (like an automobile) can be factored into the system. Selected examples of ways to measure sales performance using some of the criteria (mostly quantitative) follow.

1. Total Cost for Each Salesperson

The total costs can be computed by adding salary, commissions, bonuses, stock options, fringe benefits, and expenses, for example. Overall costs and total revenue comparisons are usual comparisons. Cost figures for each salesperson can be related to sales generated per salesperson. Management must decide what comparisons are helpful; for example, to customers served, to orders placed, or to profitability indicators. Cost norms can be established and used to flag areas and salespeople where problems may be occurring.

2. Sales for Each Salesperson and Selected Comparisons

In computing the total sales performance for the sales force members, managers must first define how and when a sale is recorded. For instance, a sale can be considered to have occurred when the order is placed, after the goods have been shipped, or when the invoice is paid. Most organizations regard a sale as the placement of an order minus any returns or cancellations. A few companies credit half the amount of the sale at the time of the order and the other half at the time of payment. Sales can be defined in alternative terms; for instance, will sales be measured as total revenue, total units, or by some other unit of measure?

Given the definition of a sale, a simple sales report would merely report total sales for a month, year, or specified time period by salesperson or territory. A comparative report might compare total sales to some other figure like a quota resulting in a sales index. A sales performance index is computed as follows:

$$\text{Performance index} = \frac{\text{Actual sales} \times 100}{\text{Quota}}$$

Index figures of less than 100 indicate the quota has not been reached. Other factors can be added to the index like the BPI to refine the computation by relating the quota to population, income, and retail sales dimensions.

Sales figures can be related to company total sales, the sales territory, or analyzed by salesperson. Additional comparisons can be made such as sales revenue and costs. Sales figures and the number of orders placed or the number of calls are often useful. The data for producing the most useful reports must be defined and integrated into the system.

3. Call Records and Selected Comparisons

Another series of comparisons included in the information system for sales focuses on the salesperson's call records. First the number of calls made in a given time period is reported. Cost per call figures for the total sales force may be reported compared to the total revenue generated. Or cost per call figures for individual salespersons are compared to the revenue generated by each salesperson. The number of calls related to the number of orders may be helpful either overall or by salesperson. The number of calls compared to average order size could be helpful. These comparisons often are expressed as ratios. Once the manager decides on the types of comparisons he needs related to the call information, the process can be built into the information system.

4. Selected Examples of Ratios Used to Evaluate Sales Force Performance

Ratios commonly used for evaluating sales force performance include the following:

Expense Ratios

$$\text{Sales expense ratio} = \frac{\text{Expenses}}{\text{Sales}}$$

$$\text{Cost per call ratio} = \frac{\text{Total costs}}{\text{Number of calls}}$$

Account Development and Servicing

Account penetration ratio

$$= \frac{\text{Accounts sold}}{\text{Total accounts available}}$$

New account conversion ratio

$$= \frac{\text{Number of new accounts}}{\text{Total number of accounts}}$$

Lost account ratio

$$= \frac{\text{Number of prior accounts not sold}}{\text{Total number of accounts}}$$

$$\text{Sales per account ratio} = \frac{\text{Total sales revenue}}{\text{Total number of accounts}}$$

$$\text{Average order size ratio} = \frac{\text{Total sales revenue}}{\text{Total number of orders}}$$

Order cancellation ratio

$$= \frac{\text{Number of cancelled orders}}{\text{Total number of orders}}$$

Call or Productivity Ratios

$$\text{Calls per day ratio} = \frac{\text{Number of calls}}{\text{Number of days worked}}$$

$$\text{Calls per account ratio} = \frac{\text{Number of calls}}{\text{Number of accounts}}$$

$$\text{Call plan ratio} = \frac{\text{Number of planned calls}}{\text{Total number of calls made}}$$

$$\text{Order per call ratio} = \frac{\text{Number of orders}}{\text{Total number of calls}}$$

5. Tracking and Computing the Cost of Lost Sales

The information system may be set up to track lost sales by salesperson, customer, and cost to the company. For instance, the cost of lost sales to the company per year may be determined as follows:

Total yearly revenue lost

= Number of customers lost to the company per year

× Total annual revenue by customer

Total annual profits lost

= Total yearly lost revenue

× % profit margin on revenue

Total closing costs per year

= Average closing cost per account

× Number of customers lost to the company per year

Total yearly cost of lost customers

= Total closing cost per year

+ Total yearly profits lost

V. COST ANALYSIS FOR SALES AND MARKETING

Cost analysis or profitability analysis is also part of managing the sales function. Cost analysis for marketing and sales requires data that are not readily reported in the accounting records of the firm. Cost or profitability analysis often is a function of the marketing and other departments rather than solely a sales function. Thus, the topic is only mentioned in this section. The three approaches to cost allocation are full costing, contribution analysis, and activity-based costing (ABC). Contribution analysis seems to be the most appropriate way to analyze the data; however, the full cost approach may be more popular because the figures are easier to obtain. The cost/profitability analysis results differ according to the method used. Unfortunately, many firms do not provide the data needed for the types of marketing cost/profitability analysis useful for sales managers. The reports are customized to provide the details needed by management. Many companies are reluctant to design and provide these reports.

Cost and sales analyses provide financial tools for controlling the sales function. Sales analyses measure the actual results achieved via sales data. Cost analyses measure the cost of producing the results. A missing factor is the assets needed to achieve the results. The return on assets managed (ROAM) formula can supply the missing information. This formula involves both the contribution margin associated with a stated sales level and asset turnover. The formula is:

ROAM = Contribution as a percentage of sales

× Asset turnover rate

The formula assumes that the return to a business unit or segment can be improved by increasing the sales profit margin or by keeping the same profit margin and increasing asset turnover. Consequently, ROAM is used to evaluate business segments or to evaluate alternate strategies.

VI. IMPLICATIONS

While the purpose of this article is to discuss the concepts involved in building information systems for personal sales and sales management instead of the specific hardware and software necessary for the information system, some basic equipment is rudimentary for setting up the system. Types of equipment and software basic to the system operations include, but are not limited to:

- Access to PC's, laptops, automated note pads, etc., for each salesperson and manager; computer networks
- Pagers, cellular phones, and other electronic communication devices
- Customized software to provide the information needed and information networks
- Software packages
- Access to various databases (scanner data, for example) and subscription services
- Access to the Internet

The technology for selling is advancing rapidly. For instance, the gains in e-commerce sales are affecting the way selling is performed. While the outcomes of technological advancements cannot be easily predicted, the concept of selling and how to sell are changing. Wireless Internet technologies also should be monitored for implications and importance. Salespersons and sales managers must be technologically current in order to adequately service customer needs in cost-effective ways.

Information systems for selling must be user friendly. They should quickly provide data, problem solutions, and reports for the salesperson and manager through the easy manipulation of text and data. They must provide currency and consistency. The parts of the information system should interface to avoid duplication of effort. For example, the call sheet becomes the sales report log from which data can be extracted for management reports. Salespersons and managers should set the parameters and specifications for establishing user-friendly systems. If the organization lacks the financial resources to build a complete system, an incremental approach is suggested. Company security and privacy issues with the information system must be addressed. Information, easily obtained, is a marketing advantage and leading companies represent the cutting edge in the use of sophisticated information systems to build competitive advantage.

SEE ALSO THE FOLLOWING ARTICLES

Advertising and Marketing in Electronic Commerce • Cost/Benefit Analysis • Electronic Commerce • Electronic Payment Systems • Marketing • Procurement • Research • Transaction Processing Systems

BIBLIOGRAPHY

ACT software information, version 2.1 (1986, 1990). Cupertino, CA: Symantec Corporation.

Churchill, G., Ford, N., Walker, O., Johnston, M., and Tanner, J. (2000). *Sales force management,* 6th ed. New York: Irwin McGraw-Hill.

DC Consulting (2001). *GoldMine essentials and power tips: Booklet (Windows 95/Windows).* New York: McGraw-Hill.

Futrell, C. M. (1999). *Fundamentals of selling,* 6th ed. New York: Irwin McGraw-Hill.

Lamb, C. W., Hair, J., and McDaniel, C. (2000). *Marketing,* 5th ed. Cincinnati: South-Western College Publishing.

Lilien, G. L., and Rangaswamy, A. (1998). *Marketing engineering computer-assisted marketing analysis and planning,* Reading, MA: Addison Wesley.

Lodfish, L. M. (December 1971). CALLPLAN: An interactive salesman's call planning system. *Management Science,* Vol. 18, No. 4, Pt. 2, 25–50.

Manning, G. L., and Reece, B. L. (1998). *Selling today,* 7th ed. Upper Saddle River, NJ: Prentice Hall.

O'Brien, J. (1995). *Introduction to information systems,* New York: Irwin McGraw-Hill.

Schiff, J. S. (April 1983). Evaluating the sales force as a business. *Industrial Marketing Management.* Vol. 12, No. 2, pp. 131–137.

Weitz, B., Castleberry, S., and Tanner, G. (2001). *Selling: A step-by-step approach,* 3rd ed. New York: Irwin McGraw-Hill.

SAS (Statistical Analysis System)

George A. Marcoulides and Laura D. Marcoulides

California State University, Fullerton

I. INTRODUCTION
II. SAS SYSTEM FILES

III. OVERVIEW OF THE SAS SYSTEM COMPONENTS

GLOSSARY

applications software Programs that are written to apply the computer to conduct a specific task.

data analysis tools Special types of programs that are used to analyze and interpret data.

decision support applications An information and planning approach that provides users with the ability to analyze data and consider the impact of decisions before they are actually made.

graphical analysis tools Special types of programs that are used to analyze and display data for planning and decision making.

statistical and mathematical analysis tools Special types of programs that are used to collect, summarize, analyze, and interpret data for planning and decision making.

I. INTRODUCTION

The SAS system is a fully integrated, modular-based, and hardware-independent system of software. It was original developed at North Carolina State University for use in statistical analysis research and is based on the acronym for Statistical Analysis System (SAS). It has evolved over the years into a widely used and extremely flexible software system for statistical applications, but also offers other procedures for data warehousing, data mining, data visualization, on-line analytic processing (OLAP), and many other decision support applications. For this reason, SAS is no longer

considered an acronym for any particular application, but rather a brand name for an entire system.

The SAS system can be thought of as a library of algorithms and application software that can be accessed by submitting sets of program commands. The syntax of a SAS program is relatively easy to learn. For example, the SAS commands

```
PROC MEANS DATA=MEASURES;
RUN;
```

would generate an array of simple descriptive statistics on all variables in the data set called MEASURES, which are provided in Fig. 1. Being able to access such a wide variety of applications with simple commands is what makes the SAS system so powerful and easy to use.

II. SAS SYSTEM FILES

Three types of system files are very important in any SAS analysis: (1) the SAS program file, (2) the SAS log file, and (3) the SAS output file.

A. SAS Program File

In general, the SAS program file contains the set of commands that describe the data to be analyzed (the so-called DATA statements) and the type of procedures to be performed (the so-called PROC statements). Consider the age, height, and weight measurements obtained from five people presented in

13

The MEANS Procedure					
Variable	N	Mean	Standard Deviation	Minimum Value	Maximum Value
AGE	5	25.800	5.119	20.000	32.000
WEIGHT	5	161.000	26.552	130.000	190.000
HEIGHT	5	66.400	6.107	60.000	75.000

Figure 1 Results generated by the PROC MEANS command.

Table I. The following program lines could be used to input these data into the SAS system:

```
DATA MEASURES;
INPUT AGE 1-2 WEIGIIT 4-6 HEIGHT 8 9;
CARDS;
30 130 60
25 185 70
20  90 65
32 140 75
22 160 62
;
```

The information does not have to begin in any particular column but each statement in SAS begins with a one-word command name that tells SAS what to do, and ends with a semicolon (;). The DATA command statement provides the name for the data set that follows. The name chosen for this data set is MEASURES. The INPUT command statement names the variables to be studied and the columns in which the data are located (free-format statements can also be used in which no column location is specified). The variable names used in the above example represent the variables included in the data set. The CARDS command statement indicates that the data lines come next. It is important to note that a CARDS command is the simplest way to tell the SAS system about the location of the data. This approach requires that the data lines follow immediately after the CARDS command. Another way to inform

Table I **Example Data Set**

Age (years)	Weight (pounds)	Height (inches)
30	130	60
25	185	70
20	190	65
32	140	75
22	160	62

the SAS system about data is to use the INFILE command statement. For example, the following lines could be used with the INFILE command statement:

```
DATA MEASURES;
INFILE 'MEASURES.DAT';
INPUT AGE WEIGHT HEIGHT;
```

The INFILE command statement indicates the file name from which the data are to be read, and the INPUT statement directs the system to "retrieve the data from file MEASURES.DAT" according to the specified free-formatted variables.

Once a SAS data set is created, all types of analyses can be performed using any number of PROC command statements. PROC refers to the procedures to be performed on data. PROC command statements are just like computer programs that read a data set, perform various manipulations, and print the results of the analyses. Although only a simple example was illustrated above, it is important to note that the SAS system contains hundreds of procedures that can be used for data analysis. The various procedures, categorized according to components embedded within the SAS system, are described in further detail later.

Once a program file is submitted to the SAS system, two types of files reporting the results of the requested analyses are created. The first is called the SAS log file, and the other is called the SAS output file. The SAS log file contains messages and other information related to the execution of the SAS program file, whereas the SAS output file contains the results of the requested analyses.

B. SAS Log File

The SAS log file is a complete listing of messages concerning the submitted program file. If the program file is executed successfully, the log file will provide a reprinting of the program file and an indication of the number of variables and observations included in the analyzed data set. If the program file does not execute successfully, the log file provides a listing and location of the errors made. For example, the above `PROC MEANS` program file would provide the log file presented in Fig. 2.

If the `PROC MEANS` statement were incorrectly spelled as 'PROC MENS,' the log file would contain the error message displayed in Fig. 3. Whenever an error message is encountered, the SAS program file must be corrected and resubmitted for analysis before proceeding to the SAS output file.

C. SAS Output File

The SAS output file provides a complete listing of the analyses generated by the SAS program file. For example, the following program lines would generate the simple statistics and Pearson correlation coefficients among variables provided in Fig. 4:

```
DATA MEASURES;
INPUT AGE 1-2 WEIGHT 4-6 HEIGHT 8-9;
CARDS;
30 130 60
```

```
25 185 70
20  90 65
32 140 75
22 160 62
;
PROC CORR;
RUN;
```

III. OVERVIEW OF THE SAS SYSTEM COMPONENTS

The SAS system is made up of numerous components for handling four commonly encountered data-driven tasks: (1) data access, (2) data management, (3) data analysis, and (4) data presentation. Table II provides a complete listing of all the currently available SAS system components. Each of the SAS system components is described next.

A. Base SAS

The Base SAS component is a key component of the total SAS system. It contains the essential procedures for

```
NOTE: Copyright (c) 1999-2000 by SAS Institute Inc., Cary, NC, USA.
NOTE: SAS (r) Proprietary Software Release 8.1 (TS1M0)
      Licensed to CSU FULLERTON-CAMPUSWIDE-TEACHING & RESEARCH, Site 0039713013.
NOTE: This session is executing on the WIN_PRO platform.

NOTE: SAS initialization used:
      real time           11.66 seconds
      cpu time             0.78 seconds

1    DATA MEASURES;
2    INPUT AGE 1-2 WEIGHT 4-6 HEIGHT 8-9;
3    CARDS;

NOTE: The data set WORK.MEASURES has 5 observations and 3 variables.
NOTE: DATA statement used:
      real time            0.79 seconds
      cpu time             0.01 seconds

9    ;
10   PROC MEANS DATA=MEASURES;
11      RUN;

NOTE: There were 5 observations read from the data set WORK.MEASURES.
NOTE: PROCEDURE MEANS used:
      real time            0.74 seconds
      cpu time             0.02 seconds
```

Figure 2   Example SAS log file.

```
12    DATA MEASURES;
13    INPUT AGE 1-2 WEIGHT 4-6 HEIGHT 8-9;
14    CARDS;

NOTE: The data set WORK.MEASURES has 5 observations and 3 variables.
NOTE: DATA statement used:
      real time              0.11 seconds
      cpu time               0.02 seconds


20    ;
21    PROC MENS DATA=MEASURES;
ERROR: Procedure MENS not found.
22      RUN;

NOTE: The SAS System stopped processing this step because of errors.
NOTE: PROCEDURE MENS used:
      real time              0.01 seconds
      cpu time               0.01 seconds
```

Figure 3 SAS log file displaying error message.

data processing, summarizing, and reporting results. For example, frequency counts, cross-tabulation tables, various descriptive statistics, including the mean, variance, standard deviation, correlation, and many other measures of association are easily generated through a few simple commands. The Base SAS component also provides extensive data access and interface capabilities and supports Structured Query Language (SQL), the ANSI-standard language that allows one to create, retrieve, and update database information.

```
                        The CORR Procedure

              3 Variables:   AGE    WEIGHT   HEIGHT


                         Simple Statistics

  Variable   N    Mean        Std Dev     Sum         Minimum     Maximum

  AGE        5    25.80000    5.11859     129.00000   20.00000    32.00000
  WEIGHT     5    141.00000   35.42598    705.00000   90.00000    185.00000
  HEIGHT     5    54.40000    28.27189    272.00000   5.00000     75.00000


                 Pearson Correlation Coefficients, N = 5
                      Prob > |r| under H0: Rho=0

                         AGE        WEIGHT      HEIGHT

        AGE           1.00000      0.18750     0.68481
                                   0.7627      0.2021

        WEIGHT        0.18750      1.00000     0.81573
                      0.7627                   0.0923

        HEIGHT        0.68481      0.81573     1.00000
                      0.2021       0.0923
```

Figure 4 Results generated by the PROC CORR command.

Table II List of SAS System Components

Base SAS	SAS/ETS	SAS/OR
Enterprise Miner	SAS/FSP	SAS/QC
Enterprise Reporter	SAS/GIS	SAS/SHARE
SAS/ACCESS	SAS/GRAPH	SAS/SPECTRAVIEW
SAS/AF	SAS/IML	SAS/STAT
SAS/ASSIST	SAS/INSIGHT	SAS/TOOLKIT
SAS/CALC	SAS/IntrNet	SAS/Tutor
SAS/CONNECT	SAS/LAB	SAS/Warehouse Administrator
SAS/EIS	SAS/MDDB Server	WebHound

B. Enterprise Miner

The Enterprise Miner component is an integrated data mining software product which, combined with the SAS Warehouse Administrator (see description below) and OLAP technologies, provides users with automated procedures for selecting, exploring, modifying, and modeling large amounts of data to uncover previously unknown patterns. The Enterprise Miner component provides a user-friendly point-and-click front-end graphical user interface to create complicated data mining process flow diagrams. Fairly sophisticated statistical analysis tools like clustering, decision trees, linear and nonlinear regression, logistic regression, and neural networks can be easily invoked. Similarly, data preparation and visualization tools can be accessed in order to examine large amounts of data. Although the Enterprise Miner component provides quantitative experts with the opportunity to control entirely the data mining process, it also provides less sophisticated users with an opportunity to take advantage of the state of the art in machine-driven data exploration.

C. Enterprise Reporter

The Enterprise Reporter component is an integrated part of the entire SAS system which, when combined with the SAS Warehousing Administrator (see description below), is designed to offer users the ability to customize reports. It is specifically constructed to look and feel like a Microsoft Office component with all the familiar graphical user interface capabilities. Besides providing traditional hardcopy output, various expanded options for output, such as HTML for web browser distribution and PDF files for e-mail distribution, are also available.

D. SAS/ACCESS

The SAS/ACCESS component is comprised of various data access engines that can translate read-and-write requests to an assortment of DBMS or file structures. For example, direct access to database and ERP systems like ADABAS, IMS-DL/I, Informix, R/3, the SYSTEM 2000 software (the user-oriented database and logical storage SAS software component for production applications) is possible, and a variety of relational databases are available. Regardless of the source or platform on which the data reside, SAS/ACCESS handles all external data as native to the SAS system and provides users with the full functionality of every SAS component available.

E. SAS/AF

The SAS/AF component is an object-oriented development tool for generating customized user-friendly interactive window applications. SAS/AF even includes its own programmable Screen Control Language designed to help users develop SAS system interactive applications and procedures. For example, customized graphical user interfaces complete with icons, pulldown and pop-up menus, and command buttons can be created for users to point-and-click their way through various applications and procedures.

F. SAS/ASSIST

The SAS/ASSIST component is a task-oriented visual interface that enables users to easily access, manage, and analyze data within the SAS system without requiring knowledge of SAS programming syntax. By using a point-and-click interface with the entire SAS System, the SAS/ASSIST component provides users of varying skill levels with the ability to activate almost all of the available SAS components through pulldown menus. The SAS/ASSIST component is also available in eight different languages in addition to English: Danish, Finnish, French, German, Italian, Norwegian, Spanish, and Swedish.

G. SAS/CALC

The SAS/CALC component is a fully integrated component that offers users complete spreadsheet-like graphical and numerical modeling capabilities that enable users to access, manage, analyze, and present data from all types of sources. SAS/CALC also offers programmers and applications developers a spreadsheet programming language for building customized spreadsheet applications that utilize the capabilities available in the entire SAS system. Two-dimensional, three-dimensional, and linked spreadsheet representations for handling groups of related data in a single spreadsheet application are also possible. In addition, graphical representations of the linked spreadsheets showing the established dependencies are easily produced.

H. SAS/CONNECT

The SAS/CONNECT component enables the sharing of data and applications across multiple computing environments. By supporting most communication protocols (e.g., APPC, TCP/IP, DECnet, and NETBIOS) and most terminal-oriented interfaces (e.g., ASYNC, TELNET, and HLLAPI), users are provided with simple and efficient remote processing and data access capabilities.

I. SAS/EIS

The SAS/EIS component is an integrated object-oriented environment for building user-friendly enterprise information systems. Using SAS/EIS, the entire SAS system can be front-ended to handle most common data processing tasks. By providing point-and-click menus with pull-down windows, the SAS/EIS component provides users access to unlimited applications such as report generating, data analysis and screening, graphical displaying, and even e-mail. The SAS/EIS component also includes numerous prewritten objects for doing data processing tasks.

J. SAS/ETS

The SAS/ETS component is an integrated part of the SAS system, specifically designed for modeling all types of dynamic systems and performing various time series analyses. The SAS/ETS component includes such forecasting methods as linear/nonlinear and dynamic regression, trend extrapolation, exponential smoothing, autoregressive integrated moving average modeling (ARIMA or Box Jenkins), and multivariate time series. Users can also call on an automatic model selection facility to select best-fitting models for each time series considered. Various estimation methods are available in the SAS/ETS component such as least squares and full- and limited-information maximum likelihood. In addition, results obtained from the various forecasting methods can be combined to create new models that produce improved time series forecasts.

K. SAS/FSP

The SAS/FSP component is an interactive full-screen information-processing component of the SAS system. Users can customize the appearance of data entry and data display windows. The SAS/FSP component also works hand-in-hand with the SAS/AF component to provide users with predefined objects for designing customized full-screen applications.

L. SAS/GIS

The SAS/GIS component offers an interactive geographic information system (GIS) within the SAS system. SAS/GIS offers users a simple interactive way to organize and analyze data that can be spatially or attribute referenced. Three types of features (points, lines, and areas) can be used to represent data in their spatial context. Spatial data can also be linked to different attribute data. In addition, various physical aspects such as roads, railways, waterways, and even political boundaries can be used to spatially organize data into layers according to their common features or attributes.

M. SAS/GRAPH

The SAS/GRAPH is a high-resolution graphics component of the SAS system. The SAS/GRAPH component offers a wide variety of color graphics capabilities that include charts, plots, maps, and pattern designs. An interactive graphics editor is also provided for importing and modifying all types of graphics-oriented information and presentation material. In addition, SAS/GRAPH provides capabilities for building different multimedia applications like video editing, image capture, processing, and playback. Many popular industry video and image file formats such as AVI, TIFF, GIF, PCX, GEN, and WAV sound files are supported.

N. SAS/IML

The SAS/IML component provides a flexible and extremely powerful interactive matrix programming language. Customized data manipulation and statistical analyses can be programmed using an extensive set of built-in mathematical functions and matrix operators.

For example, obtaining roots of polynomials, solving systems of equations, or computing eigenvalues, eigenvectors, and determinants can be easily handled with just a few simple commands.

O. SAS/INSIGHT

The SAS/INSIGHT component is a dynamic tool for examining, exploring, and analyzing data sets. By providing point-and-click menus with pull-down windows, the SAS/INSIGHT component provides users access to unlimited ways with which to explore data. The SAS/INSIGHT component also provides various modeling options to enable users to quickly build models and analyze observed relationships or patterns in selected data. In addition, simple descriptive statistics and univariate and multivariate correlational and principal component analyses can be generated to numerically confirm visually determined results.

P. SAS/IntrNet

The SAS/IntrNet component is a dynamic application tool for integrating the SAS system into the World Wide Web. By providing users with a so-called common gateway interface (CGI) and Java technologies, the SAS/IntrNet component enables the development and building of web-based applications and data services for easy access and execution of remote SAS-based analyses and programs.

Q. SAS/LAB

The SAS/LAB is a fully integrated, guided data analysis component of the SAS system. SAS/LAB operates like an expert system product designed to help a wide variety of users select and apply the appropriate statistical methods for analysis. The SAS/LAB component is especially designed for engineers and scientists and offers commonly used techniques for analyzing data from experimental design situations. For example, techniques such as analysis of variance, analysis of covariance, and regression analysis are available to users with minimal statistical expertise.

R. SAS/MDDB Server

The SAS/MDDB Server is an OLAP multidimensional database component that enables users to obtain un-

limited views of patterns of relationships in large data sets. By using innovative OLAP capabilities within a database/warehouse environment, the SAS/MDDB Server component offers high-performance access to an incredible array of methods for the analysis and writing of reports on large amounts of data. Once a database is created, it can be accessed by multiple users across various platforms, including the World Wide Web.

S. SAS/OR

The SAS/OR component is a fully integrated component that offers users complete decision support capabilities within the SAS system. SAS/OR includes a number of extremely powerful management science tools for solving complex business problems. For example, procedures for conducting mathematical programming, project management and scheduling, transportation, resource management, decision tree analysis, and networks are available to users through a complete point-and-click interface.

T. SAS/QC

The SAS/QC is a fully integrated component of the SAS system comprised of various specialized procedures for conducting total quality management improvement and quality control activities. For example, control charting, probability plots and life distributions, product reliability estimates, and analysis of data from various types of experimental designs are easily generated through a few simple commands. The SAS/QC component also provides a point-and-click graphical user interface to guide users through the various specialized quality management and quality control applications, and an interface for creating process flow diagrams through the SAS/AF.

U. SAS/SHARE

The SAS/SHARE component operates as a data server within the SAS system to allow multiple users simultaneous access to SAS files while working interactively with other system components. By permitting multiple accessing capabilities across different format and hardware platforms, SAS/SHARE provides users with endless data sharing opportunities. Of course, despite all the data sharing activities, the SAS/SHARE component maintains native host data integrity through security and password verification safeguards.

V. SAS/SPECTRAVIEW

The SAS/SPECTRAVIEW component is a data visualization and analysis tool that offers users interactive capabilities for handling multidimensional data. Users can choose to view data through two- and three-dimensional charts, cutting planes, isometric surfaces, three-dimensional volumes, or stacked contours. Several model images can be handled concurrently using four display windows. In addition, the model images can, independently or collectively, be enlarged, rotated, or modified in terms of image attributes like axis, color, and text. By using a point-and-click menu-driven interface, the SAS/SPECTRAVIEW component provides users with simple but extremely powerful data visualization and analysis capabilities.

W. SAS/STAT

The SAS/STAT component is another key component of the total SAS system. It contains all essential procedures for conducting extensive statistical analysis of data. For example, procedures for conducting analysis of variance, categorical data analysis, cluster analysis, psychometric analysis, regression analysis, survival analysis, and various other types of multivariate and nonparametric analyses are easily handled through a few simple commands. And because the SAS/STAT component is fully integrated with the entire SAS system, users can easily access data from any source, perform data management, conduct data analyses, and present findings through any available reporting or graphical option.

X. SAS/TOOLKIT

The SAS/TOOLKIT is an integrated component specifically designed for users to write customized SAS procedures, formats, functions, call routines, and database engines in one of several programming languages including C, FORTRAN, PL/I, and IBM assembler. A number of programming language debuggers like the SAS/C compiler, the VMS compiler, and the dbx debugger can all be used to assist users with the debugging of code. The SAS/TOOLKIT component also provides an extensive library of routines needed to perform commonly encountered data access, management, and analysis activities. By enabling the development and writing of customized routines and procedures, the SAS system can be tailored to the specific needs of almost any user.

Y. SAS/Tutor

The SAS/Tutor component is an interactive computer-based training course comprised of six different lessons. The SAS/Tutor lessons were written for both beginners and intermediate SAS users. The lessons cover topics beginning with simple DATA command and INPUT command statements, and continue through illustrations of the various PROC statements and SAS System components. Each lesson also offers questions, quizzes, and case studies, as well as guided hands-on practice sessions.

Z. SAS/Warehouse Administrator

The SAS/Warehouse Administrator component is an integrated database software product that, when combined with SAS components like Enterprise Miner and Enterprise Reporter, provides users with an opportunity to effectively maintain and navigate large amounts of data. The SAS/Warehouse Administrator component provides a user-friendly point-and-click graphical user interface that simplifies the visualization, navigation, and maintenance of almost any created data warehouse or data mart.

AA. WebHound

The WebHound component is a new SAS system e-commerce-related software product for monitoring web site visitors. The WebHound component also comes with a clickstream analysis capability, which is the process of measuring and analyzing navigation paths through a web site. Because every visitor to a web site leaves a sort of trail about how the site was used, the WebHound component acts as a tracking system that follows the trail of visitors. In this way, questions such as "Who is visiting the web site?" "How long did they stay in the web site?" or "Which parts of the web site are the most interesting?" can be easily answered.

SEE ALSO THE FOLLOWING ARTICLES

Data Mining • Data Warehousing and Data Marts • Decision Support Systems • On-Line Analytical Processing (OLAP) • SPSS (Statistical Package for Social Sciences)

BIBLIOGRAPHY

Hatcher, L., and Stepanski, E. J. (1994). *A step-by-step approach to using the SAS system for univariate and multivariate statistics.* Cary, NC: SAS Institute, Inc.

Marcoulides, G. A., and Hershberger, S. L. (1997). *Multivariate statistical methods.* Mahwah, NJ: Lawrence Erlbaum Associates.

Miron, T. (1994). *SAS software solutions.* Cary, NC: SAS Institute, Inc.

SAS Institute, Inc. (1990). *SAS language reference guide.* Cary, NC: SAS Institute, Inc.

SAS Institute, Inc. (1990). *SAS procedures guide.* Cary, NC: SAS Institute, Inc.

SAS Institute, Inc. (1990). *SAS/STAT changes and enhancements.* Cary, NC: SAS Institute, Inc.

SAS Institute, Inc. (1990). *SAS user's guide.* Cary, NC: SAS Institute, Inc.

SAS Institute, Inc. (1994). *SAS/STAT user's guide.* Cary, NC: SAS Institute, Inc.

SAS Institute, Inc. (1995). *SAS/INSIGHT user's guide.* Cary, NC: SAS Institute, Inc.

SAS Institute, Inc. (1998). *Getting started with Enterprise Miner software.* Cary, NC: SAS Institute, Inc.

Tilanus, E. W. (1994). *Working with the SAS system.* Cary, NC: SAS Institute, Inc.

Search Engines

Thomas M. Parks

Colgate University

GLOSSARY

crawler See spider.

lexicon A list of words. A search engine may build a lexicon of words extracted from all the documents in its database.

polysemy The property of having multiple meanings. A word is polysemous when it can have different meanings in different contexts.

robot See spider.

spamming The practice of designing Web pages to exploit the ranking methods of search engines.

spider A computer program that visits Web pages by following hypertext links.

stemming The process of removing prefixes and suffixes to obtain the basc form of a word.

stop words Frequently occurring words that convey little information.

synonymy The property of having the same meaning. Words arc synonymous when they have the same meaning.

truncation The process of removing letters from the end of a word

SEARCH ENGINES send out spiders to crawl across the Web, following links from one Web page to the next. The documents discovered by the spider are indexed in a huge database. The ever-changing nature of the Web makes keeping this database up-to-date a constant challenge. Queries entered at search engine sites trigger searches through this database. Thousands or millions of Web pages may match a query. Search engines must rank the results so that the most relevant are displayed first. If there are many irrelevant results, users must refine their queries to find the information they need.

I. INTRODUCTION

In the 1940s, Vannevar Bush envisioned hypertext as a means to record and organize "trails" through the overwhelming and growing body of scientific literature. The natural links between documents, which Bush referred to as associative indexing, would be superior to artificial indexing schemes that organize documents numerically or alphabetically. The interlinked documents of today's World Wide Web embody many of the concepts of Bush's vision. However, even with all the links that form trails for us to follow, it is still difficult to find information.

Searching the Web involves more than looking for matching keywords in the text of Web pages. The Web is not a collection of unrelated documents. There are links between these documents that imply relationships. Search engines that exploit these relationships to provide more relevant results have emerged in recent years.

Computer programs known variously as spiders, crawlers, or robots retrieve and examine Web pages, extracting the links that they find. The spiders follow these links to retrieve other Web pages with links to yet more Web pages. The Web includes not only hypertext documents formatted using the Hypertext Markup Language (HTML), but also text documents in other formats and nontext objects such as images and music. Text documents on the Web can be found in the form of word processing documents, presentation slide shows, and even spreadsheets. Search engines are expanding the file formats that they understand so that they can index text documents in formats other than HTML. Each document visited by a spider is indexed in the search engine's database.

When a user types in a query, the search engine's database is searched. Matching results are ranked and presented to the user as a list on a Web page. Search engines attempt to rank the results so that the most relevant are displayed first. However, characteristics of language can cause relevant pages to be missed and irrelevant pages to be found.

In 1997, there were an estimated 320 million publicly accessible Web pages. This grew to 800 million in 1999 and to over 2 billion in 2000. The Web grows by more than a million pages each day. Because the Web is large, growing, and in a constant state of change, search engines face a difficult task when trying to keep their databases complete and up to date.

II. CRAWLING

A spider is a computer program that crawls across the Web, retrieving Web pages by following hyperlinks. A spider can begin by visiting a single Web page. It extracts all the hyperlinks that it can find in that page, follows each of those links, and repeats the process for each of the new Web pages it visits. The ultimate goal is to discover every Web page in existence, but the structure of the Web itself can make crawling a difficult and time consuming process. This task would be difficult enough if the Web were a static, unchanging collection of documents. Unfortunately, Web pages and links are frequently added, updated, and deleted, so that the spider will have to revisit Web pages from time to time.

A spider that simply adds all the links it discovers to a list of pages to be visited runs the risk of getting trapped in the Web. A spider must remember all the links it discovers. As a spider extracts links from the pages that it visits, it should ignore those links that refer to already-visited pages. Otherwise, a spider risks crawling around in circles if it should stumble across a cluster of Web pages linked together in a cycle. Similarly, links that are already on the list of as yet unvisited pages should not be added to that list again. Otherwise, a spider will waste time on repeated visits to the same Web page. Instead, a spider should either ignore such links or keep a tally of how many times it

comes across each link. If the same link appears repeatedly in many different Web pages, then perhaps it refers to an important page that should be visited sooner than other pages. Several search engine spiders use priorities based on link count and other factors to determine which links should be followed next.

The average number of links on a Web page is between 4 and 5, and some Web pages have many more links, so that for each Web page visited, several new links are added to the list of Web pages to be visited. Clearly, this list of unvisited Web pages can grow quickly. A spider may have to prioritize to decide which of the pages in the list should next be visited. How a spider selects the next page to visit can influence the inclusiveness of the crawling process.

Spiders may give higher priority to links that are encountered more frequently. It is assumed that a Web page with many links leading to it must somehow be more important than a Web page with only a few links. One consequence of such prioritization is that spiders will gravitate toward popular Web sites while neglecting Web sites devoted to more esoteric subjects. Unfortunately, popularity does not always equate to importance.

Spiders may give higher priority to shorter links. Links with fewer subdomains in the host name (fewer dots), or with fewer segments within the path (fewer slashes) may be considered more important and could be selected before longer links. For example, <http://berkeley.edu/> is shorter than <http://ptolemy.eecs.berkeley.edu/> and <http://cs.colgate.edu/> is shorter than <http://cs.colgate.edu/courses/465/syllabus.html>. Such prioritization has several consequences. Web sites that choose to distribute their Web content across several different Web servers, which may consequently have longer names, may be penalized in comparison with those that publish all their content on one server (though there may actually be several servers under the same name with the same content in order to distribute the load of serving Web pages). Similarly, those sites that organize their content into a deep hierarchy may be penalized in comparison with those that choose a flatter hierarchy for naming their Web pages.

The penalty suffered by Web sites that use longer links is that fewer of their Web pages may be visited by a spider that prioritizes on the length of a link. However, this may not be a significant handicap for Web sites that are devoted to a single topic. If many important keywords appear in the pages with shorter links, such as the home page for the Web site, and if the Web site is well-organized and easy to navigate, then search engines will still index the site under relevant keywords, and users who are brought to the site by a search engine will be able to browse to the information that they are seeking. On the other hand, limited crawling of a Web site may be a serious penalty for some Web sites, such as <http://www.aol.com> and <http://www.geocities.com>, that host Web pages for many different individuals and organizations. At such sites, an extra layer of hierarchy results in longer links.

Some Web pages are difficult to find through crawling, and others are completely inaccessible to spiders. Some Web pages are inaccessible because a password is required to access them. Some links are difficult to interpret because they are embedded within scripts on the Web page. The link structure of the Web itself can make it difficult to reach some Web pages. If a spider begins crawling from a randomly selected Web page, there will be a significant portion of the Web that cannot be reached by following links from that starting page. In fact, about half the time a spider will hit a dead end after visiting 100 pages. The spider will be unable to find new links to Web pages that have not already been visited.

III. INDEXING

Think of the Web as a book. Each Web page is like a page in the book, and a search engine is like the index at the back of the book. Interested in a particular topic? Look up a word in the index to find a list of the pages where that topic is discussed. The index in the back of a book is a list of lists: a list of words that appear in the book and, for each word, a list of the pages on which the word appears. In essence, a search engine is an index of the Web. Search engines maintain a list of words that appear in documents on the Web, and for each word there is a list of the documents in which the word appears.

To construct a complete index of the Web, it is necessary to extract every word from every document discovered by the search engine's spider. The search engine constructs a lexicon from the words encountered as it processes the text documents retrieved by the spider. Some search engines may maintain a complete lexicon of every word encountered, while others may omit some words in order to reduce the size of the lexicon. Words such as "a" and "the," which occur frequently but do not convey much meaning, are known as stop words and may be omitted from the lexicon. Some search engines perform stemming, removing prefixes and suffixes to include only the base form of a word in the lexicon. Some search engines ignore capitalization, recording only the uncapitalized form of a word in the lexicon.

For each word in the lexicon, the search engine maintains a list of documents where that word appears. These lists are constructed as each document is processed: as words are extracted from a document, it is added to each of the lists for each of those words. Search engines also record the location within the document at which a word appears. This makes it possible to later search for words as part of a phrase, or words that appear near each other. A weight or score indicating the importance of the word relative to the other words in the document is also recorded. This weight is calculated from a combination of factors. Words that occur frequently within a document, and presumably are relevant to the main topic of the document, are given more weight than words that seldom appear. Similarly, words that appear closer to the beginning of the document, or in prominent positions such as titles or headings, are also given more weight. The precise mathematical formula used in determining this numerical weight varies from one search engine to the other and affects the ranking of search results.

Some search engines index documents that have never been visited by their spiders. Text that appears as part of a link can be associated with the document that the link leads to. In this way, a spider can collect fragments of text that describe a document that has not yet been visited. This technique also makes it possible to index nontext items such as images and music. Many search engines also store and organize information about the link structure of the Web. The location of a Web page can become another "word" in the lexicon. This "word" will appear in documents that have links to that page.

Conceptually, a search engine's index is a lexicon, or list of words. For each word, there is a list of documents in which the word appears. Each entry in the list records not only the a link to a document, but also additional information including a numerical weight indicating the importance of the word in that document. In practice, the search engine's database uses more complex data structures in order to speed up the process of searching. The database may even be distributed across many computers to take advantage of parallel processing.

Many of the techniques just described depend on knowledge of the English language. The documents on the Web are written in a variety of languages with a variety of alphabets, and it can sometimes be difficult to determine the language that a Web page is written in. A search engine that is optimized for the English language may do a poor job of indexing foreign-language documents on the Web.

IV. QUERY PROCESSING

After a spider has retrieved a vast number of Web pages and other text documents, and after an index has been constructed that, for every word in the lexicon, lists every known document that contains that word, a search engine is finally ready to accept queries from users. The user submits one or more keywords and the search engine searches through its vast index to produce a list of the documents that contain one or more of these keywords.

Sometimes few relevant documents are included in the responses to a query. Many relevant documents may be missed because they do not contain the exact keywords of the query, but instead contain related words. Increasing the number of relevant responses requires that words related to the keywords of a query be included when searching through the index. This can be done automatically, or by requiring the user to refine the query.

As mentioned previously, some search engines use stemming when constructing the lexicon. These search engines must also perform stemming on the keywords of a query in order to find matches in the lexicon. Thus, the keywords "mathematics," "mathematical," and "mathematician" would all be reduced to the stem "math" and would all produce identical search results. Thus, a search engine can automatically generalize an overly specific query to increase the number of relevant responses.

Related to stemming is truncation. With truncation, a search engine will seek keyword matches in the lexicon where one or more letters have been removed from the end of words. This can be done automatically, or the user can enter a query in a special form. For example, entering "math*" will cause the words "math," "mathematics," "mathematical," "mathematician," and other words in the lexicon that begin with "math" to be added to the list of query keywords. This new, augmented query will then cause more (hopefully relevant) documents to be included in the response. Stemming and truncation allow different forms of a word, such as singular and plural nouns or verbs in different tenses, to automatically be included in a query. Care must be taken, however, otherwise unrelated words may inadvertently be included in a query. For example, "law*" could cause the words "lawyer" and "lawn" to be included.

Another approach to increasing the number of relevant responses is to automatically add synonyms to a query. If a user enters the word "car," the word "automobile" may be added to the query so that more Web pages will be retrieved. However, not all of the additional responses will be relevant to the original query.

Sometimes the responses to a query include many irrelevant documents. The nature of human language contributes to the problem of irrelevant responses. For example, an American sports fan may search for Web pages about "football" only to find a wealth of information about the sport she knows as "soccer." A British sports fan may search for Web pages about "cricket" only to find pages about an insect. These are examples of polysemy: words that can have multiple meanings. Another example is the word "Java," which can be an island, a caffeinated beverage, or a popular computer programming language. Approaches such as stemming, truncation, and the automatic addition of synonyms to queries can increase the number of relevant responses, but these techniques can also increase the number of irrelevant responses precisely because of polysemy. The words added to the query may have additional, unrelated meanings. Decreasing the number of irrelevant responses generally requires the user to refine the query.

The best cure for the problem of too many irrelevant responses to a query is to have the user enter a more specific query. Unfortunately, the majority of users submit simple queries with only one keyword, ignoring the advanced search features described here.

Some search engines allow a user to limit responses to documents that include or exclude particular keywords. For example, responses to the query

```
Java +island
```

must include the word "island," and may also include the word "Java." Similarly, responses to the query

```
Java -coffee
```

may contain the word "Java," but must not include the word "coffee."

Another, similar approach is to allow Boolean expressions for more precise queries. The Boolean operators AND, OR, and NOT are used to combine query terms. When using OR, pages containing one or more of the keywords are included in the response. When using AND, only pages containing all of the keywords are included. The NOT operator negates the sense of a Boolean expression. For example, the query

```
Java AND (NOT coffee)
```

would return results similar to the query above. Instead of explicitly using Boolean operators, some search sites provide choices such as "any of the words" for OR and "all of the words" for AND.

Several other techniques are available for refining queries. Users may specify that keywords must appear in specific parts of a Web page, such as the title, a section heading, or the location of the page itself. Exact phrases may be entered as query terms by enclosing them in quotation marks. For example, the query

```
title:"breast cancer" domain:gov
```

might be used to find Web pages at government Web sites with the phrase "breast cancer" in the title.

V. RANKING

After a search engine has produced a list of thousands of Web pages in response to a user's query, it must rank these results before displaying them to the user. Unless the most relevant documents can be displayed at the top of the list, a search engine is useless. Because ranking algorithms often fail to place relevant documents at the top of the list of responses, it is important for users to refine their queries by taking advantage of advanced search features, such as those discussed previously, to eliminate as many irrelevant responses as possible without limiting the number of relevant responses.

Most search engines rank results by keywords. A simple ranking algorithm would give a higher rank to a document that contained all of the keywords in the query and a lower rank to one that contained only some of the keywords. This simple formula can be modified to take into account the keyword weights stored in the search engine's database. A document can be assigned a score that combines the weights for the matching keywords. If a matching keyword is one of the more important words for a document, then that document would receive a higher score. The score for a document is then determined by the sum of the numerical weights for each query keyword that appears in the document. The documents with the highest scores would be ranked at the top of the list of search results. The weights for each word in each document can be calculated in advance and stored in the search engine's index. The final rank for a document, however, can only be calculated after a query has been submitted.

The exact formulas used to calculate keyword weights and to rank documents are closely held secrets. If these details were made readily available, then it would be easier for Web page authors to design their pages so that they could easily be found in response to a relevant query. Unfortunately, it would also be easier for unscrupulous Web page authors to design their pages so that they could easily be found

in response to common (not necessarily relevant) queries. Many Web designers engage in the practice of spamming: they attempt to manipulate the ranking algorithms of search engines so that their pages will be ranked higher than other Web pages. Some techniques including repeated keywords that are not visible when users view the Web page but are visible when a search engine examines the HTML source of that page. These repeated keywords can appear in the title, in special META tags in the header, or even as normal text that is the same color as the background. It is because of the practice of spamming that details of search engine ranking algorithms are kept secret. Spammers (and other Web authors) are left to make educated guesses about how to get their Web pages noticed by search engines and ultimately by users.

More recently, some search engines have begun to use the link structure of the Web to rank search results. Web pages that are linked to by many other Web pages are ranked higher than Web pages with only a few links to them. Some search engines go a step further and take into account the importance of the page that a link comes from. A Web page with only a few links from important pages may be ranked higher than a page with many links from unimportant pages. These rankings for Web pages can be calculated in advance, before the user enters a query, and stored in the search engine's database.

Some search engines rank Web pages by how often users visit the page when it appears in a list of search results. Other search engines auction off the positions at the top of the list of results, placing a page closer to the top in exchange for a higher bid. The owner of the Web page then pays a fee each time that a user selects that page from the list of results.

VI. LIMITATIONS OF SEARCH ENGINES

Each individual search engine covers only a fraction of the Web, but combining the databases of the major search engines increases coverage significantly. Measuring the coverage of a search engine can be done by carefully studying the responses to numerous queries. By submitting the same queries to different search engines, it is possible to compare the coverage of those search engines. Up-to-date comparisons of search engines can be found at Web sites such as Search Engine Showdown (http://www.search engineshowdown.com) and Search Engine Watch (http://www.searchenginewatch.com).

Because the databases of different search engines do not overlap completely, better results can be obtained by submitting a given query to multiple search engines. Meta-search engines can do this automatically. Meta-search engines do not actually have their own database. Rather, they automatically submit your query to several conventional search engines and collect the results. This approach produces more responses because the combined coverage of several search engines can be significantly larger than any individual search engine.

Unfortunately there are several drawbacks to using meta-search engines. Because different search engines expect queries in different formats, it generally is not possible to have a meta-search engine successfully translate a complex query so that it is understood by each of the search engines that it forwards the query to. Also, it is difficult to eliminate duplicate results and to rank results combined from different search engines. Despite these shortcomings, meta-search engines can save you the work of having to manually enter your query at several search engines. Meta-search engines help most when you have a very specific query that produces only a few results at any one Web site. For searches on popular topics, meta-search engines may overwhelm you with too many results.

The databases of search engines are not only incomplete, they are also out of date. Crawling the Web is a time consuming process. A spider can visit only so many pages in a day. It can take weeks or months for a spider to discover a new Web page. Many new Web pages are created every day, and others are modified, or removed. Keeping up with the churning of the Web is a constant challenge. The database used by a search engine will always be out of date to a certain extent. With stale data, search engines can sometimes return results that turn out to be irrelevant (the page content has changed significantly since it was indexed) or results that refer to nonexistent Web pages (the page has been moved or removed since it was indexed). Some search engines now store entire copies of every Web page in their database and make these cached copies available when they return results for a query. Such cached copies can help users find the information they need, even when the search engine's database is out of date.

VII. CONCLUSION

Has Bush's vision been realized? Has hypertext made it easier to find information, or has it made it more difficult by accelerating the rate at which new information becomes available? Finding information by browsing alone is often difficult. Bush himself realized that even with hypertext, there would be a need for automated search. Our situation has undoubtedly improved since the time that Bush first published his ideas more than half a century ago. Information is much more accessible and search engines are extremely helpful in finding what we seek.

With the growing use of formats based on XML, the Extensible Markup Language, documents will become easier to search. HTML was invented to allow scientists to easily share information. It is well suited to this purpose, allowing the same headings, paragraphs, lists, tables, and figures common in printed scientific literature. However, HTML has often been used for purposes to which it is less well suited. The structural elements of HTML have been misused to control the appearance of text. For example, headings are often used to produce large, bold text. With XML, it becomes possible to invent new document formats with structural elements that are appropriate to the application. For example, a document format for bibliographic information could include structural elements for specifying authors, editors, titles, publishers, volumes, pages, and dates. Because the new formats will be based on XML, search engines will be able to easily analyze documents in these formats. Specialized search engines may emerge for different types of documents, such as medical or legal documents, or general search engines may allow users to submit advanced queries that specify XML elements in which keywords must appear, just as it is now possible to limit keywords to titles or headings. Many of these advantages may be lost, however, if users continue to use simple queries with only one or two keywords.

As the Web continues to grow, will search engines be able to keep up? There are already signs that Web growth is slowing. The computing and storage technology used by search engines will continue to improve in speed and capacity. However, lack of economic incentive may keep search engines from improving to the extent that improved technology would predict. Many search engines make money through advertising, or by selling their search services to other Web sites that make money through advertising. A relatively small database may be sufficient to handle the majority of queries on very popular topics. The size of the database would have to be increased significantly, at significant cost, in order to cover an array of obscure topics. These obscure topics would not draw many additional users, yielding little gain in advertising dollars.

SEE ALSO THE FOLLOWING ARTICLES

Artificial Intelligence Programming • Evolutionary Algorithms • Intelligent Agents • Internet Homepages • Internet, Overview • Java • Machine Learning • Search Techniques • Structured Query Language (SQL) • XML (Extensible Markup Language)

BIBLIOGRAPHY

Albert, R., Jeong, H., and Barabási, A.-L. (1999). The diameter of the world wide web. *Nature,* Vol. 401, 130–131; http://www.nd.edu/~networks/Papers/401130A0.pdf.

Brin, S., and Page, L. (1998). The anatomy of a large-scale hypertextual web search engine, in *Seventh International World Wide Web Conference, Brisbane, Australia;* http://decweb.ethz.ch/WWW7/1921/com1921.htm.

Broder, A., Kumar, R., Maghoul, F., Raghavan, P., Rajagopalan, S., Stata, R., Tomkins, A., and Wiener, J. (2000). Graph structure in the web, in *Ninth International World Wide Web Conference, Amsterdam;* http://www9.org/w9cdrom/160/160.html.

Bush, V. (1945). As we may think. *The Atlantic Monthly,* Vol. 176, No. 1, 101–108; http://www.theatlantic.com/unbound/flashbks/computer/bushf.htm.

Bush, V. (1967). Memex revisited, in *Science Is Not Enough.* New York: Morrow.

Butler, D. (2000). Souped-up search engines. *Nature,* Vol. 405, 112–115; http://www.nature.com/nature/webmatters/search/search.html.

Chakrabarti, S., Dom, B. E., Kumar, S. R., Raghavan, P., Rajagopalan, S., Tomkins, A., Kleinberg, J. M., and Gibson, D. (1999). Hypersearching the web. *Scientific American,* Vol. 280, No. 6, 54–60; http://www.sciam.com/1999/0699issue/0699raghavan.html.

Cho, J., Garcia-Molina, H., and Page, L. (1998). Efficient crawling through URL ordering, in *Seventh International World Wide Web Conference, Brisbane, Australia;* http://decweb.ethz.ch/WWW7/1919/com1919.htm.

Introna, L., and Nissenbaum, H. (2000). Defining the web: The politics of search engines. *Computer,* Vol. 33, No. 1.

Kornblum, J. (2000). More useless info: 2 billion web pages. *USA Today,* July 11, 2000; http://www.usatoday.com/life/cyber/tech/jk071100.htm.

Lawrence, S., and Giles, C. L. (1999). Accessibility and distribution of information on the web. *Nature,* Vol. 400, 107–109.

Online Computer Library Center. (2001). Web characterization project; http://wcp.oclc.org/stats/size.html.

Search Techniques

Richard E. Korf

University of California, Los Angeles

GLOSSARY

admissible A heuristic is said to be admissible if it never overestimates actual cost from a given state to a goal. An algorithm is said to be admissible if it always finds an optimal solution to a problem if one exists.

branching factor The average number of children of a node in a problem-space graph.

constraint-satisfaction problem A problem where the task is to identify a state that satisfies a set of constraints.

depth The length of a shortest path from the initial state to a goal state.

heuristic evaluation function A function from a state to a number. In a single-agent problem, it estimates the cost from the state to a goal. In a two-player game, it estimates the merit of the position with respect to one player.

node expansion Generating all the children of a given state.

node generation Creating the data structure that corresponds to a problem state.

operator An action that maps one state into another state, such as a twist of Rubik's Cube.

problem instance A problem space together with an initial state of the problem and a desired set of goal states.

problem space A theoretical construct in which a search takes place, consisting of a set of states and a set of operators.

problem-space graph A graphical representation of a problem space, where states are represented by nodes, and operators are represented by edges.

search A trial-and-error exploration of alternative solutions to a problem, often systematic.

search tree A problem-space graph with only a single path to each state.

single-agent path-finding problem A problem where the task is to find a sequence of operators that maps an initial state to a goal state.

state A configuration of a problem, such as the arrangement of the parts of a Rubik's Cube at a given point in time.

I. INTRODUCTION

Search is a universal problem-solving mechanism in artificial intelligence (AI). In AI problems, the sequence of steps required for solution of a problem are not known *a priori*, but often must be determined by a systematic trial-and-error exploration of alternatives. The problems that have been addressed by heuristic search algorithms fall into three general classes: *single-agent path-finding problems, two-player games,* and *constraint-satisfaction problems.*

Classic examples in the AI literature of path-finding problems are the sliding-tile puzzles, including the 3×3 Eight Puzzle (see Fig. 1) and its larger relatives the 4×4 Fifteen Puzzle, and 5×5 Twenty-Four Puzzle. The Eight Puzzle consists of a 3×3 square frame containing eight numbered square tiles, and an empty position called the blank. The legal operators are to slide any tile that is horizontally or vertically adjacent to the blank into the blank position. The problem is to rearrange the tiles from some random initial configuration into a particular

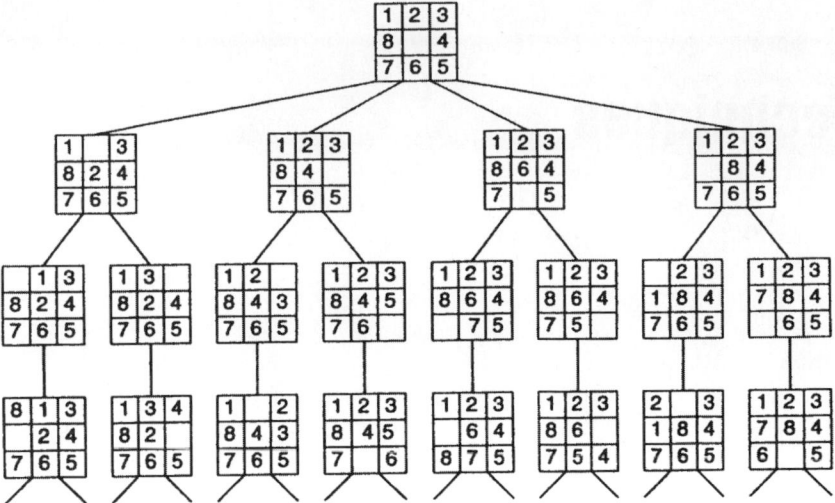

Figure 1 Eight Puzzle search tree fragment.

desired goal configuration. The sliding-tile puzzles are common testbeds for research in AI search algorithms because they are very simple to represent and manipulate, yet finding optimal solutions to the $N \times N$ generalization of the sliding-tile puzzles is NP-complete. Other well-known examples of single-agent path-finding problems include Rubik's Cube and theorem proving. Real-world examples include the traveling salesman problem, vehicle navigation, and the wiring of VLSI circuits. In each case, the task is to find a sequence of operations that map an initial state to a goal state.

A second class of search problems includes games such as chess, checkers, backgammon, bridge, or poker. The third category is constraint-satisfaction problems, such as the Eight Queens Problem. The task is to place eight queens on an 8×8 chessboard, such that no two queens are on the same row, column, or diagonal. Real-world examples of constraint-satisfaction problems are ubiquitous, including planning and scheduling applications.

We begin by describing the problem-space model on which search algorithms are based. Brute-force searches are then considered including breadth-first, uniform-cost, depth-first, depth-first iterative-deepening, and bidirectional search. Next, various heuristic searches are examined including pure heuristic search, the A* algorithm, iterative-deepening-A*, depth-first branch-and-bound, and the heuristic path algorithm. We then consider two-player game searches, including minimax and alpha-beta pruning. Finally, we examine constraint-satisfaction algorithms, such as backtracking, constraint recording, and local search algorithms. The efficiency

of these algorithms, in terms of the costs of the solutions they generate, the amount of time the algorithms take to execute, and the amount of computer memory they require, are of central concern throughout. Since search is a universal problem-solving method, what limits its applicability is the efficiency with which it can be performed.

II. PROBLEM SPACE MODEL

A *problem space* is the environment in which a search takes place. A problem space consists of a set of *states* of the problem, and a set of *operators* that change the state. For example, in the Eight Puzzle, the states are the different possible permutations of the tiles, and the operators slide a tile into the blank position. A *problem instance* is a problem space together with an initial state and a goal state. In the case of the Eight Puzzle, the initial state would be whatever initial permutation the puzzle starts out in, and the goal state is a particular desired permutation. The problem-solving task is to find a sequence of operators that map the initial state to a goal state. In the Eight Puzzle the goal state is given explicitly. In other problems, such as the Eight Queens Problem, the goal state is not given explicitly, but rather implicitly specified by certain properties that must be satisfied by any goal state.

A *problem-space graph* is often used to represent a problem space. The states of the space are represented by *nodes* of the graph, and the operators by *edges* between nodes. Edges may be undirected or directed, depending on whether their corresponding operators are reversible or not. The task in a single-agent path-finding problem is to find a path in the graph from the initial node to a goal node. Figure 1 shows a small part of the Eight Puzzle problem-space graph.

Although most problem spaces correspond to graphs with more than one path between a pair of nodes, for simplicity they are often represented as trees, where the initial state is the root of the tree. The cost of this simplification is that any state that can be reached by two different paths will be represented by duplicate nodes in the tree, increasing the size of the tree. The benefit of a tree is that the absence of cycles greatly simplifies many search algorithms. In this survey, we will restrict our attention to trees, but there exist graph versions of all of the algorithms we describe as well.

One feature that distinguishes AI search algorithms from other graph-searching algorithms is the size of the graphs involved. For example, the entire chess graph is estimated to contain more than 10^{40} nodes. Even a small problem like the Twenty-Four Puzzle contains almost 10^{25} nodes. As a result, the problem-space graphs of AI problems are never represented explicitly by listing each state, but rather are implicitly represented by specifying an initial state and a set of operators to generate new states from existing states. Furthermore, the size of an AI problem is rarely expressed as the number of nodes in its problem-space graph. Rather, the two parameters of a search tree that determine the efficiency of various search algorithms are its *branching factor* and its *solution depth*. The branching factor is the average number of children of a given node. For example, in the Eight Puzzle the average branching factor is $\sqrt{3}$, or about 1.732. The solution depth of a problem instance is the length of a shortest path from the initial state to a goal state, or the length of a shortest sequence of operators that solves the problem. For example, if the goal were in the bottom row of Fig. 1, the depth of the problem instance represented by the initial state at the root would be three moves.

III. BRUTE-FORCE SEARCH

The most general search algorithms are *brute-force* searches, because they do not require any domain-specific knowledge. All that is required for a brute-force search is a state description, a set of legal oper-

ators, an initial state, and a description of the goal state. The most important brute-force techniques are breadth-first, uniform-cost, depth-first, depth-first iterative-deepening, and bidirectional search. In the descriptions of the algorithms below, to *generate* a node means to create the data structure representing the state, whereas to *expand* a node means to generate all the children of that node.

A. Breadth-First Search

Breadth-first search expands nodes in order of their distance from the root node, generating one level of the tree at a time until a solution is found (see Fig. 2). It is most easily implemented by maintaining a queue of nodes, initially containing just the root, and always removing the node at the head of the queue, expanding it, and adding its children to the tail of the queue.

Since it never generates a node in the tree until all nodes at shallower levels have been generated, breadth-first search always finds a shortest path to a goal. Since each node can be generated in constant time, the amount of time used by breadth-first search is proportional to the number of nodes generated, which is a function of the branching factor b and the solution depth d. Since the number of nodes at level d is b^d, the total number of nodes generated in the worst case is $b + b^2 + b^3 + \cdots + b^d$, which is $O(b^d)$, the asymptotic time complexity of breadth-first search.

The main drawback of breadth-first search is its memory requirement. Since each level of the tree must be stored in order to generate the next level, and the amount of memory is proportional to the number of nodes stored, the space complexity of breadth-first search is also $O(b^d)$. As a result, breadth-first search is severely space-bound in practice, and will exhaust the memory available on typical computers in a matter of minutes.

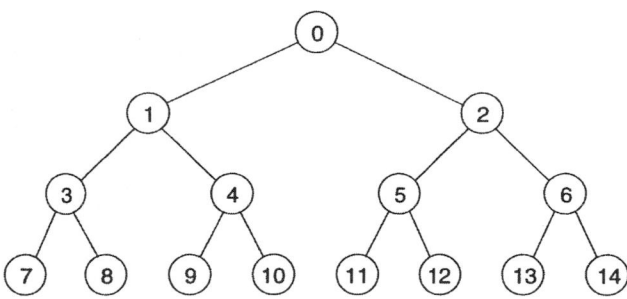

Figure 2 Order of node generation for breadth-first search.

B. Uniform-Cost Search

If all edges do not have the same cost, then breadth-first search generalizes to *uniform-cost search*. Instead of expanding nodes in order of their depth from the root, uniform-cost search expands nodes in order of their cost from the root. At each step, the next node n to be expanded is one whose cost $g(n)$ is lowest, where $g(n)$ is the sum of the edge costs from the root to node n. The nodes are stored in a priority queue. This algorithm is also known as Dijkstra's single-source shortest-path algorithm.

Whenever a node is chosen for expansion by uniform-cost search, a lowest cost path to that node has been found. The worst-case time complexity of uniform-cost search is $O(b^{c/m})$, where c is the cost of an optimal solution, and m is the minimum edge cost. Unfortunately, it also suffers the same memory limitation as breadth-first search.

C. Depth-First Search

Depth-first search remedies the space limitation of breadth-first and uniform-cost search by always generating next a child of the deepest unexpanded node (see Fig. 3). Both algorithms can be implemented using a list of unexpanded nodes, with the difference that breadth-first search manages the list as a first-in first-out queue, whereas depth-first search treats the list as a last-in first-out stack. More commonly, depth-first search is implemented recursively, with the recursion stack taking the place of an explicit node stack.

The advantage of depth-first search is that its space requirement is only linear in the search depth, $O(d)$, as opposed to exponential for breadth-first search. The reason is that the algorithm only needs to store a stack of nodes on the path from the root to the current node. The time complexity of a depth-first search to depth d is $O(b^d)$, since it generates the same set of nodes as breadth-first search, but simply in a different order. Thus, as a practical matter, depth-first search is time limited rather than space limited.

The disadvantage of depth-first search is that it may not terminate on an infinite tree, but simply go down the leftmost path forever. For example, even though there are a finite number of states of the Eight Puzzle, the tree fragment shown in Fig. 1 can be infinitely extended down any path, generating an infinite number of duplicate nodes representing the same states. The usual solution to this problem is to impose a cutoff depth on the search. Although the ideal cutoff is the solution depth d, this value is rarely known in advance of actually solving the problem. If the chosen cutoff depth is less than d, the algorithm will fail to find a solution, whereas if the cutoff depth is greater than d, a large price is paid in execution time, and the first solution found may not be an optimal one.

D. Depth-First Iterative-Deepening

Depth-first iterative-deepening (DFID) combines the best features of breadth-first and depth-first search. DFID first performs a depth-first search to depth one, then starts over, executing a complete depth-first search to depth two, and continues to run depth-first searches to successively greater depths, until a solution is found (see Fig. 4).

Since it never generates a node until all shallower nodes have been generated, the first solution found by DFID is guaranteed to be on a shortest path. Furthermore, since at any given point it is executing a depth-first search, saving only a stack of nodes, and the algorithm terminates when it finds a solution at depth d, the space complexity of DFID is only $O(d)$.

Although it appears that DFID wastes a great deal of time in the iterations prior to the one that finds a solution, this extra work is usually insignificant. To see this, note that the number of nodes at depth d is b^d, and each of these nodes is generated once, during the final iteration. The number of nodes at depth $d - 1$ is b^{d-1}, and each of these is generated twice, once during the final iteration, and once during the penultimate iteration. In general, the number of nodes generated by DFID is $b^d + 2b^{d-1} + 3b^{d-2} + \cdots + db$. This is asymptotically $O(b^d)$ if b is greater than one, since for large values of d the lower order terms become insignificant. In other words, most of the work goes into the final iteration, and the cost of the previous iterations is relatively small. The ratio of the number of

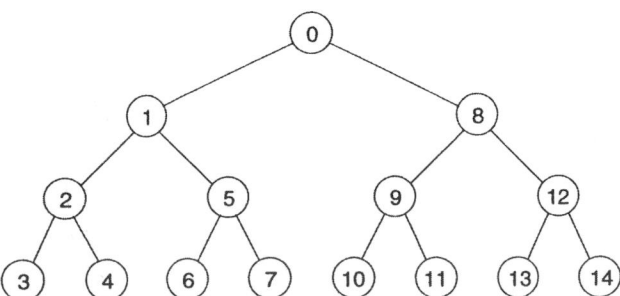

Figure 3 Order of node generation for depth-first search iterative-deepening search.

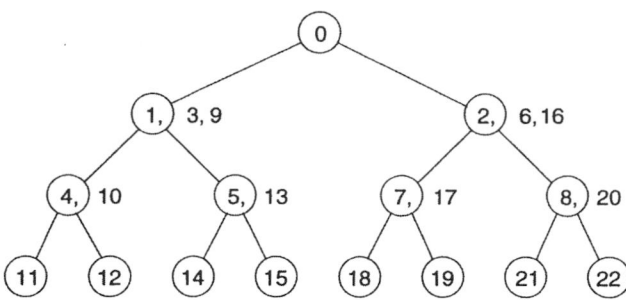

Figure 4 Order of node generation for depth-first.

nodes generated by DFID to those generated by breadth-first search on a tree is approximately $b/(b-1)$. In fact, DFID is asymptotically optimal in terms of time and space among all brute-force shortest-path algorithms on a tree.

If the edge costs differ from one another, then one can run an iterative deepening version of uniform-cost search, where the depth cutoff is replaced by a cutoff on the $g(n)$ cost of a node. At the end of each iteration, the threshold for the next iteration is set to the minimum cost of all nodes generated but not expanded on the previous iteration.

On a graph with cycles, however, breadth-first search may be much more efficient than any depth-first search. The reason is that a breadth-first search can easily detect all duplicate nodes, whereas a depth-first search can only check for duplicates along the current search path. Thus, the complexity of breadth-first search grows only as the number of states at a given depth, while the complexity of depth-first search depends on the number of paths of a given length. For example, in a square grid, the number of nodes within a radius r of the origin is $O(r^2)$, whereas the number of paths of length r is $O(3^r)$, since there are three children of every node, not counting its parent. Thus, in a graph with a large number of very short cycles, breadth-first search is preferable to depth-first search, if sufficient memory is available to store all the nodes.

E. Bidirectional Search

Bidirectional search is a brute-force search algorithm that requires an explicit goal state instead of simply a test for a goal condition. The main idea is to simultaneously search forward from the initial state, and backward from the goal state, until the two search frontiers meet. The path from the initial state is then concatenated with the inverse of the path from the goal state to form the complete solution path.

Bidirectional search still guarantees optimal solutions. Assuming that the comparisons for identifying a common state between the two frontiers can be done in constant time per node, by hashing for example, the time complexity of bidirectional search is $O(b^{d/2})$ since each search need only proceed to half the solution depth. Since at least one of the searches must be breadth first in order to find a common state, the space complexity of bidirectional search is also $O(b^{d/2})$. As a result, bidirectional search is space bound in practice.

F. Combinatorial Explosion

The problem with all brute-force search algorithms is that their time complexities grow exponentially with problem size. This is called *combinatorial explosion,* and as a result, the size of problems that can be solved with these techniques is quite limited. For example, while the Eight Puzzle, with about 10^5 states, is easily solved by brute-force search, the Fifteen Puzzle contains over 10^{13} states, and hence cannot be solved with any brute-force search techniques on current machines. Faster machines will not have a significant impact on this problem, since the 5×5 Twenty-Four Puzzle contains almost 10^{25} states, for example.

IV. HEURISTIC SEARCH

To solve larger problems, domain-specific knowledge must be added to improve search efficiency. In AI, *heuristic search* has a general meaning, and a more specialized technical meaning. In a general sense, the term *heuristic* is used for any advice that is often effective, but is not guaranteed to work in every case. Within the heuristic search literature, however, the term *heuristic* usually refers to the special case of a *heuristic evaluation function.*

A. Heuristic Evaluation Functions

In a single-agent path-finding problem, a heuristic evaluation function estimates the cost of an optimal path between a pair of states. For example, Euclidean or airline distance is an estimate of the highway distance between a pair of locations. A common heuristic function for the sliding-tile puzzles is called Manhattan distance. It is computed by counting the number of moves along the grid that each tile is displaced from its goal position, and summing these values over all tiles. For a fixed goal state, a heuristic evaluation $h(n)$ is a function of a node n, which estimates the cost from node n to the fixed goal state.

The key properties of a heuristic evaluation function are that it estimate actual cost and that it be computed efficiently. For example, the Euclidean distance between a pair of points can be computed in constant time. The Manhattan distance between a pair of states can be computed in time proportional to the number of tiles. In addition, many heuristic functions are lower bounds on actual cost, a property referred to as *admissibility*. For example, airline distance is a lower bound on road distance between two points, since the shortest path between a pair of points is a straight line. Similarly, Manhattan distance is a lower bound on the actual number of moves necessary to solve an instance of a sliding-tile puzzle, since every tile must move at least as many times as its distance in grid units from its goal position, and each move moves only one tile.

Such heuristic functions are often derived by generating a simplified version of the problem to be solved, then using the cost of an optimal solution to the simplified problem as an admissible heuristic evaluation function for the original problem. For example, in the sliding-tile puzzles, if we remove the constraint that a tile can only be slid into the blank position, then any tile can be moved to any adjacent position at any time. The optimal number of moves required to solve this simplified version of the problem is just the Manhattan distance, which is an admissible heuristic for the original problem.

A number of algorithms make use of heuristic functions, including pure heuristic search, the A* algorithm, iterative-deepening-A*, depth-first branch-and-bound, and the heuristic path algorithm. In addition, heuristic information can be employed in bidirectional search, and is used in two-player games as well.

B. Pure Heuristic Search

The simplest of these algorithms, pure heuristic search, expands nodes in order of their heuristic values $h(n)$. It maintains a *Closed list* of those nodes that have already been expanded, and an *Open list* of those nodes that have been generated but not yet expanded. The algorithm begins with just the initial node on the Open list. At each cycle, a node on the Open list with the minimum $h(n)$ value is expanded, generating all of its children, and is placed on the Closed list. The

heuristic function is applied to each of the children, and they are placed on the Open list, sorted by their heuristic values. The algorithm continues until a goal state is chosen for expansion.

In a graph with cycles, multiple paths will be found to the same node, and the first path found may not be the shortest. When a shorter path is found to an Open node, the shorter path is saved and the longer one discarded. When a shorter path to a Closed node is found, the node is moved to Open, along with the shorter path. The main drawback of pure heuristic search is that since it ignores the cost of the path so far to node n, it does not find optimal solutions.

Breadth-first search, uniform-cost search, and pure heuristic search are all special cases of a more general algorithm called *best-first search*. In each cycle of a best-first search, the node that is best according to some cost function is chosen for expansion. These best-first algorithms differ only in their cost functions: the depth of node n for breadth-first search, $g(n)$ for uniform-cost search, and $h(n)$ for pure heuristic search.

C. A* Algorithm

The *A* algorithm* combines features of uniform-cost search and pure heuristic search to efficiently compute optimal solutions. A* is a best-first search in which the cost associated with a node is $f(n) = g(n) + h(n)$, where $g(n)$ is the cost of the path from the initial state to node n, and $h(n)$ is the heuristic estimate of the cost of a path from node n to a goal. Thus, $f(n)$ estimates the lowest total cost of any solution path going through node n. At each point a node with lowest f value is chosen for expansion. Ties among nodes of equal f value should be broken in favor of nodes with lower h values. The algorithm terminates when a goal node is chosen for expansion.

A* finds an optimal path to a goal if the heuristic function $h(n)$ is admissible, meaning it never overestimates actual cost. For example, since airline distance never overestimates actual highway distance, and Manhattan distance never overestimates actual moves in the sliding-tile puzzles, A* using these evaluation functions will find optimal solutions to these problems. In addition, A* makes the most efficient use of a given heuristic function in the following sense: Among all shortest-path algorithms using a given heuristic function $h(n)$, A* expands the fewest number of nodes.

The main drawback of A*, and indeed of any best-first search, is its memory requirement. Since the Open and Closed lists must be stored, A* is severely space limited in practice, and will exhaust the available memory on current machines in minutes. For example, while it can be run successfully on the Eight Puzzle, it cannot solve most instances of the Fifteen Puzzle before exhausting memory. An additional drawback of A* is that the Open and Closed lists take time to maintain.

D. Iterative-Deepening-A*

Just as depth-first iterative-deepening solved the space problem of breadth-first search, *iterative-deepening-A** (IDA*) eliminates the memory constraint of A*, without sacrificing solution optimality. Each iteration of the algorithm is a depth-first search that keeps track of the cost, $f(n) = g(n) + h(n)$, of each node generated. As soon as a node is generated whose cost exceeds a threshold for that iteration, its path is cut off, and the search backtracks before continuing along a different path. The cost threshold is initialized to the heuristic estimate of the initial state, and is increased in each successive iteration to the lowest cost of all the nodes that were generated but not expanded during the previous iteration. The algorithm terminates when a goal state is reached whose cost does not exceed the current threshold.

Since IDA* performs a series of depth-first searches, its memory requirement is linear in the maximum search depth. In addition, if the heuristic function is admissible, IDA* finds an optimal solution. Finally, by an argument similar to that presented for DFID, IDA* expands the same number of nodes, asymptotically, as A* on a tree, provided that the number of nodes grows exponentially with solution cost. These facts, together with the optimality of A*, imply that IDA* is asymptotically optimal in time and space over all heuristic search algorithms that find optimal solutions on a tree. Additional benefits of IDA* are that it is much easier to implement, and often runs faster than A*, since it does not incur the overhead of managing the Open and Closed lists. Using appropriate admissible heuristic functions, IDA* can optimally solve random instances of the Fifteen Puzzle, the Twenty-Four Puzzle, and Rubik's Cube.

E. Depth-First Branch-and-Bound

For many problems, the maximum search depth is known in advance, or the search tree is finite. For example, consider the traveling salesman problem (TSP) of visiting each of a given set of cities and returning to the starting city in a tour of shortest total distance. The most natural problem space for this problem consists of a tree where the root node represents the starting city, the nodes at level one represent all the cities that could be visited first, nodes at level two represent the cites visited second, and so on. In this tree, the maximum depth is the number of cities, and all candidate solutions occur at this depth. In such a space, a simple depth-first search guarantees finding an optimal solution using space that is only linear in the number of cities.

The idea of depth-first branch-and-bound (DFBnB) is to make this search more efficient by keeping track of the lowest cost solution found so far. Since the cost of a partial tour is the sum of the costs of the edges traveled so far, whenever a partial tour is found whose cost equals or exceeds the cost of the best complete tour found so far, the branch representing the partial tour can be pruned, since all its descendents must have equal or greater cost. Whenever a lower cost complete tour is found, the cost of the best tour is updated to this lower cost. In addition, an admissible heuristic function, such as the cost of the minimum spanning tree of the remaining unvisited cities, can be added to the cost so far of a partial tour to increase the amount of pruning. Finally, by carefully ordering the children of a given node from smallest to largest cost, a lower cost solution can be found more quickly, pruning even more nodes.

Interestingly, IDA* and DFBnB exhibit complementary behavior. Both are guaranteed to return an optimal solution using only linear space, assuming that their cost functions are admissible. In IDA*, the cost threshold is always a lower bound on the optimal solution cost and increases in each iteration until it reaches the optimal cost. In DFBnB, the cost of the best solution found so far is always an upper bound on the optimal solution cost and decreases until it reaches the optimal cost. While IDA* never expands any nodes whose cost exceeds the optimal cost, its overhead consists of expanding some nodes more than once. While DFBnB never expands any node more than once, its overhead consists of expanding some nodes whose cost exceeds the optimal cost. For problems whose search trees are of bounded depth, or for which it is easy to construct a good solution, such as the TSP, DFBnB is usually the algorithm of choice for finding an optimal solution. For problems with infinite search trees or for which it is difficult to construct a low-cost solution, such as the sliding-tile puzzles or Rubik's Cube, IDA* is usually the best choice.

F. Complexity of Finding Optimal Solutions

The time complexity of a heuristic search algorithm depends on the accuracy of the heuristic function. For example, if the heuristic evaluation function is an exact estimator, then A* runs in linear time, expanding only those nodes on an optimal solution path. Conversely, with a heuristic that returns zero everywhere, A* becomes a brute-force uniform-cost search, with exponential complexity. In general, the time complexity of A*, IDA*, and DFBnB depends on the accuracy of the heuristic function. The effect of a good heuristic function is to reduce the effective depth of search required by approximately the expected value of the heuristic.

G. Heuristic Path Algorithm

Since the complexity of finding optimal solutions to these problems is still exponential, even with a good heuristic function, in order to solve significantly larger problems, the optimality requirement must be relaxed. An early approach to this problem was the *heuristic path algorithm (HPA)*. HPA is a best-first search algorithm, where the cost of a node n is computed as $f(n) = g(n) + w * h(n)$. Varying w produces a range of algorithms from uniform-cost search ($w = 0$), through A* ($w = 1$), to pure heuristic search ($w = \infty$). Increasing w beyond 1 generally decreases the amount of computation, while increasing the cost of the solution generated. This trade-off is often quite favorable, with small increases in solution cost yielding huge savings in computation. Furthermore, it can be shown that the solutions found by this algorithm are guaranteed to be no more than a factor of w greater than optimal, but often are significantly better.

V. TWO-PLAYER GAMES

The second major application of heuristic search algorithms in AI is two-player games. One of the original challenges of AI, which in fact predates the term *artificial intelligence*, was to build a program that could defeat the best human chess player, a goal recently achieved by IBM's Deep Blue Machine.

A. Minimax Search

The standard algorithm for two-player perfect-information games, such as chess or checkers, is mini-max search with heuristic static evaluation. The simplest version of the algorithm searches forward to a fixed depth in the game tree, limited by the amount of time available per move. At this *search horizon*, a heuristic function is applied to the frontier nodes. In this case, a heuristic evaluation is a function that takes a board position and returns a number that indicates how favorable that position is for one player relative to the other. For example, a very simple heuristic function for chess would count the total number of pieces on the board for one player, appropriately weighted by their relative strength, and subtract the weighted sum of the opponent's pieces. Thus, large positive values would correspond to strong positions for one player, called MAX, whereas large negative values would represent advantageous situations for the opponent, called MIN.

Given the heuristic evaluations of the frontier nodes, values for the interior nodes in the tree are recursively computed according to the minimax rule. The value of a node where it is MAX's turn to move is the maximum of the values of its children, while the value of a node where MIN is to move is the minimum of the values of its children. Thus, at alternate levels of the tree, the minimum or the maximum values of the children are backed up. This continues until the values of the immediate children of the current position are computed, at which point one move to the child with the maximum or minimum value is made, depending on whose turn it is to move.

B. Alpha-Beta Pruning

One of the most elegant of all AI search algorithms is alpha-beta pruning, first used in the late 1950s. The idea is that the exact minimax value of the root of a game tree can be determined without examining all the nodes at the search frontier.

Figure 5 shows some examples of alpha-beta pruning. Only the nodes shown are generated by the algorithm, with the heavy black lines indicating pruning. At the square nodes MAX is to move, while at the circular nodes it is MIN's turn. The search proceeds depth-first to minimize the memory required, and only evaluates a node when necessary. First, nodes e and f are statically evaluated at 4 and 5, respectively, and their minimum value, 4, is backed up to their parent node d. Node h is then evaluated at 3, and hence the value of its parent node g must be less than or equal to 3, since it is the minimum of 3 and the unknown value of its right child. Thus, we label node g as $< = 3$. The value of node c must be 4 then, because it is the maximum of 4, and a value that is less than

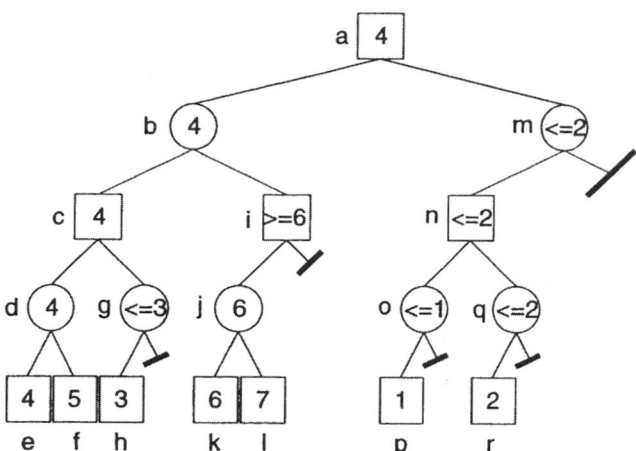

Figure 5 Alpha-beta pruning example.

or equal to 3. Since we have determined the minimax value of node *c*, we do not need to evaluate or even generate any more children of node *g*.

Similarly, after statically evaluating nodes *k* and *l* at 6 and 7, respectively, the backed up value of their parent node *j* is 6, the minimum of these values. This tells us that the minimax value of node *i* must be greater than or equal to 6, since it is the maximum of 6 and the unknown value of its right child. Since the value of node *b* is the minimum of 4 and a value that is greater than or equal to 6, it must be 4, and hence we cut off the remaining children of node i.

The right half of the tree shows an example of *deep pruning*. After evaluating the left half of the tree, we know that the value of the root node *a* is greater than or equal to 4, the minimax value of node *b*. Once node *p* is evaluated at 1, the value of its parent node *o* must be less than or equal to 1. Since the value of the root is greater than or equal to 4, the value of node *o* cannot propagate to the root, and hence we need not generate any more children of node *o*. A similar situation exists after the evaluation of node *r* at 2. At that point, the value of node *o* is less than or equal to 1, and the value of node *q* is less than or equal to 2, hence the value of node *n*, which is the maximum of the values of nodes *o* and *q*, must be less than or equal to 2. Furthermore, since the value of node *m* is the minimum of the value of node *n* and its brothers, and node *n* has a value less than or equal to 2, the value of node *m* must also be less than or equal to 2. This causes the remaining children of node *m* to be pruned, since the value of the root node *a* is greater than or equal to 4. Thus, we computed the minimax value of the root of the tree to be 4, by generating only seven leaf nodes in this case.

Since alpha-beta pruning performs a minimax search while pruning much of the tree, its effect is to allow a deeper search in the same amount of time. This raises a question: How much does alpha-beta improve performance? The efficiency of alpha-beta pruning depends on the order in which nodes are encountered at the search frontier. For any set of frontier node values, there exists some ordering of the values such that alpha-beta will not perform any cutoffs at all. In that case, all frontier nodes must be evaluated, and the time complexity is $O(b^d)$.

On the other hand, there is an optimal or perfect ordering in which every possible cutoff is realized. In that case, the asymptotic time complexity is reduced from $O(b^d)$ to $O(b^{d/2})$. Another way of viewing the perfect ordering case is that for the same amount of computation, one can search twice as deep with alpha-beta pruning as without. Since the search tree grows exponentially with depth, doubling the search horizon is a dramatic improvement.

In between worst-possible ordering and perfect ordering is random ordering, which is the average case. Under random ordering of the frontier nodes, alpha-beta pruning reduces the asymptotic time complexity to approximately $O(b^{3d/4})$. This means that one can search 4/3 as deep with alpha-beta than with simple minimax, yielding a 33% improvement in search depth.

In practice, however, the time complexity of alpha-beta is closer to the best case of $O(b^{d/2})$ due to *node ordering*. The idea of node ordering is that instead of generating the children of a node in an arbitrary order, we can reorder the tree based on static evaluations of the interior nodes. In particular, the children of MAX nodes are expanded in decreasing order of their static values, while the children of MIN nodes are expanded in increasing order of their static values.

C. Quiescence, Iterative-Deepening, and Transposition Tables

Two other important ideas are quiescence and iterative-deepening. The idea of quiescence is that the static evaluator should not be applied to positions whose values are unstable, such as those occurring in the middle of a piece trade. In those positions, a small secondary search is conducted until the static evaluation becomes more stable. In games such as chess or checkers, this can be achieved by always exploring any capture moves one level deeper, and not evaluating any position that allows capture moves.

Iterative-deepening is used to solve the problem of how to set the search horizon, and in fact predated its use as a memory-saving device in single-agent search. In a tournament game, a limited amount of time is allowed for moves. Unfortunately, it is very difficult to accurately predict how long it will take to perform an alpha-beta search to a given depth. The solution is to perform a series of searches to successively greater depths. When time runs out, the move recommended by the last completed search is made.

The search graphs of most games, such as chess, contain multiple paths to the same node, often reached by making the same moves in a different order, referred to as a transposition of the moves. Since alpha-beta is a depth-first search, it is important to detect when a node has already been searched, in order to avoid researching it. A *transposition table* is a table of previously encountered game states, together with their backed-up minimax values. Whenever a new state is generated, if it is stored in the transposition table, its stored value is used instead of searching the tree below the node. Transposition tables can also be used in single-agent searches.

Almost all two-player game programs use full-width alpha-beta minimax search with node ordering, quiescence, iterative-deepening, and transposition tables, among other techniques.

D. Special-Purpose Hardware

While the basic algorithms are described above, much of the performance advances in computer chess have come from faster hardware. The faster the machine, the deeper it can search in the time available, and the better it plays. Despite the rapidly advancing speed of general-purpose computers, the best chess machines today are based on special-purpose hardware designed and built only to play chess. For example, DeepBlue is a chess machine that can evaluate about 200 million chess positions per second. In May 1997, it defeated Gary Kasparov, the world champion, in a six-game exhibition match, achieving a long-awaited goal in artificial intelligence.

E. Multi-Player Games and Imperfect and Hidden Information

Minimax search with static evaluation and alpha-beta pruning is most appropriate for two-player games with perfect information and alternating moves among the players. This paradigm extends in a straightforward way to more than two players, but alpha-beta becomes much less effective. Games with chance elements, such as the roll of the dice in backgammon, for example,

tend to limit search algorithms because of the need to search over all possible chance outcomes. In addition to chance, card games have information that is available to some players but hidden from others, such as the cards in the different hands in bridge. Poker is a very difficult challenge in this area, combining all of the above complexities, as well as active deception and the need to model the opponents.

One technique that has been effective in handling hidden information is Monte Carlo sampling. Given a decision to be made, such as the play of a card in bridge, we can randomly generate a set of cards that could possibly be the current hands of all the other players. Given this particular set of hands, we then use perfect-information techniques, such as alpha-beta minimax, to determine the optimal play in this case. We then repeat the experiment, generating another random set of hands, consistent with all the information available, and compute the optimal move in that case. If we generate, say, 100 different random hands, we then play the card that was most often the optimal card to play over all the randomly-generated hands.

VI. CONSTRAINT-SATISFACTION PROBLEMS

In addition to single-agent path-finding problems and two-player games, the third major application of heuristic search is constraint-satisfaction problems. The Eight Queens Problem mentioned previously is a classic example. Other examples include graph coloring, Boolean satisfiability, and scheduling problems.

Constraint-satisfaction problems are usually modeled as follows: There is a set of variables, a set of values for each variable, and a set of constraints on the values of the variables. A unary constraint on a variable specifies a subset of all possible values that can be assigned to that variable. A binary constraint between two variables specifies which possible combinations of assignments to the pair of variables is legal. For example, in the Eight Queens Problem, the variables would represent individual queens, and the values would be positions on the board. The constraints are binary constraints on each pair of queens that prohibit them from being positioned on the same row, column, or diagonal.

A. Chronological Backtracking

The brute-force approach to constraint satisfaction is called *chronological backtracking*. One selects an order for the variables, and an order for the values, and starts assigning values to the variables one at a time.

Each assignment is made so that all constraints involving any of the variables that have already been assigned are satisfied. The reason for this is that once a constraint is violated, no assignment to the remaining variables can possibly resatisfy that constraint. Once a variable is reached that has no remaining legal assignments, then the last variable that was assigned is reassigned to its next legal value. The algorithm continues until either a complete, consistent assignment is found, resulting in success, or all possible assignments are shown to violate some constraint, resulting in failure. Figure 6 shows the tree generated by brute-force backtracking to find all solutions to the Four Queens problem. The tree is searched depth-first to minimize memory requirements.

B. Intelligent Backtracking

One can improve the performance of brute-force backtracking using a number of techniques, such as variable ordering, value ordering, backjumping, and forward checking.

The order in which variables are instantiated can have a large effect on the size of the search tree. The idea of variable ordering is to order the variables from most constrained to least constrained. For example, if any variable has only a single value remaining that is consistent with the previously instantiated variables, it should be assigned that value immediately. In general, the variables should be instantiated in increasing order of the size of their remaining domains. This can either be done statically at the beginning of the search, or dynamically, reordering the remaining variables each time a variable is assigned a new value.

The order in which the values of a given variable are chosen determines the order in which the tree is searched. Since it does not affect the size of the tree, it makes no difference if all solutions are to be found. If only a single solution is required, however, value ordering can decrease the time required to find a solution. In general, one should order the values from least constraining to most constraining, in order to minimize the time required to find a first solution.

The idea of backjumping is that when an impass is reached, instead of simply undoing the last decision made, the decision that actually caused the failure should be modified. For example, consider a three-variable problem where the variables are instantiated in the order x, y, z. Assume that values have been

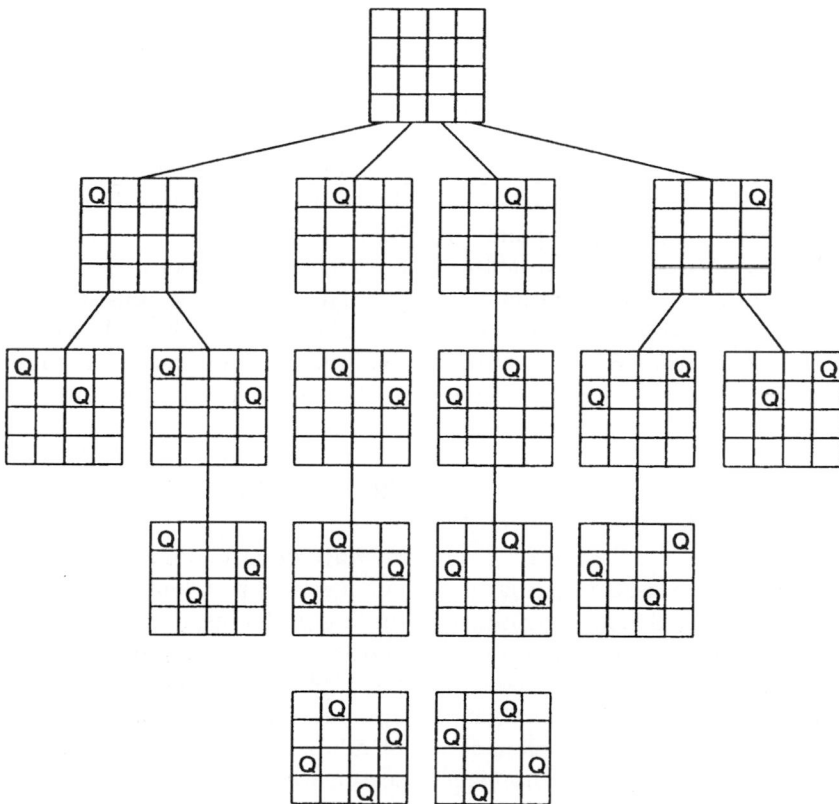

Figure 6 Tree generated to solve the Four Queens problem.

chosen for both x and y, but that all possible values for z conflict with the value chosen for x. In chronological backtracking, the value chosen for y would be changed, and then all the possible values for z would be tested again, to no avail. A better strategy in this case is to go back to the source of the failure, and change the value of x, before trying different values for y and z.

When a variable is assigned a value, forward checking checks each remaining uninstantiated variable to make sure that there is at least one assignment for each of them that is consistent with the previous assignments. If not, the original variable is assigned its next value.

C. Constraint Recording

In a constraint-satisfaction problem, some constraints are explicitly specified, and others are implied by the explicit constraints. Implicit constraints may be discovered either during a backtracking search, or in advance in a preprocessing phase. The idea of constraint recording is that once these implicit constraints are discovered, they should be saved explicitly so that they don't have to be rediscovered.

A simple example of constraint recording in a preprocessing phase is called arc consistency. For each pair of variables x and y that are related by a binary constraint, we remove from the domain of x any values that do not have at least one corresponding consistent assignment to y, and vice versa. In general, several iterations may be required to achieve complete arc consistency. Path consistency is a generalization of arc consistency where instead of considering pairs of variables, we examine triples of constrained variables. The effect of performing arc or path consistency before backtracking is that the resulting search space can be dramatically reduced. In some cases, this preprocessing of the constraints can eliminate the need for search entirely.

D. Local Search Algorithms

Backtracking searches a space of consistent partial assignments to variables, in the sense that all constraints among instantiated variables are satisfied, and looks for a complete consistent assignment to the variables, or in other words a solution. An alternative approach is to search a space of inconsistent but complete assignments to the variables, until a consistent complete assignment is found. This approach is known as heuris-

tic repair. For example, in the Eight Queens Problem, this amounts to placing all eight queens on the board at the same time, and moving queens one at a time until a solution is found. The natural heuristic, called min-conflicts, is to move a queen that is in conflict with the most other queens, and move it to a position where it conflicts with the fewest other queens.

What is surprising about this simple strategy is how well it performs, relative to backtracking. While backtracking techniques can solve on the order of hundred-queen problems, heuristic repair can solve million-queen problems, often with only about 50 individual queen moves! This strategy has been extensively explored in the context of Boolean satisfiability, where it is referred to as GSAT. GSAT can satisfy difficult formulas with several thousand variables, whereas the best backtracking-based approach, the Davis-Putnam algorithm with unit propagation, can only satisfy difficult formulas with several hundred variables.

Another technique often used with such algorithms is called random restart. If a solution is not found in a given time interval, the algorithm starts over with a different random initial state.

The main drawback of these local search approaches is that they are not complete in that they are not guaranteed to find a solution in a finite amount of time, even if one exists. If there is no solution, these algorithms will run forever, whereas backtracking will eventually discover that a problem is not solvable.

While constraint-satisfaction problems appear somewhat different from single-agent path-finding problems and two-player games, there is a strong similarity among the algorithms employed. For example, backtracking can be viewed as a form of branch-and-bound, where a node is pruned when any constraint is violated. Similarly, heuristic repair can be viewed as a heuristic search where the evaluation function is the total number of constraints that are violated, and the goal is to find a state with zero constraint violations.

VII. SUMMARY

We have described search algorithms for three different classes of problems. In the first, single-agent path-finding problems, the task is to find a sequence of operators that map an initial state to a desired goal state. Much of the work in this area has focused on finding optimal solutions to such problems, often making use of admissible heuristic functions to speed up the search without sacrificing optimality. In the second area, two-player games, finding optimal solutions is not feasible, and research has focused on algorithms for making the best move decisions possible given a limited amount of computing time. In the third class of problems, constraint-satisfaction problems, the task is to find a state that satisfies a set of constraints. While all three of these types of problems are different, the same set of ideas, such as brute-force searches and heuristic evaluation functions, can be applied to all three.

SEE ALSO THE FOLLOWING ARTICLES

Artificial Intelligence Programming • Evolutionary Algorithms • Game Theory • Intelligent Agents • Pattern Recognition • Search Engines • Structured Query Language (SQL)

BIBLIOGRAPHY

Bolc, L., and Cytowski, J. (1992). *Search methods for artificial intelligence.* London: Academic Press.

Davis, M., and Putnam, H. (1960). A computing procedure for quantification theory. *Journal of the Association for Computing Machinery,* Vol. 7, 201–215.

Dijkstra, E. W. (1959). A note on two problems in connection with graphs. *Numerische Mathematik,* Vol. 1, 269–271.

Hart, P. E., Nilsson, N. J., and Raphael, B. (1968). A formal basis for the heuristic determination of minimum cost paths. *IEEE Transactions on Systems Science and Cybernetics,* Vol. 4, No. 2, 100–107.

Korf, R. E. (1985). Depth-first iterative-deepening: An optimal admissible tree search. *Artificial Intelligence,* Vol. 27, No. 1, 97–109.

Minton, S., Johnston, M. D., Philips, A. B., and Laird, P. (December 1992). Minimizing conflicts: A heuristic repair method for constraint satisfaction and scheduling problems. *Artificial Intelligence,* Vol. 58, Nos. 1–3, 161–205.

Newell, A., and Simon, H. A. (1972). *Human problem solving.* Upper Saddle River, NJ: Prentice-Hall.

Pearl, J. (1984). *Heuristics.* Reading, MA: Addison-Wesley.

Selman, B., Levesque, H., and Mitchell, D. (1992). A new method for solving hard satisfiability problems. *Proc. Tenth National Conference on Artificial Intelligence (AAAI-92),* 440–446. July 1992, San Jose, CA.

Shannon, C.E. (1950). Programming a computer for playing chess. *Philosophical Magazine,* Vol. 41, 256–275.

Security Issues and Measures

Elizabeth Rhodenizer

Canadian Office of Critical Infrastructure Protection and Emergency Preparedness

I. NON-IT SECURITY ISSUES
II. IT SECURITY ISSUES

III. MEASURES
IV. FUTURE DIRECTIONS

GLOSSARY

asset Information or computing resources that require protection from modification, disclosure, or destruction.

authentication The validation of a user or process, verifying they are who they say they are.

authorization The permission given to a user or process to access the resource.

availability The ability of an authorized user or process to access and use a protected resource when requested.

biometrics The analysis and quantification of human biological characteristics to digital format.

computer security incident response teams (CSIRT) A team that has predetermined policies and procedures in place for responding to security incidents reported by its the user base.

confidentiality The ability to ensure that a protected resource is not legible by an unauthorized user or process.

configuration management A process that provides control and traceability of changes in the design, development, and maintenance phases of software, hardware, and firmware.

integrity The ability to ensure that a protected resource has not been modified since it left the originator.

list-based access control (LBAC) Access granted to resources given that the user's identification corresponds to the list of authorized users associated with the requested resource.

malicious hacker, attacker, intruder A person who attempts, either successfully or not, to obtain unauthorized access to information or computing resources.

nonrepudiation A service that can be used as proof of origin, proof of delivery, and for auditing purposes in order to prevent users from denying their participation in secure communications.

role-based access control (RBAC) A user is granted access to resources if the role associated with the user's identification corresponds to the role(s) authorized to access the requested resource.

social engineering The act of manipulating people into revealing privileged information, which would result in a breach of the protected assets.

user A user or process that utilizes computer-associated resources.

WHEN IT COMES TO SECURITY and data communications, there is no quick fix. There is no one product that can take care of all security requirements and there most likely never will be. The requirements of ensuring information technology security (ITS) for systems and communications are dependent on the systems and services to be protected and there is no end to the number of permutations of this combination available, now or in the future.

The two broad categories of ITS are those requirements that address the nontechnical aspects of ITS and requirements that address the technical aspect of ITS. The non-IT security requirements include *physical security, social engineering, personnel security, process management,* and *software security.* The IT security requirements include *authentication, authorization, confidentiality, integrity, availability,* and *nonrepudiation.* These requirements are not likely to change with advances in technology, although the

45

means by which they are delivered and performed most likely will.

When evaluating what technical or nontechnical security measures should be implemented in a system or product, the value of the assets being protected must be considered. The cost of security implemented should not be greater than the actual value of the assets. Specific methods are available for evaluating and identifying the security measures that should be applied to a product or system in order to help mitigate, resolve, or accept the security risks.

I. NON-IT SECURITY ISSUES

The security issues covered in this section are not implemented through technology. They focus on policies, which once implemented and adhered to should result in best practices.

A. Physical Security

The physical security of the system being protected is as important as any security technology that may be used on the system. Physical security entails properly securing a system's physical surroundings to mitigate the risk of unauthorized physical access. Unauthorized physical access can lead to the modification, disclosure, destruction, or theft of an asset.

The immediate physical surroundings of the protected system should be scrutinized for structural integrity. Structural integrity of the room is achieved when the walls extend from the floor to the ceiling to prevent physical or visual access into the room. The walls should be constructed of a suitable material such as wood, stone, concrete, or steel. The selection of the material should be commensurate with the value of the assets being protected. The floor and ceiling should not be an alternative means of entry. If the floor is raised or the ceiling is lowered to accommodate for ventilation and wiring, it should not be possible to use either of these as an alternate access route into the room. The type and quantity of security mechanisms put in place at the doorway, such as locks or card readers, should be chosen with regard to the value of the assets to be protected. The windows of the room should be secured to prevent access from the outside. The windows should also dictate the positioning of the monitors or overhead projectors in order to prevent visual eavesdropping.

Physical access control to the room will depend on the layout of the system's room(s), floor(s), and building. The described model in the following assumes the protected system is located in a room with one doorway. Appropriate locks on the door may be adequate to ensure access control. A physical key may be appropriate for a small group of people, all requiring access to the room, to protect assets that are not of high value. A keypad requires an access code in order to enter the room. A card pad, which simply reads the card as it passes over the reader, can log which employee entered the room and match that information on the card with the access control list for the room. A combination of these methods can provide a significant amount of physical security if implemented with due diligence. Again, depending on the value of the asset being protected, further measures may be necessary and could include biometric devices.

The same consideration should be given to the main entry point of the building or floor that houses the protected asset. A security surveillance system, using either personnel or automatic equipment or a combination of both, could, if warranted, be implemented for the building. It could involve security personnel, identification cards for employees, which are easily distinguishable from ID cards for visitors, or restricted floor and building access if plausible.

B. Social Engineering

Social engineering is a means of deception that is limited only by the imagination of the manipulator. Potential intruders who want to manipulate people into revealing privileged information that would result in a breach of the protected assets use social engineering to their advantage.

Social engineering is usually carried out in conversation either in person or via a medium such as phone or e-mail but mailing lists, bulletin boards, and web sites can provide just as much information as an overly trusting employee.

From one posting in a news group the following information was extracted: the person's name, the company they worked for, their e-mail address, and in this instance something resembling a user name. Continuing through the posted message, the description of the problem revealed system information as well as a vulnerability in the current configuration. An employee of a major financial institution posted this message.

Another situation that raises concern for the prevention of impersonation is the request for a password change over the telephone. If standard procedure simply calls for the user to submit a user name over the phone to the help desk, then there is a high probability that this system would be tested and possibly circumvented by a potential intruder. A challenge and response mechanism would provide more security and, depending on the system and assets being protected, it may be beneficial to require an in-person request for forgotten passwords.

Social engineering can also be carried out through dumpster diving, desk rummaging, and recycle box surfing. Dumpster diving can prove to be very valuable to a potential intruder. It can provide design documentation, financial statements, personnel information including address and salary information, and patent information, to name just a few. Any information that is important to a company, its employees, or its clients should be discarded in a secure manner. An effective method would be to shred the information or, depending on the sensitivity, incinerate the refuse. Desk rummaging can also leave the information listed above vulnerable to prying eyes and sticky fingers. Proper storage containers including lockable filing cabinets, cupboards, and safes can prevent unauthorized access to these valuables. Recycle box surfing is similar to dumpster diving. Although it is important for organizations to recycle paper, it is just as important for employees to be educated as to what information should be recycled and what information should be disposed of according to policy.

To stop social engineering, employees have to be educated. This education should not necessarily focus on the methods of manipulation but on the information that should not be revealed to unauthorized personnel.

C. Personnel Security

The most important aspect with regard to non-IT security for any corporation, agency, or organization is the people. The people that design, develop, and manufacture a product, including maintenance and janitorial staff, are the key to the success of an organization. It is through their cooperation and adherence with company policies that the organization is kept secure from internal and external threats. Investing time into the hiring and continual education of employees is essential. Personnel security planning and policy should be applied to new hires, employed personnel, and personnel leaving an organization.

The hiring process is the first step toward securing an organization. Several precautionary and procedural steps should be performed during the hiring process depending on the nature of the position. Consideration must be given to the duties of the position and the exposure to sensitive resources. The preventive measures taken during the hiring process will be dependent on the resources available to the company and legal jurisdiction. As always in the protection of IT, the value of the mechanisms and or procedures

put in place to secure assets should never be more than the value of the asset itself.

The information on a prospective employee's resume, including the address, education, previous employment, experience, and references, is the starting point in matching the best candidate to the duties of the position and the mission of the organization. A resume should always be verified. With the aid of outside agencies and again, depending on the position, organization, and legal jurisdiction, it may be necessary to do a credit check, background check, criminal record review, and polygraph on the potential new hire. All new hires in the course of signing their employment agreement or contract should be made to review and sign an acknowledgment of understanding and acceptance of the organization's security policies.

Once measures have been taken to hire the most qualified candidate, all personnel should be subject to continuous education throughout their employment. The education should contain information and guidance on all policies, which include but are not limited to password guidance, physical security, material management, social engineering, and e-mail and Internet etiquette.

It is inevitable that every employee will leave an organization either through termination, retirement, or otherwise. An organization should be prepared and have policies in place to carry out the end-of-employment procedures of co-op, term, contract, or indefinite positions. A termination of employment interview should be a standard organizational security policy for an organization. Some other considerations would be policies and procedures to ensure that future and past e-mail addressed to that person are accessible, proprietary documentation is not destroyed, compromised, or released, and that company resources are not extorted before the employee is removed from the premises.

D. Process Management

Process management is an organized and well-thought-out plan for the design, development, and maintenance of a system or products. Through configuration management and incident response, an organization can be better prepared for everyday and unexpected events.

1. Configuration Management

Configuration management provides control and traceability of changes in the design, development, and maintenance phases of software, hardware, and firmware. It allows for variable degrees of how much identification, control, accounting, and auditing are carried out during each phase.

Configuration management specifies the goals, scope, and procedure while identifying the controls for additions, deletions, and changes to the product or system's base whether hardware, software, or firmware. It is important to have a consistent and identifiable labeling system. The system can aid in identifying whether any particular change is necessary, redundant, or required and ensure that any modifications do not inadvertently affect the expected functionality of the system.

As specified in the 1988 National Computer Security Center's *Guide to Understanding Configuration Management,* the inputs to manage include detailed design specifications, other design data, user manuals and administration guides, source code, latest version of the object code, integration test documentation, system test documentation, and security test documentation.

Configuration management helps to evaluate the impact of the impending change. When the changes are implemented, the documentation is mapped to the code associated with the current version providing assurance throughout the design, development, and maintenance phases.

2. Incident Management

Incident management is an approach to planning for a rainy day. Whether the computer security incident response system is an in-house operation or provided by a third party, the functionality will be similar. Either way, having an incident management plan is key to a successful operation. Intrusions on systems are just as likely to occur to a home office as to a Fortune 500 corporation. The information for prevention and protection against intrusions relies on a well-implemented incident management system.

A *computer security incident response team (CSIRT)* is a team that has predetermined policies and procedures in place for responding to security incidents reported by its user base. The user base it services could be focused on commercial, corporate, government, general Internet populations, or a combination thereof. For a more in-depth look at a CSIRTs, consult RFC 2350.

The CSIRT has three general responsibilities to its respective user base. The first would be to define the services it provides and how those services are fulfilled. This would be covered in detail through the CSIRT's policies and procedures. The second would be to inform the user base about what relationships the CSIRT will rely on in the predetermined resolution plan. Finally, the CSIRT would have to inform

the user base of the method of communication that will be used to exchange the sensitive data surrounding the incident.

The definition of services would be communicated through published policies and the concept of operation provided by the CSIRT to the user base. The medium could be an operational framework, FAQ, white papers, newsletters, or the team's information server. This information will educate the user base on how to best report incidences, maintain the required chain of incident evidence, and what form of action to expect from the team. Some of the information that should be considered for distribution by the CSIRT, as stated in RFC 2350, to the user base is listed in Table I.

Incidences can cross over domains from internal systems to external systems, which may be public or shared. In a crossover, the incident can either have the malicious action coming from the outside and causing an adverse reaction on the inside, or the ma-

Table I   **Information to Be Distributed by a CSIRT**

Information source	Details
Document information	Date of last update
	Distribution list for notification
	Locations where the document may be found
Contact information	Name of the team
	Address
	Time zone
	Telephone number
	Fax number
	E-mail address
	Public keys and encryption information
	Team members
	Points of customer contact
Charter	Mission statement
	User base
	Sponsorship and/or affiliation
	Authority
Policies	Types of incidents and level of support
	Cooperation
	Interaction and disclosure of information
	Communication
	Authentication
Services	Incident response
	Proactive activities
Other	Incident reporting forms
	Disclaimers

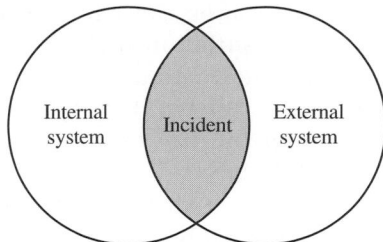

Figure 1 Affect of internal and external incidents.

licious action may come from the inside and cause an adverse reaction on the outside (Fig. 1).

In both instances, a large knowledge base exists when affected parties in public systems share experiences. Due to the extremely sensitive nature of the information reported during an incident, the user base must understand and comply with any established partnerships the CSIRT may have. Depending on the circumstances surrounding the incident, information exchanges may be necessary between CSIRTs or with government agencies, law enforcement, corporations, and companies that may not have dedicated CSIRTs. RFC 2350 notes the importance for the user base to be aware of the differences between sharing information corresponding to a working agreement and sharing information through a simple cooperation. A working agreement can imply that a nondisclosure agreement (NDR) exists between the parties, while working in cooperation implies that the parties are working in good faith.

The methods for transmitting the sensitive information, from the CSIRT's policies and procedures to reporting and disseminating information about security incidents, must be secure. The means of communication will vary between CSIRTs but the authentication, authorization, confidentiality, integrity, and availability of the communications must be preserved.

The means of publishing the CSIRT's policies and procedures should provide assurance that the information was posted by the CSIRT. That is, the person or persons whom posted the information can be verified and were authorized to post, modify, or delete the information on behalf of the CSIRT. The integrity of the information must also be maintained. For example, a digital signature would ensure that the posted information was not altered since it was signed and, if it had been altered, the comparison of signatures would fail. Using public key cryptography in combination with an access control mechanism (role-based access control or list-based access control) will ensure that only authorized individuals or groups of the CSIRT's user base can access the policies and procedures.

When reporting incidents, it is important again that the user base can verify that the connection is terminated at an authorized individual or reporting mechanism. This could be achieved via secure telephony if there is a large resource base, or via a symmetric secret (pass phrase) for a smaller resource base. The same is true for responding to an incident for the CSIRT. A protective mechanism should be in place when reporting to the user base.

On the resolution side, it is equally important that the CSIRT exercise due diligence and protect the incident information with the best means possible when collaborating with parties outside of the CSIRT team. The user base should be informed and understand that there may be a possibility for a breech in confidential information while searching for a collaborative resolution.

E. Software Security

Incorporating concepts of security into the development of software ensures a better product both for quality and quantity. The quality of the product will be exemplified in a bug-free product, which will be evident in the lack of security patches that have to be released. The fewer security patches that have to be released the happier clients will be with the product. Additionally, fewer resources will have to be expended on patches and fixes, thus providing more overall revenue for the company.

1. Robust Coding Practices

One of the best defenses against security issues is to have strong security software products that work and interoperate as expected—securely. This is easier to do than one would initially assume. The concept of security should start at the drawing table when the engineers, developers, and product managers are conjuring ideas for new and advanced technologies.

The process for stable security code is to think, design, and develop. Significant thought must be given not only to the desired functionality of the product but also to how that product will be used and integrated in multiple-user environments. The big picture is the key to the design at the drawing board. The user base and the environment will affect the functionality of the product. It is the interactions between these that have to be analyzed in order to anticipate and thus in turn produce robust code.

The following are the *security design principles*, as stated by Mat Bishop, that should be adhered to. The *principle of least privilege* gives the process the minimum amount of privilege in order to carry out its function. The *principle of fail-safe defaults* has the process returning to the last known secure state after failure occurs. The *principle of the economy of mechanism* promotes the simplest form of design. It is not necessary to have complex code if it can be represented in a simplified form. The *principle of complete mediation* lends itself to the task of checking return values and interface inputs. The *principle of open design* supports clear security mechanisms. It is not advantageous to perform security through obscurity. This is often simple and, in turn, simply broken. The *principle of separation of privilege* leads to clear and identifiable roles, which have a set of resources allocated accordingly. The *privilege of least common mechanism* implements security in a straightforward manner that is user friendly. When security becomes an annoyance to the user base, the users will try to circumvent the security mechanism. Finally the *principle of physiological acceptability* lends itself to the concept that approval is acceptance and therefore will be utilized.

2. Delivery

The security of software or information is the responsibility of the originator until it is in the possession of the end user. So although the design and development of the resource may have occurred under a controlled and secure environment, the same considerations are required for the delivery of the resource in order to maintain its integrity. Regardless of the means of delivery, integrity must be preserved through the packaging, transport, and distribution of the resource.

II. IT SECURITY ISSUES

The six services essential to the security of systems and data communications are authentication, authorization, confidentiality, integrity, availability, and non-repudiation. In the following sections, each service is reviewed. In many instances, no one service is selected in isolation but rather incorporated with other services to provide a robust infrastructure for the protection of assets.

A. Authentication

The authentication service ensures that the user's identification is valid. The three forms of authentica-

tion are (1) authentication through something that the user knows, (2) authentication through something that user has, and (3) authentication through something the user is. The typical standard of identity verification through the use of a password covers something the user knows but it is insufficient in most environments to allow a system to utilize a password as the only form of authentication. A combination of two or three forms of authentication would provide more strength depending on the mechanisms used and the system being protected.

The IT mechanisms that can be incorporated into securing authentication services include passwords, software and hardware tokens, and biometrics. This list is not limited to these specific mechanisms since the field of IT is continuously growing and expanding.

1. Passwords

A password associated with a user name is not secure enough for all applications. Some factors that strengthen the protection of a password authentication method include the length, the variability, and the randomness of the password. The length and variability of the password directly affect the number of permutations. The variability includes the number of different selections that can be chosen for each segment of the password. Table II shows that, as the length of the password and number of permutations increase, the number of different password possibilities increase.

Having a large number of possible permutations is no longer enough with the current computing power that is available. It is now essential to a system's security to have the password run through a number of hashes in order to make the task of cracking the password more difficult. The difficulty in cracking this hashed password will lead to longer computational times. Table III shows how many days it would take to run through all possible permutations assuming a computing power of 75 passwords per second for a password that has been hashed 5000 times.

Table II Number of Password Permutations

Password length X	Alpha 26^x	Alpha/ numeric 36^x	Uppercase/ alpha/numeric 62^x
6	3.09^{E8}	2.18^{E9}	5.68^{E10}
8	2.09^{E11}	2.82^{E12}	2.18^{E14}
10	1.41^{E14}	3.66^{E15}	8.39^{E17}

Table III Time to Try All Possible Password Permutations[a]

Number of password combinations	Time (days) for 1 hash	Time (days) for 5000 hashes
3.09^{E8}	0.01	47.69
2.18^{E9}	0.07	1051.31
5.68^{E10}	1.75	8765.43
2.09^{E11}	6.45	32253.09
2.82^{E12}	87.04	435185.19
2.18^{E14}	6728.39	33641975.31
1.41^{E14}	4351.85	21759259.26
3.66^{E15}	112962.96	564814814.81
8.39^{E17}	25895061.73	129475308641.98

[a]Assuming computing power of 75 passwords per second for a password that has been hashed 5000 times and a computing power of 375,000 passwords per second for a password that has been hashed once.

2. Software and Hardware Tokens

Software and hardware tokens strengthen an authentication method when used in conjunction with a password. Tokens incorporate something the user has with the password, something the user knows. This provides not only strength in the access method but increases the difficulty of having an attacker masquerade as the user. The attacker would need to take possession of the token as well as crack the associated password. This attack should be mitigated by policies and procedures, which dictate due diligence with respect to the storage of the token and selection of a password.

3. Biometrics

Biometrics is the analysis and quantification of human biological characteristics to digital format. The physical characteristics typically used, as stated in the InfoSysSec Security Portal, include finger, face, iris, retina, hand, and voice. Each characteristic focuses on the associated unique traits in order to perform a biometric scan as listed in Table IV. There are four steps to a biometric scan, which differ slightly for registering and authenticating a user to a system.

On registration of a user in a biometric system, the person's identification and authorization must be verified in a secure and undisputable manner. This method will be dictated by an organization's policies. Once the identity is validated, the biometric image must first be captured; this process is called enrollment. This image should not be held in the device beyond the time that is required to extract the unique characteristics of the physical attribute. The extraction would use predetermined points of the characteristic as input data. The unique characteristics extracted will depend on the attribute used for authentication. The digital format must be stored securely for future comparisons. On authorization of a user to the biometric system the user submits the required characteristic to the scanning device. The unique characteristic is scanned, processed, and represented in a digital format. A comparison between the secure repository and the digital format of the physical trait is performed. Access is granted or denied given a match or a failure, respectively. For more information about biometrics refer to the InfoSysSec Security Portal at *http://www. infosyssec.com/infosyssec/biomet1.htm.*

B. Authorization

The *authorization* service ensures that the user is authorized to have access to a particular resource. Authorization can be done through *role-based access control (RBAC)* or *list-based access control (LBAC)*.

RBAC will grant a user access to a resource if the role associated with the user's identification corresponds to the roles associated with the requested resource. LBAC will grant a user access to resources if the user's identification corresponds to the list of authorized users associated with the requested resource.

Table IV Physical Characteristics and Corresponding Unique Traits

Physical characteristic	Details
Finger	Finger print
Face	Upper outline of the eye socket Cheekbone Sides of the mouth
Iris	Rings Furrows Freckles Cornea
Retina	Blood vessels in the back of the eye
Hand	Length Width Thickness Surface area of the hand and fingers
Voice	Voice print

Although authorization is commonly implemented through software, no one aspect of technology is responsible for its successful operation. Encryption for confidentiality can also be seen as an authorization mechanism (see discussion of confidentiality next).

C. Confidentiality

The confidentiality service ensures that protected resources are not legible by unauthorized users or processes. Public key and symmetric key encryption can secure resources for both confidentiality and authorization. The confidentiality is provided by the encrypted text, and only the person authorized to have the corresponding private or secret key can decrypt the information. Public key encryption utilizes a public and private key pair, which is unique for each user. A user's public key is made available to the public usually through a repository in the form of a certificate. The certificate's integrity is guaranteed through the use of a digital signature applied to the certificate by a trusted third party. User A secures a resource to User B by encrypting the resource with User B's public key. User B is the only party who is able to decrypt the resources by using the private key associated with the public key used to encrypt the resource, User B's private key.

Symmetric key encryption utilizes a shared secret between two parties. The shared secret would have to be communicated securely, either via a secure protocol or out-of-band, between the two parties before any encrypted communication could proceed. Symmetric key encryption has two drawbacks. The secret has to be communicated in a secure method and there must be a unique secret between each originator and receiver.

D. Integrity

The integrity service ensures that the resource was not altered since it left the originator. For example, the use of a digital signature ensures integrity. To apply a digital signature, the originator performs a one-way hash of the text. The hash is then encrypted with the originator's private signing key. The original text along with the digitally signed hash is sent to the recipient. The recipient verifies the integrity of the message by performing the same one-way hash function on the original text. Then the recipient decrypts the signed hash with the originator's public digital signature key, which was retrieved from a trusted repository. The hash of the text and the hash that was encrypted are compared. If the hashes match the integrity of the message is intact. If they differ, the text was altered since the originator digitally signed it and the integrity is compromised.

E. Availability

The availability service ensures that authorized users or processes can access and use resources in an acceptable manner. The acceptable manner may include time to access mail servers, repositories, computational resources, memory address space, and internal and external networks. Any restrictions on resources should be made known to the user base, which relies on access to the resources. Availability is implemented through the services mentioned above, that is, authentication, authorization, confidentiality, and integrity.

F. Nonrepudiation

The service of nonrepudiation ensures that the communication between users cannot be denied and the technology verifies which users participated in the communication. Nonrepudiation is carried out through the services of authentication, authorization, confidentiality, and integrity when implemented with a secure time stamp. A secure time stamp is the secure application of the current date and time, which is retrieved from a trusted time source, to a resource. Nonrepudiation can be used as a proof of origin or proof of delivery and for auditing purposes. Nonrepudiation is technology's version of a notary public.

III. MEASURES

Understanding the basic concepts of non-IT-related security issues and IT-related security issues is the first step to securing data communications. Use of measures such as *threat risk assessments (TRAs)*, third-party and internal evaluations will aid in identifying where to apply these basic concepts. TRAs can focus on the big picture, or specific components, services, or communications between them, whereas evaluations focus on certain components of a system and determine the strength and weaknesses with respect to ITS.

A. Threat Risk Assessment

A TRA is an analysis of an organization's IT assets that identifies existing or potential threats and how to accept, minimize, or avoid risk by means that are acceptable to management. A TRA will lead to recommendations for safeguards that will reduce the risk to an acceptable level. To determine the scope of the TRA, a boundary must be laid out. The boundary will identify the components, connectivity, and user base of the environment that encompasses the assets.

Either a team or an individual may conduct the TRA. If a team conducts a TRA, the team should represent the various groups in the organization. If a select few will be carrying out the TRA, it is essential for a cross-representation to be captured through one-on-one interviews and discussions with key individuals across the organization.

Once a boundary is established, the organizational assets that require protection are then identified, keeping in mind any special needs the organization operations may have. An asset is any information or resource that requires protection from modification, disclosure or destruction. The values of the asset will always be more than the cost of the mechanisms put in place to protect the asset. For more information on TRAs, consult Communications Security Establishment (1999).

B. Evaluation

Security evaluations can add enormous value to a product or system for the effort required. Although both third-party and internal security programs have a resource cost associated with them, the benefit can far outway the cost.

Incorporating security evaluations into the development of the product can prevent and mitigate risks before the distribution of the software to the public. This results in a more stable product and fewer security patches released to the clients. This is the benefit provided by internal programs such as security reviews and penetration testing.

1. Third Party

Third-party evaluations are standards or schemes that have been developed by an external party. In the following three examples, government bodies have developed and currently run third-party evaluation programs. Government departments head the Common Criteria

and Federal Information Processing Standard programs but the evaluations are actually performed by privately owned independent and accredited laboratories.

a. COMMON CRITERIA

The *Common Criteria (CC)*, ISO/IEC Standard 15408, is an internationally recognized evaluation standard applied to ITS products and systems. The CC certificates are recognized in Australia, Canada, Finland, France, Germany, Greece, Italy, the Netherlands, New Zealand, Norway, Spain, the United Kingdom, and the United States at the time of this publication.

The CC evaluates a specific system or product against a protection profile or a security target. A protection profile is usually written by an organization with specific ITS requirements in mind but no specific system or product in mind. A security target is typically written by the vendor of a system or a product and lists how the specific ITS requirements are satisfied by their product.

b. FEDERAL INFORMATION PROCESSING STANDARD

The *Federal Information Processing Standard (FIPS)* is developed and maintained by the U.S. federal government agency, the National Institute of Standards and Technology (NIST). In collaboration with international and national organizations and agencies, NIST produces standards for the federal government when the requirements for security and interoperability exist yet no acceptable industry standards or solutions are available.

The standards produced can be either voluntary or involuntary. That is, voluntary standards provide guidance to best practices but it is not mandatory for federal government sectors to coincide. On the other hand, NIST also has the authority to make the standards involuntary. All federal government agencies must adhere to an involuntary standard unless the agency submits a waiver. The waiver must show that by following the standard, the mission of the agency would suffer a tremendous impact or the overall savings of the federal government would not offset the financial cost to the agency.

NIST provides guidance to the vendors that wish to comply with the standard as well as guidance and test criteria for accredited laboratories to evaluate the vendor and product against. The categories of FIPS publications include hardware and software standards/guidelines for database, electronic data interchange, information interchange and modeling techniques; data standards/guidelines for representations and codes; and computer security standards/guidelines for access control, cryptography, general computer security, risk analysis, contingency planning, and security labels.

2. Internal Programs

Third-party programs provide a structured evaluation of a product, which results in an evaluation certificate for marketing and partnership requirements. In many instances, such a certificate may not be necessary for certain categories of products. Internal evaluation programs provide tremendous value to a product and the overall organization. With an internal evaluation program that is run in cooperation with the development cycle, a more robust security product will result. This process can save organization resources, including development time and money, by avoiding the release of maintenance and bug patches. An internal program consists of a *security review* and *penetration testing*. Penetration testing is done in conjunction with the security review.

a. SECURITY REVIEW

A security review should be done in cooperation with the design and development process. At the time a product or system is first conceived at the drawing table, security should be at the forefront with other requirements.

A *vulnerability analysis* is a review that focuses on security-relevant issues that either moderately or severely impact the security of the product or system. A vulnerability analysis should be done on all design documentation, source code, test cases, and user and administrator documentation. During the analysis, recommendations should be made for improving the inputs if areas were inadequately documented.

A system should be in place for the classification and resolution of the vulnerabilities found. The classification would rank the vulnerabilities in order of severity, ranging from moderate impact on the system's security to an unacceptable impact, which would compromise the system. There can be any number of levels in the classification of the vulnerability, but the more levels that exist, the priority of resolving the vulnerability may be lost and seen as unimportant.

Any security issue that is found is important and should be resolved or mitigated. With a classification system in place, the identification of issues is addressed but a resolution plan and tracking system should also be put into place in order to assign developers and designers to the problem in a timely manner. A tracking system should document the issue and the solution but due to the sensitivity of the vulnerabilities found, the system should be accessible only on a need-to-know basis.

As technologies change, it may be necessary to improve the inputs used for a vulnerability analysis or change the process by which a resolution is implemented. A process improvement recommendation can be as simple as suggesting a new impartial section of the company be involved in the process or a better means of communication be put in place between the groups.

b. PENETRATION TESTING

Penetration testing focuses on how the system or product can be manipulated and in essence be broken or hacked. Of course, because the vendor of the system or product would have requested the security review, it would be considered ethical hacking. Penetration testing is done in conjunction with the vulnerability analysis. If individuals or teams are working on either, they should work in close collaboration to achieve the most thorough analysis. The documentation and configuration information should be analyzed to see if any of the information reveals vulnerabilities or could be used to compromise the security of the product. During penetration testing, the products' functionality, interoperation, and source code should be placed under close scrutiny to ensure the robustness of the product's security.

One common concern of internal security reviews and third-party reviews is the effect of the interoperation of evaluated products with products that are not evaluated. In the commercial industry this is an issue. The mitigation to this concern is to clearly identify any assumptions made during a security review including what is considered to be in the scope of the evaluation. Although it is unlikely that every commercial product will attain an evaluation status, data communications would be more secure than they are today if security were initiated at the drawing table where concepts and products are designed.

IV. FUTURE DIRECTION

Security for data communications and the Internet is seeing only a portion of the attention it deserves. A tremendous amount of work remains to be done to educate the government, business, and general public communities.

Currently, companies that invest resources into security programs have confidence in the security offered by their products but can only make assumptions about the products produced by other vendors on which they rely. The security of data communications would be augmented if all vendors would incorporate general security issues, both technical and nontechnical, into their design and development processes. Although added assurance is obtained when products undergo third-party evaluations, such as the CC and FIPS, such evaluations may not always be necessary or applicable.

Data communications and Internet traffic are growing by the minute; more and more people are discovering the opportunities the digital world presents and the possibilities it holds. The majority of users do not understand the security issues and risks associated with the Internet. If users are educated they will request secure communications from governments and vendors. The future direction of ITS should focus more on education. The more the user communities understand the issues of today, the more interested parties will collaborate in order to achieve secure and interoperable data communications for tomorrow.

SEE ALSO THE FOLLOWING ARTICLES

Computer Viruses • Crime, Use of Computers in • Electronic Mail • Encryption • End-User Computing, Managing • Ethical Issues • Firewalls • Human Side of Information, Managing the Systems • Privacy • Software Piracy

BIBLIOGRAPHY

Adams, C., and Lloyd, S. (1999). *Understanding public key infrastructures: Concepts, standards and development considerations.* (Engelman L. R., ed.) Indianapolis, IN: Macmillan Technical Publications.

Bishop, M. (2000). *Attacking programs, and writing more secure programs for Unix.* Davis: Department of Computer Science, University of California–Davis.

Brownlee, N., and Guttman, E. (1998). *RFC 2350: Expectations for computer security incident response.* Internet Engineering Task Force, Network Working Group.

Common Criteria, Version 2.1. Available at http://www.commoncriteria.org.

Communications Security Establishment (1999). *Threat and risk assessment working guide.* Ottawa: Government of Canada.

InfoSysSec Security Portal (2000). Available at http://www.infosyssec.com/infosyssec/biomet1.htm.

National Computer Security Center (1988). *The rainbow books: A guide to understanding configuration management in trusted systems.* Fort George G. Meade, MD.

National Institute of Standards and Technology (2000). *Federal information processing standards.* Available at http://www.itl.nist.gov/fipspubs.

National Security Agency Information Assurance Solutions Technical Directors (2000). *Information assurance technical framework release 3.0.*

Server Classifications

Shu Zhang
Computer Science Corporation, Los Angeles

Ming Wang
California State University, Los Angeles

GLOSSARY

centralized system Computers are hosted in data centers and users access the host computers through terminals.
distributed system Client/server system consisting of many autonomous servers.
network operating systems Operating systems designed for and dedicated to network servers.
servers Computers on the network that serve multiple users.

A **SERVER** is a networked computer that serves the requests from multiple computers. Servers play very important roles in information systems today, especially in distributed client/server computing environments. Network operating systems have crucial impacts for server performances. In today's competitive market place, all aspects of servers evolve rapidly. Functionalities of servers are reviewed. Servers are classified based on functionality.

I. SERVERS

A server is a networked computer that serves the requests from multiple computers. Servers play very important roles in information systems, especially in distributed computing environments and client/server architectures. A common example would be a database server serving many users over a network simultaneously. In this case, users might use a desktop PC (personal computer) with a graphical display to com-

pose and send a request, and receive and display the result of the request from the server. Since a server might serve hundreds or even thousands of users at the same time, it needs a more powerful CPU (central processing unit), possibly multiple CPUs, and faster and redundant data storage devices, like a RAID (redundant array of inexpensive disks) device. Because a server might store shared critical data, usually it has a tape drive, or it can connect to a networked tape drive device to archive data for ensuring data safety and integrity.

A. From Hosts to Servers

1. Centralized System

The concept of network computer architecture is evolutionary. The origin of the centralized computer dates back to the 1940s. During that time host computers were very large and expensive machines, like the famous MARK I, ENIAC, and EDVAC, etc. Even after computers were commercialized around the 1950s, most computers were "hosted" in highly secured data processing centers, and users accessed the host computers through "dumb" terminals. By the late 1960s, IBM became a dominant vendor of large-scale computers called a "mainframe" host. In the mid-1970s, minicomputers started challenging mainframe computers. In many cases, minicomputers could host applications and perform the same functions as mainframes, but with less cost. Since the host is the center of this system architecture, it is called a centralized system. In the early 1980s, most computers, no matter whether they were large-scale mainframes or smaller minicomputers, were operated as application hosts, while terminal users had limited access to their hosts; in fact, most terminal users never have any physical access to host computers. Generally speaking, a host is a computer designed for massive parallel processing of large quantities of information connected with terminals utilized by end users. All network services, application executions, and database requests are hosted in this computer, and all data are stored in this host.

Basically, minicomputers and mainframe computers were the de facto standard of enterprise centralized computing systems before PCs entered the professional computing area. Figure 1 shows a typical centralized system.

2. Distributed System

A distributed system consists of a collection of microcomputers connected to one or more computer servers by a computer network and equipped with network operating system software. Network operating system software enables computers to coordinate their activities and to share the resources of the system—hardware, software, and data. It also can coordinate activities among servers to achieve better over all performance for network tasks. A well-designed distributed system could provide users with a single, integrated computing environment even though the computers are located in geographically separated facilities.

The development of distributed systems followed the emergence of high-speed LAN (local area computer

networks) and WAN (wide area networks) in the early 1980s. Ever since IBM introduced IBM PC into the computing market, the enterprise computing system has changed dramatically, as computers have become more and more affordable to users. The availability of high performance microcomputers, work stations, and server computers has resulted in a major shift towards distributed systems and away from centralized computing systems. People are no longer being tied to high-end and expensive centralized computing environments. The trend has been accelerated by the development of distributed system software such as Oracle Server and SQL server packages, designed to support the development of distributed applications. It is very common now to see a distributed application running collaboratively among some servers. For a well-designed distributed application, any task could be executed by more that one server, so a single faulty server won't bring down the applications. For example, a state wide hospital system's IS (information system) department might have to support tens of medical centers scattered state wide and have tens of departmental information systems (like a UNIX based RIS for Radiology and a Windows NT based Dietary system, etc.) running on Windows 2000/NT servers and different UNIX platforms, while the HIS (Hospital Information System) and CIS (Clinical Information System) are on mainframe computers. Only a distributed computing environment could bring so many autonomous departmental systems together and make them work collaboratively.

Enterprise computing systems differ in significant ways from centralized and distributed systems. Since the late 1980s, a move has occurred from mainframe

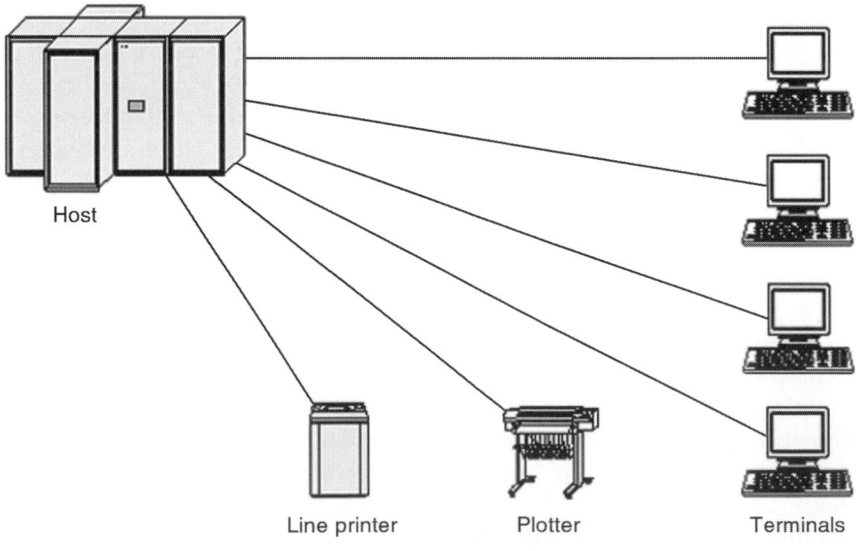

Host

Line printer   Plotter   Terminals

Figure 1 Centralized system.

systems to networked personal computing systems, with network software providing such functionality as shared data storage and electronic mail. Despite the interconnectivity of distributed systems, they remain largely independent: each user runs his or her applications on their own microcomputers, and any interactions between systems are through shared files and mails. Client-server architecture has become common in such a distributed system. A number of client computers are configured as a sort of ring around the server, which provides database functionality and file management. Again, the client computers interact indirectly through shared servers. Figure 2 shows a typical distributed system.

B. Servers for Client/Server Computing

Client/server computing is a phenomenon that has developed in the past decade. The inexpensive and powerful PC took over previously "dumb" terminal-oriented enterprise desktops as quickly as people could think. To use the excessive computing capacity of desktop PCs or workstations, many organizations began downloading data from those enterprise host computers for local manipulation at the user's fin-

gertips. In this client/server model, the definition of the server will continue to include what those traditional hosts and servers have, but people can envision the placement of network and application services on many different operating system platforms.

1. Servers for "Thin" Clients

a. "FAT" CLIENTS VERSUS "THIN" CLIENTS

Client-server computing architecture refers to the way in which software components interact to form a system. As the name suggests there is a client process, which requires some resource, and a server, which provides the resource. There is no requirement that the client and server must reside on the same machine. In practice, it is quite common to place a server at one site in a local area network and the clients at the other sites. Clients can be categorized into two types: fat clients and thin clients. A "fat" client requires considerate resources on the client's computer to run effectively. This includes disk space, RAM, and CPU power. It has significant client-side administration overhead. A "thin" client requires fewer resources on the client's computer and is responsible for only simple logic processing, such as input validation. It has less expensive hardware because the client is thin.

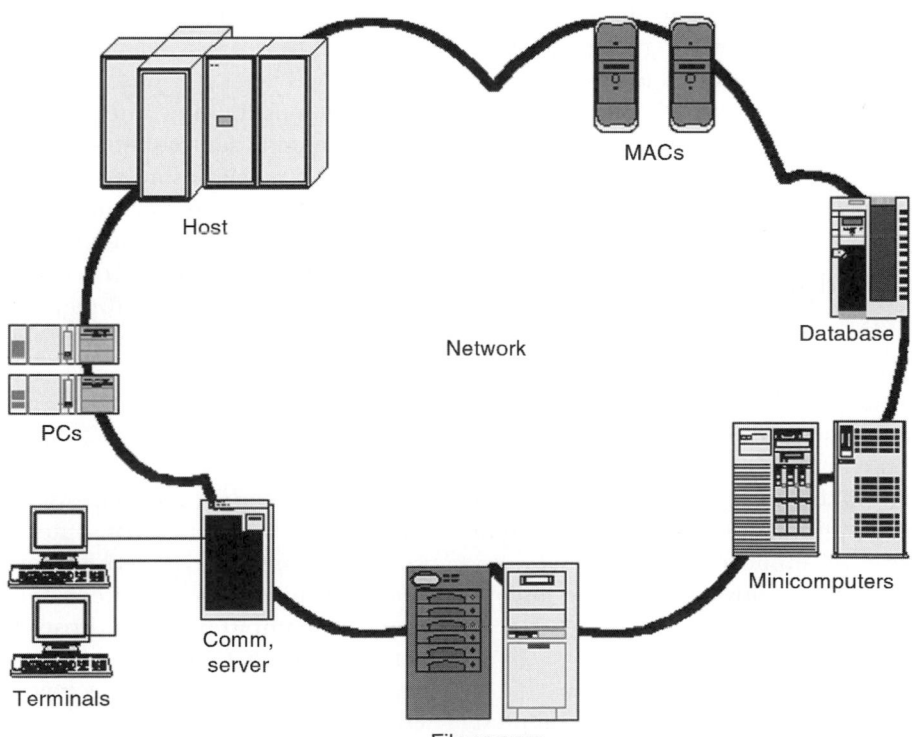

Figure 2 Distributed system.

b. Thin Clients

In the thin-client/server computing model, applications execute 100% on the server. The client computers are just ordinary desktop PCs running one or more terminal programs to access servers over LAN or WAN. The thin-client/server involves connecting thin-client software or a thin-client hardware device with the server side using a highly efficient network protocol. The thin-client/server architecture enables 100% server-based processing, management, deployment, and support for mission-critical productivity, Web-based, or other custom applications across any type of connection to any type of client hardware, regardless of platforms. The client hardware can include desktop PCs, network computers, handhold computers, wireless PDA, and Windows-CE devices.

c. Advantages of "Thin" Clients

Though it appears to be a very primitive approach for client/server computing since it simply replaces one or more dumb terminals with a desktop PC, the thin-client/server model has regained some ground recently because of the TCO (total cost of ownership) consideration for IS operation and the appearance of lower-powered client devices like a PDA (personal data assistant) for palmtop computing. For the thin-client/server computing model, there is no need to purchase or upgrade client hardware—just run the latest software on servers instead. The client can let it comfortably evolve, leveraging existing hardware, operating systems, software, networks, and standards. Thin-client/server computing extends the life of the organization's existing computing infrastructure considerably and might reduce TCO if it is planned and implemented carefully with well-scaled servers.

2. Servers for Multiple Tiers of Client/Server

In a typical client/server based application, the client process and server process can be on the same computer, or distributed in two or more computers. A single-tier client/server application consists of a single layer that supports the user interface, the business rules, and the data manipulation processes all on one computer. This kind of application is rarely used today because it will not take advantage of the distributed computing environment.

a. Two-Tier Client/Server Architecture

The two-tier client/server structure is the simplest client/server structure that is still in use for many applications today. In a two-tier application, the business rules and user interface remain as part of the client application on the client's computers. The traditional two-tier client/server architecture provides a basic separation of tasks. The client (tier 1) is primarily responsible for the presentation of data to the user, and the server (tier 2) is primarily responsible for supplying data services to the client. The client handles user interface actions and the main business application logic. The server provides server side validation, data retrieval, and data manipulation. This separate application could be a RDBMS (relational database management system), which is functioning as a data storage/retrieval system for the application.

b. Three-Tier Client/Server Architecture

The need for enterprise scalability challenged the traditional two-tier client/server architecture. In the mid-1990s, as applications became more complex and potentially could be deployed to hundreds or thousands of end-users, the client side presented the problems that prevented true scalability. Because two-tier client/server applications are not optimized for WAN connections, response time is often unacceptable for remote users. Application upgrades require software and often hardware upgrades on all client PCs, resulting in potential version control problems.

By 1995, three new layers of client/server architecture were proposed, each running on a different platform:

1. Tier one is the user interface layer, which runs on the end-user's computer.
2. Tier two is the business logic and data processing layer. This middle tier runs on a server and is often called the application server. This added middle layer is called an application server.
3. Tier three is the data storage system, which stores the data required by the middle tier. This tier may run on a separate server called the database server. This third layer is called the back-end server.

In a three-tier application, the user interface processes remain on the client's computers, but the business rules processes are resided and executed on the application middle layer between the client's computer and the computer which hosts the data storage/retrieval system. One application server is designed to serve multiple clients. In this type of application, the client would never access the data storage system directly.

c. ADVANTAGES OF THREE-TIER CLIENT/SERVER ARCHITECTURE

Since there are three physically separated layers for the application, the added modularity makes it easier to modify or replace one tier without affecting the other tiers. Application maintenance is centralized with the transfer of the business logic for many end-users to a single application server. This eliminates the concerns of software distribution that are problematic in the traditional two-tier client/server architecture. An additional advantage is that the three-tier architecture maps quite naturally to the Web environment, with a Web browser acting as the thin client, a Web server acting as the application server, and a data/database system server as the back-end.

d. MULTITIER CLIENT/SERVER ARCHITECTURE

The three-tier architecture can be extended to *n*-tiers, with additional tiers added to provide more flexibility and scalability. Some distributed computing systems have more than three layers, but the basic rules are the same as those for three-tier applications. For example, the middle tier of the three-tier architecture could be split into two, with one tier for the Web server and another for the application server. More than one server used in the second and third layers will usually increase overall application effi-

ciency as needed. Figure 3 shows a typical multiple tier client/server architecture.

II. NETWORK OPERATING SYSTEMS FOR SERVERS

Servers works best when they are configured with an NOS (network operating system) that supports shared memory, preemptive multitasking, and application isolation. To handle massive data processing load and multiple applications efficiently, servers need to use an OS that provides a multithread environment and scalability for multiple CPUs. Since servers are tied to networks to provide a variety of network services, some operating systems are dedicated to the servers and are called an NOS (network operating system). They are introduced in the following sections.

A. Novell NetWare

For a number of years, NetWare was synonymous with networking. NetWare, an exceptionally fast file-and-print server, allows desktop clients to share files, data, and printers. From its inception, Novell's redirector implementation strategy reflected the need for speed.

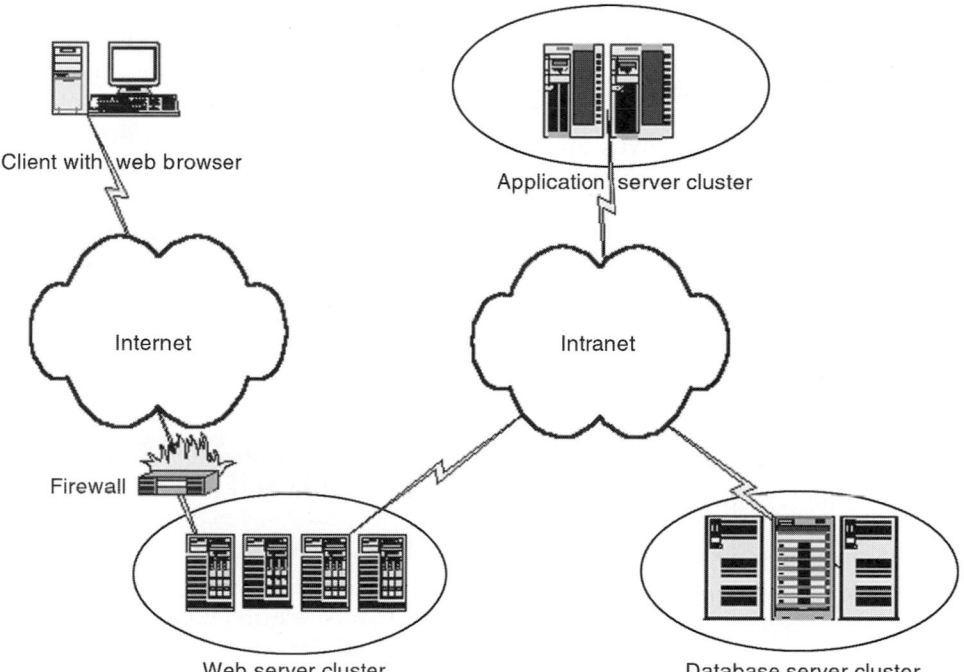

Figure 3 A multitier client/server diagram.

The NetWare redirector was designed to intercept and redirect system calls for disk access. However, Windows 2000/NT operating systems are giving NetWare some stiff competition because of their native API functionalities with desktop operating systems such as Windows 2000 Professional and Windows XP/ME/98/95 systems.

B. Microsoft Windows 2000/NT

The Microsoft Windows 2000/NT Server is a very commonly used 32-bit operating system. The Windows 2000 Server kernel has evolved directly from its predecessor Windows NT Server. The Windows 2000/NT Server leverages the Windows GUI into the world of networking. The Windows 2000/NT Server uses the same user interfaces as Windows XP/ME/98/95 with true multithreading, built-in networking, security, and memory protection. The Windows 2000 Server has three editions to address different market requirements, namely Standard Server, Advanced Server, and Data Center Server. The Windows 2000 Server provides exceptional portability, scalability, and distributed computing capacities with built-in DCOM components, as well as POSIX compliance and C2 security.

C. UNIX Families

UNIX is an interactive time-sharing operating system that was invented in the 1960s. UNIX has powerful multiuser capabilities because of its architecture and features. Among the many features of UNIX are 32-bit and 64-bit architectures, preemptive multitasking, robustness, and networking capability. There are many UNIX vendors such as Solaris from Sun Microsystems, AIX from IBM, and UX from HP. In comparison to other network operating systems such as NetWare and Windows 2000/NT, UNIX is quite expensive to maintain and support with the exception of Linux. Though UNIX was the most widely used multiuser general-purpose operating system in the enterprise level computing world in the 1990s, it has yielded more and more to the Windows 2000/NT operating system.

D. Some Proprietary Systems

1. IBM's MVS

Though IBM mainframe computers have acted as a traditional application host for many years, there is a commitment made by IBM to provide support for networking services running under its MVS (multiple virtual storage) environment. This is an attractive option for organizations with a large investment in MVS applications under IBM System 370-compatible mainframe computers. MVS provides a powerful database server using DB2. With MVS networking services, users can issue SQL requests from a client/server application to the target databases as part of the view and make this implementation viable for high-performance tasks. IBM also makes a similar commitment to its middle range computers, the AS/400 systems under the OS/400 operating system.

2. DEC's VMS

DEC (Digital Equipment Corp.), now a division of Compaq, provides VMS as its server OS platform. VMS has a long history in the distributed computing environment arena and includes many of the features necessary to act as a server in client/server models. VMS support for DBMS products such as Oracle, SyBase, RDB, and Ingres allow this platform to execute effectively as database servers for client/server applications. DEC has made its VMS, Digital-UNIX, and PathWorks products well integrated to provide a networking environment that covers its own middle range systems, RISC (reduced instruction set computing) based minicomputers, and CISC (complex instruction set computing) based Intel CPU servers. However, after Compaq Computers acquired DEC, that commitment may have some changes to be in alliance with the Compaq strategies.

There are many other proprietary network operating systems, and most of them have their own domains for either historical reasons or very special needs. However, people will see more and more reliance and strategy changes among those proprietary network operating system vendors in the rapid advancement of high-tech industries and very competitive market place of today.

III. SERVER CLASSIFICATION BY FUNCTIONALITY

A. File Servers

File servers are network computers that store programs and data files for shared access and that may control access to remote network printers, providing spooling spaces for printer queues. File servers also provide record level data services to nondatabase applications, acting like a remote disk drive. File servers manage allocation of shared storage space, and either deny or accept a user request for a file according to the user's privilege. File servers have file catalog functions to support file operation and directory structure. The maximum length of a file name usually ranges up to 256 characters, depending on the network operating system. A stored program file is typically loaded from a file server for execution on a client or an application server. The difference between a file server and an application server is that the file server stores the programs and data, while the application server runs the programs and processes the data.

A file server supports one or more file sharing protocols. If a client wants to have access to multiple file servers running different protocols, either the client supports the protocol of each server or the server supports the protocol of each client. Client software that adds this capability is very common and allows interoperability between Windows, Macintosh, NetWare, UNIX, and other platforms. The most commonly used protocols for file servers are TCP/IP, SPS/IPX, and NETBEUI. Usually file servers use a hierarchical file system that stores data in a top-to-bottom organization structure. All internal access to the data starts from the top to the bottom.

1. Novell NetWare Family

The NetWare family of network operating systems supports DOS, Windows, OS/2, and Macintosh clients. UNIX client support is available from third parties. In the early 1990s, NetWare was the most popular LAN operating system. Until NetWare 5, which natively supports TCP/IP and Java, NetWare always used its own proprietary protocols (IPX/SPX/NCP). Its hard disks are in the NetWare format. Although DOS and Windows applications reside on the server, they cannot be run on the server unless they have been compiled into NetWare Loadable Modules (NLM) using Novell libraries.

Novell Directory Services (NDS) is Novell's flagship directory service that is included in NetWare beginning with Version 4. It is also available for Windows NT and Solaris. NDS maintains a hierarchical database of information about the network resources within a global enterprise, including networks, users, subgroups, servers, volumes, and printers. Unlike the bindery, which was the directory service in NetWare 3.x, NDS users log onto the network as a whole, not a specific server, and NDS determines their access rights. NDS is based on the X.500 directory standard and is LDAP compliant. Novell provides the NDS

source code free of charge to developers that wish to integrate it into their products. In NDS, every network resource is called an "object," and each object contains properties (fields). For example, a user object would contain login ID, password, name, address, telephone, and node address.

NetWare 4 (1993) was the first NetWare version to use the much-acclaimed Novell Directory Services (NDS), which provides directory services for a global enterprise. NetWare 5 (1998) fully supported TCP/IP and Java and includes a kernel that natively supports symmetric multiprocessing (SMP). Introduced in 2001, NetWare 6 adds disk pooling and Novell Internet Printing (NIP), which enables documents to be printed over the Internet.

2. Windows 2000/NT File Servers

Windows 2000 is known as Microsoft "WIN2K" or "W2K." It is a major upgrade to Windows NT 4. Launched in February 2000, the Windows 2000 server came in one client version and three server versions. It added support for Plug and Play, which made adding peripherals considerably easier than in NT 4. Windows 2000 uses Active Directory, which replaces NT's domain system and makes network administration simpler. This is a major redesign of the directory structure for companies. Windows 2000 is more stable than Windows NT and is designed to eliminate erroneous replacement of DLLs when applications are installed.

Windows 2000 Advanced Server is a replacement for the Windows NT 4.0 Server Enterprise Edition. It supports clustering and automatic fail-over in the event of a system failure. Windows 2000 Data Center Server supports more advanced clustering and is targeting enterprise data service offering. Windows 2000 supports multiprocessing systems (SMP), adds extensive security and administrative features, and offers a dual boot capability. Designed for enterprise use, each application can access 2GB of virtual memory. With terminal service and IIS service options, Windows 2000 Server makes application deployment much easier and straightforward.

3. NFS File Servers

a. NFS
Network File System (NFS), developed by Sun Microsystems, is a file sharing protocol and a de facto UNIX network standard. It is widely known as a "distributed file system." Almost all NIX vendors implement NFS as part of their offerings, as well as Network

Information Service (NIS) developed by Sun. The advantages of such centralization include allowing unified user access to network resources and making the distributed file system more secure and manageable.

b. WEBNFS

WebNFS is derived from NFS. As a Web version of the NFS distributed file system from SunSoft, WebNFS enabled Web server browsers to access Web pages as much as 10 times faster than the standard HTTP protocol. Unlike HTTP, which drops the connection after each tiny file is downloaded, WebNFS downloads multiple files with a single connection.

4. Network Attached Storage (NAS) Systems

Network Attached Storage (NAS) systems are another file service device. The NAS is connected to the LAN just like a file server. Rather than containing a full-blown OS, it typically uses a slim microkernel specialized for handling only I/O requests such as NFS (UNIX), CIFS/SMB (Windows 2000/NT), and NCP (NetWare). Adding or removing a NAS system is like adding or removing any network node. For example, it doesn't get much simpler than the Meridian Data Snap server—containing only an on/off switch and an ethernet port. It provides an instant storage boost by simply plugging it into the network switch or hub port. However, the NAS is subject to the variable behavior and overhead of the network, which makes NAS less desirable in many cases.

B. Database Servers

1. Description

Database servers are networked computers on a network dedicated to database storage and data retrieval from the database. The database server is a key component in a client/server computing environment. It holds the database management system (DBMS) and the databases. In the database context, the client manages the user interface and application logic, acting as a sophisticated workstation on which to run database applications. The client takes the user's request, checks the syntax, and generates database requests in SQL or another database language. It then transmits the message to the server, waits for a response, and formats the response to the end-user. The server accepts and processes the database requests, then transmits the results back to the client. The process in-

volves checking authorization, ensuring integrity maintaining the system catalog, and performing query and update process.

2. Advantages of Using Database Servers

(i) It enables wider access to existing databases
(ii) It increases performance. If the clients and server reside on different computers then different CPUs can process applications in parallel.
(iii) Hardware cost may be reduced. It is only the server that requires storage for the database and processing power sufficient to store and manage the database.
(iv) It increases database consistency. The server can handle integrity checks, so that constraints need to be defined and validated only by the server.

3. Oracle Server

The Oracle database was the first DBMS to be ported to a wide variety of platforms. Oracle offers a variety of application development tools and is a major promoter of the network computer. Its Network Computer subsidiary defines the specifications for a compliant platform. ORACLE 9 is the newest relational database management system (RDBMS) with extended object-relational database features. The current version of Oracle's flagship product includes such features as replication and high availability. Oracle 9 runs on more than 80 platforms.

The new ORACLE enterprise server package includes many Internet enhancements. Noteworthy features are increased performance and support for XML and JDBC applications. JVM (Java Virtual Machine) is built into the RDBMS so that triggers and stored procedures can be written and executed in Java directly. It enables Internet developers to write applications and database procedures in the Java language. In addition, the JVM can also execute Enterprise JavaBeans (EJBs), turning the DBMS into an application server.

4. Microsoft SQL Server

SQL Server is a relational DBMS from Microsoft that runs on Windows 2000/NT servers. It is Microsoft's high-end client/server database and a key component in its BackOffice suite of server products. SQL Server was originally developed by Sybase. After Microsoft bought it in 1992, the company began developing its own version. Today, Microsoft SQL Server and Sybase

SQL Server are independent products with some compatibility. SQL Server 2000 is the newest version release in 2000. Along with Microsoft's other BackOffice products, like Microsoft Transaction Server (MTS), SQL Server is targeting the enterprise computing arena with almost all the features that its competitors have, plus native Windows interface. However, Microsoft SQL Server only operates under Windows 2000/NT systems.

5. DB2 Servers

DB2 is a RDBMS from IBM that was originally developed for its mainframes. It is IBM's major database product with the fully featured SQL language. Known for its industrial strength reliability, IBM has made DB2 available for all of its own platforms, including OS/2, OS/400, AIX-RS/6000, and OS/390, as well as for Solaris on Sun systems and HP-UX on HP 9000 workstations and servers.

DB2 Universal DataBase (UDB) is an enhanced and very popular version of DB2 that combines relational and object-relational database technology as well as various query optimization techniques for parallel processing. Also geared for electronic commerce, DB2 UDB provides graphical administration, Java, and JDBC support. DB2 UDB runs on mainframes, Windows NT, and various versions of UNIX.

6. Informix Servers

Informix is a relational database management system originally from Informix Software. It was acquired by IBM in 2001. Informix runs on most UNIX platforms, including SCO UNIX for x86 machines and NetWare. Development tools from Informix include INFORMIX-4GL, a fourth-generation language, and INFORMIX-New Era, a client/server development system for Windows clients that supports INFORMIX and non-INFORMIX databases. It is expected that either Informix will be tightly integrated with the IBM DB2 production line, or migrated into DB2 in the near future.

7. Sybase SQL Server

Sybase SQL Server is a relational database management system from Sybase that runs on OS/2, Windows NT, NetWare, VAX, and UNIX servers. It was designed for the client/server environment and is accessed by applications using SQL or via Sybase's own QBE and decision-support utilities. After SyBase acquired Powersoft, a maker of the PowerBuilder application development software in 1995, and NEON Software, an Enterprise System Integration service vendor in 2001, it offered a variety of application development tools, compilers, middleware, and database and data warehousing products for its Sybase SQL Server, as well as for other RDBMS.

C. Application Servers

Application servers are network computers that store and run an application for client computers. Application servers, whatever their function, occupy a large chunk of computing territory between database servers and the end user. Most broadly, this is called "middleware" which tells us something about what application servers do. First and foremost, application servers connect database information (usually coming from a database server) and the end-user or client program (often running in a Web browser). There are many reasons for having an intermediate player in this connection, including a desire to decrease the size and complexity of client programs, the need to cache and control the data flow for better performance, and a requirement to provide security for both data and user traffic.

In the early days of application servers, it was realized that applications themselves, the programs people were using to get work done, were becoming bigger and more complex, both to write and maintain. At the same time, pressure was increasing for applications to share more of their data and sometimes functionality. More applications were either located on a network or used networks extensively. It seemed logical to have some kind of program residing on the network that would help share application capabilities in an organized and efficient way, and make it easier to write, manage, and maintain the applications.

These designated application servers first appeared in client/server computing and on LANs. At first, they were often associated with "tiered" applications, when people described the functionality of applications as two-tiered (database and client program), three-tiered (database, client program, and application service), or *n*-tiered (all of the above plus whatever). This was (and still is) a complex model of application development, and it resisted wide-scale implementation. Then along came the Internet application. The Internet application is automatically three-tiered (usually consisting of a database, client program, and Web servers). Managing data along with application functionality suddenly became not only an esoteric exercise in better program design, but also a downright necessity. This vaulted the application server from ob-scurity to the top of a pedestal, and literally scores of companies jumped in to develop products. Not sur-prisingly, people do not consider or think of the role of the application server in the same way, so applica-tion servers have different roles and functionalities as different companies build from their requirements and understanding. Scalability is a good example. Some companies might want an application server that simply helps them organize their applications for the Web, give them better control over the business logic they contain, and make it easier to monitor and secure the data. They do not need thousands of servers. Other companies, especially big ones, do need to manage thousands of servers. For them, the scala-bility of an application server is crucial. So some ap-plication servers feature scalability, others feature other things, and some try to do everything. Also, ap-plication server products belong to a variety of pro-gramming domains: some are Java based, while oth-ers are written by C++; one might support CORBA, and another could be implemented through Microsoft DCOM. It is relatively important to consider these servers in light of an organization's programming preferences.

D. Web Servers

1. Description

A Web server is a network server that manages access to files, folders, and other resources over the Internet or a local Intranet via the HTTP (hypertext transfer protocol). HTTP is a client/server protocol that de-fines how clients and servers communicate. It trans-mits information between servers and clients. In ad-dition, Web servers possess unique Web networking characteristics. They handle permissions, execute programs, keep track of directories and files, and com-municate with the client computer. These client com-puters make requests for files and actions from server computers using HTTP. Web servers serve content over the Internet using HTTP. The Web server ac-cepts HTTP requests from browsers like Internet Ex-plorer and Netscape Communicator and returns the appropriate hypertext markup language (HTML) doc-uments, images, and Java Applets. A number of server-sided technologies can be used to increase the power of the server beyond its ability to deliver standard HTML pages. These include CGI scripts, Active Server Page (ASP), Java Server Page (JSP), and Java Servlet.

2. Development

Initially, Web servers served static content to a Web browser at a very basic level, and many new Web servers are still starting in the same way. This means that the Web server receives a request for a Web page like http://www.anyname.com/ and maps that uni-form resource locator (URL) to a local default start-ing page file on the host server. In most cases, the file is "index.html" or "default.html" as configured by Web masters. The server then loads this file from server storage and serves it out across the network to the user's Web browser. The browser and server use HTTP for this entire exchange. Users could access any file by name under that URL directly if the file on the server is accessible for the users, for example, http://www.anyname.com/anydir/anypage.html. Per-haps the most important expansion of this was the concept of dynamic content, in which Web pages gen-erated by CGI, ASP, JSP, and Java Servlet could re-spond to a user's input, whether directly or indirectly. A Web server could run those programs locally and transmit their output through the Web server to the user's Web browser that is requesting the dynamic content.

The second important advance, and the one that makes e-commerce possible, was the introduction of hypertext transmission protocol, secure (HTTPS). This protocol allows secure communication to go on between the browser and Web server. This means that it is safe for the user and server to transmit sensitive data to each other across what might be considered an insecure network using HTTPS.

3. Examples

Among the hundreds of Web servers, Microsoft Per-sonal Server (MPS), Microsoft Internet Information Server (IIS), Apache, and Jigsaw remain popular so far. Microsoft Internet Information Server (IIS) is the one most commonly used by commercial Web sites, because of its higher manageability and flexibility. However, it is also very common to see some small or nonprofit sites running a variety of free distributed Web servers.

E. Mail Servers

Mail servers are network servers that provide elec-tronic mail services for Internet users. Web servers may be the most important and ubiquitous servers on the Internet. Mail servers rank a close second because e-mail is considered the most important service provided by the Internet. For Internet mail servers, a very important factor is the support of standards. The two major protocols are SMTP (simple mail transfer protocol) for outgoing mail and POP3 (post office protocol) for incoming mail. A more recent protocol is IMAP4 (Internet messaging access protocol). IMAP offers a number of important features, including user management of mail on the server. Other Internet protocols include ESMTP (extended simple mail transfer protocol), APOP (authenticated post office protocol), MIME (multipurpose Internet mail extensions), and Ph (directory access protocol). Many mail servers are also adding S/MIME, SSL, or RSA (Rivest, Shamir, Adleman Algorithm) support for message encryption, and LDAP (lightweight directory access protocol) support to access operating system directory information about mail users. In general, the more standards a server supports, the better mail server it is.

The highly publicized viruses that attack through e-mail clients have put the spotlight on e-mail as a vulnerable point in an enterprise's firewall. In response, mail server vendors, along with major client vendors, have begun producing add-ons and built-in features that will help to scan mail, segregate questionable messages, and deal with viruses. As might be expected, this is a rapidly expanding element of e-mail servers and should be considered important when comparing products.

E-mail servers rank high in difficulty to install and manage. One reason is that they are tied to the inherently variable source–Internet connection and mail traffic. Another reason is that they require constant attention to user lists, user rights, and message storage. Thus, it is important to look for servers that provide ease of administration and ease of use. A GUI (graphical user interface) is a nice feature for user-friendly e-mail clients, but it is not necessarily the route to easy administration. This type of interface is often related to a platform (operating system), and it is important to keep in mind that many products are intended to run on a single platform (e.g., Unix or Windows).

F. Proxy Servers

Proxy servers provide a gateway for applications and filter traffic between an organization's network and the Internet for security purposes. Although proxy servers have been around for a long time (since the early days of the WAN), the Internet has transformed them. They used to be found in only the large corporations. They are now found as a critical component in small organizations with an Internet connection. They will be found running in some private homes in the future. As a key part of a network firewall system, proxy servers keep unwanted intruders, hikers, and viruses away from internal networks, while they allow approved users to access the Internet resources. Schematically, a proxy server sits between a client program (typically a Web browser) and some external server (typically another server on the Web). The proxy server can monitor and intercept any and all requests being sent to the external server or requests that come in from the Internet connection. This positioning gives the proxy server three key capabilities: filtering requests, improving performance, and sharing connections. Filtering requests is the security function and the original reason for having a proxy server. Proxy servers can inspect all traffic (in and out) over an Internet connection and determine if there is anything that should be denied transmission, reception, or access. Since this filtering cuts both ways, a proxy server can be used to keep users out of particular Web sites (by monitoring for specific URLs) or restrict unauthorized access to the internal network by authenticating users. Before a connection is made, the server can ask the user to log in. To a Web user this makes every site look like it requires a log in. Because proxy servers are handling all communications, they can log everything the user does. For HTTP (Web) proxies this includes logging every URL. For FTP proxies this includes every downloaded file. A proxy can also examine the content of transmissions for "inappropriate" words or scan for viruses, although this may impose serious overhead on performance.

It should be obvious that part and parcel of any proxy server system is the need to create policies for using it to filter Internet traffic. Few decisions can be more politically charged within an enterprise than who is allowed to do what on the Internet, and many privacy-related issues go with such decisions. It is important that the proxy server provide adequate ways not only to incorporate the rules for filtering, but also to help organize and document those rules.

The other aspect of proxy servers, improving performance, is far less controversial. This capability is usually called proxy server caching. In simplest terms, the proxy server analyzes user requests and determines which, if any, should have the content stored temporarily for immediate access. A typical corporate example would be a company's home page located on a remote server. Many employees may visit this page several times a day. Since this page is requested repeatedly, the proxy server would cache it for immediate delivery to the Web browser. Cache management is a big part of many proxy servers. It is important to consider how easily the cache can be tuned and for whom it provides the most benefit.

Some proxy servers, particularly those targeted at small business, provide a means for sharing a single Internet connection among a number of workstations. While this has practical limits in performance, it can still be a very effective and inexpensive way to provide Internet services, such as e-mail, throughout an office. There are many proxy server vendors, especially OS vendors like Microsoft, Sun Microsystems, and IBM, etc. Some proxy server vendors are targeting small businesses or the home computing market.

G. Fax Servers

A fax server is a network computer that provides a bank of fax/modems to manage the receipt and delivery of faxes. In fact, many of the functions of sophisticated fax servers involve managing limited incoming and outgoing telephone resources, which would be completely replaced by e-mail for document exchanges. In a sense, fax servers are a bridge between the old way of doing business and the new. But as long as documents continue to stampede across this bridge, the fax server market continues to breathe life vigorously.

In many respects, a fax server is similar to an e-mail server. Both types of servers are bridges between outgoing and incoming messages. Both must route incoming messages to a destination. In the case of e-mail servers, this destination is always an inbox for a particular user. Fax servers for small, single-user environments often assume that the receiving computer itself is the sole destination, so the "inbox model" does not apply. On the other hand, fax servers designed for corporate environments indeed parallel the e-mail server model, delivering incoming faxes to particular destinations assigned to individual users.

A well-designed fax server may offer extra conveniences for handling incoming faxes, such as direct-to-printer output. It may also provide outgoing specialties, such as scheduled broadcasts of a document to many recipients, and automated outgoing faxes triggered by incoming requests. Corporate fax servers must also juggle numerous outgoing faxes, possibly queued up by a number of different users. How well fax server software can effectively manage a limited number of phone lines, so as to schedule both outgoing and incoming faxes without conflict, is a major selling point for enterprise level fax servers.

Sophisticated fax servers also feature strong integration with electronic messaging systems, like Microsoft Exchange and Lotus Notes. Such features enable the fax server to become a seamless bridge between electronic documents and the anachronistic world of fax documents. Fax servers range widely in capabilities, scaled to different environments, from the home or small office needs addressed by WinFAX and RelayFax, to enterprise-level products, like RightFAX, FAXport, and Faxination, etc.

H. Management Servers

Management servers are network servers that run some dedicated network management software to monitor and manage server farms for enterprises. Almost all network management software supports the Simple Network Management Protocol (SNMP). Network management software manages computer systems in an enterprise, which may include any or all of the following functions: software distribution and upgrading, user profile management, version control, backup and recovery, printer spooling, job scheduling, virus protection, and performance and capacity planning. For example, ZENworks is a family of directory enabled system management products from Novell. ZENworks supports Windows clients, NetWare, and Windows 2000/NT servers. With ZENworks, system administration features allow users to log in from any PC and obtain their custom desktop configuration under Novell's popular NDS directory service. OpenView is Network management software from HP. Some third-party products that run under OpenView support SNA and DECnet network management protocols. OpenView supports almost all platforms either in server mode or in client agent mode and has been widely used as an enterprise-wide network management solution.

NetView is a IBM SNA network management software that provides centralized monitoring and control for SNA, non-SNA, and non-IBM devices. NetView/PC interconnects NetView with Token Ring LANs, Rolm CBXs, and non-IBM modems, while maintaining control in the host.

Systems Management Server is from Microsoft for Windows 2000/NT Server. It requires a Microsoft SQL Server database and is used to distribute software, monitor and analyze network usage, and perform various Windows network administration tasks.

Other network management server products are Sun Microsystems's SunNet Manager and Novell's NMS, which work best for their native platforms, and also have extended features to other platforms.

I. Communication Servers

Communication servers are network servers that provide network communications for remote access users either through direct dial up or through an ISP (Internet service provider) through authentication protocols. In some cases, communication servers are just regular file servers with a modem, while a dedicated server has a modem pool consisting of internal or external modems.

Windows Terminal Service is an option for Windows 2000 Advanced Edition and Data Center Edition and can be used as a communication server. Windows Terminal Service enables an application to be run simultaneously by multiple users at different remote Windows PCs. Windows Terminal Service turns a Windows 2000 server into a centralized, time-shared computer like the good old days of mainframes and dumb terminals.

Shiva's LANRover is another widely used proprietary communication software for servers, which provides secured connectivity for remote users through

either analog modems or ISDN connections. Also, some remote control software packages provide server versions, which also could be used as a communication server for remote users to access geographically separated resources.

SEE ALSO THE FOLLOWING ARTICLES

Electronic Data Interchange • End-User Computing Tools • Operating Systems

BIBLIOGRAPHY

Connolly, T., *et al.* (2002). *Database systems: A practice approach to design, implementation and management,* 3rd ed. Reading, MA: Addison–Wesley.
Coulouris, G., *et al.* (1994). *Distributed systems concept and design,* 2nd ed. Reading, MA: Addison–Wesley.
Deitel, H. M., *et al.* (2000). *Internet & World Wide Web: How to program.* Englewood Cliffs, NJ: Prentice Hall.
DeRoest, J. W. (1997). *AIX version 4: System administration guide.* New York: McGraw–Hill.
Peterson, L. L., *et al.* (2000). *Computer networks,* 2nd ed. San Mateo, CA: Morgan Kaufmann.
Russel, C., *et al.* (2000). *Windows 2000 server administrator's companion.* Microsoft Press.
Sobell, M. G. (1997). *A practical guide to SOLARIS.* Reading, MA: Addison–Wesley.

Service Industries, Electronic Commerce for

Choon Seong Leem

Yonsei University

GLOSSARY

information consulting and SI industries The industrial sector that provides the domain-dependent know-how to support business problem-solving processes with information and system integration technologies.

information contents industries The industrial sector that processes information into the value-added one for specific forms of media.

information industry Any industry which produces, manages, and processes information with suitable media or systems.

information infrastructure industries The industrial sector that produces devices or communication media which provide infrastructure of the information society.

information provider industries The industrial sector that creates value activities by providing various kinds of information or mediating information-related services.

internet business A service-oriented business which provides its customers with products or information using the internet as its main transaction channel.

internet business model The fundamental management strategy of internet business including description of its revenue model.

value proposition The main values that a company provides to its current or potential customers.

Developments in information technology (IT), along with the boom in the information industry and the elec-tronic commerce that followed, have brought much change to life as a whole and the economy. In particular, the service sector, new transaction methods and electronic commerce grew significantly based on the information industry. In turn, this has led to the overall paradigm shift in the service industry. The purpose of this article is to classify the information industries, which are the driving force behind the service industries and the changes in service itself; explain how the service industries have evolved through electronic commerce by taking examples of the actual cases of companies; understand the features and the main factors of Internet business, which has service-oriented characteristics, in order to pinpoint the change in the service industry and its types by classifying Internet business models and evaluating Internet business value.

I. ELECTRONIC COMMERCE AND INFORMATION INDUSTRIES

A. Electronic Commerce

As information technology (IT) has developed and the Internet has gained popularity, views on electronic commerce have varied. Table I puts such various definitions of electronic commerce in order.

Although there are various definitions as seen in Table I, we define electronic commerce as a transaction that processes a part or all information through computer networks for corporations, organizations, and individuals.

Electronic commerce enabled us to overcome the limitations of time and space and changed the way of

Table I Definition of Electronic Commerce

Kalakota and Whinston (1997)	Modern business methodology that improves the quality goods and service; cuts service cost and increases the speed of service delivery; and focuses on the desire of firms and consumers
Shouhong (1997)	Modern methodology that manages the performance of business by using advanced technology
OECD (1999)	Business occurring over open, nonproprietary networks such as the Internet
Becker, Farris, and Osborn (1998)	Commerce that makes information, communication, and logistic integrate along the entire value chain
Wigand (1998)	IT application that ranges from the starting point of value chain to the ending point should be designed to execute electronically business processes, and to achieve vision of enterprise
APEC (1999)	The use of computers and electronic networks to conduct business over the Internet or another electronic network

traditional transactions. In particular, such a change in transactions caused the significant paradigm shift in the service industry that provides intangible value and finally created a new paradigm in the service industry. In other words, electronic commerce became a tool that cuts service costs for firms, customers, and management, while improving the quality of service and increasing the speed of service delivery.

To fully understand the new managerial technique and paradigm in the service industry, we should first understand electronic commerce and the information industry. If electronic commerce transformed the way of transaction in the service industry, the information industry extended the realm of the service industry and changed its very essence.

Even in the manufacturing industry, the importance of marketing and sales with the Internet is being emphasized. Electronic commerce is no longer being used for production control and management only. There are even reports that say major enterprises will transform themselves into brand-holding companies in order to emphasize customer service. In other words, the boom in electronic commerce changed the way companies ran their business: companies are now focusing more than ever on customer service. However, customer service is more emphasized in the service industry than in the existing manufacturing industry.

In this regard, we should fully understand the information industries, including electronic commerce. By doing so we will be able to understand the new paradigm in the service industries. In addition, we will be able to understand how it is changing. This is

a significant approach in understanding electronic commerce for the service industries.

B. A Framework for Information Industries

Because of developments in computers and the Internet, our society and industries are going through great change, maybe the greatest change since the Industrial Revolution.

During this change, three major factors of production—land, labor, and capital—that were important in traditional industries became four major factors; information was added. Many kinds of application fields are also emerging through the technology developments in the information industry, such as IT and communication technology. This phenomenon could not be witnessed in the past industrial environment. As such, a new industrial environment was born where the manufacturing industry—the center industry in the past industrial society—gave way to the service industry. In the past industrial society, information was produced, processed, and used under the strict management from the top, but now information is being produced and processed according to the separate needs and desires of each individual. It was this very environment where the information industry was born.

Figure 1 illustrates a better and proper understanding on information industries.

The information industry consists of the industries that produce the media for production and delivery of information or that produce, manage, and process

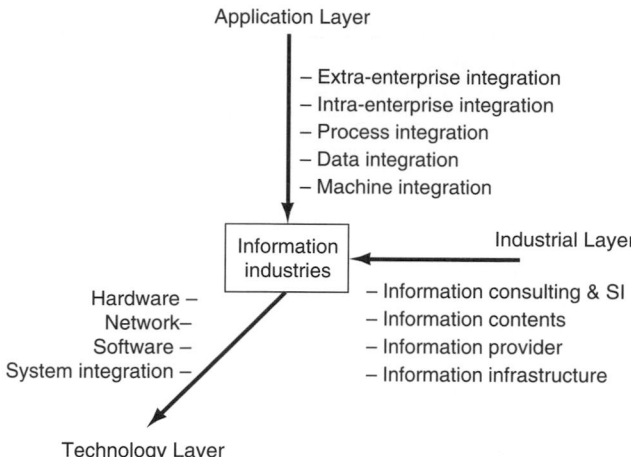

Figure 1 A framework for information industries.

information as independent goods. As seen in Fig. 1, the information industry is classified into three layers for a broader understanding of the information industry.

1. *The technology layer* (according to applied technologies) should be classified into hardware, network, software, and system integration by technology.
2. *The application layer* (according to application areas) should be classified into machine integration, data integration, process integration, intraenterprise integration, and extra-enterprise integration.
3. *The industry layer* (according to industry sectors) should be classified into information infrastructure, information provider, information contents, and information consulting and system integration (SI).

We will explain information industries around the industry layer to analyze how electronic commerce changes the paradigm of service industries with actual cases.

The standard for classifying the information industry can be derived from the variety of value. The change of value in the information industry can be explained by the change in value in IT. The value in IT originally emphasized more on hardware, but now it focuses more on software, network, and related technologies that improve the value of hardware and support a connection among them. The value structure focused on SI technology which forms and operates various services and application systems through

these software and networks. Recently, value structures that directly process information by using information infrastructure such as hardware and software and provide information to customers are being born. Especially, the consulting business that provides core business knowledge based on accumulated information is growing along with other SI growth.

The big industries called information industries consist of the information infrastructure, information contents, information provider and information consulting and SI (Table II). The following sections discuss the types of information industries.

1. Information Infrastructure Industries

"Infra" stands for "infrastructure" and means the facilities that form the basis of industrial activities such as railroads, roads, and harbors. However, infra now means devices and communication that are the foundations of value activities in the information-oriented society because of the development in the information industry.

So, information infrastructure industries are the foundation industries of IT. They are also the aggregate of vendors that develop, construct, and serve computer devices, network, system softwares, and other devices, which are needed for information providers, information contents, and information consulting and SI.

The following are subdivisions of information infrastructure:

- Computing-Infra: PC, PDA, server, storage
- Interface-Infra: input device, output device
- Network-Infra: mobile telecommunication device, telephone device, router
- Soft-Infra: browser, OS, system software

2. Information Provider Industries

Over the Internet, suppliers can now directly conduct transactions with customers for goods and services. But, as demand and supply for information increase explosively and actors of the business increase geometrically, the disintermediation—the process by which companies are being bypassed by the Internet revolution as more companies that create the goods or service interact directly with the consumer without the aid of intermediaries—becomes inefficient. In this situation, information provider industries that connect a great number of suppliers with numbers of consumers became more developed.

Table II A Classification of Information Industry and Cases

Industrial classification		Cases	
Information infrastructure industry	Computing-infra		www.ibm.com
	Interface-infra		www.hp.com
	Network-infra		www.cisco.com
	Soft-infra		www.microsoft.com
Information provider industry	Classification by revenue structure	Advertising fee	www.yahoo.com
		Information providing fee	www.gartnergroup.com
		Site rent fee	www.walmart.com
		Transaction fee	www.ebay.com
		Multiplkex fee	www.etrade.com
	Classification by contents	Various classification like Information contents industry	
Information contents industry	Social/education-information collected contents		www.britannica.com
	Personal-information collected contents		www.mp3.com
	Business-information collected contents		www.wsj.com
	Social/education-knowledge-added contents		www.imagerystudio.com
	Personal-knowledge-added contents		www.itvnews.com
	Business-knowledge-added contents		www.sap.com
Information consulting and SI industry	Consulting industry	Management or business consulting	www.mckinsey.com
		IT consulting	www.i2.com
	System integration industry		www.sap.com

From Leem C.S., and e-Biz Lab. (2000). "e-Business File," YoungjnBiz.com.

In a narrow sense, these information provider businesses mean that industries profit from contracting an information provider with the computer communication company and by providing the appropriate menu with information. However, presently they include not only organic public opinions and publishing companies, but also the on-line database industry, information provider, information brokerage, etc.

Finally, information provider industries are the set of enterprises that create value added by providing various kinds of information and services related to information.

The revenue structure and contents offered are the standard for classifying information provider industries and are divided into the following:

- Classification by revenue structure: advertising fee, information providing fee, site rental fee, transaction fee, multiplex fee
- Classification by contents: real estate information, stock information, education information, entertainment information, shopping information, etc.

3. Information Contents Industries

Information grew into contents after experiencing the days in primitive society, agrarian society, and industrial society. Contents are simply not information in itself, but are the contents accompanied with media.

Owing to the popularity of the Internet, anyone can process such contents easily, and the demand on supply of contents has continued to grow rapidly. Moreover, information contents industries, those industries processing contents appropriate to the customer, have developed.

Information contents industries are the set of enterprises that process collected information from the media and manufacture contents and software of various kinds. These include movie, television, radio, publication, etc. Recently, the on-line game industry, contents provider (CP) industry, and so forth are undergoing rapid development over the Internet, and in these industries many kinds of business models appear through the medium of the Internet.

So, information contents industries are classified

into two categories according to the level of knowledge added and the object of application.

4. Information Consulting and SI Industries

Information consulting and SI industries are the set of enterprises that provide the peculiar know-how with information-oriented strategy planning, designing, developing, and managing that can support business operations desired by customers and the solution of problems with technology of information integration and diverse information about specific areas.

Information consulting and SI industries are knowledge-intensive and technology-intensive industries that make high value added. These are basic industries that have far-reaching effects on the related industries that combine management and technology.

Information consulting and SI industries are subdivided into the consulting industry and the system integration industry. The consulting industry is further divided into business or management consulting and IT consulting.

The three categories of industry mentioned above can be referred to as service industries.

C. Electronic Commerce and Services with Information Industries

We should first understand how service-centered industries were formed in information industries for deriving factors from information industries and electronic commerce causing a new paradigm in the service industries.

The core activity in information provider industries is to analyze and combine much information in cyberspace or physical space and then provide the customers with the information. That is, it provides the service of searching for information desired by customers, processing the information, and providing customers with the information processed. Past information provider industries were small in size, which had the problem of a limited number of suppliers and consumers. However, now it has transformed into service industries that intermediate between suppliers and consumers owing to the development of network. After all, information provider industries have created various business models in service industries because of the appearance of cyberspace.

In information contents industries, contents are produced and sold. Because contents that have been produced have almost zero marginal cost and many

channels of sale and marketing, they are more popular and are emphasized in electronic commerce. The intangible goods with which vendors provide customers in service industries transform into digital goods and are sold by information contents industries. This contributes to the creation of a new service.

In information consulting and SI, companies combine lots of information with knowledge of the company themselves and produce goods and services. Although such knowledge-intensive products are offered by means of digital files, it is more important to provide services so that customers can appropriately make use of them.

Accordingly information consulting and SI industries are not industries to provide knowledge-intensive contents, but service industries to give customers the service on the basis of contents. Electronic commerce in information consulting and SI industries arranges for the foundation of providing service for lower cost and makes the diversification in the way of providing service.

Finally, as in Fig. 2, the industries creating the new paradigm of service industries through electronic commerce in information industries are information provider industries, information contents industries, and information consulting and SI that supply knowledge-based goods or services that can be transformed into digital form. Recently, in information infrastructure industries, electronic commerce is being actively conducted around the business-to-business (B-to-B) marketplace, but it is difficult to regard the new paradigm as the core trend of the industries because the activities of

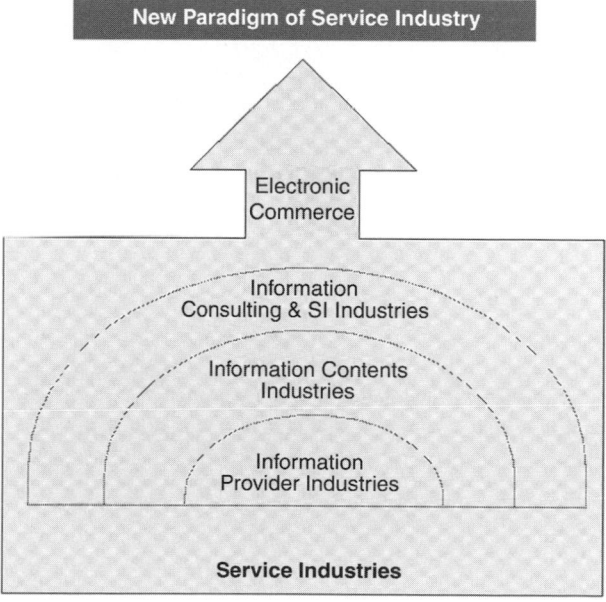

Figure 2 Electronic commerce and services with information industries.

the industries are not to service through the Internet and other network but to manufacture the goods. To make a clear assertion, we will prove with cases how electronic commerce in information infrastructure industries, information provider industries, and information contents industries contributes to the creation of the new paradigm. We will do research on Internet businesses, created through the new paradigm as the extreme form of electronic commerce in service industries by showing the classification of the Internet business model and evaluation system.

II. SERVICE INDUSTRIES TOWARD ELECTRONIC COMMERCE

Among the categories suggested, information provider, content, and consulting and SI industries are service oriented in the aspect that they provide mostly intangible values rather than physical products. Besides, many activities in electronic commerce

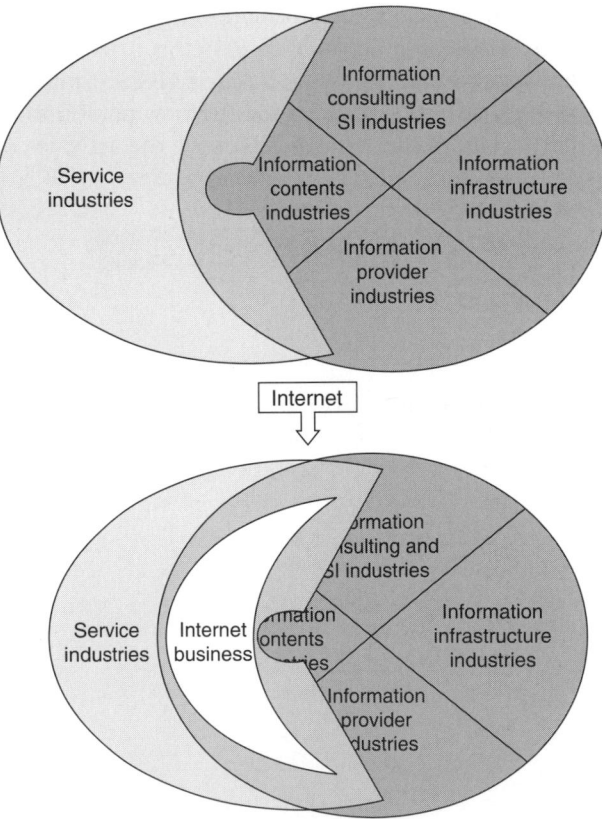

Figure 3 The change of relationships between service industries and information industries.

have service-oriented characteristics. Assuming that electronic commerce for service industries emerges as forms of information provider and information content industries, this research uses the framework of information industries, especially information provider and content industries, to figure out how traditional service industries are conducting business in electronic commerce.

Figure 3 suggests a conceptual relationship between the information industries and service industries.

A. Electronic Commerce and Services with Information Provider Industries

There is a variety of information transfer media—television, newspapers, magazines, computer telecommunications, Internet, fax, pagers, etc. Judging from past experiences and the fast development of the industrial society, there will be more various kinds of media. In the past, information consumers satisfied their desires for information with a restricted number of media such as newspapers and magazines, but as the whole social structure is transforming itself and as technologies are developing, more swift, various, and specialized information markets are in order. Today, the fastest growing information transfer medium is the Internet.

Traditional information transfer activities are being served through the Internet, and in this process, while the existing information transfer activities are simply moved to the new channel, new service business is being developed using Internet technologies.

As the most frequently used synonym of the word information provider (IP), there is content provider (CP). Like IP, CP is the industry that provides information. However, the information medium itself is based on multimedia such as sound and moving pictures. Information is not just limited in text form. IP includes all the people and companies that provide information for the users.

We will look through the categories of information industries to explain electronic commerce for service industries emerging as forms of IP industries.

1. Categorizations by Revenue Sources

According to revenue sources, the IP industry is generally categorized into advertising fee-based, usage fee-based, transaction fee-based, and hybrid models.

- **Advertising fee based.** This model provides Internet advertisements, mostly in the form of banners to the Web sites users, and makes revenue from advertisers. In a sense, it is similar to classified ads in newspapers or magazines. Advertising effectiveness, however, can be measured more accurately—such as Click-Through Rate, duration time, and response rate by banner positions. These measures enable the company to provide better services, both to users and to advertisers.

Advertisers are possibly offered with reasonable advertising cost models, and they can select their target audiences according to age, area, and desired time of day or week.

Moreover, the banners can be dynamically changed based on customer information and their interests. This service removes any ads that are not of interest to site users. We can find these cases in many portal sites such as Yahoo! and Lycos.

- **Usage fee based.** This model's revenue source is the usage fee paid by the customers who use their information. There are two price policies for this model: (1) the usage fee per unit time and (2) the usage fee per each click. Information on the Internet has been considered free. However, high value-added contents, such as reports from Mckinsey, Gartner Group, Forrester Research, and others, are willingly paid by users.

  This trend represents the service differentiation according to the contents quality. In other words, the price of the information varies according to its quality.

  As the market demands better services and contents, this model will become more feasible.

- **Site rental fee.** In this model, a company uses the Web site's brand value of the specific information-providing company. On the other hand, the owner of the Web site can profit by renting part of the site to the other company, which provides the information and services. This relationship can be easily found in the Web sites providing shopping information.

  Currently, these trends are being dominated between the sites holding partnerships, but they will grow widespread between every site, which can be mutually beneficial through this model.

- **Transaction fee.** The sites with this model provide information about digital or physical goods, earning their margins from the difference between the buying and the selling prices. This model includes Internet shopping malls, virtual shops, and Internet auctions.

  When we consider the whole framework of information industries, the reason can be explained why Internet shopping malls and virtual shops are categorized as information industries and viewed as service oriented. First of all, manufacturing and logistics belong to traditional industries; they are not among the information industries. So in distinguishing information industries from general industries, we can regard logistics as general industries. As a result, the core functions of shopping malls, except logistics, lie in providing information about the products and related services, and these industries are referred to as information-providing industries or electronic commerce for service industries.

- **Hybrid fee.** This model is a hybrid form of more than two of the previous models. For instance, there is a case where a company takes both an information usage fee and an advertising fee. In most cases, sites assume a hybrid fee model.

We have looked through information industries according to their revenue sources. If we take an example of them, the Gartner Group will be an information usage-based model.

This site provides reports on IT through updated data and research on IT. As we see in Fig. 4, users are required to pay and get their identification (ID) to look into the full materials they need. The prices are differentiated by the values of the reports. Though the information usage fee is high, many companies and individuals use the site because it guarantees high-quality reports catching the new trends and providing deep insight.

2. Categorizations by Contents

Another perspective to view electronic commerce for service industries as a form of information provider industries is contents. These categorizations are about what information a site provides, including news, entertainment, laws, stocks, shopping games, education, job opportunity, economics, etc. In addition, a huge volume of new contents is being created incessantly, and every expertise and idea in every field could be a source for this information-providing service.

We will get an idea of these categorizations by taking one outstanding example of them.

Figure 5 is a specialized shopping site providing all kinds of information needed to take good care of a garden. This site publishes gardening-related webzines to serve users with the most up to date contents, such as season's gardening skills or design information.

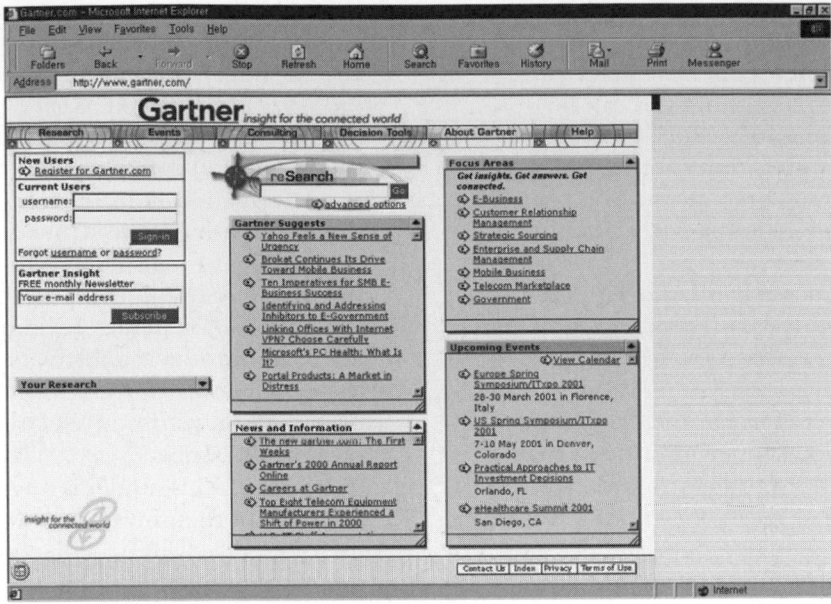

Figure 4   A case of categorization by revenue sources.

This case is a good example of creating a niche market by providing specialized services and contents.

We have examined electronic commerce for service industries with an aspect of information-providing industries. As the Internet is used by more people and the mentality for digital economy matures, information-providing industries and their markets are expected to grow exponentially. More secure and convenient paying systems such as electronic cash or credit cards-based systems will foster the rapid development of information-providing services. More enhanced bandwidth, widespread multimedia contents, and new business models will be positive factors for electronic commerce for service industries.

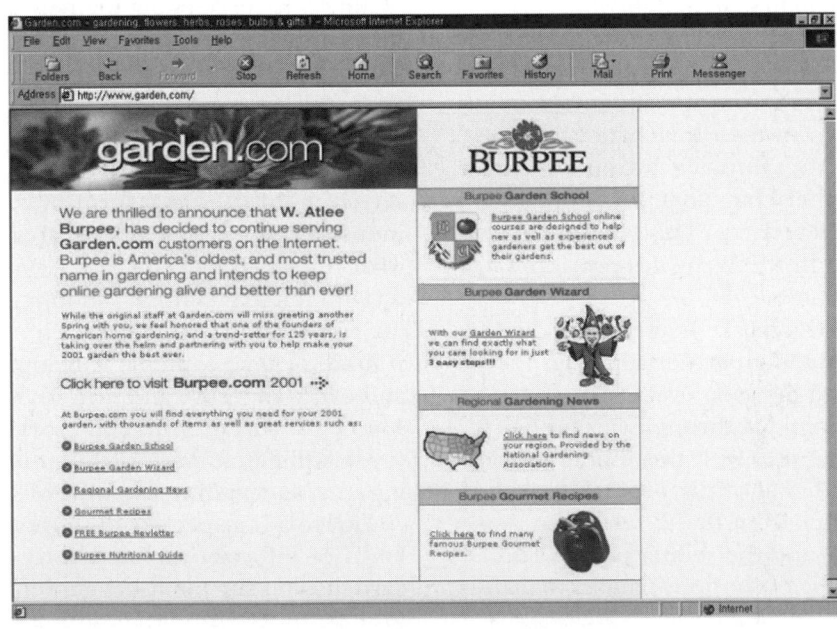

Figure 5   A case of classification by contents.

B. Electronic Commerce and Services with Information Contents Industries

Throughout the history of mankind, communication methods and media have experienced many changes. In the Industrial Age, the focus has moved to mass communications through mass media rather than person-to-person communications.

There can be a clear distinction between information producers and consumers in mass communications. Widespread use of computers and the Internet has blurred these distinctions, and both personalization and mass communication could be realized simultaneously. At this juncture, the notion of contents, which has existed throughout history, emerged with higher values.

The word "contents" means not just information itself, but it also includes both information transfer media and what they contain.

The content is created, processed, and transferred by so-called information contents industries, contributing to making profits. The information contents industries are service-oriented industries by nature in that they deal with contents which are designed to be served to users with high qualities. Therefore, now we will see how electronic commerce for service industries is emerging in the form of information contents industries.

It is necessary to categorize contents prior to examining the information contents industries' status quo.

We will consider two dimensions: information level and usage purpose. Information level refers to the level of personalization and interaction, and usage purpose is about to whom and for what the content is used. This contents categorization can be used to categorize the services provided by information contents providers. Figure 6 shows the two-dimensional categorization framework for information contents industries.

First, we will discuss information-collected contents and then proceed to knowledge-added contents.

1. **Social/education information-collected contents.** All kinds of educational materials, electronic journals, government's home pages, and the contents provided by electronic libraries are included. These contents have a wide range of users and tend to be updated more frequently.

   As the concept of "life-long education" get more pervasive, education-related digital contents are becoming essential parts served by many education programs and one of the most important services.

2. **Personal information-collected contents.** Leisure, avocation, and cultural life contents which are mostly used by individuals are mainstreams in this categorization. Personal information-collected contents are marked by their richness of multimedia services. They are divided into four categories.

   • **Game contents.** These are the most prominent field of personal information-collected

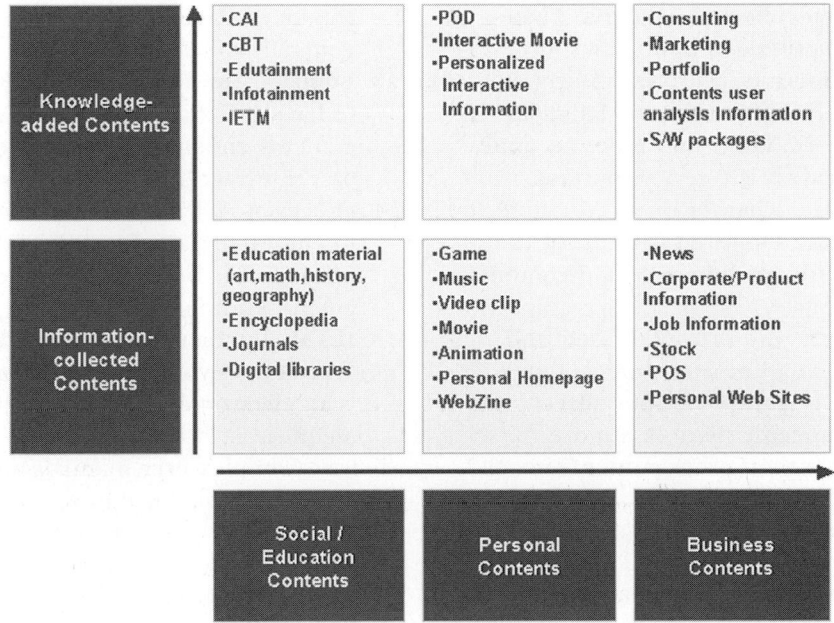

Figure 6   A classification of contents.

contents. Chances are that they make enormous profit and can be used as a test bed for advanced technologies. Game contents are moving to knowledge-added contents as they become more complex.

- **Entertainment contents.** These consist of music, films, animations, etc. and are considered as a considerable portion in the analog era. Entertainment contents have been experiencing dramatic changes in production and representation methods with the development of ITs.

- **Personal home pages.** Personal home pages are regarded as a new form of information sources, serving various contents in every interest and field. In most cases, they are non-commercial and post individual's own interests without any interference. Considering that one person provides many people with specific contents, they are a new service field enabled by Internet technologies.

- **Webzines.** For webzines it can be said that existing services are just transformed into a new channel in the aspect that they serve similar functions with traditional magazines. However, in webzines, contents are more focused on user's interactivities and participation is through graphic user interfaces and multimedia technologies. Moreover, they have different characteristics in the fact that they provide many kinds of magazines according to user's interest and tastes, in many cases, for free.

3. **Business information-collected contents.** These refer to the contents used for companies' or individuals' work processes. Business information-collected contents should provide updated information; therefore, faster and more accurate contents are required. It is a very important criterion to determine whether or not the time when the contents are delivered is right for the situation. Business information-collected contents include the following:

- **News.** Internet users are provided faster and more various information from Internet news. The recent trend is to provide specialized contents in each specific field. It is more constant and stable than other contents in providing methods and media.

- **Form/goods information contents.** Mainly from an Internet home page and its links, they provide all necessary information about companies' products such as price, inventory, functions, etc. In other cases, they play a

certain role of a company's services for users and employees, providing company introduction, job opportunities, ads, and parts of work processes.

- **Stock information.** The recent popularity and explosively growing interest in the stock market have made these contents more important. So, the quality of contents such as accuracy is more concentrated than the external factors such as graphics or design.

Until now, we have considered three categories of information-collected contents. Figure 7 is presented as an example of business information collected contents.

4. **Social/education knowledge-added contents.** Social/education knowledge-added contents are becoming more targeted and specialized for mass audience or users. Contents served to users are transforming from simple information to more specific cases and expertise. It is a recent trend to add entertaining factors to education with a purpose to encourage users to have constant interests in the contents. CAI/CBT, Edutainment, and IETM are good examples.

- **CAI/CBT.** Being education knowledge-added contents, CAI (computer assisted instruction)/CBT (computer-based training) covers right objectives of education and its specific training methods. Unlike other educational contents, the learning pace and materials are adjusted through the interaction with users. The education knowledge-contents produced through the form of CAI/CBT are generally called courseware.

- **Edutainment.** It is a new word that stands for "education" and "entertainment." Edutainment contents enhance interactivities through an easy interface and maximize education effectiveness by providing educational contents in enjoyable ways. It takes a considerable portion of infant multimedia contents and has been used in art, science, language, music, etc.

- **IETM (Interactive Electronic Technical Manual).** As you can guess from its name, this is an electronic technical manual providing technical information to users in a interactive way. Complex user manuals about military apparatus, aviation, ships, and automobiles are electronically documented, and effective document structuring, structural search, product/technology's interoperability with database can be realized. It is a very effective method in time, scale, management, and utility.

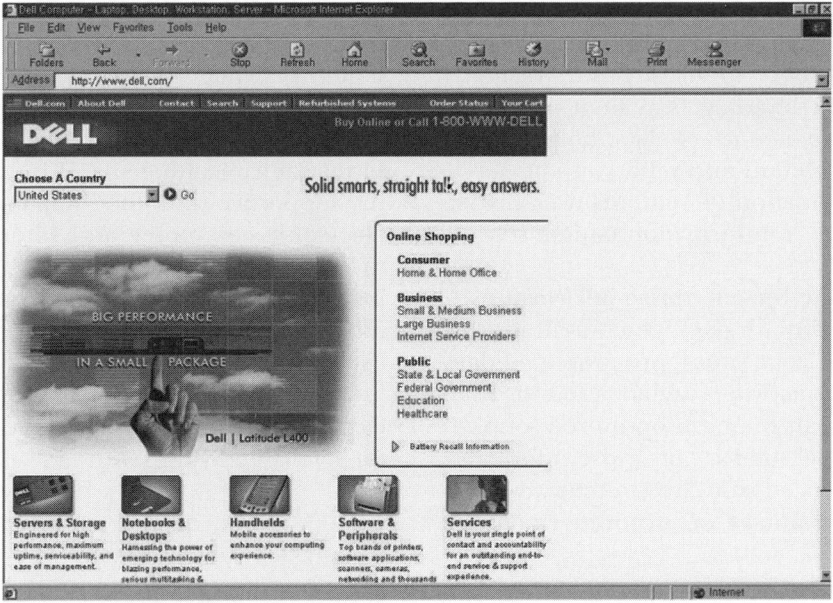

Figure 7 A case of information-collected contents.

IETM provides general services for system maintenance and an efficient working environment since it supports management functions for existing apparatus and systems.

5. **Personal knowledge-added contents.** While the analog era was dominated by fixed and fewer contents, the digital era is characterized by personalized contents representing users' interests and personalities. These personal knowledge-added contents include the following services.

- **POD (production on demand).** This is real-time-based dynamically reconfigured contents by users' needs. POD is not confined to just personal entertainment contents. It can also be applied to business software packages. Specifically speaking, if there are components needed for each work process, it is because of these customized contents services consisting of the combination of these components.

- **Interactive movie.** Unlike the traditional fixed form of scenario, users can influence the film's plot or scenario. Interactive movie is one of the most dramatic examples where the user's opinion is represented in the process of creating contents.

- **Personalized interactive information.** This provides optimally customized information according to users' personalities, tastes, and interests which are analyzed by sites. The contents can be reconfigured instantly to serve

an individual's tastes and choices. In a broad notion, it is represented as a personalization service, one of the most representative services enabled by Internet technologies. This service can be embedded in almost any business model such as Internet shopping malls, portal sites, community sites, etc. There are many solutions and techniques to support this service. Art Technology, Broadvision, and Netperceptions are a few examples of the companies providing these solutions.

6. **Business knowledge-added contents.** In many cases, business knowledge-added contents serve as a basis to create more value-added contents. Such contents include the following:

- **Consulting information.** These contents are more influential on companies' business strategies and working processes. This information is provided to solve business problems or to help achieve companies' objectives. Based on the collected information and the insights for the future, these contents are value added through information collecting and processing.

- **Marketing information.** This refers to demographic data or research data on consumer trends. To be served as marketing information, consumer tastes, product popularity, customer satisfaction, and market analysis are processed.

- **Information of contents user analysis.** This data is extracted by analyzing contents users' usage patterns. While there still exist privacy-related issues, Internet technologies make it very cheap to collect and analyze users' data, helping to provide more relevant and valid contents services. This information of contents user analysis is very beneficial to information contents providers.
- **Software package for enterprise informatization.** This is a software package content in which advanced companies' processes and data-created business activities are analyzed for a company to use in the most optimized form. The software package for enterprise informatization is high-priced software contents, used to take effective advantage of corporate resources through ITs.

    As an example of the knowledge-added contents, we introduce a software package for enterprise informatization in Fig. 8. The company in Fig. 8 ranked third in 2000 among software companies with one software package, which supports enterprise informatization.

We examined electronic commerce for service industries with the form of information contents industries in two dimensions. It is remarkable that ITs and the Internet have made critical innovations in contents' production and transfer methods. These inno-

vations are constructing a new paradigm for service industries. The previous examples have been represented to explain the paradigm shift.

Besides the IP and contents industries, information consulting and SI industries are service oriented. Information consulting and SI industries, however, play the supportive roles for companies to transform into electronic commerce and Internet business rather than be included in electronic commerce. Considering the scope and the main theme of this research, information consulting and SI industries ought to be excluded. In a sense, information consulting and SI industries can be referred to as "service industries for electronic commerce," not as "electronic commerce for service industries."

III. INTERNET BUSINESS

A. Internet Business and Service Industry

To define Internet business, we should consider its scope first (Fig. 9). It should not be regarded as the synonym of e-business or e-commerce, but as the subset of them.

Transaction of the basic operations through the Internet can be thought of as the Internet business, but the organizational operations which have nothing to do with the customer services are beside the scope of it because the basic principle of it is to contact with

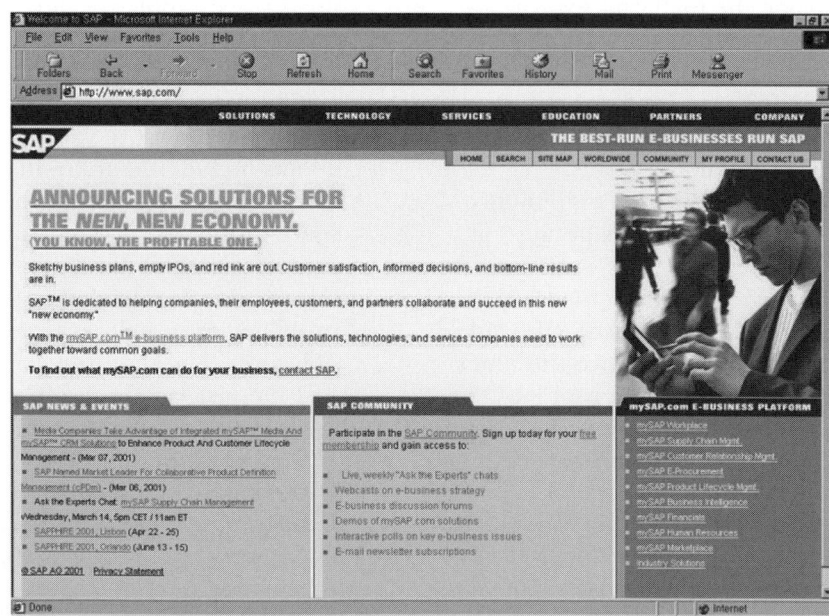

Figure 8 A case of knowledge-added contents.

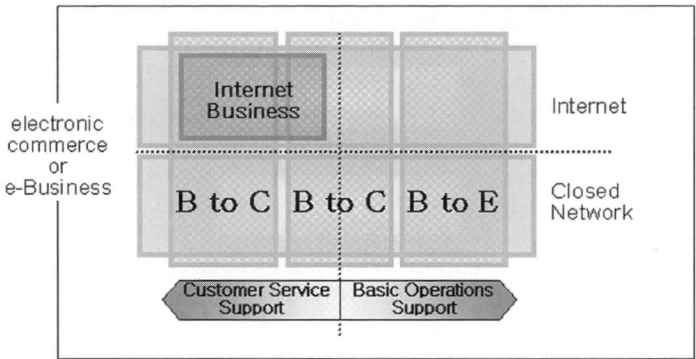

Figure 9 Scope of Internet business.

the customers through the Internet. E-business using the telephone or the private network is also out of the Internet business.

At last, it can be said that the Internet business is on the area of the electronic commerce of the business to the customer (B to C) and the part of the electronic commerce of the business to the business (B to B) among the whole range of the electronic commerce or the e-commerce.

Internet business can be defined as "the service-oriented activity, which provides the customer (the person or the company) with the product or the information through the transaction channel of the Internet." In other words, Internet business is the industry which utilizes the advantage of the information industry most efficiently through the Internet, and it is the very important matters of which service can be provided to the customer and which can be reoriented into the high value-added product.

This research will classify the various models of Internet business, which is the most customer oriented and is performed through the Internet, and will suggest the framework for Internet business evaluation to help the comprehensions and to guide the future of Internet business.

B. Internet Business Models

One should clearly define the business model when any business is set up. The model can define the vision of the business and can help the business executor decide the target market and the target customer concretely. In addition, the business model influences the design of the supportive system itself and decides the revenue creating point, especially in Internet business.

The Internet business model is the original corporate and management strategy, which is about the rev-

enue model for the customer service on the Internet, business process, and the affiliation strategy. It is composed of the revenue model which creates profits by providing the contents and the partnership which can be represented by the internal business process, affiliation strategy with other companies, etc.

We need to know the special features of the business model or its classification to understand Internet business. However, it is a business model that is very difficult to solve and is much talked about in spite of the vigorous study in progress because the criteria for the categorization are different among the scholars and the specialists and the scope of the business model is varied before anything else. Also, the openness and the connectivity of the Internet make it possible for the enterprise to transform the business model and create a new one; this makes it harder to categorize the models.

The various researches of the classification of the Internet business model have been accomplished by many consulting companies, business schools, and laboratories of universities. Table III explains the features and the critiques of the representative categorization system of the Internet business model.

This research suggests the new framework for the classification of the Internet business model for the application to the whole Internet business through the analyses and critiques of the existing frameworks (Fig. 10).

We suggest three criteria: the property of the proposed value (physical vs. digital), the scope of the proposed value (general vs. special), and the source of the proposed value (manufacturer vs. intermediary) in this research (Table IV). The ongoing Internet business enterprises are mapped by each criterion and grouped by their patterns and categorized into a business model, or each Internet business model exists in the three-dimensional framework which has three axes.

Most businesses which enjoyed the advantage of the preemption with the flourishing Internet business

Table III   Features and Critiques of the Internet Business Model

Researcher	Features and critiques
Paul Timmerce	Classified into 11 groups by the 2 criteria of the functional integration and the degree of the innovation
	Emphasized that the integration and the reconstruction of the value factors in the value chain of M. Porter can indicate the structure of the business model
	Two criteria having no discrete borders make it hard to apply to the practical classification, and the system can not reflect the characters of the floating change of the internet industry
D. Julia	Classified into e-Broker Model, Manufacture Model, Auction Model
	The reason of the division between e-Broker model and the auction model is ambiguous and so the border is not definite.
Kenneth Berryman	Classified into the seller-driven market, buyer-driven market, and the neutral market by the main possessor of the market power.
	Focus mainly on the movement of the product and the information, and do not reflect the features of the product and the information which is provided on line.
Michael Rappa	Classified into the nine models of brokerage model, advertising model, informediary model, merchant model, manufacturer model, affiliate model, community model, subscription model, utility model
	These models can be applied in a mutual benefit association by the business strategy
	However, it has the advantage of the wide conception for the definition of the business model, it lacks the approach to the other additional factors like the feature of the product and transaction function

are changing themselves into the model of providing total services, diversifying their works and varying their strategies to ensure definite revenue sources.

C. Internet Business Evaluation

In the fast growth of Internet business, the need for exact evaluation and analysis on the present and future value of the company comes to rise in order to

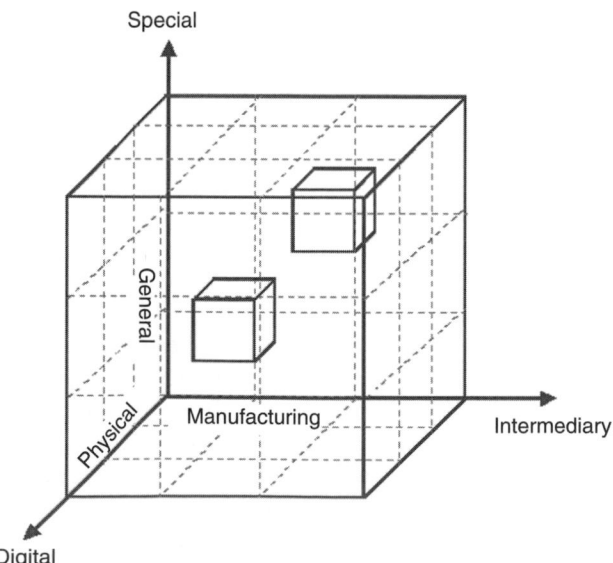

Figure 10   Business model framework.

guide the sound investment on venture and the stock market and to build the industry environment based on electronic business.

However, there are some problems in evaluating an on-line company which has some service-oriented features. Besides, Internet business advances and changes at an enormous speed. It is usually hard to apply the previous approaches which are suitable for the typical off-line enterprises.

So, this research will show the evaluation framework designed and used for the e-valuation project which was accomplished to provide the right value of the Internet business by investigating the domestic 55 companies in 2000 and to explain about the detailed domains and the items (Fig. 11).

- **Market value.** It is very important to know how the company is estimated at the present and what is able to create the future value. The capability of production of the value for tomorrow can be assessed by the brand value, the customer satisfaction, and the market share.
- **Business model.** We should consider how much profit the revenue model can create and how the business process model supports this revenue system in the area of the business model. It should be flexible to the changes in the law and the system such as the patent of the business model including intellectual properties. For example, Napster failed to manage their business in spite of their outstanding idea, the substantial

Table IV Criteria for the Internet Business Model

Criterion	Classification	Content	Sites
Property of proposed value	Physical	Provide the physical value (household electric appliances, clothing, books, etc.) through the distribution network	www.bloomingdales.com www.eddiebauer.com
	Digital	Provide the digital value (MP3, e-book, high-quality contents) of contents and services through the Internet	www.herring.com www.usatoday.com
	Hybrid	Provide both physical and digital value to the customer	www.cdnow.com www.disney.com
Scope of proposed value	General	Provide the contents and services with the wide and general areas and not special	www.travelocity.com www.aol.com
	Special	Provide the contents and services with the narrow and special areas and not general	www.deli.com www.etoys.com
	Hybrid	Provide both general and special contents and services	www.nationalgeographic.com www.personallogic.com
Source of proposed value	Manufacturing	Provide the value manufactured by itself to the customer	www.dell.com www.levi.com
	Intermediary	Mediate the value provided by the producer to the customer	www.ebay.com www.autobytel.com
	Hybrid	Provide both value manufactured by itself and provided by the producer	www.amazon.com www.lycos.com

revenue model, and the advanced business process, because they disobeyed the legal items.

Also, the mutual beneficial relation with the affiliated concern and the adaptability to the business circumstances may be estimated in this category, as well.

- **Manager.** In Internet business evaluation, the executive who manages human resources and copes with the suddenly changing environment plays a crucial role in running business because this kind of business is operated not by capital, but by the human resource.

There are many instances where the investment market regards the name value of the managers, especially the CEO, as the important factor when deciding to put money into their company because their ability of managing human resources which can create the future value is the decisive factor of the success in the unstable and immature business situation. The more a manager or a CEO is successful in harmonizing his or her company as one, the more successful leader of that corporation he or she will become.

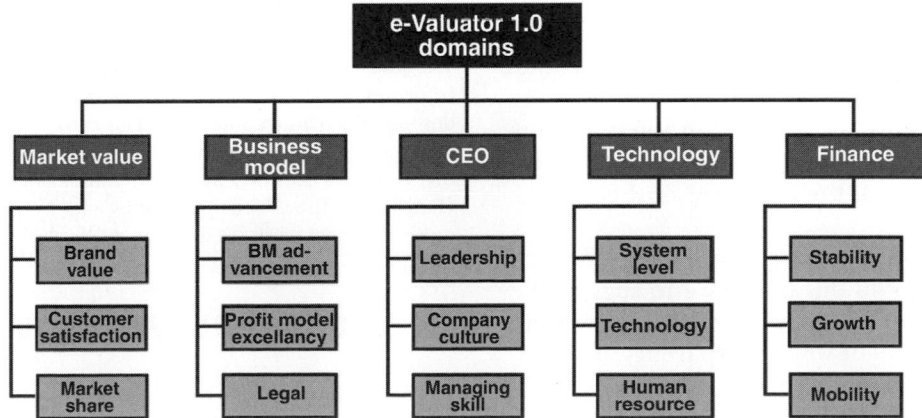

Figure 11 Framework of Internet business evaluation (e-valuator).

Table V   Ratio about the Priority of Five Areas

Domain	Market value	Business model	CEO	Technology	Finance
Ratio (%)	20	27	17	17	19

- **Technology.** Because this business is accomplished through the Internet, one of the IT, the ability to realize a business model sufficiently is a prerequisite for business. A company can get the competitive power by differentiating the value provided to the customer and the way of distribution through these techniques.

  Of course, technological power became less important compared to the first Internet business era when evaluating corporate values. This is because most companies now only possess the core technologies that they need in running their business and leave other technological problems to other companies.

  Finally, prevalent outsourcing will make it hard to judge a company's technical superiorities. But, the leading companies have invented a new business model, which sells the skills with their know-how accumulated from their business. So it is quite fair to say that existing technologies can become the opportunity of new business.

  To evaluate this domain, the service system which makes it possible to provide the services, the core technical ability which can be transferred into the revenue model, and the human resources which can manage the system should be considered.

- **Finance.** Financial strategy is of course crucial to a company regardless if it is on-line or off-line. Besides, most Internet business companies do not launch their business with a sufficient amount of capital. However, they start business with brilliant men and outstanding ideas. So the financial activity is the key factor for the specified period of growth. At that condition, most on-line companies do not have the explicit and settled revenue sources and they are just suggesting the possibility of the success, the financial ability can be the essential condition of the existence of the enterprise,

  In the end, continuous raising of capital is important, and to do this they have to suggest the vision of the company to investors and show their financial management with transparency. The financial domain should be assessed by the smooth flow of the cash, the steadiness of the capital structure, and the transparency of the

financial system based on the stability, the growth, and the mobility.

These five domains have different importance according to the adopted business model. The business model domain may be more important at the valuation of the shopping mall which is connected with a few value chains. However, at the community site network, effect between customers or the brand may have a large portion.

This research resulted in Table V from the survey conducted with the subject of the 51 investment managers of the domestic 16 investment and securities companies about the priority of 5 areas.

The business model domain got the first priority at the survey report. Its importance becomes higher as Internet business industry matures. However, the beginner of the early stage assumed an aspect of development just by their creative idea, they need the establishment of a stable revenue structure now.

The fact that brand value was measured at second means that brand recognition and the number of members are still recognized as important factors. The remaining were finance, the manager, and the technology in sequence. Especially, the importance of technology is deteriorating because as Internet business is spreading so is Internet technology. It can be said that Internet companies are becoming the size and frame of existing industries.

ACKNOWLEDGMENTS

The author would like to express gratitude to the Ministry of Information and Communication for their constant effort to develop electronic commerce. The author's gratitude also goes to Hyungsik Suh, Bumyong Kim, and Sungchul Yoon who made this research possible, and Kyungmook Kim, Sungho Yu, and Han Seo of the Electronic Times who helped the author acquire data that were used in the research.

SEE ALSO THE FOLLOWING ARTICLES

Business-to-Business Electronic Commerce • Digital Goods: An Economic Perspective • Electronic Commerce • Health Care, Information Systems and • Marketing • Sales • Service Industry

BIBLIOGRAPHY

APEC (1999). APEC SME Electronic Commerce Study: Final Report.

Bambury, P. (2000). A Taxonomy of Internet Commerce, http://www.firstmonday.dk/issues/issue3_10/bambury.

Barua, A., Pinnell, J., Shutter, J., and Whinston, A. B. (1999). Measuring the Internet Economy: An Exploratory Study. June 10. Austin: University of Texas.

Berryman, K., Harrington, L. F., Layton-Rodin, D., and Rerolle, V. (1998). Electronic commerce: Three emerging strategies. Mckinsey Quarterly. 1:129–136.

Doaln, R. J., and Moon, Y. (2000). Pricing and market naking on the internet. HBR. April 4.

ECOM. (1996). http://www.ecom.or.jp/ecom_e/index.html.

Hagel, J., and Rayport, J. F. (1997). The coming battle for customer information. The Mckinsey Quarterly. 3:64–76.

Hagel, J., and Rayport, J. F. (1997). The new informediaries. Mckinsey Quarterly. 4:54–71.

Hanson, W. (2000). *Principles of Internet Marketing*. Ohio: South-Western College Publishing.

Kalakota, R., and Whinston, A. B. (1997). *Electronic Commerce*. Reading, MA: Addison-Wesley.

Leem, C. S., and e-Biz Lab. (2001). "e-Business File," Youngjn Biz.com.

Means, G. E., and Schneider, D. M. (2000). Metacapitalism: The e-Business revolution and the design of 21th century companies and markets", PricewaterhouseCoopers.

Mesenbourg, T. L. (2000). Measuring Electronic Business: Definitions, Underlying Concepts, and Measurement Plans. U.S. Census Bureau.

OECD. (1999). The Economic and Social Implications of Electronic Commerce www.oecd.org.

Porter, M. E., and Millar, V. E. (1985). How information gives you competitive advantage. HBR. July-August.

Rappa, M. (2000). Business Models on the Web, http://ecommerce.ncsu.edu/topics/models/models_text.html.

Standing, C. (2000). *Internet Commerce Development*. Norwood, MA: Artech House.

Timmers, P. (1998). Business models for electronic markets. Electronic Markets. 8(2).

Wang, S. (1997). Impact of information technology on organization. *Human Systems Management*.

Wigand, R. T. (1998). Electronic Commerce: Definition, theory, and context. *Strategic Management Journal*.

Service Industry

Dennis Guseman

California State University, Bakersfield

I. DEFINITION OF SERVICES INDUSTRIES
II. DEFINITION AND CLASSIFICATION OF SERVICES
III. INFORMATION SYSTEMS IN SERVICE INDUSTRY
IV. APPLICATION OF INFORMATION SYSTEMS IN SERVICE INDUSTRIES
V. FUTURE PROSPECTS

GLOSSARY

contact personnel Those employees of a service firm that come into direct contact with customers during the delivery of the service.

customer service The manner of style in which a product is delivered; the personal attention given to consumers during the delivery process.

demand management Activities designed to manipulate the level of customer demand to match the available supply.

facilitating supplementary services A set of supplemental services that facilitates the use of the core service, such as order taking, billing, and payment.

frequency marketing Programs designed to motivate customers to continue patronizing a firm, such as a frequent user reward system.

hard customer standard Measurements of operational efficiency and customer service that are based on measurable, observable standards, such as the length of time required to perform a service.

high-contact service A service where the customer is present during most or all of the performance of the service.

inseparability The inability to separate the production of a service from its consumption. That is, a service must be consumed when it is produced, or its productive capacity is lost.

lifetime customer value The amount of value a customer brings to a business over all of the encounters and transactions a customer has with a business from their purchases, insight provided, and word-of-mouth-activity engaged in by the customer.

low-contact service A service where the customer is not present at all or is present for only a small portion of the performance of the service.

service failure recovery Activities to learn of and correct problems that occur during the service delivery process.

services Intangible activities or benefits provided to consumers that do not result in ownership.

soft customer standard Measurements of customer service that require subjective assessments, such as friendliness.

yield management A set of activities to obtain the highest average revenue over time per unit of capacity offered for sale.

Firms operating in the **SERVICES INDUSTRY** must develop an information system that allows the firm to meet and exceed the customers' expectations, to develop and maintain a close relationship with its customers, and to increase its productivity. This means the system must be carefully designed to provide the desired information and that the information be accurate. How a service firm can do this is discussed in this article.

I. DEFINITION OF SERVICES INDUSTRIES

The services industries are made up of those businesses that provide intangible products. A great deal of diversity exists within the various services industries, diversity in terms of the type of consumers served, including business markers, consumer markets, and governments. Diversity also exists in terms of the size of firms within the various service industries. As a rule, service industries tend to be made up of smaller, local firms, such as restaurants, laundries, and auto repair shops. However, the services industry also includes large, international firms, such as within the airline, banking, and insurance industries.

Given the diversity within the services industries, we cannot discuss each specific industry individually or discuss the particular nuances of specific services. Instead the discussion will deal with the generalities that differentiate the services sector from the manufacturing and agriculture sectors of the economy. The discussion starts with a clear definition of how services, as intangibles, differ from goods (tangibles) and provide classification systems of services. Once a firm foundation for what services are has been developed, the discussion will focus on how information systems can be applied within the services industries.

II. DEFINITION AND CLASSIFICATION OF SERVICES

A service can be defined as an activity or benefit that one party offers to another that is essentially intangible and does not result in the ownership of anything. Thus, services are distinguished from other products on two key characteristics: They are intangible and they cannot be owned.

A. Intangibility

The intangibility nature of services means services, per se, cannot be seen or felt. Rather services are experienced. The service itself may deal with or be tied to a physical, tangible product, such as providing a car (car rental) or repairing a car, but the "product" itself is intangible. In the case of a car rental a tangible is provided, but the "product" itself is the "experience" of having the car—the convenience of check-in and return, problem-free operation of the car, having the appropriate vehicle, etc. Likewise, in the case of car repair, the actual "product" is intangible—taking in a car that is not properly operating and getting it back in proper working condition. So, one major difference between services and goods is the intangible nature of the services.

B. Lack of Ownership

The second major distinguishing characteristic of services from other products is the lack of ownership—services are not owned by the person "purchasing" them. When purchased, a car would be considered a product, but if rented, the rental car would be a service. Thus, services can be distinguished from tangibles by whether the "product" is owned or not. Even though a service may involve a tangible—providing one, repairing one, or improving and altering one—unless there is ownership by the purchaser, it is a service.

C. Classification of Services

Services can be classified in many different ways, but the most comprehensive classification system is by the nature of the service act, tangible or intangible actions, and toward whom or what the actions are directed, either a person or their possessions. Table I summarizes this classification system.

1. Nature of the Service Act

Table I lists these types of services:

- *People processing services.* Tangible actions directed toward people bodies, such as health care and hotels
- *Possession processing services.* Tangible actions directed at physical possessions, such as dry cleaners and repair services
- *Mental stimulus processing service.* Intangible actions directed at people's minds, such as advertising and entertainment services
- *Information processing services.* Intangible actions directed at intangible assets, such as banking or insurance.

The role of information systems will vary across the various types of services. For example, many possession processing services can be treated as quasi-manufacturing operations, where information systems can be used to improve productivity. However, for most people processing services the consumer will be directly involved in the production process, making most manufacturing productivity models inappropriate. Yet, these people processing services do need information about individual consumers and their preferences. Mental stimulus services can benefit greatly from information systems in the delivery of the ser-

Table I Services Classified by Nature of the Service Act

What is the nature of the service act?	Who or what is the direct recipient of the service?	
	People	**Possessions**
Tangible actions	People processing (services directed at people's bodies)	Possession processing (services directed at physical possessions)
	Passenger transportation	Repair and maintenance
	Health care	Storage
	Lodging	Retail distribution
	Restaurants	Dry cleaning
	Beauty salons	Landscaping
Intangible actions	Mental stimulus processing (services directed at people's minds)	Information processing (services directed at intangible assets)
	Advertising	Accounting
	Entertainment	Banking
	Management consulting	Data processing
	Education	Data transmission
	Information services	Insurance
	Psychotherapy	Legal services
	Broadcasting	Securities investments

Source: Adapted from Lovelock, C., and Wright, L. (1999). *Principles of service marketing and management.* Upper Saddle River, NJ: Prentice-Hall, 31.

vice, allowing for higher degrees of customization and productivity. But the area of greatest potential for information systems is that of information processing services. These services by their very nature rely heavily on information systems and recent improvements in technology have greatly changed how these services can be offered, with on-line stock trading being just one example.

2. Use of Information within Service Firms

Fitzsimmons has developed a classification system for the competitive use of information within a service firm. Table II summarizes this classification system.

Information can be used either to assist in the operations of the service (internal) or externally to develop linkages and understanding of customers. Both internal and external use of information can be on-line in real time or off-line and used for purposes of analysis.

• *Customer service information—On-line information on customers.* Information of this nature is used to better serve customers and to create switching costs for the purpose of creating barriers to entry by competitors. Information is used by the firm to make a connection with the customer, thereby being in a position to better serve them. Thus the firm

Table II Competitive Use of Information within a Service Firm

	On-line (real time)	Off-line (analysis)
External (customer)	Customer service	Customer analysis
	Reservation system	Selling information
	Frequency user club	Development of services
	Switching costs	Micromarketing
Internal (operational)	Revenue generation	Productivity enhancement
	Yield management	Inventory status
	Point of sales	Data envelopment analysis
	Expert systems	

Source: Adapted and modified from Fitzsimmons, J. A., and Fitzsimmons, M. J. (1998). *Services management,* 2nd ed. Boston: Irwin McGraw-Hill, 69.

creates customer loyalties and barriers to entry for other firms. Examples of this include reservation systems, frequent user clubs, and on-line customer databases.

 • *Customer analysis information—Off-line analysis of customer information.* Information collected from customers and their transactions can be analyzed individually and collectively using data mining techniques to learn about customer preferences and to detect trends. This information can be used to improve the delivery of the service, to develop new services, and to customize the service.

 • *Revenue generation—On-line use of internal information to increase revenue opportunities.* Having information on current and expected customers' usage patterns can allow a service firm to utilize yield management tools to maximize its revenue potential. (This concept is explained more fully in a later section.)

 • *Productivity enhancement—use of off-line external information to increase productivity.* This information is especially useful for multisite services, such as franchises, to determine the effectiveness of each unit and to identify the best practice for each process that can be shared with other facilities.

Specific examples and applications of this classification system for the use of information are provided on a later section.

III. INFORMATION SYSTEMS IN SERVICES INDUSTRY

A. Objective of Information Systems in Service Industries

Every organization needs information if it is to make effective decisions and develop sound strategic plans. For many manufacturing firms this means developing information systems around its products, where product-related databases are the focal point of the information system. However, for services the product is intangible, so a different orientation is needed. For service industries the focus point has to be consumers, necessitating that information systems focus on customer databases, not product databases.

For many manufacturing firms the objective is to maximize the profitability of their products, and thus their information systems focus on measuring product-related metrics. For services industries the focus has to be on the profitability of customers—

whether measured at a mass market, customer segment, or individual customer level—dependent on the service firm's focus.

The strategic role of information systems in a service firm is as follows:

1. Allow the service firm to meet and exceed the customers' expectations. This means a service firm needs knowledge about customers' priorities and the degree to which the firm is meeting them in its various encounters with customers.
2. Allow the service firm to develop and maintain a close relationship with its customers. Part of this role involves defining who are the right customers and determining their changing expectations. Another part of this objective is knowing how the firm's performance compares to that of other service firms. Also, the service firm needs to develop information systems to learn more about its customers, to better understand them, and to be in a position to better serve them. This involves developing a longer term, lifetime customer value perspective.
3. Allow the service firm to increase its productivity. In addition to understanding the current productivity of employees and systems, information can be used to improve the effectiveness of customers interacting with the firm.

An effective service-quality information system, according to Berry in his book, *On Great Service,* offers the following benefits:

 • Encourages and enables management to incorporate the voice of the customer into decision making
 • Reveals customers' service priorities
 • Identifies service improvement priorities and guides resource allocation decisions
 • Allows the tracking of company and competitor service performance over time
 • Discloses the impact of service quality initiatives and investments
 • Offers performance-based data to reward excellent service and correct poor service

B. Characteristics of Effective Services Information Systems

Before discussing individual information systems for service firms, it would be helpful to discuss some of the design issues in the development of an information system for a services firm.

1. Information System Design

The information system design deals with the type of information needed, by whom, in what format, and when.

a. TYPE OF INFORMATION NEEDED

In general, information is needed on current customers, potential customers, employees, and the environment.

i. Current and Potential Customers For current customers you need information on their expectations, how they define value, their priorities, and their level of satisfaction with the service. For prospective customers, in addition to the above items you also need to know their attitudes about competing service firms and how your service compares on these variables.

ii. Employees For employees, you will need information on their performance, at both a technical level (providing the core service) and a function level (the manner in which the core service is delivered), and the level of satisfaction with their job. Research has shown that the level of employee satisfaction has a direct correlation on the level of customer satisfaction. Information about customers—complaints, level of satisfaction, problems, requests, etc.—should also be collected from employees.

iii. Environment To develop an effective strategy it is also necessary to collect information about changes in some crucial environments, mainly, competitive, economic, legal, and technological.

1. *Competitive environments.* Having a competitive intelligence system will provide information on changes in competitors' activities, such as adding or dropping products, increasing or decreasing level of service, changing price, and changes in promotional activity. It is also desirable to have information on the consumers the competitors are targeting and their level of satisfaction.
2. *Economic environments.* Changes in the strength of the economy and consumer finances can result in changes in the level of demand and types of services demanded, so these changes need to be monitored.
3. *Legal environments.* Changes in legislation and regulation at a local, state, or national level can create either opportunities or threats that could drastically change the way a service firm operates, so a systematic way to monitor and analyze these

changes is necessary.
4. *Technological environments.* The rapid change in technological innovations can make the cost of doing business very expensive. Technological innovations, especially those being adopted by major competitors, need to be closely monitored. A service firm also needs to monitor technological innovation in other industries, looking for potential innovation that could be used to better serve customers and create competitive advantages.

In designing the actual information system, Kotler has developed a list of 10 questions to be used for determining the type of information that needs to be captured:

1. What types of decisions are you regularly called on to make?
2. What types of information do you need to make these decisions?
3. What type of information do you regularly get?
4. What types of special studies do you periodically request?
5. What types of information would you like to get that you are not getting now?
6. What information would you want daily? Weekly? Monthly? Yearly?
7. What magazines and trade reports would you like to see routed to you on a regular basis?
8. What specific topics would you like to be kept informed of?
9. What types of data analysis programs would you like to see made available?
10. What do you think would be the four most helpful improvements that could be made in the present information system?

These questions can be asked of both managers and front-line employees, with the actual information system being a cross between what the managers and front-line personnel think they need, what they actually need, and what is economically feasible.

Berry has further refined Kotler's list of questions specifically for service industries (see Table III). Berry provides a list of questions for both the design of a new system and the refinement of an existing system. By asking these questions a service firm will be in excellent shape to understand the types of information needed to serve its customers effectively, develop relationships with customers to create competitive advantage, and to improve the effectiveness and productivity of employees. After identifying exactly what

Table III   Questions for Service Quality Information System Users

Predesign Questions

- What would you like to know about the customers you serve?
- What type of information would help you improve service in our company?
- What type of information would you like to have about your own service performance? About your work unit? About the company? About the competition?
- If you presently receive information on customer service, what type of information is most valuable to you? Why? What is least valuable? Why?
- What are your preferred ways of receiving customer service information? How often would you like to receive this information?

Postimplementation Questions

- Are you receiving the information you need to help the company improve its service? (for managers)
- Are you receiving the information you need to best serve your customers? (for front-line employees)
- What information on customer service would you like to receive that you currently do not receive? How would this information help you?
- What customer service information that you receive is most valuable to you? Why? What is least valuable? Why?
- Do you receive customer service information on a timely basis? Please explain.
- What could the company do to improve the usefulness of the customer service information it provides you?

Source: Berry, L. L., and Parasuraman, A. (Spring 1997). Listening to the customer: The concept of a service-quality information system. *Sloan Management Review,* Vol. 38, 65–76.

information is needed, a service firm must next determine where and how to collect it.

b. Sources of Needed Information

Given that the essence of a services information system is a customer information system, the majority of information collected will be from customers—both current and potential. Another major source of information will come from employees. Berry has suggested four main sources for collecting information from consumer and employees, as discussed next.

i. Transactional Surveys   These are satisfaction surveys given immediately following a customer's encounter with a service. These surveys can obtain customer feedback while the experience is still fresh, and alert the firm quickly should a negative pattern develop.

In addition to these transactional surveys, a service firm also needs to develop a transactional database that records a customer's purchase history. The transactional database can link a person's purchases (frequency and amount purchased) to their demographic and media habits so this information can be used to:

- Exchange information with the customer in future encounters. The customer will remember previous encounters with you, so you need to be in a position to remember them also.
- Provide additional sales opportunities by analyzing past purchases with the customer, and other similar customers, in order to suggest other services the customer might like. Amazon.com has used its customer databases quite effectively to suggest additional book selections based on what

other titles a customer is purchasing. Likewise Amazon.com notifies readers when their favorite author has a new book out.

- Determine the lifetime value of a customer. By analyzing customers' lifetime value, the amount and type of efforts to direct toward a customer can be differentiated by the value of the customer. For example, a bank can charge a monthly fee for checking accounts to its less valued customers but make it free to more valued clients.

ii. Customer Complaints, Comments, and Inquiries   Customer feedback, whether in the form of complaints, comments, or inquiries, can be extremely valuable in keeping customers and serving them better. Therefore, a systematic process for gathering and analyzing customer communications needs to be developed. It should be easy for consumers to provide feedback, whether in person to front-line employees, by telephone, e-mail, comment cards, or Internet web sites. Regardless of the vehicle, customer feedback needs to be captured and recorded in an information system. The information can then be analyzed looking for ways to strengthen customer relationships by either correcting mistakes or by handling problems, or by seizing opportunities to serve customers better based on their suggestions. An analysis of complaints can also identify weak links in the system that should be corrected.

iii. Total Market Survey   Total market surveys are comprehensive research projects of the entire market—current customers, former customers, and competitors' customers. A total market survey is interested in assessing the firm's service performance compared to competitors, identifying service improvement opportunities, and tracking improvements over time. Not only will a service firm gain insight into how consumers perceive the firm relative to competitors, but the firm can also see how various changes in service operations and marketing strategies influence consumers' attitudes and behaviors.

iv. Employee Surveys Two basic types of employee surveys should be conducted. One is a survey of the employee's level of satisfaction in working for the firm and the other is a survey of employees to capture intelligence about customers. The employee satisfaction survey can be undertaken to determine the level of internal service quality (i.e., how well employees are serving one another), identify employee-perceived obstacles to improved service, and track employee morale, attitudes, and overall level of satisfaction. The level of employee satisfaction is usually a good indicator of the level of customer satisfaction. By collecting and analyzing this information, managers can develop a strategy to allow employees to be more effective in their jobs.

Employees can also be surveyed as an intelligence source on customers. Front-line employees deal with many customers each day, and thus gain insight into customers' expectations, perceptions, problems, and frustrations. These insights need to be captured and analyzed through an information system.

v. Service Operating Data A system also needs to be developed to retain, categorize, track, and distribute key service performance operating data. Such things as service response times, service failure rates, operating times, and costs can be monitored to indicate problems and opportunities for improvements.

2. Information Quality

It is the quality, not the quantity, of information that is critical in the development of a service quality information system. The test of the quality of information is that it must be relevant, precise, useful, credible, and timely.

a. RELEVANT
The information gathered should focus decision-makers' attention on the most important issues. Mainly, information is needed that answers these questions:

- What are the expectations of our customers and are we meeting them?
- What are the expectations of prospective customers and what should be done to capture these consumers?

- What can be done to improve employees' performance in meeting and exceeding customer expectations?

For information to be relevant it must provide insight into these issues, otherwise there is no need to collect it.

b. PRECISE AND USEFUL
The information collected must be specific enough to allow decision-makers to take action. That is, managers need to be able to make decisions, set priorities, launch programs, and cancel projects. The information also has to be useful. That is, decision-makers must understand the format in which the information is presented and must be given the context of how the new information relates to information from the past.

c. CREDIBLE
Decision-makers also need to trust the information before they will use it. Information should be classified as to its accuracy, and multiple measures of a phenomenon can be made to try to reach a consensus of what is actually happening.

d. TIMELY
To be of use, the information should be available when needed and at the right place. Both managers and front-line personnel need to be able to access the right information, at the right time, in the right format, at the right place. Basically everyone in the organization should be able to access the information system to help them perform their jobs well and better serve customers.

IV. APPLICATION OF INFORMATION SYSTEMS IN SERVICES INDUSTRIES

As indicated in the previous section, information systems have three strategic roles within service firms:

- Allow the service firm to meet and exceed customer expectations.
- Allow service firms to develop and maintain close relationships with customers.
- Allow service firms to increase productivity.

A. Information Systems to Meet and Exceed Customer Expectations

Satisfying customers is a matter of meeting and exceeding their expectations. There are two basic questions a service firm needs to ask and answer: What are customers' expectations, and how are we at satisfying customers?

1. What Are Customers' Expectations?

Research has shown that consumers tend to use five types of variables in evaluating services:

1. *Reliability:* being dependable in providing the service as promised, over time
2. *Tangibles:* service provider's physical facilities, equipment, personnel, and communication materials
3. *Responsiveness:* the firm's employee helpfulness and ability to provide prompt service
4. *Assurance:* service employees who are knowledgeable, polite, competent, and trustworthy
5. *Empathy:* providing caring, personalized attention.

Information on the exact expectations can be obtained from total market surveys and feedback from customers' comments, inquiries, and complaints. Information from total market surveys can be analyzed to determine customer priorities and expectations. These surveys should be conducted as frequently as every quarter to semiannually, depending on the dynamics of the industry.

The information from the total market survey can be supplemented with feedback from customers. Customers can provide information in several different forms (e.g., comments, inquiries, complaints) and in different vehicles (e.g., verbally to front-line employees, telephone, mail, Internet web site, e-mail, fax). Regardless of the how the feedback is received, the information system needs to be capable of capturing, categorizing, tracking, and distributing these comments. This information should be analyzed at both an individual and aggregate level when looking for opportunities to better understand customers.

Managers will be the primary users of this information system. After the completion of a total market survey, all of the information can be reviewed with an eye toward looking for changes in consumer priorities and expectations.

2. How Well Are We Satisfying Customers?

Transactional surveys can be used to determine how well a service firm is meeting customers' expectations. Thus, a service firm needs to develop a transactional database to record each encounter a customer has with the firm. These customer databases need to be continuously updated (real time) and available to all front-line employees when dealing with customers, regardless of the nature of the interaction (in person, by phone, or Internet) or the nature of the encounter (inquiry, purchase, complaint, comment, or suggestion).

Either hard or soft service quality standards can be established in monitoring the success of a service firm in meeting customer expectations. Hard service standards are things that can be counted, timed, or observed through audits. For example, FedEx places a high priority on making no mistakes. Hard standards for FedEx would be number of packages delivered right, number of missed pickups, number of packages late, etc. A bank could track the accuracy of transactions, time required to serve customers, statements sent on time, etc.

Soft standards are things that cannot be measured and tend to be based on perceptual measures and are opinion based. Soft standards are measured by talking with customers and employees. For example, Ritz-Carlton has a set of "Gold Standards" to treat people with respect that include these guidelines: Uniforms must be immaculate, nametags must be worn, grooming standards must be adhered to, supervisor must be notified immediately of hazards, etc. American Express in the treatment of its customers expects employees to listen and do everything possible to help. General Electric expects its telephone operators to take ownership of a call.

It is easier to capture and analyze hard standards but ways must also be found to record, analyze, and distribute the results of soft standards, too. In general, high-contact services, those services where the customer is present during all or most of the service performance, such as physicians, airlines, spectator sports, and hotels, will tend to require more soft standards than hard standards. Low-contact services, those services where customers need not be present at all, or only minimally during the service performance, such as car repair, utilities, and insurance, will tend to use more hard standards than soft standards. However, every service should have a set of both hard and soft standards.

The transactional database, recording customer interactions and satisfactions, becomes the basic foundation for the other information systems. The transactional database acts as the basic monitor of how well a service firm is performing. However, the long-term viability of the firm depends on developing and maintaining a relationship with customers.

B. Information Systems to Develop Customer Relationships

Customer relationship management (CRM) is a technological initiative that focuses on building mutually beneficial customer relationships by employing technology that allows marketing, sales, and service to share information and work as a team. CRM systems can be either operational or analytical. Operational CRM systems gather customer information across various channels, such as on-site encounters, phone, Web, and call centers; organizes it; and makes it available to front-line employees so they can better serve customers. Analytical CRM systems analyze the data collected by the operational system to help improve the overall customer satisfaction and profitability of customers individually and collectively.

In general, CRM systems are used to track encounters with consumers and record communications with customers. This information can be used for purposes of segmentation and targeting of products and customer communications. The information gathered can also be used to help retain and develop customers. The CRM system can answer the following questions:

- Who are the right customers?
- What is the right customer mix by time period?
- How do we retain current customers?

1. Who Are the Right Customers?

Customers are not equally profitable to serve. Some customers generate more business, are more loyal, and are easier to serve than other customers. Some customers engage in favorable word-of-mouth activities and act like apostles for the company or provide valuable insight into how to better satisfy customers. In general, customers who generate value (produce greater benefit than cost) are the "right" customers.

One of the first uses of a CRM system is to segment and prioritize customers. The segmentation can be based on current profitability of a customer, future potential of a customer, and the potential of the customer to provide valuable referrals. The CRM should provide the necessary information to make these judgments.

2. What Is the Right Customer Mix by Time Period?

The widely fluctuating nature of demand for many services, along with the inability to inventory services, makes demand management a crucial task for service managers. Managing demand requires having information about the fluctuations in demand and understanding the nature of the demand itself.

Lovelock has suggested asking the following questions to help understand the factors that govern demand for a specific service at a given point in time:

1. Does the level of demand for the service follow a predictable cycle? If so, is the cycle duration:
   - One day (varies by hour)
   - One week (varies by day)
   - One month (varies by day or by week)
   - One year (varies by month or by season; or reflects annually occurring public holidays)
   - Some other period
2. What are the underlying causes of these cyclical variations?
   - Employment schedules
   - Billing and tax payment/refund cycles
   - Wage and salary payment dates
   - School hours and vacations
   - Seasonal changes in climate
   - Occurrence of public or religious holidays
   - Natural cycles, such as coastal tides
3. Do demand levels seem to change randomly? If so, could the underlying causes be:
   - Day-to-day changes in the weather (consider how rain and cold affect the use of indoor and outdoor recreational or entertainment services)
   - Health events whose occurrence cannot be pinpointed (heart attacks and births affect the demand for hospital services)
   - Accidents, acts of God, and certain criminal activities (these require fast response not only from fire, police, and ambulance but also from disaster recovery specialists and insurance firms)
4. Can demand for a particular service over time be disaggregated by market segment to reflect such components as:
   - Use patterns by a particular type of customer or for a particular purpose?
   - Variations in the net profitability of each completed transaction?

To help in the development of an effective demand management strategy a service manager needs information on:

- Historical data on the level and composition of demand over time, including responses to changes in price or other marketing variables
- Forecasts of the level of demand for each major segment under specified conditions

- Segment-by-segment data to help management evaluate the impact of periodic cycles and random demand fluctuations
- Good cost data to enable the organization to distinguish between fixed and variable costs and to determine the relative profitability of incremental unit sales to different segments and at different prices
- In multisite organizations, identification of meaningful variations in the levels and composition of demand on a site-by-site basis
- Customer attitudes toward queuing under varying conditions
- Customer opinions on whether the quality of service delivered varies with different levels of capacity utilization.

Information systems need to be designed to provide this information. However, this is not sufficient. Not only is it necessary for a service manager to be able to understand the nature and level of demand, but a service manager needs to manage that demand to yield the maximum amount of revenue.

Customers differ in their ability and willingness to utilize a service at a given time and also vary in the amount of money they are willing to spend. Thus a service manager must consider the yield—the average revenue received per unit of capacity offered for sale—of various strategies. For example, should a hotel accept an advance booking from a tour group at a reduced rate, or should it wait for the potential of receiving a full rate from a business traveler (not knowing for sure whether the business traveler will actually materialize)? Yield management is the strategy of obtaining the best possible yield over time from each available unit of capacity.

Yield management requires the development of mathematical models that analyze past sales data by customer segment, then factors in current market intelligence and considers various marketing efforts to arrive at an ideal customer mix. The ideal customer mix is the percent of business desired from a particular customer segment that will result in the highest revenue generation based on the amount of demand and price sensitivity of each segment.

Yield management involves the following steps:

1. Identify the principal market segments that might be attracted to the service facility and that are consistent with its capabilities and mission.
2. Forecast the volumes of business that might be obtained from each segment at specific price levels (through supply-and-demand analysis).
3. Recommend the "ideal business mix" at each specific point in time in terms of maximizing net revenues, which may not, in fact, be the same as maximizing capacity utilization.
4. Provide the sales force with specific sales targets on specific dates for each segment. This information may also be useful for planning advertising and related communication efforts.
5. Providing guidelines for the prices to charge each segment at specific points in time. For some segments, these guidelines should be adhered to rigorously; in other instances, they may simply provide targets for negotiation.

An example of yield management is where an air carrier develops different seat categories for a flight, based on the price and various restrictions placed on a ticket. Thus the most expensive seats could be purchased at the last minute with no restrictions, and the lowest ticket fares would require advance purchase and have many restrictions (Saturday night stay-over, no changes, etc.). To manage the yield, the number of seats in each category could change, based on the number of seats sold, historical ridership patterns, and likelihood of connecting passengers. If analysis shows that business travelers are buying unrestricted tickets earlier than expected, then more seats could be taken from discounted seats and reserved for last-minute bookings.

3. How Do We Retain Current Customers?

Once a service firm has established a relationship with a customer, it wants to keep and develop that customer. Research has shown that it is not only less expensive to keep current customers, but current customers who are loyal are more profitable. The longer a customer stays with a business the more profitable they are. So, retaining customers is an important activity. Retaining customers involves more than satisfying customers. A service firm must also establish an effective system for customer complaint and service failure recovery and create bonds with customers.

a. CUSTOMER COMPLAINT AND SERVICE FAILURE RECOVERY

The high variability in quality that exists for services makes quality control activities important. It also necessitates having good service failure recovery systems in place. Having a system for learning about service failures is important; as many as 90% of customers do not complain when there is a problem, and if there is a problem, consumers are less likely to return to the firm. So, learning of consumer problems and correcting them is important in a firm's efforts to retain customers.

Developing an effective service failure recovery system is basically a matter of first learning about mistakes and then having mechanisms to correct those mistakes. Mistakes in the service delivery process can be identified by:

- Actively encouraging customers to complain when there is a problem. This requires that customers be aware of complaint mechanisms and have access to them. Multiple methods for voicing complaints need to be developed, including telling the service provider or manager, comment cards, suggestion boxes, toll-free phone numbers, and the Internet.
- Training contact personnel to identify potential failures. Contact personnel need to question consumers on the level of service received and be perceptive as to when things are not right.
- Implementing quality control standards and measures. Specific measures need to be taken to ensure quality standards are being met and to alert the appropriate people when they are not met. Information systems play a vital part in monitoring the quality of the service.

Once service failure problems have been identified, steps can be taken to correct the problem. However, more needs to be done than just correcting the problem. The service firm needs to learn from the failure to prevent it from recurring. Service failures themselves need to be analyzed for their root cause. Information systems are needed to track problems so steps can be taken to prevent the problems from recurring.

The role of information systems is to capture customer complaints, analyze complaints for root cause analysis, and empower front-line workers with the information necessary to remedy the problem.

Regardless of the method used by consumers to voice a complaint—in person, via the Internet, phone, or mail—the complaint must be recorded and acted on. Analyzing complaints can provide valuable insight into how to improve the service for all customers. Front-line employees must also be able to access the information system to help them resolve the customer's problem, whether they need to track the status, as in a lost bag for an airline, or provide assistance in the steps and procedures for resolving the problem.

b. CUSTOMER MANAGERS AND CREATING CUSTOMER BONDS

Given the positive impact that retaining customers has on profitability it is wise for service firms to es-

tablish customer-managers. Just as product-managers are responsible for overseeing and managing every aspect of a particular brand, a customer-manager is responsible for overseeing and managing the relationship a firm has with a particular customer or customer segment. Some banks have personal bankers for their preferred customers. These personal bankers are the contact person for the customer, and the personal banker will handle all of the customer's needs. This provides a degree of continuity for the customer and ensures that nothing slips through the cracks. The basic job of a customer-manager is to manage and improve the relationship with the customer.

For a customer-manager structure to work the information system has to be organized around customers and not products. The customer-manager has to be able to analyze every aspect of the customer's business with the firm. Having this customer-organized database, rather than a product-organized one, allows the customer-manager to develop bonds or ties with the customer. Berry and Parasuraman have discussed four types of bonds that can be created to retain customers: financial, social, customization, and structural.

i. Financial Bonds Financial bonds create a financial incentive for the customer to continue doing business with the firm. The most common is a frequency marketing program, such as the airline frequent flier programs or hotel frequent stayer program. Frequent users receive discounted or free services based on the quantity of use. Frequency marketing programs require an information system to accurately track and report the customers' "points." Tracking customer usage becomes the basis for differentiating customer groups based on frequency and volume of usage, which in turn allows a firm to design more targeted programs for its preferred customers.

ii. Social Bonds Social bonds build on the financial incentives by creating social and interpersonal relationships with the customers. A social bond treats the customer as a client and attempts to understand and serve customers better. Establishing social bonds is especially important for professional services and personal care providers. Social bonds make the service personal by remembering the client's name and past experiences with the firm, by sending cards to commemorate special occasions, and staying in touch to learn of changing needs. This type of relationship requires the service firm to have a transactional database and CRM information systems to record, analyze, and report on all of a customer's dealings with the firm.

iii. Customization Bonds Customization involves meeting the individual needs of the customer. This means the firm must be capable of learning and remembering from each interaction the customer has with the firm. The information system needs to provide the contact person with the history and preferences of the customer. Armed with this information the firm can provide the exact service the customer desires. For example, Ritz-Carlton Hotel Company's employees are trained to input the likes and dislikes of its regular customers into a customer database. By making the database available to the entire system, a hotel can know in advance the guest's preferences and individualize the service to meet his or her particular needs.

iv. Structural Bonds Structural bonds are created when the service firm partners with its clients by linking information systems and sharing processes and equipment. For example, Allegiance Healthcare Corporation has created an integrated information system with the hospitals it supplies by linking its ordering, delivery, and billing systems with the customers' systems. Likewise, FedEx also creates structural bonds with its customers when it provides free computers to its customers to allow them to store addresses and shipping data, print mailing labels, and help track packages. These structural bonds tie the customer directly to the service firm and necessitate working closely with customer.

C. Information Systems to Increase Productivity

Meeting and exceeding customer expectations is a necessary, but not sufficient, condition for a service firm to be profitable. Profitability also means using resources efficiently. Information systems can be used to improve a service firm's productivity by increasing operational efficiency and improving how customers relate to the firm.

1. Improving Operational Efficiency

Services tend to be labor intensive and have high variability in quality due to the input and variability of employees and customers. Typical actions that a service firm can undertake to improve its productivity include the following:

- Careful controlling costs at every step of the process
- Service blueprinting to reduce wasteful use of labor and materials
- Accurately forecasting demand and matching it to capacity
- Replacing workers with automated machines

- Providing workers with equipment and databases that enable them to work faster or at a higher level of quality
- Teaching employees how to work more productively
- Installing expert systems to take on work previously performed by more experienced individuals earning higher salaries.

Service firms are starting to employ computerized performance monitoring and control systems (CPMCSs) that gather and track employee service performance data. Performance measures such as length of service calls, speed of answering, and number of abandoned calls can be documented automatically and analyzed by CPMCSs. However, care must be taken in the use of these employee-monitoring systems to ensure that employees do not focus on meeting a standard to the detriment of customer service. CPMCSs need to be used to spot problem areas that can be corrected by employee training, process reengineering, or system redesign.

Enterprise resource planning (ERP) systems, such as SAP or PeopleSoft, can be used to coordinate and streamline functions, eliminate waste, and improve service. In conjunction with ERP systems, front-office automation systems, such as Siebel Systems and Vantine Corporation, allow firms to automate their interactions with customers. For example, AT&T uses front-office automation at its call centers to identify callers by phone number and classify it by segment type to route the call to the appropriate personnel before the call is even answered. As the employee answers the call, the service provider has the customer's account history in front of him on his computer screen to expedite handing the customer's request.

Expert systems can also be provided to assist employees in dealing with customers by supplying answers to questions and details on how to perform certain tasks. For example, a call center operator for a hotel chain can select the hotel property nearest the customer's business meeting and supply detailed directions to the hotel to the customer.

2. Improving Customer Efficiency

Customers productivity is just as important as employees productivity, given the involvement of customers in the production process for many services. Customer productivity in interacting with the firm can be enhanced by facilitating the information exchange, order taking, and billing/payment process and by developing self-service technologies.

a. Information Supplemental Services

To obtain full value from a service, customers need relevant information. Information supplementary services facilitate the customer's purchase experience by telling customers about service features and performance before, during, and after the service delivery. A service firm needs to ensure customers have accurate and timely information on:

- What products will best meet the customer's needs and how to use the service
- Details on how to order the service
- Directions to the service site
- Schedules and service hours of operation
- Prices
- Documentation and confirmation of reservations
- Summary of account activity.

In addition to service providers giving out this information, it can also be provided via the Internet, touch-screen video displays, computer-accessed bulletin boards, menu-driven telephone messages, and customer controlled software. FedEx and UPS are examples of firms that have used customer-driven software. They allow customers to track movements of their packages on-line whenever they want.

b. Order Taking Supplemental Services

Information systems can also be used to facilitate the order taking process. Customers want to place orders, make reservations, or take applications in a fast, accurate, and polite manner. Information systems can be used to minimize the time and effort required to place orders. Examples include Pizza Hut's use of handheld computer devices that send the diners' orders to the kitchen, and Taco Bell is testing a system that allows customers to place their orders using touch-sensitive countertop menus. Software can also be used to facilitate order taking, such as the airlines' use of ticketless systems.

c. Billing and Payment Supplemental Services

Customers want clear, timely, accurate, and relevant documentation of the amount of money owed to the service firm. Billing can be highly computerized, even to the point of automatically withdrawing money from the customer's bank account on the delivery of the service. Some services, such as American Express, even analyze a customer's usage patterns and suggest strategies for the customer to save money. Hotels and rental car industries have highly computerized check-in/check-out procedures that make the billing process a very simple

matter. Other services are starting to employ "smart cards" to facilitate the payment process.

d. Self-Service Technologies

Customer productivity, and customer service can also be improved by employing customer self-service technologies (SSTs). SSTs, such as ATMs, pay at the pump, automated airline or hotel check-in/out, and Internet banking, allow the customer to provide her own service at her convenience and free up contact personnel to handle other customers and responsibilities. However, some customers see SSTs as intimidating, difficult to use, or unreliable. So, care must be taken to ensure that customers will use SSTs and be satisfied with them.

In developing SSTs, Meuter and Bitner suggest that a service firm answer the following questions:

- What is our strategy? What do we hope to achieve through the SST: cost savings, revenue growth, competitive advantage?
- What are the benefits to customers of providing the service on their own through the SST? Do they know and understand these benefits?
- How can customers be motivated to try the SST? Do they understand their role? Do they have the capability to perform this role?
- How "technology ready" are our customers? Do we have segments of customers who are more ready to use the technology than others?
- How can customers be involved in the design of the service technology system and processes so that they will be more likely to adopt and use the SST?
- What forms of customer education will be needed to encourage adoption? Will other incentive be needed?

V. FUTURE PROSPECTS

Changes in technology, especially in the ability to collect and analyze information on individual customers, are changing the very nature of how service firms operate and interact with their customers. Information systems have changed from being capable of only analyzing consumers in an aggregate sense to being able to collect, store, analyze, and disseminate information on each and every customer. Having detailed, accurate information on each customer and his preferences, along with his purchase histories, potentially puts a service firm in the position of better serving customers in a more efficient and effective manner.

Berry in his book *On Great Service* has suggested the following as the major impact of changing technology on services:

- Multiplying knowledge
- Streamlining services
- Customizing and personalizing services
- Increasing reliability
- Facilitating communications.

A. Multiplying Knowledge

Today's databases allow service firms to collect and store vast amounts of information on each and every customer. Through database analysis and data mining techniques, service firms will be in a position to better understand the behavior, preferences, and needs of their customers, individually and by segmented groups. Through the insights gained by analyzing these customer databases, service firms can better serve customers and thus create more loyal customers.

Managers can also analyze the customer databases to gain insight into developing new products and to create better ways of delivering existing products. Artificial intelligence programs and expert systems can be developed that will allow contact personnel to effectively and efficiently deliver a service and correct problems without having to rely on or wait for a supervisor.

B. Streamlining Services

New technology, especially information systems, will allow service firms to remove many obstacles in the current delivery systems. This will result in a more timely, reliable, productive, and valuable delivery of the service. This will be especially true for information processing services. Many services can automate activities previously requiring manual processes. Banks, for example, can automate even more, moving from ATMs to on-line banking transactions, where customers can handle their banking transactions any time and any place. Financial investment institutions will allow customers to engage in on-line trading and self-management of a person's own account.

Anywhere information is exchanged, the potential to streamline exists. Airlines are computerizing the reservation process, the ticketing process, and the check-in process. Even the medical profession is com-

puterizing its information exchanges. One example is that of doctors sending prescriptions directly to the pharmacy through handheld computers.

C. Customizing and Personalizing Services

Customer databases allow service providers to customize and personalize the delivery of service. By studying an individual's history with the firm, only the appropriate services and messages can be offered and the service can be delivered in the exact manner desired by the customer. Many hotels use information systems to customize the service its frequent stayers receive, from the type of room and amenities desired, to food preferences when ordering room service. Not only are hotels able to customize the service but they also personalize it by being able to refer to the guest by name and mention things from the guest's past visits.

The goal is to employ technology to allow for efficient delivery of the service, but to do so in a personalized manner. The result should be "high touch" delivered through "high tech."

D. Increasing Reliability

Computer information systems are allowing service firms to monitor every aspect of the service delivery process. Thus, service providers are in a better position to monitor quality and be aware of problems as they arise.

Service firms are also able to develop expert systems that allow service providers to operate at higher levels of efficiency and effectiveness. For example, auto repair shops employ computers that can diagnose problems and even provide advice on how to correct the problem.

E. Facilitating Communications

Customer databases allow contact personnel to have instant access to a customer's records and give the provider a wealth of relevant information that can be used to better serve customers. Service providers will have all the necessary information to handle almost any situation that might arise. Customers will also have access to the information systems so they can find the answer to their own questions and be in a position to inform the service of any changes in their needs or situation. The flow of information from firm to customer, and from customer to firm will be almost instantaneous, allowing for more timely delivery of the service.

Service firms should also facilitate the exchange of information from one consumer to others. Given the importance of personal sources and word-of-mouth activity in reducing risk in the purchase of services, service providers need to facilitate the exchange of information between customers. Chat rooms and bulletin boards will provide convenient mechanisms for consumers to exchange information among themselves.

F. Privacy Concerns

Customer databases allow service firms to amass a lot of information about individual customers. Much of this information will be of a personal nature. A key issue to the continuing relationship of a service firm with its customers is trust. For consumers to be willing to share information about themselves they must trust the service provider. Protecting the privacy of the customer, and only using the information gained from them to better serve the customer, are two key components of developing their trust. Therefore, a service provider must go to great lengths to protect the privacy of its customers.

SEE ALSO THE FOLLOWING ARTICLES

Benchmarking • Digital Goods: An Economic Perspective • Marketing • Sales • Service Industries, Electronic Commerce for • Supply Chain Management • Total Quality Management and Quality Control

BIBLIOGRAPHY

Bateson, J. E. G. (1995). *Managing services marketing: Text and readings,* 3rd ed. Ft. Worth, TX: The Dryden Press.

Berry, L. L. (1995). *On great service: A framework for action.* New York: The Free Press.

Berry, L. L., and Parasuraman, A. (Spring 1997). Listening to the customer: The concept of a service-quality information system. *Sloan Management Review,* Vol. 38, 65–76.

Brown, C. D. (June 2000). Is CRM in your company's future? *Trusts and Estates,* Vol. 139, No. 6, 20–22.

Fitzsimmons, J. A., and Fitzsimmons, M. J. (1998). *Service management: Operations, strategy, and information technology,* 2nd ed. Boston: Irwin McGraw-Hill.

Lovelock, C. H. (1996). *Services marketing,* 3rd ed. Boston: Upper Saddle River, NJ: Prentice-Hall.

Lovelock, C., and Wright, L. (1999). *Principles of service marketing and management.* Upper Saddle River, NJ: Prentice Hall.

Quinn, J. B., Bailly, M. N., et al. (1994). Information technology: Increasing productivity in services. *The Academy of Management Executive,* Vol. 8, No. 3, 28–40.

Rosencrance, L. Epiphany launches next-generation CRM software. *Computerworld,* Vol. 34, No. 32, 64.

Zeithaml, V. A., and Bitner, M. J. (1999). *Services marketing,* 2nd ed. New York: McGraw-Hill.

Simulation Languages

Edward J. Dudewicz
Syracuse University

Zaven A. Karian
Denison University

GLOSSARY

continuous systems simulation (CSS) Use of models with continuous variables such as time.

data mining Use of statistical procedures to find, store, and make accessible patterns in data.

discrete systems simulation (DSS) Use of models which have changes taking place at discrete instants.

general-purpose language (GPL) A digital computer programming language which can be used for many purposes (such as FORTRAN or C).

random number generator (RNG) A computer algorithm which produces numbers between 0 and 1 which appear to have a uniform statistical distribution.

simulation languages Digital computer programming languages which are specifically intended for programming of simulations (and have subroutines and commands to make the task simpler than use of a GPL).

special simulation language (SSL) Such digital computer programming languages as CSMP, a CSS language; SIMSCRIPT II.5, a CSS and DSS language; GPSS, which is a DSS language; and Arena, which is a popular interactive simulation environment that enables the user to have access to features such as animations and spreadsheets. (Witness, PROMODEL, Awesim, Automod, and @risk are other simulation environments that incorporate similar features.)

SIMULATION LANGUAGES are used to make the computer simulation of discrete systems and of continuous systems easier to implement. Discrete systems simulation (DSS) is often used in settings involving randomness, whereas continuous systems simulation (CSS) does not allow for randomness. Therefore, a DSS language should be used if the system one desires to simulate contains randomness. While there are many DSS and CSS languages, which collectively we term special simulation languages (SSLs), one can also perform simulations in general-purpose languages (GPSs) such as FORTRAN, C, etc. A simple example of deterministic motion in gravity shows the utility of CSS languages (in this case, the CSMP language). Another simple example of a single-server queueing system shows the incorporation of randomness in a language that can accommodate both discrete and continuous systems (in this case, the SIMSCRIPT II.5 language). This same queueing system is also illustrated in GPSS, a commonly used DSS language and Arena, a popular interactive simulation environment. A final example in the area of data mining illustrates how to incorporate a number of important aspects using the GPSS DSS language.

I. DISCRETE VERSUS CONTINUOUS SYSTEM SIMULATION

Simulation refers to solving problems with experimentation involving a model of the real-world system. A physical model might involve putting a scaled-down airplane wing into a wind tunnel to see the results. The forces on an airplane wing can also be modeled mathematically by a system of differential equations; one might study this model mathematically (if the equations are simple enough), or on a digital computer (if the equations are realistic, in which case they are rarely simple enough that they can be solved explicitly). Since the variables in differential equations (such as, time) are typically continuous, simulations involving them are called continuous simulations (or *continuous systems simulations*).

Simulation involving models which have changes taking place at specific time points (or discrete instants) rather than continuously is called *discrete systems simulation*. Such models date back to the French naturalist G.L.L. Buffon, who used them to estimate π (i.e., the quantity now known to be 3.14159 . . .) by tossing needles onto gridded paper in 1773. The American statistician, E.L. De Forest, was the first to use random numbers (instead of physical randomness) in such a simulation in 1876. Since the advent of the digital computer in the middle of the twentieth century, work with such models has moved largely to computers, which can process calculations rapidly. For coverage of simulation techniques, see the work of Tadikamalla, for applications in various areas such as the U.S. Census, biology and environment, electric power systems, inventory management, insurance, education, water resources, economics, system reliability, and other areas as well as modern techniques, see work by Dudewicz in 1996, 1997, and 1999.

II. DISCRETE VERSUS CONTINUOUS SIMULATION PROGRAMMING LANGUAGES

As noted in Section I, there are two basic types of simulation models: continuous (which use systems of differential equations), and discrete (which use changes at discrete time points), i.e., CSS and DSS models. There are less frequently encountered circumstances where both discrete and continuous features need to be incorporated in a simple model. All forms of simulations are, today, performed largely on modern digital computers, requiring programming in some computer programming language.

The programming of a CSS or a DSS can be done in a general-purpose computer programming language such as FORTRAN, C, etc. In fact, it has been said that more simulations are programmed in FORTRAN than any other single programming language. The advantages of programming a simulation in a general-purpose language (GPL) are that there is no need to learn a new language (if one already knows the specific language to be used), and no need to obtain new software for one's computer. The disadvantages include that one has to write routines which do well-known calculations that special simulation languages do (and do well), so one is "reinventing the wheel"; and, one may miss some of the (many) intricacies of the programming and end up with an invalid simulation.

One important caveat to bear in mind is: do not use a language that does not allow for randomness if one's real-world setting involves randomness. For example, suppose a queue with one server has service time 0.8 for all jobs, and interarrival times that average 1 (jobs do not arrive each time unit, but at random with some statistical distribution with mean 1). Then one should use a language which can allow for the randomness of job arrivals.

The above means one should not use what some have called "deterministic simulation," wherein all random quantities are replaced by their means (to simplify the model analysis). In the queueing example, one would have jobs arriving at times 1, 2, 3, 4, . . . if one replaced the interarrival times by their means. Then there would never be any queue built up (as service times are all 0.8). But this is not realistic for real-world systems where queues *do* build up. So, one should not use a language that cannot allow for randomness. While this should seem simple and clear, often systems of differential equations have random coefficients, and some suggest use of a CSS language. Such languages do not allow for randomness, so one may then be counseled to replace the random coefficients by their means, which as we have just seen is folly. In a complex system the folly will be harder to see (due to the complexity of the system), but no less real.

III. SIMULATION PROGRAMMING LANGUAGES WITH SIMPLE EXAMPLES IN CSMP, SIMSCRIPT II.5, GPSS, AND ARENA

In this section we illustrate the use of three special-purpose simulation languages and an interactive simulation environment. The first, Continuous System Modeling Program (CSMP), is appropriate for continuous systems; the second, SIMSCRIPT II.5, can be used for either continuous or discrete models; the third, General Purpose Simulation System (GPSS), is designed for simulations of discrete models; and the last, Arena, illustrates a modern interactive simulation environment.

A. A Continuous Modeling Environment—CSMP

Since the mathematical foundation for simulations of continuous systems is based on the simultaneous solution of differential equations, continuous simulation languages are designed to facilitate this process. If the system of differential equations can be solved through analytical means, then it is unnecessary to develop a simulation. Consequently, continuous simulation languages are designed to provide numerical solutions to differential equations, making them useful when analytic solutions are not available but also making them susceptible to errors due to limitations of computational precision. To show the rudiments of how a continuous simulation language functions, we choose a very simple problem, with a readily available analytic solution, and use a particular language (CSMP) to simulate the situation described by the problem.

Suppose that from a height of 1400 feet, an object is thrown vertically up with a velocity of 250 ft/sec and we wish to track the position (relative to ground level) of the object for 20 seconds. Mathematically, if we let $a(t)$, $v(t)$, and $p(t)$ be the acceleration, velocity, and position of the object at time t, respectively, then

$$a(t) = -32 \text{ ft/sec}^2, \quad \frac{dv}{dt} = a(t), \quad \frac{dp}{dt} = v(t). \quad (1)$$

Moreover, we have the boundary conditions $v(0) = 250$ ft/sec and $p(0) = 1400$ ft. The solution of $\frac{dv}{dt} = a(t)$ with condition $v(0) = 250$ gives $v(t) = -32t + 250$ and the solution of $\frac{dp}{dt} = v(t)$ with condition $p(0) = 1400$ gives $s(t) = -16t^2 + 250t + 1400$. A plot of $v(t)$ and $s(t)$ (see Fig. 1 where the parabolic curve

represents $p(t)$) gives us a detailed view of the velocity and position of the moving object at various times.

If the two differential equations in (1) had not been simple to solve, or if their solution was not available in closed form, we would resort to a simulation of the motion. A CSMP program that simulates this motion is given in Fig. 2.

The program of Fig. 2, because of its simplicity, is mostly self-explanatory. Statements that begin with "*" are comments and through the CONSTANT statement any number of constants can be specified; in the case of this program, the gravitational constant, G, the initial velocity, V0, and the initial position, P0 are defined in line 3 of Fig. 2. The next three statements form the core of the program that solves the differential equation given in Eq. (1). The INTGRL commands perform numerical integrations to obtain successive values of velocity and position at appropriate times. These times are

0, 0 + DELT, 0 + 2DELT, 0 + 3DELT, ···, FINTIM

where DELT and FINTIM are defined to be 0.01 and 20 on the subsequent TIMER statement. Following the establishment of initial values, these specifications lead to 2000 computational iterations at times

$$0.01, 0.02, \cdots, 20.$$

The PRINT statement causes the production of a three-column output consisting of time (always included), VEL, and POS. The value of 1 specified for PRDEL is the time increment that controls program output. In this case, excluding headers, there will be 21 output lines for times 0, 1, 2, . . ., 20. The TITLE statement places a heading on the program output.

The output associated with the program of Fig. 2 is given in Fig. 3. It is clear that this tabular output reflects the graphic description of the motion given in Fig. 1 (e.g., maximum height is attained near $t = 8$ and the object hits the ground at $t = 20$). An unusual

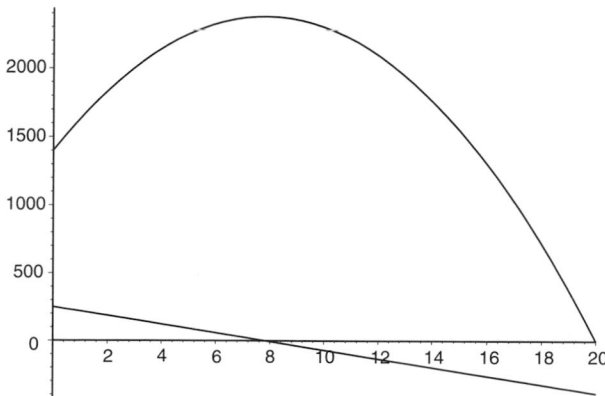

Figure 1 Velocity and position of moving object.

```
*        ACC = ACCELERATION,   VEL = VELOCITY,   POS = POSITION
*        V0 = INITIAL VELOCITY   P0 = INITIAL POSITION
         CONSTANT G = -32,   V0 = 250,   P0 = 1400
         ACC = G
         VEL = INTGRL(V0,ACC)
         POS = INTGRL(P0,VEL)
         PRINT VEL, POS
TITLE SIMULATION OF MOTION
         TIMER FINTIM = 20,   PRDEL = 1,   DELT=0.01
END
```

Figure 2 CSMP program to simulate motion.

SIMULATION OF MOTION

TIME	VEL	POS
0.000000E+00	2.500000E+02	1.400000E+03
1.000000E+00	2.180000E+02	1.634000E+03
2.000000E+00	1.860000E+02	1.836000E+03
3.000000E+00	1.540000E+02	2.006000E+03
4.000000E+00	1.220000E+02	2.144000E+03
5.000000E+00	9.000000E+01	2.250000E+03
6.000000E+00	5.800000E+01	2.324000E+03
7.000000E+00	2.600000E+01	2.366000E+03
8.000000E+00	-6.000000E+00	2.376000E+03
9.000000E+00	-3.800000E+01	2.354000E+03
1.000000E+01	-7.000000E+01	2.300000E+03
1.100000E+01	-1.020000E+02	2.214000E+03
1.200000E+01	-1.340000E+02	2.096000E+03
1.300000E+01	-1.660000E+02	1.946000E+03
1.400000E+01	-1.980000E+02	1.764000E+03
1.500000E+01	-2.300000E+02	1.550000E+03
1.600000E+01	-2.620000E+02	1.304000E+03
1.700000E+01	-2.940000E+02	1.026000E+03
1.800000E+01	-3.260000E+02	7.160000E+02
1.900000E+01	-3.580000E+02	3.740000E+02
2.000000E+01	-3.900000E+02	0.000000E+00

Figure 3 Output of program given in Fig. 2.

aspect of this output is that there are no errors due to the approximations that result from numerical integrations. Simulation of this model requires the integration of the constant function $a(t) = -32$ and the linear function $v(t) = -32t + 250$ and almost all numerical integration techniques (trapezoidal rule, Simpson's rule, Runge-Kutta, etc.) deal with linear functions without producing errors.

Obviously, as a programming language, CSMP and similar languages are far more powerful and flexible than this example shows. What they all have in common is the ability to solve simultaneous differential equations and in most cases the user is allowed considerable flexibility in choosing from a variety of numerical integration techniques and obtaining a variety of numeric and graphic output.

The simple example that we just considered does not give much of the details associated with the construction of CSMP models. For additional examples we refer the reader to Speckhart and Green and for a comprehensive discussion of CSMP we suggest the 1985 IBM publication. Among other languages for the simulation of continuous systems we mention ACSL (Advanced Continuous Simulation Language), DYNAMO (DYNAmic MOdeling), NDTRAN (Notre Dame TRANslator), and STELLA, and refer the reader to Chapter 9 of Aburdene.

B. A Discrete Model in a Mixed Simulation Environment—SIMSCRIPT II.5

There are languages that are well suited for the simulation of continuous, discrete, and mixed systems. One of the most commonly used such languages is SIMSCRIPT II.5 which, not only has features that facilitate the simulation of both continuous and discrete systems, but is also embedded within a full general-purpose programming language. A detailed exposition of SIMSCRIPT II.5 can be found in Russell's 1983 and 1993 work and the 1985 CACI manual.

We will illustrate the use of SIMSCRIPT II.5 in the simulation of a discrete model. The single-server queueing system is the simplest form of a discrete model. This situation arises when "customers" arrive at a "service station" that can serve no more than one customer at a time; the customers wait for their turn (if necessary) to obtain service and after service is rendered they leave the station and are removed from the model. Two basic properties determine the behavior of a single-server queue: customer arrival times (equivalently, interarrival times or times between successive arrivals) and the times required for customers to receive service.

Let's consider a single-server queueing system where interarrival times (in minutes) are $U(2,4)$ (are uniformly distributed on the interval [2,4]) and service times (also in minutes) are $U(0.5,4.5)$. The SIMSCRIPT II.5 simulation language has a number of features that facilitate the implementation of this model and a program for simulating it for 200 customers is given in Fig. 4.

SIMSCRIPT II.5 makes a distinction between processes (dynamic entities that cause actions) and resources (passive entities that are used by processes). It is clear that customers need to be modeled as processes, but less clear, perhaps, that the generation (initiating the arrival) of customers is also a process. The resource required in this model is the service provider.

The first segment of the program of Fig. 4, the PREAMBLE, establishes GENERATOR and CUSTOMER as processes and SERVER as a resource. Each resource has a queue attached to it and each queue has a queue size or length, in our case N.Q.SERVER, associated with it. Line 6 indicates that the program should keep a running average of N.Q.SERVER so that it will be available at the end of the simulation. Because of the ACCUMULATE directive, SIMSCRIPT II.5 will automatically keep a record of the time-weighted average of queue lengths.

```
1    ' ' A SINGLE-SERVER QUEUEING SYSTEM
2
3    PREAMBLE
4        PROCESSES INCLUDE GENERATOR AND CUSTOMER
5        RESOURCES INCLUDE SERVER
6        ACCUMULATE AV.Q.SIZE AS THE AVERAGE OF N.Q.SERVER
7    END

1    MAIN
2        CREATE EVERY SERVER(1)
3        LET U.SERVER(1) = 1
4        ACTIVATE A GENERATOR NOW
5        START SIMULATION
6        PRINT 2 LINES WITH AV.Q.SIZE(1) THUS
A SINGLE-SERVER QUEUEING MODEL
        THE AVERAGE QUEUE SIZE WAS **.***
8    END

1    PROCESS GENERATOR
2        FOR I = 1 TO 200,
3            DO
4                ACTIVATE A CUSTOMER NOW
5                WAIT UNIFORM.F(120,240,1) MINUTES
6            LOOP
7    END

1    PROCESS CUSTOMER
2        REQUEST 1 SERVER(1)
3        WORK UNIFORM.F(30,270,2) MINUTES
4        RELINQUISH 1 SERVER(1)
5    END
```

Figure 4 SIMSCRIPT II.5 program of a single-server queueing model.

Each process, since it involves action, needs to have its own program segment to describe its behavior. The third segment, PROCESS GENERATOR introduces a customer into the model (line 4), waits for a period of time with the waiting time sampled from $U(2,4)$ (line 5), and repeats this 200 times (lines 2 through 6). The use of minutes as the simulation time unit does not provide sufficient detail within the simulation since arrival and service times have to be in whole time units. Therefore, we choose to model time in seconds and sample from $U(120,240)$ rather than $U(2,4)$. The first two arguments to UNIFORM.F give the interval of the uniform distribution and the third argument specifies the random number generating stream that is to be used.

The fourth segment of the program, PROCESS CUSTOMER, describes the behavior of the customer who requests a server (line 2), "works" or occupies the server for a time sampled from $U(30,270)$ (line 3), and relinquishes the server and leaves the model (line 4). It is understood within SIMSCRIPT II.5 that if SERVER is busy, CUSTOMER is placed in a queue until SERVER becomes available. Moreover, since the preamble indicated that the server's queue size would be needed, the length of SERVER's queue is updated as needed. The "(1)" that follows SERVER on lines 2

and 4 indicates that servers of the first type are to be used—there is only one type of server in this case so this distinction is not an important one.

While the GENERATOR and CUSTOMER processes describe the logic of the model, the segment headed by MAIN, the second segment, puts things into action by establishing the presence of the SERVER resource (line 2); making sure that there is one unit (hence the U.) such resource (line 3); activating the GENERATOR process which in turn will (in time) produce 200 CUSTOMERS (line 4); and starting the simulation (line 5). At the start of the simulation the only active entity is the GENERATOR and all subsequent action flows from it. The PRINT statement (line 6), executed after the completion of the simulation, produces two lines of output in the manner described by the two template lines that follow. The output of the program (Fig. 5) is rather simple and self-explanatory.

C. A Discrete Model in a Discrete Simulation Environment—GPSS

A principal advantage of a language like SIMSCRIPT II.5 is its applicability to continuous, discrete, and mixed model simulations. If a simulation is clearly envisioned as a discrete model, as was the case with the single-server queue, then a language specifically designed for this purpose can make the modeling and programming even simpler. Languages designed for this purpose include SLAM (Simulation Language for Alternative Modeling), SIMULA, SIMAN (Simulation Modeling and ANalysis), and GPSS. See Aburdene or Banks, Carson and Nelson for a general discussion of these languages and the 1999 work of Karian and Dudewicz for a more detailed treatment of GPSS. More recently, new products such as Micro GPSS (a variant of GPSS) and Arena have been introduced to take advantage of the graphical interfaces available on many desktop computers. For a description of Arena see Kelton, Sadowski, and Sadowski.

To illustrate a discrete system modeling language we consider GPSS and apply it to the same single-server queue that was programmed in SIMSCRIPT II.5. We can see that the GPSS program of this model, given in Fig. 6, is even simpler than the SIMSCRIPT II.5 program considered earlier. In GPSS a programmer concentrates on the dynamic objects of the model called

A SINGLE-SERVER QUEUEING MODEL
THE AVERAGE QUEUE SIZE WAS 0.258

Figure 5 Output of the program of Fig. 4.

```
1                    SIMULATE
2          *
3          *         SIMULATION OF A SINGLE-SERVER QUEUE
4          *
5     1              GENERATE    180,60      Customers arrive
6     2              QUEUE       QLINE       Get in waiting line
7     3              SEIZE       SERVER      Obtain service
8     4              DEPART      QLINE       Exit the waiting line
9     5              ADVANCE     150,120     Service time
10    6              RELEASE     SERVER      Make server available for others
11    7              TERMINATE   1           Leave the simulation
12
13                   START       200         Start counter at 200
14                   END
```

Figure 6 GPSS program for the single-server queue.

transactions (the customers in our example) and describes, through a succession of commands (called blocks in GPSS), the behavior of the transactions. In GPSS lines beginning with "*" are comments and all lines as well as all blocks are numbered (by GPSS).

In the example under consideration, a customer arrives through the GENERATE block (block number 1 in Fig. 6). The 180 and 60 that follow indicate that interarrival times are to be uniform on the interval $[180 + 60, 180 - 60] = [120, 240]$. The third column or field in each block is a comment. Following the sequence of blocks, the customer gets in line (designated by QLINE) and attempts to obtain access to the server (the SEIZE block). The customer is either stuck (for some time) at this point or is able to gain access to SERVER, in which case it leaves the waiting line (the DEPART block). Conceptually, obtaining service is the same as advancing time while SERVER is busy. This is done through the ADVANCE block with time sampled from the uniform distribution on the interval $[150 - 120, 150 + 120] = [30, 270]$. Following receipt of service, the customer lets SERVER go (the RELEASE block), making it available for other customers, and leaves the simulation through the TERMINATE block.

The 1 of the TERMINATE block causes a counter that is initialized by the subsequent START statement to be decremented by 1. The SIMULATE (program line 1), START, and END statements (lines 13 and 14) do not describe transaction (customer) movements, they control the execution of the simulation. When the counter initialized by START is decremented to 0, the simulation stops.

Notice that the program in Fig. 6 has no output related statements. An implicit assumption in GPSS is that the modeler wants to have some basic informa-

tion about all the entities incorporated in the model. Consequently, such output is produced without any prompting. The output of the program of Fig. 6 is given in Fig. 7. First, the internal simulation clock, the time at the end of the simulation, is reported as 36370 units (36370 seconds or a little over 10 hours in our scale). Next, there is a listing of all the blocks with the number of transactions in these blocks at the end of the simulation and the number of transactions that "entered" these blocks during the simulation.

The block counts are followed by some reasonably detailed information about the waiting line, QLINE. We can see, for example, that on average customers waited for 47.610 seconds and if those who did not wait at all (the ZERO ENTRIES) are excluded, the remaining customers' average waiting time was 90.279 seconds. The average queue size, which was 0.258 in our SIMSCRIPT II.5 simulation of 200 jobs (see Fig. 5), is 0.263. This differs from the result of Section II.B due to a different random number generator being used.

Regarding SERVER, we can see that it was busy 83.3% of the time and the average service time per customer was 151.431 seconds.

D. A Discrete Model in an Interactive Environment—Arena

Although Arena is built on a platform of the SIMAN simulation language, it provides a much different modeling environment to the user. Models, simple as well as complex, can be developed through the proper on-screen arrangement of icons that represent the model objects and processes. Because of its friendly graphic interfaces, menus, and dialog boxes, Arena is

RELATIVE CLOCK 36370   ABSOLUTE CLOCK 36370

BLOCK	CURRENT	TOTAL	BLOCK	CURRENT	TOTAL
1	1	201			
2	0	201			
3	0	200			
4	0	200			
5	0	200			
6	0	200			
7	0	200			

QUEUE	MAXIMUM CONTENTS	AVERAGE CONTENTS	TOTAL ENTRIES	ZERO ENTRIES	PERCENT ZEROS
QLINE	3	0.263	201	95	47.3

	AVERAGE TIME/TRANS	$AVERAGE TIME/TRANS	TABLE NUMBER	CURRENT CONTENTS
QLINE	47.610	90.279		1

FACILITY	AVERAGE UTILIZATION	NUMBER ENTRIES	AVERAGE TIME/TRANS	SEIZING TRANS. NO.	PREEMPTING TRANS. NO.
STATION	0.833	200	151.431		

Figure 7 Output of the GPSS program given in Fig. 6.

easy to use. In most cases, model development consists of collecting appropriate constructs from a set of available templates, connecting them according to the logic of the model, and executing the model. The user is further assisted by the variety of output schemes (animated, graphic, or text) that are available. When necessary, the user can choose to import constructs made up of SIMAN components. In fact, it is possible to create one's own set of templates and use them whenever circumstances dictate a need.

For purposes of illustration, we again consider the simple queueing model of Sections III.B and III.C. Starting from a "blank" screen (see Fig. 8), the modeler clicks on or drags icons from those available in

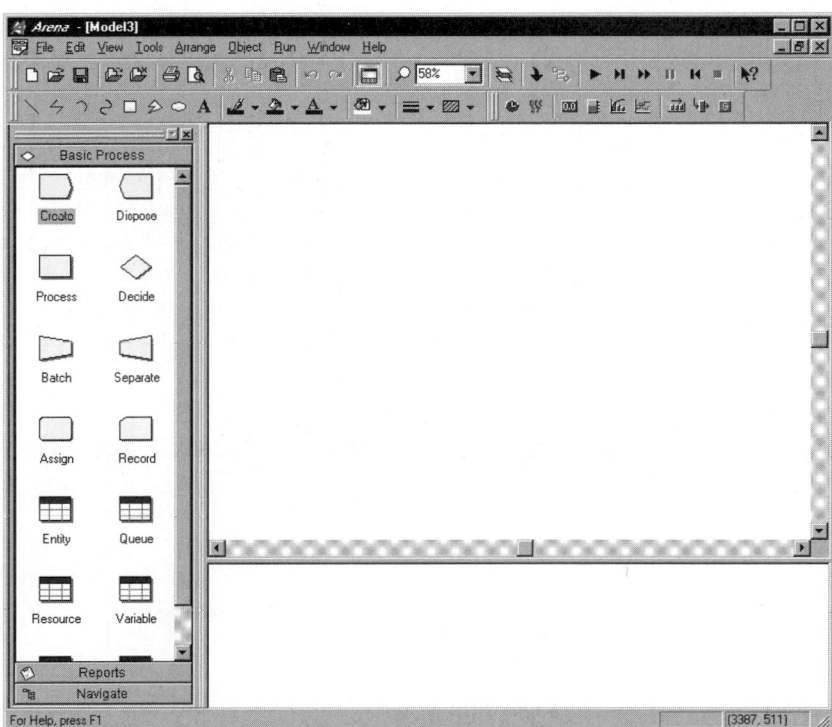

Figure 8 A "blank" arena window.

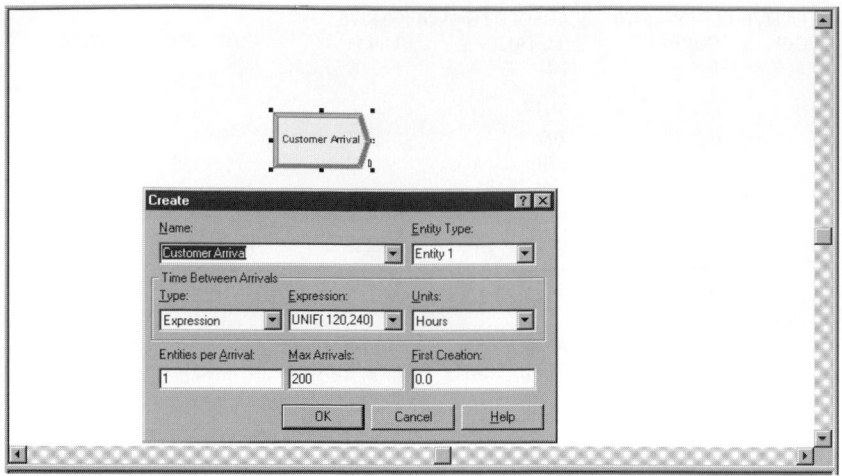

Figure 9 The Create icon and some of its specifications.

the left column to the working area (the large sub-window) of the screen. Thus, if we want to introduce customers into the simulation, we drag the Create icon to the working area and double click it to specify the arrival characteristics. Figure 9 shows the Create icon together with the window that establishes its characteristics.

When all relevant model components are brought to the working area, with their properties specified, the icons are connected in a manner that describes the flow of the model. The simple queueing model that we are considering is depicted in Fig. 10.

Arena provides several options for the output associated with a simulation run. The user can opt for animated output, graphic output, or a summary in the form of a text file. The model represented in Fig. 10 is the same as that of Figs. 4 and 6. The summary output of a single run, shown in Fig. 11, is mostly self-explanatory. The redundancies that one observes are due to the simplicity of the model where, by design, such items as the number of customers entering the

queue, or the service facility is 200 as is the number of customers who use the facility, leave the facility or leave the system. The Half Width column in the first two portions of the output is marked (Insuf) because Arena generally expects to summarize multiple runs of a simulation, and on the basis of these runs, it computes the half widths of the 95% confidence intervals for various statistics. Since Fig. 11 shows the results of a single run, (Insuf) simply indicates that there is insufficient information for the computation of half widths of 95% confidence intervals.

In the first portion of the output of Fig. 11, the first line gives results associated with service times; the second line gives the same statistics for waiting times; and the third gives information about total times (for waiting and service). In the second section of the output, the first line (Customer.WIP) gives information regarding the number of customers in the system; for example, the average of 1.2217 is the time-weighted average of the number of customers in the system and the Server.Utilization of 0.83885 indicates that

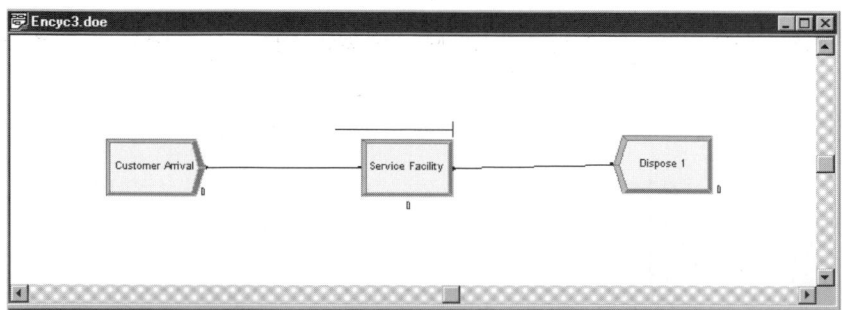

Figure 10 Depiction of the simple queueing system.

TALLY VARIABLES

Identifier	Average	Half Width	Minimum	Maximum	Observations
Service Facility.VATim	155.18	(Insuf)	30.743	269.46	200
Service Facility.WaitT	70.839	(Insuf)	.00000	485.65	200
Service Facility.Total	226.02	(Insuf)	33.678	724.43	200
Customer.VATime	155.18	(Insuf)	30.743	269.46	200
Customer.NVATime	.00000	(Insuf)	.00000	.00000	200
Customer.WaitTime	70.839	(Insuf)	.00000	485.65	200
Customer.TranTime	.00000	(Insuf)	.00000	.00000	200
Customer.OtherTime	.00000	(Insuf)	.00000	.00000	200
Customer.TotalTime	226.02	(Insuf)	33.678	724.43	200
Service Facility.Queue	70.839	(Insuf)	.00000	485.65	200

DISCRETE-CHANGE VARIABLES

Identifier	Average	Half Width	Minimum	Maximum	Final Value
Customer.WIP	1.2217	(Corr)	.00000	5.0000	.00000
Server.NumberBusy	.83885	(Insuf)	.00000	1.0000	.00000
Server.NumberScheduled	1.0000	(Insuf)	1.0000	1.0000	1.0000
Server.Utilization	.83885	(Insuf)	.00000	1.0000	.00000
Service Facility.Queue	.38292	(Insuf)	.00000	4.0000	.00000

OUTPUTS

Identifier	Value
Service Facility Number	200.00
Service Facility Accum W	14167.
Service Facility Accum V	31037.
Service Facility Number	200.00
Customer.NumberIn	200.00
Customer.NumberOut	200.00
Server.TimesUsed	200.00
Server.ScheduledUtiliza	.83885
System.NumberOut	200.00

```
Simulation run time: 0.20 minutes.
Simulation run complete.
```

Figure 11   Arena output for the simple queueing model.

the server was busy 83.885% of the time during the simulation. The third portion of the output gives some information that is accumulated through the simulation. For example, Service Facility Accum W and Service Facility Accum V give, respectively, the total amount of waiting time and service time accumulated by all customers during the simulation.

It is interesting to note the close agreement of the results shown in Figs. 7 and 11. For example, the average facility utilizations of 0.833 and 0.83885 and average service times of 151.43 and 155.18. This is due to the relatively low variability of the system, where (on average) customers arrive each 3 minutes and finish service in 2.5 minutes. On the other hand, the av-

erage queue sizes of 0.263 and 0.38292 show more variability and the need for multiple runs.

IV. AN EXAMPLE IN DATA MINING

In this section we use the topic area of data mining (see Dudewicz and Karian for more details) to show how to incorporate in GPSS such critical aspects as:

1. Use of a desired random number generator (rng) from the literature that has passed extensive statistical testing
2. A fitted distribution (such as the generalized

lambda distribution family) with generalized bootstrap methodology.

A. The Problem

An appliance repair business receives requests for repair service during an 8-hour business day and provides service by dispatching a repairman to the service site. The four repairmen, each equipped with a van that contains the necessary tools and spare parts, have an agreement that stipulates that if a repairman is available at any time during the day in which a service call is received, then that service will be rendered even if it requires working past the 8-hour work day.

From a review of business logs, the operator of the business determines that the interarrival times between service calls is exponential with a mean of 35 minutes and service times (for travel and repairs) are normally distributed with a mean of 175 min and a standard deviation of 40 minutes.

The expenses associated with running the business consist of a compensation of \$150 per day to each repairman (this includes salary and benefits, etc.), \$50 per day for the operation of each van (this includes amortization and repairs to the van), and \$300 in overhead expenses. Thus, the total expense incurred per day is $150 \times 4 + 50 \times 4 + 300 = \$1100$. The charges associated with a service call consist of an initial flat \$15 fee plus \$60 per hour for service time (including travel time).

The business operator is particularly interested in those circumstances where the daily cash flow is negative. Therefore, we are interested in determining the frequency of the days in which gross receipts fall below the \$1100 expenses of that day.

B. The Simulation

To get some insight into the situation described in Section IV.A, GPSS is used to simulate the operation of the repair service. We now give a brief overview of the GPSS program that models this business (given in Fig. 12). Minutes are used as the time units for the simulation.

The initial portion of the program (lines 1 through 20) establishes necessary conditions and definitions that will be needed in the simulation.

1. The RMULT statement of line 3 initializes the seeds of the first two random number generators that are embedded within GPSS (there are 8 such generators in GPSS).

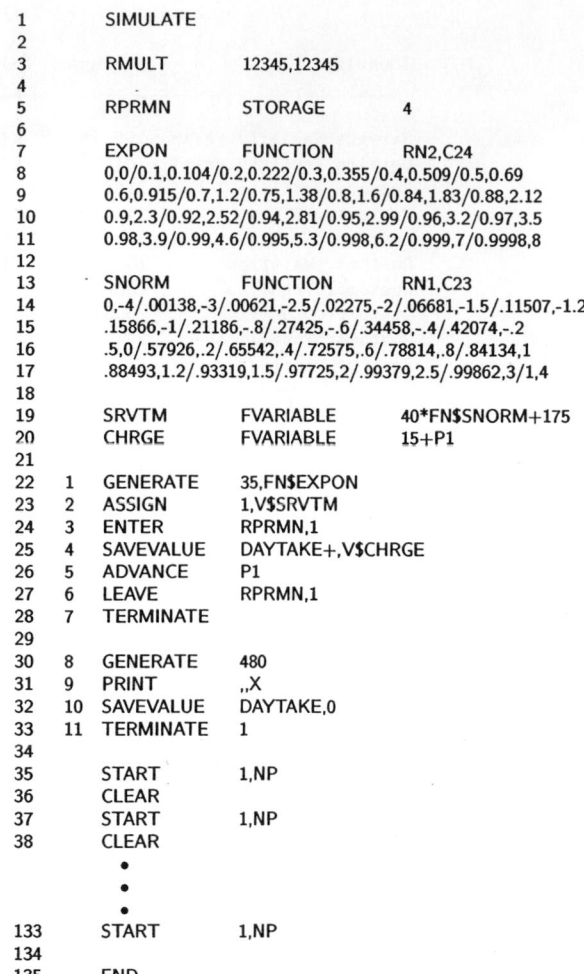

Figure 12 GPSS simulation of the repair service operation.

2. The RPRMN statement of line 5 establishes the fact that there are 4 repairmen "in storage" (i.e., available for the simulation).
3. Lines 7 through 11 define the inverse distribution function of the exponential random variable with parameter 1 (this is done through the sequence of 24 points, separated by "/", taken from the inverse distribution function of the exponential random variable); lines 13 through 17 do the same for the standard normal random variable. This is a cumbersome way of generating observations from a specified distribution and more recent implementations of GPSS have added features that simplify this process.
4. SRVTM (line 19), defined as a floating point variable, is the service time that will be required. The arithmetic operations given in this definition transform the standard normal into the random

variable specified by the problem. The charge assessed on a given service call is defined in line 20 as CHRGE and consists of $15 plus P1 which will contain the time required to render the service (recall that this charge is $60 per hour or $1 per minute).

The program of Fig. 12 has two executable segments: lines 22 through 28 and lines 30 through 33. The first of these contains the principal logical flow of the program. Following the arrival of calls at line 22, with interarrival times that are exponentially distributed with mean 35, the service time required by that call is computed and saved in P1 (line 23). Next, at line 24, a request is made for one repairman from the pool of 4 repairmen. If a repairman is assigned to the task, then that service will be performed and the storage location DAYTAKE is incremented by the charge that is applied to this specific call (line 25). Line 26, through the ADVANCE block models the passage of time associated with the service call in progress and upon completion of this service, the repairman is returned to the available pool (line 27). Now the transaction, having completed its progress through the model, leaves the simulation via the TERMINATE block.

The second executable segment of the program produces a "dummy" transaction to manage some aspects of the program. This transaction arrives into the simulation at time 480 (at the end of the 8-hour day), prints the contents of all saved data (DAYTAKE, representing the day's gross receipts, is the only item relevant in our case), and resets the value of DAYTAKE to zero (line 32). Having done its work, it decrements the termination counter of the simulation by 1 as it leaves the simulation. The subsequent START statement initializes the termination counter to 1 and through the NP designation suppresses the usual voluminous GPSS output. Since the termination counter has 1 for its initial value, the "dummy" transaction succeeds in shutting down the entire simulation.

So far we have the results of one day's simulation. Through the successive CLEAR and START statements, the simulation is cleared of all its internal values and rerun. It is important to note that when the internal conditions within the simulation are cleared the seeds of the random number generators are not reset, allowing us to obtain the results of another day's simulation that is independent of the previous day's results. Multiple repetitions of CLEAR and START can provide results for any number of days. In this case the CLEAR-START combination was repeated until 50 independent observations of the receipts for one day were obtained.

```
NON-ZERO FULLWORD SAVEVALUES: (NAME : VALUE)
DAYTAKE: 2166

NON-ZERO FULLWORD SAVEVALUES: (NAME : VALUE)
DAYTAKE: 2232
    •   •
    •   •
    •   •
NON-ZERO FULLWORD SAVEVALUES: (NAME : VALUE)
DAYTAKE: 2415

NON-ZERO FULLWORD SAVEVALUES: (NAME : VALUE)
DAYTAKE: 2330
```

Figure 13 Partial output of the program of Fig. 12.

The output of the program of Fig. 12 consists of a sequence of values of DAYTAKE, the gross receipts for one day. The results of the first and last two days are shown in Fig. 13.

C. The Analysis

We begin our analysis by first looking at the net receipts (gross receipts minus the $1100 expense per day) for the 50 simulated days; these are given in Table I. We would like to find a model, if possible, for this data.

A significant body of research and applications in many fields (e.g., see the work of Karian and Dudewicz in 2000 for references and details) has established the four-parameter generalized lambda distribution, designated by $GLD(\lambda_1,\lambda_2,\lambda_3,\lambda_4)$, as a family of distributions that can be fitted to data in a wide range of circumstances. We now briefly describe the $GLD(\lambda_1,\lambda_2,\lambda_3,\lambda_4)$ family and show a frequently used method of fitting a $GLD(\lambda_1,\lambda_2,\lambda_3,\lambda_4)$ applied to the data of Table I. The process consists of computing the mean and first four central moments of the data and finding a $GLD(\lambda_1,\lambda_2,\lambda_3,\lambda_4)$ that has approximately the same mean and first four centralized moments. These data moments $\hat{\alpha}_1$, $\hat{\alpha}_2$, $\hat{\alpha}_3$, $\hat{\alpha}_4$ (mean, variance, skewness, and kurtosis) can be obtained through

$$\hat{\alpha}_1 = \overline{X} = \sum_{i=1}^{n} X_i/n, \tag{2}$$

$$\hat{\alpha}_2 = \hat{\sigma}^2 = \sum_{i=1}^{n} (X_i - \overline{X})^2/n, \tag{3}$$

$$\hat{\alpha}_3 = \sum_{i=1}^{n} (X_i - \overline{X})^3/(n\hat{\sigma}^3), \tag{4}$$

$$\hat{\alpha}_4 = \sum_{i=1}^{n} (X_i - \overline{X})^4/(n\hat{\sigma}^4). \tag{5}$$

Table I Fifty-Day Results of the Simulation

1066	1132	967	791	865	286	842	1430	232	526
1082	1214	1050	1203	991	711	1142	852	650	1147
1363	967	1165	559	486	1334	675	903	1044	801
1125	857	1020	804	652	514	699	1259	35	701
408	702	634	715	575	969	652	841	1315	1230

The GLD family is most easily specified through its percentile, or inverse distribution, function by

$$Q(y) = \lambda_1 + \frac{y^{\lambda_3} - (1 - y)^{\lambda_4}}{\lambda_2}, \, 0 \le y \le 1. \quad (6)$$

A major advantage of using the percentile function is the simplicity it affords in generating random samples from the distribution. The actual moments, α_1, α_2, α_3, α_4 of the GLD of Eq. (6) are given by

$$\alpha_1 = \mu = \lambda_1 + A/\lambda_2, \quad (7)$$

$$\alpha_2 = \sigma^2 = (B - A^2)/\lambda_2^2, \quad (8)$$

$$\alpha_3 = (C - 3AB + 2A^3)/(\lambda_2^3 \sigma^3), \quad (9)$$

$$\alpha_4 = (D - 4AC + 6A^2B - 3A^4)/(\lambda_2^4 \sigma^4), \quad (10)$$

where

$$A = 1/(1 + \lambda_3) - 1/(1 + \lambda_4), \quad (11)$$

$$B = 1/(1 + 2\lambda_3) + 1/(1 + 2\lambda_4) \\ - 2\beta(1 + \lambda_3, 1 + \lambda_4), \quad (12)$$

$$C = 1/(1 + 3\lambda_3) - 1/(1 + 3\lambda_4) \\ - 3\beta(1 + 2\lambda_3, 1 + \lambda_4) \\ + 3\beta(1 + \lambda_3, 1 + 2\lambda_4), \quad (13)$$

$$D = 1/(1 + 4\lambda_3) + 1/(1 + 4\lambda_4) \\ - 4\beta(1 + 3\lambda_3, 1 + \lambda_4) \\ + 6\beta(1 + 2\lambda_3, 1 + 2\lambda_4) \\ - 4\beta(1 + \lambda_3, 1 + 3\lambda_4) \quad (14)$$

and $\beta(u,v)$ is the beta function given by

$$\beta(u,v) = \int_0^1 x^{u-1} (1 - x)^{v-1} \, dx \text{ for } u, \, v > 0.$$

To obtain a GLD$(\lambda_1,\lambda_2,\lambda_3,\lambda_4)$ fit, we need to solve the system of equations

$$\alpha_i = \hat{\alpha}_i, \text{ for } i = 1, 2, 3, 4. \quad (15)$$

Let us note that the A, B, C, and D defined in Eqs. (11)–(14) involve only λ_3 and λ_4 and are independent of λ_1 and λ_2. Consequently, the same is true for the α_3 and α_4 defined in Eqs. (9) and (10). Thus, solv-

ing the system of equations in (15) can be reduced to solving $\alpha_3 = \hat{\alpha}_3$ and $\alpha_4 = \hat{\alpha}_4$ for λ_3 and λ_4 and then, through appropriate substitutions, determining λ_2 and λ_1. Since it is impossible to find solutions to the simultaneous equations $\alpha_3 = \hat{\alpha}_3$ and $\alpha_4 = \hat{\alpha}_4$ analytically, numerical approximations must be employed. A comprehensive treatment of all these issues as well as detailed tables for solving $\alpha_3 = \hat{\alpha}_3$ and $\alpha_4 = \hat{\alpha}_4$ can be found in the work of Karian and Dudewicz in 2000.

For the data of Table I, through direct computation, we determine that

$$\hat{\alpha}_1 = 863.6600, \hat{\alpha}_2 = 93748.8647, \\ \hat{\alpha}_3 = -0.3621, \hat{\alpha}_4 = 2.7913. \quad (16)$$

The $\lambda_1,\lambda_2,\lambda_3,\lambda_4$ can now be determined by using the tables or, for greater accuracy, the programs provided in the work of Karian and Dudewicz in 2000. Using the latter, we obtain

$$\lambda_1 = 1039.9030, \lambda_2 = 0.0007521, \\ \lambda_3 = 0.2665, \lambda_4 = 0.084462. \quad (17)$$

A visual inspection of a histogram of the data of Table I with the fitted GLD(1039.9030, 0.00075212, 0.2665, 0.08446) indicates that we have a good fit (see Fig. 14). This is substantiated when the quantitative measure given by the χ^2 goodness-of-fit is computed by

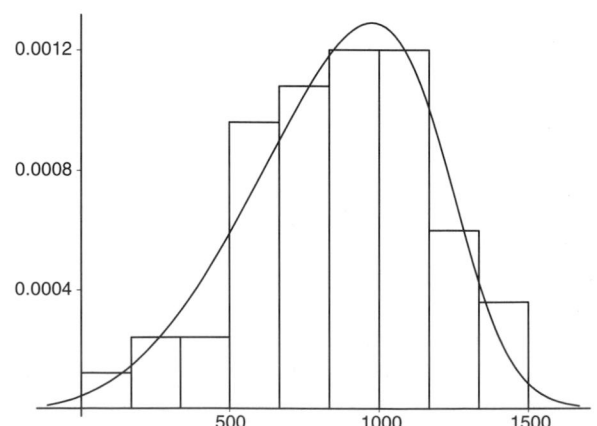

Figure 14 Histogram of the data of Table I with its fitted GLD.

Table II The χ^2 Goodness-of-Fit Statistic

Interval	Observed frequency	Expected frequency
$(-\infty, 490]$	5	6.2757
$(490, 660]$	8	6.1755
$(660, 785]$	6	6.2548
$(785, 890]$	8	6.2171
$(890, 990]$	4	6.3871
$(990, 1090]$	6	6.2686
$(1090, 1200$	5	5.8352
$(1200, \infty)$	8	6.5860

partitioning the data into the intervals indicated in Table II.

The χ^2 statistic, based on the chi-square distribution with three degrees of freedom, for the frequencies given in Table II is 2.6468 and the corresponding p-value is 0.4493.

Once a $GLD(\lambda_1, \lambda_2, \lambda_3, \lambda_4)$ model is established, we can easily sample from this distribution by generating random, pseudorandom actually, numbers $r_1, r_2, \ldots, r_n$ and substituting these for y in the GLD per-

centile function given in Eq. (6). The quality of the resulting sample will depend solely on the quality of the random number generator that is used. Of the many available generators we use the one labeled URN22 in the 1999 work of Karian and Dudewicz. This generator has been shown to do extremely well when subjected to a cluster of random number generator testing routines (see Chapter 3 of Karian and Dudewicz as above). The first 500 observations of a sample of size 25,000, generated by using URN22 and Eq. (6), are shown in Table III. Although the original data (Table I) produced by the simulation contained no negative values, we can see from Table III that the model suggests a number of negative cash flow days—we observe 5 in the first 500 days given in Table III.

From a sample of 500 observations, in which 5 show a negative cash flow, one would estimate the probability of a negative cash flow as $p_{500} = 5/500 = 0.01$. An approximate 95% confidence interval for the probability p of a negative cash flow would be (see Dudewicz, Chen, and Taneja, equation [8.4.5]) the interval

$$0.01 \pm (1.96)\sqrt{0.99} = 0.01 \pm 0.0087,$$

from which we would conclude with 95% confidence that p is between 0.0013 and 0.0187.

Table III The First 500 Observations of a Sample of Size 25000

1072	851	789	864	1131	587	886	933	301	1010
920	681	910	1012	692	712	1128	859	694	1290
899	1225	683	223	731	1186	941	1036	1049	824
1287	630	1722	659	460	959	1026	356	1159	639
981	850	456	598	328	496	530	1203	751	947
418	1002	1007	912	845	875	855	1200	−86	484
643	1163	910	804	1103	910	858	1205	332	707
949	1209	1018	769	588	928	1659	1089	835	858
1234	879	1021	286	860	908	349	1090	321	1251
1265	1104	1237	612	628	1023	1030	313	931	756
372	846	725	440	493	609	1267	1075	1347	956
811	133	403	1365	918	1163	814	726	874	108
1096	933	971	869	794	635	1162	714	1133	408
1136	1207	101	736	1022	477	1206	1145	639	923
621	828	1231	964	1273	684	899	948	470	944
442	233	527	769	494	847	316	720	1052	1009
994	781	1295	609	756	1346	735	1100	1037	1409
1180	450	1055	1139	695	777	1209	493	1056	1029

(continues)

Table III *(continued)*

796	588	784	590	1061	1194	787	670	1283	965
1082	596	396	502	1355	1288	1051	997	1501	869
685	884	716	1276	343	−73	880	978	1142	1093
929	827	598	735	1128	884	1215	970	182	1166
1072	1388	796	906	876	406	597	902	1247	1178
856	708	669	470	1253	1195	936	65	1390	1060
215	1190	1074	1308	1043	746	1251	914	1414	397
916	866	1153	374	995	725	965	823	651	671
1283	754	912	1217	593	974	1129	506	551	939
1104	568	648	989	681	649	589	1160	721	906
692	1130	570	1136	671	640	173	784	968	1145
−33	760	1283	413	362	898	933	1049	1208	731
903	504	831	969	962	1068	859	547	575	1015
987	693	1330	642	196	1178	1095	929	994	984
428	840	1033	1142	640	710	1437	296	1071	488
1191	758	1260	1281	343	1049	1001	729	1250	827
737	1226	925	654	473	1183	1281	1356	1057	1171
451	362	446	1292	1113	926	745	817	654	1397
270	956	672	903	758	1224	738	722	786	262
898	967	853	1169	1129	851	1121	450	936	1218
580	1021	983	1175	373	844	414	714	1235	462
1175	809	1061	1103	794	878	852	1036	828	765
599	128	855	475	949	308	549	930	1266	826
771	1038	1254	730	1235	596	1194	949	1048	1039
1109	719	1169	185	1274	766	748	677	937	1068
457	1211	1298	1185	648	688	1196	711	863	1130
792	629	961	1150	716	1145	623	864	1105	834
66	581	1378	518	738	527	1085	−110	123	639
1014	535	1028	274	1177	1012	1006	628	1027	969
951	360	1360	1250	710	410	835	1268	808	471
892	969	1042	475	1030	−44	847	1053	574	767
472	475	820	1175	1369	436	963	1481	1100	1364

From our total sample of 25,000 observations, one can pin down p more accurately. In these samples there were 80 negative cash flows, so p would be estimated by $p_{25000} = 80/25000 = 0.0032$. Note that this is in the interval obtained from the 500 observations, which extended from 0.0013 to 0.0187. Now we can conclude that with 95% confidence p is in the interval

$$0.0032 \pm 1.96 \sqrt{\frac{0.0032(1 - 0.0032)}{25000}}$$
$$= 0.032 \pm 0.0007,$$

i.e., between 0.0025 and 0.0039.

Note that if we had restricted ourselves to the original data, we would have been misled into thinking that negative cash flows would not occur at all (as there were none in the data of 50 days in Table I). To illustrate what would happen with the "real" simulated system upon continued simulation, we extended the GPSS simulation of Section IV.B to 250 days (see Table IV) and found 3 days in which there was a negative cash flow, giving us an estimate of p of $p_S = 0.0120$ and an interval on p between 0.0000 and 0.0255. This is consistent with a p between 0.0025 and 0.0039 as shown by the fitted GLD model.

Table IV 250-Day Results of the Simulation

1066	1132	967	791	865	286	842	1430	232	526
1082	1214	1050	1203	991	711	1142	852	650	1147
1363	967	1165	559	486	1334	675	903	1044	801
1125	857	1020	804	652	514	699	1259	35	701
408	702	634	715	575	969	652	841	1315	1230
710	1107	904	866	409	1044	750	1254	1130	1191
1040	−360	647	761	1003	874	1152	1146	875	1175
273	760	206	1171	1015	463	752	1266	940	345
593	897	343	1059	1144	910	791	1010	616	1644
967	1038	1039	960	1102	1396	573	1159	1097	1185
1172	1138	757	1120	1227	1114	573	1059	1186	1002
395	662	406	1177	1126	1530	722	1275	813	912
1207	1418	914	1045	1213	976	1235	1003	558	882
1112	1121	1128	1170	1053	661	1090	402	369	976
906	1250	881	381	1257	−85	976	1211	569	1399
1100	41	1204	917	1131	926	1080	1021	1138	1322
970	−4	1069	1140	917	1042	666	1259	758	302
1254	816	1052	646	980	231	878	1358	642	1418
1433	1054	1198	1155	600	1074	1238	1348	707	938
559	832	947	781	283	1078	1223	765	752	478
867	1009	891	803	1024	548	528	1065	1287	824
649	1269	757	701	1071	684	1412	1049	613	1213
1048	1226	938	999	1070	1141	988	789	720	987
1240	1308	1089	1004	1174	1122	1199	664	1429	1322
1336	840	1179	1010	953	78	1155	497	1337	619

SEE ALSO THE FOLLOWING ARTICLES

Continuous Simulation • Data Mining • Discrete Event Simulation • Monte Carlo Simulation • Software Process Simulation

BIBLIOGRAPHY

Aburdene, M. F. (1988). *Computer simulation of dynamic systems.* Dubuque, IA: William C. Brown Publishers.

Banks, J., Carson, J. S., II, and Nelson, B. L. (1996). *Discrete-event system simulation,* Second Edition. Upper Saddle River, NJ: Prentice-Hall.

CACI (1985). *PC SIMSCRIPT II.5: Introduction and user's manual.* Los Angeles, CA: CACI.

Dudewicz, E. J. (1996). Modern digital simulation methodology, II. *The american sciences press series in mathematical and management sciences,* Vol. 38. Columbus, OH: American Sciences Press.

Dudewicz, E. J. (1997). Modern digital simulation methodology, III. *The american sciences press series in mathematical and management sciences,* Vol. 39. Columbus, OH: American Sciences Press.

Dudewicz, E. J. (1999). Modern digital simulation methodology, IV. *The american sciences press series in mathematical and management sciences,* Vol. 40. Columbus, OH: American Sciences Press.

Dudewicz, E. J., Chen, P., and Taneja, B. K. (1989). *Modern elementary probability and statistics, with statistical programming in SAS, MINITAB, & BMPD* (Second Printing). Columbus, OH: American Sciences Press.

Dudewicz, E. J., and Karian, Z. A. (1999). The role of statistics in IS/IT: Practical gains from mined data. *Information Systems Frontiers,* Vol. 1, 259–266.

IBM (1985). *Application program: Continuous system modeling program,* GH20-0367-4. White Plains, NY: IBM Corporation.

Karian, Z. A., and Dudewicz, E. J. (1999). *Modern statistical, systems, and GPSS simulation,* Second Edition. Boca Raton, FL: CRC Press.

Karian, Z. A., and Dudewicz, E. J. (2000). *Fitting statistical distributions: The generalized lambda distribution and generalized bootstrap methods.* Boca Raton, FL: CRC Press.

Kelton, W. D., Sadowski, R. P., and Sadowski, D. A. (2002). *Simulation with Arena,* Second Edition. Boston, MA: McGraw-Hill.

Russell, E. C. (1983). *Building simulation models with SIMSCRIPT II.5.* Los Angeles, CA: CACI.

Russell, E. C. (1993). SIMSCRIPT II.5 and SIMGRAPHICS tutorial. *1993 Winter Simulation Conference Proceedings* (G. W. Evans, M. Mollaghasemi, E. C. Russell, W. E. Biles, eds.), 223–227. New York: Association for Computing Machinery.

Speckhart, H., and Green, W. H. (1976). *A guide to using CSMP,* Englewood Cliffs, NJ: Prentice-Hall.

Tadikamalla, P. R. (1984). Modern digital simulation methodology: Input, modeling, and output. *The american sciences press series in mathematical and management sciences,* Vol. 12. Columbus, OH: American Sciences Press.

Sociology

Kenneth Nyberg, Laura Hecht, and James Ross

California State University, Bakersfield

GLOSSARY

CATI operation (computer assisted telephone interviewing) Assists with data collection both in terms of sampling (either from lists or by random digit dialing and automated call back) and in conducting the interview. The questionnaire is read from a computer screen, and respondents' answers are entered as the interview progresses. Thus, data are entered as they are collected, decreasing both the time required to ready data for analysis and increasing data quality through automated data checking.

content analyses A method of social science research in which the content of communication (text, verbal, visual) is systematically recorded and analyzed to determine the intentional and implied patterns of meaning.

participant observations Also called "field observations" or "field study," a method of collecting social science data by directly observing the people under study, in their natural environment. The observations are recorded for subsequent analysis. The level of actual participation varies from discreet observation (ie in public places), to actually participating in activities, with the identity of the researcher fully disclosed.

population representation Social science attempts to know and understand a group (society, community, organization) by selecting and studying samples drawn from populations of interest. In order to generalize conclusions drawn from analyzing a sample back to the entire population from which the sample was drawn, the sample must be considered representative of that population. Random sampling techniques produce samples with the greatest likelihood of being representative of the population.

The nexus of **SOCIOLOGY AND COMPUTERS** is complex and interactive. The discipline has a long and storied history of examining the nature and impact of information technology, and yet increasingly relies on that very technology in both research and instructional missions, and for its own discourse.

This article examines each of these spheres: (1) information technology and sociological research, (2) information technology and the profession of sociology, and (3) the teaching of sociology via information technology. Each, of course, is worthy of extended treatment, and thus this article is merely an introduction to these areas of profound complexity. It is a broad stroke and should not be considered definitive.

I. INFORMATION TECHNOLOGY AND SOCIOLOGICAL RESEARCH

While some founders preceded, the discipline of sociology is predominantly a 20th century development. Most importantly, however, almost all of its major theoretical work was conceived prior to the introduction and diffusion of computing. As such, there is a primordial alienation between sociological theory and the heavily computerized practices of its current research programs. This is not inconsequential.

All research involves the collection and analysis of data, and computing has had a substantial affect on both of these elements in almost all sciences, including sociology. Sociology has often distinguished between different types of data collection and different types of data analysis, with the conspecific presumption that there are different types of data. Regardless of the conceptual merits of these distinctions, they are manifestly "real in their consequences," and thus will be treated here as such.

A. Data Collection and Information Technology

The two major types of sociological data are primary and secondary. Primary refers to the initial and original acquisition of data. Secondary refers to the acquisition and or assemblage of data collected previously, generally for another purpose. A new observation as in coding the violence content of newspapers or other media, observing children's actions on a playground or in a classroom, or a new survey are good examples of primary data; the grouping of previously recorded observations or the use of national data sets such as the census are examples of secondary data. Computing and information systems have revolutionized both primary and secondary research in sociology.

1. Primary Data Collection

The major kinds of primary data collections in sociology are surveys, observations, participant observations, and experiments.

a. SURVEYS

Computing and information technologies have had the most visible impact on surveys. While the use of technology in sociology dates back to the unit record devices of the 1940s and 1950s (worked on one card at a time; sorter/counters, accounting machines, and calculating punches), the wide diffusion of the telephone has enabled highly representative surveys without ever contacting respondents in "face-to-face" situations, and the increasingly ubiquitous presence of digital systems has substantially quickened the pace in which these can occur. Moreover, special software programs which link computers to telephones have made possible computer assisted telephone interviewing (CATI) that is highly standardized, therein reducing

interviewer effects and bias, and in which responses are immediately entered into the computer, thereby quickening data turnaround, as well as decreasing the incidence of errors associated with coding and entering data recorded on paper questionnaires. The near classic original text on these procedures is Don Dillman's Mail and Telephone Surveys from 1978, but the advance of computing and information systems in the last 20 years has necessitated a very substantial revision to address, among many other issues, the problems of answering machines, voicemails, and call blocks. Still, even this update cannot anticipate the increasing saturation of cellular telephones. Almost all surveys presume a "stationary" respondent, who is one "in place." Telephone surveys are no different, the presumption being that the number one is calling is a residence (or business), and that the person answering will be situated at their home or business. The cellular telephone invalidates this presumption, and the respondent's "place" may be their car, grocery store, or movie theater. In a time in which response rates have been steadily declining, the impact of this mobility is unknown, but the suspicion persists that this may affect the generalizability of sample data to the extent that members of particular demographic groups are less likely to respond than others. Certainly at risk is the undivided attention of the respondent; substantial issues of data reliability are in force when the respondent is being queried while driving in downtown commuter traffic, or deciding between lamb and salmon at the butchery. What technology gives, it also can take away. Regardless of these issues the cost of a CATI operation is relatively affordable and many universities have at least a small setup for applied research and research by students and faculty.

More traditional face-to-face surveying techniques, as well as mailed questionnaires, have also been impacted by computers and information systems. Computers have played important roles in formatting instruments, and the speed with which data can be entered has substantially increased the amount of information that can be requested. Prior to computing, longer instruments were impractical because of the laborious task of tabulating data. With computers, data entry (and necessary verification) is much, much quicker. Computer technology also makes it possible to enter and analyze longer open ended responses in greater detail. As a result, instrument length is now almost solely constrained by either the issues in question, or by the patience and forbearance of the respondent.

Of course, the combination of fast and inexpensive computers and Internet access has given rise to the Internet survey. Most frequently used in marketing research in which samples representative of the population at large are less important than samples representing targeted groups with disposable income, this survey method is nevertheless becoming more common in the social sciences. In some studies, population representation is not an issue, as in Heise's 2001 study of affective meanings in a variety of cultures which relies on surveying "cultural experts," in this case college students, rather than a cross section of a population. Other examples include studies of populations difficult to reach using standard random sampling techniques, such as Buxton's 2001 study of how bisexual men and their heterosexual wives maintain their marriages. Research is underway that examines the suitability of using Internet survey methodologies for collecting data generalizable to populations in the more traditional sense. The most notable of these is the Survey2000 project, an Internet survey focusing on questions of mobility, community, and cultural identity fielded by Witte *et al.* Over 80,000 respondents from 178 countries were surveyed via the National Geographic Society's home Web site. The authors compared the characteristics of U.S. respondents with those in other nationally representative surveys (General Social Survey 1996 and 1993) and Census Bureau statistics, and their results document what critics of Internet surveys have suspected: Internet users differ demographically from the general population. The findings show that the Internet sample is younger, better educated, and contains a higher percentage of males and a lower percentage of racial and ethnic minorities than occur in the population. It should be noted that the authors plan a second data collection effort, which will include both an Internet survey and a standard telephone survey using the same instrument. This effort will no doubt add much to our understanding more precisely problems of sampling bias in Internet surveys, as well as generate much discussion on the future promise of Internet-based data collection techniques in the social sciences.

b. Qualitative Research

Other forms of primary data collection include field observations, participant observations, and content analyses. Though different, these techniques are often grouped together under the rubric "qualitative research." In qualitative research, the focus on computing and information systems has been primarily concerned with issues of data analysis, which will be addressed shortly. Some researchers are beginning to make use of hand held computers for field notations, or cellular phones for linking multiple investigators

in real time, although analyses of these methodologies are not yet well examined in the sociological literature. Nor is there any discussion of the promise of what these two technologies offer when they become one device, perhaps further augmented with digital cameras and powerful directional microphones.

c. Laboratory Research

Experimental studies, though the least common in sociology, have had a much longer and more intimate connection with information technologies than other research methods. Likely, one of the first major integrations of information technology and sociological research is Richard Emerson's small groups laboratory at the University of Washington (circa 1975). Here, CRT terminals were linked to a mini-mainframe. Today, of course, similar labs are PC environments, much faster and more capable. These research environments involve a complex integration of audio and video feeds, real-time computer analysis, and very advanced programming assistance. In many situations, real interactions are recorded, mapped, and analyzed; in others, computer simulations provide both the context and actors.

One can imagine the rapidity and intensity of "events" in a six-person exchange scenario. The permutations of discourse, i.e., actor A speaks to B, B responds to A, but C and D interrupt and over speak to A, while E addresses C and F just sits glumly, looking derisively at everyone else . . . all in 15 seconds, are infinite and quick. Video and audio record these occurrences; but without computers, analysis is very laborious, if not impossible. Because the actors produce far more data than most tests require, the problem of editing is significant. Acute software programs, including those customized by the researcher, allow analysis of targeted data amid all the "noise" of interaction.

Much of this laboratory work revolves around issues of "power in social exchange networks," though other studies examine gender influences and styles of interaction, racial sensitivities, and social-sexual negotiation to name but a few. Indeed, almost any micro sociological issue can be "brought into" the lab, and in so doing, a clarity of behavior can be realized that real-life scenarios often will not permit. While the problem of "artificiality" is always present in such laboratory designs, the use of elaborate information systems—and the management that they require—provides a tantalizing counter to this weakness.

2. Secondary Data Collection

All of the above are examples of primary research methods. Computing and information systems have had a major impact on secondary data collection as well. The term "collection" is perhaps inappropriate for secondary data, simply because "secondary" requires that the data are already "collected." A better term is coordination, or organization, implying how data are assembled, grouped, and analyzed. As more and more information is collected on individuals, products, artifacts, and organizations, there is an ever-increasing overlap of context between two or more datasets, and very often, an actual linkage of discrete variables at a variety of levels of analysis, such as firms, cities, or even individuals. While there is considerable public and political concern over the increasing availability of data about individualsis, and the abuses that may prevail, there is also widespread agreement in the social scientific community that these many datasets offer a treasure trove of opportunities for important research.

Secondary analysis has existed since the early years of sociology, such as Durkheim's classic analysis, *Suicide,* first published in 1897, but it is only since the full development of computerized records that it has achieved a pronounced robustness. It remains the principle research methodology of economics and is an increasingly important source of data used in sociological research. Basically, secondary analysis involves either single data sets or multiple data sets. The classic single data set is the U.S. Census, though even here there are a multitude of large files. As more and more companies, agencies, and governments have computerized their records, there is an increasing trove of data available for secondary analysis. Some large data collection efforts were designed specifically for the purpose of providing reliable secondary data, collected from nationally representative samples, for use by the social scientific community. Examples include the national attitudinal surveys, the *General Social Survey,* an attitudinal survey conducted annually by the National Opinion Research which is affiliated with the University of Chicago; the National Election Studies, national surveys of the American electorate in presidential and midterm election years done by the Institute of Social Research at the University of Michigan; and the National Longitudinal Surveys conducted by the Center for Human Resource Research at The Ohio State University. Principal investigators of individual research projects have long made their data available for use by the research community, frequently by contributing their data to archives, and this donated data made available for other research purposes is therefore another important source of secondary data. Examples of such archives include the Inter-University Consortium for Political and Social Research at the University of Michigan (ICPSR:

http://www.icpsr.umich.edu), the Social Science Database Archive housed at California State University in Los Angeles (SSDBA: http://ssdba.calstatela.edu) and the Henry A. Murray Research Center at Radcliff College (http://www.radcliffe.edu/murray/), which archives both qualitative as well as quantitative data. By far the most comprehensive, the ICPSR is the closest we have to a national social science data archive in the United States. It is a consortium of member institutions, which include all the major universities in the United States and Canada and many universities throughout the world. The ICPSR data holdings serve a broad spectrum of disciplines including political science, sociology, history, economics, demographics, gerontology, public health, criminal justice, education, international relations, business, and education. Over 45,000 data files are included in the ICPSR including the General Social Survey, the American National Election Studies, U.S. Census data from 1790 to the present, the World Values Survey, Current Population Surveys, the Panel Study of Income Dynamics, U.S. election returns from 1788 to the present, the Monitoring the Future Surveys, the National Survey of Black Americans, National Crime Victimization surveys, the Household Survey on Drug Abuse, and the National Health Interview Surveys. The ICPSR also provides a variety of services to the research community and is a leader in training in quantitative analytic techniques through its Summer Training Program.

Having repositories for data is exceedingly important. Nearly as important is the ease of access to those data. Prior to the expansion of the Internet, identifying and accessing useful secondary data typically took a series of months, involving perusing printed catalogs, ordering data on magnetic tapes, and once the data arrived, going through a laborious process of extracting the data and downloading it to a local mainframe system. Now, those catalogs have been replaced by search engines and magnetic tapes with CDs or files downloaded from a Web site. Currently the direction is to download directly, cutting the data acquisition time to the limits of the connection speed, minutes or hours not days. This is exemplified by the new direct service of the ICPSR (http://www.icpsr.umich.edu/OR-PUBLIC/direct-access.html) and the similar download facility of the Social Science Data Base Access of the CSU (http://ssdba.calstatela.edu/).

B. Concatenation and Linking

The real power of computing and information systems for secondary analysis comes into play with multiple data sets. Here, there are two kinds: concatenation and linking. Concatenation is the simple process of adding more records to a data set, while linking adds more variables to the data set. If, for example, you had yearly attendance figures for seven schools, and then added similar records from three additional schools, you would have concatenated the data set. On the other hand, if you incorporated the attendance records of children from seven schools to juvenile arrest records in their respective counties, then you would have "linked" the two data sets.

Relational databases allow researchers to link records contained in different data files and are really only practical in a sophisticated information technology environment. Absent of computers, and solid software, the task is simply too cumbersome and expensive. There are two ways to link computerized records. The easiest, and most accurate, linkage occurs when there exists a single, common identifier, or "key," across two or more datasets which contain data on the same units (i.e., individuals, schools, counties, etc.). The most common example of an individual identifier is the social security numbers, although data made available to the research public use arbitrary identification numbers assigned to case records to protect the privacy of the respondents. A second way to link records, when unique identifiers are not available, is by finding patterns across several variables that increasingly affirm one individual, or unique record. Here, if we can identify the gender, race, age, and education of one individual in a data set and match them with a person of exactly the same characteristics in another data set known to contain data on the same individuals, there is a modest probability that they are the same individual. If we can also add their names to these identifiers, we increase the probability that they are the same individual.

Of course, this all sounds so simple. Yet, it is not. Among the many problems with data linking is incompatibility of hardware, operating systems, and software. Succinctly, if one type of computer is powered by an Intel processor, and another by Motorola, then the computers are hardware incompatible, and thus data from one machine cannot be read by the other. Hardware incompatibility is almost always associated with incompatibility of operating systems and firmware, as in the Macintosh operating system being incompatible with IBM. These are becoming less salient, however, as statistical, database, and spreadsheet software increasingly allows users to save files in a variety of standardized formats, easing their transfer across different systems. Increasingly, however, researchers confront "upward incompatibility," as cur-

rent generations software (and in some cases, hardware) no longer read or access data in older file formats of storage media. With regard to software, most programs will read at least a few versions back, but eventually, data which have been archived for a long time may not be easily accessible if stored in an obsolete format. Generally, this problem is solved by storing data in simple formats (i.e., text files). The problem with obsolescence of hardware on which files are stored is still more difficult to overcome—few computing systems, even at large universities, still maintain functional hardware capable of reading the magnetic tapes or the even older punch cards so prevalent not much more than one or two decades ago (this is of course the same issue as that record collectors have with 78, 45, and 33 LP records).

Despite the technical challenges, secondary analysis of multiple, and often linked record, databases affords the sociologist tremendous access to information that was largely unavailable 25 years ago. As computers and information systems expand, both to different organizations and groups within the U.S. and to additional countries, this data resource will take on even greater promise and utility. Given the problems of response rate with surveys, it is entirely likely that most sociological research will soon be grounded in the secondary analysis of large, linked databases, mimicking the "big science" so characteristic of physics and the marketing research of large business.

C. Data Analysis and Computing

The major advances in sociological data analysis have all depended on computers for capacity and speed, and software for ease of use. Today, most sociological research involves one or both of these innovations. Sociology often distinguishes between "quantitative" analysis and "qualitative" analysis, the former characterized by statistical applications and mathematical modeling, the latter by textual and contextual analysis not subject to statistical and mathematical treatments. Both, however, are increasingly informed by computers and software.

Statistics, used in quantitative analyses, is a basic tool of a modern social scientific enterprise traditionally requiring a high degree of mathematical training and a great deal of time in making computations. This substantially restricts the use of statistical techniques to a very few well-trained analysts working with quite small datasets. In the early 1960s, to compute and verify a simple Chi Square for a crosstabulation (a commonly used statistic for that time) took a knowledgeable individual at least 2 to 3 hours. Computers and statistical software programs completely changed this equation and a typical Chi Square for a table can be calculated almost instantaneously by modern computer applications. There are a number of statistical applications used by sociologists (SPSS, STATA, SAS, MINITAB, LIMDEP, etc.) but for historical reasons SPSS remains the major choice of sociological analysis, although SAS and STATA are also widely used.

Computers permit the storage of a great amount of information, and the means for organizing and analyzing this information. Complex statistical interpretations, such as event history analysis or qualitative analyses facilitated by software such as Nudist, are simply impossible absent of advanced computing. No innovation has so changed the power and prospect of sociology as has computing.

II. INFORMATION TECHNOLOGY AND THE PROFESSION OF SOCIOLOGY

While there are many studies of computer-based teaching and testing in sociology, and a solid empirical literature dating back to the 1970s, there is little empirical evidence on the use of information technology by sociologists qua sociologists. Sociology, as with all sciences, is fundamentally a collaborative endeavor, typically involving two or more principal scientists, distant consultants and colleagues, technical and support staff, and student research assistants. On some larger studies, upwards of 30 e-mails a day may be received on that project alone, with each requiring a reply. Correspondence, questions, data transfers, and budget issues that used to take weeks to traverse are now completed in minutes, and the construction of listserves and other "groups" has greatly expanded the network of colleagues. This collaborative effort is very similar for all sociologists with active research programs, and indeed, all such scientists.

A. Anecdotes, Not Data

The aforementioned observations are, at best, anecdotal and do not speak at all to the more mundane uses of technology by sociologists—routine communication. The American Sociological Association promotes some of this by providing the e-mail addresses of sociologists grouped by their areas of interest, e.g.

Research Methodology, Social Psychology, Theory, etc., but this is only for those who are members and join special interest groups. Also, for $60 members of the ASA can access archived American Sociological Review and other ASA publications online. Whether or not sociologists only marginally invested in their profession would enroll in these features, or the ASA itself, is an open question, and we have no empirical data on the extent of use by those who are enrolled. Still, the twin functions of speed and capacity that define all computer-based functions are offered in these realms as well.

The now ubiquitous e-mail offers promise for quickly expanding and accelerating communication within departments of sociology, though as with all organizations, there are latent functions at work here of some concern. Collegiality has often been preserved not by the presence of communication, but rather by its absence. Ill-formed opinions that used to languish for lack of a fast means of delivery are now routinely vented as they are prematurely conceived, perhaps with no more attention to writing well than thinking well. The close study of e-mail communication on the fragile bases of "working relationships" has not been studied, but the oft-repeated anecdotes—perhaps because they are anecdotes—bespeak confrontations and reputational injuries far more often than supportive endorsements in sociology, and elsewhere.

B. Home Computing

As elsewhere, sociologists have taken their professional technologies home, so that not simply the sheltered acts of scholarship are accomplished outside the office or lab, but the very business of the office and lab as well. Access to computing, data sets, statistical packages, and the like are not restricted to campuses any more. Small computers have very large capacities and powers, and the sociologist who wishes can access data, arrange it, and analyze it all from locations remote from the campus, the lab, or the firm and then communicate findings and questions quickly and easily to colleagues any place where they, too, have Internet access. As such, for sociology as a profession, "virtual" describes not just a classroom, but the office, lab, library, and university, itself. Several interesting questions can be fashioned out of this potential, superficially about how much "work" is done by sociologists in this virtual network, and more deeply regarding productivity and the quality born of such a virtual profession.

III. THE TEACHING OF SOCIOLOGY VIA INFORMATION TECHNOLOGY

Just as with most disciplines, sociology has entered an era of teaching enhanced by information technology. These enhancements range from use of technology in traditional classroom presentations and a modicum of student exercises and assignments that are facilitated by IT, to the complete integration of technology in the form of a "virtual classroom."

A. Technological Imperative

There is no evidence that either instructor or student dissatisfaction has driven the use of technology in the classroom. Rather, it appears that the existence of the technology has promoted its use—the classic "technological imperative" and, it should be noted, an evident hope on the part of higher education officials that this technology will provide discernible cost-savings.

After the use of presentation tools, the most common use of informational technology for teaching is e-mail. Typically, instructors give students their e-mail address and students can "mail" queries to the instructor regarding assignments, examinations, and term papers. In this way, an office-hour dialogue is created between the student and professor, even though it is discontinuous. At present, there appears no systematic large-scale study of this "virtual office hour," regarding its prevalence, effectiveness, or efficiency. Anecdotal evidence suggests it is ubiquitous, but not especially dense with activity. Some students engage professors in this way, occasionally with much correspondence, but most do not. Perhaps the next most common use of IT in the sociology classroom is the construction of course or instructor homepages in which syllabi, assignments, and other informational material is archived. Students can access these materials via the Internet at their leisure, provided their leisure is not too far from assignment due dates. Scanning technologies, which can input text, graphs, pictures, and even videos quickly, have greatly enhanced the kind of material that can be readily stored on these homepages. There is very little systematic evidence regarding these homepages of either a qualitative or a quantitative nature. Some are wondrously elaborate, most appear to be "under construction," and there is no information on the extent to which faculty access the homepages of colleagues—either at "distance" or their home institution, let alone the extent to which students visit the sites of distant faculty.

Newer applications of IT technology center on "active learning" assignments for students. In contrast to uses of technology that simply offer more sophisticated media for presentation and communication, technologically based active learning techniques show promise in facilitating learning experiences difficult to achieve without technological resources. Examples of these uses include individual assignments using technology to conduct empirical analyses, complex searches, and student created Web projects. Some teachers are beginning to design in-class projects where students create and solve problems using networked computers in the classroom. Thus, students actually participate in creating the content and sometimes the topic and structure of the classroom experience. This teaching technique is not yet ubiquitous, as it requires rather different teaching skills from the more typical lecture method, as well as skills in the use of technology, but it is likely that these practices will become more widespread in the future. To date, the relationship between teaching and technology has not been an active area of study by sociologists. Indeed, the entire arena of technology enhanced teaching at the collegiate level seems ripe for exploratory research.

B. Smart and Virtual Classrooms

The aforementioned technologies are somewhat different than the construction and use of "smart" and "virtual" classrooms. Smart classrooms are ordinary university classrooms augmented by informational technologies. Robert Wazienski in 1998 found that only 24% of sociology department chairs reported their students had access to computer technology in the classroom; there was no mention of frequency of use of this technology. This, of course, is different than the provision of computer-heavy lab facilities, where almost all sociology programs offer access to students. Rather, it reflects the integration of IT into "ordinary" classrooms typically using a lecture format. Technologies here may include networked computers (wireless portable labs is a current technology used in some classrooms) with Internet capability, projection technologies for "Power Point" and other types of media-enhanced presentations, access to digitized maps (GIS), and data (e.g., GSS attitude questions or NES party affiliation) and films allowing "searchable teaching"—e.g., when the instructor is discussing an issue such as global trade between Europe and Latin America, a student may ask about the Mideast and Australia, and data can be brought up immediately to examine that variant. With computer facilitated classes active learning and problem solving can done in groups using Web and library sources. The Social Science Research and Instructional Council of the CSU with Professor Ed Nelson of the Sociology Department at California State University, Fresno, and Dr. James Ross of California State University, Bakersfield, have considerable expertise in these matters and offer online documentation (http://www.csubak.edu/ssric/ and http://www.csub.edu/~jross/projects/infocomp/) and regular workshops throughout California for faculty interested in integrating IT into the classroom.

The virtual classroom is yet another development made possible by computing technology. It allows students to participate in learning, using networked computers, from a variety of locations, including a university campus, home, or even work. The virtual classroom (VC) differs substantially from the smart classroom (SC) and traditional classroom (TC), most notably because the virtual classroom is fully disembodied with its "location" being an electronic network, not a physical place. The major use of the VC has been in "distance education," providing opportunities for students to take collegiate classes when their location is far from university campuses, or just because physical attendance would be inconvenient. The VC is different from other distance education modalities, such as instructional television, or "classes by mail," though it shares with them the eschewment of "face-to-face" instruction. Typically, the virtual classroom makes extensive use of computer-mediated communication systems and linking software that creates an independent but course-paced learning environment for students. There is much data on this at the secondary school level, far less at the collegiate level. The best empirical study of the virtual classroom in sociology was by Hiltz and Meinke in 1989. They found only small and inconsistent learning and enjoyment differences in a comparative study of VC and TC sociology courses.

IV. CONCLUSION

Sociology is much impacted by information technologies, primarily in the scope and complexity of its research endeavors, but also in the manner of its teaching and the ways in which sociologists work. Still, for a science that has studied technology for so long and productively, we have not turned our research attention to the present, or inward to our use of technology in research and teaching. Information technology offers the promise for, and anecdotal evidence of, substantial change in the manner, speed, and complexity of human interaction—including that of sociologists in all their professional roles—and, yet, we have little research on this at this point.

With information technology, we are involved in "the present of things future," for capacity is a concept that defines us in the moment. New technologies will afford us different opportunities, just as they sweep away things upon which we have often relied. The very floating stations of communication which free sociologists from the rigid places of the lecturn, offices, libraries, and labs will also free our students and subjects—other men and women—such that we will not so readily find them by traditional survey techniques. As teachers, we were principally just that, and gave no concern to constructing, maintaining, or cleaning the classrooms in which we lectured and cajoled. In the virtual classroom, indeed in just the smart classroom, architecture, engineering, and custodial care become the instructor's responsibilities as well and the teaching process becomes very dynamic.

In all that defines the work of sociology, much applies to technology. Issues of stability and change, the evolution and actions of networks and groups, the differences of access and allocation, and the implications for human interaction and order are all at play with regard to information technology. This is also true of sociology itself. Do different information technologies impact—and promise to impact—different sociological activities (i.e., research, teaching, community involvement, etc.), and do differing types of sociologists engage these impacts correspondingly? And, if so, which social structures and forces mediate these differences?

SEE ALSO THE FOLLOWING ARTICLES

Library Applications • Psychology • Research

BIBLIOGRAPHY

Buxton, A. P. (2001). Writing our own script: How bisexual men and their heterosexual wives maintain their marriages after disclosure. *Journal of Bisexuality*, Vol. 1, 155–189.
Groves, R. (1990). Theories and Methods of Telephone Surveys. *Annual Review of Sociology*, Vol. 16, 221–240.
Heise, D. R. (2001). Project Magellan: Collecting cross-cultural affective meanings via the Internet. *Electronic Journal of Sociology*, Vol. 5, No. 3.
Hiltz, S., and Meinke, R. (1989). Teaching sociology in a virtual classroom. *Teaching Sociology*, Vol. 17, 431–446.
Joerges, B. (1990). *Images of technology in sociology: Computer as butterfly and bat.* New York: Society for the History of Technology.

Markovsky, B., Lovaglia, M., and Thye, S. (1997). Computer-aided research at the Iowa group processes center. *Social Science Computer Review,* Vol. 15, No. 1, 48–64.

Nyberg, K., and Sanchez, A. (1998). Seldom a discouraging word: The coming of E-mail and Internet to rural California, in *Annual Meeting of the American Sociological Association, San Francisco.*

Trent, R., and Furbee, P. (1987). Techniques of computerized record linkage in applied sociology. *Journal of Applied Sociology,* Vol. 4.

Witt, J. C., Amoroso, L. M., and Howard, P. E. N. (2000). Method and representation in Internet-based survey tools—Mobility, community, and cultural identity in survey 2000. *Social Science Computer Review,* Vol. 18, 179–195.

Software Piracy

A. Graham Peace
West Virginia University

GLOSSARY

Business Software Alliance (BSA) An industry trade group working to eliminate piracy worldwide.

copyright A legal mechanism whereby the creator of a work is permitted to control its dissemination and use.

softlifting The illegal copying of software, in violation of a copyright, for the purpose of individual benefit or entertainment.

Software and Information Industry Association (SIIA) An industry trade group working to eliminate piracy worldwide.

software piracy The illegal copying of software, in violation of a copyright, for the purpose of completing business tasks.

World Intellectual Property Organization (WIPO) A worldwide organization made up of member countries attempting to create unified intellectual property protection legislation.

SOFTWARE PIRACY is the illegal copying of computer software. Although several legislative and enforcement mechanisms were developed during the 1980s and 1990s, software industry estimates indicate that the practice of software piracy is still widespread and costs software manufacturers billions of dollars annually. While many industry groups promote the goal of eliminating piracy, the prevalence of personal computers and the Internet, and the ease with which software can be copied, make this a relatively simple crime to commit and a difficult action to detect. The fact that the crime may appear victimless to the perpetrator makes it easier to carry out than a typical transgression. Purely technical means of preventing illegal copying have gained limited success, at best, and have been shown to potentially reduce software company profits. Further complicating matters is the fact that laws and ethical norms differ across cultures. This article discusses the basic nature of piracy, including what constitutes piracy, the estimated damages, the legal issues involved, theories of why people pirate, industry responses, and possible future trends.

I. THE SOFTWARE INDUSTRY

During the 1980s and 1990s, the software industry became a major force in the world economy. According to a recent report by the Business Software Alliance, an industry trade organization, approximately 75% of the world's software is produced in the United States, where sales of software products and services topped $140 billion in 1998, a 17.8% increase over 1997. From 1993–1998, software sales increased at a rate of more than 15% per year. More than 800,000 people are employed directly in the U.S. software industry, earning an average income of over $68,000 per year. It is predicted that more than 1.2 million people will be employed by the software industry by 2008. The software industry also has an effect on other areas of business and society. Approximately 1.5 million people are indirectly employed, due to the industry, and more than $28 billion in tax revenues were collected in 1998 by various government agencies.

Internationally, the figures are similar. The software industry outside of the U.S. is expected to create revenues of more than $116 billion in 2001, while employing over 1,000,000 people and providing more than $20 billion in tax revenue. None of these figures takes into account the economic impact of the software on those using it. Software packages increase the productivity of business operations, allow for new and novel approaches to problem solving, and provide educational and entertainment opportunities to individuals. Clearly, the software industry is a major contributor to the U.S. and international economies and societies, and any threat, such as that posed by software piracy, is taken very seriously.

II. WHAT IS PIRACY?

All software is simply bits and bytes (0s and 1s) stored on some form of recordable media (e.g., CD-ROM, floppy disk, magnetic tape). An individual or a software manufacturer creates the bits and bytes through some form of programming. Under most copyright laws, the software producer owns the rights to that code and has the right to distribute it as he or she sees fit. In most cases, the software is sold in individual packages or via site licenses that allow the purchaser to use the software on a specified number of machines at any one time. In some cases, the software is rented. When the purchaser or renter acquires the package, a license agreement is included that explicitly states the rights granted to the user by the copyright holder. If a person copies a copyrighted software package from one medium to another, without the permission of the copyright holder, then an act of software piracy has been committed. This could be an intentional action to steal the software, or an unintentional act committed through accident or ignorance. In either case, software piracy has taken place.

With today's technology, it is a simple task to make an exact duplicate of any software package, at relatively little cost. CD recorders give every home PC user the ability to make perfect copies of CD-ROMs, and the Internet contains many sites from which software can be freely downloaded to a computer. The act of copying in no way degrades or uses up the original resource, and an infinite number of perfect copies can be created from a single source.

Although this article classifies all illegal software copying as software piracy, in most of the academic lit-

erature on the topic, illegal software copying is broken down into two categories: software piracy and softlifting. Both are illegal and do damage to the software manufacturer, but each has its own unique aspects.

A. Software Piracy

Software piracy refers to the illegal copying of software for the purposes of completing business tasks. For example, illegally using a single CD-ROM of the Microsoft Office Suite to install the software on more than the allowed number of PCs in a business office would be considered an act of software piracy. This may take place as an intentional act designed to reduce expenses and increase profits, or could be an unintentional act created by poor record keeping of software licenses.

B. Softlifting

Softlifting refers to the illegal copying of software for personal purposes. An individual downloading a copyrighted video game from the Internet for use on a home PC, in violation of the manufacturer's purchase contract, is an example. In some cases, the pirate may not realize the severity of her actions, because she may not be aware that a software package so easily obtainable on the Internet is, in fact, a copyrighted program. As more and more individuals gain access to the Web, the probability that softlifting is committed unintentionally due to ignorance is increased.

III. METHODS OF COMMITTING PIRACY

Software piracy can take many forms, the most obvious of which is the simple copying of software from a CD-ROM or floppy disk. In most cases, this is a deliberate act designed to deny the software manufacturer payment for the use of the package. As described above, this could also be unintentional. In either case, the individual and, if applicable, the organization for which he works, can be held liable for criminal and civil penalties.

A similar form of piracy can occur when an individual sells a computer with software loaded on it but keeps the original disks and loads the software onto a new PC. The purchaser of the PC may not realize that she does not own the license agreement to the preloaded software. This can also occur when a dealer loads software onto a PC and sells it without the proper licenses in place.

Counterfeit software is another form of piracy in which the purchaser may not be aware of the illegality of the situation. This is more prevalent in Asia, and involves the fraudulent creation of a copy of a legitimate software package. With today's scanning and printing technologies, the illegal copy can appear almost identical to the original product, complete with manuals.

Most software companies sell their products to educational institutions and students at a discount. This can lead to a type of piracy, when an organization or individual purchases a discounted package and then uses the software for nonacademic purposes. In each of these cases, the key fact is that the software is copied against the wishes of the software copyright owner and, therefore, piracy is committed.

A. Internet Piracy

The Internet has given rise to a new distribution mechanism for software pirates, and has created a serious threat to copyright legislation. The increased bandwidth, increased number of users, and anonymity of Internet traffic has created an opportunity for piracy to flourish. Pirates can now easily distribute illegal software copies, advertise products, transmit technologies for breaking anticopy software, and share tactics and strategies with other pirates. Several specific Internet technologies have led to increased piracy, including bulletin boards, e-mail, newsgroups, and auction sites. Those individuals who are using the Internet to commit software piracy for profit are subject to all of the same laws as non-Internet-related pirates. However, as discussed in Section V, a loophole existed in which pirates distributing software for purposes other than profit may not have been subject to prosecution. The No Electronic Theft Act now makes it possible to prosecute anyone distributing pirated software, regardless of the motive.

Note that the Internet has also led to the pirating of other intellectual property, such as movies and music. The International Intellectual Property Alliance (IIPA) estimates that billions of dollars of non-software-related intellectual property are also now pirated on an annual basis, in large part through the Internet.

IV. WHO COMMITS PIRACY?

Software piracy is committed by a surprising cross section of society. Studies of U.S. businesspeople indicate that 50% of managers have copied software illegally. Information technology students and professionals have been shown to be more tolerant of software piracy, but this may be due to the fact that they are more familiar with the technologies involved. Approximately half of the college student population also admits to copying software illegally. These percentages have been decreasing in recent years, but are still significant. Note also that many of these individuals may have never had the chance to pirate software. Therefore, the actual number of people who would commit the act, if given the opportunity to do so, may be higher than the statistics report. The Internet provides an easy-to-use, readily available mechanism for piracy to take place, thus giving many more individuals the opportunity to pirate easily.

Differences are seen in cross-cultural, age, and gender comparisons. Older individuals are less likely to have pirated software than younger people, but this may be simply due to the fact that older individuals are less likely to understand and use the technology. Women are less likely to allow their software to be copied than their male counterparts, and females have been found to commit less software piracy. There is little research into the cause of this difference between the genders. When looked at globally, striking differences exist between the Western World and Asia. Software piracy is much more accepted in Asia, most likely due to the cultural traditions of that part of the world. This is discussed further in Section V. Also, piracy is more prevalent in those countries with lower per capita GNPs and smaller domestic software industries. Finally, individuals who know of people who have been caught committing piracy have also been found to be less likely to pirate than the general population.

V. LEGAL ISSUES

As stated in Section I, approximately 75% of the world's software is manufactured in the United States. Consequently, the U.S. government has been at the forefront of antipiracy legislation. Initial efforts focused on domestic copyright protection, but the global nature of business and the spread of piracy throughout the world have led to an extensive effort to create internationally enforceable copyright laws. The following subsections discuss the state of software piracy legislation as of 2001.

A. U.S. Legislation

The United States, throughout history, has defended the rights of authors and inventors to protect and profit from their creative works. Since 1964, software has been considered a form of literary expression and, therefore, copyrightable under U.S. law. A copyright gives the creator the right to govern how the software is used. Title 17, Section 106, of the United States Code makes it illegal to copy a software package without the express consent of the copyright holder, although it is legal to make a backup copy of the software for archival purposes. In 1980, the law was amended to specifically include software. An individual or organization found to be in violation of the law can be subjected to two forms of punishment. The violated party has the right to recover damages incurred by the copyright infringement (for example, lost sales), up to $150,000 per work. The software copyright owner can also demand that all illegal copies of the package in question be destroyed. In addition to these civil actions, the government can pursue criminal prosecution. Penalties currently can include fines of up to $250,000 and jail terms of up to 5 years.

In 1997, President Clinton signed into law the No Electronic Theft (NET) Act, making it much easier to prosecute pirates who use the Internet. This law amended Section 506 of the Copyright Act and removed a possible loophole, known as the "LaMacchia loophole," in the then-current legislation. Under that law, pirates who distributed software via the Internet for no financial gain, or possibly in exchange for other pirated software, may not have been prosecutable. The NET Act clearly removes any uncertainty and provides law enforcement agencies with the necessary legislation to prosecute anyone using the Internet to distribute over $2500 of pirated software, even if there is no financial gain on the part of the distributor.

The Digital Millenium Copyright Act (DMCA), signed into law by President Clinton in 1998, implemented two international treaties in U.S. law, the WIPO Copyright Treaty and the WIPO Performances and Phonograms Treaty. These regulations ensure that software created outside of the U.S. is given equal protection under U.S. law as software created domestically. These treaties are discussed in more detail below.

Although one might assume that piracy is an individual act and that only individuals are punished, organizations are surprisingly vulnerable. Under Sections 504 and 506 of the Copyright Act of 1976, a company may be held liable for the actions of its employees (within the scope of their employment), even if management had no knowledge of the action. Therefore, ignorance of the employees' actions may not be used as a defense by the organization involved. Because Congress, in 1980, amended the 1976 act to make it explicit that computer software programs could be copyrighted under the statute, there is a

great deal of exposure. Organizations must be aware of the actions of the computer-using professionals they employ.

On the international front, the Omnibus Trade and Competitiveness Act of 1988 gives the United States the power to impose trade sanctions on countries that do not enforce copyright laws and intellectual property rights. Because approximately 75% of the world's software is produced in the United States, this is an increasing area of emphasis in U.S. trade negotiations. Although piracy levels in the United States are declining, a majority of the software in most Asian countries, the Middle East, and Eastern Europe is pirated, costing U.S. software manufacturers billions of dollars in potential profits.

B. Legislation in Other Countries

Many other countries have established antipiracy legislation of varying degrees. In Canada, as in the United States, software is automatically protected by federal copyright laws from the date of its creation. The Canadian Copyright Act gives the holder of the copyright the exclusive right to reproduce the software as she sees fit. An individual or organization is prevented from copying the software without the express consent of the copyright owner. Violators may be subject to up to 5 years in prison and a $(Cdn)1,000,000 fine, even if they did not realize that the copyright infringement was a crime. The violated copyright holder may also sue for damages. Several prosecutions have been carried out under this legislation.

The majority of European Union (EU) countries have adopted the EU Computer Programs Directive (CPD), which grants copyright protection to intellectual property creators. While member nations have varying civil and criminal laws in place, the basic protection is similar to that found in the United States. For example, in the United Kingdom, software is classified as a literary work and is covered by the 1988 Copyright, Designs and Patents Act. Penalties for piracy can include a prison sentence of up to 10 years and an unlimited fine. Since the general adoption of the CPD, piracy in Western Europe has decreased by almost 50%.

Most other countries have some form of legislation in place. For example, in Australia, a pirate is subject to a $(Aus)500 fine for each unauthorized copy, up to a maximum of $(Aus)50,000. Companies are subject to more severe penalties. Interestingly, individual countries have been found to develop and enforce intellectual property legislation in accordance with the development of their domestic software industry. The more developed the domestic software industry, the more likely it is that the country has created and enforces software piracy legislation. As discussed in the following section, continuing efforts by international groups such as the World Trade Organization are helping to establish laws around the globe that are consistent in both scope and enforcement.

C. International Legislation

In 1996, the World Intellectual Property Organization (WIPO), made up of representatives of 171 countries, developed two treaties: the WIPO Copyright Treaty and the WIPO Performances and Phonograms Treaty. These treaties require member countries of the WIPO to provide protection to intellectual properties created by other member countries that is no less stringent than protection granted to domestically created intellectual property. Specifically, member states are obligated to prevent the circumvention of technical antipiracy mechanisms built into software, the unauthorized access to copyrighted materials, the unauthorized duplication of copyrighted materials, and acts that are not authorized by the copyright holders of the software in question. There are some minor exceptions in the law. For example, government agencies are allowed to violate copyrights in cases of national defense, and reverse engineering is allowed, to ensure that a software package is interoperable with another software package.

The World Trade Organization (WTO) has also been active in the intellectual property rights area. In 1995, the WTO negotiated the Agreement on the Trade-Related Aspects of Intellectual Property Rights (TRIPS), which included provisions protecting copyrights and specifically included software as intellectual property. As with the WIPO Copyright Treaty, the TRIPS agreement requires member nations to extend to non-nationals the same copyright protection granted to nationals. In 1996, the WTO and WIPO agreed to cooperate in their future initiatives. The anticipated membership of China in the WTO will require adherence to the TRIPS agreement and should be a major weapon in combating piracy in that country, where piracy rates exceed 90%.

VI. ETHICAL ISSUES

Software piracy involves several ethical aspects. The nature of software is that it is replicable with virtually no cost, thus making the definition of property difficult to assign. It is also separate from the medium on which it is stored. However, there are clear ethical implications to copying intellectual property against the wishes of the creator.

A. Ethical Theories

In very simplistic terms, ethical theories can be broken down into two main categories: deontological and utilitarian. The deontological approach focuses on the action itself as being either ethically "right" or "wrong." For example, killing someone is always wrong, stealing is always wrong, etc. Acts are governed by universal laws that distinguish between ethical and unethical. Utilitarianism focuses on the consequences of the act. Killing is wrong if an innocent civilian is murdered for no good reason, but killing an ax-wielding maniac about to attack your family may not necessarily be wrong, since the act saves the lives of innocent people. What is important in utilitarianism is that the greatest good is achieved for the greatest number of people. Each of these theoretical perspectives can be used to study the act of illegally copying software.

In the deontological view, the act of piracy can reasonably be deemed to be unethical. No one is forced to use a particular software package. A contract is voluntarily entered into, in which the purchaser agrees to pay a certain price to the software manufacturer for the right to use the software in accordance with the rules contained in the license agreement. Software piracy involves the breaking of this contract; a clearly unethical act, in the eyes of most deontologists. If the contract contained some wording deemed unethical, then it may be possible to justify the breaking of the contract, but this is not the case in the vast majority of software purchases. Therefore, from a deontological perspective, software piracy is, most likely, unethical.

The utilitarian perspective is not as clear-cut. In this view, the consequences of the action are what are important. If an action causes greater total benefit than harm, then it is ethically correct. In the case of piracy, it is difficult to measure the damage done. Because no resources are consumed when software is copied, there is no direct harm to the original owner of the software. However, the software manufacturer is losing a potential sale when software is used illegally by a consumer. If a purchase would have occurred in lieu of the piracy, then revenue is being denied to the manufacturer. As discussed in Section VII, losses are seen in tax revenue, employment, and development of more advanced products. The benefit of piracy is also difficult to measure. The user of the software clearly benefits. If the piracy allows for more efficient business operations, then the employees and stakeholders of the company may also be benefactors. This may even lead to a benefit to the society, if the piracy is widespread. If the illegal act is identified, damage will be done to the pirate, including potential fines and jail terms. Damage will also be done to the organization's reputation. These potential benefits and damages are very hard to quantify and measure, making it very difficult to come up with a definitive answer as to whether or not piracy is ethical, from the utilitarian viewpoint.

B. Cross-Cultural Ethical Issues

The ethical discussion becomes more confusing when the issue of cross-cultural ethical norms is considered. Different social groups develop different sets of social and ethical mores. For example, bribery is considered an unethical act in many Western nations, but is a common part of business in other areas of the world. Does that make bribery unethical? It depends on the standards being applied. It is important to consider the different ethical norms of the world's varying cultures when piracy is discussed.

A dichotomy exists between the norms of the Western World toward intellectual property and the norms of the East, particularly Asia. In the West, creativeness is valued greatly, and expressions of ideas are patentable and copyrightable. The individual is the focus—people are trained to do what is in their best interests, within certain confines of morality and law. In Asia, however, the focus is very much on the benefit of the society, as a whole. Individual focus is downplayed. In a country where the local software manufacturing industry is relatively small, society clearly benefits when pirating is undertaken. Businesses benefit from the use of the software, and the low number of local manufacturers leads to little economic suffering. In this scenario, a utilitarian focus can easily determine that software piracy is an ethical act and is clearly in keeping with the norms of the society.

Consequently, great care must be taken when Asian countries are accused of behaving unethically in the area of intellectual property. By Western standards, this may be the case, but when judged by local ethical norms, the actions may be justified. As the software industry, and the world in general, moves toward a global business environment, this conflict in cultural norms may lead to difficulties in solving the software piracy problem.

VII. DAMAGES OF PIRACY

When a piece of software is illegally copied, the software manufacturer is denied a potential sale, thus leading to economic damages. The Business Software Alliance (BSA) estimates that more than $12 billion dollars of software were pirated in 1999, the latest year for which figures are available. Worldwide, more than 36% of all software in use was illegally copied. This represents a consistent yearly decrease in the percentage of pirated software, but with an increasing number of software packages on the market, the dollar costs remain significant. This has a far-ranging impact on society. Software companies are being denied revenue streams that would be used to develop more advanced products and pay employees. Also, sources of government revenue, such as sales taxes, are left uncollected. While pirates may view the act as being victimless, this is not the case.

A. United States

In the United States, the total dollar loss for 1999 has been estimated to be $3.2 billion, due to a piracy rate of 25% (the percentage of pirated software in use). This represents a steady decrease in the rate of piracy, although the dollar loss remains consistently high, and actually increased from a level of $2.9 billion in 1998. In 1999, North America represented 25% of total worldwide losses, with the United States yielding the highest total dollar loss of all countries in that year's survey. Piracy is estimated to have cost over 100,000 software industry jobs, and could cost almost double that amount in the next decade. More than $8 billion dollars of employee wages may be lost by 2005, along with $1.5 billion worth of tax revenue, thus impacting society as a whole. Software piracy also cost U.S. businesses more than $4.5 million in fines and legal fees in 1998.

B. Europe

In Western Europe, piracy rates are also dropping, although dollar figures remain high, as more and more software is used. In its most recent analysis, the BSA found that the piracy rate in Western Europe had dropped to 34% in 1999, from a high of 78% in 1990. This resulted in a loss of approximately $3.6 billion in the software industry alone, a $900 million increase from 1998, and $23 billion in legitimate economic activity overall. EU members may lose as much as $9.5 billion in annual tax revenues, due to piracy, and over

200,000 jobs. Germany incurred the largest losses ($652 million), although Greece was found to have the highest piracy rate, at 71%.

The geographic area with the highest rate of piracy in the world in 1999 was found to be Eastern Europe, at 70%. Russia and the former countries of the Soviet Union each exhibited levels around the 90% mark. The low level of software use led to only $505 million in damages. However, as the westernization of the area increases, so does the use of software, indicating that this may be a serious problem area in coming years. Software usage has increased more than 88% from 1994.

C. Asia

One of the most problematic areas is Asia, which accounted for $2.7 billion dollars in losses in 1999, down from $3.9 billion in 1997. While the piracy rate declined from 68% in 1994 to approximately 47% in 1999, countries such as China and Vietnam consistently report piracy rates over 90%. In 1999, China alone accounted for $645 million in losses, with a piracy rate of 91%, although this was a significant drop from 1997's highs of $1.4 billion in losses and a piracy rate of 96%. Japan, with perhaps the most advanced economy of the Asian countries, utilizes 47% of all software in the region. However, it accounted for just 36% of the region's total dollar losses ($975 million), with a reported piracy rate of 31% in 1999.

D. Other Regions

While Europe, North America, and Asia account for the bulk of software use and software piracy, other global regions are active in this area. The piracy rate in Latin America was found to have declined to 59% in 1999, with Brazil reporting the highest dollar losses, at $392 million. The Middle East and Africa had the second highest piracy rate among the regions analyzed, with 63% of software being pirated. However, this figure represented a significant decline from 1994's level of 84%.

VIII. REASONS FOR PIRACY

In recent years, there has been a concerted effort by academic researchers to determine the cause of piracy. What makes an individual decide to illegally copy a software package when he would never consider stealing an automobile or committing other forms of crime? It is most likely a combination of factors, including the ease with which software can be pirated, the cost of software, the victimless appearance of the crime, and the unlikelihood of detection. Very few other crimes meet these specifications, although speeding in an automobile is similar, and anyone who has driven on a major freeway knows that a majority of drivers exceed the speed limit. A comprehensive model has yet to be developed, but strides are being made. Most models focus on three different theories: the theory of reasoned action, the theory of planned behavior, and economic utility theory.

A. Theory of Reasoned Action

The theory of reasoned action (TRA) developed from a stream of research in social psychology that suggests that a person's behavioral intention toward a specific behavior is the major factor in whether or not the individual will carry out the behavior. Behavioral intention is, in turn, predicted by the individual's attitude toward the behavior and subjective norms. The individual's attitude is her perception of the consequences and outcomes of the behavior, on a continuum from positive to negative. If the individual believes that an action will lead to positive results, she will have a positive attitude toward the behavior. This will positively affect intention, which will lead to the committing of the actual behavior.

Subjective norms are the pressures that the individual feels from friends, peers, authority figures, etc., to perform or not perform the behavior in question. This is the individual's perception of the pressures from the social environment and is often referred to as peer norms. Much support has been found for the predictive ability of this theory, although it has also been found lacking in the explanation of ethical decision making in situations involving computer issues.

B. Theory of Planned Behavior

The theory of planned behavior (TPB) is an extension of the TRA framework. TPB posits that behavior is determined by the intention to perform the behavior, which is predicted by three factors: attitude toward the behavior, subjective norms, and perceived behavioral control (PBC). PBC refers to the perception of the subject as to his ability and opportunity to commit the behavior. A person with a high level of PBC would have confidence in his ability to successfully carry out the action in question. This is an important element, because the Internet provides an easy-to-use platform for obtaining pirated software. It may be that, in the past, potential pirates were dissuaded from illegally copying software by their perceived inability to carry out the act. However, the Internet allows almost any user to find and download pirated software with just the click of a mouse.

Much research has been done to validate TPB empirically, and it has been found to be a good predictor of an individual's behavior, including software piracy.

C. Expected Utility Theory

Economic issues, such as costs and benefits, are also commonly claimed to be factors in a person's decision-making process. For example, lack of financial resources has been cited as a reason for software piracy behavior. Expected utility theory (EUT) posits that, when faced with an array of risky decisions, an individual will choose the course of action that maximizes the utility (benefits minus costs) to that individual. Different variants of this model exist, but each supposes that a rational individual will analyze the benefits and costs involved. Where probabilities exist, the individual will factor the probability of each outcome into the decision-making process.

In most cases, computer-using professionals have three possible courses of action, when faced with a situation in which software can be used: purchase the software, do without the software, or pirate the software. It is possible to describe these choices in terms of EUT. To do so, it is necessary to determine the costs and benefits involved. Some benefit will most likely be gained through the use of the software. However, a purchase cost is involved, if the software is legally obtained. The expected utility of purchasing the software is the expected benefit gained from the use of the software, less the expected cost of the software.

In the case of software piracy, costs result not from purchasing the software but from the punishment level and the probability that the punishment will be incurred. The expected utility of pirating is the expected benefit gained from pirating less the expected cost (calculated using the punishment probability and punishment level). The individual will pirate the software when the expected utility of pirating is greater than the expected utility of not pirating. If the individual perceives that the chances of a significant punishment are low, then it is more likely that the individual will pirate the software. This may be a partial explanation of why piracy rates are so much higher in areas of the world such as Asia and Eastern Europe,

where the chances of punishment are more remote, as opposed to the United States, where the risk of punishment is much more severe.

A key aspect of economic utility is the price paid for the software. This is commonly noted as a factor in the decision to pirate. Ram Gopal and Lawrence Sanders have developed an interesting stream of research into software piracy issues, yielding several useful results regarding pricing issues. Among their findings, Gopal and Sanders discovered that piracy rates are related to per capita GNP. The lower a country's per capita GNP, the higher the level of piracy. This lends credence to the argument that price is a factor, because a lower per capita GNP would translate to relatively higher software costs, if prices are held constant throughout the world. As stated in Section X, this has led to suggestions that software companies utilize price discrimination as a tool for reducing piracy. This would involve basing software prices partially on the ability of the potential purchaser to afford the cost.

D. Comprehensive Theory of Piracy Behavior

Each of the above theories is useful in predicting the piracy behavior of an individual. Recent research has focused on combining these and other factors into a comprehensive model of behavior. Evidence that all of the factors discussed above influence the decision whether or not to pirate has been found, although different models provide different levels of importance for each factor. Punishment and the probability of punishment are consistently found to be deterrents to undesirable behavior. The relatively high level of piracy in the world may be due to the fact that people perceive the chance of prosecution and punishment as minimal. This would fit with the EUT model. Similarly, as posited by TRA and TPB, peer norms and attitude toward piracy have been demonstrated to be significant influences on a person's decision to pirate. If an individual works in an organization where piracy is accepted, she is more likely to commit the crime. The attitudes toward the behavior may be related to the ethical outlook of the individual. If the person perceives software piracy to be unethical, she will have a more negative attitude toward piracy and will be less likely to carry out an act of piracy.

Much research remains to be done in the development of a useful predictive model of piracy behavior. However, the work to date does give some indication as to what can be done to deter individuals from illegally copying software. Detection and punishment are useful deterrents, as is education, to the immoral and damaging nature of the act. Also, influencing an individual's peer group and changing the culture of an organization to be more antipiracy in nature are both important factors in controlling the problem. Discriminatory pricing practices may be a potential antipiracy tool. Each of these is discussed further in Section X.

IX. INDUSTRY RESPONSES

Software manufacturers have been very active in the area of piracy, because it is a direct threat to the nature of the industry. Several trade organizations have been created to combat the problem through a variety of educational, legal, and investigative measures.

A. The Business Software Alliance

The BSA was founded in 1988 and is made up of many of the world's software manufacturers, including such companies as Adobe, Apple, Autodesk, Corel Corporation, IBM, Microsoft, and Network Associates. The organization operates in 65 countries and is very active in publicizing the damage done by piracy, collecting statistical information on piracy, and promoting and enforcing piracy laws.

One of the BSA's main activities has been the establishment of piracy hotlines, operated in more than 50 countries as of 2001. Using these toll-free phone numbers, individuals can report instances of piracy for BSA investigation. Web sites provide similar facilities. The hotlines average over 50,000 calls per year, mostly made by disgruntled employees of pirating organizations. The BSA also provides software that makes it easier to identify pirated software in an organization.

The BSA is very active in prosecuting pirates. From 1993–2000, the BSA collected more than $47 million in damages from U.S. companies. Legal action was taken against 2100 European companies in 1998 alone. In one coordinated raid in England and Germany, more than 300,000 illegal CDs were confiscated.

B. Software and Information Industry Association

The Software and Information Industry Association (SIIA) was created in 1999, when the Software Publishers Association (SPA) merged with the Informa-

tion Industry Association (IIA). The SPA had been active in antipiracy campaigns since 1985, and the SIIA has continued those efforts in a fashion similar to the BSA, including a piracy hotline that receives more than 200 calls per week. From 1995–2000, the SIIA was involved in more than 2000 cases against software pirates. Almost all of the money collected is used to fund further antipiracy campaigns. Currently, the SIIA represents more than 1400 members.

On the international front, the SIIA annually submits a report to the Office of the United States Trade Representative identifying software piracy problems throughout the world. In 1999, the SIIA singled out China for special monitoring under Section 306 of the Trade Act of 1994, due to its failure to meet the standards of the TRIPS agreement (discussed in Section V) and the continuing high level of piracy in that country. Also, SIIA Europe, an SIIA affiliate, performs activities in the European market.

C. Other Organizations

Various other organizations exist on the national level. The Federation Against Software Theft (FAST), a nonprofit organization operating in the United Kingdom, was formed in 1984 by U.K. software manufacturers to lobby the Parliament for changes in the copyright law. They have since been active in enforcing laws and educating users with regard to software piracy, and currently have more than 1200 members. FAST has been successful in combating pirates and was instrumental in the sentencing of a pirate to a 2-year prison sentence in 1999. The organization carries out antipiracy campaigns and played a large part in creating Europe's first integrated antipiracy hotline, which provides a single contact point for copyright information regarding software, music, and video, including facilities to report piracy.

In Canada, the Canadian Alliance Against Software Theft (CAAST), created in 1990, provides very similar efforts to those described above, including an antipiracy hotline. CAAST works closely with the BSA, as do many of these organizations.

X. PIRACY PREVENTION

Software manufacturers, industry groups (such as those just discussed), and law enforcement agencies have made concerted efforts to reduce the amount of piracy around the globe. These efforts have focused on four main areas: technical, legal, educational, and the development of codes of conduct, each of which is aimed at altering the potential pirate's behavior. A fifth possibility, discriminatory pricing, is also discussed in this section.

A. Technical Measures

An initial response by the software industry to the threat of software piracy behavior was the development of technical protection. Software packages incorporated piracy protection software into their code. However, this failed to have the desired effect, because pirates were able to break the code. The protection also took up valuable storage space, had to be constantly updated to stay ahead of the pirates, and was sometimes annoying to consumers. Some studies indicate that software piracy protection does little to increase a company's profits.

The advent of the Internet makes this type of prevention strategy even less feasible, because once a pirate has broken the protection code, she can make the software available to large numbers of people with the click of a button.

B. Deterrence Measures

The earlier EUT discussion of expected costs with respect to punishment levels and probability of punishment is closely linked to deterrence theory. The punishment probability factor and the punishment level factor described above are referred to in the deterrence theory literature as punishment certainty and punishment severity, respectively. As with EUT, deterrence theory proposes that, as these factors are increased, the level of illegal behavior should decrease. The unwanted behavior can be deterred through the threat of punishment. Many crimes against property are related to the expected gains of the crime versus the expected costs at the margin. The perceived low probability of being caught may be a major reason in the decision to pirate software. The legal system, in most countries, is founded on the concept described above.

Punishment, such as fines or prison sentences, is heralded as a deterrent to unwanted behavior. This is also true in the software piracy arena. As discussed earlier, many legal mechanisms now exist to punish software pirates. Clearly, the goal is to deter pirates through the threat of both financial and physical punishment. However, these mechanisms are only useful if actually enforced. While pirates are regularly prosecuted and punished in the United States, this is not the case globally. The failure to enforce copyright laws has been a source of conflict in trade negotiations between the U.S. and countries such as China, where piracy is rampant and enforcement of international antipiracy agreements is minimal. Because the vast majority of software is produced in the United States, there is little incentive in other countries for the governments to enforce laws that are aimed at protecting foreign interests while harming local businesses. As stated in Section V, there is evidence that the development and enforcement of software piracy legislation is directly related to the existence of a domestic software industry. Those countries that have a domestic software industry are more likely to develop and enforce legislation designed to protect intellectual property rights.

Numerous examples of legal punishments are being handed out in many countries. In the U.S., the first software pirate convicted using the 1997 NET Act (described in Section V) was sentenced in 1999 to 2 years probation for using the Internet to pirate software. He could have been sentenced to up to 3 years in prison and a maximum fine of $250,000. Similarly, a Virginia man faces up to 1 year in prison, after pleading guilty to setting up a web site that made illegally copied software available for easy downloading. The BSA has collected more than $47 million in damages in the United States in the past 7 years, including a judgment of $80,000 against the city of Issaquah, Washington, which admitted to using unlicensed software on its computers. In Europe, there is a direct correlation between the adoption of the EU Computer Programs Directive and the decreasing level of software piracy, indicating that deterrence measures have been an effective tool in combating piracy.

C. Educational Measures

If the perception of pirates is that antipiracy laws are not enforced, then there is little deterrent effect. Similarly, if individuals are not aware of the damages done by piracy, or have not seriously considered the unethical nature of the act, then it is more likely that they will commit piracy. Consequently, several industry groups and software manufacturers have spent much effort and money on educational campaigns. For example, the BSA and SIIA regularly produce publications and videos that can be used to educate everyone from teenagers to high-level executives on the issues surrounding piracy.

D. Codes of Conduct

A respected code of conduct can be an effective way to influence an individual's behavior. Initially, the code of conduct makes the individual aware of potential ethical and social issues that may be encountered. As previously stated, one reason for piracy may be the lack of realization by individuals that piracy is an unethical and illegal act. Even if the issues are understood and the individual is still considering committing piracy, the agreement to adhere to a code of conduct may have an influence over his decision, because it represents a form of social norms. At a minimum, the agreement to adhere to a code of conduct eliminates any claims of ignorance, if some form of prosecution is necessary.

Several organizations and institutions have created codes of conduct that govern the use of software. Perhaps the most well known is the Association for Computing Machinery (ACM) Code of Ethics. The ACM, founded in 1947, has more than 80,000 members and is the premier educational and scientific computing organization. The ACM Code of Ethics explicitly prohibits the violation of copyright agreements and demands respect for intellectual property rights. All members of the organization are expected to adhere to the code.

Individual organizations are also utilizing codes of conduct to control employee behavior. Many companies now require new employees to read and sign codes of conduct, and internal punishments for failing to adhere to the code can be severe. Organizations such as the BSA help companies by providing sample codes.

E. Pricing

As stated in Section VIII, price is often found to be a significant factor in the decision to pirate. The higher the price of the software relative to the individual's ability to pay, the more likely the individual is to pirate the software. Consequently, one mechanism for fighting software is discriminatory pricing. Focusing purely on legislative methods has been shown to have limited success in countries where a domestic software industry does not exist. In many cases, these countries are less developed than the United States or Western Europe, and have lower per capita GNPs. Consequently, people cannot afford software at the same price levels as in the U.S. and Western Europe. Because there is no domestic software industry to protect, there is little incentive for a government to enact legislation that will harm the majority of individuals (who cannot afford the software) while doing little

to protect the country's citizens.

Consequently, it can be argued that software manufacturers would do better to explore other avenues of piracy prevention, including developing pricing strategies that are based on the value of the software product to the consumer, as opposed to single pricing strategies. This could increase software producers' profits while reducing piracy rates in less developed countries. Price discrimination is already used in many industries, including some aspects of the computer industry.

XI. FUTURE TRENDS

The future is always hard to predict, especially in the area of technology. However, some trends are clear. Efforts to combat piracy will continue to increase and piracy will be a focus of future international trade negotiations.

A. Piracy Trends

Piracy rates are decreasing in the industrialized Western World, partially due to the increase in awareness and the enforcement of punishment mechanisms. However, dollar figures still remain high, as the amount of software in use has increased. In Asia and Eastern Europe, piracy rates remain high, and enforcement of international laws, while increasing, is still minimal. China's potential inclusion in the World Trade Organization will require greater adherence to the WIPO treaties and may have an impact on piracy in that country.

B. Software Distribution

One area where changes may occur is in the way that software is sold and distributed. Two recently introduced approaches are currently making some headway: shareware and meterware.

1. Shareware

Shareware is software that is freely distributed, often via the Internet. The user is given a set period of time to use and preview the software. If the individual wishes to continue to use the software package, she is asked to send a prespecified amount to the manufacturer. If the individual does not wish to continue to use the software, it is expected that she will remove the package from her system. This form of software distribution relies on the honesty of the user, but also makes the individual very much aware of the fact that a manufacturer took time and effort to create the package, and now wishes to be fairly compensated for its efforts. This plays on the fairness of the user. One cause of piracy may be the lack of understanding of the user of the contract situation regarding the average store-bought software package. The concept of shareware, on the other hand, is easy to understand. Clearly, some pirates will simply ignore the request for payment. However, software manufacturers are counting on the fact that the majority of users will follow the instructions and behave ethically.

2. Meterware

Meterware is a new way of billing for software. Currently, a package is purchased and can then be easily copied onto multiple machines. In the meterware paradigm, the user is billed for the use of the software, not for the package itself. In one form of this technique, the user would be required to dial up the manufacturer via modem from the network on which the software is installed. The software keeps track of how often it is accessed, and the user is billed using a formula involving the usage of the package. This is a "pay-as-you-go" scheme.

Problems exist with this payment mechanism, however, that may be difficult to overcome. Users are much more familiar with the traditional one-time payment format and may not adapt easily to this new technique. It also requires the user to actively participate, which may be both inconvenient and difficult to enforce. Third, the user may be charged for accidentally starting an application, leaving a program running overnight, etc. These issues may prove too problematic for meterware to become common.

The evolution of the Internet may provide answers to some of these problems. Application service providers (ASPs) provide software applications for companies, usually through the Internet. Customers can outsource some of their software applications to the ASP. The ASP is responsible for the software licensing involved, and can work out a payment scheme with the customer. Users at the customer location utilize standard Internet browser technology to access the software over the Net.

XII. CONCLUSION

In conclusion, software piracy is a violation of copyright laws that are designed to protect the creativity and financial gain of the creators of intellectual property. Rates of piracy around the world vary, from more than 90% in some Asian countries, where the ethical nature of piracy may be viewed much more leniently, to much lower levels in Western Europe and North America. Antipiracy legislation and the action of organizations such as the BSA and SIIA have clearly had an impact. However, the level of piracy is still significantly high and does great damage to the software industry. The Internet has expanded the possibility for software piracy to easily occur on a large scale, and this is a development that will require international cooperation to combat.

SEE ALSO THE FOLLOWING ARTICLES

Computer Viruses • Copyright Laws • Crime, Use of Computers in • Ethical Issues • Psychology • Security Issues and Measures

BIBLIOGRAPHY

Business Software Alliance (1999). *Forecasting a robust future: An economic study of the U.S. software industry.* Washington, DC.

Business Software Alliance (1999). *Software piracy in the European Union.* Washington, DC.

Business Software Alliance (2000). *1999 global software piracy report.* Washington, DC.

Eining, M., and Christensen, A. (1991). A psycho-social model of software piracy: The development and test of a model. *Ethical issues in information systems,* R. Dejoie, G. Fowler, and D. Paradice (Eds.). Boston: Boyd & Fraser Publishing Co.

Gopal, R., and Sanders, G. L. (1997). Preventive and deterrent controls for software piracy. *Journal of Management Information Systems,* Vol. 13, No. 4, 29–47.

Gopal, R., and Sanders, G. L. (1998). International software piracy: Analysis of key issues and impacts. *Information Systems Research,* Vol. 9, No. 4, 380–397.

Gopal, R., and Sanders, G. L. (2000). Global software piracy: You can't get blood out of a turnip. *Communications of the ACM,* Vol. 43, No. 9, 82–89.

Peace, A. G. (1997). Software piracy and computer-using professionals: A survey. *Journal of Computer Information Systems,* Vol. 38, No. 1, 94–99.

Peace, A. G., and Galletta, D. (1996). Developing a predictive model of software piracy behavior: An empirical study. *Proc. 17th International Conference on Information Systems,* J. DeGross, S. Jarvenpaa, and A. Srinivasan (Eds.). December 17–19, 1996, Cleveland, OH, 209–222.

Software Process Simulation

David L. Olson
University of Nebraska, Lincoln

GLOSSARY

capability maturity models System of five levels of increasing software development process maturity.

discrete event simulation Simulation oriented around the timing of specific events, especially appropriate for systems involving queuing.

Monte Carlo simulation Sampling experiment based upon a system simulated with events determined by functions of random numbers with the purpose of estimating the distribution of an output variable.

simulation Mathematical or logical model of a system that can be used for experimentation with the intent of gaining insight into the system's behavior.

software process Methods and techniques used to develop software products, or systems used to make computers function.

systems dynamics Continuous simulation model in terms of stocks and flows especially suitable for incorporating feedback relationships.

waterfall model Simple network of sequential processes in a computer system project, including feedback.

SOFTWARE PROCESSES are critical to the productivity of the information technology industry, a key force in the growth of the world economy for the past few decades. It is critically important to the continued success of this industry to increase efficiency and effectiveness, to improve the quality of software products, and to provide more useful and productive technology tools. Simulation is a quantitative tool that has

proven very useful in the analysis of many fields involving complexity and uncertainty. In the past decade, systems dynamics, discrete event simulation, and other forms of simulation analysis have been applied to the assessment and improvement of software processes. The ways in which this simulation support has been applied to the software industry are presented within the framework of capability maturity model levels, representing different stages of software development maturity.

I. DEFINITION OF SOFTWARE PROCESS SIMULATION

Software processes are the methods and techniques used to develop software products or the systems used to make computers function usefully. Simulation is the use of models to reflect a real situation, with the intent of studying system behavior under various imposed conditions. Simulation models usually involve the introduction of measured uncertainty through pseudo-random numbers. Various types of simulation models were developed in the 1990s to analyze the risk elements of software processes.

Software process simulation models try to identify structural relationships in the processes used to develop software. Software process simulation is emerging as an effective tool for the evaluation of changes in software projects as well as in development organizations. A level of detail is required in such simulation models to support process improvement activities, the primary purpose of most such models. Other goals include gaining understanding and communication and investigating the expected benefits of automation of parts of the process.

II. SOFTWARE PROCESSES

A software process cited by Kellner, Madachy, and Raffo in 1999 is defined as a set of activities, methods, practices, and transformation that people use to develop and maintain software and associated products such as project plans, design documents, code, test cases, and user manuals. A process is a logical structure of people, technology, and methods organized into work activities that have the purpose of transforming inputs into desired outputs.

A. Software Process Purpose

Software processes are intended to develop quality software products efficiently in terms of time and resource expenditure. There are many methodologies seeking to attain these beneficial features. There are a number of factors that can affect final software quality, including the methodology used to develop the system, the quality of personnel assigned to the process, and the allocation of defect detection resources throughout the project life cycle.

Software processing models have been used for a variety of purposes. First, they provide a platform to study strategic management options in software development. Second, they provide a tool to compare process improvement proposals. Third, they are useful in software project management training.

B. Issues in Software Process Management

Software processing models have been used for planning studies. At the control and operational level, software process models provide tools to compare process improvement proposals.

One of the major issues in applying simulation to software process modeling is data. It is often difficult to obtain data with the accuracy required for simulation models (especially for discrete event simulation). Sometimes there is difficulty in obtaining data at all, or at least to the degree allowing accurate determination of distributions and variability.

Therefore, studies often must be conducted with the data that is available. If measures of factors such as the distribution of time overruns for various phases of the software process are not available, the expertise and experience of people who have worked in this area can be tapped through interviews. This, of course, introduces a level of subjectivity and error into the data, but that is a starting point for a model, which can be improved as real data based upon accurate measurements made in future projects become available.

As with simulation models applied to other fields, the level of detail to model depends on the questions to be answered. All simulation models are abstractions leaving out a lot of the complexity of the real system. The key to sound simulation modeling is to include the key activities and tasks, the primary factors at issue, and important dependencies and work flows. In software process simulation, input parameters often include work to be done (often measured in lines of codes or in function points), the effort required to accomplish activities of a given size, how defects are detected, and the amount of reworking required when defects are identified. Alternative models need to be built to reflect policy options, such as different staffing levels; the possibility of outsourcing, including productivity tools; the impact of training; and resource constraints. Sound simulation practice also calls for the use of controlled random number streams to make simulation model debugging easier and to make analysis of results more accurate.

C. Capability Maturity Model Levels

The capability maturity model (CMM) was developed by the Software Engineering Institute at Carnegie-Mellon University in Pittsburgh as a paradigm for the levels of maturity in software development. The CMM describes five levels of process maturity:

- Level 1 organizations are characterized by little systematic method.
- Level 2 organizations are characterized by individual control, with key processes including software configuration management, quality assurance, subcontract management, project planning, tracking and oversight, and requirements management.
- Level 3 organizations institutionalize processes, including peer reviews, intergroup coordination, software product engineering, integrated software management, training programs, and organization process definition and focus.

- Level 4 organizations incorporate process measurement and apply quality management as well as process measurement and analysis.
- Level 5 organizations obtain feedback for improvement through process change management, technology innovation, and defect prevention.

Higher CMM levels involve increased structure for the way in which software products are developed. The benefits of moving up to higher CMM levels are contended to be much less variance in software project outcomes, as well as more efficient average performance.

Simulation can be applied to software processes at all levels. In level 1 organizations, role-playing simulation can be useful in better understanding of software development. However, level 1 organizations do not have any key processes and are very unlikely to have accurate data meriting systems dynamics or discrete event simulation. In level 2 organizations, baseline models of processes using gross measures based upon experienced opinion can be applied, generally to cost and schedule models. It is hard to model defect characteristics because the data will usually not be available. In level 3 organizations, there is increased emphasis on product engineering and formal definition of processes. Data can be collected from observations of engineering processes to include data on requirements changes, defects in design phases as well as in coding, and the distribution of results from testing. Validation of simulated processes becomes possible, and the predictions obtained from simulation are superior to those based on human judgment. In level 4 organizations, more accurate data is available, and the focus of simulation is on operating processes within quantitative performance limits. Simulation can be used to determine what these quality control limits should be. It also becomes possible to conduct tradeoff analysis on various design options. Finally, at level 5, validated models can be used to track and manage processes in greater detail, allowing greater confidence in simulation results to the point that new and improved methods can be compared, thus supporting process change management.

III. TYPES OF SIMULATION MODELS

Any simulation model is a set of assumptions representing complexity and or probabilistic inputs. Despite these shaky foundations, simulation models are quite valuable in sorting out what is expected to happen. In this sense, simulations are predictions. It is therefore critical to validate the accuracy of a simulation model by observing the real process. Simulation models consist of parameters representing quantifications of how the modeler expects the real world to behave.

A. Systems Dynamics Models

Systems dynamics models are continuous simulation models using hypothesized relations across activities and processes. Systems dynamics was developed by Forester in 1961 and was initially applied to dealing with the complexity of industrial economic systems and world environmental and population problems. These models are very closely related to the general systems approach and allow modelers to insert qualitative relationships (expressed in general quantitative forms). Like all simulation models, all results are contingent upon the assumed inputs. General systems theory views assemblies of interrelated parts as having feedback loops that respond to system conditions and provide a degree of self-correction and control.

Abdel-Hamid and Madnick in 1991 applied systems dynamics models in their pioneering work on software process simulation. Their models captured relationships between personnel availability, productivity, and work activities. Process details were not required. Systems dynamics continues to be a very popular mode of software process modeling and has also been applied in interactive simulations of projects for training project managers.

Continuous simulation model advantages include its ability to capture project level and systems-related aspects of software process projects. Higher level issues such as learning curve effects, differential production rates, and the impact of using different members of the workforce are more naturally modeled with continuous simulation models than with discrete event models. However, details relating to tasks and activities are more naturally dealt with through discrete event simulation models.

B. Discrete Event Simulation

Discrete event simulation involves tracing state conditions of processes over time. This form of simulation is very good for modeling input details and identifying detailed system outputs. Discrete event simulations are entity driven, with entities typically representing customers arriving at some service facility or work arriving at a manufacturing machine. In a project environment, one entity can be created to represent the project which passes through the various sequential software processes. Monte Carlo analysis of such a discrete event system can be applied by rerunning the one-entity simulation from project start to project completion hundreds or thousands of times and by using the results to describe the distribution of time, cost, and/or defect outcomes.

C. Other Techniques

There have been a number of other approaches applied to software process simulation. Rule-based simulations apply pattern-directed inferencing implemented through production rules much in the manner of expert systems. This type of simulation may be completely deterministic and thus involves solution of a complex numeric problem.

Another commonly used simulation technique is behavioral, where individual subjects play roles that interact. This form of simulation is often effectively applied in training environments.

D. Demonstration Models

To demonstrate different types of simulation models, we assume a waterfall model of a software process. A simplified version of the waterfall model shown in Fig. 1 involves standard activities.

A project begins with the specification phase. Once a project has been specified, it moves on to the design phase. Each of the phases of this model has the potential for recycling back to prior phases. During the design phase, it might well be possible that there is re-

alization that the specifications are lacking in some sense, thus the finely dashed line leading back from design to specification. Projects may be cancelled at any phase. After successful completion of design, the next phase is production of code and finally testing. In reality, software projects are, of course, much more complicated than this. (Testing, for instance, is generally applied throughout the production coding phase, and sometimes it makes sense to begin production coding prior to finalization of systems design.) However, what we need is a simple example to demonstrate the potential of different types of simulation models in support of software process planning.

The data required for simulation of this system is ideally based on comprehensive record keeping to include measures of how long a project would be expected to spend in each phase, how often recycling occurs (from each phase to each prior phase), and the distributions of each of these measures.

1. Monte Carlo Simulation

The first simulation model we will present is simply an extension of the critical path model, listing each activity (phase) as if it went according to plan. Such a model might be applied by CMM level 1 or 2 organizations, focusing on project planning at the level of critical path modeling. This simple simulation is easily modeled, providing the level of complexity of PERT (Project Evaluation and Review Technique) models (with the added flexibility of allowing any type of distribution on activity duration). Spreadsheet models are very easy to apply to this initial model. There are many software products such as @Risk (Palisade Corporation) and Crystal Ball (Decisioneering, Inc.) on the market that make simulation of such spreadsheet models more

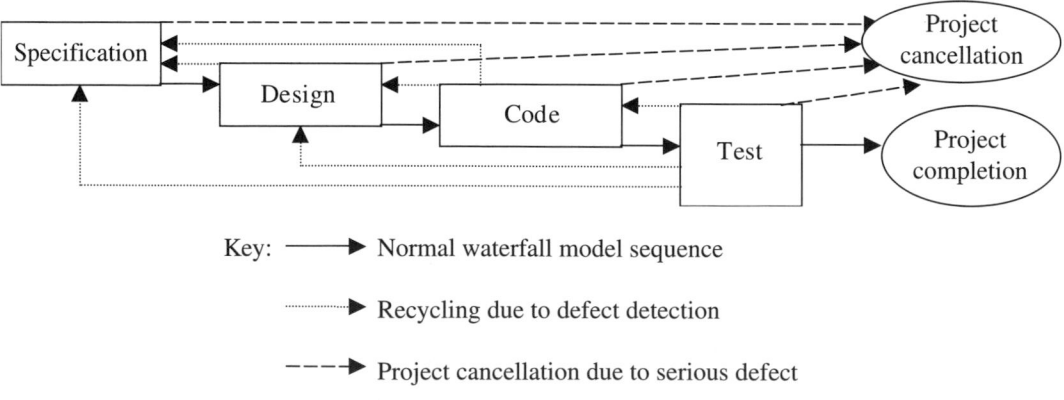

Key: ———▶ Normal waterfall model sequence

··········▶ Recycling due to defect detection

− − −▶ Project cancellation due to serious defect

Figure 1   Sketch of a basic waterfall model (simplified).

powerful. These Monte Carlo simulation systems give the ability to generate as many simulation runs as desired, which along with graphical support make it very easy to obtain a view of the distributional properties of results. Monte Carlo systems also provide the ability to easily define standard probability distributions to each activity. A Monte Carlo model of the core of the simple model given in Fig. 1 is shown in Fig. 2.

This model uses the lognormal distribution for all activities, with the standard deviation specified as one-half of the mean. The appropriate distribution and parameters should be obtained from records kept by the organization. Following standard statistical practice, a large number of observed projects would be required to be comfortable with these simulation model elements. The result of the simulation would be represented by project completion time, the maximum value in column D in Fig. 2 (cell D5 in this example). The results obtained from Crystal Ball are given in Fig. 3.

Figure 3 shows that the mean completion time is 12.21 weeks. More completely, the output demonstrates that this output ranges very widely, from 3.06 to 21.36 weeks. It also appears to be normally distributed, symmetric around the mean with declining probabilities associated with values farther from the mean. A valuable tool of Crystal Ball (and other Monte Carlo simulation systems) is the ability to assess the probability of any particular time interval. For instance, in this case, there is a 0.615 probability of project completion within 13 weeks, 0.717 probability of completion within 14 weeks, and 0.811 probability of completion within 15 weeks. There is a 0.430 probability of project completion between 12 and 17 weeks.

While Monte Carlo simulation provides very useful tools to estimate probabilities, the simulation model of the software process is far too simplified. The waterfall model includes a great potential for dynamic behavior, involving looping back from one phase to prior phases as the need for changes develop. The time until defect identification can be important, as well as what path to take when defects are detected.

This type of model element involves routing that a spreadsheet model cannot deal with easily (if at all).

2. Systems Dynamics

The perspective of systems dynamics allows more modeling of the complexity of the waterfall process. The basic sequence of planned activity is a core, leading from specification to design to coding to testing and on to project completion. This is the path that would occur if everything went according to plan. The spreadsheet model presented in Fig. 2 would consider variance in duration, but would assume only this path. However, there are possibilities of the need for changes and corrections at all phases of this model. Things could break down during the specification phase if agreement on project features cannot be obtained. During the design codes phase, it might become apparent that the specifications developed by the user are either infeasible or unrealistic. This would lead to sending the project back for respecification. Such problems could be reviewed by the funding authority, who would need to decide among the options of revising the specifications, paying for a more expensive project, or canceling the project. During the implemented codes phase, defects identified would need to be recycled back to the design code phase (and might call for recycling, in turn, back to the specified codes phase, again querying the funding authority for authorization of additional budget). During testing it is quite possible that bugs will be uncovered, calling for rework and recycling back to the implemented codes phase (and possibly further back). Systems dynamics simulations modeling the dynamics similar to those presented by this problem have been applied in many applications. They are continuous simulations, measuring the levels of effort required as well as times required to complete phases. Note that in our example many elements of possible complexity have been left out.

Systems dynamics provides a means to map the dynamic interactions of a system. For instance, a map of

	A	B	C	D
1	PHASE	Start	Duration	Finish
2	Specification	0	Lognormal(1,0.5)	=B2+C2
3	Design	=D2	Lognormal(4,2)	=B3+C3
4	Code	=D3	Lognormal(5,2.5)	=B4+C4
5	Testing	=D4	Lognormal(2,1)	=B5+C5

Figure 2 Excel spreadsheet model.

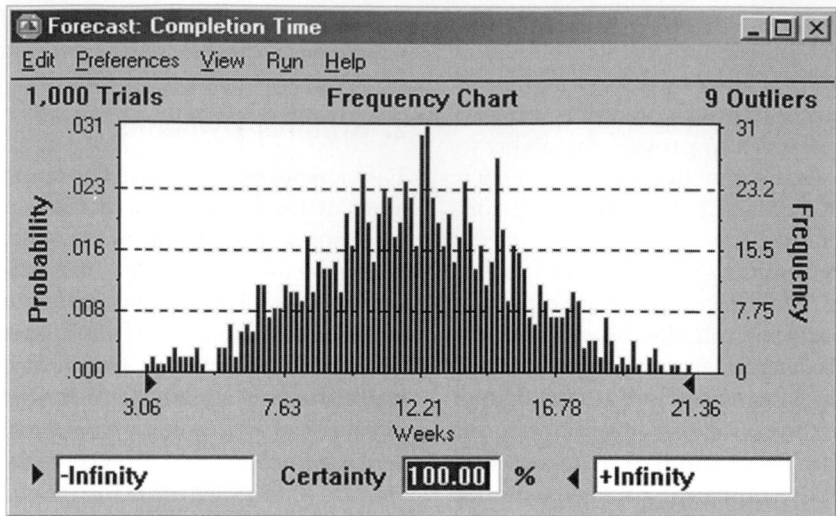

Figure 3   Crystal Ball output for a spreadsheet model.

the waterfall model with its feedback looping among and between components might be as given in Fig. 4. Systems dynamics models employ a continuous system of differential equations as their meta-model of stocks (for example, of defects to be detected) and flows (for example, lines of code completed).

Systems dynamics models focus on simulating the flow of activities. They are continuous models, and the change in states is the focus of interest. Figure 4 shows the basic flow of a project, with potential relooping when defects are encountered. Here we model defects flowing one step back, but recognize that if a defect is identified in implementing code, returning to designing code can result in further looping back to code specification. The primary benefit of systems dynamics models is the ability to include factors affecting flow,

such as the scope of the project affecting the rate of work accomplished in the specification phase. Likewise, defects identified at testing are accumulated as a variable and are fed back to implemented codes. Any loop is a bottleneck in the system. For example, if testing keeps finding defects, this prolongs the development process as shown in Fig. 5. Therefore, it clearly would be important to lower the defect rate in prior processes or the time required to correct defects. These parameters govern this systems dynamics model, and estimating accuracy would depend on experience and learning rates. The systems dynamics model requires input rates. Table 1 gives the input rates considered in this model.

In this case, we assumed a project with 10,000 lines of code. The durations of the four basic waterfall activities are the same as in the Monte Carlo model

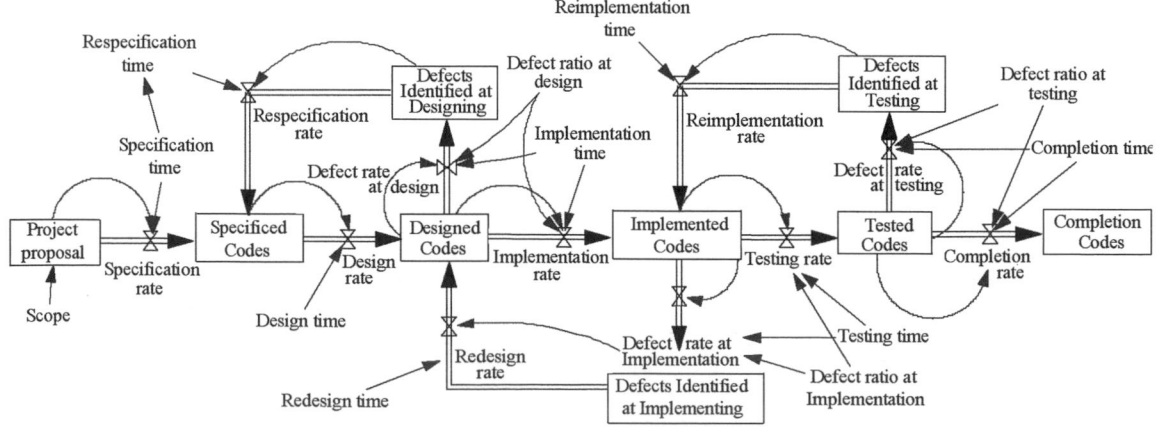

Figure 4   Systems dynamic map of a waterfall model.

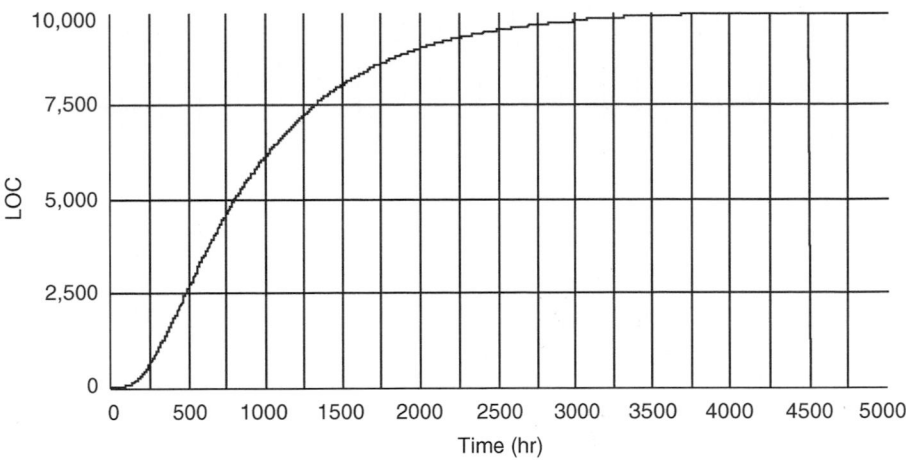

Figure 5   Systems dynamics model work accomplished over time.

given earlier. Here we used normal distributions in the software package VENSIM (which did not support lognormal distributions), although in principle lognormal distributions could be applied. The amount of time for relooping activities are given, as well as the percentage of defects detected at each phase (in terms of lines of code).

Running the simulation yielded the following output. Figure 5 shows the lines of code (LOC) accomplished over time.

Other flows could also be monitored. Figure 6, for instance, shows the experience of LOC with defects detected during testing.

Figure 7 shows another continuous measure, the rate of LOC tested per hour.

Table I   Systems Dynamics Model Input Parameter Values

Parameters	Values	Units
Scope	10,000	LOC
Specification time	40	Hours
Design time	200	Hours
Implementation time	280	Hours
Testing time	80	Hours
Respecification time	40	Hours
Redesign time	40	Hours
Reimplementation time	120	Hours
Retesting time	80	Hours
Defect ratio at design	20	Percentage
Defect ratio at implementation	30	Percentage
Defect ratio at testing	10	Percentage

Systems dynamics has proven very effective in modeling software processes where production rates in terms of LOC (or in function points) as well as defect detection rates are important. There are other aspects of interest better captured by discrete event simulation, to be presented next. Even so, systems dynamics is often applied in hybrid models along with discrete event simulation.

3. Discrete Event Simulation

Discrete event simulation focuses on the time spent by entities passing through a system of events. It is a time-focused method, especially suitable for queuing problems. It also can be very good at modeling the dynamic passage of a single project entity through a network of possibilities such as those given in Fig. 4. Attributes can be assigned to processes, such as size, complexity, and required effort. Defects can be assigned by type, consequence, and the phase in which they can be detected.

Figure 8 shows the model in the package Process-Model. This package allows the user to build the model through selection of processes connected by paths.

There are two basic elements to the model: processes and connectors. For each run of the simulation model, one entity is generated by the project icon. This entity passes to the specification process, and if all goes well the path is on to the design process, the implement process, and the test process. Table 2 gives each of these processes. There is finally a process icon representing cancelled projects. Completed projects are measured by the bottom connector leading out of the test process. The lognormal distribution was

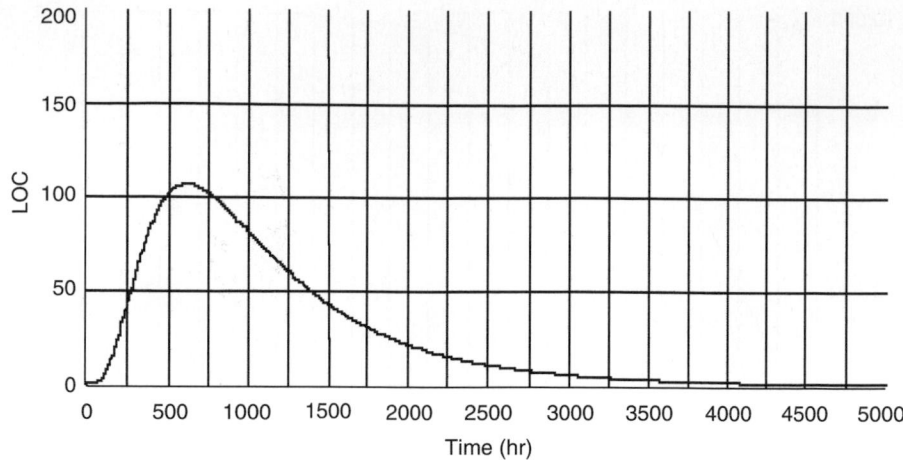

Figure 6 Systems dynamics model output—defects detected during testing.

assumed arbitrarily. All standard simulation distributions are available in ProcessModel. Time units used were hours, the largest time unit the package allows. Eight-hour working days were assumed.

The connectors in the model reflect the dynamic aspects of the system, shown in Table 3. Each of the connectors are defined as percentage arcs. This allows designation of the probability of transfer between each state. A one-day (8 hour) transfer time between states was assumed.

Table 4 gives results for this model in terms of the average number of entries on each path based on 100 simulation runs. Times are given in weeks for each phase and in total successful project completion time.

The average times can be added together to obtain an average project duration of 15.065 weeks, about

25% greater than the critical path expected times. The data indicates that 91% of the projects are successfully completed. Balance equations can be developed for each phase, as in Table 5.

There are many added complications that may be important, most of which can be added to a discrete event simulation model. A key part of the simulation would be to obtain accurate input data. Validation of the model would be accomplished by comparison of model results with actual statistics and finding a match. This important step of validation can also be used to improve the input parameters used in the model.

Models of greater complexity are not considered here. There are a number of factors that could arise that would be relatively simple to add to the last dis-

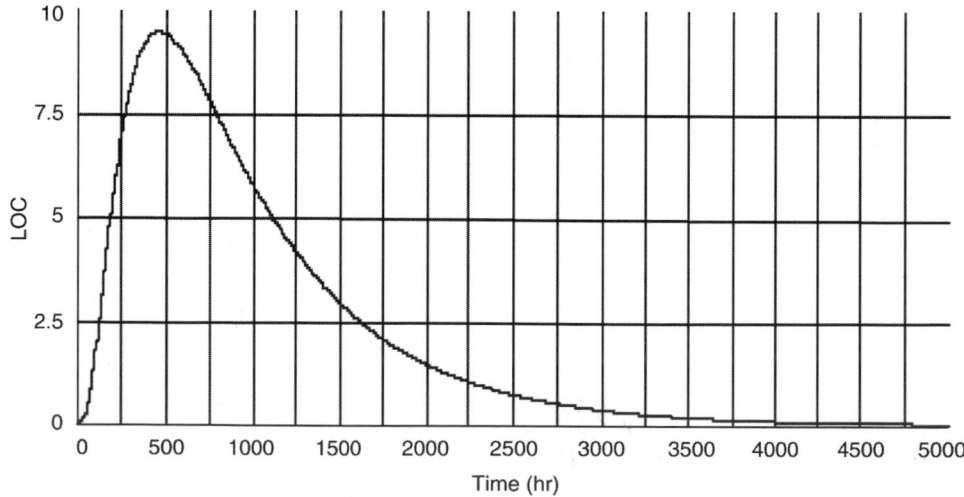

Figure 7 Testing rate in LOC per hour.

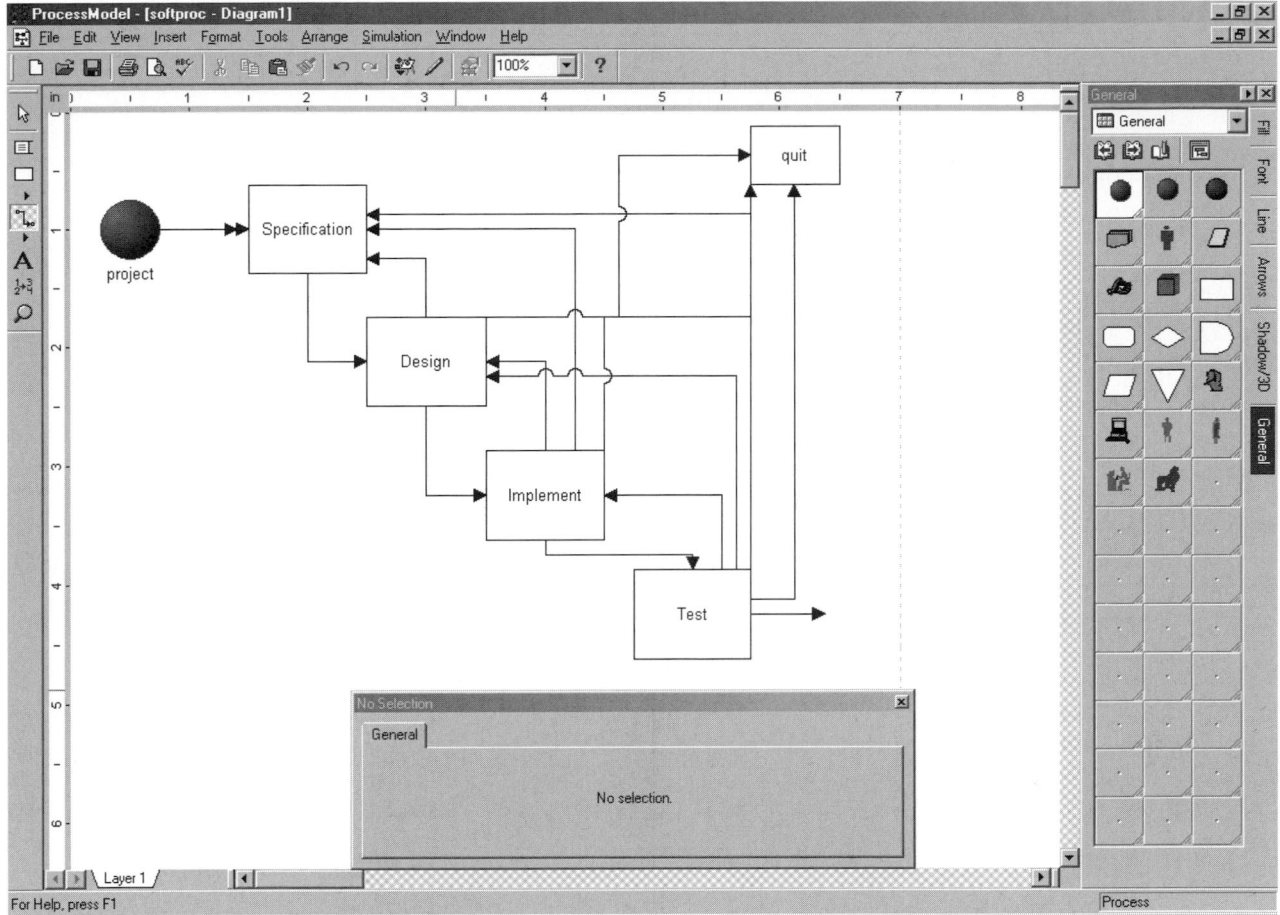

Figure 8   ProcessModel simulation of a waterfall process.

crete event simulation, such as applying distributions for durations for both classes of successful software processes, as well as those processes where defects were identified, or the duration by type of outcome. There are other complications that would call for hybrid types of simulation (combining discrete event and continuous simulation). For instance, it is harder to model partially concurrent activities, where systems design might be initiated prior to completion of specifications.

Table II   Processes in ProcessModel Simulation

Process	Capacity	Duration
Specification	1	Lognormal (40,20) hours
Design	1	Lognormal (200,100) hours
Implementation	1	Lognormal (280,140) hours
Test	1	Lognormal (80,40) hours

4. Other Types of Simulation Models

A number of other simulation systems have been developed, including hybrid combinations of systems dynamics (continuous) models and discrete event models. State-based simulation models are more formal with more complete graphical representations. State-based modeling is strong in its ability to capture details graphically, but is not as good at capturing mathematical details as discrete event models. State-based models receive productivity, error, and detection rates as inputs and predict effectiveness in terms of effort, duration, errors detected, and errors missed by process.

Knowledge-based meta-model simulations have also been developed. These employ a statistical network. Informal process descriptions are elicited and converted into a process model. The static and dynamic properties of a process model, such as consistency, completeness, internal correctness, and traceability,

Table III **ProcessModel Connectors**

Source	Destination	Type	Duration (hours)	Percentage
Project	Specification	Scheduled	0	
Specification	Design	Percentage	8	100
Design	Implementation	Percentage	8	95
Design	Specification	Percentage	8	3
Design	Quit	Percentage	0	2
Implementation	Test	Percentage	8	85
Implementation	Design	Percentage	8	10
Implementation	Specification	Percentage	8	2
Implementation	Quit	Percentage	0	3
Test	Done	Percentage	0	70
Test	Implementation	Percentage	8	15
Test	Design	Percentage	8	10
Test	Specification	Percentage	8	1
Test	Quit	Percentage	0	4

can be evaluated with this type of model. Graphic views are provided to users for interactive editing and communication.

IV. APPLICATIONS IN PRACTICE

Simulation has been among the most widely applied techniques in many aspects of manufacturing. A simulation's application in software process modeling is much more recent, with initial reports beginning in 1991 with Abdel-Hamid and Madnick. Its use has been reported in a number of cases, especially in the defense industry and in the field of overnight delivery. Simulation is a tool that directly addresses the concepts of the CMM using more accurate measures to improve software development processes systematically.

Table IV **ProcessModel Results**

		Average time (weeks)	Number
Specification		0.957	1.15
Design		5.237	1.58
Implementation		6.887	1.65
Test		1.984	1.32
Quit			0.06
Done			0.91
Design	To quit		0.03
Implementation	To quit		0.05
Test	To quit		0.01
Design	To specification		0.09
Implementation	To specification		0.05
Implementation	To design		0.23
Test	To specification		0.01
Test	To design		0.20
Test	To implementation		0.19

Table V Input/Output for ProcessModel

Phase	From	In	To	Out
Specification	Project	1	Design	1.15
	Design	0.09		
	Implementation	0.05		
	Test	0.01		
Design	Specification	1.15	Implementation	1.46
	Implementation	0.23	Specification	0.09
	Test	0.20	Quit	0.03
Implementation	Design	1.46	Test	1.32
	Test	0.19	Specification	0.01
			Design	0.23
			Quit	0.05
Test	Implementation	1.32	Done	0.91
			Specification	0.01
			Design	0.20
			Implementation	0.19
			Quit	0.01

V. SUMMARY

Simulation is one of the most flexible quantitative tools and has been widely applied across many scientific disciplines. In principle, any kind of a process can be simulated. Simulation has the advantage of being useful in sorting out complexity and uncertainty. While it has only recently been applied to software processes, it is a highly suitable tool.

While valuable, simulation limitations include data collection requirements and analysis of output. Simulation inherently requires extensive effort in data collection if accurate results are expected. This calls for accurate statistical analysis. Statistical analysis is also required for interpretation of results. Alternative analytic approaches have a relative advantage over simulation in that they have clear results. Simulation results inherently involve variation, calling upon the analyst to realize the uncertainty in output.

Systems dynamics models are useful for accurate prediction of the effects of feedback, as well as for representing complex relationships between dynamic variables. However, sequential activities are relatively difficult to model. Discrete event simulations are better for dealing with sequential activities. They also allow the use of entities with attributes and are well designed for queuing relationships and interdependent use of resources. However, discrete event models are not relatively well suited for continuous variable measurement. Continuous models such as systems dynamics tend to be more appropriate for strategic, macro-level studies, usually of longer time horizon. Studies of detailed processes are usually better supported by discrete event simulation models.

SEE ALSO THE FOLLOWING ARTICLES

Continuous Simulation • Discrete Event Simulation • Documentation for Software and IS Development • Monte Carlo Simulation • Simulation Languages

BIBLIOGRAPHY

Abdel-Hamid, T., and Madnick, S. (1991). "Software Project Dynamics," Prentice Hall, Englewood Cliffs, NJ.

Donzelli, P., and Iazeolla, G. (2001). "A dynamic simulator of software processes to test process assumptions," *J. Syst. Software* **56,** 81–90.

Evans, J. R., and Olson, D. L. (2002). "Introduction to Simulation and Risk Analysis," Prentice Hall, Englewood Cliffs, NJ.

Forrester, J. W. (1961). "Industrial Dynamics," Wiley, New York.

Kellner, M. I., Madachy, R. J., and Raffo, D. M. (1999). "Software process simulation modeling: Why? What? How?, *J. Syst. Software,* **46,** 91–105.

Law, A. M., and Kelton, W. D. (1991). "Simulation Modeling and Analysis," 2nd ed., McGraw-Hill, New York.

Raffo, D., Harrison, W., Kellner, M. I., Madachy, R., Martin, R., Scacchi, W., and Wernick, P., Guest Eds. (1999). "Introduction: the Silver Falls workshop on software process simulation modeling (ProSim'98)," *J. Syst. Software,* **46,** 89.

Speech Recognition

John-Paul Hosom

Oregon Health & Science University

GLOSSARY

channel The means by which the speech signal is conveyed from the microphone to the computer. Typical channels are microphone, land-line telephone, and cellular telephone. Each channel has properties that affect the speech signal differently.

dynamic time warping (DTW) An algorithm for aligning in time two separate utterances of the same word or phoneme sequence. DTW is useful in matching a reference template to an input speech pattern.

feature vector A vector of values, where each element in the vector represents one component of a representation of the speech signal. Each feature vector typically represents one *frame* of speech. The feature vectors are used in training a classifier to learn phonetic classes, and during recognition to determine phonetic probabilities of an input frame.

frame A short, fixed segment from a speech signal. Typical frames are 10 msec long, and the speech signal is divided into consecutive, nonoverlapping frames. At each frame, *feature vectors* are computed, and these vectors are passed to a classifier for phonetic classification.

Gaussian mixture model (GMM) A classifier that assumes that the (speech) data can be modeled by one or more Gaussian (or normal) distributions. A GMM is then specified by the mean vectors and covariance matrices of the multidimensional feature space, as well as weights that determine the relative contribution of each distribution. The number of mixtures in the GMM should be the number of distributions required to model the data. The combination of Gaussian mixtures is usually used to model a single phonetic (or subphonetic) category.

hidden Markov model (HMM) A statistical model that can be used to recognize speech. An HMM assumes that the process being modeled (such as speech) can be represented by a finite number of states, and that there are known probabilities of transitioning from one state to the next at each time frame. In automatic speech recognition, states are generally associated, at least in concept, with subphonetic categories. At each state, there are certain probabilities of generating or observing particular events (such as feature vectors in a speech signal).

phoneme An abstract representation of a basic unit of sound corresponding to a single perceived linguistic event, such as the /k/ in the word *king* or the /s/ in the word *sing*.

pitch The perceived frequency level of a voiced speech sound; the term *pitch* is often used to refer to the fundamental frequency of a sound.

resonance In speech processing, resonance refers to a region of strong energy at a particular frequency in the speech signal. Vowels can often be described by the two or three lowest resonant frequencies. These resonant frequencies are usually called *formants*.

vector quantization (VQ) An algorithm for classifying an input *feature vector* into one of a predetermined number of classes. VQ is able to learn the locations of each class in the feature space from training data.

Viterbi search An algorithm for determining the optimal sequence of states in an HMM, given an input speech utterance (represented by a number of sequential *feature vectors*) and a *hidden Markov model.*

I. INTRODUCTION

A. What Is Automatic Speech Recognition?

Speech is a natural and pervasive means of communication among humans, and highly effective over long distances (via the telephone) or when visual communication is not possible. Speech is also an efficient modality when the hands are occupied or when complementary visual information is available. The ease with which humans interact through spoken language has inspired a field of research, and now product development, in what is called *automatic speech recognition* (ASR). Automatic speech recognition refers to a computer system that is able to recognize words that are spoken to it through a microphone. ASR can be used as an input modality that complements standard input devices such as a keyboard or mouse. Current ASR systems have recognition rates that are far from perfect, with the accuracy level dependent on a wide variety of factors. ASR is related to the field of text-to-speech (TTS) synthesis, in which the computer generates a spoken sentence from text.

Most ASR systems are now implemented in software on a personal computer, although specialized hardware platforms are still sometimes employed. The recognition that is done by the computer is often restricted to identification of the sequence of words that is spoken, and does not include meaning or syntax evaluation. However, some systems incorporate a *semantic parser* component that extracts the user's intentions from the speech input. If the user says an utterance such as "I want to fly to Boston tomorrow," a standard ASR system will output only the word sequence. An ASR system that includes a semantic parser will focus on certain words or phrases and extract the knowledge that the user is requesting a flight to a certain location on a certain date. Such semantic parsing is directly related to the field of natural language processing (NLP).

Before an ASR system can be used, it must be developed, or *trained.* Training an ASR system typically involves gathering information about speech from a corpus of speech data, and using this information to construct a model that can be used to recognize new utterances. The goal of the model is to discriminate between utterances of different words while not discriminating between different utterances of the same word.

B. Capabilities and Limitations of Automatic Speech Recognition

ASR is currently used for dictation into word processing software, or in a "command-and-control" framework in which the computer recognizes and acts on certain key words. Dictation systems are available for general use, as well as for specialized fields such as medicine and law. General dictation systems now cost under $100 and have speaker-dependent word-recognition accuracy from 93% to as high as 98%. Command-and-control systems are more often used over the telephone for automatically dialing telephone numbers or for requesting specific services before (or without) speaking to a human operator. Telephone companies use ASR to allow customers to automatically place calls even from a rotary telephone, and airlines now utilize telephone-based ASR systems to help passengers locate and reclaim lost luggage. Research is currently being conducted on systems that allow the user to interact naturally with an ASR system for goals such as making airline or hotel reservations.

Despite these successes, the performance of ASR is often about an order of magnitude worse than human-level performance, even with superior hardware and long processing delays. For example, recognition of the digits "zero" through "nine" over the telephone has word-level accuracy of about 98% to 99% using ASR, but nearly perfect recognition by humans. Transcription of radio broadcasts by world-class ASR systems has accuracy of less than 87%. This relatively low accuracy of current ASR systems has limited its use; it is not yet possible to reliably and consistently recognize and act on a wide variety of commands from different users.

C. Classes of Recognition Systems

ASR systems can be grouped into several classes, depending on their intended purpose. The most basic distinction is between *speaker-dependent* and *speaker-independent* recognition. A speaker-dependent recognizer is one that has learned the voice of a single user and works particularly well for that speaker. If another person uses that recognizer, performance tends to be quite poor. A speaker-dependent recognizer is usually adapted to a single person's voice from a more general template using a process called *speaker adaptation*. The commonly available ASR dictation systems are currently speaker-dependent systems.

A speaker-independent recognizer, on the other hand, is trained on speech from many different people and is meant to work equally well on the speech of almost any user. Speaker-independent systems are often used for telephony applications, in which the user is not known to the system beforehand. Although speaker-independent systems can be used by different people, these systems have lower overall accuracy than a speaker-dependent system that has learned its target user. In addition, even speaker-independent systems are sensitive to different accents, dialects, ages, rates of speech, and degrees of enunciation or articulation. For example, a speaker-independent ASR system that has been trained on adult speech read from a textbook will have best performance on that type of speaker and speech; a child who carefully articulates individual words will likely obtain abysmal performance from that system.

A second major distinction for ASR systems is between *discrete* and *continuous* recognition. In a discrete-speech recognizer, the user must utter a brief pause between each word. The recognizer then identifies the location of each word before performing recognition on each region. In a continuous-speech recognizer, pauses between words are optional, which is more typical in conversational speech. In this case, the speech is not segmented into individual words beforehand, but the overall word sequence with the highest probability is computed. Most current systems are now targeted at continuous speech, although discrete-speech recognizers still have a place in certain applications, especially those that have strict memory or computational restrictions.

A third distinction is based on the size of vocabulary that can be recognized. In all current ASR systems, the vocabulary that can be recognized must be completely specified in advance, and the task of recognition is to identify the number, sequence, and identity of the spoken words based on the given vocabulary. Some systems, called small-vocabulary systems, are able to recognize anywhere from two words (such as "yes" and "no") to several hundred words. The restricted vocabulary size can result in higher recognition accuracy and faster response time. For other applications, a larger vocabulary on the order of several thousand words is required. Systems targeted at these larger vocabulary sizes, called medium-vocabulary systems, strike a balance between accuracy, speed, and vocabulary size. A third category is called large-vocabulary recognition, and is targeted at tens of thousands of words, with a typical vocabulary size of 64,000 words. These systems, referred to as large-vocabulary continuous speech recognition (LVCSR) systems, can require multiple top-end computers to yield results several hundred times slower than real time.

II. HISTORY OF AUTOMATIC SPEECH RECOGNITION

A. Beginnings: Radio Rex and Harvey Fletcher

Possibly the first ASR device was a toy marketed in the 1920s called *Radio Rex*. This miniature bulldog would jump from a doghouse upon hearing a person say the words "Radio Rex." Although Radio Rex was quite primitive in many ways, being able to recognize only a single phrase using simple hardware, it displayed several interesting properties, including real-time speaker-independent recognition.

From 1918–1950, Harvey Fletcher and his colleagues at Bell Labs devoted a significant amount of research effort to the requirements for communicating speech over telephone channels. They performed a large number of perceptual experiments to better understand how human speech recognition works and, based on that understanding, how the telephone channel could be optimized for signal transmission. This research resulted in a large number of results and hypotheses related to human speech recognition, from which Fletcher developed a model of human speech perception. This model is too vague to be used in development of a complete, computational ASR system, but has provided guidance to researchers who now seek to understand how it is that humans perceive speech with such apparent ease.

B. Early Years to Recent Past

Efforts at building computer-based, multivocabulary speech recognition systems started in the 1950s at companies such as Bell Labs and RCA, as well as at universities such as MIT and University College of London. Although the Bell Labs system was targeted at recognizing entire words (consisting of digits), other systems focused on a limited number of syllables or phonemes. Even in these first systems, the speech was first converted from the time domain to the spectral domain, in which the resonant frequencies that characterize speech are clearly identifiable.

In the 1960s, the existing research programs continued, and new work on ASR was begun at laboratories in Japan, the Soviet Union, and at Carnegie Mellon University in the United States. With each new decade, more companies and laboratories have entered the field. Significant progress was made in the 1970s on utilizing efficient features for representing the speech signal, using dynamic programming techniques to account for changes in duration, and developing preliminary dictation and speaker-independent systems. Most systems developed during the 1970s are referred to as *template-based* systems, because they relied on a static template of each target word or phoneme, and they matched the input speech with the existing templates using dynamic programming.

The early 1980s saw the rise of statistical approaches to ASR, specifically the use of *hidden Markov models* (HMMs). HMMs provide a probabilistic framework in which the likelihood of an utterance given a particular model can be computed; models of all phonemes or words in the vocabulary are analyzed, and the model with the greatest likelihood is selected as the recognized word or phoneme. A large amount of funding was provided for ASR research, with a significant portion of funding supplied by the Defense Advanced Research Projects Agency (DARPA) in the United States for work on LVCSR.

In the 1990s, research continued on the HMM approach, and the use of artificial neural networks (ANNs) incorporated within the HMM framework was developed for HMM/ANN hybrid systems. In addition, standardized speech corpora were collected and distributed within the speech research community. DARPA funding continued, resulting in increasing accuracy on more and more difficult tasks. Also during this time, speaker-dependent continuous speech recognition became possible on a personal computer with acceptable accuracy levels, and a number of companies developed products targeted at the consumer sector.

C. System Architectures

ASR systems can be grouped into one of four types: feature based, segmental, template based, or statistical. In a feature-based system, specific features that are known to be associated with phonetic properties are extracted from the speech signal. A feature-based ASR system extracts a large number of these features and combines the evidence over time to arrive at hypothesized phonemes, which can be further combined to arrive at hypothesized words. Although intu-

itive and in many ways well motivated, feature-based approaches suffer from a "multiplication of errors" effect: Small errors in extracting each of the features accumulate, and even low error rates in feature extraction can result in high errors at the word level.

A segment-based ASR system operates in three steps: First, the speech is analyzed to determine the likely locations of phoneme boundaries; second, the segments that result from this analysis are classified based on features taken from throughout the segment; and third, word-level results are obtained from the hypothesized phoneme segments. Segment-based systems have demonstrated performance that can be competitive with other types of systems, such as HMMs, especially on difficult tasks such as alphabet recognition. One of the difficulties in implementing a segment-based ASR system is in reliably determining the locations of phoneme boundaries; methods that work well for certain types of phonetic boundaries may not work well for other types, and in order to avoid "missing" a phoneme, many more segments are hypothesized than are likely to exist in the signal.

A template-based ASR system represents each phoneme or word using individual *templates,* or sets of time frames of features from the speech signal that are obtained from representative examples of each word or phoneme. The input speech is then matched with each of the templates, with time differences between the input and the template normalized using the dynamic programming algorithm called *dynamic time warping.* The template with the best fit to the input speech is considered the recognized word. One of the problems with the template-based approach is that it is unable to efficiently account for the wide variety of ways in which words are pronounced. A single speaker may utter the same word in a number of different ways, with variation in rhythm, relative loudness, or articulation effort. Selection of the most appropriate utterance from the training set can become a difficult issue. A speaker-dependent, word-level, template-based system may perform well in some cases, but it will be restricted to that speaker and that vocabulary; the variety of phonemes in different contexts prohibits the template-based approach from being applied to more general-purpose phoneme-level recognition. For speaker-independent ASR, the variety within and between speakers becomes insurmountable with template-based systems.

Finally, the most commonly used type of ASR system is now the statistical ASR system. In this case, the speech is divided into short, equally spaced frames (with a typical length of 10 msec), and the likelihood of a subphonetic or subword unit at each frame is computed based on statistics such as the average and standard deviation of the features for each unit found in the training set. These likelihoods are combined to arrive at phoneme-level or word-level results, typically by assuming mathematical independence between likelihoods at different frames in the signal. Statistical ASR systems, which generally use the HMM framework, are able to account for more variation than the template-based approach, do not require prior segmentation of the signal into phonetic regions as in the segment-based approach, and do not depend on accurate feature extraction required for the feature-based approach. However, the statistical approach has its own set of weaknesses, including a conflict between sufficiently complex classification units and a sufficient amount of training data, as well as certain overly simplified mathematical assumptions.

III. BACKGROUND: ACOUSTIC-PHONETICS

A. Representations of Speech

The two most common methods of representing the speech signal are in the time and frequency domains. The time-domain representation plots time on the horizontal axis and signal level on the vertical axis. Figure 1(a) shows the time-domain representation of an utterance of the word *phonetics*. In this case, the data points have been sampled at 8000 samples per second (or 8000 Hz); typical sampling rates vary from 8000 Hz for telephone bandwidth to 44,100 Hz for CD quality. It is easy to identify certain properties of the utterance, including the location of each vowel as indicated by the strong, periodic regions of the signal, as well as

other features such as the presence of the fricatives /f/ and /s/, the two bursts indicating the locations of the /t/ and /k/, and the weaker periodic region identifying the /n/. However, identification of the *type* of vowel, fricative, or burst is not easily accomplished by observing the time-domain representation.

The other common representation for speech is the *log-power spectrum* (or *log-power spectrogram*, or simply *spectrogram*), which plots time on the horizontal axis, frequency on the vertical axis, and energy (or log power) at each time and frequency point by the degree of darkness at that location. Figure 1(b) shows the spectrogram for the same utterance as in Fig. 1(a). In this case, strong energy peaks, or resonances, are quite evident in the vowel regions, and can be used to distinguish the /ax/, /eh/, and /ih/ vowels. The frequencies are also different between the /f/ and /s/, and even to some degree between the bursts in the /t/ and the /k/. The log-power spectrum at each time point can be computed by taking the Fourier transform of the signal to convert it to the frequency domain, summing the squares of the real and imaginary components at each frequency to determine the power, taking the log of these power values to determine the power in units of *bels,* and then multiplying each value by ten to arrive at units of *decibels* (dB).

B. General Descriptions of Speech

Speech is often described in terms of phonemes, but other descriptions also convey information about different aspects of the speech signal. Phonemes can be divided into a fixed number of *distinctive features*, or features that specify the manner of articulation, place

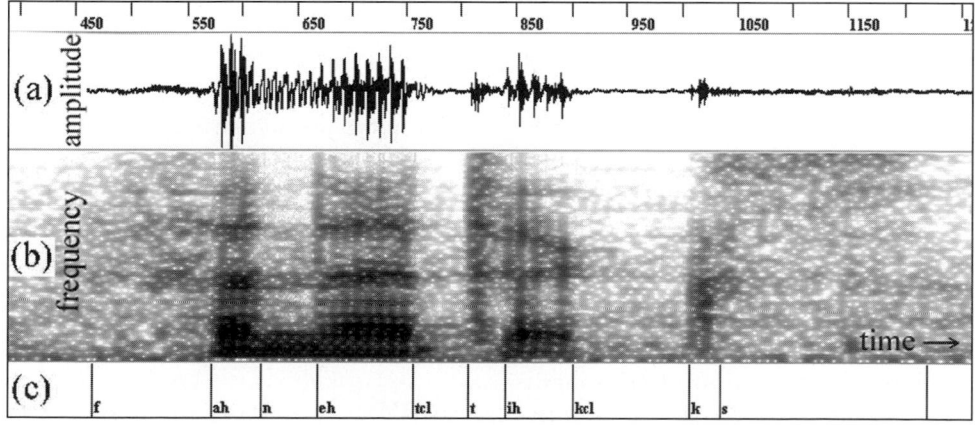

Figure 1   Displays of a speech signal. (a) The time-domain waveform for the utterance *phonetics*. (b) The spectrogram of this waveform, computed with an 18-msec window. (c) The location and identity of each phoneme in the word.

Table I Common Phonemes in English, Example Words That Contain These Phonemes, and the Corresponding Values of the Distinctive Features "Manner" and "Place"

Phoneme	Example word	Manner	Place	Phoneme	Example word	Manner	Place
iy	peat	vowel	front	p	paul	plosive	bilabial
ih	pit	vowel	front	t	tall	plosive	alveolar
eh	pet	vowel	front	k	call	plosive	velar
ae	pat	vowel	front	b	ball	plosive	bilabial
ix	roses	vowel	mid	d	doll	plosive	alveolar
ux	due	vowel	mid	g	gall	plosive	velar
ax	but	vowel	mid	m	mow	nasal	bilabial
uw	boot	vowel	back	n	know	nasal	alveolar
uh	book	vowel	back	ng	sing	nasal	velar
ah	under	vowel	back	f	fin	fricative	labial
ao	caught	vowel	back	th	thin	fricative	dental
aa	cot	vowel	back	s	sin	fricative	alveolar
er	bird	retroflex	back	sh	shin	fricative	palatal
axr	feather	retroflex	back	hh	hope	aspiration	(varies)
ey	pay	diphthong	front	v	vat	fricative	labial
ay	pie	diphthong	front, back	dh	that	fricative	dental
oy	boy	diphthong	back, front	z	zoo	fricative	alveolar
aw	out	diphthong	back	zh	azure	fricative	palatal
ow	coat	diphthong	back	ch	cheap	affricate	alv,pal
l	let	liquid	alveolar	jh	jeep	affricate	alv,pal
r	rent	liquid	palatal	em	bottom	syllabic	mid,lab
y	yet	glide	front	en	button	syllabic	mid,alv
w	wet	glide	back	el	bottle	syllabic	mid,alv

of articulation, degree of voicing, or height of the tongue within the mouth. Some typical values for the manner of articulation are *vowel* (including phonemes /ah/, /iy/, and /ow/), *glide* (/w/ and /y/), *lateral* (/l/), *retroflex* (/r/), *nasal* (the phonemes /m/, /n/, and /ng/), *fricative* (including /s/, /sh/, /th/, and /z/), *affricate* (/ch/ and /jh/), and *burst* (consisting of /p/, /t/, /k/, /b/, /d/, and /g/). *Diphthongs* consist of two separate vowels that are combined to form one phoneme, such as the /aa/ vowel in "father" combined with the /iy/ vowel in "keep" to form the /ay/ diphthong in "nine."

The place of articulation is specified by the location of the tongue tip along the roof of the mouth. Some values for place of articulation of consonants are *bilabial, dental, alveolar, palatal,* and *dorsal;* values for vowels are *front, middle,* and *back.* The height of the tongue within the mouth can be used to distin-

guish between phonemes such as the /iy/ in "sheep" and the /ih/ in "ship," and the degree of voicing indicates whether the phoneme is voiced (as in the consonants /z/ and /b/) or unvoiced (as in the consonants /s/ and /p/). Table I specifies common English phonemes and some of their distinctive features. In addition to distinctive features, speech can also be described in terms of duration, stress, and energy.

IV. OVERVIEW OF THE SPEECH RECOGNITION PROCESS: HOW DOES A TYPICAL SPEECH RECOGNIZER WORK?

An HMM-based recognition system uses a four-step process in recognizing speech. First, the input speech signal is recorded, digitized, and divided into short segments, or *frames,* by applying a windowing function. The signal is typically digitized at a rate of 8000 to 16,000 samples per second, and a frame is obtained usually every 10 msec. In the second step, each frame is analyzed and a low-dimensional representation of the speech at that point in time is computed. This representation, or *feature vector,* often emphasizes those aspects of the signal that are commonly related to phonetic identity, and de-emphasizes other aspects, including pitch and voice quality. In the third step, a classifier is used to estimate the likelihood of each phonetic category at each frame, given the feature vectors for each frame. The output of the classifier is then a matrix of likelihoods or probabilities, with P rows and F columns, where P is the number of phonetic categories, and F is the number of frames. In the fourth step, the output of the classifier is used with constraints provided by the vocabulary and grammar to determine the most likely sequence of words. The classifier outputs and properties of the vocabulary are combined using a search procedure called a *Viterbi search.* A Viterbi search is a dynamic programming algorithm that finds the optimal path based on the probabilities of phonetic categories as well as the probabilities of phonetic durations.

This general process is illustrated in Fig. 2. The first oval in this figure indicates the windowing process, which divides the signal into frames. Although frames may be computed every 10 msec, the length of the window can be larger than the length of a frame, causing overlap of the windows between successive frames. The shaded box with a dotted-line outline indicates a process

that is applied to each frame. The first step in this box is to compute a low-dimensional representation of the signal; typical feature types are *perceptual linear prediction* (PLP) or *Mel-frequency cepstral coefficient* (MFCC) features. Then, some degree of convolutional noise is removed by processes such as *cepstral-mean subtraction* (CMS) or *RelAtive SpecTrAl* (RASTA) processing.

Because speech is a dynamic process, the features that represent the speech at each frame are augmented with *delta values* that represent how the features change over time at each frame. The delta values are computed directly from the features at the current frame and from features at surrounding frames. In some cases, *delta–delta values* are also computed, which indicate the acceleration of features at each point in time. For each frame, the features (including the delta and delta–delta values, if desired) are passed to a classifier. Standard classifiers are Gaussian mixture models (GMMs) or artificial neural networks (ANNs). The classifier has been previously trained on speech that is hopefully similar in many respects (including tempo, speaker characteristics, channel and noise conditions, and topic domain) to the utterance currently being recognized. The output of the classifier is an estimation of the likelihood of each phoneme (or subphonetic category) at each frame. The Viterbi search then combines these outputs with a state-based model of the vocabulary and state duration probabilities, and determines the most likely word sequence. The output of the Viterbi search contains the most likely word and phoneme sequence, as well as their time locations.

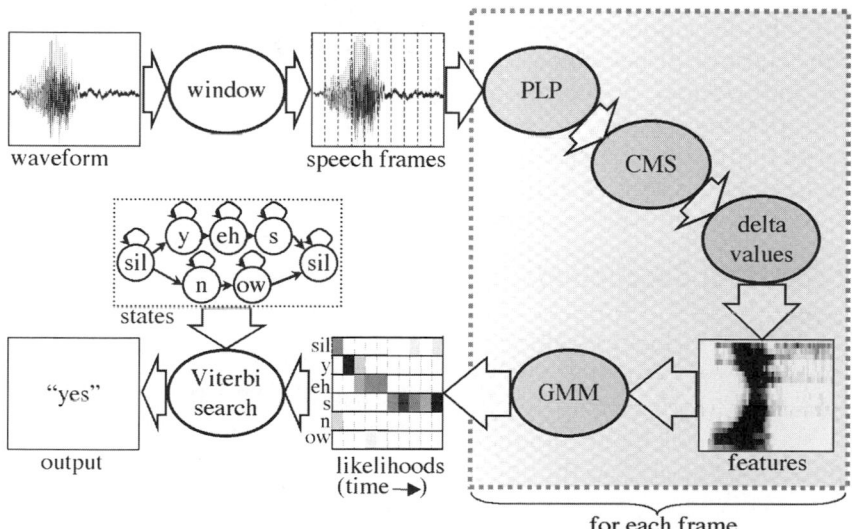

Figure 2 Illustration of the recognition process, from input waveform to output word.

V. INPUT TO A SPEECH RECOGNITION SYSTEM: FEATURES OF THE SPEECH SIGNAL

A. Motivation: What Makes a Feature Useful?

The input to the GMM or ANN classifier is a representation of the input speech signal at a given point in time. One basic question is "Why not use the time-domain signal directly?" The time-domain waveform by definition contains all of the information that can be obtained from the utterance, and so the cost of extracting special features must be justified by significant benefits. There are two primary benefits from feature extraction. First, feature extraction allows highlighting of important information in the signal and suppression of irrelevant information. For example, pitch is not strongly correlated with phonetic identity, but the energy found in different frequency bands is highly correlated with phonetic identity. The time-domain waveform varies to a large degree with the pitch, which is considered irrelevant information, whereas the power spectrum can be computed so that information about pitch is suppressed and resonant-frequency information is maintained. By using a representation based on the power spectrum, unwanted variability is reduced and the classifier can more easily learn the different phonetic classes.

A second benefit of feature extraction is in reducing the number of inputs to the classifier. As the inputs to the classifier are mapped to the phonetic outputs using statistical classification, a larger number of training samples per input value tends to yield more robust classification. By reducing the number of inputs while maintaining relevant information, a reduction can be achieved in the amount of training data required to obtain the same classification accuracy. For example, the time-domain waveform may have 256 data points per 16-msec window, but the information relevant to phonetic content can be approximated using only 13 PLP or MFCC features.

B. Mel-Frequency Cepstral Coefficients

Mel-frequency cepstral coefficient features are computed using a seven-step process. First, the signal is *pre-emphasized*, which changes the tilt or slope of the spectrum to increase the energy of higher frequencies. Next, a Hamming window is applied to the frame; a Hamming window reduces the effects of speech at the edges of the window, which is useful in obtaining a smooth spectral representation. Third, the power spectrum is computed, without taking the log operation. A filter-bank operation is applied to the power spectrum, thereby measuring the energy in different frequency bands. The frequency bands are spaced along the frequency axis according to the perceptually based nonlinear Mel scale, in which higher frequencies are represented with lower resolution. In the fifth step, the log of the energy in these frequency bands is computed. In the sixth step, the spectral-domain representation is translated into the *cepstral* domain; cepstral features can be obtained by taking the inverse Fourier transform of the log-power spectrum. The cepstral domain representation has the advantage that the features are less correlated, which is important in efficient implementation of GMM-based classifiers. Finally, the cepstral features are weighted so that the range of all feature values is approximately equal. This weighting is useful in implementation of the classifier, although theoretically not required.

C. Perceptual Linear Prediction

Perceptual linear prediction features are similar to MFCC features in several respects, but there are also significant differences. PLP features, which are motivated by knowledge of human auditory processing, can be computed using eight steps. First, the speech signal at the current frame is windowed using a Hamming window; then, the power spectrum (without the subsequent log operation) of this windowed speech is computed. The power spectrum is then warped along the Bark scale instead of the Mel scale; the Bark scale approximates properties of human auditory filters. In the fourth step, the energy in the Bark-scale frequency bands is changed to compensate for the nonuniform sensitivity of human hearing at different frequencies. In the fifth step, the amplitude of the frequency-band outputs is compressed to approximate the power law of hearing. In the sixth step, the frequency-band features are represented using linear predictive coefficients (LPC), which allows for a reduction in the number of features. Finally, these LPC features are converted to the cepstral domain and weighted in the same way as MFCC features.

D. Removing Noise: Cepstral-Mean Subtraction and RASTA

In some cases, the speech signal to be recognized is recorded in a very controlled, quiet environment. In more typical cases, the speech occurs in the presence of background noise. This noise can be *additive,* caused by addition of different sounds, or *convolutional,* caused by characteristics of the microphone or telephone channel. If the noise does not vary over time, then a technique called cepstral-mean subtraction can be effective in removing convolutional noise while preserving speech. Implementing CMS is quite simple: The mean value of a cepstral feature is computed over the duration of an utterance, and this mean value is then subtracted from each cepstral feature. By removing any constant information from the features, nonvarying noise is removed. Another technique, RASTA, filters the speech over time to remove both very slow (or constant) as well as very fast components of the signal. A modification of standard RASTA, called *lin-log RASTA,* attenuates both additive and convolutional noise.

VI. BASIC ALGORITHMS FOR SPEECH PROCESSING

A. Vector Quantization

Vector quantization (VQ) is a technique often used in the development of ASR systems, and it can be used in place of GMM- or ANN-based classification of input features. In training a vector quantization system, the feature space is divided into clusters of similar data points, and an identity or category is assigned to each cluster. In pattern classification, VQ is used to classify input features as belonging to one of the categories learned during training.

A VQ system can be trained using an iterative three-step process, given N vectors (or sets of features) in the training corpus and C categories to be learned. In the initialization step, C vectors are chosen from the N available vectors; each of the C vectors becomes one category. This initial selection can be random or based on the maximum distance between vectors in the corpus. The C categories are assigned unique "codewords" for identification, and their location is specified by the assigned vector. The search step processes all vectors in the training corpus, and computes the distance between the training vector and each of the C category locations. A common distance measure is the squared Euclidean distance, or the sum of the squared differences of corresponding feature values. The category with the minimum distance is determined, and the training vector is assigned to that category. In the update step, the location of each category is updated by averaging all of the vectors belonging to that category. The search and update

steps are repeated until there is no change in the category locations, or until the average distance falls below some predetermined threshold.

Given a trained VQ system, a feature vector can be easily classified by measuring the distance from the input vector to each of the category locations; the category with the minimum distance is the output of the classifier.

B. Dynamic Time Warping

Dynamic time warping (DTW) is an algorithm that is used to time-align two sets of feature vectors, where each set contains the feature vectors for each frame of a word or sequence of words. DTW requires a distance measure between two vectors, and the same Euclidean distance measure that is used in VQ can be used in DTW. In DTW, the frames of one utterance are assigned to the horizontal axis and the frames of the other utterance are assigned to the vertical axis. Then, at each point in the resulting two-dimensional grid, the distance (called a *local distance*) is calculated between the frames corresponding to the point on the grid.

A greedy-algorithm search is then used to trace the path with the lowest combined distance score. First, a cumulative distance is assigned to all first-row points; for the first row, the cumulative distance at a point is the same as the local distance at that point. At each point in the second row, the cumulative distances from several points in the first row to the current point are computed. The cumulative distance to the higher point is the sum of the cumulative distance to the lower point and the local distance (or sum of the local distances if a path with multiple points is considered) from that lower point to the higher point. Only points in lower rows that also have lower column values are evaluated, so that the search result always proceeds forward in time. Of the several points that are considered, the lower point with the smallest cumulative distance to the higher point is determined, and this minimum cumulative distance result is stored at the higher point. Also, a back-pointer that identifies the location of the lower point (row and column information) is recorded at the higher point. After all minimum cumulative distances are computed for the second row, the search proceeds to the third row. For each point in the third row, the cumulative distances from several lower points to the third-row point are computed, the minimum cumulative distance is determined, and this minimum distance and the back-pointer are recorded at this third-row coordinate. The search continues up through each row, determining the minimum cumulative distance to a particular point and recording the results at that point for later use.

When all rows are completed, the ending frame (or point) with the lowest total distance score is selected. The path from the ending frame to the beginning frame is then determined by inspecting the back-pointers. This path specifies the best alignment between the frames of the two speech signals.

VII. SPEECH RECOGNITION BY HIDDEN MARKOV MODELS

A. What Is a Markov Model?

A *Markov model* (MM) is a state-based model of a process such as changing weather patterns or changing speech features. A Markov model can be specified with S states and connections between some or all of the states. Each state generates a symbol or observation $\mathbf{o}^s_t$ corresponding to state s at time t, and a transition from one state to the next occurs with some specified probability. The transition from one state to the next occurs at regular clock intervals, with t increasing at each new time interval until some maximum time T. It is only possible to remain in a given state for more than one time period if that state has a state transition loop from itself to itself. The state transition probabilities are referred to using the notation a_{ij}, where a_{ij} is the probability of transitioning from state i to state j. In addition to the state transition probabilities, there are state initial probabilities, denoted π_i, of starting in state i at the first time period (when $t = 0$). Note that because the values of π are probabilities, the sum of all π_i equals 1.0, and because each state must transition to some other state (except at the final state), the sum of a_{ij} over all values of j also equals 1.0 for each state i. A Markov model is therefore a generator of events; there is an initial probability of generating $\mathbf{o}^s_0$ for each $\pi_s > 0$, and probabilities of generating subsequent observations that are dependent on the values of the previous state and a_{ij}. Because the probability of being in state s at time t is dependent only on the previous state s_{t-1}, these types of Markov models are referred to as *first-order* Markov models.

B. What Is a Hidden Markov Model?

A *hidden Markov model* is an extension of a Markov model in which both the *transitions* between states and the *observations* emitted from each state are prob-

abilistic. In this case, the probability of emitting observation $\mathbf{o}_t$ at state s is referred to using the notation $b_s(\mathbf{o}_t)$. Note that the number of types of observations now does not have to equal the number of states; each state can emit numerous types of observations, each with a given probability.

For example, in an HMM model of weather phenomena based on barometric pressure, the states may be associated with different levels of pressure, such as high, medium, and low pressure. The high-pressure state will be called H, the medium-pressure state called M, and the low-pressure state called L. State H may have an 80% chance of emitting a "sunny" observation, a 10% chance of emitting a "cloudy" observation, and a 10% chance of emitting a "rainy" observation. State M may have a 30% chance of emitting a "sunny" observation, a 40% chance of emitting a "cloudy" observation, and a 30% chance of emitting a "rainy" observation. State L may have a 10% chance of emitting a "sunny" observation, a 20% chance of emitting a "cloudy" observation, and a 70% chance of emitting a "rainy" observation. The probability of transitioning from state H back to H may be 50%, the probability of transitioning from H to M may be 45%, and the probability of transitioning from H to L may be 5%. Similar transition probabilities can be imagined for states M and L. Given state-initial probabilities, this HMM can now generate any sequence of "sunny," "cloudy," and "rainy" observations.

In a complementary manner, if we are given a sequence of "sunny," "cloudy," and "rainy" observations and an existing HMM, we can determine the probability that this HMM generated these observations. By computing the probabilities of different HMMs generating a given sequence of observations, we can select the HMM with the highest probability, and thereby perform classification of observations into a sequence of states. Because an HMM employs both observation probabilities and state-transition probabilities, the "true" underlying state sequence can never be precisely determined from a given sequence of observations; only the most likely state sequence can be computed. HMMs derive their name from the fact that the underlying state sequence is never known with certainty, or is always "hidden." For example, an observation sequence of *"sunny cloudy rainy"* in the weather phenomena HMM may have been generated by the state sequence {H, M, L}, the state sequence {M, M, H}, or any of the other possible three-state combinations. From the observed data, we can never determine the state sequence that was used to generate these observations, but we *can* determine that the most likely state sequence is, for example, {H, M, L}.

An HMM for speech recognition is shown in Fig. 3. In this figure, each state corresponds to a (nonunique) phoneme, the observations are the feature vectors at each frame, and the vocabulary is specified by only allowing certain sequences of phonemes with greater than zero probability. Some remaining issues in HMM recognition are then how the best sequence of states can be determined (search), and how the HMM parameters can be learned from the training data (training).

C. Determining the Optimal State Sequence of an HMM

The optimal state sequence of an HMM given a set of feature vectors for each time frame can be computed using a dynamic programming algorithm called a Viterbi search. The Viterbi search has two components: a forward pass, in which the likelihood of entering each state is computed, and a back-trace step, in which the optimal path is determined using back-pointers recorded during the forward pass. The forward pass proceeds frame by frame; at each state in each time frame, the likelihood of entering that state at that time is computed from information in the states at the previous time frame, the transition probabilities, and the observation probabilities. The likelihood of *transitioning into* the given state j at time t is the maximum, over all states i, of the likelihood of being in state i at time $t - 1$ multiplied by the probability of transitioning from state i to state j. The likelihood of *being in* state j at time t is then the likelihood of transitioning into this state at time t, multiplied by the probability of the observation at time t, $\mathbf{o}_t$, given state j. (The probability of observing $\mathbf{o}_t$ in state j is written $p(\mathbf{o}_t \mid j)$ and is determined from an existing classifier evaluated on $\mathbf{o}_t$.) The likelihood of being in state j at time t is recorded, as is the state i from which j was entered; the state information serves as the back-pointer for tracing the most likely path. After all states in all frames have been processed, the backward pass determines the most likely path by going from the most likely end state at time T to the state at time $T - 1$ from which the end state was entered (as recorded in the back-pointer), then from the state at time $T - 1$ to the state at time $T - 2$, and so on until the state at time 0 is reached. The output of the Viterbi search then contains the identity of each state as well as the times during which each state is occupied.

D. Initializing an HMM

Given an existing HMM, speech recognition can be performed by connecting different phoneme-specific HMM states to form words, and using the Viterbi search to determine the most likely sequence of words. However, if there are no existing HMMs, they must be created from training data. The basic training process can be divided into initialization and iterative training. It is assumed that the correct sequence of phonemes in the training data is known. To initialize an HMM, a number of methods can be used: "flat start," manual, or automatic segmentation.

The flat start technique simply divides each training utterance into P equal-length segments, where P is the number of (nonunique) phonemes in the utterance. The flat-start technique then assigns the first segment to the first phoneme in the utterance, the second segment to the second phoneme, and so on until all segments have been assigned. Another technique is to manually segment the utterance and assign the correct phonemes to each segment; this technique can be highly accurate, but is quite time and labor intensive. A compromise between flat-start and manual methods is to perform automatic segmentation, which typically uses an existing phonetic classifier and a Viterbi search to determine the most likely phonetic segmentation of a known sequence of phonetic states. (Existing classifiers can be obtained from a number of sources; for example, Japanese data can be segmented using an English HMM by providing a mapping between English phonemes and their most similar Japanese counterparts.)

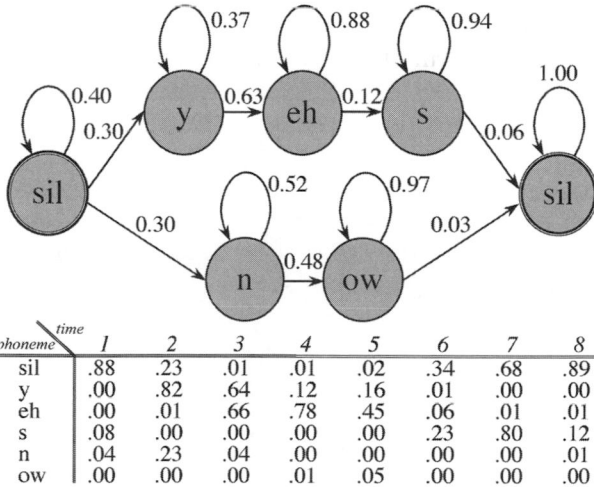

phoneme \ time	1	2	3	4	5	6	7	8
sil	.88	.23	.01	.01	.02	.34	.68	.89
y	.00	.82	.64	.12	.16	.01	.00	.00
eh	.00	.01	.66	.78	.45	.06	.01	.01
s	.08	.00	.00	.00	.00	.23	.80	.12
n	.04	.23	.04	.00	.00	.00	.00	.01
ow	.00	.00	.00	.01	.05	.00	.00	.00

Figure 3   An HMM for the isolated words *yes* and *no*, showing the probability of each phoneme at each time frame. The "sil" states model silence before and after the word.

Given an initial segmentation, initial estimates of a_{ij} and $b_s(\mathbf{o}_t)$ can be computed from the relative number of occurrences of each state, and from the feature vector means and covariance matrices. These estimates can be further refined, as explained in the next section.

E. Training an HMM: The Expectation-Maximization Algorithm

The expectation-maximization (EM) algorithm, also called the Baum-Welch algorithm, can be used to iteratively refine initial estimates of HMM parameters, so that a locally optimum model is computed. The EM algorithm relies on the computation of several probability values, including the probability of observing $\mathbf{o}_1, \mathbf{o}_2, \ldots, \mathbf{o}_t$ (where $t < T$) and arriving in state i at time t; the probability of observing $\mathbf{o}_T, \mathbf{o}_{T-1}, \ldots, \mathbf{o}_{t+1}$ and arriving in state i at time t; the overall probability of being in state i at time t; and the probability of being in state i at time t and in state j at time $t + 1$. The first of these probability values is denoted $\alpha_t(i)$ and is computed in a manner very similar to the cumulative likelihood defined for the Viterbi search, except that instead of selecting the previous state with the maximum value, the sum of all previous states is computed. The second probability value is denoted $\beta_t(i)$ and is computed in a manner similar to $\alpha_t(i)$, except that the time frames decrease from T. The last two probability values, denoted ξ (xi) and γ (gamma), can be computed from the values of α, β, the current estimates of the state transition probabilities a_{ij}, and the current estimates of the observation probabilities $b_j(\mathbf{o})$. From ξ and γ, new estimates of the model parameters π, a_{ij}, and $b_j(\mathbf{o})$ can be computed. Then, the four probabilities α, β, ξ, and γ are recomputed based on the new estimates of these HMM model parameters. This process is iterated until no further improvement in the values of the HMM parameters is obtained; the final result is a maximum-likelihood estimate of the parameters.

F. Context-Dependent Modeling

Because of constraints on the physical movements of the articulators, the effects of one phoneme can be observed in neighboring phonemes. This effect of *coarticulation* can make classification of phonemes quite difficult, as a phoneme can have very different feature values depending on its phonetic context. Most HMMs use several states per phoneme (with three states per phoneme being a typical value) to ac-

count for the change in the speech features over time, but even a multistate phonetic model does not account for the variety in the training data that is due to different phonetic contexts. As a result, many HMM systems employ what is called *context-dependent modeling*. With context-dependent models, each state in the HMM is not only associated with a phoneme, but with a phoneme with both left and right context (a triphone model). For example, a context-independent model of the word *acoustic* may be written as /ah k uw s t ih k/, with 18 unique states assuming three states per phoneme. A context-dependent model of this word may be written as /sil-ah+k ah-k+uw k-uw+s uw-s+t s-t+ih t-ih+k ih-k+sil/, where the word is assumed to occur with surrounding silence, and the format "X-Y+Z" indicates that the phoneme Y occurs with left context X and right context Z. In this case, there are 21 unique states (with three states per model), because different models of /k/ are needed for the different phonetic contexts. Thus, the context-dependent model has states that are more specific to each word.

A context-dependent model of the phoneme /eh/ in the context of a preceding /y/ and following /s/ is illustrated in Fig. 4. In this example, a GMM is used with two Gaussian distributions (mixture components) per state. The Gaussian distributions are specified by a vector of mean values ($\mathbf{\mu}$) and a matrix of covariance values ($\mathbf{\sigma}$) with the dimensions of the vector and matrix determined by the number of features. (In this figure, one-dimensional GMMs are illustrated for visual clarity.) The weight of each distribution is specified by the mixture component weight c. The transition probabilities indicate that it is more likely to remain longer in the middle state than in either of the surrounding states.

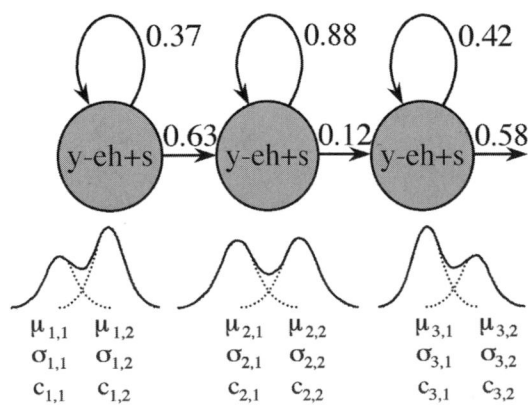

Figure 4   Context-dependent HMM of the phoneme /eh/, shown with state transition probabilities and two-component Gaussian mixture models for each state.

G. Continuous Speech Recognition

The recognition of continuous speech is, at least in theory, a simple extension of the case of recognizing discrete words using phoneme models. For recognizing continuous speech, each word in the vocabulary is specified in the same way as with isolated word recognition. The key difference is that the transitions out of each word-final state point not only to the same state and a silence model, but also to the word-initial states of all words in the vocabulary. Conceptually, then, when a word-final state is exited, the next state may be the silence model, or it may be the beginning of any other word. In implementation, several issues arise with regard to controlling the complexity of the resulting very large HMM and keeping track of word-level information. One approach to the complexity issue is to use "null" states at the beginning and ending of each phoneme HMM. These null states do not generate or record any observations, and can be entered and exited during the same time frame. The advantage of null states is that the word-end states then do not require separate transitions to each word-beginning state, but a single transition to the null state. The null states can then be easily connected from word endings to word beginnings.

H. Language Models

Until now, we have considered the computation of the probability of the observed observation sequence, given the set of HMMs for our vocabulary. If we want to compute the probability of a sequence of words given the observation sequence, Bayes' rule can be applied, along with a language model:

$$P(W|O) = \frac{P(O|W)P(W)}{P(O)} \qquad (1)$$

This equation specifies that the probability of a word sequence given an observation sequence is equal to the probability of the observation sequence given the word sequence, multiplied by the *a priori* probability of the word sequence, and divided by the probability of the observation sequence. The value of $P(O|W)$ can be computed as the output of the Viterbi search, and the value of $P(W)$ can be obtained from the language model. The value of $P(O)$ is usually ignored, as $P(O)$ is constant for all word sequences and the *relative* probability of the best word sequence will not change with $P(O)$. In most cases, *bigram* or *trigram* language models are used. These models simply compute the probability of the current word based on the occurrence of the previous one or two words. For ex-

ample, the probability of the word *day* may be relatively high when the previous word is *sunny*, but much lower when the previous word is *statistics*.

VIII. OTHER APPROACHES TO STATISTICAL ASR: HMM/ANN HYBRIDS

Traditionally, the observation probabilities in an HMM, $b_j(\mathbf{o}_t)$, are modeled using a Gaussian mixture model. In this case, the model contains the means and covariance matrices of each feature vector for specifying a single Gaussian distribution, and weights for determining the relative contribution of several Gaussians to the final model. Another approach to computing the observation probabilities uses artificial neural networks. It has been shown that, given sufficient training data, complexity of the ANN configuration, and training time, the posterior probabilities of the output classes (which are context-dependent phonemes in the case of ASR) are estimated from the input features; this posterior probability can be written as $p(c \mid \mathbf{o})$, where c is a phonetic class and $\mathbf{o}$ is a given observation vector. An HMM, however, requires estimation of $p(\mathbf{o} \mid c)$, and so Bayes' rule can be applied by dividing the neural network outputs by the *a priori* likelihood of each class to arrive at scaled estimates of $p(\mathbf{o} \mid c)$. When an ANN is used to estimate the observation probabilities, the resulting system is referred to as an HMM/ANN hybrid.

The use of ANNs in estimating the observation probabilities yields several benefits, including fast execution time and discriminative training. Furthermore, implementation of efficient GMM models requires that the input feature elements be uncorrelated; ANN training, on the other hand, allows correlation between the features. The advantages of ANNs are offset by some disadvantages, including longer training time and the inability to modify the properties of one output class without retraining the entire system. The choice of whether to use GMMs or ANNs is dependent on several factors related to the type of system that is being developed.

IX. SUMMARY

A. Successes and Weaknesses of Automatic Speech Recognition

Research during the past several decades has resulted in notable progress in the development of ASR systems. In the 1970s, recognition of isolated words was a major advance; in the 1980s, connected-word recognition was possible. Just prior to 1990, state-of-the-art performance on a 1000-word task was more than 90%, and accuracy has since increased to 96%. By the early 1990s, accuracy of more than 90% was attained on vocabularies of 5000 words. Accuracy on speaker-independent conversational speech has increased from about 10% accuracy in the early 1990s to about 80% accuracy by the late 1990s. Transcription of radio broadcasts has attained accuracy of almost 87%. Currently, speaker-dependent dictation systems on personal computers have accuracy ranging from 93 to 98%.

Despite these advances, the state of the art remains about an order of magnitude worse than human-level performance. To put the accuracy levels in perspective, an accuracy level of 95% means that 1 out of every 20 words will be incorrectly recognized; if there is an average of 7 words per sentence, with each word having a 95% chance of correct recognition, then the probability of correctly recognizing an entire sentence is only 70%. ASR systems still make errors that no human would make, and in many cases high levels of performance are only attained for specific tasks such as a well-known topic domain, speaker-dependent recognition, or small vocabularies. A system that works extremely well under one set of conditions will usually have dramatically worse performance under different conditions. As the HMM framework has been successively refined for nearly 20 years, it is not yet clear if further refinements and additional training data will be able to provide human-level robustness and accuracy, or if new models need to be considered.

B. Why HMMs Are the Dominant Technology

The field of ASR is dominated by HMM-based recognizers for several reasons. One of the primary reasons is that the accuracy levels attainable by HMM systems are often as good as, or better than, accuracy levels attainable by other architectures. One of the reasons for this higher accuracy is the ability of the HMM to account for all frames of speech when making phonetic (state) decisions; if a few frames have poor probability estimates, the remaining frames often provide sufficient evidence to make the correct classification. Another reason for the success of HMMs is in the probabilistic modeling of speech; single templates of "representative" features are not necessary, and the characteristics of a large number of training samples can be captured by the model parameters. By using a state-based framework and the Viterbi search, explicit phonetic segmentation of the signal is not required.

Furthermore, by computing phonetic probabilities directly from the speech features, the multiplication of errors found in systems that extract and combine explicit, high-level features can be avoided. Finally, development of an HMM recognizer requires understanding of mathematical concepts, but little expert knowledge about human speech production or human speech recognition processes or theories. Because our current knowledge of human spoken language processing is imprecise and incomplete, the HMM framework provides a quantifiable background for developing recognition systems.

X. FUTURE DIRECTIONS

A. "Should Airplanes Have Wings?"

In the days before heavier-than-air flight, many of the attempts at building flying machines modeled the outward characteristic of birds: wings that flapped. Of course, it was not until the Wright brothers that successful flight was achieved, and their airplane's wings were immobile. What the Wright brothers understood and implemented were the principles required to lift dense objects above the ground, and aspects that are orthogonal to the principles of flight (such as flapping) were replaced by other functions with equivalent effect, such as motors and propellers. NASA has now successfully tested airplanes such as the X-33 that have practically no wings; these airplanes are referred to as "wingless lifting bodies."

As Hynek Hermansky, a researcher in the field of automatic speech recognition, has pointed out with an airplane analogy, it is not necessary for ASR systems to mimic all of the functionality of the ear, as long as the properties important to speech recognition are preserved. Should, then, an ASR system have "ears" that mimic human hearing, in the same way that most airplanes have wings? To what degree should ASR systems mimic as much of the functionality of the ear as possible? Alternatively, should ASR be approached from a purely mathematical perspective, with no reference to existing (human) speech recognition systems? As Hermansky points out, given that human speech recognition yields performance dramatically superior to current ASR systems, it may be unwise to ignore knowledge or theories about human hearing. To continue the analogy, it is unlikely that the Wright brothers would have successfully developed a wingless lifting body based on their knowledge of aerodynamics. It is important, however, to focus on only those parts of the auditory system that are important for speech recognition, and to acknowledge that our understanding of human audition is far from complete. Until ASR systems are significantly more robust, progress might be attained by improving on and integrating our understanding of the phonetically relevant components of human hearing. However, this belief is not universally held within the community of speech researchers.

B. Possible New Areas of Research

The field of ASR is ripe for new advances in research and development; current technology is still inadequate in providing robust, high-accuracy results in all domains, and simple refinement and evolution of existing systems may not bring about sufficient improvement. ASR research may turn in several directions; some possibilities are representations of the signal that better convey information about the speech content, improved probability estimation, more efficient use of training data, incorporation of reliability measures during phoneme classification, recognition based on distinctive phonetic features rather than phonemes as the atomic units, further development of segment-based recognition, or syllable-based recognition. However, it is quite possible that major breakthroughs in performance will be achieved from research that is entirely fresh and unexpected. Research advances in automatic speech recognition will not only improve communication between humans and computers, but will also improve our understanding of how any complex information can be reliably conveyed through a noisy medium.

SEE ALSO THE FOLLOWING ARTICLES

Artificial Intelligence Programming • Pattern Recognition • Voice Communications • Word Processing

BIBLIOGRAPHY

Huang, X.-D., Ariki, Y., and Jack, M. A. (1990). *Hidden Markov models for speech recognition.* Edinburgh, Scotland: Edinburgh University Press.

Ladefoged, P. (1993). *A course in phonetics,* 3rd ed. Fort Worth, TX: Harcourt Brace College Publishers.

Lee, K.-F. (1989). *Automatic speech recognition: The development of the SPHINX system.* Boston: Kluwer Academic Publishers.

Rabiner, L., and Juang, B.-H. (1993). *Fundamentals of speech recognition.* Englewood Cliffs, NJ: Prentice-Hall.

Rabiner, L. R., and Schafer, R. W. (1978). *Digital processing of speech signals.* Englewood Cliffs, NJ: Prentice Hall.

Varile, G. B., and Zampolli, A. (1996). *Survey of the state of the art in human language technology,* R. A. Cole, A. Ronald, J. Mariani, H. Uszkoreit, A. Zaenen, and V. Zue, (Eds.). Cambridge, England: Cambridge University Press.

Waibel, A., and Lee, K.-F. (1990). *Readings in speech recognition.* San Mateo, CA: Morgan Kaufmann Publishers.

Young, S., Kershaw, D., Odell, J., Ollason, D., Valtchev, V., and Woodland, P. (1999). *The HTK book (for HTK version 2.2),* 3rd ed. Cambridge, England: Entropic.

Spreadsheets

Shashidhar Kaparthi and Daniel J. Power
University of Northern Iowa

GLOSSARY

absolute reference A cell reference in a formula whose location remains the same when copied.

cell The position created by the intersection of a column and row.

goal seeking The capability of asking the computer software model what values certain variables must have in order to attain desired goals. It is a tool that uses iterative calculations to find the value required in one cell (variable) in order to achieve a desired value in another cell.

instant recalculation The recalculation of formulas whenever values in referenced cells change.

relative reference A cell reference in a formula whose location adjusts when copied.

spreadsheet A program that allows any part of a rectangular array of positions or cells to be displayed on a computer screen, with the contents of any cell able to be specified independently or in terms of the contents of other cells.

what-if analysis The ability to "ask" the software package what the effect will be of changing some of the input data or independent variables.

I. INTRODUCTION

In the realm of accounting jargon a *spreadsheet* was and is a large sheet of paper with columns and rows that lays everything out about transactions for a businessperson to examine. It spreads or shows all of the costs, income, or taxes on a single sheet of paper for a manager to look at when making a decision. An electronic spreadsheet organizes information into software-defined columns and rows. Data can then be added by a formula to give a total or sum. A spreadsheet program summarizes information from many paper sources in one place and presents the information in a format to help a decision-maker see the financial "big picture" for a company. In general, the term *spreadsheet* is used by information systems professionals to categorize programs that allow any part of a rectangular array of positions or cells to be displayed on a computer screen, with the contents of any cell able to be specified independently or in terms of the contents of other cells.

Based on sales figures millions of managers, business analysts, and professionals around the world create spreadsheets each year. Creating spreadsheets is important in organizations and many mission-critical corporate decisions are guided by the results of large and complex spreadsheets. This article is a review, a discussion, and an exposition of spreadsheets. A brief history of spreadsheets is provided in the next section followed by a review of spreadsheet fundamentals and concepts. Then, spreadsheet applications are discussed, followed by a review of some academic research in this area.

II. BRIEF HISTORY

Spreadsheet history begins hundreds of years ago, but electronic spreadsheets are of much more recent origin. Some published newspaper and magazine stories have reported that in 1978 a Harvard Business School student, Daniel Bricklin, invented the first electronic spreadsheet called VisiCalc. Bricklin came up with the idea for an interactive visible calculator. Bricklin considers Bob Frankston a co-inventor of VisiCalc. The VisiCalc spreadsheet program was the first major application for personal computers.

In the early 1960s, Professor Richard Mattessich pioneered computerized spreadsheets for business accounting in a paper published in *The Accounting Review.* Some historical information on the computerization of accounting spreadsheets is discussed on Mattessich's web page "Spreadsheet: Its First Computerization (1961–1964)" at http://www.j-walk.com/ss/history/ spreadsh.htm. Mattessich's work influenced the computerization of spreadsheets programmed on mainframe computers, but it is unlikely that it influenced Bricklin and Frankston. Although some spreadsheet development occurred prior to the invention of VisiCalc, it began the modern spreadsheet era.

The tale of VisiCalc is part myth and part fact for most of us. The story is that Dan Bricklin was preparing a spreadsheet analysis for a Harvard Business School "case study" report and had two alternatives: (1) do it by hand or (2) use a clumsy time-sharing mainframe program. Bricklin thought there must be a better way. He wanted a program where people could visualize the spreadsheet as they created it. His metaphor was "an electronic blackboard and electronic chalk in a classroom." By the fall of 1978, Bricklin had programmed the first working version of his concept. The program would let users input a matrix of five columns and 20 rows. The first version was not very "user friendly" so Bricklin recruited an MIT acquaintance, Bob Frankston, to improve and expand the program. Frankston expanded the program and "packed the code into a mere 20K of machine memory, making it both powerful and practical enough to be run on a microcomputer." Dan Bricklin has placed his version of the history of Software Arts and VisiCalc on the Web at http://www.bricklin.com/history/ sai.htm.

During late fall of 1978, Daniel Fylstra, founding associate editor of *Byte* magazine, joined Bricklin and Frankston in developing VisiCalc. Fylstra was also an MIT/HBS graduate. Fylstra was "marketing oriented" and suggested that the product would be viable if it could run on an Apple microcomputer. Bricklin and Frankston formed Software Arts Corporation on January 2, 1979. In May 1979, Fylstra and his firm, Personal Software (later renamed VisiCorp), began marketing VisiCalc with a prerelease ad in *Byte* magazine. The name "VisiCalc" is a compressed form of the phrase "visible calculator." VisiCalc became an almost instant success and provided many businesspeople

with an incentive to purchase a personal computer. It was even available on an H-P 85 or 87 calculator from Hewlett-Packard. About 500,000 copies of the spreadsheet program were sold during VisiCalc's product lifetime. A screen shot of the first version of VisiCalc is provided in Fig. 1.

A. What Came after VisiCalc?

The market for electronic spreadsheet software grew rapidly in the early 1980s and VisiCalc was slow to respond to the introduction of the IBM PC, which used an Intel computer chip. Beginning in September 1983, legal conflicts between VisiCorp and Software Arts distracted the VisiCalc developers. During this period, Mitch Kapor developed Lotus and his spreadsheet program quickly became the new industry spreadsheet standard.

B. Lotus 1-2-3

Lotus 1-2-3 made it easier to use spreadsheets and added integrated charting, plotting, and database capabilities. Lotus 1-2-3 established spreadsheet software as a major data presentation package as well as a complex calculation tool. Lotus was also the first spreadsheet vendor to introduce naming cells, cell ranges, and spreadsheet macros. Kapor was the VisiCalc product manager at Personal Software for about 6 months in 1980; he also designed and programmed Visiplot/Visitrend, which he sold to Personal Software (VisiCorp) for $1 million. Part of that money along

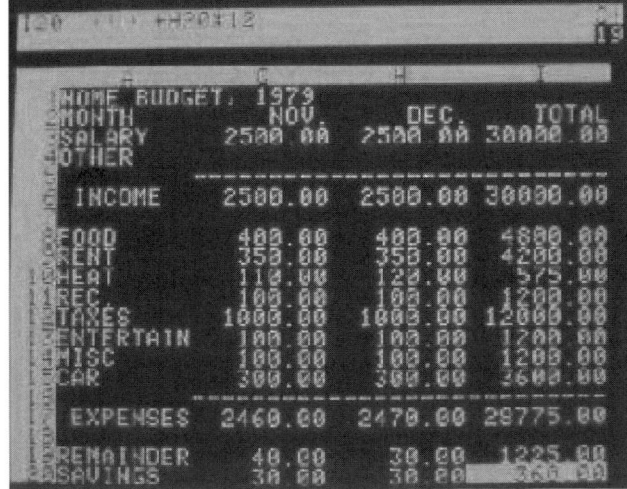

Figure 1   A screen shot of the first version of VisiCalc.

with funds from venture capitalist Ben Rosen was used to start Lotus Development Corporation in 1982. Kapor cofounded Lotus Development Corporation with Jonathan Sachs. Before he struck out on his own, Kapor offered to sell Personal Software (VisiCorp) his initial Lotus program. Supposedly VisiCorp executives declined the offer because Lotus 1-2-3's functionality was "too limited." Lotus 1-2-3 is still one of the all-time best selling application software packages in the world.

In 1985 Lotus acquired Software Arts and discontinued VisiCalc. A Lotus spokesperson indicated at that time "1-2-3 and Symphony are much better products so VisiCalc is no longer necessary."

C. Microsoft Excel

The next milestone was the Microsoft Excel spreadsheet. Excel was originally written for the 512K Apple Macintosh in 1984–1985. It was one of the first spreadsheets to use a graphical interface with pull-down menus and a point-and-click capability using a mouse-pointing device. With its graphical user interface, Excel was easier for most people to use than the command line interface of PC-DOS spreadsheet products. Many people bought Apple Macintoshes so that they could use the Excel spreadsheet.

When Microsoft launched the Windows operating system in 1987, Excel was one of the first products to be released for it. When Windows finally gained wide acceptance with version 3.0 in late 1989, Excel was Microsoft's flagship product. Excel remained the only Windows spreadsheet program for nearly 3 years and lacked significant competition from other spreadsheet products until the summer of 1992. In the late 1980s, many companies had introduced DOS spreadsheet products. Spreadsheet products and the spreadsheet software industry were maturing. Microsoft had joined the fray with its innovative Excel spreadsheet. Lotus had acquired Software Arts and the rights to VisiCalc. Jim Manzi had become CEO at Lotus in April 1986, and in July 1986 Mitch Kapor resigned as chairman of the board. The entrepreneurs were moving on. . . .

D. Legal Battles

In January 1987, Lotus Development filed suit against Paperback Software and separately against Mosaic Software claiming they had infringed on the Lotus 1-2-3 spreadsheet software. In a related matter, Software Arts, the developer of the original VisiCalc

spreadsheet software, filed a separate action against Lotus claiming that Lotus 1-2-3 was an infringement of VisiCalc. Briefly, Lotus won the legal battles, but lost the "market share war" to Microsoft. According to Russo and Nafziger, "The Court granted Lotus' motion dismissing the Software Arts' action and confirming that Lotus had acquired all rights, including all claims, as part of the earlier transaction." Most people have probably forgotten the Lotus clones called TWIN and VP Planner. TWIN and VP Planner were designed to work like Lotus 1-2-3. Advertising proclaimed that the TWIN software product "offers you so much more, for so much less."

Russo and Nafziger note "Both Mosaic's TWIN and Paperback's VP Planner had most of the same features, commands, macro language, syntax, organization and sequence of menus and messages as Lotus' 1-2-3. Their visual displays were not however identical to 1-2-3 or to each other. Both TWIN and VP Planner reorganized and placed their respective menus, sub-menus, prompts and messages on the bottom of the screen."

On June 28, 1990, Judge Keeton of the Federal District Court in Boston upheld the copyright of the Lotus 1-2-3-user interface. The Court ruled that "[t]his particular expression of a menu structure is not essential to the electronic spreadsheet idea, nor does it merge with the somewhat less abstract idea of a menu structure for an electronic spreadsheet. . . . [T]he overall structure, the order of commands in each menu line, the choice of letters, words, or 'symbolic tokens' to represent each command, the presentation of these symbolic tokens on the screen, the type of menu system used, and the long prompts—could be expressed in a great many if not literally unlimited number of ways." *Lotus Dev. Corp. v. Paperback Software Int'l,* 740 F. Supp. 37, 67 (D. Mass. 1990). Essentially, the court stated that the developers of TWIN and VP Planner products had other design choices available to them, but chose instead to inappropriately copy the Lotus 1-2-3 interface. In the late spring of 1995, IBM acquired Lotus Development and Microsoft Excel had become the spreadsheet market leader.

III. FUNDAMENTALS AND CAPABILITIES

Spreadsheet software allows users to manipulate workbooks. A spreadsheet workbook can contain one or more worksheets. A worksheet contains many rows and columns. A hierarchical overview of spreadsheet concepts is presented in Fig. 2.

Typically, the rows in the worksheet are numbered sequentially (1, 2, 3, 4, etc.) and the columns in the

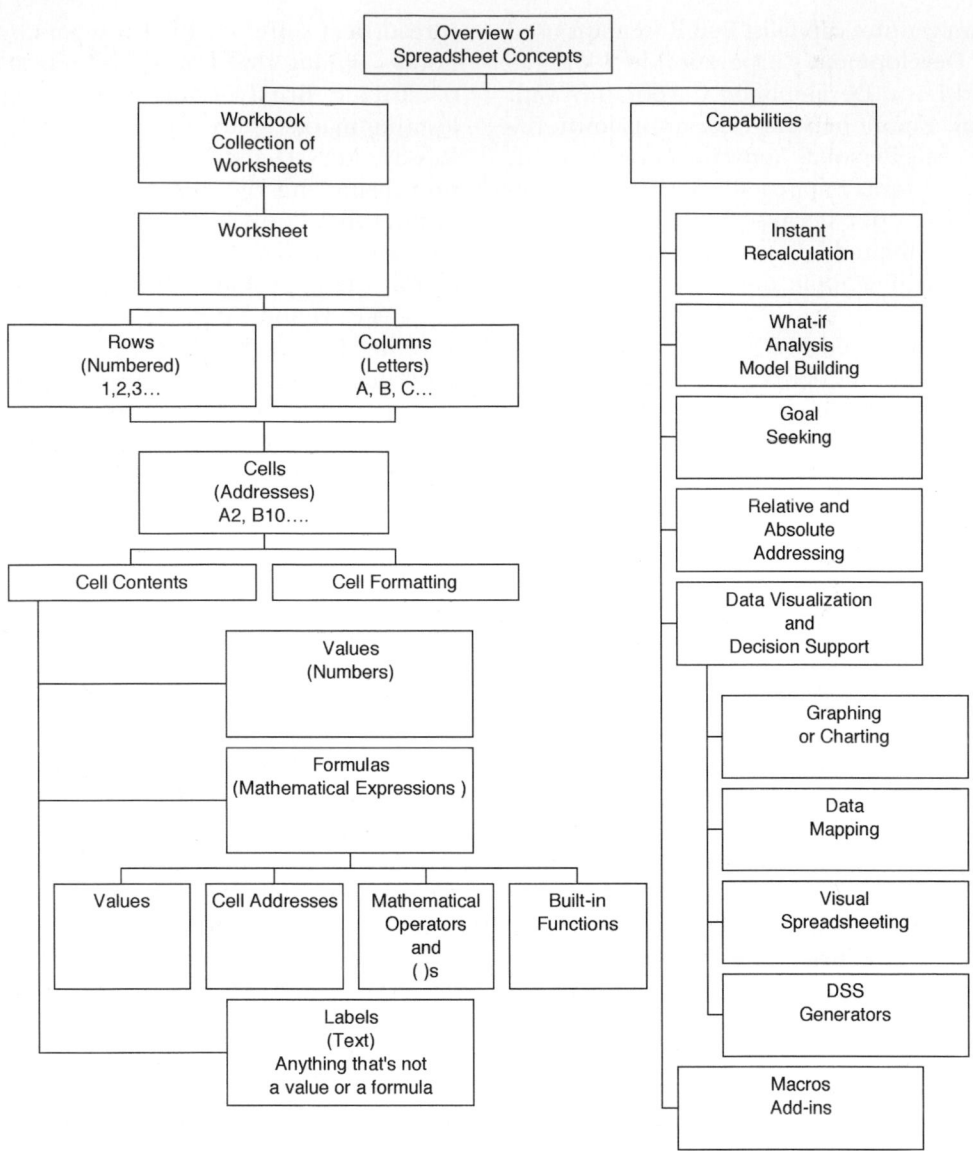

Figure 2 Overview of spreadsheet concepts.

worksheet are identified by the letters of the alphabet (A, B, C, ..., Z, AA, AB, etc.), as shown in Fig. 3. The rectangular elements formed by the intersection of columns and rows are known as cells. Each cell is unique and can be identified by its *address* or its *reference*, that is, the letter of its column followed by the number of its row. For example, in Fig. 3, the address of the highlighted cell is C5, since column C and row 5 intersect to form the cell.

A. Cell Contents

A user can type text, labels, numbers, or values into cells or, more importantly, a user can type formulas

into cells. A formula is a mathematical expression that may contain numbers, cell addresses, mathematical operators (+, addition; −, subtraction; *, multiplication; /, division; ^, exponentiation), and parentheses. When a user types a formula in a cell, the spreadsheet software computes the formula by substituting the values contained in the cells referenced in the formula and displays the result of the computation in that cell. Figure 4 illustrates this by using an example of a car loan analysis done in Microsoft Excel. In the example, the cost of the car is entered in cell C3, the down payment is entered in cell C4, and a formula (=C3−C4) is entered in cell C6. The spreadsheet software computes the formula by substituting the values contained in the cells referenced (i.e., 28000 for C3 and 4000

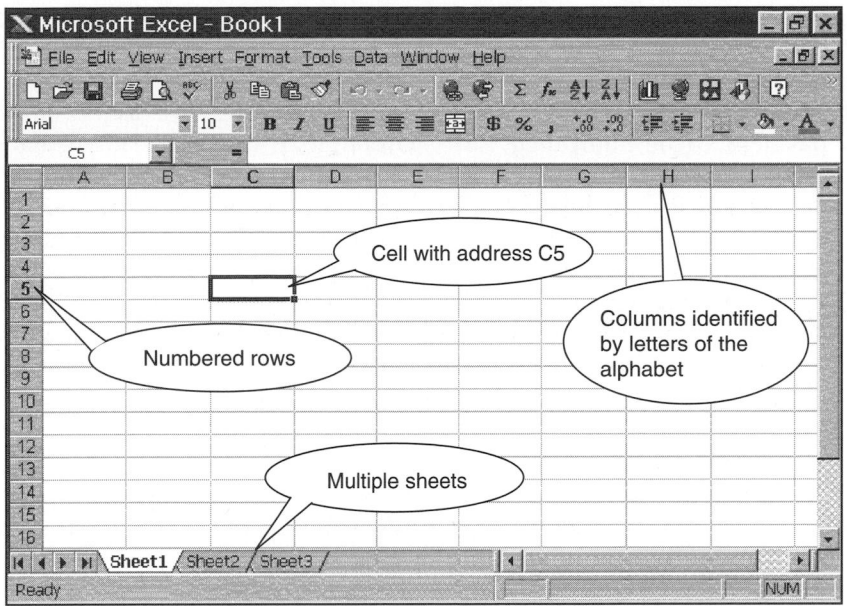

Figure 3 A screen-shot of Microsoft Excel.

for C4) and displays the result of the computation (28000 − 4000 = 24000) in cell C6.

B. Built-In Functions

To complete the car loan analysis and to compute the monthly payment, the user needs to perform a complex calculation that takes into consideration the annual interest rate as well as the time period for paying back the loan. Typically spreadsheet software has the ability to perform complex calculations through the use of built-in functions or @ functions (Lotus 1-2-3 terminology). Built-in functions process one or more values known as arguments or parameters and output a single resultant value similar to the definition of a function in mathematics. Spreadsheets provide functions for financial, date and time, math and

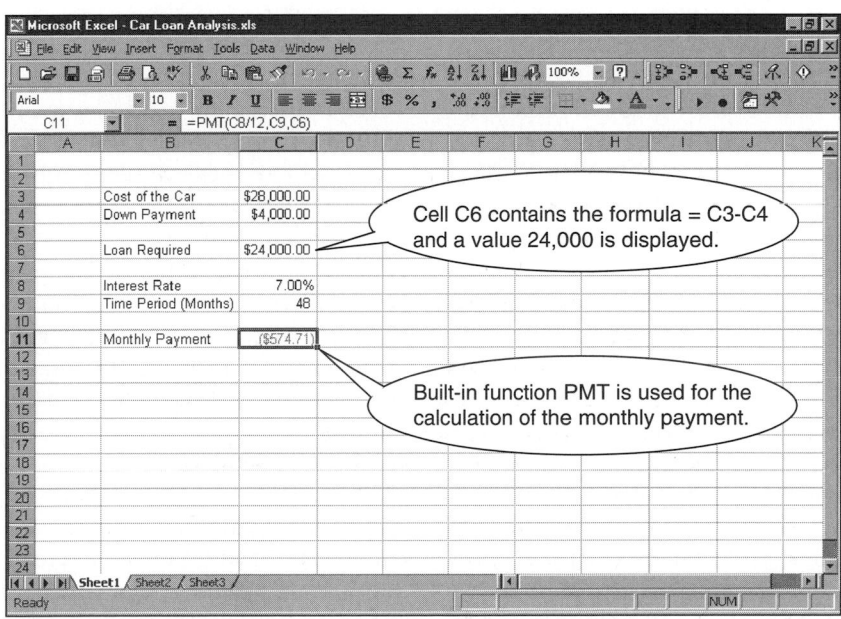

Figure 4 Using Excel to analyze a car loan.

trigonometry, statistical, lookup and reference, database, and engineering computations. Typically, built-in help features are a good source of information on the different kinds of functions available.

For the monthly payment to be computed, the spreadsheet has to process the loan required, the interest rate, and the time period for paying back the loan. In the example illustrated in Fig. 4, a built-in function is entered in cell C11 [=PMT(C8/12,C9, C6)] for computing the monthly payment. The annual interest rate is in C8, the time period in months is in C9 and the loan required is in C6. The result of the computation performed by the PMT built-in function is displayed in C11.

C. Cell Formatting

A user can format cells to better convey the significance of the contents to the audience. In the car loan analysis example (Fig. 4), the dollar amounts have been formatted using the Currency format and the cell containing the interest rate has been formatted using the Percentage format. Some of the other formats available include the text, the date, and user-defined formats. To enhance the appearance of the worksheet, a user can format the borders, patterns, colors, and fonts of cells. Column widths can be adjusted, row height can be changed, and the text can be aligned horizontally as well as vertically as needed in the cells. Modern spreadsheet software even has the ability to orient the text in the cells at any angle.

D. Instant Recalculation

Returning to the car loan example, if the user wants to reduce the monthly payment by putting more money down ($6000 instead of $4000), all the user needs to do is type the new value into cell C4. As soon as the user types the new value ($6000) into cell C4, the spreadsheet software changes the loan required to $22,000 and the monthly payment drops to $526.83. Whenever a value is changed, spreadsheet software immediately recalculates and changes the values of all formulas that depend on the new value. This is a very important feature of spreadsheet software and is known as the *instant recalculation* feature.

Even though the formulas have been set up using one particular set of values, values can be changed and the results obtained for any new situation that a user wants to examine. To put it in simpler terms, once a worksheet has been set up to analyze a partic-

ular car loan, it can be used to analyze any car loan. Hence, we have a model of a decision-making situation instead of just calculations for one particular decision-making situation. If we examine the car loan example in terms of a mathematical model, we have independent variables (cost of the car, down payment, time period), intermediate variables (loan required), uncontrollable variables (interest rate), and dependent variables (monthly payment). Spreadsheet software allow users to establish mathematical relationships between all of these variables.

E. What-If Analysis?

Once a mathematical model is built, a user can very quickly find out the impact of changes in independent variables on the dependent variables and can then make informed decisions. This is possible due to the instant recalculation capability of the spreadsheet software. In the car loan example, a user could easily determine the answer to questions like these: What is the impact of increasing the down payment by $2000? What is the reduction in the monthly payment if the loan is paid back in 5 years instead of 4 years? What is the impact of cutting the cost by going with fewer options? An analysis that allows us to change the independent variables and examine the impact on dependent variables is known in general as a *what-if analysis*. For example, a marketing executive should be able to answer the question, what is the impact of an increase in advertising expenses of 20% on sales? To summarize, what-if analysis is the capability that allows users to "ask" the software package what the effect will be of changing some of the input data or independent variables in a model.

Closely related to what-if analysis is the concept of scenario management. A scenario is a set of values that a spreadsheet saves and can substitute automatically in a worksheet. Users can use scenarios to forecast the outcome of a worksheet model. Users can create and save different groups of values on a worksheet and then switch to any of these new scenarios to view different results. Users can compare the results of several scenarios side by side and make informed decisions.

F. Goal Seeking

Goal seeking allows a user to calculate the value of an independent variable needed to achieve a certain value or goal of a dependent variable. It is a tool that uses iterative calculations to find the value required in one cell (variable) in order to achieve a desired value in another cell. A common use of the goal-seeking feature in a spreadsheet is to calculate a break-even quantity.

Examples of questions to which a goal-seeking capability would give us answers are as follows: What should the cost of the car be for the monthly payment to be $500? What should I spend on advertising to realize sales of $50,000 this quarter?

G. Relative and Absolute Addressing

Consider the car loan analysis again. The user wants to compare two car loans side by side to get a better idea of the trade-off involved. Instead of retyping the entire model, the user may use the spreadsheet software's copy operation. This allows the user to make a copy of a series of cells and place a duplicate of those cells in another area of the spreadsheet. Copying is generally a two-step process. First, a user highlights (selects) the data that should be copied and then picks the appropriate items from the menu for copying the data over to the clipboard (computer's memory). After that, the user selects the cell(s) that are to be the destination for the data and then picks the appropriate menu items for pasting the data from the clipboard. Figure 5 illustrates the car loan example after the user has copied data to column D.

If the second car costs $30,000, all the user needs to do is to type in the new cost in the cell for the cost

of the new car (D3). As soon as the user enters the value of 30000 into cell D3, the loan required in cell D6 and the monthly payment in the cell D11 are instantly recalculated as $26,000 and $622.60. Even though the user had initially designed the model in column C, when the cell contents are copied over to column D, a model independent from the initial model is copied into column D. The dependent variable in column D depends on the independent variables and the intermediate variables in column D but not column C. If one examines the formula in cell D6, it is now actually (= D3 − D4), even though the original formula copied was = C3 − C4. The spreadsheet software has modified the formula when copying, according to the concept of *relative addressing*.

For the purposes of copying, the concept of relative addressing interprets a formula in terms of the relative positioning of the cells referenced in the formula with respect to the cell containing the formula. This relative positioning is maintained when the formula is copied into the new cell. Obviously, this feature is very important for increasing the productivity with which a user can build a complex worksheet. In certain situations a user may want a formula to contain a cell reference that should not change when the formula is copied to other cells. A user can do this by using absolute cell references. Figure 6 illustrates examples of formulas containing relative addressing and absolute addressing and the resulting formulas when these are copied to other cells.

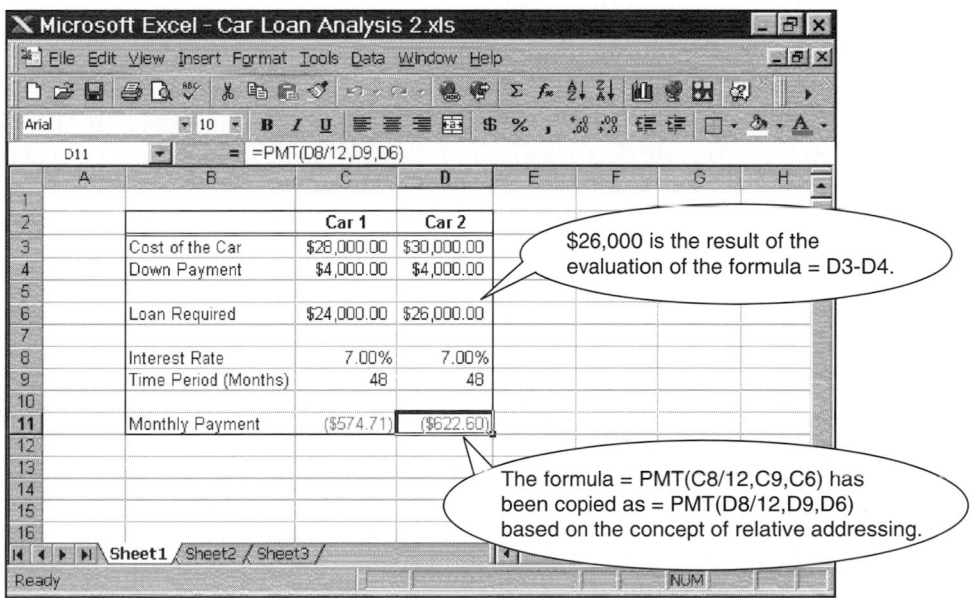

Figure 5 Car loan analysis illustrating the concept of relative addressing.

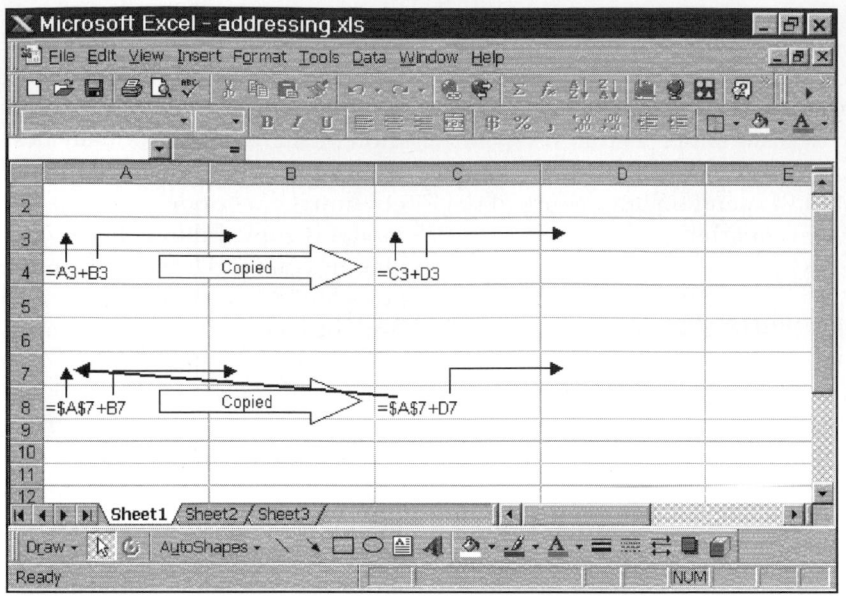

Figure 6 Relative and absolute addressing.

H. Data Visualization and Decision Support

Modern spreadsheets make use of graphical user interfaces and allow users to perform sophisticated data visualization. Data visualization is an important technique for gathering "information" from data and assisting decision making. Some of the data visualization techniques that modern spreadsheets allow users to perform are graphing, data mapping, and visual spreadsheeting. These techniques are briefly described in the following subsections.

1. Graphing or Charting

Electronic spreadsheets allow us to visualize data in a lot of ways. One of the most important ways of visualizing data is by means of charting. Charting or graphing in spreadsheets is very simple. A user selects the data that have been graphed and then picks the appropriate commands from either the menu or the toolbar. Very often, user-friendly wizards guide the user through the process of setting up the graph. These wizards show a preview of the graph while providing dialog boxes for users to manipulate the settings of the graph.

A user can choose from several graph types including column, bar, line, pie, XY, area, surface, and bubble. The user can also combine some of these graph types. A user can pick the graph type that most effectively conveys the inherent nature of the data. For example, it is useful to visualize trends in time series data by using a line graph. XY graphs are useful for depicting statistically related data. Pie graphs are useful for the visualization of percentage-based allocations. Certain spreadsheets even offer the capability of drawing three-dimensional charts.

Typically, independent variable data to be graphed on the horizontal axis are specified as X-Series data. Dependent variable(s) data are specified as data series 1, 2, 3, and so on. The user can enter a chart title, subtitles, axis titles, and legends. Scales, major ticks, minor ticks, the order of the data, and the positioning of the titles can be specified too. Sophisticated spreadsheet software like Excel allows the user to add trend lines and perform linear regression on the data by using just a simple right-click of the mouse on the chart data.

After a graph is set up, if the user changes any data in the worksheet, the instant recalculation feature of the spreadsheet recalculates all the formulas in the worksheet and updates the graph to reflect the new values. This capability allows users to conduct what-if analyses and study the impact of changes in the independent variables on a series of dependent variables to gain valuable insight into a situation. Such capabilities are enormously useful for sound decision making. Figure 7 contains a graph that has been created using the Microsoft Excel software. It depicts the stock price of Amazon Corp. over a 3-month period. The daily high, low, and closing stock prices are plotted using the stock graph type.

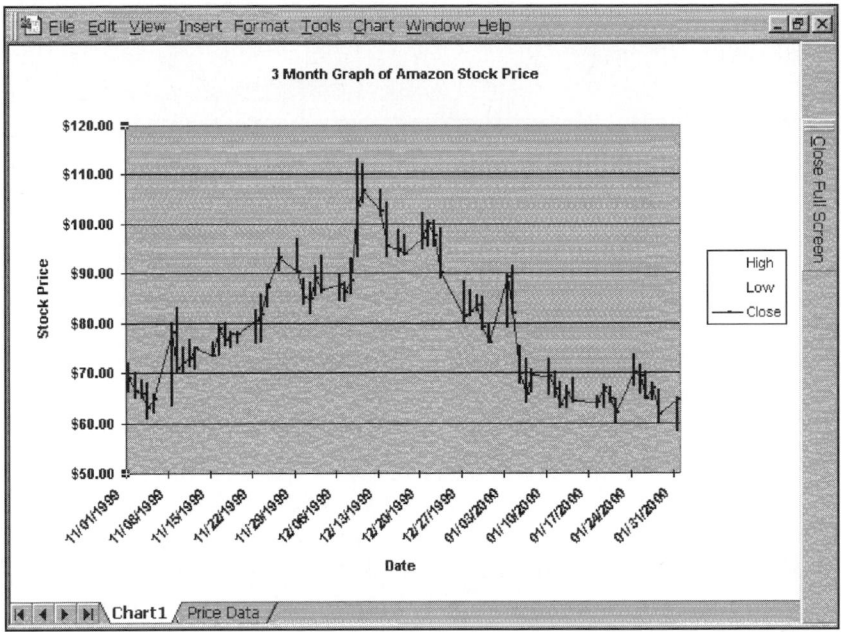

Figure 7 Graph created using Excel.

2. Data Mapping

A simple geographic information system (GIS) or a spatial decision support system can be implemented using a sophisticated spreadsheet like Microsoft Excel. Data mapping is as simple to perform as data charting. A user should enter labels for geographic regions like state names, county names, or zip codes and the regional data values in a tabular form. Once the appropriate data are selected, simple clicks on the menu or the toolbar will lead to user-friendly dialog boxes that guide the user through the process of setting up the maps. A gray-scale map of the United States depicting the population in the year 1990 is presented as an example in Fig. 8.

3. Visual Spreadsheeting Using Influence Diagrams

An influence diagram provides a graphical presentation of the relationships in a model. Arrows are used to depict the influence of certain variables on other variables. The direction of the arrow indicates the direction of the influence. Typically, rectangles are used to represent independent or decision variables, circles are used to represent uncontrollable or intermediate variables, and ovals are used to represent dependent or outcome variables. An influence diagram can be drawn using the drawing toolbar that allows users to superimpose geometric shapes on a work-sheet. Such diagrams allow the visualization of relationships between variables in a model that would normally be hidden inside formulas. An influence diagram for the car loan analysis previously discussed is presented in Fig. 9.

4. Spreadsheets as DSS Generators

Computer-based information systems that combine models and data to enable users to solve semistructured problems with extensive interactivity are typically referred to as decision support systems (DSSs). An integrated software package that provides capabilities for building specific DSSs quickly, inexpensively, and easily is known as a DSS generator. Two broad approaches can be identified in the evolution of DSS generators: one is that of special-purpose languages initially developed for mainframes and second is that of PC-based integrated software systems.

Many commercial DSS generators evolved from financial planning systems with special-purpose languages modeled on natural language processing, such as Interactive Financial Planning System (IFPS) and Encore! Some others have roots in database management systems (DBMSs) such as Nomad and Encore.

Spreadsheets are DSS generators in the sense that they allow decision situations to be modeled quickly, inexpensively, and easily. Data can be manipulated by using models, what-if analyses can be performed, and

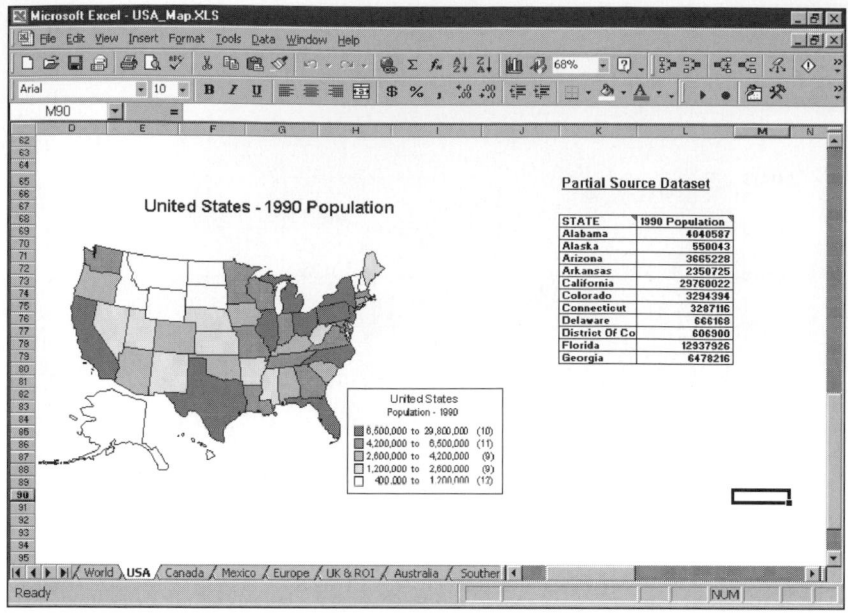

Figure 8 Gray-scale map of the United States depicting 1990 population.

results can be visualized in tables or by using graphs and maps. Users with spreadsheets can solve semi-structured problems using all of the capabilities described earlier.

I. Macros and Add-Ins

To increase the productivity of a person using a spreadsheet, spreadsheet software allows automation of tasks through the use of macros. A user records a macro by turning the macro record feature on and then performing the steps that are to be recorded. Once a macro is recorded it can be played back to make the computer perform as if the user is repeating the tasks again. Sophisticated users can write their own macros in the spreadsheet software's macro programming language or edit the macros that have been recorded. Once the macros are recorded or written, they can be saved as templates or add-ins and then imported into other workbooks.

Visual Basic for Applications (VBA) is the common development language and environment found throughout Microsoft Office including Microsoft Excel and other VBA-enabled third-party applications. By providing a common development language and environment, Microsoft and other software vendors who license VBA for their applications enable developers to focus on the functionality of the applications instead of learning a new language for each application they incorpo-

rate into their solutions. Visual Basic for Applications is very similar to the Visual Basic programming language that developers use for developing applications for the Windows operating system and to VBScript that people use for server-side scripting of active server pages and client-side scripting in Internet Explorer.

In addition to allowing developers to write macros in the macro program language, certain spreadsheets even allow modules written in other programming languages to be included as add-ins to enhance its capabilities. This capability of spreadsheet software to "add in" modules has spawned an entire industry that develops software designed to enhance the functionality of spreadsheets. Table I lists some add-ins that are available for Microsoft Excel spreadsheet along with the functionality enhanced or provided.

According to Fylstra *et al.,* since its introduction in February 1991, the Microsoft Excel Solver has become the most widely distributed and almost surely the most widely used general-purpose optimization modeling system. A brief description of the capabilities of this popular and useful add-in along with an illustrative example are provided in the following subsection. The subsection after that describes the use of the Analysis ToolPak statistical data analysis add-in.

1. Solver

Solver is an add-in that can be called from the menu of the spreadsheet program to determine the maxi-

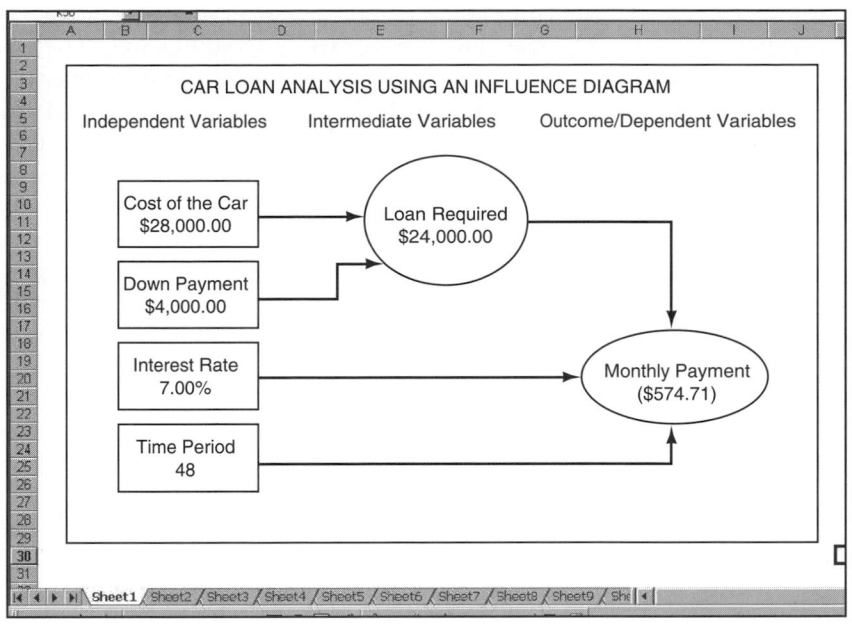

Figure 9 Influence diagram of a car loan analysis model.

Table I **Partial List of Add-Ins Available for Microsoft Excel**

Add-in	Description
Access Links Add-in	Allows you to use Microsoft Access forms and reports with Excel data tables.
Analysis ToolPak	Adds financial and engineering functions, and provides tools for performing statistical and engineering analyses.
Analysis ToolPak–VBA	Adds Visual Basic functions for the Analysis ToolPak.
AutoSave	Saves workbook files automatically.
Conditional Sum Wizard	Helps you create formulas to sum selected data in lists.
File Conversion Wizard	Converts several spreadsheet files to Excel format in one step.
Internet Assistant Wizard	Converts Excel tables and charts to HTML files.
Lookup Wizard	Finds values at the intersection of a row and column based on known values.
Microsoft Query	Retrieves data from external database files and tables using Query. [This add-in is used only when saving files in Microsoft Excel 97 and 5.0/95 (Windows) or Microsoft Excel 98 and 5.0/95 (Macintosh) format, or for backward compatibility for Visual Basic.]
ODBC	Adds worksheet and macro functions for retrieving data from external sources with Microsoft ODBC. [This add-in is included in Excel 97 (Windows) or Excel 98 (Macintosh) only for backward compatibility; for programmatic data access, use DAO.]
Report Manager	Prints reports based on views and scenarios.
Solver Add-in	Calculates solutions to what-if scenarios based on adjustable cells, constraint cells, or cells that must be maximized or minimized.
Template Utilities	Contains utilities used by Excel templates.
Template Wizard with Data Tracking	Creates a template to export worksheet data to a database.
Update Add-in Links	Updates links in Excel version 4.0 add-ins to directly use Excel 97 (Windows) or Excel 98 (Macintosh) functionality.
Web Form Wizard	Helps you create an HTML form based on an Excel spreadsheet.

mum or minimum value of one cell by changing another cell or a group of cells. For example, a user may ask Solver to figure out the advertising expenditures that generate the most profit. The cells that are selected must be related through formulas on the worksheet. According to its on-line documentation, Microsoft Excel Solver uses the generalized reduced gradient nonlinear optimization code developed by Leon Lasdon, University of Texas at Austin, and Allan Waren, Cleveland State University. Linear and integer problems use the simplex method with bounds on the variables, and the branch-and-bound method, implemented by John Watson and Dan Fylstra, Frontline Systems, Inc.

Figure 10 illustrates an example of a product-mix decision that has been solved using Excel's Solver. The decision involves choosing the amounts to produce of two different products (cases of juice glasses,

cases of wineglasses). The demand for juice glasses is forecasted at 800 units and the demand for wineglasses is forecasted at 1200 units. The production quantities should not exceed these forecasts (constraints). The net contribution from producing and selling each of these glasses is given. The decision-maker has taken into consideration two capacity limitations: the warehouse area where the products are stored and the machining time available. The decision-maker wants to figure out the quantities to produce of each product to maximize the profit generated without violating the capacity and the demand constraints. Figure 10 shows the Solver parameters where all this information is specified and also depicts the solution generated. Setting up the parameters is a simple exercise wherein a user clicks the relevant text box in the dialog box and selects the appropriate cells in the worksheet.

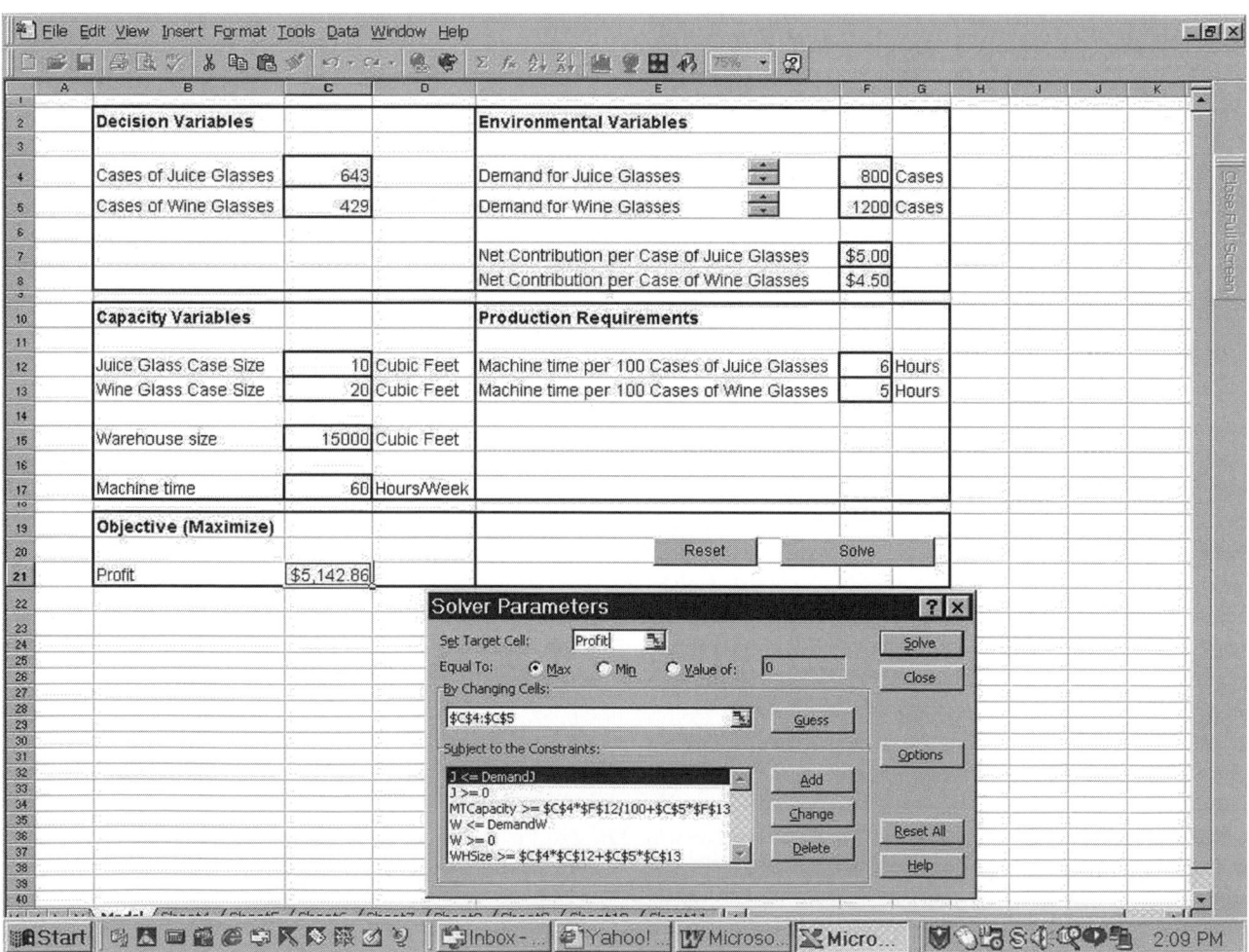

Figure 10 Solution to a product-mix problem generated by Excel's Solver.

2. Analysis ToolPak

Microsoft Excel provides a set of data analysis tools—called the Analysis ToolPak—that can be used to develop complex statistical analyses. A user provides the data and parameters for each analysis; the tool uses the appropriate statistical or engineering macro functions and then displays the results in an output table. Some tools generate charts in addition to output tables. Model specification is simple and is done by using wizards. Figure 11 illustrates the use of multiple regression analysis on bread sales data. A user is studying the relationship between the price of bread, amount spent on advertising, and the sales.

IV. APPLICATIONS

Decision support including resource allocation, estimation, budgeting, and mathematical optimization account for the majority of spreadsheet applications. In addition, spreadsheets can be used for other business, government, and personal applications. Common examples of applications developed in spreadsheet software include these:

- Financial investment analysis
- Pro-forma financial statement preparation
- Expense calculation and reporting
- Tax records and calculation
- Sales reporting and analysis
- Cash flow analysis
- Cost–benefit analysis.

As mentioned in the introduction, millions of business analysts, managers, and professionals around the world create spreadsheets each year. To get an idea of some of the current applications, a search was performed in the ABI/INFORM Global database covering periodicals

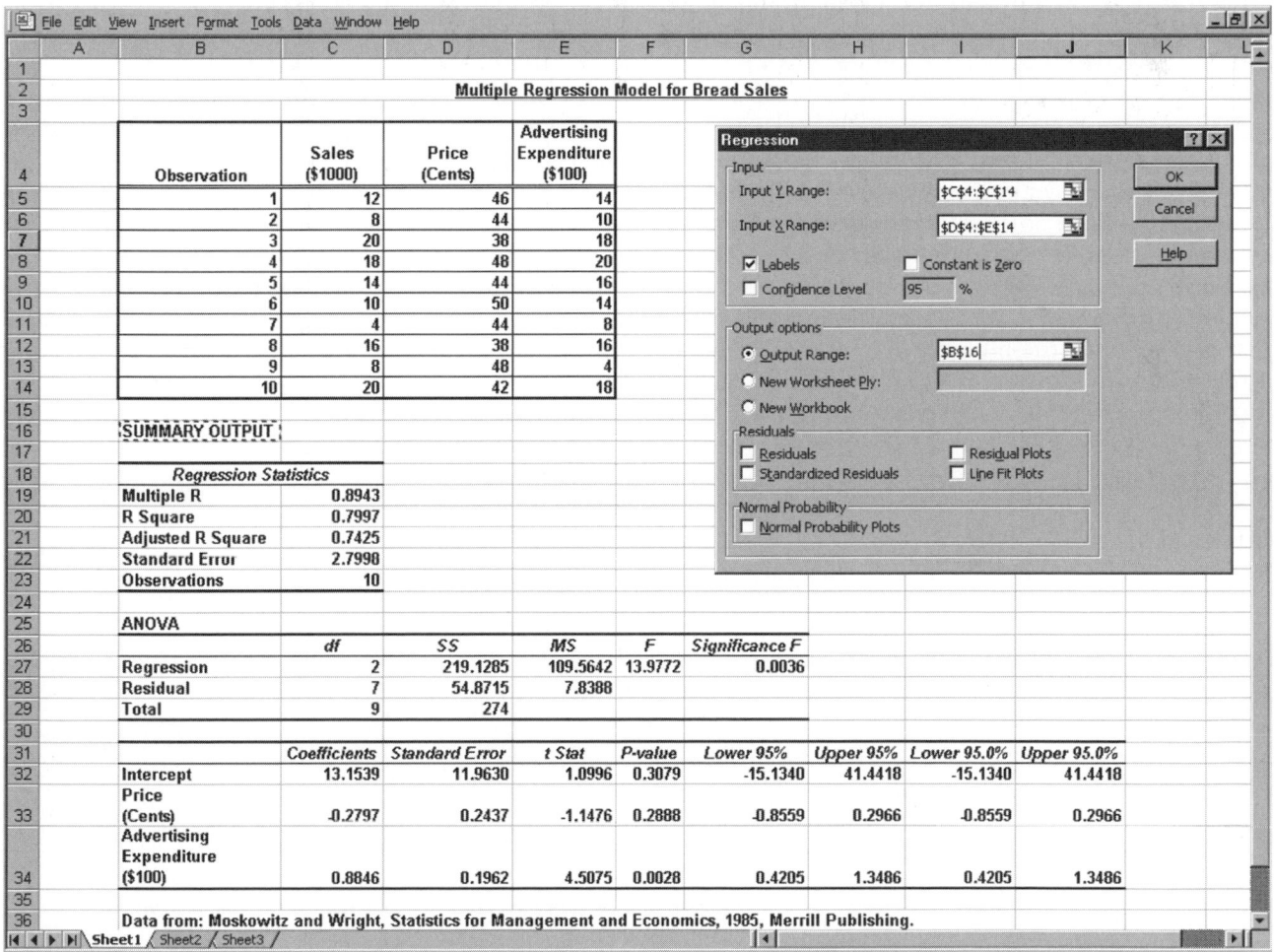

Figure 11   Multiple regression using analysis ToolPak add-in.

published in 1998–1999 for the criteria "spreadsheets and applications" in the citation and abstract fields. Some representative applications resulting from the search are summarized below. Table II contains the citations to the works described below.

Jackson and Staunton describe two applications of quadratic programming in finance. They show how, in the presence of inequality constraints, Excel's Solver can be used to find the optimal weights in both quadratic programming applications. A direct analytic solution is implemented for generating the efficient frontier when there are no inequality constraints using the matrix functions in Excel. They show how Visual Basic for Applications can be used to program such tasks, confirming that techniques that were the preserve of dedicated software only a few years ago can now be easily replicated using Excel.

Friend and Ghobbar demonstrate that spreadsheets provide a low-cost alternative to businesses interested in implementing materials requirements planning systems. The effective use of MRP is shown as a first step in the search for continuous improvement in maintenance and inventory control. The design for these MRP spreadsheets is based on data received from an airline inventory system survey.

According to Vellani, crime analysis is the study of crime information to assist in decision making and to enhance crime prevention and security programs. For the property manager, crime analysis is the logical examination of crimes that have penetrated a property's preventive plans and the application of revised policies and preventive measures that will hopefully lessen the recurrence of these crimes. Once the collection of relevant information is complete, it is time to conduct the crime analysis. The simplest method for data analysis is to use a spreadsheet software program, allowing for easy maintenance of the data and avoiding paper clutter.

Baker describes the application of spreadsheets to the assortment problem. Similar items of different sizes are required on a regular basis, but it is impractical to stock each of the different sizes. Demands for a size that is not stocked must be met by supplying the nearest acceptable size that is stocked, resulting in increased cost of trim wastage. A spreadsheet model is used to solve the problem in such a way that showing precedents on the spreadsheet results in the basis tree for the shortest or longest path solution being drawn without the need for special software.

Ruggiero argues that the versatility of a spreadsheet makes it a useful tool for market analysis. Spreadsheets allow complex calculations to be performed with market data and provide the ability to quickly test, chart, and print the results of many what-if scenarios. Using the programmability of the modern spreadsheet, it is possible to mechanize complex ideas and prototype these applications quickly. This paper illustrates how to use a simple spreadsheet program (Microsoft's Excel) to test ideas and help build trading systems.

Erenguc and Erenguc describe an optimization-based audit-planning model, which was developed and implemented to formulate a biennial audit plan for the University of Florida. The model's objective is to formulate an audit plan that maximizes the total risk coverage while satisfying system constraints such as available auditor hours, minimum number of audits to be conducted, and the distribution of total audit effort between various types of audits. The objective function to be optimized is obtained by performing a risk analy-

---

Table II   **Representative Works of Spreadsheet Applications**

1. Jackson, M., and Stanton, M. D. (December 1999). Quadratic programming applications in finance using Excel. *The Journal of the Operational Research Society.*
2. Friend, C. H., and Ghobbar, A. A. (1999). Extending Visual Basic for applications to MRP: Low budget spreadsheet alternatives in aircraft maintenance. *Production and Inventory Management Journal.*
3. Vellani, K. H. (September/October 1999). Crime Stoppers. *Journal of Property Management.*
4. Baker, B. M. (April 1, 1999). A spreadsheet modeling approach to the assortment problem. *European Journal of Operational Research.*
5. Ruggiero, M. A., Jr. (April 1999). Trading in a spreadsheet. *Futures.*
6. Erenguc, N. S., Erenguc, S. S. (July/August 1998). Optimization-based audit planning: A spreadsheet modeling approach. *Internal Auditing.*
7. Gyorki, J. R. (February 5, 1998). Simulating motor performance. *Machine Design.*
8. Hegji, C. E. (1998). A spreadsheet application of Dorfman and Steiner's rule for optimal advertising. *Managerial and Decision Economics* 19.
9. Haussmann, W. (January 1998). Custom control runs instruments from Excel. *Test & Measurement World.*

sis. The constrained optimization model is formulated as a spreadsheet application and solved using the Solver module of Microsoft's Excel.

According to Gyorki, when selecting motors, designers typically refer to manufacturers' data sheets. However, designers can enter manufacturer-supplied data into a spreadsheet application to calculate additional parameters, simulate motor performance graphically, and compare motor efficiency under varying conditions.

A paper by Hegji shows how a computer spreadsheet can be used to demonstrate the Dorfman and Steiner rule for optimal advertising. In their article, Dorfman and Steiner link optimal advertising to product price by a rule relating marginal advertising revenue to price elasticity of demand. The rule provides a simple guide for the overall utilization of firm resources.

Haussmann describes a situation wherein a spreadsheet macro language is programmed to control instruments and move data directly into a spreadsheet. With a VB add-on, ASCII command strings can be sent to control instruments through serial or other ports. The custom code allows the tester to pass I/O parameters and controls more than one instrument.

V. ACADEMIC RESEARCH

The premier source for information on spreadsheet research is edited by Ray Panko of the University of Hawaii at http://panko.cba.hawaii.edu/ssr/. His site, called Spreadsheet Research, is a repository for research on spreadsheet development, testing, use, and technology. It has detailed abstracts for papers and some full papers. Most of the research focuses on spreadsheet errors because this is a very active research area and Panko's area of expertise.

What do we know about spreadsheet errors? Panko summarizes results from more than 20 research studies including field audits, cell entry experiments, development experiments, and code inspection experiments. Uncorrected errors seem to occur in about 10% to 25% of spreadsheet applications.

Panko summarizes a number of studies. The following two seem the most important. Davies and Ikin examined 19 spreadsheets from 10 developers that were being used in 10 different firms. Four of the spreadsheets (21%) were found to have serious quantitative errors; 74% had structural problems; 68% had inadequate documentation. One error resulted in an inappropriate $7 million funds transfer between divisions. Cragg and King inspected 20 spreadsheets that were being used in 10 firms. Their audit found seri-

ous errors in 5 of the spreadsheets (25%). Developers and managers are generally overconfident about the accuracy of spreadsheets.

Some research has been done on the prevention and detection of spreadsheet errors. A web site at http://www.gre.ac.uk/~cd02/iirg/webspred.htm maintained by David Chadwick reports a pilot study that found error awareness, improved spreadsheet building methodologies/techniques, improved administration/control of spreadsheet developments, improved methods of costing errors, and audit time helped prevent and detect spreadsheet errors.

Research indicates spreadsheets often have errors. Many consulting and accounting firms caution clients about end-user-developed spreadsheet applications. A marketing-oriented web page at KPMG UK concludes "reports based on spreadsheets, databases and PC based systems may be unreliable and thus decisions based on them may be incorrect."

Most prescriptions for improving spreadsheet development and reducing errors have focused on modular construction, having an assumptions section for inputs, and using cell protection. Some controversy surrounds whether an assumption section reduces or increases errors. Clearly, linking data from an assumptions section makes the spreadsheet more complex and hence more subject to inadvertent errors. A related prescription by Panko is to "require developers to write out and critique all non-trivial formulas, doing calculations by hand, and then replicating these calculations with the formula typed into the spreadsheet." Finally, proper documentation seems to reduce the likelihood of errors in spreadsheets.

Interactive visible calculators have changed how managers, business analysts, and many professionals perform their jobs. The quality and quantity of fact-based analyses have increased in the 1980s and 1990s. Spreadsheets are an accepted tool that all business students learn and many professionals need to master.

SEE ALSO THE FOLLOWING ARTICLES

Accounting • Desktop Publishing • End-User Computing Tools • Marketing • Public Accounting Firms • Sales • Service Industry • Word Processing

BIBLIOGRAPHY

Cragg, P. G., and King, M. (1993). Spreadsheet modeling abuse: An opportunity for OR? *Journal of the Operational Research Society,* Vol. 44, No. 8, 743–752.

Davies, N., and Ikin, C. (1987). Auditing spreadsheets. *Australian Account,* 54–56.

Fylstra, D., Lasdon, L., Watson, J., and Waren, A. (September 1998). Design and use of the Microsoft Excel Solver. *Interfaces,* Vol. 28, No. 5, 29–55.

Mattessich, R. (July 1961). Budgeting models and system simulation. *The Accounting Review,* 384–397.

Microsoft Excel Architecture. Available at http://www.microsoft.com/Office/ORK/036/036.htm.

Panko, R. (Spring 1998). What we know about spreadsheet errors. *Journal of End User Computing's Special Issue on Scaling Up End User Development,* Vol. 10, No. 2, 15–21

Panko, R. (Fall 1999). Applying code inspection to spreadsheet testing. *Journal of Management Information Systems,* Vol. 16, No. 2, 159–176.

Power, D. J. *A brief history of spreadsheets.* Available at http://dss-resources.com.

Russo, J., and Nafziger, J. (1993). Software 'look and feel' protection in the 1990's. Available at http://www.computer-law.com/lookfeel.html.

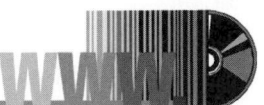

SPSS (Statistical Package for the Social Sciences)

M. L. Plume
Framingham State College

GLOSSARY

data Information, especially information organized for analysis or used as the basis for a decision.

data analysis Usually the statistical processing of information, especially the handling of information by computer in accordance with strictly defined systems of procedure.

database Typically an application software that allows for the input and/or importation of information that is arranged for ease and speed of retrieval.

data screening The process of verifying the correctness and completeness of data files by using a variety of statistical and/or graphical techniques.

module A piece of software that is added on to the SPSS Base System to enhance statistical or graphic capabilities of the user's SPSS system. Many of the modules have a specific application utility.

SPSS (Statistical Package for the Social Sciences) A statistical software package for entering, storing, and analyzing various types of data and constructing tables, graphs, and charts.

statistic An estimate of a parameter, as of the population mean or variance, obtained from a sample.

STATISTICAL PACKAGE FOR THE SOCIAL SCIENCES (SPSS) is a modular data management and analysis application created and produced by SPSS, Inc., in Chicago, Illinois. Among its features are modules for statistical data analysis, including descriptive statistics such as plots, frequencies, charts, and lists, as well as

sophisticated inferential and multivariate statistical procedures like analysis of variance (ANOVA), factor analysis, cluster analysis, and categorical data analysis. Currently SPSS is supported by a number of platforms including Windows, Mac, Mainframe/Mini, and Unix. SPSS is designed generally for the storage and manipulation of alpha-numeric data and specifically for, but not limited to, use with social science data. SPSS allows users to input, store, manipulate, and analyze alpha-numeric data. Originally designed for use with powerful mainframe computing systems, SPSS is now available for use with both Windows and Macintosh platforms. Owing to the advancement in microprocessor capabilities, the power of SPSS data storage and analysis capabilities are now available to students and others on their personal workstations without the intense support of mainframe computers or sophisticated technical staff.

I. A BRIEF HISTORY OF SPSS

The forerunner to today's versions of SPSS was developed in the late 1960s. By 1968 three Stanford University graduate students, Norman H. Nie, C. Hadlai Hull, and Dale Bent had developed their first version of SPSS. Operating exclusively on large mainframe computing systems through the late 1960s and the 1970s, SPSS was not compatible for use with personal computers until 1984. In 1984 SPSS, which was now a growing corporate entity headquartered in Chicago, introduced SPSS/PC+, a useful but underpowered version of its mainframe self. While this version made sophisticated statistics available on a desktop platform it was limited by the speed and capabilities of math coprocessors installed in early personal computers. Additionally, the software was limited by the number of variables and cases it could store and manipulate. However, SPSS, Inc., released several versions of SPSS/PC+ which became more and more powerful. Coupled with the increased power of the personal computer throughout the 1980s came increased variable and case number capabilities within the SPSS software which grew more powerful and more popular especially within the academic environment.

In 1992 a Microsoft Windows version of SPSS was introduced. This Windows version was, and remains, extremely user friendly. This and subsequent Windows versions (Windows 95 version introduced in 1995, Windows 98 version in 1998, and Windows2000 introduced in 2000) have greatly expanded the accessability of desktop workstation statistical capabilities to a range of students and private sector workers who until these versions were released were dependent on either mainframe computing applications or underpowered DOS based statistical software. SPSS has a worldwide footprint offering the Windows version in 9 separate languages. With 40 offices worldwide, SPSS, Inc., has permeated not only the scientific research field but the corporate worlds of telecommunications, banking, finance, and healthcare delivery. SPSS is not simply a tool for academics from whence it came but rather a powerful tool for interpreting and forecasting major business and social policy issues.

II. OVERVIEW OF THE DEVELOPMENT OF SPSS

Developed essentially as a response to the growing need of survey researchers in the social sciences SPSS allowed these researchers to enter, store, and analyze relatively large data sets. Survey research by its nature demands large amounts of variables to be gathered on large numbers of subjects. The onus on any statistical software package was then to be able to store large data sets and be able to manipulate those sets statistically. SPSS versions in the 1960s and 1970s were slow and cumbersome by today's standards. However, they did allow researchers to maintain electronic records in a logical way versus large handwritten or typed spreadsheet-like tables.

As the presence of computers increased on college campuses during the 1960s, researchers naturally gravitated to them in an attempt to organize, manage, and analyze cumbersome data sets. However, early

computing systems were clunky, crashed easily, and had very limited storage and mathematical processing power.

As hardware improved during the 1960s so did software. By 1962 the programming language FORTRAN (formula translation) emerged. FORTRAN allowed scientists from many disciplines to write programs for data analysis on a variety of computer platforms. While FORTRAN was being adopted by many universities and colleges, most scientists during the 1960s were writing their own programs and much of the development of software use was made through informal sessions between faculty, graduate students, and undergraduates.

These professional grapevines greatly advanced computer-based capabilities for social scientists and others. However, the nonstandardization of computer protocol, programs, and data sets made across the board or intradisciplinary use almost impossible. The private sector also saw a fierce increase in the need for and use of both hardware and software and made many of its movements forward using university-based research facilities and staff. For example, the Xerox labs at Stanford University were working with GUI (graphical user interface) systems as early as the mid-1970s.

By the late 1960s and into the early 1970s the need for standardized programming protocol was evident. Researchers at the University of Chicago and the University of Michigan as well as other schools and private sector labs began to focus on the specific needs of scientists by their particular discipline. SPSS was originally developed for sociologists and other social scientists. Other packaged programs focused on other disciplines. For example, biomedical data processing (BMDP) was developed for use with clinical biomedical data storage and analysis. This production of "program packages" became popular and useful across many disciplines. Packaging software which is developed specifically around the requirements of given disciplines or business needs became popular through the 1980s and 1990s. As of the writing of this article, targeted software development is the convention in the software industry.

This packaging was a direct response to the needs of academic and private sector programmers. While there was a growing need for packaged or targeted software in the private sector, most software development through the 1960s and 1970s was being done in the academic world. Microsoft, SPSS, and BMDP were all software projects that were first developed by undergraduate and graduate students who eventually moved their products into the private sector and ultimately served both industry and academia.

The specific needs of social scientists were the original impetus for the development of SPSS. Through the mid-1980s most large statistical packages were available only for mainframe computer platforms. SPSS was originally designed to run on mainframe computers. The target market for SPSS remained academic and institutional users focusing mainly on social variables and data. However, the development of more powerful personal computers through the 1980s and 1990s allowed SPSS to became more broad in its application, both across platforms and users.

By the late 1980s SPSS was available for use on mainframe and personal computers, with the introduction of SPSS/PC+ for IBM and IBM clone personal computers. However, this was limited by the number of variables it could handle and the relative lack of power of early personal computers. SPSS became usable on personal computers for moderate-size data sets and limited statistical analysis. The development of SPSS during the 1990s accelerated to meet the demand of the growing power of all computer platforms, number of users, and the demand across applications. In 1992 the first Windows version of SPSS was introduced, by 2000 SPSS supported Windows95, Windows98, Windows2000, and Macintosh as well as Mainframe computing systems.

III. SPSS COMPARED AND CONTRASTED WITH OTHER SOFTWARE

A. SPSS vs Other Statistical Packages

SPSS varies from other statistical packages in its modular construction. In order to increase the power or diversity of procedures one only has to find the appropriate module and add it to the Base System. SPSS can be customized in a sense to any particular data file or analysis application. For example, insurance industry researchers may need results displayed in geographical terms. That is, distribution of data across a map of the state of California can be created using SPSS Maps Module.

There are many other statistical application programs available but most do not offer the power of case and variable capability nor the flexibility of modular design. Statistical software such as SYSTAT, STATA, or MINITAB can handle few cases and variables and has a limited range of analysis features. Additionally, SPSS is available across platforms making it useful for large data sets that may need to be stored on mainframe computing systems as well as small data files that can be created, stored, and analyzed on one's home computer or laptop. SAS Institute's SAS (Statistical Analysis Software) is a powerful, full functioning statistical software system that is constructed similarly to SPSS. SAS is available in a number of platforms and is modular in its design. SAS stands alongside SPSS as the conventional software in the social and behavioral sciences at many colleges and universities.

Ultimately SPSS has become so popular and profitable because as a powerful, modular software package it is flexible enough to accommodate the demands of a wide variety of industries. Also, SPSS stays current with operating systems, offers lease/purchase plans, and provides the user with intensive training and support.

B. SPSS vs Database Programs

Database programs such as dbase, Fox Pro, Access, Paradox, and others offer some similar features as SPSS but have far fewer capabilities. Database programs are designed essentially to allow users to input or import data. Once these data are stored most database programs have limited sets of functions such as editing the data files, transforming them with simple equations, or performing basic descriptive statistics. Databases are meant as storage and management facilities for data to be retrieved and analyzed at a later date. This is not to presume that all databases are passive and inefficient. Oracle is an excellent example of a powerful database system that can maintain complex and fluid databases. However, it cannot perform the powerful statistical analysis nor produce the complex two- and three-dimensional graphing of SPSS.

C. SPSS vs Spreadsheet Programs

Spreadsheet programs such as Lotus 1-2-3, Microsoft Excel, and Quattro allow users to array large data sets in worksheet fashion. Early versions of spreadsheet software were designed for accounting applications and were simple in their capabilities. Newer versions have enhanced their capabilities including basic descriptive statistics functions.

Typically spreadsheet programs afford users the ability to enter and store numeric data in large worksheet formats. These worksheets, while similar in appearance and function to the SPSS data editor, have the additional ability to embed equations in the worksheet. These equations are used to do computations between and within cells. SPSS is a full functioning software system that is more complex and comprehensive than spreadsheet software.

IV. OVERVIEW OF SPSS CAPABILITIES

A. The Modular Nature of SPSS

SPSS is a modular software product. The Base System module must be installed in order to run subsequent modules which roughly correspond to increasingly higher order statistical operations and graphing capabilities. Table I shows a list from the 1999 SPSS Applications Guide of the modules available and their corresponding functions and capabilities.

B. Entering Data in SPSS

Central to any analysis are variables and their values. Using SPSS you can import data from other sources such as spreadsheets, databases, and text files, or simply enter new data directly into SPSS using the Data Editor (see Fig. 1). Regardless of the structure of your imported data file, data in the SPSS Data Editor are presented in the rectangular arrangement required by SPSS and most other data analysis systems. In this rectangular format rows represent CASES and columns represent VARIABLES. A CASE contains data for a single unit of analysis such as a single respondent, a business, or a country. A VARIABLE is the information collected for each unit of observation such as nationality, profit/loss, or population (see Fig. 2). SPSS allows the user to store alpha-numeric data. Both the data stored (raw data) and the variables assigned to the data can have either alphabetic (called STRING variables) or numeric values. The variable name is limited to eight characters so researchers must be succinct and creative in titling their variables. For example, if a researcher were examining differences in responses between American women and Canadian women, he or she would create a variable titled NATIONLT and its variable label would be the nationality of respondent. Then the researcher could

Table I   SPSS Modules Available to Addition to the Base System

Module	Description
Base system	This module is needed to run SPSS and any subsequent modules added to the system. Allows the user to enter, store, manipulate, and analyze data with limitations. Provides ability for report writing, descriptive statistics, cross-tabs, t-tests, correlation, analysis of variance, regression, cluster analysis, factor analysis, and nonparametric stats.
Regression Module (formerly known as the Professional Statistics Module)	Provides user the ability to analyze data that do not fit traditional linear statistical models. Included are procedures for probit analysis, logistic regression, weight estimation, two-stage least-squares regression, and general nonlinear regression.
Advanced Models (formerly known as the Advanced Statistics Module)	Includes procedures for general linear models (GLM), variance components analysis, loglinear analysis, actuarial life tables, Kaplan–Meier survival analysis, and basic and extended Cox regression.
Tables	Easy to use and powerful table building applications which are presentation and camera ready. Capabilities include one-, two-, or three-dimensional tables. Complex stub-and-banner as well as multiple response data area available.
Trends	Allows for time-series analysis, estimation, forecasting, and diagnostic tools. Also contains multiple curve-fitting models, smoothing models, and methods for estimating autoregressive functions.
Categories	Performs optimal scaling procedures, including correspondence analysis. Categories include ANACOR, HOMALS, PRINCALS, and OVERALS. Many procedures allow for an alternating least squares (ALS) method for parameter estimation.
Conjoint	Specifically designed to allow the user to perform conjoint analysis.
Exact Tests	This module performs calculations of exact p values for statistical tests when small or very unevenly distributed samples could make the usual tests inaccurate.
Missing value analysis	Can describe patterns of missing data, impute values for missing observations, and allow the user to estimate means and other statistics based on those imputations.
Maps	Can transform geographically distributed data into high-quality maps with symbols, colors, bar charts, pie charts, and combinations of themes to present not only what is happening but *where* it is happening.

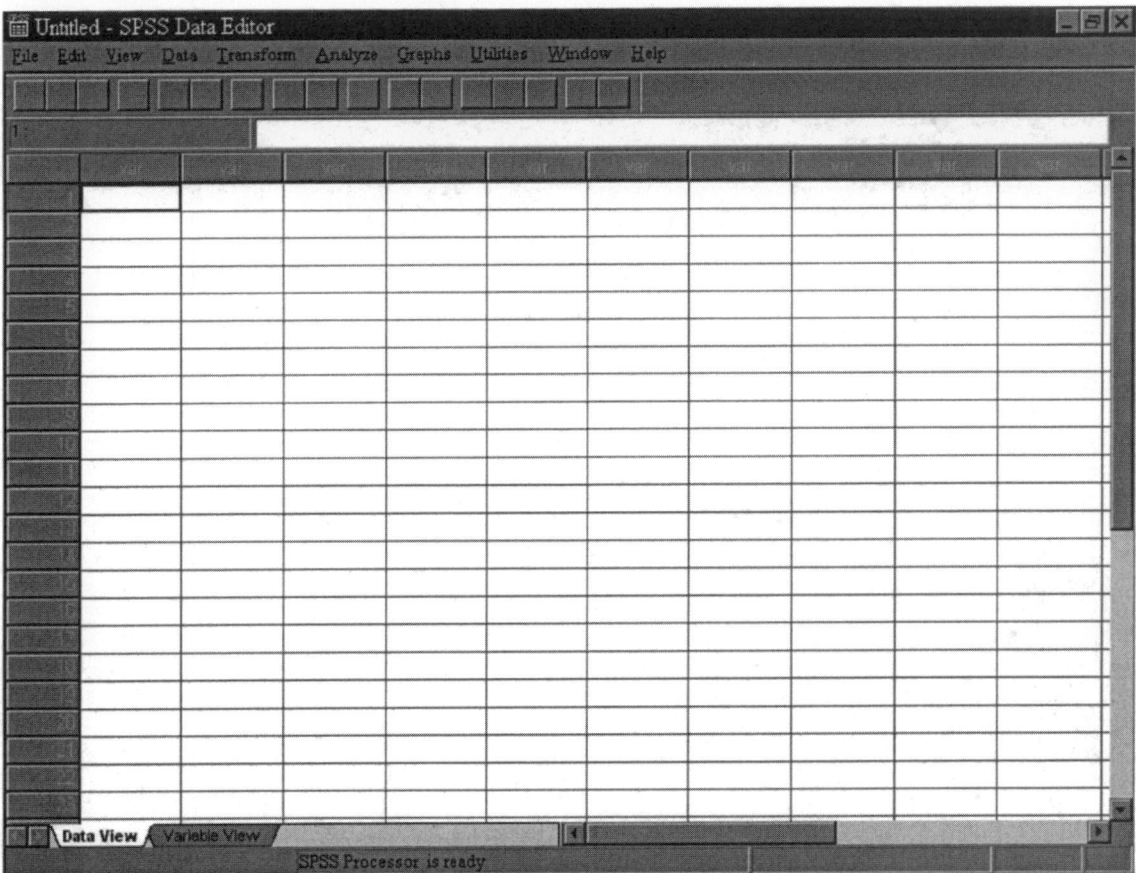

Figure 1 SPSS Data Editor, Data View, used to enter data.

enter either the value of American or Canadian, 1 or 2, where 1=US and 2=CANADA See Figs. 3 and 4. Figure 5 shows the Value Label window where values can be assigned labels.

Additionally, data can be transformed using the Transform menu. This menu allows the user to compute new values, create a set of random values, replace missing values, and more. Also, optional descriptive labels may be added to each variable and to the values of each variable. From the Data menu you may choose commands which allow you to define and sort variables, work with templates, go to a specific case, merge and aggregate files, and weigh cases. Data may also be entered in calendar form, currency, scientific notation, or a variety of other forms.

1. Missing Data

Missing values are often a problem in data sets. When a value is not supplied for a particular variable, SPSS Base System supplies a system missing value. However, most researchers code for missing or unknown responses to variables with values such as 9, 99, or 98 typically assigned to missing data. These values must be defined as missing values in the Data Editor so that those assigned values are excluded from calculations.

C. Screening Data

Once data have either been imported from another file source or entered directly into SPSS, the completed data file should be *screened* or *cleaned*. This process involves screening the data for missing values, inaccurate value assignment, and transpositional or typographical errors. Data entry errors should be identified first then further steps can be taken to be sure that the data file is sound. SPSS offers several steps one can take to screen the data.

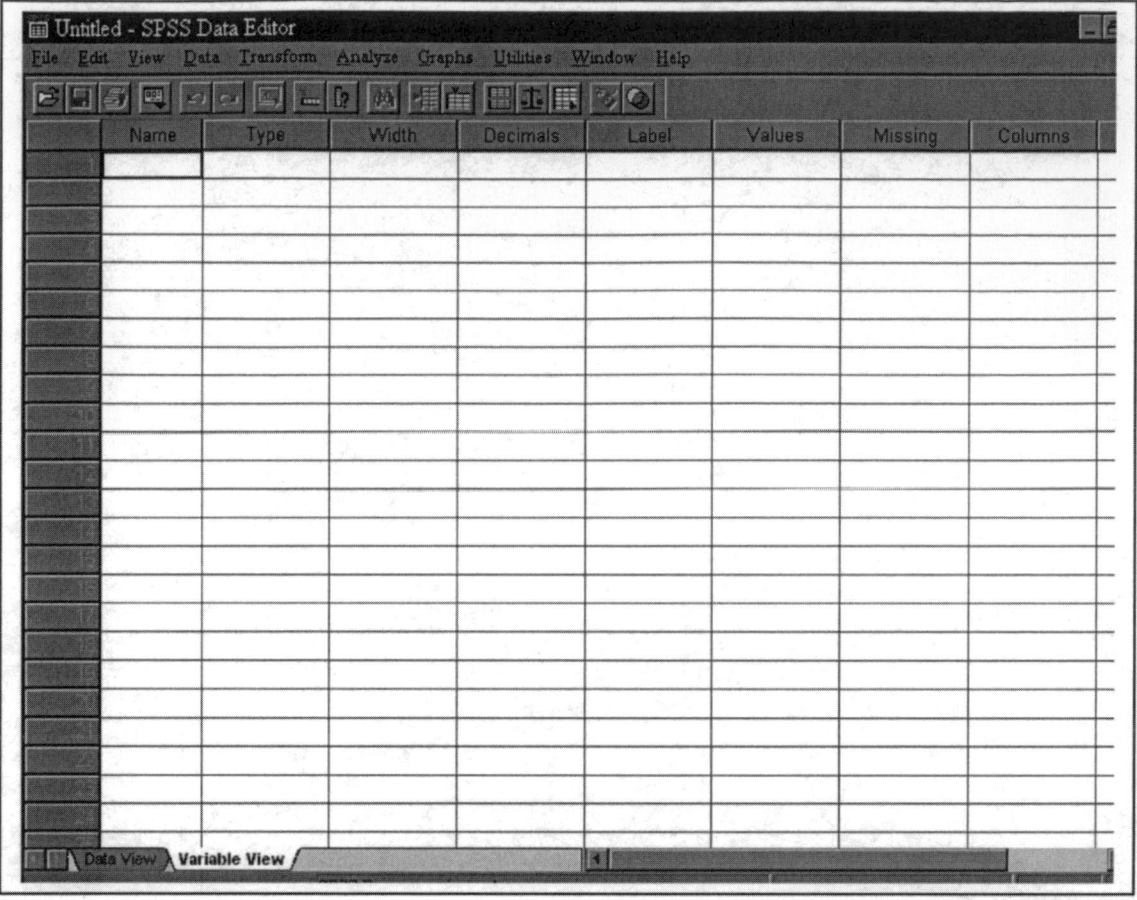

Figure 2   SPSS Data Editor, Variable View, for entering variable characteristics.

1. Outliers

In order to identify outliers and rogue values, SPSS suggests that the first step in cleaning data be to find values outside the reasonable range for a variable and to determine whether they are true outliers or simple errors.

- Obtain a frequency count on the occurrence of each unique value. Many times typos and unexpected values and codes appear in data sets. Also, look for missing values that appear as valid values.
- For quantitative variables, use histograms in the Frequencies or Explore procedure and boxplots and stem-and-leaf diagrams in the Explore procedure. Note the information on outliers in the Explore plots.
- For large data sets, scan minimum and maximum values displayed in procedures like descriptives and means. Values outside the coding scheme may be discovered or coded missing values (such as 9, 99, or 98) may be treated as valid data.
- Use case Summaries to list data. Choosing a grouping variable to list the cases by category may help. Sorting data by a variable of interest may be useful.
- For categorical data, cross-tabulations may reveal unlikely or undesirable combinations in the data.
- Use the graphical power of SPSS to display scatterplots. These Scatterplot matrices may reveal unusual combinations or values.

2. Distributional Assumptions

When assessing distributional assumptions, it must be remembered that many distributions are not normal or symmetric. These skewed distributions will affect statistical results.

- Generate histograms, compare the data with normal probability plots, and compare means; 5%

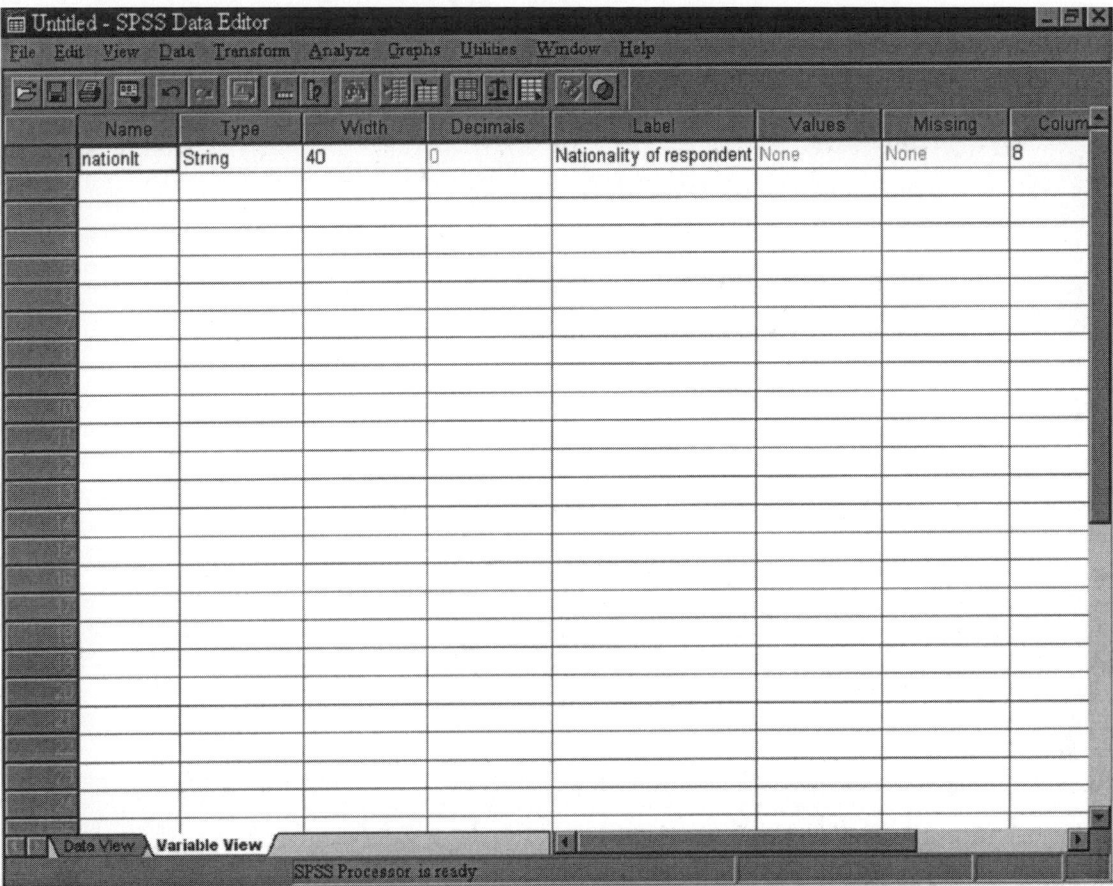

Figure 3 Data Editor, Variable View, showing NATIONLT entered as a string variable.

trimmed means and medians may help in discovering skewed data or individual variables.
- Try a formal test of normality such as the Kolmogorov–Smirnov test or the Shapiro–Wilk test found in the Explore menu.
- To detect distribution problems across groups use boxplots, Levene's test of homogeneous variances, or One-Way ANOVA.

Once satisfied that the data are clean, contain no invalid outliers or superfluous data points, are distributed normally or within normal bounds, and are not

Figure 4 Data Editor, Variable View, showing the variable NATIONLT as numeric.

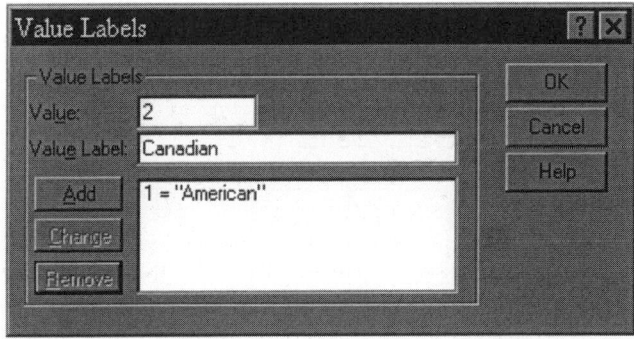

Figure 5 Value Label screen displaying values for the labels American and Canadian.

violating distributional assumptions, one can proceed to data analysis.

D. Analyzing the Data

Once the data are inputted and screened, decisions about calculating statistics or creating tables or charts must be made. This process begins with understanding the type of variables present in the data set so the appropriate statistic or procedure can be selected.

Unordered categories—String variables such as Canadian and American
Ordered categories—Likert style variables that range from "very likely" to "very unlikely"
Counts—The number of new immigrants from Canada this year
Measurements—Values measured on a scale of equal units such as IQ, weight, etc.

The next step in analysis would be selection of variables for analysis. It is extremely infrequent that all variables in a study be examined at once. Therefore, decisions for variable inclusion are based on the particular research question or hypothesis being tested.

Figure 6 shows what Green *et al.* in 2000 described as the "meat and potatoes menu." The Analyze menu offers 16 different options ranging from simple descriptive statistics to complex multivariate analyses. SPSS offers a vast selection of analyses to accommodate nascent users as well as seasoned researchers.

E. Output

The SPSS output window displays statistical procedures in tabular or graphical formats. Once analysis procedures are chosen and performed by the SPSS processor, the output from the various procedures is displayed in the output window. Users can choose to display the output in tabular form, the default, or graphical form. Figure 7 shows sample output using Frequencies data and Fig. 8 shows the same data in graphical form.

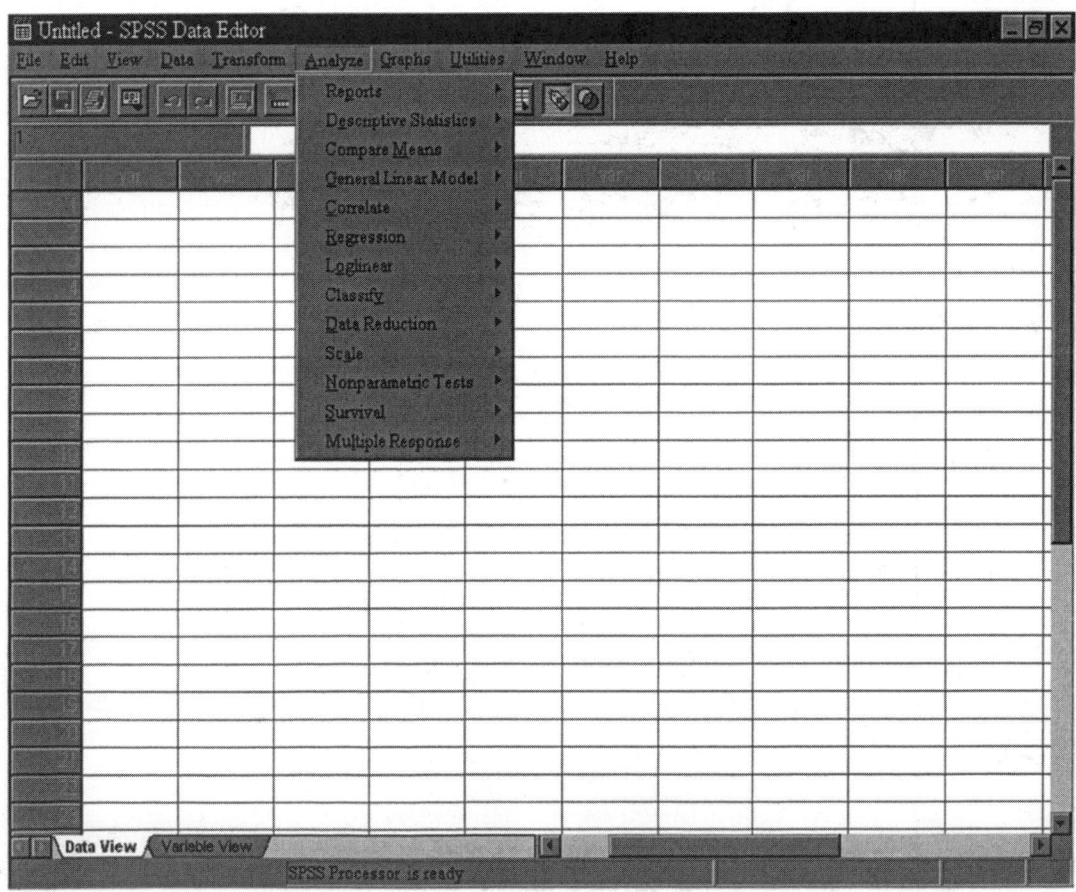

Figure 6 The Analyze Menu.

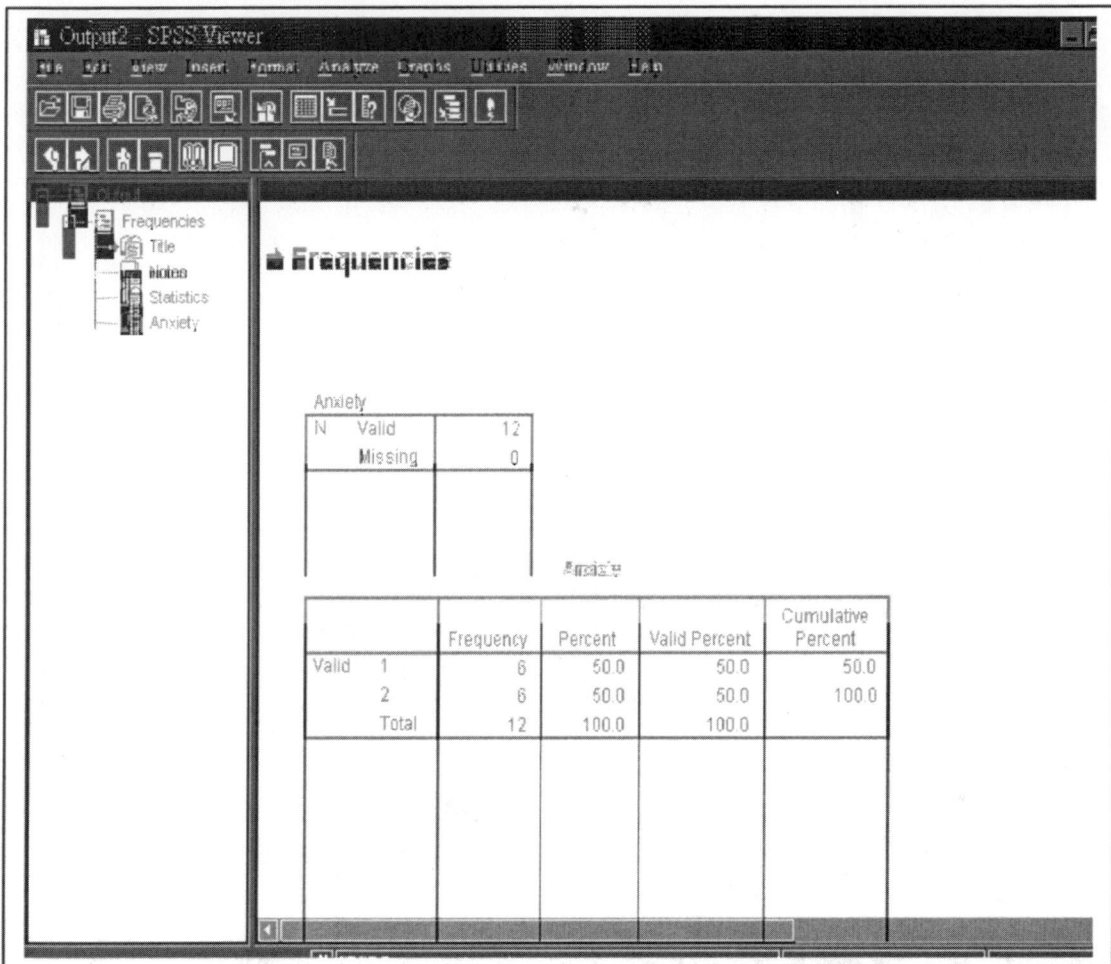

Figure 7 SPSS Viewer windows showing output using simple statistics.

V. OTHER FEATURES OF SPSS

Originally designed as a tool for social scientists, economists, sociologists, political scientists, etc., SPSS with increased power and functioning currently has a broad appeal. Advanced Modules allow psychologists to perform Analysis of Variance (ANOVA) and Graphing Modules allow businesses to illustrate trends and forecast earnings and/or losses. Consequently, many businesses have adopted SPSS as a powerful analysis tool.

A. Platform Availability

As of the writing of this article SPSS is available for use on several platforms.

1. SPSS[x] mainframe version typically runs on such systems as IBM, Honeywell, and Unisys

2. SPSS/PC+ for use on personal computers that run DOS or OS/2
3. SPSS for Windows for use on personal computers that run Windows95, Windows98, WIndows2000, or WindowsNT.
4. SPSS for use on Macintosh systems

B. Studentware

Additionally, SPSS comes in several student versions that are simply scaled down versions of those mentioned above. SPSS Student Version is targeted for undergraduate social and behavioral science students. This version is essentially the base system with limited variable capacity. The SPSS Graduate Pack is designed to accommodate the needs of doctoral students. This version affords a presumably more advanced user greater variable capacity and access to more advanced statistics.

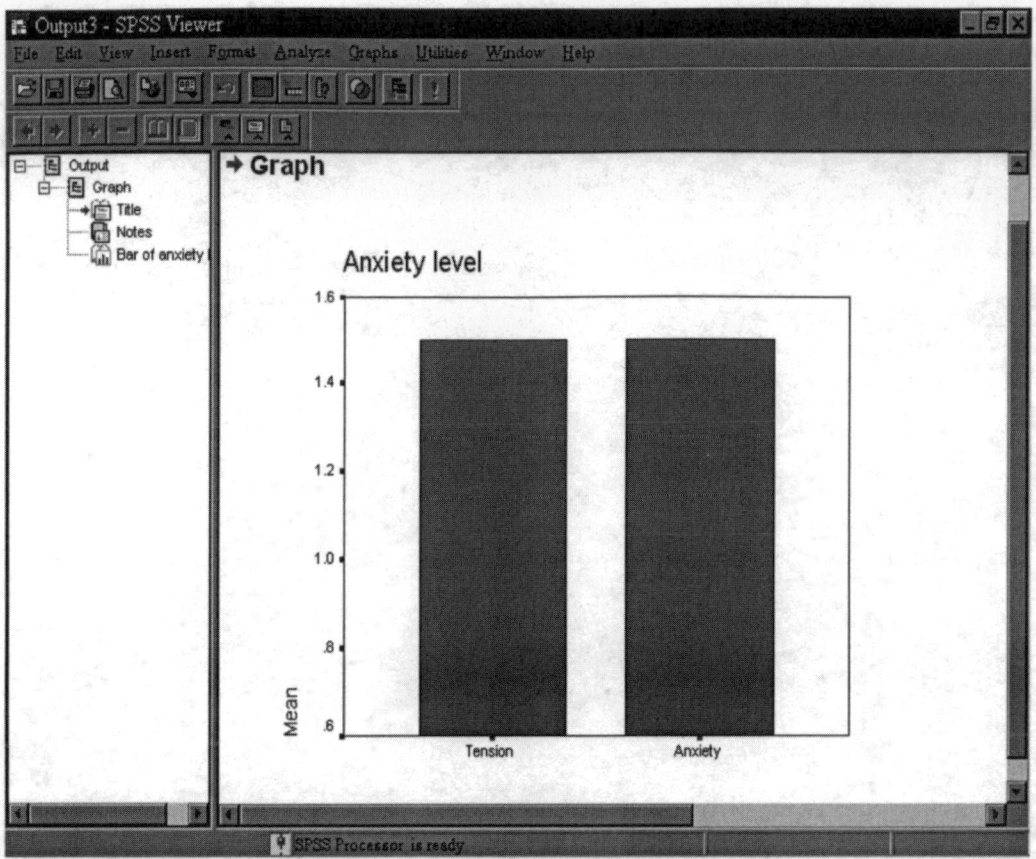

Figure 8   A simple bar graph.

VI. CONCLUSION

Earl Babbie and Fred Halley in 1995 wrote that "there is hardly a social scientist who has earned a graduate degree in the past 20 years who has not had some contact with SPSS." In the final analysis SPSS is a powerful statistical package that has transcended its social and behavioral science roots. The current versions of this software afford accessability, power, and broad application. SPSS allows users to store, manage, and statistically and graphically manipulate and present data. Users range from undergraduate sociologists to government officials to Wall Street investment bankers. While SPSS is considered the convention in the social and behavioral sciences it is a powerful data management and analysis tool that supports the type of research that informs social policy, legislation and business decisions.

SEE ALSO THE FOLLOWING ARTICLES

Library Applications • Psychology • Research • SAS (Statistical Analysis System) • Sociology

BIBLIOGRAPHY

Babbie, E., and Halley, F. (1995). *Adventures in social research: Data analysis using SPSS for Windows*. Newbury Park, CA: Sage.
Babbie, E., and Halley, F. (1998). *Adventures in social research: Data analysis using SPSS for Windows*. Newbury Park, CA: Sage.
Green, S. B., Salkind, N. J., and Akey, T. M. (2000). *SPSS for Windows*. 2nd ed. Englewood Cliffs, New Jersey: Prentice Hall.
SPSS Base System Applications Guide. (1999). Chicago: SPSS Inc.
SPSS Syntax Reference Guide. (1999). Chicago: SPSS Inc.

Staffing the Information Systems Department

Magid Igbaria
Claremont Graduate University

Conrad Shayo
California State University, San Bernardino

GLOSSARY

career orientation Also called career anchor, this term refers to a cluster of self-perceived needs, values, and talents that give shape to an employee's career decisions. Since this forms the core component of an employee's self-concept, an employee will be unwilling to relinquish it, even if forced to make a difficult choice.

diversity in the workplace Refers to a work environment that recruits, develops, retains, and promotes its productive employees without regard to gender, race, age, or sexual orientation.

employee turnover The departure of an employee from one organization to another in search of better opportunities.

IT/IS The terms information systems (IS) and information technology (IT) are taken to be synonymous. Information technology includes hardware, software, networks and workstations of all types, robots, and smart chips.

A shortage of information systems (IS) professionals is being experienced worldwide. There is a gap between the number of positions available for IT workers and the number of qualified workers to fill them. As the IS personnel staffing crisis deepens, many organizations are searching for appropriate mechanisms for recruiting, selecting, placing, and retaining IS professionals. This article explores the critical problems organizations must address in order to develop strategies that will contain the IS staffing crisis. Problem

areas that have contributed to the IS staffing crisis include (1) lack of understanding of the career orientations of IS personnel, (2) high IT staff turnover, (3) lack of diversity in the IS profession, (4) the IS profession as a young discipline, and (5) lack of coherent strategies for recruitment, development, and retention of IS personnel. Strategies for dealing with each problem area are provided.

I. INTRODUCTION

Studies have shown that some CEOs are spending up to 60% of their time headhunting for top information technology (IT)[1] talent. The general consensus in the literature is that although the demand for IT professionals is expanding, a corresponding supply of IT talent is lacking. An IT staff shortage is being experienced worldwide. The term *IT staff shortage* refers to the gap between the number of positions available for IT workers and the number of available qualified workers to fill them. In the United States alone, it is estimated that the IS staff shortage will grow from 200,000 in 2000 to about 1.3 million in 2005. In the United States, the gap is estimated to be between 25 and 35%. Worldwide, in 1998, the IT staff shortage gap is estimated to be between 15 and 25% or 600,000. As the IS personnel staffing crisis deepens, many organizations are searching for appropriate mechanisms for recruiting, selecting, placing, and retaining IS professionals.

---

[1] We use the terms *information technology* and *information systems* interchangeably.

Managing the careers of IS professionals has emerged as a critical element of the strategic use of IT in organizations.

Effective human resource management in the IS department requires an understanding of both the nature of IS staff and what they experience as they accomplish their assigned duties in the IS department. This article focuses on some of the major factors that have contributed to the IS staff shortage. These factors include (1) lack of understanding of the career orientations of IS personnel, (2) high IS staff turnover, (3) lack of diversity in the IS profession, and (4) the IS profession as a young discipline. The following sections cover each of these factors and show how IS managers can use this knowledge to increase the productivity and retention level of IS employees.

II. CAREER ORIENTATION OF IS STAFF

A. The Career Orientation Concept

Career orientation (also called career anchor) refers to a cluster of self-perceived needs, values, and talents that give shape to an employee's career decisions. This orientation is a core component of an employee's self-concept and an employee will be unwilling to relinquish it, even if forced to make a difficult choice. Schein identified eight career anchors that influence employee career decisions: (1) security/stability, (2) autonomy/independence, (3) managerial competence, (4) technical or functional competence, (5) entrepreneurial creativity, (6) sense of service/ dedication, (7) pure challenge, and (8) lifestyle integration. An employee's career anchor or career orientation is important because it influences the employee's choice of specific occupations and work settings, and it affects the employee's reactions to his work experiences.

- *Security/stability.* Security-oriented employees have a prevailing concern for a career that is stable and secure, in which future developments are predictable, and which allows them to feel that they have "arrived." This concern manifests itself in job security and/or geographic security. Remaining in the same organization, the same industry, or the same geographical location may satisfy the need for security. People with this orientation generally prefer stable and predictable work.
- *Autonomy/independence.* Individuals with this orientation have an overriding need to exercise independence in the way they work, in the rate at which they work, and in the standards they apply to their efforts. Such people have an innate dislike of

being restricted by organizational rules and regulations, whether these involve working hours, dress code, or any other organizational policies. They are likely to refuse promotion that would elevate them to positions of greater responsibility, but of lesser autonomy.
- *Managerial competence.* Individuals with this orientation discover that as their careers progress, they wish to become general managers rather than grow in a particular functional area within their organization. Such individuals display the ambition to rise to high positions in the organizational hierarchy and are motivated by opportunities for additional responsibility, contribution to the success of the organization, and higher earnings. They require a combination of talents in key areas in order to succeed in general management: analytical competence, interpersonal and intergroup competence, and emotional competence. They differ from other groups in that the combination of the above three skills is key to success, whereas other groups rely on the development of one skill element only.
- *Technical and functional competence.* The main concern of individuals with this orientation is the actual content of their work. They identify strongly with their area of expertise and want to remain within their technical/functional area. They normally have strong aptitude and motivation for a certain type of work. Such individuals are stimulated through the application of their technical or functional skills and knowledge. They are experts in their field. Some may become functional managers but they do so only if that permits them to remain in the specialized area.
- *Entrepreneurship.* This group's members have a predominant need to create an enterprise of their own, through the creation of a new product, service, or business that will be recognized as theirs and identified as existing entirely through their efforts. The spur that drives these individuals should not be confused with the creative urge that is experienced by certain researchers and designers. Entrepreneurs are driven to create not just something new, but something with which they can be identified with and which will produce significant earnings by which their success can be measured. Individuals in this orientation want the freedom to build and operate their own organization in their own way.
- *Service/dedication.* Service-oriented individuals are mainly concerned with a cause they feel strongly about and typically seek to improve the world in some way. They are interested in improving the lives of others, such as working in a "helping"

occupation. Professions characteristic of this are teaching, the ministry, and medicine. Though not all individuals in these careers have this anchor, personnel with this anchor can also be found in business and organizational careers.

- *Pure challenge*. These are people who derive satisfaction from facing and overcoming increasingly difficult problems and obstacles. Individuals with this anchor are not restricted to being challenged by a certain type of problem. They may enjoy managerial, technical, or even athletic challenges. Competing and winning out over others is of primary importance for them. These individuals seek novelty, variety, and challenge in their work.

- *Lifestyle integration*. Individuals with this orientation seek to achieve balance in all major areas of their lives. Specifically, they would want a harmonious integration of their family and career activities. There is a general belief that this orientation will become more common due to recent social trends in society and the unavoidable effect of dual-career families.

It is important to recognize that a career orientation does not imply limited career growth or change. Instead, it indicates that career movement and advancement occur within a specific bounded area. The career orientations of IS employees are important since they can influence work-related outcome variables such as job satisfaction, organizational commitment, and turnover intentions.

B. Career Orientations of IS Staff

A study of 464 IS employees by Igbaria, Greenhaus, and Parasuraman found that IS employees had a rich diversity of career orientations. In their study, technical and managerial career orientations received relatively higher scores. They also found that career orientation in the IS field was not related to demographic characteristics such as age, education, tenure on the job, or the type of organization, but was related to gender. More men were technically oriented than women. Moreover, employees with managerial, autonomy, or service orientations were more likely to hold managerial positions compared to those with security, technical, or pure challenge orientations. Technical positions included system programmers, application programmers, and software engineers. Managerial positions included computer managers, system analysts, and project leaders.

Other career orientations that received high scores were autonomy/independence, lifestyle integration,

and service/dedication. The autonomy orientation is consistent with the view that IS people tend to possess high needs for autonomy, dominance, and control of their environment. The lifestyle integration orientation mainly came from women who formed more than 20% of the sample. This is not surprising because of the primary responsibility carried by women for domestic and child care activities. However, as more men assume additional responsibilities for domestic and child care activities, the lifestyle integration orientation may become even more prevalent among IS employees.

Organizations should note the importance of matching career orientations and the IS job setting. If managerially oriented employees are assigned technical jobs and technical oriented employees are assigned managerial jobs, a mismatch will occur. This mismatch will cause negative job attitudes, low job satisfaction, and lack of commitment to the organization. Managerially oriented employees react positively to managerial jobs because they see opportunities for advancement, money, respect, and power in these jobs. Similarly, technically oriented employees see opportunities for reputation, enhancement, competent colleagues, peer respect, and challenging tasks in technical jobs and are more satisfied and committed in those positions. IS leaders should know that compatibility between internal career needs and external career options can produce positive outcomes among IS employees.

Another implication is that not all IS employees are driven by the same sets of values and goals. Organizations need to recognize this so that they can provide appropriate reward systems and career paths for their employees. IS employees should discuss their needs, values, and, yes, career orientations with their supervisors and jointly develop realistic and meaningful career goals. Supervisors should be rewarded for assuming this role. Because an employee's career orientation influences her value system, it is imperative that organizations provide different types of incentives for different employees.

C. Orientation with Job Types— Person–Job Fit

Igbaria and Siegel found that the future career choices of IS personnel primarily fall into one of four categories.[2] Two were within the IS area (technical and managerial), one within a more general organizational

---

[2] The study surveyed a cross section of 348 IS employees working for a cross section of Data Processing Management Association (DPMA) members in the Mid-Atlantic United States.

area (non-IS), and one outside the organization (consultant). Table I shows the relationships between the current job titles of the correspondents and their career choices in the next 1–3 years. It is noteworthy that some IS employees indicated a preference to move into other non-IS departments. For example, some programmers intended to move into senior management outside IS or consulting careers. Some employees currently in IS management would like to move into senior management positions outside the IS department.

The study also found that those employees preferring to hold technical positions were older and had longer tenure in their jobs. Highly educated employees showed a higher interest in becoming consultants and decided on the types of jobs they would like to hold more frequently than their counterparts. Less educated employees were more interested in holding technical positions.

This implies that organizations need to put higher emphasis on dual career paths for those employees interested in remaining within the IS department, and multiple career paths for employees who may want to work in non-IS-related positions. Organizations should not restrict IS employees from non-IS jobs and should consider training and educating IS managers to become senior managers in other business functions. This will encourage them to remain in the organization. The organization could identify the educational and training requirements for the non-IS jobs and determine the fit between the employee and the job position. This will bring about more motivation, productivity, and satisfaction with the job and career, as well as loyalty to the current organization, and eventually less desire to leave.

Additionally, organizations should know that highly educated employees have more options available to them and are, therefore, more mobile. Supervisors should make sure that they understand the career ori-entations and ambitions of these employees so that they can channel their career development prospects appropriately. Now we turn to the turnover problem.

III. THE TURNOVER PROBLEM

The departure of IS employees from one organization to another for better opportunities has contributed to the turnover problem. The rate of turnover of IS employees is more than twice the average for business managers and professionals. Excessive turnover in IS departments can be dysfunctional to organizations because of the shortage of experienced IS employees and the high cost of training new employees. Because IS managers are under intense pressure to recruit, hire, and retain qualified IS employees, they need to control employee turnover. To reduce excessive turnover among IS employees, it is first necessary to understand the reasons for the turnover. To the extent that specific aspects of the job situation of IS employees within the control of the organization contribute to turnover, retention of IS employees could be increased through appropriate administrative actions designed to address the problem areas.

A. Factors Affecting Turnover

A number of studies have identified various factors that may contribute to high turnover or intention to leave the IS department. Some of these factors include perceived work overload, role ambiguity, job conflict, lack of autonomy, insufficient resources, lack of rewards, age, organizational tenure, and education. Others include salary, perceived low chances of promotability, organizational career opportunities, lack of mentorship, and lack of recognition.

Table I Relationship between Current Job Title and Career Choice

| Job title | Career choices | | | |
| | Information systems | | Business | Consultant |
	Technical	Managerial		
Programmers	20	23	8	9
Analysts	0	25	1	2
Project leaders	1	16	0	1
IS managers	2	113	15	8
Consultants	0	7	2	13

Moore found that IS employees experiencing high levels of exhaustion reported higher intention to leave the job. She identified perceived work overload, insufficient resources, role ambiguity and conflict, lack of rewards and autonomy, and organizational tenure as the main factors contributing to work exhaustion, low job satisfaction, low organizational commitment, and therefore turnover. She also found that IS employees with fewer rewards and fewer acknowledgments for their work felt undervalued and unappreciated and consequently had low job satisfaction, reduced organizational commitment, and higher intention to leave the organization. The study by Igbaria and Greenhaus focused on demographic variables (age, organizational tenure, education), role stressors (role ambiguity, role conflict), and career-related variables (salary, promotability, career opportunities) that caused turnover intentions. The other dependent variables were job satisfaction, career satisfaction, and organizational commitment. They found that extra-organizational career opportunities had a positive effect on job satisfaction, career satisfaction, and intentions to leave the organization and a negative effect on organizational commitment. This meant that IS employees seemed to perceive that career opportunities outside their organization was an indicator of success in their jobs and careers.

The study also found that age and organizational tenure had positive direct effects on job satisfaction, career satisfaction, and organizational commitment, while education had negative direct effects on job satisfaction and career satisfaction. Moreover, low role conflict, low role ambiguity, high salary, and higher chances of promotability had direct effects on job satisfaction, career satisfaction, organizational commitment, and turnover intentions.

B. Implications for Managing IS Employees

1. Conduct Attitude Surveys and Act on Them

As recommended by Igbaria and Greenhaus and by Moore, IS department managers must monitor the level of employee attitudes on an ongoing basis and attempt to understand the factors that contribute to the development of positive work attitudes. A periodic administration of attitude surveys would help managers gauge current work attitudes and trace changes in work attitudes over time. IS managers should, however, be committed to act on the recommendations provided by IS employees in such surveys.

Factors thought to influence work attitudes must also be assessed so that areas for improvement in the work environment can be properly identified.

2. Identify High-Turnover Risk Employees and Address Their Needs

Employees who are young, inexperienced, and highly educated tend to hold low levels of satisfaction with their jobs and careers and tend to experience low levels of organizational commitment. These negative attitudes, in turn, are associated with their intention to leave for "greener" pastures. Employers must understand and address the sources of disaffection among their younger and more highly educated workforce. Realistic job previews must be provided to recruits so that they enter the organization with an accurate picture of their duties and responsibilities. Moreover, providing sufficient job challenge and performance feedback to the new employees can help bolster positive attitudes toward the job and the organization, and help forestall early intentions to leave.

Managers should use organizational socialization tactics that foster a fit between organizational and individual values and norms. Socialization should focus on the five most important factors, namely, (1) higher perceived value of the individual, (2) high opportunities for growth, (3) higher levels of trust, (4) communication, and (5) shared organizational values and beliefs. Managers should also use some of the top five motivating techniques reported by employees, namely, (1) providing personal thanks, (2) providing written thanks, (3) promotion for performance, (4) providing public praise, and (5) implementing morale-building meetings.

3. Beware of the Negative Impact of Role Stress

Role stress is experienced when employees face role ambiguity and/or role conflict in the performance of their job. Role ambiguity occurs when employees have insufficient information to perform their jobs adequately or when performance evaluation methods are unclear. Role conflict occurs when there are conflicting or unclear expectations of peers. IS employees who experience high levels of role ambiguity and role conflict tend to be dissatisfied with their jobs and careers and have a low commitment to their organization. Such employees hold strong intentions to leave their organization.

Managers can reduce role ambiguity by providing IS employees with a clear definition of tasks and priorities related to the job. This will provide a better understanding of task objectives and reasons for performing the task and a more clearly defined sequence in which subtasks should be performed. Managers should also provide a greater sense of task identity so that the beginning and ending of each task is readily determined, and a better understanding of the procedures by which a particular task should be performed.

Managers can reduce role conflict by encouraging their employees to attend orientation sessions where information can be provided regarding the organizational structure, resource allocation procedures, and commonly encountered conflict situations. Moreover, a frequently asked questions web site should be provided to help employees learn about the organization's culture and standard operating procedures. Managers can also make sure that the roles of IS personnel and end users are well defined. A culture of open conflict discussion and resolution should be fostered. Additionally, IS managers should pay special attention to recruiting employees who have a relatively high tolerance for ambiguity and who are capable of dealing with interpersonal conflicts effectively.

4. Equity and Career Development Are Critical

Employees with relatively low salaries and employees who perceive limited opportunities for career advancement are strong turnover candidates. IS employees want to be compensated at a level comparable to IS employees in other organizations. Moreover, studies have found that future opportunities for promotion may affect turnover intentions even more strongly than does an employee's current financial status. IS managers should make sure that their compensation package is equitable. They should also develop creative ways to enrich the jobs of IS employees. Organizations could develop dual career paths for IS employees where a technical path is created that parallels a managerial path in rank and salary. Technical IS employees who decide to enter a managerial career path should be provided with career planning opportunities and training and development experiences so that they can make an effective transition into management. Moreover, since lateral moves can provide feelings of challenge and growth, organizations should provide IS employees with flexible alternatives to the traditional emphasis on vertical mobility.

5. Keep Both Eyes on Job Satisfaction and Organizational Commitment

Igbaria and Greenhaus found that job satisfaction and organizational commitment have the most substantial and direct influence on turnover intentions of employees. The other factors such as role stress, equity, and career development operate through these two work-related attitudes.

IV. DIVERSITY IN THE IS PROFESSION

As the IT industry grew rapidly in the 1970s, 1980s, and 1990s a gender gap emerged with men dominating managerial and technical areas. This gender gap continues to grow and exists today in 2001. For example, despite impressive gains in employment in the United States during the last three decades, women continue to be underrepresented in professional and managerial positions in the IT field. This gender gap is most obvious at the senior management and executive levels. Although many women have advanced to the rank of middle management, as a group, women hold only 25% of upper level managerial jobs in the IT field. This phenomenon can be found in most countries including Canada and South America, Europe, Asia, and Australia. A number of reasons that may have created the gender gap have been suggested. These include deeply entrenched social norms such as cultural practices and ideologies of social control, lack of role models, lack of information about IT career opportunities for females, and occupational segregation. Others are lower career advancement prospects, lower IT self-efficacy for women compared to men, and work value congruence.

A. Social Norms and Culture

In general, people are influenced by the beliefs and values of people they think are important to them. A social norm is influenced by the beliefs that an individual attributes to relevant others about what their behaviors should be. Social norms therefore play a critical role in determining employee work decisions in all functional areas including IS. A number of research studies have indicated that women are more likely to be driven by social influences than men. Such influences may come from family, friends, peers, teachers, and even popular culture. For example, women may be influenced by limited TV images that showcase IS professionals with a "nerd" image of a male who sleeps in the office and lacks social skills. It is not uncommon to hear this from a young girl musing about her future career: "Mom, I don't want to become a computer nerd. I want to become a trade person and have my own business." Also IS is a young, misunderstood discipline that is easily confused with computer engineering and computer science disciplines.

B. Career Advancement Prospects

Igbaria and Chidambaram examined the impact of gender on individual characteristics (age, tenure, education, organizational level), role stressors (role conflict, role ambiguity), salary, advancement prospects, job satisfaction, organizational commitment, and intention to stay. They found that women in the IS profession tended to be younger, had shorter organizational and job tenure, and fewer number of years in the IS field than do men. This finding suggested that women, partly due to their relatively limited work experience and tenure, tended to hold lower level positions in the IS field than do men. They also suggest that the gender differences may be explained by sex stereotypes and other factors such as lack of sponsorship, lack of networking, and lack of coaching and mentoring.

Although there were no significant gender differences in role conflict or role ambiguity, women reported fewer opportunities to interact with people outside the IS department. Women were also paid lower salaries than men and had lower increases in promotion. Another study by Igbaria and Baroudi found that although women received job ratings similar to men, women were perceived to have less favorable chances of promotion than men. They note that women encounter a "glass ceiling" due to biased job performance evaluations.

C. Work Value Congruence

Work value congruence refers to the matching of the career orientations of individuals to the jobs they seek. Studies have shown that, generally, women prefer careers that provide more social interaction and have social relevance. For example, women are believed to have lifestyle integration and service orientations to a greater degree than men, while men have more technical and functional competence orientations than women. Also, since women tend to have primary responsibility for housework and child care irrespective of their employment status, it is incumbent upon IS managers who have women in their departments to help the women balance their career and family demands. This means, IS managers interested in recruiting and retaining women should consider gender differences more explicitly. A survey of employee attitudes will be a good starting point.

D. Womens' Strengths

Women are said to prefer human-oriented areas of IT where they mix communication and technical expertise. Thus, they are able to bring diverse skills that are in high demand to the IT field. Women are also said to have the ability to adapt to changing environments more than men. The women interviewed were obviously in managerial positions and therefore had a managerial career orientation.

E. Implications for Managing IS Employees

Organizations and society at large should address the main cause of gender inequalities in the IS field. Antiquated social norms and culture should be influenced and changed. Organizations should monitor the job performance evaluation process to include more objective measures of work performance for both men and women. Organizations should ensure that the performance appraisals are administered fairly. Job assignments should take into consideration the career orientations of all employees including women. An IT environment that is more attractive to women should be cultivated.

V. THE IS PROFESSION AS A YOUNG DISCIPLINE

The IT discipline has had a very short life span compared to other management disciplines such as manufacturing, finance, and marketing. In fact, the administrative knowledge of managing IT departments does not cover a period of more than three decades. Career paths in IT departments are not stable. The number of new specializations in the IT field remains relatively high compared to those of other disciplines. For example, the rapid development of the Internet has created new positions such as web master and web administrator. Other new positions include knowledge manager, manager of emergent technologies, system integration specialist, and ERP manager. Each new specialization develops its own expertise and competence and may require its own career path. Some of the IT positions that existed in the 1980s such as file librarian, job setup clerk, and key-in clerk are no longer in existence. These unique characteristics increase the challenges of staffing the IT department and managing the career orientations of IT personnel.

Each organization should have its own contingent approach to staffing and managing its IT human resources. IT managers should clearly define the job descriptions and professional qualifications of each IT employee and create new career paths for employees occupying the new specializations. Although job titles may vary from one organization to another, it is important for IT managers to study the activities performed at each job position and provide the necessary training and career promotion paths.

VI. CONCLUSION

Although academic and training institutions have a role to play in narrowing the IT skills gap, organizations must play a role to attract, recruit, hire, and retain talented IS employees. IS department managers must learn how to leverage the career orientations of all IS employees. This chapter has provided practical recommendations for action.

SEE ALSO THE FOLLOWING ARTICLES

Digital Divide • Globalization • Human Side of Information • Knowledge Management • National and Regional Economic Impacts of Silicon Valley • Organizations, Information Systems Impact on • Outsourcing • People, Information Systems Impact on • Reengineering • Sociology • Telecommuting

BIBLIOGRAPHY

Becker, A. (1986). Influence again: An examination of reviews and studies of gender differences in social influences. In *Psychology of gender: Advances through meta analysis,* J. S. Hyde and M. C. Linn (Eds.). Baltimore: John Hopkins University Press, 178–209.

Beutel, A. M., and Marini, M. M. (1995). Gender and values. *American Sociological Review,* Vol. 60, 436–455.

Crowford, M., Chaffin, R., and Fitton, L. (1995). Cognition in social context. Special issue on psychological and psychobiological perspectives on sex differences in cognition: Theory and research. *Learning and Individual Differences,* Vol. 7, No. 4, 341–362.

Field, T. (1999). Half of all tech workers are ready to jump ship. *CIO Connection,* IS Staffing Research Center. Available at http://www.cio.com/forums/staffing/edit/122199_staff.html.

Harlan, A., and Weiss, C. L. (1982). Sex differences in factors affecting managerial career advancement. In *Women in the workplace,* P. A. Wallace (Ed.). Boston: Auburn House, 59–100.

Igbaria, M., and Baroudi, J. J. (1995). The impact of job performance evaluations on career advancement prospects: An examination of gender differences in the IS workplace. *MIS Quarterly,* Vol. 19, No. 1, 107–123.

Igbaria, M., and Chidambaram, L. (1997). The impact of gender on the career success of information system professionals: A human-capital perspective. *Information Technology and People,* Vol. 10, No. 1, 63–86.

Igbaria M., and Greenhaus, J. H. (1992). Determinants of MIS employee turnover intentions: A structural equation model. *Communications of the ACM,* Vol. 35, No. 2, 35–49.

Igbaria, M., Greenhaus, J. H., and Parasuraman, S. (1991). Career orientations of MIS employees: An empirical analysis. *MIS Quarterly,* Vol. 15, No. 2, 151–169.

Igbaria, M., Parasuraman, S., and Greenhaus, J. H. (Summer 1997). Status report on women and men in the IT workplace. *Information Systems Management,* 44–53.

Igbaria, M., and Siegel, S. R. (1993). The career decisions of information systems people. *Information and Management,* Vol. 24, 23–32.

Information technology skills shortage: The impending impact on businesses in Europe, A special report by IDC commissioned for the Summit on Employment and Training in the Information Society. Available at http://www.microsoft.com/europe/skillsgap/.

Knowlton, T. (2000). IT worker shortage: Information technology worker shortage presents challenges and opportunities. Available at http://www.mainfunction.com/IT/workershortage.asp.

Lightbody, P., Siann, G., Tait, L., and Walsh, D. (1997). A fulfilling career: Factors which influence women choice of profession. *Educational Studies,* Vol. 23, 25–37.

Moore, J. E. (2000). One road to turnover: An examination of work exhaustion in technology professionals. *MIS Quarterly,* Vol. 24, No. 1, 141–168.

Rabbite, S. (June 2001). (Skills shortage takes up more than half of CEOs time. CIO: The decision maker's zone. Available at http://www.silicon.com/bin/bladerunner?30REQEVENT=&REQAUTH=21046&14001REQSUB=REQINT1=39434.

Schein, E. H. (1987). Individuals and careers. In *Handbook of organizational behavior,* J. W. Lorsch (Ed.). Englewood Cliffs, NJ: Prentice Hall.

Venkatesh, V., and Morris, M. (2000). Why don't men ever stop to ask for directions? Gender, social influence, and their role in technology acceptance and usage behavior. *MIS Quarterly,* Vol. 24, No. 1, 115–139.

Von Hellens, L. A., Pringle, R., Nielsen, S. H., and Greenhill, A. (April 2000). People, business, and IT skills: The perspectives of women in the IT industry. *Proc. 2000 Association of Computing Machinery, SIGCPR,* April 6–8, 2000, Chicago, 152–157.

Standards and Protocols in Data Communications

William Shay

University of Wisconsin, Green Bay

GLOSSARY

asynchronous transfer mode Very fast connection-oriented protocol using small fixed-sized packets optimized for multimedia use.

compression Reduction of the number of bits representing information while preserving all or most of the original meaning.

cyclic redundancy check (CRC) Error detection method based on interpreting bit strings as polynomials with binary coefficients.

digital certificate Commonly used to facilitate verification and encryption over a secure socket connection.

digital subscriber line Technology that allows information to be transmitted over a telephone line via unused bandwidth.

encryption The rendering of information into a different and unintelligible form to those without authority to view it.

error detection Process of determining whether errors occurred during a transmission.

ethernet A local area network based on the IEEE 802.3 standard.

local area network A network spanning a relatively small geographic area and typically implementing one of the IEEE 802 standards.

logical link control IEEE standard data link protocol used in local area networks that handles logical links between devices.

medium access control Lower sublayer of the data link protocol that controls access to the transmission medium.

modulation Process of using one signal to change another.

open system A set of protocols that allow any two different systems to communicate regardless of their underlying structure.

open systems interconnect Protocol standard developed by the International Organization for Standardization to implement an open system.

protocol A set of rules by which two or more devices communicate.

simple mail transfer protocol Mail protocol used on the Internet.

standard An agreed-upon way of doing something.

systems network architecture IBM's seven-layer communications protocol.

transmission control protocol/internet protocol (TCP/IP) Layer 3 and 4 protocols defining routing, flow control, error detection, and more for the Internet.

X.400 standard Standard defining an e-mail system.

X.500 directory service Standard defining a distributed directory for an e-mail system.

The world became a considerably smaller place during the 1990s. Technology evolved to provide access to a wide variety of different types of information stored in almost every corner of the world. Because of the easy access to so much information, it is easy to forget that enormous effort and cooperation is needed. It is essential that, during an exchange of information, each side understands how the other expects to send and receive information. To guarantee accurate, efficient, and secure exchanges, rules or protocols must be followed. Due to the wide variety of hardware, software, and service requirements, the number of protocols in existence is very large. It is simply not possible to cover them all, but this article will provide a brief overview of some of the more well-known protocols.

I. NEED FOR STANDARDS

The field of communications is certainly not new. People have been communicating since early humans grunted and scratched pictures on cave walls. For thousands of years people communicated using little more than words, parchments, stone tablets, and smoke signals. The primary forms of sending information were based on the auditory and visual senses. A person either heard someone speaking or saw the letters and symbols that defined a message.

As we begin the 21st century, new technologies are changing how we do things and how we see the world around us. The integration of media and communication services, along with the eventual conversion to digital broadcasts, promises to open up a whole new world of interactive entertainment and educational opportunities. Faster Internet access that cable companies are offering for home use will increase the amount of information available to us. Palmtop computers and wireless technologies will give us more flexibility to take our computing, learning, and entertainment activities to places previously not possible.

With such widespread activity, a major issue is to ensure that many different types of devices understand each other. Protocols or rules must be defined in order to allow them all to communicate. Furthermore, all must follow the rules to ensure effective communication.

Who defines the protocols that devices implement? Actually, anyone can define a protocol, but if the principal parties involved follow different protocols, they might as well follow none. If the necessary people could agree on a common protocol, it could become a standard and they could all use it. However, getting a diverse group of people to agree on anything is difficult. Different groups have different goals and ideas about which protocol best meets those goals. Consequently, many different standards have evolved and been used over the years.

II. STANDARDS AND AGENCIES

There are two types of standards. **De facto standards** are those that exist by virtue of their widespread use; that is, they have become so common that vendors know that producing products consistent with them will have a large market. The second type of standard is one that is formally recognized and adopted by an agency that has achieved national or worldwide recognition. Those who wish to see their work become a standard write a proposal and submit it to an agency for consideration. Typically, if the proposal has merit and widespread acceptance, the agency will make suggestions and send it back to its originators for modifications. After several rounds of suggestions and modifications, the proposal will be adopted or refused. If approved, the standard gives vendors a model on which to design new products.

The following agencies are important to the field of computer networks and data communications:

- American National Standards Institute (ANSI). The ANSI is a private, nongovernmental agency whose members are manufacturers, users, and other interested companies. It has nearly 1000 members and is a member of the International Organization for Standardization (ISO). ANSI standards are common in many fields and include languages (i.e., ANSI C) and the American Standard Code for Information Interchange (ASCII) used by many computers for storing information.
- International Electrotechnical Commission (IEC). The IEC is a nongovernmental agency devising standards for data processing and interconnections and safety in office equipment. It was involved in the development of the Joint

Photographic Experts Group (JPEG), a group that developed a compression standard for images.

- International Telecommunications Union (ITU), formerly called Comité Consultatif International de Télégraphique et Téléphonique (CCITT). The ITU is an agency of the United Nations and has three sectors: ITU-R deals with radio communications; ITU-D is a development sector; and ITU-T deals with telecommunications. ITU members include various scientific and industrial organizations, telecommunications agencies, telephone authorities, and the ISO. The ITU has produced numerous standards dealing with network and telephone communications. Two well-known sets of standards are the V series and X series. The V series deals with telephone communications and defines how a modem generates and interprets analog telephone signals. The X series deals with network interfaces, public networks, and e-mail and directory services. Examples include the X.25 standard for interfacing to a packet-switched network and the X.400 standard for electronic mail systems. Of course, there are many other X and V standards.

- Electronic Industries Association (EIA). The members of the EIA include electronics firms and manufacturers of telecommunications equipment. It is also a member of the ANSI. The EIA's primary activities deal with electrical connections and the physical transfer of data between devices. Their most well-known standard is the RS-232 (also called EIA-232) standard, which for many years personal computers (PCs) have used for communicating with other devices such as printers.

- Internet Engineering Task Force (IETF). The IETF is an international community whose members include network designers, vendors, and researchers, all of whom have an interest in the stable operation of the Internet and its evolution. It is divided into work groups that handle various technical aspects of the Internet, such as applications, operations and management, routing, security, and transport services. These working groups have been charged with the responsibility of developing and reviewing specifications intended as Internet standards. An important result of the IETF's work is the new Internet protocol IPv6.

- Institute of Electrical and Electronic Engineers (IEEE). The IEEE is the largest professional organization in the world and consists of computing and engineering professionals. It publishes many different journals, runs conferences, and has many groups that develop standards. Perhaps its best-known work in the communications field is its Project 802 local area network (LAN) standards, which include:
  - LAN/MAN Bridging & Management (802.1)
  - Logical Link Control (802.2)
  - CSMA/CD (Ethernet)-Based LANs (802.3)
  - Token-Passing Bus Access Method (802.4)
  - Token Ring Access Method (802.5)
  - Metropolitan Networks (802.6)
  - Broadband LAN (802.7)
  - Fiber Optics (802.8)
  - Isochronous LANs (802.9)
  - LAN/MAN Security (802.10)
  - Wireless LAN (802.11)
  - Demand Priority Access Method (802.12)
  - Wireless Personal Area Network (WPAN) (802.15)
  - Broadband Wireless Access (802.16)
  - Resilient Packet Ring Access Protocol (802.17)

- International Organization for Standardization (ISO). The ISO is a worldwide organization consisting of standards bodies from many countries, such as the ANSI from the United States. One of ISO's most significant activities is its work on open systems, which define the protocols that would allow any two computers to communicate independent of their architecture. One well-known model is the Open Systems Interconnect (OSI), a seven-layer organization of protocols. Some people once believed that OSI would be the model used for all future communications, but with the explosion of the Internet and World Wide Web (WWW) applications, it is unlikely. However, it is often studied as a model for layering protocols.

- National Institute of Standards and Technology (NIST), formerly the National Bureau of Standards (NBS). The NIST is an agency of the U.S. Department of Commerce. It issues standards the federal government uses for equipment purchases. It also develops standards for many physical quantities such as time, length, temperature, radioactivity, and radiofrequencies. One important standard with security applications is the Data Encryption Standard (DES), a method of encrypting or changing information into a form that cannot be understood. The DES standard has been manufactured in chips used in communications devices for many years.

These agencies are by no means the only standards bodies, but they are the ones most pertinent to data communications and networks.

The remainder of this article summarizes many of the most common standards and protocols, including those used for modulation, error detection, encryption, compression, local and wide area networks, interfaces, and e-mail systems and directory services. Websites at the end of each section are provided for more detail about a particular standard.

III. CODE STANDARDS

A. American Standard Code for Information Interchange

Perhaps, the most widely accepted code is the ASCII. It is a seven-bit code that assigns a unique combination to every keyboard character and to some special functions. It is commonly used on PCs and many other computers. Each code corresponds to a printable or unprintable character. Printable characters include letters, digits, and special punctuation such as commas, brackets, and question marks. Unprintable characters correspond to codes that indicate a special function such as a line feed, tab, or carriage return.

B. Extended Binary Coded Decimal Interchange Code

Another common code is the Extended Binary Coded Decimal Interchange Code (EBCDIC) used primarily on IBM mainframes. It is an eight-bit code, thus allowing up to 256 different characters. Like the ASCII code, there are printable and unprintable characters.

C. Unicode

ASCII and EBCDIC have long been in use and those familiar with them frequently use the terms byte and character interchangeably. In addition both have been used primarily to represent common control functions, letters, and characters from the English alphabet. With the internationalization of networking applications, the seven- and eight-bit codes have become much too inflexible and a new standard, the Unicode, is being developed. The Unicode supports many scripts or collections of symbols and special characters that exist in a particular language. Examples include Arabic, Latin, Greek, Gothic, Cyrillic, and, of course, many more scripts. The Unicode is still evolving as new scripts are added to its definition. At the time of this writing, Unicode 3.1 has defined codes for over 90,000 characters.

The Unicode defines a unique 16-bit number for each character independent of language and computing platform. The Unicode Consortium, a nonprofit organization that works in conjunction with the ISO, defines specifications. Members include companies such as Apple, Microsoft, Oracle, IBM, Novell, Netscape, and many others.

IV. MODULATION STANDARDS AND TECHNOLOGIES

A. Modems

Despite the trend toward all digital communications, analog signals still play an important role in communications. Probably the most visible are the analog signals used by telephones. Although much of the telephone network is digital, the signals that transmit voice to and from telephones are analog. Since many people use telephone lines to connect their computers to the Internet, they need modems (Fig. 1) to convert a computer's outgoing digital signal to an analog signal and to convert an incoming analog signal to a digital one the PC can recognize.

There are many ways to convert digital signals to analog signals. For example, one could associate any group of three bits with an analog signal having one of eight possible amplitudes. One could also use different frequencies, phase shifts, or various combinations for different bit groups. The important thing is that remote hardware interprets a PC's modem's signal accurately. To do this, it must know how the signal was converted. Ever since modems were first implemented, the ITU-T has been defining standards for the conversion process and have identified them using a V.xx designation, where xx is some identifying number. Different xx designations define bit rates, the association between bit values and an analog signal's characteristics, baud rates (frequency with which the characteristics can change), error correction, and data compression procedures. For example, many dial-up connections to an Internet service provider support a V.90 standard which defines "A digital modem and analogue modem pair for use on the Public

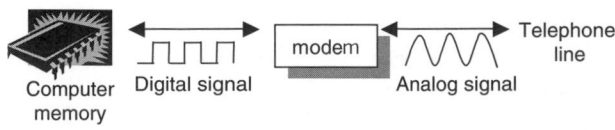

Figure 1   A modem.

Switched Telephone Network (PSTN) at data signaling rates of up to 56000 bit/s downstream and up to 33600 bit/s upstream." (For more information, go to http://www.itu.int/itudoc/itu-t/rec/v/index.html.)

Typically, the V.xx standards apply to conventional modems that, because of filters in phone company switching offices, generally limit bit rates to 56K bps (and, in practice, less than that). More recently, cable modems and digital subscriber line (DSL) technology has allowed home PCs to connect to the Internet at much higher rates. Although they represent different technologies requiring the use of a cable modem or DSL modem, the issue of using existing analog lines still exists. The IEEE has a working group (IEEE 802.14) working on cable modem standards, and the ITU-T has also adopted a recommendation (G.995.1) for DSL technology.

B. Broadband

Cable modems function similar to conventional modems except that they connect to communications lines provided by a local cable television provider. A consumer subscribes to a cable television (CATV) service and a technician routes a cable from an outsider feeder to a wall jack in a home. Inside the home another cable plugs into the wall jack and connects to a splitter (a device that takes a source signal and routes it over two or more output connections). Another cable connects one splitter output to a television or cable box. The signal from the other output is fed to a cable modem. The cable modem, in turn, has an output port that the consumer can connect via another cable to a computer's network card or USB port.

DSL refers to the technology that allows both data and voice signals to travel over analog telephone lines. It differs from conventional modem technology in that data and voice use different bandwidths and, as a result, can be used simultaneously. It also differs from using CATV lines in that a DSL line between a customer and local switching office is not shared with neighbors as is a CATV line. This is an advantage because transfer rates for DSLs do not depend on whether your neighbors are also connected. A disadvantage is that transfer rates decrease as a function of distance from the local switching office. Maximum distances for DSLs are around 3–4 miles.

There are different DSL configurations, but one uses a splitter at both the customer site and the local switching office (Fig. 2). The splitter at the customer site directs voice signals to the telephone and data to a DSL modem that connects to a PC. The splitter at the local office directs voice signals to the telephone company's voice network and data signals to a data network. There are also different variations of DSLs. For example, an asymmetric DSL (ADSL) provides higher transfer rates for downloading than for uploading. Download rates may run as high as 6 Mbps. ADSL Lite is an ITU-T standard and is similar to ADSL, but does not require a splitter at the customer site. A high data rate DSL (HDSL) provides transfer slightly above 2 Mbps in both directions. Differences are actually more detailed than described here.

V. ERROR DETECTION

Most users agree that a system that allows information to be damaged while in transit is not acceptable. However, the fact is that errors can occur. Any message transmitted electronically is susceptible to interference such as sunspots, electrical storms, or power fluctuations. The ability to detect when a transmission has been changed is called **error detection.** In most cases, when errors are detected the message is discarded, the sender is notified, and the message is sent again.

A Cyclic redundancy check (CRC) is a rather unusual but clever method that does error checking via polynomial division. It is based on the fact that, under

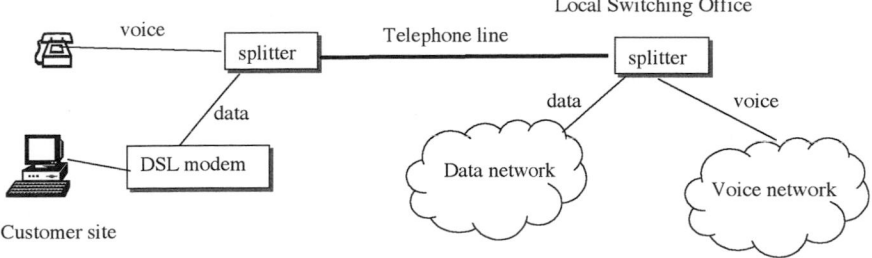

Figure 2 A DSL connection.

certain conditions, division of an arbitrary polynomial by another, fixed polynomial will almost always yield a nonzero remainder. The method interprets each bit string as a polynomial. For example, it interprets the bit string $b_{n-1}b_{n-2} \ldots b_1 b_0$ as the polynomial

$$b_{n-1}x^{n-1} + b_{n-2}x^{n-2} + \ldots + b_1 x + b_0$$

The basic steps of the CRC method are as follows with all computations done modulo 2.

- Determine a generator polynomial $G(x)$ having degree equal to n where n is a positive integer (often 16 or 32).
- Given a bit string, append n 0s to the end of it and call it B. Let $B(x)$ be the polynomial corresponding to B.
- Divide $B(x)$ by $G(x)$ and determine the remainder $R(x)$.
- Define $T(x) = B(x) - R(x)$. It can be shown that $T(x)/G(x)$ generates a 0 remainder and that the subtraction actually replaces the previously appended 0 bits with the bit string corresponding to $R(x)$.
- Transmit T, the bit string corresponding to $T(x)$.
- Let T' represent the bit stream the receiver gets and let $T'(x)$ represent the associated polynomial. The receiver divides $T'(x)$ by $G(x)$. If there is a 0 remainder, the receiver concludes $T = T'$ and no error occurred. Otherwise, the receiver concludes an error occurred and requests a retransmission.

CRC is widely used in LANs, where there are standard polynomials for $G(x)$, such as the following:

$$\text{CRC-ITU: } x^{16} + x^{12} + x^5 + 1$$

$$\text{CRC-32: } x^{32} + x^{26} + x^{23} + x^{22} + x^{16} + x^{12} + x^{11} + x^{10} + x^8 + x^7 + x^5 + x^4 + x^2 + x + 1$$

which are specified in IEEE standards such as 802.3 Ethernet and 802.15 Wireless Personal Area Networks

In general, CRC is very effective if $G(x)$ is chosen properly. Specifically, $G(x)$ should be chosen so that x is not a factor, but $x + 1$ is a factor. In this case, CRC detects the following errors:

- All burst errors of length less than or equal to n
- All burst errors affecting an odd number of bits
- All burst errors of length equal to $n + 1$ with probability $(2^{n-1} - 1)/2^{n-1}$
- All burst errors of length greater than $n + 1$ with probability $(2^n - 1)/2^n$ [the CRC-32 polynomial will detect all burst errors of length greater than

33 with probability $(2^{32} - 1)/2^{32}$; This is equivalent to a 99.99999998% accuracy rate]

VI. ENCRYPTION AND SECURITY

A. Private Key

Security and the need to disguise information to make it hard to read by unauthorized people has always been an issue, but the recent proliferation of e-commerce has raised public awareness. The NIST has produced a collection of publications called the Federal Information Processing Standards (FIPS) Publication Series that approves encryption standards to be used by federal organizations. They currently list three algorithms for encryption: DES, triple DES, and Skipjack.

1. Data Encryption Standard

The DES is an approach that uses complex procedures to encrypt the data and was developed by IBM in collaboration with the National Security Agency (NSA) and the NBS (now NIST) in the early 1970s. It was adopted as a standard in 1977 by the NIST for all commercial and unclassified information. It describes a Data Encryption Algorithm (DEA), which is defined in the ANSI standard X9.32.

The algorithm divides a message into 64-bit blocks and uses a 56-bit key. It uses a complex combination of transpositions (rearrangement of bits), substitutions (replacing one bit group with another), exclusive OR operations, and a few other processes on each block to eventually produce 64 bits of encrypted data. In all, the 64-bit block goes through 19 successive steps (Fig. 3), with the output of each step being input to the next step.

2. Triple Data Encryption Standard

Triple DES, as the name suggests, works by encrypting data three times. Based on ANSI standard X9.52, triple DES encrypts by applying three algorithms in succession to a plain text message. For example, suppose $E_k(M)$ and $D_k(M)$ correspond to DES encryption and decryption algorithms, respectively, using a key k applied to a message M. Triple DES is calculated using $E_{k3}(D_{k2}(E_{k1}(M)))$. ANSI standard X9.52 defines three options for key values: all three are independent of each other; k_1 and k_2 are independent but $k_1 = k_3$; and all are equal. Of course, in the last case, triple DES defaults to DES since the first two steps

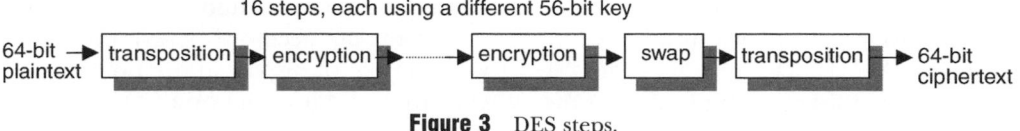

16 steps, each using a different 56-bit key

64-bit plaintext → transposition → encryption ---- encryption → swap → transposition → 64-bit ciphertext

Figure 3 DES steps.

cancel each other. This makes triple DES backwards compatible with DES.

The idea is that by using more keys one increases the number of bits used to encrypt data and, in effect, increases the key length. This, in turn, makes the encrypted code more difficult to break, and many reports have indicated that, with proper implementation, breaking triple DES should remain computationally intractable for many years.

3. Skipjack

The Skipjack Algorithm has been controversial. Designed by the NSA, details have been kept secret until its declassification in 1998, causing suspicion among some who claim the algorithm has not been subjected to stringent testing as have others whose details are freely available. Skipjack was also an integral part of the Clipper Chip (a device used for encrypting telephone conversations), itself a controversial topic. Contributing to the controversy was the fact that a backdoor was built into the algorithm that allowed law enforcement officials (assuming proper authority) to intercept and decode encrypted messages. Developed in 1987 and put into use in 1993, it was used to encrypt sensitive government data.

The algorithm has been analyzed and no weaknesses have been found, although its use of an 80-bit encryption key makes it more prone to brute-force attacks given today's increased computing power. Many now see it as an interim solution until the NIST completes work on a current project, the Advanced Encryption Standard (AES). The AES is described in a new FIPS publication and is designed to encrypt sensitive information. Based on an algorithm called Rijndael (after its developers Dr. Vincent Rijmen and Dr. Joan Daemen), it specifies key sizes of 128, 192, and 256 bits and can encrypt blocks of size 128, 192, and 256 bits. In fact, the Rijndael specification allows any of these key sizes in conjunction with any of these block sizes. Key size is significant because algorithms with smaller keys are easier to crack. For example, in the late 1990s "DES Cracker" machines were built that could determine a 56-bit DES key in just a few hours. Assuming such a machine could find a 56-bit

key in 1 s, it would still take 149 trillion years to find a 128-bit key. (For more information, go to http://csrc.nist.gov/encryption/aes/aesfact.html.)

The details of the algorithm are complex, but the Rijndael's design is based on that of another block cipher called square. (For more information, go to http://www.esat.kuleuven.ac.be/~rijmen/rijndael/.) square uses a key length of 128 bits and applies a series of steps to a 4×4 array of bytes. Rijndael can transform bytes arrays with dimensions 4×4 (128 bits), 4×6 (192 bits), or 4×8 (256 bits). Each step involves transformations, row shifting, exclusive-or operations, and substitutions via an S-box operation. Knowledge of mathematics and linear algebra is necessary to explain all the steps, and the Web site http://www.ii.uib.no/~larsr/papers/rijndael.pdf provides more detail. The AES is designed to replace the DES, which is becoming antiquated. However, most believe that triple DES will also be a viable scheme.

B. Public Key

The previous encryption schemes represent private key methods that require strict measures to keep the keys and algorithms secret. This is because the decryption method can be easily determined given knowledge of the encryption key and algorithm. By contrast, a public key method makes no attempt to keep the key secret. The methods are such that the decryption scheme cannot easily be determined even if both the encryption key and the algorithm are known.

One such public key method, the RSA Algorithm (named after its developers, Rivest, Shamir, and Adleman), uses modular arithmetic and the factorization of very large numbers. Some of the theory behind this algorithm is based in mathematical number theory, specifically in notable results known as Fermat's theorem and Euler's theorem.

A brief outline of the method is:

- Choose n to be the product of two large prime numbers p and q.
- Find a number k that is relatively prime to $(p - 1) \times (q - 1)$.

- Divide the original message into components and interpret the bit representation as a number (usually very large).
- Encrypt the message by raising each number to the power of k. However, do all arithmetic modulo n.

The process is relatively simple. In addition, knowledge of the encryption scheme requires knowing n and k. Furthermore, it can be shown that a necessary step to finding an appropriate decryption key is to factor n, an extremely difficult task, if n is very large.

C. Secure Socket Layer

With the increase of e-commerce, security has become a major concern for those conducting business over the Internet. Customers want to feel secure when ordering products and paying by credit card. One commonly used approach for protecting information is the Secure Socket Layer (SSL) protocol, which allows an exchange of encrypted information and is based on an X.509 standard for digital certificates. A digital certificate is used to verify the identity of the server site doing business. The certificate is purchased from some trusted certificate authority (CA) who verifies the identity of the purchaser and assigns a public encryption key to the server site.

When a customer's browser connects to the server, they exchange information on which encryption algorithm and key will be used for subsequent exchanges. The customer's browser downloads the server's certificate and uses the certificate to verify the server's identity with the appropriate CA. The browser also obtains the server's public key. Next, the browser defines its own encryption key that it will use to send further information. The browser also encrypts the key using the server's public key and sends it to the server. The server gets the new key in encrypted form and decrypts it. At this point it knows the key that the customer will use for sending further information and is prepared to decrypt the information it receives. Once this exchange is complete, sensitive information can be exchanged between browser and server using the encryption key and algorithm negotiated during the exchange.

VII. IMAGE COMPRESSION

One of the most significant advances in recent years is the integration of multimedia applications with computer programs and networks. With a click of a mouse we can access photographs, pictures of classic works of art on display in the Louvre, and even movie clips from the Internet or a CD-ROM. While it may at first seem a small step beyond the typical transmission of words and sentences, multimedia applications would simply not be feasible without some very sophisticated compression algorithms.

Pictures, whether they are photographs or images on a computer screen, are made up of a lot of very small dots called **picture elements** or **pixels.** The simplest images are made up of black and white dots and can be represented by using a 0 or a 1 for each pixel. Representing color images is more complex and there are different approaches. One approach uses three 8-bit groups (one for each primary color) for each pixel. The combination of the three groups can produce virtually any color in the visual spectrum.

JPEG is an acronym for the Joint Photographic Experts Group. It is a group formed as a cooperative effort by the ISO, ITU, and IEC. A compression standard, commonly known as **JPEG compression,** is used to compress both gray scale and photographic-quality color images. JPEG is *lossy*—the image obtained after decompression may not be the same as the original. Whereas information loss is unacceptable in cases such as the transfer of executable files, some loss may be tolerable if the file contains an image. The reason is that small differences in color may not even be noticeable.

JPEG compression consists of three phases: **discrete cosine transform** (DCT), **quantization,** and **encoding.** It begins by dividing an image into arrays in which each element is an 8×8 block of pixels. A DCT is applied to each array and transforms one array into another. The details are complex, but the idea is that the resulting array contains a collection of values called **spatial frequencies.** These values relate directly to how much the original pixel values change as a function of their positions in the image. In effect, they are a measure of pixel and color variation. If there is little variation, spatial frequencies have similar values. The net result is that for pictures that have little variation locally, the DCT will create an array with a lot of redundancy, a necessary characteristic for compression.

The quantization phase provides a way of ignoring small differences in an image that may not be perceptible. It defines yet another two-dimensional array by dividing each spatial frequency value by some number and rounding to the nearest integer. Because of the rounding the original values can never be recaptured exactly and this is where the loss occurs. However, if done correctly, the loss is imperceptible to the human eye. The quantization phase will take spatial frequencies that are similar and generate identical numbers, creating even more redundancy for the eventual compression.

The encoding phase finally does the compression. The main function of the encoding phase is to linearize the two-dimensional array created by the quantization phase and compress it for transmission. If done correctly and if the original picture has some compressible components, this array typically has many redundant values in it. The data can then be compressed by sending a value followed by the number of occurrences, a technique called run-length compression.

In summary, JPEG is complex, and the amount of compression depends a great deal on the image and the quantization phase, which is not prescribed by JPEG but rather depends on the application. Under the right conditions JPEG is known to produce compression ratios of 20:1 and better (meaning the transmitted file is 5% the size of the original).

VIII. VIDEO COMPRESSION

Motion, whether on the big screen, a television, a video clip from a CD-ROM, or a monitor connected to the Internet, is really no more than just a rapid display of still pictures. Standards for video differ worldwide, but a common standard defined by the National Television Standards Committee (NTSC) produces motion by displaying still pictures at a rate of 30 frames per second. This is fast enough to fool the eyes, giving the perception of true motion. Images produced at rates much slower than that produce motion that appears jerkier, which is reminiscent of some very old movies.

The group that defines standards for video compression is the Moving Pictures Expert Group (MPEG). Like JPEG, it is the result of a cooperative arrangement between the ISO, IEC, and ITU, and people often use the phrase MPEG compression when referring to video compression. MPEG, however, is not a single standard. In fact, there are several standards:

- MPEG-1, formally known as ISO/IEC-11172, was designed for video on CD-ROM and early direct broadcast satellite systems.
- MPEG-2, formally known as ISO/IEC-13818 is used for more demanding applications such as multimedia entertainment and high-definition television (HDTV) and was also adopted by the Satellite Broadcasting Industry.

- MPEG-4, formally known as ISO/IEC-14496, is intended for videoconferencing over low-bandwidth channels.
- As of this writing work is progressing on MPEG-7, which is designed to support a broad range of applications and is based on the fact that multimedia data will occupy an increasing amount of bandwidth as we progress into the 21st century. MPEG-7 will provide multimedia tools for defining and accessing content and would allow, for example, searching for songs by humming a tune into a PC's microphone, searching for images by sketching a graphic known to be in the image, or scanning a company logo and searching a multimedia database of commercials to determine which ones display the logo.
- Work is also in progress on MPEG-21. There are many players in the multimedia field and each may use their own models, rules, and procedures. MPEG-21 would define a common framework, facilitating interaction and cooperation between the different groups.

At this level we do not worry about the different MPEG variations and provide a brief overview of video compression defined by MPEG-1 (which we will, from this point on, refer to as MPEG).

Since video is actually a series of still pictures, JPEG compression or a variation of it can be used to compress each image. However, using only JPEG compression for each still picture does not provide sufficient compression for most applications.

What makes MPEG feasible is additional redundancy **(temporal redundancy)** found in successive frames. Basically, this means that no matter how much action you see in a video, the difference between two consecutive frames is usually quite small. Essentially, MPEG is based on a technique that sends a base frame and then encodes successive frames by computing the difference from the base frame and compressing and transmitting it. When differences are small, there is little data to send. The receiving end can reconstruct the frame based on the first base frame and the differences it receives.

Of course MPEG is more complex than that. Calculating differences with prior frames works well to place figures that are moving across your view, since those figures are in a prior frame. But it does not work well for images that were not in a prior frame. For example, a completely new scene cannot be compressed this way. Another example involves objects hidden behind someone who is moving. As a person moves across a scene, objects that were hidden behind the person in a previous frame come into view in successive frames.

MPEG identifies three different types of frames:

- I-frame (intrapicture frame). This is a self-contained frame that is, for all intents and purposes, just a JPEG-encoded image.
- P-frame (predicted frame). This frame is similar to what we have just discussed in that it is encoded by computing differences between a current and a previous frame.
- B-frame (bidirectional frame). This is similar to a P-frame except that it is interpolated between a previous and a future frame.

A typical sequence for frame transmission is:

I-frame → two B-frames → P-frame → two B-frames
→ I-frame.

In general, the number of B-frames can vary, but typically there will be one P-frame between two groups of B-frames. The P-frame is essentially a difference from the prior I-frame, and the B-frames are interpolated from the nearest I- and P-frames. So, for example, the first two B-frames are interpolated from the first I-frame and the P-frame. The last two B-frames are interpolated from the last I-frame and the P-frame.

IX. OPEN SYSTEMS INTERCONNECT

Some may think that the primary problem in establishing communications between two computers is simply making sure that the data get from one to the other. However, different computers are often incompatible, using different ways to represent the same information. Consequently, getting data from one computer to the other is only part of the problem. As a result, complex protocols are layered. That is, the information at one end goes through different steps where it may be changed or packaged before being sent to the other end. Protocols at the other end reverse the process and recast the data to represent the original information. Typically, each step is independent of the one above and below it, thus allowing each step to be designed, tested, implemented, or changed without knowledge of how the step above or below is implemented.

The ISO has addressed the problem of allowing many devices to communicate and has developed its Open Systems Interconnect (OSI) model. The OSI model has not been a commercial success, having been overshadowed by the protocols on which the Internet runs. Consequently, some have argued that the OSI model is dead and is no longer of use. Others counter that even though it is not a commercial suc-

cess, it does define a framework in which communication protocols can be studied and understood.

The OSI model is a seven-layer model (Fig. 4). Each layer performs specific functions and communicates with the layers directly above and below it. Higher layers deal more with user services, applications, and activities, and the lower layers deal more with the actual transmission of information.

Figure 4 shows how two sites would communicate via the OSI model. Each layer communicates logically with its counterpart at the other site. Physically, each layer communicates with the layers immediately above and below it. When a process wants to send information, it starts by handing it over to the application layer. That layer performs its functions and sends the data to the presentation layer. It, in turn, performs its functions and gives the data to the session layer. This process continues until the physical layer receives the data and actually transmits it through some network.

On the receiving end, the process works in reverse. The physical layer receives the bit stream and gives it to the data link layer. The data link layer performs certain functions and sends the data to the network layer. This process continues until the application eventually receives the information and gives it to the receiving process. The two processes appear to communicate directly, with each layer appearing to communicate directly with its remote counterpart. In reality, all data are broken into a bit stream and transmitted between physical layers.

The highest layer, the **application layer,** works directly with the user or application programs. The application layer provides user services such as e-mail, file transfers, or remote logins. For example, in a file transfer protocol the application layer on one end should appear to send a file directly to the application layer on the other end independent of the underlying network or computer architectures.

The **presentation layer** is responsible for presenting data in a format its user can understand. For example, suppose two different computers use different numeric and character formats. The presentation layer translates data from one representation to another and insulates the user from such differences. In effect, the presentation layer determines the difference between data and information. The presentation layer can also provide security measures. It may encrypt data before handing it to the lower layers for transfer. The presentation layer at the other end would decrypt the data after receiving it. The user need never know the data had been altered.

The **session layer** allows applications on two different computers to establish a session or logical con-

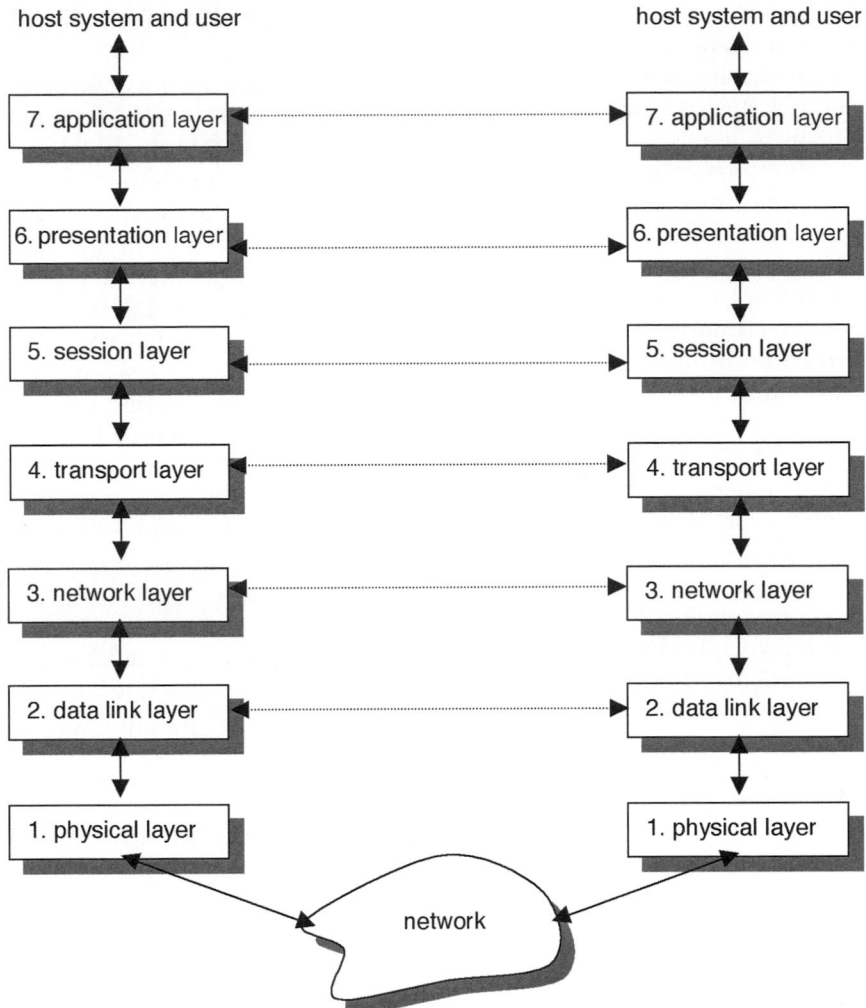

Figure 4 The OSI Model.

nection. For example, a user may connect to a remote system and communicate by alternately sending and receiving messages. The session layer helps coordinate the process by informing each end when it can send or when it must listen. This is a form of synchronization. The session layer also handles error recovery. For example, suppose a user is sending the contents of a large file over a network that suddenly fails. When it is operational again, the transfer may resume from a point prior to the failure rather than starting at the beginning.

The fourth layer is the **transport layer.** It is the lowest layer that deals primarily with end-to-end communications (the lower layers deal with the network itself). The transport layer on one side divides data into segments and sends them to the transport layer on the other side. The receiving transport layer ac-

knowledges their receipt, extracts the data, and gives them to the session layer above it.

It sounds simple, but the process is more complex. For example, since the transport layer makes no assumptions about the underlying network, it is possible for the segments to arrive out of order. The receiving transport layer must then resequence them. Lost or damage segments are also possible, and the receiving transport layer must inform its sending counterpart that these segments are missing or damaged and should be resent.

Transport layers can also implement flow control, an algorithm that controls the number of segments that can be sent before an acknowledgment for them has been received. By sending a limited number of segments at a time, the transport layer can respond to congested networks and make more efficient use of buffer space.

The **network layer** defines the communications sub-net, the collection of transmission media and switching elements required for routing and data transmission. One of the network layer's most important functions is routing. If site A needs to send information to site B (Fig. 5), then, assuming A is not connected directly to B, the information must pass through intermediate nodes. In complex networks there may be many choices. For example, in Fig. 5 there are many ways to travel from site A to site B.

Software that implements routing strategies run on routers at each intermediate node. The router receives information and determines to which node it should send it. Usually, the choice is made based on trying to find the shortest or cheapest path or trying to avoid heavily congested nodes. Many routing strategies are adaptive, which means that the best choice varies with time. A route that may be optimal at one time may become congested later.

The **data link layer** supervises the flow of information between adjacent network nodes. It uses error detection techniques to ensure that a transmission contains no errors. If the data link layer detects an error, it can request a new transmission. It also implements flow control algorithms to regulate the rate at which data is sent. This is similar to flow control in the transport layer, but is more local in scope. The data link layer also recognizes a format. Data are often transmitted in frames, which consist of a group of bytes organized according to a specified format. Frames contain necessary information such as addresses and other control information.

Finally, the **physical layer** transmits data bits over a network. It is concerned with the physical or electrical aspects of data communications. For example, is the medium copper cable, optical fiber, or satellite communications? How can data be transferred physically from one point to another? The physical layer transmits data bits received from the data link layer in streams without regard to their meaning or format. Similarly, it receives bits without analyzing them and gives them to the data link layer.

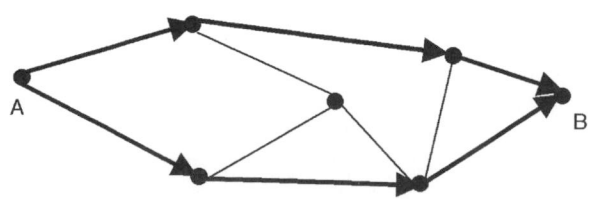

Figure 5 Network routes.

X. SYSTEMS NETWORK ARCHITECTURE

Another layered protocol is IBM's Systems Network Architecture (SNA). SNA is of interest because its 1974 release predates OSI. In addition, it was probably the most widely used proprietary network architecture. Originally it was designed to connect a single host with terminals, but was updated in 1976 to allow multiple hosts to communicate. In 1985 another update included the support of LANs and arbitrary topologies.

The SNA protocol has seven layers, but some references present SNA as a six- or even a five-layer protocol. The discrepancies occur because some people do not consider the lowest or highest layers to be part of the SNA. In some of the older versions the upper two layers were considered one. On the surface the SNA resembles the OSI model, which is not surprising, because both are designed to connect a variety of devices. SNA is preInternet and was important in mainframe environments. With the declining use of mainframe computers and heavy dependence on client-server computing and LAN/wide area network (WAN) technology, SNA is less important than it once was.

XI. TRANSMISSION CONTROL PROTOCOL/INTERNET PROTOCOL

The Internet connects many devices, each of which runs a protocol known as transmission control protocol/internet protocol (TCP/IP). TCP and IP correspond roughly to layers 4 and 3 of the OSI model, respectively, although they are not part of the OSI model. They were developed along with the Department of Defense's (DoD) Advanced Research Projects Agency (ARPA) project and have become DoD standards. TCP/IP is probably the most widely implemented protocol in the world and runs on almost anything from PCs to supercomputers.

The TCP/IP pair of protocols is part of a protocol collection called the TCP/IP protocol suite (Fig. 6). TCP provides connection-oriented services for higher layer applications and relies on IP to route packets through the network in order to make those connections. These applications, in turn, provide specific services for Internet users. For example, simple mail transfer protocol (SMTP) defines the protocol used for the delivery of mail messages over the Internet. The TELNET protocol allows users to log in to remote computers via the Internet. The file transfer protocol (FTP) allows Internet users to transfer files from remote computers. The domain name system (DNS) provides a mapping of host names to Internet addresses.

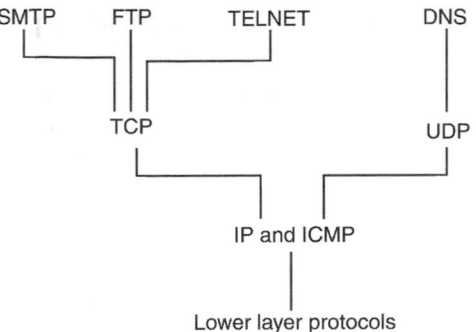

Figure 6 TCP/IP protocol suite.

TCP is a connection-oriented transport protocol designed to provide reliable communications over different network architectures. Similar to its counterpart in the OSI model, TCP implements flow control and error detection algorithms. Its predecessor in the original ARPANET was the network control protocol (NCP), which was designed to run on top of a reliable network. ARPANET was sufficiently reliable, but as it evolved into an internetwork, reliability was lost. Consequently, the transport protocol was forced to evolve as well. NCP, redesigned to run over unreliable networks, became TCP. The user datagram protocol (UDP) provides a connectionless mode of communication over dissimilar networks.

The IP is a layer 3 protocol designed to provide a packet delivery service between two sites. It is commonly used with TCP. Figure 7 shows how it works with TCP. Two sites (A and B) need a connection-oriented service requiring the transmission of some data. To begin, the TCP protocol at site A creates a TCP segment containing the user's data and "sends" the segment to site B. If all goes well site B will acknowledge what it receives. From the TCP's point of view it has made a direct connection with site B (dotted line). IP, however, intercepts the segment and creates an **IP packet** containing the TCP segment and, among other things, the destination address. It sends the packet to a router. Each router in the Internet executes routing algorithms that determine where a packet is sent next. When the packet eventually arrives at site B, the TCP segment is extracted and the transmission is complete.

Of interest is that no router knows the complete path that the packet takes. Instead, each one knows only, that given a destination, what router is the next link toward that destination. There are many routing algorithms, and there are difficulties in dealing with developing congestion or packets that circulate among routers without making progress toward their final destination. In fact, IP will not guarantee delivery of any packet, having the ability to simply discard a packet that has been circulating for too long. However, that is not usually a problem since TCP provides the acknowledgment and resending mechanisms that respond correctly if expected information does not arrive.

XII. INTERNET PROTOCOL VERSION 6

The original purpose of the Internet was to connect computers and exchange data. Consequently, protocols were developed to accomplish this primary goal. The problem is that connecting computers is not the only goal of a global network, and therefore, different protocols must emerge to meet these new goals. Just as the PC was the phenomenon of the 1980s, multimedia and video applications were and will be the phenomena of the 1990s and the early 21st century. Entertainment and digital technology continue to blend together to create new demands on global networks.

Mobility is another development. In the current Internet the vast majority of devices never change locations. They may move from one office to another, but that is a problem for local management. From the IP's perspective, they remain in fixed locations. However, this is changing. Mobile computers and satellite technology are providing the means for any two devices to communicate from anywhere in the world. The protocols must develop to allow millions of pairs of devices to make connections from arbitrary locations. Many also see current technologies such as cell phones, pagers, and portable computers eventually merging into a personal communication device that serves a variety of needs. Making telephone calls or

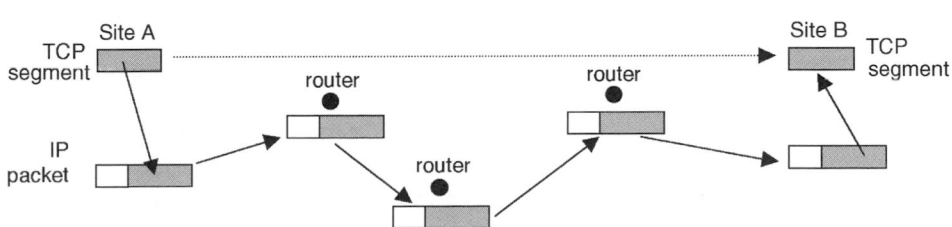

Figure 7 Relationship between TCP and IP.

being paged are obvious ones, but many see the day when such a device can do many other tasks. Homes may be equipped with computerized devices with which you can communicate. If you are getting home later than you planned, you might use a personal communication device to turn on the lights at home or start the oven. A sensor system might send a signal to you if you left without locking all the doors or turning off the lights, which, of course, you could correct using the same system. You will be able to plug the device into a portable computer and download files from any other remote computer to which you have access, all without benefit of a telephone.

Security is another issue. The IP is not secure. This is why passwords, authentication techniques, and firewalls are so important to many applications. People recognize that packets arriving on the Internet can come from virtually anywhere and that strong measures are necessary to protect their resources. The past years have seen enough examples of fraud and hacking into private computers to suggest that security will always be a concern.

People have been thinking about these ideas for many years and the concepts are certainly not new. In 1991, the IETF began looking at the issue of changing the existing IP and creating a next-generation IP informally referred to as IP next generation (IPng). In an attempt to get the computing community involved, they invited various professionals (researchers, manufacturers, vendors, programmers, etc.) to submit proposals. An appointed committee, called the IPng directorate, evaluated the proposals and rejected many because they served special interests or were just too complex. However, one proposal included a design called simple Internet protocol (SIP), which was extended to use ideas described in other proposals. The resulting protocol was named simple Internet protocol plus (SIPP).

In 1994 the IETF met in Toronto and, based on the recommendations of the IPng directorate, selected SIPP as the basis for the next-generation IP, which would be formally known as IP version 6 (IPv6). Later in the year the Internet Engineering Steering Group approved it, and the following year the group entered the protocols into the IETF standard process.

IPv6 performs the same primary functions as IPv4 (current IP protocol), providing a connectionless routing capability. However, it has added capabilities, such as authentication and encryption, not available in IPv4. It also increases the address space dramatically and simplifies the headers to make routing more efficient. There are other factors that also contribute to more efficient routing. IPv4 had to deal with frag-

menting and reassembling packets that were too large to travel some networks. Intermediate nodes under IPv6 nodes no longer fragment and reassemble packets. There is also no error detection capability in IPv6, unlike IPv4, thus relieving routers of another time-consuming task. IPv6 also defines the concept of a flow, which defines a sequence of packets that it guarantees to deliver in order. This is particularly useful in real-time applications where no time is spent rearranging packets that may have arrived out of order. The flow concept can also decrease the amount of time routers need to make routing decisions.

XIII. MEDIUM ACCESS AND LOGICAL LINK CONTROL

We now turn our attention to LANs. To fully understand IEEE LAN standards, it is important to understand where they fit in a layered design. Specifically, the data link layer is responsible for accurate communication between two nodes in a LAN. This involves frame (LAN transmission unit) formats, error checking, and flow control, some of which are independent of a specific LAN standard.

As a result, the data link layer is further divided into two sublayers, the **logical link control** (LLC) and the **medium access control** (MAC) (Fig. 8). The LLC handles logical links between the stations, whereas the MAC controls access to the transmission medium. Primarily, the LLC provides service to the network layer and calls on the MAC for specific tasks. The LLC is also a standard (IEEE 802.2) and is based on a high-level data link control (HDLC) protocol.

HDLC is a bit-oriented protocol that supports both half-duplex and full-duplex communications. It defines frame formats and implements flow control among other activities as it supervises the exchange of data between two devices. We note that there are many other protocols that are very similar to HDLC. They are:

- Synchronous data link control (SDLC). HDLC was derived from SDLC, which was developed by IBM in the early 1970s. IBM had submitted SDLC to the ISO for acceptance. ISO modified it and renamed it HDLC. Effectively, SDLC is IBM's equivalent to HDLC. (If you sit on the other side of the fence, HDLC is the ISO's equivalent to SDLC.) SDLC is part of IBM's SNA and was commonly used in IBM terminal-to-computer communications.
- Advanced data communications control procedure (ADCCP). IBM also submitted SDLC to the ANSI

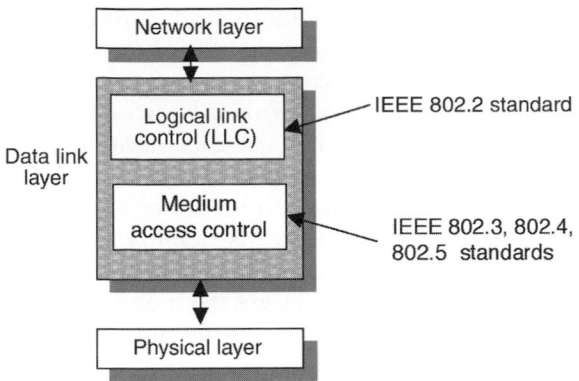

Figure 8 MAC and LLC sublayers.

for acceptance. They modified it and renamed it ADCCP.

- Link access protocols (LAPs). There are several LAPs. The ITU adopted and modified HDLC for use in its X.25 network interface standard. Originally, it was labeled LAP, but subsequently was changed to LAPB (B for balanced). It allows devices to be connected to packet-switched networks. A variation on LAPB is LAPD, the link control for the Integrated Services Digital Network (ISDN). The ISDN is an entirely digital communications system defined by the ITU that was originally designed to eventually replace the telephone system.

XIV. ETHERNET: IEEE STANDARD 802.3

The MAC sublayer is where LAN technologies differ. The IEEE 802.3 standard is a MAC protocol implementing what is commonly known as the Ethernet. Part of the Ethernet's history dates back to 1973. In his Ph.D. thesis, Robert Metcalfe described much of his research on LAN technology. After graduation, he joined the Xerox Corporation and worked with a group that eventually implemented what became known as the Ethernet. The Ethernet is named after ether, the imaginary substance that many once believed occupied all of space and was the medium through which light waves propagated.

Later, the concepts of the Ethernet were written up and proposed to the IEEE as a standard for LANs. The proposal had the backing of Xerox, Intel, and DEC. The IEEE eventually adopted it as a standard, and it is now referred to as IEEE standard 802.3. It is worth noting that two other proposals were made to the IEEE at about the same time. One was backed by General Motors and the other by IBM. They also became standards known as IEEE 802.4 Token Bus and IEEE 802.5 Token Ring.

There are many differences between the 802.3 Ethernet and the two token-based LANs, but probably the two most visible ones are the frame formats and the protocol used to access the media.

An IEEE 802.3 frame (Fig. 9) contains the following:

- Preamble. A seven-octet (byte) pattern consisting of alternating 0s and 1s is used for synchronization.
- Start of frame delimiter. The special pattern 10101011 indicates the start of a frame.
- Destination address. If the first bit is 0, this field specifies a specific device. If it is 1, the destination address is a group address and the frame is sent to all devices in some predefined group. If all bits are 1, the frame is broadcast to all devices.
- Source address. Specifies where the frame comes from.
- Data length field. Specifies the number of octets in the combined data and pad fields.
- Data field. Self-explanatory.
- Pad field. The data field must be at least 46 octets. If there is not enough data, extra octets are added (padded) to the data to make up the difference.
- Frame check sequence. Error checking using 32-bit CRC.

To access the media, Ethernet uses carrier sense multiple access with collision detection (CSMA/CD), which is summarized as follows:

- If the medium is quiet, the device transmits the frame and continues to listen.
- If the device detects a collision (another device may also send), it immediately stops transmitting and sends a short jamming signal.

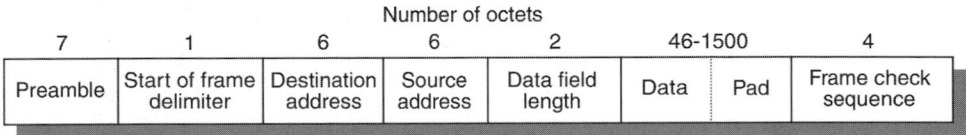

Figure 9 An Ethernet frame.

- If a medium is busy, the device waits until the medium clears. When that happens the device transmits with probability p, where $0 \leq p \leq 1$. The probabilistic transmission is used in case two or more devices are waiting. If all devices transmitted with certainty ($p = 1$) when the media cleared, then, if there are two or more devices waiting, additional collisions are guaranteed. If there is a chance that one or more of the devices will not transmit, then there is a chance that one device will transmit successfully.
- After a collision the device waits a random amount of time before trying to send again. An algorithm called binary exponential backoff is used to determine the length of time. A device may experience several collisions before it transmits a frame successfully. In theory, excessive collisions can dominate, causing a cessation of all transmissions. However, in practice, there are safeguards in place to prevent that from happening.

There are actually several different variations of the Ethernet standard as defined by IEEE 802.3. They differ, in part, by the physical connections and transfer rates. The original proposal defined a 10-Mbps transfer rate over 10Base5 cable, a 50-ohm, 10-millimeter diameter coaxial cable. Some also called it **Thick Wire Ethernet** or just **ThickNet,** a clear reference to the thick unwieldy cable. By today's standards, 10 Mbps is antiquated and gigabit transfer rates are common. To keep up with changing technology, the IEEE 802.3 group has defined many revisions of the standard to utilize thinner cables, unshielded twisted wire pairs (UTP), and optical fiber. Cables are designated by codes such as 100BASE-T, 100BASE-F, and even 1000BASE-T. The first number in the designation represents the transfer rate and the letter indicates the type of medium (F for optical fiber and T for twisted wire pair). So, for example, 1000BASE-T defines a gigabit Ethernet over twisted wire pair and is defined by IEEE 802.3z. Despite the improvements in speed and equipment, new standards must remain backward compatible with old standards to allow integration of new technologies with the old.

XV. TOKEN RING: IEEE STANDARD 802.5

Devices on a token ring LAN are connected in a ring and contention is handled through a token (a special frame) that circulates among all the devices. When a token arrives at a device, one of two things occurs. If a device does not have data to send, it passes the token to its neighbor. If a device does have something to send, it claims the token, removes it from the ring, and sends a frame in the token's place. The frame then travels along the ring and each device examines the frame's destination address. If the destination address does not match the current device's address, the device passes the frame to its neighbor. If it does match, the destination device copies the frame, sets some status bits in it, and passes the frame to its neighbor. The frame continues along the ring until it eventually arrives at the device that created it. This device removes the frame from the ring, generates a new token, and puts the token back onto the ring.

The main advantage of a token ring over the Ethernet is that there are no collisions and no bandwidth wasted as a result. A disadvantage is that a token ring requires more maintenance. Device failures can result in a token not being put on a ring or a data frame not being removed from the ring. Either case will result in a loss of communication, and procedures are built into the protocol so that it recovers from such events. Most believe that the disadvantages outweigh the advantages as token rings are rarely used anymore.

XVI. TOKEN BUS: IEEE STANDARD 802.4

The token bus standard combines features of the Ethernet and the token ring protocols. For example, the token bus operates on the same principle as the token ring. The devices are logically organized into a ring and a token circulates among them. A device wanting to send something must wait for the token to arrive. Here, however, the devices communicate via a common bus as in an Ethernet. Thus, in contrast to the token ring protocol, the token contains a destination address that specifies which device gets it. Each device monitors the bus and reads only those tokens destined for it. Also, like the token ring network, token bus networks are rarely used anymore.

XVII. WIRELESS LOCAL AREA NETWORKS

One of the more interesting emerging technologies is wireless communication. The last decade saw enormous growth in the use of cellular telephones and spawned a new generation of people who enjoy the freedom to communicate independent of their location. Although used primarily for cell phones and pager systems initially, wireless communication has now enabled the wireless network, a system that allows PCs and other typical network devices to communicate without a physical connection. It promises a whole new world of applications where cabling is impractical or for people who rarely stay in one spot. The wireless connection also allows equipment to be moved easily without worrying about disconnecting and reconnecting wires.

Two approaches are infrared and radio waves. Infrared waves are electromagnetic waves with frequencies just below those of visible light. Devices are equipped with light emitting diodes or laser diodes that emit infrared light waves. These waves may be directed toward a receiver or reflected off walls and ceilings. It is similar to using a remote control to turn on the television or change the channel. There are some advantages to infrared systems. For example, infrared signals are not regulated by the Federal Communications Commission (FCC) as radio signals are. This means that licensing is not required to use infrared-based equipment. Another advantage is that infrared signals do not penetrate solid objects such as walls. That makes them more secure from outside eavesdroppers. It also allows devices in different areas of a building to use the same infrared signal without interference. Infrared signals are also impervious to radio interference. However, nonpenetration of solid objects is a disadvantage if an application calls for communication beyond solid boundaries. Another disadvantage is that infrared signals typically provide lower bit rates than other technologies.

Wireless LANs can also use radio transmissions up to 2.4 GHz (1 GHz = 10^9 cycles per second). A common wired network such as an Ethernet forms the basic infrastructure, connecting various network devices such as PCs, printers, scanners, etc. However, another component called an access point (AP), connected to the wired network, acts as a bridge between the wired and wireless networks. The AP receives information from the wired network and broadcasts the information to other devices within its range. Various protocols are then used to ensure that the transmission reaches the proper devices.

The IEEE has developed standards designated as 802.11 [http://grouper.ieee.org/groups/802/11/index.html] for wireless networks. The standard includes a layer 2 protocol and several layer 1 specifications. The layer 2 protocol has some similarities with those found in an Ethernet. It also provides for authentication and privacy. There are actually three layer 1 specifications. Two involve communication using spread spectrum radio waves, and the other uses infrared light waves. Spread spectrum radio involves sending a radio signal over a broad frequency spectrum as opposed to a narrow one. One advantage is that it is more resistant to narrowband interference. Another is that the power level of a spread spectrum signal can be much lower than that of a conventional narrowband signal. In some cases the power level can be almost as low as background noise. Spread spectrum signals also result in a secure transmission because only devices that know how the signal was spread over the frequency spectrum can receive and decode it.

Most of the above discussion has assumed the use of typical network devices such as PCs, printers, scanners, etc. However, some developers are developing technologies that could forever change the way we view network devices. Few people would think of their wristwatch, oven timer, or videocassette recorder as being network devices, but developers of the **Bluetooth** technology hope to change that. Bluetooth is named after Harald Blatand (Bluetooth), a Viking king who lived in the 10th century and unified Denmark and Norway.

The Bluetooth concept refers to a technology in which a microchip containing a radio transceiver is embedded in an electronic device. The intent, of course, is to allow these devices to communicate without wires or cables. Bluetooth began at Ericsson Mobile Communication in 1994 when researchers studied ways to define a low-power, low-cost interface between mobile phones and their accessories. In 1998 they formed a special interest group with IBM, Nokia, Intel, and Toshiba, and today that group has grown into an alliance of nearly 2000 companies. The IEEE is working on a standard for wireless personal area networks (IEEE 802.15) based on the Bluetooth technology. It would allow communication among handheld personal computers, personal digital assistants, headsets, microphones, cell phones, and almost anything that could be carried. Some even foresee the potential of transferring information from one person to another via physical contact using natural conductive properties of the human body.

XVIII. X.25 STANDARD

In the 1970s many European countries began to develop **public data networks** (networks available to anyone with a need for network services). The problems they faced were different from those in the United States where public networks could be developed in large part by leasing existing telephone lines. In Europe this could not be done easily due to problems inherent in traversing communications systems across international boundaries. Thus, instead of developing separate and incompatible standards, European countries worked under the auspices of the ITU to develop a single standard. One result was the public data network service interface referred to as the X series of protocols.

The ITU X.25 standard defines the protocol between two devices. The traditional names for these devices are data terminal equipment (DTE) and data circuit-terminating equipment (DCE), which are connected to a public data network. Early versions focused mainly on the asymmetric DTE–DCE relationship, but later versions recognized the need for peer-to-peer communications between two DTEs. X.25 defines a synchronous transmission analogous to the three lowest layers of the OSI. However, since most of the world uses the Internet, X.25 is no longer common.

XIX. X.400 E-MAIL

The ITU-T issued its own standards for e-mail in 1984. They are referred to collectively as the X.400 family of standards and are analogous to the OSI application layer. X.400 also forms the foundation of the ISO e-mail system, MOTIS, and is the ISO analog to TCP/IP's SMTP. It is based on a model for message handling systems illustrated by Fig. 10. The model has four main parts: user agent (UA), message transfer agent (MTA), message handling system (MHS), and message transfer system (MTS).

Superficially, the UA interacts with the user and essentially defines what the user can do. The MTAs de-

fine a collection of nodes that execute a protocol to ensure proper routing of mail. They form the backbone of the mail system, and their physical connections vary. They play a role similar to that of routers in internetworks, but operate at a higher layer. Collectively, the MTAs form the MTS. The MTAs and UAs form the MHS, which ensures the eventual delivery of mail.

The UA is the user interface. It has two main functions. First, it routes messages between the user and the local MTA, allowing the user to send and receive mail. Second, it manages the message store (MS), which is used to store messages. The UA performs its functions at the request of the user and, to the user at least, defines the system's capabilities. Common UA functions include send mail, list messages, reply, forward, store, and delete. X.400 is no longer common, but may still be found in some mail systems because it is a standard.

XX. SIMPLE MAIL TRANSFER PROTOCOL

The standard mail protocol in the TCP/IP suite (Internet) is the SMTP. It runs above TCP/IP and below any local mail service. Its primary responsibility is to make sure mail is transferred between different hosts. By contrast, the local service is responsible for distributing mail to specific recipients.

Figure 11 shows the interaction between local mail, SMTP, and TCP. When a user sends mail, the local

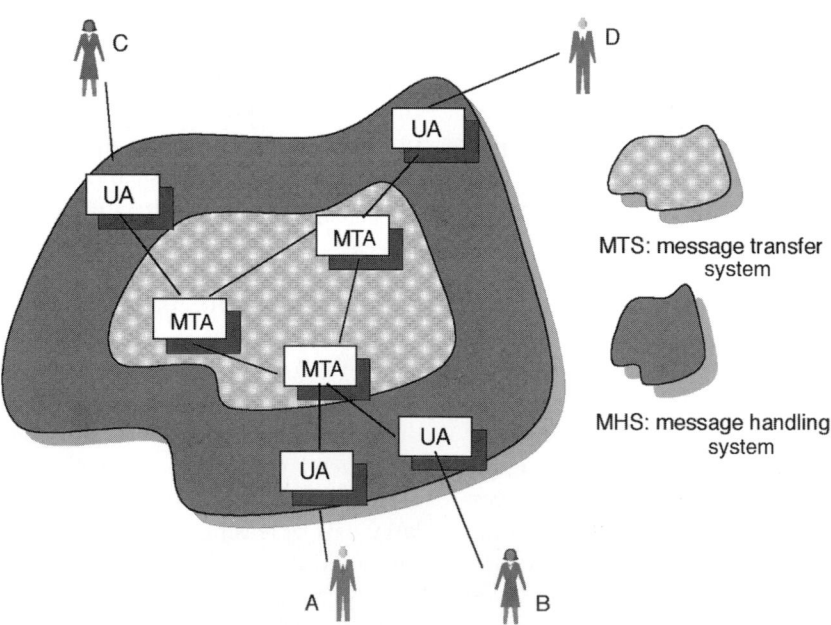

Figure 10   The X.400 e-mail system.

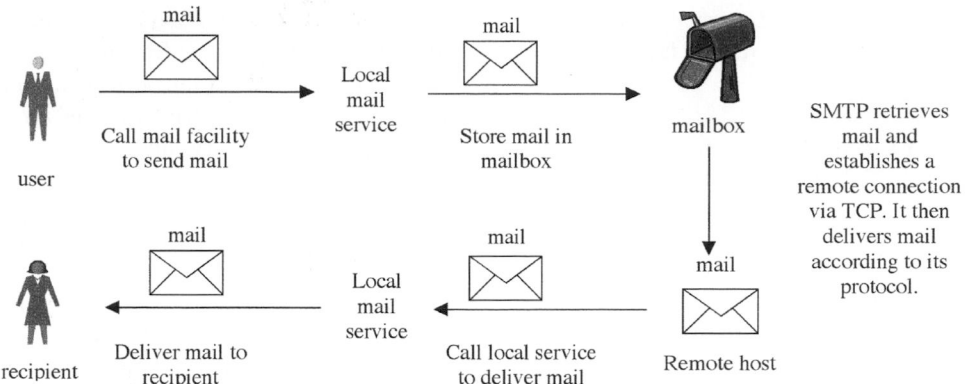

Figure 11 The SMTP.

mail facility determines whether the address is local or requires a connection to a remote site. In the latter case, the local mail facility stores the mail (much as you would put a letter in a mailbox), where it waits for the client SMTP. When the client SMTP delivers the mail, it first calls the TCP to establish a connection with the remote site. When the connection is made, the client and server SMTPs exchange packets and eventually deliver the mail. At the remote end the local mail facility gets the mail and delivers it to the intended recipient.

XXI. X.500 DIRECTORY SERVICES

As we know, e-mail systems allow users to send messages to others, but there is always one stipulation: the e-mail address must be provided. Therefore, another important issue is the **mail directory** or **directory service,** which provides the address of an individual given that he or she is unambiguously identified. It is similar to the telephone system—you can call almost anywhere in the world, but you must know the number first. If you do not know the number, resources such as telephone books or directory assistance can help, but even they are restrictive. Telephone books can be up to a year out of date. Using directory assistance requires that you first know the city in which the desired person resides.

After developing the X.400 standards, the ITU-T wanted to define standards for a directory with functions similar to those of the telephone directory. The result is the X.500 directory service standard, which has several important features:

- Distributed directory. The actual directory would be distributed across many sites throughout the

world. It appears as a single centralized directory to each user (Fig. 12), but it is located and maintained at physically separate sites.
- Hierarchical structure. This is similar to the telephone system, in which the area code defines a geographic region. Even within the region, telephones with the same three-digit prefix tend to be from the same area of town.
- Consistency. Some call it a homogeneous name space. Basically, it means that all users see the same information presented the same way. On a global scale this is a daunting requirement. Telephone numbers in the United States all have the same format, but the format changes for international calls.
- Address lookup service. Again, it is similar to the telephone service, but more general. The user could get an address by specifying a variety of items that uniquely identify a person, for example, the person's name, where he or she works, the department he or she is in, or his or her telephone extension. Services also include abilities similar to those provided by the Yellow Pages. A user could get a range of addresses for businesses

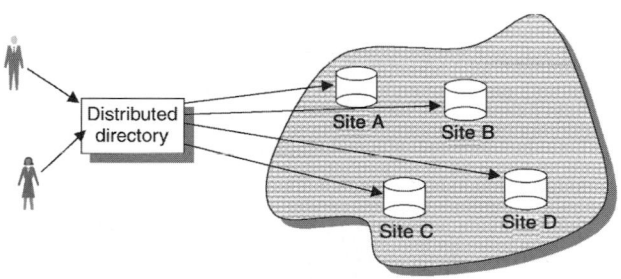

Figure 12 Distributed directory.

providing a particular type of service or addresses within a particular department in a large company.

The structure of the X.500 directory is primarily a distributed hierarchy. That is, it has a logical hierarchical structure (tree), but parts of the tree are maintained at different sites. Collectively, all of the information in the directory is called the directory information base (DIB). The DIB consists of entries, each of which contains information about a real-world entity such as a country, company, department, or person. The entries are organized in a hierarchical fashion and form the directory information tree (DIT). The distributed aspect means that different branches of the tree are maintained by different organizations, but collectively the hierarchy is maintained. Each entry contains attributes describing the object it represents. Therefore, to specify an object represented in the DIB, a user must uniquely identify attributes of the entries leading to it.

Figure 13 shows an example of a DIT. Here, second-level nodes correspond to countries, third-level nodes correspond to organizations within a country, fourth-level nodes correspond to departments within an organization, and fifth-level nodes correspond to a person within a department. The information shown means that Mary Smith works as a senior engineer in the engineering department at the ACME corporation in the United States. Thus, if someone wanted to send e-mail to Mary Smith, he or she would specify the following:

C = US, O = ACME, D = engineering,
N = Mary Smith

This format represents a keyword approach to referencing directory information, using C for country, O for organization, D for department, and N for name. The keywords and attributes define a path from the tree's root to the desired entry. If there were several Mary Smiths working in the same department, the format would require additional attributes specifying the proper Mary Smith. These could include Mary Smith's title, telephone number, or postal address. Somewhere there must be an attribute distinguishing the two Mary Smiths.

XXII. ASYNCHRONOUS TRANSFER MODE

The last protocol we discuss is asynchronous transfer mode (ATM), and it was designed, in part, to deal with a quality of service (QoS) issue. For example, some data transfers such as real-time video and voice feeds can tolerate small losses of information, but not transmission delays. Others, such as the transfer of executable files can tolerate delays in transfer, but absolutely no loss of information. The QoS issue means providing the type of service to a user consistent with needs. The ATM protocol will guarantee a QoS for real-time video and voice traffic.

To the user ATM is designed to resemble the circuit-switching technology of telephone systems in that everything appears to work in real time. However, ATM represents a complete departure from such circuit-switching technology. For example, it maintains the capability of routing individual packets of data. The following items describe the primary attributes of an ATM network:

- Connection oriented
- Packet switching
- Fixed-size packets called cells
- High-speed, low-delay transmission of cells
- Cells will not arrive out of order
- Speeds of 155.5 Mbps (this is the data rate necessary for full-motion video) or 622 Mbps (four 155.5 Mbps channels); as the technology evolves, the future no doubt will see gigabit per second rates
- Designed in large part for real-time video and voice applications

In general, ATM works by initially setting up a connection between two sites, during which a virtual circuit between them is established. In ATM terminology this is called **signaling.** It is based on the ITU-T protocol Q.2931. The virtual circuit corresponds to a specific path determined during signaling, and all cells sent through the virtual circuit follow the same path. When the transmissions are complete, ATM protocols include a disconnect phase.

One of the unique aspects of ATM is that it transmits all information in 53-byte cells (48 bytes of data plus 5 header bytes). There are several advantages of transmitting information in small fixed-size packets.

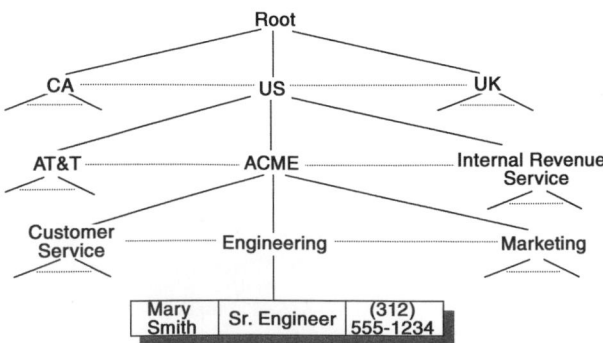

Figure 13 Directory information tree.

First, it is simpler. Programmers learn this fundamental fact early. Writing software that manipulates fixed-size units is easier than writing software that deals with variable-sized units. There are just fewer checks to make. This, of course, simplifies both the hardware and software required to do the job and also keeps the costs lower.

A second advantage of having small cells is that one cell will not occupy an outgoing link for lengthy periods. For example, suppose a switch just began forwarding a cell when another high-priority cell arrives. High priority typically means it can move to the front of an outgoing queue, but it will not interrupt transmission of a cell already in progress. Consequently, it must wait for the transmission to be complete. If that cell is large, then the time the high-priority cell must wait is longer. A smaller cell means the high-priority cell gets out quicker.

Central to ATM technology are the virtual circuit and virtual path. A **virtual circuit** represents a logical connection between two end points. For example, in Fig. 14 there is a logical connection between each of A and X, B and Y, and C and Z. However, each connection corresponds to the same path defined by the switches in the figure.

Each cell contains a 12-bit **virtual circuit ID** and a 16-bit **virtual path ID.** The ATM switches forward cells based solely on the 16-bit virtual path ID. Making decisions based on a 16-bit number instead of a full 28-bit identifier allows switching to occur more quickly. Again, this is a major goal of the ATM. Using 16-bit numbers instead of 28-bit numbers also keeps internal switching tables smaller (a maximum of 2^{16} entries as opposed to 2^{28} entries). The circuit ID is needed only when the cell arrives at the last ATM switch, which must forward the cell directly to the user.

Another advantage of using both circuit and path IDs is realized if there is a problem in a link. For example, suppose 100 connections have been established that all use the same path. If a problem develops along the path, a new one must be found. If switching were based on a 28-bit number, then the internal tables for each new switch in the alternate route would require a new entry for each connection. In this case 100 changes to each table would be made. However, since switching is based on just the path ID and all connections use the same path, each table requires just one change to accommodate all the connections.

We finish by outlining the **ATM adaptation layer** (AAL), an interface between higher layers and the ATM layer, which sits just above the physical layer (Fig. 15). It consists of two sublayers: the **segmentation and reassembly** (SAR) **sublayer** and the **convergence sublayer** (CS). The CS's responsibilities depend on the type of information the applications at higher levels generate. Generally, some application at a higher layer generates data, which we view as a byte stream. The CS extracts some of those bytes and adds a header and trailer to create its own CS packet. The SAR sublayer gets the CS packet and adds its own header and trailer to create a 48-byte payload that then gets stored into an ATM cell. It may seem that the CS and the SAR sublayer do the same things in that they add headers and trailers to data received from a higher layer. While true, there are differences in what those headers and trailers contain. Furthermore, that difference depends on the different AAL types.

AAL types differ primarily in the classes of traffic they will handle. AAL 1 deals with Class A traffic that requires a constant bit rate (CBR) and strict synchronization between sender and receiver, such as that which might be

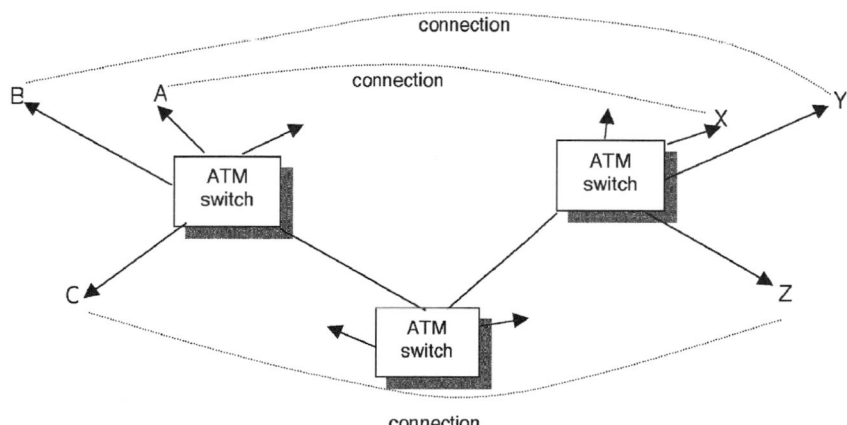

Figure 14 Virtual circuits and virtual paths. Distinct virtual circuits exist between A and X, B and Y, C and Z. All use the same virtual path.

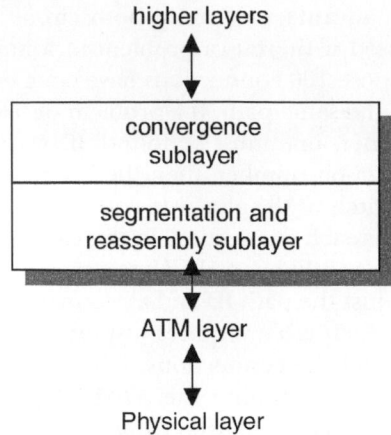

higher layers

convergence
sublayer

segmentation and
reassembly sublayer

ATM layer

Physical layer

Figure 15 AAL sublayers.

used in real-time uncompressed video. AAL 2 deals with
Class B traffic that allows a variable bit rate (VBR), but still
requires synchronization. An example is real-time compressed video. The pattern seems to suggest that AAL 3
and AAL 4 deal with Class C (connection oriented with
no time constraints) and Class D traffic (connectionless
with no time constraints). To some extent that was true,
because the ITU-T did develop an AAL 3 and AAL 4.
However, as development progressed, it became apparent
that there were no significant differences, so they elected
to combine them. One might think the result would be
labeled AAL 3½, but in fact it is called AAL 3/4. After AAL
3/4 was developed, some were concerned about what
they perceived as inefficiencies. Consequently, AAL 5 was
developed as a successor to AAL 3/4 and was also designed to be used with Class C and Class D traffic.

ACKNOWLEDGMENT

Portions of this article were reprinted from *Understanding Data
Communications and Networks, 2nd Edition*, 1999, by W. Shay with
permission of Brooks/Cole, an imprint of the Wadsworth
Group, a division of Thomson Learning.

SEE ALSO THE FOLLOWING ARTICLES

Electronic Data Interchange • Frame Relay • Integrated
Services Digital Network • Internet, Overview • Local
Area Networks • Telecommunications Industry • Transmis-
sion Control Protocol/Internet Protocol • Wide Area
Networks

BIBLIOGRAPHY

Gallo, M., and Hancock, W. (2002). *Computer communications
and networking technologies*. Brooks/Cole, Pacific Grove, CA.
Halsall, F. (2001). *Multimedia communications*. Addison-Wesley,
Reading, MA.
Kurose, J., and Ross, K. (2001). *Computer networking*. Addison
Wesley, Reading, MA.
Leon-Garcia, A., and Widjaja, I. (2000). *Communications net-
works*. McGraw-Hill, New York.
Peterson, L., and Davie, B. (1999). *Computer networks: A
systems approach*. 2nd ed., Morgan Kaufman, San Fran-
cisco, CA.
Shay, W. *Understanding data communications and networks*. 3rd
ed., Brooks/Cole, Pacific Grove, CA.
Stallings, W. (2000). *Data & computer communications*. 6th ed.,
Prentice Hall, Upper Saddle River, NJ.

Web Sites

American National Standards Institute, http://www. ansi.org
Electronic Industries Alliance, http://www.eia.org
Federal Information Processing Standards Publication,
http://www.itl.nist.gov/fipspubs/fip46-2.htm
IEEE 802 Working Group Home Pages, http:// grouper.ieee.org/
groups/802/dots.html
Institute of Electrical and Electronic Engineers, http://
standards.ieee.org
International Electrotechnical Commission, http:// www. iec.ch
International Organization for Standardization, http://
www.iso.ch
International Telecommunication Union, http:// www.itu.int
International Telecommunication Union V-series, http://www.itu.int/
itudoc/itu-t/rec/v/index.html
Internet Engineering Task Force, http://www.ietf.org
Joint Photographic Experts Group, http://www. jpeg.org
Moving Picture Experts Group, http://www. mpeg.org
National Institute of Standards and Technology, http://
www.nist.gov
Unicode, http://www.unicode.org

Statistical Models (Non-Optimization Models)

Pandu Tadikamalla and Alexandra Durcikova

University of Pittsburgh

GLOSSARY

confidence interval Gives an interval estimate of the unknown population parameter (e.g., μ) based on a random sample from that population. The confidence level (expressed as percentage) tells us how probable it is that this interval contains the unknown population parameter.

correlation A measure of the linear relationship between two variables. It is numerically expressed by the Pearson product-moment correlation coefficient. This coefficient is scaleless and can take values between -1 and $+1$. The nearer the coefficient is to $|1|$, the stronger the linear relationship between the two variables.

hypothesis testing A process to test whether a specified (unknown) parameter of a population is in a given range. Always two hypotheses are defined: the null hypothesis H_0 and the alternate (research) hypothesis H_a. The statistical procedure that leads to accept or reject the alternate hypothesis is based on the sample information.

normal distribution The probability distribution of many phenomena can be described by a bell-shaped curve. This curve is called the normal distribution. It has two parameters: mean μ and variance σ^2. Every normal random variable can be transformed to the standard normal variable with standard normal distribution whose parameters are mean $\mu = 0$ and variance $\sigma^2 = 1$.

quality control A set of statistical procedures used to monitor and detect when a process goes out of control.

random variable Assigns numerical values to the outcomes of an experiment. For each outcome only one value can be assigned. A random variable can be discrete (takes countable number of values) or continuous (takes values from an interval).

regression analysis Concerned with the relationship between a dependent variable and one or more independent variables.

statistics The science of data that involves collecting, summarizing, analyzing, and interpreting data for prediction and other decision purposes.

time series analysis A time series is a set of numbers on a variable of interest observed over successive periods of time. Time series methods use only historical data to provide forecasts for the future.

STATISTICS is the science of data. Statistical analysis involves collecting, summarizing, analyzing, and interpreting data. In our everyday life we are bombarded with data such as the baseball batting averages, the mean and median incomes of U.S. households, the latest poll numbers on the presidential elections, the consumer price index, and monthly car sales. The basic models used in statistical analysis are the descriptive statistics. Descriptive statistics try to summarize the different characteristics that a data set contains and then present them in a convenient and useful form. These descriptive statistics also help us to understand the nature and characteristics of the entire population.

Statistics plays a very important role in designing, developing, and manufacturing quality products through control charts and design of experiments. Linear statistical models are a set of statistical models that describe the mean of a variable as a linear function of one or more other variables. Regression analysis, correlation analysis, analysis of variance, and time series analysis are some of the commonly used linear statistical models.

In our everyday life we deal with different statistical models even though we may not realize it. For example:

- The U.S. Census Bureau (http://www.census.gov/hhes/income/histinc/h06.html) states that the median household income for the year 1998 was $38,885 and the mean was $51,855. Why do they need two numbers to describe the household income and what do they mean?
- Your primary care physician tells you that your blood pressure is high. How does he or she know that?
- On your way to work you like to listen to your Walkman. The manufacturer of batteries you use states that they last at least 10 hours. But you have a feeling that they last less than that. How can you find out whether the manufacturer's claim or your suspicion is correct?

All of these questions can be answered by analyzing data using statistical models. Data usually refers to a *random set* of observations (sample) from the population or universe of the variable of interest, such as the household income, the IQ of people in a community, or the blood pressure of adult males. Usually a random sample of size n values is denoted by $x_1, x_2, \ldots, x_n$. In a random sample each element of the population has an equal chance to be included in the sample, and choosing one element to be included in the sample has no influence on choosing another one. A random sample is supposed to be representative, that is, it mirrors the characteristics of the population of interest.

I. DESCRIPTIVE STATISTICS

The basic models used in statistical analysis are the *descriptive statistics*. All other models build on these basic models. Descriptive statistics summarize the patterns or different characteristics that a data set contains and then present them in a convenient and useful form. This can be in the form of tables (frequency table, stem-and-leaf display) or plots (histogram, barchart, pie chart, box-and-whisker plot).

Two of the most common and useful characteristics of data are *central tendency* and *variability*. Three of the most commonly used measures of central tendency for quantitative data sets are the (arithmetic) *mean* ($\bar{x}$), the *mode*, and the *median*. The mean is simply the average of the measurements in the data set. The median is the middle number when the measurements are arranged in ascending (or descending) order. The mode is the most frequently occurring measurement in the data set. If the distribution is nearly symmetric (bell-shaped) these three measures will be very close to one another. Otherwise we say that the distribution is skewed. Why do we need all three measures of central tendency? The mode is usually applied to nominal (categorical) data. If applied to continuous data its value depends on how we group the data (for large samples). The median is a characteristic that is not affected by extreme values (very big or very small). The mean, in contrast, is very sensitive to both high and low values but is a better estimator of the population central tendency in symmetric cases. Our first example discusses these properties of measures of central tendency very well. We can say that 50% of the population in the United States has an income lower than $38,885. This number, however, is (much) lower than the mean of $51,855. The distribution of household income is positively skewed and as we can see the mean is influenced by the very high incomes of a few households. Therefore, showing only the mean would be misleading. As opposed to income, test scores on the standardized exams such as SAT or IQ measures tend to be symmetrically distributed. In such cases the mean, the mode, and the median values would be close to one another.

To understand the characteristics of the population, in addition to the central tendency of the data, we may want to look at some measures of variability, the degree of dispersion—the *range*, the *interquartile range*, the *variance*, and the *standard deviation*. The range is the difference between the smallest and the largest value in our sample. The interquartile range is the range between the 25th and the 75th percentiles (the middle 50% of the data). The variance of a sample is defined as the sum of the squared distances from the mean divided by the sample size minus 1:

$$ s^2 = \frac{\sum_{i=1}^{n} (x_i - \bar{x})^2}{n - 1} $$

The standard deviation is defined as the positive square root of the sample variance. The first two measures of variability are easily understandable. How do we interpret the second two? If the variance (or standard deviation) is small, the distribution is compact (i.e., most of the data points are clustered around the mean) and for larger variances, the distribution is more spread out. For symmetrical distributions, approximately 68% of all data points fall within one standard deviation of the mean ($\bar{x} \pm s$), 95% of all data points fall within two standard deviations of the mean ($\bar{x} \pm 2s$), and 99.7% of all data points fall within three standard deviations of the mean ($\bar{x} \pm 3s$). The most important and most used distribution that is symmetrical is the *normal distribution*. Many statistical models are based on the normal distribution and "normality" has to be checked prior to using a model. Some of our readers may hear the term *standard normal distribution*. Its parameters are mean $\mu = 0$ and standard deviation $\sigma = 1$. Any normal distribution with mean μ and standard deviation σ can be standardized using the formula:

$$Z = \frac{X - \mu}{\sigma}$$

II. GRAPHICAL REPRESENTATION OF DATA

One of the most common graphical ways of representing univariate data is through a frequency histogram. In a frequency histogram the data are grouped into several equidistant intervals. The data are plotted with the value of the variable (widths of the interval) on the horizontal axis and the number of observations in each group on the vertical axis. The histogram reveals the shape of the distribution of the variable of interest. The shape of the distribution can be symmetrical, positively skewed, or negatively skewed as shown in Fig. 1.

A. Computer Outputs/Data Sets

Almost all of the time, data analysis is done using a computer. Several statistical packages are available for use on personal computers or mainframe computers. Sophisticated statistical packages such as Statgraphics, SPSS, and SAS provide programs to analyze a variety of statistical models. Also, the commonly used Microsoft Excel package includes modules for some routine statistical models such as descriptive statistics and regression analysis.

EXAMPLE 1

Most business schools require MBA program applicants to take a standardized test, namely, the GMAT (Graduate Management Admission Test). The scores on this test fall in a range from 200 to 800. We have collected 100 GMAT scores of all the entering stu-

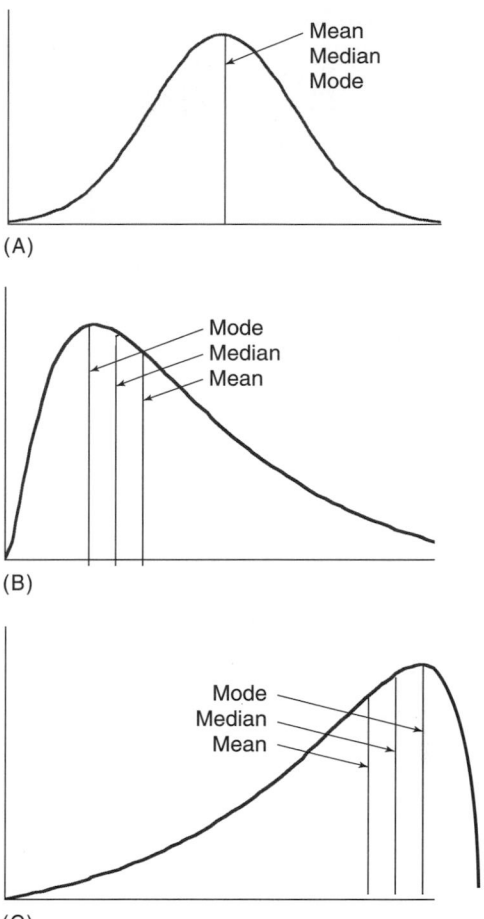

Figure 1 (A) For symmetric distributions the mean, the median, and the mode are very close to one another. (B) For positively skewed distributions, the mean is higher than the mode and the median as in the case of the household incomes. (C) For negatively skewed distributions, the mean is smaller than the median and the mode.

dents of the class of 2001 from a U.S. university. Note that this is not a random sample of all the people who took the GMAT or even of all the people who applied to this school. These are the actual scores of all the 100 students who are admitted to this MBA program. A histogram of these data is shown in Fig. 2. Also, the summary statistics from the Excel software package are given in Fig. 3.

EXAMPLE 2

Service companies such as telephone service providers always want to know how long people talk on the telephone so that they can budget their capital expenditure to provide the number of lines. One hundred people were observed at a local public telephone

Histogram GMAT_100

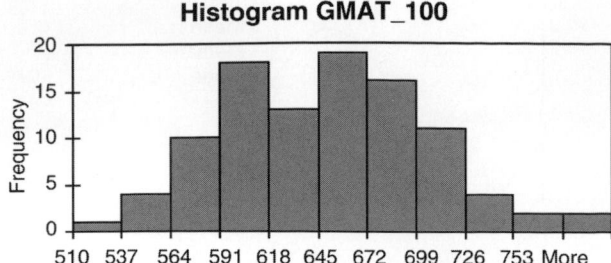

Figure 2 The data seem to be symmetrical, although one could argue that it is slightly positively skewed. In general, the test scores on standardized tests such as the GMAT would be normally distributed. In this case the data are slightly positively skewed since this business school "screened" out the low GMAT applicants.

and the time they spent in the telephone booths was measured in seconds. Figure 4 shows a histogram of the data, and the relevant summary statistics are given in Fig. 5.

Mean	623.7
Standard Error	5.558968
Median	620
Mode	610
Standard Deviation	55.58968
Sample Variance	3090.212
Kurtosis	-0.11916
Skewness	0.30793
Range	270
Minimum	510
Maximum	780
Sum	62370
Count	100

Figure 3 Some of the summary statistics are easier to understand than the others. Mean, median, mode, standard deviation, and variance have been discussed above. Minimum and maximum are intuitive. Count is the number of data points. Skewness of zero or close to zero would indicate symmetry. A large positive or negative value for skewness would indicate a nonsymmetrical nature of the data. A kurtosis value of zero would indicate the distribution is close to normal. Standard error is the standard deviation of the sample mean ($\bar{x}$).

Histogram-Phone Calls

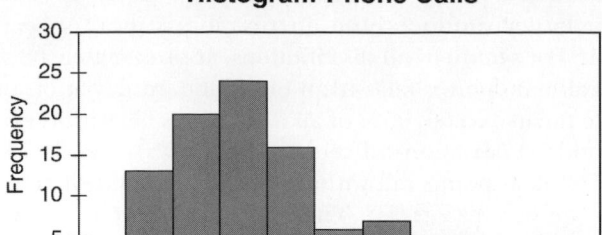

Figure 4 Histogram for lengths of telephone calls. The distribution is very highly skewed to the right. The average length of the telephone call was 167 seconds and the median was only 140 seconds. The skewness is much different from zero (1.12).

III. INFERENTIAL ANALYSIS

In our income distribution example, we knew the income of every family in the United States and therefore the average and the standard deviation that is calculated from the income are the parameters of the population distribution of income in the United States

Phone calls	
Mean	166.2279
Standard Error	11.83616
Median	140.6625
Mode	#N/A
Standard Deviation	118.3616
Sample Variance	14009.47
Kurtosis	0.915601
Skewness	1.12525
Range	499.8548
Minimum	6.17717
Maximum	506.032
Sum	16622.79
Count	100

Figure 5 Summary statistics for duration of phone calls.

in 1998. What if we did not have access to all values of the distribution of our interest, as in our second example with the blood pressure? It is impossible to measure the blood pressure of every healthy person in the United States or from all over the world. Would then the calculation of the average and the standard deviation from a random sample be good enough to describe the population? Maybe, maybe not. In "statistical terms" we call these statistics, the sample average and the sample standard deviation, *point estimates*. They have one major disadvantage and that is we do not know how "good" they are. So we need some other measure that will tell us how confident we will be in using these quantities. Statistical models give us such a measure—*confidence intervals*. We can calculate a confidence interval for many characteristics (parameter) based on our random sample.

Let us now focus on the confidence interval (CI) for the mean of the random variable of interest. The equation of CI for this parameter depends on the sample size and the population distribution. If the sample size is big enough (usually greater than 30) then according to the *central limit theorem* the sampling distribution of the sample mean is approximately normally distributed and we do not have to consider the distribution of the original (parent) population. The corresponding CI is given by the following formula:

$$\overline{x} \pm z_{\alpha/2} * \frac{\sigma}{\sqrt{n}}$$

When we have a small sample size but we know the variance of the population σ and the parent population is normally distributed we can also use the above formula. Usually σ is unknown and in the small sample case the actual CI is derived using the t_{n-1} *distribution*—*Student's distribution* with $(n-1)$ degrees of freedom. The actual formula is

$$\overline{x} \pm t_{\alpha/2} * \frac{\sigma}{\sqrt{n}}$$

This formula is correct only if we can assume that the population of interest has a normal distribution. Several questions may arise:

- What if the distribution of the population is not a normal distribution and we have a small sample size? If the sample size is big enough we can use the central limit theorem. If it is small, then our calculations are limited. We can employ, for example, *Chebyshev's inequality*.
- What do $z_{\alpha/2}$ and $t_{\alpha/2}$ mean? First, let us explain the meaning of $\sigma/\sqrt{n}$ and $s/\sqrt{n}$. They represent the standard deviation of the sample mean. Now recall the explanation of the standard deviation.

The $z_{\alpha/2} * \sigma/\sqrt{n}$ is $z_{\alpha/2}$ times the standard deviation of the sample mean. The $z_{\alpha/2}$ is the $100(1 - \alpha/2)\%$ percentile of the standard normal distribution. Let us say we want to build an interval that would contain the population mean μ, 95% of the time (5% of the time the mean will be outside this interval). Then $\alpha = 0.05$ and therefore we have to plug in the value of $z_{0.025} = 1.96$. That means that the area under the normal curve from 1.96 to the right is 2.5%. Because of symmetry, the area under the normal distribution to the left of -1.96 is also 2.5%. The value of $t_{\alpha/2}$ depends on the degrees of freedom (d.f.). If our sample size is 20, then the corresponding value for 19 degrees of freedom is $t_{0.025} = 2.093$.

- These two formulas are very similar, so what is the main difference between them? The formula using the t distribution gives you a wider interval. The t distribution is used when the population standard deviation is unknown and thus has to be estimated from the sample. This adds more "uncertainty" or "variability" to the estimation process and thus results in a wider CI. The higher the sample size, the smaller the difference between the confidence intervals using the normal and t values.
- What is the interpretation of a CI? If $\alpha = 0.05$ then we say that we are 95% confident that the population mean is in the calculated interval. If we build a large number of confidence intervals with the same sample size, 95% of those intervals would contain the unknown mean μ.

Speaking in terms of blood pressure example, let's say that your primary care physician compares your value of blood pressure with a 95% (or 90%) CI of blood pressure of healthy people. If your blood pressure is outside the CI of the population blood pressure (too high or too low) then that may suggest to the doctor that your blood pressure is abnormal and may warrant some remedial action.

If we want to build a confidence interval for other parameters, such as the standard deviation or the median, the most important thing is to find the sampling distribution of that statistic. If we know the sampling distribution we are able to find the corresponding confidence interval.

One very common application of the CI is estimating public opinion on some social issue or predicting election outcomes. National polls always solicit the opinion of potential voters as to their preferences for a particular candidate. The *margin of error* reported in these polls is the half-widths of the CI for the population proportion using a 95% level of confidence.

EXAMPLE 3

In a recent survey of 1000 likely voters in the upcoming election, 530 (53%) said that they would vote for the democratic candidate (say, candidate A). The margin of error is ±3%. Everyday in newspapers and on television we can see or hear statements of the above nature. How do we relate to these results? How did they come up with the margin of error and what does it mean?

Let us explain this problem using techniques we already described in previous sections, for example, CI calculation and distribution of the statistic. We will estimate the proportion (denoted by p) of the voters that would be voting for candidate A. A sample of $n = 1000$ voters gives a point estimate of p:

$$\hat{p} = \frac{530}{1000} = 0.53$$

A 95% confidence interval for p (using the normal approximation to the sampling distribution of $\hat{p}$) is given by the following formula:

$$\hat{p} \pm z_{\alpha/2} \sqrt{\frac{\hat{p}(1 - \hat{p})}{n}} = 0.53 \pm 1.96$$

$$\sqrt{\frac{0.53(1 - 0.53)}{1000}} = 0.53 \pm 0.031$$

The 95% CI for the unknown proportion of voters voting for candidate A is given by (0.499, 0.561). Note that the halfwidth of the confidence interval is 0.031 (3%), which is the margin of error stated in the problem.

Most often the survey sample size is around 1000 and the margin of error is about ±3%. If a smaller sample size was used, say around 700 or less, the margin of error may go up to ±4%.

IV. HYPOTHESIS TESTING

Consider the following situations.

1. A manufacturer of batteries claims that the average life of its alkaline batteries is at least 10 hours. As mentioned before in our example, you are not sure if these batteries really last 10 hours and you want to test the manufacturer's claim.
2. A corporate executive implemented a new incentive system to improve productivity and reduce absenteeism of the employees. How would we test to see whether the incentive plan has been effective?
3. Pharmaceutical companies always have to support their claim that a new drug is effective in the

treatment for a particular disease, to get approval from the Food and Drug Administration. Based on a limited clinical trial, how do they "prove" that their new drug is effective?

In these examples, we have to accept (support) one hypothesis (claim) over the other. In a statistical hypothesis testing context the established fact is called the *null hypothesis* (H_0) and the challenger's claim is called the *alternate hypothesis* (H_a).

The statistical procedure that leads us to accept or reject the alternate hypothesis is based on the sample information. Since the decision about the unknown population parameter is based on the sample, we are likely to make one of two kinds of errors, as discussed next.

In Table I, note that the Type I error (denoted by α) is the same one introduced in the confidence interval context. A Type I error is the probability of rejecting H_0 (accepting H_a) when H_0 is true. Similarly, a Type II error is the probability of rejecting H_a when H_a is true.

In the American judicial system (and in many other parts of the world as well) a person accused of a crime is innocent until proven guilty. In the hypothesis testing context the null hypothesis is that the person is innocent (not guilty) and the prosecution has to prove that the accused is guilty (alternate hypothesis). Criminal cases involve jury trial and the prosecution has to prove the accused is guilty "beyond a shadow of doubt." This implies that the value of the Type I error (α) is very low. Because of such low values of α, oftentimes the guilty person could be released on a verdict of "not guilty." The jury trial is like the test procedure (collecting data and analyzing the data to make the decision). When an innocent person is convicted of a crime, a Type II error has been committed.

The statistical test procedure involves (1) taking a random sample of size n, (2) calculating the appropriate point estimator such as the sample mean ($\bar{x}$) or sample proportion ($\hat{p}$), (3) calculating the appropriate test statistic, and (4) making the decision to accept or reject the alternate hypothesis by comparing

Table I Types of Errors That Can Occur in Hypothesis Testing

Decision	Situation	
	H_0 is true	H_a is true
Accept H_a	Type I error (α)	No error
Reject H_a	No error	Type II error (β)

the test statistic with the appropriate table value at the specified α level.

EXAMPLE 4

Do unemployed people have poor mental health? The *Journal of Occupational and Organizational Psychology* (December 1992) published a study that investigated the relationship between unemployment status and mental health. A sample of 49 unemployed men were tested for their mental health using a widely recognized test—the General Health Questionnaire (GHQ). Lower values on this test indicate better mental health and a score of 10 on this test is considered to be normal. The sample mean and the sample standard deviation were $\bar{x} = 10.94$ and $s = 5.10$. Does the sample indicate that unemployed people have poor mental health (i.e., higher GHQ values in this case)?

The null hypothesis is that unemployed people do not have poor mental health. In this case H_0: $\mu = 10$ (or $\mu \leq 10$). The alternate hypothesis we want to test is that H_a: $\mu > 10$. Usually we set the $\alpha = 0.05$. Note that the sample average of 10.94 is higher than the specified value of 10. Is this due to sampling variation? Is this difference statistically significant?

Because the sample size is big, we can use the normal approximation to the sampling distribution of the sample mean, $\bar{x}$. Also note that the alternate hypothesis is one sided and therefore we have to make a "slight" change in our decision process. Instead of using $z_{\alpha/2}$ we will use z_α to find the *critical value*. At $\alpha = 0.05$, the $z_{0.05} = 1.645$ and the test statistic is

$$z = \frac{10.94 - 10}{5.1/\sqrt{49}} = 1.29$$

Since the test statistic (1.29) is less than the table value (1.645), we conclude that there is no reason to reject the null hypothesis. In other words, we do not have enough evidence to reject the null hypothesis that unemployed people do not have poor mental health.

A controversial topic is the specification of α value. Routinely this value of α is specified as 0.05. Another approach in hypothesis testing is calculating the *observed significance level*, the *p value*. The *p* value is defined as the probability of observing a test statistic that is at least as contradictory to the null hypothesis (in support of the alternate hypothesis) as the actual value calculated from the sample data. In our case, p value $= P(z > 1.29) = 0.0985$. Note that if we had set our α value greater than the *p* value, we would have rejected the null hypothesis and accepted the alternate hypothesis. For example, if $\alpha = 0.1$, then $z_{0.1} = 1.28$ and the test statistic is greater than this

z value and we would reject the null hypothesis. In other words, the *p* value is the amount of Type I error we are willing to live with in rejecting the null hypothesis when the null hypothesis is true. For decision-making purposes if the *p* value is less than the specified α value, we will accept the alternate hypothesis.

It is very important to understand the logic behind the *p* value since every statistical software package would give you the *p* value rather than tell you to reject or not reject the H_0. The *p* value appears in regression models, in analysis of variance, etc. The computer program will give the observed confidence level but it is up to the decisionmaker to say whether there is enough evidence against the H_0 or not based on his own allowable Type I error α.

V. STATISTICS FOR QUALITY CONTROL

Statistics plays a very important role in designing, developing, and manufacturing quality products. Manufacturing processes (or any other processes) have internal variation, which is inherent in the process. For example, if we are manufacturing bolts that are 1/2 in. in length, do all the bolts produced by this process measure 1/2 in. in length? No. They will all be about this length. In fact, the mean lengths of bolts produced by this process will be 1/2 in. and the variance would depend on several factors such as the precision of the machine, the quality of raw material, the level of education, and training of employees. It is natural to assume that the lengths of the bolts would have a normal distribution.

Sometimes the process may go out of control due to failure of the manufacturing equipment, a bad batch of raw material, human error, sudden changes in power supply, etc. All of these causes are called *assignable causes*.

Statistical quality control techniques are designed to monitor and detect when a process goes out of control. One important tool in statistical quality control is the Shewart control chart. The power of control chart technique lies in its ability to separate all quality variations due to the assignable causes from natural variation.

A. X-Bar Charts and R Charts

We have stated before that the probability that a normally distributed random variable will have a value outside 3σ (three standard deviations) from the mean is about 0.003 (0.0027 to be exact). Shewart's control chart is based on this principle. If we want to use this technique, we have to periodically monitor and measure the quality characteristics. For each period a small sample of observations (usually size 3, 4, or 5) is taken and both $\bar{x}$ and the range are calculated. These are plotted separately on an $\bar{x}$ chart and R chart. Three sigma limits are also drawn on the control charts. If any of the periodic observations are outside the three sigma limits or if they exhibit any patterns, we need to go through an analysis to find out if any assignable causes exist and adjust the process accordingly. Figure 6 gives some typical $\bar{x}$ charts where some assignable causes may exist.

Statistical packages can create $\bar{x}$ charts and R charts and some of them can even tell if there are any concerns connected with them (see comments in Fig. 6). But they do not tell where the problem is and, again, it is up to the decision-maker to find the origin of the problem. The problem could be in new raw material, new employee, problems with tools, etc.

Another area of statistics that plays a prominent role in the design of quality is the *analysis of variance* or *design of experiments* that we will address under linear statistical models (see next section).

VI. LINEAR STATISTICAL MODELS

If we want to know the assessed value of a house we could collect information on the sale price of houses sold in the neighborhood (a random sample) and can estimate the price of a house using the statistical meth-

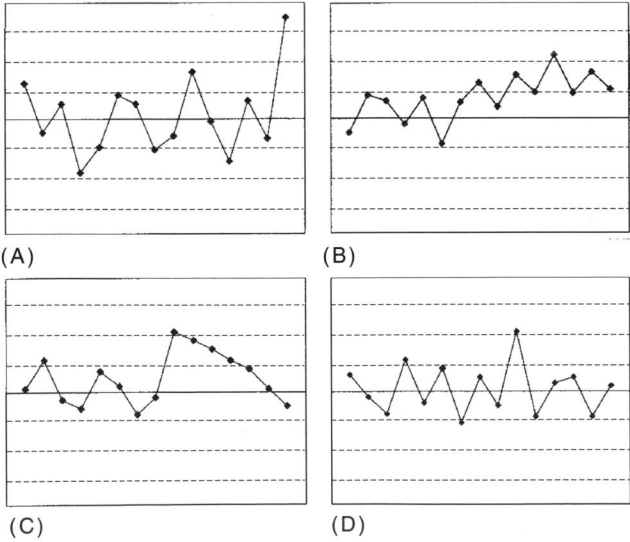

(A)   **(B)**

(C)   **(D)**

Figure 6 Examples of control charts: (A) the last point is outside the three-sigma limit; (B) 9 points in a row are on the same side of the center line; (C) 7 points in a row are constantly descending; and (D) number of center line crossings is too many.

ods described so far. A better approach would be to predict the price of a house based on the living space (square footage), number of bedrooms, the size of the backyard, etc. So far we have assumed that the mean of the variable we want to estimate is a constant. However, the mean could be a variable that depends on several other variables. Linear statistical models are a set of statistical models that describe the mean of a variable as a linear function of one or more other variables. These models include regression analysis, correlation, analysis of variance, and time series analysis.

A. Regression Analysis

In business, managers often make decisions based on the relationship between two or more variables. For example, after noting the relationship between sales and advertising, a manager may want to predict sales for a given level of advertising expenditure. In another case, a public utility company may want to predict the demand for electricity or gas based on the relationship between demand and temperatures. If data can be collected on two or more variables, regression analysis can be used to develop the equations that show the relationship between these variables.

In regression terminology, the predicted variable is called the *dependent variable,* usually denoted by Y, and the predictor variable is called the *independent variable,* denoted by X. Models containing only one independent variable are termed *simple linear regression models* and models with more than one independent variable, denoted by $X_1, X_2, \ldots, X_k$, are called *multiple regression models*. Further, if the relationship between the dependent and the independent variable(s) is assumed to be linear, the regression models used are called *linear regression models*.

Technically, regression analysis estimates the relationship between the expected value (mean) of the independent variable $[E(y)]$ and the dependent variable. In simple linear regression, the predicted value of the dependent variable is given by the equation $\hat{y} = b_0 + b_1 x$. The values of b_0 and b_1 are calculated from the data so that the line $\hat{y} = b_0 + b_1 x$ minimizes the total sum of squared errors (error is the difference between the predicted value and the actual value of y).

If there is more than one independent variable, say, $x_1, x_2, x_3, \ldots, x_k$, we will build a multiple regression model. The corresponding regression equation to predict the dependent variable will be $\hat{y} = b_0 + b_1 x_1 + b_2 x_2 + \ldots + b_k x_k$. Of course, we need to calculate the coefficients $b_0, b_1, b_2, \ldots, b_k$. Again the software packages would give us these coefficients and other information necessary for decision making.

1. Inferential Analysis: Regression Models

Several issues need to be addressed before we can use the regression equation developed above. Are the assumptions behind the regression model valid? How good is the regression equation? How much of the variability in the dependent variable is explained by the independent variables included in the equation? Are some of the variables included in the equation not significant in predicting the y value? Did we include the "right" set of independent variables in the equation?

Two of the assumptions made in linear regression models are that the errors are normally distributed (mean 0 and standard deviation σ) and the variance in the dependent variable is constant irrespective of the values of independent variables. These assumptions can be tested graphically (and statistically, of course) so that the model can be used. If the assumption of normality is not valid then all the t tests (which test the significance of independent variable) and F tests (which test the usefulness of regression model) are not valid. However, the data (the values of the dependent variable y) can be transformed [usually using (log y) or $\sqrt{y}$] so that the normality assumption can be valid. If the common variance (homoscedasticity) assumption is not valid (sometimes the log or square root transformation might fix this problem as well), we may have to develop other models such as *weighted least squares regression models.*

We can test for the significance of the individual independent variables using the t test as we did in the case of testing for the mean of the population. The t test is appropriate because we need to estimate the standard error, and the sample sizes are usually small. We can also test for the significance of the entire regression equation using an F test. Also, the strength of the regression relationship is expressed as a single number between 0 and 1 and is called R^2. A number close to 1 indicates a strong regression relationship.

The value of R^2 can be increased arbitrarily by adding variables to this equation. This deficiency in R^2 can be overcome by looking at a modified R^2 value called the *adjusted R^2.*

The selection of the best variables into the regression can be accomplished through several programs such as stepwise regression or best subset selection in standard software packages.

EXAMPLE 5

When crude oil prices rise, the gasoline prices go up "proportionately." However, when crude oil prices go down, gasoline prices go down but not necessarily in proportion to the reduction in crude oil prices. We wanted to study the relationship between gasoline prices (y) and crude oil prices (x). We collected 19 observations of the typical crude oil prices ($/barrel) and gasoline prices (cents/gallon) during the years 1975–1993 (Table II). A scatter plot of the data is shown in Fig. 7. The data and the best fitted regression line are also given in Fig. 7. We used Excel to analyze the data and the output from this program is given in Fig. 8.

The regression equation to predict the gasoline price as a function of crude oil prices can be written

$$\hat{y} = 33.4246 + 2.92782 * x$$

Thus, if the crude oil price were $18/barrel, based on the regression equation, we would expect the gasoline price to be 86.12 cents (33.4246+2.92782*18). The actual value of y may be different for several reasons. Crude oil price alone may not determine the gasoline price. Supply and demand, the state of the economy, or pure random variation in gasoline prices may be other factors that affect the gasoline prices. In fact, during the year 1987, the crude oil price used in our analysis was $17.90 and the actual typical gasoline price in 1987 was 90 cents.

Table II   **Price of Gasoline and Crude Oil from 1975–1993**

Year	1975	1976	1977	1978	1979	1980	1981	1982	1983	1984	1985	1986	1987
Gasoline price (cents/gallon)	57	59	62	63	86	119	131	122	116	113	112	86	90
Crude oil price ($/barrel)	10.38	10.89	11.96	12.46	17.72	28.07	35.24	31.87	28.99	28.63	26.75	14.55	17.9

Year	1988	1989	1990	1991	1992	1993
Gasoline price (cents/gallon)	90	100	115	72	71	75
Crude oil price ($/barrel)	14.67	17.97	22.23	16.54	15.99	14.24

From U.S. Bureau of the Census, *Statistical Abstract of the United States: 1982–1995.*

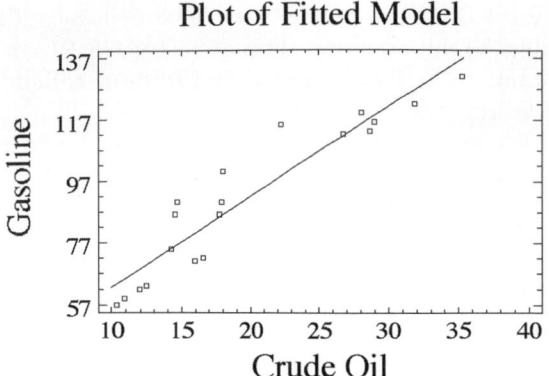

Figure 7 Fitted regression line for the crude oil and gasoline data.

Is crude oil price a significant variable in predicting the gasoline price? We can express this question in the null hypothesis that the slope of the line is zero against the alternative hypothesis that it is not zero. The t statistic corresponding to the slope b_1 is 11.3418 (see Fig. 8). The t value from the table at $\alpha = 0.05$ ($\alpha/2 = 0.025$) for 17 degrees of freedom is 2.110. Since 11.3418 is greater than 2.110, we conclude that the coefficient of x is not zero and thus is

significant. Also note that the p value is very small—$2.37 * 10^{-9}$. As discussed before, a p value smaller than the specified α value supports the alternate hypothesis. The R^2 value is 0.88327, implying that 88.327% of the variation in gasoline prices can be explained by this regression equation using just one independent variable, crude oil price.

The t test showed us that the slope of the regression equation is significantly different from zero and therefore we can use this variable for prediction. But what does the F test tell us? The value of the F statistics is 128.6358 and the corresponding p value (significance F on the computer output) is $2.37 * 10^{-9}$. This is exactly the same p value that was given by the t test. What is the conclusion for a simple regression model? The p value associated with the t test gives enough information to find out whether the proposed linear model is good or not. The H_0 is the same for the F test and for the t test in this case. This is not true when we are trying to build a multiple regression model. Each t test would test the usefulness of each independent variable and the F test would test the usefulness of the model as a whole. Therefore when making decisions we need to work with both of these tests and not only with the t test like it was in the case of simple linear regression. If there is inconsistency in the p values, e.g. the over-

SUMMARY OUTPUT

Regression Statistics	
Multiple R	0.939824713
R Square	0.883270491
Adjusted R Square	0.876404049
Standard Error	8.458923224
Observations	19

ANOVA

	df	SS	MS	F	Significance F
Regression	1	9204.329346	9204.329346	128.6358391	2.37326E-09
Residual	17	1216.407496	71.5533821		
Total	18	10420.73684			

	Coefficients	Standard Error	t Stat	P-value	Lower 95%	Upper 95%
Intercept (b_0)	33.42457717	5.47805953	6.101535952	1.17475E-05	21.8668657	44.98228864
Crude Oil Price (b_1)	2.927816029	0.25814445	11.34177407	2.37326E-09	2.383178087	3.472453972

Figure 8 Excel printout of a simple linear regression model for the crude oil and gasoline data.

all model seems to be good but none of the independent variables is statistically different from zero, the possible explanation is that the independent variables are correlated. This is called *multicolinearity*. Therefore, prior to building a multiple regression model a correlation matrix has to be calculated and the variables that have high correlation with each other have to be investigated. We usually drop one of these variables from the model and calculate a new regression equation. Statistical packages are very useful tools in these calculations since they give us the regression coefficients and their p values almost instantly and that way we can concentrate only on the usefulness of the model and on the interpretation of our model.

2. Correlation

Simple regression analysis estimates the relationship between a dependent variable and an independent variable. However, oftentimes we may not be interested in knowing the relationship, but rather in knowing whether a statistically significant relationship exists between two variables.

Correlation, denoted by r, measures the strength of the *linear* relationship between two variables (Fig. 9). Correlation between two variables can be negative or positive and is a number between -1 and $+1$. Correlation values near -1 or $+1$ indicate a strong linear relationship between variables. In the regression output of the gasoline price and crude oil price problem, the correlation coefficient between these two variables was 0.9398. As opposed to regression analysis, correlation is always between two variables and only estimates the linear relationship. In a simple linear regression model, if the regression relationship is statistically significant, then the correlation between y and x is also significant. Regression analysis is used most commonly to study the relationships between quantitative variables in business, engineering, medicine, etc. Correlation is often used to study the relationships between variables encountered in social sciences such as the relationship between the level of education of parents and children.

B. Analysis of Variance and Design of Experiments

Analysis of variance (ANOVA) statistical models, just like regression models, are also concerned with the statistical relationship between a dependent variable and one or more independent variables. In the case of regression analysis, more often, the independent variable and the dependent variables are quantitative variables. Although both regression models and ANOVA models are appropriate for observational data and based on formal experiments, ANOVA models are more often used with experimental data. Also,

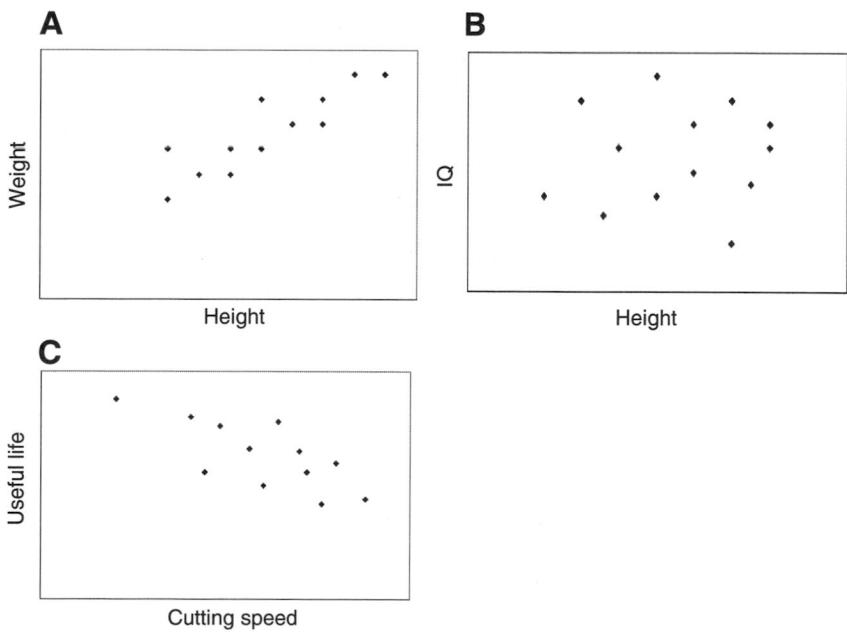

Figure 9 Examples of correlation between different pairs of variables: (A) there is a strong positive correlation between height and weight; (B) there is no correlation between the height and the IQ of individuals; and (C) there is a strong negative correlation between cutting speed and useful life of a cutting tool.

ANOVA models are more appropriate when the independent variables are qualitative. Unlike in the regression models, ANOVA models do not assume any functional relationship between the dependent variable and the independent variables. Typical examples of ANOVA applications are:

1. Does gender (male or female) have an effect on income?
2. Are there significant differences among the several advertising campaigns being considered for a product promotion?
3. Do the levels of education and type of experience have an effect on the sales volume of salespeople?

In ANOVA terminology, the dependent variable is called the *response variable* and the independent variables are called *factors*. The different values of the independent variables are called *factor levels*. An experiment (or an observation) at a specified level of all factors is called a *treatment*.

Single-factor ANOVA models (also called one-way ANOVA models) amount to testing the equality of several means and is accomplished through an *F* test. It is very important to realize that ANOVA will not tell us (1) which treatment is the best or (2) the relation between the factors and the response variable. It merely tells us whether there is a significant difference between factors and factor levels.

One of the most commonly used ANOVA models is the two-way ANOVA (with two factors). Here we can not only test for the significance of the factors, but we can also test for an interaction between the factors. Most statistical software packages will give us the complete ANOVA table that contains every important component we need in order to make the decision about whether there is a difference between the treatment means or not. By *treatment means* we mean the combination of every level of one factor with every level of a second factor. We can represent our results in graphical form and from these charts determine whether there is an interaction or not, and whether there is a main effect from the first or the second factor.

EXAMPLE 6

Consider a two-factor analysis where a marketing manager wants to study the effects of two factors, the advertisement campaign and the package design of the product, on sales volume. We are considering two levels of advertisement campaign (factor A) and three different styles of packaging (factor B). For each treatment (particular combination of a level for A and for B) we observe the sales. The sales could be af-

fected by factor A, factor B, and the interaction between factors A and B. Figure 10 shows the possible effects of these factors on the sales.

Software packages can create charts like those shown in Fig. 10, but the interpretation of these charts is very important. In Figs. 10(A), 10(B), and 10(C), we can say that level 2 of the advertisement campaign is better than level 1 for every level of package design. However, in Fig. 10(D), where an interaction between factors is present, we cannot make such a conclusion. If we want to implement package design 1 or 2, then we should choose level 2 advertising; for packaging style 3 we should choose level 2 advertising because this combination of factor levels gives us the highest mean response. Furthermore it is important to test whether the difference in mean responses, let us say in Fig. 10(B), is significant because visually it does not seem to be significant. If the test tells us that there is no significance, then the conclusion would be that it does not make a difference which advertisement campaign is employed and therefore choosing the less expensive one could be appropriate.

We can also conduct ANOVA with more than two factors. However, the more factors built into a model, the more difficult it is to interpret the interaction effects and the more difficult it is to collect data for a very big ANOVA experiment. Note that if we have four factors each at three levels, we have 3^4 (81) different treatment combinations. To study the effect of all main factors and all combinations of interactions, we need more than one experiment for each treatment level. Many researchers suggest that a three-factor, three-level experiment is the highest one that can be intelligibly interpreted. If we need to study a large number of factors at a large number of levels, statisticians have designed *fractional factorial experiments* in which all combinations of all levels of all factors do not have to be experimented with but only a fraction of them have to be. Of course, with the fractional factorial experiments we cannot study some higher order interaction effects.

C. Time Series Analysis and Forecasting

Blood banks want to forecast the demand for blood for the next few weeks. Business managers want to forecast the demand for their products for the next four quarters. Oil drillers and refiners want to forecast the demand for oil for the next few years. Regression models can be used to "predict" the response variables based on one or more independent vari-

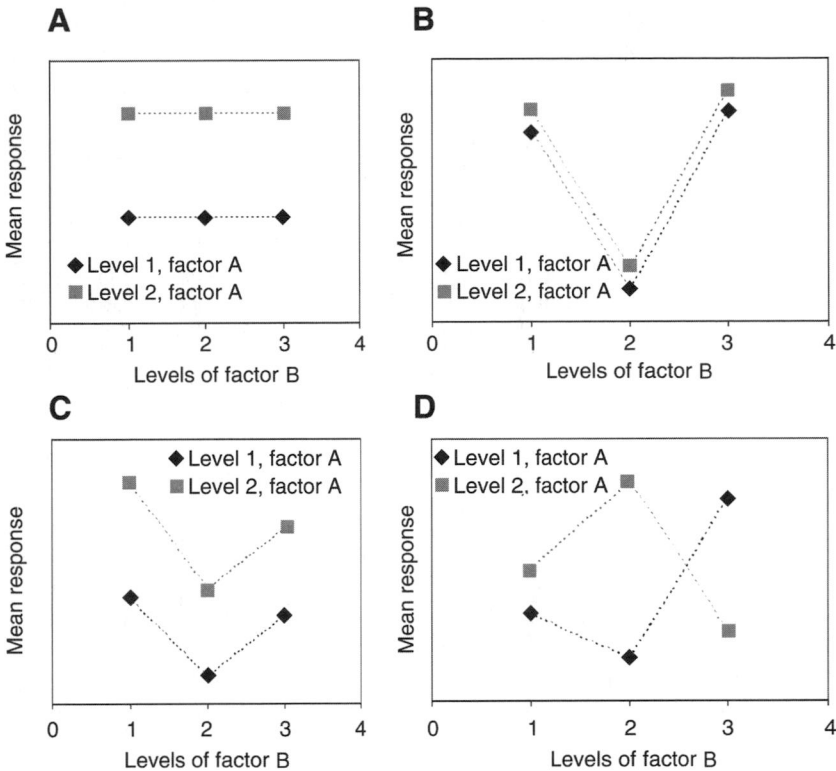

Figure 10 Possible treatment effects on sales: (A) there is no effect from factor A; only factor B has a main effect. There is no interaction between these two factors; (B) there is no effect from factor B; only factor A has a main effect. There is no interaction between these two factors; (C) both factors A and B have a main effect. There is no interaction between them; and (D) there is an interaction between the two factors.

ables. However, we may be able to forecast the demand by analyzing the historical demands for the last few periods. By reviewing historical data, we can develop models that would give us a better understanding of the patterns of past demand and would lead to better prediction of future demand.

Historical data form a *time series*. A time series is a set of numbers on a variable of interest observed over successive periods of time. Time series methods use just the historical data to provide forecasts for the future. In contrast to regression analysis, where the data have to be independent, in time series the correlation between data points is welcomed. Without such dependence we would not be able to make any prediction.

The pattern of the data in time series can have trend, cyclical, seasonal, and random components.

1. *Trend component.* The time series data may show gradual shifts to higher or lower values over a long period of time (Fig. 11).
2. *Cyclical component.* In addition to the trend component, time series data may exhibit a cyclical nature. Any recurring sequence of data

observations above or below the trend line over a long period can be attributed to the cyclical nature of the data. Crude oil prices, gold commodity prices, and stock market returns tend to contain a cyclical component. Typical time series data with an upward trend and a cyclical component are shown in Fig. 12.
3. *Seasonal component.* The seasonal component of time series data is easy to notice and to capture. Sales of air conditioners, department store sales by each quarter, and sales of winter clothing tend to exhibit seasonality. It is common to think of seasonal movement in a time series as occurring within 1 year. However, the seasonal component can be for any period of time such as the traffic pattern during different hours in a day. Typical time series data with seasonality of 1 year and upward trend are shown in Fig. 13.
4. *Random component.* The random component of time series data is the residual factor that accounts for the deviations of the actual observation values from those expected due to trend, seasonality, and cyclical components. Its

Linear upward trend

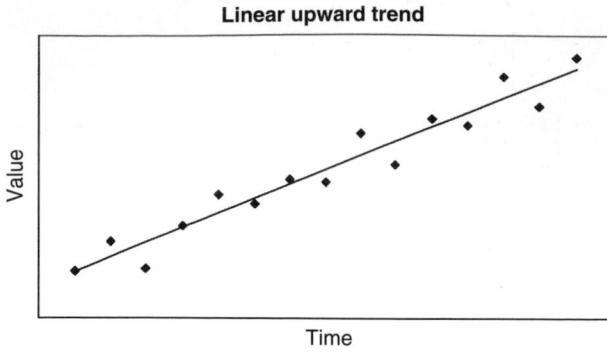

Linear downward trend

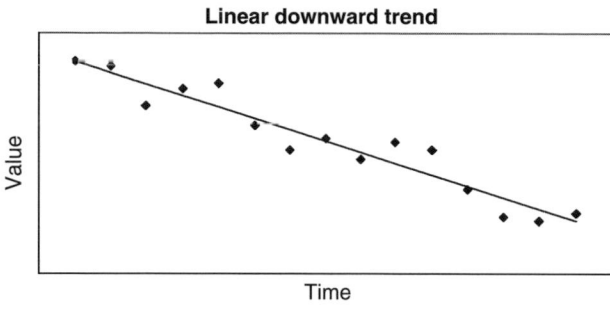

No trend

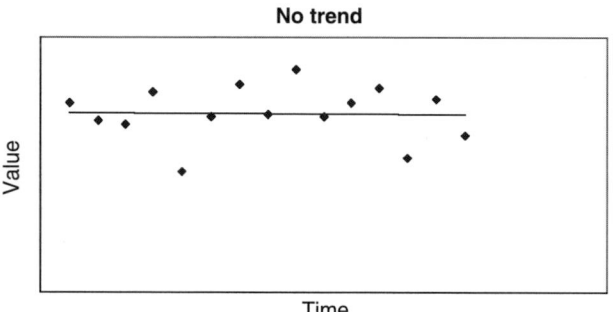

Figure 11   Examples of different trends in time series.

value is unpredictable and we cannot attempt to predict its impact on the time series.

Several sophisticated and complex methods are available for analyzing time series data to make predictions such as Box-Jenkins and autoregressive moving average (ARMA) models. But the most commonly used and easy to understand are the smoothing methods such as the moving average method and exponential smoothing. Time series data when presented along with their moving averages, approximately forecast the trend. Most technicians on Wall Street look at the stock prices along with the 200-day moving averages.

Statistical packages have been created specifically to do time series analyses. For example, ASTSA and e-views (econometric-views), which contain ARMA models, can be very helpful in an analysis of time series data.

Cyclical component in time series

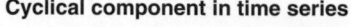
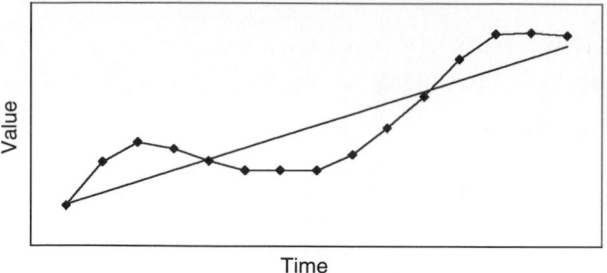

Figure 12   Cyclical trend in time series.

VII. CONCLUSIONS

Statistical models are becoming part of our everyday life, and a proper computer software package can tremendously decrease the time we spend creating and analyzing these statistical models. Building a useful statistical model is an iterative process and the computer and statistical software play significant roles in this process. However, without proper knowledge of the theory behind the statistical models the computer has almost no use. Computers cannot substitute creative thinking and will not request a change in a proposed model even if the proposed model were inappropriate and inadequate.

In building a statistical model, it is crucial to understand what questions a chosen model can answer. We also have to know the assumptions about the input data that have to be satisfied so that the model can be properly used; if these assumptions are not met, the model is not useful. Knowledge of these assumptions is not only important for the model builder but also for the decisionmaker who is going to make use of these models because improper use of models can lead to wrong conclusions. Statistical models can help people to make the right decisions.

Seasonal component in time series

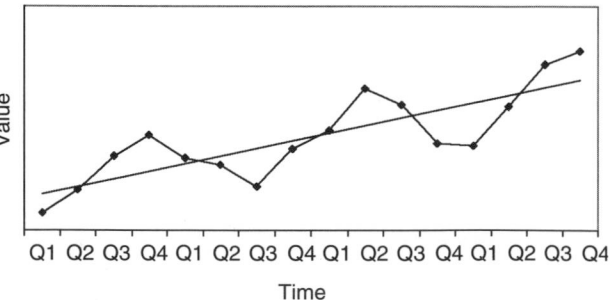

Figure 13   Seasonal component in time series.

SEE ALSO THE FOLLOWING ARTICLES

Goal Programming • Optimization Models • Uncertainty

BIBLIOGRAPHY

Moore, D. S., and McCabe, G. P. (1999). *Introduction to the practice of statistics.* San Francisco: W. H. Freeman.
Pearson, E. S. (1990). *Student—A statistical biography of William Sealy Gosset.* Oxford, England: Clarendon Press.

Rao, C. R. (1973). *Linear statistical inference and its applications.* New York: John Wiley & Sons.
Shewart, W. A. (1931). *Economic control of manufactured product.* New York: D. Van Nostrand Company.
Stigler, S. M. (1988). *The history of statistics.* Cambridge, MA: Harvard University Press.
Stuart, A., and Ord, J. K. (1991). *Kendall's advanced theory of statistics.* Oxford, England: Oxford University Press.
Tanur, J. M., Nosteller, F., Kruskal, W. H., Link, R. F., Piders, R. S., Rising, G. R., and Lehmann, E. L. (1972). *Statistics: A guide to the unknown.* San Francisco: Holden-Day.

Strategic Information Systems

Yehia Mortagy

University of La Verne

I. INTRODUCTION

A. Definition of Strategic Information Systems

Wiseman coined the term strategic information systems (SIS) to identify systems that shape or support the competitive strategy of an organization. He underscored the importance of viewing information technology utilization from a strategic perspective rather than the traditional information systems perspective. The strategic perspective views the systems as tools that shape or support the strategic vision of the organization, while the traditional perspective views information technology as systems designed as a means of achieving one or more of the following three objectives: (1) automating organizational processes, (2) monitoring and controlling the organizations, and (3) improving the decision making process in the organization. This latter view classifies systems as transaction processing systems (TPS), management information systems (MIS), decision support systems (DSS), and artificial intelligence systems (AI).

In this article we define SIS based on how the systems are used. Strategic information systems are information systems used to create and maintain an organization's competitive strategy. SIS are also systems that are used to prevent the organization's competitors from gaining a competitive advantage. Classic examples include American Airlines' SABRE, the first online reservation system; ASAP from American Hospital Supply Corporation that automated customers orders; the automatic teller machine (ATM) network by Citibank; and the ATM alliances that smaller banks developed to prevent larger banks from gaining and sustaining a competitive advantage. The Appendix contains brief descriptions of the SIS discussed in this article.

Strategic information systems are not related to a decision making level in an organization, i.e., strategic level, nor are SIS an additional type in the traditional information systems classification (TPS, MIS, DSS, and AI). SIS are often traditional systems used in a creative manner to give organizations a competitive edge. ASAP from American Hospital Supply is a transaction processing system, while Digital's XCON, which assisted customers and sales representatives in designing and correctly configuring a computer system that meets the customer's needs, is an example of an SIS that utilizes DSS and AI techniques. Neumann in his book *Strategic Information Systems* conveyed this best when he titled Chapter Two, "Strategic Information Systems are conventional information systems used in innovative ways."

The remainder of this article explains the terms used in defining strategic information systems (e.g., competitive strategy and competitive advantage) and presents frameworks used to identify opportunities for developing them. This is followed by a discussion of competitive strategies and types of SIS, followed by sections on their sustainability and risks. The last section concentrates on recent advances due to the Internet and other developments in IT.

B. Competitive Strategy and Competitive Advantage

The definition of strategic information systems is based on utilization of the systems (to create, maintain, or prevent competitors from gaining competitive strategy). However, researchers offer different definitions for the terms "competitive strategy" and "competitive advantage."

Strategies are long-term policies adopted by an organization to differentiate itself from its competitors. The implementation of a strategy requires the development and execution of processes and activities. Competitive strategies are strategies that allow an organization to gain and ,for as long as possible, sustain a competitive advantage or to prevent competitors from maintaining their competitive advantage. Porter defines competitive advantage as the ability of an organization to achieve better returns than the industry thus outperforming its competitors.

Wiseman argued that Porter's definitions of competitive strategy and competitive advantage are too restrictive. Organizations compete in areas. For example, they compete through better customer service. At the same time organizations, while competing in one area, may form an alliance in another. For example, IBM and Apple compete in the personal computer area, while they cooperate on developing the microprocessor that powers the Apple personal computer. Wiseman used the term "competitive arena" to mean a competitive area where an organization competes. Arenas may be linked or independent. Improving supplier relations may result in improving internal efficiency, while it may not improve customer relations. A typical organization competes in more than one arena. This set of arenas is called a "competitive space." A competitive advantage, therefore, is the ability of an organization to achieve superior performance in an arena, in contrast to Porter's better than average return for the whole organization. A competitive strategy is a strategy to gain or maintain an advantage, or reduce the edge of adversaries in an arena.

Three attributes of both competitive advantages and strategies are duration, vulnerability, and value. Duration is the length of time of an advantage (e.g., short, medium, or long); vulnerability is the susceptibility of the advantages to competitors' actions; value is benefit derived from possessing an advantage. Since these attributes are often used when measuring the

risk and sustainability of an SIS, further discussion will be included in the appropriate sections.

II. FRAMEWORKS AND APPROACHES TO IDENTIFY POTENTIAL AREAS OF COMPETITIVE ADVANTAGES

In order to develop a strategic information system, an organization must determine which approach to adopt in order to determine the area(s) and/or activities that present the best opportunities to create an effective SIS. Several frameworks have been proposed to assist a firm in determining the appropriate approach. Earl in 1989 classified the frameworks into three types: awareness frameworks assist managers in understanding the importance of strategic systems; opportunity frameworks include tools to identify specific opportunities; and positioning frameworks assist managers in assessing the strategic systems in their organizations. Table I includes the purpose, scope, and use of each framework as suggested by Earl.

The remainder of this section presents four widely used approaches in defining strategic systems, while additional approaches that take into account recent development in information technology, i.e., the Internet, are discussed in later sections. Porter and his colleagues developed three of the four approaches (the competitive forces, the value chain, and the information matrix). The approaches study the organization at different levels, thus offering insights at all levels as well as insights on interactions between levels. The fourth approach was developed by Wiseman: the theory of strategic thrusts and the strategic option generator.

A. Competitive Forces

The competitive forces model looks at an organization as a member of an industry and studies its interaction with the other members (see Fig. 1). It defines

Table I Earl's Frameworks[a]

Framework attribute	Awareness	Opportunity	Positioning
Purpose	Vision	Ends	Means
Scope	Possibility	Probability	Capability
Use	Education	Analysis	Implementation

[a] From Earl, M. (1989). *Management Strategies for information technology.* Englewood Cliffs, NJ: Prentice Hall International.

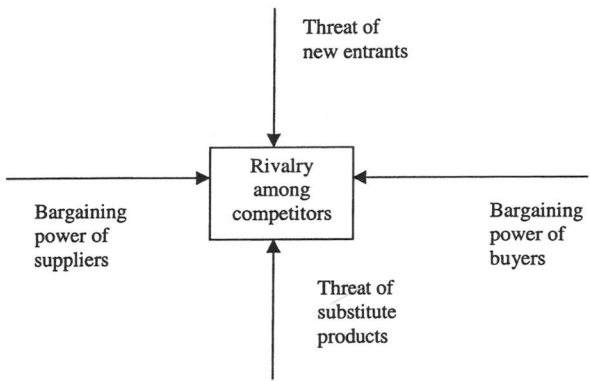

Figure 1 Determinants of industry attractiveness.

five major forces that have a relation with the organization and that determine the structure of the industry and its profitability. The forces are competitors, suppliers, buyers, new entrants, and substitute products. By studying the relationship between each of these entities, an organization may identify opportunities for developing an SIS that will present the organization with strategic advantage.

The model identifies the determinants that influence the relationship between an organization and the five forces. An organization can then develop policies that will result in convincing others to behave in a manner that will benefit the organization from these relations or reduce the potential of threats from these forces. These determinants include buyers switching costs and bargaining powers. An organization may adopt policies that change the switching cost to its advantage or increase the switching cost of buyers. Thus it increases the bargaining power of the organization with its buyers. Information technology may be used to achieve this objective. Take the case of American Hospital Supply Corporation (AHSC). Through the use of their order entry system, Analytic Systems Automatic Purchasing (ASAP), the ordering process was simplified and the ordering accuracy increased. This led to an increase in customers' dependency on AHSC, increased order size, and increased switching costs.

B. Value Chain

Organizations perform activities to transform inputs into products. These activities add value to the products. The value added is measured in terms of customers' willingness to pay for the product. If the value added by the organization exceeds the cost of creating this value, then the firm can be profitable. The model identifies two views: the value system and the value chain. The value system studies the firm as a member of a stream of activities linking the organization to its suppliers, channels, and buyers (see Fig. 2). An organization may create competitive advantages by studying and improving the links. Recent developments in supply chain management, logistics, and in multivariable optimizations underscore the importance of these links.

The value chain framework studies an organization as an entity that performs several internal activities that add value to the product (see Fig. 3). Activities are classified as primary or secondary activities. Primary activities are those that are directly involved in the production (i.e., creation) of a product, while secondary activities supply primary activities with the needed resources. Links between activities exist when one activity affects the performance of another activity. An organization can create a competitive advantage by outperforming the competition in executing all the activities.

An activity consists of a physical and an information component. Changing the mixture needed to execute the activity results in changing the performance envelope of the activity. For example, a typical athlete today performs better than a typical athlete from the past; i.e., today's runners and swimmers are fasters than their forebears. This is attributable to the knowledge gained of the activity including muscle movement, friction and drag, and characteristics of material used in shoes and swim suits (changing the information component), thus allowing an athlete with the same physical characteristics to achieve better performance.

Information technology's effects on activities are not limited to the mixture of the physical and information components of an activity. Information technology relaxes some of the assumptions and prerequisites of performing the activity that were essential in the past. One example is business meetings. In the past, a meeting demanded certain prerequisites such as fixed meeting times and places, while today, through the use of information technology a meeting may be held across continents and without place constraint.

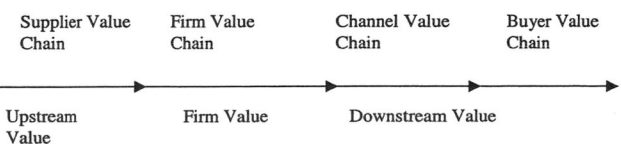

Figure 2 The Value System. Source: Porter, M., and Millar, V. (1985). How information gives you competitive advantage. *Harvard Business Review*, July–August.

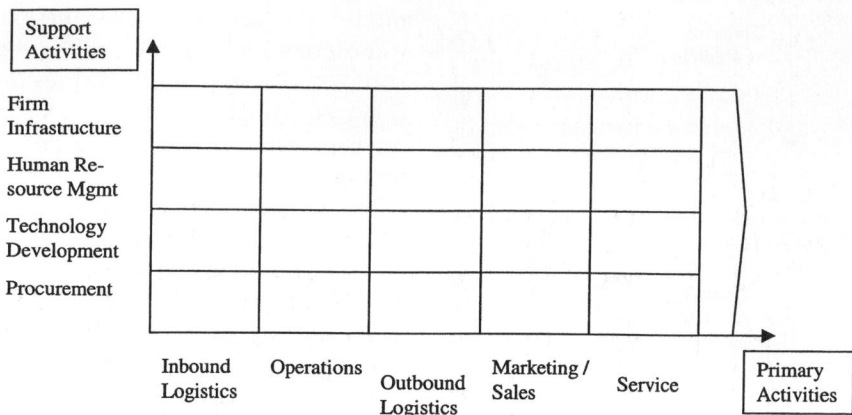

Figure 3   The Value Chain. Source: Porter and Millar (see Fig. 2).

In addition, information technology affects and re-laxes the prerequisites for the relationship between activities. Today, there is no strong connection between where a newspaper is composed and where it is printed. *USA Today, The Wall Street Journal,* and many other newspapers are printed in several geographically dispersed locations.

C. Information Intensity Matrix

Porter and Millar suggest that the information component of an activity may be divided into two elements: information intensity and information content (see Fig. 4). The information intensity measures the amount of information needed to produce the product, while the information content measures the amount of information in the product. They further suggest that by changing the mixture of the two components one may achieve an advantage over the competition.

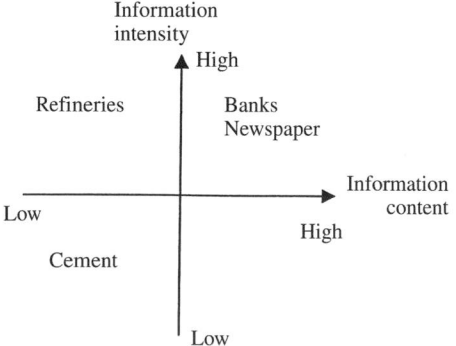

Figure 4   The Information Matrix. Source: Porter and Millar (see Fig. 2).

Most traditional banking services are examples of products that have high levels of both information content and information intensity. The industry relies heavily on information technology to produce the services, i.e., a high level of information intensity. Online banking services change the mixture of information components and supply banks with a competitive advantage due to increased savings from a reduction in transaction costs.

D. Theory of Strategic Thrusts and the Strategic Option Generator

Wiseman identified strategic thrusts (or opportunities) as actions that support or shape an organization's competitive strategies. He identified five types of thrusts: differentiation, cost, innovation, growth, and alliance, all of which are discussed in the next section. In general thrusts exhibit a set of properties, which include:

• Strategic polarity occurs because thrusts may assume opposing attributes such as using one strategy either offensively or defensively.
• Strategic thrusts occur in combinations so that more than one strategy is implemented at the same time. Though this may be beneficial, it also may require the organization to use opposing sets of properties.
• Strategic thrusts reflect a variety of ordering or degree of relation such as level of intensity or duration (long versus short term or high, medium, or low).

The strategic option generator is a tool used to identify strategic opportunities. The tool (see Fig. 5) iden-

Strategic Thrust		Strategic Target									
		Competitive Arena				System					
		Supplier	Channel	Customer	Rival	Enterprise	Supplier	Channel	Customer	Rival	
	Differentiation										
	Cost										
	Innovation										
	Growth										
	Alliance										

Figure 5 Strategic option generator. Source: Wiseman, C. (1988). *Strategic information systems.* Homewood, IL: Irwin.

tifies targets and thrusts. Targets are either system or competitive arena based. System targets are entities that use the strategic information system, while competitive arena targets are an organization's competitors whose competitive position will be affected by the implementation of an SIS. The tool user identifies strategic opportunities and develops a strategic information system that applies a thrust and influences a target. The approach is effective in determining the opportunities where information technology may be used to achieve competitive advantage.

III. STRATEGIES AND THRUSTS FOR COMPETITIVE ADVANTAGES

Strategy and thrusts are long-term policies that an organization adopts to achieve a position, and competitive strategies are those that assist the firm in achieving a competitive advantage. There are five strategies / thrusts for competitive advantages. SIS and information technologies may support these strategies. The strategies and how information technology may support each one are presented in the next few paragraphs.

A. Differentiation

An organization may develop a product that is percciccd to be different. Differentiation is not limited to the actual characteristics of the product, but includes the organization's relationship with other entities such as customer services.

B. Cost Leadership

An organization with the least total costs in an industry has an advantage over competitors because they can offer the lowest price to customers. Information technology may reduce costs by changing the organization's activities in terms of their physical or information components. For example, Boeing reduced

the cost of developing aircrafts by reducing the need for costly prototypes.

C. Innovation

An organization may achieve advantage by introducing new products or processes that cause a transformation in the way business is conducted. One such example is the dynamic pricing system tested by Amazon.com. The system allowed the organization to charge different customers different prices for the same product. The charges are based on Amazon's perception of a customer's willingness and ability to pay based on that customer's history.

D. Focus/Growth

An organization may achieve advantage by changing the volume or geographical area that it serves. It may also achieve advantage by growing vertically in either direction, or by changing its product lines. *The Wall Street Journal* and other leading newspapers increased the size of their markets by printing different editions serving different areas of the globe. Southwest Airlines achieved its competitive edge by limiting its product offerings and focusing on improving each offering.

E. Alliances

An organization may achieve advantage by forming alliances and relations with business partners. Alliances create synergy by allowing the organization to concentrate on its core competency, while benefiting from the core competency of the partners. One such example is Yahoo.com. Yahoo concentrates on customer service, while using business partners to create and supply products. For example, Yahoo acquires news items from various news organizations and concentrates on packaging the items in different layouts to satisfy customers' preferences.

IV. CHARACTERISTICS OF STRATEGIES

Strategy is a long-term commitment. It must cover several years. As such, it is important to understand how we can improve the chances of success in developing a competitive strategy. Organizations often forget this and adopt policies that contradict their strategies thus losing sight of what gave them a competitive advantage in the first place. There is no one successful strategy at all times in all organizations. A strategy that may have been successful for an organization may not be successful for another organization. Opposing strategies may be successful at the same time at different organizations. The same successful strategy may be a failure at another point in time for the same organization.

In addition, organizations often confuse strategies with efficient execution of one or more activities. Porter differentiated between operational effectiveness and strategies. Operational effectiveness means performing the same activities better than the competition, while strategy means the creation of a unique and valuable position by performing different activities, or performing the activities differently.

Strategic positioning emerges from three sources:

- Variety-based positioning. An organization produces specific products and performs them well.
- Needs-based positioning. An organization serves the needs of a specific segment of the market. The activities required to meet these needs must be different than those required to meet the needs of a different segment of the market.
- Access-based positioning. An organization segments its customers according to the different ways in which they may be accessed.

A unique position is not enough since competitors may copy it and improve upon it, or adopting it while continuing to support their old position. One example is Dell's build-to-order model, which is currently superior to Compaq's selling-through-dealers model. Compaq is attempting to copy Dell's approach and sell online while keeping the traditional outlets. Another example is Continental Airlines' attempt to copy Southwest's approach while keeping its traditional service. Neither organization succeeded.

For the unique position to be sustainable it must include trade-offs with other positions and it must fit the organization. Many factors create trade-offs: inconsistencies in image or reputation required by a strategy; activities associated with executing a strategy that may differ from one strategy to another; and priorities, internal coordination, and controls that may

differ from one strategy to another. Compaq's dilemma is that it did not consider these factors when attempting to copy Dell. Compaq lost its leadership position, and Thurow in 2001 estimated that Compaq's new policy may cost it 6–12 months' worth of sales, which may result in economic disaster.

A strategy must fit the organization's vision, policies, and culture. When considering if a strategy fits an organization, one must consider all the activities (not individual activities or a subset). Since it is more difficult to copy several activities than it is to copy one activity, fit is a factor in the sustainability of a competitive advantage. Higher levels of fit are more difficult to copy than lower levels. Performance declines when only a subset of activities is copied. Finally, the fit between activities creates operational effectiveness.

It is sometimes difficult to implement a strategy even when it is known to be better than what the organization is currently pursuing. The implementation of a strategy may cause short term losses in the immediate future, while postponing gains until much later. One example is Compaq's dilemma. Dell's build-to-order model is currently superior to Compaq's selling-through-dealers model. Compaq is losing market share to Dell and is facing declining profit margin. However, a change in strategy may cost Compaq 6–12 months' worth of sales and may result in economic disaster.

V. TYPES OF STRATEGIC INFORMATION SYSTEMS

SIS may be classified into three types: internal, external, and alliances (local and global). This section discusses each type, giving examples and identifying their impact on the organizational structure and processes.

A. Internal

Internal SIS are systems used within the organization. They enhance the organization's competitive position by improving the internal operations and productivity. One such example is the system used by Boeing in designing airplanes such as the 777, which is the first jetliner to be 100% digitally designed using three-dimensional solids technology. Throughout the design process, the airplane was "preassembled" on the computer, eliminating the need for a costly, full-scale mock-up, and expensive testing. When Boeing designed the 777, which is made up of 3 million parts, its computers simulated crashes, flight anomalies, and nasty weather scenarios before a single piece of fuselage was constructed.

Another example is the internal portion of the multiyear IT project adopted by Caterpillar in its attempt to return to profitability. During the first half of the 1980s Caterpillar faced labor unrest and stiff competition from Komatsu of Japan, which offered a comparable product at 40% less than CAT. Caterpillar's losses approached one billion dollars in 1985. To offset their losses, CAT set up three systems including a computer integrated manufacturing system, a computer-aided design system, and a Material Requirement Planning II system. These systems resulted in a reduction of the in-process inventory by 60%, reduced the lead time required to build a product from 45 days to 10, and increased on-time delivery to customers by 70%.

B. External

External SIS improve the organization's relations with its customers, suppliers, and buyers. ASAP from American Hospital Supply Corporation, SABRE from American Airlines, and APOLLO from United are examples of external systems. SABRE and APOLLO allowed both airlines to assess the impact of fare changes and to monitor their competition. The systems were the basis for an investigation by the Department of Justice and for a monopolistic practices lawsuit brought about by other airlines.

C. Alliances

Alliances evolve as more than one organization realizes that there is a benefit from combining their efforts to achieve an objective. Certain SIS create strategic alliances between organizations resulting in the creation of a competitive advantage or in preventing competition from acquiring/maintaining its competitive advantage. One example is the ATM network that allowed smaller banks to offer the same services as larger banks such as Citibank. This alliance not only put smaller banks on equal footing as larger banks that could afford to create their own network, but also network externalities[1] eliminated the need for regional and private networks developed by the larger banks.

---

[1]The product value is a function of the number of customers, while in network internalities the value of a product is inversely proportional to the number of customers.

VI. SUSTAINABILITY OF COMPETITIVE STRATEGIES AND SYSTEMS

Strategic systems do not last forever. Competitive strategies and competitive advantages in organizations often change to become the acceptable norm. In the same manner that unstructured problems turn into structured ones as a better understanding of the problem evolves, competitive strategies often are studied by other organizations and similar activities are implemented. Examples include ATM cards in banks and frequent flyer programs in airlines, which spread to other industries such as hotels and supermarkets.

The sustainability of strategic systems is an issue that must be considered when planning to develop one. Building an SIS is a large and expensive undertaking. They are often the first in an application area and may be based on new technology. All of these factors suggest that SIS are costly and that the organization should get equivalent return on investments. As such the sustainability of an SIS is important.

Christensen has identified several sources of competitive advantages and argued that these sources evolve over time. As such, when developing an SIS system today it is insufficient to consider what worked for a company in the past. Firms must also consider why and under what conditions certain sources work while others fail. In addition, it is important to consider how the industry is changing and how these changes may cause the advantages to dissipate. According to Christensen the sources are economy of scale, economy of scope, integration, and core competencies as the main sources of competitive advantages.

There are several frameworks that measure the sustainability of SIS. Feeny and Ives developed a framework to assess the sustainability of IT competitive advantage. The approach defines three sets of questions to evaluate sustainability. The first set, generic lead time, includes time-related questions such as: How long before a competitor can duplicate the system and what are the unique resources required by the competitor to develop an SIS? The second set, competitive asymmetry, includes questions that assess the difficulties each competitor must resolve to develop a similar project such as: What are the barriers that must be overcome? The third set, preemption potential, measures the unique characteristics or resources that the organization has and that will prevent competitors from duplicating the SIS.

Nakatani studied factors that influence the sustainability of SIS and presented a framework to measure it. He listed five questions that assist in identifying the degree of sustainability and for each question he identified the main variables that must be evaluated. A potential SIS is evaluated based on these variables and a score is given. Based on the answers to the questions an index number is generated that measures the sustainability. The questions are: (1) What makes duplication of an SIS application difficult? (2) What nontechnical factors delay the duplication? (3) What makes it possible for a firm to maintain a lead? (4) What makes the duplication of an SIS useless?

Kettinger reviewed the sustainability literature and identified several factors that determine the sustainability of strategic information systems. The analysis correctly classifies the sustainability of 82.14% of the investigated SIS. The factors are grouped into three sets: environmental factors, foundation factors, and action strategies. Environmental factors include unique industry characteristics, changes in regulatory and political environment, and political factors. Foundation factors include unique organizational characteristics such as size, geographic scope, product scope, vertical scope, organizational base, learning curve, and technological and information resources. Action strategies include preempting, managing risk, developing response strategies, and creating switching costs.

VII. STRATEGIC INFORMATION SYSTEMS RISKS

Risk in SIS projects must be studied and managed. Risk is defined as the degree of uncertainty regarding the deviation of the actual outcome of an activity from a desired outcome, or the inability of determining the future value of an activity. SIS are systems that attempt to chart new frontiers. They are often accompanied by uncertainty. As such, they are often accompanied with high risk. In 1988, Bank of America scrapped an accounting system that was to be released in 1984 at a cost of millions of dollars. However, the system was released in 1987 with problems. It was scrapped less than 1 year later, in 1988, after an announced cost of 80 million dollars. This is an example of a strategic information system project that did not consider the risk.

Risk management is carried out by understanding the types and sources of risk. The organization should take steps to prevent or reduce the effects of these types and sources. Sources of risk may be associated with the development effort, with the underlying assumptions used in determining the strategy and the system, and in the response of the environment, internal and external, to the organization. Similarly, a number of types of risks have been identified. Keen defined six types of risks including market concept risk, technology risk, implementation risk, economic risk, organizational risk, and regulatory risks. Neumann defined two types of risk: intrinsic, under the control of the organization; or extrinsic, outside the control of the organization. Intrinsic risks include size of project, familiarity of the organization with the information technologies involved, and the degree of structuredness of the effort. Extrinsic risks are unique to each SIS project and measure how well the project met its strategic business objectives. Extrinsic risks stem from competitors and government responses, and from changing the market conditions that previous assumptions are rendered obsolete. Extrinsic risks include risk of being first, risk of legal action, risk of changing the basis of competition, risk of losing proprietary information, and risk of lowering switching costs.

VIII. OTHER ISSUES

A. Internet and Strategic Systems

Recent years have seen the growth of the Internet and its expansion into various aspects of the business world. Some argued that the Internet set new rules, that existing business models do not apply, and that new models are needed. Some organizations attempted to suggest that it is acceptable to sell product for less than the cost of goods. The zero profit margin of buy.com is an example of such an approach. However, more recent events, which some call the bursting of the Internet bubble, suggest that a more reasoned approach is needed.

The Internet is a communication media. Information technology has developed a set of tools based on the utilization of the Internet that presents organizations and individuals with opportunities to perform the same activities faster and at less cost. These opportunities may result in changing the structure of organizations, in creating a different set of expectations, and in identifying new ways of performing processes. However, they do not present new business objectives nor do they make strategies obsolete. In other words, the so-called zero profit margin model, which does not work in brick and mortar organizations, will not, and it did not work, in the cyber world. The Internet, as Porter stated, provides better opportunities for companies to establish distinctive strategic positionings.

Though the frameworks discussed in this article are still valid, it is often necessary to consider other frameworks that stress some of the characteristics of the environment. One such approach was developed by Cartwright and Oliver. It includes two structures: the Value Cluster Analysis (VCA), which concentrates on the organization's value activities and the Value Web Analysis (VWA), which studies the entire industry. The VCA suggests that some of the value activities in the Internet environment are often unrecognized using the value chain model. These include human capital, organizational learning, and the network of relationships internal and external to the organization. The model represents value activities as hexagons to avoid the implicit sequence suggested by the value chain model. Different colors are used to differentiate between internal and external activities. The VWA represents the multiple horizontal and vertical relationships between the entities in the environment (e.g., suppliers, customers, competitors, complementors, regulatory agencies). Since the relationships between different entities are dynamic and may take different forms at the same time, e.g., two firms may compete in one area while cooperating in another, the graph is complicated and informative.

B. The Changing Nature of Information Systems

There are dangerous aspects to technology. Information systems have passed several phases in their relation to organizations:

- During the early phases, IS supported the organizational processes. That is, the shape of the organization determined the shape of the software.
- This was followed by IS that determined the shape of the organization. A good example supporting this statement is the use of ERP that often results in organizational changes.
- The near future will show us that information systems will determine what business an organization is in, for example, Amazon.com and others. Experience gained from using software and developing new areas of business often results in developing new organizational businesses.

This point of view seems clear in identifying where we are going. However, the question should be: Is this where we want to go? Technology is increasing the operational effectiveness of organizations. However, as discussed earlier, this is not a sustainable advantage. Technology is also, and more dangerously, making organizations look alike. That is, we are converging into one image. The purpose of a competitive strategy is

to differentiate the organization, to find that unique position that adds value to the organization's products. As such, when developing strategic systems we must consider the objective. It is not to cut cost; it is to create value and make us unique.

IX. CONCLUSION

Most of the examples used in this article share two characteristics. The first characteristic is that they were classified as strategic information systems after they were implemented and proved successful. The reasons for the existence of these systems did not include many of the benefits that we attribute to them today. For example, American Airlines' frequent flyer program was using two unused inventory systems, while ASAP from American Hospital Supply Corporation was an attempt to cut the cost of serving smaller customers. In brief, a firm does not schedule a meeting to develop the next strategic information system. It needs visionary individuals and a great deal of luck.

The second characteristic is that they were developed years ago, during the 1960s–1980s. There are few new strategic information systems. One possible explanation is that the advancement in technology has reduced the time it takes to duplicate new systems. Another explanation, which is related to the first, is that new systems concentrate on operational effectiveness and not on supporting a competitive strategy as defined in this article. As such it seems appropriate to redefine terms used with the hope that these new definitions will give the reader new insights on strategic information systems.

A competitive strategy is one that supplies the organization with a unique position that creates a value for the product that is difficult to replicate and that fits the organization. Therefore, strategic information systems are systems that support the strategy; they are not systems to achieve operational effectiveness.

APPENDIX 1: CLASSICAL SIS

A. American Hospital Supply Corporation ASAP (Based on information from Neumann in 1994)

American Hospital Supply Corporation (AHSC), which was acquired by Baxter International later, had a problem serving Stanford Medical Center. The center developed their own part numbering system that they used in ordering parts from their suppliers. Since the system was different than the one used by AHSC, the translation, from Sanford's system to AHSC's, was a cause for error. In order to resolve the problem, AHSC supplied Stanford with prepunched cards. The cards had the Stanford part number handwritten in ink, and the AHSC part number punched. The cards for the parts to be ordered were selected and read by a machine in Stanford connected to another in the AHSC office. This approach reduced the processing errors and increased the sales volume.

The success of the system resulted in developing Analytic Systems Automatic Purchasing (ASAP) in 1967, while competitors waited until 1986 to introduce similar systems. ASAP is credited with turning AHSC into a market leader. It contributed to AHSC increase in market share, sales, and earnings. The system processed close to 50% of the orders in 1984. In addition since customers found it easier to use the system, the system is credited with locking in customer loyalty.

B. SABRE

SABRE, developed by American Airlines, is the first online reservation system. It replaced the very thick (many inches) schedules that were placed on the desks of travel agents. In 2001 SABRE, which was spun off from American Airlines in 2000, has market capitalization of over 6.9 billion dollars, while American Airlines is 5.7 billion dollars.

C. Southwest Airlines

Southwest concentrates on short haul air travel (average aircraft trip length is 509 miles with an average duration of about 1 hour and 30 minutes). It has a limited number of routes between midsize cities and secondary airports, utilizes smaller and less congested airports surrounding large cities, and has one type of aircraft, the Boeing 737. It does not offer baggage handling, passenger ticketing, advance seating reservations, or hot food. These policies resulted in several advantages including cost leadership differentiation. Southwest has reduced turnaround time between flights from 30 to 15 minutes, thus saving approximately $175 million in capital expenditures alone through more efficient utilization of its aircraft. It emphasizes shuttle flights that efficiently utilize an aircraft on repeated trips between two airports, rather than using the hubs and spokes of the full-service carriers. Greater aircraft utilization (an aircraft flies an average of 8 flights per day, or about 12 hours per day) enables the airline to offer more flights, thus a greater selection and availability of arrival and departure times. Ensuring such tight turnarounds requires superb coordination among several value chain activities, including ticketing, catering, baggage handling, fueling, maintenance, weight and balance calculations, flight plans, and local clearances. Using one type of aircraft allows it to reduce the costs of maintenance and training.(Based on information from the Southwest Web Site http://www.southwest.com/about_swa/press/factsheet.html).

SEE ALSO THE FOLLOWING ARTICLES

Decision-Making Approaches • Decision Support Systems • Globalization and Information Management Strategy • Industry, Artificial Intelligence in • Management Information Systems • Strategic Planning for/of Information Systems • Transaction Processing Systems

BIBLIOGRAPHY

Boeing Web Site. (2001). http://www.boeing.com/commercial/777family/cdfacts.html.

Cartwright, S., and Oliver, R. (2000). Untangling the value Web. *Journal of Business Strategy, Boston,* Jan/Feb.

Christensen, C. (2001). *The past and future of competitive advantage.* Cambridge: MIT Sloan Management Review.

Earl, M. (1989). *Management strategies for information technology.* Englewood Cliffs, NJ: Prentice Hall International.

Feeny, D. F., and Ives, B. (1990). In search of sustainability: Reaping long-term advantage from investments in information technology. *Journal of Management of Information Systems,* Vol. 7, No. 1, 27–46.

Kettinger, W., Grover, V., Guha, S., and Segars, A. (1994). Strategic information systems revisited: A study in sustainability. *MIS Quarterly,* March.

Moukheiber, Z. (Jan. 8, 2001). The virtual patient. *Forbes,* New York, 234–236.

Nakatani, K. (1992). *Strategic information systems and competitive advantage: An index of sustainability.* A Master of Business Administration Thesis, San Diego State University, Spring.

Neumann, S. (1994). *Strategic information systems: Competition through information technologies.* New York: Macmillan College Publishing.

Porter, M. (1996). What is strategy? *Harvard Business Review,* November–December.

Porter, M. (2001). Strategy and the Internet? *Harvard Business Review,* March.

Porter, M., and Millar, V. (1985). How information gives you competitive advantage. *Harvard Business Review,* July–August.

Thurow, L. (2001). *Does the "E" in e-business stand for "exit"?* Cambridge: MIT Sloan Management Review.

Wiseman, C. (1988). *Strategic information systems.* Homewood, IL: Irwin.

Strategic Planning for/of Information Systems

William R. King

University of Pittsburgh

GLOSSARY

benchmarking A process of studying the "world class" business processes of other organizations in order to establish a practical understanding of what it is possible to achieve and the mechanisms that can be used to achieve such performance levels.

business process The cross-functional set of "horizontal" activities that a business conducts to achieve a customer-oriented output (e.g., new product development process or order fulfillment process).

business process reengineering The total redesign of a business process to improve its performance in terms of such measures as cost, efficiency, quality, cycle time, or customer satisfaction.

critical success factor (CSF) A capability that is necessary, but not sufficient, for success in a business.

mission The definition of the domain of a business; i.e., what it does and is willing to do and what it does not, or will not, do.

strategic business planning An organizational process for establishing the future mission, objectives, and strategies of the organization.

strategy The "general direction" in which an organization pursues its objectives.

value chain The set of sequential activities that an organization, its suppliers, and customers conduct in order to add value to inputs (e.g., raw materials in the hands of suppliers) to create outputs (e.g., finished goods in the hands of customers).

STRATEGIC PLANNING FOR INFORMATION SYSTEMS (SPIS) is the process of envisioning the desired future of the organization; defining the role that information technology (IT), information systems (IS), other information resources (IR), and IT-related policies will play in achieving that desired state; and designing the appropriate IT, IS, and information architectures and programs that will enable the role to be implemented and the organization's goals to be achieved.

Thus, SPIS is both a creative and a decision-making process because it involves the envisioning of the future and the invention of the options that might be employed to achieve future goals as well as the specification of those options that will actually be implemented.

I. EVOLUTION OF IS STRATEGIC PLANNING

In the early days of the computer era, there appeared to be little need for formalized planning for the information systems organizational activity, or the "Data Processing Department" as the organizational function was then termed. In this period, a widespread process of automation—particularly of administrative processes—was the primary focus of IS. Throughout organizations, computerized systems and processes were substituted for activities that had previously been done manually.

The only planning that was then being done was that involved in prioritizing and sequencing automation projects and in formulating budget requests. Typically, the IS annual budget rose substantially from year to year, but overall IS expenses, as a proportion of total organizational expense and as a proportion of total capital expenditures, were relatively modest.

The modest expense levels, coupled with the unfamiliarity of most business managers with the IS function, often led to a "hands off" attitude of business managers toward IS. IS was not generally subjected to the same basic management planning and controls as were most of the other elements of the organization.

The IS function thereby became a major locus of organizational slack—a term that is used to describe resource levels that are in excess of those that are strictly necessary to "do the job." Such slack-laden contexts can be good environments for creativity and innovation, but they also are prone to waste. Both of these were characteristic of the IS function in these early days of computerization.

As computer systems became more ubiquitous in organizations, the proportion of total organizational expenses and of total capital expenditures that were attributable to IS inexorably increased. The organizational slack in the IS function became easier to recognize and business managers became more familiar with the issues involved in managing IS.

As a result, "good management practices" were slowly imposed on this undermanaged organizational function. Among these management practices was formalized planning that went beyond the rudimentary planning that had previously been done.

The evolution of IS strategic planning may be described in terms of four eras. Each of these eras represents the planning methods and practices that were being used by relatively sophisticated organizations in that era. However, each of these planning modes is also reflective of the ways in which some organizations perform IS strategic planning today. As a result, a review of these areas is not merely a history lesson; it provides a basis for understanding the varieties of SPIS that exist today.

The four SPIS eras may be described as:

1. Prestrategic IS planning era
2. Early SPIS era
3. Late SPIS era
4. Era of business and IS planning integration.

A. Prestrategic IS Planning Era

In the prestrategic era of IS planning, IS managers were primarily concerned with assessing the future computing needs of the business and ensuring that adequate and appropriate computing capacity was available to fulfill those needs. An associated planning task was that of evaluating and selecting the application and systems development projects that would be funded and implemented. At the project level, project plans were developed to ensure that appropriate milestones were identified and that specific activities and tasks were assigned to appropriate IS professionals.

1. IS's Service Role

During this era, IS operated primarily in a service role—doing the processing of data within the organization so that it could operate efficiently, meet its reporting requirements to shareholders and government agencies, and provide some aggregate information to managers who might use these data to make better decisions. However, this service role for IS relegated it to a position of low strategic importance, analogous to that which the accounting function and the heating/air conditioning systems might have. At the time, many IS professionals who believed that IS should have greater organizational importance could be heard to say plaintively that the business would be required to shut down its operations if its computer systems did not operate. However, the same could have been said of the electrical supply system, which clearly is necessary, but not strategically important, to the organization.

2. Systems Development Life Cycle

The systems development life cycle (SDLC) was the primary conceptual basis for planning in this era. The SDLC for information systems evolved from the basic life cycle notion for complex systems. This theory postulated that the development of all complex systems naturally evolved through a sequential series of phases that were appropriately managed in different ways, and each of which demanded different mixes of resources to proceed effectively and efficiently. The classic SDLC for a single system is shown in the central portion of Fig. 1. There, it is depicted as consisting of three phases—system definition, physical design, and implementation. Other more elaborate versions of the SDLC specify many subphases of these three phases.

3. Cost Avoidance Criterion

Cost avoidance was the major criterion for IS development project evaluation in this prestrategic era. Project selection was relatively straightforward, primarily involving the estimation of the costs that could be avoided if manual systems were to be automated; other criteria such as feasibility and risk were used to identify projects that might not successfully achieve their predicted level of cost avoidance.

The primacy of the cost avoidance criterion tended to result in the approval of IS development projects that were primarily at the operational or operational control levels. Those projects that substituted computer systems for human operatives or those that directly measured or controlled the performance levels

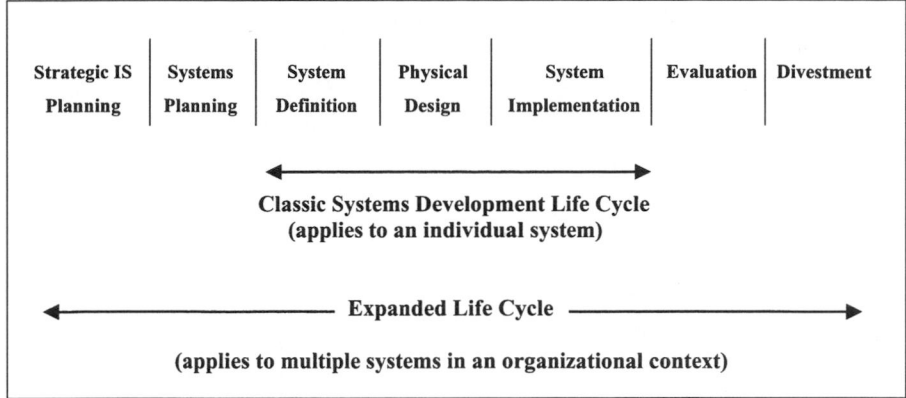

Figure 1 Classic and expanded systems development life cycles.

of operations were accepted as being worthwhile for the organization. Projects whose rationale depended on the benefits (e.g., increased revenues) that might be produced were difficult to justify because of the primacy of the cost avoidance criterion.

4. IS Master Plan

The highest level plan that came into being in some firms during the latter part of this prestrategic era was the IS master plan. This plan demonstrated the intended relationships among the various systems and subsystems that the organization operated or planned to develop. The need for a master plan was first recognized by firms that had developed multiple independent and incompatible computer systems. Although these systems may have been individually effective, they could not readily be integrated to provide comprehensive information that might be of use to management. Illustrative of this situation were the many banks that had developed expensive and operationally effective product-oriented computer systems. Their checking account systems, loan systems, and trust systems, for example, had databases that could not easily be cross-referenced to enable a marketing manager to readily determine which of the bank's various services were utilized by a given customer.

The master plan was intended to ensure effective systems integration. The adoption of this notion by the IS function was the precursor to the IS strategic planning era.

B. Early SPIS Era

During the late 1970s and the 1980s, strategic business planning became increasingly popular as a for-

mal activity in U.S. corporations. Most major firms had large strategic business planning staffs and conducted extensive annual planning processes that comprehensively examined strategic choices involving the firm's business missions, objective, strategies, and strategic programs.

These strategic business planning processes were typically a combination of top-down and bottom-up processes in the sense that they were initiated when general policies, guidelines, and environmental assessments were promulgated by top management and their corporate planning staffs, while the plans themselves were typically prepared at business unit levels and sent upward for review and consolidation. In most corporations, all business units and most key functions were involved in this process.

Because the IS function had by this time become a significant cost center and a provider of ever-more-critical services to all elements of the organization, the methods of strategic business planning began to be applied to the IS function as well.

During this era, the strategic business planning process was first conducted in order to envision the desired future of the organization and to select the best business strategies. Then, an IS strategic planning process was subsequently conducted in order to determine the role that IS might play in achieving these goals.

Although it may appear that the role of business strategy in driving IS strategy is so obvious that it could never have gone unrecognized, in fact, since the IS function had been primarily driven by the cost avoidance criterion and a "service" mentality, in this era many organizations found that mismatches existed between their business strategies and their IS strategies. For example, some businesses that were following diversification business strategies had no computer support or access to databases that would facilitate the identification and evaluation of merger or acquisition candidates, and some firms that were following niche business strategies had no data or computerized processes that would allow them to identify the market segments (niches) that might have the highest profit potential.

The simple idea of deriving the IS strategy directly from the business strategy and of then developing the IS resources that best supported the business strategy had a profound effect on IS planning and on IS development activities. When IBM incorporated the idea into its widely known business systems planning (BSP) methodology, these notions came into widespread use.

1. Enabler Role of IS

In this era, IS came to play more than a service role in the organization; its new role was that of an enabler of business strategy. For instance, companies that had chosen a cost leadership business strategy began to explore new ways, beyond the simple automation of administrative processes, to use computer systems to lower costs. Other firms began to differentiate their products by incorporating information processing capabilities into them, such as through the development of the self-diagnosis systems that enable elevator systems and other equipment to anticipate failures and to call in maintenance crews before failure has occurred.

2. More Sophisticated Criterion

The expanded role for IS necessitated a change from the simple cost avoidance IS project selection criterion that had been in common use in industry to more sophisticated criteria that gave greater consideration to a variety of potential benefits that might result from an IS project. Because cost remained a necessary consideration, and because benefits were often intangible and difficult to quantify, the net result was a multidimensional criterion that was conceptually similar to those that had been in use in R&D project selection for some time.

For the first time in the history of many firms, IS applications whose benefits were multidimensional, and sometimes intangible, and which did not promise merely the need for fewer clerks or the disposal of filing cabinets came to be given high priority. The result was that business managers developed a greater appreciation of the IS function as a potential contributor to the business rather than viewing IS merely as a service function that could be treated much like the company's other service systems.

3. System Implementation

This growing importance of the IS function to the business caused, or occurred concurrently with, an increasing emphasis on system implementation. The term *implementation* had been used, and still is used, in computer circles to mean the achievement of the specified technical operationality for a system. A system that is "implemented" in this sense is one that is performing appropriately from a technical and operational perspective.

However, the new emphasis on system implementation reflected a broader practical view that included both technical operationality and organizational fit. Thus, according to this expanded notion of system implementation, a system was not successfully implemented unless it met its technical goals as well as its organizational usage goals. Thus, a system was to do what it was supposed to do technically and was to be *used* in the fashion in which it was intended to be used in the organization in order that it be considered to be successfully implemented. The early days of the computer era were filled with anecdotes concerning systems that were implemented in the technical sense, but not in the organizational usage sense, because they were not used to the extent and in the manner that they were intended to be used, even though their technical functioning was adequate.

This increasing emphasis on the extent and nature of actual systems usage and system usefulness, rather than an exclusive focus on whether systems performed according to technical specifications, led to more complex and sophisticated criteria for evaluating systems.

4. Expanded Life Cycle

The expanded nature of IS planning and the emphasis on assessing and evaluating systems in more sophisticated ways may be conceptualized in terms of the expanded life cycle shown in Fig. 1.

There, a simple version of the classic SDLC is shown, in the central portion of the figure, to be imbedded in a broader life cycle that also includes strategic planning, systems planning, system evaluation, and system divestment phases. These phases serve to extend the traditional SDLC, which applies to a single system, to a broader organizational context.

The systems planning phase primarily involves the sort of systems integration assessments and planning that defined the earlier notion of a master plan. The strategic planning phase involves the development of an IS strategy that is derived from, and which directly supports, the business strategy.

In Fig. 1, the two phases that are shown on the right to begin subsequent to the traditional SDLC—evaluation and divestment—reflect the growing attention that was being paid to the formal evaluation of systems. Measures such as user satisfaction, systems use, and system usefulness were introduced to complement traditional evaluative metrics.

The divestment phase further recognized that an IS, like any complex system, has a finite useful life. The divestment phase not only reflects the need to phase out systems, but the need to plan for the phasing out, replacement, and decommissioning of systems. In the earlier eras, little attention was given to planning for divestment, leading many firms to make the implicit assumption that systems would function forever. This assumption inevitably leads to decisions concerning systems maintenance, updating, and modification that might be significantly different from those that would be made under the assumption of a finite useful life span for systems. The Y2K problem that was so costly for organizations to address as the 21st century was about to dawn resulted largely from failures in developing divestment plans for systems and illustrates the difficulties that can ensue in the absence of such plans.

C. Late SPIS Era

In the 1980s and 1990s, the role of SPIS as a means of implementing business strategy was expanded in recognition of the potential for IS to influence business strategy as well as to be guided by it.

1. Strategic Role of IS

Various terminologies such as *strategic systems,* and *competitive weapons,* are used to describe information systems that have the potential to impact the product-market strategies and performance levels of businesses. A large number of systems of this variety have been developed. Most familiar are Merrill Lynch's Cash Management Account (CMA), a product whose core technology is information processing, and the American and United Airlines reservation systems, which were employed to achieve competitive advantages in the marketplace rather than to merely serve as operational systems.

2. Sustainable Comparative Advantage Criterion

The evolution of the criteria used to evaluate and select systems moved toward a focus on "sustainable compar-

ative advantage" in the era of strategic systems. Systems that have the potential to produce an identifiable advantage over competition, sustainable over time, are those that were given highest priority. Systems that promise cost avoidance or temporal competitive advantage would generally be less highly valued.

D. Era of Business and IS Planning Integration

In the 1970s and 1980s, centralized planning in both the business and IS domains was the modal situation in organizations. Subsequently, strategic business planning became more decentralized within many organizations. The recognition of the increasing importance of information resources coupled with the general trend toward decentralized business planning led, in this era, to a greater level of integration of strategic business planning and IS planning.

1. Information Resources Concept

The concept of *information resources,* as contrasted with *information systems,* reflects both the greater strategic importance of computer-related entities and the rapid development of a wide variety of technologies that transcend the traditional computer hardware and software dimensions of IS. Local-area networks, intranets, wide-area networks, extranets, database management systems, and various Internet and telecommunications systems and many other technology-based entities must be thought of as a set of information resources that must be planned for and managed. The IR concept also includes data, information, and knowledge as organizational assets that may be even more valuable than hardware, software, and systems.

Associated with the IR idea are IS-related organizational policies and practices that came into being in this era. For example, telecommuting began to be explored as a means of increasing organizational effectiveness and efficiency while allowing some employees to better meet their personal and family obligations. Other IT-related policies such as controls on usage of the Internet, ensuring the security of the organization's sensitive data, and issues involved in the encryption of communications further broadened the scope of IR.

Thus, during this era, information resources became recognized as a set of assets whose deployment must be planned for and managed in much the same way as has traditionally been done for human, financial, and physical resources.

Many companies now conduct a single business planning process in which information resources are treated as an important constituent element of a set of assets that must be effectively employed if the enterprise is to prosper. In this integrated process, IS can be viewed in any or all of its roles as a backroom service, as an enabler of strategy, or as a strategic asset.

II. MODEL OF THE SPIS PLANNING PROCESS

Figure 2 shows a model of SPIS in terms of the various elements that must be considered and integrated in a strategic planning process for IS in the organization. In effect, the elements on the left side of Fig. 2 represent multiple starting points for an SPIS process that is concluded, as shown on the right side of the figure, when choices have been made concerning IS's desired organizational role, mission, capabilities, architectures, and strategic programs and when implementation plans have been developed.

The SPIS model of Fig. 2 consists of six key elements:

1. Assessment of external environments
2. Assessment of internal environments
3. Assessment of IS/IT environment
4. Generation and assessments of options for IS/IT change
5. Specification (choice) of IS strategic elements
6. Development of implementation plans.

A. Assessment of External Environments

One of the major inputs to the SPIS process is a set of assessments that are performed of external environments. Of particular interest, as shown in Fig. 2, are assessments of:

- General business and economic trends
- Industry and compctitive trends
- Supplier and customer trends
- Non-IT technological trends
- Government and regulatory trends.

Each of these assessments may have initially been done in the strategic business planning process. However, even if that is so, these assessments need to be analyzed to discern their IS-relevant content. It is almost never adequate for SPIS process managers to

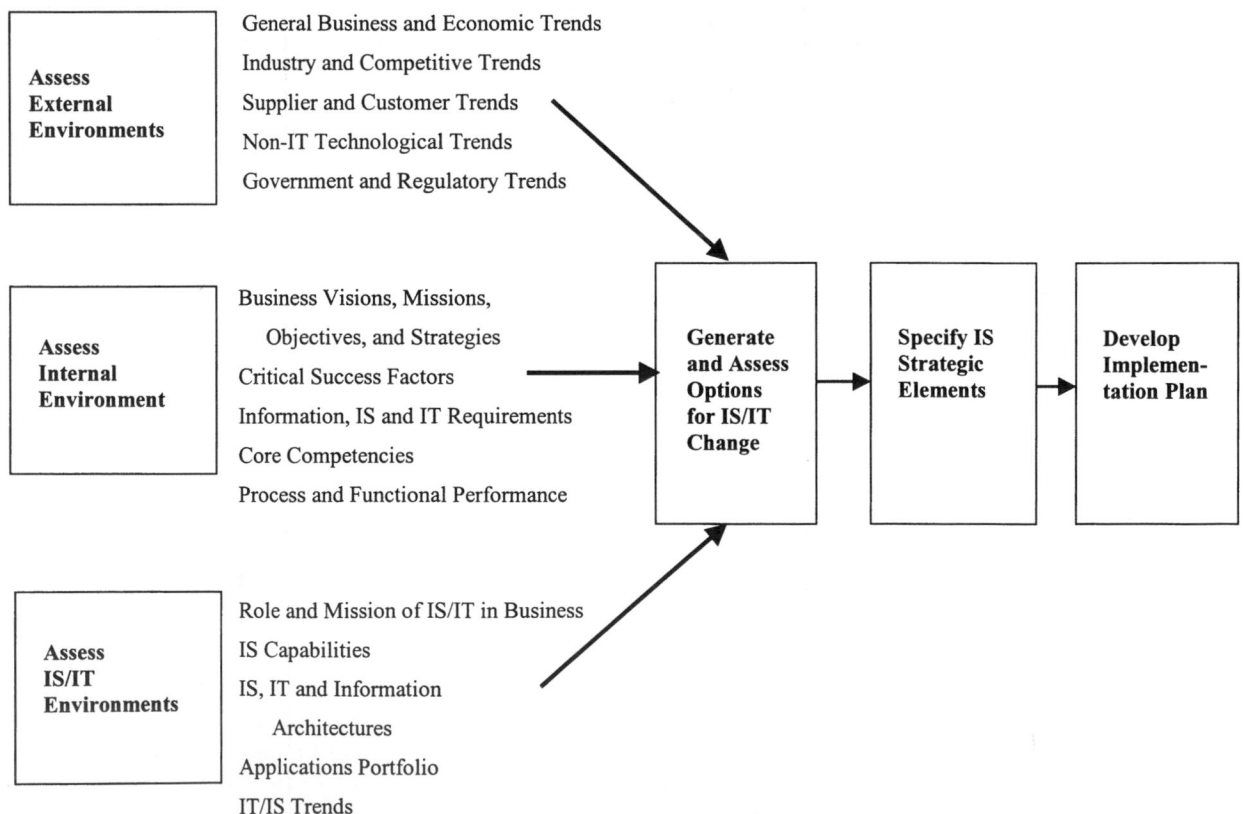

Figure 2 A general model of the SPIS processes.

merely circulate the external environmental assessments that have been performed by business planners because they will generally not focus on the aspects of these environments to which IS is most sensitive or which are most sensitive to IS.

Each of these external contexts must be assessed as potential sources of opportunities or threats. Evolving trends may indicate new opportunities for IS or they may suggest new constraints on the evolution of IS.

1. General Business and Economic Trends

Forecasts of the future business and economic climate will give some indication of whether the economy is in an expansionary or contraction mode and how long the current situation is expected to continue. This will enable IS planners to "scope" the opportunities that may exist for greater or lesser degrees of change for IS in the organization in the future. For instance, if the economy is expected to go into recession, IS planners may be less aggressive in proposing major investments in new systems and IS capabilities.

Specific forecasts of such economic factors as productivity improvements that are gathered in this phase may specify what may be expected of IT, since most productivity improvements are enabled by IT.

2. Industry and Competitive Trends

The assessment of industry and competitive trends permits the IS planner to focus on what is happening with regard to technological adoption by firms in the same industry or firms in other industries that might become future competitors.

In making such assessments, it is necessary to recognize that the traditional boundaries of industries are changing. For instance, banks, brokerage firms, investment managers, and other financial firms have been merging and developing new products that blur the traditional definitions of the banking and financial services industries. Firms such as General Electric and General Motors are now heavily involved in financial services. Firms like IBM, which traditionally provided hardware and software, now derive major portions of their total revenues for consulting services and services provided as an outsourcing vendor. So, the questions of "What is, or will be, our industry?" and "Who will be our competitors?" are of fundamental importance to effective SPIS.

3. Supplier and Customer Trends

Supplier and customer trends permit a focus on the changes taking place in the value chain on both the input and output sides. What will our customers and suppliers expect of us in the future? What is the most appropriate and profitable role that our organization can play in the overall value chain? What are the trends in using IT for supply chain management and for promoting and selling products?

For instance, for some time many firms have been implementing enterprise resource planning (ERP) systems that integrate data reflecting the various functions and processes of the organization. With the rapid development of the Internet, most such firms were forced to address the question of how their ERP systems could be integrated with supply-side systems that would provide them with the opportunity to buy through electronic auctions and to take advantage of other Internet-based purchasing options as well as to implement the promotion or sale of their products and services via the Internet. The Internet became a major factor in doing business so rapidly that many firms were unprepared for the opportunities that it offered and the threats from competitors that it may pose. Those firms that had conducted good external environmental assessments were certainly better prepared than those who did not do so.

4. Non-IT Technological Trends

As new technologies such as neural networks or nanotechnologies in materials science become practical or as new production technologies are developed, the demands placed on the IS function within an organization and the opportunities afforded to IS are likely to change. An assessment of such potentially important non-IT technological areas can help IS managers to foresee these changing demands and opportunities.

In some firms, the business strategic planning process involves an assessment of the major technologies that may be relevant to the firm's future success. Because IT is an enabling technology for other technologies, such assessments can be very useful in forecasting future IT issues and requirements.

5. Government and Regulatory Trends

Only a short while ago, IS managers may have thought this environmental area to be of only modest relevance to IS. However, recent government attempts to utilize or limit IT, such as through the establishment of data encryption standards and the implementation of electronic telecommunications surveillance software, have made it clear that the IS function in an organization must be conversant with changes in governmental actions and regulations. In the domain of IT, the IS function must be the "eyes and ears" of the firm. In addition, IS must use such assessments as a basis for determining how future systems will be developed, how the firm's intellectual property rights and trade secrets can be best protected and whether the value of IT investments may be affected by government-imposed constraints on their use. For instance, firms that invest in communications infrastructure may be concerned with the possibility that government will require them to provide open access, thus constraining their opportunity to gain a competitive advantage through such investments. The assessment of such trends can be very useful in establishing a sound basis for such investment choices.

B. Assessment of Internal Environments

Because IS cannot "do everything" that might be possible for it to do, part of the SPIS process is to select those areas within the organization on which IS can most usefully focus. Just as is the case with external environmental assessments, these areas may be thought of as either opportunities that may be addressed or as problems that may be solved using IR. The starting points for making such determinations in the internal environment are assessments of the following:

- Business visions, missions, objectives, and strategies
- Critical success factors
- Information, IS, and IT requirements
- Core competencies
- Functional and process performance levels and gaps.

3. Business Visions, Missions, Objectives and Strategies

Although SPIS must be conducted in a manner that takes into account IS-enabled opportunities to influence business strategies, an important starting point is still a clear understanding of the vision that top management has for the future of the enterprise, the business missions that have been established, and the business strategies and objectives that have been enunciated.

Sometimes, these are the products of a strategic business planning process; in other instances, they will be best reflected by assessing the past strategic programs that have been prescribed; in still other instances, they may need to be inferred from past strategic actions that top management has taken.

2. Critical Success Factors

In order for SPIS to be cost effective, concern must be given to identifying the critical success factors (CSFs) for each business and for the overall enterprise. CSFs are those activities that the organization must do well and the capabilities that it must possess in order to have a chance to be successful. They are the necessary, but not sufficient, conditions for success.

For instance, for an original equipment supplier to the auto industry, one CSF is typically the ability to produce and deliver parts on a "just-in-time" basis. Without such an ability, the parts firm has little chance to be successful. With this capacity, it has the chance to take actions that may lead to success.

Typically fewer than 10 CSFs can be identified for a business. A primary role of IS is to enable and support the development and refinement of capabilities related to these CSFs. Thus, identifying them is an important starting point for the SPIS process.

3. Information, IS, and IT Requirements

Although the idea of identifying information resource requirements—whether these requirements are for information, knowledge, systems, services, hardware, or software—is not nearly as practical a notion as it might first appear to be, a survey of perceived information resource needs can be a useful input to the SPIS process.

The notion of requirements is not as practical as it might at first appear to be, however, because managers and users of IS resources are not always capable of identifying their requirements, sometimes because they lack an understanding of the latest technologies and sometimes because they cannot conceive of that which might be provided to them and therefore cannot "require" that which they cannot conceptualize.

At some point in the SPIS process, managers and other system users may be provided with suggestions or information concerning what might be available or what might be feasible to have provided to them by IS. This may be done at an early stage of IS planning or it may be done later in SPIS when various options are being seriously considered.

4. Core Competencies

The SPIS process must give consideration to the past and potential core competencies of the organization. Core competencies are complex and sophisticated "bundles" of capabilities, processes, systems, and procedures that the organization has developed over time and which give it a unique ability to achieve a competitive advantage in the marketplace. For instance, a firm's core competency might be its capacity to rapidly develop and market new versions of existing products and new products. Such a competency would be likely to encompass good market research, concurrent design processes, effective competitive intelligence, and a variety of other organizational activities and systems.

Just as the CSF notion separates out a relatively small number of activities for special attention, the core competency notion identifies a core of activities that are absolutely critical to the future success of the organization. These assessments became important inputs to making strategic choices for IS for the same reasons that CSFs are important in SPIS.

5. Process and Functional Performance

The level of performance of various business processes and business functions must be assessed in order to determine which are operating at peak performance and which may be performing inadequately. The term *gap* is widely applied to differences between desired and actual performance levels.

Most enterprises have clearly defined business functions—marketing, operations, human resources, finance, etc.—and most routinely collect performance data for these functions such as the market share achieved by various products or business units and the operating efficiency of the production function. These performance data may be compared with those of competitors using data available through trade associations or vendors of such data. In this fashion, functional performance may be assessed relative to the levels achieved by others and assessments may be made of any gaps that might exist.

Similarly, in business processes such as new product development and order fulfillment, metrics may be available to permit the assessment of process performance. Illustrative of such metrics are cycle times for order fulfillment, levels of customer satisfaction, and quality indicators. Process performance data may not be so readily available for competitors and other firms as are functional performance data. Thus, comparisons across time may have to be relied on to indicate whether progress is being made in each process. It may sometimes be valuable to conduct benchmarking assessments of companies that are acknowledged to be "world class" in some key business processes in order to establish standards of performance that are high, but achievable.

These functional and process performance assessments and identification of gaps can provide insight

into areas of opportunity for the application of innovative information systems and technology.

C. Assessment of IS/IT Environment

The third major category of inputs to the SPIS process involves assessing the IS/IT that already exists in the enterprise in terms of:

- Role of IS/IT in the business
- Mission of the IS function
- IS capabilities
- IS, IT, and information architectures
- Applications portfolio
- IS/IT trends.

With the exception of IS/IT trends, these are strategic decision elements of SPIS—the areas in which choices must subsequently be made in the SPIS process. As such, their current status may have been specified as the result of prior periodic SPIS processes. However, it is inadequate for IS planners to assume that choices made in SPIS in prior years actually have been implemented, because it is not uncommon to discover failures in implementing the results of planning. Alternatively, the current status of these elements may simply reflect the aggregate of many minor choices that have been made throughout the organization over many years rather than a state that is the result of a comprehensive prior choice. In either case, it is important that the IS planner adequately assess the actual current situation with regard to each of these factors.

1. Role of IS/IT in the Business

An assessment must be made of the present role played by IS and IT in the business. This may vary from a service role, in which IS is viewed merely as a service that is provided to other areas of the organization, to a strategic role in which IS is viewed as something that is crucial to future success.

2. Mission of the IS Function

The mission of an organizational entity describes what is expected of it in practical terms that enable its managers to make choices that are sensible, focused toward clear objectives, and internally consistent.

A clearly defined mission enables managers to develop tactics that are consistent with strategies and goals and to choose what they will not do as well as what they will do. In the area of IS, this is of particular significance because there are so many opportunities for adopting new technologies, developing new systems, and taking initiatives that it is important for the enterprise's top managers to specify an IS mission that will guide IS managers in making the myriad tactical choices that they face on a routine basis.

3. IS Capabilities

An organization's IS capability consists of its hardware and software and the shared services, such as e-mail or group support systems, that it provides to organizational participants and the organizational skills and processes that the IS function possesses. These skills may be those possessed by individuals, such as programming skills or project management skills, or they may be elements of IS's "social capital"—skills that reside in groups rather than in individuals—such as the ability of IS-based teams to rapidly design and implement new applications systems. The IS processes are those that amplify these people skills, such as the availability of systems development techniques and software, the existence of standard templates for successful project management, and SPIS itself.

These capabilities identify the base on which the future of the IS function must be constructed. As such, having a clear understanding of existing capabilities is critical to effective SPIS.

4. IS, IT, and Information Architectures

The existing architectures related to information and to IS in the organization will either enable or inhibit change. If the organization has made expensive commitments to particular architectures, it may be reluctant to suffer the costs—both financial and psychological—of change. Thus, existing architectures may impede progress, or if they are scalable and adaptable, they may facilitate change. As a result, a delineation of existing architectures for data, systems, and networks is a fundamental input to the SPIS process.

5. Applications Portfolio

The existing portfolio of applications is another baseline that may enhance or inhibit the opportunities for change. For instance, an organization that has implemented ERP in order to integrate data from its business functions may not be willing to consider IS projects that do not conform to its ERP. Even though such a constraint may not be rational in a theoretical sense, some organizations have found that the commitment of time and energy to implement major systems such as ERP is so great that they are not psychologically prepared to consider large-scale additional changes. If this is the case, such factors must be considered in the SPIS process or it will deteriorate into an impractical exercise.

6. IS/IT Trends

Trends in new technologies and applications of IT must be assessed so that the opportunities for future IS developments in the organization can be fully appreciated. This may vary from the application of neural networks applications for the creation of new products for the business to the development of new methodologies for systems development.

D. Generation and Assessment of Options for IS/IT Change

The next level of the SPIS model of Fig. 2 involves the generation and assessment of options that may be required, or desired, for changing the IS function in manners that will best serve the organization. Some options will naturally evolve from the assessments that have previously been described. For instance, a critical success factor that is not being effectively supported or developed or an information requirement that is not being met will specify options to be considered rather readily.

Similarly, a performance gap in a function or process may readily identify an opportunity for the application of IT in improving performance. An important approach to such improvements has been business process reengineering (BPR), which involves the radical redesign of business processes to achieve significant improvements in process performance. IT typically plays a major role in such process redesigns.

Even at the broadest level of IS's role in the organization, it is necessary to periodically consider change. For instance, if IS has operated in a service role, a turnaround may be indicated to be appropriate by evolving trends in IS as well as in the assessments that have been made of other internal and external environmental factors.

Other options may need to be creatively generated based on the assessments. For instance, a functional performance deficiency coupled with a newly recognized technology may identify an option for remedying the deficiency using a technology that was not previously available. Such options may make the addressing of a problem feasible for the first time or it may present a particularly cost-effective way of doing so.

Other options can be generated through the use of brainstorming or other creativity-enhancing techniques or through the use of logical approaches such as the identification of the most significant areas in which performance gaps exist.

1. Option Assessment Criteria

Once options have been generated, they must be assessed. This may be done judgmentally, using some formal scoring technique or through some combination of subjective judgment and formality. Some of the criteria that are often used in assessing options are listed here:

1. Is this change *required* (such as because of new government reporting requirements)?
2. Is it *urgent* (such as it might be if the implementation of an IS/IT change is extremely sensitive to a deadline that is not subject to change)?
3. Is it *critical* to business success (such as it might be if it were an element of a business critical success factor or if it would significantly enhance a core competence)?
4. Does it have the potential for *high business impact?* (Will it make a real difference? Does it have the potential to improve some aspect of business performance by a significant increment?)
5. Is it *innovative?* (Does it represent a truly new way of doing something?)

E. Specification of IS Strategic Elements

Once options for changes in IS/IT have been generated and evaluated, the SPIS process, like any planning process, becomes an exercise in decision making. Decisions must be made and general specifications must be delineated for IS/IT strategic elements:

- Role of IS in the enterprise
- Mission(s) of IS
- IS capabilities that are to be developed or enhanced
- IS strategic programs
- IS/IT architectures
- Applications portfolio.

Any annual or periodic SPIS process may not result in significant changes in all of these elements. For instance, the role and missions of IS might be expected to change only infrequently. Other of the elements may require changes even more frequently than the SPIS process is formally conducted.

Ultimately, the choice of these IS strategic elements is a matter of the judgment of top IS and business managers. However, the conduct of the environmen-

tal assessments and the option generation and evaluation phases of SPIS ensures that these judgments can be made on the basis of comprehensive information concerning the options and the likely ramifications of choosing each. As such, the core of SPIS is a process of choice that is based on informed judgment.

F. Development of Implementation Plans

While the making of strategic choices is often portrayed as the end of a planning process, it is well recognized that in modern organizations, the choices made in any planning process may not be enacted. There are many reasons for such strategy implementation failures ranging from a lack of understanding as to who has responsibility for implementation to reluctance on the part of lower level managers to truly accept the choices made in the SPIS process, perhaps because they disagree with them or they do not fully understand them.

If these strategic implementation failures are to be avoided, clear implementation plans must be developed. These plans should indicate who is responsible for the implementation of each element of the plan; they should identify specific "milestones" and schedules for the reporting of results to those who are responsible and to top management, and they should specify clear performance goals for each milestone.

Such implementation plans cannot be prepared until the desired changes in the major strategic IS/IT elements have been approved by top management, but they should be developed immediately thereafter and their development should be considered to be an integral part of the SPIS process.

III. ALTERNATIVE MODES OF SPIS

The earlier description of the evolution of SPIS may be used as a basis for portraying four significantly different modes of performing SPIS. These modes importantly reflect the relationship between business strategic planning and SPIS in terms of the nature and level of integration between the two processes.

A. Administrative Integration

As shown in Fig. 3, the least integrated mode, termed "Administrative Integration," is one in which there is two-way flow between the two planning processes, but only concerning planning administrative matters such as the scheduling of various events in the planning process, the providing of planning information, the

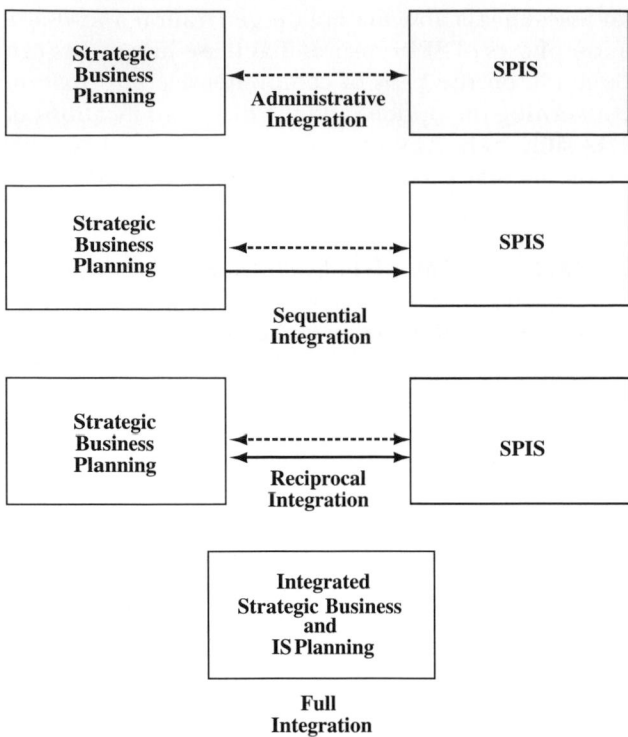

Figure 3 Alternative modes of SPIS.

formatting of plan submissions, etc. This administrative flow is depicted by the dashed arrow that shows flows in both directions in Fig. 3.

B. Sequential Integration

The second mode in Fig. 3 is termed "Sequential Integration." In addition to the two-way flow of administrative information, the primary flow of substantive information is from left to right. This describes the situation in which decisions are made during the strategic business planning process concerning such matters as business strategies and objectives. These choices become inputs to the SPIS process. In this mode, the IS function is envisioned to primarily be implementer of business strategy, and as such, the business strategy and other business information must first be provided so that the SPIS process can focus on the development of the IS infrastructure and IR programs that are best suited to the business strategy.

C. Reciprocal Integration

In the mode labeled "Reciprocal Integration" in Fig. 3, there is a two-way flow of both substantive and ad-

ministrative information. This reflects a view of IS that recognizes that the organization's IT resources may be drivers of business strategy as well as facilitators and enablers of business strategy. For instance, if an organization has an IT capability that is complex, sophisticated, and difficult for others to imitate, the business might wish to develop a business strategy in which this IT capability plays an important role. If a firm can provide access to customer data in a unique manner, the business strategy may be adapted to take advantage of this information capability.

D. Full Integration

The last mode in Fig. 3 is that of "Full Integration." This suggests that the processes for business strategic planning and SPIS are not separate, but rather that they are conducted in an integrated and concurrent manner. This represents the recognition that IS is of such critical importance to the enterprise that IS issues must be considered concurrently with other functional issues in the formulation of business strategy.

There is ample evidence that each of the four modes of SPIS depicted in Fig. 3 is in current use in a variety of organizations. Thus, the historical evolution of SPIS, as described earlier, which may be loosely thought of as going from a total lack of integration and passing through the four modes from top to bottom in Fig. 3, does not imply that all organizations will follow an evolutionary path or that all will find it useful to move to the level of full integration. Some firms may determine that the mode that best suits their needs is one that has less-than-full integration.

However, there is evidence that the more "proactive" planning modes—full integration and reciprocal integration—do result in better planning performance and outcomes than do the other, more "reactive" modes. This suggests that while all firms may not find it desirable to move to full integration, there is reason to expect better planning performance from the more advanced SPIS modes.

IV. CONCLUSION

Strategic planning for information systems is an organizational process that has as its goal the most effective and efficient employment of information resources in creating a desired future for the organization. It is both a creative and a decision-making process in that it involves the "invention" of options as well as the making of choices among them.

A variety of levels of integration between strategic business planning and IS planning can be employed for SPIS. Most organizations will begin SPIS using one of the less-integrated approaches and evolve their SPIS process toward more advanced forms. However, some organizations may choose a role for IS that does not require them to use the more sophisticated varieties of SPIS.

Whatever mode for SPIS is deemed to be appropriate, strategic IS planning is important for all organizations because it enables managers to make sensible decisions concerning the way in which the organization will employ its increasingly important and expensive information resources.

SEE ALSO THE FOLLOWING ARTICLES

Benchmarking • Corporate Planning • Decision-Making Approaches • Future of Information Systems • Globalization and Information Management Strategy • Management Information Systems • Systems Design • Systems Science

BIBLIOGRAPHY

IBM (July 1981). *Business systems planning: Information systems planning guide* (3E), GE 20-0527-3.

King, W. R. (March 1978). Strategic planning for management information systems. *Management Information Systems Quarterly,* Vol. 2, No.1, 27–37.

King, W. R., and Cleland, D. I. (August 1975). A new method for strategic systems planning. *Business Horizons,* Vol. 18, No. 4, 55–64.

King, W. R., and Zmud, R. (December 1981). Managing information systems: Policy planning, strategic planning and operational planning. *Proc. 2nd Int. Conf. Information Systems.*

Teo, T. S. H., and King, W. R. (Summer 1997). Integration between business planning and information systems planning: An evolutionary-contingency approach. *Journal of Management Information Systems,* Vol. 14, No. 1 185–214.

Structured Design Methodologies

Konrad Morgan
University of Bergen, Norway

GLOSSARY

cohesion A measure of how well a single module performs only a single task.

control constructs The pseudo code or structured English produced within structured design should limit itself to using the three basic control constructs of sequence, selection and repetition.

coupling A measure of how much two modules within a design are linked.

data dictionary A text based description of all data (and often modules) used in a system.

data flow diagrams (DFDs) A visual design method that focuses on data transformations that occur as data passes through a system.

entity relationship diagrams (ERDs) A visual design method that shows details of all data items, data structures and their relationships in a system.

function A type of sub-program that returns a single result that is based upon the internal logic within the sub-program and any variables passed to the sub-program in its parameters.

modules A set of design solving actions or data transformations that can be tested and verified independently of their use in a larger design.

modularization A concept to help the designer and later the programmer to break a complex design into smaller sub-designs often called modules (see also procedures and functions).

procedure A type of sub-program that returns multiple results, usually by means of the variables included in the parameters passed to the procedure.

pseudo-code A text based design method that represents the logical structure of a system in terms that can then be used as the basis for translation into software (also called program design language (PDL) or structured English).

structure chart A visual design method that expresses the logical structure of the system design in terms of a tree like diagram where each module is shown as a single element of the tree structure.

top-down design Specifying the solution to a problem in general terms, then dividing the solution into finer and finer details until no more detail is necessary to show a complete solution for the design (also called functional decomposition and stepwise refinement).

This article summarizes the history and major principles involved in structured design. After a definition of structured design, the article reviews the technical and social background which prompted the creation of structured design methods. Finally, by means of simplified examples the article gives brief descriptions of some of the recognized methods and features which make up structured design.

I. DEFINITION: STRUCTURED DESIGN

Structured design is a series of guiding principles which are applied through formalized methods (described later in this article) to ensure that a system design is built up from logically derived sub-components in such a way that the final overall system is self-documenting and constructed from smaller self-contained subdesigns. The name of each subcomponent of the overall system reflects the purpose of that subcomponent, and each subcomponent can be viewed and tested as a separate system which makes up the whole system. This method allows for clearer understanding of the system and also encourages compartmentalization of the design and implementation and testing among large analyst and programmer teams.

II. WHY STRUCTURED DESIGN METHODOLOGIES?

Structured design methods form the basis of almost all modern information system designs, but this was not always the case. In order to be able to understand the reasons for the development of structured design methods, we must first examine the methods used in the 1950s and 1960s.

III. EARLY SYSTEMS DESIGN

Computer systems in these periods were vastly more expensive and less widely available than they are today. The people who could afford these systems employed highly trained and specialized people to work on designing the software systems which controlled these early computers. Most designers were mathematicians or scientists who needed to have access to systems which could repeat rather simple instructions many times. The systems themselves were very large and unreliable, requiring around the clock support and maintenance. Typical users were governments and large corporations who could afford these very expensive systems.

Each computer system was quite unique and therefore had software systems specially written for it by dedicated teams of designers. Computer memory was very limited, and therefore, vast amounts of time and energy were devoted to creating complex software programs which were difficult to understand but which could make the very best use of the limited computing resources. It is important for us to realize that these programmers and designers were not de-liberately producing incomprehensible software designs, they were merely trying to make the most memory and resource efficient systems.

This state of affairs in design continued until mass production and miniaturization in the late 1960s started to make computers faster and more powerful in terms of memory and other resources. Once mass production of computers became established, the computer manufacturers had no alternative but to supply standardized software systems with each computer. In addition, software companies saw the benefits of selling "off the shelf" software solutions to the growing numbers of companies that now owned a computer.

Software companies and computer manufacturers tried to apply mass production methods to software development and rapidly found that the highly individualistic designs which had been used in the past were disastrous when applied to large software development projects.

Design team members found it impossible to understand designs or programs which had been developed by other programmers. The other problem which emerged was that as computer memory became cheaper, software systems could become more complex, and soon the required complexity exceeded the ability of designers using individualized and ad hoc designs.

This problem was so extreme that several large computer companies and software developers nearly became bankrupt. Industry and academia then set about working on identifying a set of design principles which would allow designers to create solutions for extremely large or complex computing problems in such a way that the designs could be shared and understood by a team of different designers. The method would also use a design process which documented the design decisions so they could be understood by other designers should the original designers be replaced at some time during the software production.

IV. STRUCTURED SYSTEMS DESIGN

The fundamental concepts for this new method were drawn from varied sources: engineering, programming, human psychology, and project management. The most basic component of structured design is the concept of "functional decomposition" or "top-down design." This concept is common to all the techniques within structured design and is the key to the success of structured methodologies within modern systems design.

As we have seen in the history of computer science, various techniques have been developed to try to help people in the design of software. These have ranged from techniques where the users express their design by symbols (for example, flowcharts, structure charts, or data flow diagrams) to where the users express their design ideas in a structured form of language.

Since most computer programs will also be expressed in some formal language structures, it often makes more sense for the designers to express their ideas in the form of language. Language has the advantage of being able to express an almost infinite range of concepts and ideas; we can see this simply by reminding ourselves of the range of ideas which have been expressed in literature. The fact that this book also adopts language as its major method of explanation means that it may be easiest to explain the principles of structured design using the text-based techniques of structured design (called "structured English" or "pseudo-code") than with some of the more graphical techniques.

As with all the techniques within structured design, structured English uses what is termed functional decomposition or a top-down approach. Although this sounds very formal and complex, in fact it is just an attempt to convert the natural human tendency of reducing problems into manageable parts into a formal method. Obviously, the simpler the design the easier it will be to understand, to implement (put on a computer), and to adjust if any part of it needs to be altered later.

A. Using Top-Down Design Solutions to Problems

One of the errors which occurs when people try to produce solutions to problems is often that they cannot keep all of the problem in their short-term memory at the same time. If we are honest, the second error is simply that they try too hard. The "best" solutions are often those which are so obvious that once found they seem so natural and comfortable that we cannot imagine how the solution had ever been unknown.

If a design solution is "forced" or "unnatural," then the system may also be forced and unnatural to use. The other enemies of the human problem solver are the elusive nature of creative moods and the inhibiting effect which fear or uncertainty have upon the logical processes of problem solving. The human mind has a tendency to "freeze" when doubts appear in the mental processes of the problem solver. Ideally, we need a method which will enable us to be creative in problem solving, even when we are not feeling particularly inspired, and which minimizes the risk of doubt or uncertainty entering our minds during the creative process.

Often, the less we try the better we perform, and conversely, the more we think about the processes we are undertaking the worse our performance is likely to become. This does not mean that we should not be concentrating or that we should lose concern about the acts we are performing; actually, the reverse is true. However, what a good designer must try to avoid in problem solving is being too involved in the process of expressing a solution. The key point (from a software design point of view) is that humans tend to be bad at concentrating on lots of things at the same time, while in contrast they tend to be very good at dealing with a few connected things and seeing the patterns within those few things. We can take advantage of this natural ability by splitting problems down into small parts and then concentrating on each of those parts in turn. This is the key method in top-down design or functional decomposition and forms the basis of structured systems design.

As an example to try and clarify the technique, let us try to express the logic involved in making a cup of coffee, since it is a problem which most readers will be familiar with in their daily lives. Since we are using a book format we will use structured English or pseudo-code as our structured technique, but the principle is the same for all techniques within structured design and only the notation differs. We will consider alternative notations (such as structure charts and data flow diagrams) toward the end of this article.

The following is an example of functional decomposition (pseudo-code for making a cup of coffee):

```
Making_A_Cup_Of_Coffee;
  Begin
      Prepare_All_The_Things_We_Need;
      Make_The_Cup_Of_Coffee;
      Drink_The_Cup_Of_Coffee;
  End; { Making_A_Cup_Of_Coffee }
```

In this example we have identified three major elements in the solution, but have made no effort in actually trying to define all the processes involved. As the next stage in our example we can take each one of these and expand them into more detail.

```
Prepare_All_The_Things_We_Need;
  Begin
      Get_A_Cup;
      Get_A_Spoon;
      Get_Some_Instant_Coffee;
```

```
    Get_Some_Milk;
    Get_Some_Sugar;
    Get_Some_Boiling_Water;
  End; { Prepare_All_The_Things_
    We_Need }

Make_The_Cup_Of_Coffee;
  Begin
    Put_Instant_Coffee_In_Cup;
    Pour_Boiling_Water_In_Cup;
    Pour_Milk_In_Cup;
    Stir_Contents_With_A_Spoon;
  End; { Make_The_Cup_Of_Coffee }

Drink_The_Cup_Of_Coffee;
  Begin
    Pick_Up_Cup_And_Drink_Contents;
  End; { Drink_The_Cup_Of_Coffee }
```

Hopefully, it is apparent that all we are doing in this method is expressing the parts of a solution at a high level and then taking each of these high-level solutions and expanding them until we have totally defined a solution to the problem.

B. Visual Representations within Structured Design

As we have already indicated, in addition to structured English or pseudo-code there are several design techniques associated with structured design that employ visual formats. The two most common formats are data flow diagrams and structure charts.

Of these two visual representations, structure charts are usually most closely linked to structured English or pseudo-code. It is therefore most natural that we discuss them at this point in this article.

1. Structure Charts

Structure charts are intended to give visual representations of the logical processes identified within the

design. There are some variations to the exact notation used in structure charts, but all include an inverted tree structure with boxes showing each of the main logical actions. If we continue our coffee making example, the first and highest level of the structure chart would look like the diagram in Fig. 1.

We can see from this simple chart that each box represents a major item of the design. These items are also called "modules" and are another key aspect of structured design. Modules allow the system design to be split into a series of subproblems, each of which can be split in turn into submodules and so on until the larger problem is solved when all the smaller submodules are working correctly. The concept of modularization also allows work to be split between individuals in large teams, provided that they all agree on what each module does and how it can be used. Typically, modules in large software designs have data items passed to the module and then expect other data items to be passed back at the end of the module's operation.

Splitting the software design into modules also allows the modules to be tested separately to ensure that they work correctly, provided that they have a single exit and entry point to the module.

In theory, should anything go wrong with the system or if it ever needed to be updated, the use of modules permits the person maintaining the system to know where each function is performed within the hierarchy of modules that make up the structure chart. It is not uncommon for the structured English or pseudo-code to be written in each of the module boxes that make up the structure chart. Whatever way the pseudo-code and structure chart are represented when combined, they should show the detailed design of the system.

C. Links between Modules: Coupling and Cohesion

At this point it is appropriate to highlight that simply splitting the system design into subcomponents does

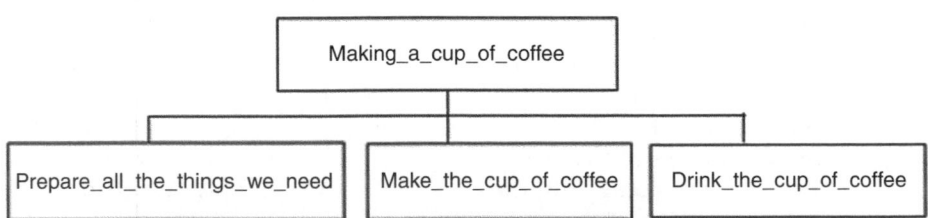

Figure 1 Structure chart for a coffee making example.

not automatically produce a "good design" which is easy to understand and, more importantly, easy to maintain. Early computer scientists who developed structured design methods rapidly found that the ways in which submodules interacted had a powerful impact on the quality of the final structured design. As a simple example imagine a situation where there is a system where the logic in one module uses or assumes the logic in another module to help perform its function. Such a link between modules within a design is known as "coupling" between the two modules and generally is regarded as a potential weakness in the system design.

Taking our simple coffee making example, imagine that in the module `Prepare_All_The_Things_We_Need` we have decided that we will be lazy or clever (depending on your viewpoint) and in the subcomponent `Get_A_Spoon` we will ensure that the spoon is clean by filling the kettle with water, boiling the water in the kettle, and then pouring the boiling water over the spoon before we use it. There is nothing wrong with such a process, provided we are careful where we pour the boiling water; however, if during the later modules in the coffee making system we assume that in the module `Get_Some_Boiling_Water` we already have a kettle full of preboiled water, problems can emerge.

To try and show a very simple example of such a problem we will quickly examine one of the possible unintended results of such a "coupled" module.

```
Prepare_All_The_Things_We_Need;
  Begin
   Get_A_Cup;
   Get_A_Spoon;
   Get_Some_Instant_Coffee;
   Get_Some_Milk;
   Get_Some_Sugar;
   Get_Some_Boiling_Water;
  End; { Prepare_All_The_Things_
   We_Need }

Get_A_Spoon;
  Begin
   Open_Kitchen_Draw;
   Pick_Up_Spoon;
   Fill_Kettle_With_Water;
   Boil_Kettle;
   Pour_Small_Amount_of_Boiling_
    Water_Over_Spoon;
  End; { Get_A_Spoon }

Get_Some_Boiling_Water;
  Begin
```

```
   { note we assume that the
    kettle is already full
    of water! }
   Boil_Kettle;
  End; { Get_Some_Boiling_Water; }
```

Now if at some later date in the system life the system is amended in either `Get_A_Spoon` or `Get_Some_Boiling_Water`, there is a possibility that the system will no longer function correctly. For example, a new programmer could look at the logic in `Get_A_Spoon` and decide that all spoons will be assumed to be clean and will remove the lines

```
Fill_Kettle_With_Water;
Boil_Kettle;
Pour_Small_Amount_of_Boiling_
  Water_Over_Spoon;
```

The system would then be

```
Get_A_Spoon;
    Begin
      Open_Kitchen_Draw;
      Pick_Up_Spoon;
    End; { Get_A_Spoon }
```

Assuming that the programmer making the amendment does not look in the module `Get_Some_Boiling_Water` since the programmer has no reason to do so, the code would remain

```
Get_Some_Boiling_Water;
    Begin
      { note we assume that the
       kettle is already full of
       water! }
     Boil_Kettle;
    End; { Get_Some_Boiling_Water; }
```

As a result of this change, sooner or later the system would fail to produce coffee since the kettle would sometimes be empty of water—depending on when it was last filled. Such changes as illustrated in this very simple coffee making example typically make errors or "bugs" in the system which are extremely difficult to correct since they are intermittent and do not always occur every time the system is run. A comprehensive study of these types of errors in modularization produced recommendations for designers to avoid coupling between modules and to produce modules which focused on performing only a single task. This last recommendation is often referred to as the "cohesion" of the module. Like all aspects of structured design, coupling and cohesion are complex topics and interested readers are referred to the references in the Bibliography for more information.

D. Logical Operations within Structured Design

Structured design does not just provide a notation in which to describe the design itself, it also provides some rules for coding and variable use which increase the ease with which designers can understand each other's software designs.

Part of the research that helped form structured design found that most of the logical operations (that is all the things we might want to perform on a digital computer) can be achieved by the use of three different types of operations:

- Sequence: Doing something in a specific order
- Selection: Making a decision
- Repetition: Doing something a number of times

In order to further understand structured design, we can look at each of these logical structures in greater detail.

1. Sequence

When I said "Doing something in a specific order" earlier, what I meant was that we were performing a series of actions which have to be done in a specific order. An example of this might be making a cup of coffee. In this example it would be wrong to try to perform one of the actions in the sequence out of order. For example, we could end up drinking cold water if we had not boiled the water before we poured it into the cup.

2. Selection

This is making a choice between a number of alternatives. Real-world systems spend a large amount of their time making such decisions. In fact, one of the most fundamental aspects of intelligence is thought to be the ability to decide among alternatives. Apart from such abstract considerations, you will probably find that the more complex your designs become, the more selections will become necessary.

Within our design the major selection mechanism is called the "If-Then-Else" statement.

It takes the form of

```
IF conditional_expression THEN
    Statement1
ELSE Statement2
```

Statement1 is executed (executed simply means that the computer will obey that statement) if the Condi-

tional_expression is true, otherwise Statement2 will be obeyed and Statement1 will be ignored. It is important to realize that either Statement1 or Statement2 will be executed, but never both.

3. Repetition

These are where a series of statements are repeated a number of times. These so-called looping constructs (or statements) have three main variants: the Repeat Until, While Do, and For loops.

a. The "Repeat Until" Loop

```
Repeat
    Statement1
Until Conditional_expression
```

This looping construct obeys the statements inside the keywords "Repeat" and "Until." Each time the program reaches the "Until," the Conditional_expression is evaluated, and if it is false the program goes back to the Repeat part of the code. However, if the Conditional_expression found at the end of the loop is found to be true, the program leaves the loop and continues to the next statement after the Until.

An example will probably be the best way of demonstrating this process. Assume that we are using pseudocode to express a situation where a lecturer continues to talk until the end of the lecture, which for convenience we can assume is 4:15 p.m. We could express this in the following way.

```
Program Lecturer;
Begin
    Enter_classroom;
    Repeat
        Talk;
    Until Time = 4:15pm
    Leave_the_class_room;
End; { Program Lecturer }
```

In this example the lecturer enters the classroom and immediately begins to talk, after each utterance he checks his watch to see if it is time for the lesson to end (4:15 PM). If it is not 4:15 PM the lecturer continues to talk, and this process repeats until the lecturer's watch displays the value 4:15 PM.

b. The "While Do" Loop

```
While Conditional_expression Do
Begin
    Statement1;
End; { While Conditional_expression
  Do  }
```

The other major looping mechanism (or method) is called the While Do loop. This loop tests the terminating condition before it starts repeating the statements contained inside the loop (note that this is in contrast to the Repeat Until loop which checks the terminating condition after it has obeyed the contents of the loop at least once). In the While Do loop the beginning and end of the section of logic that will be repeated is denoted by the keywords "Begin" and "End." If when the Conditional_expression is evaluated (or tested) the result is true, then the program enters the loop and obeys all the statements inside that loop. When it reaches the end of the loop it returns to the beginning and checks the Conditional_expression again. So long as the result of this test is true, the statements within the loop will be executed again and again. It is only when the Conditional_expression produces a false value that the program will stop obeying the statements within the While loop. For an example of the While Do loop we could revisit the lecture example above and contrast the previous lecturer with one that continues to talk as long as there are people listening, regardless of the time.

```
Program Lecturer2;
Begin
    Enter_classroom;
    While Someone_Listening Do
    Begin
        Talk;
    End; { While Someone_Listening
       Do } Leave_the_class_room;
End; { Program Lecturer2 }
```

In this example the lecturer will enter the classroom, but will only start talking if there is someone to listen. The lecturer will talk and continue to talk as long as there is someone listening. However, as soon as they stop listening, the lecturer will stop talking and leave the classroom.

c. THE "FOR" LOOP

```
FOR Variable_Name = Initial_value TO
   Terminating_Value Do
Begin
    Statement1;
End; { FOR Do }
```

The For loop is rather different from the other examples we have been looking at, because when we use the For loop we know in advance exactly how many times we want to execute the statements inside the loop. It is also different because it involves (and therefore introduces) the use of a counter or variable. This variable can best be described as the counter which the program will use to count how many times the statements inside the loop will be obeyed. Before the program can perform a For loop it has to know some other items of information, as you would if I told you to repeat a set series of actions. The programmer and the program need to know how many times to perform the actions. To give the program this information, the For loop insists that the programmer tell it how to use the variable it will use as a counter for the loop. The easiest way to do this would be to say to the program "obey this loop a number of times, using a specific variable, from the value of one to a terminating value." This would be one possible way of specifying a For loop, but we would lose a large amount of the usefulness (called functionality) of the For loop if we did specify it in this way. For example, often we will want to start and finish the For loop counter at specific values, say counting from the initial value 6 to the terminating value 24, which would make the statements in the loop be repeated a total of 18 times. As always, an example might be helpful, so imagine that we have a lecturer who has a habit of asking members of his class questions. However, he wants to be sure that he never picks on any one member of the class more than any other. To do this he has given each member of the class a number, and he starts his questions with the student he associates with number one, then two, and so on until the whole class has been asked a question and has replied. We could show the logic involved in this by the following pseudo-code:

```
Program Lecturer3;
Variables
    Student_Number = 0; Integer;
    Starting_Student_No = 1; Integer;
    No_of_Students = 16; Integer;
Begin
    Enter_classroom;
    FOR Student_Number = Starting_
      Student_No TO No_of_Students Do
    Begin
        Ask_Student_a_question
           (Student_Number);
    End; { FOR Do }
    Leave_the_class_room;
End; { Program Lecturer3 }
```

V. VARIABLE TYPES IN STRUCTURED DESIGN

In the previous example we introduced a name for the counter. This is called a variable (a name which has a value associated with it), so-called because the value it holds varies. In this case the variable is called Student_Number, and the For loop controls the way in which the value associated with the name varies. We can see that this variable starts at the value 1 (Starting_Student_No) and then proceeds by increments (additions) of the value 1 until it reaches the value 16 (No_of_Students). The statements between the Begin and End are therefore obeyed 16 times.

The For loop is often described as being like a While loop where the counter is tested for equality with a value greater than the terminating condition. Of course, this assumes that the counter is incremented by the value 1 inside the While loop, as is the case in the following example:

```
Program A_For_Loop;
Variable
    For_loop_counter = 0; Integer;
Begin
    For_loop_counter = Initial_value;

    While For_loop_counter NOT=
       (Terminating_Value + 1) DO
    Begin
        Do_Something;
        For_loop_counter = For_loop_
           counter + 1;
    End; { While DO}
End; { Program A_For_Loop }
```

VI. VARIABLE TYPES AND STRUCTURED DESIGN

The For loop forced us to encounter things called variables. These are best described as being like containers which have a unique name. The container can hold a value, and the values held inside these containers can be made to vary. Variables allow us to become much more detailed in our design solutions.

We imagine that each variable is like a container into which we can place a value, which we can inspect or change when we refer to that variable name. The similarity to a container allows us to introduce "types" of variable. The type of a variable is determined by the characteristics of the container, just like any other container. If we had a wire basket we could place certain objects such as bread inside it, but it would be unsuitable to try to store water within it. It is just the same with computer variables.

Prior to structured design most designers used any type of data location in computer memory as a storage location for any and all data within their program. This was very efficient in terms of memory us-

age, but it made the programs very difficult to understand. One of the breakthroughs in structured design was the idea of unique variable names and data types for each variable used in the design. The basic types of variables we need to know about at this stage are the following:

- Integer: Variables which are of this type can hold whole numbers without decimal places, i.e., 1, 2, 3, 4, etc., but not any numbers with decimal places.
- Real: Variables of this type can hold numbers with decimal places, i.e., 35.75734, 6.2, 23.33, etc. They can also hold whole numbers, but only in the form 1.000, 2.000, etc.
- Strings: Variables of this type can hold text, but not numbers (either real or integer) unless they are text, in which case you cannot perform arithmetic on them, i.e., "James Kirk," "Degree in Information Science," "My age is 123," etc.
- Boolean: Variables of this type can hold one of two values, either "True" or "False."

Now that we have the major elements needed to design solutions, we can proceed on to an example of a more complex problem since we can then illustrate some more advanced features of structured design.

VII. THE COINS IN STACKS EXAMPLE

Assume that we have the task of sorting coins which we have taken from our savings. We can assume that we are fortunate in that we only collected the following coins: 10 pence, 20 pence, 50 pence, and 100 pence or 1 pound, respectively. The task for your program is to collect the coins into stacks of like coins.

One possible solution to this would be the following:

```
Program Coins_Into_Stacks;
 Begin
    While Not(End_of_Coins) Do
    Begin
       Pick_Up_Next_Coin;
       If 10p Then
            Put_In_10p_Stack;
       Else If 20p Then
              Put_In_20p_Stack;
          Else If 50p Then
                 Put_In_50p_
                    Stack;
             Else If 1_Pound
                Then
                    Put_In_1_
                       Pound_
                       Stack;
```

```
      End; { While Do}
   End; {Program Coins_Into_Stacks}
```

Note that when we have a series of If statements all chained together (called nesting) we indent them on the page. This is quite important since it makes it much easier to read and understand. However, even though we have successfully placed the coins into stacks, we still have no idea of the value of the coins. To do this we need variables. Compare the two design solutions (provided above and below), and try to see how variables allow us to calculate the exact value of the coins.

```
   Program Coins_Into_Stacks2;
   Variables
      Ten_Pence_Stack = 0; Real;
      Twenty_Pence_Stack = 0; Real;
      Fifty_Pence_Stack = 0; Real;
      One_Pound_Stack = 0; Real;
   Begin
      While Not(End_of_Coins) Do
       Begin
         Pick_Up_Next_Coin;

         If 10p Then
          Begin
           Ten_Pence_Stack =
             Ten_Pence_Stack + 1;
           Put_In_10p_Stack;
          End
         Else If 20p Then
             Begin
              Twenty_Pence_Stack =
                Twenty_Pence_
                Stack + 1;
              Put_In_20p_Stack;
             End
            Else If 50p Then
               Begin
                Fifty_Pence_
                  Stack =
                  Fifty_Pence_
                  Stack + 1;
                Put_In_50p_
                  Stack;
               End
              Else If 1_Pound
                  Then
                 Begin
                  One_
                  Pound_
                  Stack =
                  One_
                  Pound_
                  Stack + 1;
                  Put_In_
                  1_Pound_
                  Stack;
                 End
      End; { While Do}

   Ten_Pence_Stack = (Ten_Pence_Stack /
     100) * 10;
   Twenty_Pence_Stack = (Twenty_Pence_
     Stack / 100) * 20;
   Fifty_Pence_Stack = (Fifty_Pence_
     Stack / 100) * 50;
   One_Pound_Stack = (One_Pound_Stack
     / 100) * 100;

   End; {Program Coins_Into_Stacks2}
```

This example introduces a few extra features of our design method that we have not needed in our previous solutions. First, we have made our variables of the type "Real," as opposed to "Integer." Real numbers are numbers which allow the specification of decimal places, while integers are only whole numbers without any decimal places. For example, the value 4.23 would be a real number, and the value 4 would be an integer number.

In the previous example we used decimal or real numbers to allow us to calculate the value of the coins in the different value stacks. One of the things you will notice if you study the calculations after the end of the While Do loop is that they are all very similar. In fact, they share the basic components of their calculations. If we had a large number of stacks to total we would find ourselves duplicating the basic components of our calculations. Obviously, this would be a waste of time and effort.

Instead, we can use something called a function, which will hold the basic parts of our calculation and will hand us back the answer every time we hand it the basic information it needs to perform that calculation. These items of information which we pass to the function are known as parameters and are shown within brackets when we call the function name. So if we wished to rewrite the last lines from the coin stack calculations we would define a function and call it in the following way:

```
   Function Convert_Count_To_
     Pence(Count_Value, Coin_Value_
     In_Pence) : Real
   Begin
     Convert_Count_To_Pence =
       (Count_Value / 100) *
       Coin_Value_In_Pence;
   End { Convert_Count_To_Pence }
```

Notice that the name of the function (the first line of the function) ends with the declaration of the type of result it will return when it is called. In this case that type is "Real." Within the function the names of the parameters (the names provided in the first line of the function) are used within the function as if they were variables. When the function is called, the values you hand to the function as parameters are substituted into the names you have defined within the function. It is very important that you realize that these names only exist inside the function. You cannot use them as variables anywhere else, otherwise you will be introducing coupling into your module design (see Section IV.C to understand why coupling is considered an error in structured design). So if we wished to use (or call) the function "Convert_Count_ To_Pence" in our program, we would substitute each of the old lines of calculation for new calls of the function. The following is an example which will try to show this by providing the old calculation and then the new function call.

Old way of calculating values:

```
Ten_Pence_Stack = (Ten_Pence_Stack /
    100) * 10;
```

New way using a function:

```
Ten_Pence_Stack = Convert_Count_To_
    Pence(Ten_Pence_Stack,10);
```

Old way of calculating values:

```
Twenty_Pence_Stack = (Twenty_Pence_
    Stack / 100) * 20;
```

New way using a function:

```
Twenty_Pence_Stack = Convert_Count_
    To_Pence(Twenty_Pence_Stack,20);
```

Old way of calculating values:

```
Fifty_Pence_Stack = (Fifty_Pence_
    Stack / 100) * 50;
```

New way using a function:

```
Fifty_Pence_Stack = Convert_Count_
    To_Pence(Fifty_Pence_Stack,50);
```

Old way of calculating values:

```
One_Pound_Stack = (One_Pound_Stack /
    100) * 100;
```

New way using a function:

```
One_Pound_Stack = Convert_Count_To_
    Pence(One_Pound_Stack,100);
```

VIII. FUNCTIONS AND PROCEDURES

There is another similar concept to the function and it is called the procedure. Procedures and functions are the major building blocks designers try to use when they are producing structured pseudo-code solutions. In all our previous examples we have been using both functions and procedures whenever we named a part in our design, an example would be "Make_The_Cup_Of_Coffee."

In the proceeding sections we have tried to outline some of the fundamental aspects of structured systems design.

A. Data Flow Diagrams

So far in our discussions about structured design we have limited ourselves to those aspects of structured design which focus on the procedural or logical design of systems. This is because for most designers such aspects are the most critical in the design of a computer software system. However, any discussion of structured systems design would not be complete without mention of another alternative view of systems design, namely, data flow diagrams.

Data flow diagrams take a completely different view of systems than that of the strictly logical and procedural which we have considered in the preceding sec-

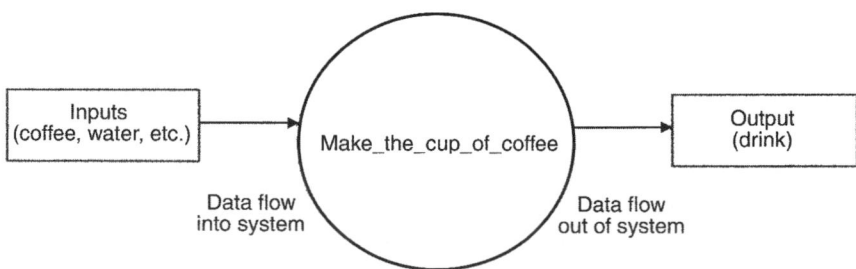

Figure 2 Data flow diagram for a coffee making example.

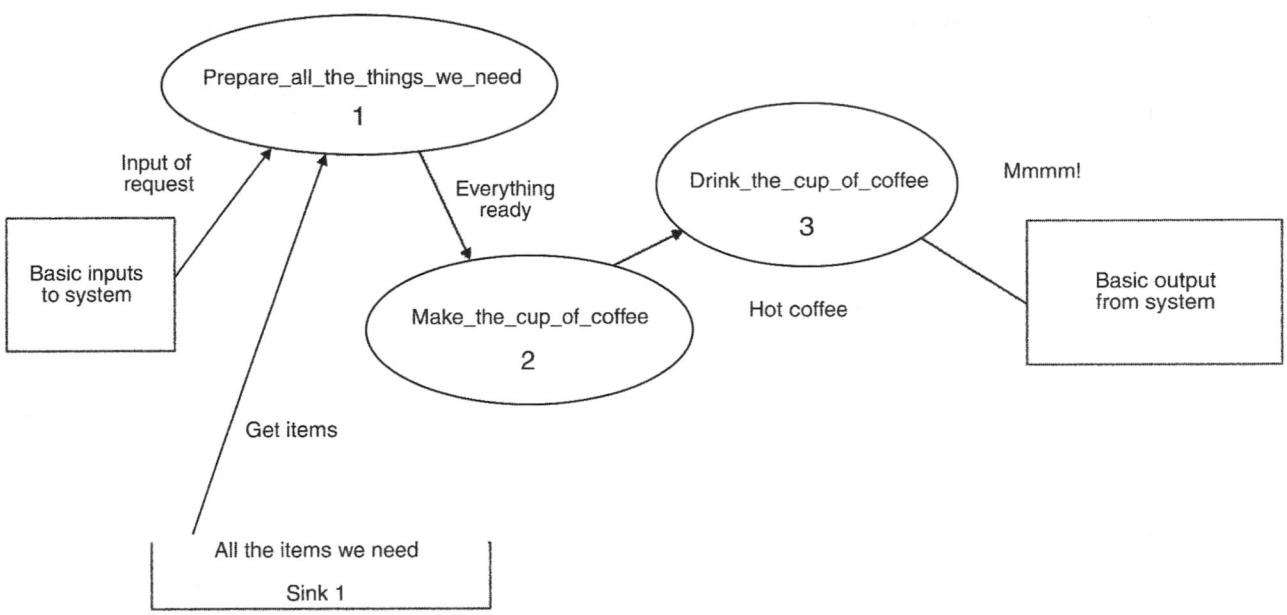

Figure 3 Detailed data flow diagram.

tions on structured English and structure charts. Instead of focusing on the sequence of operations which need to be performed in order to solve a problem, data flow diagrams attempt to describe a systems design in terms of the transformations to data and the data flows which occur within the system.

Although these are two quite different ways of viewing systems, they can compliment each other extremely well. Often a design for a system is described using both notations in order to confirm that the designer has a firm understanding of the problem to be addressed by the design.

Taking our original problem of making a cup of coffee, the same problem can be expressed using data flows (as in Fig. 2). This clearly shows that the problem, if broken down into data flows and processes, still uses a structured or top-down approach.

More detail is only considered as the data flow diagram develops in more and more detail at lower levels (as in Fig. 3). Data flow diagrams are most often used in conjunction with database design to allow the designer to identify where in the system access is needed to files and data stores. When combined with structured English and the structure chart, the designer has a complete view of the system.

IX. SUMMARY

As we have seen, structured design is a disciplined approach to information systems design based on a series of techniques for factoring information systems design into independent modules. In the process of functional decomposition of top-down design, the major logical components or data transformations within the system are identified and relationships between them are established.

Designs are developed using a semiformal notation, usually in terms of either the logical processes (pseudo-code or structured English) or the data flows (data flow diagrams) within the system in a top-down hierarchy of modules or processes. Design decisions are based on what the problem is and not on how it is to be solved. Structured design uses tools and formal notations, especially graphic ones, to render systems understandable.

The following are design techniques common to all structured design methodologies:

- Top-down design (functional decomposition): Top-down design specifies the solution to a problem in general terms and then divides the solution into finer and finer details until no more detail is necessary.
- Modularization: This is a concept to help the designer and later the programmer to break a complex design into smaller sub-designs often called modules (see also procedures and functions).
- Modules: This is a set of design solving actions or data transformations that can be tested and verified independently of their use in a larger design. Well-designed modules have hierarchical

relationships made up of a series of modules, each with their own function (cohesion) and with a simple control path which features a single entry and exit point (no or low coupling).

- Use of the three control constructs: The pseudocode or structured English produced within structured design should limit itself to using the three control constructs of sequence, selection, and repetition.

X. CONCLUSIONS

The goals of using structured design are to produce effective correctly functioning systems which are easily understood, easily modified, easily updated, and easily tested.

Due to the success of structured design methods many commercial companies offer their own variants of these principles in a complete off the shelf package.

XI. THE FUTURE

Although structured design is not given great emphasis in many popular textbooks or design courses, the good design principles pioneered by structured design are the basis for many of the aspects of object-orientated design methods.

Object hierarchies and object typing are the logical extensions of top-down design, variable typing, and modularization. Software reuse and libraries are the logical extension of modularization and sub-routines. Thus, we can see that structured design has formed the principles of good design which will continue to influence design in the foreseeable future.

SEE ALSO THE FOLLOWING ARTICLES

Computer-Aided Design • Data Flow Diagrams • Error Detecting and Correcting Codes • Flowcharting Techniques • Program Design, Coding, and Testing • Prototyping • Pseudocode • Systems Design • System Development Life Cycle • Systems Implementation

BIBLIOGRAPHY

DeMarco, T. (1982). *Controlling Software Projects.* Englewood Cliffs, NJ: Prentice-Hall.

DeMarco, T. (1978). *Structured Analysis and System Specification.* Englewood Cliffs, NJ: Prentice-Hall.

Dijkstra, E. (1968). Go to statement considered harmful. *Communications ACM.* 11(2), February: 147–148.

Gane, C., and Sarson, T. (1979). *Structured Systems Analysis.* Englewood Cliffs, NJ: Prentice-Hall.

Hatley, D. J., and Pirbhai, I. A. (1987). *Strategies for Real-Time System Specification.* New York: Dorest House Publishing Co.

Page-Jones, M. (1980). *The Practical Guide to Structured Systems Design.* Englewood Cliffs, NJ: Prentice-Hall.

Yourdon, E. (1991). *Modern Structured Analysis.* Englewood Cliffs, NJ: Prentice-Hall.

Yourdon, E., and Constantine, L. (1975). *Structured Design.* Englewood Cliffs, NJ: Prentice-Hall.

Ward, P. T., and Mellor, S. J. (1985). *Structured Development for Real-Time Systems, Volume 1: Introduction & Tools; Volume 2: Essential Modeling Techniques; Volume 3: Implementation Modeling Techniques.* New York: Yourdon Press.

Structured Query Language

Catherine M. Ricardo

Iona College

GLOSSARY

ANSI (American National Standards Institute) A United States based organization that develops and publishes national standards in several areas, including information processing.

candidate key An attribute or set of attributes that uniquely identifies tuples, and that therefore could be used as the primary key of a relation.

DDL (data definition language) The commands used to create the structures of a database.

DML (data manipulation language) The commands to insert, retrieve, update, and delete data in a database.

domain The set of allowable values for an attribute.

foreign key An attribute or set of attributes within a relation that matches the primary key or candidate key of some, usually different, relation.

index A method used to speed up access to records on the basis of the value of a field (or fields) called the indexed field. A file is constructed containing those values and the locations of records having those values.

ISO (International Standards Organization) An international organization that develops and publishes international standards in areas such as information processing.

join An operation on two (or more) tables that involves comparing values of specified attributes in tuples of each. If they satisfy the join condition, the tuples are concatenated and placed in the results table.

natural join A join operation on two tables having common columns in which tuples having the same values for the common columns are concatenated, with the common column(s) appearing only once in the result.

primary key An attribute or set of attributes used to uniquely identify tuples of a table.

query A question or enquiry that requires retrieving data from the database.

relational schema The structure of a relational database, including its domains, tables, views, character sets, constraints, authorizations, and other related information.

tuple A row of a table, corresponding to a single record.

I. INTRODUCTION

SQL, structured query language, is the standard language for creating and maintaining relational databases. Most relational database management systems, even those with proprietary languages of their own, support some version of SQL. The language allows users to create and modify the schema of a relational database using the data definition language component. Users can insert, delete, and update the data in the database and perform queries on the data using the SQL data manipulation language component. The database administrator can control access to the database using the SQL data control language component. Since its inception over 30 years ago, SQL has undergone many changes, and the language is still evolving to keep pace with new requirements.

II. HISTORY OF SQL

E. F. Codd, the originator of the relational model, described the model in a seminal paper, "A Relational Model of Data for Large Shared Data Banks," published in 1970, while he was employed at the IBM Research Laboratory in San Jose, California. D.D. Chamberlin and others working at the laboratory subsequently created a language called SEQUEL, or structured English query language, for the relational model. The original language was described in a 1974 paper and a later version, called SEQUEL2, was described in a 1976 paper. The language was implemented in a prototype relational database management system called System R, developed at the laboratory in the mid-1970s. Its name was changed to SQL when it was discovered that the acronym SEQUEL was already in use. An early commercial database management system, ORACLE, was developed in the late 1970s using SQL as its language. IBM also developed SQL/DS, a commercial relational database based on System R and released in 1981. IBM's DB2, also using SQL as its language, was released in 1983. Since then, dozens of relational database management systems have incorporated SQL.

The American National Standards Institute (ANSI) adopted specifications for the SQL language and published them in 1986. This standard, generally referred to as SQL1 or SQL-86, was also adopted by the International Standards Organization (ISO) at that time. A minor revision, SQL-89, was published 3 years later, followed by a major revision, SQL2, in 1992, approved by both ANSI and ISO. Work has continued on the language, with major developments, such as inclusion of user-defined data types and object-oriented data management capabilities, incorporated in the SQL3 standard, the first parts of which were published in 1999 and referred to as SQL:1999. Most vendors of relational database management systems use their own extensions of the language, creating a variety of dialects around the standard.

III. SQL DATA MANIPULATION LANGUAGE

SQL can be described as a declarative query language, which means that it indicates the data to be retrieved without specifying the procedures for retrieving it. It can be used as an interactive language supporting ad hoc queries, as an embedded language in a host programming language, or as a computationally complete language in itself using SQL/PSM (persistent stored modules). The fundamental SQL data manipulation language (DML) commands include the SELECT, UPDATE, DELETE, and INSERT statements. Of these, the SELECT is the most complex, having many options. We will illustrate ad hoc SQL commands using the small sample database, OrderSystem, shown in Fig. 1. The tables are

Customer(CustID, CustName, CustCity, CreditRating)

Item(ItemNo, ItemName, Price, Supplier, QtyOnHand)

Order(OrderNo, *CustID, ItemNo,* QtyOrdered)

We have underlined the primary keys in each relation and noted the foreign keys in the Order table, CustID, and ItemNo, by using italics.

A. The SELECT Statement

The SELECT statement is used to define queries. Its general form is

SELECT	[DISTINCT] col-name [AS newname], [,col-name..]...
FROM	table-name [alias] [,table-name]...
[WHERE	predicate]
[GROUP BY	col-name [,col-name]...[HAVING predicate]]

or

[ORDER BY	col-name [,col-name]...];

Applying a SELECT statement to a relation results in a table that may have duplicate rows. Since duplicates are allowed in such a table, it is not a set in the strict mathematical sense, and therefore it is not a relation. It is referred to as a multiset or a bag. As indicated by the absence of square brackets, the SELECT and the FROM clauses are required. The following examples provide an overview of some of the variations of the statement.

1. Retrieval with a Condition

EXAMPLE

Find the names and Ids of all customers in New York.

SELECT	CustName, CustID
FROM	Customer

Customer	CustID	CustName	CustCity	CreditRating
	C101	Martinez	New York	20
	C105	Jones	London	20
	C110	LeBlanc	Paris	15
	C118	Wright	New York	10
	C125	LeBlanc	Montreal	18

Item	ItemNo	ItemName	Price	Supplier	QtyOnHand
	I1001	widget	2.99	Ace	200
	I1004	manifold	5.50	Acme	
	I1010	widget	3.75	Wright	150
	I1015	brace	6.80	Ace	16

Order	OrderNo	CustID	ItemNo	QtyOrdered
	O10101	C101	I1004	50
	O10102	C105	I1010	30
	O10103	C118	I1015	5
	O10104	C101	I1001	30
	O10105	C125	I1015	10

Figure 1 The OrderSystem Database.

WHERE   CustCity = 'New York';

Result:

CustName	CustID
Martinez	C101
Wright	C118

Note that we can optionally include the table name before the column name, using dot notation, as in SELECT Customer.CustName, Customer.CustID... .

2. Use of * to Denote "All Columns"

EXAMPLE
Find all details of orders for item number I1015.

SELECT   *

FROM   Order

WHERE   ItemNo = 'I1015';

Result:

OrderNo	CustID	ItemNo	QtyOrdered
O10103	C118	I1015	5
O10105	C125	I1015	10

3. Retrieval with No Condition; Use of DISTINCT

EXAMPLE
Find the item numbers of all items that have been ordered by customers.

SELECT   ItemNo

FROM   Order;

Result:

ItemNo
I1004
I1010
I1015
I1001
I1015

Notice that we have duplicates in the result. To prevent duplicate rows, we use the word DISTINCT in the SELECT clause, as in

SELECT   DISTINCT ItemNo

FROM   Order;

This eliminates the last row of the results table shown above, so that I1015 appears only once.

4. Retrieving an Entire Table

EXAMPLE
Find all the information about all items.

SELECT   *

FROM   Item;

The result is the entire Item table.

5. Using ORDER BY; Using AS

EXAMPLE

Get Ids, names, and credit rating of all customers in New York, in decreasing order by credit rating.

SELECT   CustID AS CustomerNumber, Cust-Name, CreditRating

FROM   Customer

WHERE   CustCity = 'New York'

ORDER BY   CreditRating DESC;

Result:	CustomerNumber	CustName	CreditRating
	C101	Martinez	20
	C118	Wright	10

Note that if we wanted increasing order we could have written ASC in place of DESC, or left it out, since ASC is the default. We could also specify a second column for minor order, to be used in the event of a tie in values of the first column. In this example, we also illustrated the use of AS, which allows us to rename a column for display in the results table.

6. Using Complex Conditions; Testing for Null Values; Using BETWEEN

EXAMPLE

Find the names and item numbers of all items with price over 3.00 and quantity on hand at least 200.

SELECT   ItemName, ItemNo

FROM   Item

WHERE   Price >3.00 AND QtyOnHand >= 200;

There are no tuples that satisfy both parts of the condition, so the result multiset is empty. Comparison operators in SQL are $=, <, >, <=, >=, <>$, or $!=$. The logical connectives AND, OR, and NOT are also used. The standard order of operations is used in evaluating complex expressions. An attribute cannot be tested for null values by using the standard equality or inequality operators. Instead, we use IS NULL or IS NOT NULL. For example, to find records of all items where the QtyOnHand is null, we write

SELECT   *

FROM   Item

WHERE   QtyOnHand IS NULL:

This query retrieves the record of item I1004. BE-TWEEN can be used to specify that an attribute's value must be within a range of values, or NOT BETWEEN to specify that it is outside that range. For example, if we wanted to find customers with credit ratings between 15 and 19 in descending order, we could write

SELECT   CustID, CreditRating

FROM   Customer

WHERE   CreditRating BETWEEN 15 AND 19

ORDER BY   CreditRating DESC;

Result:	CustID	CreditRating
	C125	18
	C110	15

Note that the end values of the range are included.

7. Natural Join

Queries often involve choosing from two tables the rows that have matching values on a common column.

EXAMPLE

Find the OrderNo, CustID, and ItemNo of all orders placed by customer Martinez of New York.

SELECT   OrderNo, Order.CustID, ItemNo

FROM   Order, Customer

WHERE   CustName = 'Martinez' AND CustCity = 'New York' AND Customer.CustID = Order.CustID;

Result:	OrderNo	Order.CustID	ItemNo
	O10101	C101	I1004
	O10104	C101	I1001

Notice that we must include the final condition, stating that the CustID columns of the two tables are equal. Since the names of those columns are the same, we need to use both table names and column names to specify which table we are referring to. However, for any column that appears on only one of the two tables listed in the FROM clause, we can give the attribute name only. If we omit the equality condition in the WHERE clause, we get the Cartesian product instead of the natural join. We can do the more general theta-join by substituting any desired predicate in the WHERE clause.

Joins can also be performed on three or more tables.

EXAMPLE

Find the order information and the names of the suppliers of all the parts ordered by any customer with a credit rating below 20.

```
SELECT    Order.*, Supplier

FROM      Customer, Order, Item

WHERE     CreditRating < 20      AND

          Customer.CustID = Order.CustID
          AND
          Order.ItemNo = Item.ItemNo;
```

		Order.	Order.		
Result:	OrderNo	CustID	ItemNo	QtyOrdered	Supplier
	O10103	C118	I1015	5	Ace
	O10105	C125	I1015	10	Ace

8. Using Aliases

It is sometimes necessary to compare a table with itself. In that case, it would be useful to have two different names for the same table, so that we could refer to them as if there were two copies of the table. An alias allows us to do this. We introduce the alias for the table by simply writing the new name immediately after the actual name in the FROM clause.

EXAMPLE

Find the ItemNo and names of all the pairs of items that have the same name as each other.

```
SELECT    A.ItemNo, A.ItemName, B.ItemNo

FROM      Item A, Item B

WHERE     A.ItemName = B.ItemName AND
          A.ItemNo < B.ItemNo;
```

Result:	A.ItemNo	A.ItemName	B.ItemNo
	I1001	widget	I1010

Here, A and B are aliases for Item. Note that the WHERE clause, A.ItemNo < B.ItemNo, was included so that the results record I1010, widget, I1001, with the same items reversed, would not appear.

9. Using a Subquery

A join can sometimes be replaced by a nested query, called a subquery. For example, suppose we want to find the names of all customers who have ordered part I1015. We know how to write this as a join, namely

```
SELECT    CustName

FROM      Customer, Order

WHERE     ItemNo = 'I1015' AND

          Customer.CustID = Order.CustID;
```

Instead of doing this query as a join, we could break up the process into two queries. For the first query, we would examine the Order table, locate the rows where the ItemNo is I1015, and note the CustID. Then we would query the Customer table to find the rows with those Ids and display the customer names. An SQL subquery lets us sequence these queries so that the results of the first are available to be used in the second. The first query is nested inside the second, using parentheses. The form of this query is

```
SELECT    CustName

FROM      Customer

WHERE     CustID  IN  (SELECT  CustID

                       FROM    Order

                       WHERE   ItemNo = 'I1015');
```

The inner, nested query is done first and the results are stored in a temporary table that can be accessed by the main, outer query. Because a set of values may be returned, we have used the word IN before the subquery. However, we could use any of the relational operators instead of IN provided the subquery will return a single value.

The result of the nested query is

CustID
C118
C125

The result of the main query is

CustName
Wright
LeBlanc

Subqueries can be nested several levels. Not all join queries can be replaced by subqueries. There are several rules governing their use, including the rule that only one column name or expression can follow the SELECT clause in the subquery if you are comparing values. Another difference is that a join query keeps duplicate names, while a subquery eliminates them.

10. Using EXISTS and NOT EXISTS

Suppose we want to find the name and city of all customers who have ordered item I1015. We could write this as a join or a subquery. A different way of writing the query would be to use the existential quantifier, EXISTS, with a subquery. We could phrase the question as, "Find the name and city of those customers for whom there exists an Order record with ItemNo of I1015." The query is

SELECT   CustName, CustCity

FROM   Customer

WHERE   EXISTS (SELECT   *

                 FROM   Order

                 WHERE   ItemNo = 'I1015'

                 AND Customer. CustID = Order. CustID);

Note that here we can refer to the outer table, Customer, within the subquery. This is called a correlated subquery. The result is

CustName	CustCity
Wright	New York
LeBlanc	Montreal

A more interesting question is to find the names and cities of those customers who have no orders for item I1015, which could be rephrased as, "Find the name and city of those customers for whom there exists no Order record for item I1015." The query is

SELECT CustName, CustCity

FROM Customer

WHERE NOT EXISTS (SELECT *

                 FROM   Order

                 WHERE   ItemNo = 'I1015'

                 AND Order. CustID = Customer. CustID);

Result:	CustName	CustCity
	Martinez	New York
	Jones	London
	LeBlanc	Paris

11. Scalar Functions

Each of the aggregate functions, COUNT, SUM, AVG, MIN, and MAX, operates on a single column of data at a time and returns a single value for that column. The functions appear either in the SELECT clause or the WHERE clause of an SQL statement. The values returned are as follows:

COUNT returns the number of values in a column

SUM returns the sum of the values of a numeric column

AVG returns the average (mean) of the values of a numeric column

MIN returns the smallest value in a column

MAX returns the largest value in a column

EXAMPLE

Find the highest credit rating of customers.

SELECT   MAX(CreditRating)

FROM   Customer;

Result: 20

Except for COUNT(*), each of the aggregate functions eliminates null values first and operates on the remaining values in the column. For example, if we write

SELECT   AVG(QtyOnHand) AS AverageQty

FROM   Item;

we obtain

AverageQty
122

because the total of the nonnull values, 366, is divided by 3, not 4. If we wish to eliminate duplicates before applying one of these functions, we use the word DISTINCT before the column name. For example, to find the number of different customer names that exist, we write

SELECT   COUNT (DISTINCT CustName) AS count

FROM   Customer;

Result:	count
	4

The function can also appear in the WHERE line. For example, to find the records of customers whose credit rating is below average, we write

SELECT   *

FROM   Customer

WHERE   CreditRating < (SELECT AVG(CreditRating FROM Customer);

Result:	CustID	CustName	CustCity	CreditRating
	C110	LeBlanc	Paris	15
	C118	Wright	New York	10

To find the Id and name of the customer(s) with the lowest credit rating, we would write

SELECT   CustID, CustName

FROM   Customer

WHERE   CreditRating = (SELECT MIN(Credit Rating) FROM Customer);

Result:	CustID	CustName
	C118	Wright

The COUNT(*) is a special use of the COUNT function. It counts the number of rows in a table, regardless of whether they are null or duplicates. For example, to find the number of rows in the Order table, we write,

SELECT   COUNT(*)

FROM   Order;

Result: 5

We can apply this function even if a WHERE clause is specified. For example, to find the number of customers in New York, we write

SELECT   COUNT(*) AS NYCustomers

FROM   Customer

WHERE   CustCity = 'New York';

Result:	NYCustomers
	2

We use the GROUP BY clause to group together all the records with a single value in a specified field. We can then apply any function to any field in each group, provided the result is a single value for the group. For example, to find the total of quantity ordered for each item, we would write

SELECT   ItemNo, COUNT(ItemNo) AS CountOrders, SUM(QtyOrdered) AS NumberOrdered

FROM   Order

GROUP BY ItemNo;

Result:	ItemNo	CountOrders	NumberOrdered
	I1004	1	50
	I1010	1	30
	I1015	2	15
	I1001	1	30

The HAVING clause can be added to a GROUP BY clause to specify a property for the groups that appear in the results table. For the previous example, if we wished to find the total of quantity ordered for each item, provided there is more than one order for the item, we would write

SELECT   ItemNo, COUNT(OrderNo) AS Count Orders, SUM(QtyOrdered) AS Number Ordered

FROM   Order

GROUP BY ItemNo

HAVING   COUNT(OrderNo) > 1;

This time the result is

ItemNo	CountOrders	NumberOrdered
1015	2	15

SQL3 supports a number of other scalar functions, including CURRENT_DATE, CURRENT_TIME, CURRENT_TIMESTAMP, CURRENT_USER, SESSION_USER, SYSTEM_USER. For example, the query

SELECT CURRENT_TIMESTAMP;

displays the date and time. SQL3 also includes additional numeric and string handling functions.

12. Using LIKE for Strings

We can use a pattern string in the condition when we search character fields to find records that match the pattern, using the LIKE clause. In the pattern string, special symbols used are

% which stands for any sequence of zero or more characters
_ which stands for any single character

Any other characters in the pattern represent themselves. For example, to find names of all suppliers with names beginning with A, we write

SELECT   DISTINCT(Supplier)

FROM   Item

WHERE   Supplier LIKE 'A%';

Result:	Supplier
	Ace
	Acme

To find customer names containing the letter r write

SELECT   DISTINCT(CustName)

FROM   Customer

WHERE   CustName LIKE '%r%';

Result: <u>CustName</u>

Martinez

Wright

13. Calculated Expressions

The SELECT clause may contain a calculated field. For example, we could compute the total value of the stock of an item by multiplying the price by the quantity on hand.

SELECT   ItemNo, Price, QtyOnHand, QtyOn-Hand*Price as TotalValue

FROM   Item

WHERE   QtyOnHand IS NOT NULL;

Result:

ItemNo	Price	QtyOnHand	TotalValue
I1001	2.99	200	598.00
I1010	3.75	150	562.50
I1015	6.80	16	108.80

14. Set Operators—UNION, INTERSECT, EXCEPT

SQL supports the operations of set union, set intersection, and set difference. For these operations to be defined, the tables must be union compatible, which means they must have the same structure. Although no two of our sample tables have the same structure, we can use queries to create results tables that have the same structure and apply the set operations to those. For example, suppose we want to find the names of all items that either cost more than 5.00 or are supplied by Ace. Although we could write this directly using an OR condition, we can also do it using a UNION.

(SELECT   ItemName

FROM   Item

WHERE   Price >5.00)

UNION

(SELECT   ItemName

FROM   Item

WHERE   Supplier = 'Ace');

Result: <u>ItemName</u>

widget

manifold

brace

To find names of items that cost more than 5.00 and are supplied by Ace, we could use set intersection

(SELECT   ItemName

FROM   Item

WHERE   Price >5.00)

INTERSECTION

(SELECT   ItemName

FROM   Item

WHERE   Supplier = 'Ace');

Result: <u>ItemName</u>

brace

To find the items that cost more than 5.00 but are not supplied by Ace, we could write

(SELECT   ItemName

FROM   Item

WHERE   Price >5.00)

EXCEPT

(SELECT   ItemName

FROM   Item

WHERE   Supplier = 'Ace');

Result: <u>ItemName</u>

manifold

15. Recursive Queries

A notable addition to SQL3 is the inclusion of recursive queries, which execute repeatedly until no new results are found. To illustrate a recursive query, consider the EMPLOYEE table shown in Fig. 2. Its structure is

EMPLOYEE(<u>EmpID</u>, LastName, FirstName, Salary, *Manager*).

The Manager attribute shows the EmpID of the manager of each employee. We note that this is a foreign key for the EMPLOYEE table, even though it is itself an attribute of the same table. The recursive query is

WITH RECURSIVE

MANAGERS (EmpID, Manager) AS

(SELECT EmpID, Manager

FROM EMPLOYEE

UNION

EMPLOYEE	EmpID	LastName	FirstName	Salary	Manager
	E101	Jones	Robert	60000	E105
	E104	Smith	Mary	65000	E105
	E105	Adams	Leslie	70000	E120
	E110	Chin	Bill	65000	E120
	E120	Lee	Stuart	80000	NULL

Figure 2 The EMPLOYEE Table.

```
SELECT (COPY1.EmpID, COPY2.Manager

FROM MANAGERS COPY1, EMPLOYEE
       COPY2

WHERE COPY1.Manager = COPY2.EmpID)
SELECT *

FROM MANAGERS

ORDER BY EmpID, Manager;
```

The result table will show, for each employee, all of that person's managers, including the manager's manager. There are many other variations of the SELECT statement, both in the SQL3 standard and in various implementations of the language.

B. The UPDATE Statement

The UPDATE command is used to modify values in records that are already stored in the database. Its form is

```
UPDATE table-name

SET col-name = value1 [,col-name = value2] ...

[WHERE condition];
```

Depending on the condition, zero, one, many, or all records of the table can be updated by a single UPDATE command.

EXAMPLE 1
Change the price of item I1015 to 7.50.

```
UPDATE   Item

SET      Price = 7.50

WHERE    ItemNo = 'I1015';
```

EXAMPLE 2
Increase all customer credit ratings by 5.

```
UPDATE   Customer

SET      CreditRating = CreditRating + 5;
```

EXAMPLE 3
Change the Price of Item I1004 to 6.00 and the QtyOnHand to 100.

```
UPDATE   Item

SET      Price = 6.00,

         QtyOnHand = 100

WHERE    ItemNo = 'I1004';
```

C. The DELETE Statement

The DELETE command has the form

```
DELETE FROM   table-name

WHERE         condition;
```

The statement can target zero, one, many, or all records.

EXAMPLE 1
Delete the record of customer Wright of New York.

```
DELETE FROM   Customer

WHERE         CustName = 'Wright' AND
              CustCity = 'New York';
```

EXAMPLE 2
Delete records of all orders from customer C101.

```
DELETE FROM   Order

WHERE         CustID = 'C101';
```

EXAMPLE 3
Delete all records from the Order table.

```
DELETE FROM   Order;
```

Note that the effect of this command is to remove all rows from the table. The table structure still exists, and we could add new records to it later.

D. The INSERT Statement

The INSERT statement is used to place new records in a table. Its form is

INSERT INTO   table-name [column-list]

VALUES   (data-value-list);

EXAMPLE 1
Add a new Customer record, supplying values for all columns.

INSERT INTO   Customer

VALUES   ('C130', 'Rossini', 'Melbourne', 15);

EXAMPLE 2
Add a new Item record, leaving out the QtyOnHand

INSERT INTO   Item (ItemNo, ItemName, Price,
                Supplier)

VALUES   ('I1005', 'bracket', 4.00, 'Acme');

A second form of the INSERT allows rows to be copied from one table into another using a SELECT clause. For example, suppose we have previously created a table

OrderTotals(OrdNo, CustNo, ItemNo, Qty, Price,
                                            TotalPrice)

and we wish to fill it by selecting the appropriate information from Order and Item. We would write

INSERT INTO   OrderTotals(OrdNo, CustNo,
                ItemNo, Qty, Price, TotalPrice)

SELECT   OrderNo, CustID, ItemNo,
                QtyOrdered, Price, QtyOrdered
                *Price

FROM   Order, Item

WHERE   Order.ItemNo = Item.ItemNo;

If we had started with an empty OrderTotals table, that table would now be

Order Totals	OrdNo	CustNo	ItemNo	Qty	Price	Total Price
	O10101	C101	I1004	50	5.50	275.00
	O10102	C105	I1010	30	3.75	112.50
	O10103	C118	I1015	5	6.80	34.00
	O10104	C101	I1001	30	2.99	89.70
	O10105	C125	I1015	10	6.80	68.00

IV. SQL DATA DEFINITION LANGUAGE

A. CREATE SCHEMA, DROP SCHEMA Commands

A relational schema is a set of relational tables and associated items that are related to one another. All of the base tables, views, indexes, domains, user roles, stored modules, and other items that a user creates to fulfill the data needs of a particular enterprise or set of applications belong to one schema. SQL provides a statement to define a schema. Its form is

CREATE SCHEMA [schema-name]
[AUTHORIZATION user-name];

For our sample database, we could write

CREATE SCHEMA OrderSystem
AUTHORIZATION User111;

This statement permits User111 to create the tables and other structures in OrderSystem, and to write authorization statements allowing others to have access to them.

There is also a statement to destroy a schema, with the form

DROP SCHEMA schema-name
[RESTRICT|CASCADE];

If the user chooses RESTRICT, which is the default, all of the tables, views, and other items in the schema must be empty before the schema itself can be dropped, or the operation fails. For CASCADE, the system drops the associated schema items as well as the data.

B. CREATE TABLE, CREATE DOMAIN, ALTER TABLE, DROP TABLE, DROP DOMAIN Commands

A commonly used form of the command to create a table in the schema, called a base table, is

CREATE TABLE table-name

(column-name, data-type [NULL|NOT
    NULL[UNIQUE]] [DEFAULT data-value]

[CHECK search-condition], column_name...

...

[UNIQUE (column-name [,column-name]...),

[CONSTRAINT constraint-name constraint
    definition],

[CHECK search-condition],

[[CONSTRAINT constraint-name] PRIMARY KEY
(column-name [,column-name]...)],

[[CONSTRAINT constraint-name] FOREIGN KEY
(column-name [,column-name]...)

REFERENCES table-name(column-name [,column-
name]...) [ON UPDATE action]

[ON DELETE action]];

[[CONSTRAINT constraint-name] FOREIGN
KEY...]...)

As each attribute is defined, its data type must be specified, and any constraints on the attribute can be defined. SQL data types include numeric types INTEGER, SMALLINT, FLOAT, REAL, DOUBLE PRECISION, DECIMAL(i,j), and NUMERIC(i,j). Character-string types may be fixed length, denoted CHAR(n), or varying length, denoted VARCHAR(n). Bit-strings of fixed length, BIT(n), or varying length, BIT VARYING (n) are permitted. DATE, TIME, TIMESTAMP, and INTERVAL are also standard. Before writing the CREATE TABLE command, users can define domains, and then use the domain name in place of the data type in the CREATE TABLE command. SQL3 added four fundamental data types, namely LOB, BOOLEAN, ARRAY, and ROW. LOB, short for LARGE OBJECT, has variants BLOB for BINARY LARGE OBJECTS, and CLOB for CHARACTER LARGE OBJECTS. LOBs cannot be used as primary or foreign keys, and they allow comparisons only for equality or inequality. They cannot be used for ordering or in GROUP BY or ORDER BY clauses. Once stored in the database, LOBs are generally not transferred again, but can be manipulated by using a LOB locator, a binary surrogate for the actual value. An attribute such as a customer's signature might be stored in LOB format. SQL3's BOOLEAN data type allows values true, false, and unknown. In the Item table, we might use a boolean attribute to indicate whether an item has been reordered or not. The ARRAY[n] type allows an ordered collection of n values of the same data type to be stored as an attribute. For example, we could store the available colors for an item in an attribute that we declare as Colors VARCHAR(10) ARRAY[5]. The ROW type is a sequence of field name and data type pairs, similar to a traditional table definition. This data type can be used to represent rows of a table, allowing them to be passed as parameters to routines or returned from function calls. An attribute of a table can itself have a row-type value, allowing nested tables.

In SQL2 format, following the attribute list, any table constraints are listed, including uniqueness for combinations of attributes, conditions involving relative values of different attributes, and so on. Many database designers choose to provide their own descriptive names to help them to enable or disable specific constraints when it is convenient to do so; otherwise, the constraints are given system-generated names. A single primary key and any foreign keys are specified. The primary key can be a composite one, consisting of more than one column. The foreign key clause enforces referential integrity. It should be included in the dependent, child table. The table it references, which is the independent or parent table, has a column or set of columns that forms the primary key or candidate key of that table. Referential integrity requires that the value of the foreign key in the dependent table must either match a value in the parent table or be null. The ON UPDATE option permits the user to specify an action for the dependent tuples of the child table when the corresponding tuple of the parent table is updated. Options are CASCADE, which means the child tuples are updated to the new value of the parent, NO ACTION which means the update of the parent is not permitted, SET NULL, which means the value of the dependent attribute in the child tuples will be set to null when the parent is updated, or SET DEFAULT, which inserts the default value for the child tuples when the parent is updated. The same actions are available for the ON DELETE clause. The uniqueness constraint for other attributes or combinations of attributes can be used for candidate keys, attributes that could have been used as the primary key.

Rather than specifying the data type and constraints for each attribute in the CREATE TABLE command, SQL allows us to define domains, including an underlying data type, a default value, a check condition, and other specifications. The form of the statement is

CREATE DOMAIN domain-name AS data-type

[DEFAULT default-value]

[CHECK search-condition];

For example, we could create a domain for possible CreditRating values by writing CREATE DOMAIN ratingsType AS INTEGER

DEFAULT 1

CHECK (VALUE IN (1, 5, 10,15, 18, 20, 25));

SQL3 allows a user-defined data type, DISTINCT. If two such types have otherwise equivalent type declarations, the user can specify that they are distinct. For example, if we had written

CREATE DISTINCT TYPE ratingsType AS
INTEGER;

and also

CREATE DISTINCT TYPE quantityType AS
INTEGER;

then any attempt to compare a ratingsType attribute with a quantityType attribute would result in an error, even though both are integers.

To create the tables for the OrderSystem database in SQL92 form, we could write

CREATE TABLE Customer

(CustID	char(5) not null unique,
CustName	varchar(15) not null,
CustCity	varchar(25),
CreditRating	ratingsType,
primary key (CustID));	

CREATE TABLE Item

(ItemNo	char(6) not null unique,
ItemName	varchar(15) not null,
Price	real default 0.0 check(Price>=0.0),
Supplier	varchar(15),
QtyOnHand	quantityType,
primary key	(ItemNo));

CREATE TABLE Order

(OrderNo	char(8) not null unique,
CustID	char(5) not null,
ItemNo	char(6) not null,
QtyOrdered	quantityType not null check (QtyOrdered >=0),
primary key	(OrderNo),
foreign key	(CustID) references Customer (CustID) on delete restrict,
foreign key	(ItemNo) references Item (ItemNo) on delete restrict);

In addition to the standard built-in data types—the LOB, BOOLEAN, the ARRAY types, the ROW types, and the DISTINCT user-defined type mentioned earlier—SQL3 supports objects. Objects include named

row types, reference types, and structured data types, which are similar to classes in object-oriented languages and support inheritance and operator overloading in much the same way. Structured types may have several attributes and methods. Unlike SQL functions, methods are defined for a single user-defined type, while functions, such as the COUNT mentioned earlier, may be used for many types. Each attribute can be any SQL type, including the built-in types, ARRAY or ROW types, or other structured types, nested arbitrarily deeply. Attributes can be either stored or virtual, which means they are derived using a defined method for the type. Following the object-oriented paradigm, the attributes are encapsulated, accessible only through the type's own observer (GET) and mutator (SET) methods that are defined automatically. Unlike other functions and methods, observers and mutators cannot be overloaded, but they can be overridden if the user redefines them. The behaviors of structured types are determined by their methods, functions, and procedures. The user can define equality and ordering relationships to permit comparisons to be done. Structured types can participate in type hierarchies. Subtypes inherit all attributes and routines of their supertypes, but they may have additional attributes and routines of their own. SQL:1999 does not allow multiple inheritance. A type can be declared as FINAL, meaning no subtypes can be defined for it, or NOT FINAL, allowing subtypes. Types may be instantiable, which means instances of the type can be created, or not instantiable, similar to abstract types in other object-oriented languages. For instantiable types, a default constructor function is automatically provided to allow new instances of the type to be created. This constructor has the same name and type as the user-defined data type, takes no parameters, and assigns default values to the instance attributes. Users can create their own constructors as part of the definition of the user type. Although no instances can be created from noninstantiable types, instances of their subtypes can be created. An example of a structured type definition for CustType is

CREATE TYPE CustType AS

(CustID	char(5),
CustName	varchar15),
CustCity	varchar(25),
CreditRating	ratings)

INSTANTIABLE

NOT FINAL;

The Customer table is then created by the command

CREATE TABLE Customer of CustType
(Primary Key (CustID));

Values can then be inserted in the usual way, or, preferably, by using the type constructor, as in

INSERT INTO Customer

VALUES(CustType('C101', 'Martinez', 'New York', 20));

We could define a subtype, CorporateCustType, for CustType by writing

CREATE TYPE CorporateCustType UNDER
CustType AS (

contactPerson   varchar(25),

title   varchar(40),

CREATE FUNCTION contactIsCFO
(c CorporateCustType) RETURNS
BOOLEAN

BEGIN

IF c.title = "Chief Financial Officer"

THEN

RETURN TRUE;

ELSE

RETURN FALSE;

END IF;

END;

INSTANTIABLE

FINAL;

CorpCustomerType has attributes CustID, CustName, CustCity, and CreditRating inherited from CustType, as well as contactPerson and title. It also inherits all routines from CustType, as well as having its own method, contactIsCFO.

SQL supports dynamic database definition. The CREATE TABLE command may be used at any time during the life cycle of the schema. It is not necessary to create all the tables at the same time. If the user wishes to change the definition of a table after creation, it can be done with an ALTER TABLE command. Its form is

ALTER TABLE table-name

[ADD [COLUMN] column-name data-type ...]

[DROP [COLUMN] column-name [RESTRICT|
CASCADE]]

[ALTER [COLUMN] column-name SET DEFAULT
data-value]

[ALTER [COLUMN] column-name DROP
DEFAULT]

[ADD [CONSTRAINT] [constraint-name]
constraint]

[DROP CONSTRAINT constraint-name]

For example, we might change the specifications for the ORDER table by adding an OrderDate field having date data type, as

ALTER TABLE Order ADD COLUMN
OrderDate date;

A table can be dropped at any time using the command

DROP TABLE table-name;

This command deletes the entire structure as well as all the rows of the table. Any indexes or views that were defined on the table will also be deleted. If the user wishes to delete the rows but keep the structure, he or she should use the DELETE command instead. A domain can also be dropped at any time using the form

DROP DOMAIN domain-name
[RESTRICT|CASCADE];

C. CREATE INDEX and DROP INDEX

After a table has been created, the user can create indexes on any of the columns or combinations of columns, whether unique or not. The most common command to do so is

CREATE [UNIQUE] INDEX index-name ON
table-name (col-name [ASC|DESC] [,
column-name [ASC|DESC]...

If no order is specified, ASC is the default. To create an index on CustName for the Customer table, we could write

CREATE INDEX xCustName
ON CUSTOMER (CustName);

Some implementations of SQL permit the user to add the keyword CLUSTER for exactly one index per table. The effect of this specification is to ensure that tuples with the same value in the indexed field are placed on the same physical page of the database on disk, resulting in improved performance for retrieval by the indexed field. To remove an index that has been created, the user writes

> DROP INDEX index-name;

D. CREATE VIEW and DROP VIEW

An SQL view is a virtual table, dynamically constructed for a user by extracting data from actual base tables. The form of the statement to define a view is

CREATE VIEW view-name [(view-column-name [,view-column-name]...)]

AS subselect [WITH CHECK OPTION];

No data are retrieved when the CREATE VIEW is written, despite the fact that it contains a SELECT statement. Instead, the definition is stored in the data dictionary, and the user can refer to its name in a FROM clause of a SELECT statement. At that time, the virtual table is materialized for the user. The subselect is a standard SQL SELECT statement, possibly including a join, a subquery, grouping, or a function. Columns may be renamed in the view, by specifying a view-column-name for each. If the subselect contains a WHERE clause, thereby choosing only tuples that have specified values for one or more attributes, the view is said to be value-dependent. If there is no WHERE clause, the view is value-independent. Views may be used as a security device, a means of restricting access to the base tables by displaying only rows and columns that the end-user should be permitted to see. They can be thought of as windows into base tables. Views that are derived from a single table and that do not use grouping or functions may be updatable. If the CHECK OPTION is specified, any view updates that result in changes to the base table will not be permitted if they create rows that do not satisfy the conditions to be included in the view. For example, if we defined a view of the Customer table as follows

CREATE VIEW NYCustomers

AS   SELECT *

               CUSTOMER

               WHERE CustCity = 'New York'

WITH CHECK OPTION;

we would not be able to execute the following update

UPDATE   NYCustomers

SET   CustCity = 'Los Angeles'

WHERE   CustID = 'C101';

because this update would result in a tuple that is not included in NYCustomers. The view can be dropped by writing

> DROP VIEW view-name [RESTRICT|CASCADE];

This statement causes the view definition to be dropped from the data dictionary. If CASCADE is specified, any items that depend on the view are also dropped. For example, if the view has been used to create a derived view, that view is also dropped. If RESTRICT is specified, and any other items that depend on the view still exist in the database, the DROP will not be permitted. RESTRICT is the default.

V. SQL AUTHORIZATION LANGUAGE

SQL includes statements to extend privileges to users and to revoke those privileges. Privileges are the actions a user is permitted to perform on database objects such as base tables and views. The statement for granting privileges has the form

GRANT {ALL PRIVILEGES | privilege-list}

ON   object-name

TO   {PUBLIC | user-list} [WITH GRANT
          OPTION];

The privilege list for tables includes SELECT, DELETE, INSERT, UPDATE [col-list], or REFERENCES [column-name]. The REFERENCES privilege allows the user to refer to columns in specifying constraints. The WITH GRANT OPTION clause allows the newly authorized user to pass his or her privileges to others. If PUBLIC is specified, all users are given the privileges specified in the GRANT statement.

As an example, we could write

GRANT SELECT, INSERT, UPDATE ON Order TO
U1002 WITH GRANT OPTION;

User U1002 would then be permitted to write SELECT, INSERT, and UPDATE statements for the Order table and to pass that permission on to other users. The SQL statement to remove privileges has the form

REVOKE {ALL PRIVILEGES | privilege-list}

ON object-list

FROM {PUBLIC | user-list}

[CASCADE | RESTRICT];

SQL3 incorporates the specification of a role, which can be thought of as a set of operations that might be performed by an individual or a group of individuals. A set of privileges is granted for each role, and then user accounts can be assigned to the role. For example, the role of administrative assistant might be given SELECT authorization on certain views and that role might be assigned to several administrative assistant accounts. As an individual moves into the job, the role is assigned to his or her account and removed when the person moves out of the job.

VI. INTEGRITY CONTROL IN SQL

The ability to specify domains, to specify uniqueness for the primary key and any candidate keys, to indicate required values by NOT NULL, to enforce constraints by the CHECK clause, and to enforce referential integrity are all examples of SQL's integrity control mechanisms that can be used when database tables are created. There is also a statement that can be used independently of table creation, the CREATE ASSERTION command. Its form is

CREATE ASSERTION assertion-name

CHECK (search-condition);

The condition specified in the check must always be true, both when the assertion is first created, and when the database is updated. Any update that would violate the condition will be rejected. For example, we might write the following assertion to ensure that no customer has more than 10 orders

CREATE ASSERTION limitOrders

CHECK (NOT EXISTS (SELECT   CustID

    FROM Order

    GROUP BY CustID

    HAVING COUNT(*) > 10);

Some versions of SQL support triggers, which are actions to be performed when certain conditions arise. The form is

CREATE TRIGGER trigger-name

{BEFORE|AFTER} triggering-event ON table-name

WHEN condition

action(s);

The triggering event might be an insert, update, or delete on a table. The action might be the execution of an SQL statement or other procedure. For example, let us assume we want to be sure there are enough items in inventory to cover an order before we process it. If not, we want to call a procedure Insufficient_ Stock, passing the relevant order information as parameters. We could write

CREATE TRIGGER   SufficientStock

BEFORE INSERT ON ORDER

FOR EACH ROW

WHEN (NEW.QtyOrdered > (SELECT QtyOnHand

        FROM Item

        WHERE NEW.ItemNo
        = Item.ItemNo)

INSUFFICIENT_STOCK(NEW.OrderNo, NEW.ItemNo, NEW.QtyOrdered));

In the WHEN clause, the NEW refers to the tuple that is about to be inserted. If the operation is an UPDATE or DELETE, OLD is used to refer to the tuple to be removed or modified. The trigger can be specified to be tested for each row, or only once for the entire statement, which may modify several rows.

VII. SQL PROGRAMMING

A. Embedded SQL

SQL statements can be used within a general-purpose programming language such as Java, C, C++, Ada, and others. The host language provides the control structures, while the SQL statements, embedded or interspersed within the host language statements, provide the database access. An SQL statement can appear wherever an executable host language statement could appear. To distinguish it from host language statements, each SQL statement starts with a prefix identifier such as the keyword EXEC SQL, and ends with a terminator such as a semicolon, depending on the host language. The source code, containing a mixture of host language statements and SQL statements, is sent to a precompiler, which replaces the SQL code with function calls to DBMS routines. The host language program can then be compiled as usual, and linking is done in the normal way. Figure 3 illustrates this process.

An impedance mismatch between SQL and the host language arises due to differences between the language's data structures and the relational model, which is based on sets. Attributes of database records provide values for program variables in the host language or receive their values from those variables.

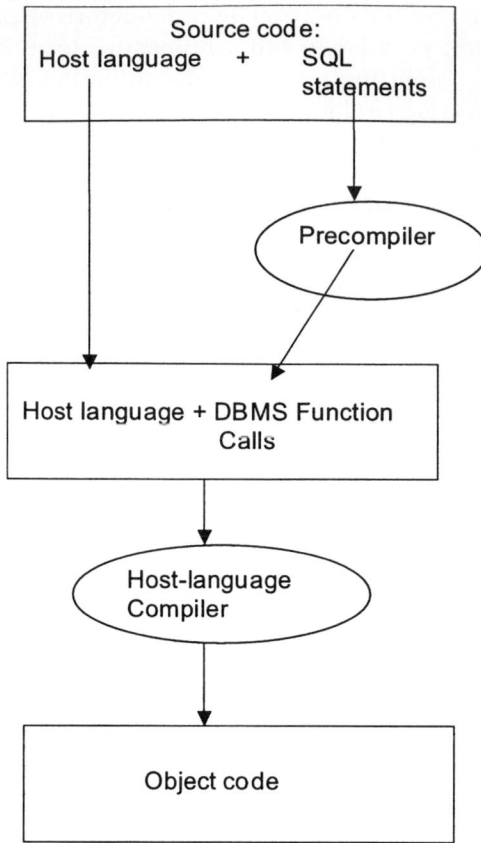

Figure 3 Processing embedded SQL programs.

The shared variables must be declared in an SQL declaration section within the program. However, there may be a mismatch between data types of the host language and those of the database attributes. A type cast operation may be necessary when passing values between SQL attributes and program variables. The language bindings in SQL'99 specify the correspondence between SQL data types and the data types of each host language. In addition to shared variables, the SQL declaration section includes a declaration of SQLSTATE, an array of five characters that is used to communicate error conditions to the program. A typical declaration section is

EXEC SQL BEGIN DECLARE SECTION;

char c_CustID[5];

char c_CustName[15];

char c_CustCity[25];

int c_CreditRating;

char SQLSTATE[6];

EXEC SQL END DECLARE SECTION;

A value is placed in SQLSTATE whenever an SQL library function is called, indicating which error condition may have occurred when the database was accessed. For example, a value of 00000 indicates no error, while a value 02000 indicates no tuple was found for a query. Host language statements may use the value of SQLSTATE as part of the control statements; for example, some processing may be performed provided the value is 00000, or a loop may be written to read a record until the value of 02000 is returned. For SQL statements that refer to a single row of a table, the embedded statements are very similar to the statements described previously. For example, a SELECT statement that retrieves a single tuple is modified for the embedded case by specifying the shared variables in an INTO line. Note that within an SQL statement, shared variables are preceded by colons. The following example begins with a host-language statement assigning a value to the variable c_CustID, and then uses an SQL SELECT statement to retrieve a row from the Customer table and place its values into three shared variables:

c_CustID = 'C101';

EXEC SQL SELECT Customer.CustName, Customer.CustCity, Customer.CreditRating

    INTO   :c_CustName, :c_CustCity, :c_CreditRating

    FROM   Customer

    WHERE Customer.CustID = :c_CustID;

This segment should be followed by a host-language check of the value of SQLSTATE. An INSERT statement can be used to insert a tuple whose values are taken from the host variables, as

EXEC SQL INSERT INTO Customer (CustID, CustName, CustCity, CreditRating)

VALUES(:c_CustID,:c_CustName, :c_CustCity, :c_CreditRating);

To address the impedance mismatch due to SQL's set orientation, a cursor is used to run through the tuples of a relation or the results of a query, allowing values to be provided tuple-by-tuple, as required by the host language. A cursor is positioned so that it points to one row in the table or in the multiset at a time. The cursor must be declared using the form

EXEC SQL DECLARE *cursorname* [INSENSITIVE] [SCROLL] CURSOR FOR *query*

[FOR {READ ONLY | UPDATE OF *attributeNames*};

For example,

EXEC SQL DECLARE custCursor CURSOR FOR

    SELECT CustID, CustName, CreditRating

    FROM Customer

    WHERE CreditRating > 15;

Once declared, the cursor must be "opened," which executes the query and positions the cursor just before the first tuple of the results table. For example, we write

    EXEC SQL OPEN custCursor;

We then use the FETCH command to retrieve the first row, using the form

    EXEC SQL FETCH *cursorname* INTO *hostvariables;*

as in

    EXEC SQL FETCH custCursor INTO :c_CustID,
        :c_CustName,:c_CreditRating;

This statement may be placed within a loop controlled by the value of SQLSTATE so that additional rows are accessed. The loop does whatever processing is required in the host language. After all data have been retrieved and the loop is exited, the cursor is closed in a statement such as

    EXEC SQL CLOSE custCursor.

For multiple-row updates, the cursor must be declared as updatable, by using a more complete declaration such as

EXEC SQL DECLARE CustRatingCursor CURSOR
  FOR

    SELECT CustID, CreditRating

    FROM Customer

FOR UPDATE OF CreditRating;

Any attribute that is updatable using the cursor must be listed in both the SELECT statement and the update attribute list. Once the cursor is open and active, the tuple at which the cursor is positioned, called the current of the cursor, can be updated by writing a command such as

EXEC SQL UPDATE Customer

SET CreditRating = 25

WHERE CURRENT OF CustRatingCursor;

Similarly, the current tuple can be deleted by a
  statement such as

EXEC SQL DELETE FROM Customer

WHERE CURRENT OF CustRatingCursor;

The type of embedded SQL discussed thus far is classified as static, but there is also a dynamic version, which allows the type of database access to be specified at run time rather than at compile time. For example, a graphical front end might prompt the user for a query that can be used to generate SQL statements that are executed dynamically, much like the interactive SQL described earlier. Two of the important commands in dynamic SQL are PREPARE and EXECUTE. For example, the user may be prompted to enter an SQL command that is then stored as a host-language string. The PREPARE command tells the database management system to parse and compile the string as an SQL command and assign the resulting executable code to a named SQL variable. The EXECUTE command is then used to run the code. For example, in the following segment an update command is assigned to a program variable, c_userstring, the corresponding code is prepared and bound to the SQL identifier user_command, and then the code is executed.

char c_userstring[]={"UPDATE Customer SET
  CreditRating = 25 WHERE CustID = C101"};

EXEC SQL PREPARE user_command FROM
  :c_userstring;

EXEC SQL EXECUTE user_command;

B. ODBC and JDBC

When SQL is embedded in a host language, the precompiler for the DBMS translates the SQL code into function calls in the host language, creating an object code that works only with that DBMS. ODBC (open database connectivity) and JDBC (Java database connectivity) are standards that take a different approach to integrating SQL code and general-purpose languages. In this approach, the DBMS must provide an application programming interface (API) which includes a set of standard library functions for database processing. This common interface allows applications to access multiple, heterogeneous databases. Because of the standardization, a single application using ODBC (or JDBC) can use the same code, without recompilation, to access different databases. Database drivers, programs that translate the ODBC or JDBC calls to DBMS-specific calls, are used to link the application to any one of several databases that could be used as the data source. A driver manager is used to load and unload drivers and to pass the ODBC or JDBC calls to the selected driver, which then establishes the connection with the targeted data source. ODBC/JDBC architecture requires four components—the application, driver manager, driver, and data source. The application performs processing, submits data requests as SQL statements to the DBMS, and retrieves the results, all using the standard API. The driver manager loads and unloads drivers at the application's request and passes ODBC/JDBC function calls to the appropriate driver. The driver connects to the database being used as the data source, submitting the data requests and returning the results. It may also do any translation necessary because of differences in the syntax of the DBMS's data sublanguage and that of the ODBC/JDBC standard. The data source is the database being accessed, along with its environment, consisting of its DBMS and platform. The standard provides a high degree of flexibility, allowing development of client-server applications that work with a variety of DBMSs, instead of being limited to a particular vendor API. Most vendors provide ODBC or JDBC drivers that conform to the standard.

C. SQL PSM

SQL itself has been extended to provide complete programming language facilities, including declarations, assignment statement, and control structures that can be used to write SQL routines that can be saved as persistent stored modules (PSMs). In contrast, programs written in a host language are referred to as external routines. The SQL assignment statement permits the value of an expression to be assigned to a variable. For example, using the user-defined CorporateCustType described earlier, we can write

DECLARE CFOflag BOOLEAN;

DECLARE company CorporateCustType;

CFOflag = company.contactIsCFO;

The selection control structure is illustrated by the following segment that uses the CustType described earlier

DECLARE cust CustType;

IF cust.CreditRating > 20

    THEN

        ...

    ELSE

        ...

END IF;

The CASE statement provides selection based on the value of a variable or expression. Using the CustCity attribute of the Customer table in Fig. 1, we could write

DECLARE shippingMethod varchar(10);

CASE City

    WHEN 'New York' THEN SET shipping Method = 'ground';

    WHEN 'London'   THEN SET shipping Method ='air';

    ...

END CASE;

Repetition is controlled by WHILE... DO END WHILE, REPEAT...UNTIL...END REPEAT, and FOR ...DO END FOR structures. For example, we could write

WHILE (SQLCODE = '00000')

    DO

        ...

END WHILE;

Procedures are invoked by a CALL statement, and a value is returned from a procedure using a RETURN statement. The language also provides exception and other condition handling mechanisms.

    Work is continuing on many aspects of SQL, including development of new standards, extending the object-oriented capabilities of SQL, developing additional language bindings, and providing specifications for secure remote access to SQL databases.

SEE ALSO THE FOLLOWING ARTICLES

Database Administration • Database Development Process • Database Machines • Database Systems • Distributed Databases • Network Database Systems • Object-Oriented Databases • Relational Database Systems

BIBLIOGRAPHY

ANSI/ISO/IEC 9075. (1992). Information technology—Database languages—SQL.

ANSI/ISO/IEC 9075-1. (1999). Information technology—Database languages—SQL Part 1. Framework (SQL/Framework).

ANSI/ISO/IEC 9075-2. (1999). Information technology—Database languages—SQL—Part 2. Foundation.

ANSI/ISO/IEC 9075-3. (1999). Information technology—Database languages—SQL—Part 3. Call-level interface (SQL/CLI).

ANSI/ISO/IEC 9075-4. (1999). Information technology—Database languages—SQL—Part 4. Persistent stored modules (SQL/PSM).

ANSI/ISO/IEC 9075-5. (1999). Information technology—Database languages—SQL—Part 5. Host language bindings (SQL/Bindings).

ANSI/ISO/IEC 9075-5/Amd1. (2001). On-line analytical processing (SQL/OLAP).

ANSI/ISO/IEC 9075-10. (2000). Information technology—Database languages—SQL—Part 10. Object language bindings (SQL/OLB).

ANSI/ISO/IEC 9579. (2000). Information technology—Remote database access for SQL with security enhancement.

ANSI/ISO/IEC 9579-2. (1998). Information technology—Open systems interconnection—Remote database access—Part 2. SQL Specialization.

Codd, E. F. (1970). A relational model of data for large shared data banks. *Communications of the ACM,* Vol. 13, No. 6, 377–387.

Connolly, T., and Begg, C. (2002). *Database systems,* 3rd ed. Harlow, England: Addison–Wesley.

Date, C. J. (2002). *An introduction to database systems,* 7th ed. Reading, MA: Addison–Wesley.

Date, C. J., and Darwen, H. (1994). *A guide to the SQL standard,* 3rd ed. Menlo Park, CA: Addison–Wesley.

Dietrich, S. W. (2001). *Understanding relational query languages.* Upper Saddle River, NJ: Prentice Hall.

Eisenberg, A., and Melton, J. (1999). SQL standardization: The next steps. *SIGMOD Record,* Vol. 29, No. 1, 63–67.

Eisenberg, A., and Melton, J. (1999). SQL:1999, formerly known as SQL3. *SIGMOD Record,* Vol. 28, No. 1, 131–138.

Elmasri, R., and Navathe, S. (2000). *Fundamentals of database systems,* 3rd ed. Reading, MA: Addison–Wesley.

Garcia-Molina, H., Ullman, J., and Widom, J. (2002). *Database systems: The complete book.* Upper Saddle River, NJ: Prentice Hall.

Kline, K., and Kline, D. (2001). *SQL in a nutshell.* O'Reilly.

Melton, J., *et al.* (1999). SQL and management of external data. *SIGMOD Record,* Vol. 30, No. 1, 70–77.

Ramakrishnan, R., and Gehrke, J. (2000). *Database management systems,* 2nd ed. New York: McGraw–Hill.

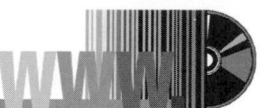

Success Measures of Information Systems

Yong Jin Kim
State University of New York, Binghamton

Edward J. Garrity
Canisius College

G. Lawrence Sanders
State University of New York, Buffalo

GLOSSARY

decision support satisfaction The degree of satisfaction a user has in the support provided by the IS tool toward the goal of planning or controlling a business process.

information system (IS) A purposeful entity composed of interdependent computer-based technology and human components that are unified by design to accomplish one or more objectives. Thus, by definition, an information system (IS) is a tool. When evaluating the success of a tool, it is imperative to assess the tool's effectiveness in a particular context and relative to its intended purpose. Therefore, IS success factors should be used to pinpoint how effective an IS tool is in a particular context toward achieving organizational and individual goals.

information systems success A measure of the degree to which the person evaluating the system believes that the stakeholder is better off.

interface satisfaction A dimension that captures the user's overall impression of and satisfaction with the interface in terms of presentation, format, ease of use, and efficiency.

management effectiveness This is measured in terms of improvement in management decision making, planning, and span of control attributed to company IS.

operational efficiency This focuses on the improvement in internal customer performance and is measured in terms of flexibility, consistency, productivity, and cycle time.

quality of work life satisfaction The degree of satisfaction users have in terms of the impact of the IS on their feelings, physical needs, personal goals, and psychological states.

SISSM (User Satisfaction-based Information Systems Success Model) An integrated IS success model consisting of four subdimensions of user satisfaction and organizational impact of IS use.

task support satisfaction The degree of satisfaction a user has in the support provided by the IS tool toward the goal of accomplishing job and task requirements.

I. THE DEFINITION OF INFORMATION SYSTEMS SUCCESS

Information systems (IS) success is a measure of the degree to which the person evaluating the system believes that the stakeholder is better off. There exist various internal and external interest groups who demand different aspects of IS performance. They include stockholders, employees, customers, managers, creditors, and government. The focus of measuring IS success is on the investigation of the effect of a system on individual performance, business process performance, and organization performance. Figure 1 is an adaptation of the classic "Leavitt Diamond" that illustrates the importance of task, technology, structure, people, and environment on IS success. This framework is fundamental to understanding IS success

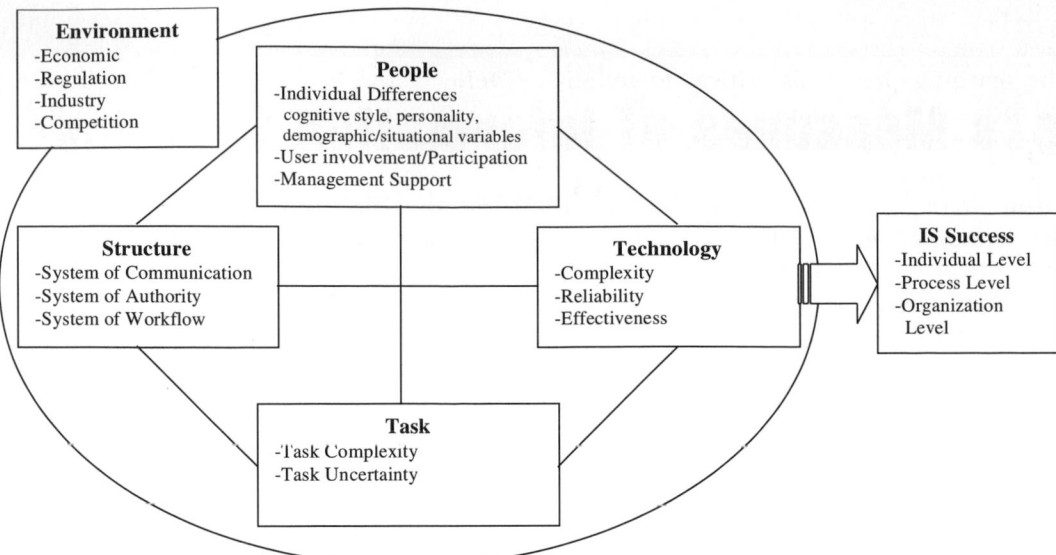

Figure 1 Framework for understanding IS success.

because incongruence among task, technology, structure, people, and environment can defeat the purpose of a technology and lead to system failure.

The effect of IS, however, may vary with situational differences. In organization research, the contingency approach may be viewed from the perspective that no one set of rules can be applied to all situations. It rejects the notion that universal principles can be applied to managing behavior in organizations. As shown in Fig. 1, the success of a system is contingent on the dynamic interplay between people, task, technology, structure, and environment. In this model, *people* refer to individuals working in an organization and their individual differences such as personality, cognitive style, attitudes, and motives. In the context of IS success, user involvement and participation in the systems development process, user attitudes, and top management support have received considerable research attention and have been shown to influence system success. The *task* factor refers to the nature of the work itself. The task can be very complex or simple, standardized or unique, or ambiguous or clear. *Technology* includes both problem solving methods and techniques and the application of process knowledge to producing products and services. Both task and system complexity play an important role in the user participation–IS success relationship. In situations where task complexity is low, the need for user participation is reduced and likely to have less impact on IS success. When the task complexity is high, the need for effective user participation is crucial. By the

same token, where system complexity is low, the need for user participation is reduced. When the system complexity is high, effective user participation will be necessary to communicate requirements, to provide feedback on usability, and to provide additional design recommendations. In the model, *structure* encompasses the system of communication, the system of authority, and the system of workflow.

A. Overview on Information Systems Success

Measuring IS success has been a major topic in IS research. The research on IS success has evolved into four main streams: the impact of individual differences on IS success, user involvement and IS, the fit between the task and the IS technology, and user information satisfaction. Individual differences have been reported to play a crucial role in the implementation of any technological innovation. Particularly in the IS domain, a relationship between individual differences and IS success has been theoretically posited and empirically tested in a large body of prior research. The individual differences include cognitive style, personality, and demographic/situational variables. The cognitive and attitudinal differences are argued to influence IS success in the context of decision performance, MIS usage, and user satisfaction. In social learning theory, individual differences are also expected to influence learning through observation and then belief formation. That is, the belief formation is essentially a learning process, and therefore, understanding the learning process is critical to understanding the formation of attitudes.

User involvement and user participation, both well-studied IS independent variables, have been used almost interchangeably for a long time within IS research. User involvement is defined as a subjective psychological state reflecting the importance and personal relevance of a system to the user. User participation is defined as a set of behaviors or activities performed by users in the system development process. User participation has been reported to significantly influence both user involvement and user attitude. The relationship between user participation and user satisfaction has also been reported to be affected by task complexity and system complexity among various contingency factors, including task complexity, system complexity, user influence, and user–developer communication.

The task-technology fit model, referred to as the correspondence between task needs and system functionality, implies that the match between technology and task explains user performance. This model is underpinned by the assumption that information systems give value by being instrumental in some tasks or collection of tasks and that users will reflect this in their evaluations of these systems. It is reported that user evaluations of task-technology fit are a function of both systems characteristics and task characteristics, and to predict performance, both task-technology fit and utilization must be included. It has also been found that mismatches between data representations and tasks would impair decision-making performance by requiring additional efforts for data interpretation.

User satisfaction, "a perceptual or subjective measure of IS success" (Ives, Olson, and Baroudi, 1983), is considered one of the most important measures of IS success. User information satisfaction has been argued to consist of three constructs: the information product, Electronic Data Processing (EDP) staff and services, and user knowledge and involvement. In the context of end-user computing satisfaction, user satisfaction consists of five subdimensions (which primarily focus on information characteristics), including content, format, accuracy, ease of use, and timeliness.

A number of researchers have reviewed and synthesized previous research in terms of IS success models. DeLone and McLean suggested a model of IS success, which consists of a six-category multilevel construct including information quality, system quality, use, user satisfaction, individual impact, and organizational impact. Seddon respecified and extended the DeLone and McLean model into a partial behav-

ioral model of IS use, an IS success model, and a process model of IS success, arguing that IS use in the DeLone and McLean model has three meanings: a variable that proxies for the benefits from use, a dependent variable of future IS use, and an event in a process model.

Garrity and Sanders adapted the DeLone and McLean model and proposed an alternative model in the context of organizational systems and sociotechnical systems. They identified four subdimensions of user satisfaction, including interface satisfaction, task support satisfaction, decision support satisfaction, and quality of work life satisfaction. It is important to note that the Garrity and Sanders model of IS success includes the impact of using information technology on the quality of work life of users, and that few studies have paid attention to this variable. Improving the users' quality of work life has been a goal of researchers who have studied and advocated participative design and user-centered approaches. The Garrity and Sanders model of IS success has been empirically tested and validated by Sherman *et al.* with data from seven different organizations and by Garrity *et al.* in an electronic commerce setting.

Davis and Davis *et al.* proposed the technology acceptance model (TAM) as a mechanism for explaining the individual's behavior to use information technology. TAM explains the relationship among beliefs, attitudes, behavioral intentions, and system usage. Perceived usefulness and ease of use represent the beliefs that affect attitude toward use and eventually lead to system usage. TAM assumes that beliefs and attitude fully mediate the effects that all other external variables may have on system usage. TAM is parsimonious and has high predictive power; however, its generality is sometimes criticized for not providing sufficient information necessary to predict user acceptance of new systems.

B. Assumptions for Understanding Information Systems Success

Assessing the success of IS should be done within the context of organizational work. Organizational work refers to human activities performed with the intention of producing something of acknowledged social value in various formal organizations. The nature of IS in the organizational setting is closely tied to providing task-related support capabilities to achieve organizational goals. That is, the extent to which IS help organizations determine objectives and support work outcomes based on system use depends upon the level of task-related support capabilities expressed by task support satisfaction, decision support satisfaction, and interface satisfaction.

System quality and information quality are antecedents to user satisfaction in the DeLone and McLean model. However, if we start with the premise that an IS is a tool, then clearly its usefulness must be judged with respect to how helpful it is in aiding users in the accomplishment of their goals. Therefore, objective features of the IS and the quality of the information become meaningless outside of the organizational context of its use. That is, a user must use an IS tool to accomplish tasks in an organizational setting. The value of a system and the information produced by it depends upon the match among the user, the task, the system, and the organizational structure. This view is consistent with Leavitt's model of implementation. From this point of view, an assessment of the quality of the IS by the user in his or her context of work is important and relevant.

As discussed above, user satisfaction is the subjective measure of IS success for the individual level of analysis. For process and organizational levels of analysis, objective measures should be developed. Existing measures include measures for operational efficiency, management effectiveness, financial performance, enhancement of products and services, and market growth. Managers must be able to measure IS success in order to obtain feedback and implement control mechanisms to ensure effective development and management of IS in organizations. This concept is embedded in the old management adage, "One cannot manage what one cannot measure."

The measurement of IS success is a fundamental activity of organization researchers. The application of the scientific method in IS research involves the devel-opment of hypotheses based on theories, the development of experiments and field studies, the measurement of variables, and empirical testing and analyses to validate the theories. Without well-understood and accurately defined measures, researchers cannot be confident in their scientific results.

II. THE DEFINITION OF INFORMATION SYSTEMS

One of the reasons for the numerous IS success measures is that there are many ways to view an IS in an organization. The DeLone and McLean model of IS success provides a visual representation of the major factors involved in the IS success concept (Fig. 2). Most of the existing success measures have focused on one aspect of this model, either system quality, information quality, system use, or user satisfaction. In general, the model depicts the notion that the quality of the IS (as either the IS artifact itself or the information produced by it) leads to system use. Higher quality systems are presumably used more frequently or more effectively, which should then produce user satisfaction with the system. The use of an effective system will then have an impact on the individual and ultimately on the organization itself.

While the DeLone and McLean model is an effective model for explaining the existing dependent measures being used by IS researchers, it may not be the best model to understand IS and their intended purposes within an organization. In order to develop a more precise definition of IS success, it is first necessary to develop a more precise definition of what an IS is and then to determine the IS's purpose in an organization.

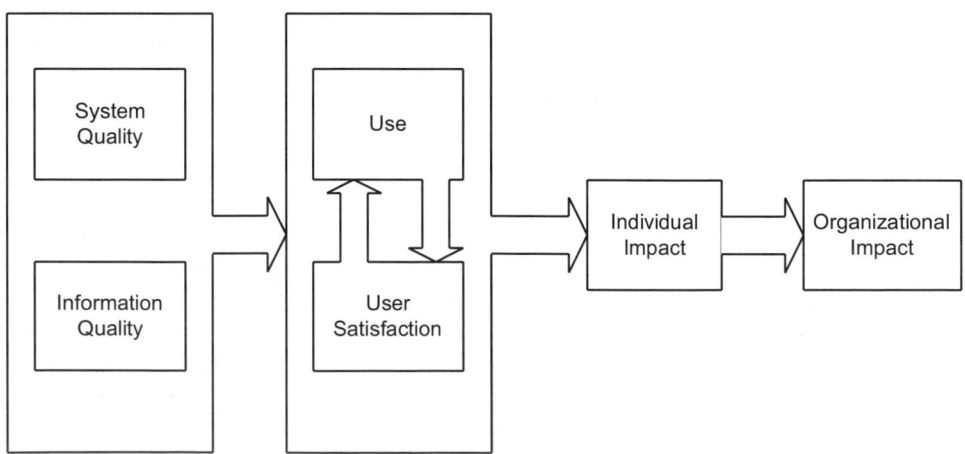

Figure 2 Delone and McLean's model of IS success.

In an abstract sense, an organization can be viewed as a complex set of interacting subsystems designed to provide a product or service to a customer in such a way as to achieve the organization's overall goal or mission. The organization's mission will typically involve product and service design, delivery, administration, and management. This viewpoint of an organization, in terms of the *organizational system,* essentially views an organization from the perspective of general systems theory (Fig. 3). Under general systems theory, a system is defined as a purposeful entity composed of interdependent components that are

unified by design to accomplish one or more objectives. The organizational system is further broken down into subsystems or functional areas. The functional areas (e.g., finance, production, etc.) act as interdependent subsystems whose goal attainment helps to achieve the goals of the organizational system. Each subsystem can be examined in a similar fashion using functional decomposition or specialization. Work is designed as groups of tasks and subtasks and is accomplished via a collaborative arrangement of human and machine (i.e., computer system and worker, or the man–machine subsystem viewpoint). In this

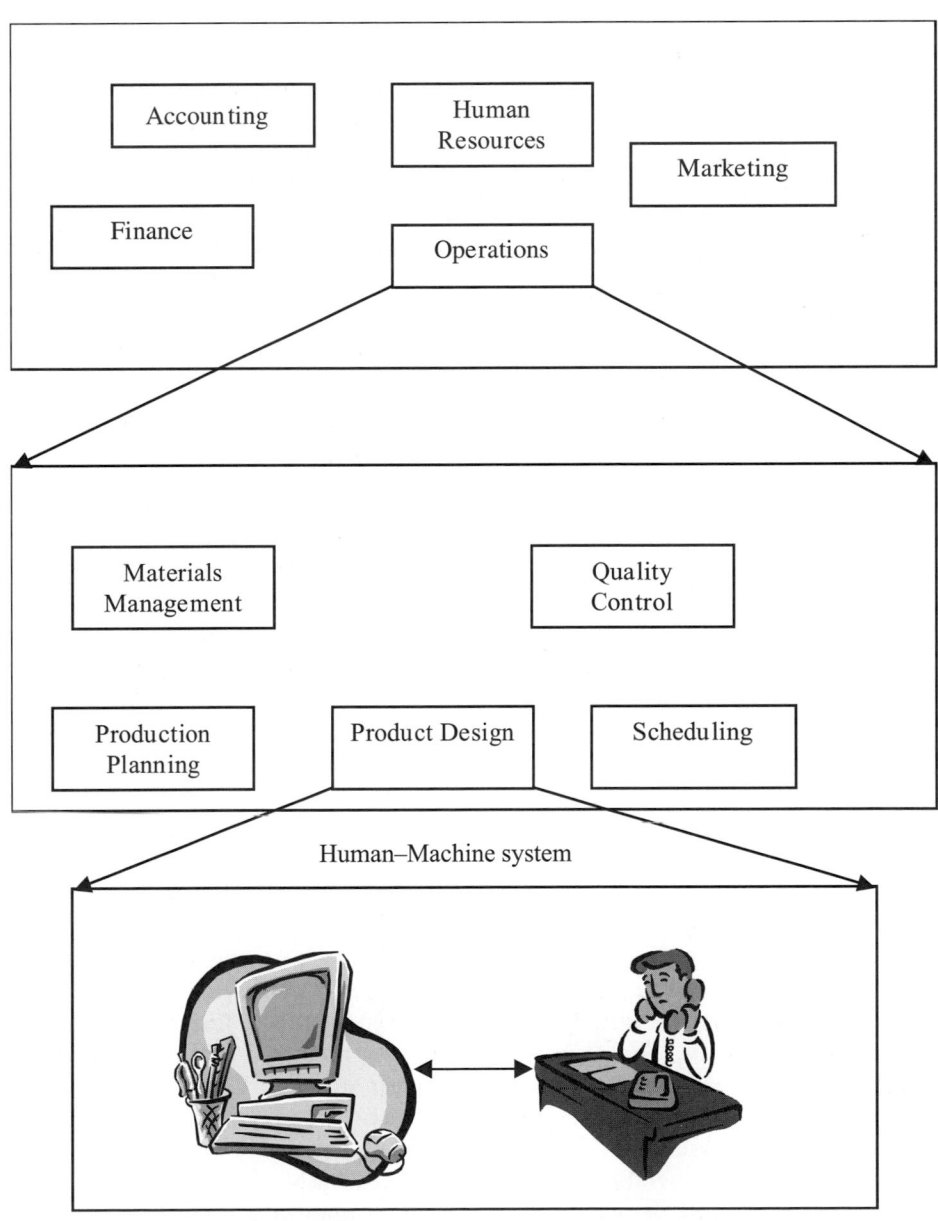

Figure 3   Organizational system viewpoint.

conceptualization of an organization, the subsystems are organizational units designed for task accomplishment and information processing. As such, IS are complementary input–process–output devices, interchangeable with human components. An effectively designed organizational system will assemble units in such a manner that work is accomplished in the most desirable way, leading to attainment of organizational goals.

A. Information Systems Goals

IS exist as components within the organizational system. In order to address the possible purposes of an IS in this context, we take an abstract view of an organizational system by borrowing the open system perspective of Bowditch and Buono (1982), where systems are composed of four interdependent subsystem components:

> "As such, organizations are referred to as multivariate social systems, composed of at least four basic components: (1) *an administrative or structural configuration,* (2) *a set of tasks* to be performed with a *related technology* or set of tools to accomplish the tasks, (3) *a human or social component* that emerges from organizational activities, and finally (4) *an informational or decision-making subsystem*" (p. 5, italics retained from the original).

An IS can be used to perform a business-related task (e.g., process an order, withdraw items from inventory, register a student for classes, or print a receipt) or to record the event or transaction for the purposes of organizational memory (subsystem component 2 from Bowditch and Buono). Essentially, the IS helps in performing the current business operations of the firm.

An IS can also be used to support the decision-making subsystem function of the organization. Essentially, all organizations must plan for future actions. After recording business activities or transactions, IS can perform decision support actions: organizing information, calculations, and re-representation, expansion, or summarizing of information (subsystem component 4).

Although IS have generally been designed to fit within the existing organizational or administrative structure, increasingly firms have achieved the most dramatic improvements in performance when they have redesigned their entire work systems to take advantage of changes in technology. Specifically, new work practices, such as decentralized decision making, self-directed work teams, and incentive systems

that encourage and reward high team performance, when combined with technology investment have been shown to provide the greatest payoff for organizations. Indeed, business process redesign can be thought of as the synergy of redesigned work structures with new technologies. In addition, computers and information technology are being used as advanced communication devices that can have a dramatic effect on organizational structure and communication patterns (thus impacting subsystem component 1).

Finally, interwoven within the organizational system is the human and social component. What makes this interdependence somewhat complex is the multifaceted and dynamic nature of humans who have their own set of goals and desires. When implementing IS to serve the needs and goals of the organization, it is imperative to take explicit account of the human and social component. The proper implementation of technology and IS requires compatibility with the sociotechnical system perspective because workers' job satisfaction and quality of work life can be negatively impacted. Alternatively, properly designed IS can increase workers' quality of work life through increased span of control and empowerment.

III. AN INTEGRATED MODEL OF INFORMATION SYSTEMS SUCCESS

The Garrity and Sanders' model of IS success adapts the Delone and McLean model by incorporating four dimensions of IS success: task support satisfaction, decision support satisfaction, interface satisfaction, and quality of work life satisfaction. The model presented in Fig. 4 is an extension of the work of Leavitt and various scholars of organization science and draws on general systems theory to provide a parsimonious representation of the major factors involved in IS success.

A. Task Support Satisfaction

The *task support satisfaction* dimension measures how well the system helps or hinders the individual in accomplishing his or her job responsibilities and fulfilling task requirements. As IS are being designed and implemented within, between, and across organizational boundaries, the implementation and use of IS can have a profound impact on a worker's ability to accomplish tasks necessary to achieve the goals of the larger organizational system. However, newly developed systems which are sound and robust in technical

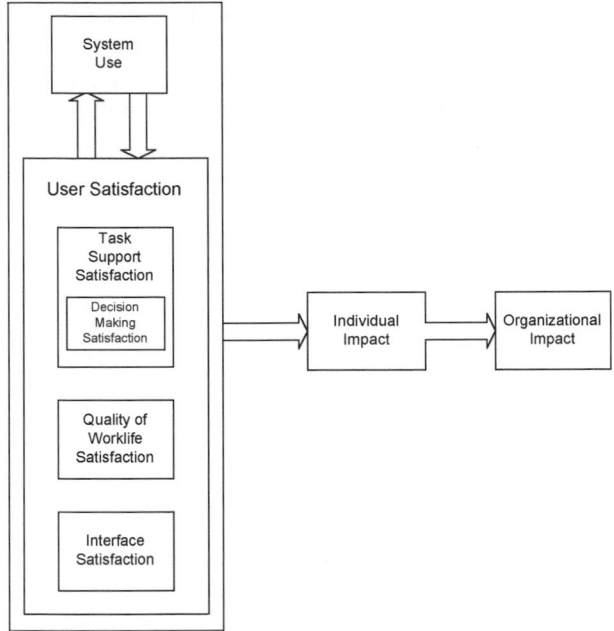

Figure 4 Garrity and Sanders' model of IS success.

ness process subsystem. The system was designed to eliminate conversations between workers and dispatchers because such conversations were thought to be "time spent off task." However, instead of increasing the efficiency of workers, the system decreased their ability to effectively troubleshoot problems. Conversations were, in fact, key ingredients to diagnosing equipment failures.

In measuring task support satisfaction, the concepts of productivity and effectiveness, and the difference between expectation and perceived quality should be incorporated because task support satisfaction is assumed to come from the individuals' perception of fulfilling task requirements. Table I shows examples of measurement items for the task support satisfaction dimension of user satisfaction.

B. Decision Support Satisfaction

Decision support satisfaction is the belief an individual has that the computer system is able to provide information and decision support toward the goal of controlling a business process. Decision support satisfaction can also be defined in terms of the capability of an IS when system intervention assists in decision making and better performance of the user's jobs. Measuring decision support satisfaction is very important because decision making is a fundamental process in organizations. The use of decision support from IS helps to simplify the decision process and make it linear, particularly when the decision-making activities are ill structured and situation specific and involve choosing from a number of alternatives.

Decision support satisfaction is viewed as a subcomponent of task satisfaction. Decision support satisfaction differs from task support satisfaction in terms of focus and detail. Jobs differ in terms of the degree of decision making involved and the composition of non-decision-making managerial or clerical tasks. For example, a job designated as managerial may still involve performing "clerical" tasks such as completing forms, generating reports, and disseminating information. On

terms frequently fail to carry out their intended roles if designers do not pay close attention to achieving a close fit with the task requirements of users and gaining a thorough understanding of how users actually accomplish work. In this context, the task support satisfaction dimension is concerned with the fit among the system, the user, and the task. This is particularly true in environments where business processes are very complex and require seamless support from IS, such as business-to-business support systems. In this context, the appropriate deployment of information technologies for each task is critical for the success of the IS.

A good example of an IS failure due to an inappropriate fit in the task support dimension is the trouble ticketing system (TTS) at NYNEX. TTS is a system which dispatches work to telephone service workers in order to schedule them and to keep an on-line record of their work. TTS was designed to make workers more productive within the context of the busi-

Table I Measurement Items for Task Support Satisfaction

1. This information system is more useful than I had expected.
2. This information system assists me in performing my tasks better.
3. This information system is extremely useful.
4. Using this information system enables me to accomplish tasks more quickly.
5. This information system makes it easier to do my tasks.

the other hand, an individual in a clerical or analyst position may perform managerial tasks such as communicating, delegating, coordinating and organizing individuals, and controlling a process or decision making at a certain organizational level. The task support satisfaction dimension captures the IS support for the overall set of tasks associated with job activities, while decision support satisfaction is more focused on IS support for decision making such as structuring, analyzing, and deciding or implementing a decision.

Measurement items for decision support satisfaction attempt to determine whether the system supports the individual in recognizing problems, structuring problems, and/or making decisions related to the goal of controlling a business process. Examples of measurement items for decision support satisfaction are shown in Table II.

C. Interface Satisfaction

Interface satisfaction is a dimension that captures the user's overall impression of the interface in terms of presentation, format, ease of use, and efficiency. According to the theory of symbolic representation in problem solving, there are three types of symbolic representation: linguistic representation, visual imagery representation, and exploratory reasoning. In most problem solving situations where information search and the evaluation of alternatives are critical stages, various combinations of these three representations help direct attention and focus on appropriate alternatives. Differences in information presentation may also result in changes in decision-making strategies. This, in turn, influences the effectiveness of decision making and also task performance.

Hence, limited menus, poorly designed navigation, and the difficulty in comparing alternatives in a effective manner all make task support and decision support activities more difficult in business organizations. In particular, high interface quality in the systems that assist in complex processes is critical in reducing cognitive overhead (i.e., additional efforts and concentration necessary to maintain several tasks or trails at one

time) and disorientation (i.e., the tendency to lose one's sense of location and direction in a set of nonlinear documents). As such, the quality of the interface is related to both task support satisfaction and decision support satisfaction. An improperly designed interface can cause users difficulty with task completion or can impair their ability to make decisions.

The focus of measuring the interface satisfaction dimension is on presentation, format, ease of use, and efficiency. Interface satisfaction is assumed to incorporate most parts of information quality because the vehicle for presenting the information (e.g., a textbox, table, graph, listbox, or form) cannot be separated from the information itself. Table III shows several examples of measurement items for interface satisfaction.

D. Quality of Work Life Satisfaction

Quality of work life satisfaction or perceived quality of work life is a set of affective beliefs directed toward the organizational work domain of life. *Quality of work life* addresses the fit between an IS and the sociotechnical work world of the respective users and involves IS's impacts on people's feelings, physical needs, and psychological states. In this view, users are not only components of the organizational system, but they are also recognized as having their own goals and aspirations separate from the directives of the organization.

Introducing a new IS changes job characteristics such as task autonomy, skill variety, task identity, task significance, and task feedback through deskilling and/or upgrading jobs. Task autonomy is defined as the extent to which the job provides individual discretion relating to the work process. Skill variety means the opportunity to use numerous and varied skills in one's personal repertoire to perform the work. Task identity is defined as the degree to which the job requires the completion of a whole, recognizable piece of work. Task significance is defined as the degree to which a job affects the lives of other people. Finally, task feedback means the well-defined opportunity to know how effectively one is performing directly from the job itself.

Table II Measurement Items for Decision Support Satisfaction

1. This information system improves the quality of my decision making.
2. Use of the information system enables me to make better decisions.
3. This information system assists me in making decisions more effectively.
4. Use of the information system enables me to set my priorities in decision making.

Table III Measurement Items for Interface Satisfaction

1. The information provided by this information system is clear and understandable.
2. Learning to use this information system was easy for me.
3. This information system is user friendly.
4. This information system is easy to use.
5. I found it easy to get this information system to do what I want it to do.
6. My interaction with this information system was clear and understandable.
7. It would be easy for me to become skillful at using this information system.

Changes in these job characteristics have been shown to have a curvilinear influence on the key indicators of the quality of work life satisfaction, including job satisfaction, job-related anxiety, and emotional exhaustion. Deskilling involves a decrease in the skill content of a particular job over time and an increase in the number of people in less skilled jobs. Upgrading involves increases in time to concentrate on conceptual and decision-making tasks by reducing much of the manual work in information processing. Likewise, introducing a new IS may alter job characteristics and, in turn, influence work outcomes.

Measurement items for quality of work life satisfaction attempt to determine whether the introduction of a new IS changes the perceived quality of work life in terms of changes in five job characteristics: task autonomy, skill variety, task identity, task significance, and task feedback. The examples of measurement items for the quality of work life satisfaction are shown in Table IV.

E. Dimensions of Information Systems Success and the Integrated Model

The four dimensions of IS success all contribute to or impact the successful attainment of goals at the organizational level. The nature of IS in the organizational setting is closely tied to providing task-related support capabilities to achieve organizational goals. That is, the extent to which IS help organizations determine objectives and support work outcomes based on system use depends upon the level of task-related support capabilities expressed directly by task support satisfaction and indirectly by decision support satisfaction and interface satisfaction. However, it is believed that task-related support capabilities alone do not account for the effect of system use on perceived organizational performance. Emotional factors such as quality of work life are inextricably intertwined with rational organizational processes such as task support and also influence organizational performance. Figure 5 provides a causal model of how the dimensions of IS success are believed to be related to one another and how they ultimately affect organizational performance.

The so-called user satisfaction-based information systems success model (SISSM) presented in Fig. 5 is related to the TAM. Specifically, task support satisfaction corresponds with TAM's perceived usefulness and interface satisfaction corresponds with TAM's perceived ease of use. However, the model extends TAM by incorporating explicit consideration of decision support satisfaction as a separate and important dimension of IS success. Furthermore, the model incorporates the assessment of a worker's quality of work

Table IV Measurement Items for Quality of Work Life Satisfaction

1. The information system has improved my overall quality of work life.
2. The information system helps alleviate time pressure.
3. The information system gives me the right level of autonomy.
4. The use of the information system makes my job more challenging.
5. The information system makes my job more important.
6. The information system makes my skills more important.
7. The use of the information system improves my relationship with other employees.
8. Learning the information system allows more promotion opportunities.

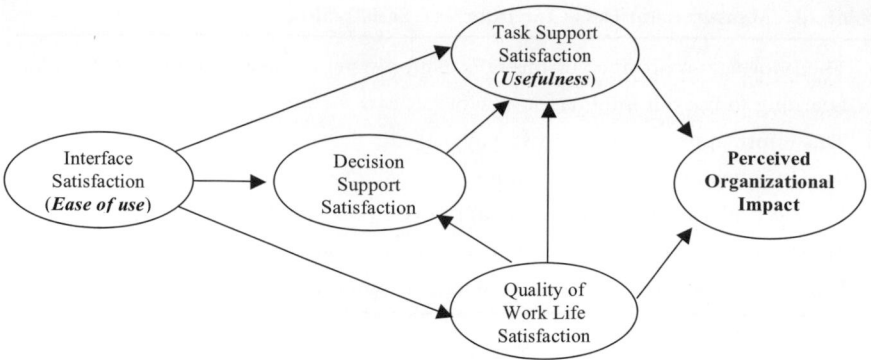

Figure 5 User satisfaction-based information systems success model (SISSM).

life satisfaction. Empirical results lend support to the model. Figure 6 shows the results of an empirical test of a structural model using partial least squares. The model is able to account for 70% of the variance in perceived organizational impact.

IV. LEVELS OF ANALYSIS

According to the Delone and McLean model of IS success, an IS contributes to or impacts the individual performance, which then leads to organizational impact. Two major questions arise from this sequence of impacts or causal chain:

1. How, precisely do individual impacts lead to organizational impact?
2. Why not measure organizational impact directly instead of individual impact or user satisfaction?

We next examine the levels of analysis in order to address these two issues. Three levels of analysis can be used to examine this causal chain: the individual level of analysis discussed earlier, the process level, and the organization level (see Table V).

A. Information System Success at the Individual Level

The vast majority of empirical studies on IS development have utilized IS success measures at the individual level of analysis. The previous sections of this article discussed the basic theoretical foundation of this research. Although too numerous to mention here, most of the dependent measures have been classified as user satisfaction, user information satisfaction, or end-user computing satisfaction or have utilized a simple self-reported "use" measure. Using DeLone and McLean's model as a guide (see Fig. 2), user satisfaction and use should lead to individual impact, which then leads to organizational impact.

B. Information System Success at the Process Level

The purpose of a business processes is to produce a product or service and to create value for various internal or external customers. Introducing a new IS may change the business process and how value is created.

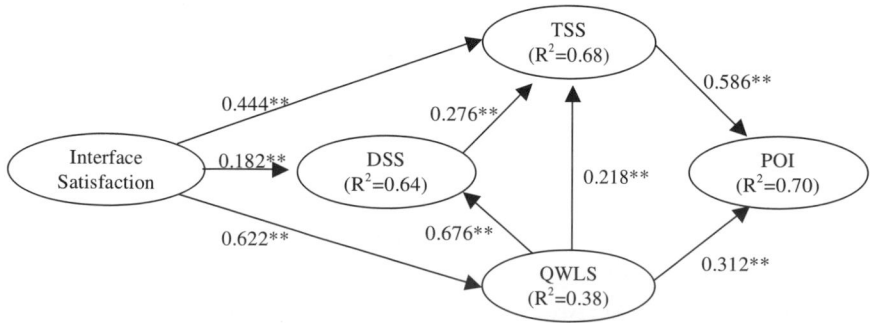

Figure 6 SISSM structural model results.*p < .01, **p < .001 (based on $t_{(172)}$, two-tailed test).

Table V Information Systems Success Measurement Across Levels of Analysis

Level	Dimension(s)	Subdimensions
Individual level	User satisfaction	Task support satisfaction Decision support satisfaction Interface satisfaction Quality of work life satisfaction
Business process level	Operational efficiency	Flexibility and scalability Consistency Productivity Cycle time
	Management effectiveness	Improvement in decision making Improvement in span of control Improvement in planning
Oganization level	Financial performance	Return on investment Return on sales Cash flow Profitability
	Enhancement of products and services	Cost reduction Quality Responsiveness Reliability
	Market share growth	Market share gains Sales growth Revenue growth

The impacts of a new IS on changes in value creation logic should be focused on four basic dimensions, including operational efficiency, management effectiveness, the establishment of market linkages, and the enhancement of products and services. The operational efficiency and management effectiveness can be viewed in the context of internal customers, while the establishment of market linkages and the enhancement of products and services can be evaluated in terms of external customers. By focusing on internal customer value, the impacts of IS on business processes can be measured using internal performance variables such as flexibility, consistency, productivity, and cycle time. The impacts of IS on business processes in the context of external customer value can be measured using external performance variables in the form of perceptions of cost, quality, responsiveness, and reliability. However, external customer value is better assessed at the organizational level of analysis since financial and external measures already exist and because these processes are designed to benefit customers and impact the organization.

1. Information Systems Contribution to Operational Efficiency

Operational efficiency focuses on the improvement in internal customer performance and is measured in terms of flexibility, consistency, productivity, and cycle time. The flexibility of a business process is defined as the adjustability to meet immediate and/or long-term customer needs as business conditions change. Information technologies such as computer-integrated manufacturing and group technology allow organizations to adopt a more flexible way of manufacturing and to increase customer responsiveness. IS also help companies cope with market conditions in a flexible manner by providing faster and more exact information regarding customer needs, prices, and costs. Scalability is defined as the ability to significantly increase or decrease capacity without major disruption or excessive costs. The increase in scalability is one of the important benefits of the technical advances in information technologies because nonscalable processes require huge capital expenditure for production system capacity changes.

Consistency in a business process means the degree to which the same desired results are obtained by applying the same techniques in the same way. IS may force organizations to do things consistently by incorporating all the work procedures in the systems. IS may also be designed to provide information that helps people perform and control business processes in a consistent manner.

Productivity in the context of business process is referred to as the relationship between the amounts of output produced by a business process and the amount of money, time, and effort it consumes. Improvement of business process productivity depends on the capability to produce more output from the same level of inputs or produce the same output from lower levels of inputs. IS help employees to work smarter and more efficiently by (1) providing the right information to allow workers to skip steps in task processing, (2) automating tasks and calculations, (3) providing support for decision making, and (4) providing support for production processing and scheduling. It is important to note that IS investments are not just the purchase price, but also all the other costs such as support, training, maintenance, administration, and time spent by end users doing programming.

Cycle time is defined as the length of time between the start of the process and its completion. It is determined by a combination of three factors: processing time, waiting time, and dependencies between steps. It was reported that in complicated manufacturing with factories producing a wide range of products, less than 10% of the total cycle time had been actually spent adding value to the material in process. IS can help in situations where long waiting times and bottlenecks exist by helping people decide on the right order of work to improve workflow. This is accomplished through various drawing tools, statistical analysis tools, and detail information.

2. Information Systems Contribution to Management Effectiveness

Management effectiveness can be measured in terms of improvement in management decision making, planning, and span of control attributed to company IS. An increased span of control can be achieved through improvements in monitoring and performance measurement, which in turn improves the time management of managers and increases their productivity. Managers can also focus more on the major issues and speed up decision making by leaving routine decisions to other individuals.

Decision-making behavior can be characterized in terms of the number of criteria used, the type of information search, sources of information used, the use of heuristics, and the number of alternatives generated. IS help decision makers specify required information and alternatives needed to be considered. This assistance from an IS increases management decision-making performance by simplifying the decision process, making it linear, and ultimately allowing managers to control the business process.

C. Information Systems Success Measurement at the Organization Level

The organizational impact of IS includes various issues from cost effectiveness to economic performance, including profit performance to product and management quality. Most variables that measure organizational impacts directly have used economic metrics.

1. Information Systems Contribution to Financial Performance

The major measurements for financial performance include return on investment, return on sales, cash flow, and profitability. Information systems contribute to the maximization of financial performance by reducing internal costs or increasing productivity and by providing information needed for better decisions such as pricing decisions. IS can support pricing decisions in many different ways. The most direct way is simply to provide immediate results to the relationship between price and sales. Another way is to maximize profits through market segmentation, dividing the market into different customer groups willing to pay different amounts for different types or levels of service.

2. Information System Contribution to the Enhancement of Products and Services

The impact of new IS on the enhancement of products and services results in a higher level of perceived value by customers. This perceived value of customers can be measured in terms of cost/price, quality, responsiveness, and reliability. Cost is argued to be a primary determinant of customer satisfaction. IS reduce costs to a customer by reducing the cost of acquiring and using the product.

Quality is defined as the degree of excellence or superiority in kind and as the totality of features and characteristics of a product and service that bears on its ability to satisfy given customer needs. It is not just about meeting specifications or agreed upon goals, but also about satisfying customers' expectations better than the competitors. IS can be applied in many different ways to improve product or service quality. Major approaches to increasing product or service quality through IS are based on increasing the accessibility to information regarding product/service features and providing additional information that can increase the product's usefulness. This is because customers purchase a service when they buy a product. Furthermore, in many cases, to buy a product means only to access a service.

Responsiveness is referred to as the degree to which a service or product provider takes timely action based on what a customer wants. IS help companies give customers timely and useful responses, as well as provide a way to achieve market presence through Web-based technology.

Finally, the reliability of a product or service is defined as the likelihood it will provide the promised functionality without experiencing significant operational failures. Systems can also make output more reliable by reducing dependence on the personal knowledge of specific individuals and by increasing the amount of explicit organizational knowledge. Likewise, systems that bring expert knowledge to help people make decisions may increase reliability by making the best knowledge available for whomever is making a decision.

3. Information Systems Contribution to Market Share Growth

IS impacts on market share growth can be measured in terms of market share gains, sales growth, and revenue growth. A new IS may help increase product awareness, support the sales force, improve product availability, and facilitate payment. IS that establish and use marketing databases can promote product awareness by exploiting "addressability"—the ability to direct specific messages to specific individuals or groups. By providing information such as purchase patterns, affiliations, and age, these databases make it possible to focus marketing resources on the individuals with a higher probability of making a purchase.

IS can support various steps in the sales process, including designing the sales program, identifying prospects, negotiating prices, order taking, and follow-up contacts to maintain the relationship. IS such as inventory systems also provide an effective way for businesses to maximize merchandise availability without excessive inventory levels by tracking the quantity on hand of every item and allowing quick replenishment. Facilitating payment is another way to increase sales volume by helping customers purchase products. IS that allow credit card, debit card, and smart card transactions all facilitate payment for consumers by making cash or checks unnecessary, thereby increasing convenience and sales volume.

V. LEVELS OF ANALYSIS AND CURRENT INFORMATION SYSTEMS SUCCESS MEASUREMENT

Viewing IS success across the levels of analysis gives us a broad perspective on how IS contribute to organizational success. Since IS can be defined as components within the organizational system and since their ultimate purpose is to enhance organizational goals, it is tempting to measure IS success using broad organizational measures. However, isolating the specific contribution of IS to the attainment of organizational goals is difficult. Since organizational level measures are so broad, it is very difficult to control for and measure other impacts on profitability, market share, and enhanced product or service levels.

Because of these long-standing difficulties in macrolevel measurement, researchers and practitioners alike have relied on user satisfaction measures. However, increased precision and insight can be obtained by unlocking the hidden dimensions of IS success, which can then lead to insights on relationships between IS features and organizational impacts.

Specifically, task support satisfaction measures the degree of satisfaction a user has in the support provided by the IS tool toward the goal of accomplishing job and task requirements. IS that support users in their specific tasks will improve operational efficiencies at the business process level (see Figs. 3–5). Increases in operational efficiency will lead to market share growth via lower prices and potentially will contribute to enhanced products and services and the ability to establish and maintain market linkages (e.g., arrangements with suppliers and external firms are enhanced when companies have greater market power, more efficient operations, etc.).

Decision support satisfaction will increase management effectiveness at the business process level. As discussed earlier, improved decision support can increase the span of control of managers by improving monitoring, decision quality, decision speed, and performance measurement and thereby increase managers' productivity. Increased management effectiveness can have a deep and broad impact on all aspects of organizational performance measurement. More effective management decision making can lead to improved levels of service, enhanced products (e.g., via better product positioning, improved features), increased market share, and more and better market linkages.

Perhaps the most profound and significant changes in organizations occur when IS, work systems, and business processes all change in unison, which then result in significant changes in organizational performance. These simultaneous work system and IS changes will result in improved sociotechnical systems because when work system and human systems are both improved together and in harmony, a synergistic effect occurs that then results in significant and simultaneous improvements in quality of work life and in organizational goal achievement (Garrity, 2001). Business process redesign is the study of business process changes and how best to achieve dramatic improvements in organizational performance through the redesign of work practices. Recently, researchers have called for IS development practices that take into account the codesign of work systems and IS. It is believed that improved business processes will lead to better organizational performance.

The interface satisfaction dimension of IS success captures the IS specific design characteristics that enhance or negatively impact task support, decision support, and quality of work life satisfaction (see Fig. 3, the human–machine system viewpoint). By measuring IS success at the individual level of analysis, we can determine the direct affect of IS characteristics (interface satisfaction) on people and examine how these effects ultimately influence perceived organizational impacts. Ultimately, users are best able to assess IS success from their vantage point, as components of the organizational system, the sociotechnical system, and the human–machine system.

The use of general systems theory (GST) provides a unified vision of the multiple systems and system components involved in complex organizations. GST considers systems from an abstract perspective, thus allowing us to envision work systems, IS, and human or sociotechnical systems using the same paradigm. It is clear that organizations are best viewed from a GST perspective so that we may consider how IS can best fit within the structure of work systems, business processes, and human systems.

Since GST uses simple, abstract definitions and concepts, understanding IS success using this framework can be extended regardless of changes in technology. In other words, GST uses notions of systems, components, goals, and design and thus ignores *how* systems accomplish their goals. Changes in technology can easily be incorporated into new dimensions of IS success.

VI. THE FUTURE OF COMPUTING AND THE EVOLUTION OF INFORMATION SYSTEMS SUCCESS

Trends in information technology and electronic commerce are providing IS planners with both opportunities and problems because it is not currently clear how these technologies can be best applied to affect firm performance. However, the development of IS success measurement constructs can aid practitioners

by providing empirical evidence to substantiate strategic applications of new technology. One can extend the current success model through the identification of new, major areas of potential impact that can then be developed into IS success dimensions.

While the dimensions of IS success presented here (task/decision support satisfaction, interface satisfaction, quality of work life satisfaction) cover the contribution of IS success to organizational goals, the IS used earlier as examples may be thought of as internal IS. However, increasingly IS may be developed and included as components of corporations' products and services. In order to account for new types of systems, the IS success model must be adapted to include new major areas of potential impact.

The new major areas of impact we have identified and their corresponding success dimensions are: (1) IS that support and that are components of products and services (product and service support satisfaction), (2) IS that support and link to external organizations (market linkage support satisfaction), and (3) IS that support and alter communication within organizations (communication and structural support satisfaction). Each of these dimensions is discussed later.

A. New Dimensions of Information Systems Success

As IS become important components of other facets of organizations, new dimensions of IS success can be incorporated into the IS success framework. As discussed earlier, IS are becoming an important tool for differentiating products and services. This can be done in a number of ways, including providing IS as an actual part of the product (e.g., automobiles with geographic map support) and through product customization. Customization is the creation or modification of a product or service based on a specific customer's needs, thereby increasing the product's value for that customer and ultimately company profits. The Internet is one technology that has provided the capability to customize products to customers. Customer tracking technologies such as writing cookies to the user's computer, database marketing, and the use of intelligent agents can allow for increased customization. No doubt ubiquitous computing and newer technologies will provide even greater capabilities.

Recall that from the perspective of GST that an organization is a set of components (i.e., the organization structure, departments, or functional areas) arranged by design to accomplish one or more objectives such as profitability and other organizational goals. The open systems view of an organization takes an additional step and allows for many possible structural arrangements outside the organizational system boundary. In the current business environment, traditional company boundaries are beginning to blur as IS are increasingly being used to forge strategic alliances with external organizations.

Finally, revisiting Bowditch and Buono's multivariate, open system framework of organizations, we can also imagine how future IS will likely affect the administrative and structural configuration. As is already apparent, recent Internet-based technologies have served to alter communication patterns and, in some cases, allowed organizations to assume flatter structures. With the peer-to-peer models of computing, it is likely that future organizations may evolve into hybrid organizational structures that leverage this technology to its fullest.

The analysis of IS using GST provides an ideal framework for understanding the role of IS in organizations. GST considers systems from an abstract perspective, thus allowing us to envision work systems, IS and human or sociotechnical systems using the same paradigm. It is clear that organizations are best viewed from a GST perspective so that we may consider the multiple and sometimes conflicting goals of work systems, business processes, human systems, and IS. Indeed, one may view the fundamental concepts of IS simply as a special case of a work system. Understanding the fundamental concepts of IS and how they relate to the larger context of organizational systems and human systems allows us to have a better understanding of the goals of IS. Understanding IS goals is fundamental toward understanding IS success.

SEE ALSO THE FOLLOWING ARTICLES

Decision-Making Approaches • Decision Support Systems • Information Measurement • Prototyping • Quality Information Systems • Structured Design Methodologies • Systems Implementation • Total Quality Management and Quality Control

BIBLIOGRAPHY

Bowditch, J. L., and Buono, A. F. (1982). *Quality of Work Life Assessment: A Survey-Based Approach.* Boston, MA: Auburn House Publishing Co.

Davis, F. D. (1986). "A Technology Acceptance Model for Empirically Testing New End-User Information Systems: Theory and Results," unpublished Ph.D. Dissertation, MIT.

Davis, F. D. (1989). Perceived usefulness, perceived ease of use, and user acceptance of information technology. MIS Quarterly 13(3), 319–340.

Davis, F. D., Bagozzi, R. P., and Warshaw, P. R. (1989). User acceptance of computer technology: a comparison of two theoretical models. Management Science 35(8), 982–1003.

DeLone, W. H., and McLean, E. R. (1992). Information systems success: the quest for the dependent variable. Information Systems Research 3(1), 61–95.

Doll, W. J., and Torkzadeh, G. (1988). The measurement of end-user computing satisfaction. MIS Quarterly 12(2), 259–274.

Garrity, E. J. (2001). Synthesizing user centered and designer centered IS development approaches using general systems theory. Information Systems Frontiers 3(1), 107–122.

Garrity, E. J., and Sanders, G. L. (1998a). Introduction to information systems success measurement, In *Information Systems Success Measurement,* E. J. Garrity and G. L. Sanders, Eds., pp. 1–12. Hershey, PA: Idea Group Publishing.

Garrity, E. J., and Sanders, G. L. (1998b). Dimensions of information systems success, In *Information Systems Success Measurement,* E. J. Garrity and G. L. Sanders, Eds., pp. 13–45. Hershey, PA: Idea Group Publishing.

Garrity, E. J., Glassberg, B., Kim, Y. J., Sanders, G. L., and Shin, S. (2001). An experimental investigation of electronic commerce success factors for web-based information systems. Working paper.

Ives, B., Olson, M. H., and Baroudi, J. J. (1983). The measurement of user information satisfaction. Communications of the ACM 26(10), 785–793.

Leavitt, H. J. (1964). Applied organization change in industry: structural, technical, and human approaches, In *New Perspectives in Organizational Research,* pp. 55–71. Chichester: Wiley.

Seddon, P. B. (1997). A respecification and extension of the DeLone and McLean model of IS success. Information Systems Research 8(3), 240–253.

Sherman, B. A., Garrity, E. J., Kim, Y. J., and Sanders, G. L. (2001). A model of information system success based on user satisfaction. Working paper.

Supply Chain Management

Mo Adam Mahmood, Leopoldo A. Gemoets, and Adriano O. Solis

University of Texas, El Paso

GLOSSARY

electronic commerce (e-commerce) technologies The Internet, World Wide Web, intranets, and extranets.

electronic data interchange (EDI) The direct computer-to-computer exchange between two business partners (e.g., a manufacturer of finished goods and a supplier of raw materials) of standard business documents such as purchase orders and invoices.

enterprise application integration (EAI) A framework for integrating enterprise software applications and business processes that run on different computer systems.

enterprise resource planning (ERP) system An enterprise-wide information system that facilitates the flow of transactional data relating to manufacturing, logistics, finance and accounting, marketing and sales, and human resources in the firm.

logistics That part of the supply chain process that plans, implements, and controls the efficient, effective flow and storage of goods, services, and related information from the point of origin to the point of consumption in order to meet customers' requirements.

materials management A coordinating function responsible for planning, coordinating, and controlling materials flow from supplier through production to consumer; as an organizational concept, typically involves purchasing and supply management activities, inventory management, receiving activities, stores and warehousing, in-plant materials handling, production planning, scheduling, and control, and traffic and transportation.

supply chain Encompasses all activities associated with the flow and transformation of goods and services, as well as the attendant information flows, from suppliers down to the end user.

SUPPLY CHAIN MANAGEMENT involves integrating and managing the key business processes associated with the flow and transformation of goods and services, as well as the attendant information flows, from the sources of raw materials to the end user.

I. WHAT IS SUPPLY CHAIN MANAGEMENT?

The past couple of decades have seen much attention given to *supply chain management* (SCM). The term was first introduced by consultants in the 1980s, and its definition has undergone some fairly significant evolutions since then.

The fierce competition in global markets, increasingly shorter product life cycles, and increasingly higher customer expectations with respect to product capability and reliability, delivery lead times, flexibility, and service have all led business firms to focus on their supply chains. In an industrial setting, the *supply chain* (see Fig. 1) encompasses all activities associated with the flow and transformation of goods and services, as well as the attendant information flows,

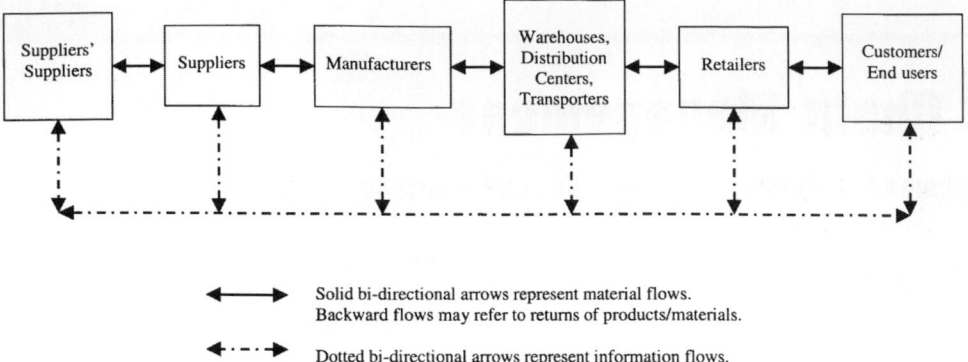

Figure 1 Supply chain: entities and flows.

from suppliers of raw material and components, through manufacturing/assembly plants, through the distribution chain (transporters, warehouses, distribution centers, retailers), and down to the customers/end users. Managing the supply chain involves transcending the traditional, legal boundaries of entities along that chain—such as between the manufacturer and its suppliers, or between the manufacturer and its distributors.

The early literature defined SCM as the planning and control of total materials flow from suppliers through customers. Later literature referred to the management not only of the materials flow, but of both materials *and* information flows. However, some confusion has arisen between the terms *SCM* and *logistics*. Until recently, SCM was generally understood by practitioners, consultants, and academics to be the integration of logistics across the supply chain, inclusive of customers and suppliers. This understanding had largely been consistent with the definition of *logistics management* appearing in previous literature (circa 1986) of the Council of Logistics Management (CLM):

> The process of planning, implementing, and controlling the efficient, cost-effective flow and storage of raw materials, in-process inventory, finished goods, and related information flow from point-of-origin to point-of-consumption for the purpose of conforming to customer requirements.

The CLM eventually issued in October 1998 a revised definition explicitly stating the position that logistics management is only a part of SCM:

> Logistics is that part of the supply chain process that plans, implements, and controls the efficient, effective flow and storage of goods, services, and related information from the point-of-origin to the point-of-consumption in order to meet customers' requirements.

SCM, therefore, is not just another name for logistics, but involves elements that extend beyond logistics.

The Supply-Chain Council—which was organized in 1996–1997 by representatives of a number of companies including, among others, Procter & Gamble, Lockheed Martin, Texas Instruments, Compaq, and Bayer—defines the supply chain as encompassing "every effort involved in producing and delivering a final product or service, from the supplier's supplier to the customer's customer." Accordingly, the Supply-Chain Council emphasizes that SCM includes key business processes such as supply and demand management, sourcing of raw materials and parts, manufacturing and assembly, tracking of warehousing and inventory, order entry and management, distribution across all channels, and delivery to the customer.

On the other hand, the Global Supply Chain Forum (GSCF)—a group of practitioners and academic researchers that has been meeting since 1994, and whose stated objective is to improve the theory and practice of supply chain management—defines SCM as "the integration of key business processes from end user through original suppliers that provides products, services, and information that add value for customers and other stakeholders." The key supply chain processes identified by the GSCF are (1) customer relationship management, (2) customer service management, (3) demand management, (4) order fulfillment, (5) manufacturing flow management, (6) procurement, (7) product development and commercialization, and (8) returns.

Definitions do vary from one source to another in terms of exact wording. Nevertheless, the understanding of SCM has gone beyond merely integrating logistics across the supply chain. SCM is currently understood in terms of integrating and managing the key business processes associated with the flow and transformation of goods and services, as well as the attendant information flows, both within and between the various organizations along the supply chain.

As cited in early literature, the stated goal of SCM is to meet customer service objectives, while at the same time minimizing inventory and related costs. Underlying this goal has been the need to boost competitiveness and profitability in increasingly tougher global markets. This rationale continues to be as relevant today as it had been when SCM was first being discussed in the 1980s. Current literature would refer to the supply chain as consisting of all stages involved, directly or indirectly, in fulfilling a customer request, and SCM as involving the integration of all activities along a supply chain to achieve a sustainable competitive advantage, minimize system-wide costs, satisfy service level requirements, and maximize the overall value generated. The value generated by the supply chain—which refers to the difference between what the final product is worth to the customer and the effort expended in fulfilling the customer's request—would be correlated with the profitability of the supply chain. Apparently, while goals and objectives of SCM are stated somewhat differently in various sources, they all lead back to the same rationale for SCM as declared early on.

This article is organized as follows: The next section discusses the difficulty in supply chain integration. The following section on supply chain management decisions describes decisions that managers are required to make in the context of SCM at the strategic, tactical, and operational levels. The fourth section discusses the dimensions along which integration and coordination of supply chain processes and activities need to take place. This is followed by examples of SCM success stories. The sixth section discusses the importance of information flow in the context of SCM. The next section explains enterprise resource planning systems, which facilitate the flow of information in SCM. The eighth section addresses EDI and its problems. The following section details the role of e-commerce technologies in SCM. This is followed by a review of emerging technical and managerial issues in SCM. The final section concludes the article by providing suggestions for future research.

II. DIFFICULTY OF SUPPLY CHAIN INTEGRATION

The early papers on SCM stressed that the key to managing a supply chain efficiently is to view it as a single entity, instead of relegating fragmented responsibility to the various functional areas (e.g., purchasing, man-

ufacturing, distribution, and sales) and entities (e.g., national, regional, and subregional warehouses and distribution centers) in the chain. Three elements were cited as being necessary in integrating/coordinating the supply chain: (1) recognizing customer service level requirements, (2) determining where inventories should be positioned along the supply chain and how much stock to carry at each point, and (3) developing appropriate policies and procedures for managing the entire chain as a single entity.

Traditional inventory theory suggests that a supply chain will use increasing amounts of resources (e.g., inventory, manufacturing/transport/storage facilities, funds, people) to satisfy greater service levels and customer needs. Integration of the supply chain is aimed at lowering the total amount of resources needed to provide the required customer service levels. However, supply chain integration is difficult for two main reasons.

In the first place, the various entities along the supply chain will have different, often conflicting objectives. For instance, car dealers will prefer to have a wide variety of automobile models and option configurations actually present on their premises. On the other hand, a car manufacturer would find it very costly to maintain huge dealer-based inventories. Likewise, suppliers' deliveries of subassemblies, components, and accessories will have to address the car manufacturer's need to address the wide variety of models and options that car buyers expect. However, suppliers may prefer to deliver materials in larger lot sizes in order to achieve production, handling, and transportation economies. It is certainly important to recognize that supply chain management involves minimizing system-wide costs and maximizing the overall value generated by the supply chain. It will be doomed to failure if costs were simply shifted from one entity to another along the chain—which may happen when entities have conflicting objectives and only the entity that wields more power is favored by a certain decision.

Secondly, the supply chain is a dynamic system. Customers' expectations and customer demand change over time, as with suppliers' and distributors' capabilities. Undoubtedly, the entities and relationships between entities along the supply chain will also evolve over time. After World War II, there was a dearth of products in domestic markets, while customers exhibited fairly homogeneous, predictable product preferences. Mass production was an appropriate competitive strategy. Eventually, however, customers have become more sophisticated and demanding, expecting not only increasingly lower prices and higher levels of quality and reliability in the products that they purchase, but also greater customization. Mass customization imposes operating concerns and pressures on the various entities along the supply chain that are totally different from those under a regime of mass production. Computer vendors like Dell and Gateway now allow customers to select, using the Internet, from among many possible configurations and options for personal computers listed in on-line catalogs, and ship the customized orders direct to buyers' offices or homes within a matter of days. This constitutes a significant departure from the traditional supply chain for the personal computer industry, which has included distributors and retailers. Similarly, global markets are characterized by increasingly shorter product life cycles. Personal computers, for instance, have life cycles currently estimated at 6 months or even less. The pressure to drastically reduce time to market underscores the importance of such relatively new approaches as early purchasing involvement and early supplier involvement in the product development process.

III. SUPPLY CHAIN MANAGEMENT DECISIONS

SCM requires making decisions at various levels of a firm's activities: strategic, tactical, and operational.

Strategic supply chain decisions pertain to how to structure the firm's supply chain. These include the number, locations, and capacities of manufacturing and warehousing facilities, types of products to be manufactured and stored at the various facilities, and the modes of transportation of materials through the logistics network, as well as the type of information system to be used. For instance, associated with its distribution strategy, which is discussed below, Wal-Mart Stores has had to decide on the number and locations of its distribution centers (62 locations reported as of May 10, 2001). Such strategic decisions are long-term in orientation and involve relatively significant costs. Moreover, changes would tend to be very costly. Hence, strategic supply chain decisions should take into consideration uncertainties in the marketplace over the next several years.

Tactical supply chain decisions relate to defining operating policies that govern short-term operations. These policies may be updated anywhere between once quarterly and once yearly, and would pertain to such decisions as, among others, purchasing and inventory replenishment policies, which markets to be supplied from which locations, aggregate production volumes by product category at each manufacturing plant, and

the planned buildup of inventories. Such tactical decisions establish the parameters or bounds within which the supply chain will function over a given time period. At the tactical level, firms would try to take advantage of any flexibility built into the supply chain design (at the strategic level) to optimize performance within the shorter time horizon involved.

The *operational* level involves day-to-day or weekly supply chain decision making. With the supply chain configuration fixed and operating policies already in place, decisions are made with respect to placing replenishment orders, scheduling production, allocating product to individual customer orders, establishing required lead times, specifying the shipping date and the appropriate shipping mode for each order, and packing and loading each order, among many others.

IV. DIMENSIONS OF SUPPLY CHAIN MANAGEMENT

The key supply chain processes identified by both the Supply-Chain Council and the Global Supply Chain Forum clearly indicate the need to coordinate across various entities along the supply chain, both within and between organizations. Integration and coordination of supply chain processes and activities need to take place along three dimensions: intrafunctional, interfunctional, and interorganizational (see Fig. 2).

Intrafunctional coordination pertains to managing activities within the firm's logistics or materials management function. The coordination is strictly between activities under the direct responsibility of a logistics or materials manager and could be relatively easy. Intrafunctional coordination would generally involve trading off costs against each other (e.g., inventory carrying costs versus production setup or purchasing costs, inventory carrying costs versus transportation costs, warehousing costs versus transportation costs). Analysis and optimization of activities and costs that are in conflict, being within the responsibility and authority of the logistics manager, are possible and have been major contributors to cost reductions in product flow activities.

Managing supply chain activities within the same firm also involves functions other than logistics or materials management: marketing, production, finance, etc. Changes in practices or levels of activity in purchasing, transportation, warehousing, and inventories would have implications on the other organizational functions, and vice versa—and would require *interfunctional coordination,* which makes managerial con-

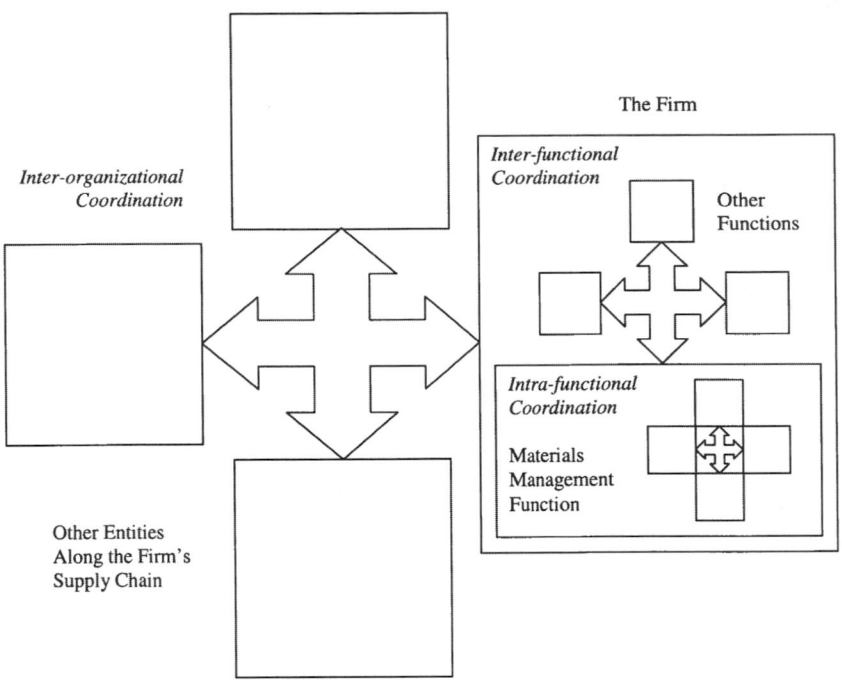

Figure 2 Dimensions of supply chain coordination.

trol relatively more difficult. For instance, reducing inventory levels or using lower cost, but slower transport services may reduce materials management costs, but also adversely affect the marketing objective of maximizing sales revenues or the firm's customer service level objectives. Opting for more frequent, but lower volume deliveries of raw materials or supplies may reduce inventory carrying costs, but also adversely affect a production department's objective of minimizing unit processing costs or a service department's customer service level objectives. Adding new warehouses and trucks may reduce per-unit logistics costs, but also adversely affect the finance department's objective of minimizing capital requirements. There is a need to balance the effects of such changes on the other functions in a manner that would most benefit the organization as a whole. This interfunctional coordination takes place within the firm, but outside of the logistics function.

Finally, the supply chain includes separate legal entities (suppliers, manufacturers, distributors, retailers, and customers), and calls for *interorganizational*—or *interenterprise*—*coordination*. It is this dimension of SCM, being relatively uncharted territory for most supply management professionals, that presents perhaps more significant opportunities for improvements in service levels and costs—improvements that cannot be achieved if entities along the supply chain were to act independently and focus on optimizing their own cost structures. Interorganizational coordinating mechanisms that transcend the traditional, legal boundaries and benefit the entities in the supply chain that are involved, such as early supplier involvement in new product development, just-in-time systems, or vendor-managed inventories, need to be developed and implemented.

V. SOME SUCCESSES IN SUPPLY CHAIN MANAGEMENT

A. Wal-Mart Stores

Perhaps one of the most commonly cited success stories in supply chain management (SCM) is that of Wal-Mart Stores, which reported total sales of $191.329 billion and a net income of $6.295 billion during the fiscal year ended January 31, 2001. These figures represent a 15.9% growth in total sales and a 17.1% increase in net income over the immediately preceding fiscal year. International sales accounted for $32 billion of the total sales figure, increasing 41% over the previous year. Wal-Mart, which opened its first store in Arkansas in 1962, has retail stores in all 50 states of the United States and in the U.S. territory of Puerto Rico, as well as in Mexico, Canada, the United Kingdom,

Germany, Brazil, Argentina, China, and South Korea. As of May 10, 2001, the company reported having 3153 operating units (Wal-Mart discount stores, Super-centers, Sam's Clubs, and neighborhood markets) in the United States and 1088 Wal-Mart international units—with more than 962,000 employees ("associates") in the United States and 282,000 internationally.

Wal-Mart has been an innovator in SCM, which has allowed it to provide low-cost merchandise to its customers and undercut its competitors. An article in the *Harvard Business Review* reported back in 1992:

> In 1979 Kmart was one of the leading companies in the retail industry. . . . At that time, Wal-Mart was a small niche retailer in the South with only 229 stores and average revenues about half those of Kmart stores. . . . Today Wal-Mart is the largest and highest profit retailer in the world. How did Wal-Mart do it? The starting point was a relentless focus on satisfying customer needs; Wal-Mart's goal was simply to provide customers with access to goods when and where they want them and to develop cost structures that enable competitive pricing. The key to achieving this goal was to make the way the company replenishes inventory the centerpiece of its strategy. This was done by using a logistics technique known as *cross-docking*. In this strategy, goods are continuously delivered to Wal-Mart's warehouses from where they are dispatched to stores without ever sitting in inventory. This strategy reduced Wal-Mart's cost of sales significantly and made it possible to offer everyday low prices to their customers.

The traditional distribution strategy in U.S. retail chains involved keeping inventory at warehouses. An alternative strategy would be for goods to be shipped from suppliers directly to the retail stores. Cross-docking has resulted in lower unit transportation and inventory costs, relative to cost of goods sold, through the supply chain. It relies on a well-developed computer information system—utilizing point-of-sale bar-code readers and electronic data interchange—which links Wal-Mart stores, distribution centers, and a large number of major vendors. Moreover, Wal-Mart maintains its own fleet of truck-tractors that deliver multi-item shipments of goods to any store from one of its distribution centers in the United States within 48 hours from the time a consolidated replenishment order is placed. Wal-Mart further cuts costs by using its own trucks to pick up merchandise from manufacturers, after having delivered goods to the stores. The back-haul rate (i.e., the proportion of Wal-Mart trucks picking up goods on their way back from the stores to the distribution centers) has been reported to average more than 60%.

B. Procter & Gamble

Procter & Gamble (P&G), founded in Cincinnati in 1837, manufactures and markets worldwide more than 300 brands of packaged consumer goods in the following product segments: baby care, beauty care, fabric and home care, feminine care, food and beverage, health care, and tissues and towel. P&G, which employs some 110,000 people worldwide, had net sales of $39.951 billion and net earnings of $3.542 billion during the fiscal year ended June 30, 2000.

P&G began, as early as 1985, a retailer-supplier partnership with Wal-Mart involving a *vendor managed inventory* (VMI) system. Under such a system, the vendor—subject to bounds previously agreed on with the retailer—decides on the appropriate levels of inventory to carry at the retail stores, as well as the corresponding inventory policies to maintain such levels. In the P&G and Wal-Mart partnership, P&G committed to the development of a dedicated team to handle the Wal-Mart account. A primary objective of this team is to facilitate information-sharing between the two firms and address logistics, supply, management information systems, accounting, finance, and other issues. Under this arrangement, Wal-Mart shares point-of-sale information from retail outlets directly with P&G, giving the latter easy access to information on consumer transactions and buying patterns. P&G's dedicated Wal-Mart account team effectively takes responsibility for the marketing and sales of P&G products within Wal-Mart stores. Similar VMI partnerships with other giant retailers have been established by P&G. These partnerships have been acknowledged to dramatically improve P&G's on-time deliveries to Wal-Mart and the other retailers while increasing inventory turnovers.

C. Dell Computer Corporation

Founded in 1984, Dell Computer Corporation is the world's leading direct computer systems company and is second worldwide in market share in the global computer systems industry, rising from number 25 a decade earlier. Dell ranks number 1 in the United States, where it is the leading supplier of personal computers to business organizations, government agencies, and educational institutions, as well as consumers. It reported net revenues of $31.888 billion for the fiscal year ended February 2, 2001—representing a hefty 26.2% increase over the immediately preceding fiscal year—and a net income of $2.177 billion. Net revenues and net income were $5.296 billion and $272 million, respectively, only 5 years earlier (for the fiscal year ended January 28, 1996). Dell currently has approximately 40,000 employees around the globe.

Dell sells its computer systems directly to end users, bypassing distributors and retailers. Its supply chain, therefore, involves only three stages—suppliers, the manufacturer (Dell), and customers—excluding transporters. Dell's direct contact with customers allows it to properly identify market segments, analyze the requirements and profitability of each segment, and develop more accurate demand forecasts. Over the phone or via the Internet, Dell steers its customers toward computer configurations that may be built from components that are available, thereby allowing Dell to match supply and demand.

Dell's is an assemble-to-order manufacturing strategy, and there is no finished product in inventory. Computers are manufactured "one at a time, as ordered" at manufacturing facilities in the United States (Austin, Texas, and Nashville, Tennessee), Brazil, Ireland, Malaysia, and China. Dell attributes a significant part of its success to how it handles product and information flows along its supply chain. A recent account by Chopra and Meindl states:

> . . . Dell carries only about 10 days' worth of inventory; in contrast, the competition, selling through retailers, has been carrying in the vicinity of 80 to 100 days. If Intel introduces a new chip, the low level of inventory allows Dell to go to market with a PC containing the chip faster than the competition. If prices suddenly drop, as they did in the early part of 1998, Dell has less inventory that loses value relative to its competitors. For some products, such as monitors manufactured by Sony, Dell maintains no inventory. The transportation company simply picks up the appropriate number of computers from Dell's Austin plant and monitors from Sony's factory in Mexico, matches them by customer order, and delivers them to the customers. This procedure allows Dell to save time and money associated with the extra handling of monitors. . . . The success of the Dell supply chain is facilitated by sophisticated information exchange. Dell provides real-time data to suppliers on the current state of demand. Suppliers are able to access their components' inventory levels at the factories along with daily production requirements. Dell has created customized Web pages so that its major suppliers can view demand forecasts and other customer-sensitive information, thus helping suppliers to get a better idea of customer demand and better match their production schedules to that of Dell.

VI. IMPORTANCE OF THE FLOW OF INFORMATION

The definition of SCM includes information flow as one of the two major flow components of the supply chain. The need to share information across the various entities along the supply chain is definitely of paramount importance.

As already pointed out, Wal-Mart has used point-of-sale bar-code readers feeding data into an information system that links stores, distribution centers, and vendors. Under its VMI partnerships, Wal-Mart shares point-of-sale information from its retail outlets directly with a large number of its major suppliers. Other retailers may fear that the willingness to share information would result in losing power within such partnerships. It actually allows the suppliers, given the easy access to information on consumer transactions and buying patterns, to themselves take responsibility for the sales and marketing of their own products within Wal-Mart stores. This saves Wal-Mart a significant amount of managerial and other resources. At the same time, these VMI partnerships have improved the suppliers' on-time deliveries while increasing their inventory turnovers and demonstrate how information sharing leads to mutual advantage for both parties in such partnerships.

In all the information sharing that takes place in SCM, however, there is a need to ensure that the information flow is accurate and reliable. P&G started to explore, after experiencing erratic shifts in ordering along the supply chain for its popular brand of disposable diapers, a phenomenon referred to as the *bullwhip effect*. This phenomenon results in the flow of distorted information from one entity to another along the supply chain. In particular, it was found that distributors' orders showed more variability than that of sales (customer demand) and, further along the supply chain, P&G's orders to its supplier exhibited the greatest variability. Managers at every link in the supply chain tend to magnify even slight demand uncertainties and variabilities, and will tend to make ordering and inventory decisions in their own entity's interest. The phenomenon can give rise to excessive inventories, poor customer service, and lost revenues, among others. It is not unique to P&G or the consumer packaged goods industry.

It is worth noting that both the interfunctional and interorganizational coordination dimensions of SCM have made significant strides forward as a result of developments in the field of information technology, particularly the growth of interorganizational information systems. Enterprise resource planning systems have facilitated interfunctional coordination. Interorganizational systems, also known as extranets, are application systems linking various entities along the supply chain using public or private telecommunications infrastructure. The wide use of EDI, especially during the last 10 years or so, has helped improve interorganizational coordination in SCM.

VII. ENTERPRISE RESOURCE PLANNING SYSTEMS AND ENTERPRISE APPLICATION INTEGRATION

An enterprise resource planning (ERP) system is an enterprise-wide information system that facilitates the flow of transactional data relating to manufacturing, logistics, finance and accounting, marketing and sales, and human resources in the firm. The integration, which allows the firm to achieve "end-to-end connectivity," is accomplished through a database residing on a common platform and shared by the various application programs. Manufacturing is made immediately aware of any new customer order as soon as it is entered by sales. Likewise, purchasing is made aware of material requirements associated with the new customer order. Accounting records are automatically updated as transactions occur. The status of every customer order—whether being planned for assembly, in process, just completed, being prepared for shipment, in transit, or received by the customer—is available to the sales personnel. The shared database not only allows the various functional departments access to up-to-date information, but also enables the firm to avoid unnecessary duplication and the attendant potential for error associated with posting the same information all over. It is evident that an ERP system can facilitate and strengthen the interfunctional dimension of supply chain coordination.

General Mills, one of the largest food companies in the United States, reported record financial results during the fiscal year ended May 28, 2000, arising from total sales of $6.7 billion and net earnings of $614 million. It marked the third consecutive year of double-digit earnings per share growth. In an interview with the *Journal of Supply Chain Management*, the vice president of purchasing for General Mills, declared:

> We have a fully integrated ERP system, so we have been able to significantly reduce the amount of our transactional activities, as well as the associated costs. We have a low-cost supply chain relative to our competitors, which has been a direct benefit.

Case studies have shown that firms that have implemented ERP systems have made improvements in interfunctional coordination and business performance at various levels, helping them reduce cycle times, reduce inventories, and share information readily across the organization. Because flexibility, speed of delivery, and responsiveness to preferences of individual customers have become order winners in today's marketplace and traditionally "make-to-stock" manufacturing operations have switched to "make-to-order" mode, ERP systems have proven very useful for, among others, incorporating new sales orders and order changes into production scheduling, materials management, and logistics planning.

It is worth noting, however, that many companies have experienced unexpected difficulties in implementing ERP systems. Hershey Foods Corporation began its *1999 Annual Report* citing problems in implementing its ERP system:

> There is no doubt that 1999 was a most difficult and disappointing year for Hershey Foods Corporation. While the year got off to a slow start due to excessive retail inventories, we fully expected a strong finish in the second half of the year. Instead, the implementation of the final phase of the Corporation's enterprise-wide information system created problems in the areas of customer service, warehousing and order fulfillment. These difficulties were exacerbated by our growth in recent years which had resulted in shipping capacity constraints. As a result, Hershey's sales and earnings fell well short of expectations for the year.

Hershey's consolidated net sales of $3.94 billion in 1999 represented a 2.8% decline from 1998, while earnings before interest and taxes (excluding gains from the divestiture of its pasta business) declined 8.7%.

In some cases, implementation projects may be poorly managed, with the company having inadequately trained personnel to install and customize the system.

Often, an ERP system is unable to provide all of the functionality provided by custom applications that have been written during the past 30 years. As a result, such "legacy" applications must be kept in operation alongside the ERP system. For example, Whirlpool Corporation, one of the world's largest manufacturers of household appliances, while utilizing SAP's R/3 system as its ERP platform, has continued to use its "best-of-breed" pricing and promotion system from Trilogy Software. MMS, a Utah-based maker of vitamins and minerals, also selected the SAP R/3 ERP system, but decided to keep its warehouse management system (WMS) from Catalyst International. Similarly, Fujitsu PC, which chose Oracle Applications as its ERP system, implemented a separate application package for product configuration and a custom-built manufacturing execution system (MES).

However, the ERP system acquired from the primary vendor may not be capable of communicating directly with the legacy system. This has prompted the emergence of enterprise application integration (EAI) as a framework for tying an ERP system with other applications needed for SCM, by way of providing the messaging and data transformation tools that link the applications. For instance, Whirlpool selected CrossWorlds Software to create an interface between its SAP R/3 ERP system and its Trilogy pricing and promotion system. MMS, the vitamins and minerals manufacturer, turned to Oberon Software's Prospero to integrate the Catalyst WMS with SAP R/3. Fujitsu PC chose Vitria Technology's BusinessWare for integration of its Oracle ERP system with the product configuration and MES applications.

Moreover, mergers and acquisitions lead not only to various legacy applications, but also multiple ERP packages within the same enterprise. In such cases, EAI needs to address links between the multiple ERP packages, in addition to those between ERP systems and legacy systems.

While EAI does address interfunctional coordination—i.e., the need to integrate systems internally—it may also address the interorganizational dimension of supply chain coordination and integration by way of enabling interfaces with suppliers' or customers' ERP systems and other SCM applications. For example, Extricity's Alliance EAI framework has allowed a company that provides outsourced semiconductor foundry services to hundreds of customers worldwide to integrate the company's custom, mainframe-based order management system with the disparate ERP and legacy systems of its customers.

VIII. EDI AND ITS PROBLEMS

Presently, electronic data interchange (EDI) is primarily used to facilitate coordination and communication among supply chain partners—e.g., Wal-Mart and its major vendors, as discussed earlier. Thus, EDI addresses information flows that apply principally to the interorganizational dimension of supply chain coordination.

EDI is the direct computer-to-computer exchange between two business partners (e.g., a manufacturer of finished goods and a supplier of raw materials) of standard business documents such as purchase orders and invoices. Others define EDI as the transmission of standard business documents in a standard format

between industrial trading partners from computer application to computer application. EDI messages can be transmitted directly between two business partners or through a third-party value-added network.

EDI can help businesses save time and money by reducing transaction processing and data entry costs while gaining faster access to information. Studies suggest that EDI reduces the human element in communication while improving both speed and accuracy of data flow. EDI can also help lower inventory costs by reducing the time raw materials spend in inventory. Reductions in both leadtimes and inventory levels, using EDI, have been reported.

Unfortunately, EDI is not living up to its promise for a number of reasons. First, the participating companies must agree on the format of a standard, which is not as easy for them to do since many of them are using different standards. The American National Standards Institute (ANSI) developed the X.12 data interchange protocol as a flexible standard, but different industries have developed different versions of this standard.

Second, software is too expensive and too proprietary. Specialized software must be developed by participating businesses to convert incoming and outgoing messages in a common format that is understandable to other businesses, but only large businesses can afford to do that. This makes EDI less affordable to smaller organizations. Traditional EDI works better between two large organizations with a high volume of transactions.

Third, the transaction fees are too high. Again, only large organizations can afford EDI. For instance, EDI has been used to support the automotive and retail industries.

Fourth, EDI optimizes various links in the supply chain without holistically tackling the problem of end-to-end efficiency. This is mainly because the efficiency in some parts of the overall links is improved due to e-commerce technologies and these technologies may not be available to some supply chain partners, especially smaller businesses.

Fifth, while timely and accurate information exchange facilitates closer manufacturer and supplier relationships, and such closer relationships can improve leadtime performance, some studies have shown EDI to appear to have little effect on either relationships or leadtime performance.

The bottom line is this: EDI will remain in SCM, at least for the time being, since it has the advantage of higher data security than the Internet and it can carry large transaction volumes. In spite of concerns about security over the Internet, a growing number of experts agree that the economics of the Internet versus EDI appear overwhelming. Some argue that EDI simply does not have the flexibility to survive and will die a very slow death. EDI is inflexible and limited in the sense that it is a one-to-one technology that can only handle large transaction volumes.

IX. ROLE OF E-COMMERCE TECHNOLOGIES IN SCM

The development of electronic commerce technologies such as the Internet, World Wide Web, intranets, and extranets has created innumerable opportunities for businesses to streamline their supply chains. However, many companies have not been very successful in taking advantage of these opportunities for reducing costs and adding value along the supply chain, mainly because of the fact that these technologies are fairly new and the use of these technologies in SCM is a relatively recent phenomenon. Nevertheless, the benefits offered by EDI pale in comparison with those available via e-commerce-based technologies. Some may even view the Internet's impact on SCM as rivaling that of the interstate highway system on the transportation industry. Businesses are now realizing the superiority and benefits e-commerce technologies have to offer in SCM, looking to these technologies to accomplish what EDI has fallen short of delivering. The e-commerce-based technologies are capable of delivering a holistic system that incorporates what EDI is already capable of accomplishing—combining it with broad-based access and cost-effective, real-time document transmission and distribution.

More specifically, the objectives of supply chain management include, among others, minimizing costs, improving service levels, improving communications among entities along the supply chain, and improving flexibility and speed of delivery. This section discusses how e-commerce technologies can help achieve these and other objectives, and how some businesses are actually using these technologies to realize these goals.

The evidence of e-enabled SCM is especially visible in the high-technology environment where product life cycles are often measured in months or even days. According to an article appearing in the *Journal of Business Strategy* in 2000, corporations like Cisco, Dell, and IBM lead the revolution by developing comprehensive and global supply chains characterized by low inventory levels, lean production, demand collaboration, and deferred assembly—resulting in lower costs and greater responsiveness to changing market conditions.

A case in point is IBM. It has realized significant benefits from e-enablement. The same article reported that, since 1994, IBM has reduced inventory write-offs by $800 million, increased on-time delivery from 90% to 98%, and reduced order time from two weeks to real-time. On the supply side, the Big Blue has reduced the cost of purchasing goods and services by $4.2 billion.

Extranets link various partners in the supply chain using a public or private communications infrastructure. The availability of the Internet to electronically transfer massive amounts of information over the extranets with minimal time and effort has resulted in efficient and effective sharing of information among business partners. Companies have used the Internet and extranets to, among others, reduce delivery costs and increase the number of deliveries.

A case in point is General Electric. An article published in 2000 in *Industrial Marketing Management* reported that GE has used the Internet to schedule shipments out of its warehouses in metropolitan areas. The goal is to allow the company to more accurately and cost effectively deliver its products on time. The number of deliveries per hour has increased significantly while transportation costs per order have dropped dramatically.

Firms would benefit from increased use of the Internet in purchasing activities, and the potential for significant cost savings and productivity improvement suggests so. E-commerce technologies can also increase the value of the information that can be transmitted back and forth in the context of SCM.

A case in point is, again, General Electric. The same, previously cited article in the *Journal of Business Strategy* reported that GE decided in 1996 to streamline, using the Web, its procurement process for certain products that require a formal request for proposal (RFP). GE believed that it can use the Web to reduce both the time and cost involved in the process. In fact, cycle time for the RFP process dropped from 29 days using the manual process down to 4 to 12 days over the Web. The company's material acquisition cost also dropped 20%.

E-commerce technologies increase the value of the information that can be exchanged. Previously, via EDI, only transactions could have been transmitted back and forth. Now, using the Internet, rich exchange of information has become fairly common. Corporations now have access to details of product or service availability, as well as price and term negotiations, at a significantly reduced cost. E-commerce technologies are helping SCM become more of a global business-to-business phenomenon by greatly increasing the size of the audience that can be reached. The one-to-one nature of EDI in SCM has definitely been superceded by the many-to-many capabilities of e-commerce technologies.

A case in point is the Automotive Network Exchange (ANX) recently established by the big three automakers: General Motors Corporation, Ford Motor Company, and Daimler-Chrysler AG. Even though the project is presently still in its infancy, it still makes the point. An article published in 2000 in *Hospital Materiel Management Quarterly* explains that the goal here is to create a very large virtual marketplace using a reliable, secure, highly efficient extranet where all automakers can conduct business with suppliers and other business partners. The goal reflects the auto industry's belief that this collaborative work will provide the greatest leverage in reducing time and cost for their supply chains.

X. EMERGING MANAGERIAL AND TECHNICAL ISSUES

Supply chains will continue to be challenged to increase responsiveness, effectiveness, and efficiency. This section identifies some of the managerial and technical issues corporations will face in developing and managing their supply chains and in e-enabling their SCM.

A. Managerial Issues

The emerging competitive environment in today's global marketplace is one where businesses no longer compete with each other as autonomous, individual firms. Rather than simply brand versus brand or store versus store, competition is now on a supply chain versus supply chain basis. The supply chain cannot be viewed merely as a series of one-to-one, business-to-business links between the entities along the chain. Even the early papers had emphasized that the entire supply chain needs to be viewed as a single entity—albeit a network of multiple legal entities and relationships. Management of the individual business firm should learn to identify, develop, and exploit synergies offered by intrafunctional, interfunctional, and interorganizational coordination and integration throughout this network of entities and relationships along the firm's supply chain.

A major challenge will lie in coordinating activities of the various management groups involved in managing the supply chain. Coordinating activities within the firm itself is considered a prerequisite to successful SCM. Key business processes need to be identified, and these ought to be managed using cross-functional teams. In this regard, it is necessary to develop a set of common goals that the various management groups involved in these key processes can all work toward. Within the firm, the marketing and logistics/materials management functions are considered the most influential in supply chain operations. The former traditionally seeks to satisfy customers and maximize sales, and may accordingly stress operating flexibility, product proliferation, and high inventory levels, while the latter traditionally seeks low inventory levels, product standardization, and shipment consolidation—goals that are apparently inconsistent across functions. Needless to say, top management should develop performance measures, goals, and reward systems in such a way that the various management groups having to do with supply chain operations would jointly address customer satisfaction and the overall competitiveness and profitability of the firm.

The people using the new e-commerce technologies and their willingness and ability to embrace changes may pose the biggest barrier to e-SCM collaboration. A detailed survey of Fortune 500 executives found that three main barriers to SCM are lack of functional expertise, lack of management expertise, and ineffective change management. Top management can play a big role in alleviating these barriers by hiring people with appropriate technical, functional, and management expertise and by providing guidance and training to those employees who may have difficulty with organizational changes induced by e-SCM.

In addition, even when a firm does have the appropriate personnel needed to implement a new e-commerce technology, the other entities along the supply chain, which should also be involved in implementing such technology, may not. This may happen, in particular, when some supply chain partners are relatively small. In such a case, the larger firm should consider providing technical assistance to the smaller supply chain partners when implementing the new technology. In many supplier–buyer partnerships—for instance, under a just-in-time systems environment—technical assistance provided by a buyer (manufacturer) to a smaller supplier has been observed to be beneficial to both parties.

One of the biggest obstacles in making SCM more efficient and effective is that a lot of links are reluctant to swap information back and forth. One of the basic premises of successful e-SCM is that organizations are willing to share information with their business partners on their internal operations including inventory, orders, and shipments. E-commerce technologies can help swap enormous amounts of information back and forth quickly, but cannot do so without help and approval from top management. Top management must help create a climate of trust and true partnership among the partners.

To encourage interorganizational coordination and collaboration, it is necessary for the other firms along the supply chain to recognize that the application of e-commerce technologies would benefit not only the firm advocating the use of such technologies across supply chain entities. In particular, supply chain managers should ensure that the other entities involved do perceive the implementation of new technology as being not merely an added burden in terms of effort and cost, but actually translating into benefits that outweigh the additional cost. More importantly, suppliers/vendors must recognize a true system-wide reduction in costs, rather than one where the manufacturer or retailer merely passes costs upstream along the supply chain by way of the implementation of new technology.

B. Technical Issues

Many strategic managers have not embraced e-enabled management practices as a management concept. As a result, working toward an e-enabled supply chain management is being hindered by the lack of proper vision. Strategic managers should accept and encourage development and deployment of e-enabled management practices. These practices should facilitate deployment of business processes to sense and take advantages of opportunities to increase values in the supply chain.

The majority of businesses do not yet have an e-strategy. E-business is opening the door to unprecedented opportunities for increasing revenues by expanding geographic scope, reducing operating costs, and improving procurement, productivity, and efficiency. To succeed in e-business, corporations must have an integrated e-business strategy that considers both customer needs and corporate business objectives. The e-strategy must be integrated with the overall business strategy. Because many brick-and-mortar companies are also becoming click-and-mortar companies or at least developing a click-and-mortar presence on the Web, it is imperative that these businesses develop internal and external strategies in order to effectively use e-commerce technologies for deploying and utilizing supply chains.

Many businesses do not also have an e-SCM strategy. Since e-commerce technologies are being used more

and more in enhancing what supply chains have to offer, it is important for businesses to develop an e-SCM strategy especially if they want to play a proactive role in using e-enabled supply chains that take advantage of some of the benefits these technologies have to offer. This is particularly true for small and mid-sized companies since supply chain collaborations are even less likely among these companies. To operate effectively, organizations moving to e-SCM will require access to a wide range of e-commerce technologies including intranets, extranets, and access to the Web. Among these, extranets probably play the most important role by providing the technology infrastructure to facilitate the flow of information along the supply chain. Top management must be willing to spend enough money to put the E-commerce technological infrastructure in place.

Security protection is still an issue in using e-commerce technologies. Before e-SCM reaches its full potential security must, therefore, be in place to give suppliers and other trading partners the confidence that their information and communication are securely handled. Businesses must develop a strong information technology infrastructure that will establish appropriate security measures such as a "firewall," network integrity, authentication, and authorization. Top management must help develop such a strong IT infrastructure.

XI. DIRECTIONS FOR FUTURE RESEARCH

This article concludes by providing a number of suggestions for conducting future research.

Current literature acknowledges that academia has been following, rather than leading, business practice in SCM. There is a declared need for research to build theory and to develop normative tools and techniques that can guide managers in SCM practice.

Empirical studies have been, for the most part, exploratory in nature. The theoretical approaches thus far identified need further empirical verification.

Exploring and demonstrating opportunities that SCM provides, particularly given the emphasis on management across functional and organizational boundaries, has been popular as a research area. However, much research work still needs to be done on how to achieve the expected benefits of interfunctional and interorganizational coordination in SCM—especially since such dimensions of supply chain coordination involve either managerial functions within the same firm which have different goals, priorities, and reward structures or altogether separate legal entities.

Moreover, the parties involved in interfunctional or

interorganizational coordination in SCM must benefit from their cooperation. Therefore, the search for normative models that could be used for balancing such benefits across functional or organizational boundaries is a major challenge for future SCM research.

As use of the e-commerce technologies becomes more prevalent, researchers should reexamine traditional EDI-based versus e-commerce-based systems to develop an understanding of the nature of changes an organization might have to go through to successfully convert an EDI-based SCM to an e-commerce technology-based SCM. Future research might also look into identifying the conditions under which an organization is most likely to benefit from e-SCM. Research efforts should especially focus on how top management can properly manage these changes.

Future research should help top managers recognize and develop strategies for successfully adopting e-SCM. They should especially investigate how the new technologies are likely to impact organizational behavior and how best to manage this impact.

Suppliers and other business partners play an important role in bringing about successful SCM. Future research should investigate the impact of e-commerce technologies on suppliers and other business partners, with a focus on not merely passing costs upstream along the supply chain as e-commerce technologies are implemented.

SEE ALSO THE FOLLOWING ARTICLES

Control and Auditing • Cost/Benefit Analysis • Enterprise Resource Planning • Executive Information Systems • Global Information Systems • Globalization and Information Management Strategy • Operations Management • Procurement • Total Quality Management and Quality Control • Value Chain Analysis

BIBLIOGRAPHY

Ballou, R. L., Gilbert, S. M., and Mukherjee, A. (2000). New managerial challenges from supply chain opportunities. *Industrial Marketing Management,* Vol. 29, No. 1, 7–18.

Chopra, S., and Meindl, P. (2001). *Supply chain management: Strategy, planning, and operation.* Upper Saddle River, NJ: Prentice-Hall.

Cooper, M., Lambert, D. M., and Pagh, J. D. (1997). Supply chain management: More than a new name for logistics. *International Journal of Logistics Management,* Vol. 8, No. 1, 1–14.

Cross, G. J. (2000). How e-business is transforming supply chain management. *Journal of Business Strategy,* Vol. 21, No. 2, 36–39.

Handfield, R. B., and Nichols, E. L., Jr. (1999). *Introduction to supply chain management.* Upper Saddle River, NJ: Prentice-Hall.

Houlihan, J. B. (1985). International supply chain management. *International Journal of Physical Distribution and Materials Management,* Vol. 15, No. 1, 22–38.

Jones, T. C., and Riley, D. W. (1985). Using inventory for competitive advantage through supply chain management. *International Journal of Physical Distribution and Materials Management,* Vol. 15, No. 5, 16–26.

Lambert, D. M., and Cooper, M. C. (2000). Issues in supply chain management. *Industrial Marketing Management,* Vol. 29, No. 1, 65–83.

Lancioni, R. A., Smith, M. F., and Oliva, T. A. (2000). The role of the Internet in supply chain management. *Industrial Marketing Management,* Vol. 29, No. 1, 45–56.

Larson, P. D., and Kulchitsky, J. D. (2000). The use and impact of communication media in purchasing and supply chain management. *Journal of Supply Chain Management,* Vol. 36, No. 3, 29–39.

Larson, P. D., and Rogers, D. S. (1998). Supply chain management: Definition, growth and approaches. *Journal of Marketing Theory and Practice,* Vol. 6, No. 4, 1–5.

Peters, L. R. R. (2000). Is EDI dead? The future of the Internet in supply chain management. *Hospital Materiel Management Quarterly,* Vol. 22, No.1, 42–47.

Reese, A. (2000). An interview with David L. Sorensen: One on one. *Journal of Supply Chain Management,* Vol. 36, No. 3, 2–3.

Shapiro, J. (2001). *Modeling the Supply Chain.* Pacific Grove, CA: Duxbury.

Simchi-Levi, D., Kaminsky, P., and Simchi-Levi, E. (2000). *Designing and managing the supply chain: Concepts, strategies, and case studies.* New York: McGraw-Hill.

Skjoett-Larsen, T. (1999). Supply chain management: A new challenge for researchers and managers in logistics. *International Journal of Logistics Management,* Vol. 10, No. 2, 41–53.

Stalk, G., Evans, P., and Shulman, L. E. (March–April, 1992). Competing on capabilities: The new rule of corporate strategy. *Harvard Business Review,* 57–69.

Walton, S. V., and Marucheck, A. S. (1997). The relationship between EDI and supplier reliability. *International Journal of Purchasing and Materials Management,* Vol. 33, No. 3, 30–35.

System Development Life Cycle

Constantinos J. Stefanou

Technological Educational Institution of Thessaloniki

I. INFORMATION SYSTEMS AND THE NEED FOR
   DEVELOPMENT METHODOLOGIES
II. SDLC
III. PHASES OF THE SDLC

IV. SYSTEM DEVELOPMENT TOOLS AND TECHNIQUES
V. ALTERNATIVE APPROACHES TO INFORMATION SYSTEM
   DEVELOPMENT
VI. SUMMARY

GLOSSARY

big bang An approach to system development which advocates delivery of the complete information system in contrast to the incremental process aiming at producing new software releases improved incrementally over the previous ones.

CASE tools A general term describing the technology that facilitates developers and end users to build applications by automating system analysis and design.

life cycle The fundamental phases or stages of the evolution a product or activity passes through from its creation to its maturity and retirement.

milestones End points of system development activities helping monitoring the progress of the project.

prototype A working pilot version of a system to be developed providing a tool for identifying system specifications.

spiral model An evolutionary process aiming at rapid development of more complete versions of software by taking into account the technical and managerial risks associated with each evolutionary level.

use case A set of sequence of possible actions or a system usage scenario used to define the functional and operational requirements of a system.

V-shaped model A top-down model of information system development with testing phases matching the development phases.

waterfall model A formalized procedure of developing information systems through a number of successive phases.

THE SYSTEM DEVELOPMENT LIFE CYCLE (SDLC) can be defined as the formal process of developing information systems through a number of successive stages or phases. Each phase, comprised of several subphases or steps, has to be completed to a great extent before subsequent phases can begin, although feedback loops, mainly between successive development phases, are explicitly proposed in the original specification of the model. There is no agreement among authors, consulting companies, government agencies, and authorities proposing SDLC models regarding the optimum number and the names of the phases. In general, the objectives and the linear sequence of the basic phases (system analysis, system design, and system implementation) of the SDLC models are common. The objective of the whole approach, which is essentially a project management technique, is to reduce the complexity of the development project by establishing manageable phases and deliver a complete information system by completing successively each phase in a controlled, integrated, and systematic way. In practice, linear approaches to information system development may be difficult to be achieved. Overlapping and iteration between all stages is usually inevitable. This traditional approach of developing information systems, first presented in the mid-1950s, is still relevant today as it provides the basis of numerous variations and other modern methodologies. The SDLC is also known as information system development, conventional or traditional system analysis, Waterfall or V Model, Linear Sequential Model, Classic Life Cycle, and applications development.

I. INFORMATION SYSTEMS AND THE NEED FOR DEVELOPMENT METHODOLOGIES

Information is a corporate resource contributing significantly to the competitive position of the organization. Therefore, organizations need useful information systems aiming at supporting user needs in a continuously changing and competitive environment. An information system can be defined as a formalized set of interrelated components aiming at providing information effectively and efficiently in order to continuously support business and management activities within the organization and its transactions with the external environment and the users of the system, at every level of the organization, in their decision making and action taking. Today, information systems are computer-based and their main components are hardware, software, and people.

The development or procurement and the implementation, maintenance, and replacement of information systems are complex, costly, and high-risk activities, since a wide range of technical, business, managerial, strategic, organizational, and social issues are involved. Due to the high costs involved, information system failure can affect even the existence of an organization. Organizations, therefore, need proven methodologies, which systems developers can follow in order to build successful and quality information systems. Non-systemic, randomly chosen actions to develop a system hardly produce acceptable results.

The term methodology, derived from the Greek words "method" and "logos," in its original sense means the scientific analysis and study of method. Methodology also alludes to the nature of a set of methods applied in a particular science. However, it is usually used interchangeably with the terms "method," "framework," or "approach." In its current sense of use, methodology can be defined as a set of related concepts, techniques, tools, and procedures, which can be applied in a rational and structured plan of action to solve a particular problem.

Information system development methodologies were devised in order to provide management with a planning and control device for building effective, efficient, and adaptable information systems. The formalization of the development process provides project's management with a useful mechanism to ensure the delivery of a system according to user specifications and quality standards. Methodologies are general by nature and some of them may be more appropriate for certain types of projects than others. A *pragmatic* approach to information system development, choosing and applying methodologies to suit the size, type, and scope of the project, without discarding their fundamental guiding principles, may be more appropriate for developing successful systems.

Methodologies alone cannot guarantee system success or even delivery of information systems on schedule and within budget. Information systems are sociotechnical systems and a range of factors needs to be managed carefully. User/customer participation and communication with developers during the whole development process, continuous top management support, developers' commitment to teamwork, integration of information systems into the business plan, change management, and leadership with a vision to transform the organization are the most common decisive factors cited for developing effective and efficient information systems.

II. SDLC

The SDLC can be defined as the formalized process of developing information systems through the following successive phases:

- Feasibility study
- System investigation
- System analysis
- System design
- System implementation
- Review and maintenance

This generic SDLC model, designed by the National Computing Center of the United Kingdom in the late 1960s, was described in 1971 by A. Daniels and D.A. Yeates (Fig. 1).

Each phase of the model consists of subphases and each stage must be completed to a great extent before moving to the next one. The segmentation of the SDLC into logical phases aims at facilitating information system development by focusing on one manageable subset of the whole project at a time. The term "life cycle" can have various interpretations according to the context in which it is used. Basically, it denotes the fundamental phases or stages of the evolution a product or activity passes through from its creation to its maturity and retirement. There are numerous variations of information system development methodologies based on the life cycle concept, such as the *waterfall* or the *V-shaped* model. The original waterfall model is generally considered to have been defined by Winston Royce in 1970 (Proceedings of the IEEE WESCON) and proposes the following seven phases:

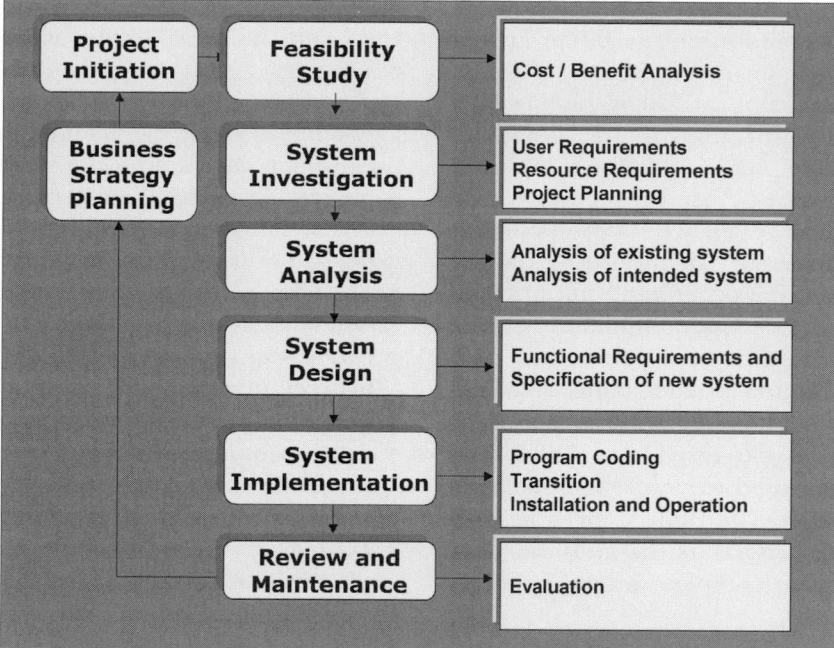

Figure 1 The conventional SDLC model. [Adapted from Daniels, A., and Yeates, D. A. (1971). *Training in Systems Analysis,* 2nd ed. London: Pitman.]

system requirements, software requirement, analysis, program design, coding, testing, and operations.

This model, treated usually as purely linear, explicitly accommodates iteration by proposing that feedback loops should ideally take place between the preceding and succeeding phases, but rarely with the more remote phases in the sequence in order to scale down the change process into manageable limits and minimize development costs. It also makes provision for simulation, that is, prototyping, proposing that the version of a computer system delivered to the customer for operational deployment should be the second version, at least as far as critical design or operation areas are concerned. It should be noted, however, that remarkably similar conceptions about the stagewise approach to information systems development had been published back in the mid-1950s. At the symposium of the United States Office of Naval Research (ONR) in June 1956, Herbert Benington described a nine-phase model for the production of large program systems, which proceeds from a general operational plan through system operation and evaluation. The phases of this model are the following:

- Operational plan (broad design requirements prepared jointly by systems engineers and users)
- Machine specifications and operational specifications
- Program specifications

- Coding specifications
- Coding
- Parameter testing (testing of component subprograms according to coding specifications)
- Assembly testing (program assembled and tested using simulated and real data)
- Shakedown (completed program testing in operational environment)
- System evaluation

It can be seen that testing is a main consideration in Benington's model of information system development. Another variation of the SDLC model, where project verification and evaluation of each phase is also required, is the V-shaped model. In contrast to the original waterfall model, where the testing phase occurs at the end of the development cycle, the V-shaped model explicitly requires the definition of criteria for testing the progress of the development process at each phase. Extensive testing may result in an increase of development costs and extension of the completion time of a project, but it is useful for risky and unfamiliar projects contributing significantly to system quality and performance. In contrast, the waterfall model may be more appropriate for low-risk projects where requirements are well understood and potential bugs can be identified more easily.

It should be noted that the life cycle models require extensive documentation to be produced within each phase. Each major stage of the life cycle models produces an output or a deliverable, which provides the basis for the next phase. Thus, the model assumes that one phase should be completed, at least to a great extent before proceeding to the next one, which is often restrictive, as it does not accommodate any changes occurring during the development process. On the other hand this provides a rigorous approach to system development. A series of milestones should also be established at the outset. Milestones are defined as end points of system development activities and help monitor the progress of the project. GANTT bar charts and PERT flow-diagram charts can be used to depict the phases of the project and the associated milestones, the concurrent phases, the critical path, and the time elapsed and required to complete project's phases, subphases, and tasks.

A. SDLC and System Life-Cycle

In the information systems domain, the terms SDLC and system life cycle are often used interchangeably. It has been suggested that information SDLC should not be confused with system (the delivered product) life cycle. The system life cycle begins when the SDLC delivers the final product, that is, when the implementation phase begins. Therefore, some authors consider that the final stage of the traditional SDLC, Review and Maintenance (see Fig. 1) should not belong to the system *development* life cycle but instead it should be considered as an activity related to the maturity stage of a *system* life cycle. The objective of this activity is to extend as long as possible the life cycle of an existing system. When this is not longer feasible or efficient, the system life cycle terminates and a new SDLC commences.

III. PHASES OF THE SDLC

A. Feasibility Study

The feasibility study investigates existing systems in view of new requirements and considers alternative solutions. System analysts determine whether an identified need for a new system or application is necessary for the organization, cost effective, and compatible with the organization's IT architecture and business strategy. This preliminary project feasibility study contains the following aspects:

- *Technical feasibility:* Examines whether the new system can be developed and implemented using existing technology
- *Economic feasibility:* Is concerned with the availability and cost effectiveness of resources needed to complete the project
- *Legal feasibility:* Examines whether the proposed system conforms to legal requirements
- *Operational feasibility:* Pertains to the compatibility between organizational procedures, existing systems, and operations of the new system
- *Schedule feasibility:* Examines whether the system can be developed on time and identifies alternative options
- *Organizational and social feasibility:* Examines whether the system is acceptable for the organization and its people at all levels
- *Strategic feasibility:* Examines whether the recommended system fits into the strategic business and information technology plan of the organization and whether it contributes to the competitive advantage of the organization

It should be noted that a complete feasibility study is not possible at this stage, since the analysis phase has not even started and the full scale of the project is not yet known. For this reason some authors place this activity after the system analysis phase. Obviously, in practice, some overlapping between the three first phases of the SDLC is inevitable.

1. Feasibility Study Report

The next subphase of the feasibility study is to propose a recommended solution for approval by the management. The feasibility report recommends a project plan for developing and acquiring new systems or applications. It is the outcome of project initiation specifying the objectives of the project, the cost and the expected benefits on a technical, organizational, and business basis, and the associated risks. If this is accepted a more detailed system investigation activity takes place.

B. System Investigation

System investigation is the thorough examination of the functional requirements, the performance, and restrictions of the existing system, if there is one currently operating, and the requirements of the intended system. At this stage, a more detailed analysis will be conducted, taking into account data types, volumes, and transactions, which the new system needs to process.

The requirements documentation, that is the recording of the requirements in any form, such as a computer file or a document, ensures that all people involved in the development project take into account user information needs and other requirements, such as system friendliness and ease-of-use. The investigation process can be documented by using a number of aids, such as flowcharting describing data flows and processes in the system, organization charts depicting responsibilities of the people in the organization, and grid charts showing the interaction of the elements of the system. Although requirements never stay still, at some point of time the development process has to begin. Subsequent requirements will have to be implemented at a later stage.

1. Tools and Techniques

The achievement of good requirements definition is essential for designing and building useful information systems. To this end the analysis team uses a number of techniques, such as observation, document study, interviewing, questionnaires, and prototyping:

- *Observation:* One technique for collecting data on a function or business process is to observe crucial data and information flow pertaining to this function or process. Graphical techniques are used subsequently to document data flows and the logic of the processes.
- *Document Study:* The search and study of documents may provide useful information and identify existent problems.
- *Interviewing:* Interviews can be fairly unstructured in the beginning or semistructured and structured during the final phase of interviewing the system users. It is a useful technique for obtaining first-hand data about user requirements, views, and opinions.
- *Questionnaires:* Questionnaires are used extensively for collecting data from a large number of people and for postimplementation system audits. The questionnaire is designed in such a way as to be capable of being completed by the respondents alone.
- *Prototyping:* Prototypes, that is, working models of systems to be developed, provide a useful tool for

identifying system and software specifications. Prototypes are constructed quickly according to user requirements and iteration occurs as the model is redesigned to meet user needs.

C. System Analysis

At this phase, the information gathered during system investigation is meticulously examined and the current system is analyzed in detail in order to formally determine the functional requirements of the new system. The requirements analysis/definition phase forms a fundamental part of the SDLC methodology. Requirements specification provides the solid foundation upon which the information systems development project is based. Therefore, system developers need to make sure that requirements have been defined as comprehensively and precisely as possible.

System analysis is the investigation of a problem situation, which involves rigorous understanding and description of the existing system, leading to the identification and recording of the characteristics of the new, intended, information system. The objective of the analysis of existing information systems is to identify whether and to what extent the system is well defined and successfully operating and eventually propose how the new system will improve upon the current one.

The examination of the Input/Output (I/O) functions of the system, data, information flows, transactions, and processing required is carried out during system analysis. Tools and techniques used to facilitate the activities in both the system analysis and design phases are discussed in Section IV. System analysis is a complex activity with many difficulties. Communication between users and developers, changing user requirements, and departmental politics are among some of the issues involved.

The final product of system analysis is a report which includes the following: scope of study, problems identified with current systems, user requirements specification, resource availability, and recommendation as to whether the project should be continued in light of the analysis findings.

D. System Design

System design provides the *solution* to a problem. In this phase, alternative technical solutions are examined and the specification of the new system in terms of hardware, software, human resources, and procedures is provided. This phase consists of two basic sub-phases. The first one is the *logical* design of the system, that is, how the system fits the requirements. In some SDLC models, this may overlap to some extent with analysis performed during the system analysis phase. The second one examines the *physical* design of the system consisting of hardware, software, file, database, and program specifications. System analysts/designers follow important *design principles,* such as software modularity, extendability, maintainability, and reusability. A range of techniques providing complementary views of the information system (data-oriented view, process-oriented view, and time-dependent view) is used in both the system analysis and design phases. In addition, various software tools have been developed in order to facilitate the activities of system analysis and design. These techniques, such as data flow and entity relationship diagramming, and tools, such as CASE tools, are discussed in more detail below in Section IV.

The basic activities performed in the system design phase are related to the following:

- *Human-computer interface design:* The Human-Computer Interface (HCI) is the means by which users interact with the system. Thus, the design of the HCI, the visible part of the system to the users, is an important design activity, which is based upon the logical data flow analysis.
- *I/O design:* System analysts/designers determine the content and the format of the information processed by the system, considering user requirements and technical issues, such as access controls, output mediums, and storage devices. The content and the means of data input to the new system are also designed. Software tools are used to facilitate I/O design.
- *Software design:* If a need for developing new software applications was identified during the analysis phase, then software engineering takes place. *Software engineering* can be defined as the structured process for developing quality and reliable software programs by using a set of appropriate techniques and tools. Alternative solutions are the procurement of ready-made application packages or the outsourcing of the whole or part of the information system function.

The final output of the system design phase is a report containing the detailed specification of the new system. This is used for the construction of the system and the development of software.

E. System Implementation

System implementation is the activity of installing according to specifications and delivering into operation a computer system, which was either developed by the organization or purchased from a third party. According to the traditional SDLC model system implementation involves the following:

- Software development or programming
- Testing
- Documenting
- Delivering the system into operational use

1. Programming

During this phase, software engineers construct the programs, which might have been designed in the previous phase. Coding, debugging, testing, and documenting the software are the main subphases of this activity. Some authors include programming as the final activity of the previous phase of the SDLC, the system design phase, or as a distinct stage of the SDLC. Programming is limited when organizations choose to implement an off-the-shelf system instead of developing one in-house.

2. System and Software Testing

The testing subphase is very important in determining the quality and the performance of the developed information system. The following categories of tests are identified:

- *Unit or module:* Testing of the individual modules of the system.
- *Integration:* Individually developed components of a system may not function accordingly to specifications when combined together. In this case, system integration is performed, ensuring the functioning of interfaces between modules. Integration is the synthesis of independently developed modules or subsystems so as to form a complete system operating to specified standards.
- *Volume:* Tests whether the system can cope with the anticipated volumes of transactions and data.
- *System:* The project team tests the whole system in order to evaluate its actual performance in relation to expected functionality.

- *User-acceptance:* Users of the system determine whether and to what extent the system meets their information needs and requirements documented in the previous phases. User training is carried out and upon user acceptance the system development project team installs and puts the new system into operation.

3. System Documentation

System documentation is usually generated automatically by using computer aided software and system engineering tools. Documentation facilitates the understanding of the operation and the maintenance of the system after implementation

4. Going Live

After successful testing, the system is finally installed and put into operation. This is a complex activity as a range of organizational, behavioral, and technical issues are still involved. Implementation of large and complex systems can be very costly and time-consuming. Some of the problems the implementation team has to manage are they following:

- Hardware and software installation
- Necessary file conversions
- User resistance to the introduction of the new system
- Coexistence of the new system with existent systems for a period of time for testing the performance of the new system before discarding the current one
- User training regarding the operation of the new system and the possible changes in normal work routines induced by the new system
- Integration, which refers to resolving the remaining incompatibilities of the new system with existing systems that will continue to operate

F. Review and Maintenance

The postimplementation audit and review activities are important in order to determine the usefulness of the system, the required modifications and the extent at which the system meets the project objectives. There are no generally accepted measures that can be used to evaluate the performance of the implemented system. System usage statistics, system failure rates, user satisfaction, information quality, and return on investment are among the measures that have been used to evaluate information system performance.

The new system should be constantly monitored by developers, users, and management to ensure it performs according to intended functionality and meets expectations and standards. The enhancement of the system extends its life and postpones its replacement. According to the Central Computing and Communication Agency (CCTA) in the United Kingdom, there are four types of maintenance:

1. *Preventive:* Aims to make subsequent maintenance of software more efficient; it is essentially a design and coding activity
2. *Corrective:* Aims at error fixing or correcting performance shortfalls; it is usually carried out at the early stages of a system's life cycle
3. *Perfective:* Refers to enhancements due to changes in requirements; most common in the mid and late life of a system
4. *Adaptive:* It is used for accommodation of environmental changes, such as new technical platforms or software infrastructure; most common in the mid and late life of a system

Maintenance represents a significant cost in the total budget of information systems development. When this phase ends, in the sense that it is no longer possible, economically or otherwise, to maintain and enhance further the current system to meet changing user needs, a new SDLC begins.

G. Potential Strengths and Weaknesses of the Life Cycle Approach

The adherence to the stages of an SDLC methodology does not guarantee systems success. Many projects based on the SDLC methodology have failed while others have been entirely successful. The rigid nature of the approach provides system analysts and designers with the necessary control to complete the development task, but at the same time it can be a restrictive factor in allowing users to participate in every stage of the life cycle. The development of a system is based on user requirements as stated in the early stages of development and, thus, the resulting system is not flexible enough to adapt to changing user needs and functionality required by organizations. Many alternatives to this conventional approach of designing information systems have pointed out the role of user participation in the whole process of analyzing,

Table I   Potential Strengths of the SDLC

Disciplined approach to system development

Logically (to a great extent) defined steps

Simple and easy to use by systems developers

Straightforward approach, easily understood by users/customers

Partitioning of project into smaller parts which can be handled by separate specialized individuals or teams

Testing can be established for each phase before proceeding to the next one

Milestones can be established for each phase for reviewing the progress of the project

Deadlines dates can be more easily defined and met

Well–tried methodology

designing, and implementing information systems, the iterative nature of the information system development function, and the concurrency of the system analysis and design activities.

Tables I and II summarize the potential strengths and weaknesses of the SDLC, respectively.

IV. SYSTEM DEVELOPMENT TOOLS AND TECHNIQUES

System development tools and techniques assist developers in building and delivering as rapidly as possible better information systems by speeding up and facilitating the activities in the analysis, design, software development, and implementation phases. Some of these tools are discussed below.

A. Flowcharts, Data Flow, and Entity-Relationships Diagrams

1. Flowcharts

Flowcharting was the first system analysis and design tool proposed in the 1960s. System flowcharts depict graphically the processes of a system while program flowcharts depict graphically the steps executed by a

Table II   Potential Weaknesses of the SDLC

Requires users to explicitly and completely define requirements; this cannot always be achieved as users may be either unable or unwilling to do so or may confuse requirements with solutions

The specific description of requirements at the beginning of the project may result in limited system functionality and adaptability to change

Limited user involvement throughout the development process may result in lack of system ownerships, user acceptance and user satisfaction

Linear sequential flow (when followed) is contrary to the iterative nature of system development

No established communication protocols between phases

Functional version of the system is not produced until very late; it is costly and difficult to fix errors not detected in the early stages

The feasibility study is undertaken before the new system is even defined

System maintenance workload and costs can be very high

It may take long time complete the project because possible delays in one stage cause delays in all the subsequent

Long-lasting development process leads to application backlog

Project inflexibility and limitation of human creativity as stages and subphases are determined at the outset

Heavy documentation is required

computer program. Flowcharts, although useful for describing processes, were not very well suited as a program-planning tool and were rarely used as such.

2. Data Flow Diagrams

Flowcharts have been replaced by data flow diagrams (DFD), which were proposed in the 1970s as a graphical tool to be used in the structured approaches of information system analysis and design. DFD depict first the general flow of system data between basic business and processes (diagram zero). Then, every process is developed in more detailed diagrams (diagram one, two, etc.). In combination with a *structured English text* describing the process and a *data dictionary,* describing data characteristics of the system databases, a dataflow diagram is a useful tool for system analysts and designers in identifying critical tasks and functions of the existing and the intended information system. Another objective of structured design is the improvement of communications between the stakeholders of the systems, such as users, managers, a steering committee, and developers.

3. Entity–Relationships Diagrams

DFD, despite its name, is a logical modeling tool focusing mainly on processes without emphasizing data relationships and flows. Entity–relationship diagrams (ERD), proposed by P. Chen in 1976, are a conceptual modeling technique emphasizing data entities of an organization and their relationships, complementing, thus, DFD. In an ERD, an entity represented by a rectangle is an external or internal element or a transaction of an organization, for example, a customer or a sale. A relationship, illustrated with a diamond, refers to the connection of two entities, such as a sale to a customer generating a sales invoice. Thus, the identification of entities and relationships offers a comprehensive view of the structure of the database of the current or proposed system and assists in both system analysis and design phases of the SDLC.

B. CASE Tools

Computer-Aided System and Software Engineering (CASE) is a general term describing the technology that facilitates developers or end users to build information systems and applications by coordinating and automating as much as possible system analysis and design. *End-user computing* refers to the activity by which users develop their own information systems or appli-

cations by using CASE tools and fourth-generation languages. Commercially available software tools simplify, automate, and improve system design quality and development process by analyzing the physical and logical specifications of the required system according to user needs, automatically generating programs code and documenting the system. CASE tools have also been developed to facilitate prototyping and object-oriented approaches to system development. Changes to models, required by users after a period of interaction with them, are more easily implemented. Therefore, CASE technology reduces the time required and the costs associated with the activities of system design and analysis. CASE tools support DFD and ERD. They are usually characterized as upper, middle, lower, and integrated CASE tools. Upper CASE tools are used by executives in the phase of the strategic planning of information systems. Middle CASE tools, such as diagramming tools and screen and report generators, automate the early stages of system analysis and design by documenting the processes and data of the existing and the new system. Lower CASE tools, such as code generators, apply to the later stages of system analysis and design and help programmers to develop and maintain code. Integrated CASE tools (I-CASE) engulf all the above categories.

C. Fourth-Generation Tools

Fourth-generation technology (4GT) software tools or fourth-generation languages (4GL) enable developers and software engineers to specify software at a higher level, automatically producing the source code required for a particular task, reducing, thus, the time associated with programming and helping users get answers to their requests faster. 4GT are general-purpose tools that can be applied to any problem and include non-procedural languages, report and code generators, query languages, web site creation languages, graphics capability, and screen interaction. Basic system development activities such as analysis and design are still required. Opponents claim that 4GL are not easier to use than traditional programming languages and they produce inefficient code.

V. ALTERNATIVE APPROACHES TO INFORMATION SYSTEM DEVELOPMENT

The conventional SDLC and its variations is the most widely used methodology for developing information systems. SDLC has assisted organizations in building information systems in a controlled and structured manner, but it has also been associated with high costs and development time underestimations. To overcome these and other potential weaknesses (see Table II) a number of alternative information system development and acquisition methodologies, techniques, devices, and mechanisms have been proposed. These are discussed below.

A. Structured Approaches to System Development

The need for a more disciplined approach to system development resulted in the development of structured methodologies. Structured design of information systems is based on the notion of business processes and functions and emphasizes the understanding of the whole system as a prerequisite for developing successful information systems. A disciplined, top-down, step-by-step approach is proposed, moving from an overview of the intended system to successive levels of detail. Well-known structured methodologies are, among others: the STRADIS by Gane and Sarson; the SASS by De-Marco; the Yourdon Systems Method (YSM); the Jackson System Development (JSD); the EUROMETHOD, which is a framework for the integration of existent European methodologies; and the Structured Systems Analysis and Design Methodology (SSADM), originated in the early 1980s. SSADM follows the waterfall approach to system development specifying the sequence of the project, the modules, the stages, the tasks, and the deliverables of each stage. This divides the life cycle into five separate modules, which are in turn divided into a hierarchy of stages as depicted in Fig. 2.

In addition, SSADM incorporates an extensive set of techniques for specifying and documenting systems, including DFD and entity-behavior and conceptual process modeling. It is essentially a system analysis and design methodology and does not cover the subsequent stages of the life cycle model, such as system implementation. The methodology has been criticized as bureaucratic, complex, restrictive, and inappropriate for rapid system development. However, it provides a logical and coherent way to design and analyze information systems and, as pointed out above, development success depends on the type of the project, the project management, and the way a particular methodology is applied.

B. Prototyping

Prototyping provides users with a simplified, working, physical model or a representation of the intended information system with the objective of defining requirements and testing the basic functional specifications of the new system before fully developing and implementing it. Typically, the functionality of the prototype is kept to a minimum for keeping its development costs down, although it is essential that the model should embody all the critical user requirements. In system development, a prototype is more likely to be a first version of a rather small system or a system component, which will eventually provide the basis for the construction of the entire system.

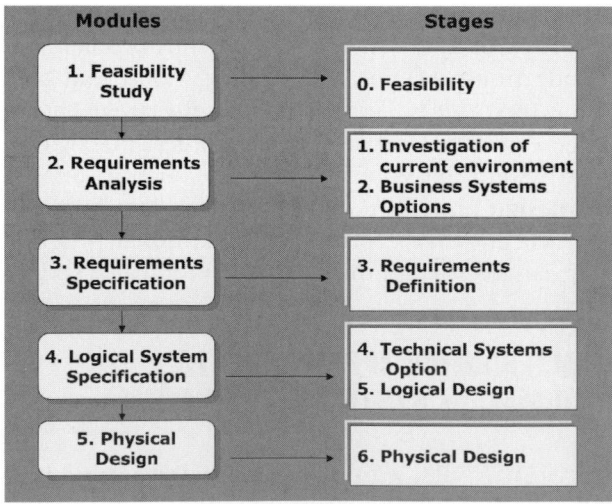

Figure 2   SSADM model.

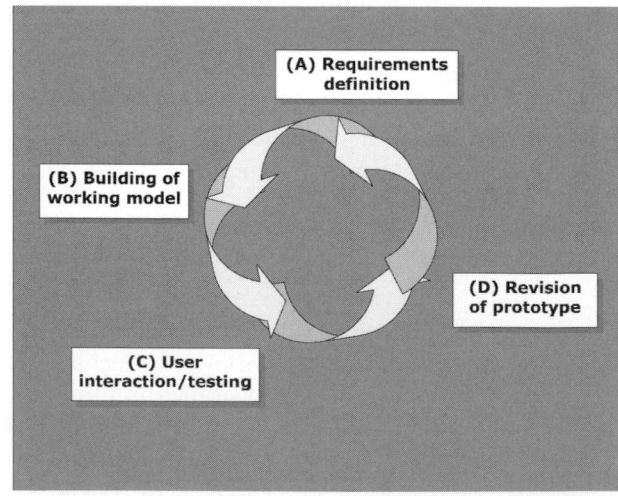

Figure 3   Prototyping.

Users interacting with the prototype, developed according to their instructions, suggest changes and developers modify or build a new prototype (Fig. 3). Two main types of prototyping are identified:

1. *Throw-away:* Once user acceptance is established, the prototype is discarded and the development of the final information system begins.
2. *Evolutionary:* In some cases, it is possible to continue the development of the accepted model until a finished system emerges.

High-level languages and other software tools are used in prototyping building, which is essentially a system analysis technique. Prototyping significantly reduces the time between the beginning of a development project and the system a user can operate, allowing significant user participation in the development process and providing crucial feedback from the users to the developers. In conventional system analysis, the need to identify at the outset user requirements is of the utmost importance. However, users are rarely able or willing to express their needs in quantifiable terms, usually they confuse requirements with solutions and have difficulty in comprehending system specifications set by developers. Prototyping overcomes these disadvantages by constantly changing the specifications, as long as costs are within budget, until the model's final approval by users. Thus, prototyping is particularly appropriate for developing information systems, in which requirements are frequently changing and cannot be clearly defined by users/customers. However, progress is difficult to measure due to the lack of established milestones and an excessive amount of development efforts, time and costs may be required as new functionalities are added to the prototype by users' requests. When system requirements are fully defined and understood prototyping may not be the appropriate development approach. Prototyping may also result in poorly structured systems consisting of large and complex applications or subsystems. Documentation can have serious limitations when a casual approach is adopted and users may have unrealistic expectations regarding the final system, especially when critical features are not addressed in the prototype.

C. Evolutionary and Incremental Approaches to System Development

Evolutionary approaches are iterative allowing developers to deliver increasingly more complete versions of a system or software application. The *spiral model*, pro-

posed by Barry Boehm in 1986, is such an evolutionary process aimed at rapid development of more complete versions of the software or system by taking into account the technical and managerial risks associated with each evolutionary level. Each loop of the spiral, representing a phase of the project, consists of the following sectors:

- Determination of objectives, alternatives, and constraints
- Evaluation of alternatives and risk assessment and reduction
- Selection of development method, e.g., prototyping or SDLC modified to incorporate incremental development, and
- Planning the next phase

The model encourages active user participation throughout the project. In its evolutionary version, the WINWIN spiral model explicitly incorporates negotiation activities between systems stakeholders for balancing systems functionality against costs and delivery time. The *incremental model* partitions the project into smaller components, which can be managed and developed more easily, aiming at producing new software releases improved incrementally over the previous ones. Users can operate earlier a subsystem or an application than they would have under the standard SDLC, which advocates a "big bang" approach. Each linear sequence of the incremental model, which may incorporate prototyping, adds new functionality and produces a deliverable component of the software or the information system. The output of the first sequence is usually the core product and, if accepted by the users, a more detailed functionality is planned and developed. The process is repeated until the complete product is delivered. Thus, both the spiral and the incremental approaches result in a formalized prototyping process by combining SDLC with prototyping.

D. Rapid Application Development

Rapid application development (RAD) is an incremental sequential software development process aimed at very short development cycles by using a component-based construction approach. To speed up the process of application development, usually more that one development team is working on separate system components or application modules. These are then integrated to form a whole system. A combination of techniques and tools such as joint applications development (JAD), joint requirements planning (JRP), CASE tools, and 4GL contribute to RAD.

JAD is an alternative to the interviewing activity of the traditional SDLC, allowing user participation in the development process. Systems developers and users attend intensive meetings discussing and documenting user needs. The specifications identified in the JAD sessions can be also used to develop prototypes.

The RAD approach is more likely to succeed when projects have a scalable scope and there is commitment by both users and developers to meet the tight time frames. Large projects require properly designed modularization and extensive human resources to create the components project teams.

E. Sociotechnical Approaches to System Development

Sociotechnical methodologies introduced the study of the social and political factors involved in the development process of information systems. Such well-known methodologies are the Soft System Methodology (SSM) proposed by P. Checkland in 1981, the ETHICS methodology by E. Mumford in 1995, and the Multiview (MV) methodology originated in 1985. These methodologies integrate human and technical aspects of information system development and emphasize the importance of such issues as human relationships, people roles, tasks, norms, values, and conflicts. The emphasis on the human aspects of the SDLC is obvious when considering the five MV stages below:

1. Analysis of human activity
2. Analysis of information
3. Analysis and design of sociotechnical aspects
4. Design of the HCI
5. Design of technical aspects

F. Object-Oriented (OO) Approach

The OO approach emphasizes system analysis and design from the perspective of the final users of the system, that is, OO approach is *use-case* oriented. A use-case encompasses a system usage scenario. It is used to define the functional and operational requirements of the system to be built by describing the way users interact with the system. The OO approach adopts the component-based development (CBD) paradigm, using the notation of the diagrammatic Unified Modeling Language (UML) for modeling the components of a system (see section below).

In OO models, systems components consist of objects, which are concepts or entities, such as inventory

and accounts. Objects are characterized by *attributes* and *methods* or operations, which contain a permissible set of procedures. Objects are autonomous but can interact by using communication means called *messages. Encapsulation* is the property that allows data and methods to be hidden from the external world allowing previously designed objects to be reused in new systems. Access to the data and methods of an object is achieved through the prescribed interfaces using messaging. The encapsulation of both data and functions within objects enables the construction of *classes* (the implementation of object type), which is an *abstract* concept for a logical grouping of related objects. This leads to the creation of libraries of reusable objects and classes. A basic property, *inheritance* means that each object inherits the attributes and methods of the class to which it belongs. Inheritance allows the extension of existing object types, the importance being that OO code modules are reusable either for extending existing applications or for rapid development of new ones. It should be noted that commercial off-the-self (COTS) components are also available which can be used in system development. The popularity of OO approaches during the 1990s is based on the concept that software constructed upon modular, reusable and self-contained objects is more maintainable, extensible, and flexible than the conventionally produced software. Systems developed with tested reusable components are reduced risk systems and developed much faster than those conventionally developed.

OO approaches are conceptually distinctly different from conventional system development methodologies. OO approaches emphasize the basic properties of the objects, encapsulation, classification, and inheritance. Conventional methodologies treat separately data and procedures applied to data adopting an information flow model in examining a particular problem. However, the basic phases of the traditional SDLC, that is, analysis, design, and implementation, still exist in OO approaches either as distinct activities or as a continuous process.

Object-Oriented Analysis (OOA)—OOA focuses on the investigation of a problem. It begins with the assessment of customer specifications and the creation of use-cases. A use-case describes alternative scenarios, that is, how user and other systems can interact with the system to be built before proceeding into creating an OOA model. A principal task of systems analysts in object-oriented analysis is to identify the objects pertaining to a particular problem, identify *instances,* which represent a single occurrence of an object within a class, and group objects into classes, providing descriptions and indicating their purposes. The *class-responsibility-collaborator* (CRC) modeling technique can be used to transform system requirements defined by use-cases into class categories and related operations. At each stage of the construction of an OOA model, system analysts, taking into account user requirements, develop, test, and document the role of each class, their interactions and the operations performed of a class object upon receipt of a message.

Object-Oriented design (OOD)—OOD focuses on the logical solution of a problem. Various modeling techniques have been proposed for the design of either systems or individual objects. OO system design (OOSD) identifies and specifies subsystems required to perform certain functions, defines a multilayered software architecture, and describes objects, classes, and communication mechanisms. OOSD aims at developing a detailed model consisting of software modules, data management, task management, and user interfacing, which can be realized by applying an object-oriented language.

Object-Oriented Programming (OOP)—This activity transforms OO design into program code using object-oriented programming. Testing of a system or application is an additional activity performed at this stage.

Object-oriented technology is of particular significance in building modern information systems on client/server architectures. Objects may be in the same or separate software modules or processors or scattered across a worldwide network. The database management system is less dependent upon programs, and the database is more easily used in distributed environments. This is useful for business and reporting activities dispersed geographically. Better audit trail of activities can also be established because operations determine how users' requests are carried out.

G. UML

UML, although it has been associated with OO models, is a general purpose notational language used to visualize, specify, construct, and document a software intensive system. UML is use-case driven, iterative, incremental, and centered on software's architecture, which is comprised of system's structural elements and their behavior and other elements such as usage, functionality, reuse, and aesthetics. According to its designers G. Booch, J. Rumbaugh, and I. Jacobson, UML permits modeling of the five distinct views of a software system, which can stand alone or interact with one another: the *use case* view of a system, the *design* view, the *process* view, the *implementation* view, and the *deployment* view.

H. The Concurrent Development Model

The *concurrent* development model is based on the notion that concurrency exists across all system or software development activities in a project. For example, although a project may be in its final stage, there are still personnel involved simultaneously in activities, such as designing, coding, and integration testing, typically associated with individual stages of development. Activities, such as analysis or design, exist concurrently in different states or modes of behavior, such as the "awaiting changes" state or the "done" state. When it is required, the model defines a series of events that will transit activities from one state into another. The model can be applied as a paradigm for the development of client/server applications. In a client/server system the system dimension includes the activities of design, assembly, and use and the component dimension includes the activities of design and realization. System and component activities occur simultaneously and the modules of the system can be designed and developed concurrently. The *chaos life cycle* is an extension of the concurrent model. This model suggests that software development is a user-developer-technology continuum. All the basic phases of system development are applied recursively to user needs and technical specification of the software. The concurrent and chaos models provide a more realistic view of system development, as they do not confine systems and software development in a linear sequential series of steps.

I. Formal Methods Model

The formal methods model proposes a mathematical specification of the information system. System design, development, and verification are specified by applying a rigorous mathematical notation, which is either algebraic or model-based using the notation of sets and sequences. Inconsistencies and incompleteness can be detected more easily through mathematical analysis but the model is difficult to understand by users, thus limiting the communication between user/customers and developers.

J. Cleanroom Software Development

The term "cleanroom," derived by analogy with semiconductors' ultraclean atmosphere fabrication units, denotes the software development iterative life cycle approach based on static verification techniques, aiming at producing reliable software. The development process has the following basic phases:

- System specification using formal methods
- Definition of software increments which are developed separately
- Structured programming
- Static verification of the developed software using mathematical correctness techniques
- Functional testing based on random selection of test data
- Statistical testing of the integrated system.

This "cleanroom" approach requires that programs are not compiled and tested only statistically. When testing fails, a feedback mechanism modifies parameters of the design process and a new development life cycle begins.

K. Business Process and Information System Reengineering

The need to reduce costs and increase product quality and service has driven many organizations to focus on the effectiveness of their business processes. Reengineering is defined by M. Hammer and J. Champy (*Reengineering the corporation: A manifesto for business revolution,* Harper Business, NY, 1993) as the fundamental rethinking and radical redesign of critical business processes in order to achieve dramatic improvement in business performance. This redesign of business processes is greatly enabled by information technology. A model of Business Process Reengineering (BPR) is depicted in Fig. 4.

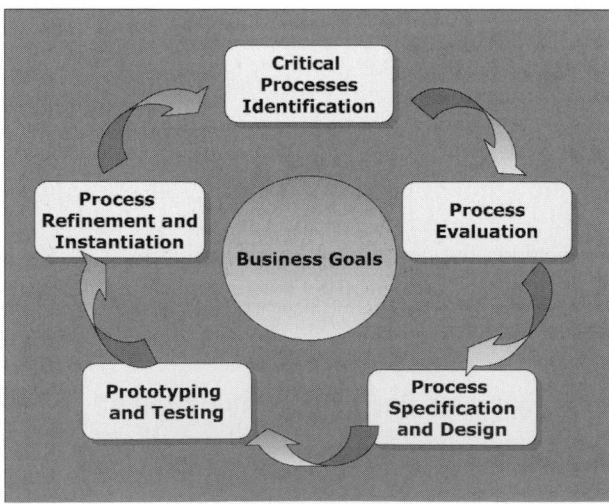

Figure 4 A BPR model.

Traditional information system development focused mainly in automating and speeding up existing procedures without questioning their impact on business performance or even the usefulness of their existence. Reengineering requires that management challenges assumptions and rethinks business processes. Reengineering projects usually result in the elimination of some processes and in major organizational change, which has a dramatic impact upon the people in the organization. Therefore, organizations adopting this action take a greater risk than those requiring only incremental improvements. Change management aimed at successfully implementing change in the organization is mainly confronted with behavioral and organizational problems. BPR requires that information systems be reengineered too in order to support the new business paradigm. This is a challenging and complex activity considering the incompatible systems and the heterogeneous and inflexible computing architectures of most organizations. However, when this iterative and evolutionary approach is well executed, it can integrate information systems into business processes. Software tools are useful for the analysis of business processes, rapid development of applications, and prototype development. A number of techniques have been proposed for *information systems reengineering,* including reverse and forward engineering:

- *Reverse engineering* is the activity of rebuilding or refining an existing system according to a design re-specification, by extracting the original design from code. This is appropriate when there have not been any drastic changes concerning the original requirements and the system can be rebuilt to conform to new information technology architecture or to new user needs.
- *Forward engineering,* assisted by CASE tools, extracts information from existing systems and uses this information to reconstruct the system and to add new functionality.

L. Outsourcing

Internal software development is generally resource consuming and can result in program duplication, application backlog, and system inflexibility. Large off-the-shelf software packages and systems can also be extremely expensive and complex to implement and operate. An alternative option is the outsourcing of a part or the whole information system function to a third party offering IT services. Organizations adopt outsourcing when they consider it to be a lower cost or better quality alternative to internal development of applications. Organizations may not adopt outsourcing when they:

- Are reluctant to share information with other firms
- Wish to have total control over their information technology and information system development function
- Do not wish to be tied-up with long-term contracts with the outsourcer

Application Server Provision (ASP) is an emerging market for outsourcing both the hosting and the management of business software applications. ASPs rent and deliver application software to their customers over the Internet. This allows companies to have access to expensive software systems by simply using a standard Web browser.

M. Application Packages

Ready-made applications packages are software programs developed by third-party vendors designed to be used by a number of organizations, usually with a minimum customization effort. These packages are general, taking advantage of the fact that many business functions are sufficiently standardized across a range of diverse organizations. In order to meet the specific needs of a variety of organizations, packages allow some customization through the use of parameters. Development costs are spread across the organizations in which they will be finally installed. Off-the-shelf packages offer a serious alternative to custom programming, which is usually more expensive and resource consuming. However, installation of more complex packages requires a great deal of customization effort and extensive company resources. The SDLC can still be used to evaluate the proposed off-the-shelf system, although some phases of the conventional SDLC will no longer be applicable, such as the coding process and debugging of the system, except in the case where interfaces are required to link the new system to existing ones. Implementation activities, such as user training and system customization, integration and testing are still required.

During the 1990s, off-the-shelf enterprise resource planning (ERP) systems emerged as the prevailing form of computing in medium and large organizations in the private and public sector. These systems, also known as enterprise-wide systems (EWS), are based on a client/server architecture providing support to integrated business processes across organizational functions. ERP software can be defined as a set of customizable and highly integrative real-time business applications software modules sharing a common database, which incorporate best business practices and support core business, production, and administrative functions, such as logistics, manufacturing, sales, distribution, finance, and accounting. Pressures of an intensively competitive global marketplace and changing customer needs have driven organizations to implement extended ERP systems, including, for example, Supply Chain Management (SCM) and Customer Relationship Management (CRM) modules.

Each module of an ERP system can access over 1000 in-built business processes based on industry best practices. Industry solutions, such as retail or hospital management are special versions of ERP software aimed at satisfying the needs of certain business sectors. ERP software is customizable in order to support critical existing processes followed by certain organizations. However, customization is costly, time-consuming, difficult, and usually requires experienced external consultants. Although some customization according to specific business needs is inevitable, major customization of the software with the purpose of adapting it to existing business processes is difficult and certainly not recommended. Most organizations need, therefore, to substantially reengineer their processes in accordance with the software's requirements and embedded industry best practices, a source of major organizational change.

In traditional information system development theory, the software has to fit in to certain business processes, probably adopting and reproducing organizational inefficiencies. In ERP systems implementation, the reverse course is usually effective. Due to complexity of the system, enterprises prefer to adapt their business processes to software's in-built best business practices, which is usually a cause for major organizational change. It should be noted that, due to the strategic nature of ERP systems, the ERP life cycle begins with the clarification of business vision and objectives. This ensures that the ERP software fits into the business strategy and the information technology architecture of the organization. The selection of the system involves the evaluation of the product, vendor, and supporting services available, such as training and consulting, according to detailed user requirements. Implementation of the system usually requires external consultants to customize the software, excessive user training, integration with existent systems,

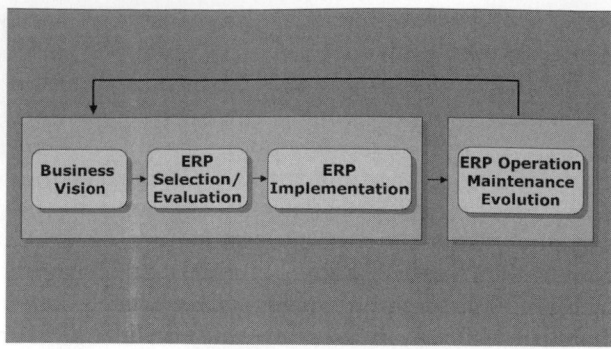

Figure 5   ERP life cycle.

and management of organizational change. Finally, the maintenance phase of the software reviews its performance and may lead to its evolution by acquiring additional functionality. Figure 5 depicts the basic phases of an ERP life cycle.

VI. SUMMARY

The SDLC is a conventional project management methodology for developing information systems, proposing a top-down sequential process. The basic phases of the methodology are (1) system analysis, (2) system design, and (3) system implementation. SDLC provides the basis that numerous variations and other modern methodologies have been built upon. Recent advances in information technology can significantly automate the linear sequence of the stages proposed by life cycle methodologies and facilitate prototyping and iteration, a necessary activity in information systems development. Alternative methodologies and techniques have been introduced in information system development aimed at building more efficient and effective information systems. Information system development is foremost a manage-

rial activity and needs to be planned as such. Given the sociotechnical nature of information systems and development projects, besides technical considerations, also taken into account should be the human aspects and organizational issues involved throughout the life cycle of the project and its final product, the information system.

SEE ALSO THE FOLLOWING ARTICLES

Computer Assisted Systems Engineering (CASE) • Control and Auditing • Database Development Process • Documentation for Software and IS Development • Error Detecting and Correcting Codes • Prototyping • Success Measures of Information Systems • User/System Interface Design

BIBLIOGRAPHY

Avison, D. E., and Fitzgerald, G. (1995). *Information systems development: Methodologies, techniques and tools,* 2nd Edition. United Kingdom: McGraw-Hill International.

Boehm, B. (1986). A spiral model of software development and enhancement. *ACM SIGSOFT Software Engineering Notes.* Vol. 11, No. 4, pp. 22–42

Booch, G., Jacobson, J., and Rumbaugh, I. (1999). *The Unified Modeling Language user guide.* Reading, MA: Addison-Wesley.

Burch, J.G. (1992). *Systems analysis, design and implementation.* Boston, MA: Boyd and Fraser.

Coad, P., and Yourdon, E. N. (1991). *Object oriented analysis,* 2nd ed. Englewood Cliffs, NJ: Prentice Hall.

Pressman, R.S. (2000). *Software engineering, a practitioner's approach,* 5th edition. United Kingdom: McGraw-Hill International.

Raccoon, L.B.S. (1995). The chaos model and the chaos lifecycle. *ACM Software Engineering Notes,* Vol. 20, No. 1, pp.55–66.

Sommerville, I. (1995). *Software Engineering,* 5th Edition, Reading, MA: Addison-Wesley.

Wu, S.Y., and Wu, M.S. (1994) *Systems analysis and design.* Minneapolis, MN: West.

Yourdon, E.N. (1989). *Modern structured analysis.* Englewood Cliffs, NJ: Prentice Hall.

Systems Analysis

Tonya Barrier

Southwest Missouri State University

SYSTEMS ANALYSIS, more correctly referred to as information systems analysis, is the process by which an individual(s) studies a system such that an information system can be analyzed, modeled, and a logical alternative (independent of technology) can be chosen. The basic systems analysis project consists of two basic steps: (1) analysis (study of the system) and (2) modeling the system and choosing the logical alternative.

The best way to fully describe systems analysis is to define the terminology used in the process. First, a system is a set of components that work together to achieve a particular goal or objective. Therefore, an information system is a set of components that work together to provide information for an organization. This information may be used to plan, make decisions, and/or manage an organization. The components of the information system are software, hardware, people, procedures, data/information, and communication networks.

The key is that the system provides information and not data. Data are simply a list of facts, while information is a group of facts organized in such a way that the facts can be used in their present format to plan, make decisions, and and/or manage an organization. Systems analysis describes a specific set of steps (methodology) for analyzing, modeling, and choosing a logical alternative for an information system, which ultimately identifies the logical (human) requirements of an information system (software specifications, people's duties, logical procedures, data required, and information produced).

I. REASONS FOR INITIATING PROJECTS

Systems analysis projects are started for three basic reasons: (1) the organization has a problem, (2) a "new" opportunity exists to make changes within the organization, and/or (3) a directive has been issued that mandates changes to be made. When an organization experiences a problem, many times an information system is developed to solve the problem and/or a current system is modified to "fix" the problem. A classical definition for a problem is the difference between what a system is doing versus what a system should be doing. Therefore, a complete study is performed of what the system is doing combined with a study of what the system should be doing. The difference between the two studies results in the logical specifications for the new system. This is a very simple description of the traditional developmental methodology.

Opportunities and directives are administered in the same way as problems. Opportunities represent new types of systems that generally result from the introduction of new technology and/or software. Directives are passed from the upper level management to the information systems area and represent new development projects. Opportunities and directives are not related to problems but represent new ways that information systems can support the organization.

II. PEOPLE INVOLVED

The individuals involved in systems analysis projects include systems analysts and nontechnical individuals (sponsors and users). The system analyst is the individual(s) that works closely with the nontechnical individuals to determine the system's requirements. Basically, it is the systems analyst's responsibility to manage the specific methodology so that the system can be developed or modified. The nontechnical people include sponsors and users. The sponsors are the individuals responsible for assigning resources (money, time, materials, and man hours, etc.) to the project. The users are the individuals that receive the benefits of the system. The user may or may not have direct contact with the system. A user could simply receive a written report or have the ability to retrieve an online report from the system.

III. PURPOSE

The purpose of systems analysis is to identify the logical requirements for a system and to choose an alternative independent of technology to fulfill those logical requirements identified. Logical requirements are the basic functional requirements of the system. These requirements include the "human needs." An example of a logical requirement would be, "We need an information system to display customers that are 10 days late paying their bills." These requirements can be summed up with the following question: What does the system need to do?

Once the logical requirements are determined the appropriate logical components are chosen and/or created. The set of tasks, techniques, and tools that are used to develop an analysis projects are referred to as the systems development life cycle.

IV. SYSTEMS DEVELOPMENT LIFE CYCLE

The systems development life cycle can be performed many ways. In fact, each organization may develop its own list of tasks, techniques, and (automated) tools, which can be referred to as "their" methodology. Each of these methodologies has common themes. The first includes ways to search for facts about the system. The basic fact finding techniques include questionnaires, interviews, observation, and document collection.

The second theme includes ways to determine the data necessary to produce the logical requirements specified by the organization. The data will be represented by a predetermined model. The most common data model used is the entity relationship diagram.

The third theme includes ways to determine the processes (actions) necessary to produce the results as defined by the requirements of the system. The processes will be represented by a predetermined model. One common process model used is the data flow diagram.

Once the themes have been identified then there are predetermined tasks and techniques to finish the project as defined by the approved methodology of the organization.

V. METHODOLOGY CLASSIFICATION

There are three basic classifications for the methodologies used. They are the traditional, information engineering, and object-oriented methodologies. Their purpose is the same; however, the specified steps are different.

A. Traditional Methodology

The traditional methodology is the oldest. Its basic premise is that all functional requirements can be decomposed into input (data), process (actions to transform data into information), and output (information). The models used in this process represent the decomposition of input, process, and output. The model commonly used is the data flow diagram. The data flow diagrams represent the processes of the system in a hierarchically decomposed fashion. Further, the diagrams are supported by an alphabetized listing of all the items pictured in the diagram (data dictionary). Therefore, first the processes are represented by the data flow diagram and second the data are represented by the data dictionary. Figure 1 is a partial data flow diagram for a library.

The traditional methodology has distinct advantages. It uses simple models such as the data flow diagram to hierarchically represent the functional requirements (processes) of a particular system. Therefore the models become a communication tool to discuss the functionality of the system (which is important to the users). Since they are decomposed hierarchically, the analyst and user can discuss the more general functions of the system to the most detailed functions of the system as needed. The disadvantages

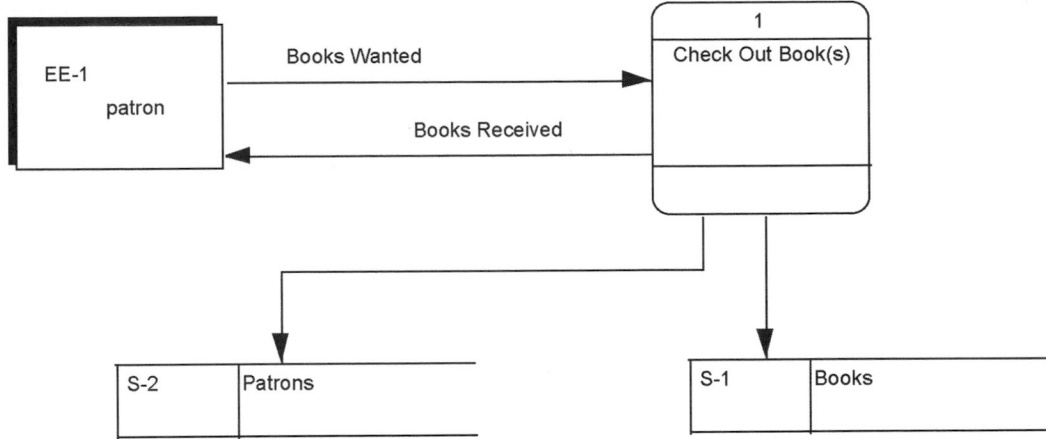

Figure 1   Partial data flow diagram.

of the traditional methodology include that users must be trained to understand the models used; and that users must be able to comprehend the decomposition of the inputs, processes, and the outputs of the system.

B. Information Engineering Methodology

The information engineering (IE) methodology's main focus is on the data of the organization. First, the data are represented by a data model such as an entity relationship diagram. Second, the processes are represented by another model such as an activity hierarchy diagram. The information engineering methodology supports an assumption that data should be the primary focus of a development methodology while traditional methodologies support processes as the primary focus. Figure 2 shows an example of an entity relationship diagram for a library.

The main difference in the traditional methodology and the information engineering methodology can be explained by order. Traditional methodologies identify the functions first and then the data. Information engineering methodologies identify the data first and then the functions. However, some researchers still insist that the information engineering methodology is better than the traditional methodology because data are the foundation (first identified)

for IE. These researchers insist that data are more stable in organizations than processes. So IE is a better methodology.

The primary advantage of the IE methodology is that data are identified first, then the functions are identified second. The IE methodology does not foster the complete decomposition of the inputs, processes, and outputs. In fact it can be argued that IE does not hierarchically decompose the functions in the same way that the traditional methodologies do; this can be seen as an advantage not to have to train users to decompose the functionality of the system.

The disadvantages of the IE methodology include the fact that users must be trained to understand the models and that users must be able to identify the data of the system first before identifying the functions of the system.

C. Object-Oriented Methodology

The object-oriented (OO) methodology is the "newest" methodology. The primary focus of this methodology is objects. In the simplest sense, objects are simply a representation of a unit of input-process-output. There is no separate data and process model as represented by the other two methodologies. The unified modeling language is used to describe a system by objects. This particular methodology appears to be more understood by the nontechnical person. This methodology uses a single model that shows both the data and the process simultaneously. The most common model is the object-oriented class (OO class) model. The OO model stresses reusability. For example, an object once built could and should be used again and again as parts of other information systems.

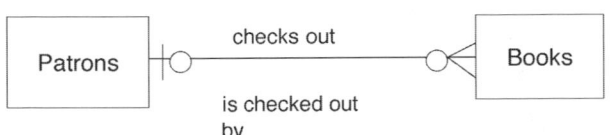

Figure 2   Partial entity relationship diagram.

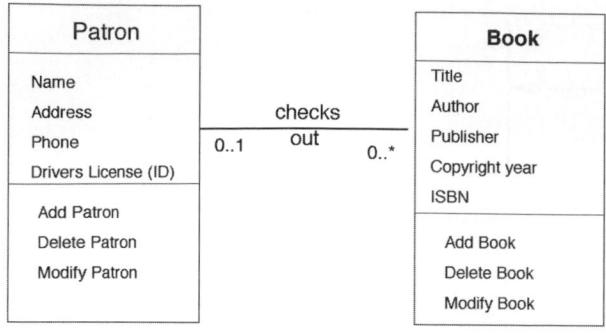

Figure 3 Partial object class diagram.

Figure 3 shows an example of a partial OO class model for a library.

The advantages of the OO methodologies include the fact that users are only concerned with one model—not two models—and that users are not required to separate the data from the processes. OO models are seen by users as simpler and easier to interpret than the traditional and IE models. Therefore users appear to be more comfortable with OO methodologies. Further, trained OO development staff can be "more" productive because the models are simpler, self-contained, and provide reusable objects. However, the disadvantages are clear to information systems department personnel. The OO methodologies are based upon OO programs such as Java and C++. If the organization has an "older" information systems department, the personnel may not feel comfortable with the "newer" technologies and therefore may be hesitant to adopt the new methodologies. Further, the information systems department may not have the tools necessary to support OO. Therefore, it would be expensive to adopt the "newer" methodology. In other words, information system personnel might need "new training" to adopt OO methodologies.

There are many other methodologies that may be hybrids of the above or simply other kinds of methodologies (for example, event driven, component-based, or Web-based methodologies). However, each methodology must ultimately represent the three basic themes as described previously. Each methodology must also list specific tasks, techniques, and (automated) tools.

VI. AUTOMATED METHODOLOGY SUPPORT

Following a methodology can be a complex and tedious process. There have been software programs created to support the process. These software programs are referred to as CASE tools. CASE stands for computer-aided systems engineering. CASE tools have been classified three ways. The first is Upper CASE. Upper CASE tools help the analyst document the logical requirements of the system. They include support for fact-finding, model building (data and process), and/or simple written documentation of the process followed.

The second classification is Lower CASE. Lower CASE tools support the development of the physical requirements of the system. They include support for software generation, network configuration, simulation, and/or physical modeling of the system.

The third classification is Full CASE. Full CASE tools support the entire development process. Full CASE tools basically combine the functionality of the Upper and Lower CASE tools. Further, some Full CASE tools have the added capability to support the management of the process as well. Full CASE tools are the most useful tools available for analysts in organizations.

Each CASE tool regardless of its classification (Upper, Lower, or Full) supports a specific methodology. For example, Excelerator , Visible Analyst, and Silverrun support the traditional methodologies. CoolGen supports the IE and component-based methodologies.

Object-oriented methodologies are supported by a variety of tools such as Java, C++, and combinations of CASE tools. Although there is not a single Full CASE tool that totally supports OO, combinations of CASE tools already available and used by organizations can be used to build the components necessary to support OO. Therefore individuals using OO methodologies may be required to become familiar with multiple CASE tools.

VII. SUMMARY

Systems analysis is the process by which an individual(s) studies a system such that an information system can be analyzed, modeled, and a logical alternative can be chosen. Systems analysis projects are initiated for three reasons: problems, opportunities, and directives. The people involved include systems analysts, sponsors, and users. The process by which systems are developed can be described by the systems development life cycle. The tasks, techniques, and tools used by the systems development life cycle can be referred as a methodology. There are three classifications of the methodologies: traditional, information engineering, and object-oriented. CASE tools are automated tools that support specific methodologies.

SEE ALSO THE FOLLOWING ARTICLES

Systems Approach • Systems Design • Systems Implementation • Systems Science

BIBLIOGRAPHY

Kendall, K., and Kendall, J. (1999). *Systems analysis and design*, 4th ed. Upper Saddle River, NJ: Prentice Hall.

Satzinger, J., and Orvik, T. (2001). *The object-oriented approach*, 2nd ed. Boston, MA: Course Technology.

Shelly, G., Cashman, T., and Rosenblatt, H. (2001). *Systems analysis and design*, 4th ed. Boston, MA: Course Technology.

Whitten, J., Bentley, L., and Dittman, K. (2001). *Systems analysis and design*, 5th ed. Boston, MA: McGraw–Hill/Irwin.

Systems Approach

Gordon B. Davis

University of Minnesota

GLOSSARY

black box A subsystem at the lowest level (input, process, output) not defined as to the process. This system is termed a black box, since the inputs and outputs are known but not the transformation process.

boundary Defines those system elements that interact together and therefore are included in the system to be studied, analyzed, or built. The environment defines that which is outside the boundary of the system.

closed system A system that is self-contained and does not exchange material, information, or energy with its environment. There are no truly closed systems in organizations and information processing. However, there are systems that are relatively isolated from the environment. These will be termed closed systems, meaning relatively closed.

clustering System simplification by grouping clusters of subsystems that interact with each other and defining a single interface path from the cluster to other subsystems or clusters of subsystems.

decomposition Process of dividing a system into a number of subsystems and then each of these into smaller subsystems. This process continues until the smallest subsystems are of manageable size. The principle that guides the definition of subsystems is functional cohesion. Components are considered to be part of the same subsystem if they perform or are related to the same function.

decoupling Use of methods that reduce coordination required between systems that send outputs and receive inputs. Decoupling reduces the need for tight interconnections and high communications between subsystems. Examples of methods are inventories, buffers, and waiting lines.

double loop learning Applies to organizational learning. In single loop learning, humans adjust the responses of the organization as new events or situations occur that are not part of existing understanding and system responses. New responses are added but there is no attempt to determine underlying changes that caused the unanticipated inputs. In double loop learning, when faced with unanticipated inputs, humans question the assumptions and values of the existing system and seek to understand the underlying reasons for behaviors represented in the new events and situations. The system is revised to reflect this new understanding.

entropy The decay of systems so that they are less and less able to meet the objectives and perform the functions intended for them. It is synonymous with decay or disorganization. Results of entropy are systems that are disordered and do not perform functions intended.

equifinality Expectation that systems for organizations can be designed in many different ways and all the variations accomplish the basic purpose. This means organizations have system design alternatives and can base choices of system design on criteria such as cost of the system, human factors, and social desirability.

feedback System regulation and control mechanisms in which measurements of the output of a system are compared with the desired output (standard), and any difference causes an input to be looped back to the process to adjust the operations, so that output will be closer to the standard. Feedback that seeks to dampen and reduce fluctuations around the standard is termed negative feedback. Positive feedback reinforces the processes that produced a favorable output, so that the processes will produce a further increase. For example, negative feedback may be employed to keep expenditures within budget; positive feedback may be employed to increase effort that has been successful in increasing sales.

interfaces The interconnections and interactions between systems and subsystems. Interfaces occur at the boundary and take the form of inputs and outputs.

negative entropy Also termed system maintenance. Systems can run down and decay or can become disordered or disorganized (an increase in entropy). Preventing entropy or offsetting an increase in entropy requires inputs of matter and energy to repair, replenish, and maintain the system.

open system A system that exchanges information, material, or energy with the environment. Exchanges include random and undefined inputs. Open systems tend to have form and structure that allow them to adapt to changes in their environment.

requisite variety For a system to be controlled under all possible conditions, there must be at least as many variations of control to be applied as there are ways for the system to get out of control. The law of requisite variety means that for a system to be controlled, every controller (human or machine) must be provided with one of the following: (1) a list of control responses (what to do in each case) to cover all possible conditions the system may face, (2) decision rules for generating all possible control responses, or (3) the authority to become a self-organizing system in order to generate control responses.

socio-technical Approach to systems analysis in which system designers, system operators, and system users participate in designing alternative technical solutions and proposing systems that meet both technical and social system objectives.

soft system An artificial system with objectives defined by human participants. The subsystems of a soft system may have conflicting, changing objectives. These can be resolved by systems analysis approaches such as Checkland's soft system methodology.

subsystem Each system is composed of subsystems which in turn are made up of other subsystems, each subsystem being delineated by its boundaries.

system dynamics Modeling of system behavior over time. The approach explicitly examines the influence of system behavior in one time period with behavior in subsequent time periods. For example, a business venture that is increasing sales rapidly will have increases in inventory, sales force expenditures, accounts receivable, etc. These factors require financial capital either from equity investments or debt, increase in workforce, etc. The model shows how these forces interact over time to limit growth or perhaps place the system in jeopardy.

The **SYSTEMS APPROACH** is an analytical and management approach in the development of organization systems such as business process systems, information technology applications, computer and communications software, and computer and communications technology systems. The systems approach is based on concepts of systems. It guides the process by which systems are analyzed, developed, combined into larger systems, implemented, enhanced, and renewed. A systems approach is followed in contexts other than organization systems, but this article will focus only on systems in organizations and especially information systems. The article explains the limited view of systems that is applied in information systems work. At the end of the article, a broader classification of systems is provided along with notes about its relevance to information systems.

I. DEFINITION OF SYSTEM AND SYSTEMS APPROACH

Systems can be abstract or physical. Information systems are physical systems, so this explanation will focus on that type. A physical system is a set of elements that operate together to accomplish an objective. A system is not a randomly assembled set of elements; it consists of elements that can be identified as belonging together because of a common purpose, goal, or objective. Physical systems display activity or behavior, and the parts interact to achieve an objective.

A physical system can be a biological living system that occurs in nature or an artificial system. An artificial system is an artifact of human design and development, i.e., a designed system. It can include a variety of elements including humans procedures and processes, and technology. Information systems are artificial systems because they do not occur in nature but are the result of human design and development effort. Examples of artificial systems are:

- Computer system—The computer and communications equipment that function together to accomplish computer processing.
- Accounting system—The records, rules, procedures, equipment, and personnel that operate to record data, measure income, and prepare reports.
- Information system application—The information technology hardware, software, procedures for input and output, database, and operating personnel to perform information processing functions required by an organization.

A. General Model of System

A general model of a physical system is input, process, and output. A system may have several inputs and outputs. The features that define and delineate a system form its boundary. The system is inside the boundary; the environment is outside the boundary. In some cases, it is fairly simple to define what is part of the system and what is not; in other cases, the person studying the system may arbitrarily define the boundaries. Some examples of systems and possible boundaries are:

- Supply chain system—System boundary includes suppliers, internal inventory, customers, systems for communications, transportation, and so forth. The boundary may exclude suppliers' suppliers, customers' customers, and so forth.
- Production system—Boundaries include production machines, production inventory of work in process, production employees, production procedures, etc. The rest of the company is in the environment.
- Financial analysis information system—Includes financial analyst users, data entry personnel, computer software, databases, desktop terminals, and procedures for performing analysis and displaying results. The environment is the organization employing the analysts, the organizations supplying the data for the databases, and so forth.

Each system is composed of subsystems which in turn are made up of other subsystems, each subsystem being delineated by its boundaries. The interconnections and interactions between the subsystems are termed interfaces. Interfaces occur at the boundary and take the form of inputs and outputs. A subsystem at the lowest level (input, process, output) is often not defined as to the process. This system is termed a black box, since the inputs and outputs are known but not the transformation process.

B. System Approach and System Thinking

The systems approach is an approach to analysis, problem solving, and design of systems that looks at the system as a unity that receives inputs, performs processes, and delivers outputs. The process by which inputs result in outputs is performed by a set of subsystems that interact. In the systems approach, an investigator defines a boundary for the system to be studied that distinguishes between the system and the environment in which the system is found. The set of possible inputs that can influence the system is defined as well as the possible outputs from the system. The process by which the system receives inputs and produces outputs is investigated by determining the subsystems within the system and the interaction of these subsystems. System control is investigated by examining how outputs can be compared to system performance criteria and differences provided as inputs to the system to influence the process. A negative feedback loop is used to keep a system within acceptable limits of output; a positive feedback is used to increase favorable performance.

Systems thinking is evident in many ancient writings and in many cultures. As a body of explicit knowledge tied to modern scientific discoveries, it can be traced to studies of the adaptive mechanisms of the human body and the recognition of principles of feedback control in nature and in the design of artificial systems. In 1955, a society was formed, the International Society for Systems Sciences. The idea behind the society was to formulate general systems theory by studying the way systems adapt and survive in a changing environment. The study of adaptation has tended to focus on living systems and open systems in artifacts such as organizations. Those who espouse general systems theory have provided interesting analyzes of systems with different objectives and different processes that demonstrate similar general systems principles. Even though general systems theory has provided interesting insights, it has been of limited use in applied areas such as information systems analysis and design. Within information systems work, system concepts are employed in the design and operation of information system infrastructures, applications, and business systems. System principles are incorporated in a variety of ways into system design approaches. Four of these are described later: hard systems analysis, soft systems methodologies, socio-technical approaches, and learning organization approaches.

C. System Goals and Objectives

An important reason for different system design approaches is the issue of system objective or goal. Systems in nature appear to have clear goals or objectives. In the design of systems in organizations, such as information systems, the goals and objectives for some systems may also be clear and well defined, but others are unclear and conflicting. An example of an information processing system with clear objectives is a software system for well-established methods of data analysis. Examples of systems with unclear and conflicting objectives are complex systems that deal with probabilistic behavior embedded in organizational or societal processes where different stakeholders have different, often conflicting objectives.

The processes for formulating goals and objectives may differ depending on the nature of the systems. Systems with clear, unambiguous goals may be defined without conflict; the system development process then focuses on how to produce a system that achieves the goals. Where conflicting objectives are found, systems analysis procedures need to spend significant effort on surfacing assumptions and creating dialogue among stakeholders to arrive at reasoned agreement for the goals.

II. TYPES OF SYSTEMS RELEVANT TO THE SYSTEMS APPROACH

Although many phenomena as different as a human and a computer program can be described in systems terms, they are still quite different. There are several ways of characterizing systems that emphasize these differences. Two such classifications are deterministic versus probabilistic and closed versus open systems. Deterministic or mechanistic systems tend to have clear objectives and tend to be simple compared to probabilistic systems that are complex and may have conflicting objectives.

A. Deterministic and Probabilistic Systems

A deterministic or mechanistic system operates in a predictable manner. The interaction among the parts is known with certainty. If one has a description of the state of the system at a given point in time plus a description of its operation, the next state of the system may be given exactly, without error. An example is a correct computer program which performs exactly according to a set of instructions.

A probabilistic system can be described in terms of probable behavior, but a certain degree of error is always attached to the prediction of what the system will do. An inventory system is an example of a probabilistic system. The average demand, average time for replenishment, etc., may be defined, but the exact value at any given time is not known. Another example is a set of instructions given to a human who, for a variety of reasons, may not follow the instructions exactly as given.

B. Closed and Open Systems

A closed system is defined as a system that is self-contained. It does not exchange material, information, or energy with its environment. There are no truly closed systems in organizations and information processing. However, there are systems that are relatively isolated from the environment but not completely closed. These will be termed closed systems, meaning relatively closed. For example, systems in manufacturing are often designed to minimize unwanted exchanges with the environment outside the system. Such systems are designed to be as closed as possible, so the manufacturing process can operate without disturbances from suppliers, customers, etc. A computer program is a relatively closed system because it accepts only previously defined inputs, processes them, and provides previously defined outputs. In summary, the relatively closed system is one that has only controlled and well defined inputs and outputs. It is not normally subject to disturbances from outside the system.

Open systems exchange information, material, or energy with the environment, including random and undefined inputs. Examples of open systems are biological systems (such as humans) and organizational systems. Open systems must have form and structure to allow them to adapt to changes in their environment in such a way as to continue their existence. A critical feature of organizations as open systems is their capability to adapt in the face of changing competition, changing markets, etc.

III. SYSTEM CONTROL

System regulation and control mechanisms are based on feedback. Measurements of the output of a system are compared with the desired output (standard), and any difference causes an input to be looped back to the process to adjust the operations so that output will be closer to the standard. Feedback that seeks to dampen and reduce fluctuations around the standard is termed negative feedback. Positive feedback reinforces the direction in which the system is moving. In other words, positive feedback causes the system to repeat or amplify an adjustment or action. For example, a programming supervisor may have learned about the use of object program structure. After trying it on a small project with good results (positive feedback), the supervisor tries it on a larger project, again with good results. The supervisor may continue this until all programming is done in that way (a steady state) or until projects are found for which it does not work.

Feedback in which the system changes its operation is not the only adjustment an organizational system may make. In response to feedback, the organization may question the assumptions and values incorporated in the existing system and revise the system (change its processes based on the new understanding). This is termed double loop learning. Single loop learning adjusts the process while double loop learning adjusts the rules or concepts that govern the process. In the example above, the positive results from use of object program structure may result in an adjustment of the standard for programmer performance.

System that are well controlled exhibit requisite variety. To control each possible state of the system elements, there must be a corresponding control state (responses to the inputs). In other words, there must be at least as many variations of control to be applied as there are ways for the system to get out of control. This means also that the controller for a system must be able to determine variations of the control variables and send system change instructions for each change. The law of requisite variety means that for a system to be controlled, every controller (human or machine) must be provided with one of the following: (1) a list of control responses (what to do in each case) to cover all possible conditions the system may face, (2) decision rules for generating all possible control responses, or (3) the authority and structure to become a self-organizing system in order to generate appropriate control responses. Enumerating all responses is possible only in simple cases. Providing decision rules works well, but it is difficult to be all-encompassing when open systems are involved. The solution for open systems such as applications involving both humans and computer hardware and software is to program decision rules to generate control responses for all normal or expected situations and to

train human decision makers to generate control responses for the unusual or unexpected.

IV. APPLYING THE SYSTEMS APPROACH

The systems approach is a way of thinking about, analyzing, diagnosing, constructing, and revising systems. The systems that result from the systems approach are human artifacts; the systems exist only because humans design and build them. The fact that they are human artifacts means that they reflect characteristics and objectives of human systems. Guiding the systems approach are the basic concepts of system boundary, system purpose, interacting parts for a system, subsystems, simplification, control (such as feedback), equifinality, and requisite variety. Techniques employed may include interviews, observation, measurement, modeling, simulation, and prototyping. The systems approach may involve management, system users, and system analysts. It usually involves a careful, phased approach.

- *System boundary.* The system to be analyzed is defined and its boundary delineated. The boundary encompasses those system elements that interact together and therefore must be included. The environment defines that which is outside the system. The environment may affect inputs and use outputs, but it is not vital to understanding the processes of the system being studied.
- *System purpose.* A clear definition of the purpose of a system is required for systems analysis. If there are different purposes specified by different stakeholders (those with an interest or stake in the system), these must be prioritized and reconciled. The essence of systems analysis is to look at an entire problem in context, to systematically investigate the objectives of the system and the criteria for system effectiveness, and to evaluate the alternatives in terms of effectiveness and cost. The results of the analysis are a questioning of the objectives and criteria and a formulation of new alternatives until the problem, the objectives, the assumptions, and the cost-effectiveness of alternatives are clarified.
- *Interacting parts for a system.* The different parts of the system must be defined and understood. How they interact is important for understanding the system.
- *Subsystems.* The system to be studied is usually too large to analyze without further reduction in the size and complexity of the parts being studied. The approach is to decompose or factor the

system into subsystems. The boundaries and interfaces are defined, so that the sum of the subsystems constitutes the entire system. This process of decomposition is continued with subsystems divided into smaller subsystems until the smallest subsystems are of manageable size. The principle that guides the definition of subsystems is functional cohesion. Components are considered to be part of the same subsystem if they perform or are related to the same function. If there are a large number of subsystems, the design can be simplified by organizing them into hierarchies.

- *Simplification.* The process of decomposition could lead to a large number of subsystem interfaces to define. For example, 4 subsystems which all interact with each other will have 6 interconnections; a system with 20 subsystems all interacting will have 190 interconnections. The number can rise quite quickly as the number of subsystems increases. Simplification is the process of organizing subsystems so as to reduce the number of interconnections and the need for coordination and communication. Some methods of simplification are clustering and decoupling.

- *Clustering.* Clusters of subsystems are established which interact with each other, then a single interface path is defined from the cluster to other subsystems or clusters of subsystems. An example is a database which is accessed by many programs, but the interconnection is only through a database management interface.

- *Decoupling.* The objective is to reduce the need for tight interconnections and high communications to coordinate subsystems. Inventories, buffers, and waiting lines are used. For example, inventories reduce the need for close coordination of raw materials, production, and shipments; data buffers compensate for different rates of input and output of data in computer systems; and standards allow subsystems to operate with less communication (because inputs and outputs are specified by the standards). The process of decoupling and allowing each subsystem some independence in managing its affairs has many benefits, but it is not without its costs. One of these is the cost of the decoupling mechanism; another cost stems from the fact that each subsystem may act in the best possible way as a subsystem, but the sum of their actions may not be optimal for the organization.

- *Maintenance (negative entropy).* Systems can run down and decay or can become disordered or

disorganized. Stated in system terminology, an increase in entropy takes place. Preventing or offsetting an increase in entropy requires organizational inputs of matter and energy to repair, replenish, and maintain the system. This maintenance input is termed negative entropy. Open systems require more negative entropy than relatively closed systems for maintaing a desirable steady state of organization and operation, but all the systems in organizations require maintenance.

- *System control.* Feedback mechanisms are usually desirable to provide for either automatic negative feedback to keep the system within control limits or monitoring systems that provide measurements to personnel assigned to monitor the system and make adjustments. System feedback may be positive and increase the process that produced a favorable output in order to further increase the output. System control is achieved by monitoring the interaction of inputs, processes, and outputs and adjusting the processes.

- *Equifinality.* Since systems for organizations can be designed in many different ways and all the variations accomplish the basic purpose, the organization can base the selection on other criteria such as cost of the system, human factors, social desirability, and so forth.

- *Requisite variety.* The need for requisite variety guides the systems approach in analyzing the allocation of functions so as to maintain a balance between automated features for routine decisions and human intervention and decision making for exceptions. Human factors may require that the human be provided with a mix of activities that will support vigilance.

Systems that are robust over time (survive well) tend to have characteristics such as functionally cohesive subsystems, hierarchical organization of subsystems, loose coupling among subsystems (simplification), system control feedback mechanisms (both single loop and double loop learning), provisions for maintenance, and requisite variety.

Techniques employed in the systems approach to systems analysis and design may include interviews, observation, measurement, modeling, simulation, and prototyping. Since it is often difficult to model complex organization systems, simulation may be employed to trace the effect of various input conditions, both normal and unusual. A somewhat simplified prototype of the system may be developed in order to study the operating characteristics of the proposed system. This allows users to study the way the system will operate and how it will affect them.

The systems approach may involve management, system users, and system analysts. There is a tendency for system analysts to get purposes and specifications from management and to not involve users to any great extent. If all the relevant stakeholders are involved in formulating the requirements, the requirements elicited by this process may be conflicting. The soft systems approach is designed to surface these differences and arrive at some resolution.

The principle of equifinality suggests that there are many possible designs that meet the intended purpose, but they may differ markedly in how they affect those who operate and those who use the system. The system may be viewed as a technical system being used in a social system (a socio-technical system). A socio-technical approach to systems analysis will involve the system operators and user in designing alternative technical solutions and proposing systems that meet both technical and social objectives.

The system approach typically involves a careful, phased approach. At the beginning, the problem is defined and the system purposes clarified. The existing system is analyzed, alternatives are examined, and cost/benefit estimates are made. Detailed analysis is performed and detailed requirements are obtained. In conjunction with management and systems operators and users, system designs are developed. The system is built and installed. After some experience with use, there is maintenance and enhancement.

V. EXAMPLES OF THE SYSTEMS APPROACH RELEVANT TO INFORMATION SYSTEMS

Analysts and designers who employ systems approaches make use of the basic concepts of systems in analysis and design. Differences in systems approaches in practice may reflect differences in views about how to deal with the combination of technical systems (procedures, technology, rules, and so forth) and humans that are part of the system, both as individuals and as groups with norms and social dynamics. Modeling that assumes the existence of well defined objectives and rational behavior by human participants in achieving the objectives is often termed "hard systems" modeling to distinguish it from soft systems modeling that views the problem of deciding on objectives as being a central difficulty of systems analysis and design. Explicit recognition of the existence of both a social system and a technical system results in a variant of the systems approach termed socio-technical analysis and

design. Since many information systems projects result in organizational design along with information system design, the learning organization concepts are useful in analysis and design effort. This section briefly describes the "hard systems" approach, the soft systems approach, the socio-technical approach, and the learning organization concepts.

A. "Hard Systems" Modeling

One approach to systems thinking is a quantitative modeling approach to systematic analysis. This "hard systems" approach reflects a functionalist view that, given system objectives, a system can be engineered to achieve the objectives. In this approach, the first problem is to define the objective of the system clearly. The second problem is to design a system that will achieve the objective. The analyst defines the system holistically by describing the system objectives, and its boundaries, inputs, outputs, and structure. The system is a coherent whole but can be analyzed in detail as subsystems.

The advantage of the hard systems modeling approach is the clarity of analysis that can be applied by using an unambiguous expert definition of objectives and other properties. The analysis can focus on system designs that achieve these results. Alternative structures and properties can be analyzed by simulation (or perhaps analytically).

System modeling can consider the system at a point in time with interactions defined or can analyze the performance of the system over time. The latter modeling is typified by system dynamics in which systems are analyzed over time. For systems that change in size and are limited by the availability of resources, the system dynamics methods identifies the effects of different growth or decline rates. Based on the relationships defined by the modeler, limiting resources are identified and effects of policies are examined. For example, many new businesses fail not because of lack of good products or services but because of growth in sales that is not supported by growth in management and availability of financing. Software packages are typically employed in system dynamics studies. The studies can be useful; however, they are very sensitive to assumptions because the posited effects can be cumulative.

B. Soft Systems Approach

Many researchers and developers have found "hard systems" approaches to be insufficient. They found the world to be complex and objectives difficult to define and often changing. The problem was often not just to solve a specified problem but to decide the objective (what to do). An alternative to hard systems thinking is "soft systems" thinking in which objectives and alternative systems designs emerge from an interactive process between system analysts and stakeholders to clarify objectives and alternatives. There is a learning process during clarification. Well-known exponents of soft systems as the relevant approach for systems analysis include Churchman, Ackoff, and Checkland. Peter Checkland in 1981 defined a multistep soft system methodology.

The soft systems approach assumes the existence of purposeful action in human affairs. The linked set of activities for purposeful action is a human activity system. The soft systems process is systemic. It employs various methods and mechanisms to clarify world views of participants, surface constraints, and build consensus. It reflects an inquiry and learning system approach to design. It supports a social process in which a group of people in a particular organizational context define the purposeful action to be taken. The result is the basis for information system design.

The soft systems methodology provides for a broad analysis that goes beyond the proposed intervention to social and political system analysis. Changes are analyzed for systemic desirability and cultural feasibility. The method begins with a naming of relevant systems. Transformation processes are elaborated by formulating root definitions based on customers, actors, transformation process, world view, owners, and environmental constraints. The core of the root definition is the combination of transformation process and world view (Weltanschauung) that makes a transformation meaningful. The other root definitions define those undertaking the system activity (actors), those who can stop the activity (owners), those benefitting or disadvantaged by the system (customers), and environmental elements that constrain the system design. Models are built with operational and control systems and evaluated. The process is designed to surface operational, social, and political considerations and to provide feedback to redesign.

C. Socio-Technical Design Approach

The socio-technical approach (which can be considered a variation on a soft system approach) in information systems is based on socio-technical research and practice in the design of production and clerical work processes. The socio-technical approach reflects systems thinking because it recognizes the interplay of the technical components of a system with the human components (both as individuals and as work groups). It is an example of systems analysis and design methods that emphasize participation by all stakeholders and focus on improving the quality of work life for those who operate and use the system. The socio-technical approach was developed by members of the Tavistock Institute in the 1940s and 1950s. In a 1951 report on a project to investigate work methods in a coal mine, Trist and Bamforth recognized the existence of both a technical system and a social system. The goal in improving work methods was to achieve joint optimization of both systems.

Since work systems are changed by the introduction of information technology, the socio-technical design approach has been found to be useful in information systems analysis and design.

The technical dimension is reflected in the design of workgroups, activities, and work flows to make use of technology for maximum efficiency and effectiveness. The social dimension is reflected in the design of workgroups, activities, and work flows to increase worker satisfaction and thereby increase productivity and commitment. The social design takes into account the unique capabilities of human workers, individual need for variety and meaning in work, and need for workgroups to have some control over their activities and influence on how their work is structured.

A fundamental proposition in the socio-technical approach is the existence of several competing designs when work systems are being changed through the introduction of new methods and new technology. This rests on the systems principle of equifinality (more than one system design will work). A systems project is organized with technical systems designers and representatives of the workers whose work is being changed. Technical and social objectives for the system are developed and various designs are proposed. The interaction of technical and social is part of the systems analysis. Competing designs are evaluated on both technical and social (quality of work life with the system design) dimensions. The process tends to produce designs that achieve technical objectives along with improved social design, when compared with designs produced from managerial specifications by technical designers.

The method was formalized by the ETHICS method of Enid Mumford. The concepts of participation by workers and evaluation of alternative system designs based on both social and technical criteria are incorporated in some development methodologies.

D. Learning Organization

In the design of information systems and related data repositories and reports, the users who specify requirements and the designers who build the systems can benefit from models of how organizations can use information to improve organization learning and performance. A useful systems-based model is the learning organization. Two variations on this model are double loop learning espoused by Chris Argyris in 1982 and the learning organization (with systems thinking as its fifth discipline) explained by Peter Senge in 1990.

Double loop learning is based on the system implications of internal and external events. In an organization, single loop learning is individual and organization learning through responses to a flow of activities, transactions, and events. The expertise that is developed by single loop learning is based on building appropriate responses to unanticipated inputs or unexpected outputs. Double loop learning is learning based on development of a deeper understanding of the system. System changes are reflected in policies, procedures, and rules. The double loop learning occurs by questioning assumptions and looking for the meaning, commonalities, and policy implications of the set of experiences. Double loop learning is a form of systems thinking, because the activities, transactions, and events are analyzed in terms of the overall system to which they apply rather than being considered in isolation. Interactions within the system are analyzed in order to improve the systems, procedures, and policies for handling similar experiences in the future.

Senge in 1990 identified five disciplines for an organization that learns and adapts well (the learning organization). Four of the disciplines are personal mastery (commitment to lifelong learning by individuals in the organization), mental models (shared mental models of the company, markets, products, competitors, etc.), building a shared vision (a set of principles and guiding practices), and team learning (dialogue among team members to achieve learning together). The fifth discipline is systems thinking. As the fifth, unifying discipline, systems thinking seeks to clarify interrelationships, patterns of change, and how to make changes effectively. There is a difference in the way management responds to events: the most common is to react to events, the next is to analyze events for trends or patterns and respond to these, while the third is to analyze the structure of the system to identify underlying causes and to generate solutions that deal with structural causes. The third way demonstrates systems thinking by seeing interrelationships and seeing processes of change rather than linear cause–effect chains and snapshots of desired results. There is an understanding of feedback that can reinforce or counteract actions. Senge advocates the use of system archetypes or common structures that occur in systems in identifying system relationships. The building blocks of the archetypes are reinforcing processes, balancing processes, and delays. One example of a system archetype is a system in which feedback is delayed, so that corrective action should also be delayed; if corrective action is taken too soon, the system process will go out of control limits. A second example of an archetype is a system structure with limits to growth; accelerating growth or expansion slows down or comes to a halt because of one or more limiting factors such as resource constraints or market saturation.

VI. BROAD CLASSIFICATION OF SYSTEMS AND RELEVANCE TO INFORMATION SYSTEMS

Systems are pervasive in nature and in artifacts created by humans. The term can be applied to a broad range of systems ranging from an abstract sets of ideas (such as system of theology) to complex social organizations. Within the activity of information systems analysis, design, implementation, and maintenance, the system concept is pervasive. However, not all uses of the concept of system are applicable to information systems. Classifications of systems have been proposed to differentiate the different types of systems included under the broad term of systems and systems theory. An example of a taxonomy of systems is one by Kenneth E. Boulding given in 1956. The taxonomy was proposed as a basis for general systems theory. The taxonomy consists of nine levels of systems arranged in a hierarchy from the most simple to the most complex (Table I).

The Boulding taxonomy of systems presents a broad overall view of systems in nature and society. Notes in Table I suggest the applicability of different levels in the taxonomy to the analysis and design of information systems. Since information systems are human artifacts, the part of the taxonomy that focuses on living systems would not be applicable, except that the information system artifacts are human–machine systems deployed in human social systems (organizations), so living system concepts are often useful in understanding and analyzing information systems.

Table I Boulding Taxonomy of Hierarchy of Systems with Comments on Applicability to Information Systems

1	Static structure	Frameworks. Organized knowledge of patterns and relationships. Simple classifications of hardware and software may fit the static structure of a framework.
2	Simple dynamic system	Clockworks. Simple dynamic systems with predetermined, necessary motions. Kinds of systems studied in physics, chemistry, and economics. Some information system applications are based on simple dynamic systems. For example, the processes for producing checks, invoices, order quantities, and so forth are simple dynamic systems.
3	Cybernetic system	Control mechanism. Example is thermostat. Transmission and interpretation of information in order to maintain system equilibrium. Homeostasis in physiology is a cybernetic system for maintaining an organism within limits for life. Information system applications for process control and budgetary control are based on cybernetic control concepts.
4	Open system	Self-maintaining system. Systems may maintain themselves with inputs and outputs of material and energy. They may reproduce themselves. Information system applications can be viewed as human–machine open systems that are maintained (kept viable) by inputs of material and energy (system changes, updates, fixes, etc.).
5	Genetic-societal system	Typified by plants. Division of labor among mutually dependent subsystems. The design of information systems with subsystems (modules) that perform different functions but are mutually dependent can be likened to this level.
6	Animal systems	System has mobility and awareness. Behavior is based not only on input of information but on system organization of prior knowledge to create structures or images. Information system applications that create structures based on the inputs received may be viewed as a primitive system at this level. An example is a recommendation system that develops a profile that is personalized to individual behaviors and produces individualized recommendations.
7	Human systems	Self reflective system. Human subsystems can generate a wide range of both anticipated and unanticipated responses to inputs from the environment. Responses may be routine or creative. Information system artifacts are not at the level of the human system. However, most applications operate as human–computer systems with interaction of human users and computer systems. The information system must therefore be designed to account for the attributes of the human compenent of the combined system.
8	Societal systems	System with interaction of humans (each human in the defined society being a subsystem of the societal system). A family can be viewed as a system with different roles by parents, children, etc. This view of systems may be applicable to complex systems such as interorganizational systems that have both human and system components.
9	Transcendental systems	The mind and its perceptions of external objects. This is not applicable to information systems.

SEE ALSO THE FOLLOWING ARTICLES

Systems Analysis • Systems Design • Systems Implementation • Systems Science

BIBLIOGRAPHY

Ackoff, R. I. (1971). Towards a system of system concepts. *Management Science*, July, 661–671.

Argyris, C. (1982). *Reasoning, learning, and action: Individual and organizational.* San Francisco: Jossey–Bass.

Boulding, K. (1956). General systems theory—The skeleton of science. *Management Science*, April, 197–208.

Checkland, P. (1981). *Systems thinking, systems practice.* New York: Wiley.

Checkland, P., and Scholes, J. (1990). *Soft systems methodology in action.* Chichester, England: Wiley.

Churchman, C. W. (1968). *The systems approach.* New York: Dell.

Churchman, C. W. (1971). *The design of inquiring systems.* New York: Basic Books.

Emery, F. E. (Ed.). (1969). *Systems thinking.* Baltimore: Penguin.

Katz, D., and Kahn, R. L. (1978). *The social psychology of organizations,* 2nd ed. New York: Wiley.

Mumford, E. (1995). *Effective systems design and requirements analysis: The ethics method.* London: Macmillan.

Senge, P. M. (1990). *The fifth discipline.* New York: Doubleday/ Currency.

Simon, H. A. (1981). *The science of the artificial,* 2nd ed. Cambridge: MIT Press.

Trist, E., and Bamforth, K. (1951). Some social and psychological consequences of the long wall method of coal getting. *Human Relations*, Vol. 4, 3–38.

Von Bertalanffy, L. (1968). *General systems theory: Foundations, development, applications.* New York: Braziller.

Weinberg, G. M. (2000). *Quality systems management: Systems thinking.* New York: Dorset.

Weinberg, G. M. (2001). *An introduction to general systems theory.* New York: Dorset.

Systems Design

Jeremy Rasmussen

University of South Florida

I. INTRODUCTION
II. MODERN HISTORY OF SYSTEMS DESIGN
III. ASPECTS OF SYSTEMS DESIGN

IV. SYSTEMS DESIGN PROCESSES
V. CONCLUSION

GLOSSARY

CASE (computer-aided software engineering) Tools that automate, manage, and simplify the software system design process.

configuration management Set of techniques used to define and control the development of a system through its concept, design, implementation, and maintenance phases.

COTS (computer off-the-shelf) Product sold, leased, or licensed to the general public.

data modeling Analysis of data objects used in a business or other context and the identification of the relationships among these data objects.

DFD (data flow diagram) A graphical notation used to describe how data flow between processes in a system. An important tool of most structured analysis techniques.

ERD (entity relationship diagram) Data modeling technique that shows a graphical representation of entities and relationships between entities, within an information system.

functional decomposition Technique for developing systems in which the problem is divided into more easily handled subproblems, the solutions of which create a solution to the overall program.

Gantt chart Horizontal bar chart developed as a system production control tool in 1917 by American engineer Henry L. Gantt.

IPT (integrated product team) Interdisciplinary team that aids in system life cycle integration.

modeling Application of techniques for analysis of various system design parameters; a means of abstracting a system for ease of study.

OOD (object-oriented design) Method of design encompassing the process of object-oriented decomposition and a notation for depicting both logical and physical as well as static and dynamic models of the system under design.

PERT (program evaluation and review technique) Method of planning, scheduling, controlling, and reviewing a series of interdependent events in order to follow a proper sequence and complete a project.

reengineering Process to recreate an existing standard product design using new technology.

sequence flow diagram Graphical tool to break up long, complex procedures into a system of smaller chunks or procedures.

six-sigma A quality engineering approach developed by Motorola within a framework of design for manufacture (DFM) and lean manufacturing.

structured analysis Method of the systems analysis that allows the analyst to represent the processes of a system in a logical and manageable way.

system Set of interrelated components designed to achieve a goal and related by flows of energy, materials, or information.

system design engineering Process of being able to define and model complex interactions among many components that comprise a system, and being able to implement the system with proper and effective use of resources

TQM (total quality management) Principles proven to improve manufacturing operations, such as quality circles and statistical process control, are applied across all business activities for the purpose of exceeding customer expectations and achieving organizational objectives.

traceability Process by which a measured value indicated by a measuring instrument (test) can be compared to the original standard (requirement) for the given measured quantity in one or several steps.

UML (unified modeling language) Standard notation for modeling real-world objects as a first step in developing an object-oriented design methodology. Its notation is derived from that of the Booch, Rumbaugh, and Jacobson techniques.

waterfall method Highly structured approach to project management that delineates distinct phases that flow sequentially from one to another.

WBS (work breakdown structure) Means of dividing a project into smaller, more manageable parts.

I. INTRODUCTION

Systems design is an interdisciplinary engineering activity that enables the realization of successful systems. A system may be defined as an integrated set of components that accomplish a defined objective. The process of systems design includes defining software and hardware architecture, components, modules, interfaces, and data to enable a system to satisfy a set of well-specified operational requirements.

In general, systems design, systems engineering, and systems design engineering all refer to the same intellectual process of being able to define and model complex interactions among many components that comprise a system, and being able to implement the system with proper and effective use of available resources. Systems design focuses on defining customer needs and required functionality early in the development cycle, documenting requirements, then proceeding with design synthesis and system validation while considering the overall problem consisting of:

- Operations
- Performance
- Test and integration
- Manufacturing
- Cost and schedule
- Deployment
- Training and support
- Maintenance
- Disposal

Systems design integrates all of the engineering disciplines and specialty groups into a team effort forming a structured development process that proceeds from concept to production to operation. Systems design considerations include both the business and technical requirements of customers with the goal of providing a quality product that meets the user needs. Successful systems design is dependent upon project management, that is, being able to control costs, develop timelines, procure resources, and manage risks.

Information systems design is a related discipline of applied computer systems, which also incorporates both software and hardware, and often includes networking and telecommunications, usually in the context of a business or other enterprise. The general principals of systems design engineering may be applied to information systems design. In addition, information systems design focuses on data-centric themes such as subjects, objects, and programs.

II. MODERN HISTORY OF SYSTEMS DESIGN

The late Rear Admiral Dr. Grace Murray Hopper, a noted pioneer of computing in the 20th century, once lamented, "Life was simple before World War II. After that, we had 'systems.'" It's true that modern systems have the following properties that can cause a burgeoning number of problems:

- They are increasingly complex.
- They are increasingly interconnected.
- They are increasingly emergent (i.e., they do things for which they may not have been originally intended).
- They are increasingly bug-ridden.

All of these aspects can lead to cost overruns, confusion, consternation, and ultimately failure, unless there is a solid process in place for controlling the design. Fortunately, just as systems have evolved, systems design engineering has also evolved.

The modern systems designer must be an adaptable individual, able to understand how to interface diverse components to each other to meet a functional or performance requirement. He or she should have some background in the fundamentals of electronic (digital and analog) systems, classical and modern control theory, and software engineering. The challenges that face today's scientific and engineering community require the ability to cross disciplines easily in order to use technology and research results to empower both individuals and entire societies.

Prior to World War II, architects and civil engineers were, in effect, the systems design engineers of their time, and they worked on large, primarily civil engineering projects such as the Egyptian pyramids,

Roman aqueducts, Hoover Dam, the Golden Gate Bridge, and the Empire State Building. However, these early systems designers operated without any theory or science of system design engineering, or without any well-defined and consistently applied processes.

After World War II, as systems became more complex, systems design engineering began to evolve as a separate branch of engineering. No doubt, the space race and arms race, with their extreme pressures to develop, test, and launch missiles, satellites, and manned spacecraft, moved along the discipline of systems design engineering. The Apollo moon mission itself comprised over 1 million subsystems and is still considered a marvel of systems design. NASA, the Department of Defense, and their prime contractors (e.g., Boeing, Lockheed, and Rockwell) were at the vanguard of developing standardized systems engineering practices and processes. In the past 20 years, commercial endeavors such as large-scale information networks (e.g., the Internet), personal computers, and personal electronics (e.g., palm-top computers) have further spurred the development of information systems design techniques.

One idea that came out of their quest to develop tools and techniques that would help them excel at system performance and project management was the program evaluation and review technique (PERT). PERT is a quasi-statistical project scheduling technique that is useful in making better estimates of the completion time of a project that has numerous series, parallel, and interdependent tasks. It provides visibility into the potential impact on the completion date of any delays or speedups in a given task.

The PERT chart (Fig. 1) complements the earlier Gantt chart, a tool developed during World War I by Henry Gantt. In a Gantt chart, each project task takes up one row. Dates run along the top of the chart in increments of days, weeks, or months, depending on the total length of the project. The expected time for each task is represented by a horizontal bar whose left end marks the expected beginning of the task and whose right end marks the expected completion date. Tasks may run sequentially, in parallel, or overlapping. Often, important project events, called milestones, are marked on a Gantt chart with a special symbol such as an upside-down triangle. Figure 2 shows a sample Gantt chart.

Some of the other systems design processes that came about during the post-World War II industrialization era include:

- *Parts traceability*—Organizations developed processes to identify all parts by their supplier and

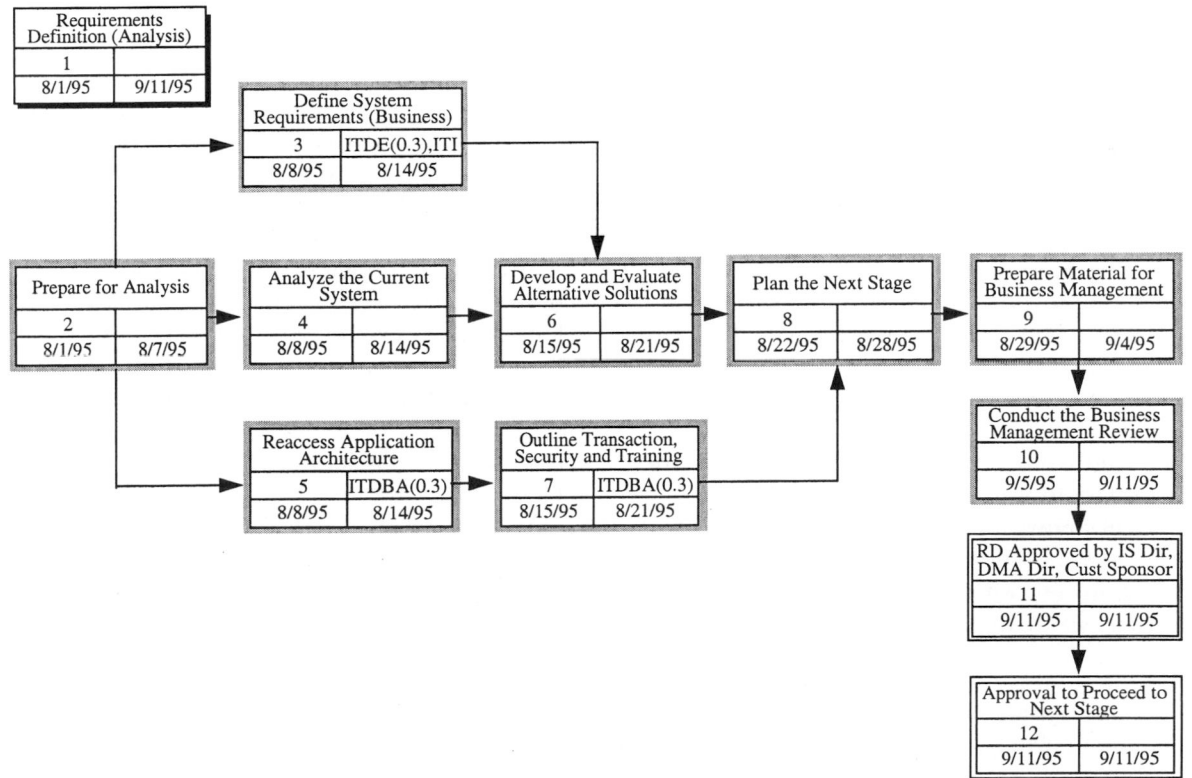

Figure 1 A sample PERT chart.

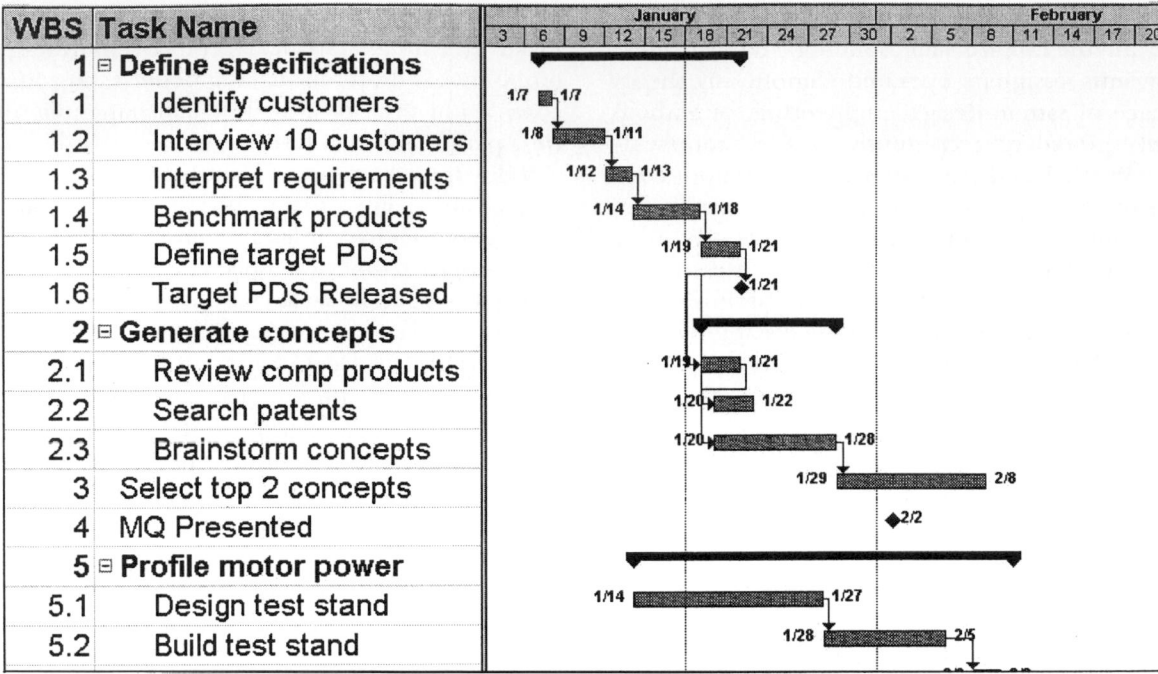

WBS	Task Name		January									February					
		3	6	9	12	15	18	21	24	27	30	2	5	8	11	14	17	20
1	⊟ **Define specifications**																
1.1	Identify customers	1/7 1/7															
1.2	Interview 10 customers	1/8 1/11															
1.3	Interpret requirements		1/12 1/13														
1.4	Benchmark products		1/14 1/18														
1.5	Define target PDS			1/19 1/21													
1.6	Target PDS Released			◆1/21													
2	⊟ **Generate concepts**																
2.1	Review comp products			1/19 1/21													
2.2	Search patents			1/20 1/22													
2.3	Brainstorm concepts			1/20 1/28													
3	Select top 2 concepts				1/29 2/8												
4	MQ Presented					◆2/2											
5	⊟ **Profile motor power**																
5.1	Design test stand		1/14 1/27														
5.2	Build test stand			1/28 2/5													

Figure 2 A sample Gantt chart.

batch number and to track them to all installation locations, so they could be replaced more quickly and efficiently if bad parts were found.

- *Materials and process control*—Organizations had to determine, specify, test, and verify materials and processes and their use by all suppliers, to ensure that failures and successes were carefully tracked for future design and process refinement.
- *Change control*—Organizations developed configuration management procedures to carefully document, review, and approve changes in advance by all affected groups. In most organizations, formal change control boards were established. This precluded "informal" design changes that typically were undocumented and led to "requirement creep" away from the original design baseline.
- *Formal interface control*—Organizations determined that early definition and strict control of interfaces between individual system elements helped alleviate the chaos that can arise during integration test, when incompatibilities are extremely costly to both budget and schedule.

The systems engineering processes that have evolved over the past 50 years encompass techniques to address potential problems represented by the above examples plus many others. In its present (and still evolving) form, systems design combines elements of many

disciplines such as operations research, system modeling and simulation, decision analysis, project management and control, requirements development, software engineering, specialty engineering, industrial engineering, specification writing, risk management, interpersonal relations, liaison engineering, operations analysis, and cost estimation.

Historical evidence has shown that if no formal systems engineering effort is included, projects run the risk of 50 to 100% development cost overruns to fix major downstream integration problems. Costs often soar due to the necessity of keeping a major portion of the project team at the ready to troubleshoot problems until they are all resolved. Anecdotal and "lessons learned" experiences from some of the large-scale programs of the 20th century (the *Titanic* being an obvious example) indicate that serious problems were caused by insufficient systems design engineering. In fact, the very feasibility of today's most demanding engineering projects may depend on the balanced insight that is needed to assemble the best combination of human and technical resources to fulfill the required objectives.

III. ASPECTS OF SYSTEMS DESIGN

In order to effectively design a complex system, it must be able to be *modeled* and subsequently understood. The process of systems design requires being able to skillfully subdivide complex processes and phenomena into meaningful and intelligible subcomponents. These components of the overall system will have well-defined interactions that can be mathematically articulated and understood by the systems design engineer. This abstract model can be rigorously represented as a mathematical system of equations, studied further with analysis software, or implemented by a combination of hardware and software. The model will have captured the important aspects of the domain under consideration, so that a tractable solution can be defined with available technologies.

Formal systems design methodology is an *iterative* process of deriving and defining requirements at each level of the system, beginning at the top (the system level) and propagating those requirements through a series of steps which eventually lead to a preferred system concept. Further iteration and design refinement leads successively to a preliminary design, a detailed design, and a final, approved design. At each successive level there are supporting, lower-level design iterations that are necessary to gain confidence for the decisions taken. During each iteration, many concept alternatives are postulated, analyzed, and evaluated in trade-off studies. There are many cross-coupling factors, where decisions on one subsystem effect other subsystems. These factors must also be evaluated.

The processes of system design go hand-in-hand with the *system life cycle*. This life cycle could be the classic "waterfall" method (see Fig. 3) in which one activity follows another, or some alternate technique. Table I depicts some of the modern system life-cycle approaches. These methodologies emphasize the incremental, iterative, evolutionary, concurrent, and situational nature of systems development.

Regardless of the life cycle approach, systems engineering is involved in all steps during project definition, requirements analysis, conceptual design, and into the subsystem level, and integrates many other activities including design, design changes, and upgrades; goals and objectives for element iteration; customer feedback; and operational support.

The activities in Fig. 3 are all balanced by techniques, tools, and controls used to track decisions and requirements, maintain technical baselines, manage interfaces, manage risks, track cost and schedule, track technical performance, verify requirements are met, and review/audit the progress.

IV. SYSTEMS DESIGN PROCESSES

The purpose of systems engineering is to provide a structured but flexible set of processes for transforming requirements into specifications, architectures, and configuration baselines. The discipline of these processes provides the control and traceability to develop solutions that meet customer needs. Systems engineering processes may be repeated one or

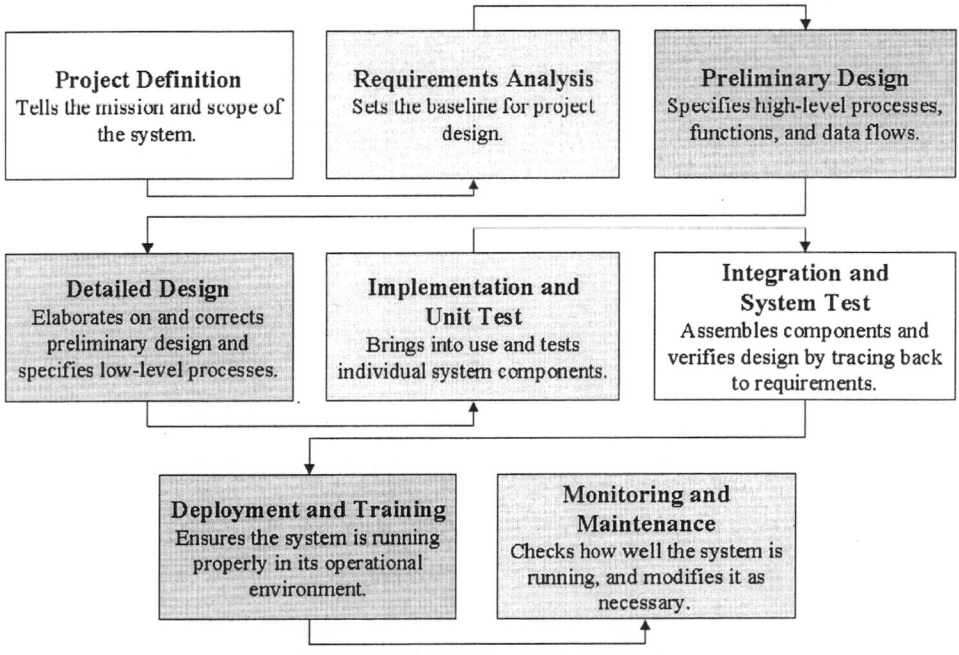

Figure 3 Waterfall system life cycle.

Table I System Life-Cycle Approaches

Waterfall
- Analysis
- Design
- Programming

Spiral
- Analysis, prototyping, risk management
- Design, prototyping, risk management
- Programming, prototyping, risk management

Incremental
- Some analysis
- Some design
- Some programming
- Repeat

Rapid prototype
- Build a mock-up system to simulate look and feel of interface
- Get feedback from user community
- Iterate: redesign and retool prototype

design work in order to consider as many alternatives as possible. As important as creative thinking is, there is also a caveat to avoid "reinventing the wheel." Having a good historical perspective will allow implementation of ideas that are already tested and true. In the final analysis, a system will likely fall between one of two extremes: (1) complete originality, and (2) an unchanged or existing design. The second change considers making choices between alternative designs. Typically systems designers are looking neither to spend too much time designing something that is not novel, nor to acquire components and have to go far out of the way to make them work together in the system. The objective is to find at least one solution that was not considered on any previous occasion.

The following sections detail what happens during each phase of the system design process, as they relate to the overall system life cycle. Note how the changes are occurring during each phase. The seven processes are summarized in Table II.

more times during any phase of the development process.

Two independent changes of emphasis occur during the course of system design. First, there is a change from creative to routine work. Second, there is a change from considering several alternative approaches to developing the detail of the preferred one.

The first change involves producing something new, or something that has not existed in that form before. The creative process is especially important to

A. Problem Definition

First, an organization begins to perceive the need for a new or modified system or service. It might perform "in-house" systems analysis studies to quantify the need and determine how best to meet it, or try to interest a government agency in funding low-level, sole-source, or competitive studies. Systems design engineers usually become involved here in some sort of feasibility study report prepared with recommendations as to what should be done next. However, often higher au-

Table II Seven Basic System Design Processes

1. **Problem Definition.** Stating the problem is perhaps the most important systems engineering task. It entails identifying customers, understanding customer needs, establishing the need for change, discovering requirements, and defining system functions.

2. **Investigating alternatives.** Through this process, alternatives are investigated and evaluated based on performance, cost, and risk.

3. **Modeling.** Running a model clarifies requirements, reveals bottlenecks and fragmented activities, reduces cost, and exposes duplication of efforts.

4. **Integration.** Integration means designing interfaces and bringing system elements together so they work as a whole. This requires extensive communication and coordination.

5. **Deployment.** This process of launching the system entails running the system and producing outputs, i.e., making the system do what it was intended to do.

6. **Testing and performance measurement.** Performance is assessed using figures of merit, technical performance measures, and metrics. Measurement is the key—if you cannot measure it, you cannot control it. If you cannot control it, you cannot improve upon it.

7. **Reevaluation.** Reevaluation of a system should be a continual and iterative process with many parellel loops.

thorities may direct a different approach, based on competitive, political, or emerging market data, intelligence data, or other sources.

Making radical, dramatic changes in a system is called reengineering. Making small incremental changes is considered total quality management (TQM). When a systems engineer analyzes or reengineers an existing system, he or she performs functional analyses to determine what the system does in order to improve its performance and performs functional decomposition to see what the system is supposed to do.

The Software Engineering Institute (SEI) at Carnegie-Melon University has developed the Capability Maturity Model (CMM), a process-based TQM model for assessing the level of an organization's software development process. The CMM also serves as a five-level improvement process by specifying steps for organizations to progress to the next level, ultimately leading to statistical (process) control and sustained improvement (see Table III).

One of the biggest challenges for systems engineers is to understand customers' needs. Unfortunately, customers seldom know exactly what they want or need. This can lead to "requirements creep" throughout the system life cycle, in which the system gradually changes scope from its original intention into something new, usually at great time and expense. A systems engineer must enter the customer's environment and find out how the customer will use the system. Flexible designs and rapid prototyping help identify aspects that might have been overlooked. The terms "customer" and "stakeholder" include anyone who has a right to impose requirements on the system, including end users, operators, owners, regulatory agencies, beneficiaries, *et al.*

The problem statement begins with a description of the top-level function that the system must perform or the deficiency that system must improve upon. It includes system requirements stated in terms of *what* must be done (as opposed to *how* it must be done). Inputs for the problem statement come from customers, end users, operators, owners, regulatory agen-

cies, marketing, manufacturing, *et al.* In a modern business environment, the problem statement starts with a reason for change followed by vision and mission statements for the company. The problem statement is one of systems engineering's most important products because an elegant solution to the wrong problem would be worthless.

The evaluation of the system concept will continue with more detailed simulations of the system and its environment; improved analysis, tradeoffs, and definition of system elements and their subsystems; and improved modeling and analysis of subsystem performance. Requirements and specifications are developed in a top-down/bottom-up fashion, with systems designers defining what they want in a top-down fashion and subsystem designers describing what they can provide in a bottom-up fashion. Alternate system and subsystem tradeoff studies are performed until the system and subsystems engineers converge on workable solutions.

B. Investigating Alternatives

Most system designs have several performance and cost criteria. Systems design engineering creates a set of alternative designs that satisfy these criteria to varying degrees. There is never a "perfect" or "optimal" solution to a problem, so typically moving from one alternative to another will improve at least one criterion and worsen at least one criterion; i.e., there will be tradeoffs. None of the feasible alternatives is likely to optimize all the criteria. Therefore, systems engineers must settle for less than optimality. While it might be possible to optimize some subsystems, when they are interconnected, the overall system may not be optimal. In addition, the best possible system may not be that made up of optimal subsystems. In general, it can be proven that a system is at a local optimum, but it cannot be proven that it is at a global optimum.

Before attempting to evaluate alternatives, it is critical to establish baseline control system requirements,

Table III SEI CMM Levels

- **Level 1: Initial.** Every project is handled differently; ad hoc and chaotic.
- **Level 2: Repeatable.** Every project is handled similarly.
- **Level 3: Defined.** Standard processes are defined and used for all projects.
- **Level 4: Managed.** A measurable basis for all improvements to the process.
- **Level 5: Optimizing.** Emphasis on defect prevention and optimizing/continually improving the process.

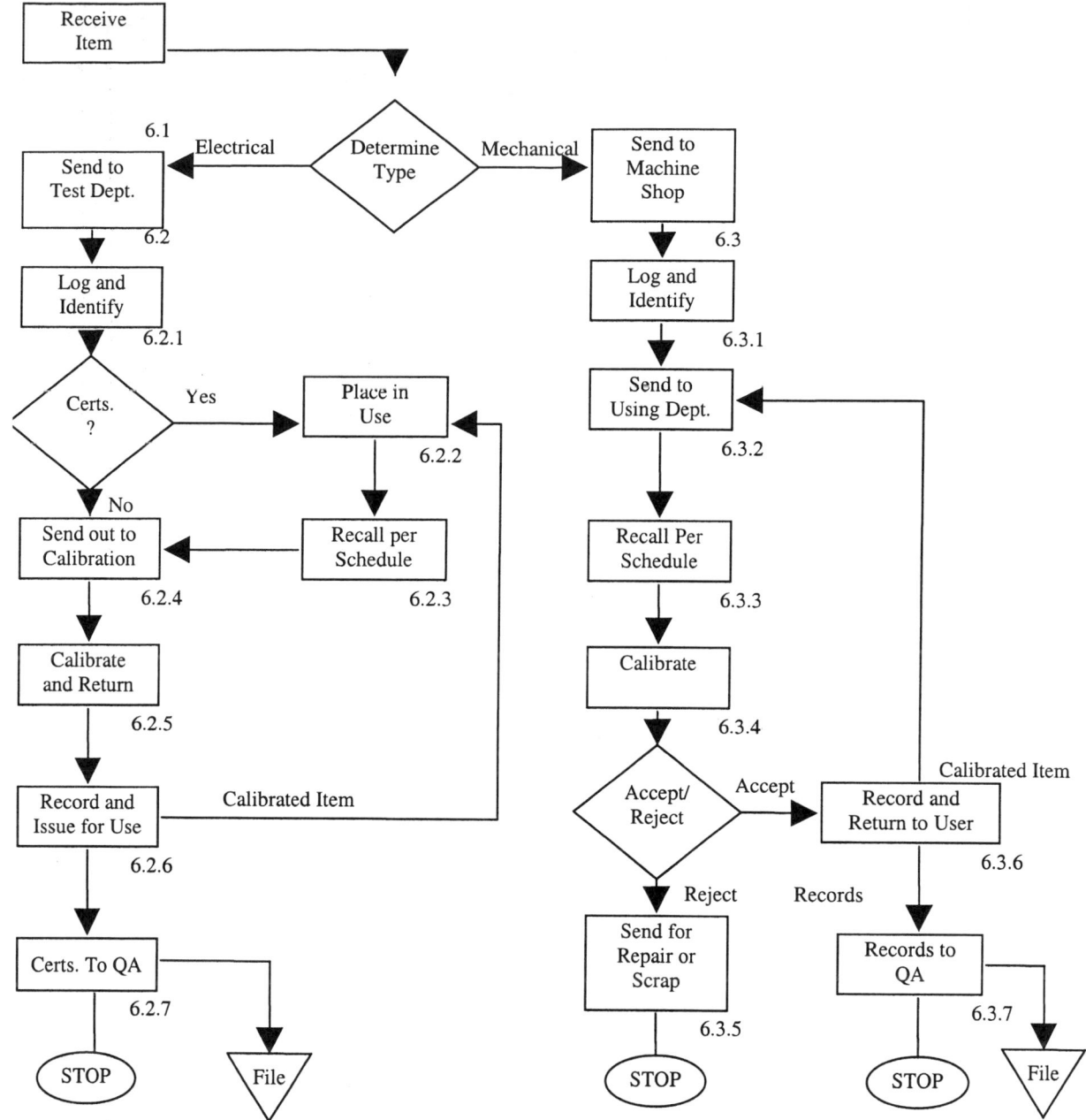

Figure 8 Sample unleveled DFD.

effect of all changes on system performance. When deviations occur, system engineering supports the determination of program adjustments to minimize or avoid program impact. After the system is built, its performance within specifications is verified through a planned series of analysis, inspection, demonstration, and test, which maps back to the requirements.

Life-cycle integration is necessary to ensure that the design solution is viable throughout the life of the system. It includes the planning associated with product and process development, as well as the integration of multiple functional concerns into the design and engineering process. In this manner, product cycle-times can be reduced, and the need for redesign and rework substantially reduced.

Life-cycle integration is achieved through integrated development—that is, concurrent consideration of all life-cycle needs during the development

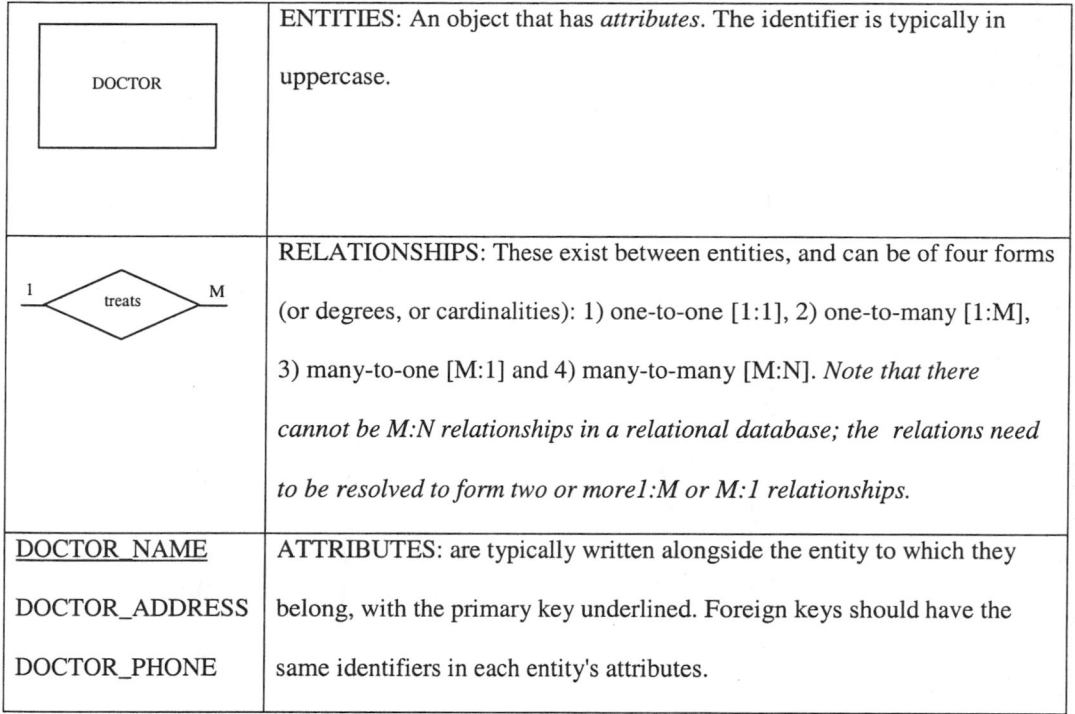

DOCTOR	ENTITIES: An object that has *attributes*. The identifier is typically in uppercase.
1 ⟨treats⟩ M	RELATIONSHIPS: These exist between entities, and can be of four forms (or degrees, or cardinalities): 1) one-to-one [1:1], 2) one-to-many [1:M], 3) many-to-one [M:1] and 4) many-to-many [M:N]. *Note that there cannot be M:N relationships in a relational database; the relations need to be resolved to form two or more 1:M or M:1 relationships.*
DOCTOR_NAME DOCTOR_ADDRESS DOCTOR_PHONE	ATTRIBUTES: are typically written alongside the entity to which they belong, with the primary key underlined. Foreign keys should have the same identifiers in each entity's attributes.

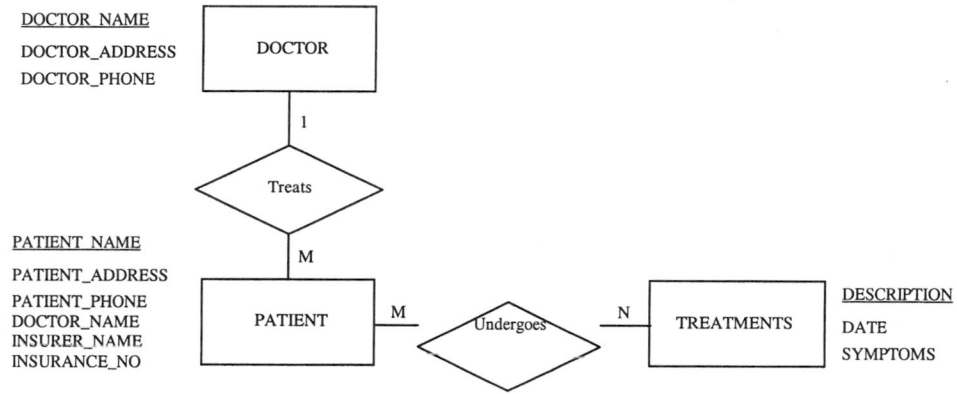

Figure 9 Entity relationship diagram (ERD).

process. This can be greatly enhanced through the use of interdisciplinary teams. These teams are often referred to as integrated product teams or IPTs (see Table VII). The objective of an integrated product team is to: (1) produce a design solution that satisfies initially defined requirements, and (2) communicate that design solution clearly, effectively, and in a timely manner.

Throughout integration, it is very important to manage and track requirements, because failure to do so costs more at every step. Quantitative technical performance measures, called "metrics," should be used wherever possible to quantify system perfor-

mance and track the progress of design and manufacturing. These can help control requirements and ensure that the design traces faithfully back to the original concept and requirements baseline.

E. Deployment

Deployment means doing what the system was intended to do, e.g., running the system and producing outputs. During production, deployment, or fielding there are still many activities requiring the attention of system design engineers. At this point, the system

Table VII Multifunctional, Integrated Product Teams (IPTs)

Functions

- Place balanced emphasis on product and process development
- Require early involvement of all disciplines appropriate to the team taks
- Include design-level IPT members who will help meet the team objectives

Competencies

- Technical management (systems engineering)
- Life cycle functional areas
- Technical specialty areas, such as safety, risk mangement, quality, etc.
- When appropriate, business areas such as finance, cost/budget analysis, and contracting.

is developed; so the focus is on solving problems which arise during manufacturing, assembly, checkout, integration into its deployed configuration, and on customer orientation and acceptance testing. Activities during this phase include troubleshooting, problem solving, design change processing, design change control, manufacturing liaison, and product sell-off and training development for the customer.

F. Testing and Performance Assessment

During the operation and maintenance phase of the system life cycle the performance of the system must be measured. Initially these measurements will be used to verify that the system is in compliance with its requirements. Later they will be used to detect deterioration and initiate maintenance.

Early in the system life cycle systems engineering should describe the tests that will be used to prove compliance of the final system with its requirements. However, most testing should be performed by built-in self-test equipment. These self-tests should be used for initial testing, postinstallation testing, power-up diagnostics, field service, and depot repair. The recipient of each test result and the action to be taken if the system passes or fails each test must be stated.

Systems design engineers should ensure that the appropriate reviews are conducted and documented. The exact reviews that are appropriate depends on the size, complexity, and customer of the project. The following set is common: Mission Concept Review, System Requirements Review (SRR), System Definition Review,

Preliminary Design Review (PDR), Critical Design Review (CDR), Production Readiness Review (PRR), and System Test. Full-scale engineering design begins after the Preliminary Design Review. Manufacturing begins after the Critical Design Review.

Systems engineers must prove that the final system satisfies each system requirement. Requirements may be verified by inspection, analysis, demonstration, test, logical argument, modeling, or simulation.

The system that is finally built must be tested to ensure that it satisfies the system requirements, and how well it meets the needs of the customer. The classic example of importance of good system testing is the Hubble Space Telescope. In order to save money, no total system test was ever done before the Hubble was launched. As a result, taxpayers footed a bill for an additional $850 million to fix a major system error.

The Department of Defense usually operates and supports its equipment with factory support from suppliers. Commercial companies, on the other hand, typically provide parts and training to factory-authorized service centers. Either way, there is a need for continuing sustainment services. Monitoring is important because no system is ever perfect, and detection and correction of operational errors can lead to increased quality over time. There are also internal and external variables to be considered. Internal changes may include wear and tear on the system. External changes may include environmental impact or obsolescence. Monitoring activities include the following:

Configuration Management—Ensures that any changes in requirements, design or implementation are controlled, carefully identified, and accurately recorded. All stakeholders should have an opportunity to comment on proposed changes. Decisions to adopt a change must be captured in a baseline database. This baseline is a time frozen design containing requirements for functions, performance, interfaces, verification, testing, cost, etc. Baselines can only be changed at specified points in the life cycle. All concerned parties must be notified of changes to ensure that they are all working on the same design. The phrase "requirements tracking" is now being used for an important subset of configuration management.

Project Management—The planning, organizing, directing, and controlling of company resources to meet specific goals and objectives within time, within cost, and at the desired performance level. Project management creates the work breakdown structure, which is a product-oriented tree of hardware, software, data, facilities, and services. It displays and defines the products to be developed and relates the elements of work to be accomplished to each other and to the end product. It provides structure for guiding team assignments and cost and tracking control.

Documentation—All of these systems engineering activities must be documented in a common repository, often called the Engineering Notebook. The stored information should be location, platform, and display independent: which means any person on any computer using any tool should be able to operate on the fundamental data. Assumptions, results of tradeoff studies, and the reasons for making critical decisions should be recorded. These documents should be alive and growing. For example, at the end of the system life cycle there should be an accurate model of the existing system to help with retirement.

G. Reevaluation

Reevaluation is arguably one of the most important tasks of systems engineering. For centuries, engineers have used feedback to control systems and improve performance. Learning from our failures (and successes) is one of the most fundamental engineering tools. Reevaluation means observing outputs and using this information to modify the system inputs, the product, or the process. Reevaluation should be a continual process with many parallel loops.

Everyone should continually reevaluate the system looking for ways to improve quality. Major tools used in this process include basic concurrent engineering, Deming's quality improvement concepts, quality function deployment (QFD), total quality management, Taguchi's quality engineering techniques, and approaches such as six-sigma.

V. CONCLUSION

In summary, systems design is an interdisciplinary engineering process to evolve and verify an integrated, life cycle balanced set of system solutions that satisfy customer needs. System design converts an approved functional specification into a detailed plan of how a system is to be built. Analysis asks the question: "What is the system to do?" Design asks: "How is the system to accomplish that?"

The systems design process is a top-down, comprehensive, iterative, and recursive problem solving process, applied sequentially through all stages of development, that is used to:

- Transform needs and requirements into a set of system product and process descriptions (adding

value and more detail with each level of development)
- Generate information for decision makers
- Provide input for the next level of development

A complete systems engineering approach involves both analysis and design, considering design alternatives, performing cost/benefit studies of alternatives, and employing a standardized modeling approach.

SEE ALSO THE FOLLOWING ARTICLES

Database Development Process • End-User Computing, Managing • End-User Computing Tools • Object-Oriented Programming • System Development Life Cycle • Systems Analysis • Systems Science • User/System Interface Design

BIBLIOGRAPHY

Blanchard, B. S., and Fabrycky, W. J. (1998). *Systems engineering and analysis.* Englewood Cliffs, NJ: Prentice Hall.

Buede, D. M. (2000). *The engineering design of systems.* New York: Wiley.

Chapman, W. L., Bahill, A. T., and Wymore, W. (1992). *Engineering modeling and design.* Boca Raton, FL: CRC Press.

Coad, P., and Yourdon, E. (1991). *Managing software development projects object-oriented analysis,* 2nd ed. Englewood Cliffs, NJ: Prentice Hall.

Connell, J., and Shafer, L. (1995) *Object-oriented rapid prototyping.* Englewood Cliffs, NJ: Prentice Hall.

DSMC. (1999). *Systems engineering fundamentals.* Defense System Management College; http://www.dsmc.dsm.mil/pubs/gdbks/pdf/systengfund.pdf.

Embley, D. W., Kurtz, B. D., and Woodfield, S. N. (1992). *Object-oriented systems analysis.* Englewood Cliffs, NJ: Prentice Hall.

Hoffer, J. A., George, J. F., and Valacich, J. S. (2001). *Modern systems analysis and design.* Englewood Cliffs, NJ: Prentice Hall.

IEEE 1220 Standard. (1998). *Application and management of the systems engineering process.* New York: IEEE Standards Dept., December.

International Council on Systems Engineering (INCOSE). (1998). *Systems engineering manual.* Seattle, WA 98133-9009.

International Council on Systems Engineering (INCOSE). (1999). *What is systems engineering?* Seattle, WA 98133-9009, URL: http://www.incose.org/whatis.html.

Rumbaugh, J., and Booch, G. (1995). *Unified method: Notation summary, Version 0.8.* Santa Clara, CA: Rational Software Corporation.

Sage, A. P., and Rouse, W. B. (Eds.). (1999). *Handbook of systems engineering.* New York: Wiley.

Schneier, B. (2000). *Secrets & lies: Digital security in a networked world.* New York: Wiley.

University of Waterloo. (2001). *What is systems design engineering?* Ontario, Canada, URL, http://sydewww.uwaterloo.ca/SystemsDepartment/WhatIsSystems/whatissystems.html.

Yourdon, E. (1994). *Object-oriented systems design: An integrated approach.* Yourdon Press Computing/ Englewood Cliffs, NJ: Prentice Hall.

Systems Implementation

Merle P. Martin

California State University, Sacramento

I. PROGRAM CONSTRUCTION
II. SOFTWARE AND SYSTEM TESTING
III. SYSTEM TRAINING

IV. SYSTEM CHANGEOVER PREPARATION
V. SYSTEM CHANGEOVER
VI. SYSTEM EVALUATION

GLOSSARY

acceptance testing The final testing stage in which users or an independent group tries to "break" the new system by using data outside the range of normal usage.

adaptability quality dimension The measure of a system's future qualities, including flexibility, reusability, and maintainability.

changeover contract A formal agreement to transfer application system responsibility from the development team to the business unit.

day-one file conversion A method that reduces file conversion efforts by converting only records that have shown recent transaction activity.

direct changeover A method by which the old system is discontinued and the new system is initiated as of a specific cutoff date.

engineering quality dimension The measure of a system's internal quality, including efficiency, testability, and documentation.

external program documentation Explanation of program logic in the form of graphic tools such as hierarchical and program flowcharts.

functionality quality dimension The measure of a system's external quality, including correctness, reliability, and integrity.

parallel changeover The method by which the old and new application systems are operated concurrently for a specified period of time.

regression testing A testing method where the application system undergoes repeated testing under similar circumstances.

staged changeover A method whereby the old application system and the new system are initiated by stages.

stress testing A method by which the system is ingested with varying volumes of data to see how it responds.

string testing A method by which several independently tested modules belonging to the same parent module are tested concurrently for data passing and navigation paths.

system success rate The number of transactions processed without system errors divided by total transactions processed.

unit testing The testing of primitive level software modules to determine how effectively they function.

usability quality dimension The measurement of a system's ease of use, including learning time, performance speed, error handling, and user satisfaction.

SYSTEMS IMPLEMENTATION is the third phase of the systems development life cycle (SDLC) following the analysis and design phases. This is the phase where logical design specifications are translated into the actual instruction code and operating specifications of the operating system. Systems implementation includes the stages of (1) program construction, (2) software and systems testing, (3) system training, (4) system changeover preparations, (5) systems changeover, and (6) system evaluation.

I. PROGRAM CONSTRUCTION

This stage converts logically designed inputs, outputs, files, processes, and their interactions into program code that drives the operational application system.

A. Logic Sources

The programmer receives design logic to be coded from one or more of the following sources:

• Pseudo-code, including structured English
• Skeleton code produced by a code generator, including computer-aided system engineering (CASE) software
• A throwaway prototype used as a model for the final system
• Logic flowgraphs such as structure charts or program flowcharts

B. Selecting an Operational Programming Language

This selection may have been made earlier in the SDLC. Often, however, the decision as to which programming language to use is finalized in the implementation phase. Choice of an operational language entails consideration of many factors. Primary among these factors is the nature of the operational system to be delivered.

1. If the final system has a large volume of input, output, and file accesses [a transaction processing system (TPS)], then the operating language probably should be a third-generation language (3GL) such as COBOL.
2. If the final system has smaller volumes, is menu driven, and is database retrieval focused, then the operating language probably should be a fourth-generation language (4GL).
3. An applications software package may be purchased or the firm may lease the application through an applications service provider (ASP). In these cases, the choice of programming language is restricted to package characteristics.

C. Relationship to Prototyping Language

If prototyping has been used as an analysis and design tool, it is tempting to extend the prototype language to the operational language. This can be dangerous, however, leading to transaction backlogs when a 4GL prototyping language is used in an operational environment best fitting a 3GL language. Figure 1 shows the proper relationship of the prototyping to the operational language.

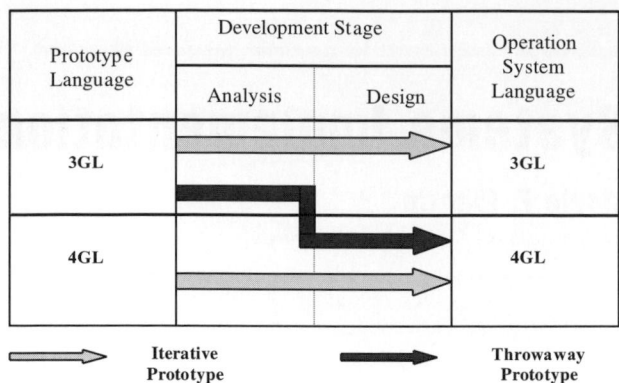

Figure 1 Relationship of prototyping to operational language.

1. The most appropriate operational language (right side) is chosen.
2. The most appropriate prototyping language (left side) is chosen.
3. The appropriate prototype path (type) connects the two languages.

D. Programming Coordination

Most information system applications are too complex to be programmed by one person. Programming teams are the norm. Three tactics aid coordination of the multiple programmers assigned to an applications project.

1. The Hierarchical Chart (Fig. 2) allows the project to be separated into small, cohesive modules, which then can be assigned to different programmers. Each individual programmer understands where his or her module fits within the total application.
2. A senior programmer is appointed lead programmer to coordinate the separate programming efforts.
3. A common terminology is used. This can be accomplished through such techniques as a data dictionary or a commonly used COBOL data division.

E. Programming Standards

A primary design goal is to maximize the ease of future programming changes (program maintenance). This requires that different programmers at some fu-

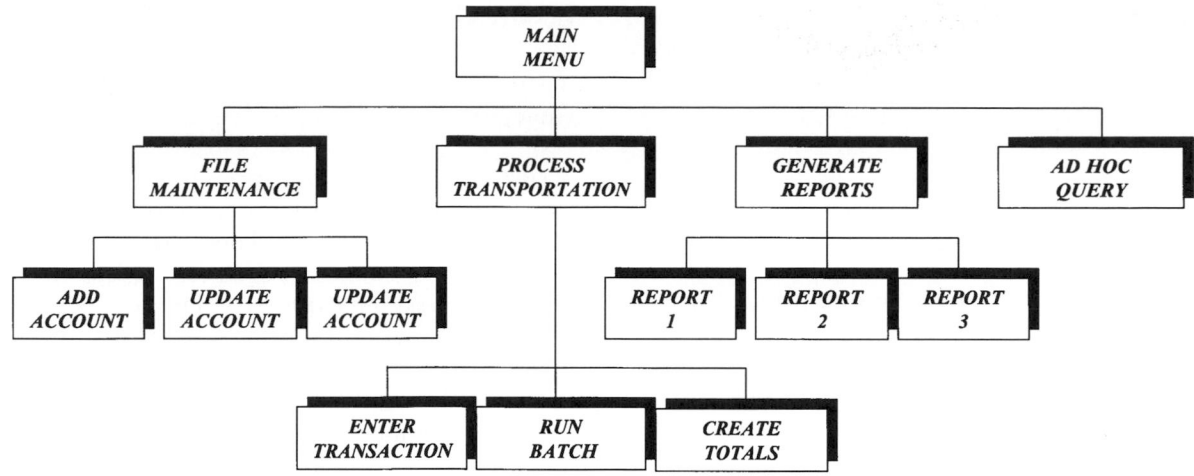

Figure 2 Hierarchical chart.

ture time must be able to understand the logic and sequence of current programming. This goal may require sacrificing program efficiency in order to optimize maintenance programming. The most effective means of emphasizing future ease of change is to establish and enforce programming standards. This entails using the following:

- A modular structure that allows future program modification with minimal interruption to the rest of the application
- Internal program documentation such as liberal use of comment statements
- External program documentation that quickly leads a maintenance programmer to the module or statement that requires modification

F. Programming Documentation

The external documentation produced in the program construction stage includes tools such as (1) hierarchical charts, (2) program flowcharts, (3) input-process-output (IPO) charts, (4) compiled listings and results, and (5) sample output based on test data.

II. SOFTWARE AND SYSTEM TESTING

"Testing is the measurement of software and system quality" (Hetzel, 1984). It is essential that thorough testing be done because the effort required to change an application can be up to 30 times greater after implementation than before.

A. Testing Dimensions

There are four quality dimensions to be tested:

1. *Functionality* measures a software system's external quality.
   a. *Correctness.* Are system outputs accurate and complete?
   b. *Reliability.* Do functions perform consistently without failure?
   c. *Integrity.* Are results consistent with user expectations?
2. *Engineering* measures the system's internal quality.
   a. *Efficiency.* Are functions performed in minimum times with minimum lines of code?
   b. *Testability.* Can modules be tested and audited easily?
   c. *Documentation.* Has the system been documented to allow easy future modifications?
   d. *Structure.* Is the software system organized logically to facilitate tailoring and training?
3. *Adaptability* measures the system's future quality.
   a. *Flexibility.* Can the system be adapted to the needs of a diverse and changing cast of users and business situations?
   b. *Reusability.* Can modules be reused in other systems?
   c. *Maintainability.* Does the organization of the system facilitate future changes?
4. *Usability* measures the system's ease of use.
   a. *Learning time.* Can users learn to use the system quickly?
   b. *Performance speed.* Does the system maximize transaction throughput?

c. *Error handling*. Does the system provide users with adequate and helpful guidance to detect and correct errors?

d. *User satisfaction*. Is the system designed so that it is not a constant source of user annoyance?

B. Testing Principles

Hetzel (1984) suggests the following principles:

1. *"Complete testing is not possible."* Suppose you wish to test the accuracy of each IF . . . THEN . . . ELSE statement in a program and that there are 15 such statements. In the simplest case where each statement has only two states (true or false), the number of tests needed is 2 raised to the 15th power, or 32,768 tests. The number of tests needed will grow exponentially with increased system complexity. You rarely have resources to test every system possibility.

2. *"Testing work is creative and difficult."* A detected error in one system output may lead step-by-step "upstream" to the real problem source. Most detected errors are merely problem symptoms. Finding the real problem involves creative and painstaking detective work.

3. *"Testing is risk (probability) based."* Because complete testing is not feasible, the limited testing resources must be applied to the most probable and important sources of failure through the following process:

   a. Identify those modules having the highest probability of failure (probably the most complex modules).

   b. Within these modules, identify those with the highest risk of loss when failure occurs (usually those that have more user visibility or dependency).

   c. Fully test the riskiest module, then the next riskiest, and so on until testing resources are exhausted.

   d. Recognize that this risk-based strategy may result in less riskier modules not being tested at all.

4. *"Testing requires independence."* A tester who finds design and programming errors will not be popular with his or her co-workers. No one likes personal errors discovered. Because of this,

   a. The same person who programmed a software module should never test the same module.

   b. A senior programmer should manage testing responsibilities with no programming responsibilities.

C. Strategies

Testing can be planned according to two different strategies:

1. *Bottom-up:* Lower level (primitive) modules are programmed and each module is tested independently. When a complete set of modules (siblings) is complete, then testing is done at the next highest level (parent). This testing approach continues in an upward direction until the entire software system is tested as a unit.

2. *Top-down.*

   a. The top-most (main menu) module is programmed and tested first. All child modules (level 2) arc "stubbcd out"; thcy contain a message such as "Module under construction—press any key to return to the last screen."

   b. The next level of modules (children) is composed of intermediate menus that are programmed and tested independently with their children modules stubbed out. Then these intermediate menu modules are "hooked onto" the main menu (parent) module and the entire group is tested as a unit.

   c. This top-down approach continues until all program modules have been programmed, tested independently, and then tested in a group.

D. Stages

For each strategy chosen, there are four testing stages:

1. *Unit testing*. This is done for primitive level modules that perform application tasks. Test data is input to each module to determine how effectively it functions. Typically, this test data is:

   a. Within a specified data range

   b. Outside that data range

   c. At the boundaries of the range

   d. At the value zero

2. *String testing.*: Several independently tested modules belonging to the same parent module are tested concurrently. Emphasis is placed on correct passing of data between modules and on a smooth navigation path through the module string.

3. *System testing*. This involves full integration of application system hardware and software. It includes stress testing and regression testing:

a. *Stress testing.* The system is ingested with (1) more data than expected, (2) no data at all, and (3) the expected data load. This is done in a short time frame to see if the application system can handle various levels of data input. System response times and data accuracy are verified.

b. *Regression testing.* The application system undergoes repeated testing under similar circumstances. New results are compared with old results and any differences are reconciled.

4. *Acceptance testing.* Ultimate system users or an independent group uses the system guided by documentation provided by the development team. Ideally, the acceptance-testing group tries to break the new system by entering data outside the range of normal usage. Acceptance testing should be designed for each of the four software quality spaces of functionality, engineering, adaptability, and usability.

E. Management

1. *Testing control.* All modules to be tested must be scheduled for a specified date by a specified person using a test control chart. This chart has the following elements:

   a. Module to be tested (list in testing order)
   b. Type of test (e.g., functionality)
   c. For each combination of module and test type:
   - Date test is to begin
   - Initials of person responsible for test
   - When test is complete
   - When retesting is required (after reprogramming)

2. *Testing documentation.* Each software or system test should be documented with information such as:

   a. Procedures—a list of all functions that users must perform in the program module
   b. Expected results for each function
   c. Pass/fail—Did test results match expected results?
   d. Comments—What went wrong?
   e. Person testing and date tested
   f. Date returned for reprogramming
   g. Programmer name and date returned for retesting
   h. Retesting person and date of retesting
   A separate documentation page should be constructed for each category of each quality software space. For example, under "functionality," there should be separate test matrices for correctness, reliability, and integrity.

3. *Testing responsibility.* Testing should be done by a senior programmer who has not done any coding on the tested module and who has sufficient status not to be swayed by pressures to "stop finding errors so that we can finish this project."

F. The Test Plan

A testing plan is prepared before testing begins. This plan includes the following:

1. A program hierarchical chart with specific identity code for each program module
2. A testing control chart
3. Success criteria that indicates when to stop testing (e.g., when all critical and 90% of noncritical modules have passed tests successfully)
4. Testing procedures that include the type approach (e.g., top-down), testing stages (e.g., regression), who will perform testing, and retesting procedures (how/who)
5. Test data to be used
6. Assumptions. For example, "We do not have the time available to test all modules fully. Therefore, we have organized the modules in the following priority sequence."

G. Test Data

Data used to test software modules emanate from one or more of the following sources:

1. *Tester generated.* The tester may have to "manufacture" certain test data. For example, there may not be any real-world transactions with quantity values of "zero," yet that value needs to be tested.
2. *User provided.* The tester can use real-world transaction data provided by system users. This allows comparison of new system with current system output.

III. SYSTEM TRAINING

Training on the developing application system must begin as early as possible. Carey (1988) demonstrated that the longer the period of time end users are indoctrinated to new system changes, the less resistance they exhibit toward these changes. In addition, early systems training leads to earlier discovery of system faults. Correction of system faults becomes more expensive the further along the SDLC the project has progressed.

A. The Shneiderman Model

Shneiderman (1987) separates computer knowledge into the two domains of semantic (conceptual) and syntactic (keyboard). He subdivides the semantic domain into task (applications) knowledge and knowledge about computers in general. The key to this subdivision is that each category of knowledge requires different training methodologies. For example, syntactic knowledge training requires a great deal of repetitive exercises. Semantic knowledge training requires that the material presented be logically included within a conceptual framework or model.

B. Training Logistics

1. *Who is the training audience?* The foremost audience is prospective system end users. Information processing specialists also must be trained on how to operate the new system. Finally, managers and executives require at least an overview of the new system.
2. *Who should conduct training?* The ideal training team is composed of (a) end users, who know the applications area, (b) information systems specialists, who know the technology, and (c) professional trainers who are experts in training methodologies and techniques.

3. *Where should training be conducted?* The three choices are (a) on-site in end-user work areas, (b) on-site in separated training facilities, and (c) off-site. On-site training is less expensive, but is subject to interruptions and distractions from the immediate work environment.
4. *When should training be conducted?* There is a tendency to postpone training in the face of "more pressing" design and implementation issues and tasks. However, the advantages of early training include (a) better preparation for new system operation, (b) a greater range of personnel undergoing training, and (c) more opportunity for end-user feedback on potential system problems. At the same time, refresher training should be conducted as close to new system operation as possible to prevent forgetting.
5. *How much and what type of training should be conducted?* Figure 3 uses Shneiderman's computer knowledge taxonomy to suggest the level and type of training that should be conducted for the three training audiences:

C. Prototypes as Training Tools

Use of prototype models in the analysis and design phases of the SDLC can facilitate early training. Early prototypes can be used for management and end-user orientation and familiarization with the system being developed. Successively refined prototype models can be used for training of increased depth. An advantage of using prototype models for system training is the similarity of those models to the user's actual operational environment.

TRAINING AUDIENCE	KNOWLEDGE LEVEL		
	SYNTACTIC (SYSTEMS MECHANICS)	TASK SEMANTIC (APPLICATIONS)	COMPUTER SEMANTIC (COMPUTER CONCEPTS)
END USERS	E	N	M
OPERATIONS PERSONNEL	E	M	N
MANAGERS AND EXECUTIVES	L	L	L
LEGEND: E = EXTENSIVE; M = MODERATE; L = LIMITED; N = NONE			

Figure 3   Suggested level and type of training.

IV. SYSTEM CHANGEOVER PREPARATION

A. Site Preparation

Often there must be physical preparation, even minor construction, to prepare the site that will house system hardware. This site preparation often is minor for small system comprising workstations, servers, or even a local area network (LAN). Site preparation can be extensive for large systems that include mainframe computers and large file servers. The key factors to consider when planning for site preparation include the following:

1. Are air conditioning and heating conditions suitable to meet equipment specifications?
2. Have environmental monitoring and control devices been installed so that computer equipment will automatically be protected when specifications have been exceeded?
3. Are sprinkler systems deactivated to prevent damage to computer equipment?
4. Do security provisions limit access to the computer site?
5. Has equipment been located with an eye to human safety and to reducing human work movement? (For example, is wiring covered so no one will trip?).

B. Hardware and Software Acceptance

Selection of a specific brand and type of hardware and software is a complex process that involves extensive testing before agreeing to buy or lease.

1. Why is testing necessary? Hardware and software can be defective in manufacture; this does not happen very often, but it can occur. More frequently, hardware or software can be damaged in the shipping process.
2. Acceptance period. Hardware and software often are operated during a period of time before formal acceptance. This acceptance period should be specified in the purchase contract.
3. Acceptance test preparation. The following issues should be decided before acceptance testing begins:
   a. How to conduct tests
   b. Length of testing period
   c. Acceptance criteria
   d. How to handle failures

C. Operating Instructions

These are procedures that explain to users how to operate the new application system.

1. *Purposes.* Operating instructions are used to (a) train new users, (b) reacquaint experienced users who have not used the system for a while, and (c) provide guidance on how to handle uncommon system occurrences.
2. *Types.* There are three sets of operating instructions to prepare:
   a. *User instructions* allow end users to learn how to operate the system and serve as a means to troubleshoot day-to-day system problems.
   b. *Technical instructions* allow information technology personnel to handle the technical aspects of the system (e.g., backing up file data).
   c. *Executive overviews* are system summaries intended for executives and managers. These overviews focus on what the system does rather than how it does it.
3. *Operating instruction guidelines.* Following are some points to consider when preparing operating instructions:
   a. Consider on-line documentation as an alternative to, or enhancement of, off-line (paper) documentation.
   b. Have the instructions previewed by the intended audience.
   c. The instructions should be professionally prepared and aesthetically pleasing in order to inspire user confidence in the authenticity of the instructions.
   d. Organize the instructions in modules with tabs and a table of contents so busy users can quickly find what they are looking for.
   e. Include an index of common problems that may be encountered and how to solve these problems.

D. File Conversion

Development of a new application system requires some degree of conversion from the old system format to the new system format. This conversion can be extensive if the old application system is manual or is using very old hardware or software.

1. File conversion process
   a. Old system files are augmented with new system file additions.

b. Programs are written to automatically convert old system file contents to the new system formats.

c. At a specified period of time, old system file contents are downloaded to an off-line medium such as magnetic tape.

d. The downloaded files and the off-line file augmentations are uploaded to new system hardware using the file conversion program.

e. This conversion process is shown in Fig. 4.

2. The day-one approach. File conversion can require considerable effort and expense. This is particularly true for organizations converting to their first automated applications. The day-one approach reduces conversion to those records that are active—that have shown recent transaction activity. In some organizations, the number of inactive records may exceed the number of active records by a factor of 4:1. The day-one approach allows file conversion to occur after rather than before changeover to the new application system. The approach includes the following steps:

a. A new transaction is received and needs to be entered in order to update a file.

b. The transaction is entered into the system.

c. The transaction entry program searches the file to find the appropriate record.

d. If that record is found, the program updates the file with transaction data.

e. If that record is not found, processing is deferred until the old record format is converted to the new system.

f. The transaction is then re-entered.

The day-one approach creates additional data entry workload immediately after cutover to the system. This may be a major deterrent to using this approach. The approach does, however, considerably reduce the amount of total file conversion required. At the end of approximately 1 month, most active records have been converted. A decision is then made whether or not to convert the remaining inactive records (often 80% of total records).

V. SYSTEM CHANGEOVER

All changeover preparations are now complete. It is time to discontinue use of the current application system and begin use of the new system.

A. Changeover Alternatives

The three changeover alternatives are direct, parallel, and phased.

1. *Direct changeover*: A cutoff date is established for the simultaneous discontinuance of the old system and full operation of the new system. The

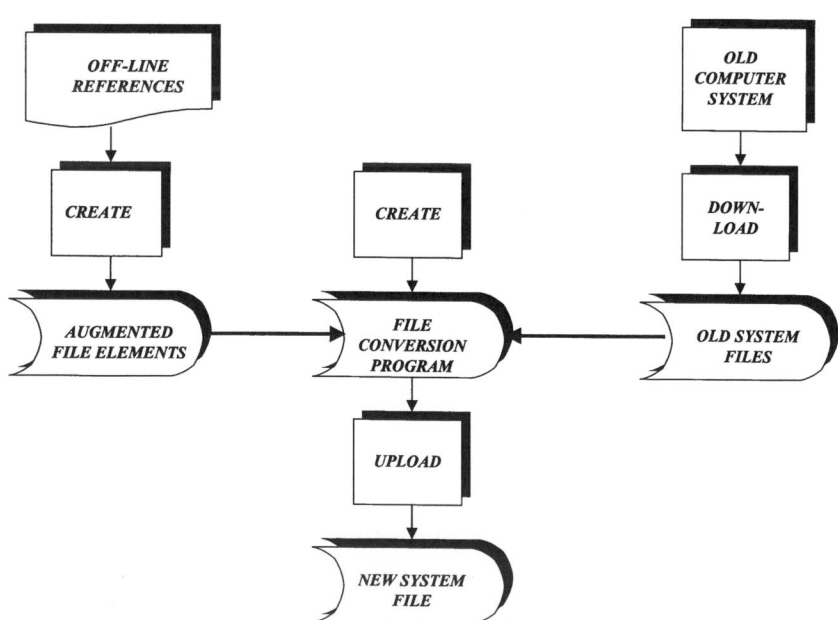

Figure 4 File conversion process.

direct changeover alternative has the following characteristics:

a. It is the least costly of the three alternatives, since there are not two separate systems operating at the same time.

b. It is the least confusing because there is only one set of inputs and outputs.

c. It has stronger user commitment, since the old system no longer exists to fall back on if the new system fails.

d. It has more thorough design and testing because analysts must ensure that the new system works well since there will be no old system to fall back on.

e. It is riskier, for if the new system fails, the old system no longer exists.

2. *Parallel changeover.* This entails operation of both the current and the new application systems for a period of time until everyone is comfortable that the new system works effectively. The parallel changeover alternative has the following characteristics:

a. It is the safest of the three alternatives, providing a safety net should the new application system not work effectively.

b. It is the most expensive, since two full applications systems must be operated at the same time.

c. It is the least conducive to committing users to the new application system since the old system still operates as a comfort zone.

d. It is the most auditable, since new system output can be compared transaction by transaction to the old system.

3. *Staged changeover.* This compromise alternative shares all the advantages and disadvantages of direct and parallel changeover, but to a lesser magnitude. The old system is discontinued and the new system is initiated one stage at a time. There are two variations of this changeover alternative.

a. Pilot. This entails implementation of a complete new application system at a single geographic location. Lessons learned at the pilot implementation are used to fine-tune the system before implementation at other locations.

b. Phased. Modules of the new application are implemented consecutively rather than concurrently. For example, the purchasing module is implemented. When it is operating effectively, then the receiving module is implemented.

B. Selecting the Changeover Alternative

Figure 5 shows tradeoffs between the three changeover alternatives. For any given application implementation, one would mark where on each criterion scale the current changeover environment falls. Often a pattern appears (e.g., most marks on the left side of Fig. 5) which will suggest the choice of one changeover alternative over the other two alternatives. If a clear pattern does not result, often the user community is consulted to determine which of the criteria are the most important. It is critical that selection of the changeover alternative be done early in

	DIRECT	*STAGED*	*PARALLEL*
CHANGEOVER CRITERIA	*CRITICAL* ⟶	*COST CONSTRAINTS* ⟶	*RELAXED*
	LOW ⟶	*SYSTEM CRITICALITY* ⟶	*HIGH*
	HIGH ⟶	*COMPUTER EXPERIENCE* ⟶	*LOW*
	LOW ⟶	*SYSTEMS COMPLEXITY* ⟶	*HIGH*
	HIGH ⟶	*USER RESISTANCE* ⟶	*LOW*

Figure 5   Changeover alternative tradeoffs.

the development process so that expectations (e.g., testing depth) can be fixed appropriately. The choice of changeover alternative should be changed later in the project only if circumstances warrant such a change.

C. Changeover Scheduling

Many problems can occur during the changeover process. These problems can adversely affect a wide range of users and customers. Therefore, a changeover schedule is designed and distributed widely. This schedule includes the following:

1. *User notification.* Notification must be far enough in advance to allow orderly user planning.
2. *Activity phase-down.* Transaction activity must be decreased so that only priority matters are handled during the changeover period.
3. *File conversion.* Old files are downloaded from the old system and uploaded (in conjunction with off-line file augmentations) to the new system.
4. *System cutover.* The old system is discontinued and the new system begins its operation.
5. *Activity resumption.* Transaction activity is resumed at normal levels on the new application system.

VI. SYSTEM EVALUATION

The new application system has been installed and is now handling day-to-day operations. There is now a period of fine-tuning and performance evaluation before responsibility for the new system can be transferred to the business unit.

A. System Fine-Tuning

There are five considerations in the fine-tuning of an application system.

1. *User expectations.* Users expect perfectly designed application systems much as they might expect their new cars or toaster ovens to operate flawlessly. However, the design of application systems is too complex to expect perfection. Designers must condition users to expect minor flaws with the promise that such flaws will be fixed expeditiously. When users expect minor

flaws, they do not lose confidence in the new system when such flaws do occur.
2. *Problem discovery.* System designers need to establish a detection mechanism so users can discover and report system problems quickly.
3. *Rapid correction.* User confidence during this stage correlates highly to how quickly reported system discrepancies are corrected.
4. *New system priority.* Correcting new system problems should have priority over other program maintenance needs. New application system users do not appreciate being placed at the end of a long line of program maintenance changes.
5. *Status reports.* Users tend to remember only failures unless they are reminded of successes. Implementation status reports are produced to include (a) problems detected, (b) problems corrected, (c) correction times, (d) parts of the application that have been operating with no problems, and (e) systems success rate which is defined as follows:

$$\frac{\text{Number of transactions processed}}{\text{Total transactions processed}}$$

B. Postchangeover Evaluation

A comprehensive evaluation is conducted at a specified time (e.g., 6 months) after system changeover.

1. *Purpose.* This evaluation determines whether or not the new application system is operating according to expectations and is ready to be transferred to the business unit. Participants in this review include designers, end-users, auditors, and management.
2. *Postchangeover evaluation report.* A formal report is produced which includes the following:
   a. Performance goals for the new system
   b. Current system performance compared to these goals
   c. Specific areas where the new system has not met the goals
   d. Actions required to improve new system performance to expected levels
   e. Estimated date when these improvements actions will be completed
   f. Date for a final review of new system performance

C. The Changeover Contract

The final step in the SDLC is creation of a formal agreement to transfer application system responsibility from the development team to the business unit. This changeover contract often is drafted before design project work is initiated as a scope of work agreement. Since the scope of work may change, the agreement usually is rewritten into a changeover contract. This contract explains to the business unit what to expect from the new application system. The changeover contract has five elements:

1. *Performance goals.* How the new system is expected to perform in terms of response time, computer downtime, report distribution time, etc.
2. *Tolerance.* How far performance can vary from goals before the system should be judged to be in poor health.
3. *Estimated system life.* When likely enhancement or replacement should be planned for.
4. *Maintenance expectations.* How long it should take from detection to correction of system problems.
5. *Future changes.* Establishment of a future file containing system needs not included in this project and any subsequent user requests or suggestions for future system enhancements.

D. System Operation

The new application system now is fully in the hands of the business unit. Any minor fixes or modifications will be the responsibility of maintenance programmers rather than application developers. This will be the case until, sometime in the future, this new application system begins to deteriorate or become dated. Then another SDLC will be initiated to build a replacement system.

SEE ALSO THE FOLLOWING ARTICLES

Prototyping • Quality Information Systems • Reengineering • Resistance to Change, Managing • System Development Life Cycle • Systems Analysis • Systems Design • Total Quality Management and Quality Control

BIBLIOGRAPHY

Carey, J. (1988). Understanding resistance to system change: An empirical study. In *Human factors in management information systems.* (J. M. Carey, Ed.), pp. 195–206. Norwood, NJ: Ablex.

Dunn, R. (1984). *Software defect removal.* New York: McGraw-Hill.

Fowler, G. (1994). *Structured programming techniques for solving problems.* Boston: Boyd & Fraser.

Hetzel, W. (1984). *The complete guide to software testing.* New York: Wiley.

Martin, M. (July 1987). The human connection in systems design: Prototypes for user training. *Journal of Systems Management,* Vol. 38, 19–22

Martin, M. (October 1989). The day-one implementation tactic. *Journal of Systems Management,* Vol. 40, 12–16.

Martin, M. (1995). *Analysis and design of business information systems,* 2nd ed. Englewood Cliffs, NJ: Prentice Hall.

Martin, M., and Trumbly, J. (February 1986). Measuring performance of computer systems. *Journal of Systems Management,* Vol. 37, 7–17

Price Waterhouse World Technology Center. (1997). *Technology forecast: 1997.* Menlo Park, CA: Price Waterhouse.

Shneiderman, B. (1987). *Designing the user interface.* Reading, MA: Addison-Wesley.

Stahl, B. (1988). The ins and outs of software testing. *Computerworld,* 63–65.

Systems Science

George J. Klir

State University of New York, Binghamton

GLOSSARY

epistemological hierarchy of systems A partial ordering of basic categories of systems.

system A set of things and a relation among the things.

systems complexity The amount of information needed either to describe a systems or to eliminate uncertainty associated with it.

systems knowledge Knowledge regarding the various categories of systems.

systems meta-methodology The study of methods for dealing with systems problems.

systems methodology A family of coherent collections of methods for dealing with the various systems problems.

systems science A science whose object of study is systems.

I. THE MEANING OF SYSTEMS SCIENCE

Scientific knowledge is organized, by and large, in terms of systems of various kinds. What, then, is the difference between systems science and classical science? To answer this question, we need to examine the meaning of the term *system* from a broad perspective. In such a situation, it is advisable to begin with a definition given by a standard dictionary. Consulting, for example, *Webster's New World Dictionary,* we find that a system is "a set or arrangement of things

so related or connected as to form a unity or organic whole." It follows from this commonsense definition that the term *system* stands, in general, for a *set of things* and a *relation among the things*. Formally,

$$S = (T, R) \qquad (1)$$

where S, T, R denote, respectively, a *system, a set of things,* and a *relation* (or, possibly, a set of relations) defined on T.

The commonsense definition of a system, expressed by the pair (T, R) seems overly simple. Its simplicity, however, is only on the surface. While the definition is very simple in its form, it contains symbols, T and R, that are extremely rich in content. Symbol T stands not only for a single set with arbitrary elements, finite or infinite, but also, for example, for a power set, a power set of a power set, etc., or any arbitrary set of sets. Furthermore, things in T may have special properties by which systems are distinguished from one another. These properties have lately been referred to as *thinghood properties.*

The content of symbol R is even richer. For each set T, with its special characteristics, the symbol stands for any conceivable relation defined on T. Formally, a relation is a subset of some Cartesian product of given sets. Even if T is only a single set, R stands for a relation from a family of distinct types of relations: $R \subset T \times T$ (binary relations), $R \subset T \times T \times T$ (ternary relations), etc. When T is a set of sets, the variety of distinct types of relations virtually explodes. For example, when T consists of just two sets, say, $T = \{X, Y\}$

the number of types of relations grows quite rapidly, including, for example, the following types:

$$R \subset X \times Y$$

$$R \subset (X \times X) \times Y$$

$$R \subset (X \times X) \times (Y \times Y)$$

$$R \subset (X \times X) \times (X \times Y)$$

$$R \subset (X \times Y) \times (X \times Y)$$

$$R \subset (X \times X \times X) \times (Y \times Y \times Y)$$

$$R \subset (X \times Y) \times (X \times Y) \times (X \times Y)$$

Although these few examples illustrate the great variety of possibilities represented by the single symbol R, they still do not capture the full richness of this symbol. The form of the Cartesian product on which a relation is defined is only one property of the relation. Other properties depend on the nature of elements of the relevant Cartesian product that are included in the relation. All of these properties of relations have recently been subsumed under the suggestive name *systemhood properties.*

The simplicity of the commonsense definition of a system is, paradoxically, its weakness as well as its strength. The definition is weak because it is too general and, consequently, of little pragmatic value. It is strong because it encompasses all other, more specific definitions of systems. Due to its full generality, the commonsense definition qualifies for a criterion by which we can determine whether any given object is a system or not: an object is a system if and only if it can be described in the form that conforms to Eq. (1).

Once we have the capability of distinguishing objects that are systems from those that are not, it is natural to define systems science as a *science whose objects of study are systems.* It is significant that this definition refers to systems, but not to any particular types of systems such as physical systems, biological systems, social systems, or economic systems. This implies that these distinctions of systems, which are expressed solely in terms of the things involved, are not significant in systems science. This means, in turn, that systems science is concerned with systemhood properties of systems rather than their thinghood properties.

Classical science, which is predominantly oriented to thinghood properties, and systems science, which is predominantly oriented to systemhood properties, are two distinct perspectives from which scientific inquiry can be approached. These perspectives are complementary. Although classical scientific inquiries are almost never devoid of issues involving systemhood properties, these issues are not of primary interest in

classical science and have been handled in an opportunistic, ad hoc fashion. There is no place in classical science for a comprehensive and thorough study of the various properties of systemhood. The systems perspective thus cannot be fully developed within the confines of classical science. It was liberated only through the emergence of systems science. Although the systems perspective was not essential when science dealt with simple systems, its significance has increased with the growing complexity of the systems of current interest.

From the standpoint of the disciplinary classification of classical science, systems science is clearly cross-disciplinary. There are at least three important implications of this fact. First, systems science knowledge and methodology are directly applicable in virtually all disciplines of classical science. Second, systems science has the flexibility to study systemhood properties of systems and the associated problems that include aspects derived from any number of different disciplines and specializations of classical science. Such multidisciplinary systems and problems can thus be studied as wholes rather than collections of the disciplinary subsystems and subproblems. Third, the cross-disciplinary orientation of systems science has a unifying influence on classical science, increasingly fractured into countless number of narrow specializations, by offering unifying principles that transcend its self-imposed boundaries. Classical science and systems science may thus be viewed as complementary dimensions of modern science.

II. THE ORIGIN OF SYSTEMS

Although the commonsense definition of systems allows us to recognize a system, when one is presented to us, it does not help us to obtain it. From whence do systems arise? This question is one of the most fundamental epistemological issues of science, and particularly of systems science. By and large, two opposing positions on this issue have been advanced and debated since the emergence of systems science. They are based on two very different views about the nature of knowledge: *realism* and *constructivism.*

According to realism, each system that is obtained by applying correctly the principles and methods of science *represents* some aspect of the real world. This representation is only approximate, due to limited resolution of our sensors and measuring instruments, but the relation comprising the system is a *homomorphic image* of its counterpart in the real world. When we use more refined instruments, the homomorphic mapping between entities of the system of concern and those of its real-world counterpart (the corresponding "real system") also becomes more refined, and the system becomes a better representation of its real-world counterpart.

Realism thus assumes the existence of systems in the real world, which are usually referred to as *real systems*. It claims that any system obtained by sound scientific inquiry is an approximate (simplified) representation of a real system via an appropriate homomorphic mapping.

According to constructivism, all systems are artificial abstractions. They are not made by nature and presented to us to be discovered, but we construct them by our perceptual and mental capabilities within the domain of our experiences. The concept of a system requiring correspondence to the real world is illusory because there is no way of checking such correspondence. We have no access to the real world except through experience. It seems that the constructivist view has become predominant, at least in systems science, particularly in the way formulated by von Glasersfeld. According to this formulation, constructivism does not deal with ontological questions regarding the real world. It is intended as a theory of knowing, not a theory of being. It does not require us to deny ontological reality. Moreover, the constructed systems are not arbitrary: They must not collide with the constraints of the experiential domain. The aim of constructing systems is to organize our experiences in useful ways. A system is useful if it helps us to achieve some aims, for example, to predict, retrodict, control, make proper decisions, etc.

III. CONCEPTUAL FRAMEWORKS AND TAXONOMY OF SYSTEMS

Because systems science is oriented to the study of systemhood properties, its aim is to understand these properties as completely as possible. The following are key steps in pursuing this aim:

1. Divide the spectrum of conceivable systems into significant categories defined in terms of systemhood properties.
2. Study the individual categories of systems and their relationship.
3. Organize these categories into a coherent whole.
4. Study systems problems that emerge from the underlying set of organized systems categories.
5. Study methodological issues regarding the various types of systems problems.

6. Study meta-methodological issues emerging from systems methodology.

A prerequisite for dividing systems by their systemhood properties into significant categories is that we develop a conceptual framework within which these properties can properly be codified. Each framework determines the scope of systems conceived. It captures some basic categories of systems, each of which characterizes a certain type of knowledge representation and provides a basis for further classification of systems within each category. To establish firm foundations of systems science, a comprehensive framework is needed to capture the full scope of systemhood properties.

Several conceptual frameworks that attempt to capture the full scope of systems currently conceived have been proposed by Klir, Mesarovic and Takahara, Wymore, and Zeigler. In spite of differences in terminology and in the way in which these frameworks evolved, they have essentially the same expressive power. As an example, a particular framework developed by Klir is described here, which is known in the literature as the *general systems problem solver* (GSPS). The kernel of the GSPS is a hierarchy of epistemological categories of systems, which represents the most fundamental taxonomy of systems. The following is a brief outline of the basic levels in this hierarchy.

At the lowest level of the epistemological hierarchy, an *experimental frame* is defined in terms of appropriate variables and their state sets (value sets). In addition, some supporting medium (such as time, space, or population) within which the variables change their states is also specified. Furthermore, variables may be classified as input and output variables. An experimental frame (also called a *source system*) may be viewed as a *data description language*. When actual data described in this language become available, we move to the next level in the hierarchy. Systems on this level are called *data systems*.

When variables of an experimental frame are characterized by a relationship among them, we move to a level that is still higher in the hierarchy. It is assumed on this level that the relationship among the variables is invariant with respect to the supporting medium involved. That is, it is time invariant, space invariant, space–time invariant, population invariant, etc. The relationship may involve not only variables contained in the experimental frame, but also additional variables defined in terms of the former by specific translation rules in the supporting medium. When the supporting medium is time, for example, we obtain lagged variables. Systems on this level are called *behavior systems*. Some of these systems can also be characterized conveniently as *state-transition systems*.

We say that a data system is represented by a behavior system if, under appropriate initial or boundary conditions, the support-invariant relation of the latter can be utilized for generating the data of the former. The generative capability of a behavior system extends, of course, beyond any given data. That is, a behavior system is capable of generating, for example, predictions or retrodictions of the variables involved. Moreover, it provides us with an explanation of the behavior of the variables within the given supporting medium.

Climbing further up the hierarchy involves two principles of integrating systems as components in larger systems. According to the first principle, several behavior systems (or sometimes lower level systems) that may share some variables or interact in some other way are viewed as subsystems integrated into one overall system. Overall systems of this sort are called *structure systems*. The subsystems forming a structure system are often called its *elements*. When elements of a structure system are themselves structure systems, we call the overall system a *second-order structure system*. *Higher order structure systems* are defined recursively in the same way.

According to the second integrating principle, an overall system is viewed as varying (in time, space, etc.) within a class of systems of any of the other types. The change from one system to another in the delimited class is described by a replacement procedure that is invariant with respect to the supporting medium involved (time, space, etc.). Overall systems of this type are called *metasystems*.

In principle, the replacement procedure of a metasystem may also change. Then, an invariant (changeless) higher level procedure is needed to describe the change, Systems of this sort, with two levels of replacement procedures, are called *metasystems of second order*. *Higher order metasystems* are then defined recursively in the same way. Structure systems whose elements are metasystems are also allowed by the framework, similarly as metasystems defined in terms of structure systems.

The key feature of the epistemological hierarchy is that every system defined on some level in the hierarchy entails knowledge associated with all corresponding systems on lower levels and, at the same time, contains some knowledge that is not available in any of these lower level systems.

The number of levels in the epistemological hierarchy is potentially infinite. In practice, however, only a small number of levels are considered. For each particular number of levels, the hierarchy is a semilattice. For five levels, for example, a part of the semilattice is expressed by the Hasse diagram shown in Fig. 1. The circles represent the various epistemological categories of systems, the arrows indicate the ordering from lower to higher categories. Symbols E, D, B denote experimental frames (source systems), data systems, and behavior systems, respectively. Symbol S, used as a prefix, stands for structure systems. For example, SD denotes structure systems whose elements are data systems. Symbol S^2 denotes structure systems of second order. For example, S^2B denotes structure systems of structure systems whose elements are behavior systems. Symbols M and M^2 denote metasystems and meta-metasystems, respectively. Combination SM and MS denote structure systems whose elements are metasystems and metasystems whose elements are structure systems, respectively. The diagram in Fig. 1 describes only part of the first five levels in the epistemological hierarchy; it can be extended in an obvious way to combinations such as S^3B, S^2MB, SMSB, M^2SB, and S^2MB.

Categories of systems captured by the epistemological hierarchy are actually categories in the strong sense of mathematical category theory. It is useful to further classify systems subsumed under each episte-

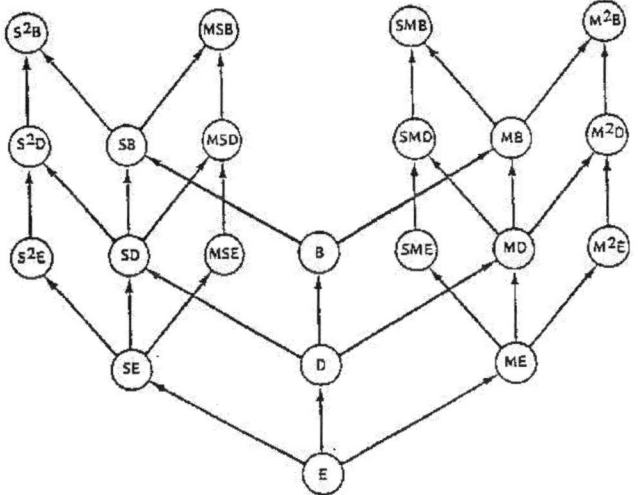

Figure 1 Epistemological hierarchy of systems categories. E, experimental frame or source system; D, data system; B, behavior system; SE, SD, SB, structure systems based on source, data, and behavior systems, respectively; S^2E, S^2D, S^2B, second-order structure systems of the three types; ME, MD, MB, metasystems based on source, data, and behavior systems, respectively; M^2E, M^2D, M^2B, second-order metasystems of the three types; SME, SMD, SMB, structure systems based on metasystems of the three types; MSE, MSD, MSB, metasystems based on structure systems of the three types.

mological category by relevant methodological distinctions. The aim of this classification is to capture the relationship between classes of systems and methods applicable to problems associated with the systems. Examples of methodological distinctions are those between systems based on discrete variables and systems based on continuous variables, between deterministic and nondeterministic systems, and between dynamic and spatial systems.

IV. HISTORICAL ROOTS OF SYSTEMS SCIENCE

Although the notion of a system can be traced to antiquity, systems science is a phenomenon of the second half of this century. It developed within a movement that is usually referred to as the *systems movement.* In general, the systems movement can be characterized as a loose association of people from different disciplines of science, engineering, philosophy, and other areas who share a common interest in ideas (concepts, principles, methods, etc.) that are applicable to all systems and that, consequently, transcend the boundaries between traditional disciplines.

The Systems movement emerged from three principal roots: mathematics, computer technology, and a host of ideas that are well captured by the general term systems thinking. Mathematics is clearly a source of the various systemhood properties. It also provides us with methodological tools pertaining to these properties. Those tools produced by mathematics prior to the 20th century, the most important of which was calculus, were capable of dealing only with rather simple problems involving deterministic systems with a mere handful of variables. They were adequate for dealing with typical problems in science and engineering until physics became concerned with processes at the molecular level in the late 19th century. It was obvious that the available mathematical methods were completely useless for investigating processes of this sort. They were not useless in principle, but because of the enormous number of entities involved. The need for fundamentally new mathematical methods resulted eventually in statistical methods, which turned out to be applicable not only to the study of molecular processes (statistical mechanics), but to a host of other areas such as the actuarial profession, designing large telephone exchanges, and the like.

While the classical (analytic) mathematical methods are applicable only to problems that involve a small number of variables related to each other in a predictable way, the applicability of statistical methods has exactly the opposite characteristics: Statistical

methods require a very large number of variables and a high degree of randomness. These two types of methods are thus highly complementary. When one of them excels, the other totally fails. Unfortunately, despite their complementarity, these types of methods cover only problems that are clustered around the two extremes of the complexity and randomness scales. Most problems are somewhere between these two extremes. They are typical in life, behavioral, social, and environmental sciences, as well as in applied fields such as modern technology or medicine.

To deal with the broader range of problems, more expressive mathematical theories were required and those required, in turn, existing theories to be generalized. The following are some of these generalizations:

- From quantitative theories to qualitative theories
- From functions to relations
- From classical (additive) measures to nonadditive measures
- From classical set theory to fuzzy set theory
- From graphs to hypergraphs
- From ordinary geometry (Euclidean as well as non-Euclidean) to fractal geometry
- From ordinary automata to dynamic cellular automata
- From linear theories to nonlinear theories
- From regularities to singularities (catastrophe theory)
- From precise analysis to interval analysis and to fuzzy analysis
- From regular languages to developmental languages
- From special algebras to universal algebra and to category theory
- From single objective criteria optimization to multiple objective criteria optimization

Each generalization of a mathematical theory usually results in a conceptually simpler theory. This is a consequence of the fact that some properties of the former theory are not required in the latter. At the same time, the more general theory always has a greater expressive power, which, however, is achieved only at the cost of greater computational demands. This explains why these generalizations are closely connected with the emergence of computer technology and steady increases in computing power.

In addition to mathematics and computer technology, systems science has also been influenced by a host of ideas for which I use the general term *systems thinking.* Perhaps the most important of them are ideas associated with *holism,* which emerged at the beginning of this century as an antithesis of *reductionism,* a methodological view predominant in science since about the 16th century. The latter claims that properties of a whole are explicable in terms of properties of constituent elements. Holism rejects this claim and maintains that a whole cannot be analyzed in terms of its parts without some residuum.

Holism, in opposition to reductionism, was undoubtedly one of the main roots from which systems movement sprang. Initially, a tendency toward a full commitment to holism and a total rejection of reductionism was quite visible in the systems movement. Over the years, this extreme position slowly moderated. Now, the two doctrines are viewed, by and large, as complementary. While holism is accepted as a thesis that is correct on logical grounds and, consequently, desirable to follow as an ideal guiding principle, it is recognized that its applicability is often limited on pragmatic grounds. For example, simultaneous monitoring of large number of variables may be impossible or impractical, computational complexity involved in dealing with a desirable overall system may exceed our computational limits, the overall system may be incomprehensible to the human mind of its user, etc. By studying the relationship between wholes and parts, current systems thinking goes far beyond the thinking emerging either from reductionism or holism. We might say that it represents a synthesis of the reductionistic thesis and the holistic antithesis.

Other developments beside holism paved the way for systems science. Among them was the increasing awareness that many phenomena and problems could not be studied within the boundaries of individual disciplines of science. This eventually led to the emergence of interdisciplinary areas such as biophysics, biochemistry, physiological psychology, and social psychology. The existence of these interdisciplinary areas was probably the first step leading to the recognition that systems may be defined across disciplinary boundaries. We may say that it was the first step in recognizing the notion of systemhood. Another step was the recognition of analogies (isomorphies) between systems describing different phenomena (e.g., mechanical, electrical, acoustic, thermal), which made it possible to construct and use analog computers and resulted eventually in the formulation of the *theory of similarity.* Further progress was made by actually identifying some fundamental systemhood properties such as information and control in Wiener's *cybernetics.*

The ideas of holism, the emergence of interdisciplinary areas in science, and the increasing recognition of the existence and utility of isomorphies between disciplines of science created a growing awareness among some scholars that certain concepts, ideas, principles, and methods were applicable to systems in general, regardless of their disciplinary categorization. This eventually led to the notions of general systems, a general theory of systems, general systems research, and the like. These notions, originated and promoted primarily by Ludwig Von Bertalanffy, formed an intellectual basis from which organized systems movement emerged.

The first organization fully devoted to the formation of the systems perspective in science, the Society for General Systems Research, was formed in the United States in 1954. This was followed by the formation of other professional societies supportive of the systems movement in different countries in the 1960s and 1970s. Since 1980, the systems movement has been united under the auspices of the International Federation for Systems Research, whose aims are "to stimulate all activities associated with the scientific study of systems and to coordinate such activities at the international level." Systems movement is now supported not only organizationally through this federation and its member societies, but also by a respectable number of scholarly journals and other publications. Furthermore, some academic programs in systems science, systems engineering, cybernetics, and related areas are well established and stable, and additional programs seem to emerge at a steady pace.

V. SYSTEMS KNOWLEDGE, METHODOLOGY, AND META-METHODOLOGY

As explained previously, systems science is not a new science in the traditional sense, but rather a new dimension in science. Yet, the two dimensions of science have significant parallels: Systems science, as is true of any of the classical sciences, contains a body of knowledge regarding its domain, a methodology for acquisition of new knowledge and for dealing with relevant problems within the domain, and a meta-methodology, by which methods and their relationship to problems are characterized and critically examined.

In every traditional discipline of science, we develop systems models of various phenomena of the real world. Each of these models, when properly validated, represents some specific knowledge regarding the relevant domain of inquiry. In systems science, the domain of inquiry consists of knowledge structures themselves—the various categories of systems that emerge from the conceptual framework employed. That is, the objects of investigation in systems science are not objects of reality, but systems of certain specific types.

Knowledge pertaining to systems science, or *systems knowledge,* is thus different from knowledge in traditional science. It is not knowledge regarding various aspects of reality, as in traditional science, but rather knowledge regarding the various types of systems in terms of which knowledge in traditional science is organized. That is, it is knowledge concerning knowledge structures. This knowledge is, of course, applicable to the processes of acquisition, management, and utilization of knowledge in every discipline of traditional science.

Systems knowledge can be obtained either mathematically or experimentally. Mathematically derived systems knowledge is the subject of the various mathematical systems theories, each applicable to some class of systems. It consists of theorems regarding issues such as controllability, stability, state equivalence, information transmission, decomposition, homomorphism, self-organization, self-reproduction, and many others.

Systems knowledge can also be obtained experimentally. Although systems (knowledge structures) are not objects of reality, they can be simulated on computers and in this sense made real. We can then experiment with the simulated systems for the purpose of discovering or validating various hypotheses in the same way as other scientists do with objects of their interests in their laboratories. In this sense, computers may be viewed as laboratories of systems science. Experimentation with systems on computers is not merely possible, but it may give us knowledge that is otherwise unobtainable.

The computer has, in fact, a dual role in systems science. In one of the roles, it is a methodological tool for dealing with systems problems. In the other role, it serves as a laboratory for experimenting with systems. The purpose of this experimentation is to discover or validate laws of systems science. In contrast to laws of nature, laws of systems science characterize properties of various categories of systems rather than categories of real-world objects. We perform experiments of some kind on the computer with many different systems of the same category. The aim of this experimentation is to discover useful properties characterizing the category of systems or, alternatively, to validate some conjectures regarding the category.

Experimentation with systems on computers to expand systems knowledge is only one of two sides of systems methodology. The other side consists of methods developed for dealing with various systems problems. These are problems that involve primarily systemhood properties. An expertise in systems

knowledge and systems problem-solving methodology may, in principle, be implemented on a computer in the form of an expert system. Such an expert system is complementary to the usual expert system, which is predominantly oriented to thinghood expertise in some special area of classical science, engineering, or some other profession. The two types of expert systems together should form a far better computer support for dealing with overall problems than either of them alone.

The principal aim of systems science is to study the phenomenon of systemhood as completely as possible. The first step in achieving this aim is to develop a comprehensive conceptual framework by which the whole spectrum of conceivable systems is divided into significant categories (Section III). The second step is to study the individual categories of systems and their relationship, and to organize the categories in a coherent whole. The third step is to study systems problems that emerge from the underlying set of organized systems categories. Finally, we address methodological issues regarding the various types of systems problems. The *primacy of problems* in systems methodology is in sharp contrast with the *primacy of methods* in applied mathematics. It is the most fundamental commitment of systems methodology to develop methods for solving genuine systems problems in their natural formulation. Simplifying assumptions, if unavoidable, are introduced carefully, for the purpose of making the problem manageable, yet distorting it as little as possible. The methodological tools for dealing with a problem are of secondary importance; they are chosen in such a way as to best fit the problem rather than the other way around. Moreover, the tools need not be only mathematical in nature. They may consist of a combination of mathematical, computational, heuristic, experimental, or any other desirable methodological traits.

To choose an appropriate method for a specific problem, relevant characteristics of prospective methods must be determined. This is a subject of systems meta-methodology—the study of systems methods as well as methodologies (integrated collections of methods). Let any particular study whose aim is to determine some specific characteristics of a method (or methodology) be called a *meta-methodological inquiry*. Examples of the most fundamental characteristics of methods, which are relevant to virtually all problems, are computational complexity, performance, and generality of the methods involved.

Computational complexity is a characterization of the time or space (memory) requirements for solving a problem by a particular method. Either of these requirements is usually expressed in terms of a single parameter that represents the size of the problem, e.g., the number of variables in the given systems. The dependence of the required time or memory space on the problem size is usually called a time complexity function or space complexity function, respectively. Either of these functions can be used for comparing different methods for dealing with the same problem type.

Performance of a method is characterized by the degree of its success in dealing with the class of problems to which it is applicable. It can be expressed in various ways, typically by the percentage of cases in which the desirable solution is reached, by the average closeness to the desirable solution, or by a characterization of the worst case solution. Methods whose performance is not perfect are usually called heuristic methods. They are employed as a means for reducing computational complexity.

Generality of a method is determined by the assumptions under which it operates, e.g., by the axioms of a mathematical theory on which the method is based. A particular set of assumptions, on which several different methods may be based, is often referred to as a *methodological paradigm.* Each assumption contained in a methodological paradigm restricts the applicability of the associated methods and, consequently, restricts the set of possible solutions in some specific way.

In some instances, characteristics of methods or methodologies can be obtained mathematically. For example, worst case complexity functions have been determined for many methods involved in systems problem solving. In many cases, however, mathematical treatment is not feasible. For example, it is often impossible to determine mathematically the performance of a heuristic method or the complexity function of a method for typical (average) problems of a given type. One way of obtaining the desired characteristics in these cases is to perform experimental investigations of the methods involved. That is, the application of the investigated method or methodology is simulated on a computer for a set of typical problems of a given type. Results obtained for these problems are then summarized in a desirable form to characterize the method or methodology and, if possible, compare it with its various competitors.

VI. COMPLEXITY AND SIMPLIFICATION OF SYSTEMS

Complexity is perhaps as important a concept for systems science as the concept of a system. It is a difficult concept, primarily because it has many possible meanings. Although various specific meanings of complexity

have been proposed and discussed on many occasions, there is virtually no sufficiently comprehensive study that attempts to capture its general characteristics.

To begin with a broad perspective, let us consult a common dictionary first. We find that complexity, according to *Webster's Third International Dictionary,* is "the quality or state of being complex," i.e.,

- "Having many varied interrelated parts, patterns, or elements and consequently hard to understand fully" or
- "Marked by an involvement of many parts, aspects, details, notions, and necessitating earnest study or examination to understand or cope with."

This commonsense characterization of complexity does not contain any qualification regarding the kind of entities to which it is applicable. As such, it can be applied to virtually any kinds of entities, material or abstract, natural or human-made, products of art or science. Regardless of what it is that is actually considered as being complex or simple, its degree of complexity is, according to the commonsense characterization, associated with the number of recognized parts as well as the extent of their interrelationship; in addition, complexity is given a somewhat subjective connotation since it is related to the ability to understand or cope with the thing under consideration.

We can see that the commonsense characterization of complexity assumes an interaction between an object (a part of the world that may have "many varied interrelated parts . . .") and a human being (or, perhaps, a computer) for whom it may be difficult "to understand or cope with" the object. This means that the complexity of an object for a particular human being depends on the way he interacts with it (i.e., on his interests and capabilities). More poetically, we may say that *the complexity of an object is in the eyes of the observer.*

In most cases, one can interact with an object in a virtually unlimited number of ways. As a consequence, the interaction is almost never complete. It is based on a limited (and, usually, rather small) number of attributes that the observer is capable of distinguishing on the object and that are relevant to her interests. These attributes are not available to the observer directly, but only in terms of their abstract images, which are results of perception or some specific measurement procedures. These abstract images are usually called *variables.* When a set of variables is established as a result of our interaction with an object of interest, we say that a system (or, more precisely, a source system) is distinguished on the object.

Because we deal with systems distinguished on objects and not with the objects themselves (in their totality), it is not operationally meaningful to view complexity as an intrinsic property of objects. While complexities of objects may exist in the ontological sense, they are epistemologically and methodologically vacuous, in contrast to complexities of systems. As explained in Section III, systems have many different faces, each represented by one of the epistemological categories of systems. These different categories give the concept of complexity different meaning, each of which requires a special treatment.

Notwithstanding the differences in complexities of the various systems types, two general principles of systems complexity can be recognized; they are applicable to any of the systems types and can thus be utilized as guidelines for a comprehensive study of systems complexity. According to the first general principle, the complexity of a system (of any type) should be proportional to the amount of information required to describe the system. Here, the term *information* is used solely in a syntactic sense; no semantic or pragmatic aspects of information are employed.

One way of expressing this *descriptive complexity* is to define it by the size of the shortest description of the system in some standard language or, alternatively, the size of the smallest program in a standard language by which the system can be simulated on a canonical universal computer. The primary advantage of this definition of descriptive complexity is that it is theoretically sound and applicable to all systems, regardless of their classification. Its primary weakness is methodological: It is rather difficult to determine in many cases the shortest description of a system.

According to the second general principle, systems complexity should be proportional to the amount of information needed to resolve any uncertainty associated with the system involved (predictive, retrodictive, prescriptive). Here, again, syntactic information is used, but that information is based on a measure of uncertainty.

Uncertainty is an inherent property of nondeterministic systems. Such systems describe situations that offer multiple choices. Several mathematical theories are now available within which various types of uncertainty can be formalized and measured. Both descriptive complexity and uncertainty-based complexity are connected with information: information needed to describe a system (descriptive or algorithmic information) and information needed to resolve uncertainty embedded in it (uncertainty-reducing information). When we simplify a system, we want to reduce both the complexity based on descriptive information and the complexity based on the uncertainty information. Unfortunately, these two complexities conflict with each other. In general, when we reduce

one, the other increases or, at best, remains unchanged. Hence, a general problem of simplification is a multiobjective criteria optimization problem.

One way of reducing the descriptive complexity of a system of any type is to exclude some variables from the system. *Excluding variables* from any relation reduces the relation in two ways. First, its dimension is reduced because some sets in its Cartesian product are excluded. Second, its cardinality is reduced because overall states that were distinguished only by the excluded variables become equivalent.

When our aim is to reduce uncertainty-based complexity, we have to involve an inverse procedure. That is, we add some input variables to the system, which contribute, at least potentially, some information that, in turn, reduces the uncertainty regarding the output variables.

Another way of reducing the descriptive complexity of a system is to partition states of some variables of the system into equivalence classes and replace each equivalence class with one state. This simplification strategy is usually referred to as *coarsening* or *quantizing* of variables; it reduces cardinalities of relations involved, but it leaves their dimensions intact. While descriptive complexity is always reduced by coarsening of variables, uncertainty-based complexity may be affected by coarsening of variables in either way.

An important strategy for reducing the descriptive complexity of a system is to break the system down into appropriate subsystems. That is, we approximate a given overall system with a structure system. The key issue in employing this strategy is to minimize the increase in uncertainty (or loss of information) while achieving the desired reduction of descriptive complexity. This issue has been investigated for the last two decades under the name *reconstructability analysis*.

Conceptualizing systems as structure systems, possibly of higher orders, is certainly an efficient way of managing complexity. Such systems are organized hierarchically: Each system consists of a network of interconnected subsystems, each of which consists again of a network of its own subsystems, and so on, until some ultimate subsystems are reached that are not further divided into more primitive subsystems.

For a long time, the power of organizing systems hierarchically has been recognized and utilized with great success in the sciences of the artificial. This organizing principle has undoubtedly been one of the basic tools of good designers, artists and managers. It has also played a key role in the process of developing efficient mass production by allowing the division of labor in manufacturing complex products.

The significance of hierarchically organized systems has also been recognized for a long time in the sciences of the natural. It has repeatedly been observed that virtually all complex systems that we recognize in the real world (that is models of the real world) have the tendency to organize hierarchically. Thus, for example, biological cells seem to group naturally into organs, while organs group into organisms, organisms group into populations of animals, and the latter group into ecosystems. The fact that we tend to perceive the world as hierarchically organized might have some ontological significance, but it may as well be solely of epistemological nature, reflecting how the human brain and mind have evolved to deal with the complexity of the real world. Regardless of its ontological significance, it is undeniable that hierarchically organized systems play an important pragmatic role in our comprehension and management of reality, be it natural or human-made.

Another way of dealing with very complex systems, perhaps the most significant one, is to allow imprecision in describing properly aggregated data. Here, the imprecision is not of a statistical nature, but rather of a more general modality, even though the possibility of imprecise statistical descriptions is included as well. The mathematical frameworks for this new modality are, as already mentioned, the theories of fuzzy sets and nonadditive measures. The two types of complexity introduced thus far, the descriptive complexity and the uncertainty-based complexity, pertain to systems. Yet another face of complexity exists, a complexity that pertains to systems problems. This complexity, which is usually referred to as *computational complexity,* is a characterization of the time or space (memory) requirements for solving a problem by a particular algorithm. Either of these requirements is usually expressed by a function, f, of a single parameter, n, that represents the size of the problem. This function is called a *time* (or *space*) *complexity function.*

The main distinction is between algorithms whose complexity function can be expressed in terms of a polynomial

$$f(n) = a_k n^k + a_{k-1} n^{k-1} + \ldots + a_1 n + a_0$$

for some positive integer k, and algorithms for which $f(n)$ is expressed by an exponential form, e.g., 2^n, 10^n, $2^{e(n)}$, where $e(n)$ is an exponential function of n, etc.

Due to the essential differences between polynomial and exponential time complexity functions, polynomial time algorithms are considered efficient, while exponential time algorithms are considered inefficient. As a consequence, problems for which it can be proven are not solvable by polynomial time algorithms are viewed as intractable, while problems for which polynomial time algorithms are known are viewed as tractable. Computational complexity has been exten-

sively investigated since the early 1970s. Many important results regarding tractability of various systems problems are covered in the classic book on computational complexity by Garey and Johnson.

From a broader and more realistic perspective, the size of a problem instance is not the only determinant of its computational complexity. That is, problem instances of the same type and size may have very different computational demands. Most studies in the area of computational complexity are oriented primarily to the characterization of the worst case problem instances. Although this orientation is theoretically sound, it usually results in estimates that are rarely reached in practice and are therefore too pessimistic. To ameliorate this situation, the worst case estimates are sometimes supplemented with average-case estimates. However, such estimates are based on the assumption that all problem instances are equally likely, which does not necessarily reflect the actual probability distribution of problem instances encountered in practice. The problem of determining the actual distribution for various problem types is predominantly an empirical problem. This problem can be studied, in principle, by monitoring and analyzing problem instances requested by users of the various systems problem packages. Any such study is an example of a meta-methodological inquiry.

VII. STATE OF THE ART

Systems science, by its very nature, contributes a new perspective to science that is complementary to the perspective of traditional science. This new perspective provides science with a counterbalance of the ever increasing division of traditional science into disciplines, subdisciplines, specializations, etc. It enables us to deal with systems and problems that transcend boundaries of the traditional science. Perhaps the most fundamental role in forming systems science as a legitimate field of inquiry was played by the various broad conceptual frameworks (Section III) through which the notion of systemhood is properly characterized and codified. Categories of systems that emerge from these frameworks delineate fairly precisely the domain of systems science.

Major progress has been made in using the computer as a laboratory. In fact, numerous laws of the various categories of systems have already been determined by properly designed experiments on computers, contributing thus to the knowledge base of systems science. Although this knowledge base is still rather small when compared with other, well-established areas of traditional science, it is slowly but steadily growing.

The progress in systems methodology during the last few decades has also been quite encouraging. On the conceptual level, it is important that systems problems are now well characterized and codified in terms of the various categories of systems. On the pragmatic level, it is clear that methodologies for some important classes of problems have advanced considerably.

In parallel with the progress in systems methodology, we can also observe progress at the meta-methodological level. For one thing, the role of the computer in meta-methodological studies (by which, for example, the performance of heuristic methods can be evaluated) has now become almost routine.

The progress in systems science can also be examined in terms of the growth of relevant publications, academic programs, and activities. In the mid-1970s, a thorough study determined that the literature pertaining to systems science had doubled approximately every 4 years since 1950. This trend was confirmed by another study made in the early 1980s. This is a good indicator of the progress in systems science. There is also some evidence, although less documented, that the number of academic programs and professional activities bearing on systems science has been slowly but steadily growing since the 1950s.

Perhaps the main visible impact of systems science on traditional science is its cross-disciplinary orientation. As a result of arguments pursued by systems science for decades, scientists are now becoming, in general, more sensitive to the limitations of their own disciplines. They tend to be considerably more aware now than a few decades ago that significant real-world problems almost always involve aspects that transcend disciplinary boundaries. This impact is, of course, only indirect and, consequently, it is virtually impossible to characterize it more specifically. Another indirect impact of systems science on traditional science is the increasingly habitual use of systems thinking in the latter. For example, it is now quite common in most areas of traditional science to think in terms of systems concepts such as hierarchy, homomorphism, regulation, feedback, stability, adaptivity, complexity, information, and self-organization.

Among the most active areas of current research in systems science is the investigation of relatively new categories of systems, whose practical utility is closely connected with advances in computer technology. Examples of these new categories of systems are cellular automata, neural networks, systems based on fractal geometry, fuzzy systems, chaotic systems, developmental systems, autopoietic systems, anticipatory systems, and self-reproducing systems. Each of these categories of systems opens a new avenue for representing knowledge.

Another active area is the ongoing research on systems complexity and simplification strategies. This inevitably involves research on nondeterministic systems and this, in turn, requires us to study the various facets of uncertainty (predictive, retrodictive, prescriptive, diagnostic, etc.), a subject that became tremendously important as a result of the emergence of fuzzy sets nonadditive measures.

With the rapidly growing knowledge and methodology of systems science, it will soon become impossible for any single person to master the whole domain of systems science. It is thus likely that systems scientists will have to specialize in the not so distant future, similar to the specialization practiced in the traditional sciences for a long time. Nevertheless, each of the emerging systems science specializations will still remain cross-disciplinary from the standpoint of traditional science.

SEE ALSO THE FOLLOWING ARTICLES

Cybernetics • Data, Information, and Knowledge • Expert Systems • Future of Information Systems • Hybrid Systems • Knowledge Acquisition • Systems Analysis • Systems Approach • Systems Design • Systems Implementation • Uncertainty

BIBLIOGRAPHY

Bertalanffy, L. (1968). *General systems theory: Foundations, development, applications.* New York: George Braziller.

Garey, M. R., and Johnson, D. S. (1979). *Computers and intractability: A guide to the theory of NP-completeness.* San Francisco: W. H. Freeman.

Klir, G. J. (1972). *Trends in general systems theory.* New York: Wiley-Interscience.

Klir, G. J. (1985). *Architecture of systems problem solving.* New York: Plenum Press.

Klir, G. J. (2001). *Facets of systems science* (Second Edition). New York: Plenum Press.

Lin, Y. (1999). *General systems theory: A mathematical approach.* New York: Kluwer/Plenum.

Mesarovic, M. D., and Takahara, Y. (1975). *General systems theory: Mathematical foundations.* New York: Academic Press.

Mesarovic, M. D., and Takahara, Y. (1988). *Abstract systems theory.* New York: Springer-Verlag.

Rosen, R. (1985). *Anticipatory systems: Philosophical, mathematical, and methodological foundations.* Oxford, MA: Pergamon Press.

Smuts, J. C. (1926). *Holism and Evolution.* London: Macmillan.

von Glasersfeld, E. (1995). *Radical constructivism: A way of knowing and learning.* London: The Farmer Press.

Weinberg, G. M. (1975). *An introduction to general systems thinking.* New York: John Wiley.

Wiener, N. (1948). *Cybernetics.* New York: John Wiley.

Wymore, A. W. (1976). *Systems engineering methodology for interdisciplinary teams.* New York: John Wiley.

Zeigler, B. P. (1976). *Theory of modelling and simulation.* New York: John Wiley.

Telecommunications Industry

Amitava Dutta
George Mason University

I. INTRODUCTION
II. COMPETITION IN THE LOCAL LOOP
III. INTERNET TELEPHONY

IV. MERGERS AND ALLIANCES
V. CONCLUSION

GLOSSARY

asymmetric digital subscriber line (ADSL) A service offered mostly by local phone companies, where the existing copper line from a residence or business can be used to provide high speed Internet access. The name asymmetric arises from the difference in upload and download speeds since most Internet applications have more data flowing to the user than in the opposite direction.

competitive local exchange carrier (CLEC) Historically, local telephone service could only be purchased from a monopoly provider. In 1996, Congress deregulated service market. CLECs are providers of local service who now compete with each other and the former monopoly provider.

incumbent local exchange carrier (ILEC) A provider of local telephony services who, until 1996, was protected from competition by law.

local loop The part of the telephone network that connects a user device, such as a telephone, fax machine or PC to the nearest access point of a service provider. It typically covers no more than a couple of miles in distance.

quality of service (QoS) This term includes multiple measures of quality of data transmission as seen by a user. Error rates, variability of delay, guaranteed bandwidth on demand are examples of some of these dimensions. QoS is becoming an important issue as users demand more from their data networks and become more dependent on them for conducting daily business.

transmission control protocol/internet protocol (TCP/IP) Collection of rules for packaging and reliably transmitting packets of data over the Internet. The original set rules were not designed to support emerging Internet applications like real time voice and video or to achieve a high degree of security in transmission.

THE TELECOMMUNICATIONS INDUSTRY is undergoing major upheaval fueled by a combination of regulatory changes, technology advances, and customer demand. These changes and resulting issues are too varied and complex to be addressed comprehensively within the scope of a single book article. Instead, we have chosen to focus on a few selected issues, which in our opinion are among those that will have a major impact on the evolution of this industry. Specifically, we discuss competition in the local loop and its impact on services, IP telephony, and telecommunications mergers/alliances. The selection is motivated by a desire to cover the three major dimensions of technology, regulation, and customer demand associated with this industry. By making it possible to send voice packets over the standard TCP/IP platform, IP telephony is forcing the industry to rethink its basic concepts of common carriers and enhanced services. Regulatory changes specified in the telecommunications act of 1996 have set the stage for competition in the local loop. Already, new services are becoming available to residential and business customers, particularly broadband services needed to obtain high-speed access to the Internet. Also, with digital convergence, customers are demanding one-stop shopping for telecommunications services. These changes in technology, demand patterns, and regulation have resulted in a spate of mergers and alliances as equipment and service providers try to reposition themselves to face the new realities. Collectively, the three issues to be discussed in this article reflect the interplay between technology, regulation and demand that is shaping this industry.

I. INTRODUCTION

The telecommunications industry is being shaped by significant changes in regulation, technology, and customer demand. The complexity and extent of these changes implies that we can only examine a limited number of issues within the confines of a single article. Historically, telecommunications was synonymous with telephony, the transmission of voice signals. Data communications evolved more or less separately as did video networks. However, today's telecommunications is characterized by so-called digital convergence, where the lines between voice, data, and video networks are increasingly blurred. Customers want integrated access to a variety of voice, data, and video services, all at a reasonable price. We use the generic network shown in Fig. 1 to identify the specific topics that are addressed in this article and to provide a motivation for their selection.

Figure 1 shows that business and residential customers communicate with one another through a telecommunications infrastructure that, currently, has two major spatial components: the local loop and the backbone network. The term *local loop*, although having its roots in telephony, generally refers to that part of the infrastructure that connects a subscriber to the first access point within a service provider's network. It generally covers a small distance—of the order of a few kilometers at most. The backbone network covers

much larger distances, generally has much higher capacities and much more complex topologies. The telecommunications industry covers both parts of this structure.

In this article, we have decided to focus on three contemporary issues affecting this industry. The first is competition in the local loop. The backbone segment of the infrastructure has been open to competition for quite some time. However, the local loop has been thrown open to competition only recently. This has had significant impact on the types of services, particularly broadband, available to customers. The local access segment of the overall infrastructure has been a choke point in the delivery of fast service to the customer. Given the increasing importance of the Internet and digital convergence, the need for broadband local access is fast becoming urgent and universal. Hence, competition in the local loop is clearly a major driver in today's telecommunications industry.

The second topic we discuss is IP telephony or, in simple terms, sending voice as data packets using Internet technology. Traditional telephony uses a completely different technology called circuit switching. Moreover, it is still subject to substantial national and international regulation, while the Internet has not been regulated as much. These technical and regulatory differences have a considerable impact on pricing. Further, it promises to have significant impact on the traditional telephone companies. Because voice transmission is such a large fraction of the overall traffic carried by telecommunications networks, IP telephony is clearly worth examining

The third and last issue to be examined here is the unprecedented consolidation that is occurring in the telecommunications industry. The extent of this activity has caused the Federal Communications Commission (FCC) to recently review its entire process for evaluating its approval process. As we shall see shortly, the telecommunications industry has evolved in a very fragmented manner. This makes it difficult for the indus-

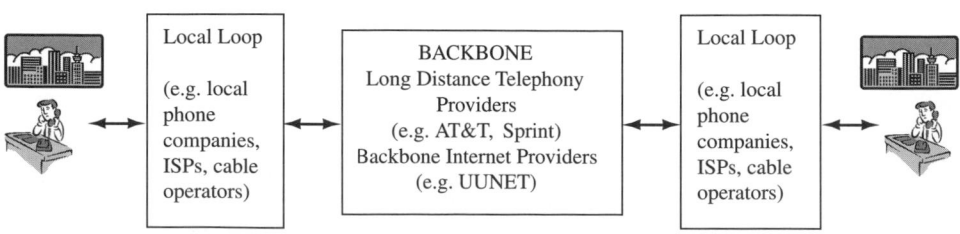

Figure 1   A generic telecommunications infrastructure.

try to respond to customer need for integrated delivery of digital services. We examine two different consolidation mechanisms, alliances and mergers, and compare their strengths and weaknesses. The three activities to be discussed here have been selected because they illustrate the interplay between technology, regulation, and customer demand that is shaping—and will continue to shape—the telecommunications industry.

II. COMPETITION IN THE LOCAL LOOP

With reference to Fig. 1, the backbone infrastructure for voice and data communications has been modernized and expanded steadily over the years. However, the local loop segment has been slow to keep up with technology and emerging needs. This situation has occurred due to a combination of technical and regulatory factors to be discussed shortly. Even though the term *local loop* has its roots in telephony, the issue of competition in the local loop is also of considerable importance for applications other than telephony.

Even though the Internet itself is largely unregulated, the on-ramps to the information superhighway, i.e., the local loops, are highly regulated. Hence, in the modern world, where access to voice and data services is becoming equally important, the capabilities of the local loop are of vital concern to customers. Regulatory relief and technical advances have, in recent times, brought remarkable improvements to the local loop. In this section, we discuss the evolution of competition in the local loop and its impact on services.

A. History of Local Competition

In 1876 Alexander Graham Bell obtained a patent for the telephone and, with Gardiner Hubbard and Thomas Sanders, formed the Bell Telephone Company in 1877. In 1882, Bell acquired a controlling interest in the Western Electric Company, which became its manufacturing unit. Gradually, Bell came to own most of its licensees. Collectively the enterprise became known as the Bell System and they enjoyed patent monopoly from 1876–1894. These Bell-licensed operating companies developed a network of users within their areas by way of a local switchboard, which became known as the *local exchange*. However, interconnection among exchanges was not easy. In 1885, Bell established American Telephone and Telegraph (AT&T) as a long-distance subsidiary, a key step in reaching interconnectivity.

In 1894, when the telephone patent expired, many competing independent telephone companies entered the market. They quickly attained dominance in several rural areas throughout the South and Midwest. However, this fragmentation made interconnection even more difficult. The government introduced regulation into the industry with a goal of "universal service." This implied the technical ability to connect all telephones independent of locality, service provider and distance. It also meant diffusion of telephone service to all parts of the United States, so that everyone could have access to telephony at a reasonable price. To give telephone companies the incentive to make the massive investments necessary to achieve this goal, they were protected from competition. The United States was broken up into mutually exclusive areas called *LATAs* or *local access transport areas*. There could only be one provider of local service within a LATA. This structure persisted for quite some time and AT&T continued to dominate the industry with more than 90% of the market.

However, even as protection from competition facilitated the goal of universal service, technological advances and business needs were generating pressure on incumbent service providers to innovate. The regulatory environment was feeling pressure to allow new entrants into the market. The MCI verdict in 1976 introduced competition into the long-distance market, but local access remained protected from full competition. The breakup of AT&T in 1984 created a major realignment in the industry. One of the consequences was the creation of seven Regional Bell Operating Companies (RBOCs), each of which comprised a collection of Bell telephone companies operating as regulated monopolies for local telephony in their regions. The remaining AT&T was free to operate in the long-distance market. Note how the industry started without any regulation, moved into an era of heavy regulation and lack of competition, and is now gradually moving back to a more competitive posture.

In parallel, the cable companies began operating as regulated monopolies, being the sole source provider of TV services in their respective areas. With technical advances in the 1990s, it became possible to send voice and data over this cable infrastructure, and regulatory changes were clearly needed. Note that, although innovations were gradually being deployed in local telecommunications, the new services were being primarily deployed in economically attractive areas. The possibility of inequality of access to information-rich services across different parts of the United States therefore needs to be addressed.

B. The 1996 Telecommunications Act

As the benefits of competition became evident in the long-distance market, service providers started to demand that the local access market should be opened to competition. Mounting pressure led to the introduction of legislation in Congress on March 30, 1995. This culminated in President Clinton signing S.652, enacting the Telecommunications Act of 1996 into law. The act has three principal objectives:

1. Opening the local exchange and exchange access markets to competitive entry
2. Promoting increased competition in telecommunications markets that are already open to competition, including the long-distance market
3. Preserving the concept of universal service as the local access market moves from monopoly to competition.

Competitive local exchange carriers (CLECs) can enter the market for local service using different mechanisms. CLECs are new organizations that would compete with the incumbent local exchange carrier (ILEC). The first mode was total service resale (TSR), a concept in which the CLEC buys local telephone service from the ILEC at bulk discount rates and then resells it under its own name. Examples of companies who pursued this avenue are McLeodUSA and USN. The second was a hybrid arrangement where the CLEC would use its own existing facilities and interconnect with the ILEC's local network using unbundled network elements (UNEs) to complement its network. Several physical components are needed to connect to the end customer. This includes transmission lines, switches, multiplexers, etc. The UNE concept simply means that these components should be available separately, i.e., unbundled, to CLECs. This approach is used by most established long-distance carriers (e.g., AT&T, MCI, Sprint) or well-funded local access start-ups (e.g., Teligent, Level 3).

A third way to enter the local market is by using a completely separate infrastructive network thus circumventing most of the ILEC's local network altogether. This strategy can be adopted by cable companies who already have access to customers' homes with an independent network or by interexchange carriers (IXCs) who have networks built-out to major business customers. CLEC activity across the nation has been impressive since the act. More than 90% of LATAs are competitive and more than 50% of the central offices in the major metropolitan areas have collocation activity.

To facilitate competition, the FCC defined seven UNEs and the way in which the ILECs had to offer them to the CLECs. The UNEs consist of the network interface device, the local loop, local and tandem switching, interoffice transmission facilities, signaling databases, operations support systems, and operator services. The incentive for ILECs to cooperate with CLECs is strong since ILECs must pass a 14-point checklist before they are allowed to offer long-distance service. To date, the FCC has approved only one application—the Bell Atlantic application for the state of New York on which a favorable decision was reached in December 1999. The act also provides for competition in the cable industry.

In short, the act has introduced a significant amount of competition into the local loop within a short period of time. We now review the more common technology and service alternatives that have emerged for the local loop from this competition.

C. Leased Lines and UNEs

Here, a CLEC leases a circuit to the customer location typically from the ILEC. The ILEC switches the circuit through its network and hands it off to the competitive provider at its point of presence (POP). UNEs were introduced with the act and gave CLECs yet another method by which to gain access to the local customer. UNE resellers can choose from the seven basic components to offer a particular service or to gain parity with the ILEC and brand the service under their name. The advantages of this approach are obvious. Leased lines have existed for a long time and while the UNE is a relatively new regulatory concept, it is simply a reselling of services and facilities that have been utilized within the Bell system for decades. In addition to being well established, the reselling of existing infrastructure provides CLECs with the option of getting into business quickly while keeping investment in facilities low.

However, while it allows rapid market entry, the reselling business is one of low margins and may be hard to sustain in the long run. The other disadvantage is that circuits remain under control of the ILEC. Thus a competitor impacts delivery times, provisioning, and support. An alternative approach is for a CLEC to gain greater control by using its own existing facilities for part of the infrastructure, and then to interconnect with the ILEC's local facilities to complete customer access.

D. Fiber Optics

With optical fiber, a CLEC typically buries its own conduit in built-up suburban and urban areas to provide ready access to potential customers. Customers have access to speeds of an optical carrier level-3 (OC-3) and above, along with virtually error-free transmission unattainable using copper or wireless transmissions technologies. However, costs are high. The average cost today to lay fiber and wire a single building is approximately $500,000. The cost is incurred due, in part, to the significant construction effort required to string the conduit to the curb. In some urban areas, disruptions caused by excavation have reached serious enough levels for city governments to enact rules and penalties. Fiber optic systems also require a higher level of sophistication in costly labor skills. Thus, for now, fiber is primarily a business solution. However, of the roughly 700,000 office buildings in major cities, only 3% have been optically wired to date. In addition, this 3% represents large businesses; typically single clients willing to take the entire fiber for themselves. Only recently have CLECs begun to offer multiple tenants a shared fiber solution. To date, companies like Qwest, MFN, and Level3 have made a name for themselves deploying fiber to the curb.

E. Digital Subscriber Line

Digital subscriber line (DSL) is a transmission technology that achieves high speeds over existing twisted-pair lines. To provide DSL service, a provider installs a digital subscriber line access multiplexer (DSLAM) at the company central office (CO). This is used to aggregate multiple customer DSL lines. At the customer location, a DSL modem is installed to terminate the DSL connection.

DSL comes in a variety of flavors and transmission speeds. To date, asymmetric digital subscriber line (ADSL) has been deployed the most. It offers speeds of up to 7 Mbps downstream but significantly lower upstream speeds. It is marketed primarily to the residential market for Internet activity. High-speed digital subscriber line (HDSL) is also available. It is a T1-like service having comparable bandwidth. Symmetric digital subscriber line (SDSL) allows for symmetrical data rates of up to 2.2 Mbps, which is adequate for small and medium-sized businesses.

The fact that DSL uses existing copper wire makes it particularly attractive to ILECs. There are, however, some limitations. Higher frequency signals attenuate faster over metallic loops. DSL service is therefore limited in distance to approximately 12,000 feet. It is adversely affected by network elements commonly found on voice copper lines, such as taps and loading coils. For these reasons, DSL service has not been deployed as rapidly and extensively as the ubiquity of twisted-pair infrastructure would suggest. Companies like Rhythms, Covad, and Northpoint have positioned themselves to sell ADSL, SDSL, and HDSL to businesses around the United States. However, they often find themselves at the mercy of the ILECs who own the existing copper loops. Analysts see vast growth in residential use of ADSL. While current penetration is approximately 1% of households, Goldman Sachs, among others, predicts that DSL will be used in nearly 44.8 million homes by 2008.

Other DSL standards are emerging. These include Very High Data Rate Digital Subscriber Line (VDSL), designed to offer capacity suitable for video, and Rate-Adaptive Digital Subscriber Line (RADSL), which is able to adjust the delivery rate based on line conditions.

F. Cable Modems

Some service providers are looking at the cable TV network as a way of providing high-speed local access. Current TV transmission to the home uses only a small fraction of the bandwidth available on TV cables, and cable modems make use of this extra capacity for data transmission. Cable TV networks operate in a simplex fashion with a "head-end" that broadcasts TV signals to homes. An upgrade of the network, specifically this head-end transmission equipment, allows signals to flow in both directions by utilizing switching technology that can handle voice and data along with the existing video transmissions. The service provider must install cable modems at customer locations to terminate the transmissions. Data flowing downstream from the service provider shares line capacity in a fashion similar to an Ethernet segment.

The advantages of this technology are significant, especially in the residential market. Speeds can go up to 36 Mbps although most current providers operate at 10 Mbps. Additionally, the near ubiquity of cable offers a large potential market—in fact, cable passes approximately 96 million homes. Analysts predict that nearly 20 million American homes will use cable modems by 2004. This is primarily a solution for the home, as coaxial connections are almost exclusively to residences. The primary service type is data, although with companies like AT&T buying cable companies, voice service will surely follow. Some cable companies, like Cox, are already offering voice over cable.

There are several limitations. Critics point to the shared bandwidth as one problem. As downstream bandwidth is shared, speed is dependent on how many users are utilizing their connection at a given point in time in the neighborhood. Typically, 500–2000 houses may share one line segment. This results in unpredictable service quality. The cable industry counters that, with continued investment in equipment, they will be able to decrease the number of shared segments served by a single head-end. There is also a security issue since everyone on one segment can technically see data packets. While encryption is used as standard procedure by cable modems, this issue continues to be of some concern.

There is also some debate on whether cable operators should provide "open access" to service providers via these cables. Much like the ILECs who monopolize the copper loops to their customers, the cable companies have been granted an exclusive conduit into millions of residences. However, just as the Telecom Act of 1996 forced ILECs to provide "open access" to their copper lines into the home, it is reasonable to expect that over time, market pressures will result in regulation that requires cable companies to do likewise. Cable operators such as AT&T/TCI see the broadband market as a whole and argue that DSL provides a major alternative to customers. Further, they argue that they should be protected from competition to protect the enormous investments required to upgrade their networks for these new services. However, CLECs and other ISPs state that they should have open access to all conduits into the home. Anything less, they argue, would make the customer worse off.

G. Fixed Wireless

Like cable, fixed wireless provides carriers a way to bypass ILECs and reach customers. Typically, fixed wireless refers to broadband, point-to-multipoint technologies such as local multipoint distribution systems (LMDS) operating in the 18–38 GHz range, or multichannel multipoint distribution Systems (MMDS) operating in the 2.2–2.4 GHz range. Fixed wireless providers install an antenna at a centralized base station and, using a hub-and-spoke approach, communicate via terrestrial microwave to antennas installed on homes or offices.

Bandwidths currently deployed run up to OC-3, and can be flexibly bundled to provide truly cus-

tomized solutions. The construction associated with a fixed wireless deployment is limited. This leads to a cost structure that is significantly lower than the wired alternatives. Typical base stations cost approximately $250,000 while the cost to "light" a single building may be as low as $50,000 compared to low-end fiber. There are limitations, of course. Because this is terrestrial microwave-based technology, the base station must have line of sight to the receiver. This may complicate deployment in dense urban and suburban settings with structural obstacles. Also, short wavelength signals can be easily affected by natural elements such as rain and snow. System designers are conservative in their deployments and allow for excess power and shorter distances. Typical applications require distances of between 1 and 10 km, and thus may call for many base stations to reach all of the potential receivers in a given geographic market.

Increasingly, fixed wireless has being targeted at small and medium-sized businesses. Due to the need for line of sight and efficient use of the hub-and-spoke approach, this technology is often deployed in downtown or campus settings around the United States, by companies like Teligent, WinStar, Advanced Radio Telecom, and Nextlink. The FCC has held several spectrum auctions for both LMDS and MMDS and analysts expect significant competition in this arena in the near future. With larger companies like AT&T and Sprint vying for fixed wireless assets it seems reasonable to assume that this is a technology that will see increased deployment in the coming years.

H. Mobile Wireless

Mobile wireless (MW) includes cellular and personal communications services (PCS). Currently, they are a complement to but not a substitute for wireline telephony. That situation will change as the price, reliability, and geographic coverage of MW improves.

MW enjoys several advantages. It can be deployed more quickly compared to wireline infrastructure and supports mobile communications. In addition, unlike fixed wireless, MW does not require uninterrupted line of sight to the customer. New and specialized data services, such as cellular digital packet data (CDPD), have been piggybacked on existing cellular infrastructure. Simple Internet services are also becoming available to the mobile customer through these technologies.

MW has certain disadvantages. The amount of spectrum available to PCS and cellular license holders is limited. This requires sophisticated ways to reuse frequency, which complicates planning and increases technical complexity. Weather can also impact performance. Overall performance is not as reliable as wireline services. Also, geographic coverage is still not universal. There are many parts of the United States, particularly rural areas, where coverage is poor or nonexistent. Last, bandwidth is still limited for delivering substantial Internet services to the handheld devices. Despite these deficiencies, the future holds the promise of one telephone number for a person that he will be able to carry with him no matter where he is located.

I. Other Technologies

Other technologies under development may also emerge as contenders. They run the gamut from satellite providers like Hughes, EchoStar, and Teledesic, to power companies who also have extensive copper connectivity into every office and residence in the United States. Both of these groups, and plenty of others, seem willing to test the waters as soon as regulatory or technological barriers fall.

The year 2000 marked the fourth year of a competitive revolution brought to this market by the Telecommunications Act of 1996. The act has created new industry players and brought about technological innovation. However, the regulation of local access is still evolving and will likely slow deployment somewhat. Nevertheless, business and residential customers can look forward to greater service variety at reasonable cost.

III. INTERNET TELEPHONY

Telephony involves the transmission of voice signal. Historically, telephone networks have used a method called circuit switching. In this method, a complete path (circuit) is established from source to destination before conversation can begin. Moreover, this path remains fixed for the duration of a call. The switches along the way do not introduce any significant delay. So, once a path is set up, the connection from source to destination can be thought of as one continuous pipe. While this switching method is good for voice, it is inefficient for data traffic that is often bursty in nature. This is what led to the development of various packet switching methods such as X.25 and Frame Relay. The Internet protocols, i.e., TCP/IP, were originally designed to carry data. However, over time, as the Internet diffused globally, there was in-

creased interest in seeing if voice could be sent effectively over this type of network.

A. Basic Mechanics of IP Telephony

Internet telephony refers to standard telephone services that are transported using packet switching, rather than the circuit switching method. At the source, the process begins by converting analog voice into a digital bit stream, which is then compressed and formatted as IP packets for transmission over the Internet. The receiving end reverses this process. Early incarnations of IP telephony required multimedia computers at the sending and receiving ends. Clearly, this was limiting in that there was no ability to use the regular telephone as end-user equipment. Besides, both the sending and receiving parties needed to use the same application software, and the conversation quality was very poor. Since that time, Internet telephony has advanced considerably, with many vendors offering software. More significantly, gateways have been developed to interface the Internet with the Public Switched Telephone Network (PSTN). This development enables computer–computer, computer–telephone, and telephone–telephone communication using Internet technology.

B. IP Telephony Drivers

Internet telephony is attracting great attention from customers because the quality of transmission has improved substantially and it can offer considerable savings over the PSTN, particularly for international calls. Nevertheless, Internet telephony still has problems due mainly to the unreliability of the Internet and limitations in compression algorithms. The technology performs much better on an Intranet where traffic patterns are more predictable and bandwidth issues are under the control of one organization. Intranet telephony allows users to save on long-distance and overseas toll charges. Say a caller in San Francisco wants to place a phone call to another caller in India. Let us assume that both callers have multimedia computers and are connected to their respective ISPs under a flat rate pricing plan. The caller's voice is digitized and electronically packaged by his machine at San Francisco, and then transmitted over the Internet to the caller in India. The voice packets are unpacked and reconverted back to analog by the machine in India. However, the caller is not paying for the call on a per-minute basis. In fact, since he is under a flat rate plan from the ISP, there is no extra charge for the phone call. This leads to tremendous costs savings. Of course, voice quality is not as good as over the regular telephone network.

Several factors contribute to poor voice quality in Internet telephony. Congestion on the Internet can lead to packets being discarded or getting lost. In addition, since the IP protocol is connectionless in nature, voice packets may arrive out of sequence at the destination and this increases the likelihood of packet loss. Lost voice packets manifest themselves as periods of silence or interruptions in the voice message being received. Sound quality also depends on the techniques used to encode and compress voice as well as on the voice-processing functions of the gateway servers. Currently, vendors of Internet telephony software and servers have been using different compression methods that differ in their internal mechanisms and sound quality. This lack of standardization results in performance differences across vendors as well as interoperability problems.

C. Technical Developments

Advances in packet switching technology and standardization efforts will help address these problems. As the Internet backbone is gradually converted to ATM and SONET technology, the switching and transmission infrastructure will be in place to carry voice, data, and video in a uniform manner. ATM technology uses fixed-length packets of 53 bytes enabling more predictable packet delivery times. Further, error correction and congestion control are end-to-end responsibilities. The variability of delay for real-time applications, such as voice, is minimized greatly, resulting in higher voice quality. Second, the development of standards for packetized voice transmission will relieve some of the interoperability problems. In May 1996, the International Telecommunications Union (ITU) ratified the H.323 specification, which defines how voice, data, and video traffic will be transported over IP-based local-area networks. However, industry recommendations conflict with parts of the ITU recommendation. In short, there is some convergence on the standards issue but work still remains. There is also a need for industry standards in the area of Internet telephony directory services to ensure interoperability between the Internet and the PSTN. The lightweight directory access protocol (LDAP) seems to be emerging as the basis for a standard in this area.

Despite its technical limitations, IP telephony can work reasonably well over corporate intranets and commercial extranets. These networks involve either a single or limited group of organizations that have control over network access and usage. Voice transmission over the public Internet, however, will continue in the near term to be a niche market that can tolerate the varying performance levels of that transport medium in exchange for major savings over the PSTN. However, as ATM/SONET technology is deployed in the public Internet backbone and broadband services become more available on the local loop, the public Internet will be able to carry voice over IP as well.

D. Potential Industry Impact of IP Telephony

The impact of IP telephony on the telecommunications industry promises to be revolutionary from technical, economic, and regulatory points of view. As IP telephony matures, it simply does not make economic sense for telecommunications operators to maintain separate investments in circuit switched infrastructure that is optimized for voice. With IP telephony, the long awaited convergence between telephony and computing will be a step closer to reality. The benefits of an integrated voice data network are obvious. They include simplified network management, unified support staff, and integrated applications. While TCP/IP may not be the best standard for integrating voice and data, it has a few significant advantages. It is ubiquitous and has become a corporate communications standard, thus attracting a whole host of application developers. In addition, countless companies, including giants such as Cisco, 3Com, and Newbridge Networks, are working on IP-based equipment. By contrast, only a handful of companies are making circuit switches for telecommunications providers. Packet switching equipment is improving in performance at a much faster pace than circuit switching equipment and their prices are also falling. In short, the economics are rapidly working against circuit switching.

From an industry standpoint, this means the traditional telephone carriers need to reassess their current infrastructure, build new infrastructure to support this digital convergence, and integrate this new structure with legacy components. Actually, convergence can be a potential cost saver for traditional carriers since packet switching technology is much more flexible in its use of bandwidth. In contrast, circuit switching technology divides capacity into rigid 64-Kbps channels. Carriers can also offer multiple services more efficiently by moving to a common platform. It is well known that the expected growth in traffic lies in data not voice. Traditional telephone companies are therefore building up IP infrastructure and it is natural to start offering some voice services on that platform. It also enables developers to develop integrated voice/data applications that were difficult or impossible to develop when voice and data networks were distinct entities.

In short, IP telephony is causing major changes in the underlying technological base of the telecommunications industry. The trend clearly is to progressively work up to a homogeneous data network that will also carry voice. Separate voice and data networks will be a thing of the past. Pricing issues in this new environment are also poorly understood. Before, pricing for voice calls was based on distance and time but that does not make sense with the new data transmission infrastructures where the economics of service provision are quite different.

Despite the advantages of a homogeneous IP-based network for voice and data, some roadblocks, both technical and regulatory, remain in the march toward convergence. The per-port cost of IP switching equipment is still about an order of magnitude higher than that of analog voice switches. These costs have to come down before IP equipment can be economically deployed on the scale necessary to carry significant amounts of voice traffic. Scalability is also an issue. Voice switches are available with a very large number of ports, while the largest IP switches have two orders of magnitude fewer ports. Also, voice networks have a separate signaling network—the SS7 (Signaling System No. 7) network—while IP networks do not. In IP networks, control packets use the same electronic conduits as that occupied by payload. Hence the controlling mechanism is more vulnerable to security threats and system failures. It will take time to get a full set of voice telephony features into IP equipment. IP networks also need to implement end-to-end QoS (quality-of-service) features before they can truly replace the PSTN. IP network reliability has also got to be addressed since telephone networks currently operate at around 99.999% reliability. Vendors and service providers also want more standards to be developed so that their equipment can interoperate. Given these constraints, the expectation is that convergence will first appear on intranets, and from there it will move out to extranets and the public Internet.

E. Regulatory Issues Concerning IP Telephony

On the regulatory front, IP telephony has muddied the clear separation between telephone carriers and providers of data services. The FCC has historically regulated telephony but maintained a relatively hands-off attitude toward data services. IP telephony threatens to complicate that separation. One of the reasons for the immediate interest in IP telephony is lower calling costs to the consumer. These lower prices result, in part, from the absence of regulatory mandates. However, if a data service provider now offers voice service using IP telephony, should this service offering not be regulated and taxed like that from a traditional phone company?

In 1998, the FCC told the U.S. Congress that federal telecommunication laws require treating some IP telephony services like regulated phone service and not Internet service, which has been exempt from regulation. This decision appears to foreshadow a requirement that IP telephony providers contribute to the universal access fund. Of course, this would make the services of these providers less price competitive in the market. Some of the major Internet telephony players, however, fear that this narrow regulatory effort may be just the start of government regulation of the Internet at large. In response to intense lobbying efforts, congress has asked the FCC to maintain a hands-off posture toward Net telephony.

As mentioned earlier in this article, the Telecommunications Act of 1996 has two specific statutory aims: (1) to promote competition in such a fashion as to reduce costs and improve service provision and (2) to facilitate the rapid deployment of emerging and advance telecommunications technologies. The telecommunications carriers, who are threatened by Internet telephony, argue that the first objective requires the FCC to extend its regulatory scope to Internet telephony. However, ISPs and Internet telephony software developers argue that the second objective requires the FCC to maintain the regulatory status quo. Currently, the FCC is waiting to rule on the status of IP as a telecommunications service, since it is recognized that if it is subject to regulation, and taxes, this may retard innovation.

In summary, IP telephony is here to stay and will cause profound changes in the telecommunications industry. Several technical issues, such as compression and jitter, need to be resolved, as do some major regulatory issues. However, these impediments will only delay deployment temporarily because the impetus to overcome them is strong. The biggest challenge is perhaps faced by the ILECs who have considerable investment tied up in the old circuit switched infrastructure. For them, the question is not *if* they should convert to the newer data transmission based infrastructure, but *how* and *when*.

IV. MERGERS AND ALLIANCES

As mentioned elsewhere in this article, technology advances, customer demand, and regulatory changes are pushing telecommunication companies to become more competitive and offer a broader range of services on a global scale. The World Trade Organization (WTO) negotiated an agreement in February 1998 between nations representing approximately 85% of the world telecommunications markets. This agreement, and other regional ones like NAFTA, put these national or regional markets on a path toward greater competitiveness. Although these agreements are still open to interpretation and disagreement by world governments, telecommunication companies are beginning to provide services in countries from which they have previously been excluded. For the first time in the history of the telecommunications industry, markets will truly be global in scope.

Historically, however, the telecommunications industry has evolved in a fragmented manner and has continued to do so until recently. Spatially, for example, companies did not cross national boundaries. Even within national boundaries, as in the United States, companies had monopoly privileges and did not encroach on each other's territories. Outside the United States, the government frequently owned and operated the telecommunications company for the entire country. Wireline telephone companies grew up separately from those selling wireless services. The cable television industry grew up separately in parallel with another set of technologies. This fragmented nature of the industry is inconsistent with emerging customer needs. In the age of digital convergence and global business operations, it is unreasonable to expect the customer to synthesize an integrated and global service from multiple industry organizations. As a result, major telecommunications service firms are looking for partners to enable them to offer a comprehensive suite of services from a single source. Carriers are partnering with content providers; long-distance providers are merging with local access providers, and consolidating among themselves. The pace of partnering has reached a feverish pitch and will continue in the near term. In this section, we discuss two different mechanisms commonly used for partnering: mergers and alliances. The strengths and weaknesses of each approach are illustrated using three case studies.

A. Merger and Alliance Structures

A merger is a combination of two or more organizations, after which only one continues to exist, for ex-

ample, MCI and WorldCom merged into MCIWorld-Com. It is a formal joining of previously autonomous organizations that affects all aspects of the business from leadership to employees, customers, and shareholders. Usually the leadership of the joining entities agrees at the time of the formal signing who will be running the new organization, what it will be called, and how shares will be valued. The three types of mergers are horizontal, vertical, and conglomerate. In a horizontal merger, two direct competitors in the same market segment merge. In the second, two companies from different stages of the distribution channel merge. Finally, a conglomerate merger is where two completely unrelated companies merge. Any one type has the potential to greatly change the competitive landscape of its industry. However, horizontal mergers are the most closely watched and regulated by the Justice Department because they result in fewer competitors and more concentrated power in that industry.

In an alliance type of partnership, the partnering entities each maintain their original identities, organizations, and leaderships. Rather, a new additional entity—a joint venture—is created that leverages the strengths of the participating entities. The formation of Globalone, originally a joint venture between Deutsche Telekom, France Telecom, and Sprint, is an example. In the telecommunications world, this type of partnering has been seen most commonly in the formation of global service companies. Alliances can generally be divided into two groups: pure play and converging. Pure play alliances involve the union of partners with closely related products, technologies, and markets. Converging alliances feature partners with differing but perhaps complementary resources, such as a pairing of an Internet and a radio company. Converging alliances generally hold greater promise for success and value creation given their minimal overlap of resources. However, most major global telecommunications alliances fall into the riskier pure play category.

B. Comparative Strengths and Weaknesses

In theory, mergers and alliances allow partners to quickly integrate their respective service strengths to offer a comprehensive package for customers across national boundaries. An additional benefit to providers is the economies of scale derived from the sharing of common resources. Partners can practice mutual outsourcing and share R&D costs and risks and marketing. However, alliances and mergers are viewed differently from a regulatory standpoint, the latter usually generating more scrutiny.

National regulations, trade barriers, and antitrust restrictions may prohibit outright mergers in some countries due to foreign ownership concerns. For example, no foreign company is allowed to own more than 25% of a telecommunications carrier in the United States. Alliances allow companies to minimize these concerns if not totally exempt themselves from such laws. Alliances may also defuse potential political nationalism issues that mergers would otherwise inflame because an alliance is seen as less threatening to a national phone company's culture and existence. In fact, alliances offer several benefits over mergers in today's market. The more informal structure of alliances can allow projects to be rapidly created and disbanded, can involve multiple corporate participants, and can lead to internal efficiencies. Companies seeking a merger may not always end up with the best partner because the potential partner may not be on the market. Mergers may also create a national talent drain from companies in smaller nations whose employees may feel their career opportunities would be limited in a large international corporation. Additionally, national banks may be more willing to lend money to a local alliance partner than to an international player. Last, there is less financial risk with alliances than mergers. If the partnership fails, it is easier for both parties to walk away from the relationship.

However, alliances do have their shortcomings. The multiple relationships created by many-partnered combinations can be difficult to manage. Because the companies are not fully integrated under one leadership, an inherent lack of control can exist among the partners. The central problem is that there is no clear line of authority. Each partner may have veto power over the other, thereby requiring unanimity for all decisions. This structure can lead to lengthy and damaging delays in making key decisions. Programs that must be implemented to achieve synergy in the alliance, such as integration of sales, marketing, and technical development among the partners, may not be pushed forward due to the absence of a central leader with authority. This lack of leadership coupled with the partners' natural wariness of each other makes it difficult for many alliances to live up to their potential.

In contrast, mergers, once fully implemented, do not suffer from the management control and other organizational deficiencies just noted for alliances. It is the implementation process itself that is a daunting task. First, the regulatory hurdles to overcome are more stringent. Under the Clayton Anti-Trust Act, the U.S. government tightly regulates mergers. When two companies wish to merge, they are required to produce extensive documentation for the U.S. Department of Justice (DOJ) and/or U.S. Federal Trade Commission (FTC). The DOJ investigation will seek to determine whether the merger is likely to adversely impact customers through reduced competition and approval of the merger is by no means automatic. In practice, though, the DOJ interpretation of antitrust law has become more liberal over time. The same DOJ that broke up the Bell system in 1984 has, within the last two years, permitted some of these Baby Bells to merge with each other, and with other telecom service providers. Apart from the complexities of regulatory approval, mergers sometimes create clashes of organizational culture that undermine synergies. The merger between America Online and Netscape is a good example. The merger resulted in a large exodus of Netscape employees who felt that AOL's culture would be stifling. We now illustrate these relative advantages and disadvantages with three case studies.

C. Case Studies

The first case study is an alliance called Concert. It is a global venture between AT&T and British Telecom. The second case study is Globalone, the alliance between Deutsche Telekom, France Telecom, and Sprint. This case exemplifies what can go wrong with an alliance. The third case study is the pending MCIWorldCom-Sprint merger that clearly demonstrates the formidable regulatory hurdles to be overcome.

1. Concert

These two partnering companies, AT&T and British Telecom, are well established financially. Given the similarity in their service offerings, this alliance would fall into the pure play category. However, the complementary and extensive geographic presence of each partner is what the alliance seeks to leverage. Concert is a $7 billion start-up that is targeting multinational businesses, international carriers, and Internet service providers as customers. The two companies announced the alliance in July 1998. Before the alliance could move ahead, regulatory hurdles had to be overcome. They needed the approval of the European Union (EU), U.S. DOJ, and the FCC. The EU required AT&T to loosen its ties to Telewest, the number two cable company in the United Kingdom, and sell a U.K. long-distance company before it would approve the alliance. AT&T went further by selling its stake in Mannesmann Arcor, a German phone venture. With those conditions met, the EU approved the alliance in March 1999. The process in the United States was a little easier. No divestitures were required.

The DOJ approved the partnership on June 28, 1999, and the FCC gave its sign off on October 22, 1999. AT&T and BT turned over assets and businesses going to the joint venture in November 1999. Dave Dorman heads the executive team of Concert.

Obviously, the jury is still out on whether this alliance will be a success. Many analysts have observed that although this alliance will help the two companies in building city-to-city infrastructure, they still do not control the last mile, which can prove to be a problem. Analysts are also saying that AT&T and BT are undistinguished in providing Internet service, which is becoming the lifeblood of the telecommunications industry. Only time will tell. Concert does provide a good example of how two companies can use an alliance to strengthen their global position without merging with or acquiring another company.

2. Globalone

Globalone was launched on January 31, 1996, as a joint venture of Deutsche Telekom, France Telecom, and Sprint, three well-established companies in their own nations. The motivation, once again, was to leverage each entity's technological strengths and geographic presence to offer one-stop global service to multinational customers. The Globalone partners coexisted until April 1999 when Deutsche Telekom began negotiations with Telecom Italia in a takeover bid. They did not, however, inform either partner of this activity. If Deutsche Telekom had been successful, it would have put them in direct competition with France Telecom in Italy. Ultimately Deutsche Telekom lost out to Olivetti, but the secrecy surrounding the effort did not please the other two partners in the alliance. France Telecom has filed suit alleging that Deutsche Telekom violated the terms of the alliance agreement. Sprint, meanwhile, used this dispute as an opening to look elsewhere and is engaged in talks with MCIWorldCom.

Although the secret takeover bid by Deutsche Telekom precipitated the breakup of the alliance, factors in the alliance's structure also presented major management challenges. Each of the three owners had veto power over major decisions. This caused serious delays for Globalone's implementation of its network and opened the door for competitors to step in. They also did not develop a unified sales and marketing structure for the three companies. It was not uncommon for two members to be selling the same products in the same country. Finally, the cultures of the three companies were not a good match. Deutsche Telekom and France Telecom were state-owned monopolies that

had noncompetitive cultures. Sprint, in contrast, has always been an underdog in the telecommunications industry and has had to battle for market share, making for a very different corporate culture.

Globalone had approximately 4000 employees and 1999 revenues of $1.1 billion. They had a sales presence in 65 countries with more than 1400 network centers outside of the United States, France, and Germany. It has evolved into a single-source provider of voice, data, and IP needs for its customers generating 14% revenue growth excluding Asia and Russia. On January 26, 2000, France Telecom acquired Globalone in its entirety. Despite its size, the travails of Globalone clearly illustrate the weaknesses of alliances.

3. MCIWorldCom and Sprint Merger

On October 5, 1999, Sprint and MCIWorldCom announced intent to merge and create, what they called the preeminent telecommunications company of the 21st century. MCIWorldCom is the second largest CLEC with annual local revenues in excess of $1 billion. It has local service to over 42,000 buildings in 100 metropolitan areas and has DSL services at more than 1500 POPs as of 1999. Sprint's ILEC operations cover 18 states with virtually no overlap with MCIWorldCom. Its nationwide all-digital PCS wireless network and MCIWorldCom's paging assets will give the combined company a competitive suite of wireless services. MCIWorldCom's Internet backbone and its extensive international presence complement the advanced data services offered by Sprint. While Sprint's experience with Globalone may have been a catalyst in conceiving this merger, clearly there are real synergies present. A combination of Sprint and MCIWorldCom would form a powerful force in the global telecommunications industry, with a formidable presence in local-service and long-distance markets, a substantial collection of international assets, the premier wireless company in the United States and a potentially dominant share of data and Internet traffic.

As with all mergers, the deal was scrutinized carefully by the relevant regulatory agencies. At the time of the merger announcement, most observers thought the biggest hurdle would be potential concentration in the top-level networks that provide long-haul connections throughout the Internet. MCIWorldCom and Sprint are the two largest Internet backbone providers, and their merger would result in an entity providing more than 43% of Internet service providers with interconnection services. When WorldCom bought MCI in 1998, Sprint was one of the many parties that complained to regulators that the merger constituted a severe threat to the competition within the Internet service provider market. FCC Chairman William E. Kennard expressed skepticism about the merger's benefits in a statement: "American consumers are enjoying the lowest long-distance rates in history and the lowest Internet rates in the world for one reason: competition. Competition has produced a price war in the long-distance market. This merger appears to be surrender. Their parties will bear a heavy burden to show how consumers would be better off."

There were several anticompetitive concerns in the merger between MCIWorldCom and Sprint:

1. Undue concentration in long-distance markets. The merger would combine the second and third largest U.S. long-distance companies in an already highly concentrated market.
2. Monopoly in the Internet backbone market. The merger would combine the largest and second largest Internet backbone providers, with approximately half of the long-haul Internet market. As precedent, DOJ had required MCI to sell its entire Internet business before approving its merger with WorldCom.
3. Anticompetitive impacts in international markets. According to one analysis, 85% of all intra-European Internet traffic travels through the MCIWorldCom network exchange point in Washington, D.C. Sprint is in direct control of the other major network exchange point for intra-European traffic. MCI has control of Embratel, Brazil's long-distance carrier, and Sprint owns 25% of Intelig, the company being developed to compete with Embratel.
4. Postmerger employment cuts. MCI and WorldCom laid off several thousand employees after their merger, despite statements to regulators to the contrary.
5. Service quality problems in local telephone markets. Sprint has local telephone operations in 18 states. State regulators were concerned that MCIWorldCom's focus on global business customers would drain resources from Sprint's local operations.
6. Federal telecommunications contracts. Sprint and MCIWorldCom had each been awarded multimillion dollar contracts to serve as competing providers of telecommunications services to federal agencies. These contracts would need to be modified in the context of the merger.

Ultimately, these concerns were sufficient to scuttle the agreement. On July 13, 2000, Joel I. Klein, assistant attorney general in charge of the department's Antitrust Division issued the following statement after MCIWorldCom and Sprint announced they were abandoning their merger plans:

> We welcome this decision to abandon the transaction. The merger would have led to higher prices, lower service quality, and less innovation for millions of American consumers and businesses. America's consumers and businesses will continue to reap the benefits of competition in the long distance, Internet backbone and data network services businesses.

However, despite such regulatory hurdles, the spate of mergers and alliances in the telecommunications industry continues unabated and is likely to continue as business users continue to demand one-stop shopping and simplify their network management responsibilities.

V. CONCLUSION

We began this article by noting that customer demand, technology, and regulation continue to shape the telecommunications industry. Despite some friction and inertia produced by legacy infrastructures and regulatory problems, the industry is surely moving in a direction that will enable it to better support the notion of digital convergence. In other words, companies that used to be thought of as telephone companies will become providers of integrated services. Conversely, companies that started out as data service providers will gradually take on voice services as voice-over-data technology matures. In our view, consolidation in the telecommunications industry will continue. The DOJ must continue to scrutinize each new deal carefully because excessive concentration of market power might otherwise result. As more economies across the world become liberalized, and their telecommunications sectors in particular, it will become easier to set up alliances and mergers that span multiple countries. This should enhance the availability of one-stop shopping for global services.

For the residential customer, the evolution of the telecommunications industry may be a confusing period in the short run because of the increasing number of services being provided in a fragmented manner by multiple providers. Nevertheless, the one-stop shopping phenomenon is sure to extend to the residential sector as well and there is evidence that it is starting to happen already. In some parts of the United States, cable companies are also offering phone service, while phone companies are offering video service through their copper infrastructure.

It is appropriate to end this article by briefly mentioning important aspects of the industry that we have not covered here due to space constraints. The theme of this article has been on telecommunications services and we have not examined the equipment-producing sector of this industry. The physical characteristics of customer devices, their functional capabilities, and their economics will all have an important impact on the evolution of the industry. The history of the Palm Pilot provides an example of such an evolution in customer end devices.

Although not a direct component of the telecommunications industry itself, we feel that any study of the industry would be incomplete without an in-depth examination of telecommunications regulation. In particular, one needs to understand the history of this regulation within the United States and abroad and the mechanisms by which such regulations are produced. Mechanisms should cover both national and international aspects of regulation. We close by repeating that this article examines three important aspects of the telecommunications industry. Nevertheless, there are additional aspects of the industry and a more complete understanding would require their study as well.

SEE ALSO THE FOLLOWING ARTICLES

Digital Goods: An Economic Perspective • Internet, Overview • Mobile and Wireless Networks • National and Regional Economic Impacts of Silcon Valley • Speech Recognition • Standards and Protocols in Data Communications • Telecommuting • Transmission Control Protocol/Internet Protocol (TCP/IP) • Voice Communications

BIBLIOGRAPHY

ADSL Forum (1998). Fiber–Copper access to the information highway. Available at http://www.adsl.com/vdsl_tutorial.html.

ADSL Forum (1998). Twisted pair access to the information superhighway. Available at http://adsl.com/adsl_tutorial.html.

Ameritech (2000). Internet telephony public policy issues. Available at http://www.ameritech.com:1080/corporate/regulatory/internet_telephony.html.

Anonymous (May 1, 1999). Business: the battle for the last mile. *The Economist*, 59–60.

Beard, T. R., Kaserman, D. L., and Mayo, J. W. (1998). The role of resale entry in promoting local exchange competition. *Telecommunications Policy*, Vol. 22, No. 4, 315–326.

Borland, J. (July 27, 1999). Study: High-speed net bypasses rural areas. CNET News.com. Available at http://aolcom.cnet.com/news/0-1004-200-345389.html.

Branson, K. (May 1999). Is local resale a sinking ship? Voyagers prefer facilities; hope floats in UNE-P. *PhonePlus Magazine*.

Available at http://www.phoneplusmag.com/articles/951cover.html.

BT and AT&T welcome EU clearance of $10 billion global venture. Available at http://www.concert.com/whoweare/bt033099.asp.

Ciciora, W., Farmer, J., and Large, D. (1999). Modern cable television technology: Video, voice, and data communications. San Francisco: Morgan Kaufmann Publishers.

Clark, D. D. (1999). High-speed data races home. *Scientific American*, Vol. 281, No. 4, 94–99.

The concert story. Available at http://www.concert.com/whoweare/gvstory.asp.

Digital subscriber line and its variants. Available at http://acc-systems.com/whatis.htm.

Douskalis, B. (1999). *IP telephony—The integration of robust VoIP services*. Upper Saddle River, NJ: Prentice-Hall.

Fung, P. J. (April 1998). A primer on MMDS technology." *Communications Systems Design*. Available at http://www.csdmag.com/main/9804fe4.htm.

Globalone corporate overview. Available at http://www.globalone.net/about.html.

Goodman, D. J. (1997). *Wireless personal communications systems*. Reading, MA: Addison-Wesley.

Hamblen, M. (July 21, 1999). Cable modems. Quickstudy Computerworld research. Available at http://www.computerworld.com/home/features.nsf/all/990621qs.

Huttle, W. (October 1998). Asymmetric digital subscriber lines. NSWC Dahlgren Division, Code B32. Available at http://www.nswc.navy.mil/cosip/nov98/osa1198-1.shtml.

IP telephony standards portal. Available at http://www.computertelephony.org/.

ISP Planet (September 20, 1999). Voice over IP sales to reach $4 billion. Available at http://www.isp-planet.com/research/voip_growth.html.

Katz, M. L. (1997). Ongoing reform of U.S. telecommunications policy. *European Economic Review*, Vol. 41, No. 3, 681–690.

Knauer, L. T., Machtley, R. K., and Lynch, T. M. (1996). *Telecommunications Act handbook: A complete reference for business*. Rockville, MD: Government Institutes.

Langtry, B. (1998). *All connected: Universal service in telecommunications*. Australia: Melbourne University Press.

Lazar, T. D. (April 19, 2000). Cable modems lead DSL in broadband consumer race, Insight press release. Available at http://www.insight-corp.com/4_19_00.html.

Lenore, T. (October 1999). The relentless march of market forces: North America—United States. *Telecommunications Online*. Available at http://telecoms-mag.com/issues/199910/tci/usa.html.

Lieberman, D. (July 27, 1999). Fight brews over high-speed Internet access. *USA Today*. Available at http://167.8.29.15/life/cyber/tech/ctf687.htm.

Lipartito, K. (1989). *The Bell system and regional business: The telephone in the South, 1877–1920*. Baltimore: Johns Hopkins University Press.

Long, C. D., and Spinks, S. O. (1997). Alliances, mergers and acquisitions in telecommunications. *International Telecoms Review '97*. Available at http://www.coudert.com/practice/teleacq.htm.

Lorraine, S. (1997). *Failure is not an option: How MCI invented competition in telecommunications*. Santa Monica, CA: Knowledge Exchange.

Mason, C. (February 1, 1999). Can you find the wireless runners? *America's Network*. Available at http://www.americasnetwork.com/issues/99issues/990201/990201run.htm.

MCIWorldCom (2000). Corporate Overview. Available at http://www.wcom.com/about_the_company/corporate_overview/.

MCIWorldCom (2000). Merger facts: Frequently asked questions on the MCIWorldCom–Sprint merger. Available at http://www.worldcom-merger.com/merger_facts/merger_facts.htm.

Ness, S. (March 3, 1998). Why investment matters, Remarks of Commissioner Susan Ness before the Economic Strategy Conference, Washington, DC. Available at http://www.fcc.gov/Speeches/Ness/spsn804.html.

Newbridge Networks. Extending the reach of broadband: Services symmetric digital subscriber line. Available at http://www.newbridge.com/ads_keyword/dsl/index.html.

Noll, A. M. (1999). *Introduction to telephones and telephone systems*. Norwood, MA: Artech House.

Olivetti savors Italia spoils: Underdog outlines strategic plans after $65 billion victory over Telecom Italia, May 24, 1999. Available at http://207.25.71.63/1999/05/24/europe/ italia/.

Ono, R., and Aoki, K. (1998). Convergence and new regulatory frameworks. *Telecommunications Policy*, Vol. 22, No. 10, 817–838.

Personal Communications Services, National Telecommunications and Information Administration. Available at http://www.ntia.doc.gov/opadhome/mtdpweb/povrview.htm.

Pleasance, C. A. (1989). *The spirit of independent telephony: A chronicle of the accomplishments, intrigue, and the fight for survival that accompanied the independent telephone movement in the United States*. Johnson City, TN: Independent Telephone Books.

Powell, M. K. (December 2, 1998). FCC commissioner speech presented at local competition . . . CLECs in the midst of an explosion convention, Las Vegas. Available at http://www.fcc.gov/Speeches/Powell/spmkp819.html.

Reuters (October 7, 1999). Will MCI WorldCom's buy of Sprint escape EU review? *CNET.com news*. Available at http://aolcom.cnet.com/news/0-1004-200-809984.html.

Reinhardt, A., Moeller, M., and Siklos, R. (May 24, 1999). As the web spins. *Business Week*, 30.

Shooshan, H. M., III. (1984). *Disconnecting Bell: The impact of the AT&T divestiture*. New York: Pergamon Press.

Stuart, D. (1998). Competitive local exchange carriers (CLECs) in the U.S.: Overview. Datapro. Available at http://163.18.14.55/datapro/05981-1.htm.

Tarjanne, P. (1999). Preparing for the next revolution in telecommunications: Implementing the WTO agreement. *Telecommunications Policy*, Vol. 23, No. 1, 51–63.

Thyfault, M. F. (April 13, 1998). Voice-data integration: Resurgence of convergence. *Information Week Online*. Available at http://www.informationweek.com/677/77iuvoi.htm.

U.S. Department of Justice Announcements. Available at http://www.usdoj.gov/atr/public/press_releases/2000/5142.htm.

U.S. Department of Justice and FTC (1997). Horizontal merger guidelines. Available at http://www.usdoj.gov/atr/public/guidelines/horiz_book/hmg1.html.

van Cuilenburg, J., and Slaa, P. (1995). Competition and innovation in telecommunications: An empirical analysis of innovative telecommunications in the public interest. *Telecommunications Policy*, Vol. 19, No. 8, 647–664.

VIP calling—One of telco industry's best-kept secrets. *Packet*™ *Magazine Archives*, Third Quarter 1999. Available at http://www.cisco.com/warp/public/784/packet/july99/16.html.

World Trade Organization basic telecommunications agreement, 2000. Available at http://infoserver.fcc.gov/ib/wto.html.

Yoffie, D. B. (Ed.) (1997). *Competing in the age of digital convergence*. Cambridge, MA: Harvard Business School Press.

Telecommuting

Sathiadev Mahesh
University of New Orleans

GLOSSARY

computer-mediated communication (CMC) The use of technologies such as e-mail, synchronous chat, discussion boards, instant messengers, electronic whiteboards, multimedia messaging, and e-conferences for communication.

last mile The final segment of the telecommunications link to the home. This could be the cable loop to the home or the telephone wire to the wall socket from the exchange.

telecenter A satellite office located away from the main office, often close to the employee's residence, that is used to counter the isolation of home-based telecommuting.

telecommuting The use of computer-mediated communication (CMC) to perform work at locations other than the main office, thereby reducing commute time.

telework Work done at a remote location, which could be a satellite work center, including those in other countries with lower wage rates.

total cost of operations (TCO) The complete cost of operating a system; the hardware, software, personnel, training, debugging, security, and other maintenance costs of the system.

TELECOMMUTING is the use of computer-mediated communication (CMC) to perform work at locations other than the main office. The term is used when an employee is expressly paid for work done at a work site other than the main office, often the employee's home, and the employee's total commute time is thereby reduced.

I. INTRODUCTION

Advocates of telecommuting claim it will revolutionize work, with work coming to people rather than people going to work, and that this will lead to a transformation of organizations. Telework is a term often used interchangeably with telecommuting. *Telework* refers to work done at a remote location, which could be a satellite work center, including those in other countries with lower wage rates. Telecommuting can refer to work at remote locations such as vacation homes and hotels, or mobile offices in cars, where work is accomplished using CMC with the main office. Telecommuting does not refer solely to jobs requiring computer work such as software development or data entry. Any job that can be performed at a location other than the primary place of work, using CMC to facilitate interaction with managers, co-workers, customers, and suppliers, can be effectively telecommuted. A list of organizations that promote telecommuting and support businesses considering telecommuting as an option is provided in Table I.

A. Survey of Telecommuting

A survey of 2000 Americans, age 18 or older, completed in July 1998 by the International Telework

Table I   Telecommuting Reference Web Sites and Trade Organizations

Name	Web address	Description
JALA	*http://www.jala.com*	A telecommuting support site with reports, links, and information on telecommuting by Jack Nilles, who coined the term *telecommuting*.
AT&T Telework Center	*http://www.att.com/telework/*	A guide for telework programs.
Langoff's Center	*http://www.langhoff.com*	Site maintained by author of telecommuting books with FAQs, tips, calendar of conferences, and news.
Network World Fusion	*http://www.nwfusion.com/research/tele3.html*	Network world research site on telecommuting.
British Telework	*http://www.eto.org.uk/faq/faq02.htm*	List of terms used in teleworking and a large archived discussion group.
Electronic Commerce and Telecommuting Trends (ECaTT)	*http://www.ecatt.com/ecatt/*	European site with statistics, case studies, and country reports from the European Community about e-commerce and telework.
Federal Interagency Telecommuting Centers	*http://www.gsa.gov/pbs/owi/interim.htm*	Interim report, U.S. General Services Administration, Office of Workplace Initiatives, Washington, DC, August 2, 2000.
Gil Gordon's Site	*http://www.gilgordon.com/telecommuting/*	Numerous reports on telecommuting, *Telecommuting Review Magazine*, trade tips.
CIO Virtual Workplace Research Center	*http://www.cio.com/forums/remote/teleresource_content.html.*	Resources for telecommuting programs, October 2000.
Interagency Telecommuting Program, GSA	*http://www.gsa.gov/pbs/owi/telecomm.htm*	October 8, 2000.
International Telework Association and Council (ITAC)	*http://www.telecommute.org/*	Nonprofit organization dedicated to promoting the economic, social, and environmental benefits of teleworking
Telecommuting Site	*http://telecommuting.about.com*	A guide to telecommuting with links, articles, discussion groups, products.
Telework, Colorado	*http://teleworkcolorado.org/*	A site to support telecommuting in Colorado. Information for businesses to set up and manage telecommuting programs. Case studies and support. A large list of links for telecommuting related information is provided *http://teleworkcolorado.org/links.htm*.
TMA group	*http://www.telework-connection.com/*	A guide to managing telecommuting with news, links, and reports.
TManage	*http://www.tmanage.com/*	A telecommuting ASP working with telecommunications providers to manage telecommuting programs for business.
US DoT Telecommuting Agreement	*http://dothr.ost.dot.gov/Telecommuting/forms_work_agreement.htm*	
US DoJ Telecommuting Agreement	*http://www.usdoj.gov/jmd/ps/flexiplaceform.htm*	Format of agreement between employee and department for telecommuting.
US West—Extended Workplace Solutions Page	*http://www.uswest.com/largebusiness/products/ews/*	Site with papers, many telecommuting studies, review of technologies to support telecommuting, and *extended workspaces,* a US West term for remote and mobile offices.

Association and Council, showed that nearly 15.7 million people in the United States telecommuted to a job with an outside employer, during normal business hours, a minimum of 1 day per month or more. While many of these individuals were only part-time telecommuters, the size and willingness to use telecommuting has become more significant with Internet availability and the growth of information processing jobs. The same study also pointed out that nearly half were full-time employees, who telecommuted half their work time. An earlier Bureau of Labor Statistics survey, from the May 1997 Current Population Survey of 50,000 households, shows that 21 million people in the United States telecommuted for part of their job (http://www.bls.gov/opub/mlr/ 2000/03/precis/htm, http://www.bls.gov/news.release/homey.nws.htm). This study shows that while the total number who worked at home did not grow dramatically between 1991 and 1997, the number being expressly paid to work at home did. In the earlier study in 1991, many white collar workers did work at home. However, they were not expressly paid for this work. In the later study employers compensated some of the teleworkers for work done at home. While about half the teleworkers were not expressly paid for work done at home, 17% were paid for the hours worked. The remaining 33% were independently employed. A European study by Electronic Commerce and Telecommuting Trends (EcaTT) showed that almost one-third of European establishments were using telework with a 50% penetration in Finland and Denmark. This study found that nearly 6% of the European Community workforce telecommutes on at least a partial basis, with Finland the standout, having one-sixth of the workforce telecommuting.

B. Perceptions about Telecommuting

Many managers are uncertain about embracing a telecommuting strategy. Telecommuting is often seen as a solution to a particular employee's commuting problem, rather than as part of business strategy. Managers often confuse telecommuting with virtual organizations, and assume that extensive telecommuting will lead to an amorphous organization and reduce the ability of mangers to control the organization. Because communication with co-workers and managers plays a major role in organizations, managers fear that widespread telecommuting will disrupt established communications channels and lead to a breakdown of communications across the organization. Studies have focused on the lack of social contact and the dangers of anonymity as negative social consequences of telecommuting, and the reduction of gridlock on highways and urban sprawl as positive social consequences. Telecommuting is often used on a limited scale to meet the requirements of a few employees for flexible work schedules, rather than on a large

scale for all employees. Most telecommuting programs mandate office attendance for a few days each week to maintain the human touch.

One view of telecommuting is that individual autonomy is enhanced and family relationships are enriched when employees are allowed to work away from the confines of the office. This view is prevalent because CMC technology limits the level of control and interaction. This creates a very different work environment for the telecommuter and the employee at the office. Managers are advised to shift their focus from managing employee time to results of the employee's work. This makes managing employees more difficult, since it is easier to check attendance and physical presence in the workplace, than it is to monitor the quality and quantity of work, especially in a knowledge-oriented workplace. Many reports and web sites have proposed telecommuting as the future of the workplace. The other view is that ongoing improvements in CMC technology, and changes in the workplace, will create an environment for telecommuters that is not very different from that of the office. Improvements to CMC technology have made it possible to exercise a significant degree of control over telecommuting employees, and the shift to knowledge work has made it more feasible to manage telecommuting employees effectively. However, merely providing the technology does not ensure its acceptance or its effective and widespread usage. A longitudinal study of desktop videoconferencing conducted by Webster in 1998 shows that social influences, experience with the medium, fit to the job, and ease of use resulted in acceptance, while a failure on these factors caused a low level of usage/nonusage. This study argues that universal access is a prerequisite for new media usage, since a lack of access to the new media for some employees positions the new CMC tool as one of limited reach, in the minds of employees, and discourages widespread usage of the tool. This means that access to the CMC tools and good training must be provided to the employees in order to make the tool widely used.

II. INFORMATION PROCESSING JOBS

Jobs in which the primary inputs and outputs are information can be performed effectively by telecommuters. Jobs that involve the production of tangible goods or services, requiring physical raw material, are more difficult to telecommute. An assembly line task involving physical material handling and specialized machines cannot be telecommuted. However, the shift in the economy from manufacturing to services, and an increasing emphasis on information processing, means that most of the jobs in the new economy can be telecommuted with the right CMC tools. In the same manufacturing plant the jobs of the product designers, production planners, forecasters, and many others can be telecommuted. Data collection devices can record parameters from various locations to capture quality, production, labor usage, and other information. These data can be provided in real time to employees via the information system. The development of enterprise requirements planning (ERP) systems has placed most of the numbers needed by the managers of the organization at their fingertips. While the numbers may fail to capture valuable shop floor data, that is not because of an inherent incapability of the ERP system; rather it is because the systems have been designed to capture too few of the parameters, or capture them erroneously, due to measurement instrument biases. Often the instruments are designed to capture easily quantifiable data and fail to capture, record, or transmit subjective data. This is a shortcoming of most ERP systems and the problem with management by numbers. This problem is not unique to telecommuters, since managers in the office who receive their data via the ERP are in the same situation. The telecommuting employee must have access to a rich set of multimedia data. This includes the quantified data available via the ERP system, text messages via e-mail, public and private chat rooms, and threaded discussion groups, as well as voice and video interaction with shop floor employees. Many of the jobs, even in a manufacturing environment, can be effectively telecommuted if CMC tools provide all of these features.

For example, a quality control system can capture the quality test results and provide the manager with the number of items sampled, the number defective, and the batch size. However, it does not provide the manager with related data that may be used for effective control, such as employee absenteeism and skills available in a separate database. A good ERP is designed to overcome this limitation and provide all the quantitative data via the computer. This still does not address employee morale, which may be judged by talking to the employees, observing their interactions and work habits, and viewing the physical condition of the shop floor. The CMC for effective telecommuting must include tools to support all of these features. If the quality manager interviews employees on a regular basis and uses an on-line chat room with live videoconferencing where needed, he will have the qualitative data needed to make a quality assessment. Telecommuting programs need to ensure that all of the employee's data needs are met.

A. Telecommuting for Manufacturing

Telecommuting can be applied to the production of physical goods or the provision of information services on a piece rate basis by independent contractors working at home. In some cases these individuals are part-time employees of the organization and work on a contract basis. The use of part-time employees or independent contractors impacts the quality of the work, employee loyalty, and organization structure. The primary focus of this section is on the use of information systems to support CMC for telecommuting by full-time employees of the organization. However, the issues discussed here can be applied to contract and part-time employees. Many telecommuters are in fact independent contractors or part-time employees. The reasons for this are that these individuals have the most to benefit and the least to lose from telecommuting. Since they often do not work a complete 8-hour workday, the proportion of time spent on commuting to work is excessive, and they save significantly from telecommuting. Since they are not full-time employees, they do not have many of the perks of the job, such as a nice office or established relationships with co-workers, that they would lose by telecommuting.

B. Telecommuting Case Study

A company that provides marketing and sample distribution services for the pharmaceutical industry implemented a successful 4-year telecommuting program, in which 24% of the workforce of 150 persons telecommuted by 1998. This study by Watad and DiSanzo showed that since the jobs were primarily information-based tasks, the telecommuting employees could successfully perform their jobs at remote locations over an extended period of time. The company reengineered many processes to meet the needs of telecommuting employees. Paper-based procedures were converted to automated procedures and voice communications were replaced with on-line communications. This study also shows that telecommuting does not necessarily reduce the amount of travel. Many of the telecommuting employees were salespeople who contacted clients and telecommuting enabled them to meet clients more often. Total travel did not decline. It was reallocated to meeting customers more frequently.

III. PREDICTIONS ABOUT TELECOMMUTING

A review of the history of telecommuting shows many predictions of the coming boom in telecommuting that have been largely unfulfilled. Although technology has been a problem in the past, the recent improvement in Internet and related technologies for CMC have made telecommuting technically and economically feasible. However, many organizational issues need to be addressed as part of a successful telecommuting program for an organization.

The Bureau of Labor Statistics (BLS) notes that federal worker telecommuting levels are seen to have leveled off at 25,000, well short of a 60,000 goal in 1999, and only 4% of workers said that they report for fewer hours at the office as a result of telecommuting. Use of the Internet to work at home has increased due to an increase in the number of work hours rather than in a reduction of the number of commutes. A study of telecommuters in the U.S. South by Gupta, Karimi, and Somers was based on a sample of 363 individuals and showed that the use of telecommuting was stronger among those with higher education levels and higher age. Females used it more than males, and it was more likely to be used in the knowledge-based industries such as finance and real-estate than mining or manufacturing. The study supports the view that knowledge-based jobs are more likely to be telecommuted, and employees who are familiar with the organization through more years of experience are more likely to use telecommuting as an alternative to a long commute. Many current users of telecommuting are small-office/home-office (SOHO) owners who use telework to avoid a daily commute to an office and save the cost of maintaining an office outside the home. While many jobs can be telecommuted and many individuals state a preference to telecommute, actual use of telecommuting lags behind stated preference for telecommuting. Mokhtarian and Solomon point out that a good forecast of telecommuting levels must be based not on stated preferences to telecommute, but on behavioral models. These must include preferences for working at home, technical support, loss of co-worker companionship, managerial views, and employee attitudes. Forecasts of telecommuting will be incorrect if these factors are not built into the forecast models. Telecommuting levels remain low even though many jobs are knowledge based and can be effectively telecommuted using available CMC tools. Kaifa and Davidson studied the reason for low levels of telecommuting usage and present the argument that behavioral attitudes of the parties involved, per-ceived consequences of telecommuting, social factors, and facilitating conditions drive the decision to telecommute. Technology is seen in this study as only a facilitating condition and not sufficient to cause employees to telecommute. Behavioral attitudes are shaped by industry and regional standards. Telecommuting is accepted in Silicon Valley, but it is not as widely accepted in other parts of the country. Hence predictions of telecommuting need to take into account regional preferences, and the growth that occurs in one area may not occur in other areas.

IV. TECHNICAL ISSUES

The technical challenge facing a telecommuting program is the provision of effective CMC for remote employees. This means the provision of parallel, multimodal communication channels between remote users and the office. Parallel channels need to be provided so that telecommuting employees are not limited to a single link to the main office. This does not necessarily mean redundant lines; it refers to separate channels. Technology such as DSL on home telephone lines permits multiple communication links on the same line. An employee can talk on the phone and work on the computer at the same time. Satisfactory assistance often requires multiple computer links for multiple services. Rich communication is multimodal. Employees discuss matters using conversations, gestures, diagrams, and models. Hence the CMC for telecommuting must support rich communication. A detailed study of e-mail use among 36 teleworkers in a software company in Japan by Higa, Liu, Shin, and Figuerdo shows that strong management support and employee perception of e-mail as a rich communication medium are factors supporting perceived productivity gains. Early e-mail adopters developed emoticons to enrich the text medium available for e-mail. Attachments, including voice files and sketches, are now available with e-mail. Employees can use these features to conduct rich on-line communications with co-workers and managers. The technical issue facing IS is to provide for the use of these attachments and the development and adoption of standards for these features.

A. Home Personal Computer Installation

Although many employees in knowledge jobs already possess a PC at home, effective telecommuting programs need to ensure that the PC at home has the capability to run the required programs. A PC running a different version of the OS will not look and feel exactly like the one at work and the resulting confusion can cause numerous problems. For example, a large screen on the office workstation may show the complete application screen, while a lower resolution and smaller screen at home may cut off a part of the application's screen. Large client applications may not run fast enough on the home PC and licensing limitations may restrict giving the employee a copy of the client application to install on a home computer. Some organizations give powerful laptops to employees and provide docking stations at work to ensure that the same interface is available at home and work. This avoids reinstallation of the software and limits the number of licenses required since the same machine is used at home and the office. Adequate support for the office PC and the home PC is necessary for telecommuting programs to be successful.

An employee working on a program needing assistance is generally at a disadvantage when working at a remote location. At the office a co-worker with the right skills can walk the employee through the steps to fix the program at the employee's desktop PC. Online the same assistance requires PC screen mirroring software, which in turn requires a working (not frozen) PC to function. Telecommuters need to be trained to use manuals and fix problems on their own. Telecommuters will place a greater demand on the network bandwidth and support. A Gartner group study shows that remote users generate four times more network and security help requests than office workers. The bandwidth problem is greater for telecommuters since many of the applications will work more slowly than at the office.

B. Telecommunications Link

Early telecommuting programs provided voice-grade telephone lines and analog modems to link the remote employee's computer to the office network. The bandwidth limitations of these early systems restricted the communication to e-mail and Telnet to remote systems. It was difficult to maintain this link reliably for the entire workday. Many studies of telecommuting cost-effectiveness focused on the cost of providing this link and the related productivity enhancement. ISDN (Integrated Services Digital Network) provided the first reliable digital links via phone lines. The system had many configuration complexities and never became a significant method of providing digital links to the home. The delivery of a robust digital link for the last mile, the link from the branch office to the

home, remained a problem for many years and stalled many telecommuting programs.

Two currently popular approaches to providing digital links for the last mile are DSL (Digital Subscriber Lines) and cable modems. DSL uses existing telephone wiring, and conditioning of the line to provide bandwidths of up to 512 Kbps to the home. However, the technology works only for a short hop from the branch office to the home and is dependent on the quality of the wiring. After many stumbling blocks DSL services are slowly being rolled out across the country. Cable modems use the coaxial cable delivering TV to the home. This cable is intrinsically capable of much higher bandwidth than telephone wires. The problem here is that cable wiring is designed to broadcast multiple TV channels to all the households in a loop. This means that the individual user does not have a private line to the branch office; rather the individual shares the cable bandwidth with other customers in the loop. As a result available bandwidth varies with the number of users on a loop. Both technologies do provide vastly improved bandwidth to users and eliminate the need to make the connection required with analog telephone lines. This means that maintaining a broadband connection to an office for the entire workday (or longer) is no longer a challenging feat in much of the country.

A third approach does away with the wires altogether by using wireless access. Because communications between the user and the central office are very bursty in nature, the bandwidth in a dedicated connection is used only for short intervals. Hence, a well-designed system can manage to provide continuous links using a shared wireless link.

C. Internet-Based Telecommuting

The Internet and net-based applications have become a reliable and global platform for business and individual interaction. IS managers now have a readily available suite of hardware and software that can be used to set up CMC for telecommuting employees. These systems satisfy corporate security and reliability standards while providing links to corporate software and facilitating rich interaction between employees and managers.

Many of the latest enterprise software applications have been designed to work on the Internet. In the past telecommuting employees had to log on to the corporate information systems via a telephone modem and a remote access application such as Telnet or RAS. These remote access systems were slow and often lacked proper security features. Many of these applications did not offer encryption to secure passwords and mission-critical data transported over the public network. Client/server systems need complex client software containing business processes to be loaded on to the user's home machine. This restricted telecommuting since IS managers raised security, licensing, and maintenance concerns. The maintenance of client software became a major issue even for client machines on the local-area network (LAN), and products such as Terminal Server and Citrix Metaframe allowed centralized servers to deliver the client application on demand, to client workstations via a thin client. This meant that the user's machine only had a small software program that allowed screen displays, navigation, and data entry, while the major part of the client software with the business processes worked on a centralized server. The server ran multiple instances of the client and delivered the screens to the user's machines. Proprietary technologies gave way to the web browser as the thin client application and made implementation of remote access from the telecommuter's home simple. Newer ERP applications are being designed with web browser access as the primary user interface. This makes telecommuting extremely simple to manage from a technical standpoint. The extensive cost–benefit analysis for establishing and maintaining remote access has become less necessary since the system is already web enabled and broadband net access has dropped to under $50 per month.

Ubiquitous and broadband net links for the last mile make it simpler to provide anytime and anyplace access to remote employees. The Wireless Access Protocol (WAP) allows appliances to talk to net-based servers using a common set of communication standards. The permits a user to view and enter robust information via a variety of devices such as cell phones, PDAs, and laptops. The need to be at a physical location to ensure the receipt and transmission of accurate information is lifted and telecommuting becomes more feasible.

D. Telecommuting Security Issues

Many corporate IS managers hesitate to open up their systems to the Internet because of security concerns. Good security policy enforcement is essential for all information systems, whether they are limited to the office network or allow for net-based access. Some telework programs like one at the California Franchise Tax Board have required that employees work at remote telework centers rather than at home to minimize security risks and the City of Los Angeles issued smart cards to telecommuters who accessed personnel and payroll data from home. As corporate IS managers realize the seriousness of internal threats and the need for establishing and maintaining good security in all systems, the risks posed via net-based access diminish. The use of virtual private networks (VPNs) rather than dial-up connections, or open Internet connections, improves security by creating a secure tunnel for traffic between the teleworker and the organization. However, this does pose a major configuration problem for IS departments. VPNs do not automatically eliminate the security problem, since a compromise of the home computer itself can lead to a breakdown of security. This is especially true if the home computer is connected to a DSL line and is open to hacker attacks. Remote users must set up a firewall between the computer and the DSL line/Internet. The home system should be set up by the IS department rather than by the user to ensure that security precautions and standards are met.

E. Information Systems Department Support for Telecommuting

The IS department needs to consider the problem of linking a very large number of devices to the corporate network as telecommuting becomes widespread. The sheer number of IP addresses used by mobile, home, and office computers creates a shortage of IP addresses. While the IP2 standards will alleviate this by making many more IP addresses available, current systems need to ration out addresses and dynamic IP addressing needs to be supported in many cases. This is in many cases an added burden for IS departments when telecommuting programs are put in place.

The technology used for a telecommuting program must be reliable and robust. Bleeding edge technology can and will have bugs that cause disillusionment with telecommuters, their mangers, co-workers, and customers. The software applications and business processes need to be developed and modified to meet the needs of telecommuting. A business that uses an ERP for its financial, production, human resources (HR), and sales management needs to web enable the applications so that telecommuting employees can "view" the system data from remote locations. This is not limited to the specific application they use for their job. All applications and procedures that are used must be available to the telecommuting employee. An employee in sales may use order and customer data most of the time. However, production schedules may be reviewed just once a day, and payroll and HR information from the HRIS accessed once a month. If only one part of the system is web enabled and the other parts that may be used on a intermittent basis are not available from home, the employee will feel cut out of the loop and prefer to be at "work" to ensure the availability of all tools. Often telecommuting programs are designed for one employee and limit the availability of information to the primary task performed by the employee. Technology to web enable applications is fast becoming standard because the deployment, upgrade, and maintenance of client applications has increased the total cost of operations (TCO) significantly. The TCO of managing client software has further increased with the spread of IS applications into all areas of the business and increasing use across the organization. This has led IS to seriously focus on developing and deploying web-based applications that almost eliminate the TCO for client workstations. A fully web enabled application suite requires only a compatible browser to be operating on the user's workstation. Telecommuting is very easy to implement if the IT department has already web enabled all applications. In that case the only roadblock to remote access is the issue of security for web-based access, and the movement from an Intranet to the Internet for client access.

F. Cost of Technical Support for Telecommuting

Watad and DiSanzo classify the technology improvements into three categories or layers. The first layer is the development of network systems including hardware and software to ensure the complete reach of PCs/workstations to the desktop, network administration, and training in end-user applications. In their study they calculate this to be the largest cost factor amounting to more than $28,000 per employee over a 4-year period. However, note that this cost will be incurred even if the employees do not telecommute, since it is the cost of maintaining a LAN in the office, and providing today's knowledge worker with all the necessary information at the desktop. The second layer is the telecommuting technology and includes the cost of remote communications such as laptops, teleworker training, remote access software, and security systems. They calculate this to be $9000 per telecommuter over a 4-year period. Finally, layer 3 refers to the development of remote sales force applications and this is calculated to be $7000 per telecommuter over a 4-year period.

An earlier survey of 1000 large companies by Forrester Research calculated the cost to a company to support a telecommuter to be $4000 for setup and over $2000 for annual maintenance. Many companies have robust legacy systems that provide the necessary information and do not plan to replace these systems with web-enabled applications. In this situation the IS department needs to configure remote access technology and contract for remote access. User system configuration, network enhancements, security, and troubleshooting take significant time and effort. Often the IS departments may lack the skills to manage this operation. The complexities of managing telecommuting have caused many IS departments to turn to application service providers (ASPs) to manage the telecommuting operation.

V. ECONOMIC ISSUES

Economic costs associated with telecommuting include the cost of providing the telecommunications link, hardware at the remote site, installing and maintaining the CMC system at the office to support telecommuting, and training for managers and employees. In the past the cost associated with providing a second telephone line or upgrading it to digital lines was significant enough to reduce the economic benefits of telecommuting. Moore's law has impacted not only processors, but all components of networking. Configuration and maintenance of an ISDN link often ran to more than a couple of hundred dollars a month and cost–benefit analyses had to take this into account. The decreasing cost and increasing performance capabilities of computer hardware and networking have made the cost of providing home office links far less than the commuting cost for employees. Hence the telecommunications link cost has become an almost insignificant part of the total cost of telecommuting. Unlike in the past, extensive cost computations for this component are unnecessary. Hardware requirements at the remote site are also minimal. Because most new applications are web based and even older applications are being web enabled, all the user needs is a browser and a link to the Internet. PC costs are continually declining and PCs are fast becoming appliances. Web-enabled systems reduce the need to maintain a dedicated client application on the user's machine.

A. Training Costs for Telecommuters

Significant costs are associated with training employees and mangers for telecommuting. This component has outstripped the direct hardware and telecommunications link costs. Employees who telecommute need to be good at motivating themselves and maintaining a focus on the job. They need to know how to separate home and work. They must learn to use CMC tools to maintain their relationships with co-workers. The organization needs to profile the employees to find out their aptitude for successful telecommuting and provide them with up-front and ongoing training that deals with these issues. The training programs start with tests and interviews with the employees to find out the reasons for telecommuting and their approach to work. This is followed by an educational program that highlights the need for organizing the workday and techniques for doing that when not working at the office. A BLS study shows that employers provided between 8 and 15 hours of training for telecommuters. This is insufficient for managing a long-term telecommuting program. In most cases this time can be used to review only the technical issues regarding the use of remote access technology.

An employee who has problems coming to work on time may present a case for telecommuting by arguing that the elimination of commute time will enable the employee to put in the necessary hours. However, the reason for not coming to work on time may be a poor work ethic or problems at home. Offering telecommuting to this employee will exacerbate this problem since the need to get started on time diminishes, and the domestic problems get worse interfering not only with coming to work but with the entire day's work.

B. Training Program Features

The training program must monitor the productivity and job satisfaction of the employee over time. New intervention programs may be needed to keep the employee on track. The managers of telecommuting employees need a similar program to enable them to manage the telecommuting employee. The program for managers focuses on the special needs of the telecommuting employee and ways for managers to evaluate the work performance of the telecommuting employee. Since telecommuting employees cannot be directly observed, traditional measures for performance measurement such as attendance do not work very well. It must be noted that the continuing improvement in CMC tools makes remote monitoring possible and the employee can be required to log in and connect a video camera to the home PC. This will enable the manager to "see" the employee at work. These improvements in CMC do not mean that training is unnecessary for the manager and the employee.

The training needs to go into the effective use of these tools and the impact of these tools on perceptions. The organization needs to establish a policy regarding telecommuting and acquaint managers and employees with the details of this policy.

High costs are associated with telecommuting if the telecommuting employees or their managers and co-workers are unable to use the CMC technology. This can cause problems in work quality and customer perceptions. Typically telecommuting has been used by back-office employees, such as those in the IS department, and the customers affected have often been internal customers. These internal customers have been the managers and co-workers of the telecommuting employee. However, as telecommuting moves into jobs that deal with customers, such as call center employees, the effect on customer perceptions of the service needs to be measured. A poorly managed telecommuting operation that results in customers receiving poor quality or unprofessional service can have a serious cost effect.

A help center employee who telecommutes from home must make sure that a customer calling for assistance gets quality help, delivered in a professional manner. A noisy telephone line and interference from family present a very poor interface to the customer. The employee must be able to access all the records necessary from the home office and transfer the call to other employees at any location in a seamless manner. Business processes need to be studied to understand the impact of telecommuting on the performance of the job.

On the other hand, a well-managed telecommuting operation can have a positive effect on quality. An empirical study of 316 telecommuters working for 18 companies in Europe, by Venkatesh and Speier, showed that supervisor characteristics, employees, tasks, work environment, management support, and technical issues were the six major factors for the success of telecommuting programs. Employees freed from arduous daily commutes can focus more of their efforts toward customer satisfaction. Telecommuting works well for customer-focused jobs where employees deal directly with customers. The employee may in many cases go directly to the customer's site to deliver a service and need not be burdened with a daily office commute. Reporting tasks, job assignments, and interaction with managers can be carried out using CMC tools. The commute is not eliminated, rather the commuting effort is directed toward enhancing customer satisfaction. The telecommuting program needs to calculate the costs involved to the company from all of these factors when judging the total cost of the telecommuting operation.

C. Economic Benefit Studies

The economic benefits of telecommuting are reductions in commuting costs and office space costs and compliance with urban pollution control laws in some areas. The elimination of commuting time and travel cost is a major benefit to telecommuters. Significant savings in office space in prime urban areas and pollution control programs in some urban areas support telecommuting programs that reduce commuter traffic at peak hours. Many regional agencies, such as Telework Colorado, promote telecommuting to reduce traffic and pollution. The federal government's reports on telecommuting by the U.S.-GSA on August 2, 2000, and October 8, 2000, focus on the commuting time savings and the savings in energy usage and traffic as a result of telecommuting. Many of the web sites promoting telecommuting focus on the environmental benefits of telecommuting, especially the reduction of commuter traffic. However, studies have shown that most telecommuters today do not eliminate their commutes. They shift their commuting to direct contact with the customer from travel to the home office. One study shows that 6.1% of the workforce telecommutes with 1.5% of these individuals telecommuting on any given day. Because telecommuters run other errands, the total reduction of vehicle miles was calculated to be less than 1% in a study conducted in 1998.

1. Commute Time

Commute time in large metropolitan areas can easily run to more than a couple of hours a day and this has provided the major incentive to employees' desire to telecommute. The cost of driving or taking public transit and more importantly the opportunity cost of the lost commuting time provides the major cost benefit to telecommuters. Enhancements to user interfaces, reduction in size and increased portability of hardware, and the growth of wireless alternatives to wired networks has worked toward decreasing the opportunity cost of lost commute time. When commuters can use a laptop to work on their proposals or write code on a commuter train, they find a way to use this otherwise "lost" time effectively. Cell phones allow commuters to stay in touch with their co-workers and customers, thereby making it possible to use some of their commute time. Voice input devices have made it very convenient to work while on the move, even though they endanger the safety of both the commuter and other travelers. The ability to work while on the move has reduced the net benefit derived from

commuting time savings. Employees often avail themselves of telecommuting programs to stay at home and take care of family members needing attention such as children or sick relatives. While this does provide a benefit to the telecommuter in the form of savings of caregiver costs they do impose a burden on the employee, and could affect the performance level of the telecommuting employee. Hence, this approach to telecommuting has been used only sporadically and accounts for the large number of telecommuters who telecommute less than 1 day a week.

2. Office Costs

Office space costs are significant in major metropolitan areas, amounting to more than $50,000 per employee in some areas. The reduction in office space from an effective telecommuting program is a clear and measurable benefit to the organization. While most telecommuting programs require a few days a month of physical presence in the office, this space can be rotated among employees to reduce the need to have dedicated space for each employee. For example, if an office allows 10% of its employees to telecommute, and no more than half of them need dedicated office space at any time, there is a 5% reduction in necessary office space. Watad and DiSanzo calculate cost benefits for a telecommuting project, and show that real estate savings can add up to meet half the cost of running the program. IBM saves 40% to 60% of real estate costs for its sites by limiting office space to only essential employees and Northern Telecom estimates $2000 per person per year savings in real estate costs from telecommuting.

3. Pollution Control

Urban pollution control programs aim to reduce smog levels in cities, caused by commuter traffic, and some urban areas notably Los Angeles and Phoenix, Arizona, have programs aimed at reducing traffic during rush hours. Telecommuting programs have helped many large organizations meet these goals, by reducing the number of employees driving to the downtown offices during rush hour. The federal Clean Air Act mandates that large companies in areas that do not meet clean air standards must develop an Employee Commute Options Plan. Telecommuting is one of the many ways to meet these standards. The average passenger occupancy (APO) is calculated as the ratio of employees reporting for the 6 A.M. to 10:00 A.M. shift to the number of vehicles used. Telecommuters reduce this number, since a telecommuter is counted as an employee who arrives for the shift, but does not use a car. Such programs have not been very successful, given the desire of most metropolitan areas to encourage job growth, at the expense of traffic and gridlock. As a result these programs have had a very limited impact on the establishment of telecommuting programs outside a few metropolitan areas.

4. Reengineering

Finally, companies that institute major telecommuting programs can benefit from improvements that reengineer procedures and enhance efficiency. A reengineered reporting system that permits salespeople to report contacts when recording client interaction and uses this for performance appraisal can ease the reporting burden of filing separate contact and performance reports. The development of intranet-based applications with visibility provided via the intranet to other related applications often provides a convenient starting point for a telecommuting program. A study by El Sawy *et al.* of 400 field sales employees who access sales data from customer sites via laptops shows that in-house applications designed to foster greater integration of disparate systems can support an effective telecommuting program. The same study also shows how the use of CMC technology to set up on-line meetings that bring together potential customers and suppliers to design new products can be used for telecommuting. Mangers will learn to use the information system to monitor employees more effectively only when telecommuting becomes pervasive in the organization. Automatic logs of client meetings, times, and sales data, will allow a manger to view reports on sales activities and ensure quality performance. Better data collection mechanisms allow an organization to use data mining and detect patterns in performance that might have remained invisible for a long time.

VI. ORGANIZATIONAL ISSUES

In spite of these technical and economic advantages, productivity gains from telecommuting have been noted in only a few studies, and even the gains that have been documented have not been adequately demonstrated to be sustainable in the long run. Many of the studies that have shown gains in productivity have been conducted by communications companies that actively promote telecommuting and not by independent researchers. US West reported that telecommuter productivity increased by as much as 40%, and reported savings of $4000–$21,000 per telecommuter in office space costs. Additionally the study showed that telecommuting contributed to reduced absenteeism and supported the retention of qualified individuals who might otherwise have sought employment elsewhere. A good telecommuting program should enhance employee morale and lead to higher job satisfaction. A recent study by AT&T and ITAC showed that more than half of teleworkers report higher job satisfaction after beginning to work from home. Only 7% of those surveyed reported less job satisfaction after beginning to work at home. While this study was conducted by a council that is a strong advocate of telecommuting, analysis of these studies shows that the numbers have steadily increased with better CMC tools and more information-oriented jobs. The AT&T study also showed that in many cases the employees were supportive of telecommuting while employers did not offer the program. IBM claims a 15–40% productivity improvement and Hewlett Packard doubled its revenue per salesperson after moving its salespeople to visit customers' workplaces. One of the key incentives for business to try out telecommuting is the need to hold on to a valuable employee who moves out of town. The tight labor market provides a strong incentive to hold on to a valuable employee so managers end up trying out a pilot telecommuting program. In fact, many reports of successful telecommuting refer to the retention of a valuable employee who needed to move out of the region. Success here leads to more such openings.

A. Reasons for Failure

Why could a telecommuting program fail to provide these benefits? Often failures are due to organizational issues such as employee motivation at remote sites, the management of remote personnel, workplace ergonomics and the home work environment, and interpersonal relations between telecommuting employees and on-site employees.

1. Organizational Learning Losses

The loss of organizational learning is often cited as a problem with telecommuting. While on-line communities have been created for a variety of topics, and telecommuters can create and access the communities, true organizational learning often occurs during shared problem-solving exercises. Goodman and Darr have shown that a computer-aided problem-solving system is only capable of eliciting simple solutions, and not very successful in helping solve problems requiring high levels of tacit knowledge. Their study shows that communities with well-specified and narrow niches work more effectively than organization wide communities. Telecommuting programs need to support the creation of focused problem-solving communities to ensure that organizational learning is not hampered by the lack of physical proximity among employees.

2. Employee Motivation

Employee self-motivation is essential for telecommuting and the employee must meet the psychological profile for effective work at home since interaction is constrained by the technology. While studies show many telecommuters reporting an improvement in productivity when working outside the traditional office, the improvements are generally not sustained in the long run. While improvements in technology can provide for monitoring and motivation via multimodal, multimedia interfaces in the future, the link between the manager, co-workers, and employee are sufficiently restrictive today and require a high level of employee self-motivation. When employees commute to an office there is a clear separation between home and work and between personal time and work time. Monitoring the workplace is a supervisory activity and, combined with peer pressure in the workplace, makes the employee perform at an acceptable level. The flip side of this problem is the failure to stop working, with some telecommuters becoming workaholics who are unable to "get home." Some telecommuting sites recommend the use of a computer-generated alarm that starts and stops work by the telecommuter to create the feel of a managed workplace. There is a high attrition rate of telecommuters and more than 50% give up full-time telecommuting after 9 months. Most telecommuters commute no more than 1 day a week.

The major problem faced by telecommuters when the link was limited to a slow and often less than 56 Kbps telephone modem was that there was no pressure to start work or work at an accepted pace. Employees with limited ability to motivate themselves found their output slowing down and having a negative impact on performance appraisals. Workplace motivation arises from the distinctive "feel" of the workday, and from environmental, co-worker, and supervisory influence. The availability of convenient tools to monitor employee performance makes it possible for managers to check on—and influence—employee work patterns from a remote setting. The same is true for chat rooms and on-line meetings with co-workers. However, until the technology improves further, telecommuting employees will need to motivate themselves more effectively than employees who are in an office. Tools have been developed that can support time management and reporting work hours for teleworkers and that allow managers to plan and monitor telecommuting employees. These tools can integrate with workflow management software, and extend process management to telecommuters.

B. Strategic Benefits from Telecommuting

Senior executives considering telecommuting as part of corporate policy need to consider the program as part of the employee benefit package. Companies with telecommuting programs can attract and retain key employees in a tight labor market. However, they need to understand and evaluate the cost and benefits of managing the cultural changes in the organization, and the technical issues in implementing a successful telecommuting program. An analysis by Gainey, Kelley, and Hill of the impact of long-term and broad-based telecommuting recommends that managers do the following before implementing a telecommuting program. They must first identify corporate culture and see if it is heavily dependent on social interaction. They must monitor the strength of corporate culture and identify its specific norms. Managers need to consider the impact of telecommuting for new employees if the corporation puts new employees through a period of intense training/learning/socialization where they are indoctrinated into the corporate culture. Finally, managers need to watch for cultural transformations that take place among the employees since telecommuting employees may spend less to no time at the office. The main idea of this analysis is that managers cannot consider telecommuting as nothing more than a van pool for employees. It can lead to significant cultural changes in the organization.

C. Manager Training and Skills

Managers need training on how to use available technology to create a remote work environment that provides the motivational support offered by the office environment. This includes managerial observation and feedback about performance on a regular basis and extensive interaction with co-workers to enhance creativity in problem solving and learning new skills.

In most scenarios, managers are less aware and fluent in CMC than employees, since they were educated and trained in a non-IT environment. This means that they need to learn how to manage telecommuting employees effectively, and they are generally not fluent in the required technologies. The telecommuter achieves benefits from telecommuting through a reduction in commute time and cost, and the option of meeting home work/care needs. The organization benefits from a reduced need for office space and ability to hire/retain a skilled employee. The manager does not directly benefit from telecommuting. Often the manager is forced to learn new technologies and use them for remote management. The learning includes the technical skills and the more important managerial skills for managing with CMC technology.

From a technical standpoint managers need to know how to use computer log files to identify employee attendance and activities. In the physical office managers use attendance data and employee activities to measure performance. These measures can be more conveniently tracked in cyberspace if the managers know how to use the right tools. In a classroom professors evaluate student class participation using attendance, interaction in classroom discussions, and other related activities. In the on-line classroom there are automatic logs of system usage and all the comments by each student in the discussion groups can be evaluated at any time. The on-line class retains a permanent log of all contributions made by the student and the relevance and originality can be judged very effectively. The professors need to learn how to access and analyze this rich source of information. Training in the use of these class management and evaluation tools become a key to running the on-line course effectively. The same is true of a telecommuting program. "Invisible" workers are more difficult to manage than "visible" workers.

Improvements in employee and managerial abilities in using CMC tools has led to a decline in the problems of isolation and communications problems for telecommuters. A study of 170 telecommuters and 60 conventional workers in nine organizations showed that there is not a significant statistical difference in overall satisfaction with office communication, managerial ability to evaluate performance, keeping up with office gossip, belonging to a team, or getting help with co-workers. While this study by Watson-Fritz, Narasimhan, and Rhee does not demonstrate any improvements with telecommuting, it does show that there are no major problems with communication for telecommuters. This study however deals with telecommuters who mostly work 1, 2, or less than 1 day a week out of their homes and the effect of telecommuter isolation may be weak due to the intermittent nature of telecommuting.

D. Job Selection for Telecommuting

Jobs with a high degree of task identity are those that are completely accomplished by a single individual. Such jobs can be effectively judged based on measured output. The manager need not monitor all the inputs to the job, rather the output can be measured and job performance evaluated. This type of job is very suited to telecommuting. The employee works alone, at a remote site, and the performance is measured based on the output. A clerical employee who transcribes medical records is a good example of such a job. The number of lines transcribed and the error rate are measures of performance. However, many jobs require teamwork and it is difficult to measure the output of a poorly monitored and remotely located employee. What was the contribution in the team discussion or the type of help given to co-workers? These evaluations are made by managers and based on their observations in personal meetings and casual conversations with employees. While the availability of better technologies for monitoring remote work eases this problem, most managers are not well trained in using these tools for measuring the performance of remote employees. Telecommuters are generally evaluated like contract employees based on measured outputs. These jobs generally have no career advancement. Employees who telecommute find that they are locked out of growth opportunities and remain at the same level.

E. Home Office Standards

1. Workplace Ergonomics

Workplace ergonomics contributes to improved productivity and the remote work environment must be properly monitored to ensure quality and output. The manufacturing sector has paid a great deal of attention to workplace ergonomics to ensure high productivity, quality, and safety. While offices have not emphasized workplace design to the same level, most modern offices are designed to enhance employee morale, work quality, and safety. Filing cabinets are selected to improve record filing, safety, and retrieval. Cubicles are designed to promote the desired level of interaction, privacy, and comfort. These are not trivial issues and studies have shown the importance of workplace design on productivity, quality, safety, and morale. It is therefore not a trivial issue for telecommuting. Business needs to ensure that the home workplace design meets the requirements for productivity, quality, safety, and morale. The Occupational Safety and Health Administration issued a ruling (http://www.osha-slc.gov/OshDoc/Directive_data/CPL_2-0_125.html) requiring employers to ensure safety of the home workplace and be liable for any defects. An uproar over these regulations led to their being rescinded in a couple of days. While the ruling had some serious problems such as making an employer liable for a faulty basement ladder in the employee's home, the core concept of ensuring a safe, productive, quality-focused, morale supportive environment is an important issue for telecommuting. It is generally a good practice to ensure that a telecommuter has a separate work area (a room), which can simulate the "at work" experience. This means a room with a office decor, furniture, and privacy.

A company can provide preapproved PCs and contract for high-speed lines to ensure a viable link between the telecommuter, manger, co-workers, and customers. The company can make recommendations for furniture and lighting to ensure a safe and comfortable workplace. Data storage technology can be provided to ensure that data losses and corruption are eliminated or in the worst case minimized. The need for good workplace design does not stop at the office and telecommuters need to make sure that the home office is a suitable place for quality work.

2. Work Environment

Telecommuters in many cases choose to work at home so that they can meet child care or other home care requirements. Such a work environment is often unsuited to high-quality work. Constant interruptions and multiple demands on the employee can make telecommuting very stressful. Telecommuters need to get child or home care for their dependents during their work hours and home care is a poor reason for approving telecommuting work agreements. Telecommuting programs need to monitor employee home-work conditions through interviews and ongoing performance appraisals to ensure that the home-work environment has not deteriorated to unacceptable levels. An unfriendly work environment at home, due to addition of child care and other tasks for the telecommuter, has reduced the productivity of telecommuting. A study of 199 telecommuters by Dixon in 1998 found that telecommuters and nontelecommuters did not have different

levels of stress. However, the sources of stress were different and the type of stress faced by telecommuters depended on the family structure. Well-managed telecommuting programs helped reduce employee stress. Education for the telecommuting program must provide techniques for the telecommuters to manage family responsibilities, and for the family to understand the dual role of the telecommuter. A study by Venkatesh and Speier shows game-based training facilitates the training process for teleworkers, by increasing users' extrinsic motivation to increase their desire to use technology. Teleworkers and their managers need hands-on training to use new technology. A strong desire to use technology is a prerequisite for a successful telework program, and the training program needs to build that desire on the part of the individuals involved.

F. Telecommuter Isolation

Employees have a need to be accepted by peers as a co-worker, and the lack of micro-flow activities and shared experiences for telecommuters affects their job performance. Many telecommuters feel that they miss out of career advancement due to the loss of interaction, weaker evaluations due to the way job performance is judged, a loss of "inside" information including on-the-job training, and their isolation from the organization. The John J. Heidrich Center for Workforce Development at Rutgers University found that 45% of American workers believed that telecommuting would reduce their chances for career advancement. Satellite offices have been used to counter the isolation of home-based telecommuting. In this approach, small offices are located close to residential areas and equipped with high-quality CMC to the main office. Such *telecenters* permit employees to socialize with some co-workers and work in a social setting rather than the totally isolated home environment.

Telecommuting programs require attendance at the workplace on a periodic basis to maintain the cohesiveness of the team and the organization. It is possible that a more net-savvy workforce in the future and strong support for rich communications in CMC will make the workday more pleasant for the telecommuting employee.

VII. POLICIES FOR TELECOMMUTING

Telecommuting has slowly gained acceptance in many businesses. Rather than full-fledged telecommuters, who work all the time out of their home offices, most telecommuters use it on an intermittent basis. However, the skills gained in utilizing CMC tools to perform remote work enable more telecommuting over a period of time. In many businesses top management may not even realize the extent of telecommuting. Many part-time telecommuters learn how to use e-mail, conference calls, and chat rooms to stay in touch with one another when telecommuting. Managers gain the ability to manage remote employees more effectively over time. Since most of these telecommuting programs are intermittent, with some requirements for office work, the organizational problems that arose from early and full-time telecommuting have been avoided. Simultaneously the improvement in quality of CMC tools and the increasing capabilities of employees and mangers to use these tools effectively has contributed to the viability of long-term telecommuting.

A. Approval Process

The business can allow individual employees on a case-by-case basis to request and gain approval for telecommuting. Many businesses use this approach and require documentation demonstrating need, cost–benefit analysis, and agreements from the employee and the manager before approval. Such an approach restricts telecommuting to employees who have a special need such as family requirements or health issues and are willing to make the extra effort to get approval for telecommuting. Broader telecommuting programs are those that offer training to managers and employees and offer it as part of a commute reduction program, office space savings program, or a systematic organization change program. In these cases the organization actively promotes telecommuting as part of business strategy. This promotion may be because the organization is in the telecommunications business and wants to use its in-house telecommuting program to promote telecommuting as an alternative to other businesses. Many sites dealing with telecommuting are hosted by telecommunications organizations.

The telecommuting program could be critical to the attraction and retention of key employees. Many businesses in Silicon Valley offer telecommuting to attract and retain key employees in a tight labor market. The program can be part of a strategy of placing employees closer to the customer. Rather than have the employee commute to the office and talk to customers over the phone, the employee could work at home and travel to the customer's office to discuss matters. Many telecommuting programs are exploiting the benefits of mobile computing by creating a mobile office and providing connectivity via wireless networks. A framework for telecommuting programs is presented by Kurland and Bailey. This framework classifies these programs into four groups: home-based telecommuting, satellite offices, neighborhood work centers, and mobile work and provides recommendations to mangers on how best to achieve benefits from each of these four classes of telecommuting.

B. Telecommuting Agreement

A good telecommuting program will have a clearly laid out telecommuting agreement, which lays out the requirements for the employee and the supervisory personnel. While many small companies often are reluctant to adopt a formal policy for telecommuting, a good program needs to be based on a formal agreement between the telecommuter, the telecommuter's manager, and the organization. The agreement will lay out rules regarding remote access, security, logging work hours, physical presence in the office, performance appraisal, and program review. While home office inspection is recommended for long-term telecommuting, many employers do not inspect the home office. In some cases the home office inspection is an employee filled-out checklist. This is primarily due to liability problems that could arise if the workplace is inspected by the employer and there are subsequent accidents or other problems at the site. The U.S. Department of the Treasury Telecommuting Agreement is available at http://dothr.ost.dot.gov/ Telecommuting/forms_work_agreements.htm and the U.S. Department of Justice Telecommuting Agreement is available at http://www.usdoj.gov/jmd/ ps/flexiplaceform.htm. The Florida State Employees Telecommuting Agreement is at http://fcn.state. fl.us/dms/hrm/telecom/telagree.html, and the GTE Telecommuter Agreement, *GTE Solutions for Business—GTE Telecommuting Solutions Book,* is available at http://www.gte.com. These documents provide a format for an agreement between an employee and the organization for telecommuting.

VIII. IMPACT OF TELECOMMUTING

Telecommuting is gradually gaining acceptance in the business world and many jobs are at least partially telecommuted. In fact, many employees may not even realize that they are telecommuting, when cell phones, PDAs, and the home computer enable them to do their work, anytime and anyplace. The conventional 8-hour workday is giving way to almost continuous contact with work, and the defining line between work and rest has been shattered. Telecommuting impacts the separation between work and play, the role of central cities, and as it becomes more ingrained in our work habits, it supports the creation of virtual organizations.

A. Labor Issues

The labor issues become more important as a broader pool of the workforce telecommutes. The Fair Labor Standards Act requires keeping good records of work hours, and ensuring compliance with minimum wage legislation. Many telecommuters are professionals, and relatively few will fall below these standards. However, the broadening reach of telecommuting will create situations where organizations will fail to meet these standards. Systems need to be put in place to ensure reliable reporting of work hours. Office safety and work design are other issues that need to be considered as telecommuting moves into the mainstream. Unions have been concerned about telecommuting leading to a dispersal of office workers making it more difficult to organize them. However, this is a sector of the workforce that has not been effectively organized even in concentrated office buildings. Unions have objected to telecommuting and home-based work because they fear that these jobs will essentially convert full-time employees to contract employees paid on a piece-rate basis. An early issue regarding home-based work during the 1970s was over a Depression era law restricting home-based garment manufacturing and women who knit sweaters in Vermont. Unions have generally opposed home-based work over the potential for piece-rate payments, violation of minimum wage laws, and workplace safety regulations. The intrusion of work into leisure time and the 24-by-7 electronic linkages with work conflict with many of the work regulations of unionized shops and are a matter of grave concern for unions.

B. Urban Impact

The impact of telecommuting on central cities has been referred to in the federal report on telecommuting. Since the long commutes are often from suburbs to the central city where major offices are located, telecommuting will reduce the need for centrally located office space. This will accelerate the loss of jobs in the inner cities and eliminate a major source of revenue for central cities. A study of the experience of telecommuting in Europe by Grimes shows that while CMC and widespread network access can reduce the impact of distance from urban areas, and support knowledge work

in rural areas, telecommuting has remained largely a suburban phenomenon, with technology not becoming a substitute for entrepreneurship. This means that merely wiring an area, whether inner cities or rural areas, will not automatically convert them into successful entrepreneurial zones. However, such network access is a prerequisite to economic growth in the knowledge economy. An efficient network supporting rich CMC will reduce the impact of distance and enhance the learning capacity of these areas.

C. Transnational Telecommuting

The effective use of telecommuting can lead to telework that crosses national boundaries and open up an array of new opportunities and problems. If employees can commute from across town via the Internet and manage their job without physical presence in the office, it is possible for employees to commute across the country or across the globe. This opens up a vast pool of labor for information processing jobs and will have a major impact on business. The vast differences in labor costs in different countries mean that telecommuting can transfer knowledge jobs to low wage countries. The flight of manufacturing jobs to low-wage countries can be repeated with knowledge jobs. While telework has in the past been limited to IS jobs, typically programming, improvements to the net have made it possible to transfer many clerical jobs across national boundaries in real time.

D. Teledemocracy

Teledemocracy and televoting have been held up as an alternative to conventional voting and a solution to the perceived problem of low voter turnout in the United States. Allowing voters to cast their ballot from home can create an electronic town hall, and fundamentally shift government from the constraints of a manufacturing type of environment. Rather than limiting voting to the selection of representatives, televoting can allow for on-line discussions, and votes on most issues, helping to eliminate a layer of representatives between voters and legislation.

E. Telemedicine

Telemedicine is use of CMC to provide medical information and services over a distance. The consultation can be interactive and in real time or on a batch basis with data transmitted to a remote site for diagnosis. The savings in travel costs and time are augmented by providing the patient, especially those in isolated and small communities, with a wider selection of specialists.

IX. SUMMARY

Telecommuting has steadily gained acceptance in the business workplace. The impact of telecommuting on employees and management is discussed in this article. Information processing jobs have grown and these jobs possess the characteristics for effective telecommuting. Technology improvements in computer-mediated communication have made telecommuting more applicable for a variety of tasks. Many of the predictions about fast telecommuting growth have not occurred and the reasons for this are discussed. Effective telecommuting programs need to consider technical, economic, and organizational issues to ensure the success of the program.

SEE ALSO THE FOLLOWING ARTICLES

Digital Divide • Electronic Mail • Ergonomics • Future of Information Systems • Globalization • Group Support Systems and Electronic Meeting Systems • National and Regional Economic Impacts of Silcon Valley • Outsourcing • Reengineering • Security Issues and Measures • Staffing the Information Systems Department • Virtual Organizations

BIBLIOGRAPHY

Apgar IV, M. (May–June 1998). The alternate workplace: Changing where and how people work. *Harvard Business Review*, Vol. 76, No. 3, 121–136.

Cascio, W. F. (August 2000). Managing the virtual workplace. *Academy of Management Executive*, Vol. 14, No. 3, 81–90.

Christenson, K. (Summer 1991). Managing invisible employees: How to meet the telecommuting challenge. *Employment Relations Today*, 133–143.

Dannhauser, C. (June 1999). Who's in the home office? *American Demographics*, Vol. 21, No. 6, 50–56.

Davenport, T., and Pearlson, K. (Summer 1998). Two cheers for the virtual office. *Sloan Management Review*, Vol. 39, No. 4, 51–65.

Dixon, T. (1998). Family structure and the telecommuter's quality of life. *Journal of End User Computing*, Vol. 10, No. 4, 42–50.

El Sawy, O., Malhotra, A., Gosain, S., and Young, K. (September 1999). IT intensive value innovation in the electronic economy: Insights from Marshall Industries. *MIS Quarterly*, Vol. 23, No. 3, 305–355.

Farrah, B., and Dagen, C. (July 1993). Telecommuting Policies that work. *HR Magazine*, Vol. 38, 64–71.

Gainey, T. W., Kelley, D. E., and Hill, J. A. (Autumn 1999). Telecommuting's impact on corporate culture and individual workers: Examining the effect of employee isolation. *SAM Advanced Management Journal*, Vol. 64, No. 4, 4–10.

Goodman, P., and Darr, E. (December 1998). Computer-aided systems and communities: Mechanisms for organizational learning in distributed environments. *MIS Quarterly*, Vol. 22, No. 4, 417–440.

Gupta, Y., Karimi, J., and Somers, T. (February 2000). A study on the usage of computer and communication technologies for telecommuting. *IEEE Transactions on Engineering Management*, Vol. 47, No. 1, 26–39.

Harrington, S. J., and Ruppel, C. P. (December 1999). Telecommuting: A test of trust, competing values and relative advantage. *IEEE Transactions on Professional Communication*, Vol. 42, No. 4, 2223–239.

Higa, K., Liu Sheng, O., Shin, B., and Figuerdo, A. (May 2000). Understanding relationships among teleworkers' e-mail usage, e-mail richness perceptions and e-mail productivity perceptions under a software engineering environment. *IEEE Transactions on Engineering Management*, Vol. 47, No. 2, 163–173.

Huston, T., and Huston, J. (June 2000). Is tele-medicine a practical reality. *Communications of the ACM*, Vol. 43, No. 6, 91–95.

Igbaria, M., and Tor, G. (Summer 1999). Exploring differences in employee turnover intentions and its determinants among telecommuters and non-telecommuters. *Journal of Management Information Systems*, Vol. 16, No. 1, 147–164.

Jacobs, S. M., and Van Sell, M. (Winter 1996). Telecommuting: Issues for the IS manager. *Information Systems Management*, Vol. 13, No. 1, 18–21.

Kaifa, M., and Davidson, R. (March 2000). Exploring the Telecommuting Paradox. *Communications of the ACM*, Vol. 43, No. 3, 29–31.

Kurland, N., and Bailey, D. (1999 Autumn). Telework: The advantages and challengers of working here, there, anywhere, and anytime. *Organizational Dynamics*, Vol. 28, No. 2, 53–68.

Mokhtarian, P., and Solomon, I. (Oct. 1996). Modeling the choice of telecommuting. *Environment and Planning*, Vol. 28, No. 10, 1877–1894.

Nilles, J. M. (1994). *Making telecommuting happen*. New York: Van Nostrand Reinhold.

Ruppel, C., and Howard, G. (Summer 1998). The effect of environmental factors on the adoption and diffusion of telework. *Journal of End-User Computing*, Vol. 10, No. 4, 5–14.

Tor, G., and Dallow, P. (March 1999). Empirically testing the benefits, problems, and success factors for telecommuting programmes. *European Journal of Information Systems*, Vol. 8, No. 1, 40–54.

Venkatesh, V., and Speier, C. (June 2000). Creating an effective training environment for enhancing telework. *International Journal of Human–Computer Studies*, Vol. 52, No. 6, 991–1005.

Watad, M. M., and DiSanzo, F. J. (Winter 2000). The synergism of telecommuting and office automation. *Sloan Management Review*, Vol. 41, No. 2, 85–95.

Watson-Fritz, M., Narasimhan, S., and Rhee, H. (Spring 1998). Communication and co-ordination in the virtual office. *Journal of MIS*, Vol. 14, No. 4, 7–28.

Webster, J. (1998). Desktop videoconferencing: Experiences of complete users, wary users, and non-users. *MIS Quarterly*, Vol. 22, No. 3, 257–286.

Temporal Data Model and Query Language Concepts

Michael H. Böhlen and Christian S. Jensen

Aalborg University

I. INTRODUCTION
II. TEMPORAL DATA SEMANTICS
III. TEMPORAL DATA MODELS

IV. TEMPORAL QUERY LANGUAGES
V. SUMMARY
VI. OUTLOOK

GLOSSARY

bitemporal relation A relation with exactly one system-supported valid time and exactly one system-supported transaction time.

calendar Provides a human interpretation of time. As such, calendars ascribe meaning to temporal values where the particular meaning or interpretation is relevant to the user. In particular, calendars determine the mapping between human-meaningful time values and an underlying time-line.

chronon, time instant, time point A (one-dimensional) chronon is a nondecomposable time interval of some fixed, minimal duration. An n-dimensional chronon is a nondecomposable region in n-dimensional time. Important special types of chronons include valid-time, transaction-time, and bitemporal chronons. This article uses *time instant* and *time point* as synonyms to chronon, and, in keeping with the literature on which the article is based, we generally prefer the latter term.

snapshot equivalent Two tuples are snapshot equivalent if the snapshots of the tuples at all times are identical. Similarly, two relations are snapshot equivalent if at every instant their snapshots are equal.

snapshot relation Relations of a conventional relational database system incorporating neither valid-time nor transaction-time timestamps.

span A directed duration of time. A duration is an amount of time with known length, but no specific starting or ending instants. For example, the duration "one week" is known to have a length of seven days, but can refer to any block of seven consecutive days. A span is either positive, denoting forward motion of time, or negative, denoting backward motion in time.

temporal element A finite union of n-dimensional time intervals. Special cases of temporal elements include valid-time elements, transaction-time elements, and bitemporal elements. They are finite unions of valid-time intervals, transaction-time intervals, and bitemporal intervals, respectively.

temporal expression A syntactic construct used, e.g., in a query that evaluates to a temporal value, i.e., an instant, a span, a time interval, or a temporal element.

time interval Two different definitions are used in the literature. In the first definition, it is the same as a time period. In the second definition, which is used in SQL standards, it is the same as a span. This article generally uses the first definition and resorts to the second in only a few situations where predefined query syntax requires this.

time period The time between two instants. In a system that models a time domain using chronons, a time period may be represented by a set of contiguous chronons.

timestamp A time value associated with some object, e.g., an attribute value or a tuple. The concept may be specialized to valid timestamp, transaction timestamp, instant timestamp, span timestamp, interval timestamp, bitemporal-element timestamp, etc.

transaction time A database fact is stored in a database at some time instant, and after it is stored, it is current until the instant it is logically deleted. The transaction time of a database fact is the time when the fact is current in the database and may be retrieved. Transaction times are consistent with the serialization order of the transactions. They cannot extent into the future. Also, as it is impossible to change the past, (past) transaction times cannot be changed. Transaction times are system-generated and -supplied. While valid times may only be associated with "facts," statements that can be true or false, transaction times may be associated with any database object.

transaction-time relation A relation with exactly one system-supported transaction time. As for valid-time relations, there are no restrictions as to how transaction times may be incorporated into the tuples.

valid time The time when the fact is true in the modeled reality. A fact may have associated any number of instants and time intervals, with single instants and intervals being important special cases. Valid times are usually supplied by the user.

valid-time relation A relation with exactly one system-supported valid time. There are no restrictions on how valid times may be incorporated into the tuples; e.g., the valid times may be incorporated by including one or more additional valid-time attributes in the relation schema, or by including the valid times as a component of the values of the application-specific attributes.

I. INTRODUCTION

A wide range of database applications manage time-varying data. The area of temporal databases characterizes the semantics of temporal data and provides expressive and efficient ways to model, store, and query temporal data. This article introduces the reader to temporal data models and query languages. It concisely introduces fundamental temporal database concepts, surveys state-of-the-art solutions to challenging aspects of temporal data management, and offers a look into the future of temporal databases.

Indeed, most applications of database technology are temporal in nature. Examples include financial applications such as portfolio management, accounting, and banking; record-keeping applications such as personnel, medical-record, and inventory management; scheduling applications such as airline, train, and hotel reservations and project management; and scientific applications such as weather monitoring. Applications such as these rely on *temporal databases,* which record time-referenced data.

In contrast, the support for temporal data management offered by commercially available software tools and systems is quite limited and leaves much to be desired. As a result, temporal database management is a vibrant field of research, with an active community of several hundred researchers who have produced some 2000 papers over the last two decades. Many of these papers are listed in a series of seven cumulative bibliographies. The newest, listed in the bibliography, provides pointers to its predecessors. The field has produced a comprehensive glossary of terminology (the glossary at the outset of this article borrows from this glossary), an edited volume which captures state-of-the-art circa 1993, and three workshop proceedings. These are all listed in the bibliography. The topic of temporal databases is now also covered in many textbooks, and Snodgrass has written the first book dedicated entirely to temporal databases (again, listed in the bibliography).

This article provides an introduction, readable by the nonexpert, to central concepts and issues in temporal data models and query languages. More specifically, the article examines in turn the semantics of temporal data, temporal data models, and temporal query languages, which are central areas of temporal database management. Each area is first motivated, and then sample contributions are surveyed, to give the reader a feel for the challenges and issues that are faced in each particular area. The article concludes with a summary and a look into the possible futures of temporal databases.

The presentation is by no means complete in its coverage of areas, let alone contributions within areas. The article does not cover the issues related to the representation of the time domain such as whether time is assumed to be continuous or discrete. Further, the article does not cover the many issues related to the support for multiple time granularities (e.g., day, week, month, and year), calendars (e.g., national, solar, lunar, financial, and business calendars), indeterminacy (e.g., from between 14.00 and 15.00 until between 21.00 and 22.00), and the unique temporal notion *now.* Finally, the article focuses on the recording of phenomena that have a duration in time. It largely avoids issues specific to the recording of instantaneous events and also time series.

The bibliography contains works that either survey the area or are compilations of research contributions.

II. TEMPORAL DATA SEMANTICS

Before we proceed to consider temporal data models and query languages, we examine, in data model-independent terms, the association of times and facts, which is at the core of temporal data management.

Initially, a brief description of terminology is in order. A database models and records information about a part of reality, termed either the *modeled reality* or the *mini-world*. Aspects of the mini-world are represented in the database by a variety of structures that we will simply term *database entities*. In general, times are associated with database entities. We will employ the term "fact" for any (logical) statement that can meaningfully be assigned a truth value, i.e., that is either true or false.

The facts recorded by the database entities are of fundamental interest. Several different temporal aspects may be associated with these. Most importantly, the *valid time* of a fact is the collected times—possibly spanning the past, present, and future—when the fact is true in the mini-world. Valid time thus captures the time-varying states of the mini-world. All facts have a valid time by definition. However, the valid time of a fact may not necessarily be recorded in the database, for any of a number of reasons. For example, the valid time may not be known, or recording it may not be relevant for the applications supported by the database. If a database models different possible worlds, the database facts may have several valid times, one for each such world.

Next, the *transaction time* of a database entity is the time when the entity is current in the database. Like valid time, this is an important temporal aspect. Transaction time is the basis for supporting accountability and "traceability" requirements, which exist in many applications, e.g., financial and medical applications.

Note that transaction time, unlike valid time, may be associated with any database entity, not only with facts. For example, transaction time may be associated with objects and values that are not facts because they cannot be true or false in isolation. To be more concrete, the value "5" may be stored in a database, but does not denote a logical statement. It is meaningful to associate transaction time with 5, but not valid time. Thus, all database entities have a transaction-time aspect. This aspect may or may not, at the database designer's discretion, be captured in the database. This is dependent on the requirements posed by the applications to be supported.

The transaction-time aspect of a database entity has a duration: from insertion to deletion, with multiple insertions and deletions being possible for the same entity. As a consequence of the semantics of transaction time, capturing this aspect of database entities renders deletions purely logical. Deleting an entity does not physically remove the entity from the database; rather, the entity remains in the database, but ceases to be part of the database's current state.

Transaction time captures the time-varying states of the database, and, as mentioned, applications that demand accountability or "traceability" may use databases that record transaction time.

Observe that the transaction time of a database fact, say *F*, is the valid time of the related fact, *F is current in the database*. This would indicate that supporting transaction time as a separate aspect is redundant. However, both valid and transaction time are aspects of the content of all databases, and recording both of these is essential in a wide range of applications. In addition, transaction time, due to its special semantics, is particularly well behaved and may be supplied automatically by the database management system (DBMS). Specifically, the transaction times of facts stored in the database are bounded by the time the database was created at one end of the time line and by the current time at the other end. This provides the rationale for the focus of most temporal database research on providing improved support for valid time and transaction time as separate aspects.

In addition, some other times have been considered, e.g., decision time. But the desirability of building decision time support into temporal database technologies is less clear, because the number and meaning of "the decision time(s)" of a fact varies from application to application and because decision times, unlike transaction time, generally do not exhibit specialized properties.

The valid and transaction time values of database entities are drawn from some appropriate time domain. There is no single answer as to how to perceive time in reality and how to represent time in a database, and different time domains may be distinguished with respect to several orthogonal characteristics. First, the time domain may or may not stretch infinitely into the past and future. Second, time may be perceived as discrete, dense, or continuous. Some feel that time is really continuous; others contend that time is discrete and that continuity is just a convenient abstraction that makes it easier to reason mathematically about certain discrete phenomena. In databases, a finite and discrete time domain is typically assumed, e.g., in the standard query language (SQL) standards. Third, a variety of different structures have been imposed on time. Most often, time is assumed to be totally ordered, but various partial orders have also been suggested, as has cyclic time.

An aspect of time that has been intriguing philosophers for centuries and that is difficult to describe fully is the concept of the current time, which we term *now*. This concept is unique to time; indeed, there really does not exist any other notion quite like it.

Among its properties, the current time is ever-increasing, all activity is trapped at the current time, and the current time separates the past from the future. The spatial equivalent, *here*, simply fails to enjoy the properties of *now*. The uniqueness of *now* is one of the reasons why techniques from other research areas are not readily, or not at all, applicable to temporal data.

Much research has been conducted on the semantics and representation of time, from quite theoretical topics, such as temporal logic and infinite periodic time sequences, to more applied questions such as how to represent time values in minimal space. Substantial research has been conducted that concerns the use of different time granularities and calendars in general, as well as the issues surrounding the support for indeterminate time values. Also, there is a significant body of research on time data types, e.g., time instants, time intervals (or "periods"), and temporal elements.

Temporal data management can be very difficult using conventional (nontemporal) data models and query languages. Accommodating the time-varying nature of the enterprise is largely left to the developers of database applications, leading to ineffective and inefficient ad-hoc solutions that must be reinvented each time a new application is developed. The result is that data management is currently an excessively involved and error-prone activity. Temporal database research has produced several proposals for temporal data models and query languages to remedy this situation. Section III considers temporal data models, and Section IV then covers query languages based on these models.

III. TEMPORAL DATA MODELS

A first step in providing support for temporal data management is to extend the database structures of the data models supported by a conventional DBMS. Assuming a relational data model, mechanisms must be provided for capturing the times of the facts recorded by the relations, leading to temporal relations. Throughout, we focus on the valid-time aspect of the facts.

More than two dozen temporally extended relational data models have been proposed. We consider the main types of models that have been proposed. In order to exemplify these, consider a video store where customers, identified by a CustID attribute, rent video tapes, identified by a TapeNum attribute. We consider a few rentals during May 1997. On the 3rd of May, customer C101 rents tape T1234 for three days. On the

5th, customer C102 rents tape T1245. The tape is returned on the 7th. From the 9th to the 12th, customer C102 rents tape T1234. Customer C102 rents tape T1245 from the 19th to the 20th and again from the 21st to the 22nd. The video store keeps a record of these rentals in a relation termed CheckOut.

A. Points

The most basic type of temporal data model uses tuple timestamps that are instants, or *points*. Under this view, each fact is associated with a time point that indicates when the fact is valid. Multiple tuples are used if a fact is valid at several points in time. The resulting CheckOut instance is illustrated in Fig. 1.

A distinguishing feature of this approach is that (syntactically) different relations have different information content. Next, timestamps are atomic values that can be easily compared. Assuming a totally ordered time domain, the standard set of comparison predicates, $=$, $\neq$, $<$, $>$, $\leq$, and $\geq$, is sufficient to conveniently compare timestamps. As we will see in the next section, this simplicity is lost when moving to more compact representations of time, which has the effect of making some conceptually simple queries cumbersome to formulate. The conceptual simplicity of time points comes at a cost, though. In general, it is impossible to reconstruct the original intervals from the points. Additional attributes, such as the SeqNo attribute in CheckOut in Fig. 1, must be used for this purpose. The reader can easily verify that it becomes impossible to represent the 2- and 4-day rentals described in the running example if the SeqNo attribute is omitted.

SeqNo	CustID	TapeNum	T
1	C101	T1234	3
1	C101	T1234	4
1	C101	T1234	5
2	C102	T1245	5
2	C102	T1245	6
2	C102	T1245	7
3	C102	T1234	9
3	C102	T1234	10
3	C102	T1234	11
3	C102	T1234	12
4	C102	T1245	19
4	C102	T1245	20
5	C102	T1245	21
5	C102	T1245	22

Figure 1 Snapshots of the CheckOut instance at times 4(a), 5(b), and 8(c).

It is important to note that the point model is an *abstract* view of a temporal database and is not meant for physical representation. For all but the most trivial time domains, the space needed when using the point model is prohibitive.

The combination of conceptual simplicity and computational complexity has made the point model popular for theoretical studies while there is a lack of implementations. Only recently have some implementation issues been considered.

B. Intervals

From an implementation perspective, the most popular type of data model is the one that uses time *intervals*. This type of model associates each fact with an interval that captures the valid time of the fact. Multiple tuples are needed if a fact is valid over disjoint intervals. Figure 2 illustrates the approach.

When employing intervals rather than time points as timestamps, two timestamps satisfy precisely one of the following thirteen relationships, first enumerated by James Allen: before, meets, overlaps, during, starts, finishes, and equal, in addition to the inverses of the first six of these relationships. Allen's pioneering work in this area has inspired designs of many of the collections of interval predicates available in temporal query languages. While well-chosen interval predicates are more convenient to use than relationships over interval start and end points, such predicates alone turn out to not be sufficient to provide comprehensive and easy-to-use support for temporal data management in general and the point-based view in particular (see Section IV.A).

The notion of *snapshot equivalence*, which reflects a point-based view of data, establishes a correspondence between the point based and interval based models. Consider the relations in Fig. 3. The relations are different, but snapshot equivalent. Specifically, the relation in Fig. 3b is a coalesced version of the relation in Fig. 3a. (In *coalescing*, tuples with the same nontimestamp values, termed value-equivalent tuples, and adjacent or overlapping time intervals are merged.)

SeqNo	CustID	TapeNum	T
1	C101	T1234	[3,5]
2	C102	T1245	[5,7]
3	C102	T1234	[9,12]
4	C102	T1245	[19,20]
5	C102	T1245	[21,22]

Figure 2 An interval model of the CheckOut instance.

a

CustID	TapeNum	T
C101	T1234	[3,5]
C102	T1245	[5,7]
C102	T1234	[9,12]
C102	T1245	[19,20]
C102	T1245	[21,22]

b

CustID	TapeNum	T
C101	T1234	[3,5]
C102	T1245	[5,7]
C102	T1234	[9,12]
C102	T1245	[19,22]

Figure 3 Different but snapshot equivalent CheckOut instances.

Clearly, the two relations are different. However, in some temporal data models, the relations are taken to contain the exact same information because they contain the same snapshots, some of which are illustrated in Fig. 4. These models adopt a point-based view and are only interval-based in the weak sense that they use time intervals as convenient representations of (contiguous) sets of time points.

It then also makes sense for such models to require that their relation instances be coalesced. This requirement ensures that relation instances that are syntactically different are also semantically different, and vice versa.

In our example, the requirement rules out Instance 1 in Fig. 3. This implies that it is not possible to distinguish two consecutive 2-day check-outs from one four-day check-out, unless an additional attribute is used to uniquely identify check-outs. For such weakly interval-based models, the CheckOut instance in Fig. 2 is thus the appropriate representation of the rental scenario.

In an inherently interval-based model, intervals are not merely representational devices—they carry meaning beyond denoting a set of points. Returning to the example, it is easy to imagine a scenario where the average rental price per day decreases as the check-out span increases. It then makes a difference whether a customer checks out a tape for two short, consecutive intervals (see Fig. 3a) or for one longer interval (see Fig. 3b). Interval-based models do not enforce coalescing and capture this distinction naturally and are in this sense more expressive than point models. They require no additional attribute to identify the check-outs, and the CheckOut instance in Fig. 3a is the appropriate representation of the rental scenario.

C. Temporal Elements

A frequently mentioned shortcoming of intervals is that they are not closed under all set operations. For example, when subtracting the interval [5,7] from the

a

CustID	TapeNum
C101	T1234

b

CustID	TapeNum
C101	T1234
C102	T1245

c

CustID	TapeNum

Figure 4 Snapshots of the CheckOut instance.

interval [1,9], we do not get an interval, but a set of intervals: {[1,4], [8,9]}. This has led to the proposal that *temporal elements* be used as timestamps instead. These are finite unions of intervals.

In the definition, the unions are restricted to be finite in order to ensure that temporal elements can be represented conveniently in a database. It should also be noted that the definition is meaningful for both a discrete and a continuous time domain. In this article, we generally assume a discrete and bounded time domain, as does probably most data model research.

With temporal elements, the same two semantics as for intervals are possible, although models that use temporal elements seem to prefer the point-based semantics. Figure 5a uses temporal elements to capture the rental scenario assuming the interval-based semantics. Under this view, intervals are perceived as atomic units. Under the point-based view, an interval is identical to a set of points. This implies that the instance in Fig. 5a is equivalent to the one shown in Fig. 5b, as the tuples of the two relations then have timestamps that denote the same time points. Under this assumption (and recalling our assumption about the time domain), "a (finite) set of time points" is an equivalent definition of a temporal element.

We consider next the bitemporal conceptual data model (BCDM), which has been used to TSQL2, to be discussed in Section IV.F. This model adopts the point-based view. So the SeqNo attribute is introduced in Fig. 6, which shows the BCDM relation instance that captures the rental scenario.

The BCDM timestamps facts with values that are sets of time points. (We used the valid-time variant of the BCDM.) This is equivalent to temporal elements because the BCDM adopts a discrete and bounded time domain.

Because value-equivalent tuples are not allowed (this corresponds to the enforcement of coalesced relations as discussed in the previous section), the full history of a fact is contained in exactly one tuple, and one tuple contains the full history of exactly one fact. In addition, relation instances that are syntactically different have different information content, and vice versa. This design decision reflects the point-based underpinnings of the BCDM.

Note that the BCDM is intended for the conceptual level and as the basis for a query language. When it comes to the physical representation and the display to users of temporal information, the BCDM is impractical. The varying length and voluminous timestamps of tuples are impractical to manage directly, and the timestamp values are hard to comprehend.

D. Attribute Value Timestamping

With temporal elements, the full history of a fact is contained in a single tuple. The information in a relation that pertains to some real-world object may still be spread across several tuples, though. To capture all information about a real-world object in a single tuple, attribute value timestamping has been introduced. We use the parametric model of Gadia and Nair for illustration. This is a typical non-first-normal-form data model. The name of the model derives from the view that a temporal database is a time-varying nontemporal database. In other words, a temporal database is a nontemporal database that is time parameterized.

The relation in Fig. 7 is thought of as recording information about some types of objects. It records information about customers and thus holds one tuple for each customer in the example, with a tuple containing all information about a customer. An obvious consequence is that the information about a single tape cannot be contained in a single tuple. Another observation is that a single tuple may record multiple

a

CustID	TapeNum	T
C101	T1234	[3, 5]
C102	T1245	[5, 7] ∪ [19, 20] ∪ [21, 22]
C102	T1234	[9, 12]

b

CustID	TapeNum	T
C101	T1234	[3, 5]
C102	T1245	[5, 7] ∪ [19, 22]
C102	T1234	[9, 12]

Figure 5 Temporal element representation of the CheckOut instance.

SeqNo	CustID	TapeNum	T
1	C101	T1234	$\{3, 4, 5\}$
2	C102	T1245	$\{5, 6, 7\}$
3	C102	T1234	$\{9, 10, 11, 12\}$
4	C102	T1245	$\{19, 20\}$
5	C102	T1245	$\{21, 22\}$

Figure 6   Using the BCDM to model the CheckOut instance.

facts. In the example, the second tuple records multiple facts: rental information for customer C102 for the two tapes, T1245 and T1234, and four different check-outs.

It should also be noted that different groupings of the information into tuples are possible for this attribute-value timestamping model. For example, Fig. 8 illustrates a relation instance that is snapshot equivalent to the one in Fig. 7. This new instance is "grouped on" the TapeNum attribute, indicating that it is now the tapes, not the customers, that are the objects in focus. (Section IV.H elaborates on this.)

IV. TEMPORAL QUERY LANGUAGES

This section illustrates and discusses central query language concepts that have emerged after years of temporal database research and are representative for the field. To be specific, these concepts are discussed in the contexts of specific query languages that are all extensions to variants of the SQL query language. Because the aim is to communicate the essential principles, we gloss over semantic variations among temporal constants and predicates (e.g., overlaps), and introduce additional functions (e.g., duration) as needed.

We first motivate the need for temporal query languages, then extend the video rental example for use in this section. This is followed by discussions of six different approaches to temporal query languages.

A. Motivation

Given the prevalence of applications that currently manage time-varying data, one might question the need for a temporal query language. Is the existence of all this SQL code of ostensibly temporal applications not proof that SQL is sufficient for writing such applications? The reality is that in conventional query languages like SQL, temporal queries *can* be expressed, but often only with great difficulty.

To illustrate the issue, we use the relations Check-Out in Fig. 2, which records check-out intervals for video rentals, and CheckOutSnap in Fig. 4b, which records the check-outs at time 5. Using SQL, it is straightforward to express the number of check-outs from CheckOut-Snap. For example, this can be expressed as follows.

```
SELECT COUNT (TapeNum) AS Cnt FROM
    CheckOutSnap
```

The temporal generalization of this query, asking now for the time-varying count of tapes checked out, as recorded in relation CheckOut, is nontrivial. The reader may verify that the result in Fig. 9 is correct. Although possible, expressing this query in SQL is quite difficult. The authors are aware of one stepwise and systematic solution that consists of six steps and takes up 35 lines of complex SQL code.

As another example, specifying a key constraint on relation CheckOutSnap is trivial in SQL.

```
ALTER TABLE CheckOutSnap ADD PRIMARY
    KEY (TapeNum)
```

This key constraint may be generalized to apply to a valid-time relation, now meaning that TapeNum is a key at each point in time or, equivalently, is a key in each snapshot that may be produced from the valid-time relation. Specifying this constraint on relation CheckOut in SQL is again difficult. Expressed as an SQL assertion, it may easily take more than 10 lines.

The lesson learned is that quite reasonable queries can be difficult to express on temporal relations using a query language such as SQL. Even SQL experts

SeqNo		CustID		TapeNum	
[3, 5]	1	[3, 5]	C101	[3, 5]	T1234
[5, 7]	2	$[5, 7] \cup [9, 12] \cup [19, 22]$	C102	$[5, 7] \cup [19, 22]$	T1245
[9, 12]	3			[9, 12]	T1234
[19, 20]	4				
[21, 22]	5				

Figure 7   Parametric representation of the CheckOut instance.

SeqNo		CustID		TapeNum	
[3,5]	1	[3,5]	C101	[3,5] ∪ [9,12]	T1234
[9,12]	3	[9,12]	C102		
[5,7]	2	[5,7] ∪ [19,22]	C102	[5,7] ∪ [19,22]	T1245
[19,20]	4				
[21,22]	5				

Figure 8 Parametric representation of the CheckOut instance.

would be hard pressed to express the examples above in SQL. Given also the ubiquitous nature of temporal information, this indicates a strong need for temporal support beyond what SQL offers today.

B. Video Rental Example

The following queries together with their intended results build on the video rental example and will serve for illustration in the subsequent sections.

Query $Q1$ asks for all available information about check-outs that overlap the interval [7,9]. Returning the nontemporal information of a check-out is straightforward. Returning the temporal information is more subtle, as we will see Section IV.E.

$Q1$ *All check-outs that overlap the time interval* [7,9].

C102	T1245	[5,7]
C102	T1234	[9,12]

Query $Q2$ constrains the number of time points included in a time interval. This query teases out the difference between time points and intervals. Only if a model gives an interval a meaning beyond a set of time points or if auxiliary attributes are used will it be possible to distinguish a four-day check-out from two consecutive two-day check-outs.

$Q2$ *All 2-day check-outs.*

T1245	[19,20]
T1245	[21,22]

Cnt	T
0	[−∞,2]
1	[3,4]
2	[5,5]
1	[6,7]
0	[8,8]
1	[9,12]
0	[13,18]
1	[19,20]
1	[21,22]
0	[23,∞]

Figure 9 A time-varying count.

Query $Q3$ is an ordinary query that, conceptually, must be applied to each state of a temporal database. In this case the nontemporal query is a (self-)Cartesian product.

$Q3$ *Which tapes were checked out together with tape T1234?*

T1245	[5,5]

Query $Q4$ is another example of an ordinary query that must be applied to each state of a temporal database. The only difference with respect to query $Q3$ is the actual nontemporal query. In this case the nontemporal query is an aggregation.

$Q4$ *What is the number of tapes that have been check out?*

See Fig. 9.

Like Query $Q4$, Query $Q5$ is an aggregation. However, the aggregation is to be applied independently of any temporal information. Instead of a time-varying count of the check-outs, we want to determine the total number of check-outs.

$Q5$ *How many check-outs were made in total?*

5

The final query refers to the (constantly moving) current time. (We assume that the current time is 5.)

$Q6$ *List all (current) check-outs.*

C101	T1234
C102	T1245

This type of query can come from two sources. First, applications that are time-aware might ask for the current status of the check-outs. Second, time-unaware applications might ask it as a legacy query.

C. Approach I: Abstract Data Types

The earliest and, from a language design perspective, simplest approaches to improving the temporal data management capabilities of query languages have simply introduced time data types and associated predicates and functions. This approach is attractive because it has limited impact on the language, e.g., SQL, that it is applied to and because the addition of new data types, predicates, and functions is fairly well understood. To illustrate this approach, we assume that the video rental data is represented by the interval-timestamped CheckOut instance in Fig. 3a.

Formulations of predicates on time-interval data types have been influenced by Allen's 13 interval relations: any two intervals are related by precisely one of these. With reference to these, different sets of practical proposals for predicates have been proposed. For example, the overlaps predicate can be used to formulate query *Q*1.

$Q1^{SQL}$: `select * from CheckOut`
`    where T overlaps [7,9]`

The result of this query depends on how the rental information is represented—see Fig. 3, which illustrates that the same information (from a point-based view) may be represented in more than one way.

A selection that limits the duration of an interval follows the same approach:

$Q2^{SQL}$: `select TapeNum, T`
`  from CheckOut where duration(T) = 2`

The third query can be expressed using selection, projection, and join. Its formulation is simplified if predicates and functions on intervals are available:

$Q3^{SQL}$: `select b.TapeNum,`
`      intersect(a.T, b.T) as T`
`  from CheckOut as a,`
`     CheckOut as b`
`  where a.TapeNum = T1234`
`    and b.TapeNum <> T1234`
`    and a.T overlaps b.T`

As mentioned in Section IV.A, expressing a time-varying aggregation is possible, but exceedingly complicated. There exists no reasonable SQL solution for counting the number of check-outs at any point in time (*Q*4).

In contrast, counting the check-outs independent of the temporal references is easily possible:

$Q5^{SQL}$: `select count (*)`
`  from CheckOut`

Retrieving the current check-outs is stated as follows:

$Q6^{SQL}$: `select CustID, TapeNum`
`  from CheckOut`
`  where T overlaps [now]`

In summary, the availability of appropriate time data types aids in the formulation of several of the example queries considered, but falls short when it comes to formulate temporal aggregation queries such as *Q*4.

Let us consider this point in a bit more detail, as it indicates the limits of the abstract data type approach and motivates the consideration of other approaches. Queries *Q*3 and *Q*4 are related in the sense that, conceptually, both generalize a simple snapshot query to becoming time-varying, i.e., to be applied to all states of the database. The only difference is in the snapshot query, a join (*Q*3) versus an aggregation (*Q*4). In spite of their close relationship, the temporally extended language offers no systematic way of formulating the two queries when starting from their snapshot formulations. The techniques that are applied to formulate *Q*3 may not be reused when formulating *Q*4 and vice versa. Rather, new solutions must be thought out for each new kind of query. So although the availability of abstract data types for time do aid in formulating temporal queries, they fall short in offering means of conveniently formulating a wide range of queries on interval-timestamped temporal relations such as the time-varying aggregation and the primary key constraint mentioned in Section IV.A. Indeed, more than 20 years of temporal database research has not produced an abstract data type that allows one to conveniently express temporal queries.

D. Approach II: Folding and Unfolding

Being of fixed size, interval timestamps are very convenient when representing the temporal aspects of information. In some respects, the most straightforward and simplest means of capturing temporal aspects is by means of an extra interval timestamped attribute in each relation. On the other hand, one might suspect that the difficulty in formulating temporal queries in the previous section is caused by the intervals. SQL comes unprepared to support something (intervals) that represent something (sets of consecutive time points) that they are not.

In response to this, it has been proposed to equip SQL with the ability to *normalize* timestamps. The idea is to split or merge interval timestamps so that they are *aligned* (identical or disjoint) and can be treated as atomic entities.

Advanced most prominently by Lorentzos, the earliest and most radical approach is to introduce the two function *unfold* and *fold*. The unfold function decomposes an interval timestamped tuple into a set of point timestamped tuples, one for each point in the original interval. The fold function "collapses" a set of point timestamped tuples into value-equivalent tuples timestamped with maximum intervals. Thus, unfolding the relations in Fig. 3 yields the relation in Fig. 1 (modulo the sequence number attribute), which may be folded to yield the relation in Fig. 3b. The idea is to use the interval-based representation of temporal information while being able to manipulate it as if the point-based representation was used, thus obtaining the representational benefits of intervals while avoiding the problems they seem to pose in query formulation.

The fold and unfold functions have been integrated into IXSQL, which we use for illustration. IXSQL inherits and extends the semantics of SQL. Thus, each

SQL query statement is also an IXSQL query statement. For instance the IXSQL formulations of the first three queries are essentially those given for SQL in the previous section. (There are minor differences in the syntax of temporal predicates and functions, which are not relevant for our discussion. For example, cp is an IXSQL predicate that is true if the argument intervals have common (time) points. It corresponds to the overlaps predicate used in Section IV.C.) We assume the CheckOut relation in Fig. 3a.

```
Q1^IXSQL: select * from CheckOut
    where T cp [7,9]
Q2^IXSQL: select TapeNum, T
    from CheckOut
    where dur(T) = 2
Q3^IXSQL: select b. TapeNum,
        intervsect (a.T, b.T) as T
    from CheckOut as a,
        CheckOut as b
    where a.TapeNum = T1234
      and b. TapeNum <> T1234
      and a.T cp b.T
```

The fold and unfold functions become useful when we consider temporal aggregation. Here, unfold is used to explicitly convert the interval-based representation into its point-based representation; then the point-based representation is used in query formulation; and, the final interval-based result is produced by applying fold. Query Q4 illustrates this:

```
Q4^IXSQL: select count (*), T
    from (select *
            from CheckOut
            reformat as unfold T)
            as a
    group by T
    reformat as fold T
```

Thus, the general pattern for queries using unfold and fold is to (1) explicitly construct the point-based representation by unfolding the argument relation(s), (2) compute the query on interval-free representation, and (3) fold the result to end up with an interval-based representation.

The standard SQL solution can be used to count the check-outs independently of time, and to retrieve the current state of the CheckOut relation.

```
Q5^IXSQL: select count (*)
    from CheckOut
Q6^IXSQL: select CustID, TapeNum
    from CheckOut
    where T overlaps [now]
```

In summary, a language enriched with folding and

unfolding may offer a systematic approach to formulating temporal queries, in particular temporal queries that generalize nontemporal queries.

The efficient evaluation of queries formulated using fold and unfold has yet to be resolved. Unfolding has a worst case exponential space complexity; and for the time domains available in current systems, unfolded relations are so large that storing them is impractical.

A more subtle observation is that IXSQL adopts a view on relations instances that is neither purely point-based nor interval-based. It is not purely point-based because it is sensitive to the specific interval representation chosen for the data. Thus when different, but snapshot-equivalent, relations are used, the same query generally returns different results. In contrast, the fold and unfold functions only preserve the information content in a relation up to that captured by the point-based view. For example, unfolding and then folding the relation instance in Fig. 3a yields the instance in Fig. 3b.

E. Approach III: Point Timestamps

A more radical approach to designing a temporal query language is to simply assume that temporal relations use point timestamps—fold and unfold are then not needed. The temporal query language SQL/TP advanced by Toman takes this approach to generalizing queries on nontemporal relations to apply to temporal relations. The semantics of SQL/TP is defined with respect to the point-based representation, and we thus assume the CheckOut relation instance in Fig. 1 in the following. The restriction to point timestamps yields a simple and unambiguous semantics that avoids many of the pitfalls that can be attributed to interval timestamps.

Q1 calls for a comparison of neighbor database states. The point view, which separates the database states, does not easily support this type of query. The straightforward approach is to use a disjunction of equality predicates: select CustID, TapeNum from CheckOut where T = 7 or T = 8 or T = 9. This query does not yield the intended result. The query restricts the time of the original check-out interval to the time points 7, 8, and 9, and it fails to report the original check-out intervals as intended. A more complicated query that involves a join is needed.

```
Q1^SQL/TP: select a.*
    from CheckOut a,
        CheckOut b
    where a.SeqNo = b.SeqNo
```

```
      and a.CustID = b.CustID
      and a.TapeNum = b.TapeNum
      and (b.T = 7 or b.T = 8
          or b.T = 9)
```

In SQL/TP, duration queries are formulated as aggregate queries. (Remember that the semantics of queries is defined with respect to the point representation.)

```
Q2^{SQL/TP}: select SeqNo, TapeNum, T
      from CheckOut
      group by SeqNo
      having count(T) = 2
```

As explained before this query can only be answered if an attribute is available to distinguish individual check-outs. Note that if this additional attribute is omitted from the final projection, the two-day intervals will generally not follow from the results. The result might consist of four tuples timestamped with time points, one tuple timestamped with an interval spanning four time points, or two tuples with intervals spanning two time points.

The strength of SQL/TP is in its generalization of queries on snapshot relations to corresponding queries on corresponding temporal relations. The general principle is to extend the snapshot query with equality constraints on the timestamp attribute of the temporal relation, to separate different database snapshots during query evaluation.

```
Q3^{SQL/TP}: select b.TapeNum, b.T
            from CheckOut as a,
                CheckOut as b
            where a.TapeNum = T1234
                and b.TapeNum <> T1234
                and a.T = b.T
Q4^{SQL/TP}: select count(*), T
      from CheckOut
      group by T
```

In the first query we use a self-join to determine the time points when tape T1234 was checked out together with another tape. In the second query, the grouping takes care of isolating the database states from each other. The second query is restricted to bounded time domains, to avoid infinite relations.

In a sense, SQL/TP and SQL are opposites when it comes to the handling of temporal information. In SQL, intervals have no special meaning—they are treated as atomic entities. On the other hand, SQL/TP effectively decomposes intervals into sets of points. This difference becomes clear when considering aggregate queries. In SQL, time-varying aggregation ($Q4$) is poorly supported, while SQL/TP needs an ad-

ditional attribute in the argument relation to support time-invariant aggregation ($Q5$). Note that the SQL/TP query `select count(*) from Check-Out` counts the number of time points (possibly multiple times) when tapes were checked out and thus does not give the intended result. However, if an attribute is available that identifies the real-world facts, counting the facts is possible:

```
Q5^{SQL/TP}: select count(distinct SeqNo)
      from CheckOut
```

The current state of the CheckOut relation is retrieved as follows:

```
Q6^{SQL/TP}: select CustID, TapeNum
      from CheckOut
      where T = now
```

In several of the examples, we have used relations with sequence numbers in order to be able to capture the intended information and express the desired queries. While the introduction of sequence numbers appears to be a minor issue, it is worth noting that these do not offer a systematic approach to obtaining point-based semantics *and* a semantics that preserves the intervals of the argument relations. The query *When was tape T1245, but not tape T1234, checked out?* may serve to illustrate this point. The expected answer is the intervals {[6,7], [9,12], [19,20], [21]22]}. The following formulation, using a temporal difference, seems plausible.

```
select T from CheckOut
where TapeNum = T1245
except
select T from CheckOut
where TapeNum = T1234
```

This query does not guarantee that fragments of individual check-out intervals are returned because the sequence numbers that are used to identify check-outs are not included. On the other hand, if we add the sequence number attribute to the select lists, the temporal difference will effectively be disabled, and the returned result would simply be the intervals of the original check-outs of tape T1245. The problem here is that set operations are sensitive to any additional attributes and essentially do not permit such attributes. This issue is not germane to SQL/TP, but applies equally to all approaches that use a point-based data model.

In summary, the strength of SQL/TP is the restriction to time points to ensure a simple, unambiguous, and well-defined semantics. As intervals are still to be used in the physical representation of the temporal information as well as when presenting the results of queries to the users, one may think of SQL/TP as a variant of IXSQL where, conceptually, queries must always apply unfold as the first operation and fold as the last. A compilation technique has been supplied for SQL/TP that avoids this unfolding, thus offering hope that SQL/TP queries can be evaluated efficiently in practice.

F. Approach IV: Syntactic Defaults

Along with the introduction of temporal abstract data types, what may be termed *syntactic defaults* have been introduced that make the formulation of common temporal queries more convenient. The most common defaults concern access to the current state of a temporal database and for handling temporal generalizations of nontemporal queries, e.g., joins. The most comprehensive approach based on syntactic defaults is the TSQL2 language, which we use for exemplification. We assume the CheckOut instance in Fig. 2.

In TSQL2, a default valid clause, placed after the select clause, computes the intersection of the valid times of the argument relations mentioned in the from clause, which is then returned in the result. With only one relation in the from clause this yields the original timestamps.

$Q1^{TSQL2}$: select * from CheckOut
           where valid(T) overlaps
                 period '7-9'

The cast function is available to map between intervals and time spans. (Note the terminology: in TSQL2, a period (e.g., [7-9]) is an anchored interval, and an interval (e.g., 4 days) is an unanchored time span.)

$Q2^{TSQL2}$: select SeqNo, TapeNum, T
         from CheckOut
         where cast(valid(T) as
               interval) = 2

Note that the returned result must include the SeqNo attribute in its projection list to properly show the two-day check-outs (see Section IV.E).

The default for the default behavior of the valid clause was designed with snapshot reducibility in mind. This shows nicely if we consider the snapshot reducible join.

$Q3^{TSQL2}$: select b.TapeNum
         from CheckOut as a,
           CheckOut as b
         where a.TapeNum = T1234
           and b.TapeNum <> T1234

The implicit default valid clause is here valid intersect(valid(a), valid(b)). If two tuples have valid times that do not overlap, they do not contribute to the result. Tuples with empty timestamps are not allowed in TSQL2's data model.

$Q4^{TSQL2}$: select COUNT(*)
         from CheckOut
$Q5^{TSQL2}$: select snapshot COUNT(*)
         from CheckOut

The default behavior of TSQL2 is to return temporal relations. The snapshot keyword is used to retrieve nontemporal relations. Thus, to retrieve the current state of the CheckOut instance, the following query is issued:

$Q6^{TSQL2}$: select snapshot *
         from CheckOut
         where valid(CheckOut)
           overlaps [now]

TSQL2 is a large language with many parts and an informally specified semantics. It provides syntactic defaults that simplify the formulation of temporal queries over point-based temporal databases. The problem with syntactic defaults relates to lack of the "scalability" over language constructs. When defining a language that uses syntactic defaults, one must explicitly specify a large number of defaults. It becomes challenging to be comprehensive and systematic in the specification of such defaults, and to ensure that the defaults do not interact in unanticipated ways. This approach tends to yield a language where, although it may be possible to formulate common queries concisely, the language itself is complex and therefore difficult to understand and use.

G. Approach V: Semantic Defaults

ATSQL introduces temporal statement modifiers to add temporal support to SQL. In contrast to syntactic defaults, statement modifiers are *semantic defaults* that indicate the intended semantics without specifying how to compute it.

The basic idea in statement modifiers is to offer a systematic means of constructing temporal queries from nontemporal queries, the motivation being that queries that are easily formulated in SQL on nontemporal relations are very difficult to formulate on temporal relations, as discussed in Section IV.A. With statement modifiers, one thus formulates a temporal query by first formulating the corresponding nontemporal query (i.e., assuming that there are no timestamp attributes on the argument relations) and then applies a statement modifier to this query.

For example, to formulate a temporal join the first step is to formulate a nontemporal join. Next, a modifier is prepended to tell the database system to use temporal semantics. The modifier ensures that the argument timestamps overlap and that the resulting timestamp is the intersection of the argument intervals. If the enclosed query is simply a selection, the timestamps do not have to be transformed, and the only task of the modifier is to ensure that the original timestamps are returned as the timestamps of the result. If the enclosed statement is a difference, the modifier ensures that the intervals are appropriately subtracted.

While ATSQL supports both valid time and transaction time, we consider only valid time. Unlike the languages that consider intervals as compact representations of sets of points, ATSQL gives more meaning to intervals. Reflecting this, relations in ATSQL consist of interval timestamped tuples, and value-equivalent tuples with adjacent or overlapping intervals are permitted. Thus, CheckOut as given in Fig. 3a is assumed in the following.

The first and second queries can be formulated almost as in SQL. The seq vt modifier ensures that the original timestamps are returned as intended. The seq vt is short for "sequenced valid time" and indicates that the semantics is consistent with evaluating the nontemporal query on a sequence of nontemporal relations, see Section IV.E. Note that the seq vt modifier does not limit the possibility to, e.g., use Allen's interval predicates, to constrain the timestamps, which is otherwise typical for point-based languages. For example, it is perfectly natural (and easy to understand) to have a temporal join between relations p and q *and* to restrict the temporal join to tuples in p with a timestamp that spans at least two time points.

```
Q1^ATSQL:  seq vt
    select * from CheckOut
    where T overlaps [7,9]
Q2^ATSQL:  seq vt
    select TapeNum
    from CheckOut
    where duration(T) = 2
```

The next two statements are temporal generalizations of nontemporal queries. Thus, they can be formulated by prepending the nontemporal SQL queries by the seq vt modifier.

```
Q3^ATSQL:  seq vt
    select b.TapeNum
```

```
    from CheckOut as a,
       CheckOut as b
    where a.TapeNum = T1234
      and b.TapeNum <> T1234
Q4^ATSQL:  seq vt
       select count(*)
       from CheckOut
```

Query $Q5$ is to be evaluated independently of the time attribute values of the tuples. This is achieved by using the nseq vt modifier (short for "nonsequenced valid time"), which indicates that what follows should be treated as a regular SQL query.

```
Q5^ATSQL:  nseq vt
    select count(*)
    from CheckOut
```

The design decision to make a query without any modifiers considers only the current state of the argument relations aids in ensuring that legacy queries on nontemporal relations are unaffected if the nontemporal relations are made temporal by the addition of a timestamp attribute. The last query may then be formulated as follows.

```
Q6^ATSQL:  select * from CheckOut
```

In summary, semantic defaults offer systematic support for writing temporal queries that can be evaluated on all sets of concurrent states of the argument relations in isolation. This language mechanism is independent of the syntactic complexity of the queries that the modifiers are applied to, which is very desirable. While statement modifiers offer attractive means of formulating the example queries, it should be noted that a language based on statement modifiers represents a much more fundamental change to the language than, e.g., a language based on temporal abstract data types.

H. Approach VI: Temporal Expressions

The notion of temporal expression was originally advocated by Gadia and is supported in his TempSQL language, which is based on the data model described in Section III.D. Relations in TempSQL thus consist of tuples with attribute values that are functions from a subset of the time domain to some value domain (specified as a pair of a temporal element and a value). The functions in the same tuple must have the same domain. Figure 7 exemplifies these relations.

In addition, relations are keyed. A set of attributes being a key means here that no two tuples are allowed to exist in the relation that have the same range values for those attributes. In our example, we are not interested in customers, but in check-outs. Therefore, the key should be SeqNo, not CustID as in Fig. 7. This can be achieved by applying a special restructuring operation to the CheckOut instance on SeqNo, thus obtaining the result in Fig. 10.

The first two queries can be formulated using temporal expressions. If X is an expression that returns a function from time to some value domain then $[\![X]\!]$ is a temporal expression. This expression returns the domain of X, i.e., returns the time when X is true.

$Q1^{TempSQL}$: `select *`
      `from CheckOut:SeqNo`
      `where` $[\![$ `TapeNum` $]\!]$ $\cap$ `[7,9]` $\neq$ $\emptyset$
$Q2^{TempSQL}$: `select TapeNum`
      `from CheckOut:SeqNo`
      `where duration(`$[\![$ `TapeNum` $]\!]$`)` `= 2`

The result of the second query is the relation {<[19,22] T1235>}.

For the third query, the while clause can be used to specify a temporal element to which the time domain of the result tuples is restricted.

$Q3^{TempSQL}$: `select b.TapeNum`
      `while` $[\![$ `a.TapeNum` $]\!]$ $\cap$
         $[\![$ `b.TapeNum` $]\!]$
      `from CheckOut a,`
         `CheckOut b`
      `where a.TapeNum = T1234`
         `and b. TapeNum <> T1245`

The fifth query may be formulated as a simple aggregate, where the argument relation is keyed on the sequence number. (The authors have been unable to formulate the fourth query based on the available documentation.)

$Q5^{TempSQL}$: `select count(*)`
      `from CheckOut:SeqNo`

TempSQL offers built-in support for accessing the current state of a database. Users that wish to query

SeqNo		Cust ID		TapeNum	
[3,5]	1	[3, 5]	C101	[3, 5]	T1234
[5,7]	2	[5, 7]	C102	[5, 7]	T1234
[9, 12]	3	[9, 12]	C102	[9, 12]	T1245
[19, 20]	4	[19, 20]	C102	[19, 20]	T1245
[21, 22]	5	[21, 22]	C102	[21, 22]	T1245

Figure 10 Relation CheckOut:SeqNo.

only the current states of temporal relations are specified as so-called *current users,* upon which the argument relations are always assumed to be the ordinary snapshot relations that contain the current states of the temporal relations.

$Q6^{TempSQL}$: `select * from CheckOut`

In summary, TempSQL timestamps attribute values with temporal elements and permits the use of so-called temporal expressions in this context. This combination simplifies some queries.

V. SUMMARY

This article has introduced the reader to temporal data management with an emphasis on temporal-data semantics and temporal data model and query language concepts.

Based mainly on the three central notions of *fact, valid time,* and *transaction time,* we offered a conceptual understanding of a temporal database that records either when facts are true in the modeled reality or when database entities are or were part of the current database state, or records both. With this understanding as the basis and restricting our attention to the valid-time aspect of data, we then surveyed, discussed, and compared different proposals for the temporal relations that serve as the starting points for temporal query languages. This led the foundation for an exploration of important approaches to the querying of temporal data. With the purpose of illustrating diverse query language concepts, we considered the formulation of six queries in concrete language contexts that embody the concepts.

Although temporal relations capture the temporal aspects of data using time points, time intervals, and so-called temporal elements, this article shows that this is not the most important distinction. Rather, some relations are designed to capture collections of time-indexed snapshots, which may be done using all three types of timestamps. In this case, time intervals are merely compact representation of sets of time points. In contrast, other models give more semantics to time intervals and may thus be termed interval based. These models require intervals or temporal elements for timestamping. In addition, they allow uncoalesced relations. We have seen that the interval semantics may to some extent be simulated in point-based models by using an additional "sequence number" attribute.

The different query language concepts explored assume different relation constructs, although they may make sense for other relation constructs than the ones used for illustrating them in this article. The abstract data type approach to querying temporal data is simple, but also limited in the support offered. The fold and unfold functions convert between corresponding relations with time point versus time interval timestamps. Point timestamps make the formulation of some queries easier, while interval timestamps are convenient for other queries, as well as for physical representation of relations and user display of query results. Fold and unfold imply a point-based view. The approach that solely uses point timestamps assumes that representation and display are beyond the scope of the query language. This leads to a clean, point-based query language. Next, with syntactic defaults, typical queries may be given very short formulations. However, it is challenging to design a query language with comprehensive support for syntactic defaults that is also easy to understand. The notion of statement modifiers offers what may be termed semantic defaults: modifiers are introduced that control the semantics of any query language statements. The strong point is the support for intervals and the ability to easily construct temporal queries that generalize snapshot queries. Finally, the concept of temporal expressions was explored. These constructs extract the time when a logical expression is true and are quite convenient in formulating a range of queries.

VI. OUTLOOK

Although many important insights and results have resulted from the research in temporal database management, many challenges remain. Some of these are considered here.

The lack of consideration of some of these challenges has reduced the potential of earlier results, including those described in this article. In many cases, core concepts have been established, but it remains to be shown how they may be combined and applied, to simplify and automate the management of time-referenced data in practice.

There is a need for increased *legacy-awareness* in a number of areas within temporal databases. Research is needed that takes into account the reality that most databases are in fact legacy temporal databases and that the applications running on them are in fact legacy temporal database applications. In contrast, most research so far has assumed that applications will be designed using a new temporal data model, implemented using novel temporal query languages, and run on as yet nonexistent temporal DBMSs. In

the short to medium term, this is an unrealistic assumption. Indeed, perhaps in part because of this and despite the obvious need in the marketplace, as yet no prominent commercial temporal relational DBMS exists.

The recent growth in database architectures, including the various types of middleware, prompts a need for increased *architecture-awareness*. Studies are needed that provide the concepts, approaches, and techniques necessary for third-party developers to efficiently and effectively implement temporal database technology while maximally exploiting available architectural infrastructure, as well as the functionality already offered by existing DBMSs. The resulting temporal DBMS architectures will provide a highly relevant alternative to the standard integrated architecture that is generally assumed. As a next step, research is needed on how to exploit existing and novel performance-improving advances, such as temporal algebraic operator implementations and indices, in these architectures. Finally, approaches for transitioning legacy applications will become increasingly sought after as temporal technology moves from research to practice.

Also, there has been little work on adding time to so-called fourth-generation languages that are revolutionizing the user interfaces of commercially available DBMSs. There is a clear need for ways to *visualize temporal data*. Scrolling down a relation with additional timestamp attributes is not an effective means of visualizing the temporal variation in the data.

The results on the *conceptual design* of temporal databases as reported in the literature have potential for finding application in practice, but additional research is needed. When database designers actually understand the core temporal database concepts, perhaps most prominently valid and transaction time, they are able to design better databases using existing models and tools. A central challenge is to provide complete conceptual models, with associated design tools, that cover all aspects of designing a temporal database; empirical evaluation of these by real users is needed to provide essential insights. Reengineering of legacy databases is also a very relevant challenge in this context.

Concerning *performance,* more empirical studies are needed to compare techniques, and to possibly suggest even more efficient techniques. Indexing techniques is an important aspect. While preliminary performance studies have been carried out for all or most of the proposed temporal indexes in isolation, there has been little effort to empirically compare them. More work is also needed on exploiting temporal indexes in algebraic operations other than selection. Finally, there has been little work in refining and validating cost models of temporal operators, or of developing and maintaining database statistics.

A number of research areas that are either separate within temporal databases, overlap with this area, or take temporal databases as their point of departure also pose important challenges. Although not mentioned exhaustively in the coverage below, these areas are slated to offer sample challenges.

In the area of *active databases,* rules responding to database changes and external events are a focus. These may be extended to take into account prior history and temporal trends. For example, an absolute temperature reading in a nuclear power plant may be acceptable if it is part of a decreasing trend, but may signal a problem if it represents an increase. Some initial work has been reported in this area, but as yet there has been little integration of rule constructs and temporal constructs.

The area of *spatiotemporal databases* is becoming increasingly important. Providing built-in support for both space and time makes it convenient to manage objects with extents in physical space and time, enabling new database applications.

For example, many *moving objects* such as people, animals, cars, aircraft, and ships will be equipped with wireless devices (e.g., GPS) that track their positions and make these available for storage in databases. The continued advances in wireless communications and other key technology areas constitute powerful drivers for such applications. While we are already witnessing the appearance of some transportation-related systems, a very substantial growth can be expected in the number, sizes, diffusion, and diversity of moving-object applications.

Next, *multimedia* presentations and *virtual reality* scenarios are in fact special breeds of spatiotemporal databases. And, again, there are powerful enablers of these kinds of spatiotemporal database applications. We are witnessing continued advances in data storage, processor, network, and user interaction technologies. In short, the integration of temporal databases with spatial databases offers exciting new challenges and promises to become an important research area in the future.

The area of *temporal data mining* is relatively new. While extracting static associations from a mass of data is an important goal, more effort needs to be focused on associations that capture time-varying behavior.

The focus among vendors, users, and researchers alike on *data warehousing* has brought new prominence to temporal databases. W. H. Inmon, known as the founder of data warehousing, mentions time vari-

ance as one of four salient characteristics of a data warehouse, and there is general consensus that a data warehouse is likely to contain several years of time-referenced data.

Being temporal, data warehouses are thus prime candidates to benefit from the advances in temporal databases. But cross-fertilization between temporal databases and data warehousing is largely absent. In fact, some of the original impetus for a separate data model and query language for data warehouses arose from a perceived lack of temporal support in the relational model and SQL. Few attempts have been made to exploit the advances in temporal databases in the context of data warehousing, although exceptions do exist. The special architecture of a data warehouse and the emphasis on supporting advanced query functionality, e.g., application-specific time-series analysis, bring novel challenges to temporal database researchers. Reconciling the differences between general relational database schemas and specialized star schemas would help enable users and developers achieve an integrated view of an enterprise.

Adopting a longer term and more abstract perspective, it is likely that new database management technologies and application areas will continue to emerge that provide "temporal" challenges. Due to the ubiquity of time and its importance to most database management applications, and because built-in temporal support generally offers many benefits and is challenging to provide, research in the temporal aspects of new database management technologies may be expected to continue to be needed.

SEE ALSO THE FOLLOWING ARTICLES

Data Modeling: Entity-Relationship Data Model • Data Modeling: Object-Oriented Data Model • Structured Query Language (SQL) • Transaction Processing Systems

BIBLIOGRAPHY

Clifford, J., and Tuzhilin, A., eds. (1995). *Recent advances in temporal databases: Proceedings of the international workshop on temporal databases.* Workshops in Computing Series. New York: Springer-Verlag.

Etzion, O., Jajodia, S., and Sripada, S., eds. (1998). *Temporal databases: Research and practice.* LNCS 1399, New York: Springer-Verlag.

Jensen, C. S., and Dyreson, C. E., eds. (1998). *A Consensus Glossary of Temporal Database Concepts,* 2, pp. 367–405.

Jensen, C. S., and Snodgrass, R. T. (1996). Semantics of time-varying information. *Information Systems,* 21(4):311–352.

McKenzie Jr., L. E., and Snodgrass, R. T. (1991). Evaluation of relational algebras incorporating the time dimension in databases. *ACM Computing Surveys,* 23(4):501–543.

Özsoyoglu, G., and Snodgrass, R. T. (1995). Temporal and real-time databases: A survey. *IEEE Transactions on Knowledge and Data Engineering,* 7(4):513–532.

Roddick, J. F., and Patrick, J. D. (1992). Temporal semantics in information systems—A survey. *Information Systems,* 17(3):249–267.

Snodgrass, R. T., ed. (1993). *Proceedings of the International Workshop on an Infrastructure for Temporal Databases.* Arlington, TX.

Snodgrass, R. T. (1995). Temporal object oriented databases: A critical comparison. In *Modern database systems: The object model, interoperability and beyond* (W. Kim, ed.), pp. 386–408, Reading, MA: Addison-Wesley/ACM Press.

Snodgrass, R. T., ed. (1995). Ahn, I., Ariav, G., Batory, D., Clifford, J., Dyreson, C. E., Elmasri, R., Frandi, F., Jensen, C. S., Käfer, W., Kline, N., Kulkarni, K., Leung, T. Y., Lorentzos, N.,

Roddick, J. F., Segev, A., Soo, M. D., and Sripada, S. M. *The TSQL2 Temporal Query Language.* Dordrecht: Kluwer Academic Publishers.

Snodgrass, R. T. (1997). Temporal databases. Part II. *Advanced Database Systems* (C. Zaniolo, S. Ceri, C. Faloutsos, R. T. Snodgrass, V. S. Subrahmanian, and R. Zicari, eds.), San Mateo, CA: Morgan Kaufmann Publishers.

Snodgrass, R. T. (2000). *Developing time-oriented database applications in SQL.* San Mateo, CA: Morgan Kaufmann Publishers.

Tansel, A., Clifford, J., Gadia, S., Jajodia, S., Segev, A., and Snodgrass, R. T., eds. (1994). *Temporal databases: Theory, design, and implementation.* Redwood City, CA: Benjamin-Cummings.

Theodoulidis, C. I., and Loucopoulos, P. (1991). The time dimension in conceptual modelling. *Information Systems,* 16(3):273–300.

Wu, Y., Jajodia, S., and Wang, X. S. Temporal database bibliography update, pp. 338–366.

Total Quality Management

Bengt Klefsjö

Luleå University, Sweden

GLOSSARY

capability index A measure, independent of scale, to judge the capability of a process. One of the suggested indices is the ratio between the length of the tolerance interval and 6σ, where σ is the standard deviation of the characteristic we measure.

customers The people or the organizations we and our activities should give benefit and value to.

improvement cycle or **PDSA-cycle** A mental model for continuous improvement consisting of the four phases "Plan–Do–Study–Act." Its popularity is due to Edwards Deming, but he in turn was inspired by a similar cycle by Walter Shewhart.

process A network of activities which is repeated, the aim of which is to create value to its customers.

process capability The ability of a process, production process, or other type of process to produce units within the set tolerance limits.

process management A methodology to focus on and improve the processes in an organization.

quality The ability to satisfy, or preferably exceed, the needs and expectations of the customers.

quality system A management system to direct and control an organization with regard to quality. It consists of the organizational structure, responsibilities, procedures, processes, and resources for implementing quality management.

self-assessment A methodology aimed at measuring how well the core values have contributed to the culture in the organization and how systematic and comprehensive the work is with total quality management.

six sigma An improvement program with a focus on processes and variation. It is based on a project-by-project basis and each project should be beneficial.

total quality management A management system consisting of core values, methodologies, and tools with the aim of satisfying external and internal customers with as small amount of resources as possible.

In this article we discuss the **CONCEPT OF QUALITY** from different aspects. We also discuss the four phases of the quality movement: quality inspection, quality control, quality assurance, and quality management. In particular, the emphasis is on total quality management, which is discussed from the perspective of a management system consisting of core values, which should constitute the quality culture, and different methodologies and tools needed to support the values. Finally some quality awards are described and how the quality award criteria can be used for self-assessment within the organization is discussed.

I. THE CONCEPT OF QUALITY

The word "quality" is derived from the latin "qualitas" meaning "of what" and was used during ancient times. The Roman orator and politician Cicero (106-43 BC) is considered to be the first person who used the word.

For a long time the word quality was used in the meaning of "characteristics," and it is still used sometimes in that sense. As an example, within the steel industry people sometimes talk about steel qualities meaning steel with different strengthes. However, the word quality has come to encompass a much broader and deeper interpretation during the last decades (see Figs. 1 and 2).

Figure 1 The Japanese character for the concept of quality. The upper half is pronounced "hin" and roughly means "product." The lower half is pronounced "shitsu" and roughly means "quality." Originally this lower character depicted two axes on top of a mussel and could be interpreted as "a promise of money or the value of money." Now the combination of the signs denotes the concept of quality and not only "product quality."

A. Some Definitions of Quality

Over the years several definitions of the concept of quality have been suggested. Some of these can be found in Fig. 2. One, often too narrow, definition is due to the American consultant Philip Crosby (1926–2001) as "conformance to requirements," a definition which focuses on the tolerances set. This definition has a producer's perspective.

The American quality guru Joseph Juran (born 1904) formulated during the 1950s the more user- and customer-focused definition "fitness for use." Ed-

wards Deming (1900–1993), who together with Juran had a large impact on the quality development in Japan, had in a sense an even stronger customer focus when he said that "quality should be aimed at the needs of the customer, present and future." In his definition he also points at the importance of thinking of the customers of tomorrow.

The Japanese Genichi Taguchi (born 1924) defined product quality, or more accurately the lack of product quality, as "the costs caused to the society by the product after its delivery." Although Taguchi formulated his definition of quality for goods it is suitable for services as well. Taguchi focused in an obvious way on the consequences of our products, even for those who do not primarily use the product but still are affected by the product. This definition, in that way, establishes a close relation to environmental issues and today's thoughts of sustainable development and a sustainable society.

In the international standard ISO 9000:2000 of quality management systems, quality is defined as "the degree to which a set of inherent characteristics fulfils requirements, i.e., needs or expectations that are stated, generally implied, or obligatory."

As illustrated by Fig. 2 the most common interpretation of the quality concept during some decades, although formulated with slightly different words, has been that "quality of a product is its ability to fulfil the customers' needs and expectations." A product here consists of either goods or services or combinations thereof. We strongly believe that this definition needs

> The degree to which a set of inherent characteristics fulfills the requirements, i.e. needs or expectations that are stated, generally implied, or obligatory.
> ISO 9000:2000

> Lack of quality is the costs to society by a product after its delivery.
> Genichi Taguchi

> Conformance to requirements.
> Philip Crosby

> Fitness for use.
> Joseph Juran

> Quality should be aimed at the needs of the customer, present and future.
> Edwards Deming

> Quality is a state in which value entitlement is realized for the customer and provider in every aspect of the business relationship.
> Mikel Harry, Six Sigma Academy

> There are two common aspects of quality. One of these has to do with the consideration of the quality of a thing as an objective reality independent of the existence of man. The other has to do with what we think, feel, or sense as a result of the objective reality. In other words, there is a subjective side to quality.
> Walter Shewhart

Figure 2 Some definitions of the concept of quality.

to be more progressive and suggest the definition of the concept of product quality given by Bergman and Klefsjö in 1994:

> The quality of a product is its ability to satisfy, or preferably exceed, the needs and expectations of the customers.

This definition means that it is not always sufficient to fulfil the needs of the customers. We must strive to exceed them. When the customer is surprised, delighted, and fascinated we get loyal customers, who in return buy more and also speak highly of the company and its products.

The degree of customer satisfaction depends on the correlation between the customers' expectations and their experiences with the product and the company. It is therefore influenced by such things as the image of the company, the promises from the company, and past experiences.

It is important here to emphasize that needs and expectations are two different things. Sometimes we, as customers, have expectations that we do not need. But we also have needs, which we do not expect to get fulfilled, for instance, because we are not able to realize our own needs. Sometimes people talk about "requirements, needs, and expectations." However, we think that requirements should be looked upon as a part of needs and expectations and do not see the need to mention requirements explicitly.

B. The Kano Model

In order to establish long-term loyal customers it is very important to really understand the needs and expectations of those customers. The Japanese Noriaki Kano (born 1940) presented in 1984 a model, called *the Kano model*, which explains the customer needs; see Fig. 3.

The basic needs are almost unconsciously expected to be there by the customer. They are so obvious to the customer that he or she usually would not describe these needs if asked. If dissatisfied with respect to these needs the customer will be most unhappy. We cannot, however, get a satisfied customer by only fulfilling the basic needs. Expected needs are such needs as the customer is aware of and wants to have fulfilled, but they are not always absolutely necessary. The unconscious needs, however, are related to characteristics the producer has to find out by himself. They are surprises to the customer, who sometimes cannot imagine them. Innovations, such as a Sony Walkman, mobile phone, or a PC, make it possible to satisfy needs the customer is not even aware of. Here we may find opportunities to delight our customers. Of

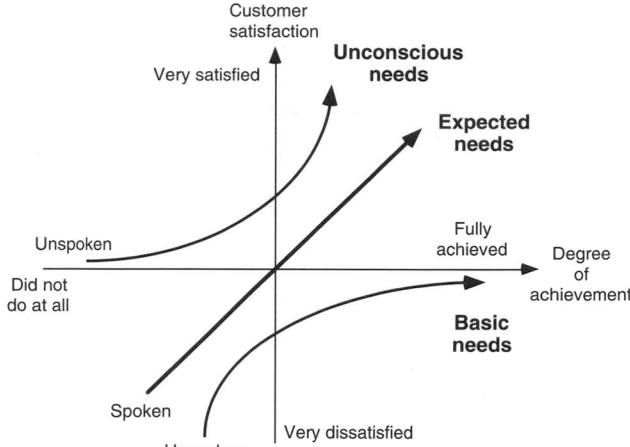

Figure 3 The Kano model illustrating the different types of customer needs. From Bergman, B., and Klefsjö, B. (1994). *Quality from customer needs to customer satisfaction.* London: McGraw–Hill.

course, these surprises may also be different types of well-performed and surprising services.

When we order a hotel room, for instance, a basic need is a bed, which is carefully made up. Among expected needs are perhaps a TV set, a piece of soap, and a toothbrush. Unconscious needs may include a dressing gown, a bowl of fruit, or personal greetings from the manager.

It is also important here to realize that the customer requirements change with time. As an illustration of this we may think of the self-starter of a car. It was an exciting experience in the 1920s, an expected need in the 1940s, but a very basic standard today. A similar development has occurred with color televisions, for instance.

Sometimes it is possible to change dissatisfaction to satisfaction, and even to excitement. By treating a disappointed customer very well you can win a loyal customer. To catch such an opportunity it is important that people on the front lines have sufficient knowledge and also the authority to act rapidly and take corrective action when faults and mistakes occur. For instance, a car rental company often gives you the very best car if some trouble occurs.

C. The Concept of Customer

From the definitions of quality it follows that the concept of "customer" is very important. The concept of customer is sometimes hard to accept, not the least in the public sector. The main reason is that many people associate some form of economic relation to a customer.

However, here the customer concept is used as the best way to summarize "those people or organizations we and our activities should give benefit and value to." To immediately focus on established groups of customers, as students for universities, subscribers for newspapers, or patients in health care, is unwise. The reason is that we in most cases have several groups of customers which need to be identified. Often too, the different groups have different views on their needs and expectations and we have to identify these and then prioritize. To work systematically with quality improvements means to discuss and try to answer the following questions:

- Who are the customers of our organization?
- What needs and expectations do they have?
- How do we fulfil these needs and expectations, or even better, try to exceed them?

Each one of these questions might be hard to answer, but still, this must be the process to follow.

Finally, we want to emphasize that we as customers not only judge the product we buy or use but the whole impression of the relations we have with the organization. When we judge the quality of a car, for instance, we also think of possibilities to obtain spare parts and their cost, the service we get, and how we are treated. The product quality is then a part of our total impression. As a consequence of this widened view there is today a large interest in brands, and the concept of brand relationship management has been well established.

II. THE FOUR PHASES OF THE QUALITY MOVEMENT

People have from time immemorial been concerned about faults and their consequences, the quality of products they have bought, and the work they have done. Some old examples are the law by Hammurabi,[1] the pyramids of Egypt, and the Roman aqueducts.[2]

Soon after World War II, quality work was dominated by *quality inspection* in most western countries. People inspected produced units and sorted out, reworked, or scrapped those with deficiencies or faults or which in other ways did not fulfil the requirements set by the production. This reactive methodology has during the last decades to a large extent been substituted by more

progressive ideas. One of these is *quality control*, the idea of which is to catch signs and signals already in the production process indicating that deficiencies are going to be produced and make the necessary adjustments. We often talk about process control or statistical process control as a methodology for quality control (see Section II.B). The next step in the development of quality work is to create conditions before production starts so that deficiencies can be avoided. This focuses on the formulation of routine procedures, for instance, how to handle incoming material, how to deal with complaints, procedures for calibrating instruments, and how responsibility should be organized. These routines are put together in quality systems or quality manuals. These activities together are called *quality assurance*.

Developments during the last decades have led to more and more emphasis being put earlier and earlier in the product development process. Recent developments have very clearly focused on activities before the production starts. By systematically trying to catch the needs and expectations of the customers, by using well-planned experiments to create robust designs, and by focusing on the processes and not the products, it is possible to avoid bad-quality products, which are unprofitable, getting delivered to the market. This concept is called *quality management* and contains all the other phases of quality. It constitutes an integrated part of the organization's activities and deals with the continuous work with improvements in which all the employees are allowed to participate. The four phases are illustrated in Fig. 4.

A. Quality Inspection

It was not until the breakthrough of industrialism in connection with mass production that systematic

---

[1] Hammurabi was a Babylonien king living about 1792–1750 BC, who established Codex Hammurabi containing 282 paragraphs.

[2] For instance, Pont du Gard in the South of France was built more than 2000 years ago and can resist winds up to 215 km/h, which is twice as much as have been registrated in that area.

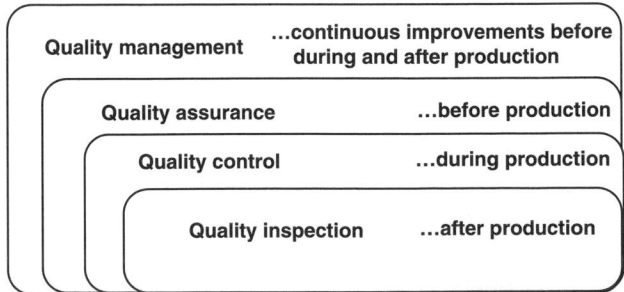

Figure 4 Illustration of the concepts of quality inspection, quality control, quality assurance, and quality management. At the same time the figure gives a common description about the development of quality work.

methods were used to control quality. In particular in the U.S. quality issues came to the forefront during World War II. Among other things, methods for quality inspection based on statistical techniques were developed. This development had already begun during the 1920s on the initiative of Harold F. Dodge (1893–1976) and Harry G. Romig (1900–1989). They both worked at Bell Laboratories. Important contributions to sequential testing were developed by the American Abraham Wald (1902–1950). His Sequential Probability Ratio Test is set up so that after every tested unit from a lot the cumulative number of defective units is compared to the cumulative number of tested units and a decision is made either to accept or reject the lot or to test another unit. Wald's results were considered so valuable that they were kept secret until the war was over.

In modern quality philosophy, activities are guided towards process improvement in order to avoid that defective units will be produced. The practice of inspecting incoming goods is therefore now of limited interest. In the past, however, *acceptance sampling* was considered very important within the quality field.

Let us briefly discuss a situation where no partnership has been established with the supplier and therefore some kind of inspection on incoming batches is considered necessary. The aim is to decide whether the batch shall go straight into production or if the units of the batch first must be checked. What decision we make depends among other things on the consequences of letting a batch of inferior quality pass into production.

Suppose that we have a lot with N units and have to decide if it fulfills the requirements with respect to a certain characteristic such as color, diameter, or time to failure. Here we measure the quality of a lot by *the lot fraction defective p*, i.e., the fraction of defective units in the batch. Please observe that when we say "a lot," it may refer to what has been produced during one shift or one day and not necessarily to the contents of "a box." We evaluate the contents of the lot by randomly selecting units and then checking them with respect to the characteristic of interest. Each inspected unit is then classified as "correct" (acceptable) or defective. Depending on the number of defective units among those selected, we *accept* the lot (i.e., we consider the contents of the lot as acceptable) or we *reject* it.

This process of selecting and making decisions can be done in several different ways. We can for instance select a certain number of units out of the lot, which we denote n, and based on the number of defective units among these decide on either rejection (if $d > c$)

or acceptance (if $d \leq c$); see Fig. 5. This is called a *single sampling plan*.

Another way would be to first select a smaller sample of n_1 units. If the number of defective units, say d_1, in this sample is small, say $d_1 < c_1$, the lot is accepted and if it is large, say $d_1 > r_1$, the lot is rejected. If $c_1 \leq d_1 \leq r_1$ we take one more sample and base the decision of acceptance or rejection on the total number of defective units in the two samples. This is called a *double sampling plan*.

Acceptance sampling is still used to some extent in different companies, for instance as a means to check deliveries from suppliers. Most of the standards for acceptance sampling, still in use, were in fact developed during or just after World War II.

B. Quality Control

1. Variation

Every process produces more or less varying results. Behind this variation there is an extensive system of causes. If enough information about the process is acquired, it is often possible to distinguish and identify some of the sources of variation and then eliminate these causes, when it is suitable from a quality and cost point of view.

Examples of causes of variation in a manufacturing process are play in bearings or spindles, vibrations, varying lighting conditions, inhomogeneous materials, and varying temperature or humidity. In a service process, information uncertainties and individual differences are important sources of variation. In each situation there are often many various causes of the variation. Therefore, it can be hard to identify the contribution of the individual cause. If, on the other hand, we have a maladjusted machine, tool wear, or defects in material lots, these causes may contribute so much to the variation that they become *assignable causes*; i.e., they can be identified and separated from the general noise. The other causes contributing to the noise are, in general, called *common causes*.

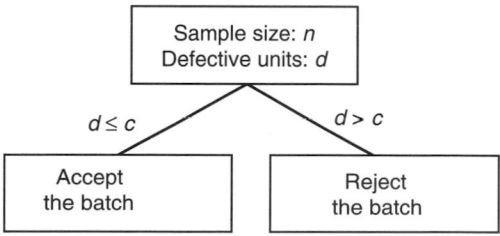

Figure 5 The principle of a single sampling plan.

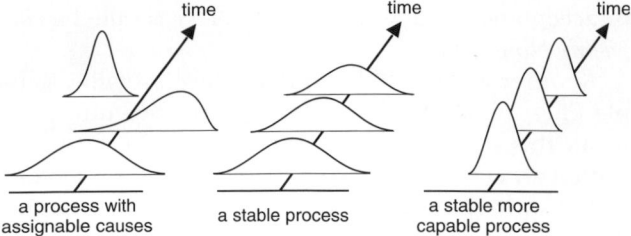

time   time   time

a process with   a stable process   a stable more
assignable causes   capable process

Figure 6 By eliminating assignable causes we get a process in statistical control, a stable process. By gathering more information about the process we can eliminate more causes of variation and the process is further improved. A capable process is a process with a sufficiently small variation compared to the requirements.

The variation occurring from assignable causes is often called *systematic variation,* whereas the other part of the variation caused by common causes is called *random variation.* However, there is no clear distinction between these two types of causes. What is an assignable cause and what is a common cause depends on the information acquired from the process.

When we have eliminated, or at least compensated for, the effect of the assignable causes, only the random variation remains in the process. As long as only this variation contributes to the dispersion, and no systematic variation occurs, we say that the process is in *statistical control* or that we have a *stable process;* see Fig. 6.

When the process is stable we can predict its future results. Walter Shewhart[3] (1891–1967) states this in the following way: "A phenomenon will be said to be controlled when, through the use of past experience, we can predict, at least within limits, how the phenomenon may be expected to vary in the future." The limits are set by the natural, random variation, which the common causes bring about.

2. Statistical Process Control

The purpose of *statistical process control* (SPC) is to find as many sources of variation as possible and then eliminate them. When a stable process with small variation is achieved, the target is to maintain or, if possible, improve the process even further. In these cases it is often not possible to make improvements by eliminat-

---

[3] Walter Shewhart (1897–1967) was employed at Western Electric in 1918 as a recently examined physicist. He worked later at Bell Telephone & Telegraph (now AT&T). He was the first to have a statistical view on the manufacturing process and he suggested in 1924 what now is called the control chart. If just one person should be named the father of the quality movement, we believe that he should have that name.

ing sources of variation. Instead, a creative change in the process structure is needed.

The purpose of statistical process control is, on the basis of data from the process, to

- Identify assignable causes in order to eliminate them
- Supervise the process when it is in statistical control so that no further assignable causes are introduced without the knowledge of the operator
- Continuously give information from the process, so that new causes of variation can be identified as assignable and eliminated

Statistical process control is a vital part of the continuous improvement work. Using information from the process, new causes of variation can be identified as assignable and eliminated, or at least compensated for. Thus, the variation of the process will decrease, the costs of quality defects will decrease, and quality will be improved.

Quite often people do not have a statistical approach to the process. They are misled by the random variation they observe and believe that the observed variation is systematic. They then try to compensate for the variation in different ways. Instead, this results in increasing variation in the process. Decisions are not based on facts, but merely on misguided ambition. By using principles from statistical process control this kind of *overcontrol* can be avoided. Deming calls this problem *tempering.*

An important tool in statistical process control for finding assignable causes and for supervising a process is the use of *control charts.* The idea is that we take a number of observations at certain time intervals in the process. Using these we calculate some form of a *quality indicator,* which we plot in a diagram. A *quality indicator* is an observable quantity based on the observations indicating the status of the process. It can, for example, be their arithmetic mean, the standard deviation of the sample, or the total number of defective units in the sample. A manufacturing process is sometimes supervised by using several quality indicators simultaneously.

As a process quality indicator we can use every quantity that in some way indicates the value of the process characteristic or how it may change. Consequently, it does not have to be based on measurements on the product itself. Instead it is an advantage if it is based on measurements in the process itself, since the long-term planning then will be larger.

As long as the plotted quality indicator remains within prescribed limits, the process is considered to

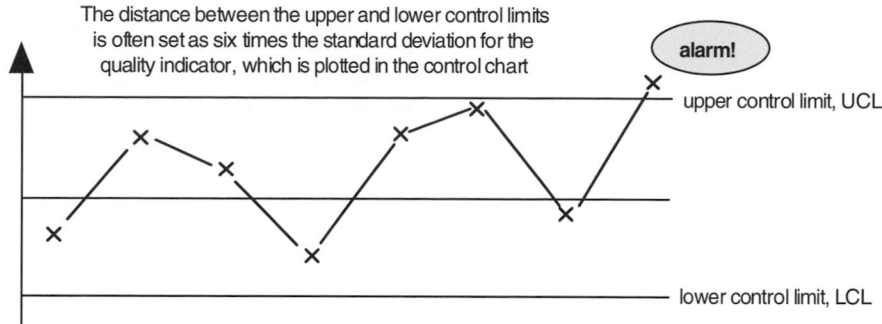

Figure 7 The principle of a control chart. The quality indicator, based on a number of observations, e.g., the mean or the sample deviation, is plotted in the diagram. If "three-sigma limits" are used, it means that the distance between the upper and lower control limit is six times the standard deviation of the quality indicator. If an observation of the indicator is outside any of the control limits it is an indication that new causes of variation have appeared in the process.

be *in statistical control*. These limits are called *control limits*. Very often an ideal level between the control limits is indicated by drawing a *central line*. A plotted point outside any of the control limits strongly indicates that assignable causes have been added to the process. See Fig. 7.

A control chart should meet the following requirements:

- With its help you should quickly be able to detect systematic changes and by that contribute to finding assignable sources of variation.
- "False alarms" should be rare; i.e., the risk must be small that a plotted point is outside the control limits when no systematic change has occurred.
- It must be easy to handle.
- In the control chart it should be possible to estimate the time of a change and the type of change to facilitate error detection work.
- It has to function as a receipt proving that the process has been stable.
- It has to function as a receipt proving that the improvement work has been successful.
- It should strengthen motivation and continuously bring attention back to variations in the process and to quality issues.
- It has to serve as a basis for evaluation of process dispersion, i.e., its capability (see Section II.B.4).

The first two items above give rise to a conflict. If the sensitivity of the diagram is increased by narrowing the distance between the control lines, the risk of a false alarm tends to increase. As a rule this problem is solved in the following way. The random dispersion of the observed quality indicator is reduced by using

several observations and not marking an isolated value. Furthermore, the control limits are usually set so that the difference between the upper and lower control limit is six times the standard deviation for the plotted quality indicator when the process is in statistical control.

3. Process Improvement

When we are looking for the causes of systematic variation, i.e., assignable causes, it is important to tackle the problems systematically and accurately. There are often several problems or causes present. It is a matter of first tackling the problem that is the most serious. When that problem is solved we move on to the next. Figure 8 illustrates *the improvement cycle:* Plan–Do–Study–Act. The phases of that cycle are commented upon as follows.

Plan. When problems are detected the first thing we have to do is to identify the main causes of the problem. Large problems have to be broken down into smaller, manageable ones. The decision concerning changes must be based on facts. That means that we have to look systematically for different plausible causes of the problem using, say, the seven QC-tools.[4] An Ishikawa diagram (see Fig. 9) can often give a hint as to the possible causes. Getting a group

---

[4] The seven QC-tools (QC, quality control) were compiled by the Japanese Kaoru Ishikawa (1915-1989) to stimulate activities in the Japanese QC-circles. The different tools differ slightly between different authors, but they are in most cases data collection with Check Sheets, Histogram, Pareto Charts, Ishikawa Diagrams (also called Cause-Effect Diagrams), Stratification, Scatter Plots, and Control Charts; see also Fig. 19.

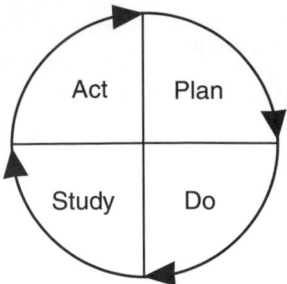

Figure 8 The improvement cycle is applicable to every process. The cycle, which is inspired by Edwards Deming, is sometimes referred to as the Deming cycle and occasionally the PDSA-cycle, where P = plan, D = Do, S = Study, A = Act. Deming himself usually refers to this cycle as the "Shewhart cycle" to honor Walter Shewhart, who earlier presented a similar cycle. Deming earlier used "check" instead of "study." The cycle was then called the PDCA-cycle.

of people together, preferably with different backgrounds and skills, for a brainstorming session where fantasy and ideas can flow freely without being criticized is often productive.

After that we have to compile data in such a way that we can detect causes of error and variation. In such cases, a histogram and other simple ways of illustrating statistical data, Pareto diagrams, stratification, and scatter plots, will be of great help. It is vital not to "overreact" in such a way that the solution of a problem becomes a costly experience based on trial-and-error.

Do. When an important cause of a problem is found, an improvement team is given the task of carrying through the appropriate steps. It is of great importance to make everyone involved fully aware of the problem and of the improvement steps decided upon.

Study. When appropriate steps have been taken we investigate the result to see if the implementation of the improvement program actually was successful. Again, several of the seven QC-tools are important and useful tools. When we are convinced that the steps taken have had a positive effect and that the quality level has been raised, we have to make sure that the new improved level is retained. Sometimes this can be made by utilizing a control chart.

Act. It is an ongoing process to learn and gain experience from the improvement process in order to avoid the same type of problem in the future. If the steps taken were successful the new and better quality level should be made permanent. If we were not successful we have to go through the cycle once more. It is also very important to analyze the entire cycle of problem solving once again in order to learn and also strengthen the improvement process.

Then we go on with improvement by moving on to the next problem in the same process or proceed to the next process and repeat the improvement cycle once again.

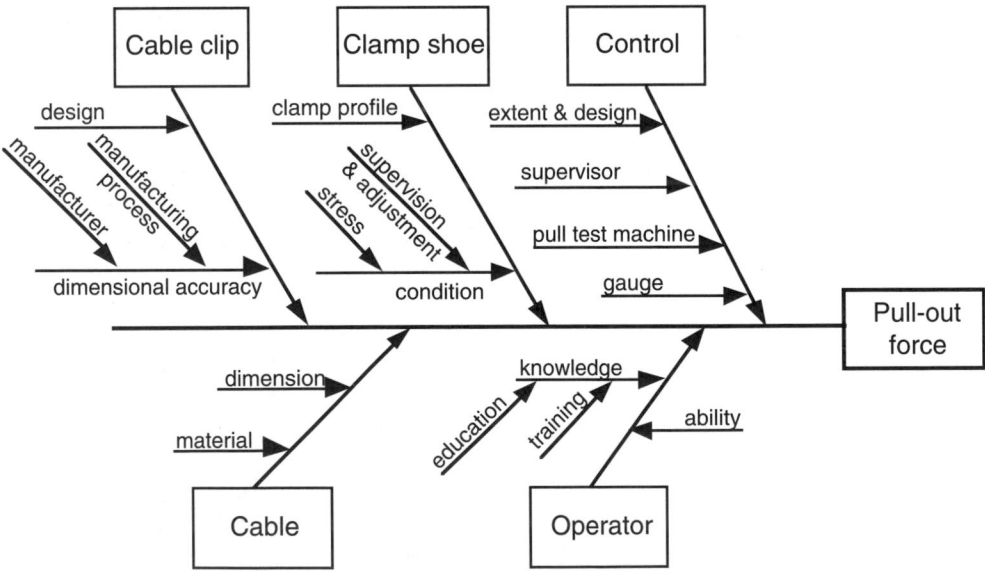

Figure 9 An Ishikawa diagram illustrating a problem with inadequate pull-out force after the clamping of a connector to a clamp-shoe. The Ishikawa diagram is one of the seven QC tools compiled by Kaoru Ishikawa. The Ishikawa diagram gives a structured picture of the cause and their effects. The diagram is sometimes called a Cause–Effect Diagram, but also, due to the appearance, a Fishbone Diagram.

Kaoru Ishikawa (1915–1989) has systematically and persistently advocated the use of statistical techniques for problem solving. Joseph Juran has also done a lot to spread the message of continuous quality improvement. "The Juran Trilogy: Planning–Control–Improvement" is an important part of his message.

4. Capability

The primary purpose of statistical process control is to reduce variation in the process and then supervise the process, so that new assignable causes do not appear. The ability of a process to produce units with dimensions within the tolerance limits is called its *capability* (with respect to the characteristic in question). Utilizing the information obtained from statistical process control we can formulate various measures of this capability.

The capability of the process is determined by the statistical distribution of the product characteristic being studied. When the process is in statistical control this distribution can often be described, at least approximately, by a normal distribution. The capability is then determined by the corresponding average value (expectation) μ and standard deviation σ together with the upper tolerance limit T_U and the lower tolerance limit T_L. This is illustrated in Fig. 10. We would, however, like to point out that several situations may arise where the outcome hardly is normally distributed. The distribution can presumably be skewed when, for example, we are studying a resistance or surface smoothness, but also in other situations when we study nonnegative variables.

A simple and widely used measure of the ability of the process to produce units between the set tolerance limits is the *capability index*

$$C_p = \frac{T_U - T_L}{6\sigma}.$$

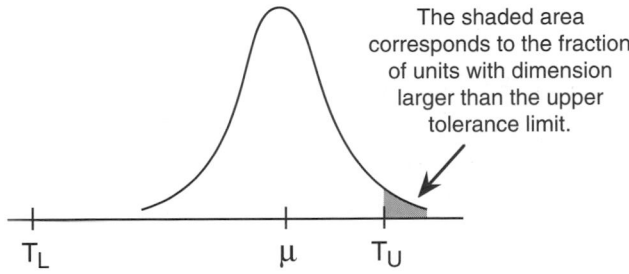

The shaded area corresponds to the fraction of units with dimension larger than the upper tolerance limit.

Figure 10 The capability to produce units within the tolerance limits T_U and T_L depends on the dispersion σ of the process and how the process is centered, i.e., where the average value μ is located.

The index C_p assigns a value to the part of the *natural variation* of the process, a common name for 6σ, which is occupied by the tolerance interval. A large value for this capability index C_p implies that the process, if well centered, will produce units with measurements within the tolerance limits. But if C_p is too small, good centering is not enough (see Table I). Far too large a part of the production will have measurements outside any of the tolerance limits; see Fig. 11. Usually a value of C_p with $C_p \geq 4/3 = 1.33$ is recommended, but higher values are also common now.

Since capability is affected not only by dispersion but also by centering, a measure is required that takes into account how well centered the process is. A measure taking care of both the dispersion of the process and its centering is *the adjusted capability index*

$$C_{pk} = \min\left(\frac{T_U - \mu}{3\sigma}, \frac{\mu - T_L}{3\sigma}\right)$$

which measures the distance between the average value of the process and the nearest tolerance limit in relation to 3σ. When the target value does not lie in the middle of the tolerance interval, other measures have to be considered.

Today, many companies all over the world focus very hard on the processes and their capability through the improvement program called *Six Sigma*. Six Sigma was first launched in the 1980s by Robert Galvin, former CEO at Motorola. More recently Jack

Table I The Number of Defective Units for Different Values of the Capability Index C_p, Assuming a Stable and Perfectly Centered Process

$(T_U - T_L)/\sigma$	Value of C_p	Defects per million units
4	0.67	46,000
5	0.83	12,500
6	1.00	2700
7	1.17	500
8	1.33	60
9	1.50	7
10	1.67	0.6
11	1.83	0.04
12	2.00	0.002

Note. The fraction of units with a measurement outside one of the tolerance limits is under these circumstances equal to $2(1-\Phi(3C_p))$, where Φ is the cumulative distribution function of $N(0,1)$.

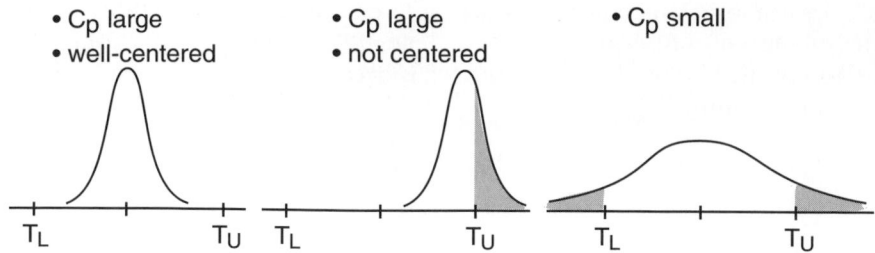

Figure 11 (a) A process with a large value of the capability index C_p will produce units within the tolerance limits if the process is well-centered. (b) A process with a large value of the capability index C_p will produce a lot of units with measurement outside the tolerance limits if the process average is too far from the center of the tolerance interval. (c) A process with too small a value of the capability index C_p will produce units with measurement outside the tolerance limits even if the process is perfectly centered.

Welsh at General Electric, Laurent Beaudoin at Bombarider, Lawrence Bossidy at AlliedSignal (now Honeywell), and several others focus on Six Sigma. The name symbolizes the goal that very seldom, and not more than 3.4 times per one million possibilities, should an important characteristic to the customer be unsatisfactory. Even if the process average moves away from the target, up to 1.5σ from the target value, the distance from the process average to the nearest tolerance limit will be at least 4.5σ.

The Six Sigma program has a clear focus on processes, process improvements, and cost reduction. Several companies have been very successful and have reaped large savings. As examples, General Electric states that the Six Sigma program alone saved them 2 billion dollars during 1999, and AlliedSignals (now Honeywell) saved half a billion dollars in 1999.

C. Quality Assurance

In recent years it has become common to talk about a company's *quality system, quality assurance system, or quality management system.* Many companies demand their suppliers to have a documented quality system. A quality system[5] contains the organizational structure, responsibilities, procedures, processes and resources for implementing quality management.

A quality system should be a base for steering and improving the quality of the company's products and processes. In other words, it is composed of most of the methods and routines as well as organization and distribution of responsibility. It is important that the system is well documented in a suitable way. The documentation is both a support and a basis for the quality audit of the company.

Already during the 1930s military customers in the U.S. and also the military alliance NATO created standards showing how a supplier should be assessed with respect to the work with quality. These standards, and later the British standard BS 5750, were the inspiration to the international series of standards for quality systems, which now is called ISO 9000. The International Organization for Standardization, which is responsible for ISO 9000, is a standardization organization with its administrative center in Geneva. As of December 2001, more than 100 countries are affiliated with this organization through their national standardization organizations. Great Britain, for instance, is affiliated through the BSI (British Standards Institute) and the U.S. through the ANSI (American National Standards Institute).

The ISO 9000 series was established as an ISO-standard in 1987 and new versions have been published in 1994 and 2000. The series has been translated into national standards in more than 100 countries. The ISO 9000 series has different names in different countries. For instance, the term ANSI/ISO/ASQC 9000 is used in the U.S., JIS Z 9900 in Japan, BS EN ISO 9000 in Great Britain, DS/EN ISO 9000 in Denmark, DIN EN ISO 9000 in Germany, and NF EN ISO 9000 in France.[6]

What is usually called ISO 9000, or in its most recent version ISO 9000:2000, is in fact a series of standards. The version ISO 9000:2000 includes standards with the numbers[7] 9000, 9001 and 9004 together with ISO 19011 (a standard for auditing quality systems). The standard ISO 9000:2000 contains basic definitions, explanations, values, and principles. ISO

---

[5] According to ISO 9000:2000 it is "a management system to direct and control an organization with regard to quality."

[6] EN means "European Norm," which in turn means that it is a European standard from CEN, CENELEC, or ETSI.

[7] The somewhat strange numbers result from an earlier version in 1994 which consisted also of standards with the numbers 9002 and 9003.

Table II　The Quality Management Principles Which Are the Basis for ISO 9000:2000

Customer	Organizations depend on their customers and therefore should understand current and future customer needs, should meet customer requirements, and strive to exceed customer expectations.
Leadership	Leaders establish unity of purpose and direction of the organization. They should create and maintain the internal environment in which people can become fully involved in achieving the organization's objectives.
Involvement of people	People at all levels are the essence of an organization and their full involvement enables their abilities to be used for organization's benefit.
Process approach	A desired result is achieved more efficiently when activities and related resources are managed as a process.
System approach to management	Identifying, understanding, and managing interrelated processes as a system contribute to the organization's effectiveness and efficiency in achieving its objectives.
Continual improvement	Continual improvement of the organization's overall performance should be a permanent objective of the organization.
Factual approach to decision making	Effective decisions are based on the analysis of data and information.
Mutually beneficial supplier relationships	An organization and its suppliers are interdependent and a mutually beneficial relationship enhances the ability of both to create value.

9001:2000 contains the requirements of a quality system. This version of the standard has much more focus on management and customers and it also has a clearer process view than the earlier two versions. The requirements of ISO 9001:2000 are based on eight quality management principles; see Table II. These are similar to the core values, or cornerstones, of total quality management, which are discussed in Section III.A. ISO 9004 is intended to give guidelines and support for the internal work in building a quality system.

In order to facilitate communications between suppliers and customers and give confidence to quality work many companies certify their quality systems. Third-party certification according to ISO 9000 means that an independent body assesses the quality system and judges if it is in agreement with the requirements of ISO 9001. This certification should be performed by a body which is accredited according to ISO 45012.

At the end of 2000 there were about 410,000 companies from all over the world with a third-party certification. More than 50% of these could be found in Europe. Different countries have attained different levels in their work on certification of companies according to ISO 9000. Great Britain, which has made the most progress, has about 64,000 companies certified by the BSI (British Standards Institution) or other certification institute. One reason for the large number of certified companies in Great Britain is that the Department of Trade and Industry has a Grant Aid Program financing a large portion of the costs for the implementation of an ISO 9000 quality system. At the end of 2000 there were about 48,000 certified companies in the U.S.A., about 21,000 in Japan, and 26,000 in China.

Other types of standards for quality systems have been established in different industrial areas. For instance, the car industry has established the standard QS-9000 and more recently ISO-TS 16949, telecommunications has its TL 9000, and the space industry has its own standard, AS 9000. These standards have great similarities with ISO 9000, but are more comprehensive in different ways with applications directed to the particular requirements of the industrial area.

D. Quality Management

After the above quality phases, where the beliefs were to inspect quality, control quality and build quality, respectively, the phase of quality management deals with "managing quality." Quality management, or total quality management, is often described as a management philosophy based on a number of core values such as top management commitment, focus on customers, base decisions on facts, improve continuously, and focus on processes.[8] What are called core values here are also called in the literature principles, dimensions,

---

[8] The number of core values differs slightly among different authors and models. For instance the Malcolm Baldrige National Quality Award, which often is considered as a model of TQM, is based on 11 core values and the European Quality Award is based on 8.

elements, or cornerstones, which indicates that the terminology is somewhat unclear and inconsistent.

Quality management looks at quality as a competitive opportunity with a strong focus on the market and the customers. Quality is considered everybody's responsibility and through management commitment, processes, and activities such as strategic planning, goal-setting, and motivation, all members in the organization should get an opportunity to contribute to the continuous improvement of the processes of the organization.

III. TOTAL QUALITY MANAGEMENT

A. The Cornerstones of Total Quality Management

A quality strategy in a company must be built on continuous and consistent commitment from top management regarding questions of quality. Top management has to include quality aspects in the company vision and support activities regarding quality financially, morally, and with management resources. Top management must also actively take part in the improvement process. If the management do not show by their actions that quality is as important as, say, direct costs and delivery times, the rest of the staff in the company will not make such a valuation.

With a strong commitment from management as a base a successful work with quality improvements can be built. Total quality management rests on an organizational culture, which in turn is based on certain core values. In our opinion these values, or cornerstones, as we prefer to call them are (see Fig. 12):

- Focus on customers.
- Base decisions on facts.
- Focus on processes.
- Improve continuously.
- Let everybody be committed.

1. Focus on Customers

In today's view of quality we have to focus on the customers. Quality has to be valued by the customers, and it has to be put in relation to their needs and expectations. This means that quality is a relative term, which to a large extent is set by the competition in the market. The quality of products, both goods and services, can be experienced as having deteriorated significantly if a competitive alternative with better properties turns up on the market. The crisis of the

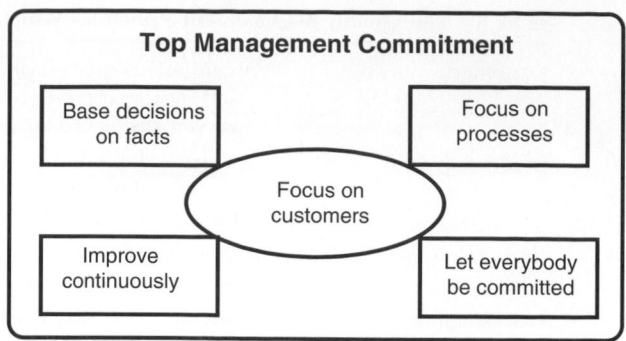

Figure 12 The cornerstones of total quality management as presented by Bergman and Klefsjö in 1994. There are also other similar groups of core values; see, e.g., The Malcolm Baldrige National Quality Award and the Quality Management Principles in ISO 9000:2000.

American car industry some years ago is a good example of this.

To focus on the customers means finding out, in different ways, what the customers really want and need, e.g., by conducting market research. Then we have to fulfil the expectations by systematically developing and manufacturing the product. To focus on the customers does not mean that the customers are always right. However, we have to understand the customers and understand why they have the stated opinions and expectations. We are the experts on our products. If we can see through our customers' stated opinions and understand the background we have the opportunity of supplying our customers with products that fill them with surprise and delight.

Focusing on the customers does not only apply to the external customers, the buyers, and final users. Every employee has customers within the company, internal customers. Their needs, in order to do a good job, also have to be satisfied. In order to be able to satisfy the external customers (high external quality) we also have to satisfy our internal customers (high internal quality); see Fig. 13. Low internal quality means disturbances in the form of redesigns, reprocessing, scrapping and delays with losses of productivity and high costs as a consequence. Trying to reach high external quality with low internal quality is bound to be unsuccessful in the long run.

2. Base Decisions on Facts

An important element in modern quality philosophy is to make decisions based on facts, which are well founded, and not allow random factors to be of decisive importance. International surveys show that be-

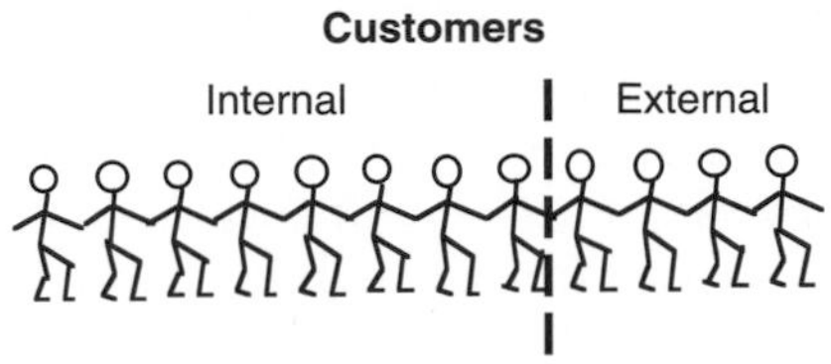

Customers

Internal | External

Figure 13 We have to satisfy both the internal customers within the company and the external customers outside the company. It is impossible to get high external quality without creating high internal quality.

tween 20 and 95% of all product development projects commenced are failures from a business point of view. A possible explanation is that there has not been a thorough examination of what the customers actually want and how much they are prepared to pay for it. Decisions have not been based on facts about market elements. These facts could have been obtained through well-performed market analyses.

It is becoming more and more important to create conditions for high quality already during the development of products. Facts have to be considered early in the product life cycle and should not come as a surprise later on. A change at an early stage of product development is much less expensive than changing a product which has already been produced or, even worse, a product which is already on the market. Another strong factor in favor of early activities regarding quality is the fact that the life cycles of products are getting shorter and shorter. The shortness of life cycles is the reason why it is impossible to make successive improvements and in this way test the product on the market. The product has to be completely developed when introduced on the market in order to yield a profit right from the sales growth.

It is also important to have a strategy for making decisions based on facts in connection with production of goods and services. Early on, many facts are collected and a lot of measurements are made. It rarely occurs that the most important conclusions about the production process are drawn from these data. Measurements are made to evaluate single units and not to evaluate and improve the manufacturing process in which the units are produced. Collected data are stored in files, later on tapes or discs, without ever being used. Simple statistical methods, e.g., those in the seven QC-tools in Fig. 19, are not used to process and analyze the data. Such an analysis could serve as an excellent basis for variation reduction of the manufacturing process and thus for achieving improved quality.

Data also have to be collected for support processes, i.e., processes which support the main processes of

the company, for instance various administrative processes. This should be done in order to continuously improve these processes too.

3. Focus on Processes

Most activities in an organization has certain elements, which are repeated, whereas others are unique at a single occasion. In a Research and Development Department unique items are designed. However, the same development facilities, the same kind of testing activity, the same type of design of experiments, and the same inspection routines are used time and time again. Furthermore, it is the same people who are doing the job. When acquiring material, the same routines are used on various occasions, even if each and every one of these acquisitions may be unique. In a project, unique decision matters are discussed, but with a similar handling of the items and with the same kind of decision support. The underlying structure of the repeated sequence of activities is called a *process*. Without a process it is difficult to talk about improvements. It is the process that ties history and future together, thus making future activities predictable. Awareness of the significance of process thinking is essential in modern leadership for quality (see Fig. 14).

The process transforms certain input, like information and material, into certain output in the form of various kinds of goods or services. From the process, data are generated. These data, including measurements of the results, indicate how well the process satisfies the needs of the customers.

Using statistics from the histories of the processes it is possible to draw conclusions regarding their future results. Also, and more importantly, it is possible to obtain the information needed to improve the process. The process view means not looking upon every single piece of data, for instance a measurement result or a complaint from a customer, as something unique. Instead it should be looked upon as a part of the statistics which can give information about how well the process is working and how it can be

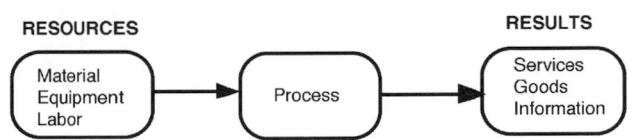

Figure 14 A process transforms certain resources into results that should satisfy the customers of the process by using the smallest amounts of resources possible.

improved. To focus on the processes means that the focus is moved from the particular products to the chain of activities that creates them. Furthermore, the process focus leads to the question of, "How do we produce the results?" becoming more important than, "Who is doing what?". The process focus also creates better possibilities to reach a common vision, since it is more clear how the different employees contribute to the final result.

An often fruitful way to separate different processes is to structure them according to their purposes; see Fig. 15. Often the following three types of processes are used for classification:

- *Core processes,* whose aim is to fulfil the need of the external customers and give value to the products the organization offers. These processes have external customers. Examples of this type of processes are product development processes, with the aim to create value to future customers, and production and distribution processes, which will create value to the customers of today.
- *Support processes,* whose aim is to support resources to the core processes. These processes have internal customers. Examples of this type of processes are recruit processes, maintenance processes, and information processes.
- *Management processes,* whose aim is to decide about goals and strategies and to perform improvements of the other processes in the organization. Also these processes have internal customers. To this group belong strategic planning, goal setting, and auditing.

The aim with each process is to satisfy its customers with the smallest amount of resources possible. Driving a process needs resources in the form of information, energy, and working time. Careful planning and sufficient resources are also necessary to drive the process. It is also necessary to identify and inform the suppliers of the process and see that they get clear signals about what is necessary.

Resources and energy should be devoted to continuous process improvement instead of using considerable resources for "fire-fighting," i.e., taking temporary steps in order to save critical situations. It is important not to react to "exceptionals." However, each separate error and each separate deviation from the expected result provides vital information about the process and must, therefore, be utilized and compiled. This information will be helpful to improve our knowledge of the underlying causes of variations in the result of the process. We will be able to identify new sources of variations. These can then be eliminated, thus further reducing variation. In this way we can improve the process and achieve improved customer satisfaction.

The importance of a process view and of continuously improving business processes has created the methodology of *process management.* The process management procedure consists of the following steps; see Fig. 16.

- *Organize for improvement.* Define ownership and a process improvement team.
- *Understand the process.* Define the boundaries, and investigate who are the customers and suppliers. Document the different activities in the process.
- *Control the process.* Establish control points and measure regularly.
- *Improve the process continuously.* Use the information from the measurement for analysis to improve the process.

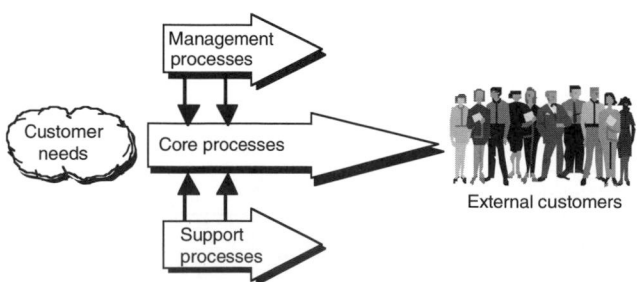

Figure 15 Illustration of the different types of processes of an organization related to the purpose of the process.

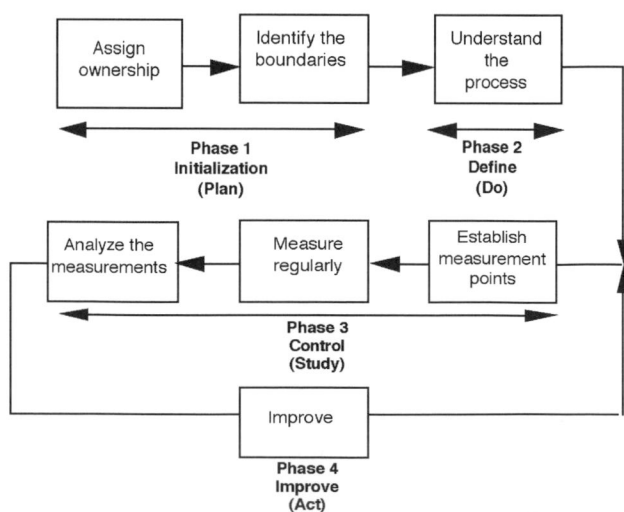

Figure 16 The steps in the process improvement process.

Within Process Management there are at least two important roles, namely process owner and process leader.

The *process owner* is responsible for strategic decisions. These decisions concern infrastructure, scope and dimensions. The process owner has the responsibility for all the resources and has to use a strategic leadership to give directions, frames, and rules to the operational activities. If the process ownership is unclear the consequences from a process orientation can be an internal fight for power. Functions, such as Marketing, Information Technology, and Personal, are examples of support functions to the process owner. They are not owned by the process owner, but are important suppliers of internal services.

The *process leader* has the operational responsibility. He is responsible for how the process is controlled on an operational level, which means that the process fulfils the goals which are set. In most important processes there are claims for fast decisions on reprioritizing and sudden requests of resources. The process leader is responsible for where that support should be put and is in that way the right hand of the process owner. The process leader is also the leader of the improvement team for that process.

In large processes there might be a need for several process leaders, since the process may need to be broken into subprocesses. There is, on the other hand, no process owner on the subprocess level; see Fig. 17. If the organization does the same work at several places there can be process leaders at the different places but the process owner has the central, strategic role. Insurance companies and banks with local offices illustrate this situation.

Benchmarking is a way of finding opportunities for process improvements. It has become frequently used in recent years by many companies. Benchmarking means "the search for the best practices that will lead to superior performance." In Japanese, the corresponding concept is called *dantotsu* which means roughly "striving to be the best of the best." The basic idea is to make a careful comparison of a process of one company with the same or similar process at another company, or another division of one's own company and benefit from the comparison.

The first known formalized benchmarking process was carried out in 1976 by Xerox when they evaluated their warehouse operation by comparing it with the legendary catalogue and retail giant L.L. Bean, with headquarters in Freeport, Maine. In fact, much of the success at Xerox has been ascribed to their systematic work on improving their processes by using benchmarking. When for instance they wanted to improve their invoicing process, they looked for a company that was good at that very process, not necessarily a company in the same business. Invoicing processes look almost the same irrespective of what product or service is to be invoiced. At Xerox they found a company, American Express, which was well known for good invoicing service and precise invoicing. By comparing the invoicing processes of the two companies they could immediately find suggestions for improvements.

It is important to emphasize that benchmarking is far more than copying. It requires deep self-assessment, and the ability to translate practices that work in another context into a process appropriate to one's own organization. It is the essence of creativity. A basis for successful benchmarking is that one's own company has adopted a process view. Benchmarking, in the sense that we use it here, means that we check not our competitors products, but their processes (see Table III).

The benchmarking process can be described by six steps: plan, search, observe, analyze, adapt, and improve (see Fig. 18). Note the similarities between these steps and the improvement cycle: Plan–Do–Study–Act. The goal is to continuously improve the processes with the objective of achieving customer satisfaction that exceeds the satisfaction delivered by our competitors.

4. Improve Continuously

A third cornerstone is working towards continuous quality improvements. The external demands for quality are continuously being increased. Therefore, continuous quality improvement of goods and services produced by the company is necessary. Competitive advantages can thereby be achieved.

Even without any external pressure continuous improvement of quality is well justified from a cost point of view. Costs due to defects and other nonquality contributions are still large. It is not unusual for them

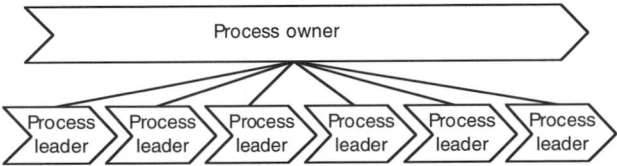

Figure 17 In a large process and when the corresponding process exists at several geographical different places within the same organization there is a need for process leaders with operational responsibility. The order process is usually comprehensive and might, for instance, consist of the subprocesses of sales, specification, design, planning, delivery, and installation, each one with a process leader.

Table III   **Different Types of Benchmarking Depending on Where the Comparison Process Is Found**

Internal benchmarking	Comparing site to site, department to department, country to country within the organization
Competitor benchmarking	Comparing our own performance to that of our direct competitors
Functional benchmarking	Comparing ourselves, not just against our competitors, but against the best organizations operating in similar fields or performing similar activities
Generic benchmarking	Comparing ourselves against the best from all industry groups

to amount to between 10 and 20% of the sales price, and up to 30% in a service company. In most cases defects, faults, and mistakes also cause other costs. If a high rate of disturbances has been accepted in a manufacturing company, this has to be compensated for by many products in production and a big buffer in stocks. Furthermore, in all organizations, different types of "fire-fighting" mean losses in time, energy, and enthusiasm. The corresponding costs are not usually registered as costs due to poor quality. Their contributions can however amount to a considerable part of the costs that have to be paid due to the fact that far too low a quality level has been accepted and in fact organized for.

Important tools in the continuous drive for better quality are simple statistical methods such as the seven QC-tools; see Fig. 19. Here QC stands for quality control. Also the improvement cycle in Fig. 8 is a mental model for the continuous improvement of production.

The basic rule of quality improvement is

It is always possible to improve quality and at the same time reduce costs.

This simple basic rule is surprisingly often applicable. In many cases very simple steps can bring about dramatic effects in terms of improved quality and reduced total costs. Many people earlier talked about "optimal" quality. They believed that there was an upper level of quality, indicating that work in order to improve the product above this level would not be profitable. They did not realize that there are an infinite number of possibilities to improve quality without increasing the costs by using knowledge gained.

Let us finally comment on the popular slogan, "Do it right the first time." This slogan must be interpreted very carefully. In order to delight our customers we have to change in order to improve. Therefore, we have to dare to make some mistakes in the improve-

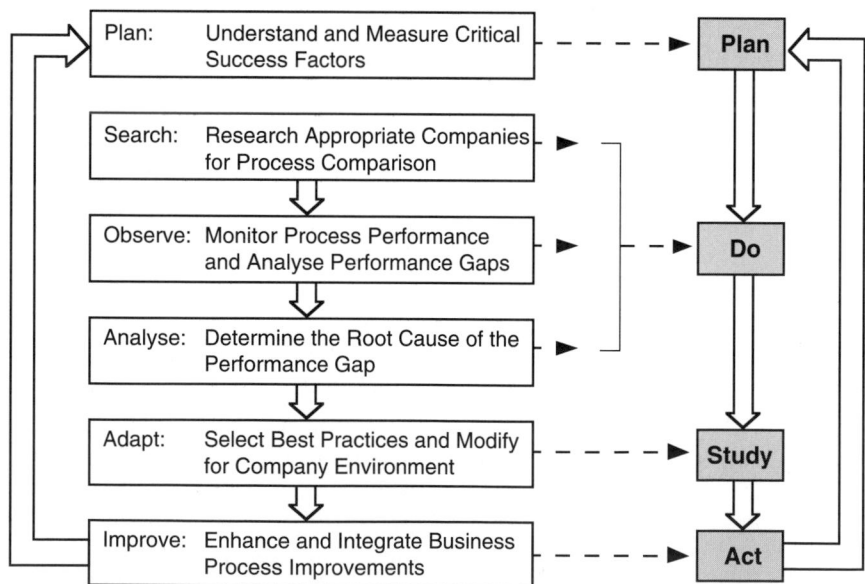

Figure 18   The benchmarking process according to Xerox. From Watson, G. H. (1992). *The benchmarking workbook.* Cambridge, MA: Productivity Press.

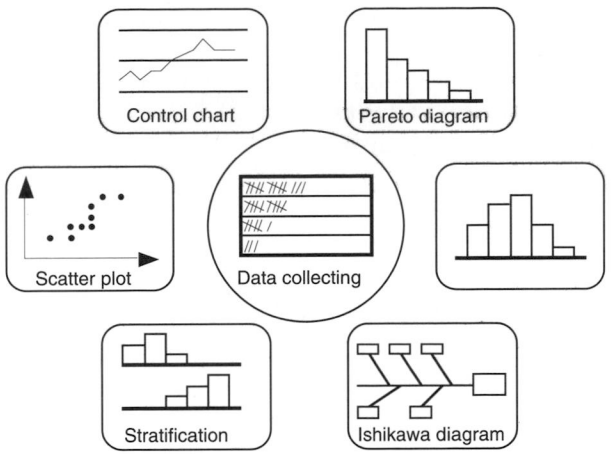

Figure 19 The seven QC tools compiled by Kaoru Ishikawa are important tools for a structured work with quality improvement.

ment process. However, it is a deadly sin not to learn from these mistakes.

5. Let Everybody Be Committed

In order to ensure that the work with quality improvements is successful it is important that possibilities are created to establish everybody's commitment. An important cornerstone therefore is to facilitate everyone having an active role in the improvement of production.

Jan Carlzon, formerly President of Scandinavian Airlines Systems (SAS), in his book from 1987, tells a story about two stonemasons who make granite blocks squared. When asked what they were doing one of them answered tiredly that he was making the granite blocks squared, while the other one enthusiastically answered that he was building a cathedral. The employees must have the chance to feel commitment, professional pride, and responsibility to be able to do a good job. They have to be a part of the building of a cathedral. Those who have been given a chance to do a good job and to feel professional pride, and who are recognized when they have done a good job, will also be committed to their job. This leads in turn to improved quality.

Not only everybody within the company, but also all the suppliers of material have to be involved in the quality improvement work. An obvious trend today is that large companies drastically reduce the number of suppliers. These companies choose to tie down a small number of suppliers even if these do not offer the lowest prices. The aim of big companies is to in-

crease the commitment, responsibility, and quality awareness of the suppliers. The employee who is making a screw for a seat in a car probably does not feel that he is building a car. However, the supplier who is responsible for the whole seat probably does. This idea to create a larger system view by including the suppliers, and sometimes also the customers, is based on a win–win strategy, meaning that all parts within the system can benefit from cooperation.

Once more we want to emphasize the fact that a basic condition for a company to succeed in its overall efforts to improve quality and to lower costs is that management show a strong commitment to questions regarding quality. Only then can a quality strategy focusing on the customers and built upon the cornerstones described above be successful. The quality strategy has to involve all the activities in the company, not only those which are directly involved in the manufacturing of the product.

B. Total Quality Management as a Management System

Some people see TQM as something necessary to reach competitiveness and emphasize the relation between TQM and success. A recent investigation showed that organizations that received quality awards in the U.S. are considerably more successful than comparable organizations. Others claim TQM to be merely a management fad and point out that many companies have failed to implement TQM. There are several reasons for the different opinions about TQM. One is that the gurus, who often are seen as fathers of TQM, did not like the concept. For instance, Deming never used the term TQM. He said, "The trouble with Total Quality Management, the failure of TQM, you can call it, is that there is no such thing. It is a buzzword. I have never used the term, as it carries no meaning." Also Juran criticized the concept and said, "It is astounding how the term TQM is tossed about without defining what it means." This resistance to the term TQM from some gurus might have resulted in people getting confused and doubtful.

Another reason is that there are several similar names for roughly the same idea, such as total quality control, total quality improvement, company wide quality control, and strategic quality management. The difference, if any, between these and other concepts is often unclear and creates confusion.

A third reason, which may be the most severe, is that there are many vague descriptions and few definitions of what TQM really is. These reasons are of course partly related to each other.

We can often see formulations such as TQM is "a way to . . . ," "a philosophy for . . . ," "a culture of . . . ," "an approach for . . . ," "a business strategy that . . . ," and so on. The absence of a clear definition of TQM is probably the most important negative factor.

To us TQM means a culture based on core values, or cornerstones; see Fig. 12. However, TQM is much more than the core values. It can be interpreted as a management system, a system in the sense of Deming, i.e., as "a network of interdependent components that work together to try to accomplish the aim of the system."

One of the components consists of the core values. The core values constitute the base for the culture of the organization. Another component is methodologies, i.e., ways to work within the organization to support the values. A methodology consists of a number of activities performed in a certain order. The third component consists of tools, i.e., rather concrete and well-defined tools, which sometimes have a statistical basis, to support decision making or facilitate analysis of data. These three components are interdependent on each other and support each other; see Fig. 20. Just to illustrate the different levels, we can think of doing joinery as a methodology and the hammer as a tool within that methodology.

We believe that it is important to classify different terms related to TQM according to any of the three components. As an example, the control chart (see Fig. 7) is a tool to be used within Process Management or Process Control, which both are methodologies. As another example, the core value of, "Let everybody be committed" cannot be implemented without suitable methodologies. Some of these might be "improvement groups" or "quality circles." However, these methodologies will not work efficiently without use of suitable tools. Examples of such tools might be the Ishikawa diagram, Pareto diagram, and histograms. Another core value is "focus on processes." One technique to establish process orientation is Process Management. Some tools, which are useful when working with Process Management, are process maps and control charts. The booklet with criteria related to a quality award, such as the Malcolm Baldrige National Quality Award or the European Quality Award, is a tool. That tool can be used within self-assessment which is a methodology supporting many different core values. In particular self-assessment will support "let everybody be committed" if many people in the organization are involved in the self-assessment process.

By consistently using a terminology based on core values, methodologies, and tools, the "concepts" used within TQM will be clarified, which certainly simpli-

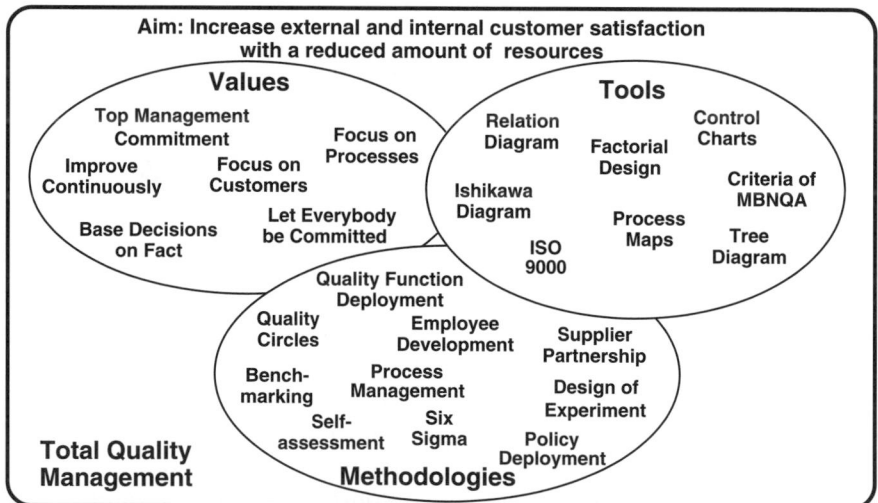

Figure 20 Total quality management (TQM) seen as a continuously evolved management system consisting of values, methodologies, and tools, the aim of which is to increase external and internal customer satisfaction with a reduced amount of resources. It is important to note that the methodologies and tools in the figure are just examples and not a complete list. In the same way the values may also vary a little between different organizations and over time. From Hellsten, U., and Klefsjö, B. (2000). *Total Quality Management,* Vol. 12, No. 4, 238–244.

fies the problem for organizations working with TQM since it gives a picture and structure of what TQM is about. One of the things which is important to note is that TQM really should be looked upon as a system. The values are supported by methodologies and tools to form a whole.

Any system should have an aim. "Without an aim there is no system," according to Deming. The aim of the TQM system is, in our opinion, to increase external and internal customer satisfaction with a reduced amount of resources. Accordingly, the system has a focus on external customers, but also an internal focus on employee satisfaction and effectiveness.

However, the TQM system is also continuously evolving. Over time, some core values might change, and in particular the interpretation of some of them might be developed. As an example we can consider the change in the interpretation of the concept of "customer" from "buyer" to include several categories of external customers and also internal customers. Also methodologies will appear or be transferred from other management theories.

There are several benefits of the system view of TQM. One is that it emphasizes the role of top management. Many of the organizations that have failed with TQM have not had sufficient top management commitment. Another is that it focuses on the totality and hopefully decreases the risk that an organization will pick up only parts of the system. We believe that one reason why several companies have failed with implementing TQM is that they just use small parts from the system. They pick up a few tools or methodologies and believe that these will solve their problems. They do not see TQM as a whole system. Illustrations of this are the use, or maybe we should call it the abuse, of control charts and quality circles some decades ago.

We have to start with the core values and ask: Which core values should characterize the culture in our organization? When that is decided we have to continuously identify methodologies that are suitable for our organization to use and which support our values. Finally, from that decision suitable tools have to be identified and used in an efficient way to support the methodologies. As an example, benchmarking should not be used without seeing the reason for using that methodology and control charts alone should not be used without seeing the core value behind the choice and a systematic implementation of the methodologies and tools. It is, of course, important to note that a particular methodology can support different core values and the same tool can be useful within many

methodologies. If we can use such methodologies and tools we support several values, which of course is of benefit to the culture.

IV. TOTAL QUALITY MANAGEMENT AND QUALITY AWARDS

To support work with total quality management and to give inspiration to other companies, a number of quality awards, both national and international, have been established during the last decades. We will here briefly outline some of these awards and the ideas and criteria behind them.

The assessment base for these awards is similar and consists of a model for the organization's work based on a number of criteria. In each criterion there are a number of questions related to the improvements cycle:

- How do we find out . . . (approach)
- To what extent do we do that? (deployment)
- What results can we explore? (results)
- How do we improve the approaches and deployments? (assessment and improvements)

The application consists of answering the different questions and then analyzing the obtained description. The questions, and also the evaluation dimensions, are based on core values, such as, or similar to, those in Fig. 12.

Although the models, the structure of the questions, and the core values differ slightly among the different awards, the similarities are much stronger than the differences.

A. The Deming Prize

The Deming Prize was instituted in 1951 to honor W. Edwards Deming's contribution to quality development in Japan. There are individual Deming Prizes and Deming Prizes for different kinds of companies. In 1984 the prize committee decided to open the Deming Prize to companies outside Japan as well and created "The Deming Application Prize for Oversea Companies" which was announced for the first time in 1987. Alltogether the following prizes exist:

- The Deming Application Prize
- The Deming Application Prize for Small Enterprise
- The Deming Application Prize for Division

- The Deming Prize for an Individual Person
- The Deming Application Prize for Overseas Companies

Among about 150 companies which have received a Deming Prize up to the year 2000, there are many companies well known in the West, i.e., Nippon Electric Co., Kawasaki Steel, Hitachi Ltd., Fuji Photo Film Ltd, Nissan Motor Co., Toyota Motor Co., Texas Instrument Japan Limited, Bridgestone Tire Company, Kansai Electric Power Company, and Fuji Xerox Co. So far only 3 companies have received the Deming Application Prize for Overseas Companies. One is Florida Power & Light in the U.S., which received the prize in 1989 after a quality program starting in 1981 under the name of QIP (quality improvement process). It is described as a never-ending journey based on the principles of customer satisfaction, plan–do–study–act, management by fact, and respect for people. The second award was given in 1991 to Philips Taiwan, an all-round electronic product manufacturer headquartered in Taipei with about 8200 workers. Philips Taiwan introduced Total Quality Control from Japan in 1985. The third award was given in 1994 to AT&T Powers Systems in Dallas, Texas, which is a part of AT&T Microelectronics. When receiving the award the CEO Andrew Guarriello emphasized that the quality work at AT&T originated with three quality pioneers who worked earlier at AT&T, namely Walter Shewhart, Edwards Deming, and Joseph Juran.

Among the people who have received the Deming Prize for Individuals are Kaoru Ishikawa, Shigero Mizuno, Yoshio Kondo,[9] and Noriaki Kano.

The assessment of a company is done from an overall picture where the Japanese CWQC (company wide quality control) concept is focused, see Table IV.

5. The Malcolm Baldrige National Quality Award

The Malcolm Baldrige National Quality Award was instituted by President Ronald Reagan in August 1987 in the "Malcolm Baldrige National Quality Improvement Act (Public Law 100-107). The work had already started, however, in 1982 on the initiative of President Reagan, who had strong support for his ideas from the American Society for Quality (ASQ).

---

[9] Mizuno is one of those behind the concept of Quality Function Deployment, a methodology for a systematic translation of customer needs to product properties. Kondo has made large contributions to, for instance, the theory of motivation.

Table IV Checklist for the Deming Application Prize

1. Policy
2. Organization and its management
3. Education and dissemination
4. Collection, dissemination, and use of information on quality
5. Analysis
6. Standardization
7. Control
8. Quality assurance
9. Results
10. Planning for the future

The main aim of the award is to increase quality awareness within American companies. As a part of the rules it is required that the companies that receive the award in various ways should inform other companies about their work with successful ventures within the quality field through publication and lectures. In that way an increased awareness of quality and distribution of knowledge will result. The assessment criteria are created to give a complete picture of the activities. This is illustrated by Joe Rocca, one of those behind the quality work at IBM Rochester, who said,

"In our experience with companies that use Baldrige criteria to improve, people who examine their organizations from a Baldrige perspective acquire a discipline for seeing wholes, for seeing interrelationships rather than things, for seeing patterns of change. They become systems thinkers."

The award is named after Malcolm Baldrige, who was Secretary of Commerce from 1981 until his death in a rodeo accident in 1987. He is considered to have had a great influence on the improvement and productivity of work in the government administration. He was also a strong proponent of the award idea. The award is given in five categories:

- Manufacturing
- Service
- Small-business, meaning a manufacturing or service company with not more than 500 employees
- Education (since 1999)
- Health care (since 1999)

No more than two companies in each category are awarded per year.

The Malcolm Baldrige Award model rests on "the 11 core values and concepts": visionary leadership, customer driven, organizational and personal learning, valuing employees and partners, agility, focus on the future, focus on results and creating value, managing for innovation, systems perspective, management by fact, and public responsibility and citizenship. The 7 criteria in the model, whose aim is illustrated in Fig. 21 consist in turn of 18 items.

The criterion "Business Results" has been given 450 points of 1000 total. This criterion includes results in the form of customer satisfaction, financial results, employee satisfaction, and process efficiency. This is an evident change towards financial and other results compared to the older model.

Table V illustrates the organizations which have received the Malcolm Baldrige National Quality Award up to the year 2001.

C. The European Quality Award

In 1992 the European Foundation for Quality Management (EFQM), with support by the European Organization for Quality (EOQ) and the European Commission established *The European Quality Award*. That award rests on what now is called *The EFQM Excellence Model;* see Fig. 22.

Key factors in the assessment criteria are leadership, quality strategy, and improvement work for all processes within the company; how the employees'

knowledge is supported and developed; and the satisfaction among customers as well as the employees. The assessment criteria are similar to those for the Malcolm Baldrige National Quality Award, although the questions in the criteria are more open in their formulation.

A matrix is used to evaluate the answers. It is built on the four dimensions results, approach, deployment, and assessment and review, which gives the acronym RADAR. The idea is that an organization should

- Decide which results should be reached.
- Plan and develop the approaches which are needed.
- Deploy these approaches systematically.
- Assess, review, and improve the approaches and deployments.

D. Quality Awards and Self-Assessment

The different quality awards and their criteria have as one aim to identify successful organizations, but the most important aim is to stimulate organizations to work with TQM in a systematic way by using the criteria for self-assessment.

Self-assessment is a methodology aimed at measuring how well the core values, which are the base of total quality management, have contributed to the culture in

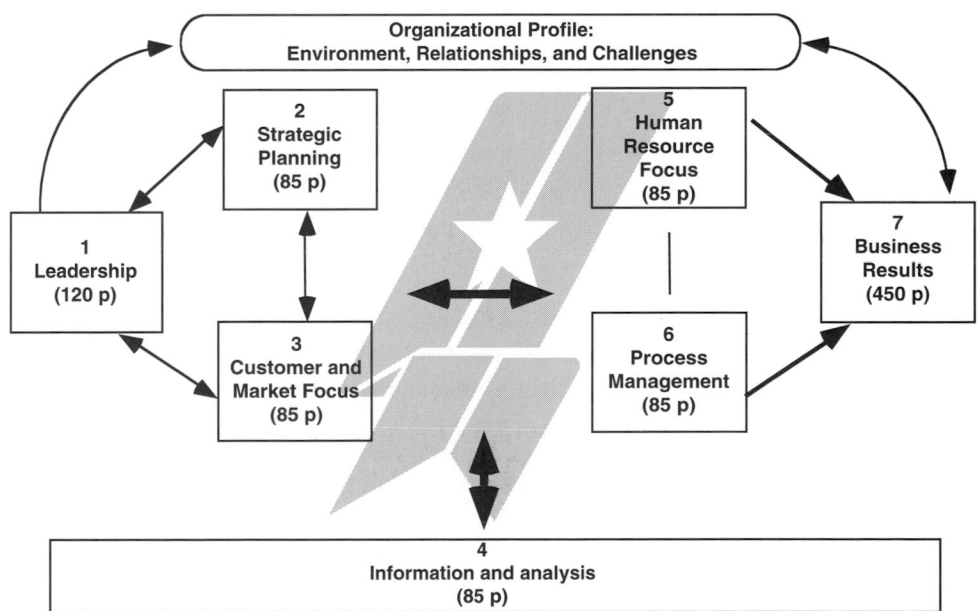

Figure 21 The model for the Malcolm Baldrige National Quality Award. The model was changed in 1997. The assessment criteria are called "Criteria for Performance Excellence."

Table V   The Organizations Which Have Received The Malcolm Baldrige National Quality Award

Year	Manufacturing companies	Small companies	Service companies
1988	• Motorola Inc. • Commercial Nuclear Fuel Division of Westinghouse Electric Corporation	• Globe Metallurgical, Inc.	(None)
1989	• Milliken & Company • Xerox Business Products and Systems	(None)	(None)
1990	• Cadillac Motor Car Comp • IBM Rochester	• Wallace Co., Inc.	• Federal Express Corporation
1991	• Solectron Corp. • Zytec Corp.	• Madowe Industries	(None)
1992	• Transmission Systems Business Unit • Texas Instruments Defense Systems & Electronics Group	• Granite Rock Company	• AT&T Universal Card Services • Ritz-Carlton Hotel Group
1993	• Eastman Chemical Company	• Ames Rubber Corporation	(None)
1994	(None)	• Wainwright Industries	• GTE Directories • AT&T Consumer Services
1995	• Armstong World Industries • Telecommunications Division of Corning Inc	(None)	(None)
1996 ·	• ADAC Laboratories	• Trident Precision Manufacturing • Custom Research Inc	• Dana Commercial Credit Corp
1997	• 3M Dental Products Division • Solectron Corp	(None)	• Merrill Lynch Credit Corp • Xerox Business Services
1998	• Boeing Airlift & Tanker Programs • Solar Turbines Inc.	• Texas Nameplates Company	(None)
1999	• STMicroelectronics	• Sunny Fresh Foods	• BI • The Ritz-Carlton Hotel
2000	• Dana Corp-Spicer • Driveshaft Division KARLEE	• Los Alamos National Bank	• Operations Management International Inc.
2001[a]	• Clarke American Checks	(None)	• Pal's Sudden Service

[a]Besides those in the figure also Chugach School District, University of Wisconsin-Stout, and Pearl River School District received the award during 2001 within the category Education (see www.nist.gov).

the organization and how systematic and comprehensive the work with TQM is. As for several other concepts within the quality area there is not one definition of what self-assessment really is. The definition we prefer is that "self-assessment is a comprehensive and systematic assessment of an organizations activities and results based on a model for business excellence."

In our interpretation self-assessment consists of four phases; see Fig. 23. First you plan the work with self-assessment. Then some form of description of how the work is done today should be created—a map of today's way of work. This description is then ana-

lyzed and strengths and improvement possibilities are identified. From this analysis an action plan is established for improvement work. This action plan is the basis for a more comprehensive business plan in order to avoid improvement work being something separate from other business activities.

Before starting with self-assessment it is important to prepare the work. Among other things it is important to discuss why the work should be done and how it should be performed. It is also important to communicate that in the organization.

Some arguments for self-assessment might be

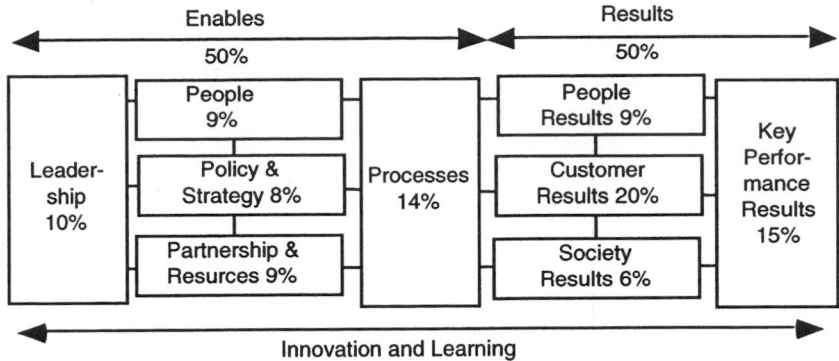

Figure 22 The model which since 1999 is the basis for The European Quality Award (EQA) and which was established by and organized by EFQM (European Foundation for Quality Management). The model is called the EFQMs Excellence Model. Of the assessment points 50% is put on approaches, or enables, and 50% on the results.

- Create a shared picture of how we work today.
- Create a shared language.
- Create a platform for improvement work.
- Create commitment in the organization.
- Introduce a systematic way to improve quality.

How the work should be performed depends on which values the work shall support and the reasons to perform the assessment. If, for instance, it should support "everybody's commitment" it is important that the employees get possibilities to participate in the work. In a small organization, maybe all the staff might be involved; in a larger organization at least one representative from each department or unit should participate. By involving people in the work a common picture of the work today is created, but also a common language. Experiences show that this is very valuable to future work. Education is probably as necessary for self-assessment as a methodology but it is also a tool which is chosen as a basis for that description. In order to create credible results it is important that

the gathered facts be trustful and actual and that the description shows "how we work today" and not "how we worked earlier" or "how we want to work." It is therefore important that the assessment procedure does not take too long. In particular in a smaller organization with limited resources it is wise to start with lower ambitions although this might imply that you limit that part of the business which is being studied. To perform a self-assessment in a useful way it is necessary that an assessment tool be used, which rests on the values and principles of TQM. Therefore, the description of how we work today preferably should be based on one of the different award models.

When the description is ready it should be analyzed and assessed. The analysis can be performed in somewhat different ways. However it is performed, it should lead to a written document with strengths and improvement possibilities within the areas which are studied. In an award simulation, the description is first analyzed individually by the members in a group of examiners. Then the group meets and agrees on a

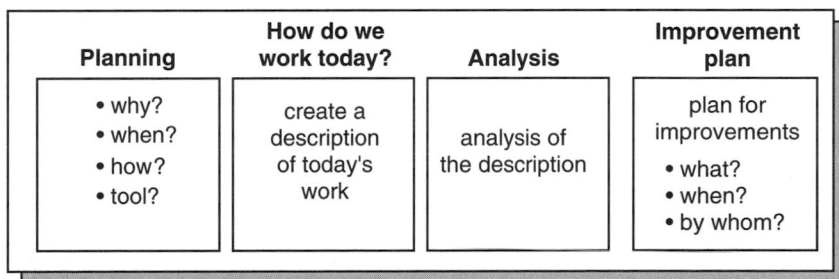

Figure 23 Self-assessment consists of four phases. First the work should be planned. Then a description of how we work today should be created. Then that description should be scrutinized and analyzed and finally an action plan should be created as a base for the improvement work. Note that the four phases have a close relation to the four phases of the improvement cycle. A self-assessment procedure corresponds to one cycle on the organizational level.

common judgment. The group of examiners should consist of 3–5 people, and at least one of the members should be external in order to get credibility.

Of course we should be pleased with our strengths but it is, of course, important to focus on the improvement areas we have found and create an action plan with concrete improvements. For this work the two tool boxes of the seven QC tools (see Fig. 19) and the seven management tools[10] are very efficient.

SEE ALSO THE FOLLOWING ARTICLES

Benchmarking • Cost/Benefit Analysis • Goal Programming • Operations Management • Productivity • Project Management Techniques • Prototyping • Quality Information Systems • Reengineering • Service Industry • Supply Chain Management • Value Chain Analysis

BIBLIOGRAPHY

Bergman, B., and Klefsjö, B. (1994). *Quality from customer needs to customer satisfaction.* London: McGraw-Hill.

Brassard, M. (1994). *The memory jogger plus+.* Methuen: GOAL/QPC.

Carlzon, J. (1987). *The moments of truth.* Cambridge, MA: Ballinger.

Crosby, P. (1979). *Quality is free.* New York: McGraw–Hill.

Deming, W. E. (1986). *Out of the crisis.* Cambridge, MA: Cambridge Univ.

Deming, W. E. (1993). *The new economics for industry, government and education.* Boston: MIT Center for Advanced Engineering Study.

Feigenbaum, A. V. (1951). *Total quality control.* New York: McGraw–Hill.

Garvin, D. A. (1988). *Managing quality.* New York: The Free Press.

Grönroos, C. (1990). *Service management and marketing in the service sector.* Cambridge, MA: Marketing Science Institute.

Hellsten, U., and Klefsjö, B. (2000). TQM as a management system consisting of values, techniques and tools. *Total Quality Management,* Vol. 12, No. 4, 238–244.

Hendricks, K. B., and Singhal., V. R. (1999). Does implementing an effective TQM program actually improve operating performance? Empirical evidence from firms that have won quality awards. *Management Science,* Vol. 43, No. 9, 1258–1274.

Ishikawa, K. (1982). *Guide to quality control.* Tokyo: Asian Productivity Press.

Juran, J. M. (1964). *Managerial breakthrough.* New York: McGraw–Hill.

Juran, J. M. (1989). *Juran on leadership for quality.* New York: McGraw–Hill.

Juran, J. M., and Godfrey, A. B. (Eds.) (1999). *Juran's quality handbook.* 5th ed. New York: McGraw–Hill.

Kano, N. (1995). Upsizing the organization by attractive quality creation, in *Proceedings the First World Congress for Total Quality Management,* April, Sheffield, pp. 60–72.

Kondo, Y. (1994). Kaoru Iskikawa: What he thought and achieved, a basis for further research. *Quality Management Journal,* Vol. 1, No. 4, 86–91.

Kotter, J. P. (1996). *Leading change.* Boston: Harvard Business School Press.

Lillrank, P., and Kano, N. (1989). *Continuous improvement. Quality control circles in Japanese industry.* Ann Arbor, MI: Center for Japanese Studies, University of Michigan.

Magnusson, K., Kroslid, D., and Bergman, B. (2000). *Six sigma. The pragmatic approach.* Lund: Studentlitteratur.

Montgomery, D. C. (2001). *Introduction to statistical quality control,* 4th ed. New York: Wiley.

Oakland, J. (1999). *Total quality management.* 2nd ed. London: Butterworth-Heinemann.

Park Dahlgaard, S. M., Bergman, B., and Hellgren, B. (2001). Reflections on TQM. Part I. A historical perspective; Part II. The evolution of core principles, in *Best on quality* (M. Sinha, Ed.). Milwaukee: ASQ Quality Press.

Shiba, S., Graham, A., and Walden, D. (1993). *A new American TQM: Four practical revolutions in management.* Portland: Productivity Press/The Centre for Quality Management.

Taguchi, G., and Wu, Y. (1979). *Introduction to off-line quality control.* Tokyo: Central Japan Quality Control Association.

Watson, G. H. (1992). *The benchmarking workbook.* Cambridge, MA: Productivity Press.

---

[10] The seven management tools are very useful for structuring and analyzing verbal information. The different tools are affinity diagrams, relation diagrams, tree diagrams, matrix diagrams, matrix data analysis, process decision program charts, and arrow diagrams.

Transaction Processing Systems

Sasan Rahmatian

California State University, Fresno

I. THE LARGER FRAMEWORK
II. TRANSACTION DEFINED
III. TPS DEFINED

IV. TPS AND DATABASE REQUIREMENTS
V. VIEWS OF TPS
VI. STRATEGIC SIGNIFICANCE OF TPS

GLOSSARY

ACID properties A transaction is characterized by four properties referred to as the ACID properties: atomicity, consistency, isolation, and durability.

database update The real effect of a transaction; it takes one of three forms: add, change, and delete.

logical conception A view of a TPS that focuses on *what* information flows into/out of it, and *what* processes are performed on that information. It is relatively stable and permanent.

master file A file that contains data about permanent entities, such as customers, products, suppliers, and employees. Its contents are updated by a transaction file.

physical conception A view of a TPS that focuses on the technology used in entering the data, producing the information, and performing the processes. It is dynamic and transient due to frequent technological advances.

ripple effect Occurs when transaction data travel to all the other parts of the organization where they are needed.

scalability The ability of an application or platform to be expanded in terms of capacity to accommodate a larger number of users or transactions than originally planned without requiring significant changes in procedure.

transaction A business event whose relevant attributes need to be recorded internally (in the corporate database) as well as externally (for the benefit of external stakeholders, such as customers, suppliers, business partners, and regulators) due to

the impact this information will later have on other operations of the organization.

transaction file A file that contains data about a particular class of transactions, such as sales, reservations, returns.

A TRANSACTION PROCESSING SYSTEM (TPS) is a system that captures, enters, stores, retrieves, and processes the relevant details of business events and generates the information and documents necessary for running the business. As such, it is a subset of the operational subsystem of the organization, recording the work done. The data captured and stored by a TPS serve two purposes. First, to support day-to-day, routine operations by being made accessible to those parts of the organization (as well as to external entities) where they are needed. Second, to feed the management reporting system and produce performance reports about the effectiveness and efficiency of the operations. The usefulness of transaction data goes beyond mere operations because large volumes of detailed data can be used as a historical reference for forecasting, identifying trends, and measuring performance. Understanding a TPS can be accomplished along two different dimensions: externally versus internally, and logically (what it does) versus physically (the technology based on which it works). Although a TPS is primarily concerned with day-to-day operations, it does play a critical strategic role in the organization, for it is with the operational level of the organization that customers and suppliers interact, and if the TPS is not working satisfactorily, then those external relations tend to suffer.

I. THE LARGER FRAMEWORK

Any organization—regardless of size, industry, and profit orientation—exists to serve its clientele by adding value to the resources obtained from its external environment. The operational level of the organization consists of those activities that perform the value-adding work on a day-to-day basis. The management control level consists of those activities that compare the results accomplished with the goals set by management in order to identify and correct any possible variances between the two. The data captured and stored by a TPS serve two purposes. First, to support day-to-day, routine operations by being made accessible to those parts of the organization (as well as to external stakeholders) where they are needed. Second, to feed the management reporting system and produce performance reports about the effectiveness and efficiency of the operations. Regardless of which purpose is served, a TPS stores the data it captures in a database for later use. As such, the database is a buffer (1) between the TPS and the management reporting system, and (2) between the TPS at one time and the TPS at a later time (Fig. 1).

II. TRANSACTION DEFINED

Trans means "beyond," as in *transatlantic*. A transaction is the action that an entity performs beyond it-

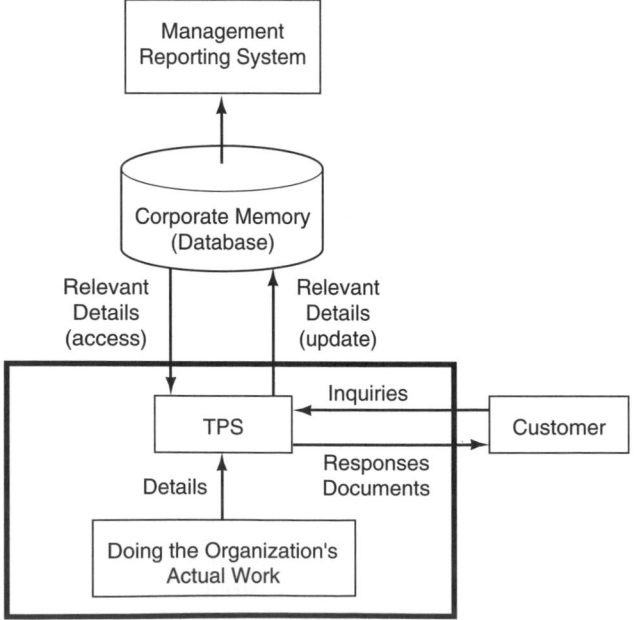

Figure 1 The larger framework of TPS.

self, i.e., on another entity. Hence a transaction, at the simplest level, can be defined as an event involving the action of one entity on another. The word *exchange* is often used to characterize a transaction.

In earlier, simpler times, when business operations were run on a small scale, it was not necessary to use information technology to get accurate status information about business processes. No technology was needed to mediate between the users and the physical reality they were trying to measure or manipulate. For instance, when a customer walked into a store and asked about the availability of a certain item, it would be possible for the clerk to go to the storage room, look up availability, and then report that information back to the customer in a matter of seconds. As this organization grew larger and larger, the size of its warehouse increased accordingly. Beyond some critical threshold point, it would take too long to check the item availability manually.

This is the point at which technology comes in to mediate between humans and the reality they are trying to control (Fig. 2). In a computer-mediated environment, the relevant details of all the sales and shipments received are entered into a computer system. The computer system then automatically updates quantity on hand of any item sold or purchased. Hence, the old scenario would be replayed as follows: When a customer walks into the store and asks about the availability of a certain item, the clerk has to look up its availability on the computer. In other words, the computer has now become the clerk's window into the real world. The picture of the world provided by the system is the only practical way of knowing what is happening in the world. What the system says is real—and only that—can be considered real.

From the above picture emerges the importance of capturing and recording events that impact other parts of the organization, and thus need to be retrieved at a later time. But an event has many different attributes. Only those attributes relevant to later retrieval and use need to be captured and stored. This is the basis on which the concept of transaction is defined as *a business event whose relevant attributes need to be recorded internally (in the corporate database) as well as externally (for a customer, a supplier, a business partner, etc.) due to the impact this information will later have on other operations of the organization and its stakeholders.* Being an event, a transaction takes place in time. It always has a date and time stamped on it. This is significant for reporting purposes, because management can later measure performance down to any unit of time desired ("How many Big Macs are sold per hour?").

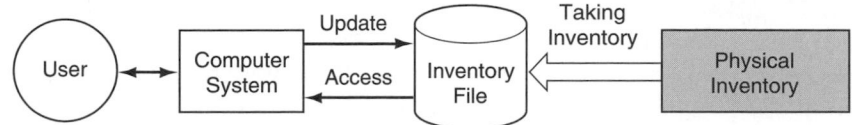

Figure 2 The computer system mediating between the humans and physical reality in an inventory application.

Updates brought about by a transaction are of three types:

- Adding a new record, such as when a new customer signs up
- Changing an existing record, such as changes in credit available for a customer when that customer makes new purchases or returns already purchased products
- Deleting a record, such as when a product is discontinued

Thus defined, transactions are an ancient concept, as old as the beginning of writing. In the Fertile Crescent, archeologists have found clay tablets written with cuneiform symbols that record commercial transactions such as sale of slaves. Some of these tablets are thousands of years old.

In a world in which the virtual is regarded as the image of the physical, what is beginning to matter more and more is not what actually happened, but what the system recorded as having happened. In Fig. 3, four scenarios can be distinguished:

1. *An event happened and it was recorded.* This is a case in which the virtual accurately reflects the physical.
2. *An event happened but it was never recorded.* Consider a customer complaint that was never recorded, or was recorded and later erased (intentionally or otherwise). Because this event was not recorded, it would not leave a trace on the organization's collective memory (i.e., the database), hence failing to set in motion the actions that a customer complaint is supposed to trigger, such as a letter of apology to the customer and an investigation into the internal processes that were responsible for the complaint (defective product, discourteous employee, etc.). Unless the customer complained again, this information would not be acted on because of the organization not remembering it.
3. *An event that never happened was mistakenly recorded as having occurred.* This could take place due to fraud or forgery, but more often it may be due to incorrect processing. Hence, items may actually exist in stock but are shown by the computer system not to be there. Thus a salesperson, checking inventory on-line, could mistakenly see an item as not available and thus forego a sale while the item actually exists in inventory.
4. *An event that never happened was not recorded.* Again, in this case, the virtual accurately reflects the physical.

In short, in the TPS mind-set, if it was not recorded, it did not happen; if it was, it did.

Three important points need to be made about the concept of transaction. One subtlety associated with the concept of event is that *sometimes certain occurrences*

	It was recorded	**It was not recorded**
It really happened	**1. OK** Example: A rental item is returned on time and is recorded as having been returned on time	**2. It did "not happen"** Example: A rental item is returned on time but is mistakenly stamped as having been returned late.
It really did not happen	**3. It "happened"** Example: A rental item is returned late but is mistakenly stamped as having been returned on time.	**4. OK** Example: A rental item is returned late and it is stamped as having been returned late.

Figure 3 What happened versus what was recorded. The event: Returning a rental item (such as a videotape) on time.

that do not happen but are expected to happen constitute events. For instance, a customer's failure to make a payment on his credit card against an assigned deadline may appear as a nonevent. Yet, because of the expectation of the receipt of the payment by the deadline, that nonevent will become an event, triggering finance charges on the next account cycle.

The second subtlety is associated with the concept of relevance. Transactions record the relevant attributes of events, but relevant to what? Two types of relevance can be distinguished: operational and managerial.

The *operational relevance* of an event is derived from other operations in the organization that use the data captured about this event. The simplest way to bring out the operational relevance of an attribute of an event is to ask. "What operations in the organization will later use this piece of information, and how?" For instance, consider the business event in which a salesperson takes a prospective customer to lunch. The amount spent would be relevant because it will be used to later reimburse that salesperson.

The *managerial relevance* of an event is derived from controls set by management to assure that things go according to plan. Returning to the above example, the amount spent on lunch would also have a managerial relevance in that it should not exceed an upper limit preset by management. But more to the point would be the managerial relevance of the *purpose* of the lunch. If that piece of data is not captured, how will management be able to ascertain whether that expenditure was worth it?

The managerial type of relevance can be extended beyond control to include strategic objectives. It used to be that as soon as a customer walked through the door of the corner shop, the proprietor knew who he was and what he wanted. With the scale of business operations increasing immensely over time, organizations have become more impersonal. Strategic conceptions of TPS aim at bringing those days back. Retailers are trying to bring back the "personal touch" using technology to compensate for impersonal contact. Regardless of the scale of an organization's operations, it is good business to know who the organization's customers are and what they want. The problem for large organizations is that they do not even know who their customers are. A large supermarket might know how many units of which item it sold when, but it usually knows much less about the people who buy them. A strategically conceived TPS allows for *micromarketing*—the ability to identify small groups of customers, even individuals, and sell them a product they need, or motivate them to buy such a product by sending them a customized coupon. In terms of customer

recognition, this is possible through special-privilege cards that entitle the customer to discounts on selected items. When the customer swipes the card in the machine, his name comes up on the monitor, and he is greeted by the supermarket staff by name.

The third subtlety has to do with the notion of update versus access. Accessing a database to perform a query or produce a report does not ordinarily constitute a transaction because it does not involve an update to the database. However, *a query is considered a transaction if the query itself is meant to be tracked.* For instance, when a customer inquires into the availability of an item, this would ordinarily count as a read/access operation. However, management may at some point realize that the inquiries themselves are a way of tracking demand. At that point, each inquiry would be tracked in terms of the items requested and their availability. A high level of unavailability of an item would signal management to order or produce a higher level of it.

III. TPS DEFINED

Having defined transaction, we can now proceed to define the term TPS. TPS is a system that captures, enters, stores, retrieves, and processes the relevant details of business events, and generates the information/documents necessary for running the organization and interfacing with external entities, such as customers. The *processing* part of the TPS has to do with the various activities involved in running it, such as the following:

- Capturing the data as close to the source as possible
- Entering them into the system in a manner as effectively and efficiently as possible
- Storing them in the database
- Retrieving them from the database for further processing
- Transforming them from the raw form to information useful to the intended user.

The *systems* part of the TPS has to do with planning and designing the above elements so that they work in sync to produce the organizational objectives behind the TPS. The *transaction* part of the TPS is somewhat more complicated. TPSs are characterized by

- Large amounts of input/output
- Large number of users
- Huge storage requirements
- Low computational complexity

- Fast input/output as well as processing capabilities
- A high degree of concern for potential security-related problems
- A high degree of concern for reliability and fault-tolerance.

A TPS is the lifeblood of an organization. For any business-related event occurring in an organization, a number of design decisions need to be made, such as these:

1. Is the event worth recording? If so, why? Customers calling to ask questions about their bill—is this event worth capturing? Yes, if (among other reasons) the organization is trying to find the most common reasons for customer calls, in order to automate responses to the most frequently asked questions.
2. If the event is worth recording, what attributes need to be captured, and why? Is the identity of the customer service representative (CSR) handling the customer's question in the above example worth documenting? Yes, if (among other reasons) the organization is trying to track customer satisfaction and train those CSRs who need more training.
3. In what form(s) should the event be documented? When a customer returns a product, there is a need to record this event not only internally (the database) but also externally (a credit memo issued to the customer).
4. How should the event be recorded? It used to be that prices were either stamped or tagged on products in supermarkets. The checker would then manually key this price into the cash register. This was both slow and prone to errors. With the advent of bar codes, this event was automated, thus making data capture faster as well as more accurate.

Picture the above design decisions being applied to the thousands and millions of events occurring in a large organization everyday and you get a sense of the enormity and complexity of TPSs.

The inner workings of a TPS are driven by the rules on which the organization runs. For instance, the inner workings of a hotel reservations system are dictated by the business rules and policies governing the reservation operation. Consider a hotel that has adopted the following policy: If a prospective guest cannot be accommodated in terms of the type of room requested, and if during the requested period a higher price room is available, then the guest will be accommodated in that higher price room while being charged the rate for the original room. The design of the reservations TPS of this hotel has to incorporate the above policy into it in order to work as desired. Not all rules are of an internal nature; they may be driven externally, such as by regulatory agencies.

There are few absolutes when it comes to the inner workings of a TPS. Business process reengineering has challenged age-old assumptions about business practices. Consider the practice of issuing invoices to customers. Some redesigned processes have made this practice obsolete. Or consider the practice of issuing purchase orders to suppliers. Continuous replenishment processes have made this practice obsolete too.

IV. TPS AND DATABASE REQUIREMENTS

As pointed out earlier, a transaction captures the relevant attributes of an event for later use by other units in the organization or by external entities. This may be referred to as the *ripple effect* of transactions: Transaction data travel to all the other parts of the organization where they are needed. For instance, the news of customers returning the same defective product needs to travel to production, R&D, or purchasing, depending on where the cause of the defect may lie.

Transaction data are also used to update master files—where data about permanent entities (such as customers, products, suppliers, and employees) are stored. A customer returning a product will trigger a credit event that will update the field "credit available" in that customer's record in the customer file.

Because a transaction sets in motion the ripple effect discussed above, there must be a way to "de-ripple" those effects if the transaction is canceled. That is why a transaction is sometimes defined as *a set of operations that must be executed together, of which none are performed if any one of them is not performed*. In other words, a transaction either *commits*, meaning the changes are all made, or *aborts*, meaning any changes in progress are undone. For instance, in the example of a customer returning a defective product, if later it turns out that the product was really not defective (the customer just didn't know how to use it) and it is returned to her, then any updates that may have already taken place need to be undone.

A transaction is characterized by four properties referred to as the ACID properties: atomicity, consistency, isolation, and durability.

- *Atomicity* means that actions can be grouped together, and either all actions in that group will occur or none will. In other words, if some work is started and a system failure occurs, the state of the system reverts to its state prior to the actions rather than the system being left in an intermediate, corrupted state. Consider, for example, the effects of doing only part of a financial transfer; a TPS should not be able to debit one account without crediting another.

- *Consistency* means that the transaction must represent a correct transformation from one state to another. For example, if a TPS credits one account in a financial transfer, it must debit the other by the same amount.
- *Isolation* means that actions do not interfere with each other. Multiple, simultaneous transactions must be made to appear as if they are actually a series of sequential transactions. If several users want to access the same bank account at the same time, the requests must be serialized and treated independently. Even if actions appear to happen simultaneously to the end users, they must be serialized and isolated internally.
- *Durability* means that once a change is made, it is not undone by a system failure. Changes to data must remain permanent once they are made.

Two of the most exciting uses of transaction data stored in a database are data warehousing and data mining. To avoid endangering an organization's operations, data are pulled from the operational system and placed in a separate data warehouse for the users to access. In data mining, mathematical modeling (in the form of statistical algorithms) is used to identify patterns in data and to analyze past transactions. For instance, data mining can be used to predict which customers are likely to switch to a competitor, or which transactions are most likely to be fraudulent.

V. VIEWS OF TPS

Having explained some of the basic concepts associated with a TPS, we will now discuss ways of viewing a TPS.

A TPS can be viewed along two independent dimensions (Table I). First is the external/internal dimension. From the outside, a TPS looks like a machine that takes certain inputs and produces certain outputs. The external view captures events taking place between the organization and its external environment. To understand how those inputs are converted to outputs, one needs to open up the box and look at the internal view. The internal view captures events taking place within the organization

Second is the logical/physical dimension. The logical understanding of a TPS has to do with *what* information flows into/out of it, and *what* processes are performed on that information, and why. It is relatively stable and permanent. The physical understanding has to do with the technology used in entering the data, producing the information, and carrying out the processes. It is dynamic and transient due to rapid technological advances.

In what follows, we explore the logical and physical views and, within each, the external and internal views.

A. External Logical View of a TPS

This view is concerned with the interactions between the organization and its external environment. We will focus on the interaction between an organization and its customers only. The interactions between an organization and its suppliers are just the mirror image of the interactions between the organization and its customers. The following is a general model of the information exchanges between an organization and its customers (Table II). It may be reminiscent of a game of ping-pong: For every action, there is a reaction.

Typically, the interaction starts with the customer's preliminary request for functionality (i.e., whether the organization produces the types of products or services that would solve the customer's problems), price, availability, and transaction alternatives (method of payment, delivery date, etc.). The orga-

Table I The Two Dimensions of a TPS

	Logical	Physical
External	The information exchanged between the external entity (especially customer) and the organization	The technology (media) used for exchanging the information
Internal	The flow of the information within the organization	The technology (media) used for supporting the information flows within the organization

Table II   External Logical View of a Typical Sales TPS

Customer ⟶ TPS	TPS ⟶ Customer

Preliminary request for information
    Functionality
    Price
    Availability
    Transaction alternatives	

	Preliminary information
	    Functionality
	    Product name/number
	    Price
	    Availability
	    Transaction alternatives

Order details
    Product
    Quantity
    Transaction specifics	

Customer details
    Name
    Address
    Financial details
	Confirmation of receipt of
	    order

	Confirmation of details

	Request for payment
	    Amount
	    Payment alternatives

Payment	Confirmation of receipt of payment

	Confirmation of shipment
	    Order number
	    Date to be shipped
	    Date shipped

Request for delivery status	
	Delivery status

nization's response, of course, would be to provide this detailed information for the customer. Once the customer has done sufficient "shopping around," the order is placed. This involves the specification of order details:

• Product
• Quantity
• Transaction specifics (expected delivery time, method of payment, etc.)

as well as customer details (for new customers):

• Name
• Address
• Phone
• Etc.

The organization's response to this is typically a confirmation (echoing) of the details received. The order is then processed and, as a result, the following may be communicated to the customer: order number, expected shipment date, and actual shipment date.

Depending on the details of the terms of trade, once the requested shipment is made, there is a request for payment (invoice). In response, the customer makes the payment. In response, the organization may produce a receipt of payment. In the process of waiting for the shipment, the customer may want to inquire into its status. The organization's response will be to provide this information.

The above model is generic. As pointed out earlier, not every organizational TPS involves those transactions. In fact, the proponents of business process reengineering would argue that some of the elements listed above, such as invoice, are unnecessary and may be reengineered out of existence.

B. Internal Logical View of a TPS

This view is concerned with the interactions within an organization that support the exchanges discussed above. It shows the various internal functions (processes) performed by the TPS as well as the data flows among them. As such, a data flow diagram is a suitable tool for showing the inner workings of a TPS. Figure 4 shows an example of the internal view of a TPS. It is meant to be representative, not complete. The major subsystems of this TPS are:

• Sales
• Shipping
• Billing
• Accounts Receivable (A/R)
• Production
• Inventory
• Purchasing
• Receiving
• Accounts Payable (A/P)
• Payroll.

As can be seen from Fig. 4, an organization's TPS typically consists of several interconnected cyclic systems with the output of one system often serving as input to another system. This interdependence serves to highlight the truly systemic nature of a TPS: What happens in one subsystem tends to impact other subsystems. For instance, if incorrect sales data are sent to billing and shipping, those functions are later haunted by returned goods and irate customers. The most integrated TPSs

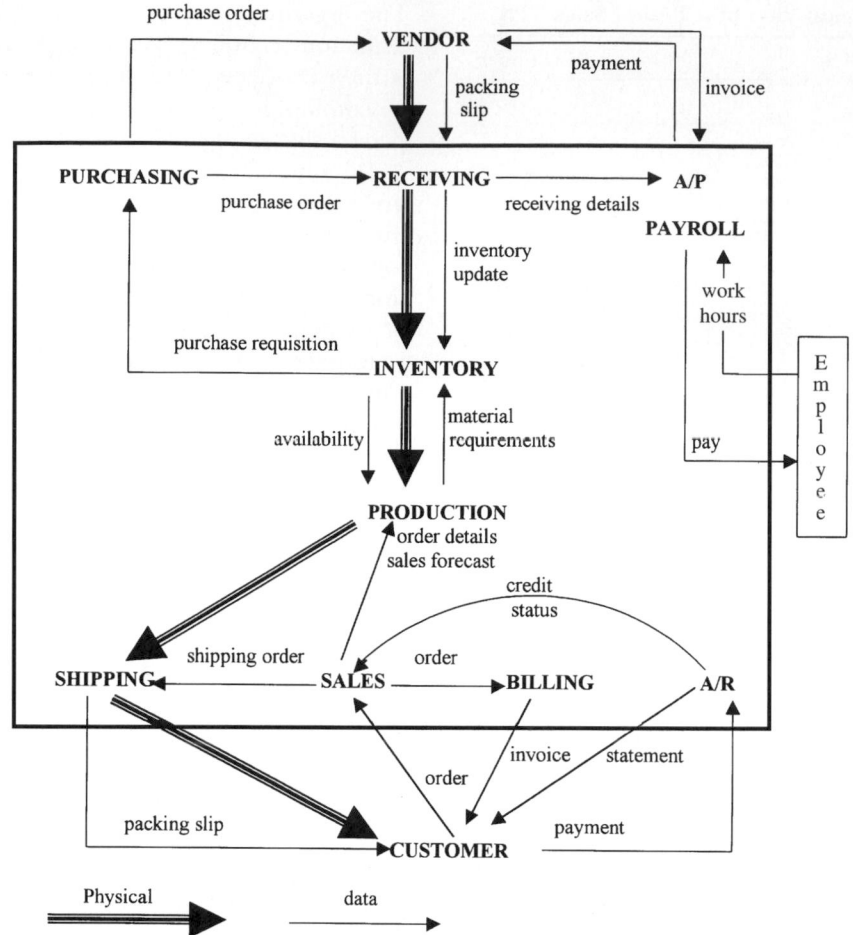

Figure 4 A partial view of the internal, logical flows within a TPS. *Note:* In a retail environment, there is no production subsystem sitting between sales and inventory.

can be found in enterprise resource planning (ERP) systems, which aim at tightly linking the various subsystems of a TPS. ERP systems integrate not only the various operational areas of an organization but, more importantly, they integrate the operational level with planning and decision making needs.

Figure 4 is somewhat misleading in that it does not show the data stores corresponding to the various processes performed. The outputs from a process are not sent directly to other processes. Rather, they are stored in that part (file) of the database that is designed to store data indigenous to that process. Hence the sales process would update the sales file, the shipping process would update the shipping file, etc.

C. External Physical View of a TPS

Recall that the physical view of a TPS focuses on the technology used in implementing it. Thus the exter-

nal physical view is concerned with all technologies used in providing input and producing output. Rather than list the various input/output technologies, we will discuss the broader categories into which TPS input/output technologies commonly fall:

- *None.* This is the oldest TPS interface. The direct face-to-face communication between the organization and its customers without any technology used as the medium still works in some industries, such as retail.
- *Mail.* This is the second oldest model, where the traditional postal system is used for sending orders and payments, and receiving invoices.
- *Fax.* While very popular during the past 20 years, fax is a feasible TPS technology only in certain ways, such as sending in orders.
- *Phone.* This is also a traditional TPS technology that works more for the front end of the TPS cycle, namely, the customer's preliminary request

for functionality, price, availability, and transaction alternatives.

- *Electronic.* This is the most advanced form of communication. As such, it takes two different forms: free-format, and structured.
  - *Free-format.* E-mail communication falls in this category. Because e-mail contents are not governed by any standardized formatting rules, e-mail is not the optimal way of conducting customer-organization interactions.
  - *Structured.* Electronic data interchange (EDI) and Internet-based electronic commerce (whether business to business or business to consumer) fall in this category. In either case, predesigned procedures are used to regulate the electronic flow of information between the customer and the organization. When the customer-organization communication is completely structured, it can be automated. Automated customer service representative systems and automated teller machines are examples of this principle.

D. Internal Physical View of a TPS

The internal physical view is concerned with all technologies used in converting the TPS inputs into outputs. In other words, they are processing technologies. Transaction volume is a major consideration in processor selection. An application that does not respond well to increased transaction volume is said to lack scalability. *Scalability* is defined as the ability of an application or platform to be expanded in terms of capacity to accommodate a larger number of users or transactions than originally planned without requiring significant changes in procedure.

Regardless of how technically advanced a processing technology is, if a TPS handles transactions one at a time immediately on request, then it is referred to as an on-line transaction processing (OLTP) system. The opposite of on-line transaction processing is batch processing. Instead of handling one transaction at a time, batch processing systems work on a group of transactions assembled for processing at a specific time, such as at the end of the day or the end of an accounting period. Payroll is a common batch processing application.

OLTP can also be viewed as a system of programs that facilitate and manage transaction-oriented applications, typically for data entry and retrieval in a number of industries, including banking, airlines, mail-order, supermarkets, and manufacturing. The classic example of a commercial OLTP product is IBM's CICS (Customer Information Control System).

Today's on-line transaction processing increasingly requires support for transactions that span a network and may include more than one company. For this reason, new OLTP software programs use client/server processing that allow transactions to run on different computer platforms in a network. Despite the recent shift to the client/server model, many legacy TPSs are still in use running on mainframe or midrange computers.

Regardless of the specific platform or architecture being used, the electronic medium has by itself revolutionized transaction processing. The difference between the electronic medium and the manual one is not just quantitative (faster, more accurate) but also qualitative (doing it versus not doing it). By hitting a single key on the specialized order entry keyboard of a point-of-sale system in a fast food chain, the order taker enters into the system a wealth of data (date, time, order details, employee ID, etc.) that are stored in the system for later use. Capturing this wealth of information in a low-tech, manual environment would not be feasible. A TPS that does not capture detailed data about the operation it is intended to support does not give its managers a clear picture of how effectively and efficiently that operation is performed.

VI. STRATEGIC SIGNIFICANCE OF TPS

A customer's satisfaction with an organization is composed of two elements:

- The satisfaction with the *product* (service) acquired—its functionality/quality
- The satisfaction with the *process* involved in acquiring the product or service.

The latter is a function of the effectiveness and efficiency of the organization's TPS. An organization is typically represented in the form of a triangle/pyramid to show the management hierarchy. The TPS, being a subset of the operational system, is typically shown as the lowest level. Whether consciously or subconsciously, we associate more status and significance with higher levels and less with the lower ones. Most of those running the TPS, at the lowest level of the organization, are clerks of lower education and pay. But it is precisely with this level of the organization that customers interact in their day-to-day business dealings. It is this level—not the higher management levels—that customers "see" as the XYZ organization.

Even if the organization offers the highest quality product or service at the lowest price, the customers have to go through the labyrinth of the customer cycle (inquiry, ordering, paying, shipping, etc.) before they receive the actual product or service. With the slightest dissatisfaction occurring in this preliminary interaction, customers may change their minds, cancel the order, and switch to a competitor. At its best, the strategic significance of the TPS lies in its ability to offer a pleasant purchasing experience to customers; one that would satisfy them enough to make them want to come back again and again. At its worst, the strategic significance of the TPS is revealed when it fails to work, thus bringing the inner wheels of the organization to a disastrous halt.

The strategic significance of a TPS goes beyond mere efficiency in that a TPS can incorporate features aimed at attracting and keeping customers. The field of strategic information systems is replete with examples of mundane types of TPSs that were given a strategic thrust. An example of a mundane transaction processing subsystem is order processing. A typical order processing system is based on the following logic. Order data are received, verified, and entered into the system. The system then verifies the customer's credit status and product availability. If both are positive, the relevant information is sent to inventory (or production as the case may be), shipping, and billing. If the requested item is not in stock, the customer is asked if he wants to backorder the item. If he does, that sets in motion a whole series of actions. Along the way, some exception reports and documents are generated also. Regardless of the complexity and number of steps involved, there is a clear-cut structure to this process.

If most order processing systems follow the above logic, then how can one stand out as strategically superior to others? The classic example of revolutionizing order entry was the American Hospital Supply Corporation's ASAP (Analytic Systems Automatic Purchasing). Order entry terminals were placed in hospitals and linked to AHSC's computers. Using these terminals, hospitals could place orders with a great deal of peace of mind, being assured of cost, availability, and delivery in advance. With a system offering this level of service, it is unlikely that a client hospital would switch to AHSC's competition.

With the increasing popularity of the Internet and electronic commerce, this model has now become pervasive and improved on by pioneers such as Amazon.com and Drugstore.com. The more value a TPS offers the customer, the more customers will be attracted and kept loyal. Therein lies the strategic promise of a TPS.

SEE ALSO THE FOLLOWING ARTICLES

Accounting • Electronic Data Interchange • Manual Data Processing • Marketing • Operations Management • Procurement • Sales

BIBLIOGRAPHY

Escalle, C. (February, 1999). Enterprise resource planning. *Harvard Business Review.*
Francalanci, C. (June, 1994). State Street Boston Corporation: Leading with information technology. *Harvard Business Review.*
Hammer, M. (July, 1990). Reengineering work: Don't automate, obliterate. *Harvard Business Review.*
Hopper, M. (May, 1990). Rattling SABRE—New ways to compete on information. *Harvard Business Review.*
Ives, B. (September, 1995). J.C. Penney: Fashioning a retailing nervous system for the future. *Harvard Business Review.*
Konsynski, B. (February, 1991). Baxter Healthcare Corporation: ASAP express. *Harvard Business Review.*
McKenney, J., and Clark, T. (March, 1995). Proctor & Gamble: Improving consumer value through process redesign. *Harvard Business Review.*
Nolan, R. (September, 1999). Drugstore.com. *Harvard Business Review.*
Rogers, T. J. (July, 1990). No excuses management. *Harvard Business Review.*

Transmission Control Protocol/ Internet Protocol (TCP/IP)

Ray Hunt

University of Canterbury, Christchurch, New Zealand

GLOSSARY

address resolution protocol/reverse address resolution protocol (ARP/RARP) A protocol used in TCP/IP networks to bind an IP address to a physical hardware address (e.g., a MAC address). RAPR operates in reverse.

classless inter-domain routing (CIDR) A way to allocate and specify the Internet addresses used in inter-domain routing more flexibly than with the original system of Class A, B, C, D . . . addresses. As a result, the number of available IPv4 addresses has been greatly increased.

directory name service (DNS) A distributed database system used to map IP addresses to their domain names. Because maintaining a central list of domain name/IP address correspondences would be impractical, the lists of domain names and IP addresses are distributed throughout the Internet in a hierarchy of authority.

file transfer protocol (FTP) A standard Internet protocol and is the simplest way to exchange files between computers on the Internet. FTP is an application protocol that uses the TCP/IP protocols and is commonly used to transfer Web page files from their creator to the computer that acts as their server.

hypertext transport protocol (HTTP) The set of rules for exchanging files (text, graphic images, sound, video, and other multimedia files) on the Web. Relative to the TCP/IP suite of protocols HTTP is an application protocol.

International Standards Organisation A worldwide federation of national standards bodies from around 100 countries. Among the standards if fosters is Open Systems Interconnection (OSI), a universal reference model for communication protocols. Many countries have national standards organizations such as the American National Standards Institute (ANSI) that participate in and contribute to ISO standards making.

Internet Assigned Number Authority (IANA) The organization under the Internet Architecture Board (IAB) that, has overseen the allocation of IP addresses to ISPs. It also has had responsibility for the registry for "unique parameters and protocol values" for Internet operation such as port numbers, character sets, and MIME media access types.

Internet Control Message Protocol (ICMP) A message control and error-reporting protocol between a host server and a gateway to the Internet. ICMP uses IP datagrams, but the messages are processed by the IP software and are not directly apparent to the application user.

Internet Engineering Task Force (IETF) The body that defines standard Internet operating protocols such as TCP/IP. It is supervised by the Internet Society Internet Architecture Board (IAB) and its members are drawn from the Internet Society's individual and organization membership. Standards are expressed in the form of Requests for Comments (RFCs).

Internet Gateway Message Protocol (IGMP) An Internet protocol that provides a way for an Internet computer to report its multicast group membership to adjacent routers. Multicasting allows one computer on the Internet to send content to multiple computers that have identified themselves as interested in receiving the originating computer's content.

Internet Protocol (IP) See TCP/IP.

Internet service provider (ISP) A company that provides individuals and other companies access to the Internet and other related services such as web site building and virtual hosting. An ISP has the equipment and the telecommunication line access required to have a POP (point-of-presence) on the Internet for the geographic area served.

internetwork packet exchange (IPX) A Netware's layer 3 connectionless datagram network layer protocol equivalent to IP. It is Novell's IP equivalent that interconnects NetWare clients and servers.

maximum transmission unit (MTU) The largest size packet or frame that can be sent in a packet- or frame-based networks. TCP uses the MTU to determine the size of each packet in any transmission. Most computer operating systems provide a default MTU value that is suitable for most users. For many operating systems the default MTU is 1500 octets, mainly because this is the Ethernet standard MTU. The Internet de facto standard MTU is 576, but ISPs often suggest using 1500.

network service access point (NSAP) A hierarchical address used to implement OSI network layer addressing. The NASP is the logical point between the network and transport layers where network services are delivered to the transport layer; the location of this point is identified to the OSI network service provider by the NSAP address.

open system interconnection (OSI) A standard description or reference model for how messages should be transmitted between any two points in a telecommunication network. Its purpose is to guide product implementers so that their products will inter-work. The reference model defines seven layers of functions that take place at each end of a communication.

protocol data unit (PDU) Used by the ISO-OSI protocol specifications, PDUs are units of data used to exchange information (user and control) between entities in a network. Common units include bit (layer 1), frame (layer 2), packet (layer 3), segment (layer 4).

quality of service (QoS) On the Internet and in other networks, QoS is the idea that transmission rates, error rates, and other characteristics can be measured, improved, and, to some extent, guaranteed in advance. QoS is of particular concern for the continuous transmission of high-bandwidth video

and multimedia data as transmitting this kind of content dependably is difficult in public networks using ordinary best effort protocols.

request for comment (RFC) A formal document from the Internet Engineering Task Force (IETF) that is the result of committee drafting and subsequent review by interested parties. Some RFCs are informational in nature. Of those that are intended to become Internet standards, the final version of the RFC becomes the standard and no further comments or changes are permitted. Change can occur through subsequent RFCs that supersede or elaborate on previous RFCs.

simple message transfer protocol (SMTP) A TCP/IP protocol used in sending and receiving e-mail. However, since it is limited in its ability to queue messages at the receiving end, it is usually used with one of two other protocols, POP3 or IMAP, that let the user save messages in a server mailbox and download them periodically from the server.

simple network management protocol (SNMP) The protocol governing network management and the monitoring of network devices and their functions. It is not necessarily limited to TCP/IP networks although this is its primary focus. SNMP exists in three versions and is described formally by the IETF RFCs.

transmission control protocol (TCP/IP) The basic communication language or protocol of the Internet. It can also be used as a communication protocol in a private network (intranet or extranet). TCP/IP is a two-layer program. The higher layer (TCP), manages the assembling of a message or file into smaller packets that are transmitted over the Internet and received by a TCP layer that reassembles the packets into the original message. The lower layer, internet protocol, handles the address part of each packet.

transport service access point (TSAP) OSI terminology used to identify the end points of the connection (i.e., the source and destination port fields in TCP protocol).

trivial file transfer protocol (TFTP) An Internet software utility for transferring files that is simpler to use than FTP but less capable. It is used where user authentication and directory visibility are not required. TFTP uses the connectionless UDP rather than connection-oriented TCP.

user datagram protocol (UDP) Is a connectionless communications protocol that offers a limited amount of service when messages are exchanged between computers in a network that uses IP. UDP is an alternative to the connection-oriented TCP and, together with IP, is sometimes referred to as UDP/IP.

TCP/IP (TRANSMISSION CONTROL PROTOCOL/INTERNET PROTOCOL) has become the most widely used protocol architecture for transporting application data over local and wide area networks. In fact TCP/IP is found in almost every installation and business sector both nationally and internationally and is now considered the *de facto* standard for OSI Reference Model layer 3 and 4 architectures. Virtually all local and wide area networking infrastructures carry IP traffic and most applications expect to be carried by TCP/IP. More recent TCP/IP networks have been enhanced to carry voice traffic in a large number of business and consumer applications.

TCP/IP has its roots in the United States Department of Defense APARNET and was designed to operate as a reliable protocol over an unreliable lower layer network. It is a protocol architecture designed for the datagram environment, where the network layer may lose, duplicate, or shuffle information unpredictably.

Unfortunately current TCP/IP bears many of the hallmarks of protocols designed over 25 years ago and indeed one not suited to today's systems. For example, it lacks adequate address space for what is currently expected of it (particularly with respect to the new range of data mobiles coming onto the market) and it has no useful performance or security facilities—issues central to the satisfactory operation of the Internet and intranets today.

This chapter traces the development and use of TCP/IP also discussing briefly its successor—IPv6. It looks at the architectural aspects of connection-oriented TCP as this provides end-to-end flow control, error control, connection setup, and status exchange as well as IP which provides a datagram-oriented (connectionless) gateway service between subnetworks. Also discussed are the links to the underlying architectures such as Ethernet, frame relay, etc., as well as architectures such as simple message transfer protocol (SMTP), hypertext transport protocol (HTTP), file transfer protocol (FTP), and others which run over TCP/IP. For these upper layers, TCP/IP was designed to present a program-layer interface that was relatively independent of any architectural features of the host, including memory, performance, etc.

A very important aspect of IP is addressing and the construction of routed subnetworks typical of those found in business practice today. This chapter will examine the IP addressing structure and subnetting in some detail and indicate the improvements that have been made pending a full implementation of IPv6.

I. INTRODUCTION

TCP/IP comprise two specific protocols existing within a protocol stack often referred to as the TCP/IP protocol suites. IP and TCP follow layered networking concepts and map to the Open System Interconnection (OSI) Reference Model layers 3 and 4, respectively. TCP provides a virtual circuit (connection oriented) communications service which—although functionally a "block" oriented protocol—appears as a "stream" to the application which it supports. As such, it provides end-to-end flow control, error control, connection setup, and status exchange while IP provides a datagram-oriented (connectionless) gateway service between subnetworks.

At layer 4 (transport layer) of the OSI model there are two key protocols of interest—TCP (connection-oriented) and user diagram protocol (UDP) (connectionless). At layer 3 (network layer) IP is the primary (connectionless or datagram) protocol but is supported by other protocols at the same level. These include address resolution protocol/reverse address resolution protocol (ARP/RARP) for address discovery, Internet gateway message protocol (ICMP) for ping, error reporting, etc., and IP routing protocols.

TCP/IP has been implemented on nearly every type of computing and networking platform in use today. It represents a communications service's "lowest common denominator," providing peer communications at layers 3 and 4 of the OSI model. The network layer of TCP/IP is the connectionless IP and is designed to route packets through a network while TCP provides the reliable end-to-end connection-oriented service. TCP/IP has supplemented older proprietary protocols such as Netware and AppleTalk by various interoperability kludges.

II. TCP/IP INFRASTRUCTURE AND ARCHITECTURE

A. Virtual Circuit versus Datagram Networking

Figure 1 shows an ISO Model connection, with each layer and peer protocol indicated. It can be seen that layers 1 through 3 of the protocol define "local" procedures, which have peer layer members in each network element or on both sides of any connection.

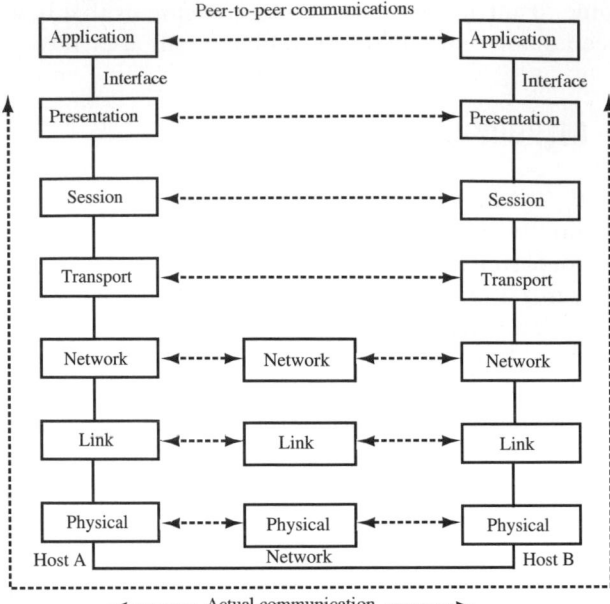

Figure 1 OSI 7-layer model showing actual and peer-to-peer communication.

Layers 4 through 7 represent "end-to-end" procedures—protocols which serve the end user directly and reside in equipment serving that user. Layer 2 is responsible for transmission of data frames or cells of information between any two communicating points. Layer 3 is responsible for the routing of data packets among the nodes of the network. Layer 4 is responsible for the reliable end-to-end communication between the applications.

In a datagram environment an application transmits a data packet into the network using the destination IP address. Routing algorithms within each node establish a route to the next node by the use of metrics such as hop count, delay, bandwidth, etc. There is no formal call setup and this procedure resembles a postal system.

Datagram networks have the following characteristics:

- There is no fixed route between nodes, so no special action is needed to reestablish a path if a link or node fails. If each node knows which output links are operating, it transmits only on those links. If any path at all can be found from source to destination, communication is possible. There is no fixed route between logical nodes, however, physically, of course, static routes between adjacent nodes (e.g., leased lines) are very much a necessity.
- Because consecutive information elements may take different routes to the destination, they may arrive out of sequence and duplicate packets can

occur if two or more possible paths exist to the destination.
- Datagrams may be "broadcast routed" where every node receiving a datagram sends it out on all available links. Broadcast routing is wasteful, but it does simplify network architecture. Further, broadcast networks (e.g., Ethernet) suffer from scalability problems.

In a virtual circuit network the nodes establish a virtual path between communicating parties when a connection is established, and subsequent data units follow that path. In a datagram network each packet is addressed to its destination and sent to the network nodes to be routed by the best path available to the destination.

Virtual circuit networks have the following characteristics:

- The network nodes must maintain a table of addresses and destination routes so that the applications can be linked. These addresses are commonly defined by "ports" or "sockets."
- A break in the routing chain disrupts the connection, because the destination address has been discarded and an alternate route cannot be looked up.
- Virtual circuits are established by a "handshake procedure" in a similar manner to which a circuit-switched telephone call is established. Once this connection is established no addressing is required as the path through the network is defined by the virtual circuit table in each node across the network.

TCP/IP was designed for the datagram environment where the network layer may lose, duplicate, or re-order information unpredictable. Thus the connection-orientated TCP protocol turns the unreliable connectionless IP protocol into a reliable end-to-end application-interconnection service where IP has the facilities to find alternative paths through the network when overload or faults occur as shown in Fig. 2.

The ISO protocol model demonstrates that there are two interfaces at any layer—one below and one above. At the *upper* layer, TCP/IP was designed to present a program-layer interface that was relatively independent of any architectural features of the host, including memory, performance, etc. At the *lower* interface TCP/IP was designed to make the application interconnection independent of underlying copper, fiber, satellite, wireless access, or core network infrastructure.

It is the combination of these features—independence of host architecture at the higher layer interaction points and of communications protocols and

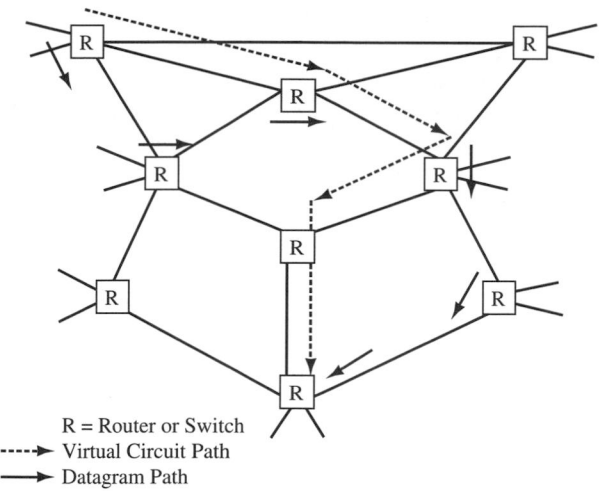

R = Router or Switch
----▶ Virtual Circuit Path
——▶ Datagram Path

Figure 2 Virtual circuit and datagram paths through a network.

facilities at the lower layer interaction points—that forms both the design basis and the commercial justification of TCP/IP.

B. TCP/IP Architectural Framework

The TCP protocol is responsible for reliable, simultaneous, full-duplex connections. TCP takes care of transmission errors by resending data received in error or any data not acknowledged in a certain time period. The application layers that use TCP do not have to be concerned with reliability of data transmission because this task is handled by TCP.

TCP also provides for simultaneous connections. Several TCP connections (virtual circuits) can be established and data can be sent simultaneously, independent of data on other connections. Thus TCP forms an excellent software-based multiplexing protocol providing full-duplex data transfer.

TCP/IP is almost always referred to in this unified form, when, in fact, each element (TCP and IP) is a unique, functional layer of protocol:

- TCP provides a virtual circuit-like, byte stream-oriented communications services for programs using application layer protocols, including end-to-end flow control, error control, connection setup, and status exchange. TCP operates independently of any routing provided by the underlying network and at any time, the route between two hosts engaged in a TCP conversation could change.

- IP provides a datagram-oriented gateway service between subnetworks, so that hosts can interwork. IP does not enhance the reliability or accuracy of the datagrams—it only lets them be routed from one subnetwork to another. IP also provides fragmentation and reassembly so that large IP datagrams can be transferred over networks with small maximum transmission unit (MTU) sizes. Figure 3 shows the position of TCP/IP in relation to protocols running below and above as well as those which support its operation.

C. TCP/IP Protocol Multiplexing and Demultiplexing

TCP provides a multiplexing/demultiplexing service as can be seen in Fig. 4. Hosts at both ends are running TCP/IP application services such as FTP, Telnet, trivial file transfer protocol (TFTP) and simple network management protocol (SNMP) for example.

Several sessions exist between the hosts that use FTP. The networking software on each host distinguishes between multiple applications or protocols at a given layer. For example, Ethernet carries IP and ICMP protocols and potentially other protocols such as Netware's IPX. Therefore the Ethernet frame must specify whether a packet arriving from a network interface is destined for IP or IPX. To make this distinction, Ethernet uses a 2-byte Ethertype field that is part of the Ethernet frame, as shown in Fig. 5. This field at the data link layer makes it possible to

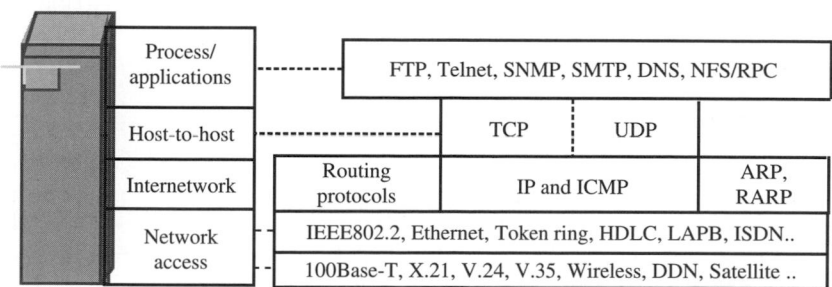

Figure 3 TCP/IP implementation layered hierarchy.

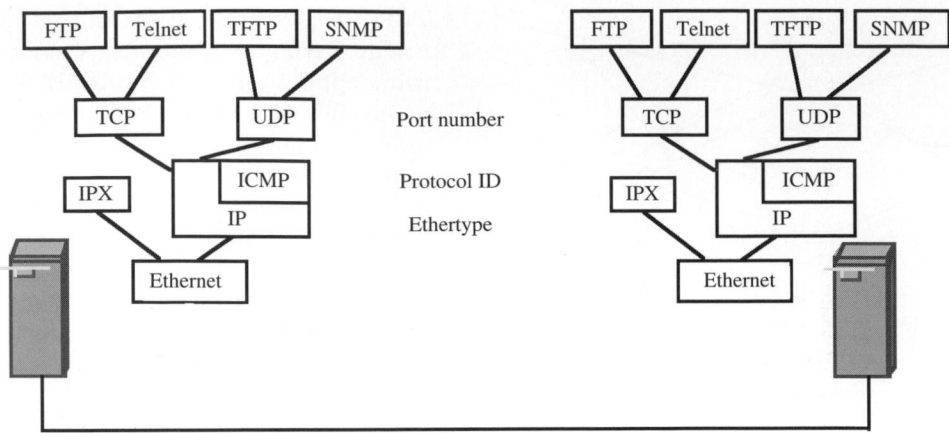

Figure 4 Protocol multiplexing and demultiplexing.

multiplex several network protocols at the sender and demultiplex them at the receiver.

D. IP [RFC 791 (IP), RFC 792 (ICMP), RFC 950 (Subnetting)]

IP is used to encapsulate TCP and UDP segments as shown in Fig. 6. It provides a logical network address for the hardware network interface. This logical address (32 bits) can be used to identify separate physical networks interconnected by routers. The IP address identifies the destination network and host address on that network.

Closely associated with IP is the ICMP which is used to report problems encountered with the delivery of a datagram, such as an unreachable host or unavailable port. ICMP can also be used to send an echo request packet to a host to test its presence on the network (ping test). On receiving an ICMP echo request, the host sends back an ICMP reply packet if it is functioning correctly. ICMP also can be used by routers to send an ICMP redirect message to other devices indicating alternative path availability.

For IP devices to communicate at layer 3 on a subnetwork, underlying layer 2 Ethernet addresses need to be resolved. Additional protocols such as ARP and RARP are used to resolve these mappings. In the following example the sender broadcasts an ARP request which specifies its own Ethernet (layer 2) and IP (layer 3) addresses as well as the destination IP address. It awaits a response in which the destination station recognizes its IP address and responds with its own Ethernet and IP address as shown below.

```
ARP_RARP: Sender's Hardware Address =
00A0C9A23CF5
ARP_RARP: Sender's Protocol Address =
132.181.13.14
ARP_RARP: Target's Hardware Address =
000000000000 (looking for an Ethernet
address)
ARP_RARP: Target's Protocol Address =
132.181.13.103

ARP_RARP: Sender's Hardware Address =
0000C065A3D2 (Ethernet address now
resolved)
ARP_RARP: Sender's Protocol Address =
132.181.13.103
ARP_RARP: Target's Hardware Address =
00A0C9A23CF5
ARP_RARP: Target's Protocol Address =
132.181.13.14
```

6 bytes	6 bytes	2 bytes	max of 1600 bytes	4 bytes
Destination address	Source address	Ethertype field	Info field	CRC

Figure 5 Ethertype filed used for multiplexing/demultiplexing.

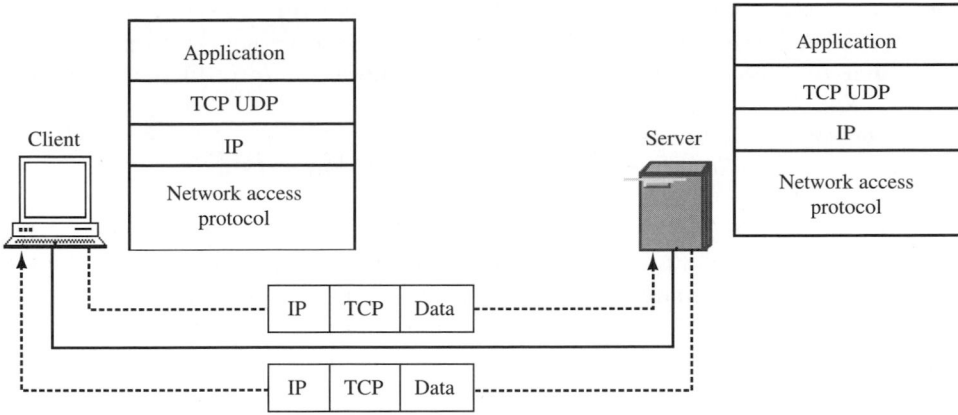

Figure 6 The IP protocol transporting TCP or UDP data segments.

1. Format of the IP Packet

An IP datagram consists of a header part and a text part. The header has a 20-byte fixed part and a variable length optional part as shown in Fig. 7.

- The *Version* field identifies IPv4 or IPv6—the only two versions in practical use.
- The *header length* specifies the length of header in 32-bit words.
- The *Type of service* field allows the host to tell the subnet what kind of service it wants. Various combinations of reliability and speed are possible. For digitized voice, fast delivery is far more important than correcting transmission errors. For file transfer, accuracy is far more important than speedy delivery.
- The *Total length* includes the total contents of the datagram (header and data). The maximum length is 65,535 bytes (the minimum length is 576).

- The *Identification* field is needed to allow the destination host to determine to which datagram a newly arrived fragment belongs. All the fragments of a datagram contain the same *identification* value.
- *DF* means do not fragment the datagram. It is an order to the gateways not to fragment the datagram because the destination is incapable of putting the pieces back together again or when the sender does not wish to use fragmentation such as with TCP path MTU discovery.
- *MF* means more fragments. All fragments except the last one must have this bit set. It is used as a double check against the *Total length* field, to make sure that no fragments are missing and that the whole datagram is reassembled.
- *Fragment offset* specifies where in the current datagram a fragment belongs. Since 13 bits are provided, there is a maximum of 8192 fragments per datagram, giving a maximum datagram length

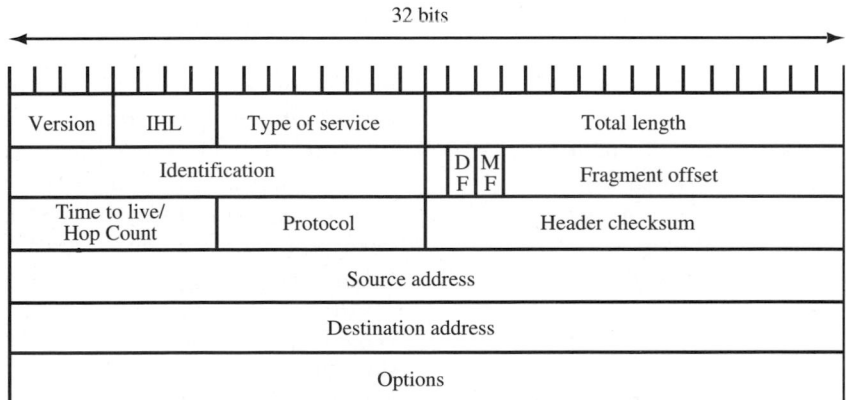

Figure 7 IP header.

of 65,536 bytes, in agreement with the *Total length* field. The fragment offset is measured in units of 8 octets (64 bits). The first fragment has offset zero.

- The *Time to live* or *hop count field* is a counter used to limit packet lifetimes. When it becomes zero, the packet is discarded. Effectively this field is now used as a hop counter.
- The *Protocol* field specifies the various transport processes to which the datagram belongs. Sample values include: TCP = 6, UDP = 17, ICMP = 1. The full list is defined in RFC1700—Assigned Numbers.
- The *Header checksum* verifies the header only. Such a checksum is useful because the header may change at a gateway (e.g., fragmentation may occur).
- The *Source and Destination Addresses* indicate the network number and host number and are further discussed below.
- The *Options* field is used for security, source routing, error reporting, debugging, time stamping, and other information.

In summary IP provides the following functions:

- *Addressing:* IP assumes an Internet-wide addressing convention generated by combining a network ID assigned by the network administrator and a local host address.
- *Status translation and communications:* IP's supporting protocol—ICMP—provides four types of status messages: destination unreachable/invalid, time-out, parameter error, and redirect requested.
- *Routing:* The IP suite provides for the exchange of messages to determine the status of gateways and their related hosts. IP provides a time-to-live (hop count) parameter, a number that is decremented as the IP datagram is processed by a router. Once it reaches zero, the datagram is discarded. This is an effective method of stopping a datagram from endlessly looping on the network.
- *Fragmentation and reassembly:* IP is capable of routing datagrams into networks that are incapable of handling the datagram's size via fragmentation. The original datagram is subdivided into pieces small enough for transmission over the destination network.
- *Type of service:* This indicates that a datagram would prefer any or all of the following services: low-delay path, high-bandwidth path, and high-reliability path. This field has not been used but is

now receiving attention as the industry demands quality of service (QoS) parameter specification pending the introduction of IPv6.

E. TCP [RFC 793]

A TCP transport entity accepts arbitrarily long messages from upper layer applications, breaks them up into segments <= 64 KB, and transmits each segment by encapsulating it in an IP datagram. The network layer provides no guarantee that datagrams will be delivered reliably, so it is up to TCP to time out and retransmit these segments if necessary. Datagrams may in fact arrive out of order and it is up to TCP to reassemble them into messages in the correct sequence.

Every byte (octet) of data transmitted by TCP has its own sequence number. The sequence number space is 32 bits and ensures that old duplicates vanish by the time the sequence numbers have wrapped around. TCP does explicitly deal with the problem of delayed duplicates when attempting to establish a connection, using the three-way handshake for this purpose, i.e., it can handle simultaneous and aborted connection attempts.

TCP provides a reliable full-duplex connection-oriented link between two hosts—analogous to a telephone connection. This is similar to a virtual circuit in concept although without saving state information at each intermediate node. Figure 8 shows such a TCP connection between two hosts which is established using a three-way handshake. After the connection is established, port numbers act as logical identifiers to identify the virtual circuit. On a TCP virtual circuit, data can be transmitted in full-duplex. The TCP connection is maintained for the duration of data transmission and is closed when the upper layer application signals the TCP layer by setting the FIN (finish) flag, for example. This releases operating system resources such as memory and state tables needed to keep the connection alive.

TCP provides reliable data transmission and segments not received at the destination are automatically resent when a time-out interval expires. The time-out interval is dynamic and takes into account factors such as changing delays caused by network congestion and alternate routes being used by underlying network services. The TCP protocol thus provides reliable connections between hosts.

Although TCP is suited to applications that require reliable data transmission, it is not suited for applications that require broadcast traffic. To send a multicast datagram to multiple destinations, TCP would require the establishment of a virtual circuit to each

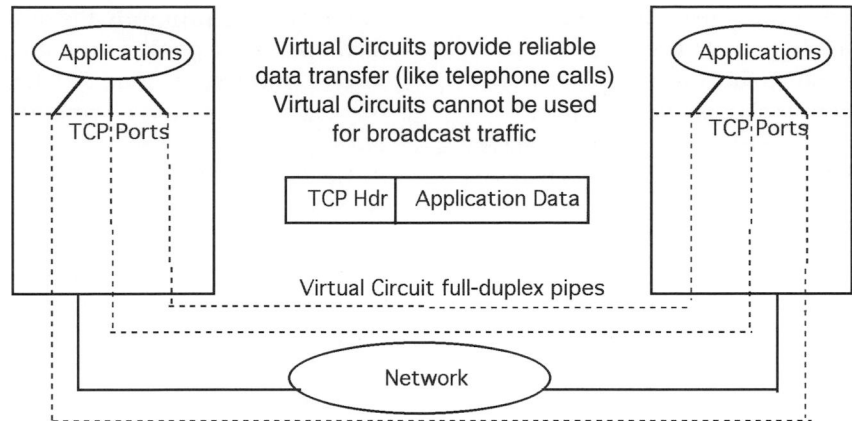

Figure 8 TCP connection used to transmit data.

destination host and then to send the datagram on each one of these virtual circuits. This would be an inefficient process. For applications that depend on broadcasts, UDP is a more suitable transport layer protocol and this is discussed in the following section.

1. Format of the TCP Segment

The format of a TCP segment is shown in Fig. 9. The header length is at least 20 bytes.

- *Source port* and *Destination port* fields identify the end points of the connection (TSAP, transport service access point addresses in OSI terminology). Some ports are defined by the application process being established while others can be dynamically assigned from a specific range. For example a TCP segment carrying an FTP

application will use a dynamic port at the client end (e.g., 1049) but predefined ports (20 and 21) at the server end. The full list of ports is defined in RFC 1700—Assigned Numbers.

- *Sequence number* and *Piggyback acknowledgment* fields (32 bits) act as pointers and keep track of transmitted and acknowledged data.

- *TCP header length* specifies how many 32-bit words are contained in the TCP header. This information is needed because the *Options* field is variable length. Note that the list of options may be shorter than the data offset field might imply. The content of the header beyond the end-of-option option must be header padding (i.e., zero).

- Flow control in TCP is handled using a variable-size sliding window. A 16-bit field is required since *Window* specifies how many bytes may be sent beyond the byte acknowledged.

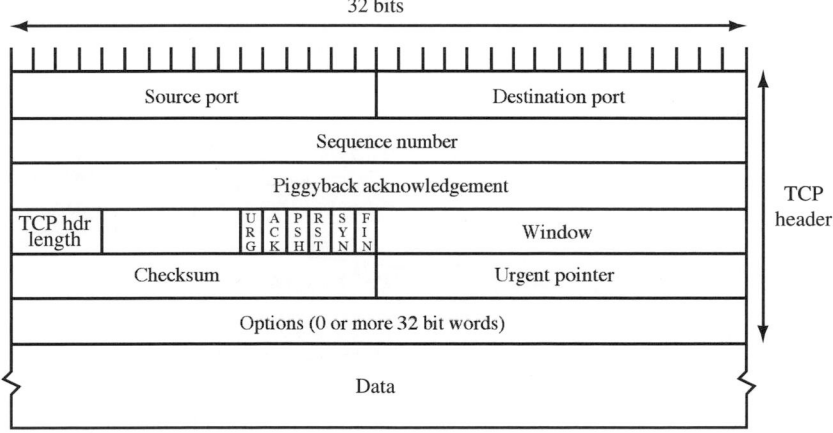

Figure 9 TCP header.

- A *Checksum* is provided for reliability and forms the 16-bit one's complement of the one's complement sum of all 16-bit words in the header and text. The checksum also protects against misrouted packets via a prefixed imaginary header with lower-level address and protocol information. This is further discussed in RFC1624 (Computation of the Internet Checksum).

The following six 1-bit flags are also defined:

- *URG* is set to 1 if the *Urgent pointer* is in use. The *Urgent pointer* is used to indicate a byte offset from the current sequence number at which urgent data are to be found.
- The *SYN* bit is used to establish connections. The connection request has $SYN = 1$ and $ACK = 0$ to indicate that the piggyback acknowledgment field is not in use. The connection reply has an acknowledgment, so $SYN = 1$ and $ACK = 1$. Essentially the *SYN* bit is used to denote *CONNECTION REQUEST* and *CONNECTION CONFIRM,* with the *ACK* bit used to distinguish between those two. The *FIN* bit is used to release a connection. It specifies that the sender has no more data but after closing a connection, a process may continue to receive data indefinitely.
- The *RST* bit is used to reset a connection that has become confused due to delayed duplicate *SYN*s or host crashes.
- If the *PSH* (Push) flag is set, data must be transmitted promptly to the receiver. Sometimes users need to be sure that all the data they have submitted to the TCP layer has been transmitted. The push function is therefore used to assure that data submitted to TCP is actually transmitted and the sending user indicates that it should be "pushed" through to the receiving user. This

results in TCP promptly forwarding and delivering data up to that point to the receiver.
- The *Options* field is used for miscellaneous options, for example to communicate buffer sizes during the setup procedure.

In summary TCP provides the following functions:

- Data transfer, providing a virtual circuit connecting the called and calling user, regardless of the lower layer delivery system—IP is a datagram service
- Error checking, including detecting lost data, duplicate, and out-of-sequence segments
- Flow control between source and destination
- Multiplexing and demultiplexing of the application layer connections
- Status and synchronization control, including the ability to set up and break connections, mark significant points in the dialog, etc., this includes the ability to signal an unusual event (interrupt)

2. TCP Connection Establishment

As discussed above, a connection is established using a *three-way handshake* procedure. The flow of data in each direction of a connection is controlled independently so as to avoid ambiguity with initial sequence numbers. These are in turn acknowledged as part of the handshake procedure. Figure 10 shows this three-way handshake establishment.

The initiating side sends a segment with the SYN flag set and the proposed initial sequence number in the sequence number field ($SEQ = X$). On receipt of this, the responding side notes the sequence number setting for the incoming direction and then returns a segment with both the SYN and ACK flags set with the sequence number field set to its own assigned value for the reverse direction ($SEQ = Y$) and a piggy-

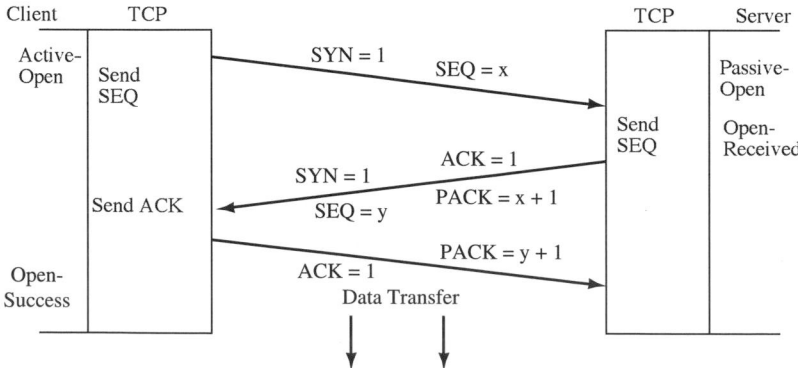

Figure 10 TCP connection establishment.

backed acknowledgement field of $X + 1$ (PACK = X + 1) to confirm it has noted the initial value for its incoming direction. On receipt of this, the initiating returns a segment with the ACK flag set and a piggy-backed acknowledgement field of $Y + 1$.

3. TCP Data Transfer

The error and flow control procedures associated with the data transfer phase are based on the "Go-back-N" error control strategy and a sliding window flow control mechanism. Figure 11 shows an example of such a data transfer.

The client issues a request message of N octets and, to force delivery, sets the PSH flag. The client sends this in a segment with the SYN and PSH flags set and a sequence number of X as shown in Fig. 11. On receipt of this segment, the receiving side detects the PSH flag set and delivers this directly and returns a segment with the ACK flag set and an acknowledgement number of $X + N + 1$—indicating the next octet it expects to receive—as well as a window value of N so as to return the window to its original setting.

If the server sends a response message which is assumed to be *three* times the maximum segment size W, TCP must send it as *three* segments. To illustrate the window mechanism, assume that the send window is

equal to $2W$—sufficient for two maximum segments to be sent. After sending two segments, the server must wait until it receives an acknowledgement with a further credit allocation in its window field.

On receipt of each segment, the client TCP then returns a segment with the ACK flag set; on receipt of the second segment, the server delivers the contents of its buffer—containing the two segments—to the client application. At the server, on receipt of the first ACK, the server TCP increments its credit value and sends the third segment.

4. TCP Connection Termination

In Fig. 12 the client protocol has finished sending all its data and wishes to terminate the connection. On receipt of the CLOSE primitive, the client sends a segment with the FIN flag set. On receipt of this segment, the server issues a CLOSING primitive to the server protocol and returns an ACK segment to the client acknowledging receipt of the FIN segment.

The connection can only be totally closed when both ends agree that they have no further data to send. Assume that the server protocol has also finished submitting data (CLOSING primitive received from application). If the server TCP still has outstanding data to send, then this gets transmitted in a

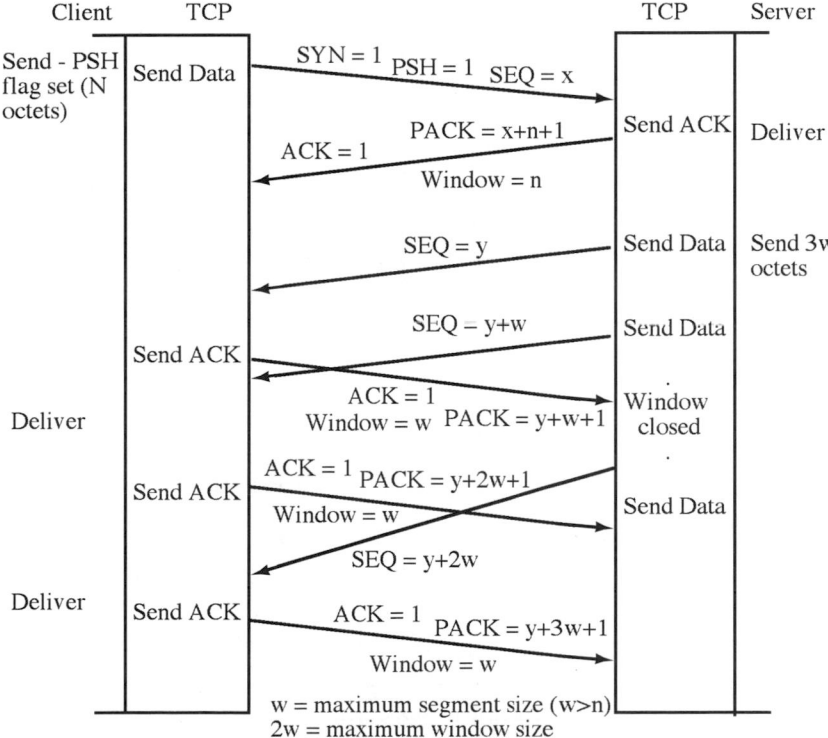

Figure 11 TCP data transfer example.

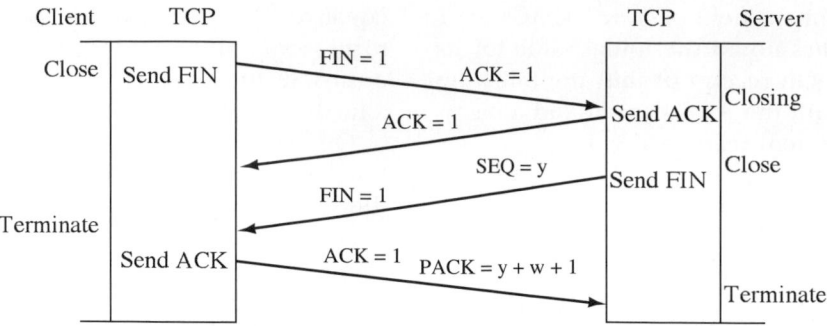

Figure 12 TCP connection termination.

segment together with the FIN flag set (which consumes a sequence number). On receipt of this segment, the client TCP issues a TERMINATE primitive and returns an ACK for the data just received. When it receives the ACK, the server TCP issues its own TERMINATE to the server protocol.

F. UDP [RFC 768]

The UDP protocol provides a connectionless service similar to IP and is therefore not as robust as TCP. It is used by applications that do not require the reliability of TCP at the host-to-host layer. UDP can send data without requiring that a virtual circuit be established. Each segment is sent by encapsulating it in an IP packet which contains complete source and destination IP addresses and port numbers that identify the application-level processes involved in the exchange. UDP is similar to ordinary postal services because complete addressing information is sent with each UDP message. UDP is called a *connectionless* transport protocol because it does not use a preestablished connection to transmit data. Figure 13 shows the use of UDP to exchange data between two hosts.

UDP has less protocol overhead than TCP and it does not guarantee that data will arrive in the order in which it is sent. TCP guarantees that messages are assembled in the order in which they are sent. UDP includes an optional checksum that can be used to ensure data integrity of the message being sent. If sequenced delivery is required, then the application-level protocol has to provide for it in this case. An important advantage UDP has over TCP is that it is more suited for applications that require broadcast data—a single datagram can be broadcast onto the network by specifying a broadcast address in the destination address field.

UDP is popular in many LAN-based applications that are broadcast-based and do not require the complexity of TCP. Applications which use UDP are primarily Directory Name Services (DNS), SNMP and TFTP. The WINS server in NT which is used for resolving names and addresses also uses UDP.

When TCP or UDP protocol modules receive a packet from the IP layer, they have to distinguish between packets that need to be processed by an application service such as FTP, Telnet, SMTP, SNMP, etc. TCP and UDP protocol modules do this by reading their respective 16-bit port number fields. Some ports are applicable to TCP, others to UDP, and some to both. Port numbers supported on a system can be found in the \winnt\system32\drivers\etc\services file on Windows NT computers and /etc/services file on UNIX hosts. Figure 14 shows the format of the UDP data segment.

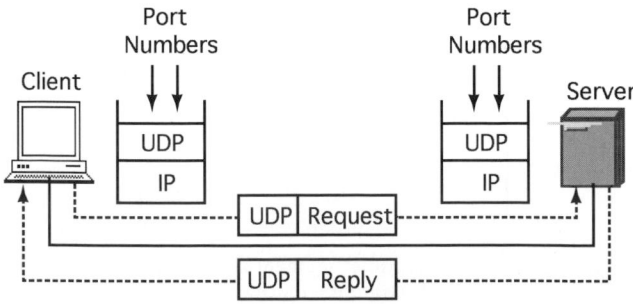

Figure 13 UDP Connection used to transmit data.

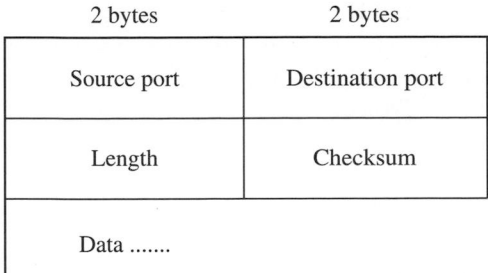

Figure 14 UDP header.

The following table shows a summary of which application protocols use TCP, UDP, or either TCP or UDP.

Process/application layer	Primary transport protocol
FTP	TCP
TELNET	TCP
SMTP	TCP
HTTP	TCP
SNMP	UDP
TFTP	UDP
DNS	UDP or TCP
NFS	TCP and/or UDP

G. Structure of TCP/IP When Encapsulated by Ethernet

Figure 15 shows a very common scenario of an Ethernet frame carrying an IP packet, which in turn carries a TCP segment which in turn carries upper layer application data. The TCP segment is encapsulated within the IP packet. In turn, the TCP segment will hold other protocol data units (PDUs) created in a format specific to an application program or service running at the session and presentation layers of the ISO model. Examples include: SMTP, SNMP, FTP, Telnet, HTTP, etc.

III. IPV4 ADDRESSING STRUCTURE AND SUBNETTING

A. Background to IP Address Classes

IPv4's addressing scheme is integral with how IP datagrams are routed through a TCP/IP network. An IP address is 32 bits long and is divided into a network identifier (netid) and host number identifier (hostid). The host number portion can be further segmented into a subnet number portion and a host portion.

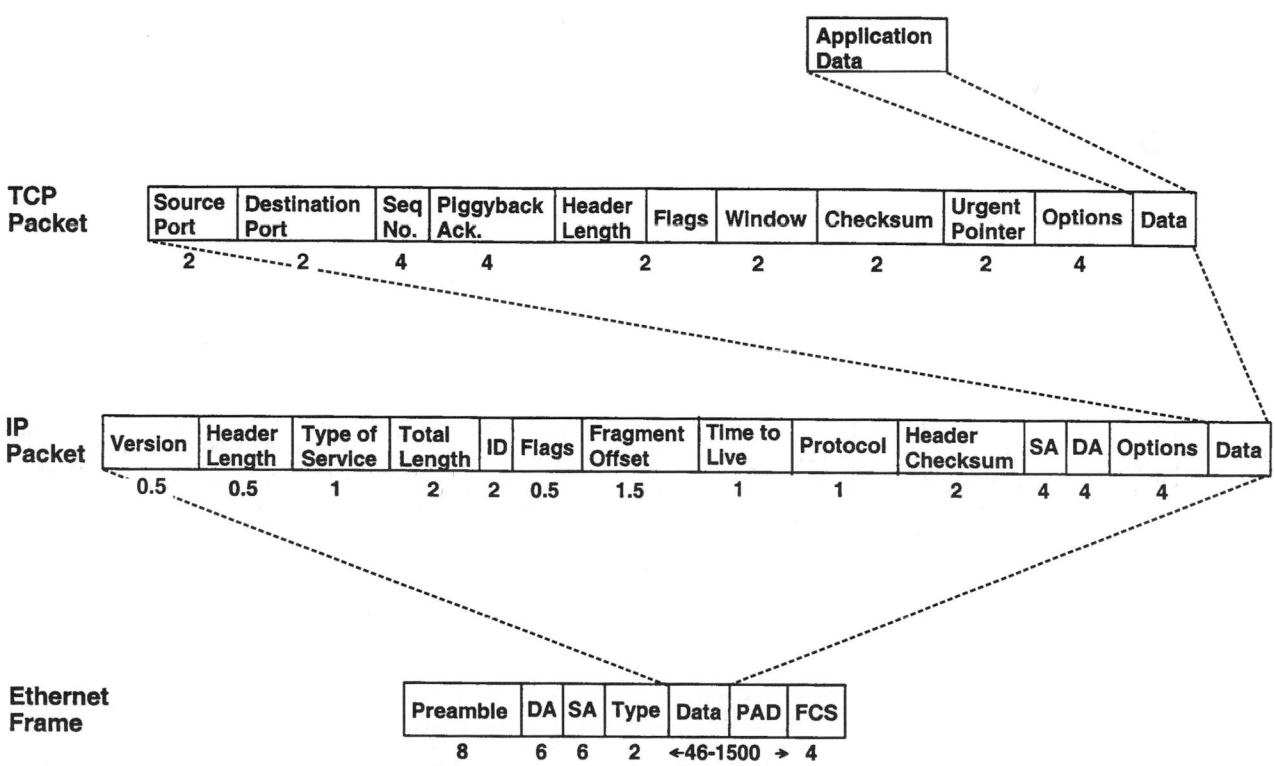

Figure 15 Encapsulation of TCP by IP by Ethernet.

Subnetting allows a network administrator to build multiple networks of hosts and yet localize each host's traffic to specific subnets.

Each network interface in a node that supports an IP stack normally has an IP address assigned to it—either temporarily or permanently. The IP address is a logical address independent of the underlying network hardware or network type. IP addresses are expressed as four decimal numbers ranging from 0 to 255 with each number separated by a dot.

IP addressing supports five unique network classes. The leftmost bits of any IP address indicate its network class. IP network numbers are assigned by the Internet Assigned Numbers Authority (IANA) and will fall into one of the following classes based on the network size requirements.

- Class A networks are reserved for very large organizations and for countries. The first octet is assigned by the IANA, and the remaining three octets are available for hosts and/or subnets. Class A networks have network numbers from 1 through 127 (2^8-1). For example, 107.122.0.230 is a Class A address because the first octet is in the range of 1 through 127.
- Class B networks allocate the first two octets to the network number, leaving the two remaining octets for host and/or subnet assignment. (Actually the first two bits define Class B networks and the remaining 14 bits define the network number.) Class B network numbers are very popular because up to $2^{16}-2$ (65,634) hosts and/or subnets can be assigned. Over two-thirds of the available Class B network numbers have been assigned by the IANA which now requires organizations requesting class B addresses to prove why a class B address is justified.
- Class C networks allocate the first three octets ($2^{24}-3$) to the network number, leaving the last octet for hosts and/or subnets. (Actually the first three bits define Class C networks and the remaining 21 bits define the network number.) This means only 256 hosts and/or subnets can be assigned. Typically organizations request multiple Class C addresses to ensure they have enough address space for future growth.
- Class D addresses are reserved for multicast groups which enables a single address to be used to define a group of receivers. Some multicast addresses are used by supporting protocols, for example, the routing protocol RIP-2 has a reserved multicast address of 224.0.0.9, while all routers on the subnet are defined by the multicast address of 224.0.0.2.
- Class E is also reserved.

Each host on the Internet will have a globally unique IP address. This IP address is typically configured into the operating system of the host by a network administrator.

In summary therefore, the number of networks and hosts possible for each call can be described as follows:

Class A: 127 (2^7) networks with 16 million (2^{24}) hosts each

Class B: 16,383 (2^{14}) networks with up to 64K (2^{16}) hosts

Class C: 2 million (2^{21}) networks—LANs with up to 256 (2^8) hosts

Class D: This is reserved for multicasting and is used by special protocols to transmit messages to a select group of nodes.

The structure of the IP address fields for each class is shown in Fig. 16.

The netid portion of the IP address identifies the network uniquely. Interconnected networks must have unique netids. If a network is to be connected to public networks such as the Internet, it is necessary to apply to the IANA in a specific country to obtain a netid (network number) not used by anyone else.

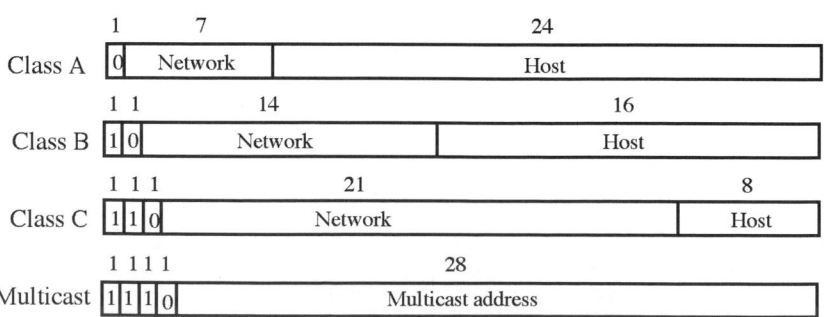

Figure 16 Source and destination address formats for various IP classes.

B. Dotted Decimal Notation and Address Classes

The 32-bit number is represented for convenience as four decimal numbers corresponding to the decimal value of the four bytes that make up the 32-bit IP address. The decimal numbers are separated by periods (.). This shorthand notation for IP addresses is called dotted decimal notation. The following shows an IP address in its binary form and in dotted decimal notation:

IP Address = 10000100 10110101 00010011 00001100
IP Address = 132.181.19.12

Given an IP address in the dotted decimal notation form, it is important to determine the address class to which it belongs. This can be determined by the number of bits assigned to the hostid field which limits the number of hosts that can be on the network. A second reason for knowing the address class is to determine how to divide a network into smaller networks, called *subnets* appropriate for structural groups in an organization.

The most significant bits of an IP address determine the IP address class. From the table below it can be seen that if the most significant bit of the IP address is a 0 and it is therefore a Class A address. If the first two most significant bits of the IP address are 10, the IP address is a Class B address and if the first three most significant bits of the IP address are 110, then the IP address is a Class C address.

Consider an IP address of 137.65.4.1. If it is converted to its binary representation, the following 32-bit pattern is obtained:

1001001 01000001 00000100 00000001

The most significant two bits of this bit pattern are 10 thus 137.65.4.1 is a Class B address. This, however, is a slow way to determine the IP address class because it involves converting the IP address to a bit pattern. A simpler way works as follows.

Consider a Class B address—the two most significant bits are 10. The minimum value of the first 8 bits occurs when the remaining 6 bits are 0; the maximum value occurs when the remaining 6 bits are 1. The minimum value of the first 8 bits of a Class B address is therefore 10000000 and the maximum value is 10111111. These minimum and maximum values correspond to a decimal value of 128 and 191. This means that if the first decimal number of an IP address in the dotted decimal notation is a number between 128 and 191 (inclusive), the IP address is a Class B address. In the preceding example of an IP address of

137.65.4.1, the number 137 is between 128 and 191, and is therefore a Class B address.

Using the same reasoning, the minimum and maximum for the first decimal number of a Class A and Class C address in its dotted decimal notation form can be determined as follows:

- Minimum value of first decimal for Class A = 00000000 = 0
- Maximum value of first decimal for Class A = 01111111 = 127
- Minimum value of first decimal for Class C = 11000000 = 192
- Maximum value of first decimal for Class C = 11011111 = 223

The table below shows the range of values for the first decimal number of an IP address in the dotted decimal notation. This table can be used to determine the IP address class by checking the first decimal number of an IP address.

IP address class	Most significant bits	Minimum	Maximum
Class A	0	0	126 (notice that 127 is missing)
Class B	110	28	191
Class C	110	192	223
Class D	1110	224	239

C. Loopback and Reserved IP Addresses

The IP address 127.0.0.1 is called a loopback address. Packets sent to this address never reach the network but are looped through the network interface card only. This can be used for diagnostic purposes to verify that the internal path through the TCP/IP protocols is working. From the table above the number 127, which should be in the Class A range of values, is missing. This number is reserved for the software loopback address. Any packet sent by a TCP/IP application to an IP address of the form 127.x.x.x, where $0 < x < 255$ results in the packet returning to the application without reaching the network, i.e., the packet is copied from transmit to receive buffer on the same machine. Although any address of the type 127.x.x.x indicates a loopback address, Windows NT servers use the IP address 127.0.0.1.

A hostid value of 0 or all 1s is never assigned to an individual TCP/IP node. An IP address with a hostid value of 0 indicates the network itself. The IP address of 132.181.0.0 indicates the Class B network 132.181.

If the hostid value contains all 1s in the bit pattern, it indicates a directed broadcast address which is sent to all nodes in the network. For the network number 132.181, the broadcast address is 132.181.255.255. The network number 132.181 is a Class B address and has 16 bits in the hostid field. If 1s are used for the 16 bits of the hostid, they correspond to a decimal value of 255.255.

Another type of broadcast, called the local broadcast, is specified by the value of 255.255.255.255. This type of broadcast address is used in LANs, since a broadcast never crosses a router boundary. It is used by the broadcast name resolution method in Windows NT.

An IP address of 0.0.0.0 is used to refer to the network itself. The Windows NT dynamic host configurable protocol (DHCP) clients on requesting IP parameter information from a DHCP server use a source address of 0.0.0.0. The 0.0.0.0 address is also used in routing tables to indicates the network entry for the default router's (often called default gateway) IP address.

D. Subnet Masks

Once the network number has been assigned by the IANA, the hostid can be assigned locally. Consider an IP network number of 132.181.0.0. 16 bits are assigned for the network number which means a unique number out of a pool of $2^{16} = 65536$ is possible. Out of 65536 combinations, the pattern consisting of all 1s (broadcast) cannot be used. In addition, the pattern consisting of all 0s (the network itself) should not be used for host number assignments.

Figure 17 shows the network number 132.181.0.0 (Network 1) connected to the Internet using a router and all traffic for network 132.181.0.0 is sent to the router for that network. It is possible (but unrealistic) to have 65534 hosts on this network.

If the company decides to segment this network to better fit the business units then a new numbering structure for the hostid field is required. A different network number assignment that belongs to Class A, B, or C could be used, but this involves applying for a new network number assignment even though many hostid bit patterns on network 1 are not in use. Therefore some of the bits from the hostid field are used to distinguish between the two networks and leave the rest for the host number assignments. This is called *subnetting*, and the resulting networks are called subnets. The scheme for subnetting is documented in RFC 950.

Figure 18 shows that a second network (Network 2) can be connected using the same router if it has an unused port. The first byte of the hostid field is used

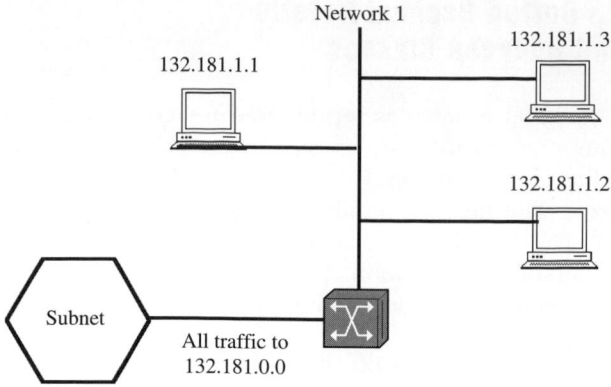

Figure 17   Class B network connected to the Internet.

to specify this subnet number. Network 1 has a subnet number of 1, Network 2 a subnet number of 2.

Subnetting enables a network to be broken into smaller networks using the same network number assignment and has the following advantages:

* Simplified administration
* Improved security
* Restructuring of internal networks without affecting external networks

Simplified administration results from the capability to use routers to partition networks using logical boundaries and allows smaller networks to be administered independently and more efficiently.

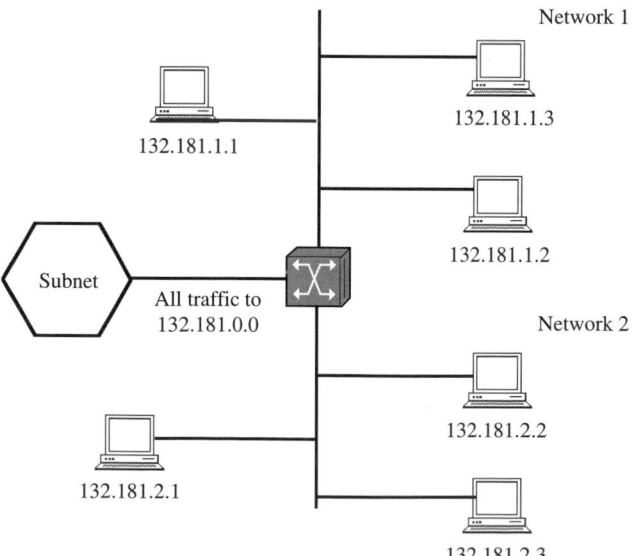

Figure 18   Class B network connected to the Internet using subnetting.

Subnets allow the network to be structured internally without the rest of the network being aware of changes in the internal network structure. In Fig. 18 the internal network has been divided into two subnets, but traffic arriving from the external network still is sent to the network address 132.181.0.0. It is the responsibility of the router that belongs to the organization to make a distinction between IP addresses belonging to its various subnets. An important benefit of the internal network being "invisible" to external networks is that an organization can achieve this internal restructuring without having to obtain an additional network number from the IANA which further conserves this scarce resource. Also because the structure of the internal subnetworks is not visible to external networks, use of subnets results in improved network security.

Figure 19 shows the relationship between different fields of an IP address and its subnetworks. Routers are used to interconnect these subnets. The routers must also know how many bits of the hostid field are being used for subnets. Thus it can analyze the hostid filed in conjunction with the "subnet mask." The subnet mask is required at the time that an IP address is also specified and is expressed in dotted decimal notation like the IP address.

The subnet mask is used by routers and hosts to interpret the hostid field in such a way that they can determine how many bits are being used for subnetting. The mask is a 32-bit number that divides the hostid field into the subnet number and the host number according to the following rules:

- 1s in subnet mask correspond to position of the netid and subnet number in the IP address.
- 0s in subnet mask correspond to the position of host number in the IP address.

Figure 20 shows an application of this rule to a Class B network number used for subnetting. Eight bits of the hostid field are being used for the subnet number while the remaining 8 bits are used to specify the hostid on a particular subnet. The subnet mask is a 32-bit pattern and is written in a dotted decimal notation. A group of 8 1s corresponds to a decimal value of 255, thus the subnet mask can be written as 255.255.255.0

If a subnet mask of 255.255.0.0 is used for a Class B address, then no subnetting is being used. A Class B address has 16 bits of netid field. This netid field is accounted for by the first two 255s (255.255) in the 255.255.0.0 subnet mask value. The remaining value of 0.0 must correspond to the host number. No 1s are in the subnet mask for the subnet number or field, thus no subnetting is being used.

If the same subnet mask value of 255.255.0.0 is used for a Class A address, it shows that subnetting is being used as a Class A address has 8 bits of netid field. This netid field is accounted for by the first 255 in the 255.255.0.0 subnet mask. The remaining 255 must correspond to the subnet number, which is 8 bits long.

If a subnet mask of 255.255.255.0 is used for a Class C address, then no subnetting is being used. A Class C address has 24 bits of netid field which accounts for by the first three 255s (255.255.255) in the 255.255.255.0 subnet mask. The remaining value of 0

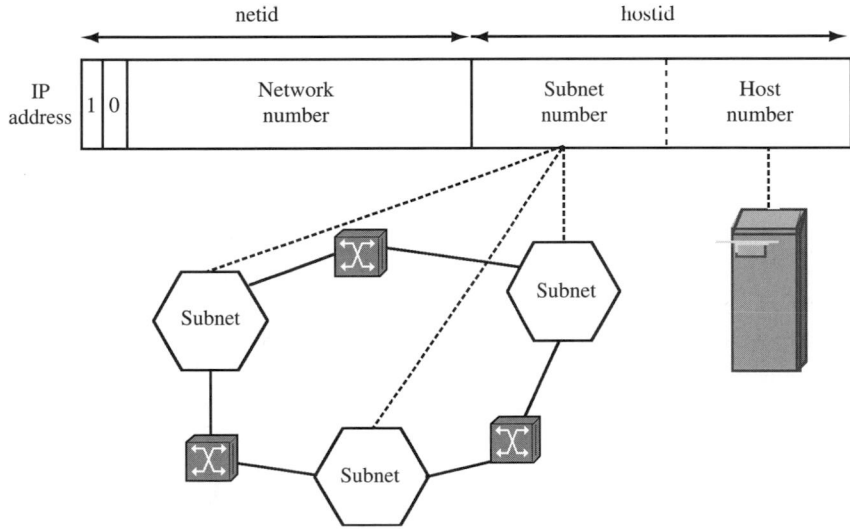

Figure 19 Subnets and subnet numbers.

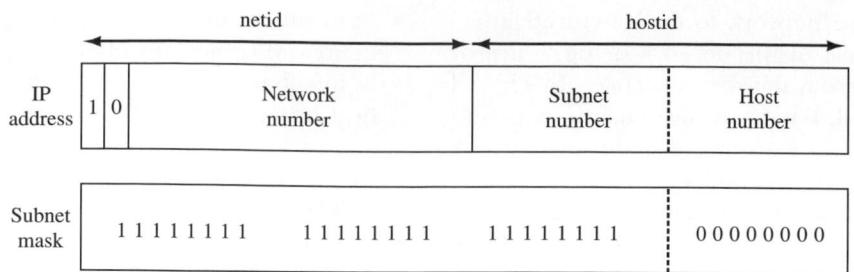

Figure 20 Subnet mask representation.

must correspond to the host number. No 1s are in the subnet mask for the subnet number field, thus no subnetting is being used.

A subnet mask of 255.255.0.0 for a Class C address is illegal as a Class C address has 24 bits of netid field, but the first two 255s in 255.255.0.0 account for only 16 bits of the netid. At least another 255 are needed to cover the remaining 8 bits of netid.

An IP address and its subnet mask can be represented in "slash" notation. For example, an IP address of 192.55.12.120 and subnet mask of 255.255.255.240 can be combined and expressed as 192.55.12.120/28 where 28 represents the number of 1s in the mask starting from the left. The following table specifies the equivalence between the binary and decimal values for subnet masks.

Subnet size (bits)	Bit pattern	Decimal value
1	10000000	128
2	11000000	192
3	11100000	224
4	11110000	240
5	11111000	248
6	11111100	252
7	11111110	254

Consider the following example:

Given an IP address of 192.55.12.120 and subnet mask of 255.255.255.240. Determine the values of: Subnet number, Host number and Directed broadcast number

The network address is formed from the binary AND of the IP address and mask, viz:

11000000 00110111 00001100 01111000

AND

11111111 11111111 11111111 11110000

=

11000000 00110111 00001100 01110000

(192.55.12.112)

The host address is formed from the binary AND of the IP address and the NOT mask, viz:

11000000 00110111 00001100 01111000

AND

00000000 00000000 00000000 00001111

=

00000000 00000000 00000000 00001000 (0.0.0.8)

The broadcast address for this subnet is formed from the binary OR of the IP address and the NOT mask, viz:

11000000 00110111 00001100 01111000

OR

00000000 00000000 00000000 00001111

=

11000000 00110111 00001100 01111111

(192.55.12.127)

E. Classless Inter-Domain Routing (CIDR) and Supernetting

The problem with global routing tables is that each network requires its own individual routing entry, which causes routing tables to be very large, particularly in the backbone network. As the Internet evolved it has become evident that several serious scaling problems had to be faced. These include:

- Exhaustion of the Class B network address space. One fundamental cause of this problem is the lack of a network Class of a size that is appropriate for medium-sized organization. Class

C, with a maximum of 254 addresses, is too small, while Class B, which allows up to 65534 addresses, is too large in most cases.
- Massive growth of routing tables in routers causing scaling problems
- Eventual exhaustion of the 32-bit IP address space

CIDR was introduced to solve this problem by changing the view of addresses from "classfull" to "classless." This method of viewing network addresses is also known as *aggregation*. CIDR eliminates the idea of Class A, B, and C networks and replaces this with a generalized IP prefix such as 172.16.0.0/12 and explained below.

The shortage of Class B addresses has required sites with multiple networks to obtain multiple Class C network addresses, instead of a single Class B network address. Although the allocation of these Class C addresses solves the problem of running out of Class B addresses, it introduces a secondary problem—every Class C network requires a routing table entry. CIDR or *supernetting* is therefore a way to prevent this explosion in the size of the Internet routing tables (RFCs 1518-9).

The term "Classless" is used because routing decisions are made on the basis of masking operations of the entire 32-bit IP address. It therefore makes little difference whether the IP address is Class A, B, or C. This change slowed down the growth of the Internet routing tables, but did nothing for all the existing routes. CIDR is the short-term solution for IPv4 until IPv6 is implemented.

The basic concept in CIDR is to allocate multiple IP addresses in a way that allows *summarization* into a smaller number of routing table entries. For example, if a single site is allocated 16 Class C addresses (192.24.16.0 through 192.24.16.15) and those 16 addresses are allocated so that they can be summarized then all 16 can be referenced through a single routing table entry such as 192.24.16.0/28. Routing protocols must carry the 32-bit mask in addition to the 32-bit address and modern routing protocols such as OSPF, RIP-2 and BGP Version 4 are all capable of carrying this 32-bit mask.

1. Example of CIDR (Supernet) Address Allocation

Consider the block of 2048 Class C network addresses beginning with 192.24.0.0 and ending with 192.31.255.0 allocated to a single network provider. In order to express this block of Class C addresses as a group with a single routing table entry then a super-

net specification would be 192.24.0.0 with mask of 255.248.0.0. The CIDR supernet representation of this group of Class C networks is 192.24.0.0/13 as shown in Fig. 21.

F. Private IP Numbering [RFC 1918]

With the proliferation of TCP/IP—including outside the Internet itself—an increasing number of nonconnected organizations use this technology and its addressing capabilities for sole intraenterprise communications (intranet), without any intention to ever directly connect to other organizations or the Internet itself.

It is therefore likely that when the organization connects to the Internet it may be necessary to renumber IP addresses for all of its public hosts that require Internet-wide IP connectivity. The IANA has reserved the following three blocks of the IP address space for private internets:

Class	Starting number		Ending number	CIDR representation
A	10.0.0.0	↔	10.255.255.255	10/8
B	172.16.0.0	↔	172.31.255.255	172.16/12
C	192.168.0.0	↔	192.168.255.255	192.168/16

The first block is referred to as a "24-bit block,"—i.e., the address range is expressed with 24 bits (0.0.0 ↔ 255.255.255) while 8 bits are used to specify the network address (10).

The second block is expressed as a "20-bit block,"—i.e., the address range is expressed with 20 bits (16.0.0 ↔ 31.255.255) while the remaining 12 bits are used to specify the network address (172.16 ↔ 172.31).

The third block is expressed as a "16-bit block,"—i.e., the address range is expressed with 16 bits (0.0 ↔ 255.255) while the remaining 16 bits are used to specify the network address (192.168).

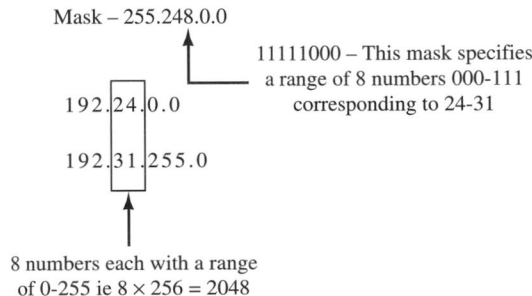

Figure 21 Example of CIDR (supernet) addresses structure.

Note that (in pre-CIDR notation) the first block is nothing but a single Class A network address, while the second block is a set of 16 contiguous Class B network addresses, and the third block is a set of 256 contiguous Class C network addresses.

An organization that decides to use IP addresses out of the address space defined for private IP numbers can do so without any reference to the IANA. The address space can thus be reused by many organizations. Addresses within this private address space will only be unique within the organization, or the set of organizations which choose to cooperate over this space so they may communicate with each other in their own private Internet (intranet). An organization that requests IP addresses for its external connectivity will *never* be assigned addresses from the blocks defined above.

In order to use private address space, an organization needs to determine which hosts do not need to have network layer connectivity outside the organization and thus could be classified as private. Such hosts will use the private address space defined above. Private hosts can communicate with all other hosts inside the organization, both public and private but cannot have IP connectivity to any host outside of the organization. While not having external IP connectivity private hosts can still have access to external services via firewalls.

Moving a host from private to public or vice versa involves a change of IP address and subnet mask, changes to the appropriate DNS entries, and changes to configuration files on other hosts that reference the host by IP address.

IV. TCP/IP'S COMMERCIAL SUCCESS STORY

TCP/IP product vendors agree that the protocol's technical characteristics have little to do with its market success. When the problems of local area network (LAN) communications among dissimilar computers were becoming critical, there were fewer solutions than are available today. Further use of TCP/IP as the backbone protocols for the Internet meant that other WAN architectures such as xDSL, frame relay, ATM, etc., needed to carry TCP/IP as well. TCP/IP's acceptance at the commercial level is attributed to *four* significant events:

1. Microprocessor and memory technology advanced to the point where protocols such as TCP/IP could be implemented on nearly any type of product without crippling financial effects

2. DARPA funded the development and integration of TCP/IP into the UNIX operating system, ensuring that TCP/IP would be widely deployed
3. Proprietary protocols at a similar level in the architecture suffered from inter-working and compatibility problems across different vendors' equipment
4. The explosive growth of the Internet

LANs have other common elements with the Internet environment, including the need to support multiple-vendor environments. LANs are linked into internetwork environments, which is the very thing that IP was designed to do in the original APPANET. Further, TCP/IP's coding was developed with public funds—its specifications and many implementations being in the public domain. Thus licensing costs for vendors are not significant.

In many ways, TCP/IP is suffering from its own success. Currently, two critical issues face the TCP/IP industry and the resolution of these will be key to the future of TCP/IP:

- The IP address space is being exhausted at a rate few would have considered possible only a few years ago
- Routing tables on many routers are becoming excessively large with the result that more time is spent in route maintenance and conversely, less time forwarding packets

Recognizing these problems, the Internet Engineering Task Force (IETF) formed a group to make a recommendation on the direction of IP which includes:

- Estimating the life expectancy of the IP address space of the current version of IP
- Determining the features and functions that a new IP protocol must provide
- Developing a migration plan for the new IP into the Internet. This activity also addressed interoperability issues and formal testing procedures

The result is IPv6 (IP version 6) which is a set of standards discussed in the following section.

V. IPV6 (INTERNET PROTOCOL—VERSION 6) [RFC 2373, 2374, 2375]

The changes from IPv4 to IPv6 fall primarily into the following categories:

- *Expanded addressing capabilities:* IPv6 increases the IP address size from 32 bits to 128 bits, thus supporting more levels of addressing hierarchy, a much greater number of addressable nodes, and simpler autoconfiguration of addresses. The scalability of multicast routing is improved by adding a "scope" field to multicast addresses. A new type of address called an "anycast address" is defined, which is used to send a packet to any one of a group of nodes.
- *Header format simplification:* Some IPv4 header fields have been dropped or moved to optional extension headers, thus reducing the processing cost of packet handling and to limit the added bandwidth cost of the IPv6 header. Fragmentation and reassembly are limited to the source and destination.
- *Improved support for extensions and options:* Changes in the way IP header options are encoded allow for more efficient forwarding, less stringent limits on the length of options, and greater flexibility for introducing new options in the future. Among the improvements is a flexible format for the carriage of explicit routing information.
- *Flow labeling capability:* A new capability is added to enable the labeling of packets belonging to particular traffic "flows" for which the sender requests special handling. Such IP QoS features are becoming important as ISP's address IP network performance.
- *Authentication and privacy capabilities:* Extensions to support authentication, data integrity, and (optional) data confidentiality (e.g., digital signatures).

The requests for comment (RFCs) specify the basic header as well as extension headers including Hop-by-Hop Options, Destination Options, Fragment Header, Security Options, and Routing Header. Authentication and Encapsulating Security Payload (privacy) extension headers for IPv6 are defined in RFCs 2401, 2402, and 2406.

TCP and UDP processing are directly affected by IPv6 and "Version 6" specifications of TCP, ICMP, ping, FTP, DNS, etc., have been specified also.

A. The IPv6 Addressing Architecture

This recommendation specifies the addressing architecture of the IPv6 protocol. It defines the three types of addresses, *unicast, anycast,* and *multicast,* and their uses. It specifies the use of a variable length Format

Prefix, and allocates a small fraction of the total IPv6 address space for provider addresses, local use addresses, and multicast addresses. Space is also reserved for NSAP, IPX, geographic and other special addresses.

B. The ICMPv6 for the IP Version 6

IPv6 uses the ICMP as defined for IPv4 (RFC 792), with a number of changes. The Internet group membership protocol (IGMP) specified for IPv4 (RFC 1112) has also been revised and has been absorbed into ICMP for IPv6. The resulting protocol is called ICMPv6. Other IPv6 specifications including Neighbour Discovery and Stateless Address Autoconfiguration introduce additional ICMPv6 messages, subject to the general rules for ICMPv6 messages given in this specification.

C. DNS Extensions to Support IPv6

This specification defines the changes that need to be made to the Domain Name System to support hosts running IPv6. The changes include a new resource record type to store an IPv6 address, a new domain to support look-ups based on an IPv6 address, and updated definitions of existing query types that return Internet addresses. The extensions are designed to be compatible with existing applications and, in particular, DNS implementations themselves.

D. An Architecture for IPv6 Unicast Address Allocation

This document describes ways in which CIDR address allocation and routing techniques can be used with IPv6.

VI. CONCLUSIONS

TCP/IP was developed in the 1970s and it is remarkable that such an old protocol suite has become the basis of the world's networking architecture. In many ways the proprietary architectures equivalent to TCP/IP were just as inefficient and cumbersome to use. Certainly the growth of the Internet and related architectures—intranets and extranets—was the major push for the industry to use TCP/IP in spite of its inadequacies and inefficiencies. Various efforts were made to fix TCP/IP's deficiencies, particularly with respect to the very limited address space as well as the lack of security features. The introduction of IPv6 and its related protocols is timely and appropriate now that careful consideration has been given to IPv4's deficiencies. IPv6 will provide a very important packet layer service for local area, wide area, fixed and mobile networks in the future.

SEE ALSO THE FOLLOWING ARTICLES

Frame Relay • Integrated Services Digital Network • Internet, Overview • Local Area Networks • Network Environments, Managing • Standards and Protocols in Data Communications • Voice Communications • Wide Area Network

BIBLIOGRAPHY

Comer, D., and Stevens, D. L. (1999). *Internetworking with TCP/IP,* 3rd edition. New York: Prentice Hall.

Gatrell, G., Karas, J., and Peschke, R. (2001). *TCP/IP Tutorial and Technical Overview,* http://www.redbooks.ibm.com.

Miller, M. A. (1999). *Troubleshooting TCP/IP,* 3rd edition. Foster City, CA: M&T Books.

Stevens, W. R., and Wright, G. R. (1996). *TCP/IP illustrated.* Reading, MA: Addison-Wesley.

Uncertainty

George J. Klir

State University of New York, Binghamton

GLOSSARY

conflict Type of uncertainty that is manifested by the conflict among evidential claims regarding a given set of alternatives.

fuzziness Type of uncertainty that results from the vagueness of linguistic expressions.

fuzzy sets Sets that are not required to have sharp boundaries.

monotone measures Set functions that are monotone with respect to subsethood relation.

nonspecificity Type of uncertainty that results from the lack of specificity in characterizing the true alternative among a given set of alternatives.

rough sets Approximations of subsets of a given universal set in terms of equivalence classes induced by a given equivalence relation.

I. INTRODUCTION

Traditionally, science, mathematics, and engineering showed virtually no interest in studying uncertainty. In fact, eliminating uncertainty was viewed as one manifestation of progress. This negative attitude toward uncertainty, prevalent prior to the 20th century, was seriously challenged by some developments in the 20th century. These developments include the emergence of statistical mechanics, Heisenberg's uncertainty principle in quantum physics, and Gödel's theorems regarding consistency and completeness of formal systems. In spite of these developments, the traditional

attitude toward uncertainty changed too little and too slow during the first half of the century. While uncertainty became recognized as useful (e.g., in statistical mechanics), it was for long time tacitly assumed that probability is the only way to deal with uncertainty.

The assumption that probability theory is capable of capturing any kind of uncertainty was challenged only in the second half of the 20th century by the emergence of two important generalizations in mathematics. One of them is the generalization of classical set theory to *fuzzy set theory,* introduced by Lotfi Zadeh in 1965. The second one is the generalization of classical measure theory to the theory of monotone measures, first suggested by Gustave Choquet in 1953–1954 in his *theory of capacities.* These generalizations enlarged substantially the framework for formalizing uncertainty and allowed us to formalize numerous new types of uncertainty. To explain this enlarged framework, we need to explain the two underlying concepts first: fuzzy sets and monotone measures.

II. FUZZY SETS AND MONOTONE MEASURES

A. Fuzzy Sets

Fuzzy sets are defined on any given universal set of concern by functions analogous to characteristic functions of classical sets. These functions are called *membership functions.* Each membership function defines a fuzzy set on a given universal set by assigning to each element of the universal set its membership grade in the fuzzy set.

The set of all membership grades must be at least partially ordered, but it is usually required to form a complete lattice. Depending on the form of the membership function, several types of fuzzy sets are distinguished in the literature. The most common fuzzy sets, usually referred to as *standard fuzzy sets*, are defined by membership grades in the unit interval [0,1]. Due to the limited size, this article is restricted to standard fuzzy sets.

Two distinct notations are most commonly employed in the literature to denote membership functions. In one of them, the membership function of a fuzzy set A is denoted by μ_A, and, assuming that A is a standard fuzzy set, its form is

$$\mu_A : X \to [0,1]$$

where X denotes the universal set of concern. In the second notation, the membership function is denoted by A and has, of course, the same form

$$A : X \to [0,1]$$

According to the first notation, the symbol of the fuzzy set involved is distinguished from the symbol of its membership function. According to the second notation, this distinction is not made, but no ambiguity results from this double use of the same symbol since each fuzzy set is completely and uniquely defined by one particular membership function. The second notation is adopted in this article; it is simpler and, by and large, more popular in the current literature on fuzzy sets.

Contrary to the symbolic role of numbers 0 and 1 in characteristic functions of classical sets, numbers assigned to relevant objects by membership functions of fuzzy sets have a numerical significance. This significance is preserved when classical sets are viewed (from the standpoint of fuzzy set theory) as special fuzzy sets, often referred to as *crisp sets*.

An important property of fuzzy sets is their ability to express gradual transitions from membership to nonmembership. This expressive capability has great utility. For example, it allows us to capture, at least in a crude way, the meaning of expressions in natural language, most of which are inherently vague. Crisp sets are hopelessly inadequate for this purpose. However, it is important to realize that meanings of expressions in natural language are strongly dependent on the context within which they are used.

Among the most important concepts associated with standard fuzzy sets is the concept of an *α-cut*. Given a fuzzy set A defined on X and a number α in the unit interval [0,1], the α-cut of A, denoted by $^\alpha A$, is the crisp set that consists of all elements of A whose membership degrees in A are greater than or equal to α; that is,

$$^\alpha A = \{x \mid A(x) \geq \alpha\}$$

It is obvious that α-cuts are classical (crisp) sets, which for any given fuzzy set A form a nested family of sets in the sense that

$$^\alpha A \subseteq {}^\beta A$$

when $\alpha > \beta$.

Many researchers have contributed to the development of foundations of fuzzy set theory, but perhaps the most important role in its development, not only in its founding, was played by Lotfi Zadeh. Fortunately, this role is now well documented by two volumes of his selected papers in the period 1965–1995, edited by Yager *et al.* and Klir and Yuan.

B. Monotone Measures

Given a universal set X and a nonempty family C of subsets of X (usually with an appropriate algebraic structure), a *monotone measure, g,* on (X, C) is a function

$$g : C \to [0,\infty]$$

that satisfies the following requirements:

(g1) $g(\varnothing) = 0$ (vanishing at the empty set);

(g2) for all $A, B \in C$, if $A \subseteq B$, then $g(A) \leq g(B)$ (monotonicity);

(g3) for any increasing sequence $A_1 \subseteq A_2 \subseteq \ldots$ of sets in C,

$$\text{if } \bigcup_{i=1}^{\infty} A_i \in C, \text{ then } \lim_{i \to \infty} g(A_i) = g\left(\bigcup_{i=1}^{\infty} A_i \right)$$

(continuity from below);

(g4) for any decreasing sequence $A_1 \supseteq A_2 \supseteq \ldots$ of sets in C,

$$\text{if } \bigcap_{i=1}^{\infty} \in C, \text{ then } \lim_{i \to \infty} g(A_i) = g\left(\bigcap_{i=1}^{\infty} A_i \right)$$

(continuity from above).

Functions that satisfy requirements (g1), (g2), and either (g3) or (g4) are equally important in the theory of monotone measures. These functions are called *semicontinuous* from below or above, respectively. When the universal set X is finite, requirements (g3) and (g4) are trivially satisfied and may thus be disregarded.

For any pair $A, B \in C$ such that $A \cap B = \varnothing$, a monotone measure g is capable of capturing any of the following situations:

1. $g(A \cup B) > g(A) + g(B)$, which expresses a cooperative action or synergy between A and B

2. $g(A \cup B) = g(A) + g(B)$, which expresses the fact that A and B are noninteractive
3. $g(A \cup B) < g(A) + g(B)$, which expresses some sort of inhibitory effect or incompatibility between A and B.

Observe that probability theory, which is based on classical measure theory, is capable of capturing only situation (2). This demonstrates that the theory of monotone measures provides us with a considerably broader framework than probability theory for formalizing uncertainty. As a consequence, it allows us to capture types of uncertainty that are beyond the scope of probability theory. For some historical reasons of little significance, monotone measures are often referred to in the literature as *fuzzy measures*. This name is somewhat confusing because no fuzzy sets are involved in the definition of monotone measures. To avoid this confusion, the term *fuzzy measures* should be reserved to measures (additive or nonadditive) that are defined on families of fuzzy sets.

III. FRAMEWORK FOR FORMALIZING UNCERTAINTY

The emergence of fuzzy set theory and the theory of monotone measures considerably expanded the framework for formalizing uncertainty. This expansion is two dimensional. In one dimension, the formalized language of classical set theory is expanded to the more expressive language of fuzzy set theory, where further distinctions are based on special types of fuzzy sets. In the other dimension, the classical (additive) measure theory is expanded to the less restrictive theory of monotone measures, within which various branches with different special properties can be distinguished.

The two-dimensional expansion of possible uncertainty theories is illustrated by the matrix in Table I. In addition to classical sets and fuzzy sets, listed under the formalized languages in this table are also rough sets and their combinations with fuzzy sets. *Rough sets,* which were introduced by Pawlak, are basically imprecise representations of classical sets in terms of a partition induced by an equivalence relation defined on the universal set involved. Elements of the universal set are considered equivalent in the context of rough set theory when they cannot be distinguished due to limited resolution of perception or measuring instruments involved or, alternatively, when it is not desirable to distinguish them (as in knowledge discovery from data). Each rough set represents a given set by two subsets of blocks (equivalent classes) of the partition: a *lower approximation,* which consists of all blocks of the partition that are included in the represented set, and an *upper approximation,* which consists of all blocks that overlap with the represented set.

Fuzzy sets and rough sets model different types of uncertainty. Because both types are relevant in some applications, it is useful to combine them. Rough sets based on fuzzy equivalence relations are usually called *fuzzy rough sets,* whereas rough set approximations of α-cuts of fuzzy sets in terms of given crisp equivalence relations are called *rough fuzzy sets.* Again, these two combinations model different aspects of uncertainty and, consequently, have different domains of applicability.

Under the entry of nonadditive measures in Table I, only a few representative types are listed. Some of

Table I Classification of Uncertainty Theories

	Formalized languages				
		Nonclassical sets			
Monotone measures	Classical sets	Fuzzy sets	Rough sets	Fuzzy rough sets	Rough fuzzy sets
Additive					
Classical numerical probability	1	2			
Nonadditive					
Possibility/necessity	3	4			
Belief/plausibility	5	6			
Capacities of various orders	7				
Coherent lower and upper probabilities	8				
Closed convex sets of probability distributions	9				

them are presented as pairs of dual measures employed jointly in various uncertainty theories, such as possibility and necessity measures in possibility theory, or belief and plausibility measures in the Dempster-Shafer theory of evidence.

An uncertainty theory of a particular type is formed by choosing a formalized language of a particular type (classical set theory, fuzzy set theories based on various types of fuzzy sets, etc.) and expressing relevant uncertainty (predictive, prescriptive, diagnostic, etc.) involved in situations described in this language in terms of a monotone measure (or a pair of measures) of certain type. This means that each entry in the matrix in Table I represents an uncertainty theory of a particular type. For example, the labeled entries in Table I represent the following theories:

1. Classical probability theory
2. Probability theory based on fuzzy events
3. Classical (crisp) possibility theory
4. Fuzzy set interpretation of possibility theory
5. Dempster–Shafer theory of evidence
6. Fuzzified Dempster–Shafer theory
7.–9. Various formalizations of imprecise
      probabilities.

To develop a fully operational theory for dealing with uncertainty of some conceived type, a host of issues must be addressed at four distinct levels:

- *Level 1:* We need to find an appropriate *mathematical representation* of the conceived type of uncertainty.
- *Level 2:* We need to develop a *calculus* by which this type of uncertainty can be properly manipulated.
- *Level 3:* We need to find a meaningful way of *measuring* relevant uncertainty in any situation formalizable in the theory.
- *Level 4:* We need to develop methodological aspects of the theory, including procedures for making the various *uncertainty principles* operational within the theory.

Among the many uncertainty theories emanating from the conceptual framework depicted in Table I, this article is restricted to those theories that are developed at least at levels 1–3. These are the Dempster-Shafer theory of evidence and possibility theory. Classical theory of numerical probability is not explicitly discussed since it is subsumed under the Dempster-Shafer theory.

IV. THEORIES OF UNCERTAINTY

A. Dempster–Shafer Theory

Dempster–Shafer theory (DST) is based on a monotone measure that is called a *belief measure*. Given a universal set X (usually referred to as the *frame of discernment* in DST), let $P(X)$ denote the power set of X (the set of all subsets of X).Then, a belief measure, Bel, is a function

$$\text{Bel}: P(X) \rightarrow [0,1]$$

such that $\text{Bel}(\varnothing) = 0$, $\text{Bel}(X) = 1$, and

$$\text{Bel}(A_1 \cup A_2 \cup \ldots \cup A_n) \geq \sum_j \text{Bel}(A_j)$$
$$- \sum_{j<k} \text{Bel}(A_j \cap A_k) + \ldots$$
$$+ (-1)^{n+1} \text{Bel}(A_1 \cap A_2 \cap \ldots \cap A_n)$$

for all possible families of subsets of X. Due to this inequality, belief measures are also called *monotone capacities of order* ∞ when characterized in terms of Choquet theory of capacities. When X is infinite, function Bel is also required to be *continuous from above*.

For any given belief measure Bel, a dual measure, Pl, is defined by the equation

$$\text{Pl}(A) = 1 - \text{Bel}(\overline{A})$$

for all $A \in P(X)$, where $\overline{A}$ denotes the complement of A with respect to X. This measure, which is called a plausibility measure (or *alternate capacity of order* ∞ by Choquet), satisfies the inequality

$$\text{Pl}(A_1 \cap A_2 \cap \ldots \cap A_n) \leq \sum_j \text{Pl}(A_j)$$
$$- \sum_{j<k} \text{Pl}(A_j \cup A_k) + \ldots$$
$$+ (-1)^{n+1} \text{Pl}(A_1 \cup A_2 \cup \ldots \cup A_n)$$

for all possible families of subsets of X. Moreover, $\text{Pl}(\varnothing) = 0$, $\text{Pl}(X) = 1$. When X is infinite, function Pl is also required to be *continuous from below*.

The pair of a belief measure Bel and its dual plausibility measure Pl are conveniently characterized by a function

$$m : P(X) \rightarrow [0,1]$$

which is required to satisfy two conditions:

1. $m(\varnothing) = 0$
2. $\sum_{A \in P(X)} m(A) = 1.$

This function is called a *basic probability assignment*. Given a particular basic probability assignment m, the corresponding belief measure and plausibility measure are determined for all sets $A \in P(X)$ by the formulas

$$\text{Bel}(A) = \sum_{B \mid B \subseteq A} m(B)$$

$$\text{Pl}(A) = \sum_{B \mid A \cap \neq \varnothing} m(B)$$

The three functions, Bel, Pl, and m, are alternative representations of the same evidence. Given any of them, the other two are uniquely determined. For example,

$$m(A) = \sum_{B \mid B \subseteq A} (-1)^{|A-B|} \text{Bel}(B)$$

for all $A \in P(X)$, where $|A - B|$ denotes the number of elements of X that are in A but not in B. Given a basic probability assignment, every set $A \in P(X)$ for which $m(A) > 0$ is called a *focal element*. The pair (F,m), where F denotes the set of all focal elements induced by m, is called a *body of evidence*. Given two frames of discernment, X and Y, a basic probability assignment of the form

$$m : P(X \times Y) \rightarrow [0,1]$$

which expresses evidence pertaining to the frame of discernment $X \times Y$ (a Cartesian product of X and Y), is called a *joint basic probability assignment*. Each focal element induced by m is a subset R of $X \times Y$. When R is projected on set X and on set Y, we obtain the sets

$$R_X = \{x \in X \mid (x,y) \in R \text{ for some } y \in Y\}$$

$$R_Y = \{y \in Y \mid (x,y) \in R \text{ for some } x \in X\}$$

respectively. These sets are then used for defining *marginal basic probability assignments*, m_X and m_Y, of m via formulas

$$m_X(A) = \sum_{R \mid R_X = A} m(R) \quad \text{for all } A \in P(X)$$

$$m_Y(B) = \sum_{R \mid R_Y = B} m(R) \quad \text{for all } B \in P(Y)$$

Bodies of evidence (F_X, m_X) and (F_Y, m_Y) are, according to DST, noniterative if and only if for all $A \in F_X$ and all $B \in F_Y$:

$$m(A \times B) = m_X(A) \cdot m_Y(B)$$

$$m(R) = 0 \quad \text{for all } R \neq A \times B$$

When all focal elements in a given body of evidence are singletons, the associated belief measure and plausibility measure collapse into a single measure, a classical probability measure, which is additive.

B. Possibility Theory

Possibility theory is based on two dual semicontinuous fuzzy measures—possibility measures (lower semicontinuous) and necessity measures (upper semicontinuous). The theory may be characterized in terms of either of these measures, which are usually viewed as functions from the power set, $P(X)$, of a given universal set X to the unit interval $[0,1]$. In a more general formulation, which is not followed in this article, these measures are viewed as functions from an ample field on X (a family of subsets of X that is closed under arbitrary unions and intersections, and under complementation in X) to a given complete lattice.

Given a universal set X, a *possibility measure*, Pos, is a function

$$\text{Pos: } P(X) \rightarrow [0,1]$$

that satisfies the following axiomatic requirements:

(Pos 1) Pos $(\varnothing) = 0$
(Pos 2) Pos $(X) = 1$
(Pos 3) for any family $\{A_i \mid A_i \in P(X), i \in I\}$; where I is an arbitrary (possibly uncountable) index set,

$$\text{Pos} \left(\bigcup_{i \in I} A_i \right) = \sup_{i \in I} \text{Pos} (A_i)$$

Given a universal set X, a *necessity measure*, Nec, is function

$$\text{Nec : } P(X) \rightarrow [0,1]$$

that satisfies the following requirements:

(Nec 1) Nec $(\varnothing) = 0$
(Nec 2) Nec $(X) = 1$
(Nec 3) for any family $\{A_i \mid A_i \in P(X), i \in I\}$, where I is an arbitrary index set,

$$\text{Nec} \left(\bigcap_{i \in I} A_i \right) = \inf_{i \in I} \text{Nec} (A_i)$$

As is well known, these two formulations are dual in the sense that

$$\text{Nec} (A) = 1 - \text{Pos} (\bar{A})$$

for all $A \in P(X)$. It is also well known that any given function

$$r : X \rightarrow [0,1]$$

such that

$$\sup_{x \in X} r(x) = 1$$

characterizes a unique possibility measure Pos via the formula

$$\text{Pos }(A) = \sup_{x \in A} r(x)$$

for all nonempty sets $A \in P(X)$. Function r is called a *possibility distribution function* and the required property that the supremum of r is 1 is called a *possibilistic normalization*. Clearly, $r(x) = \text{Pos }(\{x\})$ for all $x \in X$.

When r is a joint possibility distribution function defined on a finite Cartesian product $X \times Y$, marginal possibility distribution functions, r_X and r_Y, are determined by the formulas

$$r_X(x) = \sup_{y \in Y} r(x,y)$$

for each $x \in X$ and

$$r_Y(y) = \sup_{x \in X} r(x,y)$$

for each $y \in Y$. The marginal bodies of evidence are viewed as noninteractive in possibility theory when

$$r(x,y) = \min[r_X(x), r_Y(y)]$$

for all $x \in X$ and all $y \in Y$. The most comprehensive coverage of possibility theory was prepared by Dubois and Prade and De Cooman.

Possibility theory is a natural mathematical framework for representing and manipulating uncertainty associated with fuzzy propositions. Consider a fuzzy proposition "X is F," where X is a variable whose values are in set X and F is a standard fuzzy set defined on X. According to the well-established interpretation, this proposition induces a possibility distribution, r_F, that is defined for each $x \in X$ by the formula

$$r_F(x) = F(x) + 1 - h_F,$$

where

$$h_F = \sup_{x \in X} F(x)$$

This possibility distribution captures the uncertainty associated with the proposition. The corresponding possibility measure, Pos_F, is then determined for all $A \in P(X)$ via the formula

$$\text{Pos}_F(A) = \sup_{x \in X} \{\min[F(x),A(x)]\}$$

At level 1 (representation), possibility and necessity measures are special plausibility and belief measures, respectively, whose focal elements are nested. This nested structure of focal elements is comparable with the nested structure of α-cuts of fuzzy sets, which makes the fuzzy set interpretation of possibility theory natural. At level 2, DST and possibility theory are not comparable since they use distinct calculi.

V. UNCERTAINTY MEASURES

A measure of uncertainty of some conceived type represented within a given mathematical theory (probability theory, possibility theory, DST, etc.) is a functional that assigns to each representation of evidence in the theory (a probability distribution, a possibility distribution, a body of evidence, etc.) a non-negative real number. Intuitively, numbers obtained by this functional should be inversely proportional to the strength and consistency in evidence, as expressed in the theory employed: The stronger and more consistent the evidence, the smaller the amount of uncertainty.

Uncertainty measures are distinguished from one another by the mathematical representation employed and by the type of uncertainty involved. Although each uncertainty measure should make sense on intuitive grounds, it is even more important that it satisfies certain axiomatic requirements. In the rest of this section, the most fundamental requirements are described. Because the mathematical form of each of these requirements depends on the uncertainty theory employed, they are described in generic terms, independent of the various uncertainty calculi.

The following requirements are essential in the sense that they apply to all uncertainty theories:

1. *Subadditivity:* The amount of uncertainty in a joint representation of evidence (defined on a Cartesian product) cannot be greater than the sum of the amounts of uncertainty in the associated marginal representations of evidence.
2. *Additivity:* The two amounts of uncertainty considered under subadditivity become equal if and only if the marginal representations of evidence are noninteractive according to the rules of the uncertainty calculus involved.
3. *Range:* The range of uncertainty is $[0,M]$, where M depends on the cardinality of the universal set involved and on the chosen unit of measurement.
4. *Continuity:* Any measure of uncertainty must be a continuous function.
5. *Expansibility:* Expanding the universal set by alternatives that are not supported by evidence must not affect the amount of uncertainty.
6. *Branching/consistency:* When the amount of uncertainty can be computed in more ways, all intuitively acceptable, the results must be the same (consistent).

The remaining two requirements are applicable only to some theories of uncertainty:

7. *Monotonicity:* When evidence can be ordered in the uncertainty theory employed (as in possibility theory), the relevant uncertainty measure must preserve this ordering.

8. *Coordinate invariance:* When evidence is described within the n-dimensional Euclidean space ($n \geq 1$), the relevant uncertainty measure must not change under isometric transformation of coordinates.

It is recognized that two types of uncertainty coexist in DST as well as in possibility theory. They are usually referred to as nonspecificity and entropy-like uncertainty. Basic issues regarding measures of these uncertainty types are summarized in this section.

A. Nonspecificity

Perhaps the most fundamental type of uncertainty is expressed in terms of a finite set of possible alternatives. To describe this uncertainty, let X denote the set of all alternatives under consideration (predictions, retrodictions, diagnoses, etc.), and let it be called a *universal set.* In each situation, only one of the alternatives is correct, but we do not necessarily know which one. Assume that we only know, on the basis of all available evidence, that the true alternative is in a subset A of X. This means that only the alternatives in A are considered as *possible* candidates for the true alternative.

It is well established that the only sensible way to measure the amount of uncertainty associated with any finite set A of possible alternatives is to use functional H defined by the simple formula

$$H(A) = \log_2 |A|$$

where $|A|$ denotes the number of elements in A (cardinality of A), provided that the measurement unit is a *bit*. One bit of uncertainty is equivalent to uncertainty regarding the truth or falsity of one elementary proposition. This formula was originally derived in 1928 by Hartley, and it is thus usually referred to as the *Hartley measure of uncertainty*. Its uniqueness was later proven in several different ways on axiomatic grounds.

The type of uncertainty quantified by the Hartley measure is well captured by the term *nonspecificity*. Indeed, this uncertainty results from the lack of specificity in characterizing the true alternative. The larger the set of possible alternatives, the less specific the characterization. Full specificity is obtained when only one alternative is possible.

Viewed from the standpoint of DST, the nonspecificity quantified by the Hartley measure is derived from simple bodies of evidence, each with one focal element. To measure nonspecificity of arbitrary bodies of evidence in DST, we need a functional by which values of the Hartley measure for all focal elements can be properly aggregated. The most natural way of aggregation in this case is to take the average of these values, weighted by the associated values of the basic probability assignment function m. The general measure of nonspecificity in DST, N, is then defined for each given m by the formula

$$N(m) = \sum_{A \in P(X)} m(A) \log_2 |A|$$

If all focal elements are singletons, which means that the body of evidence represents a probability measure, then $N(m) = 0$. If all focal elements are nested, then it is convenient to replace function N with a special function, which is usually denoted in the literature by U. Assuming that $X = \{x_1, x_2, \ldots, x_n\}$ and ordering $r(x_i) \geq r(x_{i+1})$ of possibility values for all $i = 1, 2, \ldots, n$, the possibilistic measure of nonspecificity U is defined by the formula

$$U(r) = \sum_{i=2}^{n} [r(x_i) - r(x_{i+1})] \log_2 i$$

where $r(x_{n+1}) = 0$ by convention. When employing the fuzzy set interpretation, $U(r)$ measures the amount of nonspecificity in evidence expressed by the proposition "X is F," where X is a variable whose values are in X and F is a fuzzy set. Then,

$$U(r_F) = \sum_{i=2}^{n-1} [F(x_i) - F(x_{i+1})] \log_2 i + [F(x_n) + 1 - h_F] \log_2 n$$

The measure of nonspecificity N in DST and its possibilistic counterpart U have been proven unique under well-justified axiomatic requirements.

The Hartley measure is applicable only to finite sets. A *Hartley-like measure,* HL, for convex subsets of the n-dimensional Euclidean space $R^n (n \geq 1)$ was recently proposed by the formula

$$\mathrm{HL}(A)$$
$$= \min_{t \in T} \ln \left[\prod_{i=1}^{n} [1 + \mu(A_{i_t})] + \mu(A) - \prod_{i=1}^{n} \mu(A_{i_t}) \right]$$

where μ denotes the Lebesgue measure, T denotes the set of all isometric transformations of orthogonal coordinate systems, and A_{i_t} denotes the ith one-dimensional projection of A in coordinate system t.

The Hartley-like measure HL was proven to satisfy all properties that such a measure is expected to satisfy (monotonicity, continuity, subadditivity, additivity, coordinate invariance, and appropriate range), but its uniqueness under these properties has not been established as yet. The measure can be extended to fuzzy sets via the fuzzy set interpretation of possibility theory. This results in a new function, UL, a counterpart of function U, which for each convex fuzzy set F is defined by the formula

$$UL(F) = \int_0^{h_F} HL(^\alpha F) \, d\alpha + (1 - h_F)HL(X)$$

where $^\alpha F$ denotes the α-cut of F ($\alpha \in [0,1]$).

B. Entropy-Like Uncertainty

Nonspecificity is not the only type of uncertainty in DST and possibility theory. This follows directly from the fact that nonspecificity is not applicable to probability measures at all. Shannon entropy, which is a well-established measure of uncertainty in probability theory, measures uncertainty of a different type. This means that two types of uncertainty coexist in DST. The Shannon entropy, S, which is applicable only to probability measures, is expressed within DST by the formula

$$S(m) = -\sum_{x \in X} m(\{x\}) \log_2 m(\{x\})$$

This functional, which forms the basis for *classical information theory*, has been proven in numerous ways to be the only sensible measure of the average uncertainty in predicting outcomes of a random experiment.

Attempts to find a well-justified generalization of the Shannon entropy in DST have not been successful thus far. Although several functionals have been proposed in the literature for this purpose on intuitive grounds, none of them satisfies all of the mathematical properties expected of such a functional. In most cases, the proposed functionals do not satisfy the property of subadditivity.

C. Aggregate Uncertainty

In the early 1990s, the unsuccessful attempts to find a generalized Shannon entropy in DST were replaced with attempts to find an aggregate uncertainty measure. Such a measure should capture the total amount of uncertainty for each given body of evidence in DST. After some initial failures, these attempts were eventually successful. An aggregate measure of uncertainty in DST that satisfies all required properties was found independently by several authors. This *aggregate uncertainty measure* is a functional AU that for each given body of evidence based on belief measure Bel is defined as follows:

$$AU(Bel) = \max_{P_{Bel}} \left[-\sum_{x \in X} p(x) \log_2 p(x) \right]$$

where the maximum is taken over the set P_{Bel} of all probability distribution functions p that are consistent with the given belief measure, which means that they satisfy the following constraints:

1. $p(x) \in [0,1]$ for all $x \in X$ and $\sum_{x \in X} p(x) = 1$

2. $Bel(A) \le \sum_{x \in A} p(x)$ for all $A \subseteq X$

Because the common defect of all other functionals proposed in the literature to measure entropy-like uncertainty or aggregate uncertainty in DST is the lack of subadditivity, it is significant that functional AU satisfies all required mathematical properties, including subadditivity.

Because functional AU is defined in terms of the solution to a nonlinear optimization problem, its practical utility was initially questioned. Fortunately, a relatively simple and fully general algorithm for computing the measure was soon discovered.

D. Recent Developments

Although functional AU is acceptable on mathematical grounds as an aggregate measure of uncertainty in DST and possibility theory, it is rather insensitive to changes in evidence that seem significant on intuitive grounds. To illustrate this undesirable feature of the functional, let us examine a very simple example. Let $X = \{x_1, x_2\}$ and $m(\{x_1\}) = a$, $m(X) = 1 - a$. Then, Bel $(\{x_1\}) = a$, Bel$(\{x_2\}) = 0$, Bel$(X) = 1$, and AU(Bel) = 1 for all $a \in [0,0.5]$. Increasing evidence focusing on the alternative x_1 from 0 to 0.5 is thus not captured by the value of AU.

One additional undesirable feature of the aggregate measure AU should be mentioned. The measure does not take into account differences in convex sets of probability distributions that are consistent with the various bodies of evidence. Thus, for example, the situation of total ignorance, when $m(X) = 1$, has the same value of AU as the situation characterized by the uniform probability distribution $m(\{x\}) = 1/|X|$ for all $x \in X$. However, these two situations are associated with very different sets of probability distributions. In the first situation, the set consists of all probability distributions that can be defined on X; in the second situation, the set consists of a single probability distribution, the uniform one. This is an important difference, at least from the behavioral point of view.

While the second situation contains information for rational betting, no such information is available in the first situation.

This critical appraisal resulted recently in three distinct and complementary measures of total uncertainty in DST and possibility theory. To describe them, let $\bar{S}$ and $\underline{S}$ denote, respectively, the maximum and minimum Shannon entropy within all probability distributions that are consistent with the given body of evidence (hence, $\bar{S}$ = AU).

The first measure of total uncertainty, TU_1, is defined as a linear combination of $\bar{S}$ and N,

$$TU_1 = \delta\bar{S} + (1 - \delta)N$$

where $\delta \in (0,1)$ is a factor by which the situation of total ignorance is distinguished from the situation characterized by the uniform probability distribution. It seems that the proper value of δ should be determined in the context of each interpretation of DST, but this issue has not been investigated as yet.

The second measure of total uncertainty, TU_2, is defined as the pair of N and $\bar{S} - N$:

$$TU_2 = (N, \bar{S} - N)$$

Here, the difference $\bar{S} - N$ stands for the entropy-like measure.

The third measure of total uncertainty, TU_3, is defined as the pair

$$TU_3 = (N, [\underline{S}, \bar{S}])$$

where the second component represents the range of entropy values for all probability measures that are consistent with the given body of evidence.

The three measures are complementary in the sense that they express the measured uncertainty in different forms: TU_1 expresses the uncertainty by a single real number; TU_2 expresses it in terms of a pair of real numbers; and TU_3 uses a real number and an interval of real numbers.

VI. UNCERTAINTY AND INFORMATION

The concept of uncertainty is closely connected with the concept of information. In general, information in a given context is obtained by a cognitive agent whenever relevant uncertainty is reduced. Uncertainty is considered relevant in the given context if its reduction is potentially useful in some way to the cognitive agent. To obtain information, some action must be taken by the cognitive agent, such as performing a relevant experiment, searching for a relevant fact, or accepting and interpreting a relevant message.

Assume that we can measure the *amount of uncertainty* associated with a given problem situation formulated within a particular mathematical framework. Assume further that the amount of uncertainty is reduced by obtaining relevant information as a result of some action. Then, the amount of information obtained by the action can be measured by the amount of reduced uncertainty.

Information measured solely by the reduction of relevant uncertainty within a particular mathematical framework is an important, even though restricted, notion of information. It does not capture, for example, the commonsense conception of information in human communication and cognition, or the algorithmic conception of information, in which the amount needed to describe an object is measured by the shortest possible description of the object in some standard language. To distinguish information conceived in terms of uncertainty reduction from the various other conceptions of information, it is common to refer to it as *uncertainty-based information*.

The nature of uncertainty-based information depends on the mathematical theory within which uncertainty pertaining to various problem-solving situations is formalized. Each formalization of uncertainty in a given problem-solving situation is a mathematical model of the situation. When we commit ourselves to a particular mathematical theory, our modeling becomes necessarily limited by the constraints of the theory. Clearly, a more general theory is capable of capturing uncertainties in some problem situations more faithfully than its less general competitors; however, its computational complexity is likely to be higher.

Although the utility of relevant uncertainty measures is as broad as the utility of any relevant measuring instrument, their role is particularly pronounced in three fundamental principles for managing uncertainty: (1) principle of minimum uncertainty, (2) principle of maximum uncertainty, and (3) principle of uncertainty invariance.

The *principle of minimum uncertainty* is basically an arbitration principle. It facilitates the selection of meaningful alternatives from solution sets obtained by solving problems in which some of the initial information is inevitably lost in the solutions to various degrees. According to this principle, we should accept only those solutions in a given solution set for which the loss of information is as small as possible. This means, in turn, that we should accept only solutions with minimum uncertainty. Examples of problems for which the principle of minimum uncertainty is applicable are simplification problems and conflict resolution problems of various types.

The second principle, the *principle of maximum uncertainty*, is essential for any problem that involves *ampliative reasoning*. This is reasoning in which conclusions are not entailed in the given premises. Using common sense, the principle may be expressed as follows: In any ampliative inference, use all information supported by available evidence but make sure that no additional information (unsupported by given evidence) is unwittingly added. Employing the connection between information and uncertainty, this definition can be reformulated in terms of uncertainty: Any conclusion resulting from any ampliative inference should maximize the relevant uncertainty within constraints representing given premises. This principle guarantees that we fully recognize our ignorance when we attempt to make inferences that are beyond the information domain defined by the given premises and, at the same time, that we utilize all information contained in the premises. In other words, the principle guarantees that our inferences are maximally noncommital with respect to information that is not contained in the premises.

Ampliative reasoning is indispensable to science and engineering in many ways and, hence, the underlying principle of maximum uncertainty has a great utility. For example, whenever we make predictions based on a given scientific model, we employ ampliative reasoning. Similarly, estimating microstates from the knowledge of relevant macrostates and partial knowledge of the microstates (as in image processing and many other problems) requires ampliative reasoning. The problem of the identification of an overall system from some of its subsystems is another example that involves ampliative reasoning and, hence, the principle of maximum uncertainty.

The principles of minimum and maximum uncertainty are well developed and have a great utility within the classical information theory, where they are referred to as the *principles of minimum and maximum entropy*. The literature concerned with these principles is extensive.

Optimization problems that emerge from the minimum and maximum uncertainty principles outside classical information theory have yet to be properly investigated and tested in praxis. This is currently one of the most active areas of research on uncertainty.

The third uncertainty principle, the *principle of uncertainty invariance*, is of relatively recent origin. It was introduced to facilitate meaningful transformations between the various uncertainty theories. According to this principle, the amount of uncertainty (and the associated uncertainty-based information) should be preserved in each transformation of uncertainty from one mathematical framework to another.

The uncertainty invariance principle was first applied to probability–possibility transformations. Examples of other applications are probabilistic or possibilistic approximations of general bodies of evidence in DST.

VII. OPEN PROBLEMS AND UNDEVELOPED AREAS

Each of the three measures of total uncertainty introduced in Section III.D is still associated with some open problems. Measure TU_1 is mathematically well justified, but the value of δ remains an open problem. Should value of δ be unique and determined on mathematical grounds? Should it be different for different interpretations, but unique within each interpretation? Should it be determined in the context of each application?

Measure TU_2 is also mathematically well justified. The only open problem associated with it is the meaning of the component $\bar{S} - N$. Can it be viewed as the genuine entropy-like measure or is it only an artifact?

Measure TU_3 is more problematic. Although conceptually it makes good sense, it is not clear how to define a meaningful ordering for it, one that would satisfy the requirement of subadditivity. Moreover, no efficient algorithm for computing $\underline{S}$ has been developed as yet.

Considering the framework for uncertainty theories depicted in Table I, it is clear that only a small number of uncertainty theories emerging from this framework have been developed thus far, at least up to the third level. As far as level 4 is concerned, probability theory is the only uncertainty theory that is developed at this level. This means that our understanding of the broad concept of uncertainty is still rather rudimentary.

SEE ALSO THE FOLLOWING ARTICLES

Automata Theory • Data, Information, and Knowledge • Decision Theory • Game Theory • Goal Programming • Hybrid Systems • Information Theory • Optimization Models • Pattern Recognition • Systems Science

BIBLIOGRAPHY

Choquet, G. (1953–1954). Theory of capacities. *Annales de L'Institut Fourier*, Vol. 5, 131–295.
De Cooman, G. (1997). Possibility theory. *Int. J. General Systems*, Vol. 25, No. 4, 291–371.

Dubois, D., and Prade, H. (1988). *Possibility theory*. New York: Plenum Press.

Dubois, D., and Prade, H. (1990). Rough fuzzy sets and fuzzy rough sets. *Int. J. General Systems,* Vol. 17, No. 2–3, 191–209.

Grabisch, M., Nguyen, H. T., and Walker, E. A. (1995). *Fundamentals of uncertainty calculi with applications to fuzzy inference.* Boston: Kluwer.

Halmos, P. R. (1950). *Measure theory.* Princeton, NJ: Van Nostrand.

Klir, G. J. (1999). On fuzzy-set interpretation of possibility theory. *Fuzzy Sets and Systems,* Vol. 108, No. 3, 263–273.

Klir, G. J. (2001). Foundations of fuzzy set theory and fuzzy logic: A historical overview. *Int. J. General Systems,* Vol. 30, No. 2.

Klir, G. J., and Wierman, M.J. (1999). *Uncertainty-based information: Elements of generalized information theory.* Heidelberg and New York: Physica-Verlag/Springer-Verlag.

Klir, G. J., and Yuan, B. (1995). *Fuzzy sets and fuzzy logic: Theory and applications.* Upper Saddle River, NJ: Prentice-Hall.

Klir, G. J., and Yuan, B. (1996). *Fuzzy sets, fuzzy logic, and fuzzy systems: Selected papers by Lotfi A. Zadeh.* Singapore: World Scientific.

Pawlak, Z. (1991). *Rough sets: Theoretical aspects of reasoning about data.* Boston: Kluwer.

Shafer, G. (1976). *A mathematical theory of evidence.* Princeton NJ: Princeton University Press.

Smith, R. M. (2000). Generalized information theory: Resolving some old questions and opening some new ones, Ph.D. Dissertation, Binghamton University–SUNY.

Walley, P. (1991). *Statistical reasoning with imprecise probabilities.* London: Chapman and Hall.

Wang, Z., and Klir, G. J. (1992). *Fuzzy measure theory.* New York: Plenum Press.

Yager, R. R., *et al.* (1987). *Fuzzy sets and applications: Selected papers by L. A. Zadeh.* New York: John Wiley.

Zadeh, L. A. (1965). Fuzzy sets. *Information and Control,* Vol. 8, No. 3, 338–353.

Unix Operating System

Marc P. Thomas

California State University, Bakersfield

GLOSSARY

ANSI The American National Standards Institute, a private, nonprofit organization of manufacturers, common carriers, and others. The United States' representative in ISO is ANSI.

batch A batch job (or process) is a non-time-critical job which, after initiation, runs to completion without additional user interaction. Usually such jobs write their results to a file that can be examined later.

Berkeley software distribution (BSD) The variant of Unix originally written at the University of California at Berkeley primarily by William Joy and Chuck Halcy incorporating some AT&T UNIX code. The versions BSD 4.*x* (*x* = 1, 2, or 3) evolved to become competitors of AT&T's own System V distribution. BSD was sometimes referred to as "nonstandard" by AT&T spokepersons, but it proliferated rapidly at academic sites as well as in commercial offerings (e.g., Sun Microsystems' SunOS and Digital Equipment Corporation's Ultrix) in the mid- to late 1980s. A major advance was the addition (starting with version 4.2) of kernel-level support for TCP/IP and the introduction of the network socket as the application programmer's interface to the network.

binary file A file containing coded information (possibly machine code) that is not human readable without some type of decoding utility. Examples of binary files are most executable files, registry files, most picture files, and most document files produced by WYSIWYG word processors.

copylefted software A modification of the idea of public domain software in two respects: First, all contributors are copyright holders and, second, anyone modifying the program sources must pass along the freedom to, copy and make further changes to these modified sources.

daemon A background process that waits at some network service port for requests. Its complexity depends on how critical (in terms of security) the resources it is managing are and how complicated a task it will be to service the request.

descriptor A software abstraction that is essentially a handle allowing access to some physical device.

device Any item of computer hardware which, from the point of view of the kernel of the operating system, functions as an input or output unit. Examples of devices are keyboard, mouse, video monitor, disk drives, drives with removable media such as floppy disk drives and CD-ROM drives, network interface, serial port, parallel port, USB port, SCSI port, and memory.

file store The complete organization of the files of a system. The file store may include "special" files, which are paths to certain devices.

fork An operation on a process (called the *parent*) in which a duplicate (called the *child*) is created so that the environment, data area, and descriptors are a complete copy of the parent's. The child retains the same point of execution as the parent but, necessarily, has a different process ID.

GNU The recursive acronym for GNU's Not Unix. GNU is the offical name of the Unix-compatible software system project started in 1983 by Richard Stallman. GNU's C compiler, development tools, and utilities played a vital role in Linus Torvalds' early release of Linux in 1991.

International Standards Organization (ISO) A voluntary, nontreaty organization founded in 1946. Its members are the national standards organizations of the member countries.

interactive An interactive job (or process) is one that maintains a steady dialog with a user, usually through some type of log-in session.

kernel The critical inner layer of software of an operating system which executes in privileged mode, controlling the raw hardware devices, handling interrupts, and doing low-level process (and thread) management. Systems differ with regard to what else is in the kernel. A *microkernel* does not include the less hardware dependent services such as reentrant device drivers, file systems, and network services, and communicates with the other system processes via message passing. A *macro* or *monolithic kernel,* which is the norm for Unix, includes all of these in one binary image (very often in a file named "vmunix".)

latency The delay time required for the system to respond to a user action, for example, the echo of a character on the screen after a keypress. More generally, it is also used to refer to delay that occurs between an input or output request and the initiation, by the hardware, of the start of the servicing of the request.

Linux A freely distributable version of Unix developed primarily by Linus Torvalds at the University of Helsinki in Finland. The first official version was released in 1991.

Minix A small version of Unix written by Andrew Tanenbaum for the IBM PC and compatibles. The first version was released in 1987. It had a major influence on Linus Torvalds' Linux operating system.

network protocol A specification of the rules and procedures to be followed for the exchange of information on a network.

operating system The software on a computer system that controls the system, allocates resources, dialogs with hardware devices, and runs user jobs.

pipe An operating system construct that can arrange for the output of one program to be automatically directed to the input of another. Unix shells also support piping from the command line.

platform By computing platform one means a particular combination of hardware and operating system software (e.g., an IBM PC clone running Linux 2.2.5, an IBM PC clone running Windows NT 4.0,

or a DEC/Compac AlphaStation 500 running Tru64 Unix.)

port (1) Also called *software port.* When one modifies a software package that was originally written for some platform X to run on (a different) platform Y, the modified software is referred to as a *port* of the software package to platform Y. (2) Also called *network port number.* A number together with an associated network protocol that is used to reference network connections between machines. For example, the service port for Internet SMTP mail connections is port 25 with the TCP protocol for transport.

portable operating system interface for computing environments (POSIX) An IEEE standard (first version 1988) that specifies a collection of portable function calls which allow an application program to obtain important services (e.g., file, terminal, directory, and process handling) from an operating system. The POSIX function calls are primarily derived from AT&T UNIX System V and BSD Unix calls.

process An executing program together with its environment, which includes allocated memory, and descriptors, or handles, to various files, devices, and network sockets. Some operating systems make a distinction between *process* and *job* in that a job may include more than one process. Newer operating systems allow a process to contain more than one *thread.*

public domain software Software that is free to use and copy but which may also be enhanced and (re)marketed as a proprietary product.

root The user root is the privileged user or administrator on a Unix system. Anything that is critical or a security issue generally requires *root privileges* for access.

script A script is a text file that is usually used in conjunction with a command line interpreter (e.g., a Unix shell) and that consists of a sequence of logical operations and decision structures. It is similar to a program but is usually much simpler and is interpreted by the command line interpreter rather than compiled. Scripts are important tools in system administration.

shell Loosely described, this is the software that controls the direct interaction with the user. It may be as simple as a command line interpreter or as elaborate as a graphical interface with multiple desktops. The term *Unix shell* is more specific, being a command line interpreter with powerful scripting facilities.

signal The software equivalent of a hardware interrupt. A process sends a signal to another process to interrupt the normal flow of instruction execution and cause some action (e.g., reload configuration, terminate, etc.). Signals can also be used in the case of threads but usually the target has to make a specific system call first, for example, a signal could be used to "wake up" a thread which has called *sigsuspend*.

signal handler A software procedure in a process that is invoked (asynchronously) when a signal is sent to the process. A signal handler is usually written to handle a specific type of signal, and to do its work fairly quickly.

socket A software abstraction similar to a *stream file* that allows access to a network. Sockets always have an associated network protocol.

software abstraction A construct (with a precise syntax) in a programming language that allows a programmer to conveniently access some functional hardware unit or device in a standard manner, thereby avoiding differences in hardware.

spawn An operation in which a process (called the *parent*) creates a new process (called the *child*), which may or may not be the same program as the parent. One important distinction between a *fork* and a *spawn* is that a spawned process starts at the first line of executable code with a new environment and data area. Consequently, any information that the parent wants to share with the spawned offspring must be specifically coded for, whereas, in the case of a forked offspring, a copy has been made automatically of virtually all of the parent's state.

state of a process The environment, data and stack areas, current point of execution and register contents of a process; in short, all the information which would have to be saved in order to restart the process at some later time.

suid Shortened term for *Set User Id*. This is a privilege bit which, if set on a file that is an executable program, will give it the permissions of the owner (who is usually root). This is the primary mechanism in Unix for allowing a general user to execute a program that requires system privileges. It is conceptually clean and simple, but if misused (e.g., if it is possible to break out of the program to a command line shell) can be the source of very dangerous security holes.

System V The first commercial version of UNIX produced by the Unix Support Group (USG) of AT&T Bell Laboratories (now Lucent Technologies) in the early 1980s. This became the first standard version of UNIX. A number of vendors (e.g., Data General, IBM, Hewlett Packard, and Silicon Graphics) adopted this during the mid- to late 1980s.

text file A file consisting of printable characters (letters, digits, punctuation) together with some special typewriter operations such as tabs and newlines. The most common types of text files use the ASCII 7-bit character set. Examples of text files are normal Internet e-mail, most markup language documents (e.g., HTML, TeX, LaTeX, and RTF), and most "read me" files.

The Open Group A consortium, originally formed from a merger of groups of vendors supplying Unix operating systems and Unix workstation interfaces. This group now maintains a number of standards such as X/Open, Unix 98, Motif, and the Common Desktop Environment (CDE).

thread A line of execution in a process. Every process has one main thread, which may (depending on the particular platform) be allowed to start others. Multiple threads are usually more efficient than multiple processes but synchronization and security (since any thread can modify the process environment) considerations make thread programming more difficult.

throughput This relates to the number of tasks that can be serviced in a given amount of time. For official benchmarks, a selected number of standard tasks would be used.

Transmission Control Protocol/Internet Protocol (TCP/IP) The primary protocol governing the exchange of information on the Internet.

UNIX 98 An Open Group trademark for 64-bit-enabled Unix operating systems that meet specific standards of software portability and network interfaces. Linux, which has become the most widely used variant of the Unix operating system, is not, however, covered by this standard.

volatile A memory element or memory system is *volatile* if the stored information is lost when the power is turned off.

X Window System Also called by the shorter names *X11* or, simply, *X*. This is a software package that provides a complete, platform-independent graphical user interface for Unix and other systems. Originally developed by Project Athena at MIT, then handled by a group of vendors know as the X Consortium, it is currently developed and distributed commercially by The Open Group.

XENIX A third version of Unix developed by Microsoft in the early 1980s and licensed to the Santa Cruz Operation (SCO). Originally it was based on AT&T's older System III, but was substantially modified by both Microsoft and SCO (e.g., the ability to communicate with the MSLAN/PCLAN NETBIOS protocol was supported).

X/Open The current set of standards for the X Window System, maintained and licensed by The Open Group.

Strictly speaking, **UNIX** (in capitals) has been a registered trademark of UNIX System Laboratories [first owned by AT&T; then sold, in 1993, to Novell, Inc.; then sold, in 1995, to the Santa Cruz Operation (SCO)]. The Unix trademark is currently owned by The Open Group. But the word *Unix* has also come to refer to a collection of very closely related operating systems (e.g., AT&T UNIX System V, BSD 4.3 Unix, Sun Microsystems' Solaris, Silicon Graphic's Irix, DEC/Compac Tru-64 Unix, IBM's AIX, Hewlett-Packard's HP Unix, FreeBSD, NetBSD, SCO UNIX, Minix, Linux, and many others) that have found use on a wide variety of computing platforms, ranging from single-user personal computers to large network server multiprocessor machines. Many of these variants are proprietary, but others have source code freely available. Although differences and disputes have arisen concerning which version is the "standard," it is the design similarities and the wide range of computing hardware supported that are significant. For the purposes of this article, features of the Unix operating system will refer to those features which are common to almost all modern versions of Unix.

It is helpful to give a brief outline of Unix history. UNIX was the creation of a group of researchers at Bell Laboratories (now Lucent Technologies) during 1969–1970. This effort was led by Ken Thompson, Dennis Ritchie, M. D. McIlroy, and J. F. Ossanna. The desire was to produce a multiuser, multiprocessing operating system that would support research in computer science, but which had modest hardware requirements (unlike the earlier MULTICS project). Users were expected to connect to the system primarily via terminals over RS-232 serial communication lines. Additional improvements were made during the next few years. The kernel was rewritten in C in 1973. By 1974 Bell Laboratories Version 5 of the UNIX system was available for a nominal charge with full source code (but, of course, officially unsupported). Within academic computer science programs it quickly became a popular choice. The first commercial version was released as System V in 1983 and, in some sense, became the first mature standardized version of UNIX.

Interest in UNIX spread and spurred modifications that added functionality. The most successful were the modifications introduced by researchers and graduate students at the University of California at Berke-

ley during the late 1970s and early 1980s. One of the most significant milestones was the addition (in version BSD 4.2 in 1983) of TCP/IP networking via the software abstraction of a network *socket*. This made it possible for application programmers to write portable code that accessed a network. The mature version of this line of development was BSD 4.3 Unix.

Some commercial vendors chose to market Berkeley variants, two popular ones being Sun Microsystems' SunOS and Digital Equipment Corporation's Ultrix. Other vendors, including Data General, IBM, Hewlett-Packard, and Silicon Graphics, adopted AT&T's System V. A third version, called Xenix, was developed by Microsoft and licensed to SCO. It incorporated some PC-specific features such as support for the PCLAN NETBIOS protocol. This proliferation added greatly to the popularity of Unix but was at odds with software portability issues.

Unix was primarily attractive to smaller start-up ventures because the cost of writing an operating system from scratch is prohibitive to most small vendors. In addition, the Unix application programmer interface (API) is quite flexible and this saves coding time. Many of the machines marketed were in the workstation class, that is, their performance and cost put them above personal computers such as the Apple Macintosh and IBM PC but below most minicomputers. Since this was a smaller market than the rapidly growing personal computer market and since there were at least three competing standards for Unix, most Unix software was priced much higher than personal computer software. This situation tended to keep Unix out of the personal computer market where PC-DOS, MS-DOS, and later, Windows 3.1/95/98/NT would develop as the de facto standards on the IBM PC clone. Only with the growth of Linux in the 1990s did truly low-cost Unix software become available for personal computer users.

An attempt at consolidation and the adoption of a standard for Unix in the late 1980s produced two camps. One group was formed by the AT&T and Sun Microsystems agreement to merge features of both their systems as System V release 4 (SVR4). This was marketed by Sun under the Solaris name. A second group (including Apollo Computer, Digital Equipment Corporation, Hewlett-Packard, and IBM) was formed around the Open Software Foundation (OSF) agreement. By this time the line between BSD and System V Unixes had become blurred and the products of both of these groups had features drawn from both parents.

The full Unix operating system had been ported only to the top end of the early personal computer market, since Unix required CPU, memory, and disk resources that were well in excess of what was available on the majority of these early machines. However, the growing popularity of the IBM PC clone as a personal computing platform and the need to have a system that students could work on encouraged Andrew Tanenbaum to write a limited version of Unix in 1986 called Minix, for the PC platform. Although it originally supported multiprocessing with a single user and only floppy disk drives for storage, it evolved over the years to Minix 2.0, with many additional features not found in the early versions. The full source code is available. Unlike most Unix operating systems, Minix uses a microkernel-based design.

Richard Stallman had founded the GNU Project in 1983 to supply Unix-compatible compilers, development tools, and utilities under a *copylefted software* license. This excellent package of freely available software with sources (and with the encouragement to make freely available enhancements) became a mainstay to computer science programs everywhere. Even more importantly, the GNU Project enabled a new Unix operating system to rise to prominence during the 1990s.

Graphical user interfaces for Unix were available in the early 1980s but all were proprietary and communication at the graphical level between two different Unix platforms was generally not possible. This situation was remedied when the Athena Project at MIT provided a standard platform independent graphical interface for Unix and other operating systems that can be used over a network. It is usually referred to as the *X Window System, X11,* or simply *X.* In addition, it decouples display and execution, so that a remote graphics program can be run in a local graphics window.

The X Window System has continued to this day to be the main graphical interface for Unix. It was primarily enhanced and distributed commercially by the X Consortium, whose membership included most of the major vendors (including Compaq, Hewlett-Packard, Hummingbird, IBM, Silicon Graphics, and Sun). These duties have been transferred to The Open Group (which includes the above vendors but which is a larger consortium). The Open Group also licenses commercial products such as the Motif interface for the X Window System and the Common Desktop Environment (CDE). The licensing does allow the existence of free implementations such as XFree86 (which is usually packaged with Linux). Although originally developed for Unix, X is flexible enough to be used in conjunction with proprietary windowing systems (e.g., Hummingbird's Exceed product family for use with Windows 95/98/NT), thereby allowing Unix and non-Unix graphical exchange and connectivity.

The most significant development in the 1990s has been the availability of a freely distributable Unix operating system called Linux. Linux was originally ported only to the 80386 PC platform. By 1999 Linux had matured and was available on a wide range of platforms, from personal computers (with Intel Pentium family processors) to a number of RISC processor machines (e.g., Alpha processor machines, Sun SPARC processor machines, and MIPS processor machines), and supported a very wide range of boards and other hardware devices.

Linux was developed primarily by Linus Torvalds but a key factor that made possible its early release in 1991 and subsequent popularity was the suite of GNU tools. Linux also has debts to Minix, notwithstanding design disagreements between Tanenbaum and Torvalds over issues of portability and kernel type (microkernel versus monolithic). An interesting repartee took place in 1992 in the Usenet News, with several other experts joining in; it is still worth reading.

Finally, note that although sources of information on Unix are legion, one finds information scattered among articles, books, web pages, circulated notes, programming handouts, source code, Usenet news posts, and folklore. One also finds an element of strong opinion in most of these sources. This is probably due to the fact that almost all of the pioneers were programmers, interested in their subject, somewhat partisan, not inclined to waste words (nor suffer fools gladly). While this is somewhat refreshing in an industry that suffers from excessive marketing hype, it does, however, present a hurdle to those users who are interested in Unix but come from a nontechnical background. It also makes it difficult to compile a static and stable list of sources in the same way that one does for a research article in a professional journal. This will be evident from the Bibliography given at the end of this article.

I. INTERACTIVE MULTIUSER OPERATING SYSTEMS

Before discussing the features and internals of UNIX it is necessary to first have a general discussion of interactive multi-user operating systems. From the perspective of the users, any modern operating system, if it wishes to be competitive, will have to deal with all of the following issues:

- Schedule and run user processes in a fair and efficient manner so that interactive users do not experience excessive delays waiting for a response.

- Manage memory so that frequently accessed blocks of program memory stay in main memory but less frequently accessed code and data blocks are (temporarily) swapped out to disk, so that a larger number of actual users (some intensive, some occasional) can be handled than would be possible without this virtualization of memory.
- Organize files in some type of directory structure that makes user access conceptual and straightforward.
- Manage input and output so that physical devices (such as hard disks, consoles, serial ports, parallel ports, network ports, and tape drives, etc.) which dialog directly with the outside world, appear as synchronized subsystems to the user. Buffer input and output to improve the throughput of the system but not at the expense of good latency for the interactive users.
- Support a good selection of interfaces (both command line and graphical), which will enable users to conveniently dialog with the system, run programs, and communicate with other users (who may be on different machines).
- Provide an attractive development environment so that a wide range of application software will be available to users at an affordable cost.

Satisifying user requirements and expectations is a necessary step in operating system design. Other considerations are the introduction of new hardware, the scalability of the design, the long-range stability of the platform as unanticipated changes force modifications of the design, and the demands that will be put on the system administrators who will have to manage a system with growing complexity. When these factors are considered, one can list a number of desirable and more specific design features:

- There should be a consistent philosophy of design. For example, if an abstraction, such as a descriptor, can be applied to a variety of devices then the programmer will not have to handle nearly as many special cases. If the file store can be organized in a hierarchical way that conceals hardware boundaries, users will not have to make reference to *physical* entities (such as partitions) when accessing files. A consistent philosophy of design may, at times, work against backward compatibility, but, in the long run, will keep the design cleaner and more easily understood by the users and managers.

- The operating system should be written in high-level code as much as possible so that the need for assembly language coding (which is hardware specific and expensive to debug) is kept to a minimum. This will make it easier to port the operating system to a wide variety of hardware platforms and this will provide the application vendor with the incentive of a larger market.
- The operating system should have conceptually simple process control operations for creation, duplication, synchronization, and cleanup. There should be a flexible mechanism for one process to send a signal to another.
- There should be logging of both hardware and software errors. Standard mechanisms for recovery from system crashes and failures should be provided. In this light it is usually advisable to provide a privileged single-user mode for debugging system failures as well as the ability to boot a previously built kernel.
- The system should be easy to modify as new hardware and communication devices become available. The application programmer interface (API) should be designed in such a way to allow increased functionality to be added.

Each of the above five areas is discussed in a separate section with attention given to ways in which the Unix operating system is distinctive or unique (see Table I). The last section discusses users' reactions to the Unix operating system as compared to non-Unix operating systems.

Table I   **Unix System Architecture for a Monolithic Kernel**

Kernel memory	User memory	User interface
Kernel	Daemons	Shells
	User processes (fork, exec, wait, exit, SIGCHLD cycle)	sh
		csh
		ksh
		zsh
		tcsh
		bash
		and Xwindow system interface
Abstraction layer	Descriptors for files, pipes, network sockets	
Hierarchical file store	Files, pipes, process tree sockets, and other devices	/proc /etc /bin /sys /dev /mnt /usr ...

II. DESIGN OBJECTIVES OF UNIX, FILE-STORE ORGANIZATION, TEXT PROCESSING, AND PROGRAMMING

A simplified point of view is that a computer runs programs in main memory and a program accepts data in the form of input and produces results as some form of output. Because main memory is very limited and generally volatile, it was realized very early on that some form of secondary storage would be needed to keep the input data and store the output results. The modern secondary storage device of choice is usually some type of disk drive. It may have magnetic media, optical media, or magneto-optical media. The media may be removable or fixed. Disk drives themselves are usually divided into smaller chunks called *partitions*. Usually, the data are organized into *files* according to some format within some partition. The files are usually grouped into *directories* (which may have *subdirectories,* so there is usually a hierarchy of directories). Because even a small system may contain multiple disk drives, it is necessary to organize the local file structures on each partition of each disk drive into some global logical structure that will be clear and convenient from the user's point of view.

Many non-Unix operating systems still require that a file be fully referenced by a name that tells which partition (e.g., C:\winnt\system32\cmd.exe where C: indicates the partition) or which physical device (e.g. DUA1:[faculty.smith]memorandum.txt where DUA1: indicates the formatted drive) the file is on.

In contrast to this physical path naming Unix assumes that the directory structure is hierarchical (i.e., a *tree,* with the forward slash, /, used as a separator) where partitions have been mounted on various nodes or subdirectories. *Mounting* is the process whereby the local file structure on a partition gets mapped into the global file tree. For example, one partition that has a local file named quota might be mounted on /usr/faculty and another partition which has a (different) local file named quota might be mounted on /usr/student. The first file is referred to by the logical path name /usr/faculty/quota and the second by /usr/student/quota. Neither faculty members nor students need to know which physical partition these files are on because they do their work with respect to the *logical* paths rather than the physical paths. In addition, Unix allows *symbolic links* for user convenience. For example, the directory /database may actually be symbolically linked to a very long logical path name, something like/usr/ local/applications/7.5.6/database, but the symbolic path makes it easier for users to reference and work with the files in the directory. This is a feature that some newer operating systems have only recently implemented (c.f., the Single Instance Store in Microsoft Windows 2000, which is a slight modification of a symbolic link).

More importantly, the designers of Unix, as well as those who have modified the system over the years, have consistently mapped all system devices into the file store as well. For example, the /dev directory contains each physical device, raw disk drives, formatted partitions, keyboard, mouse, printer ports, serial ports, network interfaces, terminals, etc. Many of these devices require root privileges for access, but their presence in the file store makes writing system software much easier. More recent Unix ports include a /proc directory so that system configuration and process activity can be gathered very easily. In addition, the fact that most of the information about the running system can be obtained from the file store (rather than, for example, having to give students executables marked *suid* root that will be able to read and decode kernel memory) makes Unix an excellent platform for teaching operating system principles.

Unix attempts to have a consistent logical and hierarchical file store that unifies the organization of not only the files, but all of the physical devices in the system, and an application program gains access to one of these (file, pipe, network socket, etc.) by making a system call and obtaining a *descriptor* for it, thereby masking hardware differences.

A related design aspect of Unix is the use of text files whenever possible. Every operating system needs to store its configuration information somewhere. Many operating systems put configuration information in *binary* files (for example, so-called "registry" files). If this information becomes corrupted, special utilities are usually needed to correct or restore it and a utility is needed even to read the information.

With the exception of password encryption files on some systems, all configuration files in Unix are human-readable text files. In addition, the scripts which are used to build the Unix kernel are also text files. This has the following benefits:

- Configuration files can be read, printed, understood, and modified with the use of a simple text editor.
- The system configuration can be backed up by simply making a copy of these text files onto removable media.

- Fixing corrupted configuration files on a Unix system is much easier than on systems that store the configuration information in binary files.

In addition, Unix provides a selection of shells with powerful scripting capabilities (e.g., *sh, csh, ksh, bash*) and auxiliary text processing utilties (e.g., *awk, eval, find, grep, read, sed, sort, test*) so that many times one can combine these and accomplish a task in a fraction of the time needed to write a program to do the same task. This is aided by shell constructs that support input and output redirection and piping the output of one program to the input of another.

The ability to do powerful and flexible document preparation was a feature of Unix from the start. All Unix systems support *nroff* for basic document formatting and the on-line manual pages, but many users have gone to the markup languages *TeX* and *LaTeX*, especially if mathematical constructs such as equations, subscripts, and special symbols are required.

One primary design goal of Unix was to support research in computer science, so that many things in Unix are designed for the convenience of the programmer. The *make* utility is invaluable for keeping object code for the various modules up to date. This utility has proved so useful it is almost always implemented in compiler packages even for non-Unix platforms. For more elaborate software development, the Concurrent Versions System *cvs* is available from GNU. It has been very important in the development of the BSD Unix systems. Finally, there are tools for lexical analysis (*lex*) and syntactical analysis (*yacc*). This scripting, text processing, and computer science developing environment is available to both system users and general users.

III. ROLE OF THE C PROGRAMMING LANGUAGE

The common practice, prior to Unix, was for operating systems to be written in the assembly language of the given processor line. This virtually assured that the resulting code would not be portable to other systems unless the hardware was identical. One reason this was done was to keep the operating system code efficient and ensure that not too large a percentage of time was spent executing system calls (as opposed to running user programs). Most compilers for high-level languages did not produce code efficient enough to compete with that which an assembly language programmer could write. In addition, most high-level languages did not even support the low-level bit operations, arrays of typeless pointers, and other constructs all operating system code requires.

Ken Thompson had written a typeless language called *B* in 1970 for the first Unix system on the Digital Equipment PDP-7. It owed various features to another typeless language called *BCPL*, which had been written in 1967 by Martin Richards. With these influences Dennis Ritchie designed the C language to be essentially hardware independent and have the features one needed for writing portable operating system code. Ritchie wrote the first C compiler in 1972 and implemented it on a Digital Equipment PDP-11. From 1973 on, all Unix operating systems were essentially written in C (with some assembly language in the low-level device drivers).

The following specific features of C are of primary importance for writing portable and efficient operating system code:

- C uses header files which handle differences in machine architecture.
- C includes a preprocessor with logical operators which, prior to compilation, makes a pass through the source code (with included headers), thereby producing correct source code for the *specific target* platform.
- C contains bit-level operations (AND, OR, EXCLUSIVE OR, right and left shifts, and one's complement) on both machine words and individual bytes so that device driver code can be written with it.
- C allows type casts, when is it necessary to override default types, and typeless pointers. It also allows structures which may contain bit fields. Although these are certainly *not* constructs an application programmer would be advised to use, they are very necessary for handling kernel data structures or for writing a memory manager.
- C has an excellent selection of decision structures that can be used in the higher layers of the operating system. In addition, C is very flexible regarding what constitutes an expression. This allows the C programmer to handle involved calculations with relatively few lines of code.
- The formal specification for the language is designed to make it easy to optimize a C compiler to produce very efficient code.

C revolutionized not only the writing of the Unix operating system, but the writing of *all* operating systems. With the standardization of C as ANSI C in 1983, other than in a few cases where processor power and memory space were very limited (for example, the 80286 port of OS/2), it has been used to write most new operating systems introduced in the last 15 years.

IV. PROCESS CONTROL: SIGNALS AND FORK

One of the responsibilities of an operating system is to manage both the system and user processes that do the work of the system. It is necessary to have clean, efficient mechanisms for creating, controlling, and ending processes and to perform these operations at the correct times. A process always executes in the context of some environment. The environment includes variables for terminal type, paths used to search for link libraries and executable files, and system information. A process has a data area in which to store important current information (more precisely, a process has *local* data storage in a stack area and *global* data storage in a data area, but this distinction will not be needed for the following discussion). It has *descriptors* that are handles to files or devices. Finally, it has a process ID that is a unique number used to reference it. All of this information, together with the current point of execution and register contents, constitutes the *state* of the process.

Suppose, for example, that we want to have a process handling nonauthenticated requests made over a TCP/IP network such as the Internet (for example, the process, or *daemon* might be handling World Wide Web requests). It will probably be a process with system privileges so when a request is received (for example, to view a particular home page) this *parent* process will generally create a *child* process which has no special privileges (that is, it will be assigned to a nonroot user such as *nobody* and may be restricted to accessing only a portion of the full file store) that will handle the request. To handle the request, it is usually the case that some of the information known by the parent will have to be copied to the data area of the child. When the request has been fully satisfied, the child process will end itself and terminate in such a way that the parent will be informed that it has finished its task. The parent process will have to keep track of how many active child processes it has running at any given time so that system resources (such as the number of open network sockets, buffer space, and system load) are not exceeded.

Under Unix the above sequence of events would be handled as follows:

- The parent process (also called a *daemon*) would be a root-privileged process listening at a designated network socket with a well-known port number.
- When a request arrives it looks at the source address and, unless it has been configured to refuse access from that address, accepts the request obtaining a data socket for information transfer.
- It then issues a *fork* system call, which makes a duplicate process (copying all environmental values, the data area, and the descriptors), with the same point of execution but with a different process ID.
- The offspring executes a block of code that changes its privileges with the *seteuid* system call, closes off any unused descriptors (but not, of course the data socket), and possibly restricts its file store access with the *chroot* system call.
- If the task that the child has to perform is extremely simple, the parent may decide to wait by making the *wait* system call. In almost all other cases the parent makes an entry in its data area for its new offspring, closes its descriptor for the data socket, and continues. It has previously set a *signal handler* to update its offspring information whenever it receives a SIGCHLD signal indicating that some offspring has terminated.
- The next action depends on the complexity of the task to be performed. If complicated, the offspring will issue an *exec* system call to overlay itself with new program code specifically designed to handle the task (and any associated security authentication). Otherwise it will directly handle the task itself. In either case the process ID will not change.
- When the offspring is done it will call *exit* and the operating system kernel will send a SIGCHLD signal to the parent.
- The parent, on receiving the SIGCHLD signal, will invoke its signal handler, which it set previously, and update its active child information data area.

The above sequence is efficient and elegant but it may not be clear how powerful it is at first glance until one compares it to systems which lack this *fork, exec, wait, exit, SIGCHLD* cycle.

Many non-Unix systems do not use the *fork* and *exec* calls and substitute a *spawn* system call instead. A complication is that *spawn* allows a new program to be started but does not provide an *automatic* mechanism for the parent to pass its environment, descriptors, or data to the spawned offspring. Consequently, *spawn* does not recapture the full power of *fork* (not even the full power of *fork . . . exec*). To pass information from its environment, descriptors, or data to a spawned offspring it is necessary either to encode the information as text and pass it on the command line or use some operating system message passing construct, thereby increasing overhead for the call. This greatly limits how much information can be shared between parent and child processes.

Consequently, operating systems that substitute the *spawn* call tend to use multiple threads in the daemon rather than spawned offspring whenever the task requires much shared data. While this requires less operating system overhead it is also inherently less secure for these reasons:

- All threads will have the same root privileges the main thread has.
- Any thread can change the global data or environment of the daemon, so a programming mistake can be difficult to find since it may appear only after the process has run for some time.
- Signals must be used more carefully when dealing with a process that has multiple threads.

But using threads is not an option confined to non-Unix operating systems. Almost all modern versions of Unix support standard POSIX thread calls. The modern practice in Unix is to use a parent process with multiple child processes if security is the primary concern and to use multiple threads in the parent process if efficiency is the primary concern.

In summary, one can say that the Unix process control constructs, specifically the *fork, exec, wait, exit, SIGCHLD* cycle together with the option of POSIX threads, allow maximum flexibility with regard to all aspects of process control.

V. ERROR LOGGING AND RECOVERY FROM SYSTEM FAILURES

All systems crash occasionally. Very often this happens due to the upgrading of some hardware or some unforeseen interaction between privileged processes. Unix supports the following features which help to speed recovery from system failures:

- As noted above, all configuration files in Unix are text files and corruption can be fixed with a simple text editor.
- With the exception of some Unix microkernel systems, all previous Unix kernels that have been built can be saved so that if the newly built kernel fails, one can temporarily boot the previous Unix kernel, or the one before that, until the problem is found. This is not the case with operating systems that have a microkernel and a large number of associated dynamic link libraries. Replacement of dynamic link libraries during an upgrade or installation of a service pack usually

makes it impossible to recover any build other than the previous one. If it becomes necessary to apply the service pack twice, one usually cannot recover even the previous build.
- Most Unix systems support a *single-user boot,* which allows a small version of Unix to be booted. The root user can then manually mount file systems, start daemons, etc., until the exact problem is found.
- It is usually possible under Unix to log hardware faults as well as sufficient namelist and core information during a system panic so that a debugger can be used after reboot to find exactly which program caused the crash and if it was accompanied by some hardware failure. This is important since many times a system will present a problem for which it is unclear whether hardware or software is at fault.

Unix recovery procedures are quite robust by comparison to what is available from non-Unix operating systems. This has certainly been a factor when decisions have been made in choosing a server platform. It has *not* been as much of a factor in the case of client platforms for the following reason. During the past decade, rapid growth of small networks has resulted in a shortage of experienced system administrators who are able to diagnose and recover a crashed system. In the case of a client machine used primarily by a single user it may be more cost effective to simply reload and rebuild the operating system, especially if there are a large number of identical clients at the site. This has the advantage that it does not require nearly as much expertise from the system administrator; it has the disadvantage that some problems are never really solved.

VI. MODIFIABILITY AND APPLICATION PROGRAMMER INTERFACE

Most languages have a standard runtime library for routine services such as text and numeric input and output, randon number generation, mathematical functions, and text string operations. In this respect ANSI C is typical. One problem for the application programmer is that anything else may be platform dependent. A classic example of platform-dependent code is graphics software where, at the current time, a number of competing standards exist (e.g., Silicon Graphic's OpenGL, the Graphical Kernel System, and others). This is primarily due to the continual upgrading of graphics display hardware to speed up two- and three-dimensional drawing, texturing, and the use of more sophisticated lighting schemes.

We have constructed a table of additional types of functions which the application programmer needs but which may be operating system dependent (see Table II).

Historically it has always been the case that software standardization has lagged behind improvements in hardware functionality. This presents a dilemma to the applications programmer who would like to incorporate new functionality into software products as soon as possible while at the same time covering as many different platforms as possible.

Unix is not perfect in this respect, but, with the POSIX, BSD sockets, and X Window System suite of system calls, has worked more for standardization than most platforms. Unix has certainly also provided a much richer environment of function calls than most other platforms.

VII. USER'S PERSPECTIVE ON UNIX

In the end, it is usually software costs, maintenance costs, and user preferences that decide whether one operating system is adopted rather than another. The history of computing contains many examples where a technically superior solution did not succeed in the marketplace.

This is pertinent to Unix, which, although more powerful and flexible than most other operating sys-

tems, has a steep initial learning curve. This more than any other fact has worked against acceptance of Unix by the general, nontechnical user.

Users who are proficient with programming and who need to modify their systems to adapt to special needs generally prefer Unix to non-Unix operating systems. This is not surprising given the original intent of the designers that Unix be suitable for all tasks from programming on up to doing research in computer science.

However, general users, including those who insist that "I just want to get my work done," almost always prefer proprietary operating systems where the various functional units of the machine are all integrated into one desktop and many standard operations (in some configurations, only standard operations) can be done by pointing and clicking with a mouse.

This trend toward hiding implementation details has spawned much confusion in the popular press, even to the effect that, for example, Windows NT has been described as a point-and-click system and Unix as a command line system. A right click on any program icon, to `Properties` and then to the `Short-cut` tab reveals a command line in the `Target` box, showing what a delusion this point of view is. The real issue is that many users prefer an elaborate graphical interface that will, in effect, type the command line for them when they double-click on the program icon,

Table II Unix Application Programmer Function Calls

	Category	Sample function calls and constructs
ANSI C	ANSI C standard I/O	`fprintf fscanf fgets fputs unlink rewind fseek`
Not in ANSI C POSIX	Advanced file and directory ops.	`mkdir rmdir opendir readdir closedir rewinddir dup dup2`
	Special terminal I/O	`tcsetattr tcgetattr the termios struct`
	Runtime information	`getenv time localtime ctime sysconf pathconf`
	Process control	`fork exec wait exit and signal handling`
Not covered by ANSI C, POSIX BSD sockets	Networking under TCP/IP	`socket connect listen accept bind send sentto recv recvfrom`
Not covered by ANSI C, POSIX, BSD sockets X Window system	2D raster graphics and windowing	`x11 function calls`
Not covered by ANSI C, POSIX, BSD sockets, X Window System Proprietary	3D graphics, other graphics	`OpenGL, GKS, and a variety of other graphics packages`

will allow them to move files between directories by dragging icons with the mouse, and will initiate standard actions by clicking on a data icon. The X Window System, with a variety of choices of desktop (Motif, CDE, and others) and window manager, will provide this functionality under Unix, but it seems that many users find X harder to get accustomed to than many proprietary windowing systems.

If one considers the history of the automobile it is certainly the case that there are some parallels. It took almost 75 years for the general motorist to simply be able to drive an automobile with a standard control system, and not need to know anything about the underlying principles such as the thermodynamics of the Carnot cycle or the use of negative feedback in order to stabilize the handling.

Electrical systems are inherently more difficult to stabilize than mechical ones and software failure is at least an order of magnitude more common than hardware failure. Even allowing for the general speedup of technological development during the 20th century, it is probably too much to ask that computing be in the same situation of having stable, standard interfaces after only 50 years. Consequently, the prudent purchaser should demand flexibility with regard to system software, even if it requires learning something about the underlying principles of computer hardware and system software.

SEE ALSO THE FOLLOWING ARTICLES

C and C++ • Linux Operating System • Operating Systems • Transmission Control Protocol/Internet Protocol (TCP/IP)

BIBLIOGRAPHY

A brief history of Unix. Available at http://milieu.grads.vt.edu/unix_history.html.

Browne, C. Research and experimental operating systems. Available at http://www.ntlug.org/~cbbrowne/oses.html.

Comer, D. E. (1999). *Internetworking with TCP/IP*, 4th ed. Upper Saddle River, NJ: Prentice-Hall.

Darwin, I. F., and Collyer, G. (1984). A history of UNIX before Berkeley: UNIX evolution, 1975–1984. *Daemon News*. Available at http://www.daemonnews.org/199903/history.html.

Free Software Foundation. What Is Copyleft? Available at http://www.gnu.ai.mit.edu/copyleft/copyleft.html.

Free Software Foundation. Overview of the GNU project. Avalable at http://www.gnu.org/gnu/gnu-history.html.

History of Unix. Available at http://www.itech.on.ca/history_UNIX.html.

Kernighan, B. W., and Pike, R. (1984). *The Unix programming environment*. Upper Saddle River, NJ: Prentice-Hall.

Kernighan, B. W., and Ritchie, D. M. (1988). *The C programming language,* 2nd ed. Upper Saddle River, NJ: Prentice-Hall.

Lewine, D. (1992). *POSIX programmer's guide.* Sebastopol, CA: O'Reilly & Associates.

Microsoft (October 1991). White paper on Windows NT and Microsoft's Operating System Strategy.

Minix information sheet: Specification for the current version of Minix. Available at http://www.cs.vu.nl/~ast/minix.html.

Moffit, N. $7 history of Unix. Available at http://crackmon-key.org/unix.html.

Open Group. Available at http://www.opengroup.org/.

PressPass. (February 28, 2000). Single instance store and symbolic links explained, Microsoft press release. Available at http://www.microsoft.com/features/2000/02-28w2k-b.asp.

Quercia, V., and O'Reilly, T. (1993). *X Window system user's guide.* Sebastopol, CA: O'Reilly & Associates.

Ritchie, D. M. (September 1979). The evolution of the Unix time-sharing system, paper presented at the Language Design and Programming Methodology Conference, Sydney, Australia. Appears in *Lecture notes in computer science #79: Language design and programming methodology.* Berlin: Springer-Verlag, 1980.

Severance, C. A brief history of Unix. Available at http://www.hsr1.rutgers.edu/ug/unix_history.html.

Stallman, R. (1985, 1993). The GNU Manifesto. Free Software Foundation, Inc.

Stevens, R. W. (1997). *Unix network programming,* 2nd ed. Upper Saddle River, NJ: Prentice-Hall.

X.Org. Available at http://www.x.org/about.html.

X11.org. Available at http://www.x11.org/index.shtml.

User/System Interface Design

Theo Mandel

Interface Design and Development

GLOSSARY

computer–human interface (CHI) See **interface.**

graphical user interface (GUI) A user interface which presents information graphically, typically with windows, buttons, and icons that are sizable and movable, as opposed to a textual user interface, where information is presented on a text-based screen and commands are typed by the user. A GUI represents and displays a visual metaphor (such as a desktop) for a computer operating system or application.

human–computer interface (HCI) See **interface.**

human factors The discipline devoted to understanding and improving how humans interact with the world around them. Research in human cognitive and social psychology, perception, and physical and biological characteristics is used to apply that information to the design, operation, and use of products or systems for optimizing human performance, health, and safety. (*syn.* ergonomics.)

interface The place where two independent systems meet and communicate. The presentation, navigation, and interaction of information between a computer system and a user.

intranet A controlled, private network of computer systems for use by employees within a corporation.

object-oriented user interface (OOUI) A graphical user interface that also represents objects the user works with and the behaviors and interactions users have with those objects.

usability The ability of a product to be used in an effective and meaningful way by the intended user.

usability evaluation A test of either an actual program or device or a representation (prototype) of the system. Data obtained usually includes user performance (time, success, errors, and accuracy) and subjective responses of test participants.

user experience The environment encompassing all aspects of the end-user's interaction with a computer system, program, or Web site. In order to achieve a high-quality user experience, there must be a seamless merging of multiple disciplines, including engineering, marketing, graphical design, and interface design.

user interface (UI) See **interface.**

World Wide Web (WWW) A vast network of computer systems. Also called the Web and the Internet.

World Wide Web Consortium (W3C) The industry group responsible for establishing guidelines and standards for Web accessibility.

WYSIWYG An acronym meaning "what you see is what you get." WYSIWYG refers to the technology that enables users to see images on-screen exactly as they will appear when printed out. As screen and printer fonts have become more sophisticated, and as GUIs have improved their display, people have come to expect everything to be WYSIWYG. Unfortunately, this is not always the case.

The growth of the personal computer and workstation computer markets has meant that sales of computers and software, as well as sales of services and products over the World Wide Web, are more directly tied to the quality of their interfaces than ever in the past. The result has been the gradual evolution of a standardized interface architecture, from hardware support of mice to shared window systems to "application management layers." Along with these changes, researchers, designers and developers have begun to develop specification, design, and testing techniques for the production of usable interfaces.

User/system interface design is a complex discipline that draws from a number of fields. In simple terms, the basic goals are to design and build systems that are effective, are intuitive, and meet the goals of a set of users. By definition, a user, system, interface, and designer are involved.

- *User:* He or she uses the system to accomplish tasks and achieve goals.
- *System:* A set of connected things or parts that form a whole or work together. Specifically, a (computer) program designed to provide information and functionality to the user.
- *Interface:* The presentation, communication, and interaction between the user and the system.
- *Designer:* The person responsible for building the system based on his or her understanding of users and their tasks, goals, abilities, and motivations.

Because user/system interface design studies a human and a machine in communication, it draws from disciplines on both the human and the machine side. On the human side, relevant disciplines include cognitive psychology, information architecture, communication theory, graphic design, industrial design, linguistics, social sciences, and human performance. On the machine side, the fields of computer science, computer graphics, operating systems, programming languages, and development environments are relevant.

I. DEFINITIONS

The human race spends a great deal of time sitting down, whether working in an office, studying in a library, commuting by bus, car, or airplane, or eating in a restaurant. Some seats are far more comfortable than others.

Barry H. Kantowitz and Robert D. Sorkin (1983)

User/system interface design addresses a wide range of both users and systems. Human factors (HF) is the discipline that tries to optimize the relationship between technology and humans. HF discovers and applies information about human behaviors, abilities, limitations, and other characteristics to the design of

tools, machines, systems, tasks, jobs, and an environment for productive, safe, comfortable, and effective human use.

The field of ergonomics arose from studies of how humans interact with their environment, especially in the workplace. The concerns of ergonomics tend to be at the sensory-motor level, but with an additional physiological flavor and an emphasis on stress. Ergonomic studies of computers and the workplace investigate the relationship between humans and the work setting, including the effects of stress, routine work tasks, sitting posture, keyboard use, mouse usage, height and distance of computer monitors, and any other factors involved in the work environment.

Human–computer interaction (HCI; also computer–human interaction, CHI) is the discipline concerned with the design, evaluation, and implementation of interactive computing systems for human use (both hardware and software) and with the study of human interaction with computers. HCI is a subset of the HF discipline, focusing on computer hardware and software as the "system" as defined above.

The term *interface* is used commonly in the HF field and should be more clearly defined. An interface is the place at which independent systems meet and act on or communicate with each other. Narrowly defined, the user interface (UI) is composed of input and output devices, as well as the information that users see and interact with on the computer screen. More broadly defined, the UI includes everything that shapes users' involvement with the systems, information, and humans as they perform tasks using computers. This includes on-line and hardcopy product documentation, additional documentation, training, personal and remote technical support, and other tools needed to perform the task. A more encompassing description of the computer–user interface is the term "user experience." Usability guru Jakob Nielsen defines user experience on his Web site (www.nngroup.com/about/userexperience.html) as,

User experience encompasses all aspects of the end-user's interaction with the company, its services, and its products. The first requirement for an exemplary user experience is to meet the exact needs of the customer, without fuss or bother. Next comes simplicity and elegance that produce products that are a joy to own, a joy to use. True user experience goes far beyond giving customers what they say they want, or providing checklist features. In order to achieve high-quality user experience in a company's offerings there must be a seamless merging of the services of multiple disciplines, including engineering, marketing, graphical and industrial design, and interface design.

Perhaps the most common interface term used today is the acronym GUI. A graphical user interface (GUI) utilizes intuitive or familiar symbols (pictures and icons) to display system programs and files that users directly manipulate to perform user tasks and system functions. Today's computer operating systems (Microsoft Windows and Apple Macintosh) are the most familiar examples of GUIs.

II. HISTORY OF HUMAN–COMPUTER INTERFACE

HCI arose as a field from intertwined roots in computer graphics, operating systems, HF, ergonomics, industrial engineering, cognitive psychology, and computer science. The cognitive aspects of users will be discussed later in this article.

The early history of computer graphics, involving cathode-ray tube (CRT) displays and pen devices, led to the development of much of today's HCI techniques in the area of GUIs. Sutherland's 1963 MIT doctoral thesis on Sketchpad essentially marked the beginning of computer graphics as a discipline. This early work described direct-manipulation interaction techniques, where users performed actions on screen entities to represent commands. The program allowed users to draw lines, circles, and points on a computer's CRT display using a light pen. While these tasks are simple to program and use with today's computer hardware, software, and interfaces, nearly 40 years ago this was a revolutionary effort that required immense computing power. Sutherland's program assigned characteristics to graphic objects and built relationships between objects. Users could move, copy, scale, zoom, rotate objects, and save object characteristics. Although this research never was commercially developed, most software engineers credit Sutherland's Sketchpad research and designs as the first step in the evolution of GUIs.

Early research at the Xerox Palo Alto Research Center (PARC) produced a number of important building blocks for HCI, including the mouse, bitmapped displays, personal computers (PCs), windows, the desktop metaphor, and point-and-click editors. The mouse, now a critical input device for most computer users, was developed in the late 1960s. Douglas Engelbart began his work in 1964 on a handheld pointing device at SRI International in Menlo Park, CA, and carried on with his experimental designs at Xerox PARC. The culmination of this work was the first patent for the wheel mouse in 1970. Continued research and design on the mouse led to the patent for the ball mouse in 1974 by Xerox. The idea came suddenly to Ron Rider, "I suggested that they turn a trackball upside down, make it small, and use it as a mouse instead. Easiest patent I ever got. It took me five minutes to think of, half an hour to describe to the attorney, and I was done." Apple Computer redesigned the mouse in 1979, using a rubber ball rather than a metal one. Variations on the ball mouse are what GUI users mostly mouse with today.

The first operating system designed around the GUI was a Xerox in-house computer system called the Alto in the early 1970s. It had multiple, overlapping windows; used pop-up menus; and, of course, came with a mouse. Around 1976, icons were added to the on-screen desktop. The research and design of the Alto system led to the first commercial GUI product, the Xerox Star, in 1981. The Xerox Star offered both tiled and overlapping windows, a menu bar for each window, and, of course, the mouse. The Xerox Star was the first computer to follow the idea of the "desktop metaphor." The desktop metaphor is still the guiding metaphor for GUI today.

Smith *et al.* (1982) described the Xerox Star as, "Every user's initial view of Star is the Desktop, which resembles the top of an office desk, together with surrounding furniture and equipment. It represents a working environment, where current projects and accessible resources reside. On the screen are displayed pictures of familiar office objects, such as documents, folders, file drawers, in-baskets, and out-baskets. These objects are displayed as small pictures, or icons." This is the beginning of the desktop metaphor that users now see on computer screens across the world. Metaphors are further discussed later in this article.

The Xerox PARC engineers were successful at research and technology, but ultimately unsuccessful at developing commercial products. The Xerox Star was never a success, even though over 30 man-years of work went into the product. The development of the first successful GUI computer systems was left to Apple Computer. The transition of research and technology to product development from Xerox to Apple was both a friendly and profitable one, as Xerox held 800,000 shares of Apple stock when it went public in December 1980.

Steven Jobs, a founder of Apple, visited Xerox PARC and viewed their research on graphical interfaces. He returned to Apple very excited about GUIs and infused his design teams with that enthusiasm. The rest is history. The Apple Lisa, the precursor to the Macintosh, came out in 1983. Like the Xerox Star, it was not a commercial success. It took the introduction of the Apple Macintosh computer in 1984, with a revolutionary advertising approach, to successfully bring GUIs to the computer market successfully. Both the Lisa and the Macintosh had a menu bar for the entire screen and the first pull-down menus in a graphical interface. An Apple designer received a patent for pull-down menus in 1984.

Apple's success with the GUI is legendary and still remains the most familiar example of GUIs. As I try to explain what GUIs are to unknowing computer users, I often say, "You know, it's like the Apple Mac." After Apple's immense success with the Macintosh GUI, an operating system revolution was upon us, and both IBM and Microsoft went to work on PC-based GUIs of their own, along with a number of other software developers. These companies had a lot of catching up to do and had to do it on a hardware platform very different from the Apple Macintosh. One key advantage that Apple had is that they built the whole computer themselves as an integrated system. Their design philosophy followed the Xerox PARC design methodology. Jones described how the Xerox Star was built. "Star began by defining a conceptual model of how users would relate to the system. The interface was completed before the computer hardware had been built on which to run it, and two years before a single line of product software code had been written." Many other software and hardware products failed in the marketplace because they did not follow this design approach. Products and their interfaces should be designed for users, and the users should be involved in the product design process.

III. THE INTERFACE DESIGN AND USABILITY PROCESS

A. The Four-Phase Interface Design Process

Developing the UI may or may not be separate from the rest of the product development process. However, the focus is most definitely different. Focus must be on the interface elements and objects that users perceive and use, rather than on program functionality. Throughout the development process, usability test feedback and UI concerns should drive program design.

A process specifically geared toward designing and developing UIs is shown in Fig. 1. The four major phases in the process are:

- *Gather/analyze* user information
- *Design* the UI

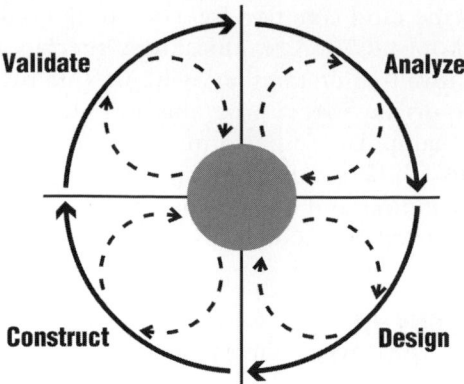

Figure 1 The elements of user interface design. [Reprinted with permission from Mandel, T. (1997). New York: Wiley.]

- *Construct* the UI
- *Validate* the UI

This process is independent of the hardware and software platform, operating system, and tools used for product design and development. Industry UI design guides all promote an iterative interface design process. The IBM Common User Access (CUA) interface design guide first described an iterative interface design process and used a car dealership sales product as a design case study.

B. Gather/Analyze User Information (Phase 1)

The interface design process starts with an understanding of the users. Before designing and building any system, first define the problems that customers or users want solved and figure out how they do their jobs. Learn about users' capabilities and the tasks they must perform. Watch and learn from people actually going about their work and using the product and other related applications and Web sites. Observe how their current computer systems (both hardware and software) restrict them. Do not limit product designs to what users currently can do with the system. Product solutions should not only satisfy the users' current needs, but also their future needs. Thorough analysis of users and their tasks in this stage is critical.

There are key questions to ask during the analysis-gathering phase. If the answers to these questions are not known, do not assume that one individual, design team, development team, or marketing or sales group knows the answers. The only way to understand how users work is to observe users and ask them questions.

Phase one's gathering and analyzing activities can be broken down into five steps:

- Determine user profiles
- Perform user task analyses
- Gather user requirements
- Analyze user environments
- Match requirements to tasks

C. Design the User Interface (Phase 2)

Designing a software UI usually requires a significant commitment of time and resources. The design phase includes a number of well-defined steps that should be followed in sequence. It is tempting to start writing code now, rather than designing the interface. Follow the steps through the design process. The design phase includes the following steps:

- Define product usability goals and objectives
- Develop user scenarios and tasks
- Define interface objects and actions
- Determine object icons, views, and visual representations
- Design object and window menus
- Refine visual designs

D. Construct the User Interface (Phase 3)

The first pass through the iterative design process should be one of prototyping, rather than constructing, the UI. Prototyping is an extremely valuable way of building early designs and creating product demonstrations and is necessary for early usability testing.

When prototyping, it is most important to remember that prototypes must be disposable. Do not be afraid to throw away a prototype. The purpose of prototyping is to *quickly* and *easily* visualize design alternatives and concepts, not to build code that is to be used as a part of the product. Prototypes may show "visualizations" of the interface—the high-level concepts—or they may show "functional" slices of a product, displaying how specific tasks or transactions might be performed with the interface.

A product prototype may take the place of (or in addition to) the product functional specification (PFS). Typically, GUI functional specifications are difficult to use, because it is difficult to write about graphical presentation and interaction techniques. It is easier and more effective to *show* a prototype of the product interface style and behavior.

Later iterations of UI construction should focus on further refinement of the product interface presentation, navigation, and interaction.

E. Validate the User Interface (Phase 4)

Usability evaluations are a critical part of the iterative development process. A usability evaluation is the best way to get a product in the hands of actual users to see if and how they use it *prior to the product's release.* Usability evaluations quantitatively and qualitatively measure user behavior, performance, and satisfaction. Some software projects do address usability testing, but only at the end of the development cycle. Unfortunately, this is too late in the development cycle to incorporate changes based on usability test results. Even if product design changes are made, the interface should be evaluated again to ensure that the product meets final product benchmarks and objectives.

Early usability evaluations include customer walk-throughs of initial designs. As pieces of the product and interface are prototyped and constructed, perform early usability evaluations on common tasks. When the product is nearing completion and all of the pieces are coming together, then conduct final system usability evaluations. Table I shows when specific usability activities should be conducted during product development stages.

Scenarios developed in Phase 2 are valuable measurement tools during usability evaluations in the validation phase. Can users perform the defined scenarios using the product? How is that known? The

Table I Usability Activities Performed during Product Development Stages

Product development stage	Usability activities
Concept definition	User requirements gathering Conceptual design definition
Concept validation	Conceptual design evaluations (paper/pencil, prototypes)
Design	Evaluations of rapid prototypes Track and fix usability problems
Develpment	Iterative tests of early designs (individual modules, key tasks) Iterative tests of final designs (integrated product, all tasks) Tack and fix usability problems

From Mandel, T. (1997). *The elements of user interface design.* New York: Wiley.

product is validated against predefined usability goals and objectives using the scenarios as the vehicle of measuring user performance.

Every product designer and developer should observe his or her product being usability tested. It is the only way, before the product is released, to see how users really work with a product. Usability activities also should not stop after a product is completed. Usability feedback should be collected from pilot participants and actual users. The Microsoft Corporation asks product users to send feedback and their wishes for future versions of its products. The "About Microsoft Works" product dialog asks users to send comments directly to Microsoft. It asks, "Help us make future versions even better by sending us your ideas and suggestions."

F. Create Design Teams

Following an iterative interface design process and design principles, and creating guidelines and standards, will help build usability into products, but they do not guarantee a usable interface. Similarly, there is not a magic design and development process that can guarantee a successful product. A product's interface design process should be tailored to the particular business, users, and development environment. A large company probably has individual departments devoted to each area of the development process. Other companies may rely upon one person or a few individuals. Regardless of the size of the company or organization, follow a *design team* approach. No one department or individual typically has all of the skills to do all of the required steps in the process. For example, does the group have the skills to gather user requirements? Is a graphics designer available? Are usability testing professionals on staff?

Baecker *et al.* points out, "Interface design and development require software engineering and programming skills, of course, but can also benefit from the skills of graphic and industrial designers; human factors engineers and psychologists who understand human cognitive, perceptual, and motor skills; technical writers and training specialists' people knowledgeable in group and organizational dynamics; and those with expertise in input devices, display technologies, interaction techniques, dialogue design, and design methodologies. . . . The growing use of sound, voice, video, animation, and three-dimensional display draw upon still other specialties."

The majority of commercial software products follow the design team approach. Sullivan describes how Microsoft Windows 95 was created, "The design team was truly interdisciplinary, with people trained in product design, graphic design, usability testing, and computer science."

IV. FUNDAMENTALS OF INTERFACE DESIGN

A. Using Real-World Metaphors

The "desktop" interface used in most of today's software applications is built on the belief that users know their way around an office. It assumes that users are familiar with the office environment, know how to use objects in that environment (folders, cabinets, a telephone, notepads, etc.), and are comfortable with an office desktop as a working space. This is an example of the use of a metaphor—it maps the way users do things on the computer to the way users would do them (in an office) if they were not using the computer. A *metaphor* (Webster's Third New International Dictionary) is "a figure of speech in which a work or phrase denoting one kind of object or action is used in place of another to suggest a likeness or analogy between them." Baecker *et al.* describe computer metaphors: "Metaphors aid users in understanding a new *target domain* (e.g., a word processor) by allowing them to comprehend it (up to the point of 'mismatch' . . .) in terms of a *source domain* they already understand (e.g., a typewriter). Metaphors aid designers because adoption of a metaphor allows them to structure aspects of the target system or interface in terms of familiar and commonly understood aspects of the source domain." Basically, metaphors allow users to transfer their real-world experiences to their use of the computer.

Metaphors fulfill a variety of important roles in computer systems. They inform users about available information, help users navigate, and create atmospheres or settings with desired tones and styles that integrate and unify the application's visual images and layouts. Intuit's Quicken financial program is perhaps the most successful example of following a real-world metaphor in a software application. If users know how to use a regular checkbook, then they already know how to use the majority of the Quicken product. Again, the basic premise of metaphors is to use familiar concepts and images to make it easier for users to understand and remember something new. Based on their understanding of the metaphor, users perform actions and tasks and have expectations about the results of their behavior.

When metaphors work well, they help users understand how information is organized based on their distinctive visual features and contexts. However, when metaphors are improperly used or extended too far, users can be confused by system behaviors that do not meet their expectations (negative transfer).

B. User Interface Models

Inconsistency among programmers', designers', and users' experiences, viewpoints, and skills with a computer system's functions and tasks causes many of the problems users experience using the system. These very different viewpoints can be viewed as different *models* of a UI. For example, a homeowner, builder, and architect have very different perspectives on the same thing they are all intimately involved in—building a house. Who they are and their role in the house-building project determine the tasks they perform, the goals they desire, the way they define success, the skills they bring to the project, the tools they use, and how they interact with each other.

The homeowners finance and live in the house—they are the real "users." The builder's role is to work with the designs and specifications of the architect to build a house that the homeowners can enjoy. The builder's skills include knowing all the regulations and codes for building an environmentally and functionally sound structure using the appropriate materials and resources. The architect studies the lifestyle of the homeowners and their family and their wishes and desires for the house. Then the architect creates visualizations and, ultimately, the design of a house that (hopefully) can be built to meet the homeowners' desires within their budget. The architect also acts as the homeowners' representative in ensuring that the builder follows the home's plans and specifications.

These three roles and viewpoints form the three models of a UI: the user's model, the programmer's model, and the designer's model. These models and their descriptions are pictured in Fig. 2. A model encapsulates the users' experiences and expectations from the world around them.

1. The User's Conceptual Model

The user's conceptual model is an internal one, based on his or her experience and expectations, so it is not easy to discover and document. A *conceptual model* is an internal representation of how users understand and interact with a system. Carroll and Olson describe mental models as, "A representation (in the head) of a physical system or software being run on a computer, with some plausible cascade of causal associa-

Figure 2 User interface models. [Reprinted with permission from IBM Corporation. (1992). Object-Oriented Interface Design: IBM Common User Access Guidelines. New York: QUE.]

tions connecting the input to the output." People are often not aware of their mental models. IBM (1992) states, "A mental model does not necessarily reflect a situation and its components accurately. Still a mental model helps people predict what will happen next in a given situation, and it serves as a framework for analysis, understanding, and decision-making." Users form mental models to:

- Predict future (or infer invisible) events
- Find causes for observed events
- Determine appropriate actions to cause desired changes
- Serve as mnemonic devices for remembering relations and events
- Help understand an analogous device
- Use strategies to overcome information processing limitations

The user's model is the basis for all interaction between the user and the computer and, therefore, is the basis for UI principles and guidelines.

2. The Programmer's Model

The programmer's model is explicit and, therefore, is the easiest to visualize and can be more formally defined. In fact, the programmer's model is usually seen in the form of a product's functional specifications. The programmer is the person(s) who actually writes the code that comprises the system or program. The product's underlying business and data objects are of critical interest to the programmer, but do not necessarily reflect how users interact with the information. A programmer works at the level of a computer's hardware and software, for example, how data is stored and retrieved as fields and records in a database. The programmer's knowledge and expertise typically includes the development platform, operating system, development tools, and programming guidelines and specifications necessary to build software programs (see Fig. 2). However, these skills do not usually give a programmer the ability to provide users with the most appropriate interface to the product. The programmer's model deals with efficient and effective use of system resources and development tools available to them in a very detailed and technical way. Users should not be subjected to platform, tool, or programming language terminology or artifacts that make no sense to them.

3. The Designer's Model

The interface designer's role is like the home architect's role in designing and building a house. The designer takes the ideas, wishes, desires, and needs of the *user* (homeowner), merges that with the skills and materials available to the *programmer* (builder), and designs a *software product* (house) that not only can be

built, but can be enjoyed by the user. The designer actually acts as the intermediary between the user and the programmer. Programmers often do not meet users of the products they develop. The interface designer and others (marketing and customer support) on the design team who work directly with product users bridge the distance between the user's environment and the programmer's world.

Figure 3 is known as the "look and feel" iceberg chart. This graphic is attributed to David Liddle, former head of Metaphor Computer Company, and it is based on early research of scientists at the Xerox Palo Alto Research Center (Xerox PARC). It shows that the interface designer's model is actually made up of three components: *presentation, interaction,* and *object relationships.* Basically, the designer's role is to describe the objects users work with, their presentation to users, and the interaction techniques used to manipulate user objects.

The tip of the iceberg is the "look" element, the presentation of information, and it should account for only about 10% of the work of the designer. Information presentation includes using color, animation, sound, shapes, graphics, text, and screen layout. Although this is the most obvious part of a UI, and often the easiest to manipulate, it does not affect user behavior and understanding as much as the other parts of the iceberg. Interface designers call this putting lipstick on the bulldog.

The second piece of the iceberg is the "feel" of the interface. This is the interaction area, and it accounts for about 30% of the designer's model. UI techniques

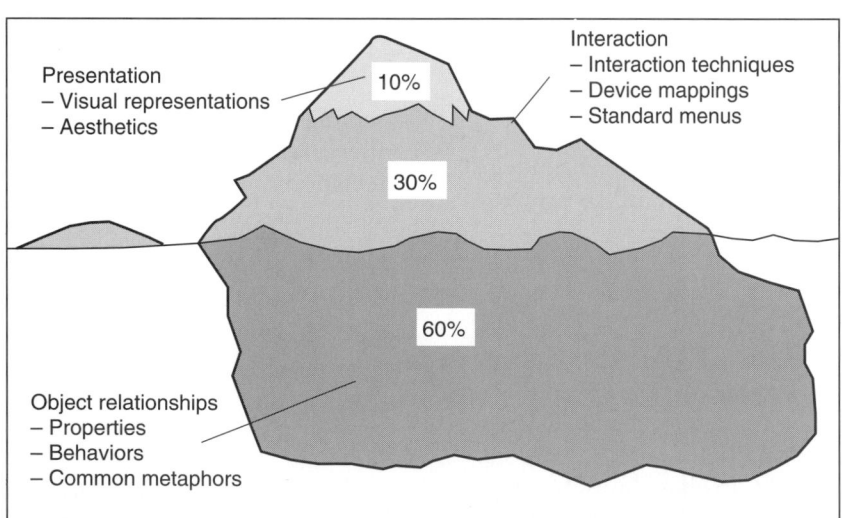

Figure 3 The look and feel iceberg. [Reprinted from IBM Corporation. (1992). Object-Oriented Interface Design: IBM Common User Access Guidelines. New York: QUE.]

involving the keyboard, function keys, and other input devices such as a mouse, trackball, or joystick are defined. Interaction also addresses how the system gives users feedback regarding their actions.

The most important part of the iceberg (around 60%) is concerned with the most critical aspects of the UI—objects, their properties, and the relationships between objects. Here, interface designers determine the appropriate metaphors to match the user's mental model of the system and the tasks they do. This part of the iceberg is submerged and not easily visible. It is not always obvious to developers to be concerned with this area of interface design. Realistically, this is also the most critical piece of the iceberg because a ship (a software product) can be hit and sunk if attention is not paid to this area. For example, do not display a flaming trash can as users discard items. If users can retrieve things from the trash can, the flaming animation is confusing; it does not match their expectation of the trash can's behavior.

V. USER-CENTERED DESIGN PRINCIPLES

A. Human Cognition and Information Processing

An understanding of users begins with the study of human information processing and cognitive psychology. This field investigates human memory, perception, motor skills, attention, problem solving, learning and skill acquisition, and motivation.

The knowledge of how people work and think helps determine the appropriate dimensions of user demographics that can impact interface design. Some of the dimensions of user characteristics are:

- Experience and knowledge of tasks
- Domain knowledge and experience
- Knowledge and experience with similar systems
- User motor skills (typing skills, mouse usage)
- Perceptual abilities: vision, color perception, and spatial visualization
- Personality traits: confidence, aggressiveness, patience, and exploration
- Social and work styles: collaboration, leadership, teamwork, and workflow

Psychology textbooks cover this area in great detail. A good on-line resource is CogLab (http://coglab.psych.purdue.edu/coglab/), an on-line cognitive psychology laboratory developed for public use by professors of Psychological Sciences at Purdue University, West Lafayette, Indiana.

B. Golden Rules of Interface Design

Many computer systems force users to adapt to the system. Instead, systems should adapt to the user. User-centered design principles are the basis for building usable systems. These principles are often called the "Golden Rules" of interface design. The UI design principles are:

- Place users in control of the interface.
- Reduce users' memory load.
- Make the UI consistent.

Computer users should enjoy successful experiences that allow them to build confidence in themselves and establish self-assurance about how they work with computers. Each positive experience with a software program allows users to explore outside their area of familiarity and encourages them to expand their knowledge of the interface. Well-designed software interfaces, like good educators and instructional materials, should build a relationship that guides users to learn and enjoy what they are doing. Based on metaphors and models (discussed in Section IV) and on our knowledge of human information and psychology, general principles of UI design have been developed. Interface design principles address each of the key components of the look and feel iceberg: presentation, interaction, and object relationships.

Rubenstein and Hersch (1984) proposed an early set of interface design principles. This classic book on HCI presents 93 design principles, ranging from "1. Designers make myths; users make conceptual models" to "93. Videotape real users."

These principles are everlasting, even as new UI technologies emerge. Jakob Nielsen noted, "The principles are so basic that even futuristic dialogue designs such as three-dimensional interfaces with Data-Glove input devices, gesture recognition, and live video images will always have to take them into account as long as they are based on the basic paradigm of dialogues and user commands."

Major software operating system vendors publish their design guidelines and reference materials as they introduce new operating systems. These guidelines show that the Golden Rules are common across all development platforms. Software design guides include Apple Computer, Inc., IBM Corporation, Microsoft Corporation, and UNIX OSF/Motif.

1. Place Users in Control of the Interface

The first set of principles addresses placing users in control of the interface. An analogy for this principle is to let users drive a car rather than force them to take a train. In a car, users control their own direction, navigation, and final destination. However, drivers need a certain amount of skill and knowledge before they can successfully drive a car. Drivers also need to know where they are going! A train forces users to become passengers rather than drivers. If someone is used to driving their own car, they probably will not enjoy a train ride, where they cannot control the schedule or the path a train will take. However, novice and casual users may enjoy a train ride if they do not know exactly where they are going. They also may enjoy relying on the train to guide them on their journey. The decision to drive a car or take the train should be the user's, not the system's. Users also should be able to change their mind and take the car one day and the train the next.

Users in control principles are listed in Table II. After each principle, a keyword is listed to help remember each principle.

The classic example of allowing users to be in control is Christopher Alexander's discussion of how to design walkways between a set of buildings. Rather than assume that an architect knew how people really used the walkways between buildings, the architect did not design and build the walkways when the buildings were completed. Rather, a grassy field was planted between the buildings. It is rumored that signs were posted saying, "Please walk on the grass." A few months after the buildings were completed, the architect observed the patterns where people wore paths through the grass. That was where walkways were eventually designed and built. This highlights how observing user behaviors is important first before building an interface that allows user to go where they want to go and how they want to get there.

2. Reduce User's Memory Load

Capabilities and limitations of the human memory and perceptual systems were discussed earlier in this section. The interface should help users remember information while using the computer. We know that people are not good at remembering things, so programs should be designed with this in mind. Table III lists the design principles in this area.

A sign that computer systems do not help users' memory is the use of external memory aids, such as sticky pads, calculators, reference books, frequently asked questions (FAQs), and sheets of paper. Often, application users must write information down on a piece of paper because they know they will need that information later in the program. Program elements such as **undo** and **redo** and clipboard actions such as **cut, copy,** and **paste** allow users to manipulate pieces of information needed in multiple places within an application and across applications.

Filling in on-line forms with common information such as name, address, and telephone number should be remembered by the system once a user has entered them or once a customer record has been opened.

Interfaces support long-term memory retrieval by providing users with items for them to *recognize* rather

Table II Principles That Place Users in Control

User in control	Keyword
Use modes judiciously	Modeless
Allow users to use either the keyboard or the mouse	Flexible
Allow users to change focus	Interruptible
Display descriptive messages and text	Helpful
Provide immediate and reversible actions and feedback	Forgiving
Provide meaningful paths and exits	Navigable
Accommodate users with different skill levels	Accessible
Make the UI transparent	Facilitative
Allow users to customize the interface	Preferences
Allow users to directly manipulate interface objects	Interactive

Table III Principles That Reduce Users' Memory Load

Reduce users' memory load	Keyword
Relieve short-term memory	Remember
Rely on recognition, not recall	Recognition
Provide visual cues	Inform
Provide defaults, undo, and redo	Forgiving
Provide interface shortcuts	Frequency
Promote an object-action syntax	Intuitive
Use real-world metaphors	Transfer
User progressive disclosure	Context
Promote visual clarity	Organize

than having to *recall* information. It is much easier to browse a list to select an item rather than trying to remember the correct item to type into a blank entry field. For example, sophisticated spell-checking techniques offer users a list of possible alternatives to select from for a misspelled word, rather than just identifying that a word is spelled incorrectly.

It is critical to continuously show users *where* they are, *what* they are doing, and *what* they can do next. These visual feedback indicators provide the context for users to understand where they are and where they can go. Early hypertext techniques allowed users to navigate between pieces of information and documents, but users got lost and could not remember why they were at their current location and how they got there!

3. Make the User Interface Consistent

UI consistency is a key element of usable interfaces. However, consistency should not be looked at as the *only* critical area of interface design. The benefit of consistency is for users to transfer their knowledge and learning to new programs after they have learned the common interface elements of the operating system and programs they use frequently. Table IV lists principles that make the interface consistent.

Consistency in *presentation* means that users should see information in the same logical, visual, and physical way throughout the product. Information that users can not change *(static text)* should be presented in the same font type and color throughout the program. If one type of information is displayed and input using a specific interface control, then the same control should be used to display and input the same information throughout the product. Consistency in *behavior* means that the way an interface element works is the same everywhere. The behavior of interface controls such as buttons, lists, and menu items should

Table IV Principles That Make the Interface Consistent

Make the interface consistent	Keyword
Sustain the context of users' tasks	Continuity
Maintain consistency within and across products	Experience
Keep interaction results the same	Expectations
Provide aesthetic appeal and integrity	Attitude
Encourage exploration	Predictable

not change within or between programs. Consistency in *interaction* technique is also important. The same shortcut keys should work in similar programs. Mouse actions should produce the same results anywhere in the interface. Keyboard mnemonics should not change for the same menus from program to program. Users expect the same results when they interact the same way with similar interface elements.

Finally, consistent interfaces encourage users to explore. Users should be able to, without fear of negative consequences, select items and navigate through the system to find out where things are and what happens when they do things.

VI. THE WEB USER EXPERIENCE

The incredible evolution of the World Wide Web (WWW) in the past few years has changed the face and scope of interface design. Although the basic principles of interface design discussed here have not changed, many things have changed for Web interfaces. Foremost, users are different. Anyone connected to the Web is a user. Users range from the very young and computer literate to the elderly, often with poor vision and dexterity and minimal computer skills. Corporations now use intranets to communicate with employees and allow them to be more productive at their jobs. Public Web sites allow individuals and companies to present information and news, gather information, and conduct business remotely. In fact, the term "user interface" has been replaced with the more global "user experience" or even "customer experience."

A. Key Differences in Web Interface Design

The well-know article "The Difference between Web Design and GUI Design" (Nielsen, 1997b) pointed out some of the main differences in Web interface design: (1) device diversity, (2) the user controls navigation, and (3) part of a whole. Web interfaces now are used across a wide array of browsers, operating systems, and even very different devices from traditional desktop PCs. Traditional GUI applications followed a WYSIWIG ("what you see is what you get") approach where designers and developers knew exactly how users would view and use their programs. The design principle of user in control has been discussed previously. The Web allows users to access sites and pages in different ways other than those intended or desired by the designer. Users can jump to a Web page directly from a search engine, therefore bypassing the site's home page and site navigation structure. Users can also leave a site or page at any time, thereby not necessarily completing the site's intended flow of information or tasks. Finally, the Web is a community of information and places. Users move between sites rapidly, often not even knowing which site they currently are on. Therefore, even though every site is different and there are no formal interface standards for the Web, it is even more important to build a common Web user experience and to follow the basic interface design principles discussed here.

Other important user/system design issues on the Web include designing interfaces for public use (Internet sites) vs private use (intranet sites). Nielsen highlights the key differences between Internet and intranet sites:

- Users differ. Intranet users are employees who may know a lot about the company, its organizational structure, and special terminology and circumstances. Customers who know much less about the company and also care less about it use Internet sites.
- Tasks differ. The intranet is used for everyday work inside the company, including some quite complex applications; the Internet site is mainly used to find out information about company products.
- Type of information differs. The intranet will have many draft reports, project progress reports, human resource information, and other detailed information, whereas the Internet site will have marketing information and customer support information.
- Amount of information differs. Typically, an intranet has between ten and a hundred times as many pages as the same company's public Web site. The difference is due to the extensive amount of work in progress that is documented on the intranet and the fact that many projects and departments never publish anything publicly even though they have many internal documents.
- Bandwidth and cross-platform needs differ. Intranets often run between a hundred and a thousand times faster than most Internet users' Web access, which is stuck at low band or mid band, so it is feasible to use rich graphics and even multimedia and other advanced content on intranet pages. Also, it is sometimes possible to control what computers and software versions are supported on an intranet, meaning that designs need to be less cross-platform compatible (again allowing for more advanced page content).

B. Components of Web Interface Design

The design of Web interfaces can be subdivided into four areas: content, interaction, navigation, and graphics. They are all important areas, and their relative importance to a Web site varies depending on the nature of the site and its intended use.

Content is king, as is often said. A site must have content that is of value to visitors or there will be no reason for people to visit the site. Depending on the type of content, it must also be timely, accurate, readable, and printable.

Interaction defines how users interface with the site. Does the site use text links, buttons, or image maps? Does the user have to log on to get information? Will the site remember the user's previous session? How can the application learn from user behavior and provide content that the user wants?

Navigation addresses how users get around within a site. Many sites provide navigation at only the top one or two levels; below those levels the user must use the browser navigation buttons. Does the site navigation structure match the user's expectation? Must users understand the company's organization to use the site?

Graphics create the interface style and metaphors for the site. They add to the aesthetics and enjoyment of the user's experience. Consumer-based sites usually maintain a high degree of aesthetic appeal, but it is not necessarily needed for the site's success. If the site is primarily information oriented, graphics can distract slow users while they scan, search, and read information. Nielsen's site, useit.com (www.useit.com), is a valuable resource for design and usability professionals and is heavily trafficked. However, Nielsen chose to use very few graphics to allow the best download time for site pages, and he admits he is not a graphic designer, so his graphics would not look very good. Useit.com is an information-intensive site, and its users are not bothered by the site's lack of graphics and attention to aesthetics.

The aesthetic and electronic commerce (e-commerce) aspects of Web design have further highlighted the need for usable designs along with more graphic and interactive designs. To enhance the consumer experience, sites strive to enhance the aesthetics and entertainment of the site, while, at the same time, hopefully enabling site visitors to easily navigate and perform their desired tasks. Thus, the skills of both interface and graphic designers are key and sometimes at odds; it is called the battle between persuading and enabling. The phrase "Cool = Usable" shows that developers are sometimes more concerned with aesthetic, persuasive, and entertainment aspects of the site rather than site's usability. From the perspective of the interface designer, however, the more appropriate phrase should be "Usable = Cool." Interface designers should strive toward enhancing the user experience by providing an interface that allows the user to read, browse, navigate, search, find, print, and purchase in an effective and usable way.

C. Making Web Interfaces Accessible

The Web is the fastest adopted technology in history. Unfortunately, for people with disabilities, the Web is often a mixed blessing. The Web displaces traditional sources of information and interaction—schools, libraries, print materials, and workplace information. Some of those traditional resources are accessible and some are not. The Web is fast becoming an essential, but sometimes inaccessible, resource for news, information, commerce, entertainment, classroom education, distance learning, job searching, workplace interaction, and civic participation (laws, voting, government information, and services). An accessible Web means unprecedented access to information for people with disabilities. Some of the barriers to avoid include:

- For users with visual disabilities: unlabeled graphics, undescribed video, poorly marked-up tables or frames, and lack of keyboard support or screen-reader compatibility
- For users with hearing disabilities: lack of captioning for audio and proliferation of text without visual sign-posts
- For users with physical disabilities: lack of keyboard or single-switch support for menu commands
- For users with cognitive or neurological disabilities: lack of consistent navigation structure, overly complex presentation or language, lack of illustrative nontext materials, and flickering or strobing designs

Companies are slowly beginning to address accessibility concerns on Internet sites, but rarely on their intranets. However, U.S. governmental regulations and international Internet standards are fast becoming the baseline (and sometimes the law) for acceptable Web site development. In "Disabled Accessibility," Nielsen states, "It would not surprise me if we start seeing money-back guarantee in design contracts that state that clients don't have to pay for sites that violate these rules." Web development tools are beginning to incorporate the accessibility standards into their tools to help Web designers build the most usable and accessible Web sites possible.

The World Wide Web Consortium (W3C) Web Accessibility Initiative (WAI) offers three levels of guidelines for developing accessible Web sites. For more information, checklists, and a complete listing of the accessibility guidelines, visit the W3C Web site (www.w3.org/WAI/). Accessibility also affects traditional applications, not just Web-based interfaces. The U.S. government has mandated legislation that addresses accessibility in the federal workplace. Section 508 requires that federal agencies' electronic and information technology be accessible to people with disabilities. The Federal Information Technology Accessibility Initiative (see www.section508.gov) is a federal government interagency effort to offer information and technical assistance to assist in the successful implementation of Section 508.

VII. NEW DIRECTIONS IN HUMAN–COMPUTER INTERACTION

How humans interact with computers is evolving rapidly. Computers themselves are constantly evolving: PCs in some form will continue to evolve and become smaller, more powerful, and more mobile. But the rapid pace of technology is drastically changing how people use computers. Some of the forces shaping future computing include:

- Decreasing hardware costs leading to faster systems with larger memories
- Hardware miniaturization leading to device portability
- Power requirements reduction leading to device portability
- New display technologies leading to new forms of computational devices
- Evolving technologies for input techniques (voice, touch, gesture, and pen, for example)
- Integrating computation abilities into existing devices and appliances (video cassette recorders, microwave ovens, and televisions, for example)
- Increased development of network communication and distributed computing
- Increased worldwide use of computers by a wider range of people
- Global social concerns leading to countries and peoples having improved access to computers and computing devices

Pervasive computing is the trend toward casually accessible, often invisible computing devices that are either mobile or imbedded in the environment. The dictionary definition of pervasive is "having the quality or tendency to pervade or permeate." The aim of pervasive computing is to allow users to perform tasks and gather information wherever they are, whenever they want. This enables people to accomplish an increasing number of personal and professional transactions using a new class of intelligent and portable devices. It gives people convenient access to relevant information stored on powerful networks, allowing them to easily take action anywhere, anytime. These devices are connected to an increasingly ubiquitous network structure. Ubiquitous computing spreads intelligence and connectivity to more or less everything in our world. The dictionary definition of ubiquitous is "existing or being everywhere, or in all places, at the same time; omnipresent." Cars, homes, aircraft, roads, bridges, tunnels, refrigerators, door handles, lighting fixtures, shoes, and even clothing will, sooner or later, have a computer chip embedded in it. The goal of ubiquitous computing is to build technology so that it recedes into the background of people's lives. This will allow people to perform their daily activities in an environment that is capable of supporting these activities without increasing the attention level or cognitive load on users in their world.

Other evolving areas affecting the future of interface design are:

- Group interfaces: Interfaces that allow groups of people to coordinate activities (meetings, projects, conversation, learning, and so on).
- User tailorability: Users will tailor programs to their own use and invent new individual applications based on their understanding of their own domains and experience. Thus, general-purpose systems will become more useful as individually tailored experiences.
- Information utilities: Public information sources (both general and specialized), such as weather, news, shopping, and finance, will continue to evolve. Their proliferation will accelerate as users interact with high-bandwidth systems and as the system interfaces improve.
- Effective use of media: Alternative media, such as video, voice, and sound, will become more integrated into the interface experience. Sound is underutilized in software and on the Web, in spite of its obvious value to other media, such as film. The performing arts has a long history of creating sound as a powerful impression on human perception and emotion and has accumulated a rich body of theories and practical insights for how this is done. These theories and insights should be explored for

their usefulness in improving sound design in computer systems. For example, sound can be used to (1) suggest physical properties of objects, (2) anthropomorphize and personalize objects, (3) judge distance and therefore size, (4) enhance the believability of images and information, and (5) change our interpretation of events.

VIII. INTERFACE DESIGN AND USABILITY RESOURCES

A. Web Resources

- HCI Bibliography: www.hcibib.org
- HCI Index: http://degraaff.org/hci
- Human–Computer Interaction (Yahoo listing): http://dir.yahoo.com/Science/Computer_Science/Human_Computer_Interaction_HCL_/
- Human–Computer Interaction, Resource Network: www.hcirn.com
- IBM Ease of Use: www.ibm.com/ibm/easy
- Interface Design and Development: www.interface-design.net
- Usability.gov (resource for designing usable, useful, and accessible Web sites and UIs): www.usability.gov
- Usability News (Software Usability Research Laboratory Newsletter): www.usabilitynews.org
- Usability Resources (STC): www.stcsig.org/usability/resources
- Usable Web: www.usableweb.com
- Useit.com: www.useit.com

B. Books, Magazines, and Bibliographies

- HCI Bibliography: www.hcibib.org
- Interactions (Association of Computing Machinery on-line and print publication): www.acm.org/interactions/frntpage/index.htm
- Suggested Readings for Usability Testing: http://www.best.com/~jthom/usability/biblio.htm
- Usable Web—Books: http://books.usableweb.com

C. Organizations

- Association of Computing Machinery (ACM): www.acm.org
- ACM Computer–Human Interaction (CHI) Special Interest Group (SIG): www.acm.org/sigchi
- British HCI group: www.bcs-hci.org.uk

- The Ergonomics Society: www.ergonomics.org.uk
- Human Factors and Ergonomics Society (HFES): www.hfes.org
- HFES Internet Technical Group: www.internettg.org
- Institute of Electrical and Electronics Engineers (IEEE): www.ieee.org
- International Federation for Information Processing: www.ifip.or.at
- National Institute of Standards and Technology: www.nist.gov
- Society for Technical Communications (STC) Usability SIG: www.stcsig.org/usability
- Usability Professionals' Association (UPA): www.upassoc.org

D. Discussion Groups

- UTEST (Internet discussion group on usability): www.upassoc.org/html/utest.html
- comp.human-factors (Usenet discussion group): news:comp.human-factors

SEE ALSO THE FOLLOWING ARTICLES

End-User Computing Concepts • End-User Computing, Managing • Human Side of Information, Managing the Systems • Internet, Overview • Intranets • Prototyping • Success Measures of Information Systems • System Development Life Cycle • Systems Implementation

BIBLIOGRAPHY

Alexander, C., *et al.* (1977). *A pattern language.* New York: Oxford Univ. Press.

Apple Computer, Inc. (1992). *Macintosh human interface guidelines.* Boston: Addison-Wesley.

Baecker, R. M., and Buxton, W. A. S., Eds. (1987). *Readings in human-computer interaction: A multidisciplinary approach.* San Mateo, CA: Morgan Kaufmann.

Baecker, R. M., Grudin, J., Buxton, W. A. S., and Greenberg, S. (1995). *Readings in human-computer interaction: Toward the year 2000.* San Francisco: Morgan Kaufmann.

Carroll, J., and Olson, J. (1988). Mental models in human-computer interaction. In *Handbook of human-computer interaction* (M. Helander, Ed.). Holland: Elsevier.

Chapanis, A. (1999). *The Chapanis chronicles: 50 years of human factors research, education, and design.* Santa Barbara, CA: Aegean Publishing Company.

IBM Corporation (1992). Object-Oriented Interface Design: IBM Common User Access™ Guidelines. New York: QUE.

Jones, M. (July 1992). Apple interface. *DESIGN,* Vol. 64.

Kantowitz, B. H., and Sorkin, R. D. (1983). *Human factors: Understanding people-system relationships.* New York: Wiley.

Mandel, T. (1997). *The elements of user interface design.* New York: Wiley.

Mayhew, D. (1992). *Principles and guidelines in software user interface design.* Englewood Cliffs, NJ: Prentice-Hall.

Microsoft Corporation. (1995). *The Windows® interface guidelines for software design.* Seattle: Microsoft Press.

Nielsen, J. (1990). Traditional dialogue design applied to modern user interfaces. *Communications of the ACM* Vol. 33, No. 10, 109–118.

Nielsen, J. (1997a). "The Difference Between Intranet and Internet Design." Alertbox for September 15, 1997, www.useit.com.

Nielsen, J. (1997b). "The Difference Between Web Design and GUI Design." Alertbox for May 1, 1997, www.useit.com.

Nielsen, J. (1997c). "Disabled Accessibility: The Pragmatic Approach." Alertbox for June 13, 1999, www.useit.com.

Open Software Foundation (1993). *OSF/Motif style guide, revision 1.2.* Englewood Cliffs, NJ: Prentice Hall.

Pake, G. (1985). Research at Xerox PARC: A founder's perspective. *IEEE Spectrum,* Vol. 22, No. 10, 54–61.

Rubenstein, R., and Hersch, H. (1984). *The human factor: Designing computer systems for people.* Boston: Digital Press.

Smith, D. C., *et al.* (June 1982). The Star user interface: An overview. *Proceedings of the AFIPS National Computer Conference,* 515–528.

Sullivan, K. (1996). The Windows® user interface: A case study in usability engineering. *Proceedings of the ACM CHI'96.*

Value Chain Analysis

Jamshid C. Hosseini and Richard J. Barnes

Marquette University

VALUE CHAIN INTEGRATION would get an international company to an even playing field with their competition. Combining the value chain process management and analysis with state of the art information technology and using an effective postponement strategy would allow a multinational corporation to rise above its competition and provide its customers exactly what they need—the right product at the right price when they need it (at the right time). Proper adoption of electronic data interchange (EDI), enterprise resource planning (ERP), advanced planning systems (APS), e-commerce, and the more localized supply chain management (SCM) such as logistic execution systems (LES) gives a global company the opportunity to streamline its value chain and manage it more efficiently and effectively.

Postponement enables demand pooling which, in turn, enhances demand forecasts, improves warehouse management, and streamlines transportation management. Managing these components of the value chain, as well as shortening lead times, gives companies an international time-based (speed) competitive advantage. This article addresses the role of information technology and postponement strategies in integrating and managing the value chain and, thereby, gaining time-based competitive advantage by multinational corporations.

I. INTRODUCTION

Can an operational strategy of integrating the value chain analysis with state of the art information technology and the postponement concept enhance a company's time-based competitiveness in the global arena? The evolution of the integration of information technology into the value chain has enabled companies to compete on a time basis in their local market. However, due to the complexity of global logistics, as well as other constraints associated with global operations, the same companies are losing this competitive edge.

Customer needs and requirements have caused manufacturers' and distributors' value chains to become integrated. Time has become the driver by which customers are selecting the companies they choose to do business with. The right product must be available when the customer is demanding it. As companies have transitioned to become time-based competitors, they have utilized the information flow through the integrated value chain to be as close to "real-time" as possible. Companies have improved their business processes by automating the information flow from the point when the customer generates a desire for a product to the point of customer fulfillment of that demand. The whole value chain has become synchronized. Information technology has enabled organizations to compete on the basis of time: the quickest to fulfill customer demands wins the business. Often, there is a premium received for winning the speed contest. Customers often pay more for the perceived value of receiving the right product at the right time.

Enterprise resource planning (ERP) tools have integrated the business transactional processes from the point of customer order through manufacturing and procurement to the release of shipping information within manufacturing and distribution companies. Warehouse management systems (WMS) have taken the shipping information and streamlined the transactional process to pick, pack, and ship the order. Transportation management systems (TMS) have been employed to control the transactions of shipping and to track the delivery of the order to the customer. Figure 1 demonstrates the use of information technology throughout the value chain.

In this article, we will address the role of information technology and electronic commerce in value chain analysis. Recent developments in these fields in terms of hardware technologies, information network, Web diffusion, and sophisticated software development have revolutionized all aspects of value chains from the design and development of the concept to the final sales service strategies. Next we will introduce global values chains followed by a discussion of the concept of postponement and its role in managing global value chains. This discussion is followed by an analysis of the operational strategy of time-based competition and the role of postponement in it. We will then present some preliminary models and measurement methodologies for value chain analysis within the context of global operations. We will continue with a discussion of global issues relevant to value chain analysis such as the advent of global pacts and bonded warehousing. Finally, we will conclude by providing some practical issues and key success factors in analyzing value chains in a global environment.

II. THE ROLE OF INFORMATION TECHNOLOGY AND ELECTRONIC COMMERCE

Electronic data interchange (EDI) has allowed the integration between IT software packages and between companies throughout the value chain. Figure 1 shows an integrated value chain with ERP packages of different functional blocks being linked through corresponding EDI transmissions between systems. The ERP packages "talk" on a virtual real time basis through EDI. The downstream ERP system then processes the information received from the upstream ERP system in a timely fashion to generate another EDI transmission to another ERP package further downstream in the value chain. ERP packages are complimented with WMS and TMS information, so that the subsequent EDI transmission carries the most appropriate information for downstream value chain partners to use to add value throughout the value chain. Some companies are even using EDI from their WMS or TMS depending on their legacy systems.

Advance planning and scheduling (APS) systems are tools that integrate control and planning support for a company across the entire value chain. Unlike the other systems mentioned above which are mostly execution based (transactional), the APS tools are planning based. The APS tool-set is made up of the following components: network modeling, demand planning, event planning, forecasting, inventory planning, and replenishment planning. The good APS tools provide collaborative methods to gain valuable information throughout the value chain.

Electronic commerce (EC) has been in existence for over 2 decades. Recently, however, electronic commerce has been brought to the manufacturing floor, the warehouse, the distribution center, the transportation fleet, and the customer through the diffusion of the Internet and the World Wide Web. Over

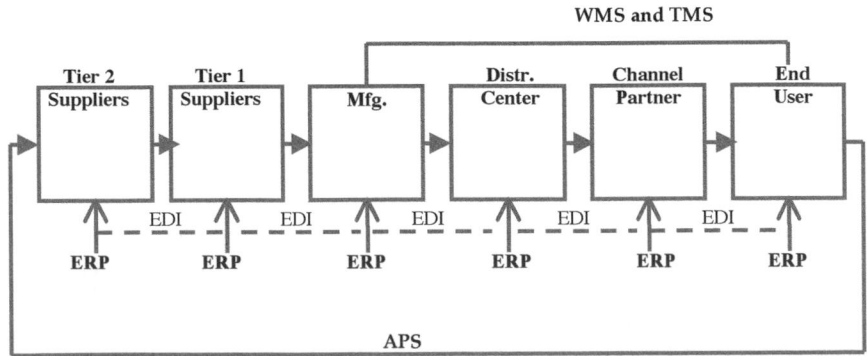

Figure 1   Integrated value chain and information technology packages.

the last few years, for instance, there has been a myriad of applications of EC spanning all facets of trade and procurement including those related to the integration and management of value chains. A combination of new solutions rooted in the network technology, thin graphical user interfaces (GUI), collaboration, and virtual interaction has deeply impacted the competitive landscape.

Electronic commerce offers the use of EDI and the development of software or smart agents that can manage the coordination and execution of value chain activities. Smart agents are designed to act autonomously on the user's behalf by continuously tracking, through other smart agents, the activities of the value chain. The agents are organized into a hierarchy and are controlled by a governing agent that executes activities based on the aggregate production plan. Each local agent executes its activities based on a set of parameters that are optimal to the domain of the activity. Higher level agents review all local execution requests and authorize decisions that are based on overall system performance. The governing agents monitor all system information using EDI and invoke algorithms and heuristics.

The diffusion of information and coordination of decision making using smart agents moves the planning and execution of value chain activities from static to dynamic and links all decisions through a hierarchy that carries out each activity based on current conditions. Static systems rely on data snapshots and are executed and later adjusted in ad hoc fashion. Real-time systems offer the benefit of analyzing information and making immediate decisions based on current conditions. Static systems rely on historical data that may or may not reflect future conditions. Furthermore, the use of smart agents allows for minimal human interaction. Smart software agents are decentralized entities that are assigned to specific products or activities (inventory levels, transportation routing, machine utilization, etc.), but are also coordinated by higher level agents that monitor overall conditions (order status, production plans, current

shipments) and authorize local decisions based on the overall objectives (service level, facility utilization, etc.) using both user based priorities and DSS logic.

By incorporating electronic commerce into value chain planning and execution the focus from local to global optimization is achieved. Several advantages are realized through integrated EC systems:

—Planning and execution moves from static to dynamic
—System execution and adjustments are based on current conditions and consider all aspects of the operation
—Ad hoc decision making is eliminated and replaced by software agents that monitor and execute activities using current and anticipate events
—Data sharing promotes free market potential in pricing that is similar to the stock market model where prices fluctuate based on current conditions and purchases are made using complex decision-making criteria (volume discounts, price hedging, etc.)

III. GLOBAL VALUE CHAINS

Global competition is experiencing the same time-frame demands from international customers. If the product they want is not available or cannot be provided in a short time frame, then the customer will look for a different supplier or a substitute product. Even if a company is beating the competition on price, features, or benefits, the customer will still not wait for most products because the time frame in international logistics to deliver that product from non-indigenous sources is very long. International transportation and customs have added uncontrollable time lags into the delivery cycle time from off shore sources. Figure 2 demonstrates this time lag up and down the value chain.

Generally, a highly variant system of cycle times cannot be overcome by better inventory planning and

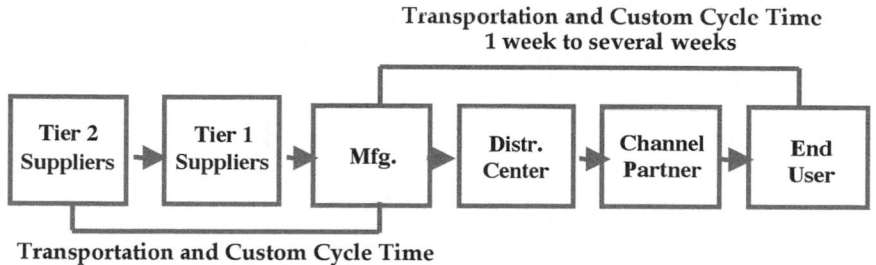

Figure 2 Lag time in international value chains.

management tools. More inventory can never solve the problem of cycle times within a system that is out of control. The best APS system cannot make up for a highly variant system of cycle times. A solution for the highly variant system of cycle times is to come up with an integrated information technology solution for controlling international transportation and custom officiating of shipments so that information can be managed to bring the cycle times under control. While these tools and methodologies are being developed, a time-based competitive company should look towards the process of postponement to add value deep in the value chain to meet global customer specifications in a timely fashion.

IV. POSTPONEMENT

We define postponement for an international customer as the process of customizing products or performing the final assembly operation of generic products in the customer's home country to meet the customer's desired specification. The concept of postponement rationalizes keeping the product as generic as possible until the point of sale and then quickly customizing or finalizing the product for sale.

When customization is performed it can greatly affect the company's inventory and service trade-offs. Lower inventory and improved service levels can be met through a postponement process. Delaying customization increases the company's flexibility to respond to changes in the mix of demands from different market segments. The company can improve its responsiveness to orders or reduce its investment in inventory. The postponement process adds variety to what a company can offer its global customers. Postponement often means better transportation economies. The manufacturer can ship generic products in bulk closer to the point of end use. Putting final configuration at the end of the pipeline improves order fill rates. For slow-moving items where manufacturing efficiency is not as critical as order fill rates, customers see better inventory turns. Postponement allows shippers to remove inventory from the pipeline instead of forcing suppliers to take up the slack. Postponement makes configure-to-order (CTO) products look like made-to-stock products to the customer, if done correctly. Customers think manufacturers and distributors have the product on the shelf, when in fact, they have an effective postponement CTO process.

Coordinating all the separate moves is the most difficult part of postponement. To do this electronically, we need enhanced software—expert systems—to take the human element out, and make it run smoothly. WMSs are being offered with work order capability. Traditional distributors can now perform CTO postponement processes just like a manufacturer can. ERP configuration modules exist so that the preengineered postponement product line can have its bill of materials (BOM) being generated from a rules-based system, cutting the engineering maintenance time of traditional BOM systems.

Postponement allows manufacturers to give customers what they want, when they want it, and where they want it, but manufacturers do not have to build it that way from nonindigenous manufacturing centers. CTO processes pose a great deal of potential in all sales opportunities, especially international opportunities where international transportation and custom delays of weeks can set back and deter customers from ordering products that are not immediately available. Postponement's goal is to reduce the time from when the customer orders the product to when the customer is using it at their site.

V. OPERATIONAL STRATEGY OF TIME-BASED COMPETITIVENESS AND POSTPONEMENT

Products are becoming less standardized and customers are demanding options that are tailored to their unique requirements. Exact quantities are being demanded, requiring a system of value chain management that is quick, precise, and provides a top quality product every time. Value chain management capabilities are required to develop a time-based competitive advantage in a global manufacturing and distribution environment. Time-based competition does not just refer to manufacturing—every link in the value chain must become involved in order to optimize the functional value added within the context of the entire chain. Time-based competitiveness has not only focused on the manufacturing component but on the whole process. It may be argued that the main strategic thrust of market competitiveness is to examine the lead time from the customer order to delivery. On average, manufacturing time consumes only 30 to 40% of total lead time. This means that most organizations can get the "biggest bang for their buck" not by focusing on reducing non-value-added activities within the manufacturing cycle, but by adopting a total value chain view of the process.

In traditional manufacturing centers variability in lead times is often due to demand variability. The variability of demand leads to the development of backlog, which is an integral part of build-to-order processes. This backlog leads to a difficult choice for value chain management of build-to-order processes: whether to orient the system around delivery speed (lead time) versus delivery reliability (on-time delivery). Delivery reliability should nevertheless be an important objective within the product/value supply chain but the greatest improvement as felt by the customer will be in lead time reduction. Lead time reductions are generated through process improvements and reengineering the value chain, and not totally realized through better planning systems. The success of lead time reduction is ultimately determined by improvements in product and process design, supplier performance, and improved material flow. Some key issues for consideration are design for value chain management, integrated databases throughout the value chain, integrated control and planning support systems, redesigned organizational incentives, and the establishment of value chain performance measurement for total lead time. Through postponement processes, which are closest to the end customer, the highly variant international transportation and custom cycle time is buffered by managing the inventory needed to turn a generic product into the customer's specified product.

What distorts the system is time: the lengthy delay between the event that creates the change of demand and the time when the company finally responds to this information. The logic behind the postponement approach is as simple as it is fundamental to competitive success: configure the product when the customer orders it and do that process as close to the customer as possible and you eliminate much of the uncontrollable delay out of the system. What this points out is that moving the value of the final product as close to the customer as possible will improve communication of the customer demand and configuring to order will allow a faster response to the customer. Another side benefit for manufacturers is that the CTO products may have components which are also sold as finished good products for maintenance and repair orders (MRO). The demand from MRO business will increase the overall demand for the stocked generic product, which will improve the product's demand. Increasing the demand and reducing variability of that demand allows the product to be accurately forecasted which would improve its fill rate from stock.

Low-volume goods, which generally produce high margins, tend to slow down or even block the path of high-volume products and components, though high-volume items generate most of the company's profit.

With a local postponement process, CTO manufacturers can retain the higher margin products while they produce them at lower costs because the components of the low volume postponement process are made at high volume manufacturing centers. Also, a typical cost structure in a postponement CTO process, which is close to the customer in the value chain, benefits from no transportation costs from the U.S., lower wage rates in-country, and lower price commodities sourced locally.

Local postponement processes are governed by a familiar strategic goal: an improved knowledge of customers integrated with a reorganized means to satisfy them. Manufacturers/distributors also benefit from demanding a premium for the improved cycle time. In general, customers are willing to pay a premium if they can get their goods and services very quickly.

VI. INVENTORY MANAGEMENT: BENEFITS OF POSTPONEMENT IN AN INTEGRATED VALUE CHAIN

Postponement processes, which customize the generic product to make the customer's specified product from standard inventory theory, would have the benefit of the risk pooling effect, and consequently, would need less safety stock in finished goods. This target inventory level for a particular product is a function of the length and variability of the lead time to replenish the stock from the factory and the level and variability of demand for the product. Analyses have shown that the inventory savings gained from changing from U.S. factory configure-to-order to an in-country postponement (CTO) process are substantial.

One of the major challenges to operational managers is product proliferation. Product proliferation makes it difficult to forecast demand accurately and, consequently, leads to high inventory investment and poor customer service. Such proliferation is often a result of the global nature of the market place. Different markets may have different requirements for the product, due to different taste, language, specifications, geographical environment, or government regulations. Another reason for product proliferation is the expansion of the customer base. Different product versions are often developed for different international market segments.

Product proliferation is often unavoidable in a global market. Design changes may require some investment in additional manufacturing capabilities, higher component costs, and additional vendor management costs. A manufacturer can deal with this environment with an intermediate (generic) stage of the product, which is built to stock, from which this intermediate (generic) product is then customized into different final products on demand. Delayed product differentiation would perhaps illustrate the importance of expanding the mind set of inventory modelers from focusing on "optimal" inventory planning and control to exploring alternative product/process designs to improve inventory and service performance. Rapid technological change and increased globalization of markets will continue to result in product proliferation as a major challenge to operations managers of global companies. Logistic issues such as inventory and customer service are critical battlegrounds for competitiveness. To this end inventory modeling tools like advance planning and scheduling have a lot to offer if properly combined with generic product postponement processes.

As companies focus more on their core competencies and outsource more value-added activities, their value chains will increasingly consist of many sites managed by third-party providers, and the flows between sites form a complex network. This complexity leads to different sources of uncertainty along a value chain. They include demand (volume and mix), process (yield, machine downtimes, transportation reliabilities), and supply (part quality, delivery reliabilities, custom clearance). Inventories are often used to protect the chain from uncertainties. A major challenge to value chain managers is to control inventories and costs along the chain while maximizing customer service performance. Because variation and distortion exist companies have a choice: They can produce to forecast or they can reduce the time delays in the flow of information and products through the system. The traditional solution is to produce to forecast. The new approach is to reduce time consumption.

Reducing time consumption will eventually enhance the forecast, because the forecast does not have to cover such a wide lead time. But especially in an international environment, when transportation times are longer and time to clear customs has greater variability, if the product can be made through a postponement process in-country it will result in a better lead time than ordering stock product from the U.S. The country's management can control the local lead time variation around a postponement process better than any process could that is hundreds or thousands of miles away in the U.S.

Because of the importance of variety, finished product inventory is almost useless in meeting customer

orders; most products can be configured only after the order has been placed. For the configure-to-order product there is no way to determine exactly what to build until the manufacturer receives an order that specifies a unique combination of options that must be converted from intermediate (base units and options) components. Forecasting such wild finished product mixes may seem futile but relating their demand to lower levels of base units and options component levels and forecasting them seems more appropriate. Nevertheless, flattening the product structure with supporting base unit and option inventory mixes seems more logical. This is especially apparent when a CTO company can assemble from stocking level base unit and option components that can be replenished within its unshipped backlog lead time. When base unit and option components are consumed from short-cycle shipments, manufacturing order lot-sizing and tracking are greatly simplified. Line stocking and replenishment tend to be covered by APS (safety stock and forecasting) "pull" techniques. Agility, flexibility, and mass customization imply a postponement process mindset. Unbalanced finished goods inventory and hardened product structuring will cease to consume precious engineering maintenance resources. In contrast, rules-based product structuring will be to customer service and engineering professionals what JIT and focused factories have been to manufacturing.

As mentioned, manufacturers and distributors will benefit from stocking to the lowest common denominator base unit and option components for postponement processes (which may also be a "sale-able" maintenance and repair order (MRO) units); see Fig. 3. It is important to point out the optimal point to design your products exists based on the many components and their characteristics that make up the product as well as the many applications or systems that the product goes into. For a traditional manufacturing company this optimal product design is usually built in one or a few locations and then exported around the world. Almost in all cases traditional manufacturing of products cannot happen in every coun-

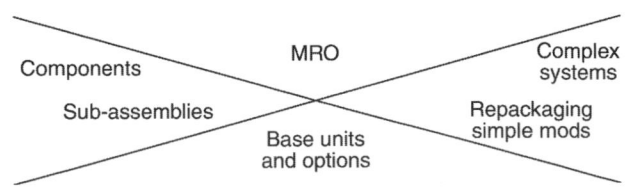

Figure 3   Lowest common denominator.

try where the company does business. There is a need for the company to pool demand and, through economy of scale and quality management, manufacture the product in a limited number of locations.

VII. MODELS

Typical international decision support models can be used to support analysis of global manufacturing policies. The objective of these models is global after-tax profit maximization through the design of the distribution network and control of material flows within the network. Its constraints include postponement process capacity, regional demand requirements, material balance, and government offset requirements. The cost structure contains variable and fixed costs for material procurement, production distribution, and transportation. These models also account for tariffs, duties, and transfer pricing. Duties and tariffs are based on material flows and hence their impact must be considered as firms determine material input, intermediate product, and finished product shipments across national boundaries. Currency exchange rates fluctuate routinely and affect profits in each country of operation. There are significant differences in corporate tax rates in each country. Global sourcing must be managed to account for tradeoffs between longer lead times, lower costs, access to new technologies, and dependence on suppliers from some nations. Market penetration strategies, local content rules, counter trade, and quotas all act to constrain the flow of product throughout the world. Product designs may vary by national market (especially for certain products such as electronic goods intended for different electrical distribution systems). Centralized control of operations is difficult in multi-

national environments and hence appropriate incentives and transfer price mechanisms must be devised. National cultural, language, and skill differences are significant and must be accounted for in human resource management. The resource deployment decisions involve both the design of the network and the management of material flow within the network of the international firm's value-added supply chain. A global policy option is a specific configuration of supply chain component substrategies where the objective is to maximize global after-tax profits. Adding a postponement CTO process to this international model eases its sensitivity to currency exchange rate fluctuations and makes the model much less complex because lead times are under control and inventory investment is minimized.

Figure 4 shows the effects of CTO in the value chain along a global customer satisfaction continuum. As the CTO process is moved closer to the international customer through postponement, the control over lead time and delivery improves customer satisfaction. The optimal product design, as discussed in Fig. 3, is applied in Fig. 4 with the result being that the optimal product design for the value chain can be configured or modified closer to the international customer through postponement. Thus, the company has more controllable lead times; cost and quality ultimately satisfy the customer more than the traditional export model. Lead times are faster and more controllable because the postponement process is closer to the customer as well as the incoming generic inventory is more accurate from the demand pooling effect. Costs are lower because of the leverage of lower transportation cost of generic products, lower local labor rate for postponement, and the potential avoidance of paying duties. Quality improves because a controllable process is demanded.

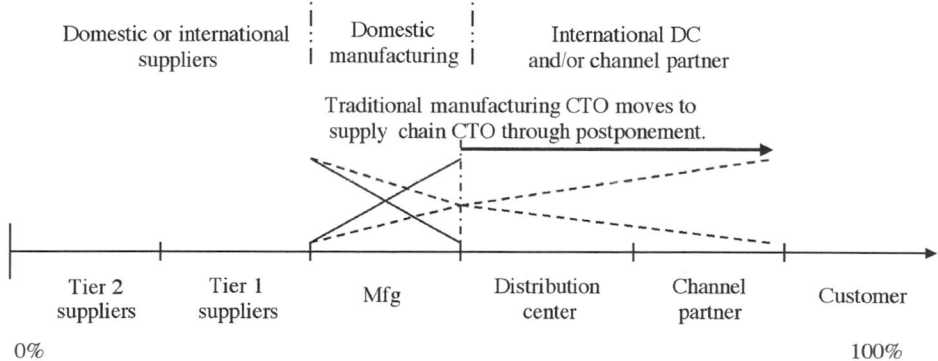

Figure 4 International value chain continuum of customer satisfaction.

VIII. MEASUREMENT METHODOLOGY—TIME VS COST (TRADITIONAL)

Time has become the overarching measurement of performance by customers. By reducing the consumption of time in every aspect of the business, companies also reduce cost, improve quality, and stay close to their customers. Time-based competitors have managed structural changes that enable their operations to execute their processes much faster. As a consequence, time has become their new source of competitive advantage. Time is a more critical competitive yardstick than traditional financial measurements. Today, time is on the cutting edge. The ways leading companies manage time—in production, in new product development and introduction, in sales, in distribution, and in delivery to the customer—represent the most powerful new sources of competitive advantage. Leading-edge companies are capitalizing on time as a critical source of competitive advantage, shortening the order to delivery time on postponement CTO processes in the international arena—managing time the way most companies manage cost, quality, or inventory. While the traditional companies track costs and size, the new competitor derives advantage from time, staying on the cutting edge, leaving its rivals behind.

In a postponement (CTO) environment, where service targets are specified not in terms of fill rates but in reliability of meeting target lead time (promise dates), manufacturers and distributors can focus on what is important from the customers' perspective: "If you don't have it on the shelf (fill rate), when will you be able to deliver it (promise date)?" At the point where time becomes an issue, the customer typically has agreed on price; they are concerned with delivery and the company's ability to do what they say (compliance to promise date). Thus, cost consciousness, quality, and reputation has gotten manufacturers/distributors the order, now results on delivery will either satisfy them and retain their faith or dissatisfy and drop their faith in postponement manufacturers/distributors.

Manufacturers/distributors need to build their measurement systems not only around financial data, but also include a heavy emphasis on time. The emphasis on time should be on how to shorten the lead time that customers are seeing when they order a product through to delivery—order to delivery lead time. This lead time is especially important when international customers order products that must be supplied from the U.S. Only a quick postponement process in-country will capture that order and satisfy the customer. Additional emphasis needs to be placed on customer service metrics: fill rates for stock products and compliance to promise date for postponement products. For either stock or postponement products, the most important metric is compliance to customer want date—manufacturers must meet customer expectations, which is the date they want it.

IX. ECONOMIC PACTS RESEARCH

The range of possible multinational strategies depends upon the structure of the world market in terms of customers and barriers to trade. For some products (such as electrical power systems or telecommunications equipment), the technology and economics of production would very strongly suggest global rationalization, but political imperatives may be so strong as to prevent it. For example, in Latin American countries, market-access restrictions are applied. Under such conditions of restricted trade and controlled market access, worldwide strategic integration is obviously difficult. Often the very nature of the goods, their strategic importance as well as characteristics such as bulky, massive equipment produced in small volumes for a few large customers reinforce the desire on the part of governments to control suppliers closely.

For example, in the Americas, there exists at least four trade blocs: NAFTA—U.S., Canada, and Mexico; Mercosur—Brazil, Argentina, Chile, Uruguay, and Paraguay; Andean—Venezuela, Colombia, Ecuador, and Peru; and the CariCom—the remaining Central American and Caribbean countries. A quick look at the Mercosur pact indicates that a local content restriction is in place. The local content restriction is that if at least 40% of the value of the product was supplied with labor or material from the specific country within Mercosur, the remaining percentage of exported value could have its duty drawn back (reimbursed). If the local content could be met and the product was sold or reexported, the duty draw back program would make the product less expensive (in Brazil, for instance, duties typically run at 32% of their imported value). If the local content could be met in one country of the Mercosur, then the other countries of the Mercosur would allow it as a duty free importation into their market. Thus, a manufacturing center in Brazil could supply the rest of the Mercosur with CTO products cheaper and faster than the U.S. could. It seems that the postponement (CTO) strategy may come to the aid of producers outside of the trade pact. A strategy which needs to be deeply explored is whether a postponement (CTO) process can contribute the required 40% local content value added.

X. BONDED WAREHOUSES

In countries or regional trading blocs where the local content restrictions cannot be met, the postponement (CTO) process should be set up at the point of a bonded facility. A bonded facility is where inventory is stored without paying the duty/tax (or nationalizing) until the product is moved from the facility. If the product is to be used in country the duties need to be paid; if the product is shipped out of the country no duties are paid.

For example, in Brazil where the duties, importation taxes, and customs processing times are the highest in Latin America, the government offers three options for bonded warehouses: distribution, virtual, and product for reexportation. The last type is self-explanatory: the product will not stay in Brazil for too long; it may be modified or changed but eventually it will be exported out of the country with no additional duty or tax levied. The distribution bonded warehouse is used for items that will eventually be used in country. The advantage is that if the product is not moved out of the bonded facility it can eventually be reexported with no additional duty or tax levied. This is advantageous for products where demand is uncertain.

In principle, the virtual bonded warehouse is exactly the same as the distribution type but the difference is in how both are administered. The virtual bonded warehouse relies on a computer system for inventory tracking and an audit system to verify its accuracy. The distribution bonded warehouse relies on posting an agent at the facility and building security around the inventory to guarantee accuracy. Any of the three types can be done within the company's facility or subcontracted to a third party. There is the added fixed expense of modifying the companies' facility to support the bonded environment and 100% of the cost of the agent. In a third-party facility, these expenses are spread across all the customers (based on volume of movement through their facilities).

To reiterate the bonded facility makes sense for products where the demand is uncertain. Thus this inventory can be returned to the supplier without any duties applied. A postponement (CTO) process helps to eliminate the need for a bonded facility because the intermediate (generic) products typically have reliable demand because of demand pooling and the extra MRO demand.

XI. CONCLUSION

Integrated value chain will only afford an international company an even playing field with their competition.

The use of postponement processes will allow them to rise above their competition and provide their customers exactly what they need—the right product at the right price when they need it (at the right time). The concept of postponement—pushing the customization of product as close to the customer as possible and delivering it to them quickly—provides demand pooling to take place. The demand pooling along with MRO demand will minimize the inventory risk and make the stock intermediate (generic) components have a more reliable demand (forecast).

Manufacturers and distributors need to analyze postponement processes to determine how their implementation of these processes fits their overall business strategies. From an international perspective, the time is right for a postponement strategy. U.S. manufacturers and distributors are at a pivotal time in their international involvement. U.S. manufacturers and distributors need differentiating logistics and a strong sales/support organization with the right set of products that will offer them competitive advantage that will come from implementing a postponement process. The following are some determining factors throughout this process.

A. Key Success Factors for Global Operational Strategy

1. Implementation of an APS or, at least, a set of transactional-based ERP, LES, WMS, etc., solutions
2. Installation and coordination of the IT system(s) across the value chain
3. Training (and continuous upgrade with regards to technology changes) for the personnel along the value chain
4. Ensure product design is conducive to a postponement process, otherwise, change the design process
5. Communicate the vision to ensure it is shared with all stakeholders
6. Obtain leadership commitment to the postponement process, otherwise, no spokesperson or advocate will help share the risk of the endeavor
7. Gain employee involvement in the design of the postponement process, otherwise, there will be no ownership and thus the attempt is doomed to failure
8. Incorporate the appropriate organizational changes with the new postponement process,

otherwise there is no integration within the organization

9. Change the performance measures looking at order to delivery cycle time as the driving metric, but balance that with the appropriate overall cost and quality metrics to ensure a balanced scorecard

SEE ALSO THE FOLLOWING ARTICLES

Control and Auditing • Cost/Benefit Analysis • Electronic Data Interchange • Executive Information Systems • Global Information Systems • Globalization and Information Management Strategy • Operations Management • Procurement • Strategic Planning, Use of Information Systems for • Supply Chain Management • Total Quality Management and Quality Control

BIBLIOGRAPHY

Chamberlain, W., and Thomas, G. (1995). The future of MRPII: Headed for the scrap heap or rising from the ashes? *IIE Solutions*, Vol. 27, No. 7, 32–35.

Cohen, M. A., and Lee, H. L. (1988). Strategic analysis of integrated production-distribution systems: Models and methods. *Operations Research*, Vol. 36, No. 2, 216–228.

Fuller, J. B., O'Conor, J., and Rawlinson, R. (1993). Tailored logistics: The next advantage. *Harvard Business Review*, May–June, 87–98.

Handfield, R. B. (1995). *Re-engineering for time-based competition: Benchmarks and best practices for production, R&D and purchasing.* Westport, CT: Quorum Books.

Lee, H. L. (1996). Effective inventory and service management through product and process redesign. *Operations Research*, Vol. 44, No. 1, 151–159.

Lee, H. L., and Billington, C. (1992). Managing supply chain inventory: Pitfalls and opportunities. *Sloan Management Review*, Spring, 65–73.

Lee, H. L., and Billington, C. (1993). Material management in decentralized supply chains. *Operations Research*, Vol. 41, No. 5, 835–847.

Lee, H. L., Billington, C., and Carter, B. (1993). Hewlett–Packard gains control of inventory and service through design for localization. *Interfaces*, Vol. 23, No. 4, 1–11.

Richardson, H. L. (1994). Cut inventory, postpone finishing touches. *Transportation & Distribution*, Vol. 35, No. 2, 38–39.

Stalk, Jr., G. (1988). Time—The next source of competitive advantage. *Harvard Business Review*, July–August, 41–51.

Stalk, Jr., G., and Hout, T. M. (1990). *Competing against time: How time-based competition is reshaping global markets.* New York: The Free Press.

Virtual Learning Systems

Maryam Alavi **Dorothy Elliott Leidner**
Emory University *Baylor University*

GLOSSARY

asynchronous communication (or interaction) A communication mode in which messages are not coordinated in time and are transmitted at different clock rates.

cognitive learning theory A theory that views learning as a process of acquisition of knowledge and change in an individual's knowledge structures that enhances his or her potential for effective performance.

cognitive structure An individual's memory and internal knowledge representations. Sometimes also referred to as mental models.

constructivist pedagogy Educational method that emphasizes the importance of a learner's active involvement in developing understanding and knowledge.

groupware Software systems designed to enable individuals and groups to communicate and interact to share knowledge and information.

hypertext Information units interlinked based on predefined associations.

synchronous communication (or interaction) A communication mode in which messages are coordinated in time and are transmitted at the same clock rate.

videoconferencing A live communication link between two or more locations involving audio, video, and textual information exchange.

videodisk An optical disk used for storage and retrieval of videos.

I. INTRODUCTION

A key trend in higher education and adult training and development is the use of virtual learning systems. Virtual learning systems (VLS) are information technology-based environments, in which the learner's interactions with learning materials (e.g., assignments and exercises), instructors, and/or peers are mediated through technology. The term "information technology" or simply "technology" is defined as a broad array of computing, communication, and multimedia technologies and their convergence. This study focuses on learning from instruction. "Learning from instruction" has been defined as an environment in which one individual tries to intentionally influence the learning process and outcomes of another individual. Virtual learning systems can be used at all levels of education from elementary through graduate school. However, this paper focuses exclusively on higher and adult education.

The increasing interest and growth of VLS can be attributed to two factors: (1) an increase in demand for learning and education from both the nontraditional and traditional sources, and (2) rapid advances in information technologies. Business, scientific, high-tech, and professional fields are faced with an explosion of knowledge. The half-life of learning grows shorter and shorter. For example, in 1997 Van Dusen stated that about half of what an engineering student learns in his or her freshman year is almost obsolete by the time that he or she graduates and enters the

Encyclopedia of Information Systems, Volume 4

561

workforce. In the introductory chapter of his book from 1998 titled *The Knowledge Economy,* editor Dale Neef states:

> . . . there is now compelling evidence that the sudden and ever-accelerating burst of growth in high-technology and high-skilled services . . . may bring about some of the most profound and unexpected changes to the way in which we live and work witnessed since the nineteenth-century transition from an agricultural to an industrial society.

This lifelong learning requirement coupled with distance, geophysical displacement of co-workers, family, and job constraints of the working adults, fuels the growth of VLS particularly in the form of distributed learning systems (which we describe later in the article).

In addition to an increasing demand for education from nontraditional students (i.e., working adult), the overall growth in the traditional student demand for postsecondary education drives the growth in VLS. According to the U.S. Department of Education statistic, the percentage of high school graduates who enroll in postsecondary education has increased from 49% in 1980 to 65% in 1995. In the meantime, according to a report published by Merrill Lynch in 1999, the education industry overall is faced with the "baby boom echo" an estimated 72 million children of the 76 million baby boomers (Americans born from 1946 to 1964).

The growth of VLS is also fueled by a rapid rate of technological progress. The pervasiveness of the Internet, the emerging high-capacity networks augmented by satellite transmission and cellular and radiofrequency communication, and the prevalence of networked personal computers at homes and businesses are creating cost-effective options for delivery of educational services to geographically dispersed participants. Information and communication technologies, which lie at the core of VLS, are advancing at exponential rates. While these technological advances have provided new options for such conventional learning environments as public and private universities, they have also led to a whole new set of competitors like corporate universities.

II. VIRTUAL LEARNING SYSTEMS: AN OVERVIEW

The variety and flexibility of modern information and communication technologies provide developers of VLS a wide array of choices. For example, one can design virtual learning such that students need not interact with each other or such that synchronous or asynchronous interactions occur. Thus, explicit choices in the design of the virtual environment must be made, choices that have likely consequences on learning and student satisfaction. Explicit design choices regarding interactivity and content delivery comprise the basic attributes of virtual learning systems. These are depicted in Tables I and II.

In terms of interactivity, courses that involve a single individual obtaining static content from a learning module delivered online constitute one extreme. In this case, the individuals do not interact. Even if there were a single individual, there could be asynchronous communication with an instructor or instructor assistant. Alternatively, multiple individuals can communicate via a list or real-time chat. Such communication can involve student to student, or student to instructor, or student with a mentor (instructor assistant). Synchronous communication can occur onsite (face-to-face) or offsite (via communications technology). Finally, courses vary in degree of interaction. Students can be required to participate and interact daily, or the interaction can be voluntary (see Table I).

Table II shows the design attributes concerning content delivery. One major attribute concerns media. Media may include text, graphics, video, and audio in some combination. Content can be delivered via linear or nonlinear modules and sequential or nonsequential navigation techniques. In either case, the designer must also determine whether the student will control progression through a module, answer periodic questions before the content material continues, or be given a choice between these two modes of control.

Virtual learning entails many choices among the above attributes. Our objective here is not to provide an exhaustive discussion of all possible approaches to development of VLS but to focus on those that have been identified as common and dominant forms in the literature.

Two primary categories of virtual learning systems can be identified: (1) virtual learning systems designed for use in classroom settings (involving onsite synchronous interactions), and (2) distributed VLS

Table I Attributes of Interactivity in Virtual Learning Systems

Time	Person	Place	Degree
Synchronous	Student–student	Onsite	Required
Asynchronous	Instructor–student	Offsite	Optional

Table II Attributes of Content Delivery in Virtual
Learning System

Media	Form	Control
Text	Linear modules and sequential navigation	Student controls progress
Audio	Nonlinear modules and nonsequential navigation	System determines progress
Video		Option between student or system control
Graphics		

designed for environments in which the learners and instructors are distributed across time and/or geographic distance (involving offsite synchronous and/or asynchronous interactions). Each category is discussed as follows.

A. Virtual Learning Systems in the Classroom

The trend in application of virtual learning systems in the classroom takes the form of electronic classrooms. An electronic classroom is a classroom equipped with advanced information technologies, which are used by instructors and/or students to store, retrieve, process, and communicate information in support of learning activities. Electronic classrooms have been used in various disciplines including science, engineering, business and management, and languages. Application of information technologies in the electronic classroom takes two primary forms: a means of *information presentation and display,* and *interactive use information technology* by students and instructor as a basis for active learning and communication during class. The *information presentation and display* feature of the electronic classroom aims at enhancing efficiency of learning and teaching processes. Examples include computer display of lecture notes, electronic note-taking by students, and access to and display of online databases. Some authors have observed that as a presentation medium only, information technology in the classroom does not fundamentally alter the dynamics of classroom interactions relative to the more traditional tools and mechanisms such as slide and overhead transparency projectors and even blackboards.

The interactive use of VLS in the classroom aims at support of student active and exploratory learning during class. For example, the interactive use of computer models and simulations by students can enhance learning through hands-on problem solving and what-if analysis (a specific example of this approach is presented in Section IV). This approach to the use of technology in the electronic classroom is based on the cognitive learning theories that view learning as an active and constructive process. Interactive use of VLS in the classroom in the form of networked computers in conjunction with specialized software tools referred to as groupware can greatly enhance communication and discussion. For example, use of these systems allows students and faculty to brainstorm and share ideas, comment on and criticize these ideas, and collaborate in solving problems and performing various learning tasks. Research by Alavi in 1994 has shown that students who routinely use interactive groupware in electronic classrooms learn more and are more satisfied with their learning experience relative to students in traditional classroom settings.

B. Distributed Virtual Learning Systems

Various forms of distributed VLS have been described in the literature. Van Dusen identified three categories of distributed VLS in 1997: the *broadcast model,* the *online model,* and the *collaborative distributed model.*

The *broadcast VLS model* is typically fashioned after a lecture-style classroom environment, in which the instructor and students are located at two or more remote locations. Sound, full-motion video, and presentation material are transmitted from a central location (classroom or studio) to remote locations. Popular examples of this model include courses delivered through videoconferencing, cable, or satellite transmission (e.g., instructional TV). In this VLS model, the instructor is viewed as the primary source of knowledge, controlling content and the rate of information transmission to students. In this distributed VLS model, the predominant pedagogical approach remains the conventional "chalk and talk" method commonly found in more traditional face-to-face classroom environments. The vision for VLS is primarily that of automation and efficiency gains. Information flow (mostly in the form of lectures and presentation materials) between the instructor and the remote students is automated. Efficiency gains involve cost savings in the form of time and resources otherwise spent on traveling (between the remote student locations, to and from the central classroom site). Economic gains to the supplier of the course include increased student coverage due to access to a relatively larger marketplace.

In some cases, this predominantly one-way broadcast model may be combined with direct synchronous and/or asynchronous communication links between the instructor and each remote student. These links serve to facilitate communication of students' feedback and questions to the instructor. Information technologies typically used to support direct communication links between students and instructor in this environment can range from telephone or online chat facilities and key response pads (for synchronous communication), to e-mail (for asynchronous communication). Use of synchronous communication devices by remote students to ask and answer questions creates some degree of interactivity in the virtual learning environment; it provides the instructor with useful feedback to gauge students' comprehension, and thus allows the instructor to adjust the presentation of material accordingly. Similarly, the use of asynchronous communication devices (e.g., e-mail) between the instructor and students facilitates student feedback and allows the instructor to answer questions beyond the scheduled class period.

In the *online VLS model*, remote students (using information and communication technologies) gain access to course content and learning resources such as simulations, computer-based exercises, demonstrations, and hypertext-based study guides. Here, the student is largely in charge of his or her learning thus providing greater flexibility in choosing the time, pace, frequency, and form of learning activities. This approach to virtual learning increases in prevalence as more interactive multimedia learning resources are made available by educational publishers via CD and other resources on the World Wide Web.

Unlike the broadcast VLS model, which treats learners as passive receivers of prepackaged information transmitted by the instructor, the online distributed learning model views the students as proactive in interpreting and constructing meaning from information by processing and filtering it through their existing cognitive structures. The role of IT in the online VLS model is to provide learners with the capabilities to access and manipulate learning materials in order to form new understandings and to create new knowledge. For example, many online VLS provide capabilities for analyzing, synthesizing, filtering, and summarizing information through simulation models.

In the *collaborative distributed VLS* model, students create knowledge and understanding primarily through social interactions across time and/or geographic distance through the use of information and communica-

tion technologies such as e-mail and online chat facilities. In the collaborative distributed VLS, learning occurs from the opportunity of the group members to be exposed to each other's thinking, opinions, and beliefs, while also obtaining and providing feedback for clarification and comprehension.

It is important to note that the three distributed VLS models described here represent the pure forms. It is quite likely that in a distributed learning program, more than one of these models would be used. For example, a program might combine a broadcast model for delivery of lectures in conjunction with the collaborative distributed VLS model to enable remote students to work on group projects.

The majority of VLS are designed and deployed in distributed learning environments. A report published in 1999 by the U.S. Department of Education indicated that in 1997–1998, about 10% of enrollments in all 2-year and 4-year postsecondary institutions in the United States were in distance (i.e., distributed) learning courses. This amounted to a total of 1.7 million enrollments in postsecondary distance learning courses. In 1997, Gubernick and Ebeling reported that only 93 postsecondary learning institutions were offering online courses in 1993. According to these authors, this number increased to 762 by 1997. The promise of flexibility and reduced downtime and travel expenses is also steadily increasing the use of VLS for employee training in the business world.

Regardless of the specific approach, however, learning is anchored in the human mind and can be supported via various configurations of virtual learning systems. In Section IV, we discuss a framework for conceptualizing the potential role of technology in the learning process and outcome.

III. LITERATURE REVIEW

Research has examined the outcomes of virtual learning systems in a variety of contexts. A relatively small number of studies have focused on electronic classrooms while most of the studies have aimed at investigation of distributed VLS. Research on electronic classrooms has aimed at evaluation of classroom settings equipped with VLS in terms of the level of student interactions and engagement in class as well as learning and student attitude. For example, studies of electronic classrooms equipped with communication capabilities have shown an increase in the level of participation and interactions among students. In 1988, Horowitz indicated that professionals who were taught in an electronic classroom and responded to instructor questions via the computers were more attentive and engaged with learning than those who were taught by a traditional lecture method. Butler in 1990 found that an electronic classroom induced student interactions. In that year, Bump observed that the electronic classroom enhanced student participation in the classroom discussions, and Slatin reported that in a class of 18 students, 100 messages was generated, with approximately 60% of these messages sent to other students in the class rather than to the instructor. Several other studies of electronic classrooms have focused on the impact of electronic classrooms on student learning and attitude. In 1988–1989, Gist *et al.* evaluated the impact of an electronic classroom equipped with an instructor computer and videodisks on students' attitudes toward the instructor and the instructional method. The study indicated that the students in the electronic classroom had more positive attitudes compared to students who were taught in a traditional classroom. Similarly, in another study of an electronic classroom in 1993, Leidner and Jarvenpaa examined the use and outcomes of computer-based instructional technology in the context of graduate business education. Their detailed case studies indicated that the use of teaching methods requiring hands-on use of computers by students in the electronic classroom enhanced exploratory analysis during class and acquisition of technical procedural knowledge by students.

In summary, studies of electronic classrooms have focused on the use and outcomes of VLS by instructors and/or students in classroom settings. These studies collectively illustrate the variety of approaches to use of VLS in classroom settings and the positive impact of these systems on classroom dynamics and learning outcomes.

A larger number of research studies have focused on the effectiveness of distributed VLS. In 1997, Moore and Thompson conducted a review of distributed virtual learning research, finding that in general, the outcomes of cognitive factors such as amount of learning, academic performance, achievement, and examination and assignment grades are generally not significantly different from the outcomes in traditional courses. This finding concurs with Brownson's review in 2000, which concluded that virtual learning and traditional classroom-based learning are not particularly different. In Moore and Thompson's study, examinations of other factors such as student satisfaction with the course, comfort, convenience, communication with the instructor, interaction and collaboration between students, interdependence, and perceptions of effectiveness showed mixed results.

While the majority of distributed learning studies find that opportunities for interaction between students and instructors seemed negatively affected in the distributed environment, in 1999, Spooner reported that several studies have found that distance learning positively affects collaboration and interdependence among students. Various factors may influence the degree of interaction virtual learning provides. In 1997, Webster and Hackley found that teaching style is the most important factor influencing student participation and interactions in virtual learning. They also found that students' comfort with their images on screen, the quality of the technology, and the perceived richness of the communication medium affected student interactions in virtual learning. The fact that the course was taught via distance was less significant than the teaching attitude and style. In 2000, Hill and Chidambaram in summarizing the findings of virtual learning research, highlighted three key findings: (1) the majority of studies have not taken into account individual differences among students (like age, attitudes, and perceptions); (2) research suggests that no single technology is as important in influencing outcomes as learner and instructor characteristics; and (3) while many studies suggest that no significant differences exist between traditional and virtual education outcomes, dropout rates have been higher for virtual education.

Until the advent of the Web, most virtual courses were highly impersonal, asynchronous, and noninteractive. Students were limited in their choice of courses by their physical location and the time it would take to send and receive materials and assignments to and from the receiving institute. As media have improved, it has become possible to develop and deliver greater interactivity at a distance. The learning in essence has become far less removed in person and time than with traditional forms of virtual education such as correspondence courses or instructional radio. No longer is the instructional package limited to that which can be mailed, or delivered via television or radio. There is now a great variety of alternatives in how courses can be developed and delivered.

Early research on virtual learning environments suggests that the learning outcomes of students using computer-based technology at a distance are similar to the learning outcomes of students who participate in conventional classroom instruction. A study published by Ahmed in 2000 compared an online course to the same course taught traditionally by the same instructor. The study indicated no difference in student performance but did find that the students in the virtual environment reported higher levels of self-efficacy and convenience. While virtual environments can offer convenience, flexibility, currency of material, increased retention, lowered costs, increased feedback, and individualized learning possibilities, in 2000 Dyrud reported withdrawal rates are significantly higher in virtual learning than traditional learning and students report that virtual learning requires more time and effort. Elsewhere, satisfaction and effectiveness of virtual learning have been perceived as lower than traditional learning.

Research has also considered the factors that influence students to choose virtual courses over their traditional counterparts. In 1992, Richards suggested that such practical considerations as distance from campus, work schedule, and family commitments affect students' choice to take online versions of courses. While such practical considerations may influence the study choices, there is growing evidence that learning and satisfaction with virtual learning depend as much upon student characteristics as upon any inherent characteristic of the virtual learning course design.

In a study published in 1998 by Salomon and Almog, individual differences that were only mildly implicated in learning in traditional settings were likely to become of central importance when computer-mediated communication was involved. One finding in this study comparing traditional classrooms with virtual ones was that although measures of ability were the best predictors of learning in the former learning environment, measures of students' disposition to engage mindfully in learning were the best predictors of the latter. According to these authors, volitional, motivated expenditure of mental effort, mindful engagement, and self-monitoring become crucial in virtual learning environments because of the general constructivist pedagogy that is naturally suited to such environments. In 2000, Robb stated virtual learning requires self-discipline for students to succeed: students have to stay on schedule with assignments, log on regularly, and participate in online class discussion, in order to achieve. In a study reported in 1994, Hiltz found that student levels of academic ability, motivation, degree of effort, and maturity all correlated positively with outcomes in online courses. Leuthhold in 1999 correlated the learning styles of 40 students in an online course with their preferences for mode of delivery. Students whose learning orientation was sequential as opposed to random preferred online courses to the traditional classroom.

It is not surprising then that aside from practical considerations, students tend to enroll in a course whose format is compatible with their attitudes and learning strategies. In fact, some researchers believe that where such a match is not made, learning outcomes are adversely affected. Ching in 1998 showed that the virtual environment may shape student learning styles: the learning style of the same individuals became more field independent after one year in a virtual learning program. We can thus distinguish between immediate and lasting benefits of virtual learning. According to Salomon and Almog, lasting benefits include improved self-discipline, improved tendency for self-regulation, or a possible change in learning style. For example, they further suggested that a more lasting cognitive effect of hypermedia content delivery might be an improved ability or disposition to construct logical cognitive structures of knowledge. In 2000, Tallman and Benson found that students who elected to take a virtual course changed their mental models of themselves as learners and their capabilities. In a new online classroom setting, students were forced into changing their patterns of learning from a need for approval for all their actions to building gradually toward self-discovery and independent learning. Students may be better able to construct interrelated networks of knowledge. On the other hand, it is also feasible that the long-term result of using hypermedia-based content delivery is that students may begin to construct rather shallow associationist cognitive structures, indicating incomplete learning.

A growing body of research investigates the degree of interactivity that can be achieved in virtual learning environments. There is an increasing consensus that online classes engage students to a greater degree than traditional classes because students are forced to write more than they talk. However, increasing interaction is insufficient to improve learning: the dialogue needs to be content focused. In 2000, Hron *et al.* suggested that content-related dialogues with minor off-task talk, coherent subject matter discussion with explanation, and equal participation of students can enhance group processes and learning in virtual environments. They studied the extent to which dialogue structuring promotes coherent subject matter discussion and symmetrical interaction in virtual learning groups engaged in synchronous communication. They found that structuring, both explicit and implicit, helps students in the virtual environment achieve more coherent subject matter discussion that was obtained in the absence of structuring mechanisms. In 1999, Hawthornthwaite reported that virtual learning environments need not restrict dialogue structuring to a synchronous exchange, but by extending interactions to times outside of class, a more sustained interaction and the creation of closer interpersonal bonds among students can occur. Thus, while one cannot totally simulate a real classroom where interaction is real-time and feedback from the instructor and other students is immediate, one can offer feedback that is better reflected and participation that is less an immediate reaction to a question and more a thoughtful reflection.

Hiltz and colleagues have extensively studied asynchronous virtual learning environments. According to reports published in 1994 and 1997, their basic premise has been that collaborative (group) learning which can be facilitated by anytime/anywhere access to the communication networks and workspace is key to achieving superior learning outcomes. The authors suggested that if collaboration rather than individual learning designs were used in an online class, students would be more motivated to actively participate and would as a result of the online social interactions perceive the medium as relatively friendly and personal. The authors found that the combination of teamwork in the online course resulted in higher perceptions of self-reported learning, whereas individuals working alone online tended to be less motivated, perceive lower levels of learning, and score lower on a test of mastery. Similarly, in 1995 Alavi *et al.* conducted a longitudinal field study of virtual learning systems in support of collaborative learning. Two types of collaborative learning environments using desktop videoconferencing were considered: one involving local student groups (i.e., nonproximate student teams on the same campus), and the other involved nonproximate students on two separate campuses. The findings indicated that both of the learning environments were equally effective in terms of student learning and satisfaction with the VLS. However, the students in nonproximate teams using the desktop videoconferencing were more committed and attracted to their groups.

To summarize, virtual learning research has covered a variety of topics and learning modes (in-class and distributed learning). Research has considered the outcomes of virtual learning in comparison with traditional learning. Research has focused on the issues that help predict why students would choose virtual learning over a traditional learning alternative. Student characteristics have been examined as moderators of any relationship between virtual learning mode and outcomes. Finally, a range of research addresses the issue of interactivity in virtual learning. This research considers the ways in which computer-mediated communication can positively enhance the learning outcomes in virtual settings. While the literature review reveals that much research focuses on learning outcomes obtainable in virtual environments, the most commonly used measures of learning focus on final task performance (on a test) or on student

perception of learning. What is missing is an understanding of how the attributes of virtual learning systems affect, or fail to affect, the underlying cognitive processing that occurs when individuals learn. The next section will present a framework for understanding these cognitive processes of learning and exploring the relationship between cognitive processes and various attributes of VLS.

IV. A COGNITIVE LEARNING FRAMEWORK AND IMPLICATIONS FOR VLS

Figure 1 depicts an input–process–output model of learning based on cognitive psychology research reported by Ausubel in 1968, Gagne and Briggs in 1979, and Mayer in 1981. This model was developed to identify the relevant variables and discuss the potential impact of technology on learning. According to the work of Reigeluth, Bunderson, and Merrill reported in 1994, the learning process is influenced by three categories of input variables: instructional strategy, learning technology, and situational factors. *Instructional strategy* refers to methods and approaches for selecting, sequencing, synthesizing, and displaying information (subject-matter content) to the learner. *Technology* refers to the means and tools used to access, process, display, and communicate content information to the learner. *Situational factors* refer to the relevant learner, instructor, and environmental variables such as learner's interest and motivation and the instructor's experience and structure of subject matter content.

Mayer defined *learning* as the process by which an individual connects new material (information to be learned) with knowledge that already exists in the memory through the cognitive processes of reception, availability, and activation. Learning involves both short and long-term memory. According to

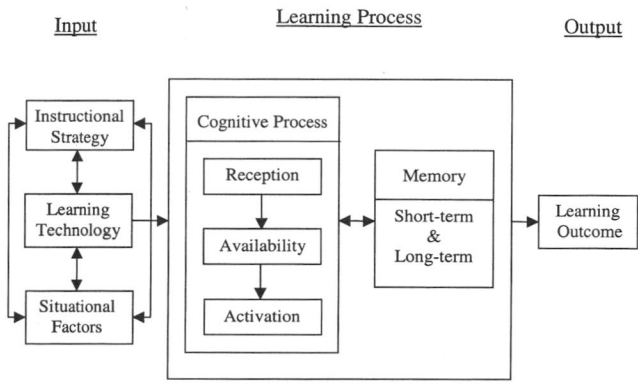

Figure 1 An input–process–output framework for learning.

Mayer, short-term memory is a temporary and limited capacity for storing and manipulating information while long-term memory is a permanent and structured store of existing knowledge. According to the assimilation theory of learning set forth in the works of Ausubel and Mayer, new information provided through instructions and delivered through technology must go through three cognitive processing steps in order for learning to occur:

1. *Reception.* The first step in the learning process requires that the learner pay attention to incoming information (the target of learning) and then transfer it to short-term memory.
2. *Availability.* Once the new information is perceived by the learner and transferred to short-term memory, it needs to be "anchored" in the relevant knowledge structures that already exist in long-term memory. Thus, existence and availability of the prerequisite concepts is a necessary condition for effective learning.
3. *Activation.* Once the prerequisite knowledge in long-term memory is located, it needs to be accessed and "remembered" by the learner. The prerequisite knowledge is transferred to short-term memory where it is actively processed and combined with the new incoming information.

The incoming information appropriately processed through the three steps of reception, availability, and activation becomes the desired *learning outcome,* which refers to *understanding* and changes in the knowledge structure of the learner. According to Mayer, understanding in this context is distinct from rote memorization and is defined as the potential for using learned information in performing new tasks that are different from what was explicitly taught.

As Fig. 1 indicates, technology applications can enhance the learning process and outcome by facilitating the implementation of the instructional strategy and by eliciting and engaging the underlying cognitive processes of learning. The following example illustrates how this was accomplished in a specific learning situation. A 1993 report by White described a virtual learning system, a computer simulation, used for teaching Newtonian mechanics. Students used the simulation to work with models of force and motion to explore relationships between these two entities in order to learn the corresponding laws of physics. The learning outcomes of the students who used the VLS were consistently superior to the learning outcomes of the students who learned in a traditional environment with the same teacher. In the simulated environment, dynamic and graphical information display

and data processing capabilities of the computer were used to develop rich visual presentations of the information stimulus (i.e., to implement an element of the *instructional strategy*) otherwise unlikely to be available to learners. The computer displays supported the reception phase of learning by eliciting a high level of the learner's interest and attention. An example was the symbolic and dynamic computer presentation of change in entities such as force vectors that correspond to formal constructs of physics and have no direct, concrete referent in the real world. Furthermore, the simulation models were designed to be progressively more sophisticated and complex. In the early models, the students worked only with motion in a horizontal plane. In the later models, the students worked with a combination of motion in both horizontal and vertical directions. The last model of force and motion incorporated a complex mix of continuous motion and various forms of force including friction and gravity. It can be argued that in this case, the computer simulation was used for sequencing and structuring the subject-matter content (two other aspects of *instructional strategy*) and supported the second cognitive phase of learning *(availability)* by providing the prerequisite concepts required for learning the more complex concepts. The students also used the computer simulation to develop the "law" that captured the relationship between the entities of the simulation model. It can be further postulated that the technology provided a forum for learners to generate and test hypothesis, make decisions, and generate responses. These activities enabled the students to explore proactively and link the new information to their existing knowledge and thus facilitated the *activation* phase of the learning process.

To summarize, this section presented a framework that identified the input, process, and output variables associated with learning and their interrelationships. This framework facilitates exploring the potential role of information technology in learning and provides a foundation for the design of virtual learning systems. In the next section, the variables of this framework are linked to specific attributes of VLS discussed in Section II.

A. Linking the Attributes of VLS to the Learning Process

Instructional strategy as defined in the previous section comprises the methods and approaches for displaying information to a learner. The attributes of virtual learning systems described in Section II would each constitute an instructional strategy decision. For example, deciding the nature and structure of interaction, attributes of virtual learning systems, is an important element of instructional strategy. This section will tie the attributes of virtual learning systems to cognitive outcomes.

As previously stated, the reception step in cognitive processing involves stimulating learner attention to incoming information. Several of the attributes of virtual learning may serve as reception catalysts. Specifically, designs that force learners to answer questions before continuing force the learner to pay attention to material in as much detail as is necessary to answer the questions. The assumption is that requiring a cognitive action on the part of the learner stimulates attention. However, it is important to consider the degree of complexity necessary to respond to a question; questions that require a simple response might engender as much boredom as attention. Questions that require the learner to extend thinking well beyond the material presented might create frustration. Thus, the design of response-soliciting systems is crucial to achieving the desired cognitive reception.

Another means of stimulating reception is the use of a range of media rather than a single media to deliver information. Multiple media are thought to increase learner attention. Certainly the dynamic and graphical information display for teaching Newtonian mechanics (the VLS example described in the previous section) was able to create greater learner receptivity than was mere talk. If students are given control over media presentation, they might be more receptive to the incoming information. For example, if students can pause a video presentation, rewind, and relisten, or control the amount of time they listen before pausing, they might be able to pay greater attention than if they are regarded as passive recipients of the information.

The availability phase of cognitive processing requires that existing knowledge structures already in memory be activated and available for interpreting new information. The virtual attributes that might have an impact on availability include the content delivery choices, regarding specifically the linear and nonlinear designs and the progression through the content. Systems that allow learners to choose which topics they will study in which order may fail to ensure that learners have the requisite knowledge to assimilate the new knowledge to which they are exposed in a given learning module. By contrast, systems that are designed in a linearly progressive fashion whereby students must demonstrate mastery of one module before proceeding to the next might be more successful in ensuring that the availability phase of cognitive processing occurs. In the Newtonian mechanics

VLS example, the fact that the simulation models were designed to be progressively more sophisticated ensured that learners mastered concepts of increasing complexity as they worked through the online simulation. The structure of content delivery is also likely to have an impact on availability. Salomon and Amog in 1998 note that hypermedia based information display may help define relations among components, so that the relationships become internalized. In essence, the hypermedia acts as tools to help learners form associative relationships among inputs in a learning event.

The activation phase of cognitive learning deals with the ability of learners to recall relevant knowledge. Of the attributes of virtual learning systems that might affect activation, it is likely that interaction has a major impact. If interaction is required and is structured to ensure that learners stay on relevant topics, then by forcing learners to compose their knowledge, to read others' insights, and to respond to those insights, one is forcing learners to recall their own knowledge and assimilate new knowledge into their existing cognitive frameworks, or at least to interpret new knowledge within their existing framework. It might be that the asynchronous arrangement is even more effective than the synchronous in that it enables learners to more thoughtfully reflect on the knowledge rather than responding with the first idea that comes to mind.

In summary, drawing from Figure 1 and Table III, we suggest that interaction influences activation, with asynchronous, required, structured interaction among students and between an instructor and students being most effective at promoting activation (see Table III). The media choices are expected to influence receptivity, as is student control of delivery. System control over delivery and a linear design are expected to influence availability with systems that require evidence of mastery of information before progression to new material expected to be more effective in ensuring availability than are designs where progression is not tied to

Table III Linking the Phases and Attributes of VLS

Phase	Attribute
Reception	Content: Media: Range of media Content: Control over progression: Student
Availability	Content: Nature: Nonlinear Content: Control over progression: System
Activation	Interactivity: Time: Asynchronous Interactivity: Person: Student–Student Interactivity: Degree: Required

evidence of obtained knowledge. As is evident, virtual learning design decisions are very important in that ultimately, they may be affecting the underlying cognitive processing that occurs during learning.

V. CONCLUSIONS

With the improved performance-price ratios of computing equipment, continued convergence of computing and communication technologies, and the increase in prevalence of the Internet and the World Wide Web, VLS can provide viable and effective educational alternatives. In addition, the increase in demand for learning at all levels and the growth in continuous and part-time learning requirements will fuel the need for development and deployment of various forms of virtual learning systems. However, in most cases, VLS have been developed without explicit consideration of the underlying learning process and contextual factors. In some cases, this approach has resulted in development of state-of-the-art VLS without clear guidelines on how these systems may be used to achieve learning improvements. Under these circumstances, despite the expenditure of resources, the opportunity is lost to create virtual learning environments that are pedagogically effective and even superior to the traditional teaching modes. Thus, it is important to continue the inquiry and investigation into the design of effective virtual learning systems. Many important research questions need to be addressed. We highlight here three important issues.

1. What Are the Enablers of Student Success in VLS?

It is clear that self-discipline is essential for students to succeed with VLS. Robb and Geffen in 2000 suggested structures to ensure that students log on regularly, stay on schedule, and participate in discussion. Aside from controllable aspects, there are also personality elements that might influence student success. The idea that field dependence vs field independence influences learning in VLS was pursued by Ching in 1998. Ching found that field-dependent types were less able to rely on their own judgments, organize their own learning activities, and maintain their own direction. Considering that the majority of VLS studies have not taken individual differences into account, it is important to now consider how individual psychological differences might influence VLS success. Moreover, students bring mental models of learning to any learning situation. In some cases, such mental models might be detrimental, as was found by Tallman and Benson in

2000 who noted that students who thrived on feedback and encouragement on a frequent basis had difficulty adjusting to the VLS environment. However, over time, these mental models can change and learners will become more self-sufficient. Nevertheless, it will be instrumental to consider those factors that help ensure student learning in VLS.

2. If IT Enables New Instructional Methods in VLS, What Are These Methods?

It is often noted that it is not the technology but the instructional implementation of the technology that determines its effect on learning. In conjunction with the implementation are such factors as instructor attitudes toward a technology, teaching styles, and control over the technology. There has been little documentation of the innovative means of using VLS. Given the various attributes of VLS, one can envision a wide array of different instructional implementations. Hence, research that examines the means of applying VLS is useful in helping define new pedagogies with potential learning gains. Related to this issue of new pedagogy is the issue of measurement: In an age of a constructivist, situated, technology-intensive learning environment, what educational achievements should we be measuring? If learning is to increasingly take place through learners' active and personally consequential interactions with peers and within particular, content-rich contexts, how do we ascertain progress and can we rely upon tests that mostly assume that students are isolated entities?

3. How Can Deeper Processing Be Encouraged?

It is widely believed that interaction can promote deeper processing, and that VLS can encourage interaction by giving learners time to think and comment. One reason that interaction is thought to promote activation is that it promotes conflict. The existence of conflict among learners is resolved through discussion and explanations. Studies such as Webb in 1982 and Baldwin, Bedell, and Johnson in 1997 have found that students who give explanations to other learners show higher levels of learning than students not involved in such interactive learning. Lim, Ward, and Benbasat in 1997 suggest that such learning environments, where learners question each other to clarify ambiguities, force learners to engage in deeper level thinking and to focus on "how and why" questions rather than simple factual questions and answers. While it is widely held that interaction has a positive impact on learning, it is worth noting that communication is not one and the same with interaction. Environments that force students to communicate do not necessarily force them to reflect upon the ideas of others, which is the hallmark of interaction. In environments that solicit communication only, there is the possibility that some learners will devote less attention to the actual cognitive activity of reflecting on the ideas of others and instead focus mostly on contributing their own ideas. In such a case, one can argue that the communication has the potential to suppress cognitive activation. Thus, it is necessary to create interaction environments where attention is devoted to designing the environment such that learners must not only communicate, but truly interact. This is especially critical in online discussion groups, where learners might feel that provided they contribute some comments, they are participating. Hence, research is needed to examine the means of eliciting interaction and the outcomes of interaction in VLS.

To summarize, past virtual learning research has largely focused on student learning outcomes in virtual learning environments and student characteristics influencing student motivation to study virtually and student ability to succeed in virtual learning. Both areas of research are critical to our understanding of the effectiveness of virtual learning. While great progress has been made in advancing our understanding of the critical enabling role of information technology in virtual learning environments, we would suggest that it is imperative to gain an understanding of how the explicit design choices one makes in developing virtual learning systems influence the learning process and outcomes. Without careful attention to these decisions, one might inadvertently develop a learning environment that is internally inconsistent. Such a system might conceivably give the learner great control in hopes of individualizing learning, yet fail to ensure that the learner actually obtains the requisite knowledge. The following section offers some suggestions for researching virtual learning systems.

A. Approaches to VLS Research

Most studies of virtual learning systems have adopted classical experimental approaches involving an independent variable (technology intervention) and then investigating and measuring its impact on one or more variables associated with learning outcomes (e.g., student achievement or perceived learning). This form of research studies may result in a limited understanding of the virtual learning systems. In 1991, Kozma stated that this is because these forms of classical experimental approaches examine the potential existence of a direct cause-and-effect relationship between technology and learning and not a potential "causal mechanism"— the underlying, interactive factors that produce events and processes that affect learning. The study of causal mechanisms in VLS is important because of the interconnected nature of various elements associated with learning as depicted in Fig. 1 and discussed in Section IV. The challenge posed by this attribute of virtual learning systems is that changes made in one element of a learning environment reverberate throughout the environment. This implies that VLS studies may need to expand to include approaches that attempt to capture the underlying processes and interactions among various underlying factors, that is, studies of the changes and events as learners interact with the technology interventions in certain ways under certain situational conditions. These processes can be captured through the inclusion of both qualitative and quantitative data. Examples include computer logs reflecting the interactions between the computer and the learners, computer-mediated communications among the learners and the learners and instructor, learner interviews, and asking learners to think out loud while they learn. Thus, inclusion of outcome and process data as well as expanding VLS studies to include both experimental and qualitative approaches will enhance our understanding of virtual learning systems and inform the design of effective systems.

With VLS expected to become ever more prevalent as continuing education needs rise and as traditional and nontraditional educational providers attempt to provide increased accessibility to their services, research that helps uncover the important attributes of VLS and their impacts on the learning process will be critical to our understanding of VLS effectiveness.

ACKNOWLEDGMENT

Work on this article by M. A. was supported by an IBM Faculty Research Award.

SEE ALSO THE FOLLOWING ARTICLES

Future of Information Systems • Groupware • Internet, Overview • Reengineering • Virtual Organizations • Virtual Reality

BIBLIOGRAPHY

Ahmed, R. (2000). *Effectiveness of Web-based virtual learning environments in business education: Focusing on basic skills training for information technology.* Unpublished Doctoral Dissertation, Louisiana State University, Baton Rouge, Louisiana.

Alavi, M. (1994). Computer-mediated collaborative learning: An empirical evaluation. *MIS Quarterly,* June, 159–174.

Alavi, M., and Leidner, D. (2001). Research commentat: Technology-mediated learning–A call for greater depth and breadth of research. *ISR,* Vol. 12, No. 1, 1–10.

Alavi, M., Wheeler, B. C., and Valacich, J. S. (1995). Using IT to reengineer business education: An exploratory investigation of collaborative telelearning. *MIS Quarterly,* September, 293–311.

Ausubel, D. P. (1968). *Educational psychology: A cognitive view.* New York: Holt, Rinehart & Winston.

Baldwin, T., Bedell, M., and Johnson, J. (1997). The social fabric of a team-based M.B.A. program: Network effects on student satisfaction and performance. *Academy of Management Journal,* Vol. 40, No. 6, 1369–1397.

Brownson, K. (2000). Distance education of health care professionals. *Hospital Material Management Quarterly,* Vol. 21, No. 2, 32–41.

Brunswic, A. (1998). Quand il suffisait d'un timbre. *Le Monde; L'education de la culture et de la formation,* September, 12–15.

Butler, W. (1990). The construction of knowledge in an electronic discourse community. Working Paper, University of Texas at Austin, Texas.

Ching, L. S. (1998). The influence of distance-learning environment on students' field dependence/independence. *The Journal of Experimental Education,* Vol. 66, No. 2, 149–160.

Dyrud, M. A. (2000). The third wave: A position paper. *Business Communication Quarterly,* Vol. 63, No. 3, 81–93.

Gagne, R. M., and Briggs, L. J. (1979). *Principles of instructional design,* (2nd ed.), New York: Holt, Rinehart & Winston.

Gist, M., Thomas, E., McQuade, R. E., Swanson, G. L., Lorenzen, S. R., Schmidt, J. R., and Fuller, R.G. (1988–1989). The Air Force Academy instructor workstation (IWS). II. Effectiveness. *Journal of Educational Technology Systems,* Vol. 17, No. 4, 285–295.

Gubernick, L., and Ebeling, A. (1997). I got my degree through e-mail. *Forbes,* June.

Hawthornthwaite, C. (1999). Collaborative work networks among distributed learners, in *Proceedings of the 32nd Hawaii International Conference on System Sciences.* Los Alamitos, CA: IEEE Comput. Soc.

Hill, T., and Chidambaram, L. (2000). Web-based collateral support for traditional learning: A field study, in *Web-based learning and teaching technologies: Opportunities and challenges* (A. Aggarwal, Ed.). Hershey, PA: Idea Group Publishing.

Hiltz, S. R. (1994). *The virtual classroom: Learning without limits via computer networks.* Norwood, NJ: Ablex.

Hiltz, S. R. (1997). Impacts of college-level courses via asynchronous learning networks: Some preliminary results. *Journal of Asynchronous Learning Networks,* Vol. 1, 2.

Horowitz, H. (1988). Student response systems: Interactivity in a classroom environment, in *Sixth Conference on Interactive Instruction Technology for the Society of Applied Learning Technology, February 24.*

Hron, A., Friedrich H., Ulrike C., and Christos G. (2000). Implicit and explicit dialogue structuring in virtual learning groups. *British Journal of Educational Psychology,* Vol. 70, 53–64.

Kozma, R. B. (1994). Will media influence learning? Reframing the debate. *Educational Technology Research and Development,* Vol. 37, No. 1, 67–80.

Leidner, D., and Jarvenpaa, S. (1993). The information age confronts education: Case studies on electronic classroom. *Information Systems Research,* Vol. 4, No. 1, 24–54.

Leidner, D., and Jarvenpaa, S. (1995). The use of information technology to enhance management school education: A theoretical view. *MIS Quarterly,* September, 265–291.

Leuthold, J. (1999). Is computer-based learning right for everyone?" in *Proceedings of the 32nd Hawaii International Conference on System Sciences.* Los Alamitos, CA: IEEE Comput. Soc.

Lim, K., Ward, L., and Benbasat, I. (1997). An empirical study of computer system learning: Comparison of co-discovery and self-discovery methods. *Information Systems Research,* Vol. 8, No. 3, 254–272.

Mayer, R. E. (1981). The psychology of how novices learn computer programming. *Computing Surveys,* Vol. 13, 121–141.

Merrill Lynch. (1999). *The book of knowledge.* New York: Merrill Lynch.

Moore, M. G., and Thompson M. M. (1997). *The effects of distance learning.* American Center for the Study of Distance Education, The Pennsylvania State University.

Neef, D. (1998). *The knowledge economy: Resources for the knowledge-based economy.* Boston: Butterworth–Heinemann.

Reigeluth, C. M., Bunderson C. V., and Merrill, M. D. (1994). Is there a design science of instruction? in *Instructional design theory* (M. D. Merrill and D. G. Twitchell, Eds.). Englewood Cliffs, NJ: Educational Technology Publications.

Richards, I. (1992). Distance learning: A study of computer modem students, in *The Annual Conference of the American Educational Research Association, San Francisco, CA, April, 20–24.*

Richardson, J., Alistair, M., and Woodley, A. (1999). Approaches to studying in distance education. *Higher Education,* Vol. 37, 23–55.

Robb, D., and Geffen, A. (2000). At home with Internet-based training. *Risk Management,* Vol. 47, No. 7, 27–34.

Salomon, G., and Almog, T. (1998). Educational psychology and technology: A matter of reciprocal relations. *Teachers College Record,* Vol. 100, No. 1, 222–241.

Slatin, J. M. (1990). InterChange: Patterns of interaction in classes using a real-time conferencing system as a medium for instruction. Working Paper, Department of English, University of Texas at Austin, Austin, TX.

Spooner, F., Jordan, J., Algozzine, B., and Spooner, M. (1999). Student ratings of instruction in distance learning and on-campus classes. *The Journal of Educational Research,* January/February, 131–140.

Tallman, J., and Benson, A. (2000). Mental models and web-based learning. *Journal of Education for Library and Information Science,* Vol. 41, No. 3, 207–223.

Tucker, R. W. (1995). Distance learning programs, models and alternatives. *Syllabus,* Vol. 9, No. 1, 48–51.

U.S. Department of Education, National Center for Educational Statistics. (1999). *Distance education at postsecondary institutions: 1997–1998,* NCES 200–013 (L. Lewis, K. Snow, E. Ferris, D. Levin, and B. Greene, Project Officer). Washington, D.C.

Van Dusen, G. C. (1997). The virtual campus, *ASHE-ERIC Higher Education,* Vol. 25, 5.

Webb, N.M. (1982). Student interaction and learning in small groups. *Review of Educational Research,* Vol. 52, 421–445.

Webster, J., and Hackley, P. (1997). Teaching effectiveness in technology-mediated distance learning. *Academy of Management Journal,* Vol. 40, No. 6, 1282–1309.

White, B. (1993). TinkerTools: Causal models, conceptual change, and science education. *Cognition and Instructions,* Vol. 1, No. 1, 69–108.

Virtual Organizations

Magid Igbaria and Pruthikrai Mahatanankoon

Claremont Graduate University

GLOSSARY

business process design The integration of a company's operations between or within enterprises to create a better product or service, achieve a faster time-to-market, increase a higher order of customization, or whatever is needed to yield a competitive edge.

information-literate population A computer-proficient population that has the ability to adapt to social and technical changes and understand the new social and physiological impacts in a virtual workplace.

telecommuting The use of information and telecommunication technology that allows employees to access their main office and to do their work remotely.

virtual Something created by information technology that exists in digital form.

virtual factory A joint operational or manufacturing capability of companies linked electronically to produce a product or service, regardless of their physical location.

virtual office Technologically enhanced office that allows employees to work remotely away from their physical offices. It is also sometimes referred to as a virtual workplace.

virtual organizations A group of companies, distributed locally or globally, forming alliances through the use of information technology to collaborate in order to achieve an objective, and dissolving when the objective has been achieved.

virtual product A product or service that exists in digital form and can be delivered through information-based channels.

virtual teams A group of people, distributed locally or globally, working together to exchange information and ideas regardless of time and place.

VIRTUAL ORGANIZATIONS are a group of companies that have forged alliances through the use of information technology in order to collaborate to accomplish a specified objective. Virtual organizations could be distributed locally or globally and are dissolved when the specified objective is attained. The obvious driving forces for virtual organizations include rapid changes in information technology and global competition. Virtual organizational structures that expand beyond traditional organizational boundaries are more complex than typical organizational structures. They also have the capability to transcend the limitations of time and place, and to permit business consortiums—alliances, partnerships, outsourcing companies, and even competitors—to cooperate in ways not previously possible. From their extended relationships, virtual organizations reap the benefits of shared skills, infrastructure, costs, and expanded markets. These benefits also allow virtual organizations to respond quickly to consumers' demands and maximize the speed with which new products are manufactured and delivered. For example, a manufacturing company may employ information technology infrastructures to strengthen its manufacturing capabilities by creating a *virtual factory*. Virtual factories are comparable to virtual organizations in the sense that they also transcend time, place, and organizational boundaries. Some of the benefits of virtual factories include the ability to foster the partners to share knowledge, research and development costs, and even production capacities. This article discusses virtual organizations in an attempt to explore the forces that drive them and to understand various issues and effects caused by these new forms of organizations.

I. WHAT IS "VIRTUAL"?

What do we mean by *virtual*? The definitions given below all describe the meaning of *virtual*.

- Being in essence or in effect though not formally recognized or admitted.
- Existing or resulting in essence or effect though not in actual fact, form, or name.
- Pertaining to a functional unit that appears to be real, but whose functions are accomplished by other means.
- Significant enhanced effects or actions, physical behavior of nonphysical entities, and the supporting use of telecommunications and computing technologies.

These definitions indicate an entity that exists in digital or in logical rather than in physical form. The last definition signifies that a virtual entity exists through the enhancement of information and communication technology. In the information world, the word *virtual* signifies the sense of being digital; something that exists in digital or logical form rather than the physical one. With recent advancements in information and communication technology, the meaning of virtual has been used extensively to represent any forms or functions that can exist without the constraints of time and place, such as virtual workplaces, virtual teams, virtual communities, etc. These virtual entities are generally established with some specific goals to fulfill. For example, a virtual team is a group of people, locally or remotely networked together via information technology infrastructures, teaming up to accomplish a specific mission. Once the mission is achieved, the virtual team is dissolved. Thus, virtuality in this meaning has spawned a new society of its own and has changed the way people live and work.

II. THE DRIVING FORCES

What are the main factors that fuel the creation of virtual organizations? Figure 1 shows the driving forces behind virtual organizations and their different virtual arrangements. After discussing these driving forces, we discuss the various present and future arrangements of virtual organizations.

A. Global Economies

Globalization has led itself to a worldwide global economy. With organizations conducting business across different countries and time zones, the need for new monetary standards has arisen. Regional agreements and organizations, such as NAFTA and the European Union, have opened new kinds of monetary exchange standards that are accepted by trading partners. Electronic money transfers are becoming common among organizations, e.g., direct deposit of paychecks, bank debit cards, and wire transfers. As trading partners carry their transactions across their national borders, much concern exists over the safety of these transactions. Newer methods of transferring money are also being implemented. For example, e-cash is used in business transactions to ensure security, anonymity, and cost reduction of trading partners. These digital monetary exchange standards are a strong force that will continue to drive virtual organizations.

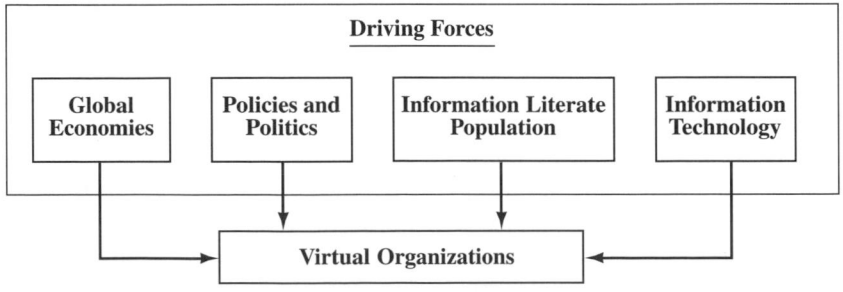

Figure 1   Driving forces of virtual organizations.

Another important force that influences virtual organizations is the adoption of a common language. To increase collaboration among organizations, virtual teams from different parts of the world must use a standardized language. While automatic language translators are being developed, English is emerging as the standard global language for exchanging ideas and information. This will significantly simplify cooperation and mutual understanding among virtual organizations.

Unfortunately, the incompatible telecommunication infrastructures in various countries hinder the adoption of virtual organizations. Active participation among trading partners requires robust telecommunication infrastructures. Not all countries are as technologically advanced as the United States and other developed countries. Countries with lower technological infrastructures will have to invest billions of dollars building telecommunication infrastructures to ensure their participation in the electronic global market. Poor telecommunication infrastructures in many countries combined with other negative factors, such as low computer literacy and high bureaucratic regulations, could impede the rapid transition toward the electronic global market.

B. Policies and Politics

Policies and politics will either encourage or discourage the adoption of virtual organizations. The concern over what should drive the IT policies is still in dispute—should the government interfere with policymaking, or should the government allow the market to drive the IT policies? Government's active role in IT implementation can improve national and business telecommunication infrastructures. By building and maintaining the nation's telecommunication backbones, the government will provide the information gateways to other nations. Furthermore, through government intervention, policies over the regulations involving privacy, security, and copyright laws can be effectively enforced. Trust among trading partners will increase growth of virtual organization settings. However, some researchers fear that if the government allows the market to drive the IT policies, large businesses with high capital will dominate the global marketplace and reduce the ability of normal consumers and small competitors to utilize the intellectual, social, commercial, and political benefits of a global economy. Clearly, effective policymaking will foster virtual organizations and their ability to compete in the global marketplace.

C. Information-Literate Populations

Virtual organizations will lead to modernized workplaces. New office arrangements, or virtual workplaces, require employees to be computer and information literate. The success of virtual organizations will depend heavily on the ability of enlightened populations to exchange ideas and information among themselves and their trading partners. They have to be adaptive to changes in labor and management relations as well. The productivity of virtual organizations also involves their ability to reconcile social and physiological impacts in virtual workplaces. Thus, they must understand and accept the consequences of the new organizational structures by reminding themselves that permanent job security, once offered by traditional organizations, is a thing of the past. This is due to the fact that the nature of virtual organizations requires them to be short lived, flexible, and easily dissolved. Information-literate populations are definitely a necessity if virtual organizations are to function. Governments of different countries must try to radically improve their educational policies and to frequently expose their citizens to information technology at an early age so they will be capable of learning and adapting to changes in the new working environments.

D. Technology

In the information age, technology, as we know it, will enhance our lives only if we know how to use it properly and wisely. Technology also has the same important role in today's businesses as an enabler. This is because technology cannot transform virtual organizations without human assistance. The organizational transformation comes from the information technology-enhanced interactions within different functional entities or among different organizations. In other words, interactive communication technology provides the foundation for organizations to do business electronically around the world. The list below describes some of the important enabling technologies used by virtual organizations:

- Electronic mail is the necessary application foundation for interactive communication.
- Groupware and videoconferencing are essential for continuous and noncontinuous communications. Groupware technology coordinates work teams by making essential information available, tracking workflows, and providing interactive discussions.

- Workflow management provides support for administering workflows, including implementing and redefining business processes.
- Data management and data warehousing are necessary to organize and to sort huge volumes of data.
- Electronic data interchange (EDI) is a mature technology that uses a collection of standard formats for exchanging and communicating data between companies.
- Internet and network infrastructures are the essential backbones that link these interactive communication technologies. Improved networking infrastructures provide the bandwidth, security, and reliability for most interactive applications.

However, not all virtual organizations use every technology as described above. The use of technology varies from one virtual organization to another. The discussion of how various technologies impact the collaborations among virtual organizations is presented later.

III. ARRANGEMENTS OF VIRTUAL ORGANIZATIONS

A. Virtual Organizations

The transformation of hierarchical, traditional organizations into flat, virtual organizations has created much management jargon. These include virtual enterprises, virtual companies, virtual corporations, and networked organizations, all of which could fundamentally be defined as *virtual organizations*. Definitions of virtual organizations include these:

- A form of product-focused partnerships and alliances, which develops a set of virtual operations to accomplish a goal and breaks up after that goal has been achieved. The collaboration requires a systematic approach to redesign work processes, people skills, and technologies.
- Organizations that are enabled by the new medium of computing and communicating developments that exist across conventional organizational structures.
- A combination of firms that possess competencies needed to create a specific product or service to quickly respond to new opportunities and dissolve in a very short period of time.

- A group of allied companies using information and communication technologies to collaborate in the production of a joint product. The location of allied companies may be distributed locally or globally but they function as a single entity.
- Temporary networks of independent companies—suppliers, customers, or even rivals—linked by information technology to share skills, costs and markets.

Obviously, these definitions have some similarities. We can see that virtual organizations are electronically linked alliances or partnerships, each with its own core competencies. These networked alliances are established for a very short period of time to create a specific product or service. Virtual organizations comprised of suppliers, customers, or even rivals are linked by communication and information technology to share essential resources. To create products or services, virtual organizations require extensive collaborative mechanisms to exchange information. They also have to be responsive to environmental changes and customer needs.

The concept of virtual organizations is continuously evolving and definitions still vary from author to author. Researchers suggest that the model of virtual organizations is composed of four variables: *connectivity* through collaboration, *purpose* of existence, *technology usage,* and *undefined boundaries*. Others have defined five essential attributes of virtual organizations: alliances for a common goal, usage of information and communication technology (ICT), undefined expansion of organizational boundaries, active collaboration among alliances, and vertical integration of core suppliers and long-term customers. These attributes help define and limit the scope of virtual organizational research. Thus, virtual organizations can be defined as a group of companies—*distributed* locally or globally—forming an *alliance* through the *use of information technology* to *collaborate* with an *objective* and dissolve when their objective has been achieved.

Smaller units of virtual entities, such as virtual teams and virtual offices, have also become parts of modernized organizations and virtual organizations. It is imperative to point out the differences of how these virtual teams and virtual offices fit into modern and virtual organizations. Figure 2 shows the comparison of the two virtual arrangements.

Modern organizations have created virtual offices (virtual workplaces) to take advantage of telecommuting. Virtual offices furnish their employees with laptops, fax machines, cellular phones, and communication software. They allow employees to work remotely

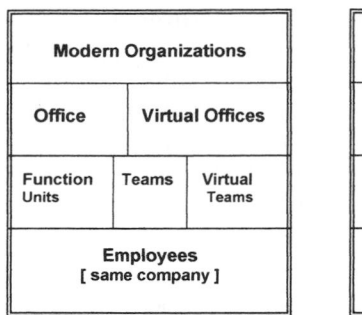 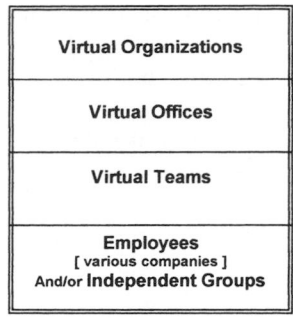

Figure 2 Comparison between modern organizations and virtual organizations.

from their physical offices, such as working from their homes, to save their commuting expenses. Companies can significantly reduce the cost of building extra physical offices by getting employees to coordinate their work with the use of information technology. Functioning units and work teams are also parts of any modern organizations. With the support of virtual offices, virtual teams can coexist with physical work teams in the same organizations. Virtual teams can exchange information and ideas regardless of time and place. They could be working from different local branch offices or overseas branch offices. As we shift toward virtual organizations, virtual teams from different companies can work and collaborate on the same project. In a virtual sense, the virtual teams will also be creating their own virtual offices environments, intentionally or not. Therefore, the main differences between modern organizations and virtual organizations are the fact that the virtual teams within virtual organizations are composed of various companies and their collaboration transcends organizational boundaries.

The arrangements in Fig. 2 imply that both modern organizations and virtual organizations utilize the benefits of information technology to support their operations. However, the technology is used differently. Note that technology acts as an enabler and differs greatly depending on the type of task, objectives, and organizations. To answer what type of organizations utilizes what technology, researchers divide the usage of technology within two categories of organizations: (1) virtual organizations and (2) government or private organizations. Generally speaking, virtual organizations use more technology for external communications and less of it for internal communications. The technologies for external communication include Internet, fax, e-mail, EDI, and teleconferencing. For private or government organizations with virtual teams, internal communication technologies like

groupware, e-mail, and intranets are preferred more than external ones. The results indicate that as the type of organizations vary, so do the levels of IT complexity. Therefore, linking of partners and alliances requires the ability to use information technology to accommodate members with different levels, while providing the members adequate functionality to access and to utilize all of the remote information resources.

1. Reuter Holdings

A good example of a virtual organization is one of the world's largest news agencies, Reuter Holdings in the United Kingdom. In an attempt to meet customer demand, the company needed to create a standardized electronic support system that would be easy to use and accepted by its customers. Customers had to be involved in various stages of the design process. However, doing so required differing expertise that the company did not possess. After conducting some feasibility studies, the company decided to create virtual teams of talented experts and customers from 12 top companies around the world to work on the project. The size of the virtual team continuously changed according to the various tasks at hand with most of the members either from independent sources or from other companies. Currently the virtual team collaborates with the use of computer-based videoconferencing.

The flexibility that the company achieves comes from the fact that most of these employed individuals are not part of its permanent staff. Therefore, it has the ability to maneuver the team's skill sets and roles according to the project or the task it needs to accomplish. Furthermore, through information and communication technologies, skills and knowledge can be learned and shared among virtual team members. It is obvious that the company is continuously reaping the savings on recruitment costs, staff benefits, and other physical overheads. With remote development staffs, the company can work closely with the customers regardless of their physical locations. Customers from various locations can actively participate in the design phase of the system. Through detailed feedback from customers in various development stages, designers and product developers can improve the design and guarantee the user's acceptance of the final system.

2. General Life Insurance

General Life, a subsidiary of General American, is a virtual insurance company that has outsourced everything except its core competencies. Having only as many people in the main office as is necessary and employing outside administrator staffs, the company has greatly lowered its fixed operational costs and now focuses more on increasing its business sales. The main office staff develops its distribution through banks, credit unions and other securities dealers, and forms joint ventures with other insurers. At the same time, it employs outside administrator staffs (normally working remotely) to handle application processing, account commissions, policyholder services, underwriting processes, and other clerical work that comes from its sales agents.

The company also employs a couple thousand mobile sale agents and shares their information via the Internet. Any individual sales agent can obtain all of the information needed to complete his or her sales, such as basic sales information, status of pending new business, daily reports, and changes in policies and product prices. With a personalized, customized home page for every sales agent, customers with a proper access can find price quotes, apply for a new policy, or even make changes to their policies by answering online questions through the agent's secured home page. The system will automatically inform the specific sales agent of such changes.

This method benefits in two ways: The customers' needs are being handled quickly, which leads to increased satisfaction, while the sales agents can spend more time and attention on increasing their sales. The virtual insurance company has gained the rewards by keeping its core competencies and has reduced the operating costs by outsourcing unnecessary operations to its alliances. In comparison with its competitors, the company is more up to date with market trends while maintaining low operational costs. In short, virtual organizations have permitted General Life Insurance to operate effectively and efficiently.

B. Virtual Factories

In contrast to virtual organizations, the term *virtual factories* applies mostly to joint operational or manufacturing capabilities with partner firms. However, the definition of a virtual factory could also be applied to virtual teams in a single company that share knowledge regarding the company's research and development process. The definitions given here convey the fundamental concept of virtual factories:

* An ever-changing network in which partner firms, whose purposes are to create mass customization

product strategy, contribute to the overall enterprise based on their core competencies and produce high-quality, feature- and information-rich products tailored to specific customer needs.
* A temporary alliance of companies coming together to produce rapidly changing worldwide product manufacturing opportunities.
* A community of electronically networked factories, each with its core competencies, that operates as one for agility and cost focus, regardless of their physical location.

The benefits of having such arrangements permit virtual factories to exchange inventory and delivery information, including allowing potential suppliers and customers to gain access to its inventory and production data. The sharing of production information electronically, e.g., computer-aided design (CAD) drawings, manufacturing-process specifications, and know-how, leads to shorter development periods and faster product launch cycles.

1. AeroTech Service Group

AeroTech Service Group, a McDonnell Douglas spin-off, has created virtual factories that join several thousands of its suppliers to the computer-manufacturing network. These interconnections of its manufacturing communities, using the Internet as the main communication platform, have accommodated the collaboration of virtual teams to efficiently build high-performance composite components and complex prototypes. To avoid security threats, computer design files are transferred via a dedicated high-speed link to secure network nodes, which are then viewed by design engineers. The files are then transferred to on-line manufacturing machines to produce the desired products. Small suppliers that could not afford high-speed links can dial into AeroTech using a modem and download designs or programs onto their computers.

Using paperless manufacturing operations, file transfers have saved the company a tremendous amount of operating costs. Other cost savings are realized from the bidding process, which can be done electronically. Instead of inviting representatives of suppliers to its office to view engineering drawings and manufacturing-process specifications, the company now e-mails its suppliers throughout the world about job biddings and lets the suppliers download the information securely through the Internet. Furthermore, to lessen schedule slippage of projects, virtual factories can remotely check on manufacturers and subcontractors via the use of on-line scheduling or project management software. Through on-line links, the company can operate sophisticated software and machinery from afar without having to send technicians to other remote sites. All in all, AeroTech's virtual factories have profited from massive collaboration among its technological partners.

Unfortunately, collaborating electronically with different sophisticated computer manufacturing systems creates integration problems for many virtual factories. A standard protocol is required before systems with various platforms and complexities can communicate. To reduce interoperability problems, the National Industrial Infrastructure Protocols (NIIP) Consortium—a group of organizations working with the U.S. government—has developed an open industry software protocol that allows virtual factories to exchange information despite their underlying platforms. The protocol is based on existing standards, object-oriented technology, and middleware. The emergence of standards will continue to enhance collaboration and create business opportunities among existing and start-up virtual factories.

C. Virtual Products

Today it is commonly imaginable that a culture once based on physical contact is being transformed to one where goods and services can be delivered and performed without the need for face-to-face contact. *Virtual* signifies the sense of being digital; something that exists in digital form rather than the physical form; the value of "products" produced by any virtual organization or any virtual factory normally has information value associated to it. When one speaks of virtual organizations or virtual factories, it is sometimes difficult to distinguish the dissimilarity between *marketplace* and *marketspace*. Marketplace is defined as any traditional physical place where physical goods and services are sold, whereas marketspace is defined as "a virtual realm where products and services exist as digital information and can be delivered through information-based channels."

In marketspace, information can be viewed as a raw material that can be manipulated or formatted to create value for the organization. The company can implement this concept by monitoring the company's operation with information technology and trying to substitute information activities for physical activities. In a typical organization, a physical value chain is a series of value-adding activities starting from raw materials acquisitions, raw materials transformation, and

ending with finished products marketing and delivery. Therefore, in creating a virtual product, the mapping of the physical value chain onto the virtual value chain would allow the company to exercise value-adding activities that turn raw information into new information-based products or services. The product delivery is done through information and communication channels. Figure 3 shows the process of *mirroring* the physical value chain onto the virtual value chain.

After the mirroring of physical activities to virtual activities, companies can create new information-based products or develop new products and services using information technology. According to Rayport and Sviokla, the value-adding processes, or *value matrix*, involves five activities: gathering, organizing, selecting, synthesizing, and distributing of information. For example, in creating a new information-based product, a data warehousing company with the sole purpose of mining essential information for its customers would have to go through the following value-adding processes:

- *Gathering phase:* Collect subject's information for information sources.
- *Organizing phase:* Establish a data repository by making data acceptable for analytical processing and manage its information databases.
- *Selecting phase:* Choose the appropriate analytical processing activities or data mining strategies.
- *Synthesizing phase:* Create new information based on existing information.
- *Distributing phase:* Output results so they can be digested by customers or end users, such as CD-ROM, reports, and web browsers.

Organizations can increase information exchange between product developers, suppliers, and contractors by moving their designs to the virtual value chain. Chrysler Corporation, an automobile manufacturer,

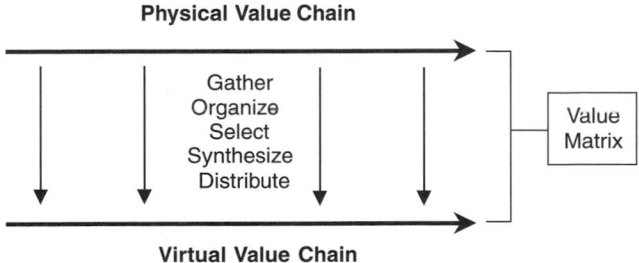

Figure 3 Exploiting the virtual value chain. [From Rayport, J. F., and Sviokla, J. J. (November–December 1995). Exploiting the virtual value chain. *Harvard Business Review*, 75–85.]

is an example of a company that has exploited the virtual value chain to develop new products. To produce automobiles, Chrysler uses a computer-based software for predictive modeling and rapid process prototyping. The CATIA computer system has the ability to replicate automobile production development processes, starting from exterior and interior designs to the final finished products. Using this technology, the company was able to cut the development time of its new automobile models by 8 months and to bring more product lines into the market.

The technology also allows the designers to look into thousands of alternative designs without having to produce a single physical prototype. When it comes to the production of its final designs, which involves multiple suppliers and contractors, the company uses information and communication technology to exchange data among various suppliers and manufacturers. This development method has saved the time and cost involved in exchanging design data.

Another important factor that leads to cost reduction is the use of computer technology to simulate the stamping process of prototype dies. On-line engineers can make modifications and create perfect dies for auto parts, such as hoods and doors, without having to create a real physical model. Its suppliers can be familiar with die specifications ahead of time and go directly to creating the physical dies. Even before final production starts, product testing and validating processes can also be done via computer simulation tools to evaluate and refine final detailed designs. This predesign testing ensures that the final products will meet federal safety requirements. In summary, the virtual product development process enables Chrysler to develop and manufacture its automobiles efficiently and with the most contemporary designs.

Typically, virtual organizations and virtual factories can also launch new virtual products or exploit new marketspace opportunities by analyzing and mapping the existing physical value chain with the virtual value chain. This mirroring of the physical world onto the digital world allows virtual organizations to lower their operation costs, save product development time, improve customer satisfaction, manipulate and reuse its digital assets, and—most importantly—find new opportunities for creating and extracting value beyond the physical value chain.

Generally, organizations establish virtual organizations for a variety of reasons:

- To share existing infrastructure.
- To spread the risk or share the risk among partners.

- To share research and development, including knowledge and know-how.
- To reduce costs.
- To link complementary core competencies for strategic advantages.
- To gain access to new markets.
- To migrate from selling physical products to selling services and solutions along with the products.
- To bring a product to market more swiftly than usual (increase product launch time).
- To share market loyalty and customer brand awareness.
- To increase facilities and perceived size.
- To improve the quality of its products and services.

Whatever their main purposes may be, the creation of virtual organizations generally consists of four distinct life cycle phases—starting from forming the partners to the termination of the relationships. The decisions and changes that virtual organizations make along the life cycle could determine the overall value-added processes that contribute to the achievement of their goals.

IV. VIRTUAL ORGANIZATIONS LIFE CYCLE

Throughout their existence, typical virtual organizations have to go through four phases: identification, formation, operation, and termination phases. Figure 4 shows the life cycle of virtual organizations.

A. Identification Stage

This is the stage that identifies the market opportunities that virtual settings will bring to organizations. The sequential processes in this stage include opportunity identification and opportunity selection. *Opportunity identification* is the process of looking for the potential advantages of forming virtual organizations. Managers need to analyze environmental threats and identify new potential opportunities in marketplace and marketspace. *Opportunity selection* involves the evaluation of potential companies' underlying information infrastructures and the feasibility study of creating and integrating an assortment of companies into new distribution networks. New market opportunities and potential partners are evaluated in detail after the initial examination.

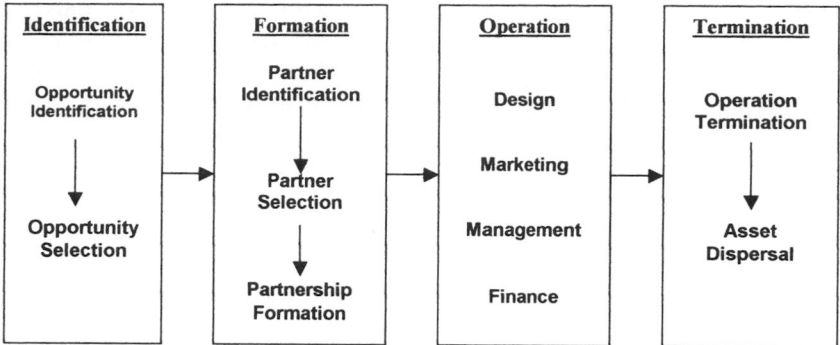

Figure 4 Virtual organizations life cycle model. [From Strader, T. J., *et al.* (1998). Information infrastructure for electronic virtual organization management. *Decision Support Systems,* Vol. 23, 75–94.]

B. Formation Stage

The formation stage or partner selection stage is comprised of three sequential processes: partner identification, partner selection, and partner formation. When prospective partners are identified, the information from the identification stage is used for in-depth *partner identification* to establish a set of potential partners. During the *partner selection* process, each potential partner is evaluated carefully for its culture, business process, information technology infrastructure, and organizational structure to ensure organizational fit among allied members. The *partner formation* process involves the actual formation of these selected partners into virtual organizations. This also includes contractual agreements of profit sharing, objective(s), and the conformity of products and services.

During the partner formation stage, virtual organizations require some kind of establishment through some of these existing collaborative mechanisms:

- Partnerships are normally two or more companies (or project teams) with the determination to share resources, such as customers, cost, and location. Partnership companies can be rivals, but they can also be partners when the circumstance permits them to cooperate competitively. There are several types of partnerships. Joint market partnerships refer to the coordination among rivalries, normally from different industries, to gain access to new customers and market shares. When competitors within the same industry cooperate, we can define the partnerships as intraindustry partnerships. Other examples of partnerships include buyer–seller partnerships (supplier–subcontractors), and IT vendor-driven partnerships that link vendors to major customers.

- Joint ventures are formed by cooperative licensing agreements of business consortiums to share investment costs and to reduce the risk of entering unknown markets. They are often found when companies are exploiting new products or services, especially when entering foreign territories.

- Strategic alliances are established due to the fact that companies need to share their focused strengths—or core competencies with others to free up their noncore activities' resources. This sharing allows the alliances to fully focus on strengthening their core competencies while leaving other noncore activities to be levered by the allied partners. Another kind of alliance is outsourcing. Through contractual agreements, outsourcing brings companies closer to their core operations and permits other competent companies to support their noncore activities. Companies usually outsource the most common functions, such as distribution, information technology, and manufacturing.

C. Operation Stage

This is the actual value-creating process in virtual organizations. Not only do they include the actual creation of products and services, but also other marketplace and marketspace value creation processes, i.e., on-line marketing, financial management, and information distribution channels. The inputs from internal and external environments, such as knowledge, organizational capital, new market opportunities, changes in customers' behavior, and industry trends, are all essential for the success of virtual organizations. The operation stage ends once the initial objective of virtual organizations has been reached or the market opportunities cease to profit from their arrangements.

D. Termination Stage

This stage occurs when virtual organizations have accomplished their goals by successfully bringing quality products or services into the market. Operation termination and asset dispersal happen at this stage. As virtual organizations' operations terminate, all of their legal documents and contracts, accounting information, and profits and losses generated during their existence will be distributed among the partnership companies. After asset dispersal has been done, the independent organizations are free to pursue newer agendas or to form new alliances.

Similarly, the life cycle of traditional organizations also progresses through these stages. However, in virtual organizations, the stages can be accomplished both physically and through information-based channels. Furthermore, while the resources of traditional organizations are generally physically oriented, virtual organizations, in addition, use information and communication technology to maneuver intangible capital, such as knowledge, design, and skills. The interrelationships between humans, technologies, organizations, and tasks have generated several impacts on organizations.

V. INTERRELATED COMPONENTS OF VIRTUAL ORGANIZATIONS

The external driving forces are transforming traditional, centralized, hierarchical organizations into virtual organizations. Globalization, electronic economy, and dynamic business environment force traditional organizations to become more flexible, agile, and responsive to the external environment. At the same time, the rapid development of information and telecommunication technology has generated newer methods of organizing work, people, and other organizational resources. The consequences could lead to the inefficient operation of traditional organizations if they are not prepared to handle continuous environmental changes. To handle these changes, researchers find that information technology not only supports communication within organizations, but also allows them to be more flexible to changes by reducing their hierarchy layers.

Furthermore, IT can be used to change the division of labor and drive autonomous decision making down to the operational level, thereby shrinking middle management and increasing the span of control. The flattening of organizational structures with empowered employees has influenced collaboration and knowledge sharing within the organizations as well. However, the impact of information technology on organizations cannot be analyzed from the perspective of information technology or organizations alone; instead, every component of the organizations must be taken into consideration. Leavitt's perspectives on organizational changes can also be a comprehensible reference model of how one should view changes in virtual organizations. It is suggested that organizations maintain a balance of tasks, people, technology, and structure.

Figure 5 shows how the components of organizations affect each other. A change in one of the components will cause changes in all components, and vice versa. Changes in one of the components, organizational structures, for example, would influence how people behave, how technology can support the structure, and how the task can be carried out. This indicates that organizations are at a constant flux with all of the components interrelated and mutually adjusting. Even if we analyze one component independently, we must not neglect the fact that all interrelated components must be taken into consideration.

A. Technology

While the structure of traditional organizations is generally defined by their physical parameters, virtual organizations use information and communication technology to create informal structures that facilitate flexibility and collaboration. Not only does technology enable new ways of doing business, but it also creates new ways of collaborating within organizations and among them. Enabled by technology and communication infrastructures, virtual workplaces create organizational and social components that give them an office-like appearance. Typical virtual workplaces furnish virtual teams with laptops, fax machines, cellular phones, and communication software that facil-

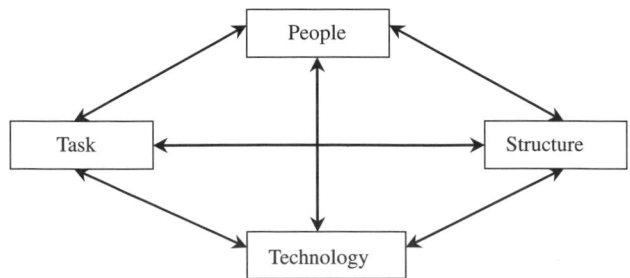

Figure 5 Leavitt's components of organizations. [From Leavitt, H. (1965). Applied organizational change in industry. In J. March (ed.), *Handbook of Organizations.* pp. 1144–1170. Chicago: Rand McNally.]

itate a variety of remote working environments without being present.

Categorized by the degree of mobility and the characteristics of working environments, the continuum of virtual workplaces includes:

- *Telecommuting.* A working environment where an employee has a fixed office at home or a nearby remote branch office.
- *Hoteling.* A working environment where an employee needs to visit the office occasionally, however, he or she is not allocated to a specific office space.
- *Tethered in office.* A working environment where an employee has some mobility but needs to report to his or her office regularly.
- *Home-based office.* A working environment where an employee works at her home equipped with information and communication tools that lessen the need to visit the office.
- *Fully mobile.* A working environment where an employee is at the customer site.

Normally, within virtual offices, virtual workers operate in teams. Virtual teams are defined as groups of people working on a specific task or goal without the restriction of place or time. Essentially, virtual teams are the core units that create value for virtual organizations by bringing together partnerships' core competencies and producing information-based products and services. Using the concepts of time and place by Johansen, we can decide on certain virtual team technologies that match any virtual team task.

In Table I, *time* refers to the synchronicity of the meeting; either a meeting can occur at the same time—synchronous, or occur at any time—asynchronous. *Place* refers to the physical place where a meeting takes place, which can be in the same place or in different places. Virtual teams may use all of the above technologies to collaborate. Normally, the team may want to start with *synchronous* face-to-face meetings in order to become familiar and to gain some trust among the members, and then later they can continue on with other *asynchronous* communication technologies.

B. Organizational Structures

Traditional hierarchical organizations rely on their structures to coordinate resources by providing rigid lines of command and control. They must deliver their products and services through the assignment and coordination of available resources. Unfortunately, organizations are now facing intensive worldwide competition that requires them to search for a more effective way of managing resources. Through the use of information and telecommunication technology, top managers are having direct control, coordination, and resources reallocation—a job that was previously done by middle managers.

As middle managers' tasks are being replaced by information technology, operational-level employees are also being empowered by their new roles and decision-making capabilities. This has resulted in flatter and less bureaucratic organizations with an expanded scope of control and empowered employees. Changes in organizational structures are not without painful restructuring, such as layoffs, reengineering, partnerships, and alliances. As organizations rely on a structure to achieve business objectives, they must also restructure themselves to correspond to market demand.

Enabled by information technology to be more responsive, virtual organizational structures have provided organizations with the agility and flexibility to meet this demand. However, since the use of information technology influences organizational structures, it is hard to identify the precise structure of virtual organizations. Some researchers define the structure of virtual organizations as "fuzzy" structures, which are appropriate for organizations to cope with environmental uncertainty. Fuzzy structures can also be described as organizations whose organizational structures follow the demand and performance requirements of their tasks. Therefore, the structures of virtual organizations are characterized by the shrinking of the middle management level, decentralization of the operational management level, high management span of control, flattened hierarchy, and fuzzy

Table I Concepts of Time and Place[a]

	Same time	Different times
Same place	Synchronous/colocated (traditional face-to-face meeting)	Asynchronous/colocated (local groupware, LAN, intranet, information centers)
Different places	Synchronous/separated (real-time text/audio/video conferencing)	Asynchronous/separated (Internet, e-mail, groupware, shared databases)

[a]Johansen, R. (1988). *Groupware: Computer support for business teams.* New York: Free Press.

structures that are flexible to meet the task and external environment uncertainties.

In addition, these characteristics require virtual organizations to restructure themselves to be more responsive to their customers and to take advantage of information sharing within virtual teams. This restructuring includes the redesigning of division of labor, power distribution, decision-making processes, motivation and rewards, sharing of knowledge and resources, and trust within virtual teams.

Some virtual organizations have gone through the process of reengineering to create greater customer focus and higher customer responsiveness by taking advantage of information technology and replacing their inefficient business processes with virtual teams. By including customers as part of their virtual teams, reengineered virtual organizations can customize their products and reduce new product development cycle time through optimized workflows. Reengineering for virtual organizations has created effectiveness with less trade-off of efficiency. Importantly, reengineered virtual organizations must not neglect the significance of empowering and training their virtual workers to be aware of their roles in the value-added business process.

C. People and Their Tasks

While the virtual workplace provides the benefits of flexibility and cost savings and improves customer relationships, the true benefits only come with the ability of the manager to assess the nature of task and business objectives along with the new approach to administering, controlling, organizing, and communicating among employees. They must also be empowered through responsibility, authority, knowledge, and tools to complete their tasks.

In order for any virtual working environment to be productive, virtual workers must be equipped with the knowledge to operate information technology tools and the know-how to boost productivity. Most importantly, employees themselves need to be computer and information literate and self-motivated. In essence, besides being proficient in technologies, the qualities of virtual workers are composed of the following:

- They must adapt their mental models to new virtual model by believing in trust, being a team player, sharing knowledge, and working for results.
- They must act proactively to seek knowledge and information.
- They must adapt to continuous learning and know

that the roles of teacher and learner are flexible and interchangeable.
- They must understand the virtual organization's commitments, processes, and goals.
- They must have the ability to handle stress.

With a common goal, a virtual team needs collaboration, socialization, and communication skills to accomplish its task. *Collaboration skills* are the ability of the team to accomplish the task by establishing ways to fulfill a given task, generate new ideas, and create a consensus that solves the problems. Team members must understand the process of conflict handling and exchange ideas without criticism. *Socialization skills* include the ability to participate, the ability to understand team's behavior, and the awareness of each member and their interdependence. Social skills promote truthful team norms, which will enhance the team's ability to sustain productive and positive interaction throughout its existence. *Communication skills* involve using a common language that everybody in the team feels comfortable with and solving the difficulties of communicating through computer-mediated media.

It is also important to emphasize the importance of managing the emerging virtual workforce. In a virtual environment, employees can now make the decision to work in a variety of locations, and as the workforce becomes dispersed, understanding and managing the human dimension—empowering employees and balancing between their work and families—still pose many great challenges for human resource personnel. The benefits of any virtual workforce come not only from the employees' understanding of information and communication technology, but also through effective management skills, which require a whole new paradigm of thinking in terms of social and technical relationships.

Therefore, management also has to embrace a new view of obscure organizational boundaries as it relies heavily on information infrastructure. On the one hand, managers need to manage the external collaboration among partners of virtual organizations, and on the other hand manage the internal working processes of virtual teams.

In managing the *external* relationships, managers need to embrace a new view of organizational boundaries. The organizational boundaries are now moving away from the physical foundations to being defined by the ability to intercommunicate electronically. This view includes being as close to the customer as possible, and performance is measured by how well the customer's requirements are satisfied. Furthermore, managers must pay much more attention to aligning the social and economic boundaries. All partners in the virtual organizations need to develop a shared vision of the organization's goals and how the organizations will function. For effective virtual organizations management, this external view resides within three management categories.

1. *Opportunity seeking* should start before any organization decides to form virtual organizations. Managers should fully grasp the foundation and the consequences of this new entity. The responsibility of seeking new opportunities are as follows:
   i. Identifying potential market opportunities by looking for potential advantages of forming virtual organizations and analyzing the environmental threats and identifying new potential opportunities.
   ii. Advertising organizational capabilities and promoting benefits to potential partners.
   iii. Identifying potential virtual organizations partners through the process of evaluation of potential firms' underlying information infrastructure, therefore, integrating potential firms into one distribution network.
2. *Customer relation* deals with creating new value for the customers by:
   i. Seeking and gathering information about the external environment, such as customers'

trends, competitors' movements, and other marketing research.
   ii. Advertising virtual products and services through traditional media and on-line media and supporting transactions between the virtual organizations and customers by creating values for on-line virtual communities.
3. *Interorganizational collaboration* is the most difficult task of managing virtual organizations. Not only do virtual managers have to coordinate activities between partners, but also their tasks of integrating business processes and designing new workflows between selected partners are quite laborious. The integration of two or more companies' processes could lead to delays or even integration failure among the partners. After the successful integration phase, virtual managers have to participate in the supporting roles of operational and collaborative functions among partners.

In managing virtual teams, managers also require a whole new paradigm of thinking about human and knowledge assets, and at the same time educate employees in the skills of collaborating, socializing, and communicating with the rest of the team members. Davenport and Pearlson have suggested five key aspects of managing and leading a virtual team. Table II shows the summary of a virtual manager's managerial tasks.

Table II Managing Virtual Work[a]

Managerial aspects	Tasks
People	• Educate on work strategies in the virtual working environments. • Assess training programs to improve skills. • Advise how to deal with work–family relationships
Information	• Educate virtual workers on the strengths and weaknesses of various technologies for collaborating. • Educate virtual workers on how to be more effective in providing and consuming shared information. • Create new information flows and/or processes in the absence of physical contact.
Teams	• Encourage and coach rather than supervise. • Handle conflict among workers. • Facilitate and train in the use of groupware tools.
Processes	• Improve key operational processes. • Monitor customers' satisfaction and demand. • Design control and supervision processes to oversee virtual workers, but allow them to work autonomously.
Facilities	• Create technical support center(s) for virtual workers. • Manage the existing traditional office or main facility. • Supervise the deployment process of virtual offices.

[a]From Davenport, T. H., and Pearlson, K. (Summer 1998). Two cheers for the virtual office. *Sloan Management Review*, 51–65.

The final criterion to be an effective virtual manager is to have strategic vision. This vision only comes from the collection and assessment of knowledge that is garnered over time. As Warner and Witzel put it, "a virtual general manager, like the virtual organization, is in fact orchestrating a highly diverse medley of tangible and intangible elements, fused together to make a harmonious whole . . . [he or she] must be someone who can feel equally at home in cyberspace and in the real world, who can work and think in real time, and who can control networks from either a single point or from distributed locations."

VI. BENEFITS OF VIRTUAL ORGANIZATIONS

The benefits of virtual organizations only come to be realized when the organizations have gone through a painstaking change of its structure, processes, value, and cultures, in addition to the high investment costs of information and communication infrastructures. There are warnings of potential drawbacks that managements have to take into consideration. These drawbacks come from the uncertain nature of virtual organizations themselves. Table III summarizes some of the potential drawbacks and solutions. However, researchers found that the benefits of virtual organizations come from:

1. *Increased competitive capabilities.* Collaborative mechanisms of various virtual organizations foster them to draw core resources from dispersed locations, even from different cultures and countries, and to compete locally and globally. Alliances of smaller companies, each outfitted with its own core competencies, can now compete with their larger rivals and build barriers to entry.

2. *Operational flexibility.* To be responsive and flexible, virtual organizations have the luxury of changing their partners after reaching the objective(s), thus, the resources can be utilized and reallocated to their optimum. Also, most work in virtual organizations is done through electronic means of communication; employees' skills, knowledge, and resources can be shared from any remote office. With customers routinely linked to the systems, product designers can work closely with them and, hence, improve customization and reduce product development time.

3. *Greater response to customer demands.* Because they may consist of virtual teams that are customers, virtual organizations get a better response from their customers. They also have few bureaucratic restrictions on business procedures. Thus, customers' demands and criticisms are handled promptly. Any questions the customers have

Table III Potential Drawbacks and Risks in Virtual Organizations

Drawbacks	Issues	Potential solutions
Organizational	• High collaboration cost. • Constantly changing organizational structures. • Inconsistent commitment of various parties.	• The relationships must be abandoned when goal(s) has been achieved. • Virtual organizations must work and agree on a consensus. • Management must create written legal contracts.
Technology	• Incompatible information and communication infrastructures. • Task and technology mismatch. • High investment cost.	• Management must perform extensive and technological feasibility study. • The sociotechnical perspective must be integrated with the redesign of business process. • Investment in technology needs cost and benefit evaluation.
Social	• Lack of trust and commitment within virtual teams. • Unclear roles between work and home life. • Increased work stress. • Socially isolated, lacking stimulus of personal contact and feedback. • Low organizational commitment and high staff turnover. • Misunderstanding due to cultural differences.	• Members of virtual teams must develop a high degree of mutual trust and understanding among themselves by initially meeting face to face. • Managers must educate virtual teams about work–family issues. • The relationships must be abandoned when trust among partners cannot be achieved. • Managers need to work as team leaders that coordinate, provide directions, and coach virtual teams. • Virtual teams have to be empowered. • Organizational and cultural differences must be addressed clearly.

regarding the products and services can be found on-line. This rapid adaptation to environmental changes and on-line services to customers will advance the relationship with the tendency to create customers' loyalty.

4. *Reduced cost.* Cost reduction not only comes from reduced traveling costs and omitted physical location, but also from reduced product development costs as well. Changing product designs and soliciting consumers' taste contribute to product development cost; however, linking customers to the earlier design phase lowers the overall cost of the product development process. Other advantages of reduced product development costs include shorter development cycles, shorter design cycle times, and a decrease in the total product design time. The agile, virtual functional structures also allow key employees to hold different positions and roles without the need to hire additional employees. Improved control over inventory and production planning are also another cost savings.

5. *Improve communication and internal control.* Working from different time zones is no longer a constraint. While utilizing appropriate information and communication technology according to the nature of the task, virtual teams are capable of communicating concurrently worldwide. Management can have more effective and efficient decision making through on-line systems. Just-in-time skill polling is done according to the task at hand.

VII. CONCLUSIONS

Globalization and competitive forces in the business world are gradually driving organizations to adapt quickly to social and economic changes. To remain competitive in the global market, the establishment of virtual organizations allows companies to be flexible and to do business regardless of time and location. This article discussed the driving forces—economy, information technology, political, and social—that influence the establishment of virtual organizations.

We presented definitions of some of the fundamental components of virtual organizations such as virtual factories, virtual products, virtual teams, and virtual offices. These components are the underlying operating engine and the essential building blocks that constitute virtual organizations. We further suggested that structure, task, technology, and people are interrelated and influence the operation of virtual organizations. Finally we identified the benefits and risks that virtual organizations may bear. The conclusion is that as technology becomes more sophisticated and permits better collaboration among organizations, the creation of virtual organizations becomes inevitable.

SEE ALSO THE FOLLOWING ARTICLES

Future of Information Systems • Outsourcing • Reengineering • Resistance to Change, Managing • Telecommuting • Virtual Reality

BIBLIOGRAPHY

Agres, C., Edberg, D., and Igbaria, M. (1998). Transformation to virtual societies: Forces and issues. *The Information Society,* Vol. 14, No. 2, 71–82.

Barnatt, C. (1995). Office space, cyberspace and virtual organization. *Journal of General Management,* Vol. 20, No. 4, 78–91.

Davenport, T. H., and Pearlson, K. (Summer 1998). Two cheers for the virtual office. *Sloan Management Review,* 51–65.

Gackenbach, J. (1998). *Psychology and the Internet: Intrapersonal, interpersonal, and transpersonal implications.* San Diego: Academic Press.

Grenier, R., and Metes, G. (1995). *Going virtual, moving your organization into the 21st century.* Englewood Cliffs, NJ: Prentice-Hall.

Hardwick, M., and Bolton, R. (1997). The industrial virtual enterprise. *Communications of the ACM,* Vol. 40, No. 9, 59–60.

Hardwick, M., Spooner, D. L., Rando, T., and Morris, K. C. (1996). Sharing manufacturing information in virtual enterprises. *Communication of the ACM,* Vol. 39, No. 2, 46–54.

Igbaria, M., and Tan, M. (1998). *The virtual workplace.* Hershey, PA: Idea Group Publishing.

Johansen, R. (1988). *Groupware: Computer support for business teams.* New York: Free Press.

Kent, A., and Williams, J. G. (1999). *Encyclopedia of computer science and technology,* Vol. 40. New York: Mercel Dekker.

Leavitt, H. (1965). Applied organizational change in industry. In J. March (ed.), *Handbook of Organizations.* Chicago: Rand McNally.

Rayport, J. F., and Sviokla, J. J. (November–December 1995). Exploiting the virtual value chain. *Harvard Business Review,* 75–85.

Shao, Y. P., Liao, S. Y., and Wang, H. Q. (1998). A model of virtual organization. *Journal of Information Science,* Vol. 24, No. 5, 305–312.

Strader, T. J., Lin, F. R., and Shaw, M. J. (1998). Information infrastructure for electronic virtual organization management. *Decision Support Systems,* Vol. 23, 75–94.

Upton, D. M., and McAfee, A. (July–August 1996). The real virtual factory. *Harvard Business Review,* 123–133.

Warner, M., and Witzel, M. (1999). The virtual general manager. *Journal of General Management,* Vol. 24, No. 4, 71–92.

World Wide Web. Available at http://www.virtual-organization.net/ and http://www.isworld.org.

Virtual Reality

William R. Sherman and Alan B. Craig

National Center for Supercomputing Applications

GLOSSARY

augmented reality (AR) A type of virtual reality in which synthetic stimuli are registered with and superimposed on real-world stimuli. Often used to make information about the real world perceptible that is otherwise imperceptible to the human system.

cyberspace The space created by technology that allows people physically located anywhere to communicate as if in one location.

experience (1) Something personally encountered, undergone, or lived through; (2) relative to VR, can be used either to describe the world created by the application authors (VR experience), or to describe a specific encounter a person has with a VW presented in VR (participatory experience).

field-of-regard A visual display property, this is the percentage of sensorial coverage that can possibly be displayed to the user in a particular sense, that is, how much the viewer is enveloped by any given sense; e.g., for visual displays a participant using a tracked HMD can see the virtual world in any direction they look (100% coverage). However, in a 3-screen CAVE, coverage is only 50% of all possible viewing directions; E.g., for force displays, a world-grounded display has only a limited amount of "reach," presenting information only within that area, and thus has a limited field-of-regard.

field of view Width of a visual display with respect to the eyes.

haptic perception Senses related to feeling the environment—combination of mechanoreceptive (tactile) and proprioceptive (force) sensations.

head-based display A (mobile) display that is physically coupled to the participant's head—this coupling can be accomplished simply by holding the device to the eyes (e.g., like a pair of binoculars) or by attaching it more directly (via a hat or helmet).

head-mounted display (HMD) A type of head-based display that is worn. It often does not include external support for bearing the weight of the device. (When this term changes to "head-worn display," it will signify a great improvement in the technology, for example, to something akin to wearing eyeglasses.)

simulation (1) A model that imitates the behavior of some process; (2) relative to VR, a computer program that describes the rules that govern a virtual world; (3) the computer model of the world of a virtual environment; (4) a computational model of a "natural" process such as atmospheric dynamics, financial fluctuations, military operations, mechanical devices, etc.

stationary display A display that is fixed with respect to the world—usually used to refer to a class of visual displays, but can also indicate other sensory displays such as speakers.

telepresence The ability to directly interact (often via computer mediation) with a physically real, remote environment from the first-person point of view. There are no restrictions on where the remote environment can be or the size of the remote interface device.

tracking The operation of sensing the position (location and/or orientation) of an object in the physical world—usually at least part of the participant's body.

virtual Indicates that an entity mimics the characteristics of another; in the context of a virtual world, any object in that world can be said to be virtual; e.g., a virtual kitchen with a virtual table mimic the appearance and perhaps function of the real counterparts.

virtual reality (VR) A medium composed of interactive computer simulations that sense the participant's position and actions, providing synthetic feedback to one or more senses—giving the feeling of being immersed or being present in the simulation.

virtual world (VW) (1) The contents of some medium; (2) a space that exists in the mind of its creator—often manifested in some medium; (3) a description of a collection of objects in a space, and the rules and relationships governing those objects.

world physics The "laws of nature" which govern a (virtual) world.

When we speak of **"VIRTUAL REALITY,"** we refer to a computer simulation that creates an image of a world that appears to our senses in much the same way we perceive the real world, or "physical" reality. In order to convince the brain that the synthetic world is authentic, the computer simulation monitors the movements of the participant and adjusts the sensory display(s) in a manner that gives the feeling of being immersed or being present in the simulation. Concisely, virtual reality is a means of letting the participant physically engage in some simulated environment which is distinct from their physical reality.

Virtual reality is a medium—a means by which humans can share ideas and experiences. We use the word *experience* to convey an entire virtual reality participation session. The part of the experience that is "the world" witnessed by the participant and with which they interact is referred to as the *virtual world*. However, the term "virtual world" does not only refer specifically to virtual reality worlds. It can also be used to refer to the content of other media, such as novels, movies, and other communication conventions.

A more formal definition of virtual reality would be a medium composed of interactive computer simulations that sense the participant's position and actions, providing synthetic feedback to one or more senses— giving the feeling of being immersed or being present in the simulation.

Note that the definition states that a virtual reality experience provides synthetic stimuli to one or more of the user's senses. A typical VR system will substitute at least the visual stimuli, with aural stimuli also frequently provided. A third, less common, sense that is

included is skin sensation and force feedback, which is jointly referred to as the haptic (touch) sense. Less frequently used senses include vestibular (balance), olfaction (smell), and gustation (taste).

There are many specialty hardware devices involved in bringing the rendered sensory images to the user from the proper perspective. A familiar VR visual display device is the head-mounted display (HMD) (Fig. 1). An HMD is a device that the user wears on their head containing a screen positioned in front of each eye. Another common technology used to display the visual part of a VR experience is to project the images onto a large screen or multiple screens that cover a sizable amount of the participant's view. Such displays date back to flight simulation projection domes and to the work of Myron Krueger (an early VR researcher) in the 1970s. This type of VR visual display is generically referred to as a large-screen stationary display.

As our formal definition suggests, an equally if not more important aspect of a virtual reality system is sensing the participant's position. Without informa-

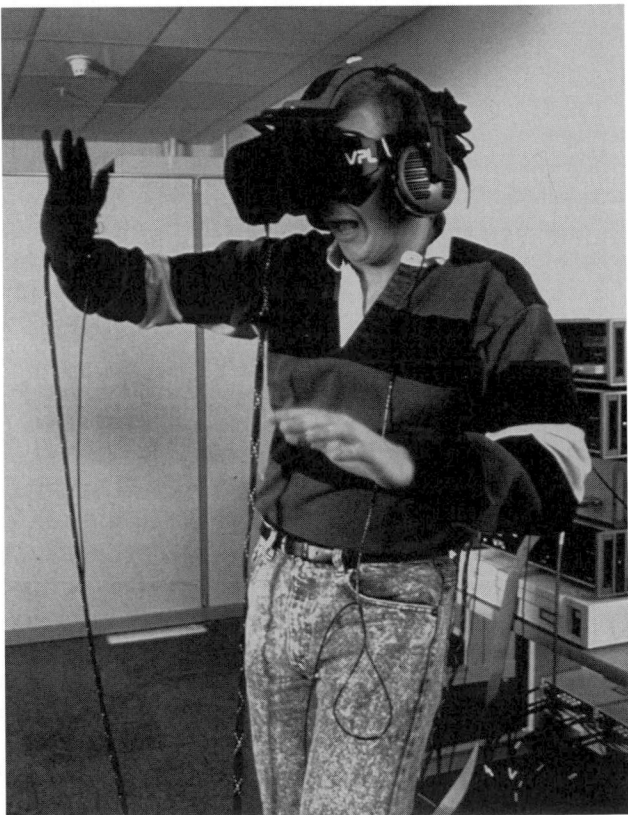

Figure 1 A virtual reality participant wearing a head-mounted display and a glove input device interacts with a virtual world. (Image courtesy NCSA.)

tion about the direction the user is looking, reaching, pointing, etc., it is impossible for the VR output displays to appropriately stimulate the senses. Monitoring the user's body movements is called *tracking*.

There are some related technological terms that are also often used in the discourse of virtual reality technology. However these terms are not necessarily restricted to VR. One such term is cyberspace. *Cyberspace* is the notion that people who are physically located in disparate physical locations can, through the use of some mediating technology, interact as if they were physically proximate. Thus, even technology such as the telephone can put two or more people in the same cyberspace.

Two other terms related to virtual reality and to one another are telepresence and augmented reality (AR). *Telepresence* is similar to VR, in that it is a means to virtually place a participant in another location in which they are not physically present. The difference from VR is that this location is actually a real place that for one reason or another is too difficult, dangerous, or inconvenient for the person to visit in person. Like telepresence, *augmented reality* gives the user an altered view of the real world. However, the view they are given is of their current physical location, and using technology with many characteristics in common with virtual reality, additional (virtual) information is added to their normal sensory input. Frequently, it is the visual sense that is augmented, providing the user with abilities such as peering through walls or seeing into a patient's body.

I. BRIEF HISTORY OF VR

If one considers virtual reality to be the simulation of an environment that allows a person to experience some place and event other than where they actually are and what is actually happening around them, then flight simulators are an early example of this medium. Flight simulators based on interactive computer displays date back to the early 1970s. Earlier flight simulators made use of mechanically driven instrument displays driven by linkages to the pilot's flight controls such as the yoke, rudder pedals, etc. Many of the pre-computer flight simulators were pedantic mechanical devices to give a future pilot the opportunity to become familiar with the flight controls and displays.

Later, by controlling the motion of a video camera over a scale model of some terrain, a sense of immersion was created. Although this did fulfill the criteria for virtual reality portrayed in the opening paragraph of this section, these early flight simulators were not general purpose environments. A different simulator had to be constructed for each type of aircraft, and additional terrain models created for new locations. General purpose simulation was only possible after the advent of advanced computer graphics and display technologies.

In the following 11 examples of research efforts of different groups in VR development one can gain a sense of how current VR technology came to be.

A. Morton Heilig's Sensorama

Early sensory display experiences included the Sensorama. The Sensorama was the brainchild of cinematographer and inventor Morton Heilig. Demonstrated in 1956, Sensorama was a scripted multimodal experience in which a participant was seated in front of a display screen equipped with a variety of sensory stimulators. These stimulator displays included sound, wind, smell and vibration. The noninteractive scenario was driving a motorcycle through an environment with the appropriate stimulators triggered at the appropriate time. For example, riding near a bus exposed the rider to a whiff of exhaust.

The Sensorama system, however, was lacking a major component of the modern virtual reality system—response based on user's actions.

B. Ivan Sutherland's Vision for Computer-Based Virtual Reality

In 1963, Harvard graduate student Ivan Sutherland demonstrated "Sketchpad," an interactive computer generated visual imagery displayed on a cathode ray tube. In 1965, he described a vision for an immersive computer-based synthetic world display system. His vision included the presentation of visual, aural, and haptic feedback in appropriate response to the user's actions. By 1968, Sutherland (as a Professor at the University of Utah) had realized and publicly demonstrated a system that accomplished the visual component of his vision.

Sutherland's system included a head-mounted display (HMD), mechanical head tracking using spooled retractable cables, and a computer program that rendered a simple stick representation of a cyclo-hexane molecule in three dimensions (Fig. 2).

Sutherland later co-founded Evans and Sutherland Computer Corporation (E&S) and developed sophisticated realtime graphics rendering hardware for the flight simulator community.

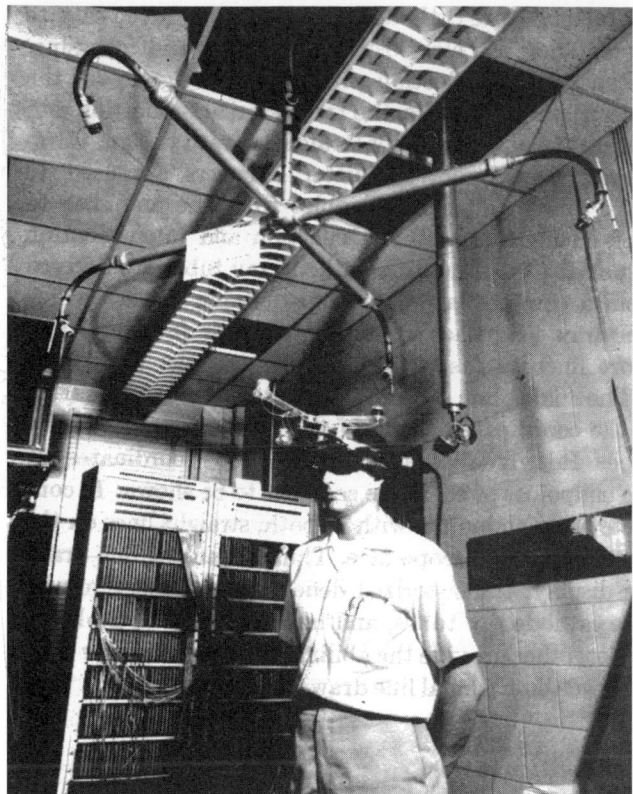

Figure 2 Ivan Sutherland demonstrates the first HMD virtual reality system. (Image courtesy Ivan Sutherland.)

Figure 3 In Krueger's *artificial reality*, a video camera is used to place an overlay of the participant's body on the virtual world. (Image courtesy Myron Krueger.)

C. Myron Krueger's Videoplace

Following Sutherland's demonstration, a variety of research and development efforts were born in university laboratories, government and military facilities, and later in the commercial sector.

In the academic community, University of Wisconsin researcher Myron Krueger was experimenting with a different perspective on virtual reality systems, which he referred to as *Artificial Reality*. Whereas Sutherland's head-mounted display was especially suited for a first person point of view in the virtual world, Krueger's artificial reality provided a second person view of a virtual world in which the participant could watch themselves within the world.

Krueger's systems also differed from Sutherland's work in that he used video camera inputs to track the user's movements. Use of video camera technology resulted in two significant differences: the machine's perspective of the user was from the second person point of view, and the user was not encumbered by any mechanical devices or other sensors attached to their body (Fig. 3).

Other universities pursued various aspects of the virtual reality problem.

D. University of North Carolina at Chapel Hill (UNC)

In the late 1960s, computer science department founder and professor Fred Brooks espoused the need to have development work geared toward specific application problems. For example, a chemist would be interested in how two molecules dock together. Brooks' team also measured the benefits and pitfalls of their various innovations.

Due to the unavailability of capable hardware at the time, UNC also had to focus on hardware development, including high performance graphics engines, head-mounted displays, and a variety of input and output devices including devices to provide haptic feedback in the form of responsive forces. Several commercial products have evolved from the innovative research at UNC.

E. Electronic Visualization Lab at the University of Illinois at Chicago (EVL)

At the University of Illinois at Chicago, Tom DeFanti and Dan Sandin co-founded the Electronic Visualization Lab (EVL) where different types of graphical representations, input and output devices, and interaction techniques were explored. Most notable among their achievements included the development of the

Sayer glove in 1977 (a glove outfitted to sense the bend of the wearer's fingers), and in 1992, the announcement the CAVE visual display system. The CAVE is a walk-in virtual reality theater typically configured as a 10′ cube with three or more of its surfaces rear-projected with stereoscopic, head-tracked, computer graphics (Fig. 4).

F. Human Interface Technologies Laboratory at the University of Washington in Seattle

The Human Interface Technologies Laboratory (HIT-Lab) at the University of Washington in Seattle has performed extensive research on visual display hardware, including a device which projects directly on the retina of the eye. They are noted for other interface technologies such as include the "magic book" concept which couples augmented reality with optical tracking. These magic books are normal books when viewed without supplemental apparatus but when viewed using their display interface additional animated 3-D graphics content emerges from the pages of the book (Fig. 5).

G. National Aeronautics and Space Administration (NASA)

In order to best serve the space and aeronautics research community, NASA often pursues new display and input technologies. Early research work at NASA

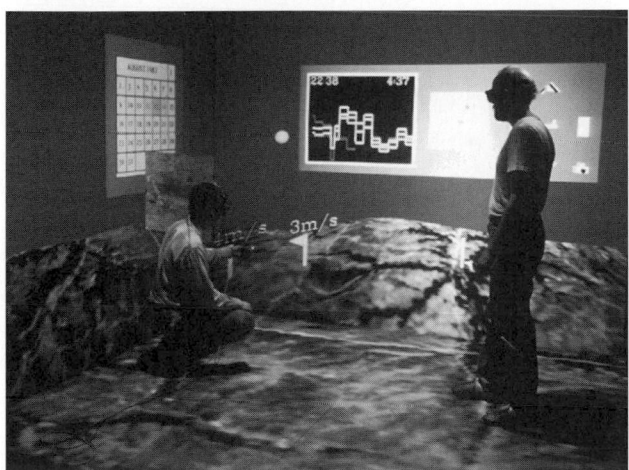

Figure 4 In the CAVE, participants stand surrounded by screens onto which the virtual world is displayed. (Image courtesy NCSA.)

led to the development of the DataGlove in 1985 (commercialized and sold by VPL Inc.) Other VR related research at NASA that has been productized in spinoff companies include the BOOM (binocular omni-orientation monitor) display device in 1987. The BOOM is similar to an HMD, but without the requirement that the user actually wear the device. The BOOM was later commercialized by FakeSpace Labs Inc. NASA also did research on the three-dimensional presentation of sounds, resulting in the Convolvotron, a sound spatialization system also developed in 1987 (sold by Crystal Rivers Engineering (CRE)).

NASA's technology research was in support of their need to provide a means to perform tasks such as interfacing with remote locations (underwater, lunar surface) and astronaut training, and visualization of aero and spacecraft design properties such as the Virtual Windtunnel project which began in 1989.

H. Military

As a leading user of flight simulation technology, military organizations have been pursuing virtual reality for multiple decades. With new possibilities in display technologies, the United States military has promoted the advance of general virtual reality by funding many early VR research and application activities. An example of this was head-mounted display design at Wright Patterson Air Force Base. In particular, this work focused on augmenting a pilot's view of the real world with target and otherwise invisible terrain information.

The military has also exploited virtual reality as a tool for training battle operations such as bringing a submarine into port (begun in 1994) and training foot soldiers in operations such as finding a sniper in a building (begun in 1993).

I. Medical Labs

Medical training is another area of interest to the military, as well as civilian medical research facilities. Some ways that virtual reality has been applied to medical training in general include surgical skill training (Figs. 6 and 7), such as suturing tubes together, needle insertion tasks, and specific physical operations (the *Surgical Simulator* from Boston Dynamics, Inc., in 1994). In addition to training applications, virtual reality has been used for visualization of medical data from MRI and CAT scan machines to give a 3-D perspective inside a patient's body (Crumbs, begun in 1994 at the National Center for Supercomputing Applications).

Figure 5 A children's book or an instruction manual can come alive through the "magic book" augmented reality concept. Here, the steps of how to assemble a chair are explained and demonstrated by looking through a head-based display system that augments the contents of the book. (Image courtesy University of Washington at Seattle.)

J. Manufacturing Industry

In the past decade, VR has migrated from the research lab to commercial use by "early adopters." Companies such as General Motors, Caterpillar, and Boeing turned to VR in search of increased productivity and decreased costs of production. For example, Caterpillar uses virtual reality to rapidly assess new designs of heavy construction equipment prior to building costly physical prototypes. Visualization of information such as financial or geological data has driven some companies to pursue virtual reality to help find hidden insight within massive datasets.

Figure 6 A medical student practices a common surgical procedure using virtual reality. (Images courtesy Boston Dynamics, Inc.)

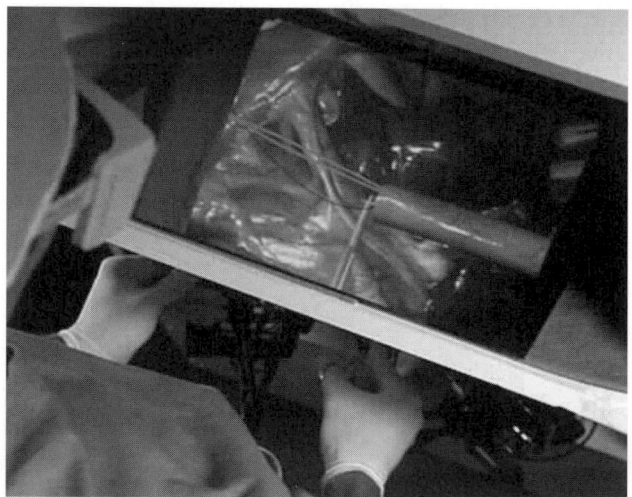

Figure 7 Another view of a surgical procedure using virtual reality.

K. Entertainment Industry

Companies such as Virtuality PLC and The Walt Disney Company have pursued the use of VR for public entertainment. In 1990, Virtuality introduced VR to the public venue with their "Dactyl Nightmare" experience designed for the video game arcade. Although it had good production quality for the era, the cost was more than the market would bear. Later, in 1998, the first DisneyQuest family arcade center was opened in Orlando, Florida. Each DisneyQuest location has a variety of traditional and innovative arcade experiences, including several virtual reality installations using different hardware configurations such as head-mounted displays and CAVE-style theaters. With an existing customer base that is charged a single entry fee for use of both the less expensive and more expensive activities, Disney has created a potentially viable means of sustaining a public outlet for virtual reality entertainment.

II. DEMONSTRATED BENEFITS OF VIRTUAL REALITY

Much like any other technology, the adoption of virtual reality as a practical tool is dependent on showing that it adds some benefit unavailable through other tools. VR has promised to aid in lowering product development times, providing cost savings, scientific insight, improved learning, and engaging entertainment. In order to assess whether VR is fulfilling these hoped for ideals, it is important to define criteria by which success is measured.

One measure is to see whether people are using the technology or not. If so, one can assume it offers something of value to the person beyond other tools they have available. If no one uses the technology, it could be because the technology is inadequate, or because it is not mature enough, still too expensive or they haven't had an opportunity to try it.

Of course one reason to not use VR for a problem is that it is not the suitable tool for the problem. In general, VR is a tool for working with three-dimensional problems. Anytime one needs to recreate the real world (which is three-dimensional), VR is often a reasonable medium in which to work. Any task that requires the simulation of a real world operation is a potential candidate for benefiting from VR. So, training in any number of areas is appropriate, including medical training and military training. VR is also useful for evaluating products and places, such as new machine prototypes, architecture, and

cars. Some fields in which VR has been adopted and has been used in the normal course of working include medical training applications, virtual prototyping, aircraft manufacturing (e.g., Boeing currently uses wearable computers with heads-up displays) and entertainment.

However, the real power of virtual reality comes from what can be done in a simulated space that cannot be done in the real world. Although VR is generally useful for imaging objects that can be represented as a 3-D physical entity—like a building or a human liver—representing a real world entity exactly as it normally appears may not make use of all the advantages provided by VR. In VR it is possible to change the surface of the objects to show additional information such as stresses, temperature, or other attributes that are not normally visible. Similar abstracted representations can be made in aural or other senses in addition to the visual.

Usefulness can be demonstrated by organizations that have already found VR to be mature enough to be useful in its present state. Uses have ranged from automobile and machinery design, visualization of scientific and medical data, engineering analysis, artistic expression, training, and entertainment.

In 1992, General Motors began investigating the use of virtual reality for aesthetic evaluation of automobiles as well as analysis of an automobile's ability to withstand crashes. Automobile designers began making regular use of the CAVE, escalating to the point where, by 2000, GM installed their fourth CAVE VR environment. Most other automobile manufacturers also now make use of CAVEs and similar technology.

In 1994 CRUMBS, an application to visualize a variety of three-dimensional scientific and medical datasets, was created at the National Center for Supercomputing Applications (NCSA). Though originally developed for a specific medical application, over the subsequent years it has been expanded and used by scientists and researchers in many different fields, including oil exploration, basic physics research, genetic research, veterinary medicine, and biomedical visualization. It has also been extended in its capabilities to allow it to be a useful application in support of education by allowing an instructor to create and share scenarios with students located at a remote facility (Fig. 8).

Nalco Fuel Tech, a company that provides engineering consulting services for operators of large boilers and incinerators, developed a prototype tool for analyzing how to improve the burn process in a way that releases fewer pollutants into the atmosphere. By visualizing the output of supercomputer simulations in a VR environment, they found that the immersive

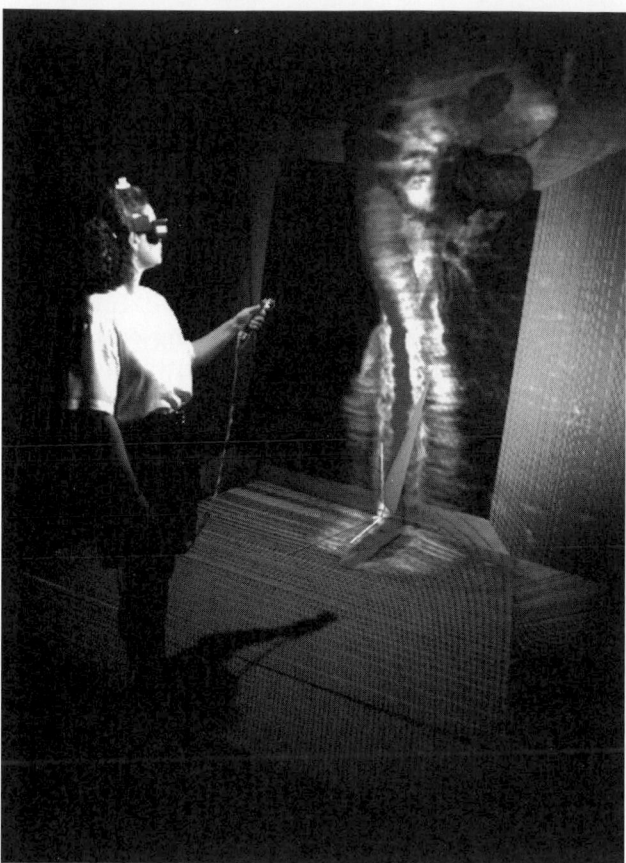

Figure 8 A user visualizes 3-D data in the CAVE using the Crumbs application. (Image courtesy NCSA.)

interaction of VR could aid the analysis and reduce the amount of time necessary to reach optimal design solutions. Their initial experimental effort with Argonne National Labs in 1995 was rewarding enough that Nalco began their own internal VR effort in 2000.

In addition to the proven benefits of flight simulation training, both the military and NASA have found VR to be suitable for training in other areas. For NASA, training for Space Shuttle Extra-Vehicular Activities (EVA, "space walk") missions such as the repair of the Hubble Space Telescope in the 1993 and 1996 missions and construction of the International Space Station have benefited from preflight exercises in a VR environment (beginning in 1998 and continuing through the present). One of the ways in which the military has used VR is training submarine officers in the seldom-performed task of bringing a submarine into port. A research project begun in 1994 at MIT has been successfully transitioned to a commercially supported tool for training this operation by 2000.

Another task that can benefit from VR training systems is surgery. Boston Dynamics, Inc. (BDI) has cre-

ated a surgical task training simulator for the commonly performed task of suturing together two tubular structures (anastomosis). In addition to training for the task, an analysis mode was also created to evaluate the progress of medical students and determine when they were ready for the next phase of their training. BDI implemented the system in such a way as to make the training system match the real world task as much as possible. The operator stood at a kiosk that mimicked standing over a patient and held on to actual surgical instruments. The instruments were connected to a haptic feedback system that displayed forces calculated from a realistic dynamics simulation. As the operator looked down, a computer-rendered stereoscopic image hid the haptic display device, showing instead the virtual ends of the instruments interacting with the simulated tubular organs.

Photographer/artist Rita Addison turned to virtual reality as a means of expression after an automobile accident in 1992 impaired the visual centers in her brain, thus reducing her ability to use a camera. After losing her ability to express herself via the camera, in 1994 she turned to virtual reality as a means of artistic expression. In particular, working with a software developer, she produced a VR experience that gave people the ability to visually experience the world through the eyes of someone suffering the aftereffects of brain injury. Many visitors of her "Detour: Brain Deconstruction Ahead" VR experience respond emotionally, stating that they can better understand what life must be like now for Rita and other sufferers of brain injury (Fig. 9). The experience is especially poignant for people who personally know others who have suffered a stroke or other form of brain trauma.

Figure 9 Vision becomes cloudy and warped in the "Detour: Brain Deconstruction Ahead" virtual reality art experience. (Copyright 2003, William Sherman.)

Although it will be a few years before VR is commonplace in the home, the graphics technology is already available, and some VR experiences have been designed purely for their entertainment value. One example migrates an experience created originally for the home video game market to high-end VR displays. Another effort creates a world designed specifically as a virtual reality experience for public consumption.

In 1997, Id software's Quake II game was adapted for use in a CAVE environment by Paul Rajlich. Although the game was developed for play on home PCs the increased immersion offered by the VR version demonstrates an added dimension of play. "CAVEQuake II" has been downloaded and installed on more CAVE and CAVE-like systems worldwide than any other application!

CAVE facilities generally do not have open public access, so for many, the DisneyQuest venue offers a more likely place to have the opportunity to experience virtual reality. The DisneyQuest family arcade centers offer a variety of interactive experiences with which families can participate. Several of the experiences consist of either head-mounted display or CAVE-like VR systems. With many of their experiences based on characters from Disney films, the creators have the opportunity to experiment with how to transition these characters from the medium of film to interactive immersive experiences (Fig. 10).

III. VR PARADIGMS

While we have already mentioned that VR systems provide synthetic stimuli to the senses, it is important to note that there are multiple ways by which this can be accomplished. Many suitable display technologies exist, but in general they can be categorized into three display paradigms. These three basic paradigms hold not only for visual displays, but also for display to other senses such as aural and touch ("haptic") display systems.

Stationary displays are fixed in place. Although the display does not move, the world is rendered in response to the user's bodily position. Examples of stationary visual displays include CAVE-type systems, single large screen systems, and desktop monitors. Loudspeakers are an example of stationary aural displays (Fig. 11).

Head-based displays move in conjunction with the user's head. Consequently, no matter which way the user turns their head, the displays move, remaining in a fixed position relative to the body's sensory inputs. Thus, visual screens remain in front of the user's eyes and headphones remain on their ears. Examples of head-based visual displays include the helmet type display often seen in popular media, and BOOM type displays which are a display box into which a user peers that can be moved around on mechanical linkages (Fig. 12). Headphones are an example of head-based aural displays.

Hand-based displays are a special case of the head-based paradigm. In this case, the user holds the display in their hand. For visual hand-based displays, monitoring both the user's head position as well as the position of the display is required, because the direction of view is important. Most often visual hand-based displays are used to overlay computer graphics imagery registered with the real world. An example of

Figure 10 A game player immerses himself into the game world. (Copyright 2003, William Sherman.)

Figure 11 The stationary CAVE visual display and loudspeaker aural display are often used together. (Copyright 2003, William Sherman.)

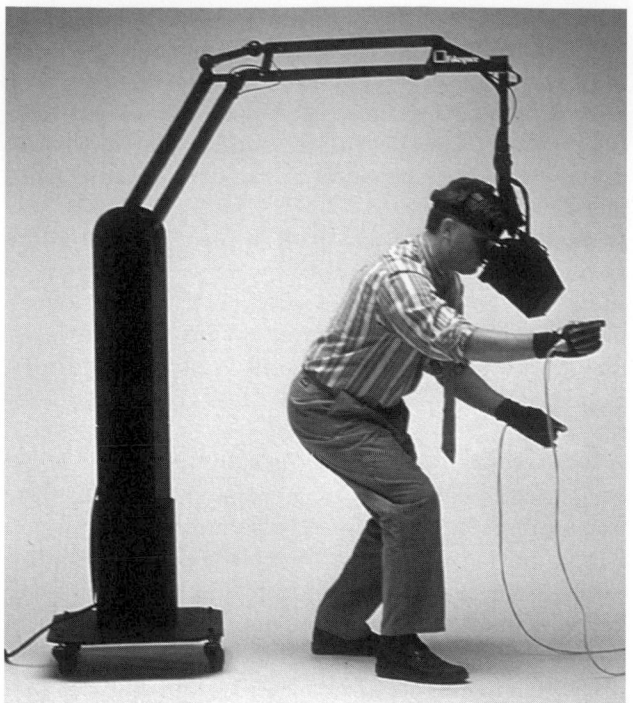

Figure 12 The BOOM head-based display mounts the screens on an arm that takes the weight from being applied to the user's head. (Image courtesy Fakespace Systems, Inc.)

a haptic hand-based display is the SensAble Technologies PHANToM arm. The PHANToM provides a dual role by mechanically tracking the user's hand as well as providing a force display to the hand.

IV. COLLABORATION

One of the strengths of virtual reality is its capability to transcend the barriers of time and space. This transcendence leads to VR being a good vehicle for supporting collaboration. VR environments can foster collaboration in a number of different ways. Space can be shared, either physically or virtually. Dialogue can be held synchronously, or in an asynchronous form.

Large-screen stationary systems such as the CAVE are the best type of VR system for collaborating in the same physical space. Many participants have a concurrent view of the virtual world, allowing them to point out items of interest to one another.

Most forms of VR systems provide a good way to collaborate in the same virtual space. A major benefit of virtual shared spaces is that they allow collaboration to take place via computer networks. Thus, not only can two workers share a space while remaining in their offices just down the hallway from one another, but they can also be an ocean away.

When working in a networked collaborative environment, each participant can be represented as a virtual entity. A virtual entity that represents a human in a collaborative environment is called an *avatar*. An avatar may be a somewhat realistic representation of the person, or an abstract representation. The mere presence of avatars can greatly improve the ability of the collaborators to communicate through nonverbal means. For example, pointing in a direction, waving an arm, or even just looking in a certain direction can convey valuable information from person to person.

Not every sense always needs to be transmitted in collaborative environments. For example, a telephone supports voice-only collaborations. VR, however, allows the option of participants sharing a three-dimensional world populated by 3-D objects which can be manipulated and worked with. Except for certain physical activities, most collaborative work relies only on the visual and aural senses, both of which are strengths of current VR technology.

Collaborators can inhabit the shared virtual world concurrently and engage in synchronous dialogue and actions, or participate asynchronously by saving the state of the system after their component of the collaborative activity. Another possibility of asynchronous collaboration is to record all the actions of the participant(s), allowing other participants to replay that experience at a later time. In fact, the collaborators can leave annotations (such as messages or virtual pictures) for others who enter the space at a later time.

V. VIRTUAL REALITY SYSTEMS

The creation of a virtual reality system requires the integration of multiple components. These components include the system hardware, underlying support software for linking the display and input hardware together, the virtual world content with which the user will interact, and a user interface design that provides a suitable means for appropriate user interactions.

A. Hardware

Hardware used in virtual reality systems can be roughly categorized as display devices, input devices that a user consciously activates, input devices that monitor the user, plus the computer(s) that support the modelling and rendering of the virtual world (Fig. 13).

Typical VR System

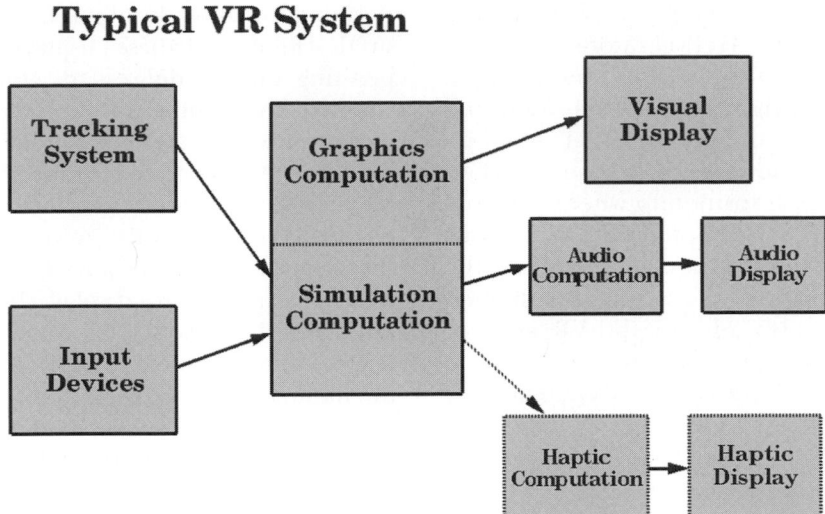

Figure 13 This diagram illustrates how the various components are integrated in a typical VR system. (Copyright 2003, William Sherman and Alan Craig.)

1. Computer/Graphics Engine

The main computing engine is responsible for calculating the physical behavior of the virtual world, and then rendering the state of the world into visual, aural, haptic, etc., representations. Because an effective VR experience requires real-time interactions, the compute system has some specific requirements.

The computational system can be implemented on a single large computer that meets all the requirements, or it can be implemented on multiple computers. In the latter case, the cadre of machines must be interconnected via a low-latency, high-speed communication network. Latency (the time delay between the time an event occurs and its results are apparent) is an important factor in any VR system. Any latency in the overall system reduces the effectiveness of the system. The use of multiple CPU components allows the system to achieve more computations both for the graphics and for the world simulation.

The primary needs that the compute system must meet include enough computational power to perform the virtual world's physics simulation calculations, sufficient graphical rendering performance from a "graphics engine" computational component, a means of rendering sounds, and perhaps rendering of other senses such as haptic (touch) information.

The specific computational needs vary based on the type of applications the system will be required to run. Representations of the real world generally require the ability to map pictures of the world onto surfaces to deliver a look of high detail (texture maps); however, an application to visualize a molecule could

be done without the use of such features requiring instead an increased geometric throughput. Some worlds, those that consist only of static objects, require no computation for world physics.

In addition to rapidly rendering the graphical representations, the graphics engine should have the capability to synchronize the display updates between multiple displays either for rendering to both eyes (stereoscopic vision) in a head-based display, multiple screens on a multiscreened projection display, or perhaps multiple-projectors projecting overlapping left and right eye images to the same screen. Many high-end graphics engines and projectors have provisions to render and display stereoscopic images through a single mechanism; however, most consumer marketed systems do not yet have this feature. The absence of synchronization between displays leads to negative artifacts such as the world appearing discontinuous between two neighboring screens.

Most modern computing systems from low cost desktop systems to high end workstations now include the ability to render sounds. If more advanced aural rendering operations are required, however, signals can be sent to an external audio processor. For example, the ability to make sound appear to come from a particular location relative to the user's head (spatialization) generally requires additional audio-rendering hardware.

The ability to perform multiple operations at the same time is also an overall requirement of VR systems. Thus, having an operating system capable of true "multithreaded" operation is a prerequisite of VR systems. The use of multiple computers is also a means of accomplishing this need.

Through the 1990s, many large VR projects have relied on the use of larger (refrigerator-sized) computer workstations with multiple CPUs, and multiple instances of high-performance graphics-rendering hardware. However, with the advent of 3-D graphics accelerators aimed at the consumer game market, we are now in a state of transition to where personal computers can be used to implement VR systems with virtual worlds of significant complexity. On the downside of this transition, the availability of such low cost systems that also address the VR need of stereoscopic rendering is limited and will continue to be so until the home market creates a demand for such features.

2. Visual Displays

The visual display portion of a virtual reality display generally has the most influence on the overall design on the virtual reality system. This influence is due to the visual system being the predominate means of communication for most people. It also tends to dominate how a VR system is defined, including which paradigm is implemented.

Each type of visual display paradigm (stationary, head-based, and hand-based) has its own specific benefits and disadvantages which are further influenced by advances in technology, and the amount of monetary resources available. In addition to these basic paradigms, all the visual displays can either display stereoscopic images or monoscopic. In general, because virtual reality often attempts to mimic the sensation of physical reality, stereoscopic display is presumed.

Large-screen stationary displays such as the CAVE, wall, and table/desk displays use fixed-position screens to fill a relatively large portion of the field of view for one or more viewers. Many of these displays (such as the CAVE and CAVE-like systems) wrap screens around the participant, surrounding them as much as possible with the visual representation of the world. Even systems with a single display surface can fill significant portions of the user's view when the user stands near the large screen.

Thus, a primary benefit of the large-screen stationary display is field-of-view coverage. Other advantages include the reduced amount of hardware worn by the user and the ability to see colleagues physically standing next to them. Because rendering latency has a somewhat reduced negative impact, the ability of the user to continue to see the physical world while viewing the virtual world improves the safety of the system.

Downsides of this style of visual display include an incomplete view of the virtual world (field-of-regard),

cost, and the difficulty of masking the real world if desired. The cost of these displays can vary greatly depending on the degree to which the user is surrounded and whether multiple projectors are used to increase the resolution of the imagery by tiling them together. An increased number of projectors also means more graphics rendering hardware will be needed. Currently, with the use of projected images, the amount of space required is also one of the costs of using a large-screen display. However, in the future, large panel displays will be available, allowing the screens to be mounted directly on a room's wall. Also, the limited field-of-regard problem is solvable with an added cost. A handful of six-sided (cube) CAVE-like facilities have already been built that entirely surround the participant by screens (one being a door). The cost of such a facility includes creating a surface on which multiple people can stand, while being projected onto from below.

Head-based displays (HBD) are perhaps the most familiar type of virtual reality display, having been popularized in movies and television. Early forms of head-based displays were often mounted onto fighter-pilot helmets, and thus were referred to as helmet-mounted displays, or HMDs. Later the acronym HMD was also used as head-mounted display. Either way, these devices were typically heavy headsets with attached screens positioned in front of the wearer's eyes. Two other types of head-based display that have also become available are a mechanical arm-mounted display that the user pulls up to their face, without any weight being placed on their body. The original of this class, the BOOM (binocular omni-orientation monitor), counterbalances the arm with the display. More recent versions of the head-based display that are attached to the head of the user use smaller screens and weigh significantly less than the original HMDs. As these displays become closer to the sensation of wearing a basic pair of sunglasses, there is an increased tendency to label them "head-worn displays", with the superior connotations that phrase implies.

A major benefit of the head-based display is that the user can turn their head to see any direction in the world. This is called 100% field-of-regard. Other benefits include being generally cheaper than the large-screen displays, requiring less space, and being much more portable.

A significant disadvantage of HBDs is that any latency in the VR system is more noticeable to the user, and thus more likely to cause nausea or a headache (thus limiting the interaction time). The currently more widely used head-mounted displays have the problem of the additional weight that the user must carry on their head, along with cables to carry the video and tracking information. BOOM and BOOM-like display armature often extend to the floor. Thus, the armature frequently causes "blind-spots" to where the user cannot move. Also, while BOOMs do not put the weight on the user's head, the weight is still there, so along with HMDs, the display has a certain amount of inertia that can affect the experience. Head-worn displays therefore sound like an optimal solution, but they typically have screens with much lower resolution than what can be provided in BOOMs, HMDs, and stationary displays. Another disadvantage of head-based displays is that they are limited to a single user at a time and generally isolate that user from the people around them, making it hard to discuss an ongoing experience.

Desktop VR displays (also known as *fishtank VR*) are similar to the large-screen displays in that they fall into the stationary display paradigm. The popular term "fishtank VR" is derived from the way one peers into a desktop VR display. A desktop VR display is basically a standard computer monitor, often augmented with the ability to display stereographically. By combining the monitor with the necessary tracking and other input devices and VR software, the scene appears to actually be inside the display—the way fish are inside an aquarium. Thus, if the viewer moves their head left or right, they can see the fish from a different perspective, and similarly for the objects in the virtual world (Fig. 14).

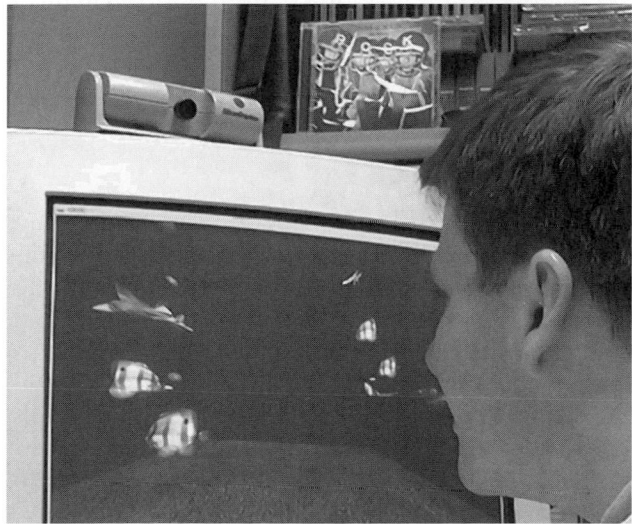

Figure 14 A computer monitor with a video camera can be a very simple VR display, referred to as "fishtank VR" due to the similarity with looking into an aquarium. (Copyright 2003, William Sherman.)

The major advantage of the desktop VR display is that it can usually make use of an existing desktop computer with a few inexpensive additions. Thus, the cost of creating such a system is not excessive. Another significant benefit is that it can be used right at the user's desk. Frequently, the more difficult it is to use a VR system, the less often it will be used, and going to another room or building to make use of the system requires that the user expect significant improvements in the experience above what a monitor, keyboard, and mouse can provide. In fact, computer hardware has progressed to the point where, with the addition of a camera for user tracking, a VR system can nearly be completely implemented on a laptop computer—except not many laptops offer stereoscopic display.

There are some big disadvantages to the desktop display of course. Namely, very limited field-of-view, and very limited field-of-regard. The user is only able to see what is immediately in front of them, and a little off to the side when they lean over, like looking through a window. Compared with the other types of visual VR displays, the cost is minimal, but there will be costs to upgrade to a stereoscopic image, along with some input hardware and software to track the user's movement. The best tracking solution is to use a video camera (which is often included with desktop computers for the purpose of teleconferencing).

Hand-based VR displays are not yet widely used by VR systems. When used, they typically have a specific VR experience that makes use of them and generally have a specific need that must be fulfilled. The most intuitive type of hand-based display is a pair of binoculars that contains two small screens instead of the typical lenses. The binoculars continuously display a magnified (computer processed) view in the direction they are pointed, and when the user holds them up they can see the processed image. Another style of hand-based display is to hold a screen approximately the size of one's palm in the hand. The image on this screen shows the virtual world from the perspective of where the user's eyes are through the small window. This form of display works well as a "magic-lens" display, giving the user an altered view of the "reality." The altered view might operate as if it were an "X-ray vision" device. The "reality" that is altered can be either physical reality or a virtual object itself. The palm-sized screen form of display is typically displayed monoscopically—in part because it is difficult to acquire small flat screens that can display stereo images.

Although not widely used, hand-held VR displays do have some advantages. In particular, they have an advantage when a VR experience has a natural interface for which the display is perfectly suited—as with the binocular, or "magic-lens" interfaces described. Because the user can choose when to look at a hand-held display, it can be combined with either physical reality (as an augmented reality display), or in a screen-based virtual reality display such as a CAVE. Thus, a virtual reality world can be augmented—*augmented virtual reality*. Another nice feature of hand-based displays is that they tend to not be very encumbering.

Where hand-based displays do not work well is when there is no other VR display and the application requires a reasonable amount of field-of-view. Both the binocular and palm-sized devices provide very limited FOV. And while the field of regard is technically 100%, it requires the user to move the device through a large spherical motion to see in all directions. In general, hand-held displays are less immersive, except when used to augment a larger view (real or virtual). One more small disadvantage is that one more item needs to be tracked in addition to the user's head—the display itself.

3. Aural Displays

The inclusion of an aural display to a virtual reality system is generally a good way of enhancing any experience for a minimal additional cost. Unlike the visual display, it cannot be assumed that the aural image is presented stereophonically. In fact, the notion of "stereo" is more complicated with the aural sense.

Many virtual reality experiences can utilize a single (monophonic) channel of sound, and still provide a deeply immersive experience. Experiences that provide just an ambient background sound, perhaps combined with some discrete sounds that mark an event in the world, seldom require more than monophonic. When this is not the case, the question becomes whether traditional stereophonic sounds should be used versus a more complex method of sound spatialization.

The trouble with traditional (prerendered) stereophonic sound display is not that it only comes out of two speakers, but rather that it is preproduced (prerendered) to seem as though particular sounds come from particular locations. Because virtual reality is interactive, it is not generally possible to know a priori where the sound will be relative to the listener. Thus, sounds that must appear to emanate from a particular location need to be processed to create this effect. The processing is referred to as *spatialization*. Spatialized sound can be rendered to function in two-speaker (binaural) or multispeaker displays.

An interesting discovery regarding spatialized sound is that it can be effectively combined with prerendered

stereo and monophonic sounds. For example, a VR experience might have a sound associated with a particular object or person in the world. That sound therefore should be spatialized to seem as if it follows the object or person. The scene might also have generic street sounds in the background presented as prerendered stereo. A monophonic, ambient orchestration to influence the mood can be added to the mix to create an overall highly immersive effect.

The two common sound display devices are loudspeakers and headphones. These two styles match well with the stationary and head-based visual display paradigms, respectively. *Loudspeakers*, the aural display of the stationary paradigm, work well with CAVE-like displays, large wall displays, and desktop displays. *Headphones*, the aural head-based display paradigm, work well with head-mounted, BOOM, and other head-based displays. Of course, it is also possible, and sometimes desirable, to use headphones in a CAVE, particularly if the sound spatialization system works best with them. Likewise, there are good reasons to use stationary speakers with a head-based system. Often, a single subwoofer is added to output loud, low-frequency sounds. Only one subwoofer is required because low frequency sounds are not easily localized anyway.

The cost of most aural displays generally pales in comparison with the cost of the rest of the VR system. Thus, neither form of aural display is more advantageous in that respect. The primary advantages of the two systems are that loudspeakers can be more easily heard by a group of participants, and headphones are generally easier to use when producing spatialized sounds. Also, headphones have a slight safety disadvantage in that if an excessive signal is presented, it will be very close to the listener's ears.

4. Haptic Displays

Roughly speaking, haptic displays relate to the sense of touch. However, not all of the haptic sensations come via the skin. Some of what is called "haptic display" is related to the muscular and skeletal systems. Therefore, haptic displays are generally discussed in two component terms: "tactile" (input through the skin), and "proprioceptic" (input through the muscular and skeletal systems). Sensing the coarseness of sandpaper or the temperature of water is a tactile sensation. Sensing how much effort is required to lift a box or knowing the current location of one's arm is a proprioceptic sensation.

Different technologies are generally required for creating forces versus creating subtle skin-response sensations. Therefore, most devices designed for haptic display focus on either tactile or proprioceptive presentation.

Like visual and aural display types, haptic displays can also be divided based on the stationary versus body-based paradigms. However, when discussing haptic displays, these characteristics are typically referred to as "world-grounded" (stationary) versus "self-grounded" (body-based) displays.

World-grounded displays are those that have a base attached to the ceiling, or perhaps sit on the desktop or are affixed in some way to some object in the real world. Typically, the user holds the end of an arm with multiple linkages leading back to the base. Each of the linkages is capable of exerting an active or resistive force in a particular direction. Thus, when the user grabs an object and tries to move it, the ease with which it can be moved can be felt allowing the user to sense the weight of the object, and the friction or viscosity of the containing medium (Fig. 15). Or, if the object is animate, such as a dog, then grabbing it (or its collar) can lead to an active force felt by the user.

Self-grounded displays are those that are somehow worn by the user. A common example is a glove fitted with some form of tactile display, such as small vibrators. Force display devices can also be self-grounded, such as a display that resists the movement of the user's arm relative to their shoulder (Fig. 16). The latter example works best, however, either by ignoring the user's movement within the virtual world or assuming that their shoulder is in a fixed location. In the latter case, the self-grounded arm display is effectively acting as a world-grounded display.

Another possible form of haptic feedback is that of the inactive prop device. In this case, the user gets tactile sensations from the skin touching a device and feeling its shape, texture, and sensing movement of buttons or other objects mounted on the prop. The prop device also provides some proprioceptive feedback by its weight and momentum. An example of an inactive prop is to use an instrumented (real) putter as an interface to a virtual golf game.

5. Other Sensory Displays

Virtual reality systems make use of visual, aural, and haptic displays in decreasing prevalence. Use of other sensory displays has also been done. Of these the vestibular sense (the sense of balance) is the most common. In fact, it has been a very common form of display for flight simulation for decades. Olfactory display (smell) has been experimented with sparingly, and computer controlled display of gustation (taste) is virtually nonexistent.

The most common form of vestibular display is the "motion platform." A motion platform is basically a large surface (the platform) mounted on top of hydraulic actuators that can raise, lower, and tilt the platform. The user (typically) sits on the platform, and in the case of flight simulators, within a cockpit mounted to the platform. Sometimes the visual display is also mounted on the platform; other times it is projected onto a large dome that can be seen through the windows of the cockpit. By tilting the motion platform; the pilot can then sense when the aircraft begins to pitch, yaw, or roll, and by how much.

Another style of vestibular display is through the use of a bladder-equipped chair. By inflating and deflating different portions of the chair, the user can feel acceleration and deceleration. For example, when undergoing strong acceleration, a pilot will feel themselves being pushed back in their chair. To recreate this, the bladder on the back of the display-seat can be filled, and thus create a similar pressure sensation on the back of the pilot. A similar effect can be implemented for sensing the effective loss of gravity while riding in a roller coaster, by deflating the seat of the chair.

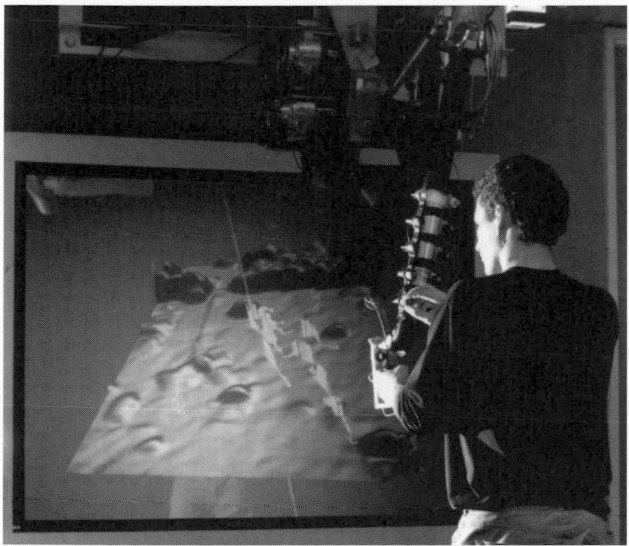

Figure 15 This world-grounded haptic force-feedback device is attached to the ceiling, allowing a user to grab the controls and interact with the molecular world. (Image copyright 1994, the University of North Carolina at Chapel Hill.)

6. Input Devices (Including User Tracking)

Without input, a computer-generated display cannot be interactive, much less be considered a virtual reality

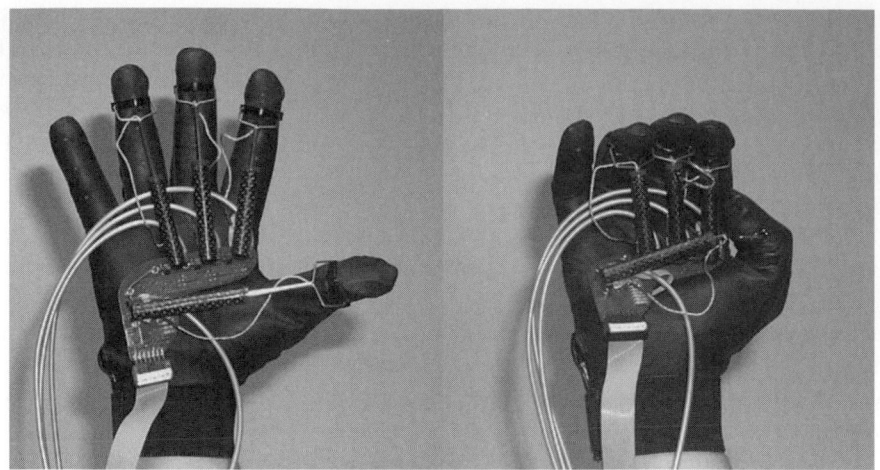

Figure 16   The Rutgers Dextrous Master II is a self-grounded display that can be used to prevent the fingers from closing all the way, simulating the effect of holding an object in the hand. (Image courtesy Rutgers University.)

system. In fact, virtual reality systems require not just a means for the user to express their intentions, but also must track at least some subset of their body. One can differentiate between these two types of input by referring to them as "cognitive input" (events specifically trigger by the user), and "user monitoring" (tracking the body movements of the user). Another way to distinguish this input dichotomy is to consider inputs that the user must specifically activate versus inputs that passively sense attributes such as the position of the user.

The *position sensor* is the most important tracking device of any VR system. There are several types of position sensors, each with their own benefits and limitations. These sensors include electromagnetic, mechanical, optical, ultrasonic, inertial/gyroscopic, and neural/muscular devices. The most crucial factor of a position sensor is the type of limitations imposed on the system. Limitations generally arise from the technological means used to determine the relationship from some fixed origin and the sensor. For example, some trackers require an uninterrupted "line-of-sight" between a transmitter and a sensor. When the "line-of-sight" is interrupted (i.e., something comes between the transmitter and sensor) the tracking system cannot function properly.

In position sensing systems, there are three factors that play against one another (discounting cost): accuracy/precision of the reported sensor position, interfering media (e.g., metals, opaque objects), and encumbrance (wires, mechanical linkages). No available technology, at any cost, provides the optimal conditions in all three of these factors. Thus, the system designer must consider how the VR system will be

used and make the optimal tradeoffs. One of the driving factors is simply the ability of the system to produce an acceptable experience. Noise and low accuracy in the position sensor reports as well as high latency decrease the "realism" or immersiveness of the experience, and often can lead to nausea in some participants.

Electromagnetic tracking systems are a popular input device for VR systems because they do not require line of sight to the tracked object. However, because they use an electrically generated and received magnetic field to determine the six degrees-of-freedom of the sensor device, metals interfere with the functionality of such a system. Ferrous metals are particularly problematic. Also, active electronic devices in close proximity to a sensor can be an issue. The magnetic properties of metals within the VR environment cause distortions in where the sensor is perceived to be with respect to the transmitter. If the interfering metals are stationary, then minor distortions can sometimes be corrected for in software.

Fortunately, the amount of metal within the environment can often be controlled. Cases where particular care must be taken to improve tracking accuracy are head-worn gear made of metal, or with internal electronics and wheelchairs. In the case of HMDs or stereo glasses with electronics, the best solution is to locate the sensor as far away from the electronics as possible. In the case of a wheelchair, a sensor mounted to the participant's head is less of a concern than for a hand-held device which will be located closer to the metallic components of the chair.

Standard electromagnetic tracking systems have wires that connect with both the transmitter and sensor units. This is somewhat encumbering, with cables tethering the participant to the VR system. For a greater cost, some of these systems connect the sensors, not directly to the VR system, but rather to a radio pack worn by the participant. The participant thus has more freedom to physically move about the space without the concern of tripping over wires (Fig. 17).

Mechanical tracking systems use transcoders mounted on physical linkages to report the movement of the linkages. The position of the endpoint can be calculated from the transcoder values. The use of transcoders provides extremely accurate and precise position readings. By improving position reports, the overall VR experience is improved by giving an increased physically immersive sensation, and perhaps also reducing the likelihood of nausea. The overriding problem of mechanical tracking systems is that there is some physical attachment between the user

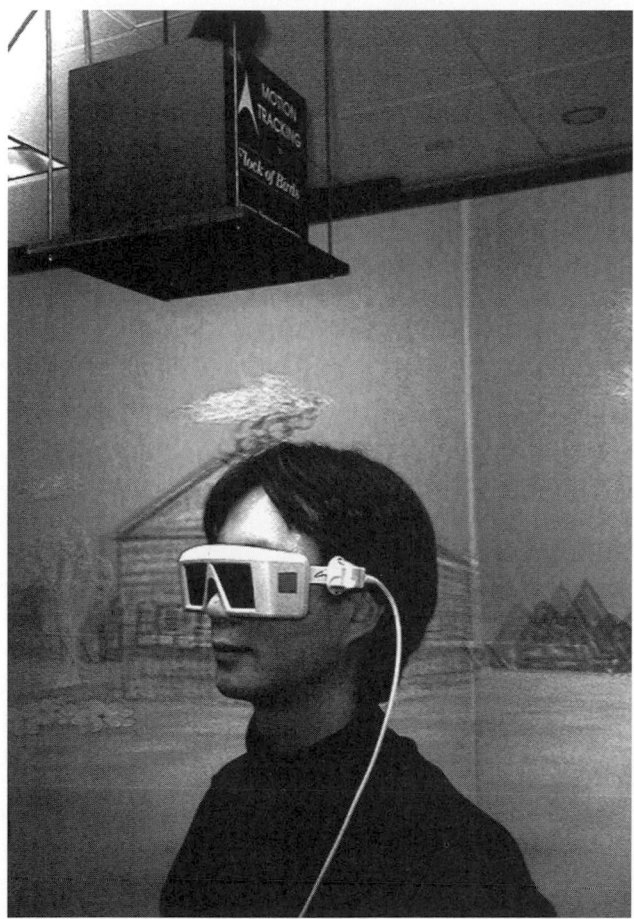

Figure 17 A low-level electromagnetic field is emitted by the large black box. The signal is sensed by a recieving antenae which allows the system to determine the location and orientation of the receiver. (Copyright 2003, William Sherman.)

and the real world. This attachment can often impede the user from moving in a natural way. However, there are some situations where the user's movement is already restricted, and therefore the mechanical system can be designed such that no additional restrictions are added—such as a pilot sitting in a cockpit.

Glove input devices generally fall within the realm of mechanical position sensor. However, it is the configuration of the hand that is measured rather than the overall location and orientation of the entire hand. To deduce the shape of the hand, sensors are placed throughout the glove to determine the amount of bend between various joints. Two common bend-sensing technologies used for hand-position sensing are optical fibers that transmit less light when bent, and metals that alter their resistance when bent.

Ultrasonic tracking systems use a collection of transducers—transmitters (speakers) and receivers (microphones)—that pass signals from one point to another (Fig. 18). By measuring the time taken for the signal to arrive, one can compute (using the speed of sound) the distance between the transducer pair. The key factors in accomplishing a proper measurement are that multiple transducer-pair measurements are required to determine the complete (X, Y, Z, roll, pitch, yaw) position, and an uninterrupted line-of-sight must be maintained between transducer pairs. Thus, hardware systems that use ultrasound to measure sensor positions typically mount several transducers on the sensor device to provide some redundancy, allowing the sensor to go through different orientations and still maintain sufficient contact with the transmitters.

Determining the orientation and/or location of a sensor requires that at least three transmitter–receiver transducer connections be made. In addition, there is a minimal distance that must exist between transducers in order to avoid ambiguous results. The number and spacing of the transducers can be cumbersome in some circumstances, such as adding significant weight to stereo-glasses, and requiring hand-held devices be large enough to accommodate the transducer distances.

Optical tracking systems can work along the same lines as ultrasonic systems—measuring distances by time and triangulation, or they may operate by attempting to discern features of a video image to recognize where certain reference markers are located, and also how they are oriented. The markers used are generally designed to contrast with the rest of the scene. This contrast can be done by using illuminated objects such as light-emitting diodes, or by creating high-contrast signature shapes such as a white square surrounded by a black square.

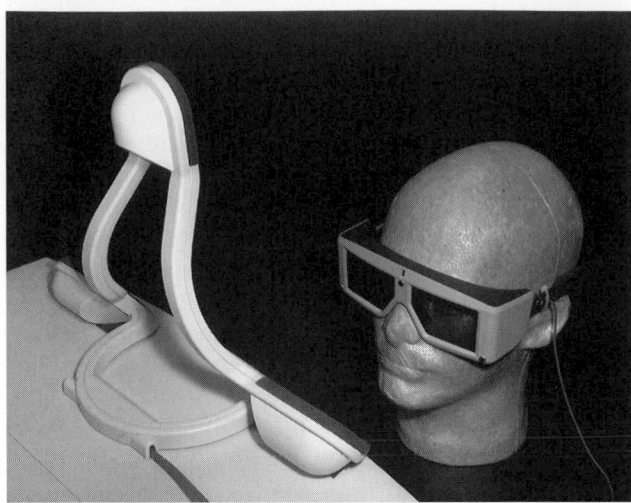

Figure 18 This basic ultrasonic tracking system uses three speakers and three microphones triangularly arranged to measure the distance between all the speaker–microphone pairs from which the location and orientation of the glasses can be determined. (Copyright 2003, William Sherman.)

Clearly, because the optical transducers work in the visual and near visual spectrum, opaque objects will interfere with the operation of the sensors—there is a line-of-sight restriction with this form of tracking. However, optical tracking systems have some significant advantages over many other tracking systems. Specifically, a reasonable system can be constructed using commodity video equipment and freely available software. Another advantage is that video tracking can be done without the need for any wires emanating from the tracked sensor. One problem with video tracking is the reduced accuracy attainable using standard video resolutions.

Inertial and *gyroscopic* tracking systems are unlike many of the previously discussed methods in that they do not directly relate themselves to a fixed reference point. The downside is that they only report relative movements, not absolute positions. The benefit of this fact is that less hardware is required to implement these types of tracking. Thus, an inertial and/or gyroscopic tracker could be mounted in a small head-based display, and no other hardware would be required to give visually immersive feedback to the user. Another important benefit of this hardware is that there is very little lag between movement of the sensor and the reported movement.

The problem with such tracking systems is that because of the lack of a fixed reference, the reported values accumulate error. After a few minutes, when the user looks forward, the system may behave as if

they are looking ten or more degrees to the left or right. Frequently, inertial and gyroscopic tracking is combined with other tracking hardware so the benefits of each can complement one another. Because some VR systems, especially head-based systems, can result in nausea when there is significant lag between user movement and the visual image, the fast response of the inertial/gyroscopic system provides a low latency response to quick movements. Electromagnetic, ultrasonic, or other type of referenced tracking is then used to continually adjust for drift.

Neural and *muscular* tracking refer to the use of transducers placed on the skin of the participant to monitor muscular and other activity within the body and make use of this information to provide inputs to the virtual reality system. For example, a sensor on the arm might be able to determine when the user clenches their fist. An example is a device called the Biomuse. When the Biomuse is attached to the user's forearm, a virtual violin can respond to the user making bowing motions with their arm.

The tracking systems above are generally used to monitor the user's general body movements. This type of activity is referred to as that which is passively transmitted by the participant. Other VR input devices are designed to give the user more active and cognitively cognizant inputs. For example, pressing a button to jump forward in the virtual world is an active form of input.

Props and *platforms* are the physical places where such active input sensors are placed. The term props comes from the theater and film industry use of the word. Short for "property," a prop is any physical object that is not part of the scenery and can be manipulated by the actors. Thus in virtual reality systems, a prop is an object that the participant can handle and use to interface with the virtual world. A prop may be embodied by a virtual object and might have physical controllers mounted on it.

Props themselves can be used for both passive and active user input. Handheld props are generally tracked in space, and thus a good indication of where one of the user's hands are located. Props also frequently have buttons, joysticks, and other inputs mounted on them, allowing the user to actively cause an action in the virtual world.

A platform is similarly used as a means of user input to the virtual world. It differs from the prop in that it is more like the scenery. Thus, a cockpit or captain's wheel of a tall ship are both part of the "scene" where the participant is located and also provide a means of controlling the virtual world (Fig. 19).

For gathering input about the real world for use in a virtual (or augmented) reality, there are many dif-

Figure 19 In this virtual reality system, a platform with a ship's wheel mounted on it provides the space where the participant takes their virtual voyage. (Image courtesy Randy Sprout.)

ferent types of data transducers. For example, MRI and medical ultrasonic scanners can produce data to recreate the internal organs of a patient. Real world objects and locations can be captured with laser scanning devices such as LIDAR. Larger scale locations and weather data can be collected by interpreting data transmitted by satellites.

Once the system has collected the input data it can further refine the data, and otherwise filter it. Two common types of filters are for calibration/registration and gestures.

In order to provide a participant with a better sense of physical immersion, it behooves the system to respond in a manner consistent with their movement. In other words, if the user moves their head 4 inches, the system should not respond with an 8-inch movement. Many systems (and especially electromagnetic trackers), produce a consistent error that can be put in a table and used to compensate for the erroneous sensor reports. Other systems might be able to combine their data with fiducial (reference) markers that can be used to correct for slight errors in the data. Either method results in more accurate reports of sensor positions, at perhaps a slight increase in latency. Augmented reality systems are especially susceptible to poor calibration and registration to the real world because any errors are glaringly obvious against the real world backdrop.

Another common form of filtering is to interpret patterns in the input from the user—gestures. For ex-

ample, if the user extends both arms out to the side and repeatedly moves them up and down, the system may generate the "flap" input. Or if the system monitors finger movements, and senses that the hand has closed into a fist, it may indicate to the virtual world that the user is attempting to grasp an object in the world. Sufficient tolerance must be built into a gesture recognition system to allow for variations from individual to individual.

Given the plethora of input possibilities, designers should consider the goals of the system and find the combination of input devices that best serve that goal.

B. Software

A variety of software components must be integrated to enable cogent VR experiences. Such software ranges from low-level libraries for simulating events, rendering display imagery, interfacing with I/O devices, creating and altering object descriptions, to completely encapsulated "turnkey" systems that allow one to begin running an immersive experience with no programming effort.

1. Laws of Nature

Many VR experiences have some programmed laws of nature that govern the behaviors and interactions carried out by the objects in the world. The exception to this is the case where the only interaction possible is changing the user's viewpoint relative to the objects in the world. In this case, the user cannot manipulate the objects, but only look at and work around them.

One option for "world simulation" is to merely allow several explicit cases of behavior to be executed under specific conditions. For example, in an architectural walk-through, the system may prevent the user from walking through walls, and constrain their vertical movement to be as if they were walking on the floor surfaces.

More advanced simulations can have global behaviors such as gravity, plus individual rules that apply only to specific objects (Fig. 20). For example, a bee could be given a rule that allows it to fly in search of a flower, gather pollen, and then return to the hive. On the other hand, a flower could be plucked with a grasping gesture, and when released, fall to the ground.

Other application simulations strive to more closely mimic the real world by adhering to mathematical descriptions of real physics. So, for a bee to fly, it would have to flap its wings sufficiently rapidly to generate

Figure 20 A simple, nonrealistic, set of rules govern this fantasy space, providing both cartoonlike renderings as well as cartoonlike laws of nature. (Copyright 2003, William Sherman.)

the needed lift and orient itself properly to send it in the desired direction.

Given that in a virtual reality experience there is no requirement that the world follow the laws of the real world, it is possible to give objects fantastic behaviors. Such behaviors might be to give the user "X-ray" vision abilities to see through objects, or to see the interior structure of an object. Another possibility is to give the user the ability to move heavy objects such as walls and furniture in an architectural (or game-world) design application, and walk through walls.

The concept of world physics also applies to how multiple users sharing the same world can interact and communicate with one another. Simple implementations of behaviors for collaboration might include representations of the other users (their "avatars"), and perhaps also an audio channel that allows everyone to communicate verbally.

2. Rendering Libraries

Rendering libraries convert the form of the world from the internal computer database to what the user experiences. The rendering library must include the appropriate rendering algorithms for whatever sense is to be portrayed. Visual images produced from graphics rendering libraries are perhaps the most common of this class of software; however, such libraries have also been developed (and used in VR) for other senses such as hearing and touch.

These libraries generally include features to render the basic elements of a "scene" along with features to enrich the display. For example, in a typical graphics library, along with the ability to render basic forms by specifying the vertices and colors of polygons, the programmer is also given options to add lighting elements and overlay photographs onto polygons to make them appear more realistic. Also, such libraries can support higher level graphical functions like hierarchical object descriptions ("scenegraphs") and collision detection.

3. VR Libraries

A complete virtual reality system is not comprised merely of rendering sensory outputs, but rather rendering appropriate outputs depending on the user's current position and actions. The paramount task of this VR library is to acquire the necessary information about the participant. This is done by interfacing with tracking and other input hardware. Information from the various sensors is integrated and provides the necessary parameters to the rendering systems. For example, the graphics (and also 3-D audio) rendering process requires knowledge of the user's head position to give the proper visual/soundscape.

Another critical requirement of the library is to operate in "real time." It must perform all the input, simulation, and rendering functions at a rate that makes the world appear to be "real" by immediately responding to the participant's actions. Using multiple processing units on VR systems can help to achieve such "real time" responsiveness. Therefore, VR libraries typically include the ability to perform multiple tasks at once.

4. Ancillary Software

The creation of a virtual reality experience also requires the use of various software apart from that required during the presentation of the experience. Examples of such tools include modeling software to aid in the construction of the form of the object's that inhabit the world, sound editing software to construct sound clips that will be heard in the experience, and image processing software to create appropriate texture maps.

Independent user interface libraries might also be linked with a VR experience to allow the operator to control parameters of the experience, for example, a mouse controlled widget panel. File formats such as VRML (a format for describing three-dimensional computer graphics objects and spaces) and other standard object formats also play an important role in the creation of virtual reality worlds.

C. Representation

There are several stages to presenting information to the user. We have stated that virtual reality is indeed a medium for communication. As such, the choice of symbols one chooses to convey is important. Depending on the goal of the VR experience one may choose to mimic the real world to a high degree of verisimilitude, or one can choose to disregard the structures and limitations extant in the real world and choose to create surreal or fantastic worlds with never seen before objects, behaviors, and beings. One can choose to present aspects of real world entities that are normally unseen, such as stresses within a structural beam, or present the world as perceived by someone who has undergone a traumatic brain injury.

Regardless of the application, a mapping must be made between concepts in the virtual world and the stimuli that will be presented to the user's various sensory organs. When choosing representations for objects and concepts, tradeoffs must sometimes be made based on the limitations of the underlying systems and the requirements of the application. The choice of representations is clearly limited to the kinds of transducers available in the system. For example, most virtual reality systems provide a visual and aural display. Beyond these two modes of presentation, in some special cases there is extra hardware available for presenting certain tactile, force, smell, and vestibular feedback.

Within the modes of presentation, tradeoffs exist regarding fidelity versus cost and performance issues. For example, a tradeoff in designing the visual aspects of an automobile lies between visual complexity/realism versus the realtime/interactive nature of the display. Limits on the realtime frame rate reduce the possible level of interactivity; however, users who require highly complex extreme realism may be willing to accept the reduction in frame rate.

Often, specialized rendering tricks are used to increase the realism. This includes techniques such as texture mapping, level of detail (LOD) culling, and polygon decimation. Sometimes these tricks lead to a tradeoff between realism in the geometric form versus realism in the surface look. The technique of texture mapping photographic images onto a simple geometry is a common method of making a world look more realistic. However, the closer one approaches a texture-mapped object (especially when presented stereoscopically), the more apparent it becomes that the form is not a true representation of the object. The object looks like a cardboard cutout or stage background of a play rather than the actual entity.

As has been stated, a user's avatar is their representation within the virtual world. There is a wide range in how one can create this personal representation. Perhaps the simplest is to restrict the avatar to a nonvisual, vocal presentation. In the realm of visual avatars, there are a variety of avatar options. The type of interpersonal communication required by the application affects the avatar representation requirements. If the capability of expressing nonverbal body language is required then having a 3-D model with articulated arms offers the ability to point, wave, and perform other gestures. If seeing the faces of other users is important to read their reactions to events, then an avatar comprised of a video representation becomes the preferred option. In a fantasy scenario, user's may not want to accurately reflect their real world counterpart at all.

D. User Interaction

Virtual reality offers the opportunity for new modes of interaction not previously available with traditional computing systems. While offering new possibilities, a downside is that there is not an established set of conventional idioms. Often interaction styles are borrowed from two-dimensional user interfaces. For example, pull-down menus can be imported into a three-dimensional virtual world (Fig. 21).

Using borrowed idioms helps the user by providing them with a familiar means of interfacing with the computer; however, it may not take advantage of the

Figure 21   The menu is an interface technique that has been adapted to the virtual reality medium from the realm of desktop computer interfaces. (Copyright 2003, William Sherman.)

potential richness of the 3-D virtual environment. Even when using borrowed paradigms questions still remain regarding where to place them, which direction they should face, and other decisions that were obvious in the 2-D worlds for which they were designed.

1. Interaction Techniques

If one starts with a blank slate, not considering previous 2-D interface styles, then one can conceive of new interaction styles that can be broken down into four major categories.

The obvious mode of interaction in virtual reality is to mimic the actions required in physical reality. Thus, to move an object, one can position their hand at the object's location, grasp it by closing their fingers, and then by moving their hand, change the position of the object. In the virtual world, this can be emulated by tracking the position of the hands and fingers. This is referred to as a *direct* form of interaction.

While *direct interaction* best mimics our methods of manipulating the real world, there are other ways in which we are accustomed to interacting with computers. These three other forms of interaction are referred to as *physical, virtual,* and *agent* interactions.

Physical interactions are those that are input to the virtual world through input devices that the user actually touches (Fig. 22). In a conventional computer system, the most common physical inputs are through the mouse and keyboard. In a virtual reality system, devices such as a hand-held wand, steering wheel, or glove input devices are examples of physical inputs.

Virtual input interactions are ones in which the "devices" with which one interacts are a part of the virtual world itself. Thus, a virtual button is one that is rendered directly in the world, and might be activated when the user moves their hand to come in "virtual" contact with the button. Many virtual interactions rely on physical or direct interactions to activate the virtual device. So in the given example, a direct interaction is used to press the virtual button. An example in which a physical input is used to activate a virtual device is when a slider is rendered in the world (or just on the screen in a traditional desktop interface) to control a parameter such as volume (Fig. 23). In both the VR experience and desktop metaphor, a physical button on the wand or mouse is pressed to manipulate the slider.

The fourth type of interaction is to express control parameters via an *agent*. In other words, by communicating with a computer entity (the agent), one lets their desires be known and expects the system to comply. For example, to travel through a solar system world, one might say the name of a planet and be taken into orbit around the specified celestial object. In the real world, we might tell our chauffeur the name of the location to which we wish to travel and expect to be taken there without any further input.

Having listed the four forms with which one can cognitively input information to the virtual reality system, it is appropriate to examine three broad categories of the types of interactions commonly performed in a virtual reality experience. These interaction categories are making selections, performing manipulations, and traveling.

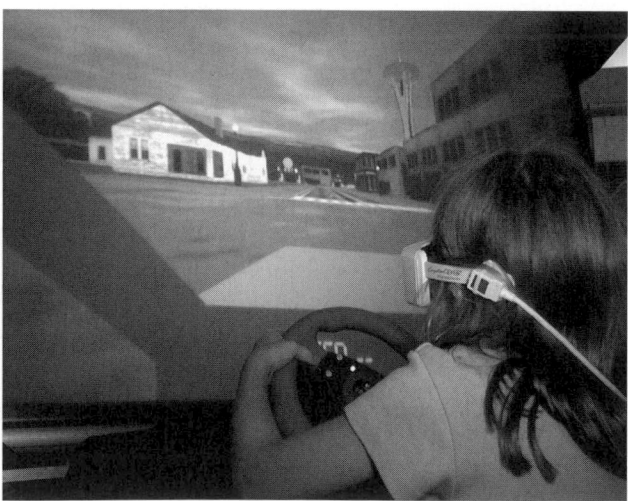

Figure 22 Steering a vehicle is one way in which the user can use a physical device to interface with the virtual world. (Copyright 2003, William Sherman.)

Figure 23 Interacting with a graphical (virtual) controller is an example of a virtual input interaction, such as moving this table using a virtual slider. (Copyright 2003, William Sherman.)

2. Making Selections

The primary selections one can make in a virtual world are selecting an object on which to act, or to select a direction in which to go.

There are a variety of ways of indicating a direction of interest. Many of these make use of the position of some part of the user's body, such as pointing with a finger, gazing with the eyes, or facing with the torso. One can also indicate direction with devices such as a joystick or steering wheel, or by referring to a coordinate system, or some landmark-based reference system.

There are many natural ways in which a VR system designer might choose to allow the user to select an item in a virtual world. In some of the previous examples, the user made contact with an item to activate it—making contact is one way to select an item. By making use of a selected direction, one can point to the object of interest. Through the use of voice recognition software, the user might just name the object, either from memory, or from a menu listing possible selections. Or, the VR system might provide a menu system that allows the user to point to the desired object or make contact with the object's name.

3. Manipulating the Virtual World

Having selected an item, the user will often want to perform some manipulation on that item. In many cases, the process of selecting an item may be incorporated directly into the manipulation process. For example, moving a box might be performed by touching or pointing at the box, pressing a button, and then moving the hand that is making virtual contact with the box.

The manipulated element of the experience can be either an object of the virtual world or an attribute of the overall virtual reality system. For example, moving a car is manipulating an object of the world, whereas choosing a filename to store the current status of the world is an attribute of the virtual reality system.

There are two ways of acting on elements of the experience: in a way that mimics the action of forces on them, or by changing attributes of objects in the world or the system in supernatural ways. So, a car in the world can be changed from blue to red, by applying virtual paint to the car (mimicking reality), or by selecting the new color from a menu (supernatural modification).

4. Navigation

Navigation describes how we move from place to place. In the real world, we navigate from place to place as we walk, drive, ski, fly, skate, and sail through the world. In a VR experience, there are several additional choices for how one might navigate through the environment.

For clarity, the term *navigation* can be divided into two subcomponents: *travel* and *wayfinding*. Travel is the act of controlling one's movement through the world, such as by physically walking or controlling an airplane yoke. Wayfinding is the use of information about the world to guide the direction and speed of travel (Fig. 24).

There are ten common travel paradigms used in virtual reality experiences.

Physical locomotion is the simplest method of travel in VR. It is merely the ability for the participant to move their body to change the position of their point of view within the virtual world. Physical locomotion travel is generally available in VR experiences, often in combination with another form of travel.

Ride-along describes a method of travel that gives the participant little or no freedom. They are taken along a predetermined path through the virtual world, perhaps with occasional choice-points. Usually the participant can change their point of view, or "look around" while on that path.

Tow-rope travel is an extension of the ride-along paradigm. In this case, the user is being pulled along a predetermined path, but with the ability to move off the centerline of the path a small distance.

Fly-through travel is a generic term for methods that give the user almost complete freedom of control, in any direction. A subset of the *fly-through method* is the *walk-through*. In a *walk-through* interface, the participant's movement is constrained to follow the terrain such that they are a natural "standing" height above it.

Pilot-through describes the form of travel in which the user controls their movements by using controls

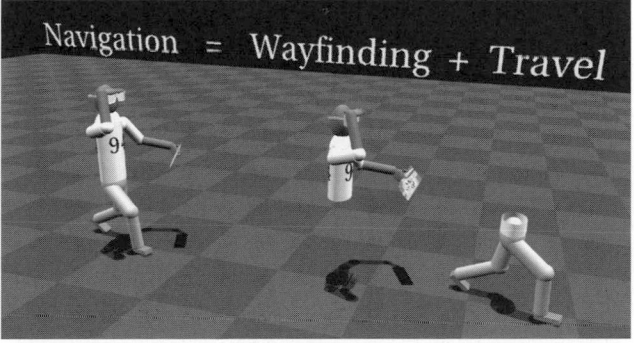

Figure 24 The task of navigating through a world can be broken into the component tasks of wayfinding (figuring out where you are and where to go) and travel (moving through the world). (Copyright 2003, William Sherman.)

that mimic some form of vehicle in which they are riding.

Move-the-world is a form of travel that is often less natural than the previous forms. Here, the user "grabs" the world and can bring it nearer, or move or orient it in any way by repositioning their hand.

Scale-the-world travel is done by reducing the scale of the world, making a small movement, and then scaling the world back to its original size. The difference between the points about which the two scaling operations are performed causes the user to reappear at a new location when returning to the original scale of the world.

Put-me-here travel is a basic method that simply takes the user to some specified position. This can be somewhat natural, like telling a cab driver your destination and arriving some time later, or this method can be totally unnatural by selecting a destination from a menu and popping there instantaneously.

Orbital-viewing is the least natural form of travel. In this method, the world (which often consists of just a model-sized collection of objects) seems to orbit about the user depending on which direction they look. When the user looks left, the object orbits to their left, allowing them to see the right side. Looking up causes the object to orbit above them showing the bottom side.

Some of the above methods of travel aid the user in their movement through the virtual world by constraining where they can go. This constrained travel is one of many ways in which a virtual world can be designed to help the user find their way around. Other "wayfinding aids" include the provision of maps, paths in the world to follow, obvious landmarks by which to site oneself, and instruments such as virtual compasses, among others.

E. Turnkey VR Applications

Presently, there are no mass market virtual reality software applications that can be purchased. A primary reason for this is due to a lack of any real standard platform for which multiple sales can be generated. However, there are some examples both of turnkey software/hardware combination packages and of freely available applications for somewhat common systems such as the CAVE. Of course, a complete package can also be purchased by hiring a firm to produce a custom application to the desired specifications.

An early example of the combined hardware/software design was the Virtuality Arcade Game system (Fig. 25). The Virtuality strategy was to create a small

Figure 25   The first complete virtual reality system on the market was the Virtuality gaming system distributed to arcades and museums around the world. (Image courtesy Virtuality PLC.)

number of standard hardware platforms and several games for each. One configuration was designed for vehicle oriented games (participants seated in a vehicle-like pod with a steering wheel and other controls). The other major hardware platform provided a ring in which the participant stood. The participant held various controllers depending on the game that was being played. For example, the "Trap Master" application made use of a toy model of a shotgun, complete with a simulated recoil force (the *Total Recoil* system). The participant used the weapon in a virtual skeet shooting scenario. Third-party game designers were encouraged to build new games using one of the standard Virtuality systems. However, the number of Virtuality installations was not large enough to generate enough interest from design companies.

Virtually Better, Inc. (VBI) provides a complete turnkey system for exposure therapy. Applications have been specifically developed for aiding psychiatrists in treating patients with various phobias. This product allows the psychiatrist to purchase a complete system that allows them to treat patients directly in the office.

Boston Dynamics, Inc. (BDI) provides a kiosk-style surgical trainer which provides haptic feedback. The appropriate (real) surgical instruments are attached to the force feedback device to allow the physician to carry out a surgical simulation under realistic conditions.

Although there are not widespread standard VR platforms, there are a few hardware environments that have enough commonality to allow application software to be shared among users of the same configuration. For example, all CAVE and most CAVE-like VR display systems can run applications that were compiled with a VR library designed for CAVE-like systems. (Some such libraries impose certain restrictions, such as the requirement of a particular tracking system and particular brand of computer.) There is a user's group of CAVE-like devices that share applications on a Web page. Two popular applications that have been downloaded by many of the facilities with CAVE and CAVE-like displays include an application for visualizing 3-D volumes of scientific and medical data (Crumbs), and a VR port of a popular PC game (CAVEQuake II).

VI. VIRTUAL REALITY APPLICATION AREAS

While the technology that supports virtual reality is interesting in its own right, the real payoff of virtual reality comes when it aids in solving real world problems, provides a creative outlet, or betters human existence in some way. The areas in which virtual reality has been applied in order to bring about edifying personal experiences is wide and varied. These range from viewing architectural (re)creations to visualization of the human body. However, virtual reality has only begun to be applied to the myriad of possible uses.

A. What Makes a Good Application Candidate for VR

A potential new user of virtual reality should consider whether their objective will gain a sufficient advantage via this medium. Many people are attracted to virtual reality simply due to the newness of the technology. This is a perfectly valid reason to make use of virtual reality if one is tasked with investigating new technology or is interested in attracting people to see your work (i.e., using VR as a means of advertising or marketing).

Apart from superficial benefits of using virtual reality, there are features of a task that can help determine whether VR can be advantageous.

Virtual reality provides a means of presenting information in a three-dimensional space, with three-dimensional input controls. Therefore, any problem that is inherently 3-D can be made to work well in virtual reality. This proficiency includes any multidimensional data that can be mapped into some 3-D form.

Much of what VR can do involves the creation of computer models of some real-world item or event. So, for real-world problems that rely on the use of models to achieve some goal, a virtual reality solution can often prove beneficial. Thus, model-based applications for which a computer construction can be created with less resources (time and/or money) than a physical mock-up would be likely to succeed as a virtual reality application. Likewise, VR is beneficial, when computer models can be generated more accurately than the corresponding physical models. For example, a building can be modelled to a greater degree of detail and more lifelike scale in a computer than can be done with a hand-crafted model.

The current technological limits of virtual reality can pose a barrier to taking (full) advantage of possible application areas. Although the computational capability of computers is always improving, some applications always seem to consume even greater computational resources. To function well as a virtual reality application, the virtual world composed of the 3-D models must be within the computer's ability to render the models in real time.

Another technological limitation that can eliminate otherwise potential applications is the degree to which the application requires input registration over a large space. Input registration refers to the ability of the hardware to maintain a stable relationship between the real world, and the sensed location of tracked objects. So, if an application requires that a user walk around a real factory and have an augmented overlay added to their real world view, that application must have good registration between the real world and the augmented data to work properly. There are techniques available for attaining good registration, but the current technology generally limits this to a smaller working volume.

B. Current Promising Application Fields

Through the examination of some of the application fields which have benefitted from the use of virtual reality, one can get a better sense of how well VR can be applied in other fields. "Genres" of VR applications can roughly be categorized into four broad groupings: virtual prototyping, visualization, training, and entertainment. Other genres can be classified as a sub-genre of these four, such as the archtectural walk-through style of application.

1. Virtual Prototyping

A classic genre of virtual reality applications that strives to save money and reduce time in bringing a product to market is *virtual prototyping*. The product can range from something small such as an appliance, to large complex machinery such as a wheel-loader or submarine.

A virtual prototype might be used to evaluate a product from a variety of perspectives: ergonomics, constructability, and aesthetics.

The ergonomics, or usability, of the product can be examined by presenting a virtual representation of the device to its intended users and allowing them to try it out. By virtually using the product, users can discover the little annoyances that might tip a purchase to another brand, and they can discover the big problems that could make the planned item unusable.

Some product designs are also tested for how easy it will be to construct them, and for mechanical products, how easy it will be to maintain them. By putting the product through a virtual assembly, with workers experiencing it in a realistic manner they can uncover trouble that might require a redesign of the assembly process. Likewise, a maintenance worker can be asked to perform many probable repair and inspection tasks to verify their ability to be successfully completed.

Many products get their edge in the marketplace primarily through their aesthetic qualities. Therefore, the design team assigned to consider the look of the product can get a good sense of how the product might appear to the customer by using virtual reality. Because realistic rendering is even more important to this aspect of product analysis, the experience is generally tuned for maximum visual fidelity, sacrificing some interactivity if necessary.

Not only is it easier to change a computer file than a piece of metal (or whatever the product is made of), it is also much easier to distribute a computer file. This feature of computer-based design makes collaboration across great distances much more feasible. In a world where companies operate on a global scale, with operations and customers spread across multiple continents, the ability to quickly pass information between sites is imperative.

2. Architectural Walkthroughs

Visualizing and demonstrating unconstructed buildings as envisioned by their designers is a widely acknowledged, appropriate, use of virtual reality. But what is it about architecture that suggests this merit? In addition to having the quality of presenting three-dimensional constructions, virtual reality improves upon traditional methods of examining a planned structure by allowing the client to experience it "first hand." They do not need to imagine walking into the building by looking at the model. The goal of reviewing the design prior to beginning construction (using either traditional methods or VR) is to find undesirable features in time to make changes inexpensively, or possibly to sell a customer on a proposed design. In this fashion, architectural walkthroughs can be thought of as a type of virtual prototyping application.

Models can also be presented using traditional computer animation renderings, which can be used to show lighting and visual esthetics of the space. However, by being immersed, the participant can also evaluate the scale, accessibility, and usability of the space.

A standard architectural VR application has an obvious three-dimensional representation—make the virtual world look like the real world. There is also a natural choice for navigation scheme—a walkthrough that allows the user to move through the space in a manner similar to how they would do so in reality. The visitor to the virtual building is constrained to walk about on the floor surfaces, but with the ability to open doors, move up and down stairs, and take the elevator.

A similar application is to create nonexistent places for reasons other than design analysis. These places might be nonexistent in time rather than space. Historical places and situations can be created as a means of allowing people to learn about the past. Here, the architectural walkthrough genre acts mostly in the realm of visualization—the exploration of data otherwise difficult to see with unaided human senses.

3. Visualization

Computer simulations and detailed sensor inputs both can provide an over abundance of data making it hard for researchers to perform a useful analysis. This trend previously led to the use of computer animations, and then to interactive tools to aid this process. By continuing this trend to the use of virtual reality, researchers can be provided a more natural way to navigate through the space into which the data have been mapped.

Although some simulated data are not three-dimensional in nature, much of it is, so it can be easily presented via 3-D VR displays. For higher-dimensional data, techniques are being developed that provide the user a glimpse of the features within.

In any case, virtual reality can provide a better interface to the data than is possible through the two-dimensional interfaces of the standard desktop mouse. This interface departure can be used with nonrealistic rendering techniques afforded via computer graphics. Nonrealistic rendering is common in scientific and medical visualization, and in VR the user can be given a natural interface to view the world through a variety of different "lenses."

4. Training

Training is also an application genre that is a rather obvious fit for VR. In fact, the oldest example of virtual reality—flight simulation—is of this genre. One basic reason for this natural fit is that mimicking the three-dimensional real world has a clear metaphor—behaving in the virtual world should simulate behavior in the real world.

Virtual reality, however, allows one to do more than merely mimicking reality. If reality imitation was the only goal, then it may be simpler to manufacture physical props with which a participant could practice some procedure. For example, much surgical training is performed on animals and cadavers. What virtual reality adds is the ability to practice uncommon, expensive, and dangerous tasks.

By practicing tasks in this computer mediated system, other benefits are realized. Specifically, the simulation operator has more control over what scenarios can be presented to the trainee and can change the scenario in response to performance. The other significant benefit is that their performance can be recorded and analyzed.

5. Entertainment

As a new medium, virtual reality has found a niche in the entertainment market. However, being new will draw people for a while, but to "keep 'em coming" requires an enhanced experience at an affordable price. A profitable, long-lived VR entertainment endeavor has yet to be demonstrated. As mentioned earlier in this article, Disney has an ongoing effort that may prove to endure.

That said, the trend in computer gaming is toward more realism with techniques to render the world from the perspective of the player. This has led to an amazing improvement in the price/performance of computer graphics hardware. If this trend continues, it is likely that the cost of hardware for physically immersive displays will become low enough for many game enthusiasts to purchase them for the home.

The added feeling of immersiveness when comparing the desktop version of a game such as Quake II to an adaptation to the CAVE VR display indicates that the computer game community is likely to embrace virtual reality. "CAVEQuake II" is perhaps the most widely distributed of all CAVE applications.

6. Other Application Genres

Virtual reality has also been applied to other areas of use, such as medical, educational, and artistic uses. However, many of these uses can be categorized as subsets of the above genres.

Medical applications chiefly fall into the two categories of visualization and training. Surgical suturing and minimally invasive surgery trainers are available commercially, and experimental work has been done on other procedures such as celius plexus block anesthesia administration. Visualization applications include analysis of CT and MRI scan data, sometimes with the ability to aid in planning for an upcoming surgery. Work has also been done at the University of North Carolina to allow a physician to visualize inside the patient's body while performing a procedure. Psychological treatment of phobias is a (clinician) controlled walkthrough of a visualization of some subset of the real world.

Educational applications can fall into the training, walkthrough, and visualization categories. The ScienceSpace application, a lesson in high school physics developed at the University of Houston and George Mason University, is an example of how physical processes can be visualized to allow the student to come to a better grasp of the 3-D nature of the subject matter than merely reading it from a book.

Architectural students supplement their education by creating virtual prototypes of their designs in the CAVE at the University of Illinois at Urbana-Champaign.

A Japanese science museum has sought to make learning important lessons about their nation's ecology entertaining, as well as educational by creating a virtual reality game that students participant in to learn about the ecological place of the dung beetle.

For art-oriented applications, rather than the utility of what can be done in a virtual reality encounter, the experience of the participant is the focus. The goal of an artistic application may or may not be to entertain the participant, but it strives to give them a chance to view the world from another perspective and give rise to intellectual stimulation. Artistic applications also differ from many visualization, training, and virtual prototyping applications which strive to closely mimic the real world. Many artistic and entertainment applications choose to focus on the surreal or fantastic rendering and interactive possibilities offered by virtual reality.

New ideas for where to apply virtual reality are continuously arising. As virtual reality becomes more commonplace, the medium will be sought as a possible answer to many new tasks and many new artistic expressions.

VII. FUTURE PROSPECTS OF VIRTUAL REALITY

The future holds great promise for virtual reality, and vice versa. The general trends of the computing industry will continue to make VR faster, better, and cheaper. The CPU and graphics-processing capabilities of low cost computers have already made significant bounds. With the ability to do low cost tracking, along with probable cost decreases in stereoscopic monitor display and head-mounted displays, virtual reality will become widely available. Of course, software is also a key necessity. Currently, there are both commercial and free open-source VR products available. Software product offerings of both types are likely to continue to increase.

Collaboration in virtual reality experiences will continue to become an important aspect, following the generic trend in all areas of computing. Experiences becoming more fully mediated lead to ramifications such as the possible anonymity of the participants, and the ability to store and therefore replay experiences from the point-of-view of any of the participants. Because the identity of the entities can be hidden, it might even be difficult to know whether one is dealing with another human, or a purely digital entity.

The reduction of encumbrances of virtual reality is already starting to occur. Encumbrances associated with both input and display components of virtual reality will improve. On the input side, methods of being able to wirelessly track the user will develop and improve. Traditional VR tracking methods such as electromagnetic technologies will use radio packs. Newer tracking methods such as video tracking are also advancing.

On the display side, encumbrances will be reduced by new methods of rendering stereoscopic visual images. In the near term, "autostereo" displays that use built-in filters to separate the left and right eye images will improve in quality and increase in size. Also under development is the ability to display computer-generated holograms in real time. Of course, for a time these will be limited in size. Another advance is in the decreasing size and weight of head-based displays to the point where they will be like putting on a pair of sunglasses.

In general, what these improvements all lead to is increased fidelity of these systems that will blur the line between what is "real" and what is not. This improvement in verisimilitude applies to not just the visual aspects of VR, but to the aural and haptic sensory displays, plus adding senses not commonly provided today. Each sense is improving in temporal and spatial resolutions. The concurrent improvement in display fidelity and reduction in encumbrance of the devices combine to offer the promise of Sutherland's vision for the "ultimate display."

Virtual reality will also be able to take advantage of the creeping of computer technology into all areas of our lives. Two current areas of computer research leading in this direction are *wearable computers* and *smart spaces* (e.g., smart houses, smart offices, smart boardrooms). As people begin to work with computers embedded into their clothing and eyewear, virtual reality and augmented reality applications will simply be assumed. Wearable computers are, after all, tools designed to augment our natural capabilities and merging the physical world more closely with the digital. So, for example, a carpenter's protective eyewear might serve also as an interface to a database of the building's design, allowing them to see more clearly what needs to be done to match the planned results. Sports gear might have a practice application built right in. A putter may work as a normal putter, or it may be linked to the owner's wearable computer and serve as a virtual reality practice putting course.

Smart spaces are the complement to the wearable computer. They embed digital augmentation into some aspect of the physical world. One goal of research into smart spaces is to have the environment change based on the preferences of the occupants, with rules to evaluate how to accommodate groups with differing preferences. As the walls of the room become the visual display, and the occupant analysis technology able to continuously track each occupant, the space itself can act as a large stationary screen display, perhaps moving the visual sweet spot from person to person as deemed appropriate. Persons wearing their own personal displays can be tied into the same virtual environment. Today's CAVE gives us a glimpse into the concept of the smart room—though with today's clumsy predecessors of the technology to come.

Another advance that can be expected in the near future is that more turnkey VR applications will be available. In addition to the current practice of selling software bundled with an entire VR system, as virtual reality hardware moves from the realm of VR researchers to the mass consumer, turnkey applications will become available as software-only products.

Games of course will be the driving force for the home VR market. Graphics, audio, and computational capabilities of home computers have already reached the level to adequately handle VR applications. A fishtank VR system can easily be developed with current commodity hardware, but no turnkey system with easy to follow instructions exists yet. Head-based displays have flirted with low price-points, but not low enough to sell enough to sustain mass production levels. The next step will likely be software that is "VR capable," but will also run in traditional desktop mode. This feature will promote the gradual adoption of VR hardware by allowing users to upgrade from a desktop interface to VR with familiar software.

As virtual reality creeps into the home market, additional genres will appear in addition to the games. Other forms of recreation such as virtual travel—sight seeing of far away and no longer existent places—will likely be an early source of applications. Education will also be a viable application wellspring, allowing home learners to experience science, geography, mathematics, and history in an entirely new way.

Certainly, virtual reality is here to stay and will find its way into more venues and more uses than one can think to enumerate at present.

SEE ALSO THE FOLLOWING ARTICLES

Artificial Intelligence Programming • Computer-Aided Design • Hyper-Media Databases • Multimedia • People, Information Systems Impact on • Robotics • Speech Recognition • User/ System Interface Design • Virtual Learning Systems • Virtual Organizations

BIBLIOGRAPHY

Billinghurst, M., Kato, H., and Poupyrev, I. (2001). The Magic-Book: Moving seamlessly between reality and virtuality. *IEEE Computer Graphics and Applications,* May/June, 2–4.

Brady, R., and Potter, C. (1995). Crumbs: A virtual environment tracking tool for biological imaging, in *Proceedings of the IEEE Symposium on Frontiers in Biomedical Visualization, Atlanta, GA, October 30,* pp. 18–25.

Brooks, F. P., Jr., Ouh-Young, M., Batter, J. J., and Kilpatrick, P. J. (1990). Project GROPE—Haptic displays for scientific visualization, SIGGRAPH 1990 Conference Proceedings, *Computer Graphics,* Vol. 24, No. 4, August.

Bryson, S., and Levit, C. (1992). *The virtual windtunnel: An environment for the exploration of three dimensional unsteady flows.* RNR Technical Report, RNR-92-013, April.

Coffin, T. (2001). CAVE research network user society homepage, http://www.cavernus.org.

Dede, C., Salzman, M., and Loftin, B. (1996). ScienceSpace: Virtual realities for learning complex and abstract scientific concepts, in *Proceedings Virtual Reality Annual International Symposium '96, Santa Clara CA, March 30–April 3.*

Emerson, T. (2001). Virtual reality knowledge base, http://www.hitl.washington.edu/projects/knowledge_base.

Krueger, M. W. (1982). *Artificial reality.* Reading, MA: Addison–Wesley.

Rheingold, H. (1991). *Virtual Reality.* New York: Summit Books.

Sherman, W. R., and Craig, A. B. (2002). *Understanding virtual reality.* San Francisco, CA: Morgan Kaufman.

Sherman, W. R. (2001). FreeVR open source VR library homepage, http://www.freevr.org.

Sutherland, I. E. (1963). *Sketchpad: A man-machine graphical communication system.* Baltimore, MD: Spartan Books.

Sutherland, I. E. (1968). A head-mounted three dimensional display, pp. 757–764. Washington, DC: Thompson.

van Dam, A., Forsberg, A. S., Laidlaw, D. H., LaViola, J. J., and Simpson, R. M. (2000). Immersive virtual reality for scientific visualization: A progress report. *Computer Graphics and Applications,* Vol. 20, No. 6, 26–52.

Zeltzer, D., and Pioch, N. (1996). Validation and verification of virtual environment training systems, in *Proc. Virtual Reality Annual International Symposium '96, Santa Clara CA, March 30–April 3.*

Visual Basic

Rod Stephens

Boulder, Colorado

GLOSSARY

application programming interface (API) Operating system and Windows functions that can be called by programs, including those written in Visual Basic, to perform operating system tasks usually impossible within the programming language itself.

active server pages (ASP) Server-side scripted web page. When a visitor requests an ASP web page, the server executes the VBScript code it contains and returns a pure HTML result.

ActiveX A technology that allows independent software objects to operate closely together. For example, an ActiveX control written in Visual Basic can be displayed in any ActiveX-enabled parent such as a Visual Basic program, a Delphi program, or even a web page displayed in Internet Explorer.

Beginner's All-purpose Symbolic Instruction Code (BASIC) The language from which Visual Basic is derived.

class A module that defines a type of object that contains related data and features. Once the class is defined, the program can make any number of instances of that class. For example, a program might define an Employee class that stores and manipulates employee data. The program could then create separate instances of the class to represent each employee in the company.

control A user interface component that allows the user to view or interact with information. The fundamental building blocks from which a user interface is built; includes text boxes, labels, and buttons.

event When certain things happen, Visual Basic raises an event. For example, when the user clicks on a button, the button raises a Click event.

event handler The code executed by a Visual Basic program to handle an event.

FileSystem object (FSO) Provides support for manipulating files and the file system.

integrated development environment (IDE) A powerful development environment that lets programmers design forms using a simple drag-and-drop interface.

method A subroutine or function provided by an object to perform actions or calculations.

modal dialog A dialog that requires the user's immediate attention. The user must close the dialog before any other part of the program will respond.

Multiple Document Interface (MDI) A program like Microsoft Word that can display several documents inside one instance of the program.

property A value that helps determine the appearance or behavior of an object.

Single Document Interface (SDI) A program like Microsoft Notepad that can display only one document at a time.

user-defined type (UDT) A group of related data fields combined in a single data structure. Similar to a struct in C.

variant array An array of Variants, each of which can contain a variety of data types including other variant arrays.

VBScript A subset of Visual Basic used in web pages and ASP programming.

Visual Basic for Applications (VBA) A large subset of Visual Basic used as a macro language by Microsoft's

Office applications. The VBA Scripting Edition allows other programs to use VBA as a macro language.

VISUAL BASIC is a powerful object-oriented programming language for developing stand-alone applications and components for use in other programs. As powerful as Visual Basic is by itself, the language's positioning in relationship to other Microsoft products may be just as important. Visual Basic is the basis for Microsoft's web scripting language VBScript and the language used for active server pages. Visual Basic for Applications is the macro programming language for all of Microsoft's Office applications: Word, Excel, Outlook, etc. Additional tools let you use VBA as a scripting language in your programs. This article briefly describes the Visual Basic programming language and explains how its positioning gives Visual Basic programmers extra flexibility not provided by other programming languages.

I. EVOLUTION OF VISUAL BASIC

BASIC (Beginner's All-purpose Symbolic Instruction Code) is an old and venerable programming language. Developed by John Kemeny and Thomas Kurtz at Dartmouth College in 1964, it was intended to be a simple introductory programming language for students to learn before moving on to more advanced languages like FORTRAN.

Over time, different versions of BASIC were released for different operating systems. Two of the most common versions were BASICA and GW-BASIC, which ran under different DOS operating systems. Other versions have included QuickBasic, TurboBasic, and PowerBASIC.

Most of these versions of BASIC produced textual output in a console window. As computers grew faster and cheaper, graphical user interfaces (GUIs) became widely available. The MacIntosh and Windows operating systems were widely adopted and users came to expect interactive graphical interfaces.

In 1991, Microsoft released Visual Basic version 1. This was followed quickly by version 2 in 1992 and version 3 in 1993. Version 3 is regarded by most as the first really useful version of Visual Basic.

Even with version 3, Visual Basic was not considered a professional language. It was seen as a language for beginners and hobby programmers. Still, this version was flexible and robust enough for programmers to build nontrivial applications.

Microsoft released Visual Basic version 4 in 1995, version 5 in 1997, version 6 in 1998, and expects to release the next version named VB.NET in 2001.

A. Improvements over Time

The biggest change with version 4 was the addition of classes. Visual Basic programmers can use classes to create multiple instances of object's packaging properties and methods together much as other object-oriented programming languages do. Visual Basic 4's classes did not provide inheritance, however, so some programmers refused to consider Visual Basic a fully object-oriented language.

Visual Basic 5 introduced ActiveX control creation. Using Visual Basic, a developer can build controls that can run in other Visual Basic programs, programs written in other languages like C++ and Delphi, and even in web pages.

Visual Basic 6 added a variety of less earth-shaking features than versions 4 and 5 did. Some of the new features included the ability to add new controls to a form flexibly at run time, easier server creation for client/server applications, a variety of new string functions such as Replace, which replaces instances of one string with another, and new support for multiple threads.

Two of the most eagerly awaited changes in VB.NET are inheritance in classes and structured error handling. This version will also completely integrate Visual Basic with Microsoft's other programming languages. These languages will all use the same integrated development environment (IDE) so a programmer can build add-ins and other IDE tools in one language and use them while building programs using any of the others. Using the IDE's debugger, a programmer will also be able to step from a Visual Basic program's code into the source code for a library or control used by the program even if the tool was written in C++ or some other language.

VB.NET will focus heavily on web programming. The intent is to shift focus from self-contained applications that do all their own work to programs that invoke the methods of web services scattered across the network. These services perform parts of the program's work and then the program ties them all together. For example, a point-of-sale system might consult an inventory service to check product availability, a pricing service to calculate prices, sales tax, and shipping cost, and a customer service to get the customer's billing information. The program would then send an order to an order fulfillment service and print a bill to be mailed to the customer.

The changes in VB.NET will be large. Microsoft is providing an upgrade wizard that loads projects written in earlier versions of Visual Basic into VB.NET, but there are many changes the wizard will be unable to handle automatically. Over the years, many companies have been left behind using older versions of Visual Basic. Quite a few still use Visual Basic 3 and 4 because they are still using 16-bit Windows and those are the most recent versions that work in 16-bit Windows. Some are using Visual Basic 5 because they feel it is more stable than Visual Basic 6 and that version 6 does not provide enough new features to justify migrating to the newer version. The changes to VB.NET are much larger than those in any previous version so it will take a substantial effort to upgrade many applications so many companies will undoubtedly continue using Visual Basic 6 rather than upgrading to VB.NET, at least in the short term.

B. Widening Scope

As Visual Basic's capabilities grew, so did its popularity. Before Visual Basic, Microsoft's popular Office applications (Word, Access, Excel, etc.) each included a simple macro language to allow users to automate basic tasks. Microsoft Word included WordBasic, Microsoft Access included Access Basic, and so forth. These languages were all variations of BASIC, but each had its own peculiarities.

As Visual Basic grew more powerful, Microsoft started merging these macro languages into one common version of Visual Basic called Visual Basic for Applications (VBA). Today all of Microsoft's Office products use VBA as their macro languages and they even use Visual Basic's IDE to edit and debug VBA source code.

Microsoft also adapted Visual Basic to create VBScript. This lightweight language runs on Web browsers to execute program code while displaying Web pages.

Active server pages (ASP), another form of VBScript, allows a server to execute VBScript code on a web server before sending a web page to a visitor's browser. The VBScript code can perform complex tasks such as accessing databases and produce pure HTML text to send to the visitor's browser.

Microsoft even has tools that let a programmer easily add Visual Basic as a macro programming language to other applications. Hundreds of commercial software products have incorporated Visual Basic in this way.

The fact that so many programs use VBA and VBScript as macro languages gives developers great flexibility. Unfortunately that flexibility is also available to hackers who write viruses. Because these programs interoperate so easily, they present few barriers to a virus written in VBA or VBScript. One of the most common forms of virus today is a VBScript file attached to an e-mail message. The file's name usually ends in ".bmp.vbs," ".gif.vbs," or ".jpg.vbs." A user who sees the "bmp," "gif," or "jpg" and assumes the file is a picture may open on it. Because the file's final extension is "vbs," the system executes it as a VBScript program. Once it is running, the virus can open Microsoft's Outlook e-mail system and forward itself to everyone in the Outlook address book.

Visual Basic's growing sophistication and its increasing adoption in other contexts has transformed it from a hobby language to an important part of a professional developer's resume. A programmer who knows Visual Basic also knows VBA and VBScript. With those tools and a little experience, a programmer can build stand-alone applications, write macros for Office programs, include VBA as a macro language in new applications, customize web pages, and generate web pages from scratch using ASP.

II. GENERAL DESCRIPTION

One of the first things a new Visual Basic programmer notices is its IDE. Using an intuitive point-and-click paradigm, the IDE lets a programmer build a running application quickly and easily. The IDE also includes powerful facilities for debugging Visual Basic programs.

A. Integrated Development Environment

Figure 1 shows Visual Basic's IDE. The IDE is highly customizable, allowing a programmer to show or hide each of its different windows and toolbars. By simply clicking and dragging, a developer can rearrange these windows, dock them to one part of the IDE or another, or detach them so they float in separate windows.

The menu and toolbar at the top provide standard tools for manipulating the Visual Basic project. These commands let the developer add forms and other objects to the project, load and save projects, step through program execution, etc. The Add-Ins menu contains tools that automate common programming tasks. For example, the Data Form Wizard helps build forms for database applications. The developer can use the standard add-ins or build and install new ones.

The IDE lets a programmer build forms using a simple drag-and-drop interface. The programmer selects a control from the window on the left side of the screen and then clicks and drags to position it on the form. Figure 1 shows a command button just after it has been created.

The Project window on the right shows the objects associated with the Visual Basic project. This example includes a single form named Form1. If the developer

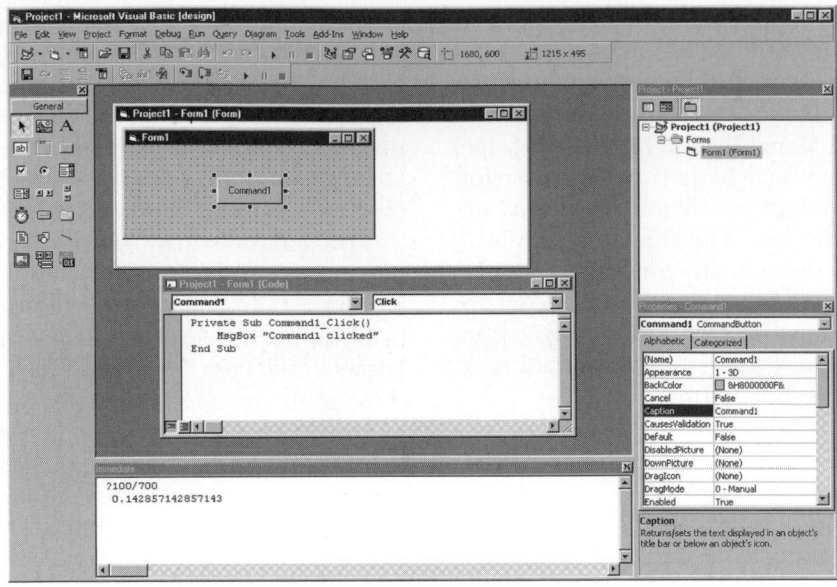

Figure 1 Visual Basic's integrated development environment.

double clicks on an object in this window, the IDE opens it up for editing. Form1 is open for editing in Fig. 1.

The Properties window sits below the Project window in Fig. 1. This area lists the properties of the object currently selected for editing. In Fig. 1, the command button named Command1 is selected so its properties are displayed. The developer can click on any of the properties and enter a new value. In this case, the developer might change the button's Caption to "Ok" and its Name to "cmdOk." Many Visual Basic programmers use the prefix "cmd" for command buttons.

Double clicking on a control makes the IDE open a code window showing the code for the control's default event handler. The developer can enter code to determine the actions the program takes when that event occurs. For example, a button's default event is the Click event. When the user clicks a button, the Click event handler executes its code.

B. Debugging

Visual Basic's IDE includes a powerful debugger. By simply clicking next to a line of code, the developer can set or clear a breakpoint. When the program reaches a breakpoint, execution stops. The developer can click on variables to see their values, modify the code, step over statements one at a time, or resume normal execution.

The developer can also execute Visual Basic statements in the Immediate window at the bottom of the IDE. For example, if the variable user_name contains the value "XXX" but should contain the value "Rod," the developer could enter this code in the Immediate window to correct it:

```
User_name = "Rod"
```

The IDE will even execute subroutines and functions in the Immediate window. This can be extremely useful for debugging routines that are hard to exercise using the program interactively. The developer can use the Immediate window to execute a routine many times, passing it different parameters. By setting breakpoints inside the routine, the developer can step through the routine and study its execution in detail.

One of the most remarkable features of the IDE is its ability to accept changes and keep running. The developer can modify the actual source code and, in most cases, continue execution. The developer can even click on a line and jump execution to that point. All of these features make the IDE a potent debugging tool.

C. Controls

Visual Basic comes with the large assortment of intrinsic controls listed in Table I. These controls are automatically included in Visual Basic programs.

Visual Basic also comes with an assortment of ActiveX controls. The programmer must explicitly load

Table I   Intrinsic Controls That Come with Visual Basic

Control	Purpose
PictureBox	Display a picture. This control has many methods and events.
Label	Display noneditable text.
TextBox	Display editable text.
Frame	Display a box around the controls it contains.
CommandButton	Perform an action when clicked.
CheckBox	Display a checked, unchecked, or grayed state.
OptionButton	Let the user select one of a set of choices at a time.
ComboBox	Let the user type a value or pick from a dropdown list.
ListBox	Let the user pick from a list.
HScrollBar	Horizontal scroll bar.
VScrollBar	Vertical scroll bar.
Timer	Execute code periodically.
DriveListBox	Let the user select one of the computer's disk drives.
DirListBox	Let the user select one of the computer's directories.
FileListBox	Let the user select one of the computer's files.
Shape	Display a rectangle, circle, ellipse, etc.
Line	Display a line.
Image	Display a picture. This control has fewer methods and events than the PictureBox but takes fewer resources.
Data	Manages database interactions. For example, you can connect this control to a database and to TextBoxes to make the TextBoxes automatically display values from the database.
OLE container	Holds insertable linked or embedded objects. For example, you can insert a Word document of Excel chart in the container.

these into a project to use them. The controls provided vary slightly in different versions of Visual Basic. Table II lists some of the most useful.

Normally a developer drags and drops controls onto a form. The program can also create new controls at runtime using one of two methods. First, the developer can create one control at design time and set its Index property to 0. That creates a control array. The program references the control using its name and its index as in:

```
txtAddress(0).Text = "1234 Main St"
```

The developer can create other controls with the same name and different indices at runtime using the Load statement.

```
Load txtAddress(1)
txtAddress(1).Top = txtAddress(0).Top
   + txtAddress(0).Height + 30
txtAddress(1).Text = "Bugville"
txtAddress(1).Visible = True
```

A program can unload controls created with the Load statement using the Unload statement:

```
Unload txtAddress(1)
```

The second way a program can load controls is by using a form's Controls collection. The program specifies the type of control, its name, and its container as in:

```
Set new_button = Me.Controls.Add("VB.
   CommandButton", "cmdNew", Frame1)
```

A program can unload controls created at runtime using the Controls collection's Remove method:

```
Me.Controls.Remove "cmdNew"
```

D. Program Compilation

After building and testing a Visual Basic application, the developer can compile it into an executable program. Visual Basic can compile the program into

Table II ActiveX Controls That Come with Visual Basic

Control	Purpose
ADOData	Manages database interactions using active data objects (ADO).
Animation	Displays AVI clips.
Common Dialog Control	Provides standard file, color, font, help, and printer selection dialogs.
CoolBar	A fancier toolbar.
DataGrid	A grid that can be bound to ADOData controls.
DataList	A list that can be bound to ADOData controls.
DataRepeater	Displays a set of controls for each record in a database query.
DTPicker	Lets the user enter a date or drop down a MonthView and pick one.
FlatScrollBar	A toolbar with a flat appearance.
FlexGrid	Displays data in a table format.
HierarchicalFlexGrid	Displays data with hierarchical details in a table format.
ImageCombo	A ComboBox that can display images as well as text.
ImageList	Holds a series of images.
Internet Transfer Control	Downloads or uploads information on the Web using the FTP or HTTP protocols.
ListView	Displays items in a list report structure similar to the one on the right in Windows Explorer.
MAPI controls	Works with the Microsoft Outlook mail system.
MaskedEdit	A TextBox that restricts the type of data the user can enter.
MonthView	Displays a calendar where the user can select a date.
MultiMedia Control	Plays multimedia files.
ProgressBar	A progress indicator.
RichTextBox	A TextBox that allows formatting (bold, italics, paragraph indenting, etc.). This control can load and save text in Rich Text Format (RTF).
Slider	Lets the user pick a value using a sliding handle similar to a scrollbar.
StatusBar	Displays messages. Usually this is at the bottom of a form.
SysInfo	Returns information about the system such as the work area dimensions and the operating system version. This control also provides some system events. For example, the SettingChanged event occurs when a system setting changes.
TabStrip	Displays clickable tabs.
Toolbar	Contains tool buttons.
TreeView	Displays items in a tree structure similar to the one on the left in Windows Explorer.
TreeView	Displays items in a tree structure similar to the one on the left in Windows Explorer.
UpDown	Provides up and down arrows the user can click on to change a value.
Various charts	Different versions of Visual Basic include different graphing and chart controls.
WebBrowser	Displays web pages.

p-code (pseudo-code) or native code. P-code is an intermediate language that encodes the Visual Basic program. At runtime, the Visual Basic runtime library translates the p-code into the computer's native code and executes it.

Visual Basic does not need to perform this runtime translation for a program compiled into native code so the code may execute faster. While a native code program does not need to translate p-code, it still needs the Visual Basic runtime libraries to provide support for other language features.

Operations closely tied to the computer's hardware may be much faster in a program compiled into native code. Arithmetic operations may be much faster depending on the hardware. Consider the following code:

```
y = 3.14159265
z = 128.75365
For i = 1 To 10000000
    x = i * Sqr(y) + z ^ 3
Next i
```

In one test, this program took roughly 84% as long compiled into native code as it did compiled into p-code. These results may vary on different hardware.

Native code programs tend to be slightly larger than p-code programs, however. In this example, the native code executable took 16 KB while the p-code version took 12 KB. This may seem like a significant difference until you take into account the Visual Basic runtime library. The Visual Basic 6 runtime library weighs in at a hefty 1.3 MB making the difference in executable size trivial. It is common to compile a program into native and p-code executables to see which produces a better result.

Visual Basic provides several options when compiling to native code. For example, you can make the IDE optimize the code for size or speed. Other options allow you to remove code that protects the program from certain types of errors. For example, you can remove code that protects the program if it tries to access an array entry outside of the array's bounds. Normally a Visual Basic program can catch this error and take special action. Without this check, the program will not realize an error has occurred. It will read and write values outside of the array's memory and that may cause obscure bugs.

Disabling these safety features can be dangerous but they can improve a thoroughly debugged program's performance. In the previous test program, disabling all of the safety checks decreased the program's runtime by almost 14%.

III. LANGUAGE ELEMENTS

Visual Basic provides many of the same features supported by other high-level languages like Delphi, C++, and FORTRAN. It provides conditional execution statements (If ... Then ...), looping statements (For i = 1 To 10 ...), subroutines, functions, classes, and all of the other features a programmer expects in a modern programming language.

Like FORTRAN, Visual Basic is a line-oriented language. That means a single programming statement usually occupies one line of source code. If necessary, a programmer can break a long statement across multiple lines. If a line ends in a space followed by an un-derscore, it is merged with the following line. The following code shows two equivalent statements.

```
A = A + B
A = _
    A + _
    B
```

A Visual Basic programmer can also place more than one statement on the same line separated by a colon. This often makes code less readable but there are times when it is useful. For example, the Immediate window can only execute code on a single line. To execute several statements, the developer must put them all in one line. For example, the following code executes a For loop that would normally occupy three lines of code.

```
For I = 1 To 10: Debug.Print Names(I):
    Next I
```

Visual Basic's comment character is the apostrophe ('). When this character appears outside a quoted string, Visual Basic ignores any text on the line after the character.

```
' Set the client's name.
client_name = "Bob's Toys"   ' Note
    the apostrophe in the string.
```

The following sections describe other Visual Basic language elements. If you have used one of the more recent versions of FORTRAN or BASIC, these may seem very familiar.

A. Program Elements

A typical Visual Basic program displays one or more forms. The forms hold controls that allow the user to view and modify data. A Visual Basic program can also include other elements such as code modules, MDI forms, and classes. The following list describes some of the more common program elements in detail.

- *Form.* A form displays controls so the user can view and modify data. A program can display a form modally as a dialog or nonmodally as a normal application window. A program can display multiple instances of the same form at the same time.
- *MDIForm.* An MDIForm holds other forms in a Multiple Document Interface (MDI) program. If a normal form's MDIChild property is True, that form sits inside the MDIForm. The MDIForm provides features to manage the child forms,

iconify them, tile them, list them in a Windows menu, etc. A Visual Basic program can have at most one MDIForm.

- *Code module.* A code module has no graphical component. It contains subroutines, functions, and variables for use by other modules. If a code module contains a special subroutine named Main, the program can start execution with that routine rather than by displaying a form. If the program can run noninteractively, it may not need to display any forms at all.
- *Class.* A class serves as a template for creating nongraphical objects that group related data and functionality. Once the class is defined, the program can instantiate the class and invoke the public methods provided by the object.
- *UserControl.* A UserControl element defines an ActiveX control. Once the control is compiled into an OCX file, any program that supports ActiveX controls can use it. For example, the control can be included in a program written in Visual Basic, C++, Delphi, or even HTML.
- *DataEnvironment.* A DataEnvironment defines one or more connections to a database. Each database connection can include one or more commands. For example, a command might be an SQL statement that selects certain records from the Customer table and orders the results by customer ID.
- *DataReport.* When connected to a data source, a DataReport generates a report. The report provides its own printing and scaling features, and can export data in text or HTML format.

B. Properties and Methods

Visual Basic's objects have properties and methods just as objects in other object-oriented languages do. The syntax for using an object's properties and methods is:

```
object_name.property_name = new_value
    ' Set a property value.
new_value = object_name.property_name
    ' Get a property value.
```

For example, suppose the emp object is an instance of the Employee class. The following code sets the emp object's Salary property to 10,000.

```
emp.Salary = 10000
```

A program invokes an object's subroutines and functions in a similar way. The following code shows how a program might call the OnDuty function to see if the Employee emp was on duty on December 31, 1999.

```
If emp.OnDuty(#December 31, 1999#)
    Then . . .
```

The programmer creates a method by defining a subroutine or function in the object's code window. If the routine is declared Public, it is available to other parts of the program. If the routine is declared Private, it is available only to other routines within the same object module. Restricting the scope of a routine like this can help reduce confusion in other parts of the program. If the main program cannot see a routine because it is declared Private in another module, it cannot misuse that routine. Later, if you change how the Private routine works, you know the main program cannot be affected because it is not allowed to use the routine anyway.

```
' This method is available to the
    whole program.
Public Function OnDuty(ByVal
    duty_date As Date) As Boolean
    . . .
End Function

' This method is available only within
    this module.
Private Sub InitializeEmployee()
    . . .
End Sub
```

The programmer can make simple properties by declaring variables in the object's code module. As is the case with methods, a property can be Public or Private. Although this kind of property is simple, it gives the rest of the program direct access to the object's data. Often it is better to encapsulate the data so the main program cannot modify it directly. That makes it easier to change the way the property is stored later without messing up the rest of the program.

Visual Basic's property procedures provide this encapsulation. The following code shows how a class might implement the Salary property using property procedures in Visual Basic 6. It stores the actual salary value in the private variable m_Salary. Property procedures give the rest of the program indirect access to the property.

```
' Private variable to hold the salary
    value.
Private m_Salary As Currency
```

```
' Public procedure to let code
   outside this module get the salary.
Public Property Get Salary() As
   Currency
      Salary = m_Salary
End Property

' Public procedure to let code
   outside this module set the salary.
Public Property Let Salary(ByVal
   New_Salary As Currency)
      m_Salary = New_Salary
End Property
```

If the main program sets an Employee object's Salary property, Visual Basic invokes the property Let procedure. The syntax is the same as it would be if Salary were a public variable.

Property procedures isolate the main program from the inner workings of the class. If the Employee class changes so it fetches the salary value from a database instead of holding it in a local variable, the main program would not need to know anything had changed.

While the different program elements described in the previous section are very different, most of them are objects. Forms, MDIForms, classes, UserControls, DataEnvironments, and DataReports are all objects that provide their own properties and methods. The developer can even add new properties and methods to Forms, MDIForms, classes, and UserControls.

C. Data Types

Visual Basic provides an assortment of data types for storing simple data. Table III lists the most useful of these. Some of these data types have features that deserve special mention.

The Currency data type is a scaled integer with four digits after the decimal point. Because it uses integer calculations, it has high enough precision for most currency calculations.

The Decimal data type can have 0 to 28 digits after the decimal point. With no digits after the decimal, values can range from roughly $-7.9E+28$ to $7.9E+28$. Values with the greatest precision possible range from roughly -7.9 to 7.9 and have precision of $1E-28$.

1. Variants

The Variant data type can hold lots of different kinds of values. A Variant variable might contain a Date, an Integer, or a String. It can also contain a variant array. A variant array is an array of Variants, each of which can contain a variety of data types including other variant arrays. The following example uses the Array

Table III Visual Basic Data Types

Data type	Size (bytes)	Range of values
Byte	1	0 to 255
Boolean	2	True or false
Integer (VB6)	2	$-32,768$ to $32,767$
Long (VB6)	4	$-2,147,483,648$ to $2,147,483,647$
Short (VB.NET)	2	$-32,768$ to $32,767$
Integer (VB.NET)	4	$-2,147,483,648$ to $2,147,483,647$
Long (VB.NET)	8	$-9,223,372,036,854,775,808$ to $9,223,372,036,854,775,807$
Single	4	$-3.402823E38$ to $3.402823E38$
Double	8	$-1.79769313486231E308$ to $1.79769313486232E308$
Currency	8	$-922,337,203,685,477.5808$ to $922,337,203,685,477.5807$
Decimal	14	$+/-79,228,162,514,264,337,593,543,950,335$
Date	8	January 1, 100 to December 31, 9999
Object	4	NA
String (variable-length)	10 + string length	0 to approximately 2 billion characters
String (fixed-length)	Length of string	1 to approximately 65,400 characters
Variant	Varies	Varies

statement to initialize a variant array of variant arrays containing employee data including strings, integers, and currency values.

```
' Declare a variant variable.
Dim employee_data As Variant

    ' Initialize the variable by
        filling it with an array.
    employee_data = Array( _
    Array("Alice", "Anderson", 2768,
        32013.37), _
    Array("Bob", "Baker", 3872,
        29850.95), _
    Array("Cindy", "Carston", 1239,
        17525.75) _
)
```

Variants can also take the special values Null and Empty. Null indicates value that does not exist as in a database field that has not been entered. A variant initially has a value of Empty until the program assigns it some value.

Visual Basic includes the IsNull and IsEmpty statements to see if a variant is null or empty. It also includes other statements such as IsDate and IsNumeric to see if a variant is another specific data type.

In VB.NET, Object variables take over the features provided by variants.

2. Objects

The Object data type holds a reference to any object. Variables can also be declared with more specific object types. For example, suppose a program contains a type of form named DataForm. The following code shows how the program might assign three variables to refer to three instances of this form.

```
' Declare three kinds of form
    variables.
Dim frm1 As DataForm
Dim frm2 As Form
Dim frm3 As Object

    ' Initialize the variables with
        new instances
    ' of the same kind of form.
    Set frm1 = New DataForm
    Set frm2 = New DataForm
    Set frm3 = New DataForm
```

All of these variables give access to their forms' properties and methods. For example, if the form has a public LoadData subroutine, the program could use this code to load the three forms:

```
frm1.LoadData
frm2.LoadData
frm3.LoadData
```

Generally Visual Basic executes methods fastest using variables with more specific declarations. In this case, frm1.LoadData would be fastest because frm1 is declared to be of type DataForm.

3. Types and Enums

A user-defined type (UDT) groups related values into a single organized data structure much as a struct does in C or a record does in Pascal. The following example creates a UDT named Employee to hold employee data. It then declares a variable emp of the Employee type and assigns values to its fields.

```
' Define an Employee UDT.
Type Employee
    FirstName As String
    LastName As String
    Extension As Integer
    Salary As Currency
End Type

' Declare an Employee UDT variable.
Dim emp As Employee

    ' Initialize the variable's fields.
    emp.FirstName = "Xavier"
    emp.LastName = "Xerxes"
    emp.Extension = 4763
    emp.Salary = 128000.01
```

An Enum statement defines a new data type that can take on one of a set of specific numeric values. The Enum definition statement can optionally specify the values' numbers. The following code defines an enumerated type listing four ways a program might start. It then declares a variable of this type and assigns it the value ct_Reboot.

```
' Define an enumerated value type.
Enum StartTypeEnum
    st_StartUp = 1
    st_ShutDown = 2
    st_Reboot = 4
    st_User = 8
End Enum

' Declare a variable of the
    enumerated value type.
Dim start_type As StartTypeEnum
```

```
' Set the variable to one of the
    enumerated values.
start_type = st_Reboot
```

4. Arrays and Collections

Arrays and collections group other variables. An array creates a group of a single variable type. The following code declares an array of integers:

```
Dim values(0 To 100) As Integer
```

VB.NET requires that all arrays begin with element zero, though earlier versions of Visual Basic allow the programmer to use any numbers for the array bounds.

A collection is an object that contains other objects. It can associate a key with each of the items it contains so a program can quickly locate an item by its key. Because a collection is an object, the program must allocate it using a New statement as shown in the following code:

```
' Declare a collection variable.
Dim payment_forms As Collection

    ' Allocate a new collection.
    Set payment_forms = New Collection

    ' Add items to the collection.
    payment_forms.Add frmRetail,
        "Retail"
    payment_forms.Add frmWholesale,
        "Wholesale"
    payment_forms.Add frmEmployee,
        "Employee"
```

D. Control Statements

Visual Basic provides several statements for controlling program flow. The If statement comes in two forms. The single-line form either executes a statement or not depending on the value of a condition.

```
If condition Then do_something
```

The multiline version can optionally contain Else If and Else statements.

```
If condition1 Then
    do_something
Else If condition2 Then
    do_something_else
Else If condition3 Then
    do_some_other_thing
Else
```

```
    do_something_different
End If
```

The Select statement works like a multiline If statement that takes different actions depending on the value of a variable. It is similar to the switch statement in C and the case statement in Pascal. The Select statement can include an optional Case Else clause to make the program do something if no other case applies.

```
Select Case variable
    Case value1
        do_something
    Case value2
        do_something_else
    Case Else
        do_something_different
End Select
```

Visual Basic's For and Do loops repeat a series of statements. The For statement determines the looping variable's start and stop values and can optionally include an increment value.

```
For i = 1 To 10
    total = total + i
Next i
For i = 100 To 10 Step -5
    total = total + i
Next i
```

A Do While statement is more appropriate when the loop should not be controlled by a simple variable. The loop's stopping test can be at the start or the end of the loop. A program will execute the code within the loop at least once if the test is at the end.

```
Do While condition
    statements
Loop

Do
    statements
Loop While condition
```

A Do Until statement is similar to a Do While statement with the condition negated. Like the Do While loop, a Do Until loop's stopping test can be at the start or end of the loop.

```
Do Until condition
    statements
Loop

Do
    statements
Loop Until condition
```

E. Error Handling

Visual Basic's error handling is quite simple. The On Error statements determine what the program does if an error occurs in the code that follows.

- *On Error Resume Next*. Makes Visual Basic ignore errors. If an error occurs, execution resumes with the next statement. The program can check the Err object's properties to see if an error occurred.
- *On Error GoTo line*. Makes the program jump to the indicated line if an error occurs.
- *On Error GoTo 0*. Cancels the previous On Error statement. If an error occurs after this statement, the program may crash.

Some programmers complain about Visual Basic's simple error handling scheme. In particular, Visual Basic does not have centralized error handling. If an error occurs and no error handler is active, the program crashes. VB.NET includes centralized error handling for catching otherwise missed errors. It also provides a more sophisticated Try . . . Catch . . . Finally . . . syntax for wrapping error handling into a more structured package.

F. System Support

In addition to statements for manipulating variables with the program, Visual Basic includes statements for interacting with a wide variety of objects that do not lie within the program itself. Some of these are provided as functions built into the Visual Basic language. For example, the FilLen statement tells the program how long a file is.

Other services are provided by objects loaded from special libraries. For example, the FileSystem object (FSO) included in the VBA library provides tools for searching the file system, copying and deleting files, creating directories, etc.

A few of the many support features provided by Visual Basic are listed in Table IV.

G. Using API Functions

In addition to these system support objects, a Visual Basic program can call most application programming interface (API) functions. That gives the program access to hundreds of other routines related to the operating system and Windows.

Table IV **System Support Features**

Service	Purpose
App	Get information about the application (company, trademark, copyright, etc.).
Client/Server Programming	Visual Basic programs can be clients or servers in a client/server environment. In particular, a Visual Basic program can use Office applications like Word or Access as servers to manipulate their special kinds of data.
Clipboard	Save and retrieve values stored in the system clipboard.
Database Access	The Jet database engine can manipulate many kinds of databases.
Drag-and-Drop	Support for drag-and-drop within a program or between programs.
Dynamic Data Exchange (DDE)	Exchange data between applications.
File System Object (FSO)	Manipulate filers and the file system.
Object Linking and Embedding (OLE)	Exchange data between applications.
Printer	Generate and print text and graphics.
Printers	List the available printers.
Resource Files	Create, edit, and load data from resource files.
Screen	Get information about the computer's screen (size, twips per pixel, etc.).
SendKeys	This function sends key strokes to the application that currently has focus. This gives Visual Basic some primitive control over applications that were not designed to be servers.
Settings	The SaveSetting and GetSetting statements let a program easily save and restore settings in the system registry.
SysInfo	This control provides system information.

For example, a Visual Basic program normally does not receive an event when a form is moved even though the form's underlying window receives a message when it moves. Using the SetWindowLong API function, a program can install a new window message processor that can watch for this message. The program can then take special action when the message arrives.

There is no room in this article to list even a small fraction of the API functions available to a Visual Basic program. For more information, consult a book on API programming.

A Visual Basic program can also use functions written in other languages and compiled into DLL files. For example, a program might use Visual Basic to display data and it could invoke functions written in Delphi to perform time-consuming calculations. This lets the program take advantage of Visual Basic's ease of use and Delphi's faster performance.

IV. COMPARISON TO OTHER LANGUAGES

There are many dimensions along which you can compare different programming languages. Some are more important than others under different circumstances. One application may require great speed. Another may be needed very quickly and place a premium on ease of construction. The following sections discuss some of the ways you can compare Visual Basic to other languages. After you understand these issues, you can select the language that best fits your situation.

A. Ease of Use

Visual Basic's point-and-click development environment makes Visual Basic extremely easy to learn and makes building user interfaces simple. Visual languages like Visual C++ and Delphi also make user interface building simple. Other languages like Java make building user interfaces painful by comparison.

Visual Basic's simple syntax is easy to learn and use. That means you can build applications quickly and with code that is easy to understand and maintain over time. Delphi is a bit more difficult to learn, though its strict type checking helps prevent some errors that can occur in Visual Basic programs. Languages like C++ and Java are much harder to learn. The resulting code is much more complicated, harder to understand, and harder to debug and maintain over time.

Visual Basic hides the most complex Windows programming issues, like building an event loop, from the developer so the program's code can focus on the application and not on Windows trivia. Some languages, like C++, require the programmer to deal directly with these complexities, creating more opportunities for errors.

B. Speed

Visual Basic 6 is slower than other compiled languages like C++ and Delphi. VB.NET will use a code base commonly shared with other Microsoft compilers such as Visual C++ so it should provide the same performance as Visual C++. Even in version 6, a Visual Basic program can call routines written in another language and compiled into a DLL. If parts of the application require high performance, you can build DLLs in other languages to handle those parts and take advantage of the other language's greater speed.

Often any speed difference is irrelevant. If the program's speed is bound by factors outside of the programming language's control, using a faster language may make no difference. For example, Visual Basic displays forms relatively quickly. If a program spends most of its time displaying data and interacting with the user, Visual Basic may not be much slower than any other language.

Similarly if a program's speed is bound by frequent database accesses, a common situation for Visual Basic programs, using a faster language may not help. If the program spends most of its time waiting for a database engine to save and retrieve data, a faster language will not make the wait any shorter.

C. Size

Compiled Visual Basic programs take more space than programs compiled in other languages. A C+ or Delphi program might only take a few kilobytes of disk space. The smallest Visual Basic programs require more than a 1.3 MB of runtime libraries making it impossible to distribute any useful application on a single floppy disk.

Those libraries only need to be installed once, however, and they can be shared by any number of Visual Basic programs. That means downloading a program from the Internet takes a long time initially but downloading new versions or other programs is much faster.

VB.NET will use the same code base as Visual C++ and C# so it will not need any additional runtime libraries. It is possible these libraries will be distributed with new Microsoft operating systems so you will not need to include any extra libraries when installing a new application.

D. Database Tools

Visual Basic provides several methods for accessing a wide variety of databases. ADO objects and controls can access most types of databases with very little trouble. Small applications can use the Jet database engine that comes with Visual Basic to use Access databases. Larger programs can use separate database products such as SQL Server, Oracle, or Informix. Most other programming languages have similar database features, though non-Microsoft languages may not be as closely related to Microsoft's Access and SQL Server databases.

E. Web Programming and Distributed Systems

A particularly interesting area for comparison is web programming. VBScript is very similar to JavaScript. Both can execute on the server to produce pure HTML output for the visitor's browser.

Java is very different from VBScript and JavaScript. Java routines are executed on the client system using a just-in-time compiler. Performance is generally better than VBScript code executing on the client's browser, though Java is much harder to program. Java and JavaScript also bear little resemblance to each other so learning one does not help you much in learning the other. When you learn any Visual Basic language, you immediately know all of the others.

Visual Basic provides compiled components on web pages via ActiveX documents, classes, and controls. These provide speed closer to that of Java. While they can work on any browser configured as an ActiveX container, making them work on browsers other than Internet Explorer can be hard enough to discourage many web visitors.

VB.NET will focus on smaller web services more than current versions of Visual Basic. Instead of using ActiveX documents and controls, VB.NET will display web forms. Microsoft says these will display using standard browser code so they should not have the same compatibility issues with non-Microsoft browsers that ActiveX controls do.

VB.NET's focus on web services should make it ideal for large-scale distributed applications. It relies heavily on the next database access tool, ADO.NET. ADO.NET uses stateless transactions much as a web page does. That may complicate traditional distributed applications that rely on synchronization among processes, but it would make scalable web solutions easier.

V. CONCLUSION

Visual Basic is a high-level programming language for developing Windows applications. Its intuitive development environment makes learning Visual Basic extremely easy. The integrated debugging facilities make finding and fixing errors relatively painless.

Perhaps one of Visual Basic's most important features is its widespread use. A developer who knows Visual Basic can program Microsoft Office applications, other programs that use VBA as a macro language, VBScript, and ASP. Using Visual Basic, the developer can easily build database and client/server applications, and ActiveX components and controls that can be used by other programs. By learning one simple language, the developer gains a wide variety of tools that can be used in all sorts of different applications.

SEE ALSO THE FOLLOWING ARTICLES

C and C++ • COBOL • FORTRAN • Java • Javascript • Pascal • Programming Languages Classification

BIBLIOGRAPHY

Appleman, D. (1999). *Dan Appleman's Visual Basic programmer's guide to the Win32 API.* Indianapolis, IN: Sams Publishing.

Connell, J. (1998). *Beginning Visual Basic 6 database programming.* Chicago: Wrox Press.

Cornell, G. (1998). *Visual Basic 6 from the ground up.* Berkeley, CA: Osborne McGraw-Hill.

Craig, J., and Webb, J. (1998). *Microsoft Visual Basic 6.0 developer's workshop.* Redmond, WA: Microsoft Press.

Kurata, D. (1999). *Doing objects in visual basic.* Indianapolis, IN: Sams Publishing.

Martiner, W. (1997). *Visual Basic programmer's guide to web development.* New York: John Wiley & Sons.

Microsoft's Visual Basic home page. Available at http://msdn.microsoft.com/vbasic.

Stephens, R. (1998). *Custom controls library.* New York: John Wiley & Sons.

Stephens, R. (1999). *Bug proofing Visual Basic.* New York: John Wiley & Sons.

Voice Communications

John Vargo and Ray Hunt

University of Canterbury, Christchurch, New Zealand

GLOSSARY

asymmetric digital subscriber line (ADSL) A form of high-speed digital service over the PSTN capable of providing simultaneous voice and data transmission. The data transmission service provides higher bandwidth downstream (1.5–9 Mbps, e.g., for downloading data) than upstream (16–640 Kbps, e.g., for sending e-mail).

asynchronous Voice communication involving the sender and receiver communicating in different times, for example voice mail.

digital subscriber line (DSL) A form of digital communication service available over the PSTN from the phone company. This service is capable of carrying both a voice call and high-speed digital data over the same line simultaneously. Examples of DSL technology are ISDN and ADSL.

integrated services digital network (ISDN) A form of all-digital service available over the PSTN from the phone company. This service is capable of carrying both voice calls and digital data over the same line simultaneously.

interactive voice response (IVR) The use of a computer-based system to respond to phone call requests. Typically involves a computer delivering voice prompts or a verbal menu to a caller which the caller responds to by selecting the desired menu item or service using their phone key pad.

modem A device for sending digital data over an analog phone system. The term comes from modulator–demodulator, the process that a modem carries out

in converting digital signals to analog signals and back again at the other end of the transmission.

public switched telephone network (PSTN) Another name for the telephone system, which describes the key elements that differentiate it. It is a public system, and it uses switches to make end-to-end circuits available for dedicated voice calls between a sender's and a receiver's phone.

synchronous Voice communication involving both the sender and the receiver communicating with each other in the same time, for example, an ordinary telephone conversation.

teledensity The number of telephones per 100 people in a region. A general measure of the availability and accessibility of telecommunications to a general population, and thus the accessibility to new communication technologies.

VOICE COMMUNICATION is the process of transmitting the human voice for the purposes of synchronous or asynchronous communication with other people or with computers. This communication may occur over telephone networks, referred to as voice networks, or over networks designed for carrying data, referred to as data networks. These networks may be at either fixed locations such as a phone or computer connected through normal landline or satellite systems, or mobile-oriented networks such as cell phone and radio telephone systems, which permit the user of the network to be on the move. Voice communication may be transported over the network in analog form or digital form and may involve a switched network, where connection is assured, or over a packetized network, such as the Internet, where the quality of the communication channel may not be assured. This communication may be person to person, as with an ordinary phone call; one person to many others, as with a conference call; be stored and handled by a computer, as with voice mail; or may be used to instruct a computer to carry out some specified function, such as retrieving a person's bank balance, or placing an order for a certain number of shares of stock at a given price.

I. INTRODUCTION

The term *telephone* had been used even prior to the U.S. Patent Office issuance of a patent to Alexander Graham Bell in March 1876. As early as the late 1600s the term had been applied to the familiar children's string phone. But since the patent issued to Bell in 1876 the term has been exclusively applied to the instrument and the system by which speech could be converted into electrical signals and transmitted over a distance for two-way simultaneous communication. This invention heralded the beginning of what we call voice communications, and now includes many refinements and related new developments. The following provides an overview of this area of voice communication, followed by a more detailed description of the various services and technologies available through voice communication systems.

A. Synchronous and Asynchronous Voice Communication

The telephone revolutionized human communication at a distance. Previously most communication at a distance took place by means of handwritten letters (still popular today, but increasingly replaced by e-mail), and by the use of the telegraph, invented in the 1830s by Samuel Morse in the United States and by Cooke and Wheatstone in England. The telegraph was aimed at distance communication of text, rather than speech. The telephone provided instant communication of the human voice over long distances in synchronous fashion. Synchronous communication occurs when the sender and receiver are in two-way communication at the same time. This is in contrast to asynchronous communication where the message is sent in one time period and received in another time period, as is typical of e-mail or letters sent by

regular post. These two modes of communication are available for voice communication for one-to-one, one-to-many, and many-to-many facilitated by a range of technologies including ordinary telephone, cell phone, radio broadcast, two-way radio, voice mail, conference phones, and voice file e-mail attachments.

B. Person-to-Computer Voice Communication

When we think of voice communication, we typically think of Bell's original conception, person-to-person voice transmission. However voice-to-computer communication is becoming increasingly prevalent for a range of applications and reasons. Person-to-person voice transmission is normally synchronous in nature, while most asynchronous voice communication will be person to computer in nature. Take voice mail as an example, with a computer-delivered voice prompting the person to leave a detailed message; the computer then records the voice message and delivers the message on request to the voice-mailbox holder. Person-to-computer (including of course computer-to-person) voice communication goes well beyond voice mail however. Voice response and voice-activated computer systems are further examples of person-to-computer voice communication, permitting the person to access computer stored information such as personal banking information or a public weather service through a voice-based interface. Some of the advantages to such voice-based interfaces to computer data are listed below:

- The universal availability of the telephone
- Simple key pad response to voice prompts
- The intuitive interface of natural voice input
- Quicker access to information than with human interaction
- Better control over confidential information
- The 24-hour, 7-day-a-week access to accurate data.

However, voice interfaces are not perfect. A more in-depth description of the benefits, services, technologies, and challenges is given in the Section III.

C. Fixed Location and Mobile Voice Communication

While fixed location voice communication has been operational since the late 1800s, mobile communication using two-way radio was not developed until the pressures of WWII required it. In WWII the German's first made effective use of two-way radio to support their highly mobile armored divisions that created the feared Blitzkrieg. This technology was based on the work of Guglielmo Marconi, with the first patent issued in 1896 for the wireless telegraph. Rapid development of this technology during the next few decades saw voice transmitted long distances by radio waves including the first transmission from England to Australia in 1918.

D. International Availability of Infrastructure and Interconnection

For a technology available for well over 100 years, the depth of penetration of telephone networks varies widely between countries. The term often used to describe this penetration is *teledensity*. Teledensity is the number of telephones per 100 people in a region, and thus describes the availability of the fundamental communication infrastructure to the general populace. Teledensity varies from less than 1 telephone per 100 people in such countries as Ghana and Uganda to more than 50 telephones per 100 people in the United States, France, and New Zealand. This measure provides insight into the availability of voice services, but also is an indicator of the potential for using modern communication technology to further develop the economy of a country.

There are a number of determinants of the teledensity of a country, including population dispersion, general state of the economy, political stability, and the interconnection with other countries. The technological issues of interconnection have largely been resolved through the efforts of the International Telecommunication Union (ITU), an international standards setting body. However, the setting of interconnection rates (the cost of settling an international call between national carriers) has been a major inhibiting factor in the spread of services for some countries.

E. Accommodating Voice and Data over the Same Network

The telegraph was designed for the transmission of text, while the telephone was designed for the transmission of voice. These two means of data and voice communication continued to be used in parallel for decades. Each was developed for long-distance use, each largely with its own infrastructure and each us-

ing analog transmission technology. The development of the facsimile telegraph in the 1930s for the transmission of graphic information is an example of a significant enhancement to the telegraph system. However the development of digital computers in the 1950s and 1960s sounded the death knell of the traditional analog telegraph system.

The development of digital communication over analog phone lines using a device called a modem (for modulator–demodulator) in the 1960s meant that digital devices could communicate directly with each other without the need for rekeying the data into a telegraph system. The development of the digital fax machine and the T1 carrier system further enhanced the ability of the Public Switched Telephone Network (PSTN) infrastructure to accommodate both voice and data.

II. TRADITIONAL TELEPHONE SYSTEMS AND MODERN ENHANCEMENTS

The telephone has been one of the most successful and influential inventions in history. The foundation that Bell provided has been enhanced by many further innovations by others. Improvements in both the basic technology for transmission and network interconnection, as well as enhanced digital features, have occurred over the years.

In order for the telephone to succeed in connecting two phones for a private call, the individual lines must be connected somehow. Individual wires are run from private homes and businesses to a phone exchange office (also called a central office or end office) where these individual lines are connected to make a calling circuit between two phones. Originally this was done by the caller phoning the exchange office, speaking to a switchboard operator and asking to be connected to someone. The switchboard operator would then literally plug one person's phone line into the other person's phone line creating a dedicated circuit for the call. This manual system was replaced as early as the 1890s with an automatic switching system in which the caller dialed a number using a rotary dial, the signals sent by the dial directed the switch to connect the caller to a particular phone number. This electromechanical style of switch remained in wide use in phone exchange offices through to the 1970s and 1980s, at which stage they were progressively replaced with electronic and digital switches capable of handling many more simultaneous calls as well as adding new features.

A. Technology

Entire books have been written on the technology supporting the telephone system! This section however, focuses on some particular aspects of modern phone technology that support the additional features we have seen come into service over recent years, including PBXs and digital exchanges.

1. PABX

The original phone system connected individual callers to each other. If two of those callers happened to work for the same organization in the same building, their call still was connected through the local exchange office some distance away, and the organization may have had to pay for the call. The private branch exchange (PBX) was developed as a result of this problem. The PBX was a local version of the original manual switchboard. You phoned your organization's phone operator, who then connected you to the extension you desired. This manual PBX was replaced by lower cost private automatic branch exchange (PABX) equipment as electronic and digital equipment fell in price. Modern PABX equipment permits you to dial an extension phone number in your organization and be automatically connected to that number. It can also permit external callers to directly dial your number, without having to go through a company switchboard operator. It also may support a range of additional computer-enhanced services, as discussed below.

2. Digital Exchanges

Digital and computer-controlled exchanges began replacing electromechanical one in the 1960s and 1970s and became the prevalent form of telephone exchange during the 1980s. This type of computer-controlled phone exchange was necessary to enable the introduction of a range of other digital technologies and services including ISDN, direct long-distance dialing, call waiting, caller ID, voice mail, and other features. Together with fiber optic cabling, digital exchanges provide the foundations for modern voice and data communication over a common infrastructure.

B. Features

Bell's original invention was delivered as a device to permit two individuals to speak to one another synchronously at a distance. However, this is only a subset of human communication with many instances of one-to-many and many-to-many voice communication occurring everyday. Meetings, speeches, homilies, and lectures are everyday examples.

1. Conference Calling

A conference call involves more than a single sender and receiver. The conference call may involve a range of setups including one sender and multiple receivers who are in the same room using a speaker phone system to permit them all to participate in the call. Alternatively it could involve multiple parties, for example three or four people, all in separate locations, being connected into a single phone conversation. This type of conference call will typically require assistance from the telecommunication provider to set up.

2. Call Forwarding/Diversion

Given the high level of mobility today, call forwarding or diversion is a popular feature of modern phone systems. This feature permits users to be at a different location and phone number and still receive their phone calls. People dialing their normal phone number will be diverted so that the phone at the different location rings instead. This feature has been made unnecessary for many users by the development of the cell phone, but is still very useful where cell phone coverage is not available or cell reception is particularly poor.

3. Caller ID

This feature involves the automatic identification of the phone number placing a call. Then using a database, the owner of that phone is looked up. The owner's phone number, and in some cases their name, will be displayed while the phone is ringing. This feature requires a special phone or attachment to permit display of the caller ID.

4. Call Waiting

This feature permits someone in the middle of one phone call to put the caller on hold so he can take an incoming call. Business phones with digital PABX services have had the "hold" feature for sometime, however this feature is only more recently available for residential users through the use of modern digital exchanges.

5. Voice Mail

Voice mail is a more flexible version of the venerable answer phone, with both providing call answering and voice messaging facilities. If the receiver is unavailable to answer the phone after a specified number of rings, the computerized voice mail system will answer with a prerecorded message, possibly tailored to the caller using Caller ID features, and permits the caller to leave a message or perhaps dial an alternative number. See Section V for more on voice mail.

6. Automated Attendant

Enhanced features for lowering the company's telecommunication bill can include an automated attendant as an alternative to direct dial numbers, whereby the caller dials into the company main number and the call is handled by an automated attendant. This computer-based system responds to the caller with a voice message asking the caller to key in the extension number if they know it, otherwise to press 0 and the operator will attend to them. See the discussion below on voice-activated systems for more on this type of technology.

7. Other Features

A range of other features have been incorporated into the modern phone system. Further examples include last number redial, speed dialing of multiple numbers from a memory in the phone, speaker phone systems, call transfer to another extension, and voice dialing. This latter along with other voice activation services are covered in the next section.

III. VOICE-ACTIVATED SYSTEMS

The most natural interface for people to use is a voice interface. Unfortunately, computer-based systems such as modern PABX systems rely instead on key pad numeric entry for their input. The development of voice-based interaction systems for person-to-person and person-to-computer communication has seen a significant step forward during the 1990s. Voice-activated systems for communication support include a range of technologies for responding to caller requests as well as for directing callers to the right extension for the person or information they are wanting. These technologies include interactive voice response systems and voice recognition systems.

A. Interactive Voice Response Systems

An interactive voice response (IVR) system involves computer-mediated communication to assist the caller in reaching the person they wish to speak to or the service they are in need of. These systems have been designed to meet two fundamental needs: (1) the need of the customer for better service and (2) the need of the company to save costs on human operators to answer phones and direct callers to the correct location or service. In a system where a human operator responds to all incoming calls, if the operator is busy the caller may have to let the phone ring many times before they get a response. If the operator is tired or irritable the caller may be greeted with a less than pleasant response when the operator does answer. A well-designed IVR system should always respond quickly, provide a pleasant greeting, and direct the customer efficiently to their desired destination, thus providing a better service to the customer.

IVR works like this. When the caller dials the main organization number a voice message greets them and gives instructions on how to proceed. In the case of an automated attendant (a form of IVR described earlier), the message will ask the caller to key in the extension they are trying to reach or 0 for a human attendant. In the case of Call Center, Information Center, or Automated Service usage of IVR, the caller will be presented with a verbal menu of items spoken by the computer-based system. For example, in the case of a Call Center the message might be: "Welcome to the XYZ Company help line. For product information please press 1, for Help with product difficulties press 2, for Customer Account questions press 3, or to speak with an operator please press 0." By pressing the appropriate key on the phone numeric pad the IVR system will then switch the caller to the appropriate phone or automated service within the company.

In some cases the IVR may direct the caller to another IVR which will then present the caller with another menu of choices. If the menu of options is too long this can be both time consuming and confusing for the caller. Some IVR systems provide "spell-by-name" directory services, requesting the caller to speak the name of the person they are trying to reach, and requesting the caller to spell the first and/or last name to clarify any uncertainty about who they are trying to reach. This feature is particularly useful for callers who are looking for a specific person, but do not know the telephone extension number, a frequent occurrence.

Although these systems have been designed to improve customer service, they do not always achieve this objective. A badly designed IVR can take a caller from one long menu of options to another three or four levels deep, and then put the caller on hold, with no one answering. This is caller "IVR limbo" or "IVR jail" and certainly does not achieve the objective of better customer service. Well-designed systems avoid this pitfall and deliver improved customer service.

B. Voice Recognition Systems

Well-designed IVR systems can provide an effective solution to some company communication bottlenecks. However, in situations where long menus of options are presented or customer needs are not easily met by a list of menu options, a voice recognition system should be considered to enhance the IVR. These systems are under development and thus are not as prevalent as IVR systems.

A voice recognition system may be used in a number of ways. It may permit the user to select from a menu with spoken words instead of a key pad response. For example when the caller dials the main organization phone number, they may get a message like the following: "Welcome to the ABC City News Information Center. You may make your selection by pressing the appropriate key on your telephone or by speaking your request clearly and distinctly. For today's breaking stories please press 1, for sports highlights press 2, for weekend activities in the city press 3, for the Editor's office press 4, for Classified Ads press 5, or for the daily weather report please press 6. Or speak your request clearly and distinctly now. Thank you." The caller then has a choice of pressing a number as the menu is read out, or at the end of the menu, if they have forgotten the number associated with their selection, they can say what they want. This approach caters to both callers who are reticent to "talk to computers" as well as those who have trouble remembering longer menu selections!

Voice recognition systems do have limitations. Some of these are technology limitations and some are social in nature. Current voice recognition systems may have difficulty with different accents and different voices as well as limits on vocabulary size. Small vocabularies are typically easier to recognize accurately across a wider range of voice types and accents and thus current systems are still constrained to recognizing a limited vocabulary or a limited number of menu items. There are also social limitations, with many people having an aversion to "talking" to a computer, thus many current systems offer dual-mode (key

pad or voice) selection. These limitations however are being overcome as more robust voice recognition engines are developed and as people become more used to such systems.

IV. VOICE OVER IP

Transporting the human voice, especially in a synchronous fashion, over the Internet, or using the Internet Protocol (IP) over private networks, is a significant technical challenge with potential for large benefits. Commonly known as voice over IP, this technology offers the promise of low-cost delivery of voice and data services over a common infrastructure, with benefits to both the caller and to the telecommunication provider (phone company, ISP or other telco). Benefits to the caller are primarily lower cost service; benefits to the service provider are primarily more efficient use of the available bandwidth, offering multiplexing capabilities (ability to carry multiple calls or voice and data simultaneously) right to the user's premises without special equipment (apart from the user's PC).

Many challenges are related to the use of this technology for voice transmission including packetizing voice streams for synchronous delivery, high bandwidth demands from voice and video, broadcasting messages to multiple users and related bandwidth problems, and quality-of-service issues arising from these challenges.

A. Packetizing Voice Streams

The IP protocol requires taking the message to be communicated and splitting it up into "packets" of data before sending. These packets includes both the data to be sent as well as information about the destination and order of the data so that they arrive at the right destination and reassembled in the right order. This works fine with e-mail and other files that might be sent over the Internet, but presents some significant challenges when transmitting the human voice, which is a continuous stream of sound. Dropped packets, delays in delivering some packets, and timely delivery of the entire message are all issues, typically referred to as quality-of-service (QoS) issues, encountered in dealing with voice over IP. How are these issues addressed? First of all the problem affects synchronous voice transmission, but is less of an issue for asynchronous examples such as sending voice mail, voice file attachments to e-mail, or delayed broadcast of voice. In each of these latter examples, the delays that are typical when using the Internet can be accommodated since it is not expected that the message will arrive in real time. So if it takes 5 or 30 minutes for a voice file attachment (asynchronous) to arrive at its destination it may not present a problem, but even a 3-second delay in a normal phone conversion would be quite a serious problem (synchronous).

Real-time transmission of voice over IP can be accomplished in a couple of different ways. First an organization may use the IP protocol on their existing leased line services, which may be an Intranet. In this case the company controls the transmission lines and can specify that voice transmission has priority over all data transmission, and thus the voice transmission is given a guarantee of first priority and of a certain amount of guaranteed bandwidth, providing strong assurance that the quality of the voice transmission will be very good. This will be evident to the user because the quality of the phone conversation will be high, the voice will not be "breaking up," no delays will occur, and a clear sound will come through on the conversation. However, most organizations are sticking with the PSTN for voice traffic because of reliability issues. The PSTN provides "5 nines" of reliability. This means that it is reliable 99.999% of the time! Unfortunately this cannot be said of most LANs, nor of the Internet. Until such high levels of reliability can be assured, this is unlikely to change in a large way.

Alternatively, real-time transmission of voice over IP can be accomplished over the public shared network (Internet), but only if similar priority and guaranteed bandwidth issues can be addressed. The most recent version of the Internet Protocol (IPv6), along with special extensions, does include the ability to set priority and guarantee bandwidth to some extent to provide such QoS. However this solution is more complicated because there also needs to be routing or switching equipment in place that is capable of utilizing the new versions of the protocol. Development of an upgraded Internet capable of providing satisfactory QoS for real-time voice and video is under way, but not yet a reality, and issues of reliability noted earlier will continue to impact organizational decisions regarding deployment of voice over IP.

B. Audio and Video Streaming Technology

Using normal asynchronous audio or video file transfer, the receiver will download the entire file (video clip, prior audio broadcast, voice or video mail, audio attachment or other multimedia file) prior to the receiver listening to or viewing it. These files can be quite large, typically in the hundreds of kilobits or even hundreds of megabits range, even when using industry standard compression algorithms such as MP3 (for audio) and MPEG-2 (for video). It may take minutes or even hours to transfer such large files over a WAN connection, depending on the speed of the receiver's connection, which could be a 56K dial-up connection through to a DSL, T1 (1.5+ Mbps) or faster connection. The receiver cannot listen to or view the item under asynchronous transfer until it is fully downloaded. With streaming technology, however, the receiver will be able to begin listening to the file shortly after it begins downloading, since with streaming only part of the file needs to be transferred before play begins, with the system playing the remainder as it is received. The receiver will need a reasonably powerful computer to run the decompression algorithm in real time as well as a fast connection to keep the buffer full. Effective streaming requires a dynamic combination of buffer size and download speed. Streaming technology attempts to overcome some of the Internet QoS problems by effectively straddling the boundary between synchronous and asynchronous communication. Streaming technology works as follows:

- The receiver requests the download of the media file they wish to listen to or view.
- A streaming media server at the sending site begins to send the streamed media file.
- The streaming media player on the receiver's computer begins to receive the media file and loads the initial packets received into the player's buffer.
- Once the player's buffer is full, the player will begin to play the audio or video clip out of the front of the buffer, while the stream of media coming over the network continues to flow into the back of the buffer.
- As long as media packets arrive quickly enough so the buffer does not empty, the media will continue to play in a continuous and quality manner.
- With a dynamic media player, as the buffer approaches empty, due to a poor flow of media packets over the network, the player will attempt to continue playing by reducing the quality of the play (thus reducing the rate at which packets from the buffer are played and increasing the time before the buffer is totally empty).

Streaming systems can still be affected by the QoS problems inherent with the traditional IP protocol and bandwidth bottlenecks experienced by Internet users, sometimes delivering poor-quality audio or video. This can be addressed in part by increasing the buffer size and the initial delay before play of the media clip begins. Much faster speeds are, of course, available in current LAN configurations and thus present fewer problems for streaming media systems. Even current high-speed LANs (for example, 100-Mbps and 1-Gbps Ethernet) can become overloaded by streamed media. An example of the load on a network using video streams with industry standard MPEG-2 compression, which may result in bandwidth demands of 2 Mbps per stream, is shown in Table I. A large organization with high levels of video streaming or videoconferencing could still saturate a 1-Gbps Ethernet LAN. See the following section on IP multicast for further information on this topic.

The advent of audio and video streaming has presented an additional challenge in the Internet environment because of the high-bandwidth requirements of multimedia. These challenges are multiplied considerably when broadcast media are considered, where a single stream is sent to multiple users (perhaps thousands or even millions). A solution to this is referred to as multicast technology and is discussed next.

C. IP Multicast

Radio and television broadcast a single signal to thousands and even millions of listeners or viewers effortlessly, but such a broadcast over the Internet can cause serious bandwidth problems. An illustration will help: The president of the United States is going to give a speech to the world on an important international issue, however there are many people who would like to hear this message but it will not be broadcast in their country, or they prefer to receive the message over the Internet. If an Internet radio station were to

Table I Bandwidth Demands of Video Streaming

Number of unique streams	Cumulative bandwidth required (Mbps)
2	4
10	20
50	100
400	800

permit 10,000 users to connect and receive this message simultaneously on unique audio streams, even at low quality (4–8 Kbps) this could amount to 50+ Mbps continuous traffic during the duration of the speech. This would be enough to shut down large portions of the Internet. IP multicast technology permits the sending of a single stream of media to all listeners, rather than a stream for each listener. IP multicasting accomplishes this by using multicast-enabled routers to replicate the media stream at any point where there are "subscribers" down an additional branch of the Internet. This results in only a single stream of the media multicast being present on any given portion of the Internet at one time.

This same concept can be used in LAN streaming applications to reduce the bandwidth demands of media streaming systems. The primary requirements of a multicast environment are routers capable of managing the multicast sessions and scheduled broadcast times, since all listeners or viewers need to be on-line at the same time.

V. VOICE MAIL

The telephone has become ubiquitous in developed countries during the last 100 years, although teledensity for many developing countries is still low. Virtually everyone in a developed country has one or easy access to one, and it is frequently the first form of communication we use for distance communication. This has created a few difficulties however; foremost is the problem that the intended receiver is often not there to receive the message, so no message is delivered. Voice mail was created to help overcome this problem.

A. Traditional Voice Mail

Voice mail typically encompasses two primary services: (1) call answering and (2) voice messaging. When a caller rings an intended receiver, after a fixed number of rings the voice mail system will pick up the call, answering with a prerecorded message stored previously on a computer. This prerecorded message will typically request the caller to leave a detailed message for the intended receiver. The caller then speaks their message into the phone, and the message is recorded by the voice mail system onto a computer. At a time convenient to the receiver, they will clear their voice mail box by phoning the voice mail system using a specified phone number or extension and then keying in their private pin number to give them access to their confidential voice mail box. The receiver can then perform a number of functions, the primary one being to listen to the messages left by callers. Other functions the voice mail system will permit them to do include listening to prior saved messages, deleting messages, and changing the security code or prerecorded message that callers hear when the voice mail system answers the receiver's phone. Additional functions of some systems also include the ability to send a voice mail message to a group of recipients, respond to a voice mail by sending a voice mail back to the sender, and transfer voice mail to another extension for someone else to reply to incoming voice mail.

One of the difficulties with voice mail is that many people still see it as a way of saying "Hi, I called. Please call me back." In other words, they still want to use the phone for synchronous communication and not asynchronous. Yet the key to effective use is in the name: voice mail. Ordinary physical mail involves sending an actual message, not just a note saying "Please write me back"! Voice mail works best if a detailed message is left, as you would with e-mail or a letter. Now the receiver will know what is wanted and can respond specifically to the need rather than playing that most annoying of games called "telephone tag." You leave a voice mail for them to call you back, they respond, but you are not there so they leave a message saying they returned your call but weren't sure what you were calling about, so you call them back but they are at lunch . . . and so on it goes. Telephone tag can be eliminated with the effective use of voice mail by leaving a detailed message of what is wanted in the first call.

B. Text Messaging

Voice mail can provide a very effective way of communicating with busy people. But many people work in the field and may not be able to talk on a phone or receive voice messages on a timely basis due to the working environment, being in meetings or for other reasons. This can be overcome by getting a text message to the receiver. Up until recently this was normally accomplished with a device called a pager using voice to text pager systems with varying processes to convert the voice message into a text message. The popularity of cellular phones and the incorporation of paging and text messaging features, however, has largely replaced pagers. Text messaging to a cellular phone may involve varying approaches including e-mail to text messages, voice mail to text messages, and pager text messages.

Voice mail to text messaging can be accomplished by a conversion service or a high-tech version using a voice recognition engine to convert the caller's message into a text message and then automatically forward the message to the recipient. This high-tech version is under development.

C. Convergence of Voice Mail and E-Mail

The convergence of voice mail and e-mail is a developing trend in the world of communication. Unified messaging systems and automatic conversion of e-mail to voice mail and voice mail to e-mail represent key aspects of this development.

A major initiative in the development of unified messaging systems involves the Voice Profile for Internet Mail (VPIM) series of standards. This standard of the Internet Engineering Task Force (IETF) has as its primary goal the communication of voice mail and e-mail messages over a common Internet infrastructure in an integrated way. This involves client applications that incorporate both e-mail and voice mail features and server/infrastructure support for the storage, retrieval, and transportation of these messages. This permits the user to choose which means of communication they prefer for a given situation.

Another aspect of this convergence involves the automated conversion of voice mail to e-mail and vice versa. The best form of communication for the sender is not necessarily the best for the receiver. With improving voice recognition engines, the seamless integration of voice mail and e-mail will become a possibility. Converting a text e-mail message into a voice mail message using a speech synthesis system is a currently available service in some areas. However, the automatic, accurate conversion of continuous speech voice mail messages to text e-mail is a very difficult task for a computer, but one that is clearly on the horizon.

D. Audio Attachments for E-Mail

An enhancement to plaintext e-mail is the use of multimedia attachments to deliver voice and video mail via the Internet. The sender simply creates an ordinary e-mail, and then attaches a prerecorded voice or video message (file) to the e-mail in the same fashion that one might attach a word processing or spreadsheet file. Naturally the sender must have a means for creating the voice or video file: microphone and/or digital camera attached to their computer as well as appropriate software and hardware for capturing the multimedia file. It is equally important that the receiver have some means of playing the media file when it arrives. Most systems today have a media player as one of the standard applications or as a plug-in to their web browser. Some problems exist with attaching media files to e-mail however. Sending an e-mail message, which usually represents a small file (a few kilobytes), is a quick and simple matter even over a dial-up line. However, by attaching a sound or video file, the few kilobytes of e-mail text can blossom to hundreds of kilobits or megabits very quickly, making the upload and download times laborious, and on overloaded networks impossible. This factor must be considered when evaluating the use of such technologies.

VI. WIRELESS AND MOBILE COMMUNICATIONS

Voice communication has come full circle. Original voice communication was short distance, face to face, and highly mobile. Along came Mr. Bell who extended the range of voice communication from face to face to around the world, but removed the mobile nature of voice communication. To make use of the distance benefits of the telephone it was necessary to be in a specified location to permit a caller to reach the intended receiver. With the development of two-way radio and then cellular phone technology the mobile nature of voice communication has been restored while retaining the distance communication benefits.

A. Two-Way Radio Technology

With the issue of a patent to Guglielmo Marconi in 1896 for the wireless telegraph, mobile long-distance communication utilizing radio waves was shown to be practicable for telegraphic messages. Early experiments demonstrated the feasibility of voice transmission using radio waves also; however, it was nearly 20 years (in 1915) before the first substantive demonstration by the American Telephone and Telegraph Company (AT&T) showed that speech could be transmitted long distance using this new technology. With that successful transatlantic transmission, mobile voice communication at a distance became a reality. Rapid development of voice-based radio during the years between the two world wars saw voice-based radio communication between ships and land stations, with airplanes and other mobile platforms. World War II saw the development of compact two-way radio systems ca-

pable of being carried by an individual to support battlefront and intelligence gathering activities.

This technology has continued to develop and is widely used today in ships, airplanes, trucks, and taxis, by police and other emergency services and is also available as handheld short-range (1–5 miles) two-way radio units for private use. The connection of mobile radio telephones to the PSTN was introduced after WWII. However, the capacity of this system was very limited, since only a limited number of nonoverlapping frequencies could be used. Thus in a large city like Chicago, there might only be 10–12 channels available, so the system was only capable of handling a few hundred customers in total. The limitations of this system led to the development of the cellular radio telephone system.

B. Cell Phone Technology

In the late 1960s the Federal Communication Commission (FCC) approved the introduction of a system of radio telephone that was based on short-range mobile radio transmission. The mobile user carried (in their car initially) a radio transceiver (transmitter/receiver) that communicated with a base station. The base station was interconnected with the PSTN using automatic dialing. This system was first introduced in Chicago in 1983 and was a great success with the customers, providing thousands of mobile connections, instead of the hundreds available with the previous radio telephone to PSTN technology.

One of the secrets of cellular technology is the use of low-power transceivers and the reuse of the limited radio frequencies available from the FCC. A city cellular system is split up into multiple base stations called *cells* to cover the entire metropolitan area. When a mobile caller dials a number from their car to place a call, the nearest cell responds and connects the call to the PSTN. When the caller drives out of range, the current cell transfers control of the call to the next cell, which now has the strongest signal, and releases the call from the original cell. This *handoff* from one cell to another happens automatically and transparently with little impact on the phone call in progress. The result of this system is that the same radio frequencies can be used in nonoverlapping cells, permitting many more simultaneous users in a given geographic location.

The technology is not perfect however. When a mobile caller approaches the edge of the serviced area, reception may become weak so that a poor-quality connection results, or they may drive out of range of the last cell and lose the call altogether. An additional problem is the multiplicity of cell technologies that are used, making some phones incompatible with some base stations. This has created a more costly and less effective infrastructure to support cell phone usage. This problem is referred to sometimes as a "roaming" problem, preventing cell phone users from roaming out of their service area. The next section talks about solutions to this problem, creating the ability to roam from service area to service area—even to other countries.

C. Roaming Capability

The lack of standards in the 1980s made using a cell phone in a service area that used a different cellular technology virtually impossible, and there were many different technologies worldwide. These differences were based on different radio frequencies in different countries, analog versus digital systems, and different modulation and compression technologies. The development of standards and continuing miniaturization of electronic componentry have helped provide roaming capability to cellular phones. One of the most influential standards was the European GSM digital standard, which provided a unified European standard so that a caller could roam from one European country to another using the same cell phone. This standard has been implemented, alongside other standards in most developed countries. However even with the GSM different frequencies are used in different places. This is being overcome by manufacturing phones that can accommodate multiple frequencies, as well phones that can operate using both digital standards like GSM or one of the more prevalent analog standards. Still, roaming on an international basis often requires organizing a separate phone in the country to be visited or special arrangements with the local telephone company to be sure the user's existing phone will work. Another way of providing roaming capability, even in areas that do not have a cellular base station infrastructure in place is to use satellite-supported phone systems. The next section discusses current systems, while the section at the end of this article discusses plans on the drawing boards.

D. LEO Satellite Networks and Low Latency Voice Communication

Satellite-based phoning has existed for a number of years from mobile platforms like airplanes and ships. Such systems require a powerful transceiver and typically work with satellites in geostationary orbit of about 22,000 miles. This means that a given satellite always provides coverage for a given part of the earth's surface. The problem with phone communication

through geostationary satellites is the need for a powerful transceiver and the annoying delay due to the long communication path.

The first significant satellite-based low-earth-orbit (LEO) communication system was the Iridium system developed by Motorola and others. This system consisted of 90 satellites orbiting at a height of 420 miles. The original plan for 66 satellites required an incremental increase to approximately 90 to provide spares and sufficient coverage of the earth. Because of the LEO satellites, small handheld satellite phones can be used and the communication delay is very small and unnoticeable by users. Unfortunately, the system has been expensive to run and unable to generate a sufficient customer base to be economically viable, with Motorola announcing plans to terminate the service. The failure of this venture is being watched closely by a number of other similar ventures including Teledesic and Globestar. It remains to be seen if this technology will supersede or even compete effectively with existing land-based cellular systems.

E. Voice Dialing

The use of cellular phones has exploded in the 1990s, and when mixed with the ubiquitous automobile yields a highly mobile platform. Unfortunately, dialing a phone and talking on it while driving can prove to be quite hazardous, with many jurisdictions passing laws to prevent it. This has given rise to a range of hands-free cell phone enhancements including microphone and speaker setups into which you plug your cell phone as well as voice dialing. Voice dialing requires a phone that is capable of this function, or a voice dialing service from the cell phone service provider. The user sets up multiple phone numbers that have been assigned a spoken key, typically the name of the person to be called. Once activated the caller needs simply to turn on his phone and then say "dial Frank Smith" and the phone will dial the preprogrammed number for Frank Smith.

F. Wireless Application Developments

The mainstreaming of wireless voice services through the increasing ubiquity of cell phones has raised the opportunity for further convergence of voice and data services by delivering Internet-available data via a mobile phone. The primary international open standard for this has emerged as the Wireless Application Protocol (WAP); however, in Japan the NTT DoCoMo-based i-mode standard accomplishes a similar function.

WAP specifies the incorporation of a microbrowser into the cell phone or other wireless device together with network deployment of WAP gateways and WAP servers. These gateways and servers take standard HTML content, filter it, and transfer it to the hand-held device's microbrowser. Thus the cell phone or connected PDA becomes an Internet client on the move. Although WAP is not a voice-based technology, it is aimed at providing text and image-based Internet content to cell phone users, thus enhancing the usefulness of the cell phone. Technology related to this is the "always on" cell phone, which can receive messages and Internet information at any time since the phone is "always on" and available to receive data.

This technology does raise some problems however. Normally IP addresses for such applications are dynamically assigned to mobile devices. If the cell phone is "always on" for data reception then it must have a permanent IP address. Under IPv4 there are insufficient addresses to meet the demand. Fortunately IPv6 rectifies this problem by significantly extending the addressing space. These enhanced cell phones are sometimes referred to as *smart phones* or *web phones* and incorporate larger screens and more memory to support mobile e-mail and the microbrowser.

VII. DATA COMMUNICATION OVER VOICE NETWORKS

Long-distance electronic data transfer, in the form of text, was originally handled by the telegraph, while voice transmission was handled by the telephone. However the development of digital computers and invention of the modem made it unnecessary to maintain two separate infrastructures. Thus the telephone system, designed for carrying voice communication using analog signaling technology, began to carry digital data. With the development of digital phone exchanges and full digital transmission services such as T1, carried over the telephone system infrastructure, the availability of digital services has continued to accelerate. A wide range of data transmission services and technologies has developed as a result.

A. Services

1. FAX

The first widely used data communications over voice-grade lines was the facsimile. A fax machine is essentially a combination of a scanner and modem. The user inserts the document to be sent into the fax machine, and dials the number of the receiving fax machine. The receiving machine answers (if it is not busy with an existing connection), establishes the communication protocol (called handshaking), and then the sending machine scans the image and transmits it to the receiving machine. All of this occurs over ordinary voice-grade phone lines in a matter of a minute or two. The development of the digital fax machine in the early 1980s increased the speed of fax services and offered the potential for dramatic cost reductions with the use of digital microcircuitry.

2. Data

The development of the modem also provided a direct benefit to computer users. As digital computers became available during the late 1950s and early 1960s, making this technology available to a wider range of users became a real challenge. Computers were very expensive and only the largest corporations, government departments, and universities could afford them. The concept of "time sharing" computers became one solution to making this very expensive resource more widely available. Using a teletypewriter connected via a modem to the computer, many others could make use of the computational abilities available. As the price of computers fell with minicomputers and then microcomputers, more computers were installed and the need to have these computers communicate with each other was also fulfilled using modems.

3. Web Browsing

The use of the telephone infrastructure to access the Internet via web browsers is a major application of data communications today. Users accessing the World Wide Web (WWW) from homes and small businesses typically use dial-up connections and modems to access the plethora of data, information, goods, and services available. The transmission of video, voice, and other multimedia data using the TCP/IP protocol is also growing rapidly.

4. Web Phones

The cellular phone system provides mobile voice services. With the development of the Internet and the wealth of information available on it, many of these same mobile phone users want to access the Internet in a mobile fashion. Web phones were discussed earlier, many using WAP services to access the Internet through a microbrowser on their cell phone.

5. PDA Web Surfing

The personal digital assistant (PDA) is an electronic equivalent of the executive diary, incorporating a calendar, address book, calculator, to-do list, and other support applications. Versions of PDAs have been developed to connect via the phone system to the Internet. In these cases the PDA will include among its applications an e-mail client and a microbrowser to permit it to access the Internet resources. The connection for these services can be via an ordinary wireline phone service or through a mobile service such as a cell phone service.

B. Technology

The technology used to permit data communication over voice-grade phone services has developed over years and accelerated recently with the explosive growth of the Internet. These technologies range from faster modems to full digital services delivered over the voice infrastructure. The whole area of bandwidth development and management has become a major issue as the telecommunications infrastructure transports increasing quantities of data, especially high-demand multimedia data. The following topics are covered here: modems, ISDN (brief overview), T1 services, and xDSL technology. Other key technologies that support ongoing development of the infrastructure include high-capacity fiber optic and microwave media, as well as multiplexing and data compression technologies.

1. Modems

Modems have been in use since the early 1960s. Modem speeds vary depending on the technology used in the modem and may range from as low as 300 bps to as high as 56 Kbps. In addition the use of compression algorithms with modern modems can significantly increase the actual throughput of data. The measure of data transfer is the bit per second (bps), requiring multiple bits (typically eight) to transmit a single character of data.

2. ISDN

Integrated Services Digital Network (ISDN) services from the telephone company were developed in the 1980s and were originally thought to replace the use of modems. ISDN services provide full digital services for voice and data over the PSTN at a basic rate of 64 Kbps per channel for two channels for a total of 128

Kbps. In the 1980s this was a very high speed for data transmission. Unfortunately, the cost of ISDN phones and other devices as well as the telco charges for ISDN services remained an expensive option at the same time modem technology continued to develop. ISDN basic rate service is rivaled by current modems with compression algorithms, making ISDN still unattractive for many individuals and small businesses. However, ISDN primary rate services consisting of 24 channels of 64 Kbps each, a total of 1.544 Mbps (equivalent to a T1 leased line), can be quite attractive to users with high bandwidth demands for dial-up services such as backup communication for T1 leased services and videoconferencing. ISDN was the first implementation of a set of standards referred to generally as xDSL and are an evolutionary step forward from the T1 carrier system. Broadband ISDN (B-ISDN) is an ISDN development aimed at reviving ISDN as a bandwidth solution for videoconferencing and other bandwidth hungry applications. The intention is to provide primary rate services at basic rate prices. However, it looks like the other DSL technologies will fill that role, raising questions about the future of B-ISDN.

3. T1 Services

The development of the T1 carrier system (E1 in Europe and elsewhere) for carrying 24 multiplexed voice streams over a single line made higher transmission capacity (1.544 Mbps for T1 and 2.048 for E1) available for services over the PSTN. This increase in bandwidth was made available two ways: as dial-up voice lines connected to the telephone company's switched voice network or as leased lines providing point-to-point connections (for example, between two offices of a company in different cities or countries) over which the customer could directly send digital data in its native form without converting to analog signals.

The T1 carrier system was developed to deal with the limited capacity of the analog-based phone system, which could only carry one phone conversation on each pair of copper wires (one wire for each side of the conversation). The T1 system took two pairs of wires, moved to a digital signaling system instead of analog, and succeeded in transmitting 24 voice or data channels over each T1 line. This produced an immediate gain of 12 times the transmission capacity and is one of the foundations for modern digital transmission.

4. xDSL Technology

Digital subscriber line (DSL) standards include a range of variations including ADSL (asymmetric digital subscriber line), HDSL (high-bit-rate digital sub-scriber line) and SDSL (single pair digital subscriber line). These standards support the transmission of high-speed digital data over voice-grade lines, often aiming to deliver T1 or E1 speeds more efficiently. This technology has become available in many areas and offers considerable benefits over the use of a modem for transmission of data. Benefits include the ability to support the simultaneous use of a single line for phone calls while transmitting data (web browsing, etc.). The technology also supports much higher data transmission rates. ADSL, for example, offers up to 640 Kbps upstream (e.g., for sending e-mail) and up to 9 Mbps downstream (e.g., for downloading from the Internet).

The technology, as always, is not without its challenges however. For most implementations of DSL technology, the user must be located reasonably close to the telco switching exchange office. The further the user is from the switch, the slower the transmission speeds. If the user is too far from the exchange she cannot use DSL at all.

VIII. LOOKING AHEAD: WHAT IS IN STORE?

Forecasting the future is always fraught with pitfalls, and yet can still be a worthwhile venture if for no other purpose than to scope new developments gathering on the horizon. This section looks at a number of particular technologies that could significantly impact voice communication during the coming years.

A. Ubiquitous Voice Recognition

Voice recognition systems in the near future will provide a totally hands-free interface for voice and data services for both wireless and wireline services. In addition to providing a friendlier interface for experienced users, it will open up voice and data services for those with limited keyboard skills. The search for speaker-independent, continuous speech with large vocabularies is likely to become a reality during the next few years. This will provide the most intuitive interface to voice and data networks and the information they contain. Talking to your cell phone will become as common as talking through it. Requesting stock quotes, weather reports, and definitions of new computer acronyms and looking up the sister-in-law's birthday will only be a verbal request away.

B. High-Speed Data and Voice over Third-Generation Cellular

Data transfer over cellular phone circuits, even digital services such as GSM, is a slow affair. GSM supports data transfer at 9600 bps, less than 20% of the speed of a standard modem for a PSTN connection. However, hope is on the way. Extensions to the GSM standard (the most widely used in the world) are expected to offer more than 50 Kbps shortly with the potential for more than 100 Kbps based on packet-switching technology in the near future. Further development of the GSM digital standard referred to as 3G (third-generation) digital cellular will permit better voice services while supporting high-speed data streams at rates of over 300 Kbps in the medium term and 2 Mbps in the longer term. This will make effective web browsing, mobile videoconferencing, and other high bandwidth demand services available in support of the rapidly developing WAP and other mobile application standards discussed earlier.

C. Ubiquitous International Roaming

The ability to simply get on an airplane in one country and be able to transparently use your cell phone in another country is a dream of all high-mileage travelers. This dream is likely to become reality during the next few years as standards mature and more cell phones are enabled to transparently support multiple standards. An alternative solution is the use of mobile satellite phones. However, the likelihood of this occurring is somewhat lower, given the failure of the Iridium venture and the rapid pace of technology development for surface-based mobile technologies.

D. Full Convergence of Phone, Computer, and Web Information Sources

The convergence of phone and computer has been projected, and its achievement grows closer with each passing year. Major developments that will hasten this convergence are critical mass for handheld computers such as PDAs, mature voice recognition, and applications delivered over the net. These developments will make powerful systems available through portable web browsers, controlled (at least in part) by voice commands. For full convergence, however, the QoS issues discussed earlier must be addressed and a faster and more robust version of the Internet is required to support this convergence.

E. Smart Device Communication Using Bluetooth Technology

Another emerging technology on the horizon is one referred to as Bluetooth. This technology is a wireless short-range LAN technology designed to support device-to-device communication, opening the way for simple communication between cell phones, cars, handheld computers, vending machines, desktop computers, digital TVs, and other office and household appliances. It is a short-range radio-frequency technology for ranges of about 10 m that will permit these devices to share information.

SEE ALSO THE FOLLOWING ARTICLES

Integrated Services Digital Network (ISDN) • Mobile and Wireless Networks • Speech Recognition • Telecommunications Industry

BIBLIOGRAPHY

Carne, E. B. (1999). *Telecommunications primer: Data, voice, and video communications,* 2nd ed., Upper Saddle River, NJ: Prentice Hall.

CommWeb Publications, previously *Data Communications Magazine* Available at http://www.commweb.com/.

Fitzgerald, J., and Dennis, A. (1999). *Business data communications and networking,* 6th ed., New York: John Wiley & Sons.

Miller, M. A. (2000). *Voice over IP: Strategies for the converged network.* Foster City, CA: IDG Books Worldwide.

PC Magazine and other on-line IT-related information resources. Available at http://www.zdnet.com/pcmag/.

Wide Area Networks

June S. Park
University of Iowa

GLOSSARY

asynchronous transfer mode (ATM) Modern packet-switched communication technology that transmits all information (data, image, audio and video) in small, fixed-size packets called cells.

broadband ISDN (BISDN) Broadband digital services provided by telephone carriers based on SONET and ATM technologies. BISDN offers speeds of 155 Mbps or higher, and is used for voice, data, and multimedia communications such as high-definition television (HDTV).

circuit-switched network The traditional telephone network infrastructure where switches connect links and establish a dedicated circuit between two telephones for each call.

digital subscriber line (DSL) Wideband communication services at speeds of 1.5 Mbps and higher offered by telephone carriers using the existing twisted-pair local loop infrastructure

fiber-to-the-curb (FTTC) Similar to HFC, but uses optical fiber trunks more extensively to have a single fiber serve about 30 homes. A twisted pair is used to connect each subscriber to the optical network unit where the fiber ends.

frame relay A connection-oriented, wide-area networking service offered by telephone carriers.

hybrid fiber-coax (HFC) As a replacement for the existing cable TV network infrastructure, this uses optical fiber trunks all the way to a neighborhood (with several hundred homes) and then coaxial cable connections to each subscriber. It provides two-way communication of digital information in addition to television signals.

integrated services digital network (ISDN) Circuit-switched, narrowband digital services mainly used for voice and data communication, provided by telephone carriers at two levels: basic interface rate (BIR) of 144 Kbps and primary interface rate (PIR) of T1 speed.

packet-switched network Computer communication networks such as ATM, frame relay, and the Internet where packets of digital information are sent one at a time, stored, and then forwarded by successive packet-switching nodes until arriving at their destination.

private digital leased lines Point-to-point digital circuits, commercially labeled as Fractional T1 ($n \times$ 64 Kbps), T1 (1.5 Mbps), and T3 (45 Mbps). These lines can be leased from telephone carriers to connect two end systems.

switched multimegabit data service (SMDS) A connectionless wide-area networking service offered by telephone carriers.

synchronous optical network (SONET) Being a standard for communication on fiber optic networks (a.k.a. synchronous digital hierarchy or SDH), and operating at multiples of 51.84 Mbps (called Optical Carrier-1 or OC-1), SONET is used for most of the long-distance telephone traffic today, replacing the old circuit-switched telephone network infrastructure.

virtual private network (VPN) Wide-area connection of offices for a corporation using public packet-switched network services

TELECOMMUNICATION NETWORKS can be classified based on the geographical coverage of the network and the kind of transmission medium used. Wide-area networks (WANs), span multiple cities, a country, or continent, whereas metropolitan-area networks (MANs) span a city, and local-area networks (LANs) a single building or even smaller area up to a few kilometers in size. In terms of the transmission medium, wireline networks use physical wires such as twisted pair, coaxial cable, and optical fiber. Wireless networks do not require a physical connection between users as in the cases of cellular telephone, cordless telephone, paging, radio, satellite, and wireless TV broadcast systems. This article focuses on wide-area, wireline digital networks. In digital networks information is converted into bits before it is transmitted from the source and reconstructed from the received bits at the other end. The next section presents fundamental concepts of digital communications that are helpful for comprehending subsequent discussions on various WAN infrastructures and services.

I. BASIC CONCEPTS OF WIDE-AREA TELECOMMUNICATION SYSTEMS

A. Principles of Telecommunication Systems

Three central features of information networks are connectivity, resource sharing, and quality of service. Connectivity allows network users to exchange information among one another. Resource sharing is the efficient utilization of networking hardware and software by many users. Connectivity and sharing are achieved by switching, multiplexing, and routing, which are discussed below. Quality of service refers to the performance characteristics of a telecommunication service such as the speed, reliability (not losing information), integrity (no errors in delivered information), and security (difficulty of interception).

The goal of a communication network is to provide services to users. A service is created by the execution of a distributed script (computer program) that performs a sequence of basic actions on network resources. Resources are basically nodes and links. Nodes include switches, routers, gateways, and end systems such as telephones, televisions, PCs, and server computers. Nodes are generally computers or controller boards. Links are wires including twisted-pair lines, coaxial cables, and optical fibers. The service script is executed jointly by a number of communicating nodes. For example, several million lines of code control a modern telephone switch.

Complex communication services are built from simpler services. The organization of services into simpler services is called the network architecture. Network architectures are layered. A layer N protocol is the distributed service script of a service of layer N. A service of layer N is executed by peer protocol entities in different nodes of a communication network. The messages exchanged by peer protocol entities of layer N are called layer N protocol data units (N-PDUs). The layer N protocol entities exchange N-PDUs via the layer $N-1$ service.

As illustrated in Fig. 1, suppose the network architecture has three layers. Assume that the protocol entity of the top layer, called the application layer, of node A wants to send a message to that of node B. The protocol entity uses a service primitive of layer 2 called *2.request*. This request is sent with some interface control information to layer 1. The control information specifies the request type, the address of the two communicating nodes, the address of the protocol entities inside the nodes, a description of the desired quality of service, etc. The service provided by layer 1 sends *1.indication* to the protocol entity in layer 2 of node B. At that time, the protocol entity receives the *2-PDU*. The protocol entity in B later sends *2.response* as a reply to *2.indication*. The reply eventually comes back to the protocol entity in layer 3 of A as *2.confirmation*.

The Open Systems Interface (OSI) reference model is the standard network architecture established by the International Organization for Standardization (ISO) to promote the compatibility of modern packet-switched network designs. It is a layered architecture as described above and has seven layers:

- Layer 1 (physical layer): Transmission of bits over a physical medium
- Layer 2 (data link layer): Transmission of frames on one given link, performing error control and flow control over the link
- Layer 3 (network layer): End-to-end routing of packets
- Layer 4 (transport layer): End-to-end delivery of a message consisting of multiple packets, enhancing the quality of service provided by the lower layers
- Layer 5 (session layer): Setup and management of an end-to-end communication session consisting of multiple messages
- Layer 6 (presentation layer): Formatting, encryption, and compression of data
- Layer 7 (application layer): Network services such as e-mail, distributed database processing, remote access to a computer, EDI, web page retrieval, and video on demand.

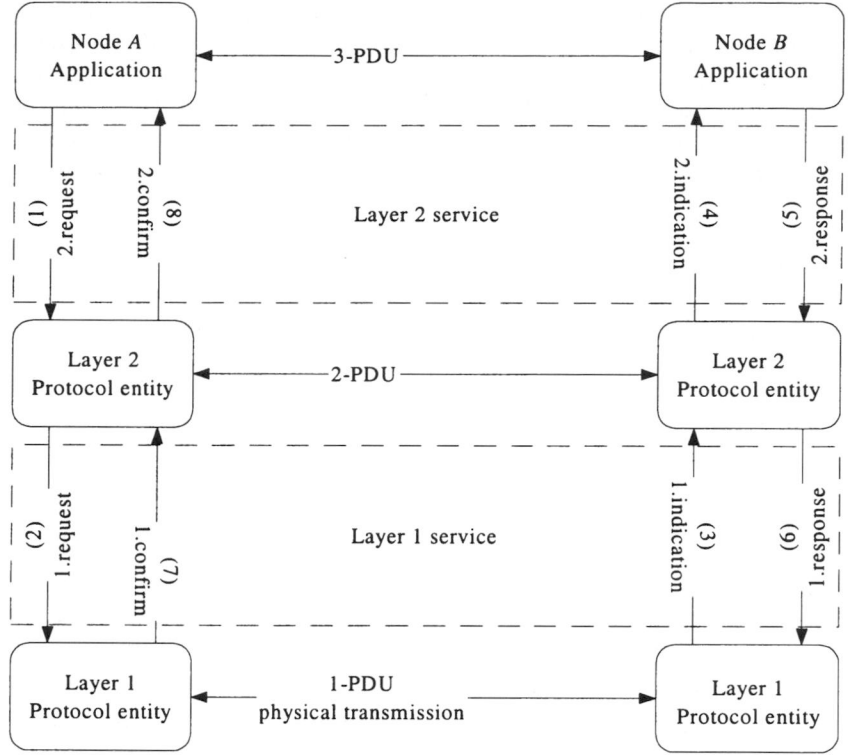

Figure 1 A layered architecture of telecommunication network.

B. Classification of Communication Services

End-to-end communication services (as seen by the users) can be classified into synchronous and asynchronous services. In synchronous communication services, information is delivered as a bit stream with a fixed delay and a given error rate. Dynamic information such as audio and video can be transmitted as bit streams. In asynchronous communication services the bit stream to be transferred is divided into packets. Packets are received by the destination with varying delays, and a fraction of them may not be received correctly. Asynchronous services are thus evaluated by their quality of service, such as the packet error rate, delay, and throughput. Static information such as data and image is organized in bit files, usually transmitted in packets, and is more error sensitive and delay insensitive relative to dynamic information.

There are two classes of asynchronous communication services: connection oriented and connectionless. A connection-oriented service delivers the packets in sequence, in correct order, and confirms the delivery. A connectionless service delivers the packets individually, out of order, and some packets may be lost.

Stream-oriented applications such as audio and video transmissions require synchronous communication services. Interactive applications that require a dialog between remote machines usually use connection-oriented services. Delay-insensitive applications such as e-mail and news distribution applications can use connectionless services.

C. Switching, Multiplexing, and Routing

A communication session between two network users creates an *information flow*—either a bit stream or a sequence of packets. At each node of a network an information flow arriving there may be sent along any one of the links connected to the node. The ability of each node to choose the next link to be followed by each information flow is called *switching*. Multiple flows of information may be transmitted on the same network link, which is called *multiplexing*.

Four basic methods are used for switching and routing information flows:

• Circuit switching
• Packet switching, permanent virtual-circuit routing

- Packet switching, switched virtual-circuit routing
- Packet switching, datagram routing.

Routing determines the path between the origin and the destination of an information flow. Different routing schemes are preferred for different communication services.

In a circuit-switched network, the bandwidth of a network link is divided into independent channels using time-division multiplexing (TDM) and each channel is assigned to an information flow. A unique path is predetermined for all information flows between a given pair of origin and destination nodes (called an *OD pair* in the sequel). When a communication session (e.g., a telephone call) starts, a channel is assigned on each link on the predetermined path forming a circuit. An information flow monopolizes a circuit for the duration of the session. If a link has n channels and all those channels are already assigned to ongoing communications, the $n + 1$st communication that needs to traverse that link is blocked. The traditional telephone network (a.k.a. POTS meaning plain old telephone service) is a circuit-switched network. Circuit-switched networks are intended for synchronous communication services.

In a packet-switched network, the information file is first decomposed into packets. Each packet is labeled with the sequence number and the destination address. Packets are sent one at a time and they are stored and then forwarded by successive packet-switching nodes (PSN). Each PSN determines the next PSN to which to send each packet. The destination node reconstructs the original information by assembling the packets according to their sequence numbers.

Unlike circuit switching, no dedicated channel is preassigned to an information flow. All the packets that need to be transmitted over a given link are stored in the same buffer even if they belong to different information flows. These packets are transmitted in some order (e.g., based on the first-in first-out policy and on some priority index) over the same link using the multiplexing technique called statistical multiplexing.

Packet switching is more efficient than circuit switching for bursty traffic, i.e., transmissions that are short and occur irregularly. Keeping a dedicated circuit idle between bursty transmissions would waste a large fraction of the capacity of the links. In a packet-switched network, the path followed by the packets of a given information flow can be changed by the user or automatically by the PSNs. It is thus easier to route information around failed links and nodes than in a circuit-switched network.

Packet-switched networks may support different routing policies. In datagram routing, each PSN determines for each packet the next PSN to send the packet to considering the destination address and the information about the congestion in other nodes. Packets belonging to the same information flow may follow different paths. In virtual circuit (VC) routing, all packets of an information flow follow the same path and are thus delivered in the correct sequence. However, they may be interleaved with packets from other information flows in each link they traverse. All packets of the same session are labeled with a unique VC number that designates the path. Each PSN stores those VC numbers in a routing table. When a packet arrives at a PSN, the PSN determines the next PSN by looking at the routing table. As a result, the PSN does not have to make a complex routing decision for each packet.

The VC routing is classified into permanent and switched VC routings (PVC and SVC, respectively). These two differ in how the virtual path is determined for each communication session. In PVC routing, a path is configured by the user for each OD pair. All communication sessions between an OD pair transmit the packets along the same predetermined path just like in circuit switching. In SVC routing, the path is determined when the connection is set up for each communication session taking into consideration the congestion of other nodes in the network. The path may change for each session between the same OD pair.

The PVC routing method is suitable for both synchronous services and asynchronous connection-oriented services. The SVC routing is suitable for connection-oriented services (e.g., for fast transmissions of relatively long durations such as database queries/replies). The datagram routing is ideal for connectionless services (e.g., for short bursty transmissions, and delay-insensitive applications such as e-mail and file transfer). The routing protocol of the Internet, called IP (Internet Protocol), uses datagram routing.

II. WIDE-AREA TELECOMMUNICATION INFRASTRUCTURE

A. Public Switched Telephone Network

Networking beyond the boundary of private property requires the use of existing public network infrastructure. The public switched telephone network (PSTN) and the cable TV (CATV) network provide the most extensive communication facilities. The telephone network is a circuit-switched network with a hierarchical structure. In the United States, there are about 20,000 end offices (also called central offices), 1000 toll offices, 200 primary offices, 50 sectional offices, and 10 regional offices. Each telephone is connected to an end office using two copper wires. The connections between an end office and individual subscribers' telephones are called local loop (or local subscriber lines). If two telephones are connected to the same end office, the area code and the first three digits of the two telephone numbers are identical. If the caller's and callee's telephones are connected to different end offices and these two end offices happen to be connected to the same toll office, the connection is established within the toll office. If the caller and callee do not have a toll office in common, the path will have to be established somewhere higher up in the hierarchy. To reduce the blocking probability for telephone calls, a routing strategy called *dynamic nonhierarchical routing* has been used where, instead of using a unique path, a sequence of paths is tried in order.

Switching offices are connected to each other via high-bandwidth trunks. Today local loops are mostly twisted pairs and use analog signaling, while trunks are fiber optics or microwave and use digital signaling.

In 1984 AT&T's monopoly was broken up into 23 Bell Operating Companies (BOCs), which were then grouped together into seven Regional BOCs (RBOCs). The United States was divided up into 160 local area and transport areas (LATAs). Within a LATA, there has been normally one local exchange carrier (LEC) that has a monopoly on telephone service within the LATA. LECs include the BOCs and about 1500 other independent telephone companies. Interexchange carriers (IXCs) such as AT&T, MCI WorldCom, and Sprint have handled the inter-LATA traffic. An IXC wishing to handle calls originating in a LATA could build a switching office called a point of presence (POP) there. The LEC was required to connect each IXC's POP to every end office either directly or indirectly via toll offices.

In 1996 a new Telecommunication Act was passed so that local telephone companies, long-distance carriers, cable TV companies, and cellular operators can enter one another's businesses. As a result, the U.S. telecommunications landscape is currently undergoing a radical restructuring.

The digital transmission of telephone calls has used the pulse code modulation (PCM) encoding with a sampling frequency of 8 kHz and 8 bits per sample. A telephone call thus requires a channel of 64 Kbps (= 8×8000), called a DS-0 channel. PCM makes it easy to time-multiplex channels. A DS-1 channel multiplexes 24 DS-0 channels and adds one bit for syn-

chronization. Its bit rate is therefore 1.544 Mbps (= 193×8000). The transmission system for DS-1 is called the T1 digital carrier system. Most telephone companies also offer the T3 carrier that is a group of 28 DS-1 channels with the bit rate of 44.736 Mbps.

B. Synchronous Optical Network

Telephone companies originally deployed fiber optics using their own proprietary TDM systems. In 1989 Bellcore (the RBOCs research arm at the time) and CCITT (renamed to ITU-T in 1993) established a fiber optics communication standard, a physical layer protocol, called Synchronous Digital Hierarchy (SDH). Three different versions of SDH exist: SDH-Europe, SDH-Japan, and SDH-SONET (Synchronous Optical Network) for North America.

Like the traditional PSTN, SONET is a synchronous system using TDM. SONET provides higher bit rates than T3 to carry mixed types of information such as data, audio, and video. SONET transmits 810-byte frames, 8000 times per second, matching the sampling rate of the PCM channels. The basic SONET channel, called STS-1 (Synchronous Transport Signal-1) or OC-1 (Optical Carrier-1), therefore has a bit rate of 51.84 Mbps (= $810 \times 8 \times 8000$). All SONET trunks are a multiple of STS-1. OC-3 trunks have a rate of 155 Mbps, and ATM to be discussed in Section III runs at this rate. SONET trunks as fast as OC-192 are available today that offer a bit rate of 10 Gbps.

In conventional fiber networks, the light signal transmitted on the fiber strand is of a single wavelength. Multiple channels are created using TDM, i.e., by allocating a specific time slot to an individual channel. Since the early 1990s a different multiplexing technique called *wavelength-division multiplexing* (WDM) has been used increasingly. Instead of using a single laser, WDM uses multiple lasers operating at different wavelengths on the same fiber. By installing WDM and SONET equipment at each end of a fiber, a LEC can gain the equivalent of many new fibers without installing a new cable. Today WDM equipment exists that can support 100 or more channels per fiber, 10–40 Gbps per channel. The advance in WDM technology has already reached a point where a single fiber can carry several hundreds of thousands of simultaneous voice and Internet connections. Virtually all long-distance telephone traffic in the United States now uses trunks running SONET.

SONET can work as the physical layer protocol for a single point-to-point circuit as well as for a ring network. Similar to the fiber distributed data interface

(FDDI) ring, a SONET ring has a dual-ring structure and is self-healing (i.e., automatically restores the traffic in case of link or node failures). If the primary ring is broken, the hardware detects the failure and uses the counter-rotating ring to reconnect. Each node on the ring uses a device known as an add/drop multiplexer (ADM). The ADM passes received frames around the ring, accepts additional bits from a local circuit, inserts them into frames passing through the node, and extracts bits and delivers them to a local station. Telephone companies have increasingly deployed SONET rings in their interoffice backbone networks to improve the network survivability.

C. Fiber Infrastructure in the Local Loop

In the United States and many other countries, most of the backbone networks connecting switching offices are now fiber based. However, the local loop portion of the public network infrastructure remains mostly copper based. To meet growing demand for multimedia communications including the Web traffic, telecommunication companies have been trying to increase the bandwidths of local connections to each home and office. Running fiber to everyone's home and office, called *fiber-to-the-home* (FTTH), would be an ideal solution. However, this is very expensive and will not happen for years.

Cable TV carriers have replaced a majority of coaxial cable in backbone trunk lines with fiber to increase bandwidth, improve services to customers, and decrease operating costs. More recently, they have been replacing coax with fiber in the local distribution network. Fiber is installed from the head end (the root of the local-distribution cable tree) to neighborhood nodes (a.k.a. junction boxes). From the junction box, a single piece of coax is routed to several hundred homes. This network is called the hybrid fiber-coax (HFC) system. Each HFC channel to a home can be of several megabits per second allowing interactive multimedia communications. Telephone companies have also adopted HFC as a way to hold market share threatened by the cable provider infrastructure, but they have lagged behind cable companies in HFC deployment.

An alternative solution more expensive than HFC is fiber-to-the-curb (FTTC). Fiber is terminated in an optical network unit (ONU) that serves about 30 homes. The final segment in FTTC is point-to-point twisted pairs (a separate link from the ONU to each home), whereas that in HFC is a shared coaxial cable. FTTC can be used for videophone and digital TV.

III. WIDE-AREA TELECOMMUNICATION SERVICES

A. Digital Leased Line

Organizations with sufficient traffic to justify dedicated communication links among distant locations can set up a private network using digital leased lines offered by telephone companies. A leased line is a permanently dedicated, point-to-point circuit connecting two sites. Leased lines are a synchronous service based on the circuit-switched network of PSTN.

Leased lines are available at many discrete levels of bandwidth. Digital data services (DDS) have rates between 2.4 and 56 Kbps, capable of supporting data communications. Voice and video applications require a leased line with a speed of at least 64 Kbps. Fractional T1 lines provide speeds at multiples of 64 Kbps, but lower than the T1 rate. One of the most common uses is the T1 circuit. T3 is coming into great use, for example, for Internet connections at large companies. IXCs also offer nondedicated line services from a POP to another at data rates between 56 Kbps and 45 Mbps. Users who need connectivity for only a few hours per day may prefer these services rather than dedicated leased lines.

The cost of connecting two sites by a leased line includes (1) the access charge for connecting the customer premise equipment (CPE) at each site to its nearest central office (CO), (2) the port charge (a.k.a. CO connection charge) for each site, and (3) the interoffice channel (IOC) charge, as can be seen in Fig. 2.

The CPE is typically a CSU/DSU (channel service unit/data service unit) device attached to a router, layer 3 LAN switch, or ATM switch. The CO connection charge is determined based on the bandwidth of the leased line and consists of a one-time installation charge and monthly recurring charges. The IOC charge is determined by both the line speed and the distance between the two COs connected. It is charged monthly and has two portions: One part determined solely by the line speed and the other determined by both the speed and the distance. For example, the IOC charge for a 64-Kbps line connecting two COs that are 100 miles apart could be \$359/month = \$332 + \$0.27/mile × 100 miles, while the IOC charge for a T3 line between the same COs could be \$27,443/month = \$22,236 + \$52.07/mile × 100 miles.

An organization setting up a private network should decide on the network topology, link capacities, and routing. For example, the private network in Fig. 2

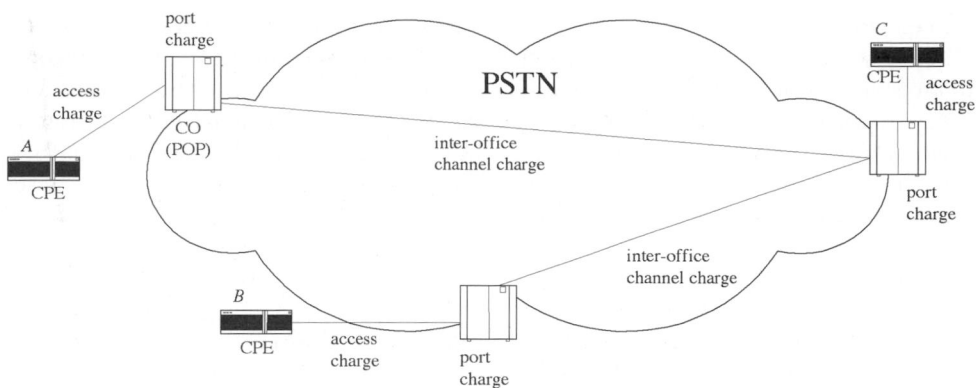

Figure 2　Private network using leased lines.

connects three sites *A, B,* and *C.* The topology has been determined to have links *AC* and *BC* (rather than *AB* and *BC,* or *AB, BC,* and *AC*). The capacity of each link must be determined based on traffic demands among the three sites and the routing of those traffic demands. Link *BC* should carry both the traffic demand between *B* and *C* and that between *A* and *B.* In a network with a greater number of nodes and links, more than one routing path is often available for each pair of nodes, thus requiring an assignment of the traffic flow to multiple routes.

B. Integrated Services Digital Network

In 1984 the world's telephone companies, under the auspices of CCITT, agreed to build a new, fully digital, circuit-switched network that can support data and video in addition to voice by the early part of the 21st century. This new system was called the *Integrated Services Digital Network* (ISDN). ISDN uses conventional copper wiring in the local loop. At present, ISDN is available to a majority of the U.S. population, but usage has been relatively low.

An ISDN line carries multiple channels using TDM. Two standard combinations of channels have been offered:

- Basic rate interface (BRI): Two 64-Kbps channels (called B channels) for voice and data, and one 16-Kbps channel (called the D channel) for signaling
- Primary rate interface (PRI): 23 B channels and 1 D channel.

The BRI can be viewed as a replacement for POTS for home and small businesses. The PRI is intended for use for businesses with a private branch exchange (PBX), a circuit-switching device on the premise (which enables, for example, five-digit phone numbers for internal calls). Because ISDN is so focused on 64-Kbps channels, it is called narrowband ISDN (NISDN).

ISDN can be used for various applications such as telephone, videoconferencing, remote access, fax, remote meter reading, and remote alarming. Unfortunately, ISDN arrived in the market a little too late while the technology in telecommunications was moving very fast. Most LANs inside businesses run at 100 Mbps. Offering 64-Kbps services to businesses for external connections is no longer a sensible proposition. On the other hand, BRI found an unexpected application—Internet access. ISDN adapters are now available that combine the 2B + D channels into a single 144-Kbps digital channel, which is much faster than using a 56-Kbps analog modem link for Internet access. In the United States, ISDN also comes with various options, including conference calling, call forwarding, voice mail, and caller ID.

C. Digital Subscriber Line and Cable Modem Technology

Another technology that enables digital services over copper wiring already in place in the local loop is called digital subscriber line (DSL). A DSL connection uses a DSL interface device on the customer premise and another at the central office. This technology permits wideband transmissions over twisted pairs at 1.544 Mbps or faster more economically and with shorter installation cycles than T1 services. However, there is a limit (of up to about 3 miles) on the distance between the customer premise and the nearest central office. Therefore, DSL has been used mainly in metropolitan areas.

There are, in fact, several DSL technologies as shown in Table I. Asymmetric DSL (ADSL) is perhaps the most widely used among home subscribers. ADSL uses a single copper pair and allows a telephone line to handle voice and high-speed data simultaneously. It offers a higher bit rate downstream (in the direction from the network to the subscriber) than upstream, which is quite suitable for web browsing. ADSL cannot guarantee a data rate because it uses an adaptive technology in which a pair of interface devices probes many frequencies on the line between them and select frequencies and modulation techniques that give optimal results on that line. Thus, the downstream rate may vary from 32 Kbps to 9 Mbps, and upstream from 32 to 640 Kbps.

Symmetric DSL (SDSL) also uses a single copper pair, but transmits data at the same speed in both directions (at roughly half the speed of a T1 line). SDSL is suitable for businesses that run a web server to provide information to others. High-speed DSL (HDSL) provides the T1 speed in both directions, and hence can replace a T1 circuit in a rather straightforward manner. However, it requires two independent twisted pairs and has a shorter distance limitation on local loops. Very high-speed DSL (VDSL) can transmit broadband traffic (at speeds ranging between 25 and 52 Mbps) over distances of less than a mile. For many subscribers the distance to the nearest central office is too long to deploy VDSL. VSDL thus requires intermediate concentration points (one in each neighborhood), with optical fiber connecting the concentration point (an ONU) to the central office. The cost estimate per subscriber for deploying VDSL is comparable to HFC.

An alternative to DSL for Internet access is cable modem. Cable TV carriers offer Internet access lines using cable modems. Usually a single frequency channel is shared by a set of subscribers in the neighborhood using TDM. Therefore the actual bandwidth for

an individual subscriber may vary from several megabits per second to a few hundred kilobits per second depending on the number of concurrent users. Since the original cable infrastructure cannot handle upstream traffic, a dual-path approach has been used where upstream traffic is sent through a dial-up modem and downstream is received through a cable modem. HFC, discussed in Section II, allows the use of a bidirectional cable modem since the carrier of HFC would have replaced all amplifiers with bidirectional devices.

D. X.25 and Frame Relay

We have discussed WAN services based on circuit-switching technologies in the three preceding subsections. In the remaining part of Section III we discuss packet-switched WAN services including X.25, frame relay, switched multimegabit data service (SMDS), and ATM services. These public packet-switched digital networks are constructed using PSTN or SONET as the underlying facility network. Packet-switched network service providers install packet switches on the nodes of PSTN or SONET and link them among one another using existing wire infrastructure. Individual organizations can use the public packet-switched network services to build virtual private networks (VPNs). It is called virtual because sites are not connected by permanent dedicated circuits, but by virtual circuits or datagrams on request.

Old public data networks follow a standard called X.25 that was developed by CCITT in the 1970s. X.25 supports permanent and switched virtual circuits as well as datagram routing. Most X.25 networks work at speeds up to 64 Kbps. Because X.25 was invented before personal computers became popular, X.25 networks were originally engineered to connect ASCII terminals to remote time-sharing computers. Those dumb terminals could not check incoming transmissions for errors or notify the sending device of an error and the need for retransmission. Moreover, copper wires were noisy and had a high propensity to cause errors on the line. Therefore, X.25 had to be designed to make packet switches perform complex error checking and correction as well as flow control (i.e., a feedback mechanism over a direct link that enables the receiver to throttle the sender into sending packets no faster than the receiver can handle the traffic).

During 1980s fiber optic networks were installed throughout the United States significantly increasing the quality of transmissions. Also with the widespread

Table I DSL Technologies

DSL	Maximum data rate	
	Downstream	Upstream
ADSL (asymmetric DSL)	9 Mbps	640 Kbps
SDSL (symmetric DSL)	768 Kbps	768 Kbps
HDSL (high-speed DSL)	1.544 Mbps	1.544 Mbps
VDSL (very high-speed DSL)	52 Mbps	2.3 Mbps

use of intelligent desktops, it no longer was necessary for the WAN to perform error recovery and flow control. On the other hand, most organizations needed to interconnect their LANs in different locations using high-speed connections. CCITT and the American National Standards Institute (ANSI) developed the frame relay standard to address this environment. The first frame relay service became available in 1991. Frame relay does not provide error recovery or flow control, thus avoiding a lot of the overhead processing. It offers data rates ranging from sub-64 Kbps to T1, and more recently up to the T3 speed.

Frame relay is a connection-oriented service supporting both permanent and switched virtual circuits. A PVC is similar to a leased line in that the communication path is predetermined between the two sites. However, there are important differences: For a leased line, the user must determine the line capacity so that it is somewhat higher than the peak transmission rate. Due to the queuing delay effect, the utilization rate of a line capacity at the peak traffic load should be, say, 80% or less. Once a certain line capacity is acquired, however, the full capacity can always be used exclusively. For a PVC the user must determine the committed information rate (CIR) that reflects the *average* traffic volume between the two sites. Data bursts above CIR can still be sent at full speed as long as the long-term average usage does not exceed the guaranteed CIR.

The carriers charge much less for a PVC than a leased line. Therefore, frame relay's PVCs are more attractive than leased lines when the traffic demand between two sites fluctuates and does not justify continuous dedicated bandwidth. SVCs establish the path on request and last only for the duration of the communication session as discussed in Section I. All major telecommunication carriers in the world provide frame relay services. Most of them provide only PVC services since PVCs are much less complex to provision while adequately handling the routing and the restoration of traffic in case of failures.

The cost of connecting a number of sites by PVCs includes (1) the access charge for connecting the CPE at each site to its nearest POP, (2) the port charge for each site, and (3) the PVC charge for each PVC as shown in Fig. 3. The port charge is determined based on the port speed, and consists of a one-time installation charge and monthly recurring charges. For each port used, the speed selected must be at least as great as the PVC speed for each PVC connected to that port. In Fig. 3 each port has four PVCs connected to it.

PVCs are simplex (one directional). Duplex (two-way) traffic requires the use of two PVCs. The two PVCs may have different speeds to support an asymmetric traffic pattern. The PVC charge also consists of a one-time installation charge and monthly recurring charges. Some carriers determine the PVC charge at each port based on the number of PVCs connected to the port, and others based on the CIR of each PVC installed. Some carriers offer an even more complex tariff, e.g., applying usage charges based on actual volumes of traffic delivered on the PVCs. Unlike the IOC charge included in leased line tariffs, the PVC charge is indifferent to the distance between the two POPs connected.

An organization setting up a VPN using frame relay services should decide the port speed at each site and the CIR of the PVC between each pair of communicating sites. It is possible to connect two sites, say, *A* and *C* in Fig. 3, indirectly via node *B* using two or more PVC links in tandem. However, the tariff structure of frame relay services provides less incentive for such a partial-mesh topology than that of leased line services. That is, the network topology and routing decisions have much less impact on the total

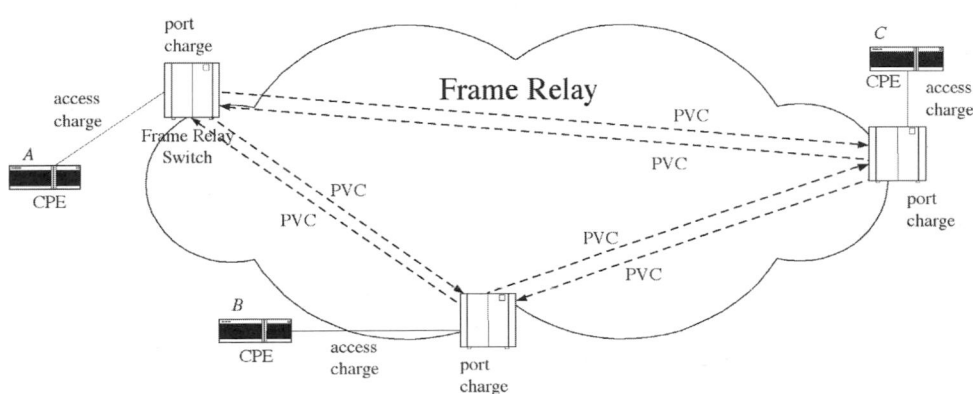

Figure 3 Virtual private network using frame relay services.

cost of a VPN using frame relay services than that of a private leased-line network.

E. Switched Multimegabit Data Service

Switched multimegabit data service (SMDS) is a high-speed, connectionless datagram service designed for LAN interconnection over a wide area. It offers speeds up to 45 Mbps. Bellcore developed the SMDS standard in late 1980s to fill the gap for broadband services until BISDN becomes widely available. SMDS service was first provided in 1991. It is presently offered by most RBOCs, MCI WorldCom, GTE, and other value-added network (VAN) service providers.

A SMDS-based VPN is composed of the following components: a number of SMDS gateways and switches inside the service provider's network, and a number of CPEs connected to the SMDS gateways via the central offices nearest to the customer's; see Fig. 4. Depending on the customer's location, the PSTN carrier who provides the connection to a central office can be the same or a different carrier than the SMDS provider.

The SMDS cells are based on CCITT E.164 standards for addressing information. This standard addressing scheme allows cells to be released into the public telephone network—just like letters get dropped off at a post office. The benefit of this connectionless any-to-any service is that new sites can be quickly added to the VPN without having to reconfigure the network.

As can be seen from Fig. 4, the cost of connecting a site to the SMDS cloud includes (1) the access charge to connect the CPE to the nearest CO and (2) the port charge per SMDS access line. The latter covers the connection from the nearest CO to the SMDS gateway as well as the SMDS port used. In addition, the customer needs special CSU/DSUs supporting the SMDS access protocol (such as DXI and SIP) on its premise.

The port charge consists of a one-time installation charge and monthly recurring charges. The monthly charge may include a fixed portion based on the guaranteed bandwidth of the access line, called the sustained information rate (SIR), as well as a variable portion based on the volume of actual transmission during each month. Only the outgoing traffic (from the CPE to the SMDS cloud) is limited to the committed SIR (which is similar to the CIR of frame relay services). The variable usage charge is also based only on the outgoing traffic volume. The SIR for each access line can be chosen from $n \times 56K$, $n \times 64K$, 1.5 M, 4M, 10M, 16M, 25M, and 34 Mbps, which represent the speeds of most popular LAN technologies. The only decision that an organization setting up a SMDS-based VPN needs to make is to choose the SIR for each site to be connected.

F. Asynchronous Transfer Mode and Broadband ISDN

Asynchronous transfer mode (ATM) is a high-speed, connection-oriented packet switching technology. It is both a technology (hidden from the user) and a service (visible to the user). ATM services provide both PVC and SVC connections at speeds of 155 and 622 Mbps. The 155-Mbps speed was chosen for compatibility with the SONET transmission system. Public ATM backbone networks operate at speeds as high as several gigabits per second. Long-distance carriers AT&T, MCI WorldCom, and Sprint already have implemented high-speed ATM backbones. RBOCs such as Ameritech, NYNEX, and Pacific Bell also offer ATM-based services.

ATM carries all types of information (voice, data, and video) using small 53-byte fixed-length packets called *cells*. Cell switching is highly flexible and can easily handle both stream-oriented traffic such as au-

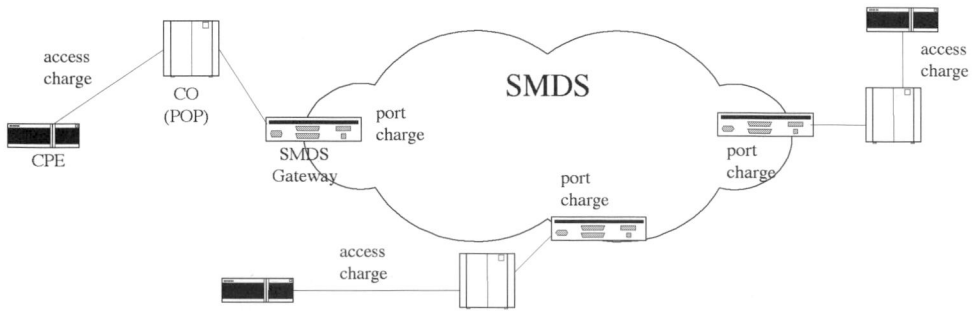

Figure 4 Virtual private network using SMDS service.

dio and voice, and bursty traffic such as data. The ATM Specification Version 4.0 defined several ATM service categories as shown in Table II.

The constant bit rate (CBR) service is intended to emulate the synchronous services used by telephone circuits and leased lines. It is also suited to interactive audio and video streams. Real-time variable bit rate (RT-VBR) is intended for traffic whose bit rate changes strongly, but requires no jitter in cell arrival rates. The interactive compressed video used in videoconferencing has such transmission characteristics because MPEG and other compression schemes work with a complete base frame followed by a series of differences between the current frame and the base frame. The nonrealtime VBR (NRT-VBR) service is for traffic where timely delivery is important but a certain amount of jitter can be tolerated. It is useful for example for displaying a multimedia e-mail from a remote server.

The available bit rate (ABR) service is suitable for most data communications where the traffic load varies significantly during the day and the range of required bit rates is roughly known. ABR is the only ATM service category in which the network provides rate feedback to the sender, asking it to slow down when congestion occurs. The ABR service does its best to provide the bandwidth required for each communication demand, but with no promise (except for the minimum bandwidth guarantee that can be optionally purchased). So it is also called best effort service. If insufficient bandwidth is available, ABR traffic has to wait until some minimal bandwidth becomes available. On the positive side, the cell loss ratio for ABR traffic is expected to be low. Finally the unspecified bit rate (UBR) service makes no promises and gives no feedback about congestion. If congestion occurs, UBR cells will be discarded with no feedback to the sender. For applications that do their own error control and flow control, UBR is a reasonable choice. File transfer, e-mail, and news distribution are all potential candidates for UBR service.

Table II ATM Service Categories

Service class	Application example
Constant bit rate (CBR)	T1 circuit
Variable bit rate, real time (RT-VBR)	Real-time videoconferencing
Variable bit rate, nonreal time (NRT-VBR)	Multimedia e-mail
Available bit rate (ABR)	Web browsing
Unspecified bit rate (UBR)	Background file transfer

To make it possible to have a concrete contract within each service category, the ATM standard defines a number of quality-of-service (QoS) parameters whose values can be negotiated between the customer and the service provider. The worst performance for each parameter is specified and the carrier is required to meet or exceed it. QoS parameters include peak cell rate, sustained cell rate, minimum cell rate, cell delay variation tolerance, cell loss ratio, cell transfer delay, and cell error rate. To meet the requirements on QoS parameters set forth in traffic contracts, ATM switches use (1) traffic shaping and policing mechanisms (such as the leaky bucket algorithm) at the source switch to control the transmission speed and delay variations, and (2) the admission control (for CBR, VBR and UBR traffic) and the rate-based congestion control (for ABR traffic) to prevent congestion at intermediate switches.

ATM removes the distinction between LANs and WANs. ATM can replace or augment LAN technologies such as Ethernet, token ring, and FDDI. ATM can be used to connect end stations or to interconnect LANs. In the WAN environment, ATM can be used in place of both synchronous (e.g., leased lines) and asynchronous services (e.g., X.25, frame relay, and SMDS). Frame relay and SMDS can use ATM networks as the backbone, in which case frames or datagrams are divided up into cells at the POP, transmitted using ATM switches, and then reassembled back into frames or datagrams at the receiving end. These services are called frame relay over ATM or SMDS over ATM.

Broadband ISDN (BISDN) is a future public telephone network based on ATM and SONET technologies—a single cell-switched network that is supposed to replace the entire telephone system and all other specialized networks, providing a universal service for all types of information transmission, i.e., voice, data, and video. While PSTN and NISDN are circuit-switching technologics, BISDN is a fabric of virtual circuits for moving information in units of cells at speeds of 155 Mbps and higher. BISDN cannot be carried over existing copper wiring in local loops and cannot use existing space-division and time-division switches. It will take some time until BISDN is available to homes.

As shown in Fig. 5, BISDN has its own reference model different from the OSI model. It consists of three layers: the physical, ATM and ATM adaptation layers, plus whatever the users want to put on top of that—including connectionless and connection-oriented data services like SMDS and frame relay, and video and voice applications. The ATM adaptation layer (AAL) provides standard interfaces for various

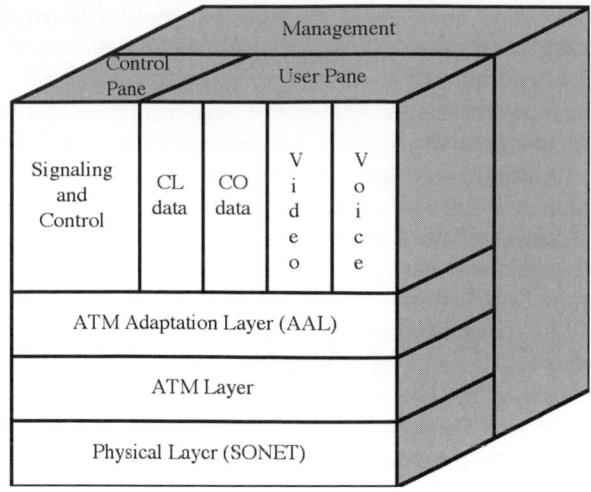

Figure 5 BISDN protocol reference model.

applications, and segments application-level messages into cells and later reassembles them back to messages at the other end.

IV. SUMMARY

In the United States, most telecommunication carriers do not expect to complete the conversion from copper to fully fiber optic system within the next 10 years. FTTC and HFC will not be widely deployed in residential markets either for the next several years. Improvements in interim technologies such as ISDN, DSL, and cable modem will allow faster transmission over copper wiring in local loops. Accelerating the speed of local loop connections will increase the demand for bandwidth in backbone networks. The long-haul fiber network carriers will continue to push innovations in WDM and the transition from TDM to WDM in order to increase their system capacity and lower the facility cost. Fiber throughput rates are expected to reach the terabit level in about 5 years as a result of improvements in WDM and SONET technologies.

Use of ATM for virtual private networks over a wide area and for private backbones (as a replacement for FDDI) within a building or campus area will increase to combine voice, data, and video traffic onto a single network. However, frame relay will continue to be more widely deployed than ATM as VPNs for the next several years due to its economic advantages. New technologies that allow companies to exploit the Internet as a VPN will gain increasing acceptance, too. Because all telecommunications providers including CATV operators see the Internet both as a threat and an opportunity, they will position themselves as Internet service providers (ISPs). Use of fixed wireless transmission will also expand to provide an alternative to wireline media, especially in areas not served by a modern, high-capacity wireline infrastructure.

SEE ALSO THE FOLLOWING ARTICLES

Frame Relay • Integrated Services Digital Network • Internet, Overview • Local Area Networks • Mobile and Wireless Networks • Network Database Systems • Network Environments, Managing • Standards and Protocols in Data Communications • Telecommunications Industry • Transmission Control Protocol/ Internet Protocol (TCP/IP) • Voice Communications

BIBLIOGRAPHY

Buckwalter, J. T. (1999). *Frame relay: Technology and practice.* Reading, MA: Addison-Wesley.

Cahn, R. (1998). *Wide area network design.* San Francisco: Morgan Kaufmann.

Comer, D. E. (1999). *Computer networks and Internets.*

Klessig, R. W., and Tesink, K. (1995). *SMDS: Wide-area data networking with switched multi-negabit data service.* Upper Saddle River, NJ: Prentice Hall.

McDysan, D. E., and Spohn, D. L. (1999). *ATM theory and application.* New York: McGraw-Hill.

Price Waterhouse. (1999). *Technology forecast.*

Tanenbaum, A. S. (1996). *Computer networks.* Upper Saddle River, NJ: Prentice Hall.

Warland, J. (1991). *Communication networks.* Chicago: Irwin, McGraw-Hill.

Word Processing

Andrew Prestage

Kern County Superintendent of Schools, Bakersfield, California

GLOSSARY

advanced capabilities Advanced word processing capabilities include sophisticated text enhancement tools, spell and grammar checking, drawing tools, voice recognition, sorting, and mail merge operations.

basic capabilities Basic word processing capabilities include simple word processing tasks such as text entry, editing, storing, deleting, and printing a document.

graphical user interface (GUI) A GUI (usually pronounced "goo-ey") is a program interface that takes advantage of the computer's graphics capabilities to make computers easier to use. A GUI frees the user from having to learn complex command languages. First designed by engineers at Xerox Corporation's Palo Alto Research Center (PARC) in the 1970s, the GUI did not gain popularity until the 1980s with the introduction of the Apple Macintosh line of computers. Later, Microsoft used many of the same ideas in their first version of the Windows operating system for IBM-compatible personal computers (PCs). A GUI requires considerably more central processing unit (CPU) power and a high-quality display screen than computers employing a text-based interface. GUIs make it easier to move data from one application to another. For example, a GUI permits the user to copy a graph created by a spreadsheet program into a document created by a word processor program. GUIs such as Microsoft Windows and the Apple Macintosh feature elements and objects such as a pointer, pointing device, icons, the desktop, windows, and menu items.

macros A saved sequence of commands, mouse clicks, or keyboard strokes that can be stored and then recalled with a single command, keyboard stroke, or mouse click. Macros are useful for executing a sequence of instructions over and over.

text-based interface Also known as a command line user interface (CLUI), a text-based interface is a computer interface that is not graphical. The term came into existence because the first interactive user interfaces to computers were not graphical; they were text and keyboard oriented. The command interface of the DOS operating system is an example of the typical user–computer interface before the introduction of the graphical user interface. An intermediate step in user interfaces between the CLUI and the graphical user interface was the nongraphical menu-based interface, which let the user interact with the computer application by using a mouse rather than by having to type in keyboard commands.

word processing Word processing is the act of using a computer to transform written, verbal, or recorded information into typewritten or printed form.

word processor A computer program that provides text layout, editing, and formatting capabilities beyond that of a text editor. Word processors typically offer a graphical user interface, creating an environment where "what you see is what you get" (WYSIWYG—see next definition).

WYSIWYG A WYSIWYG (usually pronounced "wiz-ee-wig") editor or program is one that allows the user to view the page of text as it will appear when it is printed. WYSIWYG is an acronym for "what you see is what you get."

I. AN INTRODUCTION TO WORD PROCESSING

Word processing is the act of using a computer to transform written, verbal, or recorded information into typewritten or printed form. This chapter will discuss the history of word processing, identify several popular word processing applications, and define the capabilities of word processors.

Of all the computer applications in use, word processing is by far the most common. The ability to perform word processing requires a computer and a special type of computer software called a *word processor*. A word processor is a program designed to assist with the production of a wide variety of documents, including letters, memoranda, and manuals, rapidly and at relatively low cost. A typical word processor enables the user to create documents, edit them using the keyboard and mouse, store them for later retrieval, and print them to a printer. Common word processing applications include Microsoft Notepad, Microsoft Word, and Corel WordPerfect.

Word processing technology allows human beings to freely and efficiently share ideas, thoughts, feelings, sentiments, facts, and other information in written form. Throughout history, the written word has provided mankind with the ability to transform thoughts into printed words for distribution to hundreds, thousands, or possibly millions of readers around the world. The power of the written word to transcend verbal communications is best exemplified by the ability of writers to share information and express ideas with far larger audiences and the permanency of the written word.

The increasingly large collective body of knowledge is one outcome of the permanency of the written word, including both historical and current works. Powered by decreasing prices, increasing sophistication, and widespread availability of technology, the word processing revolution changed the landscape of communications by giving people hitherto unavailable power to make or break reputations, to win or lose elections, and to inspire or mislead through the printed word.

II. MAJOR DEVELOPMENTS IN THE HISTORY OF WORD PROCESSORS

Word processors evolved from typewriters and have gained additional capabilities over the years. In fact, the earliest word processors were electric typewriters with a built-in tape recorder that offered editing capabilities. These early word processors were difficult to use and offered limited capabilities. Despite this, early word processors offered significant advantages to business users through increased efficiency. Prior to the advent of word processors, business users had to laboriously and painstakingly copy documents by hand to create additional copies. Each time a document was copied, it had to be proofread for errors, with the hope that no new errors were introduced with each retyping. The introduction of microcomputer-based word processing changed all of this forever, automating the process of creating, modifying, and printing multiple copies of the same document.

A. Selected Developments in Word Processing Evolution

Advancements in word processing capabilities came slowly at first. Major phases in the development of word processing capabilities include:

1936: The introduction of Autotypist, which enabled the storage and retrieval of common words on punched paper.

1964: The introduction of IBM's Magnetic Tape/Selectric Typewriter permitted storage and retrieval of complete documents onto magnetic tape.

1960s: The introduction of mainframe- and mini-computer-based word processors. Many large computer manufacturers entered the word processing market by marketing add-on software packages that could be attached to existing mainframes or by introducing stand-alone word processing machines. These mainframe-based word processors were large, expensive, complicated, and required special training to use.

1970s: The introduction of relatively inexpensive microcomputer-based word processors resulted in the distribution of word processing power to more users than ever before. WordStar, released in 1979, was the first commercially successful word processing software written for microcomputers. Early microcomputer-based word processors were not capable of showing on the screen exactly what the final printed output would look like. In order to see the document exactly as it would appear on the printed page, the user had to print it. This changed with the introduction of the graphical user interface (GUI). Using a GUI word processor, users benefitted from a "what you see is what you get" (WYSIWYG) operating mode. These GUI word processors allowed the user to see exactly how the printed document would look just by looking at the screen.

1980s and 1990s: In the late 1980s and early 1990s, WordPerfect became the undisputed leader among word processing applications. Microsoft Word overtook WordPerfect during the 1990s and has become the de facto standard today. As microcomputer-based word processors became more popular, additional features were added such as spelling and grammar checkers, document merging, sophisticated text enhancement capabilities, collaboration tools, and the integration of e-mail messaging and hypertext markup language (HTML) formatting capabilities for publishing documents to a Web page.

III. HISTORY AND DEVELOPMENT OF WORD PROCESSING—A CLOSER LOOK

Today's word processors evolved from writers' needs to widely distribute printed materials and the increasing sophistication and availability of inexpensive technology. The technology that authors and writers needed to reach vast audiences was not always available.

A. Introduction of the Printing Press and Manual Typewriter

With the invention of moveable type at the end of the Middle Ages, the ability to mass produce documents took a giant leap forward. Gutenberg's invention of the printing press is widely thought of as the origin of mass communication, marking Western culture's first viable method of disseminating ideas and information from a single source to a large and far-ranging audience. However, the printing press was not a technology that enabled ordinary individuals to automate the process of writing. Henry Mill, an 18th century Englishman, is credited with the first major advance in automating the writing process with his invention

of the manual typewriter. His invention, however, did not meet with immediate success.

Several improvements to the typewriter resulted in the first truly successful design in 1867. A company already made famous for firearms manufacture, E. Remington and Sons, was contracted to produce the typewriter in sufficient quantity to meet public demand for the new typewriter. Not surprisingly, users still found this typewriter somewhat difficult to use because of its design: the unit printed on the underside of the roller, making it impossible to view the work until it was finished. This drawback was not eliminated until 1880, when the typewriter was redesigned to enable printing on the upper side of the roller.

Advancements such as the addition of a "shift" key made it possible to include both upper- and lowercase letters on the same key. In 1897, the "tab" key was introduced along with the ability to set margins. These improvements made the typewriter a very attractive alternative to the laborious process of record keeping and correspondence written by hand. Not only was the new typewriter faster, it was also more legible.

B. Introduction of the Electric Typewriter

In 1872, Thomas Edison patented an electric typewriter. His device, however, was not easy to use and was ultimately replaced by the Electromatic, a much-improved electric typewriter introduced in the 1930s by IBM. The business community quickly adopted the Electromatic and the greatly increased typing speeds it offered.

C. Introduction of the QWERTY Keyboard

Patented in 1878, the name "QWERTY" for the typewriter keyboard comes from the first six letters in the top alphabet row. Inventor C. L. Sholes developed the prototype keyboard during the 1860s in a Milwaukee machine shop. Today, the QWERTY keyboard is a universal fixture used on the most advanced, sophisticated computers and word processors electronic technology can produce.

Although accused of arranging the typewriter keys in such a way as to intentionally slow typists down, Sholes' true objective was quite the opposite. Sholes found that with the keys arranged alphabetically, the typewriter would frequently jam when someone typed too fast. By rearranging the letters, Sholes determined that the number of jams could be significantly reduced.

The keys that jammed more frequently were moved farther apart so that the typebars could strike the paper without jamming as often. In effect, Sholes' efforts resulted in the ability to type faster, contrary to popular belief. Alternative keyboards have been developed, but none have been so widely used as the QWERTY keyboard. One alternative, known as the Dvorak keyboard, was developed in 1932 and arranged the vowels on one side and the consonants on the other. In theory, the Dvorak keyboard would allow typists to type about 400 of the English language's most common words without ever leaving the home row (as opposed to only 100 for the QWERTY keyboard). Despite the efficiency gains, no keyboard design has ever overcome the ubiquity achieved by the QWERTY design, derived largely by being first.

D. Introduction of Punched-Code Typewriters

Soon thereafter, the M. Shultz Company introduced the automatic or repetitive typewriter, including features that represented a transition from the manual typewriters of the day to today's modern word processors. Based on a technology very similar to that of player pianos, the repetitive typewriter punch-coded text onto paper rolls that could later be played again, creating an exact copy of the original document.

The next advance in typewriter technology was termed the Flexowriter. It retained the punched-code mechanical characteristics of the Shultz device, but employed small rolls of paper tape instead of the bulkier paper rolls. More importantly, the Flexowriter gave users the ability to edit the text in their documents. A typo, punched into the paper tape, could be "ignored" simply by punching a "nonprint" character over the tape where the typo occurred. The ability to cut text from one section of a document and paste it to another was also made possible by the Flexowriter. To cut and paste, users simply cut the paper tape section containing the text to be moved and pasted it to another location on the paper tape.

E. Introduction of the IBM Selectric and Magnetic Tape Typewriters

In 1961, IBM's introduction of the Selectric typewriter replaced the movable carriage and individual type strikers with a revolving type ball. The revolving type ball could produce text faster than typewriters based on the traditional type striker technology. Three short years later, IBM introduced a magnetic tape version of the Selectric typewriter known as the Magnetic Tape/Selectric Typewriter (MT/ST), giving users the first ever reusable storage media built into a typewriter. The ability to store, edit, cut, and paste information on magnetic tape immediately eliminated the more cumbersome method of cutting and pasting paper tape. Multiple copies of a document could be generated easily, and the tape could be erased and used for other projects as needed.

In retrospect, the MT/ST represented the first true step in the development of modern word processors. In fact, IBM marketed the MT/ST as a "word processing machine." IBM translated the term "textverarbeitung," coined by a German IBM engineer to describe the act of typing a document, to "word processing" and redefined the term to describe electronic ways of composing, revising, printing, and filing written reports.

The introduction of the MT/ST heralded a new beginning in word processing, creating profitable new markets and accelerating the pace of innovation among developers and competitors rushing to create new and alternative products in the increasingly lucrative new market. One such innovation was the MagCard, introduced by IBM in 1969. The magnetic card could be inserted into a peripheral attached to a typewriter and used to store text. The major drawback of the MagCard was its limited storage capacity, about one page of text.

A similar word processing system developed in 1972 by Lexitron and Linolex included built-in video display screens and tape cassettes for document storage. The screen enabled users to create documents, make editing corrections, and defer printing until desired.

F. Introduction of the Floppy Diskette

In the early 1970s IBM introduced the floppy diskette, and once again, an innovation in storage media technology created new ways to work and store information. Word processing systems soon incorporated the new diskette-based storage media, enabling users to store far more information than was previously possible. The new diskettes were capable of storing 80–100 pages of text. The expanded storage capability eliminated the need to store a document onto several storage receptacles.

Once the most advanced of storage media, today floppy diskettes are used for temporary data storage or for data transportation. In addition, floppy diskettes are not as reliable or fast as other internal storage devices such as hard drives. Despite these limitations, floppy diskettes provided users with an easy-to-use electronic storage media capable of storing more text than previously possible.

G. Introduction of Microcomputers

The introduction of microcomputer technology in the late 1970s revolutionized word processing forever. Although Radio Shack, Apple, and Atari had offered microcomputers previously, it was not until IBM introduced the IBM personal computer (PC) that microcomputers quickly gained immense popularity based on their increased functionality.

With a microcomputer, floppy disks could be used to store application programs, representing a significant step forward in the evolution of word processing. Before the advent of diskette-based word processing packages, word processors were large, expensive, and difficult to use "dedicated systems." These dedicated word processing systems contained "hard wired" instructions that were difficult, if not impossible, to modify. Microcomputers changed everything by separating the computer (hardware) from the brains (software) required to perform word processing functions. Floppy diskette-based word processing programs could be modified easily with new versions of the word processing software as it became available. Application vendors developed newer and more powerful applications to run on the microcomputer and thus began the "feature wars" between software vendors in their efforts to capture market share within the rapidly growing computer industry.

In the late 1970s and early 1980s, several improvements were introduced to make word processors more powerful and effective. The spelling checker, document merging capabilities, and the ability to work on more than one document at a time were significant improvements in word processing capabilities.

Word processing capabilities will continue to improve in the years to come. New features will be developed and incorporated, offering users even more effective tools for creating, modifying, and printing documents of all kinds. Each successive version of word processing software will introduce new features such as voice recognition, finer page layout and text handling capabilities, and integration with other software applications. These capabilities will ensure that word processing remains the most widely used computer application well into the future.

IV. A WORD PROCESSOR AND A TYPEWRITER: A COMPARISON

The most obvious advantage of word processing over using a typewriter is that the user can make changes without retyping the entire document. If a typing mistake is made, it can be easily corrected. Entire paragraphs can be removed without leaving a trace. Adding words, sentences, paragraphs, and even entire sections is just as easy. Word processors also make it easy to move text from one section to another within a document or even between documents. After the user has made all the changes he or she wants, the user can send the electronic file to a printer to get a fresh hard copy.

Word processing software permits editing flexibility no typewriter can match, enabling the user to revise a document before committing it to paper.

Not only do word processors eliminate the tedium of retyping, they also permit greater control over the contents of documents. Word processors can be used to quickly and painlessly perform text entry, correction, substitution, check spelling, cut, copy, paste, and page layout operations well beyond the capabilities of any typewriter. If the user makes a typing mistake, he or she simply backs up the cursor and corrects the mistake. If the user wants to delete a paragraph, he or she simply removes it, without leaving a trace. It is equally easy to insert a word, sentence, or paragraph in the middle of a document. Word processors also make it possible to print multiple copies of documents that are better reading and better looking than that which is possible from a typewriter.

A. Differences between a Word Processor and a Manual Typewriter

A word processor offers many features not found in a manual typewriter. Word processors have far more capacity than typewriters for document creation and modification. Using a word processor, it is not necessary to have a small bottle of Liquid Paper available just to erase an unwanted word. The user does not need a pair of scissors to cut and paste (rearrange) text in a document as he or she would with a manual typewriter. Everything is done electronically with a high degree of speed, efficiency, and effectiveness.

B. Differences between a Word Processor and an Electric Typewriter

While it can be argued that modern electronic typewriters contain many of the same capabilities of word processors, the major difference is in the word processor's ease of use and *huge capacity* to create and edit sophisticated documents.

V. TYPES OF WORD PROCESSORS

Word processors are either character based or contain a GUI. Character-based word processors do not display documents exactly as they will appear on the printed page. Some character-based word processors, however, include a "preview" capability, allowing the user to preview documents as they will appear on the printed page. This useful feature allows the user to verify that the appearance of the document matches the desired expectations.

The arrival of popular GUIs such as the Macintosh and Windows operating systems led to a change in the way word processors handled fonts. Word processors offering a GUI allow the user to see the document on the computer's display screen exactly as it will appear after it is printed. In other words, with a GUI word processor what you see is what you get (known as the acronym WYSIWYG).

Word processor types range from simple text editors to full-featured applications. As the name implies, a simple text editor contains very limited capabilities

such as the ability to enter, store for later retrieval, modify, and print text. In addition to these basic capabilities, a full-featured word processor permits users to use sophisticated text enhancement tools, check spelling and grammar, incorporate drawing tools, and perform sorting and mail merge operations. The following subsections explore examples of each of these types of word processors.

A. Text Editors

Text editors lack the sophisticated features of full-featured word processors. Text editors are easy to learn and use and are commonly used for creating generic American Standard Code for Information Interchange (ASCII) text files as opposed to binary files created by more sophisticated word processors. Developed by the American National Standards Institute (ANSI), ASCII is the most common format for text files in computers and on the Internet. Due to the very limited character set of ASCII text files, common text enhancement tools such as underline, bold, and italics cannot be used.

A popular example of a text editor is Microsoft Notepad, which is an accessory application bundled within the Microsoft operating system (see Fig. 1). Notepad enables the user to create, store, retrieve, modify, print, and find text within a document. In addition, certain e-mail applications also contain text editing capabilities. For example, Netscape Messenger's built-in text editor can be used to compose sim-

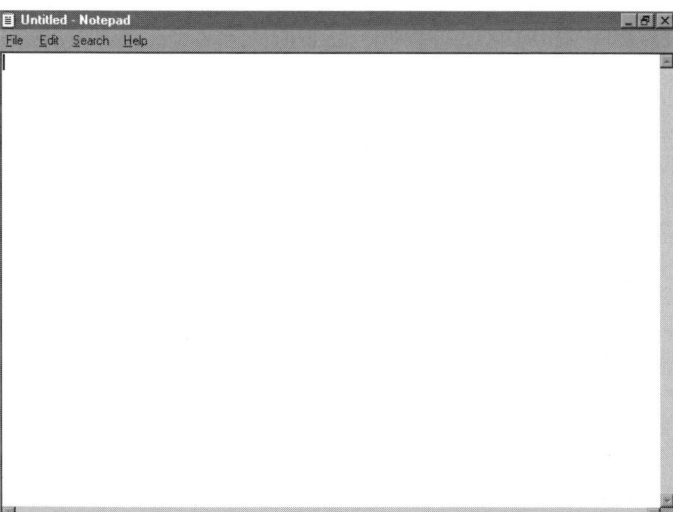

Figure 1 Microsoft Notepad, an example of a text editor.

ple, "nonrich" text e-mail messages. Text editors are good for creating text files such as program source code, e-mail messages, and other simple, unformatted text files.

B. Full-Featured Word Processors

Full-featured word processors enable users to create highly sophisticated and attractive documents. Typical features include greater control over text placement and spacing, ability to incorporate graphics, spelling and grammar checker components, search and sort capabilities, ability to create multiple columns, ability to perform mail merges, and much more. Despite considerable efforts to make these applications user friendly, the additional complexity of full-featured word processors makes them more difficult to learn than text editors. However, mastery of the basic capabilities is no more difficult than with a basic text editor. Examples of full-featured word processors include Microsoft Word and Corel WordPerfect. Figures 2 and 3 illustrate examples of these popular word processing applications.

C. Other Word Processors

Many word processors offer functionality somewhere between basic text editors and full-featured applications. For example, VEDIT is an advanced text editor that can be used to edit text, data, binary, and other file types including very large files and programming source files. Microsoft WordPad is another example, primarily due to its page layout features and ability to save text files to a number of alternative file formats, including Microsoft Word, rich text format (RTF), and text.

Finally, advanced desktop publishing (DTP) applications such as Ventura Publisher and Aldus Page-Maker are used to offer capabilities that were thought to be beyond the most advanced capabilities of word processors. In fact, brochures, books, and other complex documents that were once considered possible only through DTP applications can now be created using full-featured word processors. The increasing sophistication of word processors with respect to text placement, spacing, graphics handling, and integration with other office suite applications has blurred the line of distinction separating word processing and DTP software applications. In fact, the functional sim-

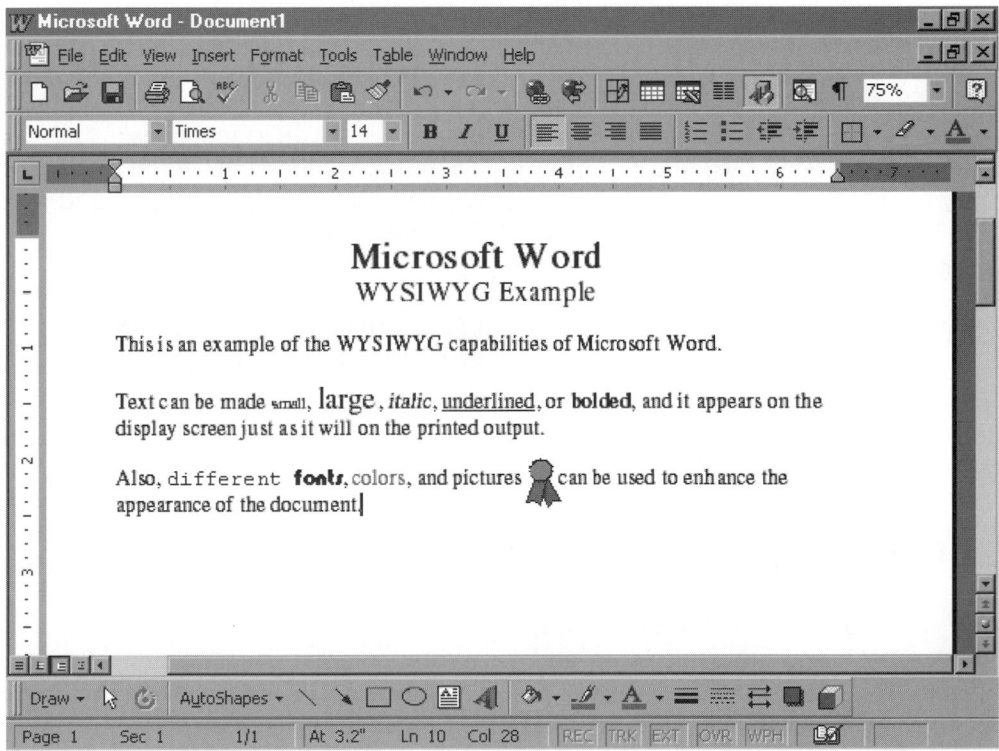

Figure 2 Microsoft Word, an example of a full-featured word processor.

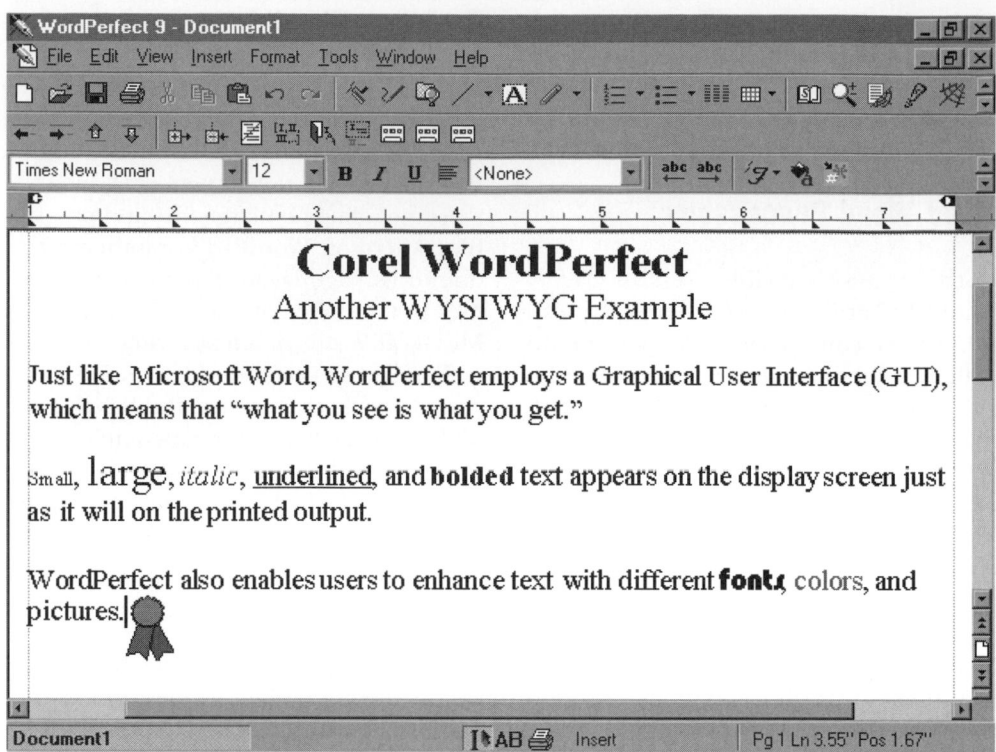

Figure 3 Corel WordPerfect, another example of a full-featured word processor.

ilarities and convergence of capability between word processors and DTP applications has resulted in the formerly separate category of DTP software being merged into the word processing category.

D. Windows Word Processors

Word and WordPerfect are the best known, but not the only choices for word processing for Windows users. Table I presents a number of alternative word processors that are compatible with the Microsoft Windows operating system.

E. Alternative Word Processors

Word processors are also available for Macintosh, UNIX, Linux, DOS, OS/2, and other platforms and languages (see Table II).

A variety of non-English word processors such as Accent Professional for Windows and The Universal Word provide multilingual capabilities. These appli-

cations include multiple character sets with support for Arabic, Chinese, Hebrew, Hindi, Indian, Lao, Punjabi, Thai, Urdu, Vietnamese, and Spanish users. These applications and add-on modules allow users to render text written right to left and provide support for multiple dialects.

VI. CAPABILITIES OF WORD PROCESSORS—A CLOSER LOOK

Although the specific capabilities of word processing applications vary considerably, all word processing applications offer the same set of basic capabilities and perform the same kinds of tasks. The following brief descriptions outline general capabilities of word processing applications.

- *Formatting/layout* capabilities reflect the application's ability to shape the content of a document through page layout features.
- *Composing/editing* capabilities provide tools for adding and modifying text within a document.

Table I Word Processors for the Microsoft Windows Platform

Microsoft Word	Probably the best known word processor for Windows. Available alone or as part of an office suite in standard, small business, professional, and premium editions.
Corel WordPerfect	Includes a variety of collaboration and productivity tools. Available stand alone or as part of a suite in standard, law office, voice-recognition, and professional editions.
Lotus WordPro	Originally the AmiPro word processor, now integrated into Lotus SmartSuite.
EasyWrite	Good for beginners, handles images, and includes spell check and a number of other useful features.
Yeah Write for Windows	A fast, small, easy-to-use, and inexpensive word processor.
Cetus CwordPad	An enchanced implementation of Windows 95 WordPad. Provides the basic functionality of WordPad, as well as a spell checker, a thesaurus, and a more complete help file.
WordExpress	A compact word processor with a variety of advanced features.
Trellix 2.0	Allows the user to publish WordPerfect documents to the Web without knowing HTML.
LetterWriter	Automates the process of phrase and letter generation.
DeScribe	Includes virtually all the features on major Windows-designed word processors and an unlimited undo per each working session.

- *File management* capabilities help users easily locate files and store them in an efficient manner.
- *Collaboration* capabilities allow users to share documents via e-mail, perform group editing, track revisions, place comments within documents, and consolidate complex documents.
- *User automation* capabilities are designed to make document creation easier via tools such as templates, macros, scripts, and mail merge features.
- *Advanced* capabilities allow users to customize the application to their particular needs through macro creation and editing capabilities, customizable keyboards and menus, drawing tools, and image handling features.

All word processors include basic capabilities such as the ability to insert, delete, cut, paste, copy, and print text. Documents can be saved onto a storage media and later retrieved for editing. See Table III for a cursory list of basic word processing terms and capabilities.

Many modern word processors contain more advanced and sophisticated features, offering the ability to manipulate and format text in a variety of ways. These full-featured word processors typically include the ability to perform file management; text enhancement; page numbering; and create footnotes, endnotes, cross-references, tables of contents, graphics, etc. Many word processors include a comprehensive spelling dictionary and grammar checking component, enabling the user to create documents that are grammatically correct and free of spelling errors. See Table IV for a description of these and other terms associated with full-featured word processing applications.

Table II Word Processors for Various Computing Platforms

Macintosh	UNIX	Linux	DOS	OS/2
Microsoft Word	Microsoft Word	Microsoft Word	Breeze	Lotus SmartSuite
Corel WordPerfect	Corel	Corel WordPerfect	Corel WordPerfect	Word Pro
Nisus Writer	WordPerfect	StarOffice	Nota Bene	Clearlook
Mariner Write	Xanthus iWrite	Maxwell	XyWrite	DeScribe
Thinker		Applix Words		
Scorpio for Mac				

Table III Terminology and Basic Capabilities of a Word Processor

Capability	Description
Insert text	Ability to insert text within previously typed material anywhere in the document without erasing the existing text.
Overstrike	Ability to substitute new text for old by typing directly over the old text.
Delete text	Ability to erase characters, words, lines, or pages as easily as crossing them out on paper.
Cut text	Ability to remove (cut) a section of text from one place in a document and insert (paste) it somewhere else.
Copy text	Ability to duplicate a section of text from one place in a document and insert (paste) it somewhere else.
Paste text	Ability to insert (paste) text that has been cut or copied from another section of the document to the current cursor location.
Page size and margins	Ability to define various page sizes and margins, and the ability to automatically readjust the text so that it fits. Pagination: automatic division of a document into pages of specified numbers of lines.
Search and replace	Ability to direct the word processor to search for a particular word or phrase and to replace one group of characters with another throughout the document.
Indentation	Ability to temporarily alter the margins within a document to something different from the primary margins.
Word wrap	Ability to automatically move to the next line when the user has filled one line with text and to readjust text if the user changes the margins.
Text adjustment	Ability to automatically realign text to accommodate new margin, tab, page layout, and/or font settings.
Alignment	Ability to automatically align text to left (ragged right margin), right (ragged left margin), full (flush left and right margins), or center alignment (ragged left and right margins).
Print	Ability to send a document to a printer to get a hardcopy printout.

VII. CONCLUSIONS

Word processors have allowed users to record their thoughts, ideas, messages, and other writings to ever-increasing audiences. Access to inexpensive, powerful, and easy-to-use word processing technology has radically altered the workplace, increased communications capabilities, and made it possible for just about anyone to publish their work. In the years to come, it is certain that word processing technology will become even more pervasive in society as more users take advantage of this technology.

The power, ease of use, and sophistication of word processors will increase, while the costs associated with its use will decrease. The features wars are far from over, evidenced by the introduction of exciting new capabilities such as fully automated formatting, voice recognition, and tighter integration with operating systems and Internet resources. Recent improvements in word processors have introduced improved data management features and the ability to search for and replace multiple word forms such as

buy, bought, and other forms of the same word with the corresponding forms of *purchase* in a single operation. Fully integrated software suites will become increasingly common, and will include extensive data sharing capabilities, natural language help systems, and eventually maybe even thought recognition capabilities. All of these exciting new capabilities will play an important role in allowing users to tap into the power of the world's most sophisticated computer—the human brain. Ultimately, word processing technology will grow even more ubiquitous as it continues to improve, becoming tightly ingrained into people's everyday lives as they communicate with those around them.

SEE ALSO THE FOLLOWING ARTICLES

Copyright Laws • Desktop Publishing • Electronic Mail • End-User Computing, Managing • End-User Computing Tools • Groupware • Multimedia • Speech Recognition • Spreadsheets

Table IV   Terminology and Advanced Capabilities of a Word Processor

Capability	Description
File management	Ability to create, delete, move, and search for files.
Font specifications	Ability to change fonts within a document. For example, the user can specify bold, italics, and underlining. Most word processors also let the user change the font size and typeface.
Footnotes and cross-references	Ability to create sequentially numbered footnotes and easily cross-reference other sections of the document at the bottom of the appropriate pages during pagination.
Table of contents	Ability to automatically generate a table of contents based on the contents of a document.
Graphics	Ability to include drawings, illustrations, and graphs into a document. Some word processors include the ability to create the graphics within the word processor, while others let the user embed an illustration produced by a different (external) program.
Headers, footers, and page numbering	Ability to specify customized headers and footers that the word processor will put at the top and bottom of every page. The word processor automatically keeps track of page numbers so that the correct number appears on each page.
Layout	Ability to specify different margins within a document, create multiple columns, and specify various methods for indenting paragraphs.
Macros	Ability to assign a series of keystrokes, mouse clicks, or any combination of keystrokes and mouse clicks to a character or word. The keystrokes can represent text or commands. The ability to create macros saves time by automating and replacing common combinations of keystrokes.
Merges	Ability to combine two documents into a third document to generate multiple copies of the final document, another file. This is particularly useful for generating many files that have the same format, but contain different data. Merging a form letter with a mailing list to generate multiple copies of the letter with the different addresses and other variable information filled in is the most common use of the merge feature.
Spell checker	Ability to check the document for misspelled words. A spell checker will highlight words that it does not recognized by comparing words in the text against an on-line dictionary, flagging items not found in the dictionary, and offering alternative spellings.
Grammar checker	Ability to check the document for grammatical errors.
Tables of contents and indexes	Ability to automatically create a table of contents and index based on special codes that the user inserts in the document.
Thesaurus	Ability to look up synonyms, antonyms, and related words within the document.
Discretionary hyphenation	Ability to insert a hyphen to break a word that ends a line. The hyphen will not print if later editing moves the word to the middle of a line.
Windows	Ability to edit two or more documents at the same time. Each document appears in a separate window. This is particularly valuable when working on a large project that consists of several different files.

BIBLIOGRAPHY

Blissmer, R. H. (1986). *Computer annual: An introduction to information systems.* New York: Wiley.

Flores, I. (1983). *Word processing handbook.* New York: Van Nostrand-Reinhold.

Kunde, B. (1998). *A brief history of word processing (through 1986).* Union City: Fleabonnet Press.

Munday, M. F. (1985). *Opportunities in word processing.* Lincolnwood, IL: Natl. Textbook Company.

Price, J., and Urban, L. P. (1984). *The definitive word-processing book.* New York: Viking Penguin.

XML (Extensible Markup Language)

Joseph C. Otto

California State University, Los Angeles

GLOSSARY

browser An application that allows the retrieval and display of Web sites located on the Internet.

data Unprocessed raw facts and figures.

DTD (document type definition) Used by an XML document to set up the definition for the document structure.

extensible Customizable; able to create code for use with data and information.

HTML (hypertext markup language) A collection of markup tags that defines how the contents of a Web site on the Internet should be displayed. It is a simple text-based markup language for creating hypertext documents, which can be read by browsers over the Internet.

hypertext Content that is easily connected to other content.

information Processed facts and figures to give some meaning or context to the data.

internet The network of computers located everywhere around the globe that allows access to many different types of information.

interoperable Standardized form of documents that are transferable between most computer systems, irregardless of application, operating system, or platform.

markup language A language that allows data or information to be displayed in a certain way or to be transferred and manipulated in a certain way.

plugin Can expand the capabilities or uses of a browser by adding extra features not included.

portable Same as interoperable; standardized form of documents that are transferable between most computer systems, regardless of application, operating system, or platform.

processor Along with a browser, allows for the access and reading of XML documents.

programming languages Code used to create applications that manipulate data, or input, and produce information, knowledge, or output.

proprietary Private or nonstandardized formats usable by only one application, operating system, or platform.

SGML (standard generalized markup language) The standard for all markup languages. It is a complex and very powerful language for defining and standardizing the structure of documents.

standardized A consistent and generally accepted form.

stylesheets Allow the creator of a Web site to separate the content and the code, or tags that describe how the content should be displayed or defined.

tag The code that is inserted into either Web site documents or data documents that defines how the content of the document should be displayed or defined for transmission from one computer to another.

Web site (Web page) A location of the Internet that contains data and/or information.

XML (eXtensible Markup Language) A markup language that allows the definition of data and its uses and/or the creation of a Web site. XML allows the user to define markup tags.

XML, OR EXTENSIBLE MARKUP LANGUAGE, is a way of defining, displaying, and transferring data and information between the computers of the same company or between the computers of different companies very easily, no matter what platform, what type of computer, what type of operating system, or what type of application. The data and information are described in a specified format and marked so that the computers, applications, and programs involved can store, transmit, and read the file data quickly and easily, identifying the data and its purpose.

I. WHAT IS XML?

A. Definition

XML is a universally accepted markup language used to describe data and how the data can be processed or displayed. A markup language is a programming language that describes data in some way through the use of code inserts or tags. XML is a standardized and structured set of rules for defining any kind of data that are to be shared on the Web or between computers. It is a method for defining, testing, and sharing documents no matter what system is being used. XML is used to create Web site pages on the Internet, similar to existing ones but able to do much more. Current Web pages are static, or limited to the code available through a markup language called HTML, hypertext markup language. Web pages generated through XML allow the user to create their own codes, making the Web pages customizable and unlimited in available features.

XML can be used to create many different types of electronic documents, such as EDI (electronic data interchange) messages, channel definitions, application descriptions, and documents that can be shared across many different platforms. For example, in the area of EDI, XML can be used to set up a standard format to describe the data and include a beginning dictionary in a relatively simple manner allowing businesses to exchange data and information in any format. In an industry, such as the banking industry, where traditionally proprietary systems were used to exchange and track transactions, XML has allowed the exchange of information, no matter what the application or platform used. The data are no longer limited to those utilizing the proprietary system, but available to everyone.

It is called an "extensible" markup language because anyone using it can invent his or her own set of markup codes for any purpose. As long as everyone uses it, it can be utilized for many different purposes. It is a markup language used to identify the parts of a document that contains both words and pictures and what the relationship and meaning of those words and pictures are to the Web site.

XML is meant to improve some the uses of the Web by allowing a more customizable way of identifying information. It is meant to provide more flexible and adaptable information identification. Because it has the ability to customize the coding of Web sites for limitless applications it is referred to as a "metalanguage"—a language for describing other languages. It is also referred to as extensible because it is an adaptable language, not a fixed language. XML allows users to design their own customized markup languages for almost any type of document.

B. Relationship to HTML and SGML

Hypertext markup language (HTML) is the most frequently used language on the Internet, and probably will be for a while. It has insertable code, or tags, that are fixed, or static—they cannot be changed. The display of the Web site is completely dependent upon the translation of the codes by the browser. The browser is the software used to translate the information of the Web site for display back to the user. HTML creates a very simple type of report-style document. The biggest limitation of HTML is that it allows only one way of describing the content of a Web site. The number of elements allowed is limited, whereas with XML, the elements are defined by the user, and are unlimited.

XML is not fixed; it is not dependent upon the browser, but instead translated by the definitions used by the applications or the stylesheets. The applications or stylesheets are separate from the content and control how the content is defined or displayed. It allows the creators of Web sites to set up their own customized markup applications, allowing the exchange of information within their own particular domain.

XML does not define, nor is it limited to, generic tags; instead it is the creator that sets up the tags needed in the document. Instead of trying to work within the limitations of HTML, the user can create their own tags with XML. This results in smarter documents, documents that can be used, manipulated, and browsed more efficiently.

XML is a small subset of SGML, written in SGML. SGML, standard generalized markup language, is the international standard metalanguage for defining the descriptions of how different types of documents are organized and for setting up Web sites. It is the mother language—a very large, powerful, and complex markup language that has been used in industrial and commercial areas for years. SGML is considered to be overly complex and too large for most common applications, therefore not appropriate for most Web site creations.

XML is an easy-to-use, "watered-down" form of the more complex SGML. XML is designed to make it easier to create and define documents, easier to transmit, and easier to create interoperable documents than possible with both SGML and HTML. Interoperable documents can be transferred between computers, no matter what type of operating system, browser, platform, or application. XML allows users to define their own document types and also to make it easier to write programs that can manipulate the created documents.

XML is closer to being an abbreviated version of SGML than an enhanced version of HTML.

XML is not meant to replace HTML. HTML will be around for a very long time to come. XML is an alternative that allows the user to define their own markup tags, allowing for more flexibility when describing the documents or data. You do not have to know HTML or SGML to learn XML but it can be useful because the syntax and terminology are similar.

C. Relationship to XHTML

XHTML stands for extensible hypertext markup language and is the bridge between the use of HTML in the past and present and the use of XML in the future. It is not the same as HTML; it is a much stricter implementation of HTML. Because of its simplicity, and small set of rules, it allows smaller computer devices, such as PDAs (personal digital assistants) and cell phones to surf the Web. It is primarily used to help with the transition from HTML to XML. It is a method of moving toward a modular and extensible Web based on the use of XML. It provides the bridge for Web designers to enter the Web of the future, while still being able to maintain compatibility with today's HTML.

D. Difference between XML and Programming Languages

Programming languages, such as C++, Java, COBOL, Fortran, Pascal, and many others, are a way of setting up customized software programs for different appli-

cations, or tasks, with a computer. They can be used to set up programs that calculate, do some type of action, make some type of decision, or dozens of other tasks for computer users. It specifies what should be done with the input data to produce output information, but does not describe the data or information. XML is a markup language that allows the user to design ways of describing information, both a text- or data-type document. XML only describes the data; it does not do anything on its own; it does not process the data. It waits for a program, application, or stylesheet to do something with it.

II. WHAT IS XML FOR?

XML is intended for several purposes. It is intended to be an easy-to-use and straightforward form of the very complex SGML. It is intended to make it easy for the author of a Web site to set up and manage a SGML-standardized document, and make it easy for users to transmit and share information included in a document anywhere on the Web. XML is a much simpler version of SGML, allowing a standardized, portable, and easy-to-transmit document to be stored, transmitted, and shared across the Internet. It has been designed for ease-of-use, easy manipulation, and for document usage compatible with both SGML and HTML.

XML is not just for Web pages. Just as important, it can be used to store any kind of structured information in a standardized and portable format, allowing for the user to organize and manipulate the information in such a way as to allow the sharing of that information between incompatible computing systems.

III. WHO IS RESPONSIBLE FOR XML?

XML can only work with the many different types of computers, operating systems, and platforms of the Internet if it is standardized by a controlling organization. Every user must use the same XML structure if the data and information are to be shared. The organization that controls the standardization of XML is the World Wide Web Consortium (W3C), which is made up of experts from various fields. This is the same organization that controls the standardization of SGML and HTML. The control and maintenance of SGML, HTML, and XML by this organization ensures that it remains in a public format and not a proprietary development of any particular organization or corporation.

IV. WHY SGML?

The information included on the Internet and all of the information stored by the different organizations and users on computers is in many different formats and types of computers. The information should not be stored in a format that is restricted to just one make or model. In order for the information to be made public it must be in a format that is accessible by all the users, no matter what platform, system, or type of computer. It is also helpful if the information can be reused in many different ways. Private, or proprietary, formats are not an option if the information is to be shared between users. The information would be incompatible, and therefore unusable, by many of the users of the documents. SGML is the internationally accepted standard for the defining of these documents, applications, and methods of organization.

V. WHY XML?

Some of the more important reasons for success of XML are that it removes some of the limitations of previous Web developments, such as the dependence on the unchangeable codes of HTML, an inflexible document type that is overburdened with many incompatible codes from many different manufacturers. It also overcomes the complexity of SGML, which allows more options, but is more complex and contains more features than the average user needs.

XML was created to allow changeable and structured documents to be stored on the World Wide Web. It allows the user to create their own markup elements, or design their own document types, instead of having to use one of the "standards" already set up. It can be used for more than just Web pages; it can be used to store any kind of information and is very convenient to pass information between incompatible platforms or computer systems. This means that the data, information, and knowledge stored can be more descriptive, richer, and much easier to manipulate, because it is being described in more detail and because the user is setting up the code to do the describing. The content of the Internet should be able to be used by any person, regardless of platform, operating system, or type of computer. This public type of information should not be restricted by the format in which it is saved, but instead in a representative format that can be used by everyone, and anyone, in many different ways. Proprietary content representations are restrictive and would not work on the Internet.

The development of XML has allowed the Web sites of the Internet to overcome two limitations. XML overcomes the dependence of Web sites upon the static and inflexible HTML code and allows creators of Web sites to program in this easy-to-use, markup language instead of the alternative, SGML, which can be very complex and cumbersome to program in, too much for the average user to create a Web site.

XML is a convenient way for both small- and large-scale Web content providers to set up Web sites that are specific to their particular industry. Because the users can set up their own code, the content can be "customizable" for the participants of that area. As long as everyone is using the same customized code, the documents can be standardized for all users. The content is not dependent upon a particular vendor, media, marketing environment, or processors. Some of the advantages of XML are:

- Allows Internet searches to be more word-meaning specific, finding only the more appropriate documents for the user. For example, if you are doing a search for Windows you will receive hits from everything from the windows of a house to the Windows operating system. With XML the searches can be more filtered to just return the desired Web sites.
- Allows the information of the Web site to be customized so it can be displayed and defined in the manner most useful for the reader or user.
- Allows information from different Web sites to be brought together very easily.
- Allows related groups of users to exchange information in their own syntax.
- Allows for instant updates of information.
- Allows for easier electronic commerce transactions.

XML is intended to meet the needs of many different sizes of Web sites, especially those large-scale content providers. It can be used to help set up industry-specific content for exchange no matter what the platform or type of computer. It can work with any type of media, in many types of marketing situations including one-on-one marketing.

VI. WHAT IS NEEDED TO RUN XML?

A. XML Parsers

A parser is not intended for use by the Web browser. The browser would never see it even though it is working in the background. A parser is a tool for those users creating Web sites or programming information. A parser reads and interprets the XML electronic document for an application. It is like a preprocessor or filter. It examines the code and indicates any errors. It must decipher and translate the unlimited number of possible tags that have been set up by the XML programmer correctly. It must also do something with the markup errors in the document—not an easy task. The parser tries to protect the applications from the possible complexities and idiosyncrasies of XML. It allows the users of XML to set up applications faster and with less effort.

B. XML Browsers

When surfing the Internet, nothing but a browser will work with XML. A browser is an application that allows the retrieval and display of Web sites located on the Internet and is needed to translate the SGML, HTML, or XML markers into something that can be displayed on the screen. Because the user is designing the code and how it describes the information, the XML document and the accompanying hypertext links are much stronger and more indicative of what the information and its purpose are, but also make it more difficult for the browser to translate.

XML is relatively new, especially when compared to HTML, and a lot of the code is still in the experimental stage—meaning that there is no single browser available that will be able to handle 100% of XML applications. Also, because it is customizable, the number of XML applications, and the accompanying code, is unlimited, meaning the browsers available will have to handle all possible code. Although there are some parts of XML that are fairly generic, such as searching and formatting, which means the browser will have an easier time translating this general-purpose markup code, much of the code is still very new. Some of the other applications usable by XML can be added by customizing for a specific industry or by using some of the available languages that work with the Internet, such as Java, to develop a plugin to allow them to work with the browser. A plugin is an added application that can expand the capabilities and uses of a browser by adding extra features not included.

When considering what will run with a particular browser, there are two major classes distinguished when considering an XML application: documents and data. This goes along with the two main uses of XML: the creation of Web sites and the defining of data documents for their easy transference between systems. The document-type applications are those

published somewhere that includes both text and images in an environment that is structured. It includes fonts and formatting for ease of reading, pleasing, effective, and efficient display to the reader. The datatype applications are where XML is used as the container to define and pass the data and information between differing or alike systems. There is usually no formatting and it is usually not seen by or presented to readers.

Because of the newness of XML the browser will encounter code it is not able to translate. When the browser encounters XML code that it cannot recognize, it simply ignores it.

Specific examples of browsers and how they handle XML include:

- Microsoft Internet Explorer 5.5 handles XML but does it in the same way that it translates and displays HTML. Internet Explorer 4 comes with a XML parser.
- Netscape 6 supports some, but not all, of the XML code.
- Opera 5.0 seems to be the most complete supporter of XML, allowing for the translation of a majority of the code.

C. XML Processor

An XML processor is used to read the XML documents and provide access to their data content and the description of their logical structure. A separate module called an application describes how the XML processor should read and process the data and information.

D. DTD (Document Type Definition)

A DTD is used to set up and define the document structure with a list of legal elements; it is a description of the syntax used in the document. It sets up the names of the elements used, where they are used, and how they can be used together. It may or may not be included with the XML document. A DTD allows the XML document to include a definition of its own format, allows independent groups of people to exchange information in a standardized, application-independent, and consistent manner through an agreed upon common DTD, and allows for the verification of external or internal data. It can be declared either internally or externally. A validating parser looks at the DTD before the document is looked at ensuring that the elements are defined correctly. A

DTD provides applications for the information needed about the XML document and confirms that all of the documents of a certain type are consistent and in the correct format as far as the elements used.

VII. WHAT IS INCLUDED IN AN XML DOCUMENT?

A. Tags, Elements, Attributes, etc.

The basic structure of an XML document is very similar to an SGML or an HTML document. The document is made up of text and codes. The text is in a generic format allowing for easy transference over the Internet, but without any formatting. The inserted codes, or markup tags, allow the inclusion of formats for the text, pictures, sounds, and many other enhancements with the text content making it a much more effective presentation of the material. The documents can range from the very complex to the very simple.

(i) Entities—Storage units, or variables, that define the common text, containing either parsed or unparsed data. These are reusable text that can appear numerable times in the document, but only have to be transmitted once. This allows for a quicker transmission of the document.

(ii) Characters—Makes up the parsed data of an XML document; includes the character content and the markup tags. The markup tags describe the presentation of the content and the organization layout.

(iii) Tags—Mark the beginning and ending of an element.

(iv) Elements—Identify the environment surrounding the content. They are the basic building blocks of the document. They can contain text, other elements, or be empty.

(v) Attributes—Added SGML, HTML, and XML code allowing for a more specific look to the displayed document. These are a way of adjusting the code to more accurately and effectively display the data and information by providing more information about the elements.

(vi) Parsed data—The text characters of the document and the accompanying markup tags. The text is the content of the document and the markup tags describe the appearance and reaction of the text characters.

(vii) Entity references—A method of allowing the inclusion of markup tags into the XML document; an alternative way of displaying characters that are normally reserved symbols in the XML markup language, such as the < symbol used to indicate the beginning of the tag.

(viii) White space—Includes linebreaks, TAB characters, and regular spaces and spaces between elements where no text can appear. Included are significant white space, which is the space that is contained in elements and can contain both text and XML markup code, and insignificant white space, which is the space that is contained in elements, and only the element content is allowed, not any text data.

(ix) Comments—To provide documentation to the document for the person or people that create or maintain the Web site.

(x) Processing instructions—Used to provide information to an external application or plugin.

(xi) PCDATA—Parsed character data. It is the text between the beginning and ending tags of an element. A parser parses it.

(xii) CDATA Sections—Character data. It tells the parser to ignore, not parse, some characters that are not considered markup characters.

(xiii) Document type declarations—Four types of declarations that allow the Web site document to relate information to the parser about the nature of its content.

    (1) Element type declarations—Identify elements and what the content is meant to represent.

    (2) Attributes list declarations—Indicates information about the attributes of an element.

    (3) Entity declarations—Used to correlate a unique name with a part of the content. These define which tags can appear in a document.

    (4) Notation declarations—Used to indicate external data, which are then processed by an application.

B. What Does a Well-Formed XML Document Look Like?

A well-formed XML document is easy for the computer and browser programs to read and translate and is defined and ready for network delivery. It should be set up correctly and be valid. Some of the attributes of a well-formed document are:

- The document starts with an XML declaration, <?xml version="1.0"?>.
- There should be an element in which all of the other elements are contained, such as <meeting>, in the example following.
- The beginning and ending tags all match up. They must be balanced, that is, every start tag should have an end tag.
- All of the attributes are enclosed in quotes and are properly and adequately documented.
- All empty elements should end with />, such as <BR/>, or have both starting and ending tags with no content between, such as
</BR>.
- There should not be any tag start characters by themselves, such as <.
- There should be no overlapping markups; all elements should nest inside each other.
- If an XML document is set up without a DTD, the elements should be of the CDATA type.
- All of the entities of an XML document that is set up with a DTD are declared.

An example of an XML document follows; it is very simple with no DTD (document type declaration):

```
<?xml version="1.0"?>

<meeting>

        <discussion>

                <question>What state are you from?
                    </question>

                <answer>I am from California!
                    </answer>

                <question>What is your name?
                    </question>

                <answer>My name is Joseph.
                    </answer>

                <question>What is your name?
                    </question>

                <answer>My name is Irene. </answer>

        </discussion>

</meeting>
```

A DTD file for the above example might look like

```
<!DOCTYPE meeting [

        <!ELEMENT discussion (question, answer)>

]>
```

The DTD file helps make sure that the XML is in the desired format. The document can be checked by a validating parser to make sure that everything within the tags acts the way it is supposed to.

The tags that are invented describe the contents and also help with the searching of documents. They are tags that are very readable by both humans and browsers.

When designing a site, there are a few things to keep in mind and a few questions to ask yourself to create the best site possible.

The *KISS* (keep it simple sweetie) principle works well for a Web page. You should always focus your ideas. Make sure that everything on your page has a really good reason for being there. Because the information, and all of the things that go with it, has to go from a server to the user's computer over communication lines, everything takes time to get there. Consider everything on your Web site. Try to take as much time picking out the images as you spend on the copy.

The content of the Web page should:

- Be as brief as possible and still get the intended information across
- Be clear and use simple language with consistent terminology throughout the site
- Be checked for spelling and for grammar
- Use hypertext links to connect to useful, current information that is not on your Web site

Planning a Web site is very important. There are many poorly designed, hard-to-read pages that do not have to be that way. The design of a Web page should include answering the following questions:

- What is the point of the site? What is the purpose of this Web site?
- Who are you? Who is your target audience?
- How is your audience going to view your page?
- When considering speed, you should also think about browsers, plug-ins, and added applications. They tend to slow down the display of a Web site.
- How do you attract visitors to your Web site, and once they are there, how do you keep them there?
- What colors should you use?
- How do I place the information on the page?
- How will I organize this information?

If you are setting up a Web site with different pages, links, or frames, it is important to follow some simple navigational rules:

- On each page include a link that returns to your main page, or the "Home page."

- Always include a way back to the top of the presentation.
- Always place your navigation links in the same place on each page so the user is not lost to other links. At the top or to the left is standard.
- If your site is large, consider including a site map. A site map is a sketch or diagram of how all of your Web pages work together.
- Always let the user know where they are.
- Avoid useless clicking and page loads.
- The most important information should always be displayed first.
- Do not place under construction signs that take a while to load on an unfinished site—it is frustrating for the user to wait just to find that nothing is there.
- Do not let links get out of date. Only include current and useful links on your Web site.
- Let the user know what is new in case they are a repeat visitor.
- Include dates to show updated information.
- Do not let pages link to a dead end with no way of going anywhere else.
- Use graphics effectively—use the same graphic, such as a logo, in multiple places.

VIII. UPCOMING FEATURES OF XML

Browsers will continue to incorporate more and more features of XML, allowing users to utilize more of the features available. For example, through VoiceXML there will be a standardized, portable, and independent way of creating speech-enabled applications. Through VoiceXML, speech-enabled Web-based content can be created and telephony-based speech recognition call center applications can be set up. Through XML tags, actions for setting up a connection between human voice and the speech recognition system can be set up.

SEE ALSO THE FOLLOWING ARTICLES

Electronic Data Interchange • Internet Homepages • Internet, Overview • Java • Javascript • Linux Operating System • Network Environments, Managing • Programming Languages Classification • Unix Operating System

BIBLIOGRAPHY

Ancha, S. (2001). Introduction to XML programming, http://www.javacommerce.com/tutorial/xmldev/index.html.

Flynn, P. (2001). The XML FAQ, http://www.uce.ie/xml/faq.xml.

Freter, T. (2001). XML: It's the future of HTML, http://www.sun.com/980602/xml/.

Jones, J. (2001). XML 101, http://www.swynk.com/friends/jones/articles/xml_101.asp.

OASIS. http://www.oasis-open.org/cover/sgml-xml.html.

Richmond, A. (2000). Introduction to XHTML: Why do we need XHTML? http://www.wdvl.com/Authoring/Languages/XML/XHTML/why.html.

Simpson, J. E. (2000). Will XML replace HTML? http://www.xml.com/pub/a/2000/12/13,xmlhtml.html.

Walsh, N. (1998). A technical introduction to XML, http://www.xml.com/pub/a/98/10/guide0.html.

W3C. http://www.w3.org/XML/.

Year 2000 (Y2K) Bug Problems

Steven H. Goldberg

Imagitas, Inc.

I. THE YEAR 2000 PROBLEM
II. RESPONSES TO Y2K

III. THE OUTCOME

GLOSSARY

compliance Under most definitions, an application system is Year 2000 compliant when it has been proved to produce accurate results when: using dates in the 1900s; using dates looking forward spanning two centuries (1900s/2000s); using dates looking backward spanning two centuries (2000s/1900s); and using dates in the 2000s. This includes accurate date comparisons, accurate date calculations, proper date sequencing, and the ability to select a range of dates for queries and receive the correct information. No system should be considered Year 2000 compliant until it has been tested and inspected by the appropriate mix of technicians and customers/users.

embedded system A phrase that refers to a device that contains computer logic on a chip inside it not independently programmable by the user. Such equipment is electrical or battery powered. The chip controls one or more functions of the equipment, such as remembering how long it has been since the device last received maintenance.

failure horizon A point in time when an application is expected to fail due to noncompliant date comparisons.

fixed window A technique of remediation that determines the century (specifically only the two high-order century digits) of a year which has been represented by only two digits (e.g., an automated record may have carried the code "78" for the year "1978"). The two-digit year is compared against a pair of hard-coded pivot points representing the low and high points of a 100-year span. Any two-digit century field is considered to be in the 20th century (19xx) if it is greater than the lower pivot point number (e.g., assume the lower pivot point is 60, a century designation of 71 would be interpreted as 1971). Likewise a century designation less than or equal to the higher pivot number is considered to be in the 21st century (20xx) (e.g., in our example the higher pivot point has to be 40, therefore a century designation of 31 would be interpreted as 2031).

noncompliant Failure to meet the requirements of "Year 2000 compliant" or "Year 2000 Ready" and where work or replacement is needed to allow correct operation.

remediate The process of making an application, system, or computerized component compliant to the Year 2000 and beyond. To remediate is to "fix" an application or process for the Year 2000 problem.

renovate A Year 2000 Strategy in which an application system is modified to become Year 2000 compliant. Resources that are not Year 2000 compliant are located, modified, and verified to ensure compliance.

sliding window A technique to determine the century (high-order digits) of a year when represented by two digits. The user specifies the number of years (both past and future) within a 100-year window spanning two centuries. For example, assume the window is set at 19 future years (1996–2014) and 80 past years (1915–1994). Dates in the range "00–14" (inclusive) are designated 21st century dates because they fall into the future window. Dates in the range "15–99" (inclusive) fall into the 20th century.

windowing solution This is a procedural solution that can be applied for dates that span less than 100 years. The data is not changed. Rather, the logic in the program interprets the century for the dates. With a fixed window, a point in time is chosen and all dates are interpreted based on that pivot year. With a sliding window, a changing point in time is used for the interpretation. For example, the pivot year may be set at the current year and extend 50 years forward and fifty years backward.

year 2000 ready The capability of a product, when used in accordance with its associated documentation, to correctly process, provide, and/or receive date data within and between the 20th and 21st centuries, provided that all products (for example, hardware, software, and firmware) used with the product properly exchange accurate date data with it.

THE "YEAR 2000" PROBLEM—popularly known as Y2K—referred to the inability of most computers to process date information later than December 31, 1999. For several decades, date codes in most programs had been abbreviated to allow only two digits for the year (e.g., "97" for 1997). Unless those programs were converted to handle the century date change, they would interpret the year 00—that is, 2000—as 1900. If that happened, some computers would not work at all and others would suffer critical calculation and other processing errors. Because of the unprecedented scope of the problem, long lead times were required to assess, correct, and test automated systems to prevent computer failures and operational disruptions.

I. THE YEAR 2000 PROBLEM

On October 19, 1998, President Clinton signed into law the Year 2000 Information and Readiness Disclosure Act, in which Congress made the following sobering findings:

> At least thousands but possibly millions of information technology computer systems, software programs, and semiconductors are not capable of recognizing certain dates in 1999 and after December 31, 1999, and would read dates in the year 2000 and thereafter as if those dates represent the year 1900 or thereafter or would fail to process those dates.
>
> The problem described [above] and resulting failures could incapacitate systems that are essential to the functioning of markets, commerce, consumer products, utilities, government, and safety and defense systems, in the United States and throughout the world.

As it turned out, the actual impact of Y2K was not significant; indeed, the outcome surpassed most best-case scenarios. Until late 1999, however, it was not possible to reasonably conclude that the problem had been brought under control. Before that time, there were compelling indications that Y2K posed very serious business and legal risks that required sweeping, aggressive, and expensive corrective measures.

A. Y2K Computer and Other Technical Failures

A simple illustration of the Y2K problem involved the calculation of someone's age, a vital piece of information for many business, government, and professional computer applications. A person who was born in 1935 turned 65 in 2000. But computers that could not correctly process 21st century dates would subtract 1935 from 1900 and calculate the individual's age to be -35 (or possibly 35). Similarly, a credit card issued for four years starting in 1998 might not work because computers would think the card expired in 1902. The problem was serious because computers use dates in many ways and for many purposes. Date information is critical to carrying out financial transactions, processing claims, establishing eligibility for various programs and services, and operating telecommunications, scheduling, and process control systems.

Reprogramming computers to achieve Y2K compliance was fairly simple as a technological matter. However, the project management demands of Year 2000 conversions posed an exceptionally difficult and expensive logistical undertaking. Y2K was maddeningly complex because virtually all computer systems, large and small, public and private, performed hundreds or thousands of date calculations, all of which had to be located, reprogrammed, and tested at enormous cost over a relatively short period of time. Moreover, Year 2000 impacts would not be isolated within information technology (IT) departments. The management challenge extended throughout the enterprise, as well as to the suppliers and service providers the organization depended upon and the business partners, customers, and clients who depended upon the organization.

1. Internal IT Systems

Internal IT systems were the most obvious source of potential Y2K failures and the risk most under the company's immediate control. Vulnerable technologies included mainframes, client/server systems, networks, intranets, personal computers (PCs), and other components of hardware and software infrastructure, as well as application programs, utilities, databases, etc. The nature of Y2K risk often depended on the extent to which components of information systems were under the company's direct control. Many firms had a combination of systems, including applications that were developed entirely in-house, plain vanilla, or modified commercial off-the-shelf (COTS) programs, and custom-built systems and applications. Many companies used software developed by third parties to provide expert application and systems development not available in-house. However, vendors often were not willing to provide the level of Y2K support required, because they were faced with risks to their own bottom line, and possible liability exposures from their noncompliant products.

Companies often depended on maintenance and support agreements with multiple vendors responsible for different parts of the system that had been strung together over time. Dealing with multiple vendors of IT products and services was difficult enough in normal times, and it was fair to assume that Y2K would stress these relationships in new and unpredictable ways. The patchwork quilt of interdependent technologies upon which most companies relied created additional difficulties because Year 2000 required assessment, remediation, and testing of an entire system for which no single vendor bore sole responsibility.

2. Embedded and Non-IT Systems

Embedded systems are devices used to control, monitor, or assist the operation of equipment, machinery, or plant. Embedded chips are nonprogrammable microcircuits hardwired into other pieces of equipment, many of which include date calculations in their programming logic. The equipment in which the chips were embedded often was not under the control of the information services department but usually was the responsibility of the vendors that supplied and maintained them for diverse operational units of the organization. The renowned Year 2000 evangelist, Peter de Jager, said of embedded systems: "Without doubt, this is the area of greatest risk. . . . They are the Achilles heel of Y2K."

Giga Information Group of Cambridge, MA, categorized embedded systems into four groups: individual microprocessors, small microprocessor assemblies with no time functions, subassemblies with timing functions, and computer systems used in manufacturing or processing control. According to Giga, only the last two groups were likely to experience Y2K failures, ranging from annoying, to aggravating, debilitating, and finally, life threatening. Embedded chip systems that needed to be tested for Year 2000 vulnerability included monitoring and control systems, including smart valves and sensors and environmental and safety equipment; fire alarm systems, including detection, sending, receiving, and suppression units; security systems, including sending and receiving units, video and surveillance systems, and badge readers; telecommunications equipment, including telephone switching equipment, call management systems, pagers and cellular phones; medical devices and equipment, including monitoring systems, dialysis, chemotherapy and radiation equipment, and laboratory, radiology, and other diagnostic systems; and building infrastructure, including heating, ventilation, and air conditioning (HVAC) equipment, energy management and lighting controls, emergency generators and lighting, uninterruptible power supplies, and elevators.

Embedded systems posed unique Year 2000 risks. Most organizations lacked the in-house technical expertise required to inventory, repair, and test these automated devices for Y2K vulnerability. In fact, most Y2K consultants had little or no expertise in this difficult area, and there were serious concerns that there was not sufficient technical capacity in 1999 and 2000 to address the problem. As de Jager suggested, "the only alternative we've left ourselves is to turn off what we're not sure of."

The other major problem with embedded chips was that they were so ubiquitous, with literally hundreds of billions of them installed in all kinds of equipment around the globe. Even if, as most knowledgeable experts believed, only a very small percentage of such devices were vulnerable to century-date failures in equipment that could be considered vital, incapacitating and even catastrophic consequences could have resulted.

3. Exchanging Data Electronically

An increasing number of commercial transactions are now handled by direct electronic communication, including electronic funds transfers (EFT); electronic data interchange (EDI) systems that place, fill, invoice, and pay for orders for parts, supplies, and finished goods; medical and other insurance claims processing and payments; and securities trading clearinghouses, and regulatory compliance reporting.

Several opportunities for Y2K breakdown existed. First, a basic prerequisite for electronic communication is that both systems must be able to talk to each other, that is, successfully send and receive information. Y2K could disrupt IT systems on either end of the wire, blocking electronic communication, and it could disable the communication linkage itself.

Second, even if both systems have achieved internal Year 2000 compliance, they still might have not been able to communicate if they had renovated their systems using incompatible methodologies. For example, if one party converted its code using a fixed window and a trading partner used a sliding window, the century designation for the data could become ambiguous after transmission.

Finally, electronic data exchange could have contaminated compliant systems with erroneous data transmitted by noncompliant, but functioning systems of their trading partners. For example, if system A generated data with financial information that was 100 years off and successfully sent that information to system B, the databases of system B could have used that data to process transactions and perform calculations that contained unknown errors.

Due to the increasing importance of direct electronic transactions, Year 2000 remediation often required large-scale end-to-end testing across many links in a supply chain, such as retailers, EDI clearinghouses, value-added networks, distributors, wholesalers, shippers, suppliers, and assemblers. Substantial technical, logistical, financial, and managerial challenges abounded, with corresponding business risk.

B. Y2K Business and Legal Risks

1. Direct Impacts

By mid-1999, the direct impacts of Y2K failures were reasonably well understood. The most likely affects were thought to be business disruptions and financial losses. Three published reports provided some insight.

A June 1999 study by International Monitoring, a London consultancy, estimated that Y2K damages in the United States would reach $114.8 billion (exclusive of insurance and legal costs), an amount that would be neither negligible nor recessionary. This estimate reflected International Monitoring's "best case conservative scenario" of 20.63 million uncorrected Y2K bugs in the United States.

Milliman & Robertson Inc., an international actuarial firm, estimated in a June 1999 report that "the cost to U.S. property/casualty insurers of Y2K-related events could range from $15 billion to $35 billion," including the legal costs of defending policyholders. Anticipated coverage claims included professionals or employers who were prevented from performing required services, companies that were forced to close for a period

of time to repair systems, personal injuries from Y2K failures, and increases in the frequency and/or severity of "normal" losses as a result of Y2K failures.

In September 1998, Capers Jones estimated the "best," "worst," and "expected" case scenarios for Y2K based on assumed bug-removal efficiency rates of 95, 75, and 85%, respectively. Under the best-case scenario (which assumed a Y2K defect removal rate that would be 10% higher than the current United States average for all software defects), the net economic effect would only be a 5% stock market correction and a 0.3%, increase in unemployment. Still, the business damage resulting from what Jones projected would be four additional months of wide-scale software repairs would have been significant.

2. External Business Dependencies

Most business organizations, public and nonprofit agencies, and institutions understood that, no matter how well prepared they may have been for the century date change themselves, they remained acutely vulnerable to Year 2000 problems if the many third parties with which they did business were not ready to process 21st century dates.

a. SUPPLY CHAIN COMPLIANCE

The problem of evaluating Y2K risks in the supply chain was a stubborn one for many reasons. The number and diversity of outside dependencies made efforts daunting. Companies often were unable to control or even reliably assess external compliance efforts. Potential failure points that could trigger and result from Y2K chain reactions were unpredictable. A large number of initial Y2K efforts had proven ineffective. All of these obstacles made it exceedingly difficult to assess supply chain compliance. For example, a group of companies that relied upon thousands of suppliers, including Sears and the big three automakers (acting through its Automotive Industry Action Group), were among the first to disseminate detailed vendor compliance questionnaires in an attempt to assess supply chain Year 2000 preparations. Despite formidable efforts, however, the initial results proved unsatisfactory because of low response rates and unreliable data.

Nevertheless, vendor surveys proliferated widely, albeit with mixed results. Common mistakes included asking for too much detail, requiring compliance "certifications" and signatures that give rise to liability concerns, and adopting an antagonistic tone.

b. CUSTOMER COMPLIANCE

There was a real risk that companies unprepared for Year 2000 would be unable to pay their bills or at least experience significant disruptions. If so, businesses providing goods and services to such companies could have taken hits to their own cash flows and receivables. For example, in September 1998, the *Boston Globe* reported that a Massachusetts technology consultant and systems integrator saw its stock price drop 22% after the company announced that many of its customers were delaying new projects to focus on Y2K work. The concern was serious enough that the Federal Financial Institutions Examination Council (FFIEC) required member banks, credit unions, and savings associations to implement customer due diligence plans to evaluate whether Y2K might prevent their material customers from repaying their loans on time.

c. INFRASTRUCTURE COMPLIANCE

Every enterprise, whether public or private, needed electric power, telephone service, water and sewer service, police, fire and ambulance service, public transportation, cargo ports, airports, and similar services and facilities. Providers of those infrastructure services and operators of those facilities faced the same Y2K risks discussed here.

In many cases, the useful life of aging infrastructure had been extended far beyond its original design by patches, workarounds, and other short-terms solutions, making Y2K assessment and remediation all the more difficult. Since most enterprises can't build their own electric generating station, sewage treatment plant, or international shipping terminal, serious Year 2000 disruptions in essential infrastructure systems posed risks that would have been extremely difficult to overcome. At the same time, no one could safely ignore infrastructure risks; to the contrary, every business was advised to formulate contingency plans so it could operate without basic services for a short or extended time.

d. INTERNATIONAL COMPLIANCE

International Y2K risk exposure was particularly uncertain. In April 1999, the United States Department of Commerce made the following observation:

> The international trading system, with its complex web of suppliers, distributors, customers, and transportation links, is supported by a critical infrastructure of products and services. The most important components of the infrastructure are energy production and distribution facilities, transportation modes, communications channels, and financial networks. These sectors are highly computerized and interdependent and are particularly sensitive to dates for the smooth exchange of goods and services. These characteristics render them especially susceptible to Y2K-related problems. Breakdowns in any part of the trade

support structure could slow or halt shipments of key imports needed to keep factories working, hospitals functioning, food in continuous supply, and people employed.

Not all countries devoted equal efforts to tackling Year 2000 problems. In fact, there were wide disparities among nations in their compliance preparations. According to the Gartner Group, which conducted a quarterly Y2K survey of 15,000 companies in 87 countries, the United States was farthest along in its preparations, followed by Holland, Belgium, Sweden, Canada, and Australia. By contrast, Gartner predicted that two-thirds of the companies in Russia, China, India, the Middle East (excluding Israel), Argentina, and Venezuela, as well as half of all companies in Japan, Germany, Mexico, and Malaysia, would have one major mission-critical Y2K failure. *USA Today* reported in April 1998, that only 8% of German companies had a formal compliance program, as compared to 80% of large American companies. Professor Richard L. Nolan believed that "probably more than 70% of Japan's CEOs are unaware of the potential of the Y2K problem to disrupt their business and are not providing any meaningful Y2K leadership." The Federal Reserve Bank expressed serious concerns about the compliance efforts of many foreign banks, in no small part because many United States banks depended on international funds flows and foreign counterparties for funds deposits and processing major financial transactions.

Outside the United States, additional obstacles were complicating Year 2000 conversion efforts. Economies around the globe were struggling to recover from failing markets, and some were converting to a single European currency. Because EMU conversions and economic difficulties had largely preempted international Y2K preparations, American companies were in danger from noncompliant overseas customers and suppliers. Unprepared international subsidiaries and affiliates of American firms also posed financial risks to those companies that maintained consolidated balance sheets.

C. Anticipated Timing and Consequences of Y2K Failures

1. Failure Horizons

There was a widely held and often unstated assumption, supported by most media coverage, that Year 2000 problems would not occur until internal computer clocks rolled over to 00 at midnight on December 31, 1999. In fact, Y2K failures were likely to occur as soon as 21st century dates were entered into non-compliant systems. The Gartner Group predicted that the majority of failures would not occur close to January 1, 2000. Specifically, the group predicted, Y2K system failures would occur in highest volumes from the third quarter of 1999 through the first quarter of 2001, with the highest volume peaks during the final quarter of 1999 and the first three quarters of the year 2000. Less than 10% of failures were expected to occur during the two weeks surrounding January 1, 2000. The Gartner Group depicted January 1, 2000, as simply the tip of a bell curve of date-related computer failures.

Indeed, a number of Year 2000 problems occurred before the date rollover:

- The Social Security Administration discovered the problem in 1989, when it was unable to perform long-range actuarial forecasts that extended into the 21st century.
- The mortgage banking industry had similar experiences when it tried to calculate payments and returns on 30-year mortgages.
- A 104-year old woman in Winona, MN, was sent a computer-generated notice to enroll in kindergarten in 1992.
- A Detroit-area grocery store filed suit in 1997 after its computerized cash register system shut down whenever it tried to process transactions using credit cards with 00 expiration dates.
- On January 1, 1998, a Chase Manhattan Bank software program that normally maintained stop-payment orders on checks for two years treated all that day's orders as "expired."
- A survey of IT directors and managers in twelve business sectors conducted by Rubin Systems for Cap Gemini America in July 1998, showed that 40% of respondents had already experienced Y2K failures, including processing disruptions (87%), financial miscalculations or loss (62%), logistics or supply-chain problems (44%), and customer service problems (38%).

It was widely anticipated that Y2K problems would increase dramatically in 1999. Many planning requirements common in business and government required computers to process information at least one year ahead: preparing budget and financial projections; procurement planning for manufactured goods; determining whether someone is eligible to drive or holds an unexpired professional license; scheduling annual appointments and follow-up visits; calculating insurance policy expiration dates; and so on.

The "time horizon to failure" could also have been foreshortened if fiscal years were used in processing date calculations. For example, most state and local governments operate on July 1 fiscal years, so FY00 started on July 1, 1999 for those organizations.

By the end of 1999, it was accurately predicted that Y2K problems would be neither widespread nor protracted. Earlier in the year, however, it was far less clear what level of compliance would be achieved. Several studies indicated that a significant number of American firms had fallen behind self-imposed Y2K project schedules. These data suggested that many organizations had a lot of ground to cover in the last three quarters of 1999.

In three separate polls conducted in late June and early July 1999 by Edward Yardeni, chief economist at Deutsche Banc Alex. Brown, between 11 and 19.5% of the respondents characterized their projects as five or more weeks behind schedule. A Morgan Stanley Dean Witter survey found that most sectors were in good shape, but described 29.8% of the 611 companies surveyed in the last quarter of 1998 as only "under way" (or worse), meaning that the "[c]ompany is in the *early stage* of renovating and testing its mission-critical systems (at least 50% of systems completed), but expects them to be Y2K ready in the 2nd half of 1999." A survey of 152 major domestic companies and 14 federal, state, and local government agencies conducted by Rubin Systems Inc. for Cap Gemini America LLC found that 74% of respondents had expected to have their code "completely tested and compliant" by January 1, 1999, but only 55% had met that goal. A study by Triaxsys Research LLC compared the planned and actual Y2K spending reported in SEC filings by 647 Fortune 1000 companies between January and April 1999. The study found that the average respondent had spent only 56% of its Y2K budget.

Moreover, Year 2000 problems were likely to continue to crop up long after 2000. Many Y2K errors would not prevent systems from operating, but would simply generate incorrect data that the system would accept and process. As a result, organizations could encounter major and minor snafus until the errors were discovered and fixed, one at a time. Also, the use of windowing, masking techniques, and other shortcuts to repairing noncompliant systems could have degraded the performance of many IT systems and created greater than usual maintenance requirements that could have adversely affected business productivity. Indeed, as companies rushed to complete and test their mission-critical remediation work by the end of 1999, there remained many important, albeit not "critical," systems that still required attention.

2. Potential Consequences of Y2K Failures

Y2K risks were categorized not only by their potential sources, but also the kinds of damage they might cause. In particular, operational disruptions, financial losses, and litigation were widely anticipated.

a. OPERATIONAL DISRUPTIONS

Serious Y2K problems from any of the sources outlined previously—internal IT systems, embedded systems, data exchanges, and external business dependencies—could have prevented a company from conducting business as usual, on either a short-term or prolonged basis. Plausible date-related failure scenarios included:

- Inability to generate invoices, pay bills, or issue paychecks
- Cancellation of customer accounts identified as 100 years past due
- Delays in just-in-time deliveries from key parts suppliers
- Malfunctioning of first-in/first-out inventory management systems
- Termination of lines of credit due to inaccurate credit reports
- Failure of robotics, calibration systems, or process control sensors
- Loss of electrical power, phone service, or Internet access
- Disruption of airline reservations and flight schedules
- Erroneous cancellation of insurance policies resulting from uncredited premium payments or miscalculation of expiration dates

b. FINANCIAL LOSSES AND BUSINESS FAILURES

Any of the foregoing operational disruptions would surely have had financial consequences. A number of credible analysts anticipated that Y2K would push some companies into bankruptcy, with potential ripple effects for customers and suppliers. For example, the respected software economist, Capers Jones, projected that Y2K problems would lead to a 5-7% business failure rate for the approximately 30,000 United States corporations that have 1000–10,000 employees. That figure would have translated to approximately 1500–2100 Y2K bankruptcies. Jones reasoned that:

> In the year 2000 context, mid-size corporations would probably be late in getting started on their year 2000 repairs, would underestimate and underbudget for their year 2000 work, would not bring in the appropriate tools and specialists, and would probably not have any contingency plans in place on what to do with applications that don't make the changes in time.

c. THE EXPECTED LEGAL FALLOUT

The projections of litigation arising from Y2K were unprecedented. Capers Jones estimated that damage awards and legal fees would total $100 billion in the United States and $300 billion worldwide. Giga Information Group puts the global cost at $1 trillion. Jeff Jinnett, a leading Year 2000 lawyer, also offered a $1 trillion estimate for United States Y2K litigation. He put the scope of the Y2K liability picture in perspective when he observed that "a $1 trillion cost for Year 2000 litigation would exceed even the estimated total annual direct and indirect costs of all civil litigation in the United States (at $300 billion per year)." Jones identified the major kinds of Y2K lawsuits that were expected:

- Litigation filed by clients whose products, finances, or investments have been damaged
- Litigation filed by shareholders of companies whose software does not safely make the year 2000 transition
- Litigation associated with any deaths or injuries derived from the year 2000 problem
- Class-action litigation filed by various affected customers of computers or software packages
- Litigation filed by companies that used outsource vendors, contractors, consultants, or commercial year 2000 tools, but Year 2000 problems still slipped through and caused damage
- Litigation against hardware manufacturers such as computer companies and defense contractors if the year 2000 problem resides in hardware or embedded microcode as well as software

While Jones focused on cost recovery suits by parties that suffered some financial or other loss that could be measured in pecuniary terms, some lawsuits could have fallen outside the cost recovery boundary. Four additional categories of potential Y2K suits also were recognized:

1. Suits to determine whether insurance companies were required to provide coverage for various Y2K claims and lawsuits
2. Enforcement actions by regulatory agencies and law enforcement authorities for civil and (much less likely) criminal violations of federal and state statutes and regulations

3. Suits to determine the validity of immunity legislation that several states adopted to insulate themselves from Y2K litigation
4. Suits by software vendors (probably in the form of countersuits against their customers) alleging that customers violated copyright laws by rewriting noncompliant computer code in breach of the terms of the software license.

II. RESPONSES TO Y2K

A. Technical Approaches

Identifying and responding to Y2K vulnerabilities comprised six recognized phases: awareness, assessment, renovation, validation, implementation, and postimplementation. The goals and objectives of each phase and a checklist of corresponding tasks illustrate the scope and intensity of compliance efforts.

1. Awareness Phase

Goals and Objectives: To raise awareness of management, the user community and external business partners to the Year 2000 issue and its potential impact to company operations.

- Executive and Senior Management Sponsors identified
- Year 2000 Project team established
- Business impact identified
- Awareness briefings for senior management conducted
- Awareness campaigns for user community initiated
- Year 2000 contacts with external business entities initiated
- Working group for the Year 2000 established including representatives from management, business partners, users, and IT communities
- Method for continued awareness building and distributing relevant Year 2000 information to other entities within company developed
- Year 2000 compliance policy developed and approved
- Year 2000 contract language developed and approved

2. Assessment Phase

Goals and Objectives: To estimate the scope and budget for the Year 2000 project.

- Determined the inventory methodology to employ
- Inventory of hardware completed
- Inventory of software completed
- Inventory of in-house application software (mainframe and desktop) completed
- Identification of users and responsible support personnel
- Schedule for new development and/or replacement
- Inventory of production control procedures
- Compliance information, including written commitments received from hardware and software vendors
- Compliance information, including written commitments from outside business partners (i.e., equipment and office suppliers, clients, financial institutions, etc.)
- Identify and perform risk rating of all applications based on estimated level of impact to organization's business functions
- Estimate of required resources for correcting all high-risk applications
- Preliminary budget for the Year 2000 project execution developed
- Senior management briefed on the results from the assessment phase
- Senior management approval of preliminary budget and commitment of the required resources to execute the Year 2000 project

3. Renovation Phase

Goals and Objectives: To perform a detailed analysis and develop detailed plans for correction, testing, and implementation of remediated applications.

- Year 2000 team has determined analysis methodology
- Initial draft for conversion sequence determined for identified applications
- Detailed analysis of each application was conducted and documented
- Method of correction for each identified application was selected
- Preliminary conversion plan, including applicable bridging, for each application developed
- Coding and naming standards for the conversion process developed
- Resource requirements for correcting, testing, and implementing each at-risk application developed
- Year 2000 compliance criteria and test plan for each application developed
- Identified and procured required external services
- Year 2000 budget adjusted as required

- Senior management is briefed on the results from the planning phase
- Senior management approval of the budget adjustments
- Executive commitment to provide required resources

4. Validation Phase

Goals and Objectives: To correct, test, and implement all applications that were identified and remediated. By the end of this phase, the project should have converted all at-risk applications and have successfully completed all Year 2000 compliance testing and regression testing for each application.

- Application code and all associated data elements were corrected (JCL, procs, datalibs, etc.)
- Software documentation was updated
- Corrected applications comply with coding and naming standards developed for the Year 2000 project
- All unit, system, and acceptance tests were successfully completed
- Testing was executed under system software releases that will be used in Year 2000
- Testing was executed using date simulation tool to represent dates (pre-2000, in-2000, post- 2000)
- Conversion phase schedule is on time
- Bridging solutions required for gradual implementation of specified applications were developed
- Data element migration plan and procedures for all data elements were developed
- Detailed implementation plan for each identified application was developed

5. Implementation Phase

Goals and Objectives: To implement all corrected applications and data elements in the production environment. By the end of this phase, the project should have completed the conversion of all at-risk applications and placed them back into production.

- All converted applications were moved into the production environment
- All system and third-party software packages were upgraded to meet Year 2000 compliance criteria as set forth in the Year 2000 Compliance Policy
- All data elements associated with identified applications were converted to acceptable Year 2000 compliance guidelines

- All operational procedures associated with new or corrected applications were implemented in the production environment
- All users were trained and ready to use the new or corrected applications as well as any upgraded third-party software systems
- Organization will have developed fall-back procedures to be implemented in case of application failure

6. Postimplementation Phase

Goals and Objectives: To identify and correct any unpredictable malfunction of information systems caused by internal and external errors associated with the Year 2000 problem.

- Clean management procedures developed
- Fall-back procedures were developed
- Functional users are prepared to conduct company business without automated systems for a specific period of time
- Disaster recovery team was assembled to deal with system failures
- Procedures for manual record keeping and follow up data entry were developed
- Contingency plans were exercised

B. Governmental Responses

1. President's Council on Year 2000 Conversion

On February 4, 1998, President Clinton issued Executive Order 13073, which created the President's Council on Year 2000 Conversion. The Council's mission was to coordinate the federal government's overall Year 2000 activities. These activities fell into three areas: ensuring that agency systems were ready for the century change; coordinating Y2K efforts with "interface partners" (primarily states) for important federal services; and promoting action among businesses and other governments, domestically and internationally.

2. Legislative Responses

The Year 2000 problem was the subject of hundreds of committee hearings, reports, and report cards on agency preparedness. In response to repeated calls for government action, Congress enacted a number of noteworthy Y2K laws, primarily to quell anticipated lawsuits.

a. Litigation Fears

Predictions of widespread litigation had been rampant ever since Y2K came to public attention. In the summer of 1997, for example, *Forbes* magazine wrote that "[t]he prospect of this mess has lawyers drooling." Between late 1996 and June 1999, more than 1200 articles about the legal implications of Y2K had been published around the world, many of which carried such lurid headlines as "Lawyers Circle Over 2000 Time Bomb," "Here Come the Lawyers," and "But First, We Kill All the Lawyers . . ."

Reports about the predicted "tidal wave" of litigation did not go unnoticed in Congress and were cited as justification for enacting legislation that would curb what was widely described as "frivolous" Y2K lawsuits. One oft-repeated story provides a cogent example. On June 20, 1997, the *San Francisco Chronicle* reported—inaccurately as it turns out—that "Lloyd's of London underwriters estimated yesterday that lawsuits arising from the dreaded 'millennium bug' would top $1 trillion in the United States alone." In its March 10, 1999, report on Senate Bill 96, the Senate Committee on Commerce, Science, and Transportation stated that "Lloyd's of London has estimated the cost of litigation which would be generated in the United States alone at over $1 trillion." The House Judiciary Committee also asserted that "the projected cost of Y2K litigation is as high as $1 trillion."

In fact, the $1 trillion figure was never "estimated" by or even attributable to Lloyd's of London at all. As explained by the dissenters in the House Judiciary Committee Report, the figure originated in earlier congressional testimony, which was then merely repeated by other speakers at a Y2K conference sponsored by Lloyd's. Indeed, Ann Coffou of Giga Information Group, the congressional witness who was the original source for the $1 trillion figure, extrapolated the estimate from two assumptions: the predicted total cost of Y2K remediation and the multiple of such costs that would be attributable to litigation costs and damages:

> The amount of legal litigation associated with Year 2000 has been estimated by Giga Information Group to be $2 to $3 for every dollar spent fixing the problems. With the estimated size of the market for Year 2000 ranging from $200 billion to $600 billion, the associated legal costs could easily near or exceed $1 trillion.

As it turned out, the Department of Commerce concluded in late 1999 that the total United States cost of Y2K repairs would be "in the neighborhood of $100 billion." That estimate was between one-half and one-sixth of the total Y2K cost on which Coffou relied in her congressional testimony. Assuming that her $2–3 litigation multiple for every dollar spent on remediation was correct, then the resulting estimate of Y2K legal costs would have been between $200 and 300 billion, substantially below the much-touted $1 trillion figure. Such a calculation would have been in line with alternative estimates of Year 2000 legal costs. For example, Capers Jones' best- and worst-case scenarios predicted that Y2K failures would drive between 47,500 and 356,250 lawsuits, at a total cost of between $25 and 300 billion. An unpublished Harvard Business School study estimated that Y2K lawsuits seeking damages of $75 billion would be filed against the directors and officers of the S&P 500.

b. The Y2K Act

Congress decided that the Y2K problem was sufficiently unique—and the consequences of unrestrained Y2K–related litigation sufficiently catastrophic—to merit federal legislative intervention. The Year 2000 Readiness and Responsibility Act (Public Law 106-37, 15 U.S.C. §§6601-6617), better known as the Y2K Act, was signed into law July 20, 1999. The Act was designed to influence virtually every aspect of Y2K litigation: the right to sue, the timing of suit, the nature of the claims, the defenses available, pleading requirements, procedural rules, evidentiary standards, and the types and amounts of damages and other relief that could be recovered. Indeed, the Act imposed these federal procedures on state court proceedings and displaced substantive rules of state law in areas where federal governmental entities had previously played virtually no role at all.

Congress understood that Y2K failures could disrupt supply chains, financial transactions, just-in-time manufacturing, professional services, and regulatory compliance, all of which could catalyze a broad spectrum of litigation that often would involve parties that were neither buyers nor sellers of technology products. Accordingly, the Act imposed new procedural and substantive rules that applied to a diverse array of potential Y2K suits. As the House Judiciary Committee observed about an earlier version of the statute, "[i]n essence, H.R. 775 is about defining rights and remedies in court to address problems presented by a particular technological problem, regardless of the type of claim that results."

The Act consisted primarily of tools for diverting, discouraging, and constraining Y2K suits:

• Subject to limited exceptions, the Act applied very broadly to all actions involving Y2K injuries, claims, or defenses. The Act expressly or implicitly preempted many kinds of inconsistent state law provisions.

- Punitive damages became harder to prove and were capped for small business defendants.
- Defendants generally would not be liable for more than their actual share of the damages they caused.
- Most Y2K actions could not be filed until a cooling-off period for remediation and alternative dispute resolution had expired.
- Plaintiffs were required to provide detailed information about their claims before investigation of their adversaries began.
- Plaintiffs could not recover damages for losses they could have avoided by preparing for Y2K problems.
- Contract terms and conditions, including limitations on liability and damages, would be strictly enforced.
- In tort cases, stringent restrictions were imposed on the recovery of economic losses, such as lost profits.
- Class actions could only be brought for Y2K defects that were "material" for most class members, and notice had to be provided to each member. The Act also expanded federal jurisdiction over Y2K class actions.

c. PRIOR STATUTES

By the time the Y2K Act was passed, Congress already had held extensive hearings on a wide range of related topics and had enacted two other statutes that helped shape the Act: the Examination Parity Act and the Year 2000 Information and Readiness Disclosure Act (IRDA).

i. Examination Parity Act   Not surprisingly, Congress' first foray into the Y2K issue concerned the banking industry, including credit unions and thrift institutions. The Examination Parity and Year 2000 Readiness for Financial Institutions Act became law March 20, 1998. As the Congressional Budget Office reported, the statute provided federal financial regulators with comprehensive authority to help the banking sector prepare for Y2K:

> H.R. 3116 would require the federal regulators of financial institutions to provide those institutions with model approaches for dealing with the year 2000 computer problem. Agencies would be required to take into account the need for different approaches for different institutions in developing guidance on year 2000 compliance. It also would give the Office of Thrift Supervision (OTS) and the National Credit Union Administration (NCUA) statutory parity with other federal banking regulators, including the Federal Deposit Insurance Corporation (FDIC), the Office of the Comptroller, and the Board of Governors of the Federal Reserve, to examine entities that provide services to financial institutions. Finally, the bill would require the federal financial regulatory agencies to hold seminars for financial institutions on the implications of the year 2000 problems for safety and soundness practices.

Although the banking sector began to focus on Y2K before the passage of the Examination Parity Act, the statute undoubtedly contributed to the tightly coordinated compliance program that the Federal Financial Institutions Examination Council established for all federally regulated financial institutions, as well as their mission-critical vendors and information technology service providers. More fundamentally, it expressed Congress' first recognition that "[t]he Year 2000 computer problem poses a serious challenge to the American economy, including the Nation's banking and financial services industries."

ii. Information Readiness and Disclosure Act   Once organizations realized that they were vulnerable to the Y2K problems of companies with which they did business, they promptly encountered considerable difficulty in obtaining information about what their suppliers and trading partners were doing to prepare themselves. In 1997 and 1998, a virtual "paper blizzard" ensued in which companies fired off letters and questionnaires to each other, producing frenzied activity but little useful information.

To resolve the impasse created by the legal uncertainties involved in exchanging compliance information across company boundaries, President Clinton introduced what was then called "The Good Samaritan Act" to protect organizations that provided such information in good faith. The purpose of the bill was to foster private-sector remediation efforts by reducing the potential for liability exposure from voluntary disclosures about Y2K readiness.

This bill ultimately was enacted Oct. 19, 1998, as the Year 2000 Information and Readiness Disclosure Act (IRDA). It created protections from liability for two types of Y2K communications, "Year 2000 Statements"—essentially any Y2K-related utterance—and "Year 2000 Readiness Disclosures"—statements specifically about an entity's compliance efforts or status. A Year 2000 statement could not be used to hold the party making the statement liable in an action covered by IRDA, even if the statement is alleged to be "false, inaccurate, or misleading," unless the claimant established by clear and convincing evidence that the statement was material and made "(i) with actual knowledge that the year 2000 statement was false, inaccurate, or misleading; (ii) with intent to deceive or mislead; or (iii) with a reckless disregard as to the accuracy of the year 2000 statement." Similarly, Year 2000 Readiness Disclosures generally were not admissible in evidence against the maker of the disclosure to prove its truth or accuracy. The evidentiary exclusion did not establish an immunity to liability related to Y2K failures, but it required plaintiffs to prove their case without using self-reported compliance information.

IRDA led directly to the widespread dissemination of disclosure information on specially designated "Year 2000 Internet Websites" and through standardized letters labeled "Year 2000 Readiness Disclosure," which were sent out to third parties that had requested compliance information. The Act also contained a temporary antitrust exemption that allowed companies, including competitors, to exchange Y2K data for the purpose of "facilitating responses intended to correct or avoid a failure of year 2000 processing . . . or communicating or disclosing information to help correct or avoid the effects of year 2000 processing failure." The exemption was intended to reduce Y2K risks associated with supply chain compliance and other external business dependencies.

III. THE OUTCOME

A. What Really Happened

In its final report, the President's Council offered the following understated observation: "There is general agreement that the Year 2000 rollover went more smoothly than expected." Perhaps the clearest indication of how far short actual Y2K failures felt of many, perhaps most, predictions, even by informed and sober professionals, was that it was possible to compile a short and finite list of the few significant problems reported during the January 1 and February 29, 2000 (Leap Day) rollovers:

- A classified Defense Department intelligence satellite system was totally inoperable for several hours during the rollover period. The problem originated not in the satellite itself but in the ground-based switching and software equipment used to download and process information from the satellite.
- Bank credit card companies identified a Y2K-glitch involving some credit card transactions. Merchants that did not make use of free upgrades provided during 1999 for a particular software package charged customers for orders every day after a single purchase was made. The problem affected primarily smaller retailers since most major retailers use their own customized software.

- A Y2K computer glitch at a Chicago-area bank temporarily interrupted electronic Medicare payments to some hospitals and other health care providers. As a work-around, Medicare contractors—private insurance companies that process and pay Medicare claims—were forced to send diskettes containing processed claims to the bank by courier or Federal Express so that the payments could be made in a timely manner.
- Florida and Kentucky unemployment insurance benefit systems encountered a Y2K glitch in an automated telephone call processing system. The Y2K glitch in customized code prevented some claimants from claiming earned income for the week ending 01/01/2000. Claimants reporting the problem had to be given an alternative means for filing their claims pursuant to state contingency plans.
- Low-level Windshear Alert Systems (LLWAS) failed at New York, Tampa, Denver, Atlanta, Orlando, Chicago O'Hare, and St. Louis airports during the date rollover. The systems displayed an error message. Air transportation system specialists at each site were forced to reboot LLWAS computers to clear the error. Fortunately, the weather was mild across the United States.
- Seven nuclear power plant licensees reported problems with plant computer systems used for supporting physical plant access control, monitoring operating data, and calculating meteorological data. The affected systems did not have an impact on the safety of operations at the plants.
- During the Leap Day rollover, several hotels reportedly were unable to issue room keys to guests because of a failure in hotel key-producing software.
- The Council Chair, traveling in March, received a car rental contract that included a $10 daily charge as an underage driver since the software indicated he was born in 2039.

In fact, Y2K proved so uneventful that the Council felt called upon to respond the widely expressed question of whether Y2K was "over-hyped":

> In the weeks since the rollover, some have expressed doubt about the magnitude of the Y2K problem and whether or not the significant investment of time and money to avoid disruptions was necessary. However, it has been difficult to find executives who worked on Y2K in a major bank, financial institution, telephone company, electric power company, or airline who believe that they did not confront—and avoid—a major risk of systemic failure.

One indication of the difficulty of the Y2K problem is the fact that many large, sophisticated users of IT revealed in regular filings with the Securities and Exchange Commission that they had been required to increase the funds allocated to their Y2K programs. These increases, which in some cases were in the hundreds of millions of dollars, were not for public relations purposes. Rather, they reflected the difficult effort of remediating large, complicated, and often antiquated IT systems.

Notably, the fears of crippling litigation were not realized. Fewer than 200 Y2K-related cases were actually filed, compared to the tens of thousands that had been predicted. Whether the passage of the Information Readiness and Disclosure Act and the Y2K Act helped increase compliance and reduce lawsuits remain a subject of debate.

Even more surprising, perhaps, was the fact that many countries that appeared to have spent little to prepare for Y2K did not experience substantially greater disruptions than the United States and other Western countries. The President's Year 2000 Council attributed this unexpected outcome to several factors:

- Difficulty in obtaining accurate international status reports
- A concentration of global remediation expenditures in the last six to nine months of 1999
- A reduced reliance abroad upon both IT generally and vulnerable legacy systems specifically
- Later-starting countries benefiting from lessons learned and remediation tools developed by industrialized countries

B. The Legacy of Y2K

The President's Council on Year 2000 Conversion was widely credited with having played an important role in coordinating an effective national and international response to the century rollover. In its Final Report, the Council offered its assessment of the lessons that had been learned in responding successfully to Y2K and that the Council believed could be applied to other large-scale technical threats, such as information security and cyberterrorism:

- Top management needs to be involved in IT decisions on an ongoing basis.
- Organizations need to do a better job keeping track of and managing the technology they use and the functions that technology performs.
- Contingency plans should be continually updated and tested.

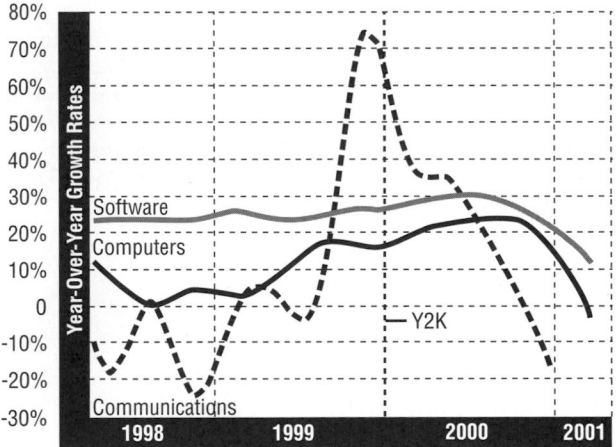

Figure 1 The real crisis. Tech spending surged before Y2K and has fallen ever since. [From the U.S. Bureau of Economic Analysis.]

- Industry National Centers are an important resource for reconstitution of critical services.
- Full disclosure is critical to sustaining public confidence in the face of possible emergencies.
- Forming partnerships across traditional boundaries can be a tremendous asset in the drive to achieve a commonly held goal.

Interestingly, Y2K remediation efforts contributed to a major spike in IT spending (see Fig. 1), particularly by companies that decided to replace, rather than renovate, noncompliant systems. There is general agreement that Year 2000 expenditures estimated in the $200–600 billion worldwide spurred economic growth during 2000 and early 2001. However, by mid-2001, once the spending surge had dissipated, the passing of the Y2K era helped exacerbate the developing economic downturn.

SEE ALSO THE FOLLOWING ARTICLES

Computer Viruses • Electronic Data Interchange • Electronic Payment Systems • Ethical Issues • National and Regional Economic Impacts of Silicon Valley • Privacy • Security Issues and Measures

BIBLIOGRAPHY

DeJager, P., and Bergeon, R. (1998). *Countdown Y2K: Business survival planning for the year 2000.* New York: John Wiley & Sons.
Goldberg, S. H., Davis, S. C., and Pegalis, A. M. (1999). *Y2K risk management: Contingency planning, business continuity, and avoiding litigation.* New York: Wiley Computer Publishing.

Johnson, C. (June 11, 2001). Y2K is finally here. *The Industry Standard.* http://thestandard.net/article/0,1902,27030,00.html

Jones, C. (1998). *The year 2000 software problem: Quantifying the costs and assessing the consequences.* Reading, MA: Addison-Wesley Longman.

Kappelman, L., ed. (1997). *Year 2000 problem: Strategies and solutions from the fortune 100.* Boston, MA: International Thomson Computer Press.

Ulrich, W., and Hayes, I. S. (1997). *The Year 2000 software crisis: Challenge of the century.* Upper Saddle River, NJ: Prentice Hall/Yourdon Press.

Ulrich, W., and Hayes, I. S. (1998). *The year 2000 software crisis: The continuing challenge.* Upper Saddle River, NJ: Prentice Hall/Yourdon Press.

U.S. General Services Administration, National Y2K Clearinghouse. http://www.y2k.gov/got.hml.

Reviewers

Frederic Adam
University College, Cork, Ireland

Carlisle Adams
Entrust Inc.

Majed Al-Mashari
King Saud University, Riyadh

Anne Anderson
University of Glasgow

Deborah Lines Anderson
State University of New York, Albany

Timothy Anderson
Portland State University

Ioannis Androutsopoulos
National Center for Scientific Research, Greece

Phillip J. Ardoin
Southern University

Kirk Arnett
Mississippi State University

Medhi Asgarkhani
Christchurch Polytechnic and Institute of Technology

Elizabeth Attree
University of East London

Massimo Aureli
International Fund for Agricultural Development

Gerald Autler
Strategic Economics

Bilal Ayyub
University of Maryland

Gojko Babic
Ohio State University

Richard J. Badham
University of Wollongong, Australia

Sebastiano Bagnara
University of Siena, Italy

David H. Bailey
Lawrence Berkeley National Laboratory

Richard E. Baker
Northern Illinois University

Richard H. Baker
Cambridge Knowledge Systems, Houston

Ganesh Baliga
Rowan University

Reza Barkhi
Virginia Polytechnical Institute

Jennifer Barr
Richard Stockton College

Adam S. Bendell
SV Technology

A. Michael Berman
Rowan University

Peter Bernus
Griffith University, Australia

Alex Berson
Entrust Incorporated

Sudip Bhattacharjee
University of Connecticut

Judith V. Boettcher
Corporation for Research and Educational Networking

Gary E. Bolton
Pennsylvania State University

Clinton Todd Brass
University of Pennsylvania

Agostino Bruzzone
University of Genoa

Janice M. Burn
Edith Cowan University, Churchlands Campus

David S. Butler
Syracuse University

John Butler
Ohio State University

Marco Cadoli
Universita di Roma

Mort Canty
Juelich Research Center

Jane Carey
Arizona State University

Erran Carmel
Kogod School of Business, American University

Suk-Gwon Chang
Hanyang University

Kaushal Chari
University of South Florida

Lawrence R. Chen
McGill University, Canada

Peter Cheng
University of Nottingham

Timothy Chenoweth
Arizona State University

David M. Chess
IBM Corporation

Roger Chiang
University of Cincinnati

Bill W. Childs
MC Informatics

Malcom Chisholm
University of Southport

Byoung K. Choi
Korea Advanced Institute for Science and Technology

Elizabeth Churchill
Xerox Corporation

Thomas Clark
Xavier University

David I. Cleland
University of Pittsburgh

David Cohn
Carnegie Mellon University

Mark Conway
PeopleSoft, Inc.

David P. Cook
Old Dominion University

William W. Cooper
University of Texas, Austin

Kenneth Corey
Michigan State University

Piero Cosi
Consiglio Nazionale delle Ricerche

Crispin Cowan
WireX Communications, Inc.

Alan Cox
Red Hat UK Limited

Walt Crawford
Research Libraries Group, Inc.

Thaddeus Reed Crews, Jr.
Western Kentucky University

Paul E. Cule
Marquette University

Gordon B. Davis
University of Minnesota

Carmen de Pablos Heredero
Universidad Rey del Juan Carlos

Anthony Debons
University of Pittsburgh

Lars Degerstedt
Linkopings University

Sarvanan Devaraj
University of Notre Dame

Klaus R. Dittrich
University of Zurich

David G. Druker
Druker Consulting

Timon Chin-Ting Du
City University of Hong Kong

Warren E. Duclos, Jr.
Tulane University

Martin Dufwenberg
Stockholm University

Robert P.W. Duin
Pattern Recognition Group, Delft University of Technology

Marlon Dumas
Queensland University of Technology, Australia

Peter E. Earl
Lincoln University

Maling Ebrahimpour
University of Rhode Island

Lauren B. Eder
Rider University

Christoph Eick
University of Houston

David England
Liverpool John Moores University

Sean B. Eom
Southeast Missouri State University

Tomaz Erjavec
Institute Jozef Stefan

Alan Brian Evans
University of California, Irvine

James R. Evans
Evans & Associates

Joseph B. Evans
University of Kansas

Jeff Ferguson
University of Western Sydney, Nepean

Richard Field
Private Attorney, New Jersey

Barry D. Floyd
California Polytechnic University, San Luis Obispo

Dennis Galletta
University of Pittsburgh

Brent Gallupe
Queens University

Blaine T. Garfolo
San Francisco State University

Eduardo Gelbstein
United Nations International Computing Center

Joey F. George
Florida State University

Zeno Geradts
Independent Consultant, The Netherlands

Jerry D. Gibson
Southern Methodist University

Jeff Gilchrist
Elytra Enterprises, Inc.

Sanjay Goil
Sun Microsystems, Inc.

Wei-bo Gong
University of Massachusetts, Amherst

Ram Gopal
University of Connecticut

Lynford Graham
BDO Seidman, LLP

John Grant
Towson University

Rebecca A. Grant
University of Victoria

Paul Gray
Claremont Graduate University

William Green
Sul Ross State University

Michael Guerriere
Healthlink Clinical Data Network, Inc.

Lou Hafer
Simon Fraser University

Richard Halapin
Indiana University of Pennsylvania

Marty Hall
Johns Hopkins University

Michael S. Hanna
University of Southern Alabama

Brian Harmer
Victoria University of Wellington

Susan J. Harrington
Georgia College and State University

Oscar Hauptman
Melbourne Business School

Mark Headington
University of Wisconsin, La Crosse

John Heinrichs
Consultant; Plymouth, Michigan

Mary Heinrichs
University of Toledo

Abdelsalam Helal
University of Florida

Jon C. Helton
Sandia National Laboratories

Jack Hogue
University of North Carolina, Charlotte

Clyde W. Holsapple
University of Kentucky, Lexington

H. James Hoover
University of Alberta

Tom Horan
Claremont Graduate University

Max Houck
Federal Bureau of Investigations

Ray Hunt
University of Canterbury

Kevin Huynh
James Irvine Foundation

Magid Igbaria
Claremont Graduate University

Jin H. Im
Sacred Heart University

Michael D. Ishman
Niagara University

Lech J. Janczewski
University of Auckland, City Campus

A. Milton Jenkins
University of Baltimore

Albert T. Jones
National Institute of Standards & Technology

K.D. Joshi
Washington State University, Pullman

Bernd Kahlbrandt
Professional School of Hamburg, Germany

Subramanyam Kasala
University of North Carolina, Wilmington

Elena Katok
*Smeal College of Business Administration,
Pennsylvania State University*

Edward G. Kennedy
IBM Corporation

John M. Kennedy
Indiana University

Martin Kenney
University of California at Davis

Jon-Lark Kim
University of Illinois, Chicago

Chris Kimble
University of York

William R. King
*Katz Graduate School of Business,
University of Pittsburgh*

Barbara D. Klein
University of Michigan, Dearborn

George Kocur
Massachussetts Institute of Technology

Laszlo T. Koczy
Budapest University of Technology and Economics

Clifford M. Koen
University of New Orleans

Rajiv Kohli
Trinity Health

Israel Korn
University of New South Wales

Stacy E. Kovar
Kansas State University

Pernille Kræmmergaard
Aalborg University

Harris Kravatz
Xcelerate Corporation

Anita M. Krsak
Lakeland Community College

David Kung
University of LaVerne

Howard Kunreuther
*Wharton School of Business,
University of Pennsylvania*

Ko Kuwabara
University of Michigan

Rachel Lander
De Montfort University

Tomas Lang
University of California, Irvine

Marc LaRoche
Entrust Incorporated

Mark Last
University of South Florida

Francis Y. Lau
University of Victoria

Kurt F. Lauckner
Eastern Michigan University

Nada Lavrac
J. Stefan Institute

Beatrice Lazzerini
Università degli Studi di Pisa

John A.N. Lee
Virginia Tech

Kunwoo Lee
Seoul National University

Merrikay Lee
Lee Publishing Services, Inc.

William H. Lehr
Massachussetts Institute of Technology

Cheryl Q. Li
University of Adelaide

Gyoo Gun Lim
*Korea Advanced Institute of
Science and Technology*

Chang-Yang Lin
Eastern Kentucky University

Karen D. Loch
Georgia State University

William Long
Massachussetts Institute of Technology

Maxima Lopez Equilaz
UNED University, Spain

Stephanie Low
College of Charleston

Sanjay Kumar Madria
University of Missouri-Rolla

George Magoulas
Brunel University

Sathiadev Mahesh
University of New Orleans

Mo Adam Mahmood
University of Texas, El Paso

Farzad Mahmoodi
Clarkson University

David Maier
Oregon Graduate Institute

Jerry Lee Maier
Middle Tennessee State University

Edward J. Malecki
Ohio State University

Timothy R. Mangan
Softricity Incorporated

Ronald J. Mann
University of Michigan Law School

Salvatore March
*Owen Graduate School of Management,
Vanderbilt University*

M. Lynne Markus
*Drucker Graduate School of Management,
Claremont Graduate School*

Merle P. Martin
California State University, Sacramento

Rose Martin
California Polytechnic, Pomona

Victoriano Martin Martin
Rey Juan Carlos University

Martin Mauve
University of Mannheim

Ketan Mayer-Patel
University of North Carolina, Chapel Hill

Donna Weaver McCloskey
Widener University

Raymond McLeod
University of Texas, Austin

Brian McNamara
California State University, Bakersfield

Novie Merchant
California State University, Sacramento

Leslie L. Miller
Iowa State University

James K. Mills
University of Toronto

Frank Mittelbach
*Anderson School of Management—University of
California, Los Angeles*

Kathy Moffitt
California State University, Fresno

Bonnie W. Morris
West Virginia University

Hiroshi Motoda
Osaka University

Todd Mowrer
*Forestry Service, United States
Department of Agriculture*

Richard R. Muntz
University of California, Los Angeles

Yi Lu Murphey
University of Michigan, Dearborn

Peter Mykytyn
University of Texas, Arlington

Thomas Myrach
University of Bern, Switzerland

Len Nadler
George Washington University

Ata Nahouraii
Indiana University of Pennsylvania

David R. Naugler
Southeast Missouri State University

Norman D. Neff
The College of New Jersey

Solomon Negash
University of California at Riverside

Robert A. Nehmer
Campbell School of Business, Berry College

Barry Nelson
Northwestern University

Peter G. Neumann
SRI International

Sandra Niehaus
Westwind Company

Erkki Oja
Helsinki University of Technology

Robert A. Orchard
*City University of New York,
College of Staten Island*

Marian W. Orlowski
Queensland University of Technology

Franko Orsucci
Rome International University

Nicholas Ourusoff
University of Maine, Augusta

Fatma Ozcan
IBM Almaden Research Center

Jonathan W. Palmer
*Smith School of Business—University of Maryland,
College Park*

Ruslan Pavlov
DMK Press

Graham Peace
West Virginia University, Morgantown

Wallace Peers
Electronic Warfare Associates, Canada

Rossella Petreschi
Università degli Studî di Roma

Wilfried Philips
University of Ghent

Mark Plume
Independent Consultant; Shirley, Massachussetts

Ken Polsson
Canadian Ministry of Forests

Jaana Porra
University of Houston

Anne L. Powell
Southern Illinois University, Edwardsville

G.K. Premkumar
Iowa State University

Andrew Prestage
Kern County School District

Roy Rada
University of Maryland, Baltimore

T.S. Ragu-Nathan
University of Toledo

R. Kelly Rainer, Jr.
Auburn University

Victor Raj
Murray State University

Hejamadi R. Rao
State University of New York, Buffalo

Donovan Rebbechi
Rutgers University, Newark

Gabor Redey
Hungarian Atomic Energy Authority

Richard T. Redmond
Virginia Commonwealth University

Mary Ann Robbert
Bentley College

Daniel Robey
Robinson College of Business, Georgia State University

Kenneth Saban
Duquesne University

Asghar Sabbaghi
Indiana University, South Bend

Matti, Saikkonen
Kuopio Institute of Technology

Kazuhiro Saitou
University of Michigan

Michael Sampson
The Institute for Effectivity

Radhika Santhanam
*Gatton College—University of
Kentucky, Lexington*

Rathindra Sarathy
Illinois State University

N.L. Sarda
Indian Institute of Technology, Bombay

Ulf Sarlén
SiF Stockholm, Sweden

Edwin Sasaki
California State University, Bakersfield

Taisuke Sato
Tokyo Institute of Technology

Jonathan Schaeffer
University of Alberta

George P. Schell
Cameron School of Business, University of North Carolina, Wilmington

Frank Schlier
Gartner Group

Homer H. Schmitz
Saint Louis University

Stephen D. Scott
University of Nebraska, Lincoln

Peter Seddon
University of Melbourne, Australia

Gad J. Selig
Sacred Heart University

Timos Sellis
National Technical University of Athens

Vikram Sethi
University of Texas, Arlington

Ramesh Sharda
Oklahoma State University, Stillwater

Conrad Shayo
California State University, San Bernardino

Peter Shenkin
City University of New York

Paul Sherman
Austin Usability

J.P. Shim
Mississippi State University

Bongsik Shin
San Diego State University

Kitae Shin
National Institute of Standards and Technology

Sung Shin
South Dakota State University

Pete Simis
California State University, Fresno

Rahul Singh
University of North Carolina at Greensboro

Sten Söderman
Sodertorn University College

Scott Springer
Arthur Andersen Consultants

Constantinos J. Stefanou
Technological Educational Institution of Thessaloniki, Greece

Friedrich Steimann
University of Hannover

Eric W. Stein
Pennsylvania State University, Great Valley

Dirk Stelzer
Technical University of Ilmenau

Rod Stephens
Rocky Mountain Computer Consulting, Inc.

Kim Styles
Monash University

G.A. Swanson
Tennessee Technological University

Earl E. Swartzlander
University of Texas, Austin

Scott Swenseth
University of Nebraska, Lincoln

Pandu Tadikamalla
Katz Graduate School of Business, University of Pittsburgh

Yutaka Takahashi
Kyoto University

Mehrdad Tamiz
University of Portsmouth

Lixin Tao
Concordia University

Wallapak Tavanapong
Iowa State University

Herman Tavani
Rivier College

Horia-Nicolai L. Teodorescu
Technical University of Iasi

Marc Thomas
California State University, Bakersfield

Daniel Tomiuk
McGill University

Mary Trauner
Georgia Institute of Technology

Richard Upchurch
University of Massachusetts, Dartmouth

Susan D. Urban
Arizona State University

Roberto Urzua
Community Medical Center—Fresno, California

Theuns Verwoerd
Independent Network Security Specialist

Roger von Holzen
Northwest Missouri State University

Index

Volume numbers are boldfaced, separated from the first page reference with a colon.
Subsequent references to the same material are separated by commas.